New Perspectives on

MICROSOFT® EXCEL 2000

Comprehensive Enhanced

JUNE JAMRICH PARSONS

DAN OJA

ROY AGELOFF
University of Rhode Island

PATRICK CAREY
Carey Associates, Inc.

MICROSOFT OFFICE USER SPECIALIST
APPROVED COURSEWARE

COURSE TECHNOLOGY
THOMSON LEARNING

Australia • Canada • Mexico • Singapore • Spain • United Kingdom • United States

COURSE TECHNOLOGY
THOMSON LEARNING

New Perspectives on Microsoft® Excel 2000—Comprehensive Enhanced
is published by Course Technology.

Managing Editor
Greg Donald

Senior Editor
Donna Gridley

Series Technology Editor
Rachel A. Crapser

Acquisitions Editor
Christine Burmeister

Senior Product Manager
Kathleen Finnegan

Production Editors
Catherine G. Dimassa, Melissa Panagos, Jennifer Goguen

Associate Product Manager
Melissa Dezotell

Editorial Assistant
Jessica Engstrom

Developmental Editor
Joan Kalkut

Text Designer
Meral Dabcovich

Cover Art Designer
Douglas Goodman

Printed in the United States of America

5 6 7 8 9 BM 04 03 02

For more information, contact Course Technology, 25 Thomson Place, Boston, Massachusetts, 02210.

Or find us on the World Wide Web at: www.course.com

ISBN 0-619-04427-6

PREFACE

The New Perspectives Series

About New Perspectives

Course Technology's **New Perspectives Series** is an integrated system of instruction that combines text and technology products to teach computer concepts, the Internet, and microcomputer applications. Users consistently praise this series for innovative pedagogy, use of interactive technology, creativity, accuracy, and supportive and engaging style.

How is the New Perspectives Series different from other series?

The **New Perspectives Series** distinguishes itself by **innovative technology**, from the renowned Course Labs to the state-of-the-art multimedia that is integrated with our Concepts texts. Other distinguishing features include **sound instructional design**, **proven pedagogy**, and **consistent quality**. Each tutorial has students learn features in the context of solving a realistic case problem rather than simply learning a laundry list of features. With the **New Perspectives Series**, instructors report that students have a complete, integrative learning experience that stays with them. They credit this high retention and competency to the fact that this series incorporates critical thinking and problem-solving with computer skills mastery. In addition, we work hard to ensure accuracy by using a multi-step quality assurance process during all stages of development. Instructors focus on teaching and students spend more time learning.

Choose the coverage that's right for you

New Perspectives applications books are available in the following categories:

Brief
2-4 tutorials

Brief: approximately 150 pages long, two to four "Level I" tutorials, teaches basic application skills.

Introductory
6 or 7 tutorials, or Brief + 2 or 3 more tutorials

Introductory: approximately 300 pages long, four to seven tutorials, goes beyond the basic skills. These books often build out of the Brief book, adding two or three additional "Level II" tutorials. The book you are holding is an Introductory book.

Comprehensive
Introductory + 4 or 5 more tutorials. Includes Brief Windows tutorials and Additional Cases

Comprehensive: approximately 600 pages long, eight to twelve tutorials, all tutorials included in the Introductory text plus higher-level "Level III" topics. Also includes two Windows tutorials and three or four fully developed Additional Cases.

Advanced
Quick Review of basics + in-depth, high-level coverage

Advanced: approximately 600 pages long, cover topics similar to those in the Comprehensive books, but offer the highest-level coverage in the series. Advanced books assume students already know the basics, and therefore go into more depth at a more accelerated rate than the Comprehensive titles. Advanced books are ideal for a second, more technical course.

Office
Quick Review of basics + in-depth, high-level coverage

Office: approximately 800 pages long, covers all components of the Office suite as well as integrating the individual software packages with one another and the Internet.

Custom Editions

Choose from any of the above to build your own Custom Editions or CourseKits

Custom Books: The New Perspectives Series offers you two ways to customize a New Perspectives text to fit your course exactly: *CourseKits*™ are two or more texts shrink-wrapped together, and offer significant price discounts. *Custom Editions*® offer you flexibility in designing your concepts, Internet, and applications courses. You can build your own book by ordering a combination of topics bound together to cover only the subjects you want. There is no minimum order, and books are spiral bound. Contact your Course Technology sales representative for more information.

What course is this book appropriate for?

New Perspectives on Microsoft Excel 2000—Comprehensive Enhanced can be used in any course in which you want students to learn all the most important topics of Excel 2000, including creating, editing, and formatting worksheets and charts, working with Excel lists and pivot tables, integrating worksheet data with various programs and the World Wide Web, working with multiple worksheets, one- and two- variable input tables, and Solver, importing data, and creating applications using Visual Basic. It is particularly recommended for a full-semester course on Microsoft Excel 2000. This book assumes that students have learned basic Windows navigation and file management skills from Course Technology's *New Perspectives on Microsoft Windows 95—Brief*, or the equivalent book for Windows 98 or NT.

What is the Microsoft Office User Specialist Program?

The Microsoft Office User Specialist Program provides an industry-recognized standard for measuring an individual's mastery of an Office application. Passing one or more MOUS Program certification exam helps your students demonstrate their proficiency to prospective employers and gives them a competitive edge in the job marketplace. Course Technology offers a growing number of Microsoft-approved products that cover all of the required objectives for the MOUS Program exams. For a complete listing of Course Technology titles that you can use to help your students get certified, visit our Web sit at **www.course.com.**

New Perspectives on Microsoft Excel 2000—Comprehensive Enhanced has been approved by Microsoft as courseware for the Microsoft Office User Specialist (MOUS) Program. After completing the tutorials and exercises in this book, students may be prepared to take the MOUS exam for Microsoft Excel 2000. For more information about certification, please visit the MOUS program site at **www.mous.net.**

Proven Pedagogy

CASE

Tutorial Case Each tutorial begins with a problem presented in a case that is meaningful to students. The case turns the task of learning how to use an application into a problem-solving process.

45-minute Sessions Each tutorial is divided into sessions that can be completed in about 45 minutes to an hour. Sessions allow instructors to more accurately allocate time in their syllabus, and students to better manage their own study time.

1.
2.
3.

Step-by-Step Methodology We make sure students can differentiate between what they are to *do* and what they are to *read*. Through numbered steps—clearly identified by a gray shaded background—students are constantly guided in solving the case problem. In addition, the numerous screen shots with callouts direct students' attention to what they should look at on the screen.

TROUBLE?

TROUBLE? Paragraphs These paragraphs anticipate the mistakes or problems that students may have and help them continue with the tutorial.

"Read This Before You Begin" Page Located opposite the first tutorial's opening page for each level of the text, the Read This Before You Begin Page helps introduce technology into the classroom. Technical considerations and assumptions about software are listed to save time and eliminate unnecessary aggravation. Notes about the Student Disks help instructors and students get the right files in the right places, so students get started on the right foot.

QUICK CHECK

Quick Check Questions Each session concludes with meaningful, conceptual Quick Check questions that test students' understanding of what they learned in the session. Answers to the Quick Check questions are provided at the end of each tutorial.

RW

Reference Windows Reference Windows are succinct summaries of the most important tasks covered in a tutorial and they preview actions students will perform in the steps to follow.

TASK REFERENCE

Task Reference Located as a table at the end of the book, the Task Reference contains a summary of how to perform common tasks using the most efficient method, as well as references to pages where the task is discussed in more detail.

REVIEW

CASE

INTERNET

LAB

Explore

End-of-Tutorial Review Assignments, Case Problems, Internet Assignments and Lab Assignments Review Assignments provide students with additional hands-on practice of the skills they learned in the tutorial using the same case presented in the tutorial. These Assignments are followed by three to four Case Problems that have approximately the same scope as the tutorial case but use a different scenario. In addition, some of the Review Assignments or Case Problems may include Exploration Exercises that challenge students encourage them to explore the capabilities of the program they are using, and/or further extend their know-ledge. Finally, if a Course Lab accompanies a tutorial, Lab Assignments are included after the Case Problems.

File Finder Chart This chart, located in the back of the book, visually explains how a student should set up their data disk, what files should go in what folders, and what they'll be saving the files as in the course of their work.

Certification Skill Activity

MOUS Certification Chart In the back of the book, you'll find a chart that lists all the skills for the Microsoft Office User Specialist Exam on Excel 2000. With page numbers referencing where these skills are covered in this text and where students get hands-on practice in completing the skills, the chart can be used as an excellent study guide in preparing for the Excel MOUS exam.

The Instructor's Resource Kit for this title contains:

- Electronic Instructor's Manual
- Data Files
- Solution Files
- Course Labs
- Course Test Manager Testbank
- Course Test Manager Engine
- Figure Files

These teaching tools come on CD-ROM. If you don't have access to a CD-ROM drive, contact your Course Technology customer service representative for more information.

The New Perspectives Supplements Package

Electronic Instructor's Manual. Our Instructor's Manuals include tutorial overviews and outlines, technical notes, lecture notes, solutions, and Extra Case Problems. Many instructors use the Extra Case Problems for performance-based exams or extra credit projects. The Instructor's Manual is available as an electronic file, which you can get from the Instructor Resource Kit (IRK) CD-ROM or download it from www.course.com.

Data Files Data Files contain all of the data that students will use to complete the tutorials, Review Assignments, and Case Problems. A Readme file includes instructions for using the files. See the "Read This Before You Begin" page/pages for more information on Student Files.

Solution Files Solution Files contain every file students are asked to create or modify in the tutorials, Tutorial Assignments, Case Problems, and Extra Case Problems. A Help file on the Instructor's Resource Kit includes information for using the Solution files.

Course Labs: Concepts Come to Life These highly interactive computer-based learning activities bring concepts to life with illustrations, animations, digital images, and simulations. The Labs guide students step-by-step, present them with Quick Check questions, let them explore on their own, test their comprehension, and provide printed feedback. Lab icons at the beginning of the tutorial and in the tutorial margins indicate when a topic has a corresponding Lab. Lab Assignments are included at the end of each relevant tutorial. The Labs available with this book and the tutorials in which they appear are:

Tutorial 1 Windows 98

Tutorial 1 Windows 98

Tutorial 2 Windows 98

Tutorial 1 Excel 2000

Tutorial 11 Excel 2000

Figure Files Many figures in the text are provided on the IRK CD-ROM to help illustrate key topics or concepts. Instructors can create traditional overhead transparencies by printing the figure files. Or they can create electronic slide shows by using the figures in a presentation program such as PowerPoint.

Course Test Manager: Testing and Practice at the Computer or on Paper Course Test Manager is cutting-edge, Windows-based testing software that helps instructors design and administer practice tests and actual examinations. Course Test Manager can automatically grade the tests students take at the computer and can generate statistical information on individual as well as group performance.

Online Companions: Dedicated to Keeping You and Your Students Up-To-Date Visit our faculty sites and student sites on the World Wide Web at **www.course.com**. Here instructors can browse this text's password-protected Faculty Online Companion to obtain an online Instructor's Manual, Solution Files, Student Files, and more. Students can also access this text's Student Online Companion, which contains Student files and all the links that the students will need to complete their tutorial assignments.

More Innovative Technology

Explore! CBT/WBT The back of this textbook contains an exciting new CBT learning product—Explore! Explore! places the student as an intern in a working company, AdZ, Incorporated. Students will gain computer skills through helping the other AdZ employees solve their business problems. The CD included in this textbook contains a CBT that teaches the basic operating system and file management skills of Microsoft Windows 2000 Professional. (Students do not need Microsoft Windows 2000 Professional to run Explore!, but the content may not match what students see on their computers if they are running Windows 95, 98, or NT.)

For more information, or to use the WBT version of Explore!, go to www.npexplore.com. Or, see the Technology Tools Appendix included in this textbook for step-by-step instructions on how to use Explore!

MyCourse.com MyCourse.com is an online syllabus builder and course enhancement tool. Hosted by Course Technology, MyCourse.com adds value to your course by providing additional content that reinforces what students are learning. Most importantly, MyCourse.com is flexible. You can choose how you want to organize the material—by date, class session, or the default organization, which organizes content by chapter. MyCourse.com allows you to add your own materials, including hyperlinks, school logos, assignments, announcements, and other course content. If you are using more than one textbook, you can even build a course that includes all of your Course Technology texts in one easy-to-use site!

Computer Buyer's Guide A comprehensive Computer Buyer's Guide is available on our Office 2000 Enhanced Student Online Companion (www.course.com/newperspectives/office2000). Simply go to the Student Online Companion and click the link for the Buyer's Guide.

Course CBT Enhance your students' Office 2000 classroom learning experience with self-paced computer-based training on CD-ROM. Course CBT engages students with interactive multimedia and hands-on simulations that reinforce and complement the concepts and skills covered in the textbook. All the content is aligned with the MOUS (Microsoft Office User Specialist) program, making it a great preparation tool for the certification exams. Course CBT also includes extensive pre- and post-assessments that test students' mastery of skills. These pre- and post-assessments automatically generate a "custom learning path" through the course that highlights only the topics students need help with.

Course Assessment How well do your students *really* know Microsoft Office? Course Assessment is a performance-based testing program that measures students' proficiency in Microsoft Office 2000. Previously known as SAM, Course Assessment is available for Office 2000 in either a live or simulated environment. You can use Course Assessment to place students into or out of courses, monitor their performance throughout a course, and help prepare them for the MOUS certification exams.

WebCT WebCT is a tool used to create Web-based educational environments and also uses WWW browsers as the interface for the course-building environment. The site is hosted on your school campus, allowing complete control over the information. WebCT has its own internal communication system, offering internal e-mail, a Bulletin Board, and a Chat room.

Course Technology offers pre-existing supplemental information to help in your WebCT class creation, such as a suggested Syllabus, Lecture Notes, Figures in the Book/Course Presenter, Student Downloads, and Test Banks in which you can schedule an exam, create reports, and more.

Acknowledgments

We would like to thank the many people whose invaluable contributions made this book possible. Our reviewers Greg Lowry, Macon Technical Institute, Rick Wilkerson, Dyersburg State Community College, Mary Dobranski, College of St. Mary, Suzanne Tomlinson, Iowa State University, and Barbara Miller, Indiana University; at Course Technology, we would like to thank Donna Gridley, Senior Editor; Rachel Crapser, Senior Product Manager; Catherine Donaldson, Product Manager; Karen Shortill, Associate Product Manager; Melissa Dezotell, Editorial Assistant; Greg Bigelow, QA Supervisor; John Bosco, John Freitas, Nicole Ashton, Jeff Schwartz, Alex White, Quality Assurance testers; and Catherine DiMassa, Senior Production Editor. A special thanks to Joan Kalkut, Developmental Editor, for her helpful suggestions and dedication to completing the text.

June Jamrich Parsons
Dan Oja
Roy Ageloff
Patrick Carey

Reference Window List

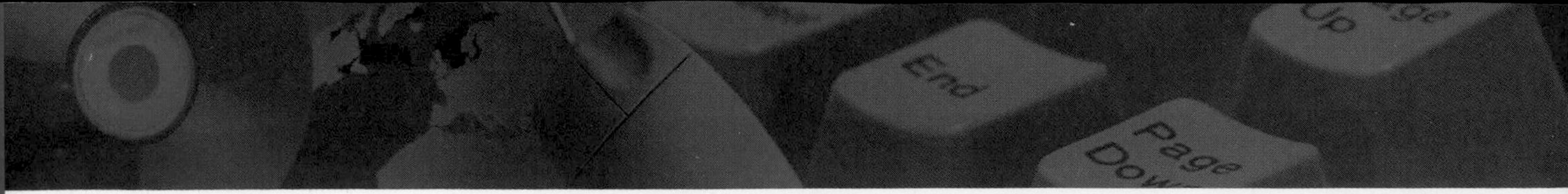

Tutorial Tips

These tutorials will help you learn about Microsoft Excel 2000. The tutorials are designed to be worked through at a computer. Each tutorial is divided into sessions. Watch for the session headings, such as Session 1.1 and Session 1.2. Each session is designed to be completed in about 45 minutes, but take as much time as you need. It's also a good idea to take a break between sessions.

Before you begin, read the following questions and answers. They will help you plan your time and use the tutorials effectively.

Where do I start?

Each tutorial begins with a case, which sets the scene for the tutorial and gives you background information to help you understand what you will be doing. Read the case before you go to the lab. In the lab, begin with the first session of a tutorial.

How do I know what to do on the computer?

Each session contains steps that you will perform on the computer to learn how to use Microsoft Excel 2000. Read the text that introduces each series of steps. The steps you need to do at a computer are numbered and are set against a shaded background. Read each step carefully and completely before you try it.

How do I know if I did the step correctly?

As you work, compare your computer screen with the corresponding figure in the tutorial. Don't worry if your screen display is somewhat different from the figure. The important parts of the screen display are labeled in each figure. Check to make sure these parts are on your screen.

What if I make a mistake?

Don't worry about making mistakes—they are part of the learning process. Paragraphs labeled "TROUBLE?" identify common problems and explain how to get back on track. Follow the steps in a TROUBLE? paragraph only if you are having the problem described. If you run into other problems:

- Carefully consider the current state of your system, the position of the pointer, and any messages on the screen.
- Complete the sentence, "Now I want to…" Be specific, because identifying your goal will help you rethink the steps you need to take to reach that goal.
- If you are working on a particular piece of software, consult the Help system.
- If the suggestions above don't solve your problem, consult your technical support person for assistance.

How do I use the Reference Windows?

Reference Windows summarize the procedures you will learn in the tutorial steps. Do not complete the actions in the Reference Windows when you are working through the tutorial. Instead, refer to the Reference Windows while you are working on the assignments at the end of the tutorial.

How can I test my understanding of the material I learned in the tutorial?

At the end of each session, you can answer the Quick Check questions. The answers for the Quick Checks are at the end of that tutorial.

After you have completed the entire tutorial, you should complete the Review Assignments and Case Problems. They are carefully structured so that you will review what you have learned and then apply your knowledge to new situations.

What if I can't remember how to do something?

You should refer to the Task Reference at the end of the book; it summarizes how to accomplish tasks using the most efficient method.

Before you begin the tutorials, you should know the basics about your computer's operating system. You should also know how to use the menus, dialog boxes, Help system, and My Computer.

How can I prepare for MOUS Certification?

The Microsoft Office User Specialist (MOUS) logo on the cover of this book indicates that Microsoft has approved it as a study guide for the Excel 2000 MOUS Expert exam. At the back of this text, you'll see a chart that outlines the specific Microsoft certification skills for Excel 2000 that are covered in the tutorials. You'll need to learn these skills if you're interested in taking a MOUS exam. If you decide to take a MOUS exam, or if you just want to study a specific skill, this chart will give you an easy reference to the page number on which the skill is covered. To learn more about the MOUS certification program refer to the preface in the front of the book or go to http://www.mous.net.

Now that you've read the Tutorial Tips, you are ready to begin.

New Perspectives on

MICROSOFT® WINDOWS® 98

Read This Before You Begin

To the Student

Make Student Disk Program

To complete the Level I tutorials, Tutorial Assignments, and Projects, you need 2 Student Disks. Your instructor will either provide you with Student Disks or ask you to make your own.

If you are making your own Student Disks you will need 2 blank, formatted high-density disks and access to the Make Student Disk program. If you wish to install the Make Student Disk program to your home computer, you can obtain it from your instructor or from the Web. To download the Make Student Disk program from the Web, go to www.course.com, click Data Disks, and follow the instructions on the screen.

To install the Make Student Disk program, select and click the file you just downloaded from www.course.com, 5446-0.exe. Follow the on-screen instructions to complete the installation. If you have any trouble installing or obtaining the Make Student Disk program, ask your instructor or technical support person for assistance.

Once you have obtained and installed the Make Student Disk program, you can use it to create your student disks according to the steps in the tutorials.

Course Labs

The Level I tutorials in this book feature 3 interactive Course Labs to help you understand selected computer concepts. There are Lab Assignments at the end of Tutorials 1 and 2 that relate to these Labs. To start a Lab, click the **Start** button on the Windows 98 Taskbar, point to **Programs**, point to **Course Labs**, point to **New Perspectives Course Labs**, and click the name of the Lab you want to use.

Using Your Own Computer

If you are going to work through this book using your own computer, you need:

Computer System Microsoft Windows 98 must be installed on a local hard drive or on a network drive.

Student Disks You will not be able to complete the tutorials or exercises in this book using your own computer until you have your Student Disks. See "Make Student Disk Program" above for details on obtaining your student disks.

Course Labs See your instructor or technical support person to obtain the Course Lab software for use on your own computer.

Visit Our World Wide Web Site

Additional materials designed especially for you are available on the World Wide Web. Go to http://www.course.com.

To the Instructor

The Make Student Disk Program and Course Labs for this title are available on the Instructor's Resource Kit for this title. Follow the instructions in the Help file on the CD-ROM to install the programs to your network or standalone computer. For information on using the Make Student Disk Program or the Course Labs, see the "To the Student" section above. Students will be switching the default installation settings to Web style in Tutorial 2. You are granted a license to copy the Student Files and Course Labs to any computer or computer network used by students who have purchased this book.

OBJECTIVES

In this tutorial you will:

- Start and shut down Windows 98
- Identify the objects on the Windows 98 desktop
- Practice mouse functions
- Run software programs and switch between them
- Identify and use the controls in a window
- Use Windows 98 controls such as menus, toolbars, list boxes, scroll bars, option buttons, tabs, and check boxes
- Explore the Windows 98 Help system

LABS

Using a Keyboard

Using a Mouse

EXPLORING THE BASICS

Investigating the Windows 98 Operating System

CASE

Your First Day on the Computer

You walk into the computer lab and sit down at a desk. There's a computer in front of you, and you find yourself staring dubiously at the screen. Where to start? As if in answer to your question, your friend Steve Laslow appears.

"You start with the operating system," says Steve. Noticing your puzzled look, Steve explains that the **operating system** is software that helps the computer carry out operating tasks such as displaying information on the computer screen and saving data on your disks. Your computer uses the **Microsoft Windows 98** operating system—Windows 98, for short.

Steve tells you that Windows 98 has a "gooey" or **graphical user interface (GUI)**, which uses pictures of familiar objects, such as file folders and documents, to represent a desktop on your screen. Microsoft Windows 98 gets its name from the rectangular work areas, called "windows," that appear on your screen.

Steve explains that much of the software available for Windows 98 has a standard graphical user interface. This means that once you have learned how to use one Windows software package, such as word-processing software, you are well on your way to understanding how to use other Windows software. Windows 98 lets you use more than one software package at a time, so you can easily switch between your word-processing software and your appointment book software, for example. Finally, Windows 98 makes it very easy to access the **Internet**, the worldwide collection of computers connected to one another to enable communication. All in all, Windows 98 makes your computer an effective and easy-to-use productivity tool.

Steve recommends that you get started right away by using some tutorials that will teach you the skills essential for using Microsoft Windows 98. He hands you a book and assures you that everything on your computer system is set up and ready to go.

SESSION 1.1

In this session, in addition to learning basic Windows terminology, you will learn how to use a pointing device, how to start and stop a program, and how to use more than one program at a time.

Starting Windows 98

Using a Keyboard

Windows 98 automatically starts when you turn on the computer. Depending on the way your computer is set up, you might be asked to enter your username and password.

To start Windows 98:

1. Turn on your computer.

TROUBLE? If prompted to do so, type your assigned username and press the Tab key. Then type your password and press the Enter key to continue.

TROUBLE? If this is the first time you have started your computer with Windows 98, messages might appear on your screen informing you that Windows is setting up components of your computer. If the Welcome to Windows 98 box appears, press and hold down the Alt key on your keyboard and then, while you hold down the Alt key, press the F4 key. The box closes.

After a moment, Windows 98 starts.

The Windows 98 Desktop

In Windows terminology, the area displayed on your screen represents a **desktop**—a workspace for projects and the tools needed to manipulate those projects. When you first start a computer, it uses **default** settings, those preset by the operating system. The default desktop, for example, has a plain teal background. However, Microsoft designed Windows 98 so that you can easily change the appearance of the desktop. You can, for example, add color, patterns, images, and text to the desktop background.

Many institutions design customized desktops for their computers. Figure 1-1 shows the default Windows 98 desktop and two other examples of desktops, one designed for a business, North Pole Novelties, and one designed for a school, the University of Colorado. Although your desktop might not look exactly like any of the examples in Figure 1-1, you should be able to locate objects on your screen similar to those in Figure 1-1. Look at your screen display and locate the objects labeled in Figure 1-1. The objects on your screen might appear larger or smaller than those in Figure 1-1, depending on your monitor's settings.

Figure 1-1 THE WINDOWS 98 DESKTOP

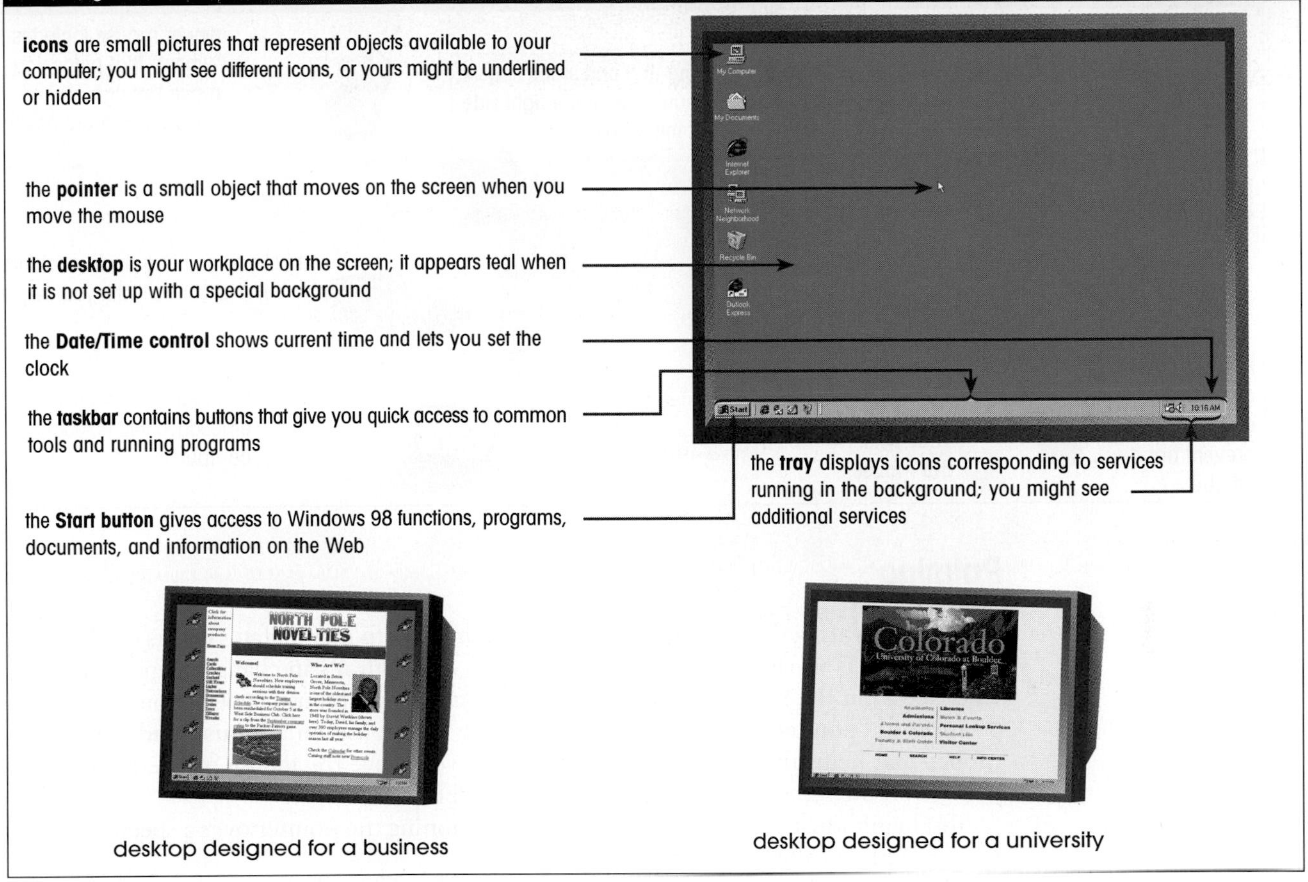
icons are small pictures that represent objects available to your computer; you might see different icons, or yours might be underlined or hidden
the **pointer** is a small object that moves on the screen when you move the mouse
the **desktop** is your workplace on the screen; it appears teal when it is not set up with a special background
the **Date/Time control** shows current time and lets you set the clock
the **taskbar** contains buttons that give you quick access to common tools and running programs
the **Start button** gives access to Windows 98 functions, programs, documents, and information on the Web
the **tray** displays icons corresponding to services running in the background; you might see additional services
My Computer
My Documents
Internet Explorer
Network Neighborhood
Recycle Bin
Outlook Express
Start
10:16 AM
NORTH POLE NOVELTIES
Colorado
University of Colorado at Boulder
desktop designed for a business
desktop designed for a university

If the screen goes blank or starts to display a moving design, press any key to restore the Windows 98 desktop.

Using a Pointing Device

Using a Mouse

A **pointing device** helps you interact with objects on the screen. Pointing devices come in many shapes and sizes; some are designed to ensure that your hand won't suffer fatigue while using them. Some are directly attached to your computer via a cable, whereas others function like a TV remote control and allow you to access your computer without being right next to it. Figure 1-2 shows examples of common pointing devices.

The most common pointing device is called a **mouse**, so this book uses that term. If you are using a different pointing device, such as a trackball, substitute that device whenever you see the term "mouse." In Windows 98 you need to know how to use the mouse to manipulate the objects on the screen. In this session you will learn about pointing and clicking. In Session 1.2 you will learn how to use the mouse to drag objects.

You can also interact with objects by using the keyboard; however, the mouse is more convenient for most tasks, so the tutorials in this book assume you are using one.

Figure 1-2 POINTING DEVICES

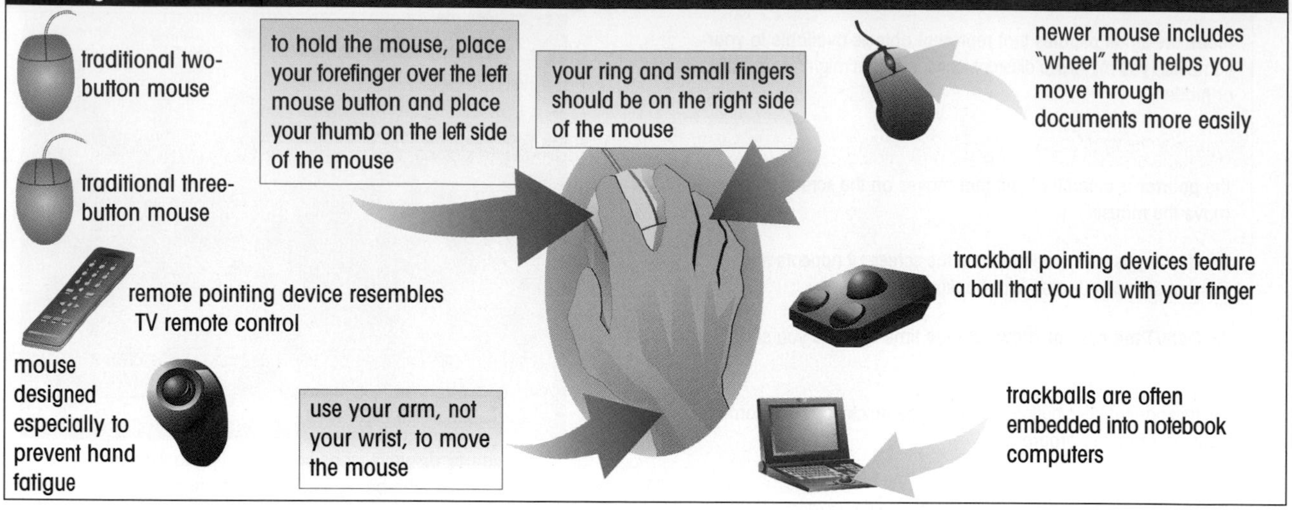
traditional two-button mouse
traditional three-button mouse
remote pointing device resembles TV remote control
mouse designed especially to prevent hand fatigue
to hold the mouse, place your forefinger over the left mouse button and place your thumb on the left side of the mouse
your ring and small fingers should be on the right side of the mouse
use your arm, not your wrist, to move the mouse
newer mouse includes "wheel" that helps you move through documents more easily
trackball pointing devices feature a ball that you roll with your finger
trackballs are often embedded into notebook computers

Pointing

You use a pointing device to move the pointer, in order to manipulate objects on the desktop. The pointer is usually shaped like an arrow, although it can change shape depending on where it is on the screen. How skilled you are in using a mouse depends on your ability to position the pointer. Most computer users place the mouse on a **mouse pad**, a flat piece of rubber that helps the mouse move smoothly. As you move the mouse on the mouse pad, the pointer on the screen moves in a corresponding direction.

You begin most Windows operations by positioning the pointer over a specific part of the screen. This is called **pointing**.

To move the pointer:

1. Position your right index finger over the left mouse button, as shown in Figure 1-2. Lightly grasp the sides of the mouse with your thumb and little fingers.

   TROUBLE? If you want to use the mouse with your left hand, ask your instructor or technical support person to help you use the Control Panel to swap the functions of the left and right mouse buttons. Be sure to find out how to change back to the right-handed mouse setting, so that you can reset the mouse each time you are finished in the lab.

2. Place the mouse on the mouse pad and then move the mouse. Watch the movement of the pointer.

   TROUBLE? If you run out of room to move your mouse, lift the mouse and place it in the middle of the mouse pad. Notice that the pointer does not move when the mouse is not in contact with the mouse pad.

When you position the mouse pointer over certain objects, such as the objects on the taskbar, a "tip" appears. These "tips" are called **ToolTips**, and they tell you the purpose or function of an object.

To view ToolTips:

1. Use the mouse to point to the **Start** button Start. After a few seconds, you see the tip "Click here to begin," as shown in Figure 1-3.

Figure 1-3 VIEWING TOOLTIPS

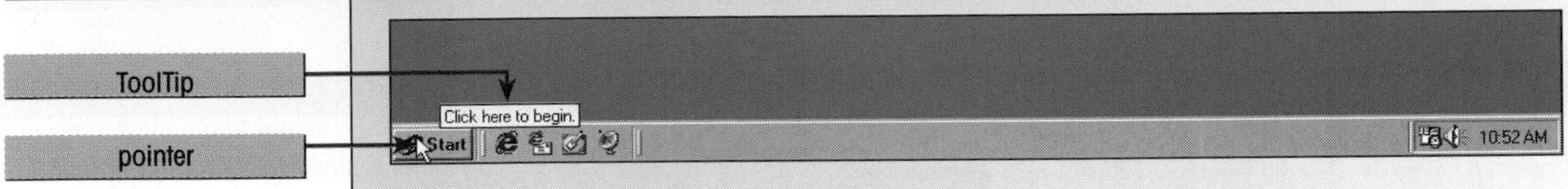

2. Point to the time on the right end of the taskbar. Notice that today's date (or the date to which your computer's time clock is set) appears.

Clicking

Clicking is when you press a mouse button and immediately release it. Clicking sends a signal to your computer that you want to perform an action on the object you click. In Windows 98 you can click using both the left and right mouse buttons, but most actions are performed using the left mouse button. If you are told to click an object, click it with the left mouse button, unless instructed otherwise.

When you click the Start button, the Start menu appears. A **menu** is a list of options that helps you work with software. The **Start menu** provides you with access to programs, documents, and much more. Try clicking the Start button to open the Start menu.

To open the Start menu:

1. Point to the **Start** button Start.

2. Click the left mouse button. An arrow ▶ following an option on the Start menu indicates that you can view additional choices by navigating a **submenu**, a menu extending from the main menu. See Figure 1-4.

Figure 1-4 START MENU

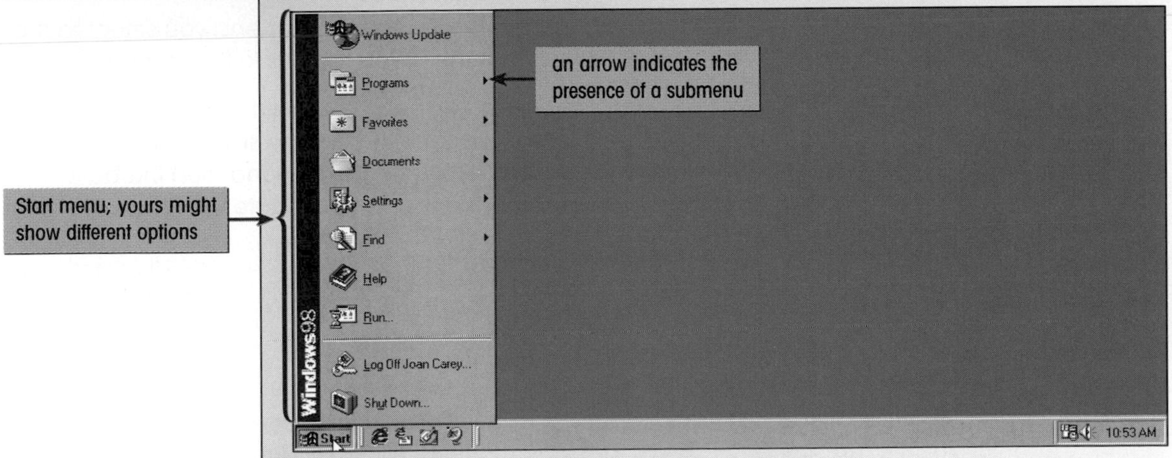

3. Click Start again to close the Start menu.

Next you'll learn how to open a submenu by selecting it.

Selecting

In Windows 98, pointing and clicking are often used to **select** an object, in other words, to choose it as the object you want to work with. Windows 98 shows you which object is selected by highlighting it, usually by changing the object's color, putting a box around it, or making the object appear to be pushed in, as shown in Figure 1-5.

Figure 1-5 SELECTED OBJECTS

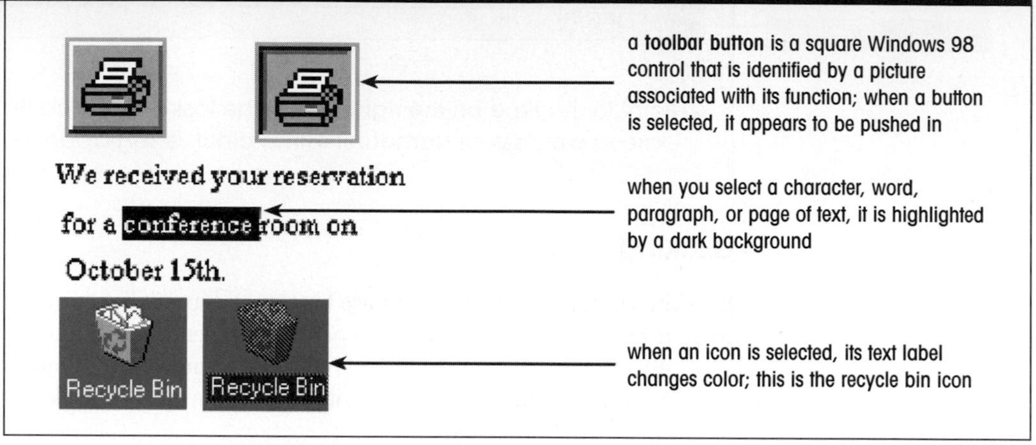
We received your reservation
for a conference room on
October 15th.
Recycle Bin
Recycle Bin
a **toolbar button** is a square Windows 98 control that is identified by a picture associated with its function; when a button is selected, it appears to be pushed in
when you select a character, word, paragraph, or page of text, it is highlighted by a dark background
when an icon is selected, its text label changes color; this is the recycle bin icon

In Windows 98, depending on your computer's settings, some objects are selected when you simply point to them, others when you click them. Practice selecting the Programs option on the Start menu to open the Programs submenu.

To select an option on a menu:

1. Click the **Start** button and notice how it appears to be pushed in, indicating it is selected.
2. Point to the **Programs** option. After a short pause, the Programs submenu opens, and the Programs option is highlighted to indicate it is selected. See Figure 1-6.

   TROUBLE? If a submenu other than the Programs menu opens, you selected the wrong option. Move the mouse so that the pointer points to Programs.

   TROUBLE? If the Programs option doesn't appear, your Start menu might have too many options to fit on the screen. If that is the case, a small arrow appears at the top or bottom of the Start menu. Click first the top and then the bottom arrow to view additional Start menu options until you locate the Programs menu option, and then point to it.

Figure 1-6 PROGRAMS SUBMENU

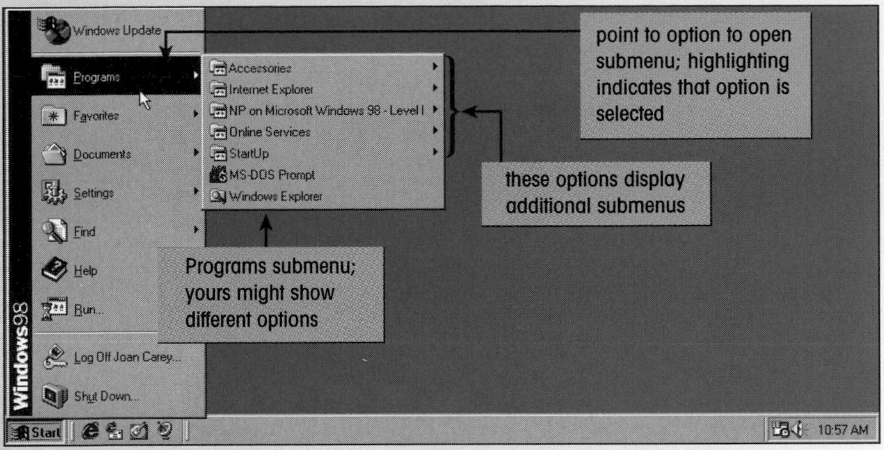

3. Now close the Start menu by clicking Start again.

You return to the desktop.

Right-Clicking

Pointing devices were originally designed with a single button, so the term "clicking" had only one meaning: you pressed that button. Innovations in technology, however, led to the addition of a second and even a third button (and more recently, options such as a wheel) that expanded the pointing device's capability. More recent software—especially that designed for Windows 98—takes advantage of additional buttons, especially the right button. However, the term "clicking" continues to refer to the left button; clicking an object with the *right* button is called **right-clicking**.

In Windows 98, right-clicking both selects an object and opens its **shortcut menu**, a list of options directly related to the object you right-clicked. You can right-click practically any object—the Start button, a desktop icon, the taskbar, and even the desktop itself—to view options associated with that object. For example, the first desktop shown in Figure 1-7 illustrates what happens when you click the Start button with the left mouse button to open the Start menu. Clicking the Start button with the right button, however, opens the Start button's shortcut menu, as shown in the second desktop.

Figure 1-7 CLICKING WITH THE LEFT AND RIGHT MOUSE BUTTONS

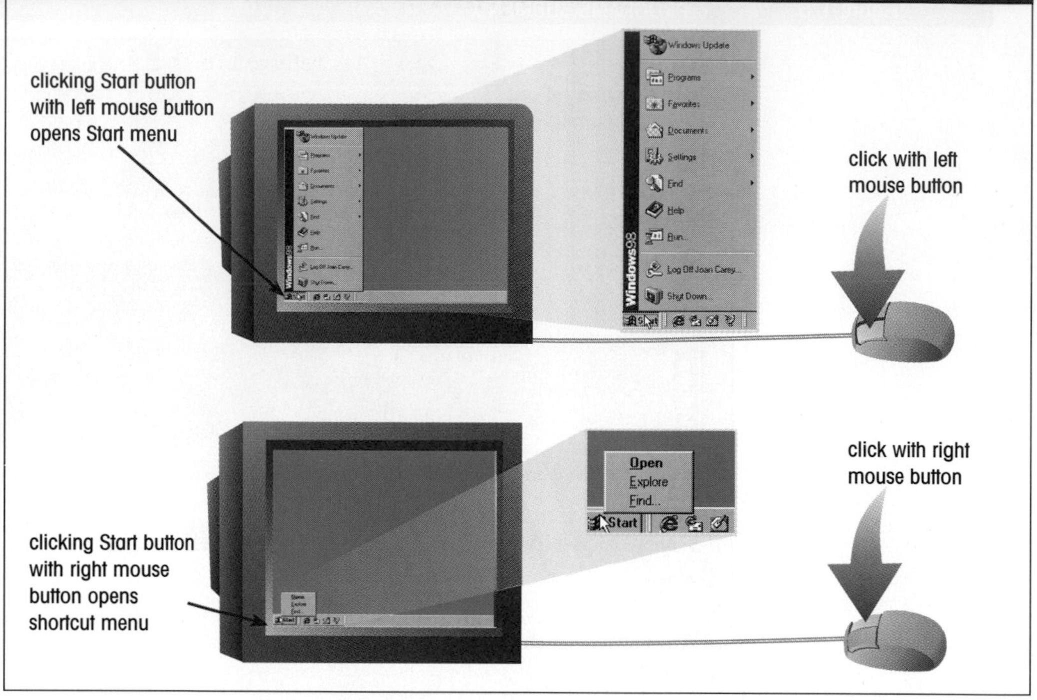

Try using right-clicking to open the shortcut menu for the Start button.

To right-click an object:

1. Position the pointer over the Start button.
2. Right-click the **Start** button [Start]. The shortcut menu that opens offers a list of options available to the Start button.

   TROUBLE? If you are using a trackball or a mouse with three buttons or a wheel, make sure you click the button on the far right, not the one in the middle.

   TROUBLE? If your menu looks slightly different from the one in Figure 1-8, don't worry. Computers with different software often have different options.

Figure 1-8 START BUTTON SHORTCUT MENU

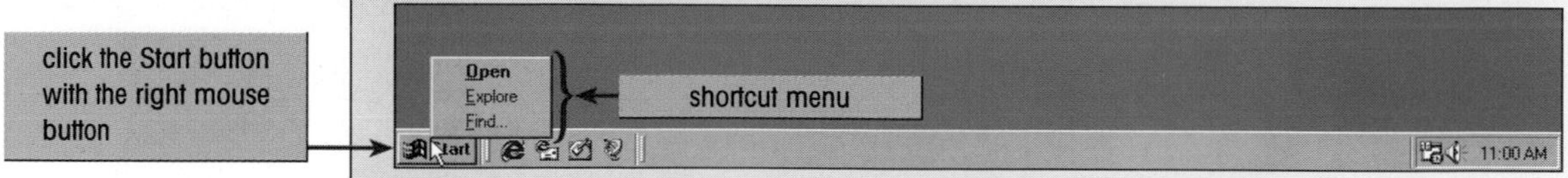

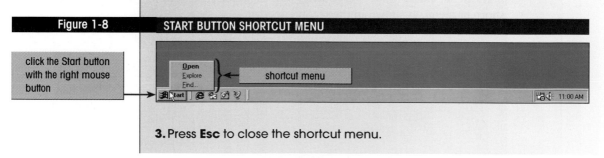

3. Press **Esc** to close the shortcut menu.

You again return to the desktop.

Starting and Closing a Program

The software you use is sometimes referred to as a **program** or an **application**. To use a program, such as a word-processing program, you must first start it. With Windows 98 you start a program by clicking the Start button.

The Reference Window below explains how to start a program. Don't do the steps in the Reference Window now; they are for your later reference.

REFERENCE WINDOW RW

Starting a Program

- Click the Start button, and point to Programs.
- If necessary, point to the submenu option that contains your program, then click the name of the program you want to run.

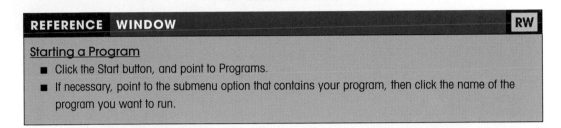

Windows 98 includes an easy-to-use word-processing program called WordPad. Suppose you want to start the WordPad program and use it to write a letter or report. You open Windows 98 programs from the Start menu. Programs are usually located on the Programs submenu or on one of its submenus. To start WordPad, for example, you navigate the Programs and Accessories submenus.

To start the WordPad program from the Start menu:

1. Click the **Start** button Start to open the Start menu.
2. Point to **Programs**. The Programs submenu appears.
3. Point to **Accessories**. Another submenu appears. Figure 1-9 shows the open menus.

   TROUBLE? If a different menu opens, you might have moved the mouse diagonally so that a different submenu opened. Move the pointer to the right across the Programs option, and then move it up or down to point to Accessories. Once you're more comfortable moving the mouse, you'll find that you can eliminate this problem by moving the mouse quickly.

Figure 1-9 START MENU

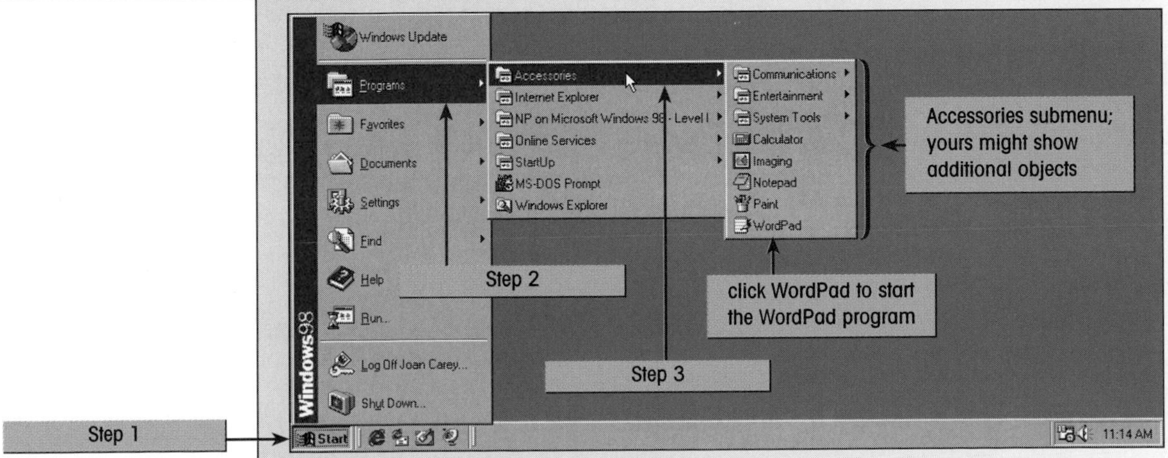

4. Click **WordPad**. The WordPad program opens, as shown in Figure 1-10. If the WordPad window does not fill the entire screen, don't worry. You will learn how to manipulate windows in Session 1.2.

Figure 1-10 THE WORDPAD PROGRAM

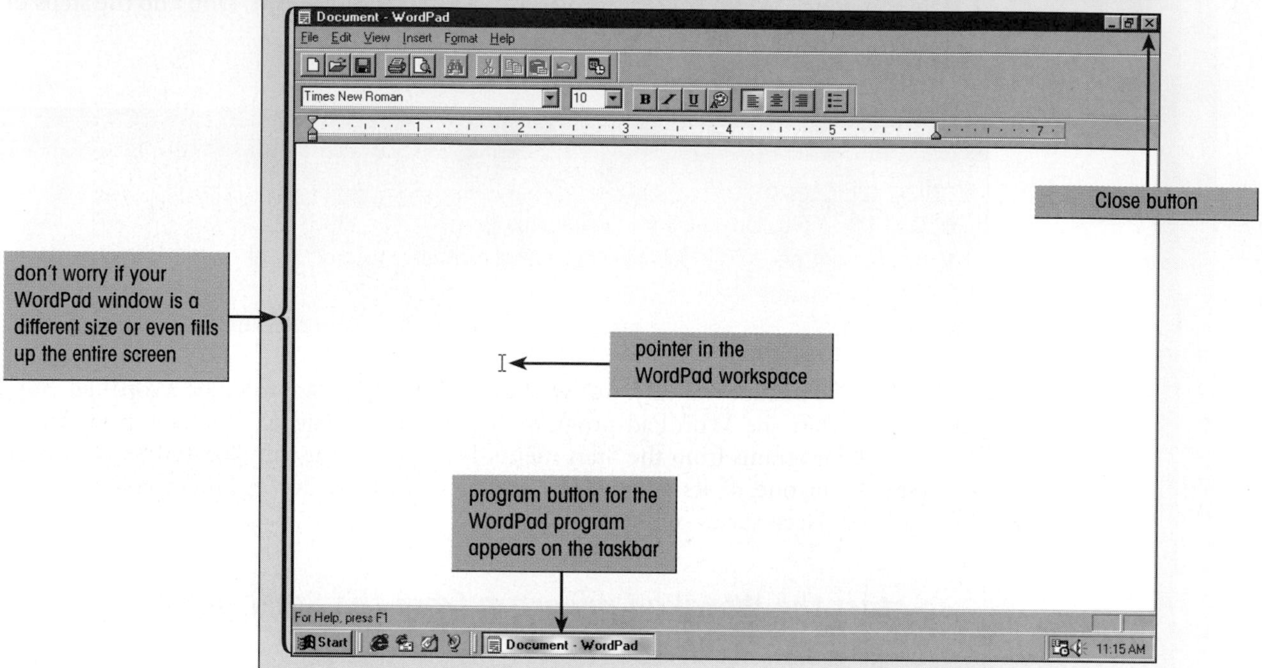

When a program is started, it is said to be **running**. A program button appears on the taskbar. **Program buttons** give you access to the programs running on the desktop.

When you are finished using a program, the easiest way to close it is to click the Close button ☒.

To exit the WordPad program:

1. Click the **Close** button ☒. See Figure 1-10. You return to the Windows 98 desktop.

Running Multiple Programs

One of the most useful features of Windows 98 is its ability to run multiple programs at the same time. This feature, known as **multitasking**, allows you to work on more than one project at a time and to switch quickly between projects. For example, you can start WordPad and leave it running while you then start the Paint program.

To run WordPad and Paint at the same time:

1. Start WordPad, then click the **Start** button [Start] again.
2. Point to **Programs**, then point to **Accessories**.

3. Click **Paint**. The Paint program appears, as shown in Figure 1-11. Now two programs are running at the same time.

Figure 1-11 THE PAINT PROGRAM

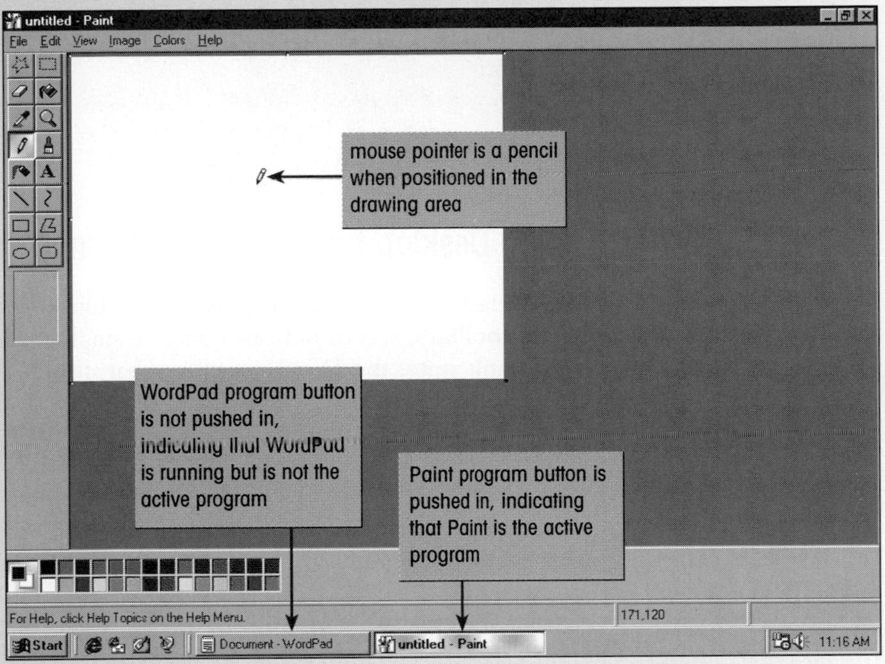

TROUBLE? If the Paint program does not fill the entire screen, don't worry. You will learn how to manipulate windows in Session 1.2.

What happened to WordPad? The WordPad program button is still on the taskbar, so even if you can't see it, WordPad is still running. You can imagine that it is stacked behind the Paint program, as shown in Figure 1-12.

Figure 1-12 PROJECTS STACKED ON A DESK

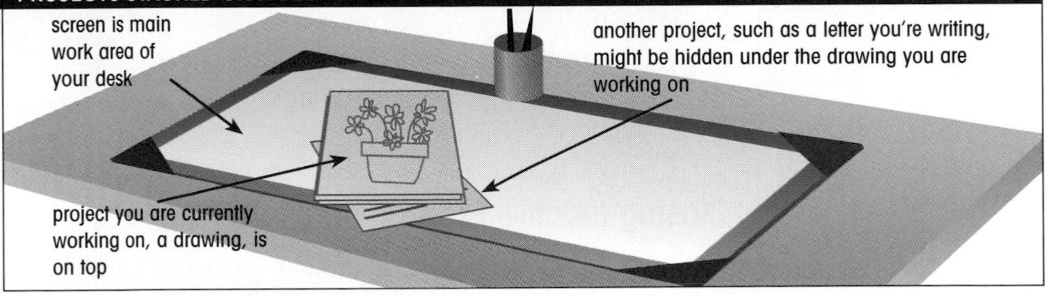

Switching Between Programs

Although Windows 98 allows you to run more than one program, only one program at a time is active. The **active** program is the program with which you are currently working. The easiest way to switch between programs is to use the buttons on the taskbar.

To switch between WordPad and Paint:

1. Click the button labeled **Document - WordPad** on the taskbar. The Document - WordPad button now looks as if it has been pushed in, to indicate that it is the active program, and WordPad moves to the front.
2. Next, click the button labeled **untitled - Paint** on the taskbar to switch to the Paint program.

The Paint program is again the active program.

Accessing the Desktop from the Quick Launch Toolbar

The Windows 98 taskbar, as you've seen, displays buttons for programs currently running. It also can contain **toolbars**, sets of buttons that give single-click access to programs or documents. In its default state, the Windows 98 taskbar displays the **Quick Launch toolbar**, which gives quick access to Web programs and to the desktop. Your taskbar might contain additional toolbars, or none at all.

When you are running more than one program but you want to return to the desktop, perhaps to use one of the desktop icons such as My Computer, you can do so by using one of the Quick Launch toolbar buttons. Clicking the Show Desktop button returns you to the desktop. The open programs are not closed; they are simply inactive.

To return to the desktop:

1. Click the **Show Desktop** button on the Quick Launch toolbar. The desktop appears, and both the Paint and WordPad programs are temporarily inactive. See Figure 1-13.

   TROUBLE? If the Quick Launch toolbar doesn't appear on your taskbar, right-click the taskbar, point to Toolbars, and then click Quick Launch and try Step 1 again.

Figure 1-13 ACCESSING THE DESKTOP

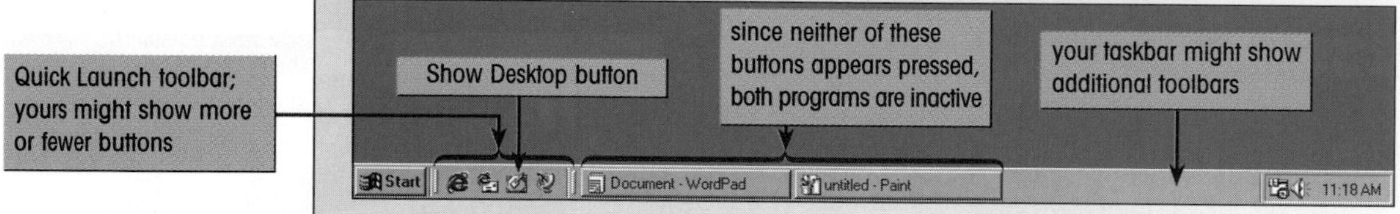

Closing Inactive Programs from the Taskbar

It is good practice to close each program when you are finished using it. Each program uses computer resources, such as memory, so Windows 98 works more efficiently when only the programs you need are open. You've already seen how to close an open program using the Close button. You can also close a program, whether active or inactive, by using the shortcut menu associated with the program button on the taskbar.

To close WordPad and Paint using the program button shortcut menus:

1. Right-click the **untitled - Paint** button on the taskbar. To right-click something, remember that you click it with the right mouse button. The shortcut menu for that program button opens. See Figure 1-14.

Figure 1-14 PROGRAM BUTTON SHORTCUT MENU

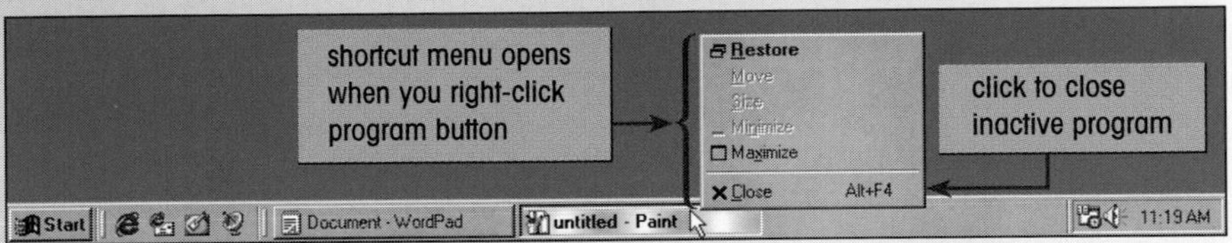

2. Click **Close**. The button labeled "untitled – Paint" disappears from the taskbar, and the Paint program closes.
3. Right-click the **Document – WordPad** button on the taskbar, and then click **Close**. The WordPad button disappears from the taskbar.

Shutting Down Windows 98

It is very important to shut down Windows 98 before you turn off the computer. If you turn off your computer without correctly shutting down, you might lose data and damage your files.

You should typically use the "Shut down" option when you want to turn off your computer. However, your school might prefer that you select the Log Off option on the Start menu. This option logs you out of Windows 98, leaves the computer turned on, and allows another user to log on without restarting the computer. Check with your instructor or technical support person for the preferred method at your school's computer lab.

To shut down Windows 98:

1. Click the **Start** button Start on the taskbar to display the Start menu.
2. Click the **Shut Down** menu option. A box titled "Shut Down Windows" opens.

   TROUBLE? If you can't see the Shut Down menu option, your Start menu has more options than your screen can display. A small arrow appears at the bottom of the Start menu. Click this button until the Shut Down menu option appears, and then click Shut Down.

   TROUBLE? If you are supposed to log off rather than shut down, click the Log Off option instead and follow your school's logoff procedure.

3. Make sure the **Shut down** option is preceded by a small black bullet. See Figure 1-15.

   TROUBLE? If your Shut down option is not preceded by a small black bullet, point to the circle preceding the Shut down option and click it. A small black bullet appears in the circle, indicating that Windows 98 will perform the Shut down option. Your Shut Down Windows dialog box might show additional options, such as Stand by.

Figure 1-15 SHUTTING DOWN

if the Shut down option is not selected, click the circle to select it

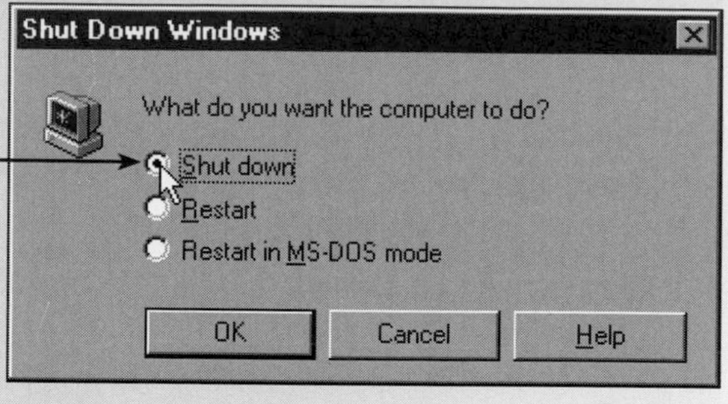

4. Click the **OK** button.
5. Click the **Yes** button if you are asked if you are sure you want to shut down.
6. Wait until you see a message indicating it is safe to turn off your computer. If your lab staff has requested you to switch off your computer after shutting down, do so now. Otherwise leave the computer running. Some computers turn themselves off automatically.

QUICK CHECK

1. What is the purpose of the taskbar?
2. The ______________ feature of Windows 98 allows you to run more than one program at a time.
3. The ______________ is a list of options that provides you with access to programs, documents, submenus, and more.
4. What should you do if you are trying to move the pointer to the left edge of your screen, but your mouse bumps into the keyboard?
5. Even if you can't see an open program on your desktop, the program might be running. How can you tell if a program is running?
6. Why is it good practice to close each program when you are finished using it?
7. Why should you shut down Windows 98 before you turn off your computer?

SESSION 1.2

In this session you will learn how to use many of the Windows 98 controls to manipulate windows and programs. You will also learn how to change the size and shape of a window; how to move a window; and how to use menus, dialog boxes, tabs, buttons, and lists to specify how you want a program to carry out a task.

Anatomy of a Window

When you run a program in Windows 98, it appears in a window. A **window** is a rectangular area of the screen that contains a program or data. Windows, spelled with an uppercase "W," is the name of the Microsoft operating system. The word "window" with a lowercase "w" refers to one of the rectangular areas on the screen. A window also contains controls for manipulating the window and for using the program. Figure 1-16 describes the controls you are likely to see in most windows.

Figure 1-16 WINDOW CONTROLS

CONTROL	DESCRIPTION
Menu bar	Contains the titles of menus, such as File, Edit, and Help
Pointer	Lets you manipulate window objects
Program button	Appears on the taskbar to indicate that a program is running on the desktop; appears pressed when program is active and not pressed when program is inactive
Sizing buttons	Let you enlarge, shrink, or close a window
Status bar	Provides you with messages relevant to the task you are performing
Title bar	Contains the window title and basic window control buttons
Toolbar	Contains buttons that provide you with shortcuts to common menu commands
Window title	Identifies the program and document contained in the window
Workspace	Part of the window you use to enter your work—to enter text, draw pictures, set up calculations, and so on

WordPad is a good example of a typical window, so try starting WordPad and identifying these controls in the WordPad window.

To look at window controls:

1. Make sure Windows 98 is running and you are at the Windows 98 desktop.
2. Start WordPad.

   TROUBLE? To start WordPad, click the Start button, point to Programs, point to Accessories, and then click WordPad.

3. On your screen, identify the controls labeled in Figure 1-17. Don't worry if your window fills the entire screen or is a different size. You'll learn to change window size shortly.

Figure 1-17 WORDPAD WINDOW CONTROLS

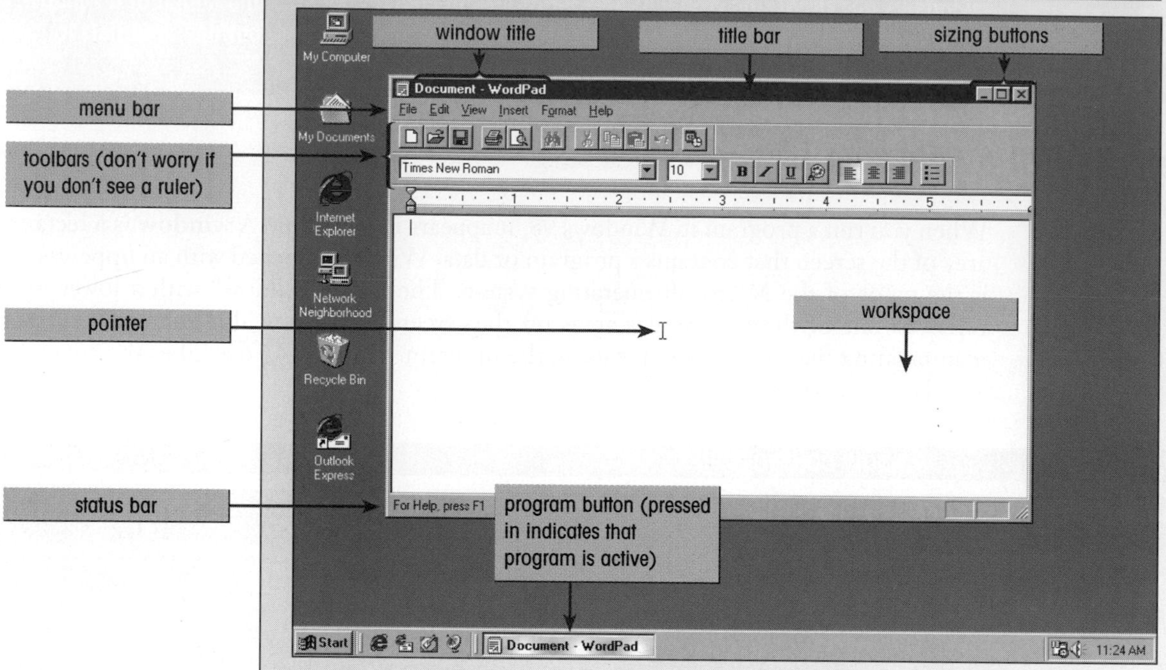

Manipulating a Window

There are three buttons located on the right side of the title bar. You are already familiar with the Close button. The Minimize button hides the window so that only its program button is visible on the taskbar. The other button either maximizes the window or restores it to a predefined size. Figure 1-18 shows how these buttons work.

Minimizing a Window

The Minimize button hides a window so that only the button on the taskbar remains visible. You can use the Minimize button when you want to temporarily hide a window but keep the program running.

To minimize the WordPad window:

1. Click the **Minimize** button. The WordPad window shrinks so that only the Document - WordPad button on the taskbar is visible.

   TROUBLE? If you accidentally clicked the Close button and closed the window, use the Start button to start WordPad again.

Figure 1-18 WINDOW BUTTONS

If your screen looks like this...	and you click this button...	your screen will change to this:

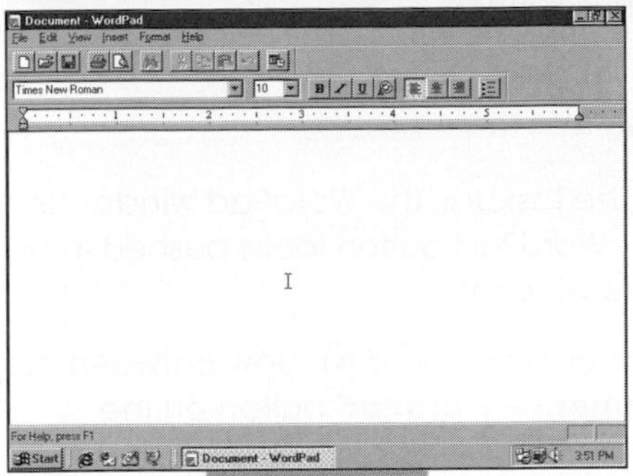

maximized

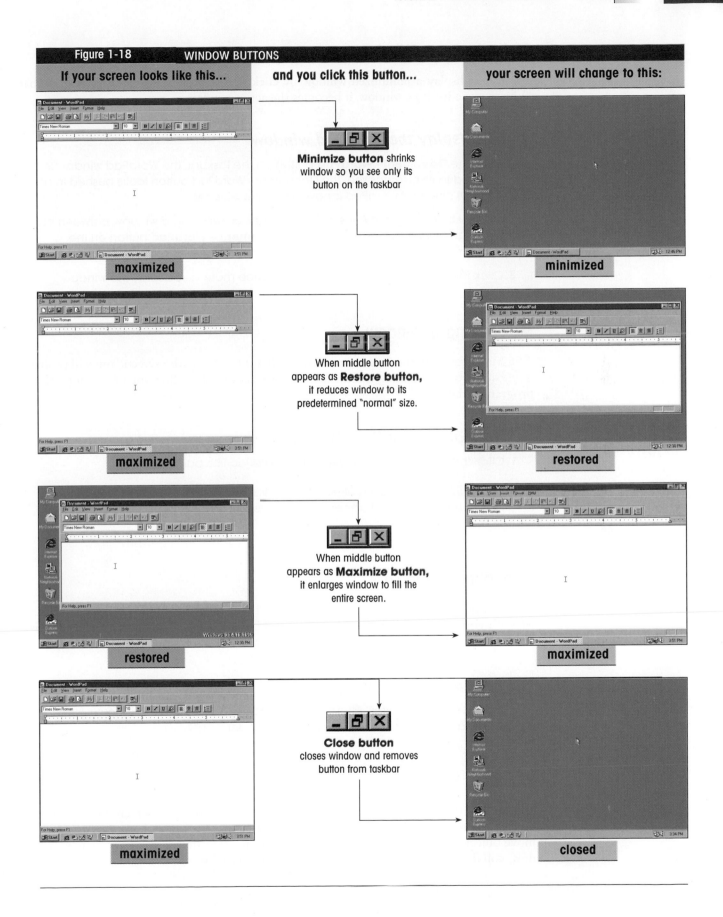

Minimize button shrinks window so you see only its button on the taskbar

minimized

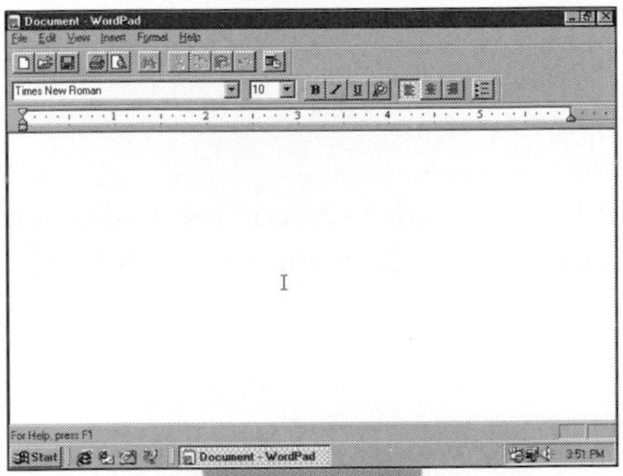

maximized

When middle button appears as **Restore button,** it reduces window to its predetermined "normal" size.

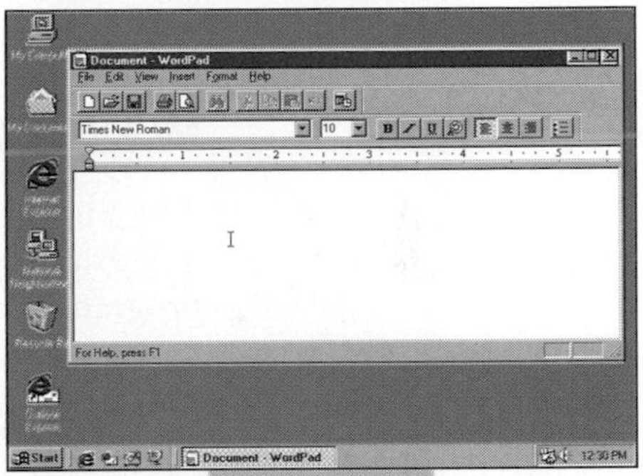

restored

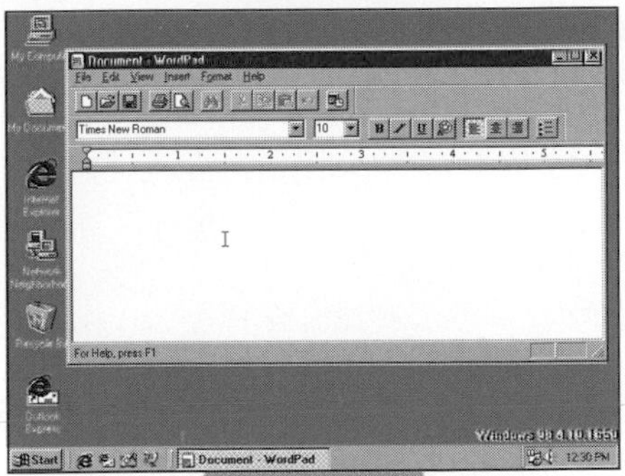

restored

When middle button appears as **Maximize button,** it enlarges window to fill the entire screen.

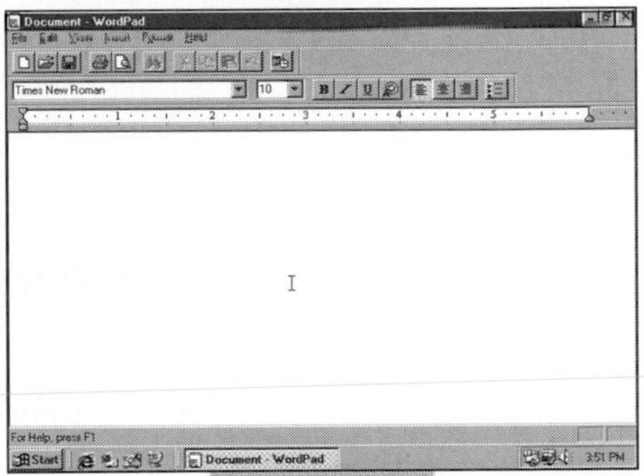

maximized

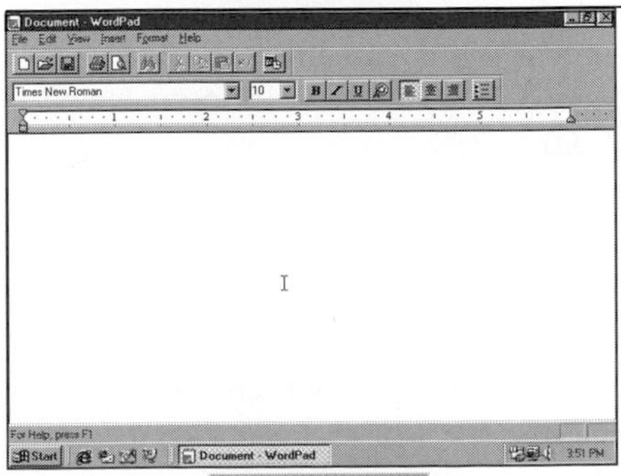

maximized

Close button closes window and removes button from taskbar

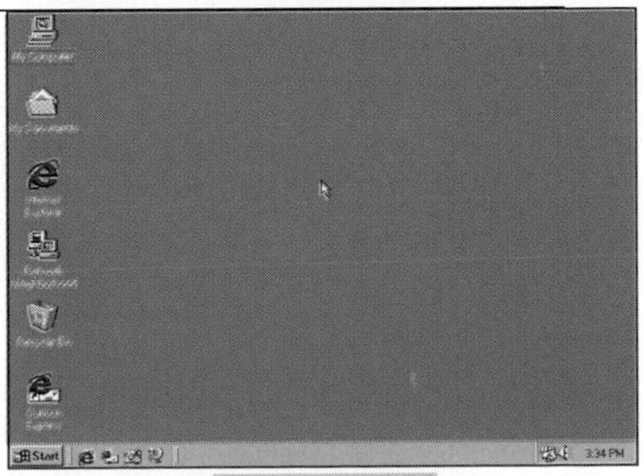

closed

Redisplaying a Window

You can redisplay a minimized window by clicking the program's button on the taskbar. When you redisplay a window, it becomes the active window.

To redisplay the WordPad window:

1. Click the **Document - WordPad** button on the taskbar. The WordPad window is restored to its previous size. The Document - WordPad button looks pushed in as a visual clue that WordPad is now the active window.
2. The taskbar button provides another means of switching a window between its minimized and active state: click the **Document - WordPad** button on the taskbar again to minimize the window.
3. Click the **Document - WordPad** button once more to redisplay the window.

Maximizing a Window

The Maximize button enlarges a window so that it fills the entire screen. You will probably do most of your work using maximized windows because they allow you to see more of your program and data.

To maximize the WordPad window:

1. Click the **Maximize** button on the WordPad title bar.

   TROUBLE? If the window is already maximized, it will fill the entire screen, and the Maximize button won't appear. Instead, you'll see the Restore button. Skip Step 1.

Restoring a Window

The Restore button reduces the window so it is smaller than the entire screen. This is useful if you want to see more than one window at a time. Also, because of its smaller size, you can drag the window to another location on the screen or change its dimensions.

To restore a window:

1. Click the **Restore** button on the WordPad title bar. Notice that once a window is restored, changes to the Maximize button.

Moving a Window

You can use the mouse to move a window to a new position on the screen. When you hold down the mouse button while moving the mouse, you are said to be **dragging**. You can move objects on the screen by dragging them to a new location. If you want to move a window, you drag its title bar. You cannot move a maximized window.

To drag the WordPad window to a new location:

1. Position the mouse pointer on the WordPad window title bar.
2. While you hold down the left mouse button, move the mouse to drag the window. A rectangle representing the window moves as you move the mouse.
3. Position the rectangle anywhere on the screen, then release the left mouse button. The WordPad window appears in the new location.
4. Now drag the WordPad window to the upper-left corner of the screen.

Changing the Size of a Window

You can also use the mouse to change the size of a window. Notice the sizing handle at the lower-right corner of the window. The **sizing handle** provides a visible control for changing the size of a window.

To change the size of the WordPad window:

1. Position the pointer over the sizing handle. The pointer changes to a diagonal arrow ↘.
2. While holding down the mouse button, drag the sizing handle down and to the right.
3. Release the mouse button. Now the window is larger.
4. Practice using the sizing handle to make the WordPad window larger or smaller, and then maximize the WordPad window.

You can also drag the window borders left, right, up, or down to change a window's size.

Using Program Menus

Most Windows programs use menus to provide an easy way for you to select program commands. The menu bar is typically located at the top of the program window and shows the titles of menus such as File, Edit, and Help.

Windows menus are relatively standardized—most Windows programs include similar menu options. It's easy to learn new programs, because you can make a pretty good guess about which menu contains the command you want.

Selecting Commands from a Menu

When you click any menu title, choices for that menu appear below the menu bar. These choices are referred to as **menu options** or **commands**. To select a menu option, you click it. For example, the File menu is a standard feature in most Windows programs and contains the options typically related to working with a file: creating, opening, saving, and printing a file or document.

To select the Print Preview menu option from the File menu:

1. Click **File** in the WordPad menu bar to display the File menu. See Figure 1-19.

TROUBLE? If you open a menu but decide not to select any of the menu options, you can close the menu by clicking its title again.

Figure 1-19 FILE MENU

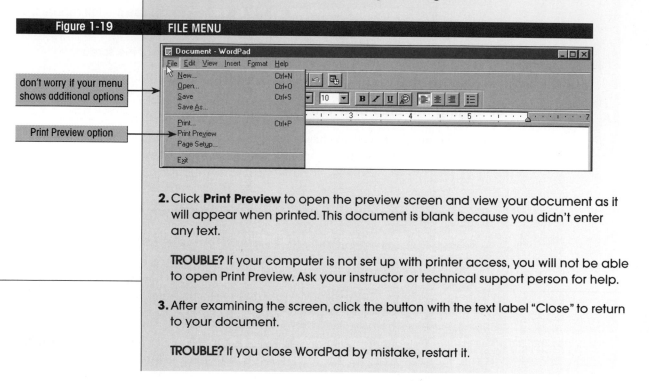

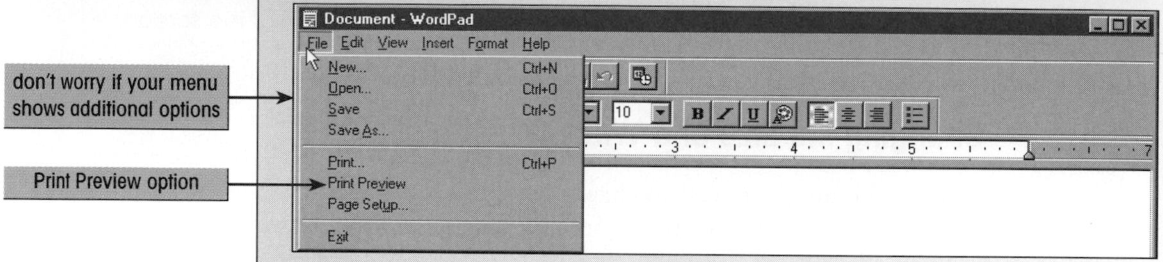

2. Click **Print Preview** to open the preview screen and view your document as it will appear when printed. This document is blank because you didn't enter any text.

TROUBLE? If your computer is not set up with printer access, you will not be able to open Print Preview. Ask your instructor or technical support person for help.

3. After examining the screen, click the button with the text label "Close" to return to your document.

TROUBLE? If you close WordPad by mistake, restart it.

Not all menu options immediately carry out an action—some show submenus or ask you for more information about what you want to do. The menu gives you hints about what to expect when you select an option. These hints are sometimes referred to as **menu conventions**. Figure 1-20 describes the Windows 98 menu conventions.

Figure 1-20 MENU CONVENTIONS

CONVENTION	DESCRIPTION
Check mark	Indicates a toggle, or "on-off" switch (like a light switch) that is either checked (turned on) or not checked (turned off)
Ellipsis	Three dots that indicate you must make additional selections after you select that option. Options without dots do not require additional choices—they take effect as soon as you click them. If an option is followed by an ellipsis, a dialog box opens that allows you to enter specifications for how you want a task carried out
Triangular arrow	Indicates presence of a submenu. When you point at a menu option that has a triangular arrow, a submenu automatically appears
Grayed-out option	Option that is not available. For example, a graphics program might display the Text Toolbar option in gray if there is no text in the graphic to work with
Keyboard shortcut	A key or combination of keys that you can press to activate the menu option without actually opening the menu

Figure 1-21 shows examples of these menu conventions.

Figure 1-21 EXAMPLES OF MENU CONVENTIONS

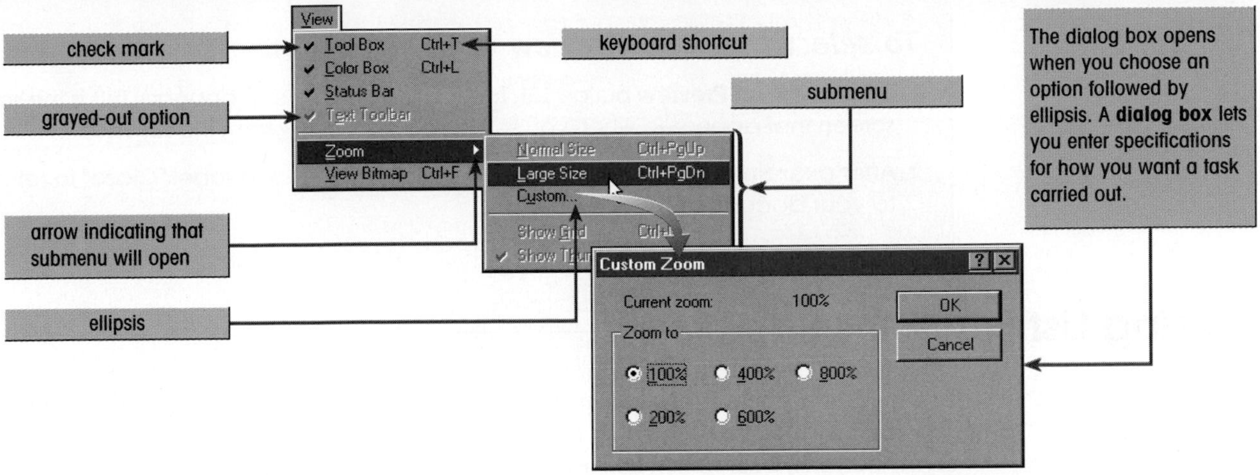

Using Toolbars

A toolbar, as you've seen, contains buttons that provide quick access to important commands. Although you can usually perform all program commands using menus, the toolbar provides convenient one-click access to frequently used commands. For most Windows 98 functions, there is usually more than one way to accomplish a task. To simplify your introduction to Windows 98 in this tutorial, we will usually show you only one method for performing a task. As you become more accomplished at using Windows 98, you can explore alternate methods.

In Session 1.1 you learned that Windows 98 programs include ToolTips, which indicate the purpose and function of a tool. Now is a good time to explore the WordPad toolbar buttons by looking at their ToolTips.

To find out a toolbar button's function:

1. Position the pointer over any button on the toolbar, such as the Print Preview button. After a short pause, the name of the button appears in a box near the button, and a description of the button appears in the status bar just above the Start button. See Figure 1-22.

Figure 1-22 TOOLBAR BUTTON AIDS

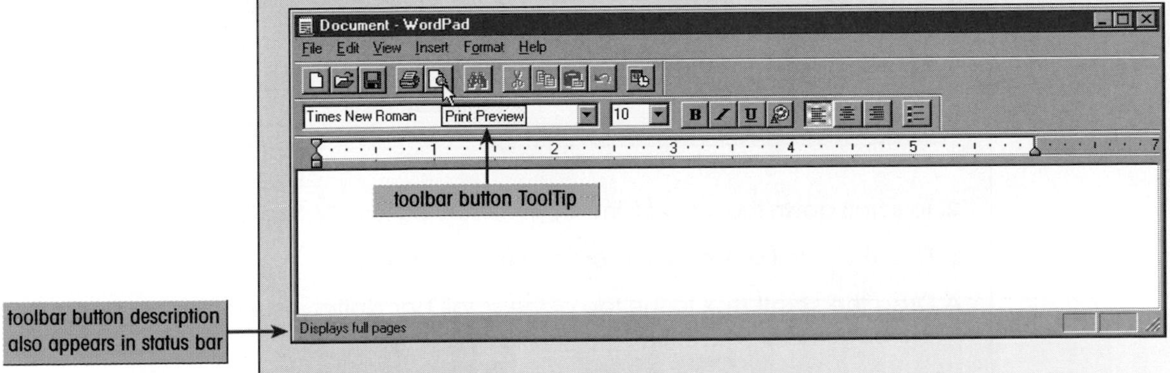

2. Move the pointer to each button on the toolbar to see its name and purpose.

You select a toolbar button by clicking it.

To select the Print Preview toolbar button:

1. Click the **Print Preview** button. The Print Preview screen appears. This is the same screen that appeared when you selected Print Preview from the File menu.
2. After examining the screen, click the button with the text label "Close" to return to your document.

Using List Boxes and Scroll Bars

As you might guess from the name, a **list box** displays a list of choices. In WordPad, date and time formats are shown in the Date/Time list box. List box controls usually include arrow buttons, a scroll bar, and a scroll box, as shown in Figure 1-23.

To use the Date/Time list box:

1. Click the **Date/Time** button to display the Date and Time dialog box. See Figure 1-23.

Figure 1-23 LIST BOX

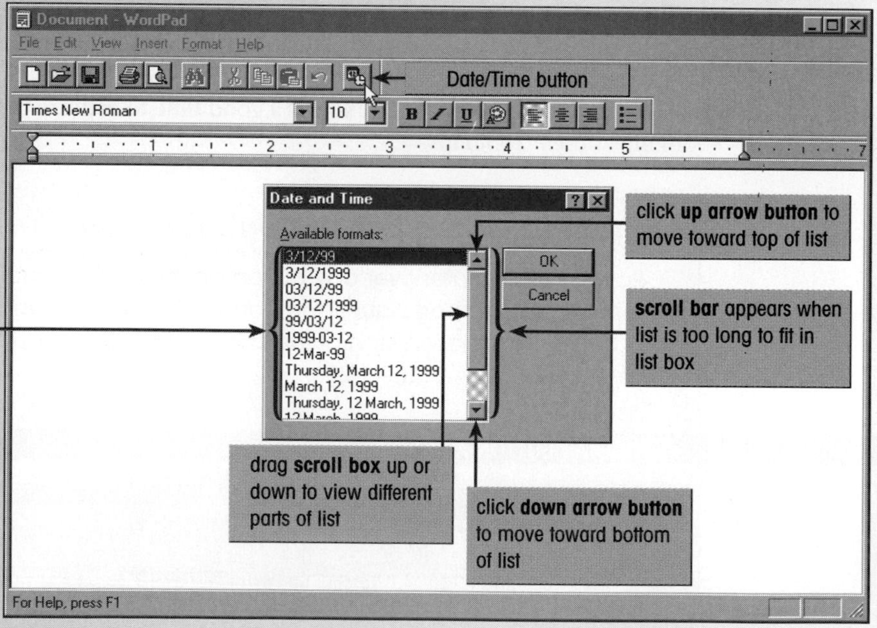

2. To scroll down the list, click the **down arrow** button. See Figure 1-23.
3. Find the scroll box on your screen. See Figure 1-23.
4. Drag the **scroll box** to the top of the scroll bar. Notice how the list scrolls back to the beginning.

TROUBLE? You learned how to drag when you learned to move a window. To drag the scroll box up, point to the scroll box, press and hold down the mouse button, and then move the mouse up.

5. Find a date format similar to "March 12, 1999." Click that date format to select it.

6. Click the **OK** button to close the Date and Time dialog box. This inserts the current date in your document.

You can access some list boxes directly from the toolbar. When a list box is on the toolbar, only the current option appears in the list box. A **list arrow** appears on the right of the box that you can click to view additional options.

To use the Font Size list box:

1. Click the **list arrow** shown in Figure 1-24.

Figure 1-24 FONT SIZE LIST ARROW

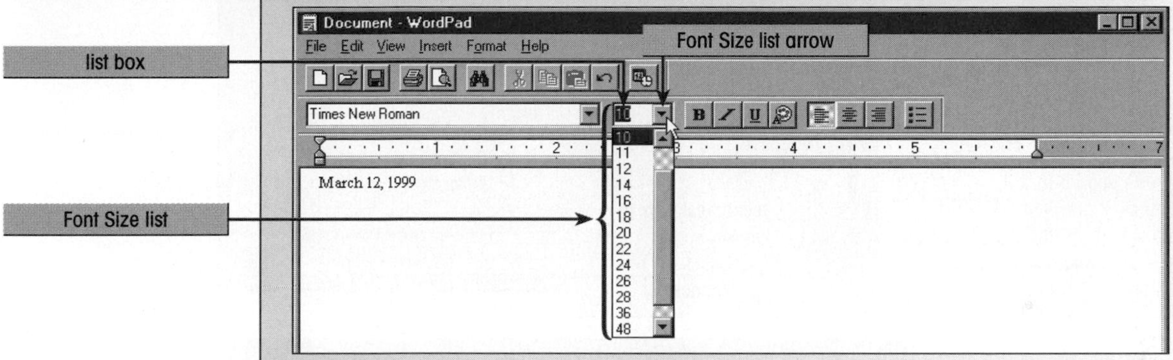

2. Click **18**. The list disappears, and the font size you selected appears in the list box.

3. Type a few characters to test the new font size.

4. Click the **Font Size** list arrow again.

5. Click **12**.

6. Type a few characters to test this type size.

7. Click the **Close** button to close WordPad.

8. When you see the message "Save changes to Document?" click the **No** button.

Using Dialog Box Controls

Recall that when you select a menu option or button followed by an ellipsis, a dialog box opens that allows you to provide more information about how a program should carry out a task. Some dialog boxes group different kinds of information into bordered rectangular areas called **panes**. Within these panes, you will usually find tabs, option buttons, check boxes, and other controls that the program uses to collect information about how you want it to perform a task. Figure 1-25 describes common dialog box controls.

Figure 1-25 DIALOG BOX CONTROLS

CONTROL	DESCRIPTION
Tabs	Modeled after the tabs on file folders, tab controls are often used as containers for other Windows 98 controls such as list boxes, radio buttons, and check boxes. Click the appropriate tab to view different pages of information or choices.
Option buttons	Also called **radio buttons**, option buttons allow you to select a single option from among one or more options.
Check boxes	Click a check box to select or deselect it; when it is selected, a check mark appears, indicating that the option is turned on; when deselected, the check box is blank and the option is off. When check boxes appear in groups, you can select or deselect as many as you want; they are not mutually exclusive, as option buttons are.
Spin boxes	Allow you to scroll easily through a set of numbers to choose the setting you want
Text boxes	Boxes into which you type additional information

Figure 1-26 displays examples of these controls.

Figure 1-26 EXAMPLES OF DIALOG BOX CONTROLS

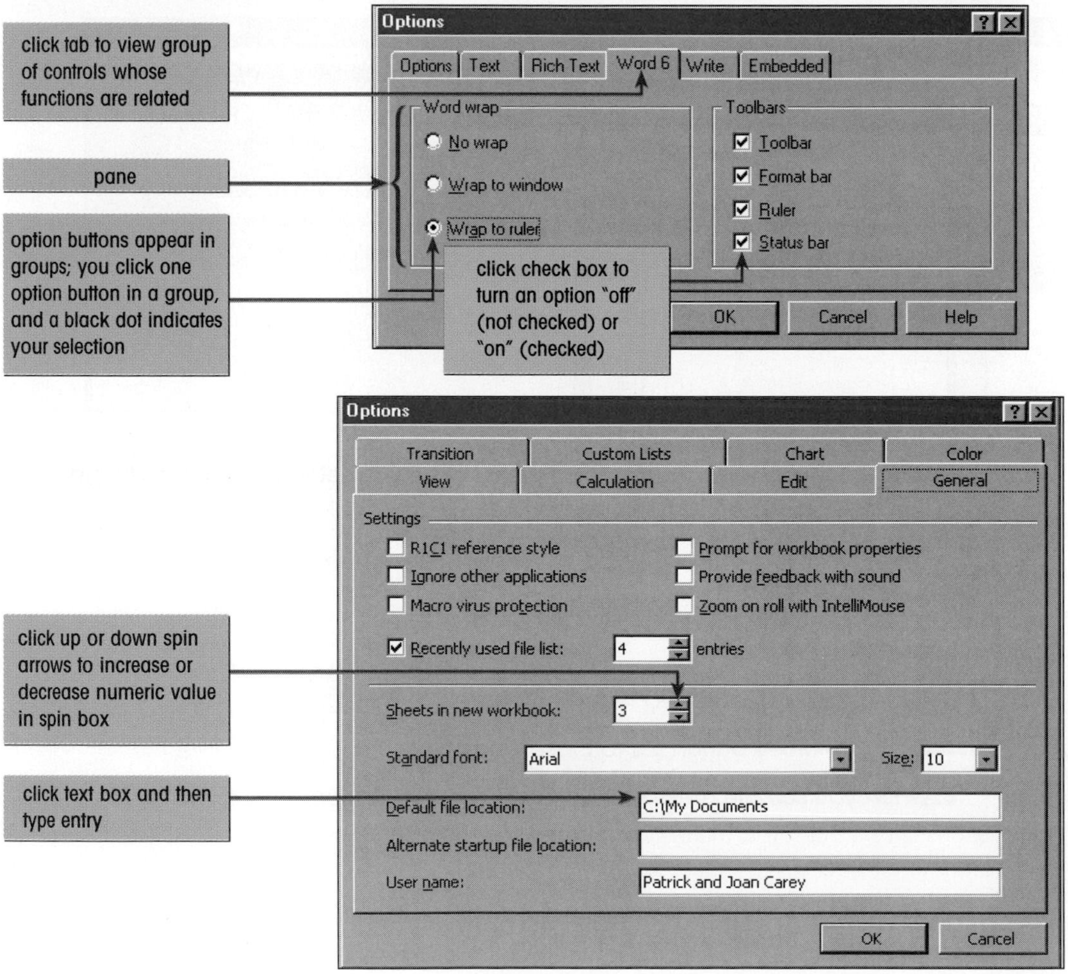

Using Help

Windows 98 **Help** provides on-screen information about the program you are using. Help for the Windows 98 operating system is available by clicking the Start button on the taskbar, then selecting Help from the Start menu. If you want Help for a program, such as WordPad, you must first start the program, then click Help on the menu bar.

When you start Help, a Windows Help window opens, which gives you access to help files stored on your computer as well as help information stored on Microsoft's Web site. If you are not connected to the Web, you only have access to the help files stored on your computer.

To start Windows 98 Help:

1. Click the **Start** button.
2. Click **Help**. The Windows Help window opens to the Contents tab. See Figure 1-27.

TROUBLE? If the Contents tab is not in front, click the Contents tab to view Help contents.

Figure 1-27 WINDOWS HELP WINDOW

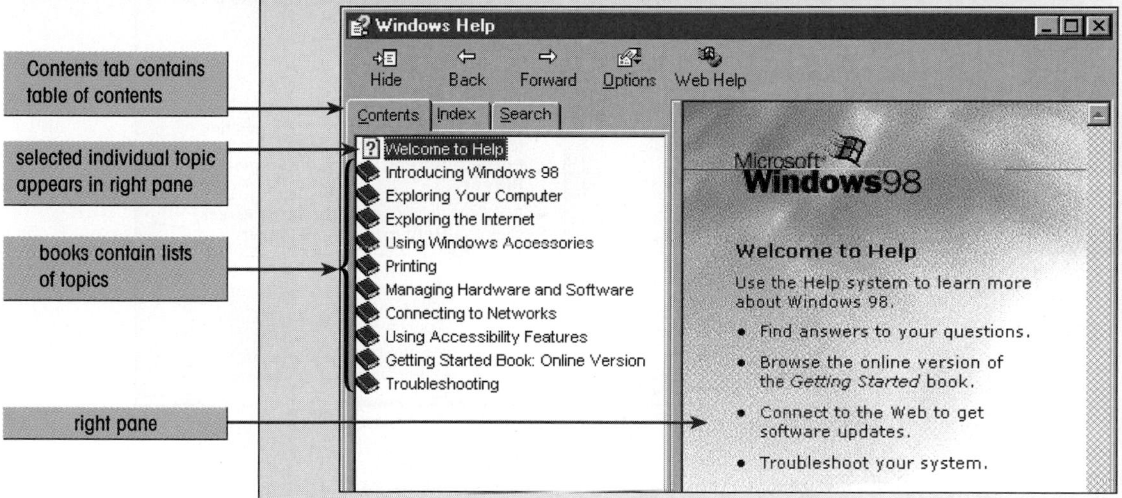

Help uses tabs for the three sections of Help: Contents, Index, and Search. The **Contents tab** groups Help topics into a series of books. You select a book by clicking it. The book opens, and a list of related topics appears from which you can choose. Individual topics are designated with the icon.

The **Index tab** displays an alphabetical list of all the Help topics from which you can choose. The **Search tab** allows you to search the entire set of Help topics for all topics that contain a word or words you specify.

Viewing Topics from the Contents Tab

You've already opened two of the Windows accessories, Paint and WordPad. Suppose you're wondering about the other accessory programs. You can use the Contents tab to find more information on a specific topic.

To use the Contents tab:

1. Click the **Using Windows Accessories** book icon. A list of topics and related books appears below the book title. You decide to explore entertainment accessories.
2. Click the **Entertainment** book icon.
3. Click the **CD Player** topic icon. Information about the CD Player accessory appears in the right pane, explaining how you can use the CD-ROM drive (if you have one) on your computer to play your favorite music CDs. See Figure 1-28.

Figure 1-28 LOCATING INFORMATION ABOUT CD PLAYER ACCESSORY

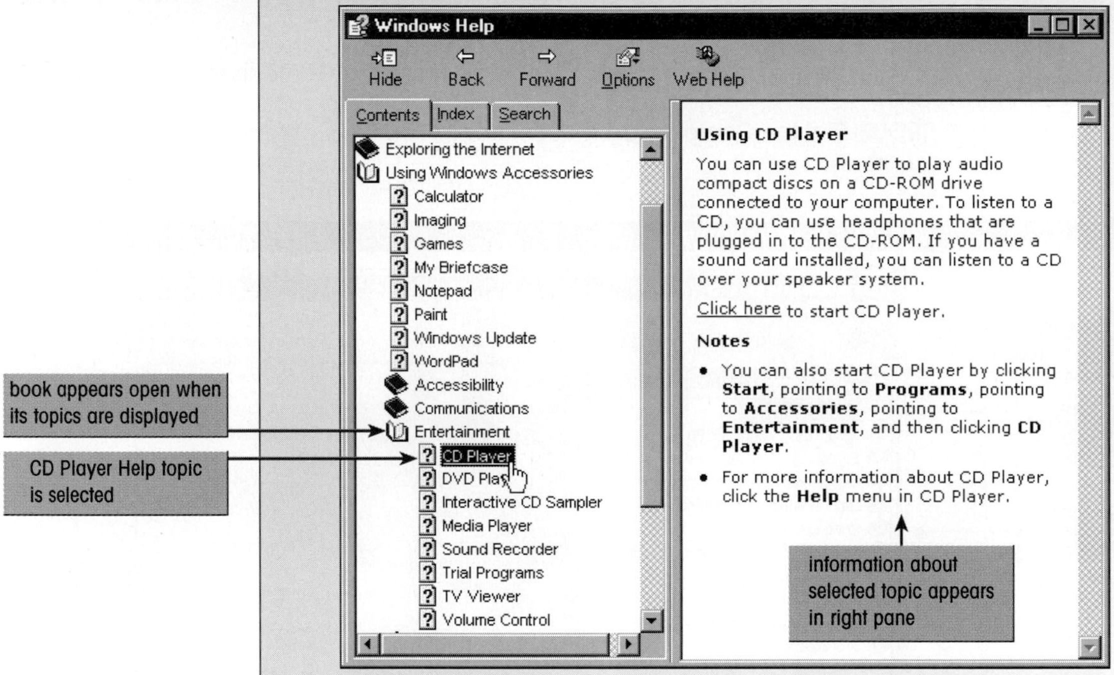

Selecting a Topic from the Index

The Index tab allows you to jump to a Help topic by selecting a topic from an indexed list. For example, you can use the Index tab to learn how to arrange the open windows on your desktop.

To find a Help topic using the Index tab:

1. Click the **Index** tab. A long list of indexed Help topics appears.

   TROUBLE? If this is the first time you've used Help on your computer, Windows 98 needs to set up the Index. This takes just a few moments. Wait until you see the list of index entries in the left pane, and then proceed to Step 2.

2. Drag the scroll box down to view additional topics.
3. You can quickly jump to any part of the list by typing the first few characters of a word or phrase in the box above the Index list. Click the box and then type **desktop** to display topics related to the Windows 98 desktop.

4. Click the topic **arranging windows on** and then click the **Display** button. When there is just one topic, it appears immediately in the right pane; otherwise, the Topics Found window opens, listing all topics indexed under the entry you're interested in. In this case, there are two choices.

5. Click **To minimize all open windows**, and then click the **Display** button. The information you requested appears in the right pane. See Figure 1-29. Notice in this topic that there is an underlined word: taskbar. You can click underlined words to view definitions or additional information.

Figure 1-29 USING THE INDEX TO LOCATE INFORMATION

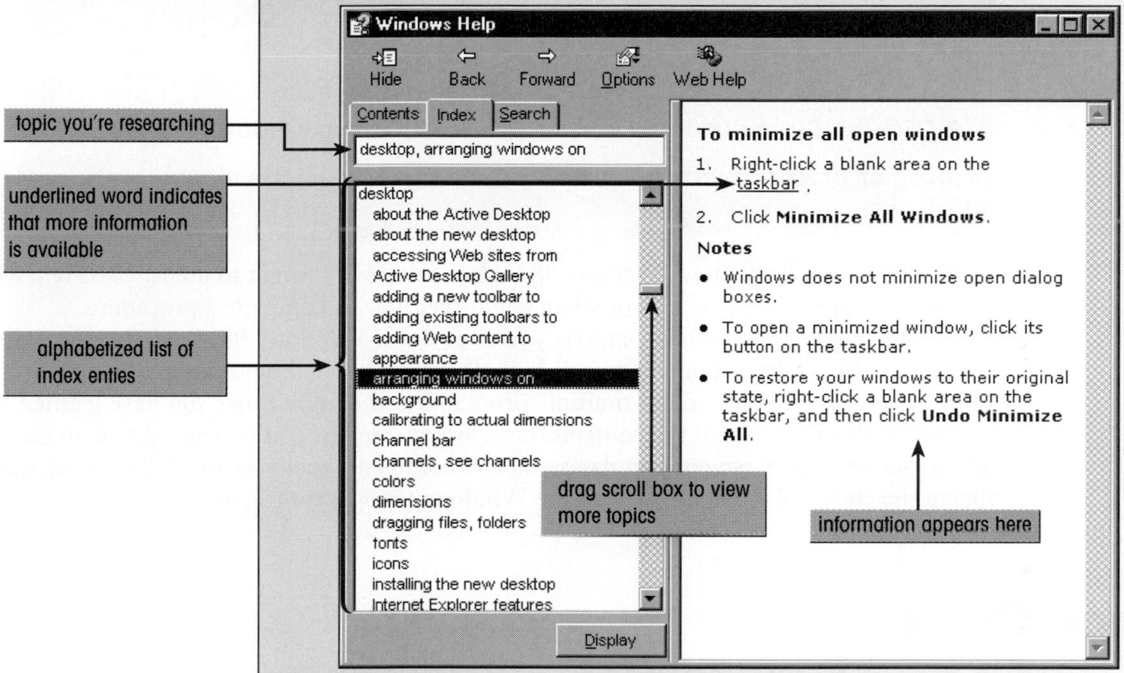

6. Click **taskbar**. A small box appears that defines the term "taskbar." See Figure 1-30.

Figure 1-30 VIEWING ADDITIONAL INFORMATION

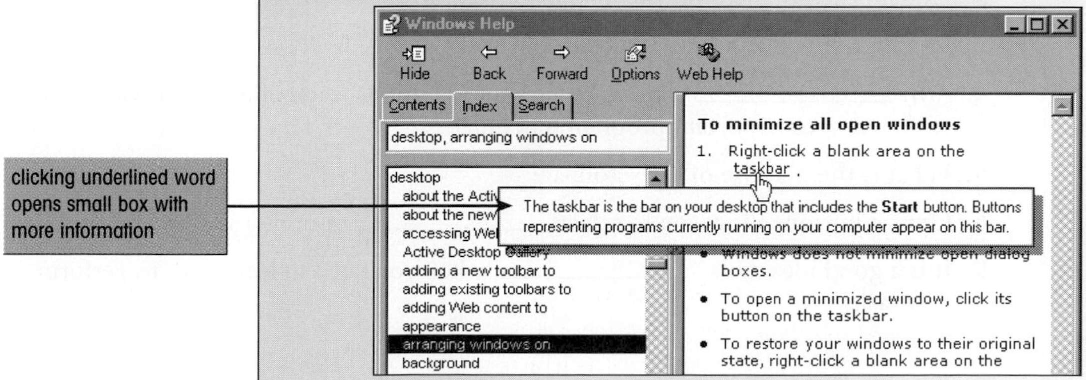

7. Click a blank area of the Windows Help window to close the box.

The third tab, the Search tab, works similarly to the Index tab, except that you type a word, and then the Help system searches for topics containing that word. You'll get a chance to experiment with the Search tab in the Tutorial Assignments.

Returning to a Previous Help Topic

You've looked at a few topics now. Suppose you want to return to the one you just saw. The Help window includes a toolbar of buttons that help you navigate the Help system. One of these buttons is the **Back** button, which returns you to topics you've already viewed. Try returning to the help topic on playing music CDs on your CD-ROM drive.

To return to a help topic:

1. Click the **Back** button. The Using CD Player topic appears.
2. Click the **Close** button ☒ to close the Windows Help window.
3. Log off or shut down Windows 98, depending on your lab's requirements.

Now that you know how Windows 98 Help works, don't forget to use it! Use Help when you need to perform a new task or when you forget how to complete a procedure.

You've finished the tutorial, and as you shut down Windows 98, Steve Laslow returns from class. You take a moment to tell him all you've learned: you know how to start and close programs and how to use multiple programs at the same time. You have learned how to work with windows and the controls they employ. Finally, you've learned how to get help when you need it. Steve congratulates you and comments that you are well on your way to mastering the fundamentals of using the Windows 98 operating system.

QUICK CHECK

1. What is the difference between the title bar and a toolbar?
2. Provide the name and purpose of each button:

   a. [minimize button] b. [maximize button] c. [restore button] d. [close button]

3. Explain each of the following menu conventions:

   a. Ellipsis... b. Grayed-out c. ▸ d. ✔

4. A(n) ______________ consists of a group of buttons, each of which provides one-click access to important program functions.
5. What is the purpose of the scrollbar?
6. Option buttons allow you to select ______________ option(s) at a time.
7. It is a good idea to use ______________ when you need to learn how to perform new tasks.

TUTORIAL ASSIGNMENT

1. **Running Two Programs and Switching Between Them** In this tutorial you learned how to run more than one program at a time, using WordPad and Paint. You can run other programs at the same time, too. Complete the following steps and write out your answers to questions b through f:
   a. Start the computer. Enter your username and password if prompted to do so.
   b. Click the Start button. How many menu options are on the Start menu?
   c. Run the Calculator program located on the Accessories menu. How many program buttons are now on the taskbar (don't count toolbar buttons or items in the tray)?
   d. Run the Paint program and maximize the Paint window. How many programs are running now?
   e. Switch to Calculator. What are two visual clues that tell you that Calculator is the active program?
   f. Multiply 576 by 1457 using the Calculator accessory. What is the result?
   g. Close Calculator, then close Paint.

Explore

2. **WordPad Help** In Tutorial 1 you learned how to use Windows 98 Help. Just about every Windows 98 program has a help feature. Many computer users can learn to use a program just by using Help. To use Help, you start the program, then click the Help menu at the top of the screen. Try using WordPad Help:
   a. Start WordPad.
   b. Click Help on the WordPad menu bar, and then click Help Topics.
   c. Using WordPad Help, write out your answers to questions 1 through 4.
      1. How do you create a bulleted list?
      2. How do you set the margins in a document?
      3. How do you undo a mistake?
      4. How do you change the font style of a block of text?
   d. Close WordPad.

Explore

3. **The Search Tab** In addition to the Contents and Index tabs you worked with in this tutorial, Windows 98 Help also includes a Search tab. You may have heard that Windows 98 makes it possible to view television programs on your computer. You could browse through the Contents tab, although you might not know where to look to find information about television. You could also use the Index tab to search through the indexed entry. Or you could use the Search tab to find all Help topics that mention television.
   a. Start Windows 98 Help and use the Index tab to find information about television. How many topics are listed? What is their primary subject matter?
   b. Now use the Search tab to find information about television. Type "television" into the box on the Search tab, and then click the List Topics button.
   c. Write a paragraph comparing the two lists of topics. You don't have to view them all, but in your paragraph, indicate which tab seems to yield more information, and why. Close Help.

4. **Discover Windows 98** Windows 98 includes an online tour that helps you discover more about your computer and the Windows 98 operating system. You can use this tour to review what you learned in this tutorial and to pick up some new tips for using Windows 98. Complete the following steps and write out your answers to questions d–j.
   a. Click the Start button, point to Programs, point to Accessories, point to System Tools, and then click Welcome to Windows. If an error message appears at any point or if you can't locate this menu option, Welcome to Windows is probably not loaded on your computer. You will not be able to complete this assignment unless you have the Windows 98 CD. Check with your instructor.
   b. Click Discover Windows 98.
   c. Click Computer Essentials and follow the instructions on the screen to step through the tour.
   d. What is the "brain" of your computer, according to the tour information?
   e. What two devices do you use to communicate with your computer?

f. What is the purpose of the ESC key?
g. What is double-clicking?
h. What is the purpose of the top section of the Start menu?
i. What is another term for "submenu"?
j. What function key opens the Help feature in most software?

PROJECTS

1. There are many types of pointing devices on the market today. Go to the library and research the types of devices that are available. Consider what devices are appropriate for these situations: desktop or laptop computers, connected or remote devices, and ergonomic or standard designs (look up the word "ergonomic").

   Use up-to-date computer books, trade computer magazines such as *PC Computing* and *PC Magazine*, or the Internet (if you know how) to locate information. Your instructor might suggest specific resources you can use. Write a one-page report describing the types of devices available, the differing needs of users, special features that make pointing devices more useful, price comparisons, and finally, an indication of what you would choose if you needed to buy a pointing device.

2. Using the resources available to you, either through your library or the Internet (if you know how), locate information about the release of Windows 98. Computing trade magazines are an excellent source of information about software. Read several articles about Windows 98 and then write a one-page essay that discusses the features that seem most important to the people who have evaluated the software. If you find reviews of the software, mention the features that reviewers had the strongest reaction to, pro or con.

3. **Upgrading** is the process of placing a more recent version of a product onto your computer. When Windows 98 first came out, people had to decide whether or not they wanted to upgrade their computers to Windows 98. Interview several people you know (at least three) who are well-informed Windows computer users. Ask them whether they are using Windows 98 or an older version of Windows. If they are using an older version, ask why they have chosen not to upgrade. If they are using Windows 98, ask them why they chose to upgrade. Ask such questions as:

   a. What features convinced you to upgrade or made you decide to wait?
   b. What role did the price of the upgrade play?
   c. Would you have had (or did you have) to purchase new hardware to make the upgrade? How did this affect your decision?
   d. If you did upgrade, are you happy with that decision? If you didn't, do you intend to upgrade in the near future? Why, or why not?

   Write a single-page essay summarizing what you learned from these interviews about making the decision to upgrade.

4. Choose a topic you'd like to research using the Windows 98 online Help system. Look for information on your topic using all three tabs: the Contents tab, the Index tab, and the Search tab. Once you've found all the information you can, compare the three methods (Contents, Index, Search) of looking for information. Write a paragraph that discusses which tab proved the most useful. Did you reach the same information topics using all three methods? In a second paragraph, summarize what you learned about your topic. Finally, in a third paragraph, indicate under what circumstances you'd use which tab.

LAB ASSIGNMENTS

Using a Keyboard To become an effective computer user, you must be familiar with your primary input device—the keyboard. See the Read This Before You Begin page for information on installing and starting the lab.

1. The Steps for the Using a Keyboard Lab provide you with a structured introduction to the keyboard layout and the function of special computer keys. Click the Steps button and begin the Steps. As you work through the Steps, answer all of the Quick Check questions that appear. When you complete the Steps, you will see a Summary Report that summarizes your performance on the Quick Checks. Follow the directions on the screen to print the Summary Report.

2. In Explore, start the typing tutor. You can develop your typing skills using the typing tutor in Explore. Take the typing test and print out your results.

3. In Explore, try to improve your typing speed by 10 words per minute. For example, if you currently type 20 words per minute, your goal will be 30 words per minute. Practice each typing lesson until you see a message that indicates that you can proceed to the next lesson. Create a Practice Record, as shown here, to keep track of how much you practice. When you have reached your goal, print out the results of a typing test to verify your results.

   Practice Record

   Name:

   Section:

Start Date:	Start Typing Speed:	wpm
End Date:	End Typing Speed:	wpm
Lesson #:	Date Practiced/Time Practiced	

Using a Mouse A mouse is a standard input device on most of today's computers. You need to know how to use a mouse to manipulate graphical user interfaces and to use the rest of the Labs. See the Read This Before You Begin page for information on installing and starting the lab.

1. The Steps for the Using a Mouse Lab show you how to click, double-click, and drag objects using the mouse. Click the Steps button and begin the Steps. As you work through the Steps, answer all of the Quick Check questions that appear. When you complete the Steps, you will see a Summary Report that summarizes your performance on the Quick Checks. Follow the directions on the screen to print the Summary Report.

2. In Explore, create a poster, to demonstrate your ability to use a mouse and to control a Windows program. To create a poster for an upcoming sports event, select a graphic, type the caption for the poster, then select a font, font styles, and a border. Print your completed poster.

QUICK CHECK ANSWERS

Session 1.1

1. The taskbar contains buttons that give you access to tools and programs.
2. multitasking
3. Start menu
4. Lift the mouse up and move it to the right.
5. Its button appears on the taskbar.
6. To conserve computer resources such as memory.
7. To ensure you don't lose data and damage your files.

Session 1.2

1. The title bar identifies the window and contains window controls; toolbars contain buttons that provide you with shortcuts to common menu commands.

2. a. Minimize button shrinks window so you see button on taskbar
   b. Maximize button enlarges window to fill entire screen
   c. Restore button reduces window to predetermined size
   d. Close button closes window and removes button from taskbar

3. a. ellipsis indicates a dialog box will open
   b. grayed-out indicates option is not currently available
   c. arrow indicates a submenu will open
   d. check mark indicates a toggle option

4. toolbar
5. Scrollbars appear when the contents of a box or window are too long to fit; you drag the scroll box to view different parts of the contents.
6. one
7. online Help

OBJECTIVES

In this tutorial you will:

- Format a disk
- Enter, select, insert, and delete text
- Create and save a file
- Open, edit, and print a file
- Switch to Web style
- Create a Student Disk
- View the list of files on your disk and change view options
- Move, copy, delete, and rename a file
- Navigate Explorer windows
- Make a copy of your Student Disk

LABS

Using Files

WORKING WITH FILES

Creating, Saving, and Managing Files

CASE

Distance Education

You recently purchased a computer in order to gain new skills and stay competitive in the job market. Your friend Shannon suggests that you broaden your horizons by enrolling in a few distance education courses. **Distance education**, Shannon explains, is formalized learning that typically takes place using a computer, replacing normal classroom interaction with modern communications technology. Many distance education courses take advantage of the **Internet**, a vast structure of millions of computers located all over the world that are connected together so that they are able to share information. The **World Wide Web**, usually called the **Web**, is a popular service on the Internet that makes information readily accessible. Educators can make their course material available on the Web.

Windows 98 makes it possible for your computer to display content in a way that is similar to the way it appears on the Web, and Shannon is eager to show you how. She suggests, however, that first you should get more comfortable with your computer—especially using programs and files. Shannon points out that most of the software installed on your computer was created especially for the Windows 98 operating system. This software is referred to as **Windows 98 applications** or **Windows 98 programs**. You can use software designed for older operating systems, but Windows 98 applications take better advantage of the features of the Windows 98 operating system.

You typically use Windows 98 applications to create files. A **file**, often referred to as a **document**, is a collection of data that has a name and is stored in a computer. Once you create a file, you can open it, edit its contents, print it, and save it again—usually using the same application program you used to create it.

Shannon suggests that you become familiar with how to perform these tasks in Windows 98 applications. Then she'll show you how to set up your computer so it incorporates the look and feel of the Web. Finally, you'll spend time learning how to organize your files.

SESSION 2.1

In Session 2.1 you will learn how to format a disk so it can store files. You will create, save, open, and print a file. You will find out how the insertion point differs from the mouse pointer, and you will learn the basic skills for Windows 98 text entry, such as inserting, deleting, and selecting. ***For the steps of this tutorial you will need two blank 3½-inch disks.***

Formatting a Disk

Before you can save files on a disk, the disk must be formatted. When the computer **formats** a disk, the magnetic particles on the disk surface are arranged so data can be stored on the disk. Today, many disks are sold preformatted and can be used right out of the box. However, if you purchase an unformatted disk, or if you have an old disk you want to completely erase and reuse, you can format the disk using the Windows 98 Format command. This command is available through the **My Computer window**, a window that gives you access to the objects on your computer. You open My Computer by using its icon on the desktop. You'll learn more about the My Computer window later in this tutorial.

The following steps tell you how to format a 3½-inch high-density disk using drive A. Your instructor will tell you how to revise the instructions given in these steps if the procedure is different for your lab equipment.

Make sure you are using a blank disk before you perform these steps.

To format a disk:

1. Start Windows 98, if necessary.
2. Write your name on the label of a 3½-inch disk and insert your disk in drive A. See Figure 2-1.

Figure 2-1 INSERTING A DISK INTO A DISK DRIVE

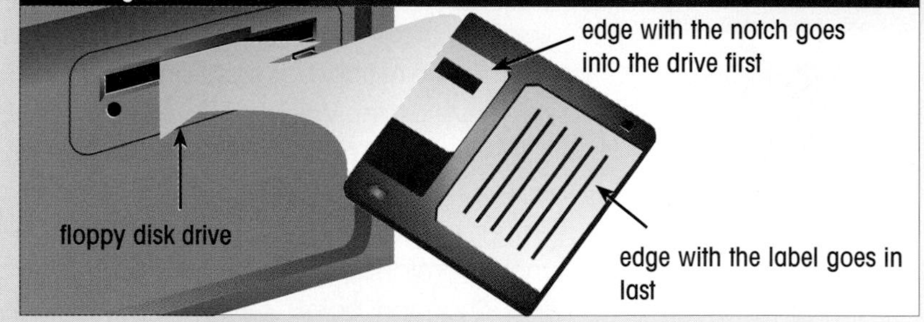
edge with the notch goes into the drive first
floppy disk drive
edge with the label goes in last

TROUBLE? If your disk does not fit in drive A, put it in drive B and substitute drive B for drive A in all of the steps for the rest of the tutorial.

3. Click the **My Computer** icon on the desktop. The icon is selected. Figure 2-2 shows the location of this icon on your desktop.

   TROUBLE? If the My Computer window opens, skip Step 4. Your computer is using different settings, which you'll learn to change in Session 2.2.

4. Press **Enter** to open the My Computer window. See Figure 2-2 (don't worry if your window opens maximized).

   TROUBLE? If you see a list instead of icons like those in Figure 2-2, click View, then click Large Icons. Don't worry if your toolbars don't exactly match those in Figure 2-2.

TROUBLE? If you see additional information or a graphic image on the left side of the My Computer window, Web view is enabled on your computer. Don't worry. You will learn how to enable and disable Web view in Session 2.2.

Figure 2-2 MY COMPUTER WINDOW

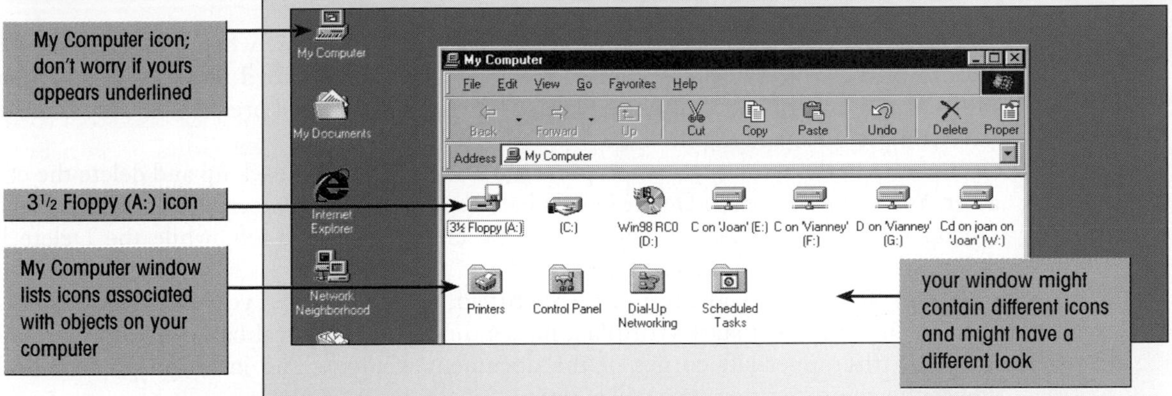

5. Right-click the **3½ Floppy (A:)** icon to open its shortcut menu.
6. Click **Format** on the shortcut menu. The Format dialog box opens.
7. Click the **Full** option button to perform a full format. Make sure the other dialog box settings on your screen match those in Figure 2-3.

Figure 2-3 FORMAT DIALOG BOX

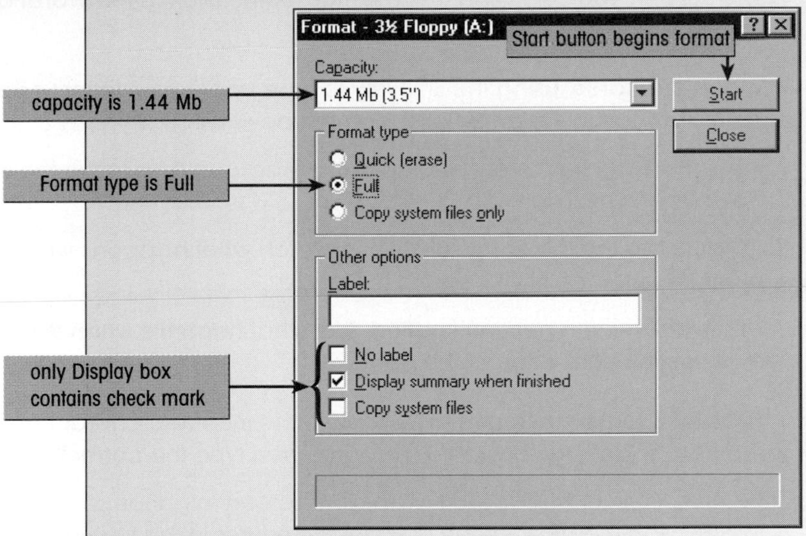

8. On the right side of the dialog box is a Start button. Click this **Start** button to begin formatting the disk. A series of blue boxes at the bottom of the Format window shows you how the format is progressing. When the format is complete, the Format Results dialog box appears.
9. Click the **Close** button, and then close any open windows on the desktop.

TROUBLE? To close the windows, click each Close button ☒.

Working with Text

To accomplish many computing tasks, you need to type text in documents and text boxes. Windows 98 facilitates basic text entry by providing a text-entry area, by showing you where your text will appear on the screen, by helping you move around on the screen, and by providing insert and delete functions.

When you type sentences of text, do not press the Enter key when you reach the right margin of the page. Most software contains a feature called **word wrap**, which automatically continues your text on the next line. Therefore, you should press Enter only when you have completed a paragraph.

If you type the wrong character, press the Backspace key to back up and delete the character. You can also use the Delete key. What's the difference between the Backspace and the Delete keys? The Backspace key deletes the character to the left, while the Delete key deletes the character to the right.

Now you will type some text using WordPad, to practice what you've learned about text entry. When you first start WordPad, notice the flashing vertical bar, called the **insertion point**, in the upper-left corner of the document window. The insertion point indicates where the characters you type will appear.

To type text in WordPad:

1. Start WordPad and locate the insertion point.

   TROUBLE? If the WordPad window does not fill the screen, click the Maximize button ☐.

   TROUBLE? If you can't find the insertion point, click in the WordPad workspace area.

2. Type your name, using the Shift key to type uppercase letters and using the Spacebar to type spaces, just as on a typewriter.

3. Press the **Enter** key to end the current paragraph and move the insertion point down to the next line.

4. As you type the following sentences, watch what happens when the insertion point reaches the right edge of the page:

   This is a sample typed in WordPad. See what happens when the insertion point reaches the right edge of the page.

   TROUBLE? If you make a mistake, delete the incorrect character(s) by pressing the Backspace key on your keyboard. Then type the correct character(s).

   TROUBLE? If your text doesn't wrap, your screen might be set up to display more information than the screen used for the figures in this tutorial. Type the sentences again until text wraps automatically.

The Insertion Point Versus the Pointer

The insertion point is not the same as the mouse pointer. When the mouse pointer is in the text-entry area, it is called the **I-beam pointer** and looks like I. Figure 2-4 explains the difference between the insertion point and the I-beam pointer.

Figure 2-4 THE INSERTION POINT VS. THE POINTER

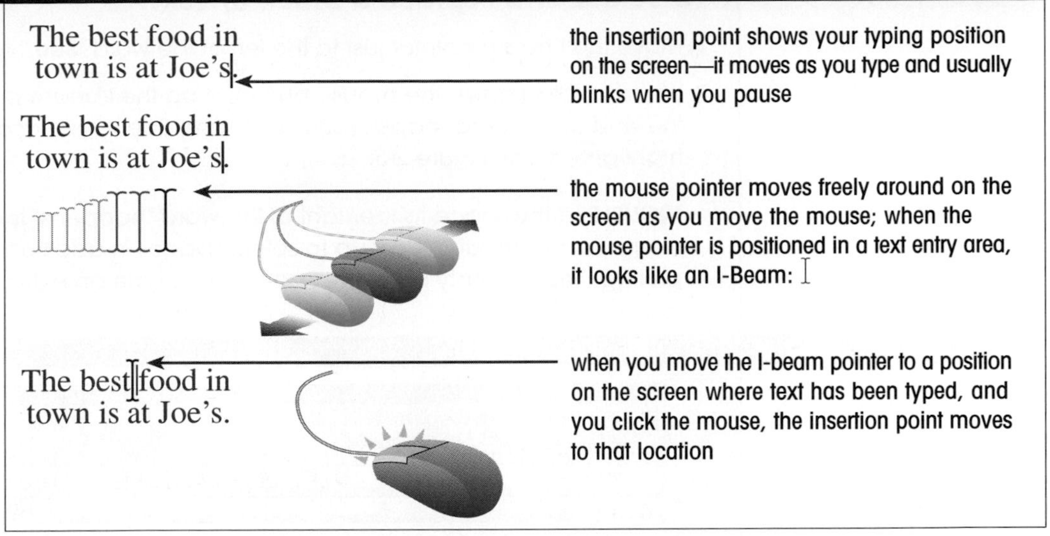
The best food in
town is at Joe's.
the insertion point shows your typing position on the screen—it moves as you type and usually blinks when you pause
The best food in
town is at Joe's.
the mouse pointer moves freely around on the screen as you move the mouse; when the mouse pointer is positioned in a text entry area, it looks like an I-Beam:
The best food in
town is at Joe's.
when you move the I-beam pointer to a position on the screen where text has been typed, and you click the mouse, the insertion point moves to that location

To enter text, you move the I-beam pointer to the location where you want to type, and then click. The insertion point jumps to the location you clicked and, depending on the program you are using, may blink to indicate the program is ready for you to type. When you enter text, the insertion point moves as you type.

To move the insertion point:

1. Check the locations of the insertion point and the I-beam pointer. The insertion point should be at the end of the sentence you typed in the last set of steps.

   TROUBLE? If you don't see the I-beam pointer, move your mouse until you see it.

2. Use the mouse to move the I-beam pointer to the word "sample," then click the mouse button. The insertion point jumps to the location of the I-beam pointer.

3. Move the I-beam pointer to a blank area near the bottom of the workspace, and click. Notice the insertion point does not jump to the location of the I-beam pointer. Instead the insertion point jumps to the end of the last sentence. The insertion point can move only within existing text. It cannot be moved out of the existing text area.

Selecting Text

Many text operations are performed on a **block** of text, which is one or more consecutive characters, words, sentences, or paragraphs. Once you select a block of text, you can delete it, move it, replace it, underline it, and so on. As you select a block of text, the computer highlights it. If you want to remove the highlighting, just click in the margin of your document.

If you want to delete the phrase "See what happens" in the text you just typed and replace it with the phrase "You can watch word wrap in action," you do not have to delete the first phrase one character at a time. Instead, you can highlight the entire phrase and then type the replacement phrase.

To select and replace a block of text:

1. Move the I-beam pointer just to the left of the word "See."
2. While holding down the mouse button, drag the I-beam pointer over the text to the end of the word "happens." The phrase "See what happens" should now be highlighted. See Figure 2-5.

   TROUBLE? If the space to the right of the word "happens" is also selected, don't worry. Your computer is set up to select spaces in addition to words. After completing Step 4, simply press the Spacebar to type an extra space if required.

Figure 2-5 **HIGHLIGHTING TEXT**

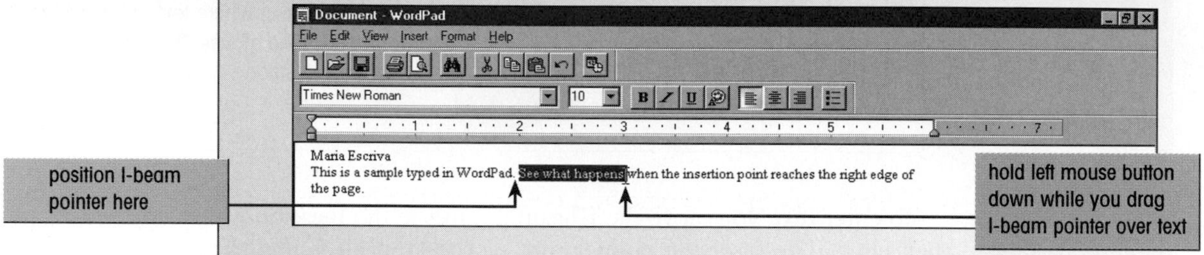

3. Release the mouse button.

   TROUBLE? If the phrase is not highlighted correctly, repeat Steps 1 through 3.

4. Type **You can watch word wrap in action**

The text you typed replaces the highlighted text. Notice you did not need to delete the highlighted text before you typed the replacement text.

Inserting a Character

Windows 98 programs usually operate in **insert mode**—when you type a new character, all characters to the right of the insertion point are pushed over to make room.

Suppose you want to insert the word "sentence" before the word "typed" in your practice sentences.

To insert text:

1. Move the I-beam pointer just before the word "typed," then click to position the insertion point.
2. Type **sentence**
3. Press the **Spacebar**.

Notice how the letters in the first line are pushed to the right to make room for the new characters. When a word gets pushed past the right margin, the **word-wrap** feature moves it down to the beginning of the next line.

Saving a File

Using Files

As you type text, it is held temporarily in the computer's memory. For permanent storage, you need to save your work on a disk. In the computer lab, you will probably save your work on a floppy disk in drive A.

When you save a file, you must give it a name. Windows 98 allows you to use up to 255 characters in a filename, although usually the operating system requires some of those characters for designating file location and file type. So, while it is unlikely you would need that many characters, you should be aware that the full 255 characters might not always be available. You may use spaces and certain punctuation symbols in your filenames. You cannot use the symbols \ / ? : * " < > | in a filename, but other symbols such as & ; - and $ are allowed. Furthermore, filenames for files used by older Windows 3.1 or DOS applications (pre-1995 operating systems) must be eight characters or less. Thus when you save a file with a long filename in Windows 98, Windows 98 also creates an eight-character filename that can be used by older applications. The eight-character filename is created from the first six nonspace characters in the long filename, with the addition of a tilde (~) and a number. For example, the filename Car Sales for 1999 would be converted to Carsal~1.

Most filenames have an extension. An **extension** is a suffix, usually of three characters, separated from the filename by a period. In the filename Car Sales for 1999.doc, a period separates the filename from the file extension. The file extension "doc" helps categorize the file by type or by the software that created it. Files created with Microsoft Word software have a .doc extension, such as Resume.doc (pronounced "Resume dot doc"). In general you will not add an extension to your filenames, because the application software automatically does this for you.

Windows 98 keeps track of file extensions, but does not always display them. The steps in these tutorials refer to files using the filename, but not its extension. So if you see the filename Practice Text in the steps, but "Practice Text.doc" on your screen, don't worry—these refer to the same file. Also don't worry if you don't use consistent lowercase and uppercase letters when saving files. Usually the operating system doesn't distinguish between them. Be aware, however, that some programs are "case-sensitive"—they check for case in filenames.

Now you can save the document you typed.

To save a document:

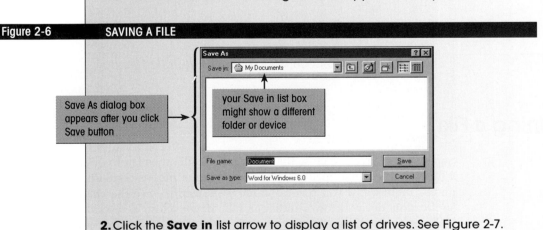

1. Click the **Save** button on the toolbar. Figure 2-6 shows the location of this button and the Save As dialog box that appears after you click it.

Figure 2-6 SAVING A FILE

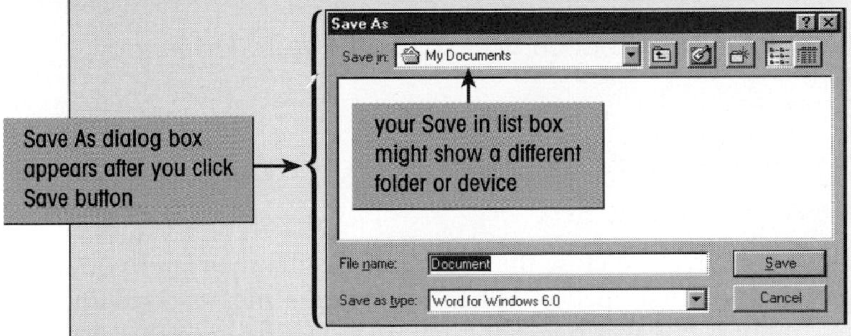

2. Click the **Save in** list arrow to display a list of drives. See Figure 2-7.

Figure 2-7 SELECTING THE DRIVE

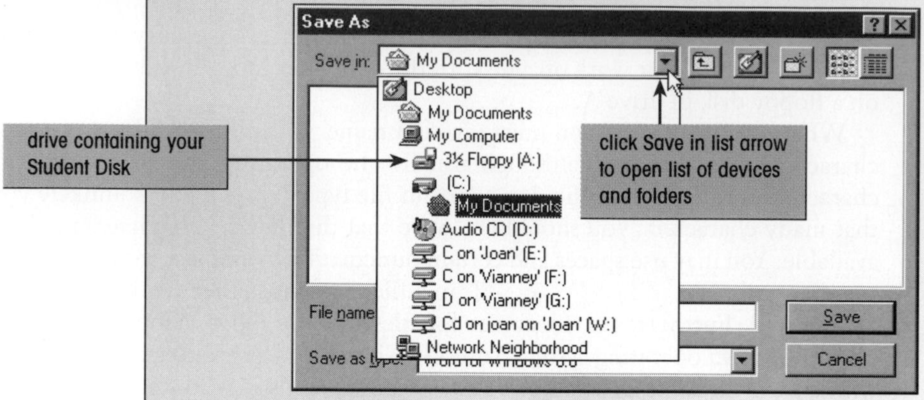

3. Click **3½ Floppy (A:)**, and select the text in the File name box.

   TROUBLE? To select the text, move the I-beam pointer to the beginning of the word "Document." While you hold down the mouse button, drag the I-beam pointer to the end of the word.

4. Type **Practice Text** in the File name box.

5. Click the **Save** button in the lower-right corner of the dialog box. Your file is saved on your Student Disk, and the document title, "Practice Text," appears on the WordPad title bar.

What if you try to close WordPad before you save your file? Windows 98 will display a message—"Save changes to Document?" If you answer "Yes," Windows will display the Save As dialog box so you can give the document a name. If you answer "No," Windows 98 will close WordPad without saving the document. Any changes you made to the document would be lost, so when you are asked if you want to save a file, answer Yes, unless you are absolutely sure you don't need to keep the work you just did.

After you save a file, you can work on another document or close WordPad. Since you have already saved your Practice Text document, you'll continue this tutorial by closing WordPad.

To close WordPad:

1. Click the **Close** button to close the WordPad window.

Opening a File

Suppose you save and close the Practice Text file, then later you want to revise it. To revise a file you must first open it. When you **open** a file, its contents are copied into the computer's memory. If you revise the file, you need to save the changes before you close the application or work on a different file. If you close a revised file without saving your changes, you will lose them.

Typically, you use one of two methods to open a file. You could select the file from the Documents list or the My Computer window, or you could start an application program and then use the Open button to open the file. Each method has advantages and disadvantages.

The first method for opening the Practice Text file simply requires you to select the file from the Documents list or from the My Computer window. With this method the document, not the application program, is central to the task; hence, this method is sometimes referred to as **document-centric**. You only need to remember the name of your document or file—you do not need to remember which application you used to create the document.

The Documents list contains the names of the last 15 documents used. You access this list from the Start menu. When you have your own computer, the Documents list is very handy. In a computer lab, however, the files other students use quickly replace yours on the list.

If your file is not in the Documents list, you can open the file by selecting it from the My Computer window. Windows 98 starts an application program you can use to revise the file, then automatically opens the file. The advantage of this method is its simplicity. The disadvantage is Windows 98 might not start the application you expect. For example, when you select Practice Text, you might expect Windows 98 to start WordPad because you used WordPad to create it. Depending on the software installed on your computer system, however, Windows 98 might start the Microsoft Word application instead. Usually this is not a problem. Although the application might not be the one you expect, you can still use it to revise your file.

To open the Practice Text file by selecting it from My Computer:

1. From the desktop, open the **My Computer** window.
2. Click the **3½ Floppy (A:)** icon in the My Computer window.

   TROUBLE? If the 3½ Floppy (A:) window opens, skip Step 3.

3. Press **Enter**. The 3½ Floppy (A:) window opens.
4. Click the **Practice Text** file icon.

   TROUBLE? If the Practice Text document appears in a word-processing window, skip Step 5.

5. Press **Enter**. Windows 98 starts an application program, then automatically opens the Practice Text file. You could make revisions to the document at this point, but instead, you'll close all the windows on your desktop so you can try the other method for opening files.

   TROUBLE? If Windows 98 starts Microsoft Word or another word-processing program instead of WordPad, don't worry. You can use Microsoft Word to revise the Practice Text document.

6. Close all open windows on the desktop.

The second method for opening the Practice Text file requires you to open WordPad, then use the Open button to select the Practice Text file. The advantage of this method is you can specify the application program you want to use—WordPad, in this case. This method, however, involves more steps than the method you tried previously.

To start WordPad and open the Practice Text file using the Open button:

1. Start WordPad and maximize the WordPad window.
2. Click the **Open** button  on the toolbar.

3. Click the **Look in** list arrow to display a list of drives.

4. Click **3½ Floppy (A:)** from the list.

5. Click **Practice Text** to make sure it is highlighted. See Figure 2-8.

Figure 2-8 SELECTING THE FILE

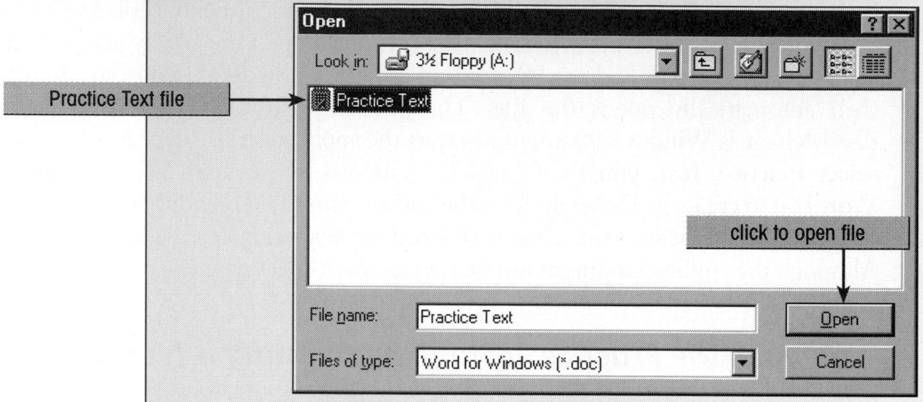

6. Click the **Open** button in the lower-right corner of the dialog box. Your document should appear in the WordPad work area.

Printing a File

Now that the Practice Text file is open, you can print it. It is a good idea to use Print Preview before you send your document to the printer. **Print Preview** shows on the screen exactly how your document will appear on paper. You can check your page layout so you don't waste paper printing a document that is not quite the way you want it. Your instructor might supply you with additional instructions for printing in your school's computer lab.

To preview, then print, the Practice Text file:

1. Click the **Print Preview** button on the toolbar.

TROUBLE? If an error message appears, printing capabilities might not be set up on your computer. Ask your instructor or lab assistant for help, or skip this set of steps.

2. Look at your print preview. Before you print the document and use paper, you should make sure the font, margins, and other document features look the way you want them to.

TROUBLE? If you can't read the document text on screen, click the Zoom In button.

3. Click the **Print** button. A Print dialog box appears. Study Figure 2-9 to familiarize yourself with the controls in the Print dialog box.

Figure 2-9 **PRINTING A FILE**

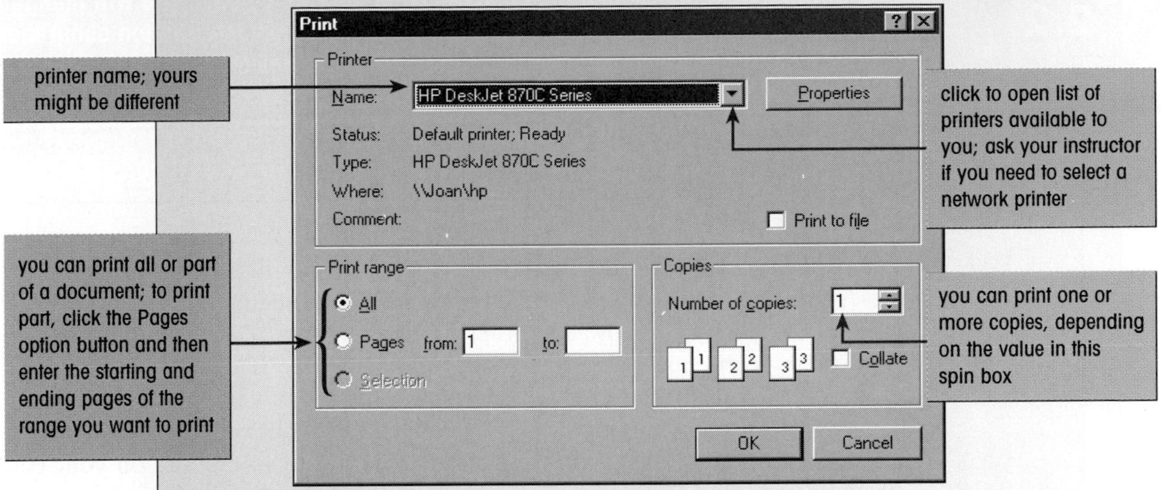
Print
Printer
Name: HP DeskJet 870C Series
Properties
Status: Default printer; Ready
Type: HP DeskJet 870C Series
Where: \\Joan\hp
Comment:
Print to file
Print range
All
Pages from: 1 to:
Selection
Copies
Number of copies: 1
Collate
OK
Cancel
printer name; yours might be different
click to open list of printers available to you; ask your instructor if you need to select a network printer
you can print all or part of a document; to print part, click the Pages option button and then enter the starting and ending pages of the range you want to print
you can print one or more copies, depending on the value in this spin box

4. Make sure your screen shows the Print range set to "All" and the number of copies set to "1."

5. Click the **OK** button to print your document.

   TROUBLE? If your document does not print, make sure the printer has paper and the printer online light is on. If your document still doesn't print, ask your instructor or lab assistant for help.

6. Close WordPad.

   TROUBLE? If you see the message "Save changes to Document?" click the No button.

You've now learned how to create, save, open, and print word-processed files—essential skills for students in distance education courses that rely on word-processed reports transmitted across the Internet. Shannon assures you that the techniques you've just learned apply to most Windows 98 programs.

QUICK CHECK

1. A(n) ______________ is a collection of data that has a name and is stored on a disk or other storage medium.
2. ______________ erases all the data on a disk and arranges the magnetic particles on the disk surface so the disk can store data.
3. True or False: When you move the mouse pointer over a text entry area, the pointer shape changes to an I-bar.
4. What shows you where each character you type will appear?
5. ______________ automatically moves text down to the beginning of the next line when you reach the right margin.
6. How do you select a block of text?
7. In the filename New Equipment.doc, doc is a(n) ______________.

SESSION 2.2

In this session you will learn how to change settings in the My Computer window to control its appearance and the appearance of desktop objects. You will then learn how to use My Computer to manage the files on your disk; view information about the files on your disk; organize the files into folders; and move, delete, copy, and rename files. ***For this session you will use a second blank 3½-inch disk.***

Changing Desktop Style Settings

Shannon tells you that in Windows 98 you work with files by manipulating icons that represent them. These icons appear in many places: the desktop, the My Computer windows, the 3½ Floppy (A:) window, and other similar windows. The techniques you use to manipulate these icons depend on whether your computer is using Classic-style or Web-style settings or a customized hybrid. **Classic style** allows you to use the same techniques in Windows 98 that are used in Windows 95, the previous version of the Windows operating system. **Web style**, on the other hand, allows you to access files on your computer's hard drives just as you access files on the Web. In Classic style, to select an item you click it, and to open an item you click it and then press Enter. In Web style, to select an item you point to it, and to open an item you click it.

Thus, if you wanted to open your Practice Text document from the My Computer window, in Classic style you would click its icon and press Enter, but in Web style you would simply click its icon.

Switching to Web Style

By default, Windows 98 starts using a combination of Classic and Web style settings, but it uses Classic click settings. Your computer might have been set differently. If you have your own computer, you can choose which style you want to use. If you want to minimize the number of mouse actions for a given task, or if you want to explore your computer in the same way you explore the Web, you'll probably want to use Web style. On the other hand, if you are used to Classic style settings, you might want to continue using them. Shannon suggests that you use Web style because you'll be able to use the same techniques on the Web, and you'll be more at ease with your distance learning courses. The next set of steps shows you how to switch to Web style, and the rest of the tutorial assumes that you're using Web-style settings.

To switch styles:

1. Click the **Start** button Start and then point to **Settings**.
2. Click **Folder Options**. The Folder Options dialog box opens.

   TROUBLE? If you can't open the Folder Options dialog box, or you can't make any changes to it, you probably don't have permission to change these settings. If your computer is set to use Classic style and you can't change this setting, you will notice a few differences in subsequent steps in this tutorial. The **TROUBLE?** paragraphs will help to ensure that you learn the proper techniques for the settings you are using.

3. On the General tab, click the **Web style** option button. See Figure 2-10.

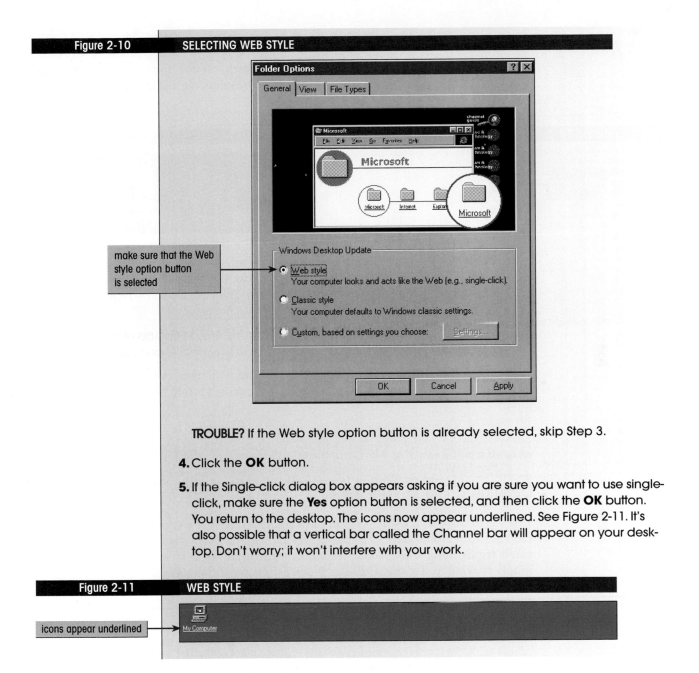

Figure 2-10 **SELECTING WEB STYLE**

make sure that the Web style option button is selected

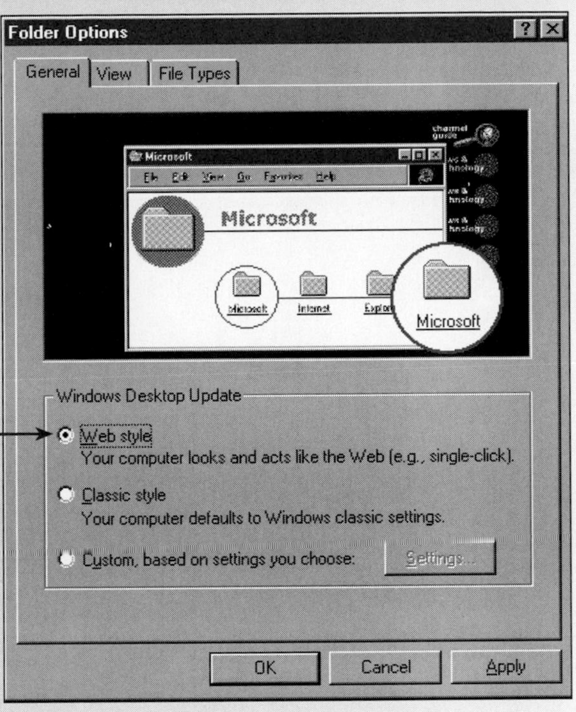

TROUBLE? If the Web style option button is already selected, skip Step 3.

4. Click the **OK** button.

5. If the Single-click dialog box appears asking if you are sure you want to use single-click, make sure the **Yes** option button is selected, and then click the **OK** button. You return to the desktop. The icons now appear underlined. See Figure 2-11. It's also possible that a vertical bar called the Channel bar will appear on your desktop. Don't worry; it won't interfere with your work.

Figure 2-11 **WEB STYLE**

icons appear underlined

You are now using Web-style settings.

Selecting an Icon in Web Style

In Web style, you select an icon representing a device, folder, or file by pointing to the icon long enough for it to become highlighted. This technique is sometimes called **hovering**. The pointer changes from ↖ to ☝ when you point to the icon. Try selecting the My Computer icon in Web style.

To select the My Computer icon in Web style:

1. Position the pointer over the My Computer icon on the desktop and notice how the pointer changes from  to 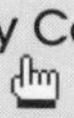 and the color of the text label changes to show it is selected. See Figure 2-12.

Figure 2-12 SELECTING AN ICON IN WEB STYLE

pointer when you point at icon in Web style

TROUBLE? If the My Computer icon is not selected when you point to it, you might not be holding the mouse steadily. You need to steadily "hover" the pointer over the object long enough for the object to become highlighted. Simply passing the mouse over an object will not select it.

TROUBLE? If in Web style you click the My Computer icon instead of simply pointing at it, the My Computer window will open. Close the window and repeat Step 1.

TROUBLE? If you were unable to switch to Web style because you didn't have permission, you'll need to click the My Computer icon to select it.

Note that the Web style selection technique only applies to icons on the desktop and icons in windows such as My Computer.

Opening a File in Web Style

You saw in Session 2.1 that you can open the Practice Text document directly from the 3½ Floppy (A:) window. The steps in Session 2.1 assumed you were using Classic style. Now you'll try opening the Practice Text document using Web style. You open an object by simply clicking it. Try opening your Practice Text file in Web style.

To open the Practice Text file in Web style:

1. Click the **My Computer** icon. The My Computer window opens.

   TROUBLE? If you were unable to switch to Web style, you'll need to press Enter after Steps 1, 2, and 3.

2. Click the **3½ Floppy (A:)** icon. The 3½ Floppy (A:) window opens.
3. Click the **Practice Text** icon. Your word-processing software starts and the Practice Text file opens.
4. Close all open windows.

Now that you've practiced working with icons in Web style, you'll learn other tasks you can perform with these icons to manage your files.

Creating Your Student Disk

For the rest of this session, you must create a Student Disk that contains some practice files. *You can use the disk you formatted in the previous session.*

If you are using your own computer, the NP on Microsoft Windows 98 menu selection will not be available. Before you proceed, you must go to your school's computer lab and find a computer that has the NP on Microsoft Windows 98 program installed. If you cannot get the files from the lab, ask your instructor or lab assistant for help. Once you have made your own Student Disk, you can use it to complete this tutorial on any computer you choose.

To add the practice files to your Student Disk:

1. Write "Disk 1 - Windows 98 Tutorial 2 Student Disk" on the label of your formatted disk (the same disk you used to save your Practice Text file).
2. Place the disk in drive A.
3. Click the **Start** button Start.
4. Point to **Programs**.
5. Point to **NP on Microsoft Windows 98 - Level I**.

   TROUBLE? If NP on Microsoft Windows 98 - Level I is not listed ask your instructor or lab assistant for help.
6. Click **Disk 1 (Tutorial 2)**. A message box opens, asking you to place your disk in drive A.
7. Click the **OK** button. Wait while the program copies the practice files to your formatted disk. When all the files have been copied, the program closes.

Your Student Disk now contains practice files you will use throughout the rest of this tutorial.

My Computer

The My Computer icon, as you have seen, represents your computer, its storage devices, printers, and other objects. The My Computer icon opens into the My Computer window, which contains an icon for each of the storage devices on your computer. On most computer systems, the My Computer window also contains the Control Panel and Printers folders, which help you add printers, control peripheral devices, and customize your Windows 98 work environment. Depending on the services your computer is running, you might see additional folders such as Dial-Up Networking (for some Internet connections) or Scheduled Tasks (for scheduling programs provided with Windows 98) that help you keep your computer running smoothly). Figure 2-13 shows how the My Computer window relates to your computer's hardware.

Figure 2-13 RELATIONSHIP BETWEEN COMPUTER AND MY COMPUTER WINDOW

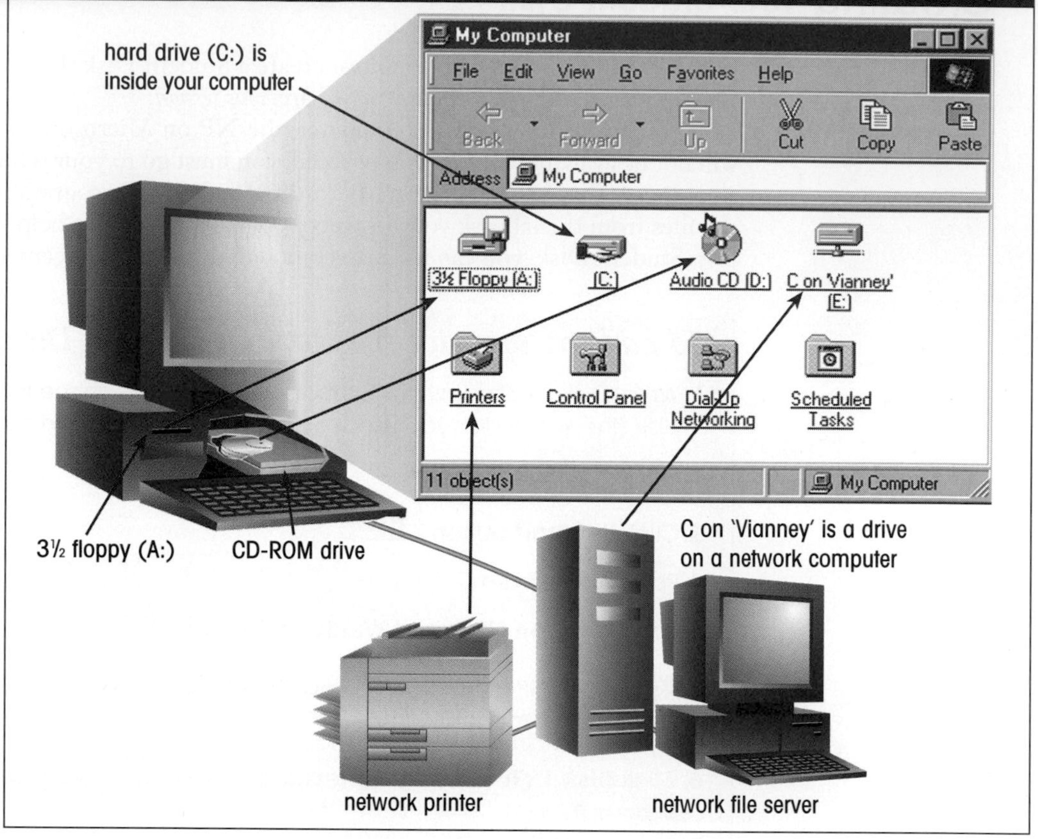

The first floppy drive on a computer is designated as drive A (if you add a second drive it is usually designated as drive B), and the first hard drive is designated drive C (if you add additional hard drives they are usually designated D, E, and so on).

You can use the My Computer window to keep track of where your files are stored and to organize your files. In this section of the tutorial you will move and delete files on your Student Disk in drive A. If you use your own computer at home or work, you will probably store your files on drive C instead of drive A. However, in a school lab environment you usually don't know which computer you will use, so you need to carry your files with you on a floppy disk that you use in drive A. In this session, therefore, you will learn how to work with the files on drive A. Most of what you learn will also work on your home or work computer when you use drive C (or other drives).

Now you'll open the My Computer window.

To open the My Computer window and explore the contents of your Student Disk:

1. Open the My Computer window.
2. Click the **3½ Floppy (A:)** icon. A window appears showing the contents of drive A; maximize this window if necessary. See Figure 2-14.

   TROUBLE? If you are using Classic style, click Settings, click the 3½ Floppy (A:) icon and then press Enter. Your window might look different from Figure 2-14; for example, you might see only files, and not the additional information on the left side of the window.

TROUBLE? If you see a list of filenames instead of icons, click View, then click Large Icons.

Figure 2-14 CONTENTS OF STUDENT DISK

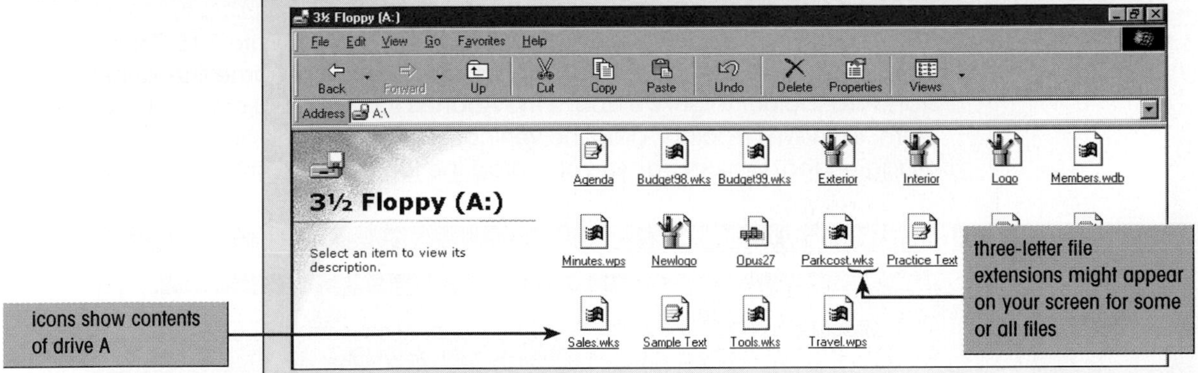

Changing My Computer View Options

Windows 98 offers several different options that control how toolbars, icons, and buttons appear in the My Computer window. You can choose to hide or display these options, depending on the task you are performing. To make the My Computer window on your computer look the same as it does in the figures in this book, you need to ensure four things: that only the Address and Standard toolbars are visible and Text Labels is enabled, that Web view is disabled, that Large Icons view is enabled, and that file extensions are hidden.

Controlling the Toolbar Display

The My Computer window, in addition to featuring a Standard toolbar, allows you to display the same toolbars that can appear on the Windows 98 taskbar, such as the Address toolbar or the Links toolbar. These toolbars make it easy to access the Web from the My Computer window. In this tutorial, however, you need to see only the Address and Standard toolbars. You can hide one or all of the My Computer toolbars, and you can determine how they are displayed, with or without text labels. Displaying the toolbars without text labels takes up less room on your screen, but it is not as easy to identify the button's function.

To display only the Address and Standard toolbars and to hide text labels:

1. Click **View**, point to **Toolbars**, and then examine the Toolbars submenu. The Standard Buttons, Address Bar, and Text Labels options should be preceded by a check mark. The Links option should not be checked.
2. If the Standard Buttons option ***is not checked***, click it.
3. If necessary, reopen the Toolbars submenu, and then repeat Step 2 with the Address Bar and Text Labels options.
4. Open the Toolbars submenu once again, and if the Links option ***is checked***, click it to disable it.

5. Click **View** and then point to **Toolbars** one last time and verify that your Toolbars submenu and the toolbar display look like Figure 2-15.

TROUBLE? If the checkmarks are distributed differently than in Figure 2-15, repeat Steps 1–5 until the correct options are checked.

TROUBLE? If your toolbars are not displayed as shown in Figure 2-15 (for example, both the Standard and Address toolbars might be on the same line, or the Standard toolbar might be above the Address toolbar), you can easily rearrange them. To move a toolbar, drag the vertical bar at the far left of the toolbar. By dragging that vertical bar, you can drag the toolbar left, right, up, or down.

Figure 2-15 CHECKING VIEW OPTIONS

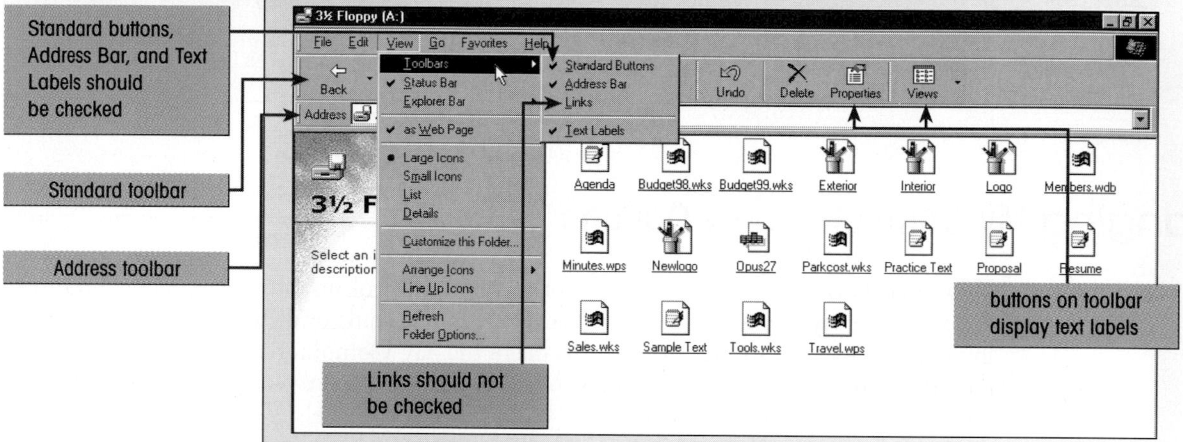

6. Click **View** to close the menu.

Web View

The My Computer window also can be viewed in **Web view**, which allows you to display and customize the My Computer window as a document you would see on the Web. Web view is automatically enabled when you switch to Web style; in its default appearance Web view shows information about the open folder or selected file, along with a decorated background. There are many advantages to Web view, including the ability to place information, graphics, and Web content in a folder window. Shannon says you'll find this feature useful once you've started your distance education courses. For now, however, you don't need to customize Web view, so you'll disable it.

To disable Web view:

1. Click **View**.

2. If the option "as Web Page" is preceded by a check mark, click **as Web Page** to disable Web view.

3. Click **View** again and ensure that as Web Page is not checked.

TROUBLE? If as Web Page is checked, repeat Steps 1 and 2.

4. Click **View** again to close the View menu.

Changing the Icon Display

Windows 98 provides four ways to view the contents of a disk—large icons, small icons, list, or details. The default view, Large Icons view, displays a large icon and title for each file. The icon provides a visual cue to the type and contents of the file, as Figure 2-16 illustrates.

Figure 2-16 TYPICAL ICONS AS THEY APPEAR IN MY COMPUTER

FILE AND FOLDER ICONS
Text documents that you can open using the Notepad accessory are represented by notepad icons.
Graphic image documents that you can open using the Paint accessory are represented by drawing instruments.
Word-processed documents that you can open using the WordPad accessory are represented by a formatted notepad icon, unless your computer designates a different word-processing program to open files created with WordPad.
Word-processed documents that you can open using a program such as Microsoft Word are represented by formatted document icons.
Files created by programs that Windows does not recognize are represented by the Windows logo.
A folder icon represents folders.
Certain folders created by Windows 98 have a special icon design related to the folder's purpose.
PROGRAM ICONS
Icons for programs usually depict an object related to the function of the program. For example, an icon that looks like a calculator represents the Calculator accessory.
Non-windows programs are represented by the icon of a blank window.

Large Icons view helps you quickly identify a file and its type, but what if you want more information about a set of files? Details view shows more information than the large icon, small icon, and list views. Details view shows the file icon, the filename, the file size, the application you used to create the file, and the date/time the file was created or last modified.

To view a detailed list of files:

1. Click **View** and then click **Details** to display details for the files on your disk, as shown in Figure 2-17. Your files might be in a different order.
2. Look at the file sizes. Do you see that Exterior and Interior are the largest files?
3. Look at the dates and times the files were modified. Which is the oldest file?

Figure 2-17 DETAILS VIEW

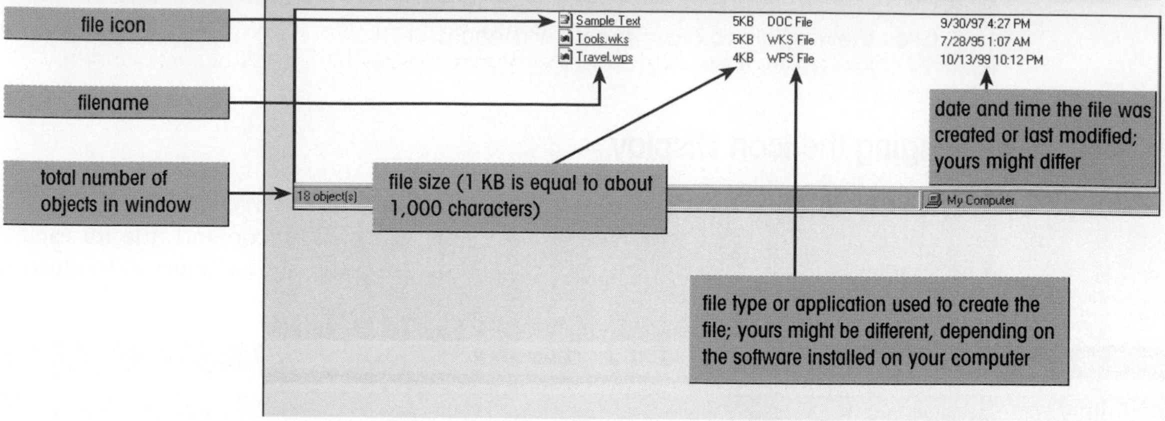

Now that you have looked at the file details, switch back to Large Icon view.

To switch to Large Icon view:

1. Click **View** and then click **Large Icons** to return to the large icon display.

Hiding File Extensions

You have the option to show or hide file extensions for file types that Windows recognizes. Showing them takes up more room but gives more information about the file. In this tutorial, however, you don't need to see file extensions, so you'll hide them. They might already be hidden on your computer.

To hide file extensions:

1. Click **View** and then click **Folder Options**. Note this is the same dialog box you saw when switching to Web style. It is accessible from the Start menu and the My Computer window.
2. Click the **View** tab.
3. Make sure the **Hide file extensions for known file types** check box is checked. If it is not, click it to insert a check mark.
4. Click the **OK** button.

The only file extensions that now appear are those whose file type Windows doesn't recognize.

Folders and Directories

A list of related files located in the same place is referred to as a **directory**. The main directory of a disk is sometimes called the **root directory**, or the **top-level directory**. The root directory is created when you format a disk, and it is designated by a letter—usually A for your floppy disk and C for your hard disk. All of the files on your Student Disk are currently in the root directory of your floppy disk.

If too many files are stored in a directory, the directory list becomes very long and difficult to manage. You can divide a directory into **folders**, into which you group similar files. The directory of files for each folder then becomes much shorter and easier to manage. A folder within a folder is called a **subfolder**. Now, you'll create a folder called Practice to hold your documents.

To create a Practice folder:

1. Click **File**, and then point to **New** to display the submenu.
2. Click **Folder**. A folder icon with the label "New Folder" appears.
3. Type **Practice** as the name of the folder.

   TROUBLE? If nothing happens when you type the folder name, it's possible that the folder name is no longer selected. Right-click the Practice folder, click Rename, and then repeat Step 3.

4. Press the **Enter** key.

When you first create a folder, it doesn't contain any files. In the next set of steps, you will move a file from the root directory to the Practice folder.

Moving and Copying a File

You can move a file from one directory to another, or from one disk to another. When you move a file, it is copied to the new location you specify, and then the version in the old location is erased. The move feature is handy for organizing or reorganizing the files on your disk by moving them into appropriate folders. The easiest way to move a file is to hold down the right mouse button and drag the file from the old location to the new location. A menu appears and you select Move Here.

REFERENCE WINDOW RW

<u>Moving a File</u>

- Locate the file in the My Compuuter window.
- Hold down the right mouse button while you drag the file icon to its new folder or disk location.
- Click Move Here.

Suppose you want to move the Minutes file from the root directory to the Practice folder. Depending on your computer's settings, this file appears either as Minutes or Minutes.wps. In the following steps, the file is referred to as Minutes.

To move the Minutes file to the Practice folder:

1. Point to the **Minutes** icon.
2. Press and hold the right mouse button while you drag the Minutes icon to the Practice folder. See Figure 2-18.

TROUBLE? If you release the mouse button by mistake before dragging the Minutes icon to the Practice folder, the Minutes shortcut menu opens. Press Esc and then repeat Steps 1 and 2.

Figure 2-18 MOVING A FILE

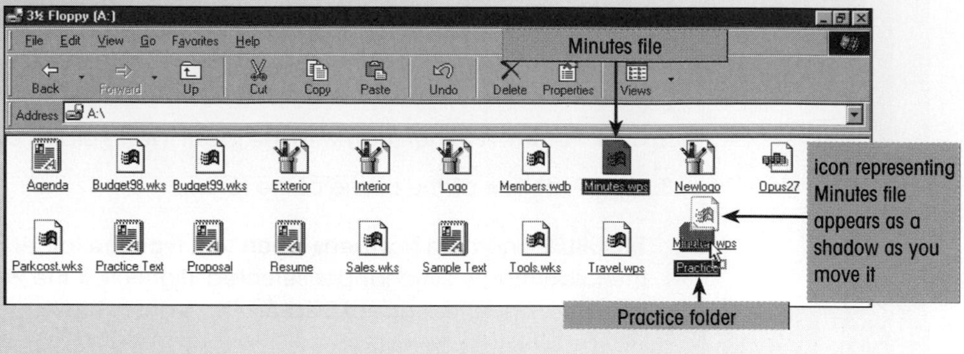

3. Release the right mouse button. A menu appears.

4. Click **Move Here**. The Minutes icon disappears from the window showing the files in the root directory.

Anything you do to an icon in the My Computer window is actually done to the file represented by that icon. If you move an icon, the file is moved; if you delete an icon, the file is deleted.

You can also copy a file from one folder to another, or from one disk to another. When you copy a file, you create an exact duplicate of an existing file in whatever disk or folder you specify. To copy a file from one folder to another on your floppy disk, you use the same procedure as for moving a file, except that you select Copy Here from the menu.

REFERENCE WINDOW RW

Copying a File

- Locate the file in the My Computer window.
- Use the right mouse button to drag the file to its new location, then click Copy Here.

Try copying the Resume file into the Practice folder.

To copy the Resume file into the Practice folder:

1. Using the right mouse button, drag the Resume file into the Practice folder.

2. Click **Copy Here**. Notice this time the file icon does not disappear, because you didn't actually move it, you only copied it.

After you move or copy a file, it is a good idea to make sure it was moved to the correct location. You can easily verify that a file is in its new folder by displaying the folder contents.

To verify that the Minutes file was moved and the Resume file was copied to the Practice folder:

1. Click the **Practice** folder icon. The Practice window appears, and it contains two files—Minutes, which you moved, and Resume, which you copied.

TROUBLE? If you are using Classic style, click Settings, click the Practice folder icon and then press Enter to open the Practice window.

Navigating Explorer Windows

The title bar of the open window on your computer, "Practice," identifies the name of the folder you just opened. Before you opened the Practice folder, you were viewing the contents of your floppy disk, so the window's title bar, 3½ Floppy (A:) (or possibly just A:/, depending on how your computer is set up), identified the drive containing your disk, drive A. Before you opened that window you were viewing the My Computer window. Windows that show the objects on your computer are called **Explorer windows** because they allow you to explore the contents of your computer's devices and folders.

You've seen that to navigate through the devices and folders on your computer, you open My Computer and then click the icons representing the objects you want to explore. But what if you want to move back to a previous Explorer window? The Standard toolbar, which stays the same regardless of which Explorer window is open, includes buttons that help you navigate through your Explorer windows. Figure 2-19 summarizes the navigation buttons on the Standard toolbar.

Figure 2-19 NAVIGATIONAL BUTTONS

BUTTON	ICON	DESCRIPTION
Back		Returns you to the Explorer window you were most recently viewing. This button is active only when you have viewed more than one Explorer window in the current session.
Forward		Reverses the effect of the Back button.
Up		Moves you up one level on the hierarchy of your computer's objects; for example, moves you from a folder Explorer window to the drive containing the folder.

Try returning to the 3½ Floppy (A:) window using the Back button.

To navigate Explorer windows:

1. Click the **Back** button to return to the 3½ Floppy (A:) window.

2. Click the **Forward** button to reverse the effect of the Back button and return to the Practice window.

3. Click the **Up** button to move up one level. You again return to the 3½ Floppy (A:) window because the Practice folder is contained within the 3½ Floppy (A:) drive.

Deleting a File

You delete a file or folder by deleting its icon. However, be careful when you delete a folder, because you also delete all the files it contains! When you delete a file from a *hard drive* on your computer, the filename is deleted from the directory but the file contents are held in the Recycle Bin. The **Recycle Bin** is an area on your hard drive that holds deleted files until you remove them permanently; an icon on the desktop allows you easy access to the Recycle Bin. If you change your mind and want to retrieve a file deleted from your hard drive, you can recover it by using the Recycle Bin.

When you delete a file from a *floppy disk*, it does not go into the Recycle Bin. Instead, it is deleted as soon as its icon disappears.

Try deleting the file named Agenda from your Student Disk. Because this file is on the floppy disk and not on the hard disk, it will not go into the Recycle Bin, and if you change your mind you won't be able to recover it.

To delete the file Agenda:

1. Right-click the icon for the file Agenda.
2. Click **Delete**.
3. If a message appears asking, "Are you sure you want to delete Agenda?", click **Yes**. The file is deleted and the Agenda icon no longer appears.

Renaming a File

Sometimes you decide to give a file a different name to clarify the file's contents. You can easily rename a file by using the Rename option on the file's shortcut menu or by using the file's label. The same rules apply for renaming a file as applied for naming a file, and you are limited in the number and type of characters you can use.

When you rename a file when file extensions are showing, make sure to include the extension in the new name. If you don't, Windows warns you it might not be able to identify the file type with the new name. Since you set up View options to hide file extensions, this should not be an issue unless you are trying to rename a file whose type Windows doesn't recognize.

Practice using this feature by renaming the Logo file to give it a more descriptive filename.

To rename Logo:

1. Right-click the **Logo** icon.
2. Click **Rename**. After a moment, a box appears around the label.
3. Type **Corporate Logo Draft** as the new filename.
4. Press the **Enter** key. The file now appears with the new name.
5. Click the **Up** button to move up one level to the My Computer window.

You can also edit an existing filename when you use the Rename command. Click to place the cursor at the location you want to edit, and then use the text-editing skills you learned with WordPad to edit the filename.

Copying an Entire Floppy Disk

You can have trouble accessing the data on your floppy disk if the disk is damaged, is exposed to magnetic fields, or picks up a computer virus. To avoid losing all your data, it is a good idea to make a copy of your floppy disk.

If you wanted to make a copy of an audio cassette, your cassette player would need two cassette drives. You might wonder, therefore, how your computer can make a copy of your disk if you have only one disk drive. Figure 2-20 illustrates how the computer uses only one disk drive to make a copy of a disk.

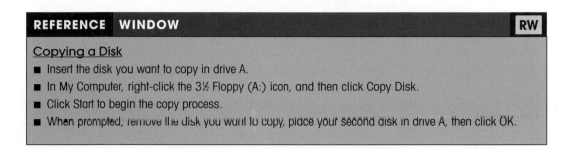

REFERENCE WINDOW RW

Copying a Disk

- Insert the disk you want to copy in drive A.
- In My Computer, right-click the 3½ Floppy (A:) icon, and then click Copy Disk.
- Click Start to begin the copy process.
- When prompted, remove the disk you want to copy, place your second disk in drive A, then click OK.

Figure 2-20 USING ONE DISK DRIVE TO COPY A DISK

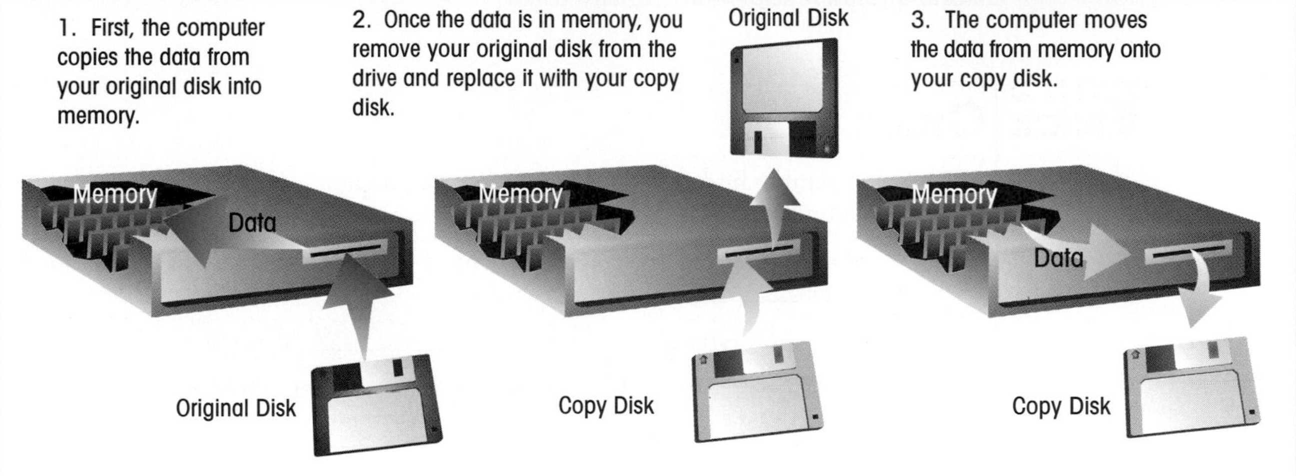
1. First, the computer copies the data from your original disk into memory.
2. Once the data is in memory, you remove your original disk from the drive and replace it with your copy disk.
Original Disk
3. The computer moves the data from memory onto your copy disk.
Memory
Data
Memory
Memory
Data
Original Disk
Copy Disk
Copy Disk

If you have an extra floppy disk, you can make a copy of your Student Disk now. If you change the files on your disk, make sure you copy the disk regularly to keep it updated.

To copy your Student Disk:

1. Write your name and "Windows 98 Disk 1 Student Disk Copy" on the label of your second disk. Make sure the disk is blank and formatted.

   TROUBLE? If you aren't sure the disk is blank, place it in the disk drive and open the 3½ Floppy (A:) window to view its contents. If the disk contains files you need, get a different disk. If it contains files you don't need, you could format the disk now, using the steps you learned at the beginning of this tutorial.

2. Make sure your Student Disk is in drive A and the My Computer window is open.

3. Right-click the **3½ Floppy (A:)** icon, and then click **Copy Disk**. The Copy Disk dialog box opens.
4. Click the **Start** button to begin the copy process.
5. When the message "Insert the disk you want to copy to (destination disk)..." appears, remove your Student Disk and insert your Windows 98 Disk 1 Student Disk Copy in drive A.
6. Click the **OK** button. When the copy is complete, you will see the message "Copy completed successfully." Click the **Close** button.
7. Close the My Computer window.
8. Remove your disk from the drive.

As you finish copying your disk, Shannon emphasizes the importance of making copies of your files frequently, so you won't risk losing important documents for your distance learning course. If your original Student Disk were damaged, you could use the copy you just made to access the files.

Keeping copies of your files is so important that Windows 98 includes with it a program called **Backup** that automates the process of duplicating and storing data. In the Projects at the end of the tutorial you'll have an opportunity to explore the difference between what you just did in copying a disk and the way in which a program such as the Windows 98 Backup program helps you safeguard data.

Quick Check

1. If you want to find out about the storage devices and printers connected to your computer, what window can you open?
2. If you have only one floppy disk drive on your computer, it is usually identified by the letter ____________.
3. The letter C is typically used for the ____________ drive of a computer.
4. What information does Details view supply about a list of folders and files?
5. The main directory of a disk is referred to as the ____________ directory.
6. True or False: You can divide a directory into folders.
7. If you have one floppy disk drive, but you have two disks, can you copy the files on one floppy disk to the other?

TUTORIAL ASSIGNMENT

1. **Opening, Editing, and Printing a Document** In this tutorial you learned how to create a document using WordPad. You also learned how to save, open, and print a document. Practice these skills by opening the document called Resume in the Practice folder of your Student Disk. This document is a resume for Jamie Woods. Make the changes shown in Figure 2-21, and then save the document in the Pratice folder with the name "Resume 2" using the Save As command. After you save your revisions, preview and then print the document. Close WordPad.

Figure 2-21

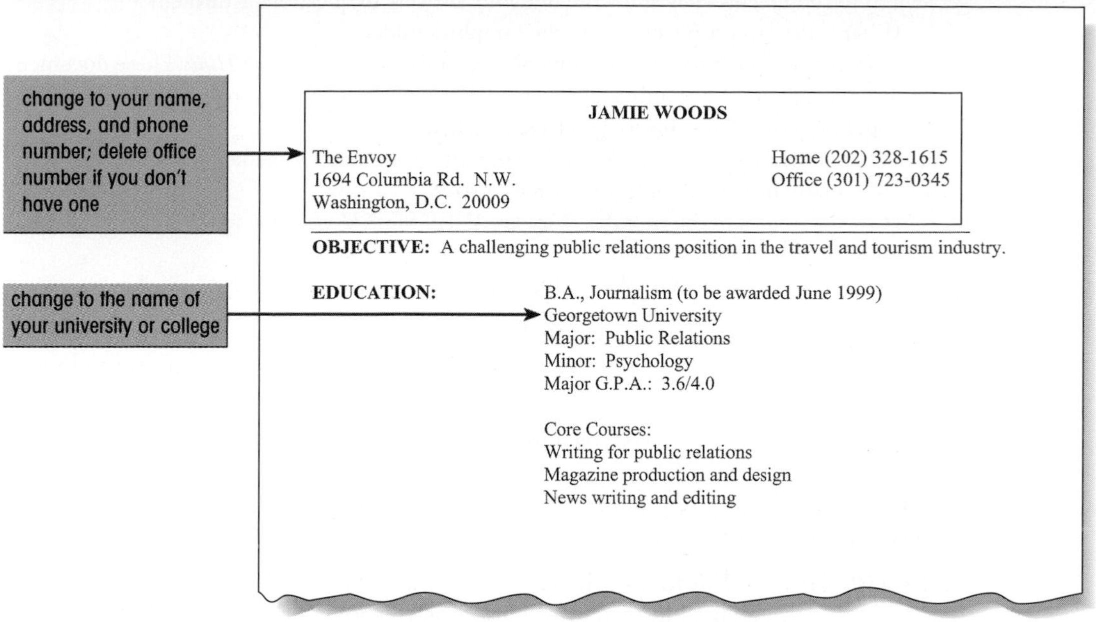
change to your name, address, and phone number; delete office number if you don't have one
change to the name of your university or college

JAMIE WOODS

The Envoy
1694 Columbia Rd. N.W.
Washington, D.C. 20009

Home (202) 328-1615
Office (301) 723-0345

OBJECTIVE: A challenging public relations position in the travel and tourism industry.

EDUCATION:
B.A., Journalism (to be awarded June 1999)
Georgetown University
Major: Public Relations
Minor: Psychology
Major G.P.A.: 3.6/4.0

Core Courses:
Writing for public relations
Magazine production and design
News writing and editing

2. **Creating, Saving, and Printing a Letter** Use WordPad to write a one-page letter to a relative or a friend. Save the document in the Practice folder on your Student Disk with the name "Letter." Use the Print Preview feature to look at the format of your finished letter, then print it, and be sure to sign it. Close WordPad.

3. **Managing Files and Folders** Using the copy of the disk you made at the end of the tutorial, complete parts a through f below to practice your file management skills.
   a. Create a folder called Spreadsheets on your Student Disk.
   b. Move the files Parkcost, Budget98, Budget99, and Sales into the Spreadsheets folder.
   c. Create a folder called Park Project.
   d. Move the files Proposal, Members, Tools, Corporate Logo Draft, and Newlogo into the Park Project folder.
   e. Delete the file called Travel.
   f. Switch to the Details view and write out your answers to questions 1 through 5:
      1. What is the largest file or files in the Park Project folder?
      2. What is the newest file or files in the Spreadsheets folder?
      3. How many files (don't include folders) are in the root directory of your Student Disk?
      4. How are the Opus and Exterior icons different? Judging from the appearance of the icons, what would you guess these two files contain?
      5. Which file in the root directory has the most recent date?

4. **More Practice with Files and Folders** For this assignment, you need a third blank disk. Complete parts a through g below to practice your file management skills.
   a. Write "Windows 98 Tutorial 2 Assignment 4" on the label of the blank disk, and then format the disk if necessary.
   b. Create a new Student Disk, using the Assignment 4 disk. Refer to the section "Creating Your Student Disk" in Session 2.2.
   c. Create three folders on the Assignment 4 Student Disk you just created: Documents, Budgets, and Graphics.
   d. Move the files Interior, Exterior, Logo, and Newlogo to the Graphics folder.
   e. Move the files Travel, Members, and Minutes to the Documents folder.

f. Move Budget98 and Budget99 to the Budgets folder.
g. Switch to the Details view and write out your answers to questions 1 through 5:
   1. What is the largest file or files in the Graphics folder?
   2. How many word-processed documents are in the root directory? *Hint*: These documents will appear with the WordPad, Microsoft Word, or some other word-processing icon, depending on what software you have installed.
   3. What is the newest file or files in the root directory (don't include folders)?
   4. How many files in all folders are 5 KB in size?
   5. How many files in the root directory are WKS files? *Hint*: Look in the Type column to identify WKS files.
   6. Do all the files in the Graphics folder have the same icon? What type are they?

5. **Finding a File** The Help system includes a topic that discusses how to find files on a disk without looking through all the folders. Start Windows Help, then locate this topic, and answer questions a through c:
   a. To display the Find dialog box, you must click the ______________ button, then point to ______________ from the menu, and finally click ______________ from the submenu.
   b. Do you need to type in the entire filename to find the file?
   c. How do you perform a case-sensitive search?

6. **Help with Files and Folders** In Tutorial 2 you learned how to work with Windows 98 files and folders. What additional information on this topic does Windows 98 Help provide? Use the Start button to access Help. Use the Index tab to locate topics related to files and folders. Find at least two tips or procedures for working with files and folders that were not covered in the tutorial. Write out the tip in your own words and include the title of the Help screen that contains the information.

Explore

7. **Formatting Text** You can use a word processor such as WordPad to **format** text, that is, to give it a specific look and feel by using bold, italics, and different fonts, and by applying other features. Using WordPad, type the title and words to one of your favorite songs and then save the document on your Student Disk (make sure you use your original Student Disk) with the name Song.
   a. Select the title, and then click the Center, Bold, and Italic buttons on the toolbar.
   b. Click the Font list arrow and select a different font. Repeat this step several times with different fonts until you locate a font that matches the song.
   c. Experiment with formatting options until you find a look you like for your document. Save and print the final version.

PROJECTS

1. Formatting a floppy disk removes all the data on a disk. Answer the following questions using full sentences:
   a. What other method did you learn in this tutorial to remove data from a disk?
   b. If you wanted to remove all data from a disk, which method would you use? Why?
   c. What method would you use if you wanted to remove only one file? Why?

2. A friend who is new to computers is trying to learn how to enter text into WordPad. She has just finished typing her first paragraph when she notices a mistake in the first sentence. She can't remember how to fix a mistake, so she asks you for help. Write the set of steps she should try.

3. Computer users usually develop habits about how they access their files and programs. Take a minute to practice methods of opening a file, and then evaluate which method you would be likely to use and why.
   a. Using WordPad, create a document containing the words to a favorite poem, and save it on your Student Disk with the name Poem.
   b. Close WordPad and return to the desktop.
   c. Open the document using a *document-centric* approach.
   d. After a successful completion of part c, close the program and reopen the same document using another approach.
   e. Write the steps you used to complete parts c and d of this assignment. Then write a paragraph discussing which approach is most convenient when you are starting from the desktop, and indicate what habits you would develop if you owned your own computer and used it regularly.

Explore

4. The My Computer window gives you access to the objects on your computer. In this tutorial you used My Computer to access your floppy drive so you could view the contents of your Student Disk. The My Computer window gives you access to other objects too. Open My Computer and write a list of the objects you see, including folders. Then click each icon and write a two-sentence description of the contents of each window that opens.

Explore

5. In this tutorial you learned how to copy a disk to protect yourself in the event of data loss. If you had your own computer with an 80 MB hard drive that was being used to capacity, it would take many 1.44 MB floppy disks to copy the contents of the entire hard drive. Is copying a reasonable method to use for protecting the data on your hard disk? Why, or why not?
   a. As mentioned at the end of the tutorial, Windows 98 also includes an accessory called Backup that helps you safeguard your data. Backup doesn't just copy the data—it organizes it so that it takes up much less space than if you simply copied it. This program might not be installed on your computer, but if it is, try starting it (click the Start button, point to Programs, point to Accessories, point to System Tools, and then click Backup) and opening the Help files to learn what you can about how it functions. If it is not installed, skip part a.
   b. Look up the topic of backups in a computer concepts textbook or in computer trade magazines. You could also interview experienced computer owners to find out which method they use to protect their data. When you have finished researching the concept of the backup, write a single-page essay that explains the difference between copying and backing up files, and evaluates which method is preferable for backing up large amounts of data, and why.

LAB ASSIGNMENTS

Using Files In this Lab you manipulate a simulated computer to view what happens in memory and on disk when you create, save, open, revise, and delete files. Understanding what goes on "inside the box" will help you quickly grasp how to perform basic file operations with most application software. See the Read This Before You Begin page for instructions on starting the Using Files Course Lab.

1. Click the Steps button to learn how to use the simulated computer to view the contents of memory and disk when you perform basic file operations. As you proceed through the Steps, answer all of the Quick Check questions that appear. After you complete the Steps, you will see a Quick Check Summary Report. Follow the instructions on the screen to print this report.

2. Click the Explore button and use the simulated computer to perform the following tasks:
   a. Create a document containing your name and the city in which you were born. Save this document as NAME.
   b. Create another document containing two of your favorite foods. Save this document as FOODS.
   c. Create another file containing your two favorite classes. Call this file CLASSES.
   d. Open the FOOD file and add another one of your favorite foods. Save this file without changing its name.
   e. Open the NAME file. Change this document so it contains your name and the name of your school. Save this as a new document called SCHOOL.
   f. Write down how many files are on the simulated disk and the exact contents of each file.
   g. Delete all the files.
3. In Explore, use the simulated computer to perform the following tasks.
   a. Create a file called MUSIC that contains the name of your favorite CD.
   b. Create another document that contains eight numbers and call this file LOTTERY.
   c. You didn't win the lottery this week. Revise the contents of the LOTTERY file, but save the revision as LOTTERY2.
   d. Revise the MUSIC file so it also contains the name of your favorite musician or composer, and save this file as MUSIC2.
   e. Delete the MUSIC file.
   f. Write down how many files are on the simulated disk and the exact contents of each file.

QUICK CHECK ANSWERS

Session 2.1

1. file
2. Formatting
3. True
4. insertion point
5. Word wrap
6. Move the I-beam pointer to the left of the first word you want to select, then drag the I-beam pointer over the text to the end of the last word you want to select.
7. file extension

Session 2.2

1. My Computer
2. A
3. hard
4. file name, size, type, and date modified
5. root or top-level
6. True
7. yes

New Perspectives on

MICROSOFT® EXCEL 2000

Read This Before You Begin

To the Student

Data Disks

To complete the Level I tutorials, Review Assignments, and Case Problems, you need 2 Data Disks. Your instructor will either provide you with these Data Disks or ask you to make your own.

If you are making your own Data Disks, you will need 2 blank, formatted high-density disks. You will need to copy a set of folders from a file server or standalone computer or the Web onto your disks. Your instructor will tell you which computer, drive letter, and folders contain the files you need. You could also download the files by going to www.course.com, clicking Data Disk Files, and following the instructions on the screen.

The following table shows you which folders go on each of your disks, so that you will have enough disk space to complete all the tutorials, Review Assignments, and Case Problems:

Data Disk 1

Write this on the disk label:
Data Disk 1: Tutorials 1-3

Put these folders and all subfolders on the disk:
Tutorial.01, Tutorial.02, Tutorial.03

Data Disk 2

Write this on the disk label:
Data Disk 2: Tutorial 4

Put these folders and all subfolders on the disk:
Tutorial.04

When you begin each tutorial, be sure you are using the correct Data Disk. Refer to the "File Finder" Chart at the back of this text for more detailed information on which files are used in which tutorials. See the inside front or inside back cover of this book for more information on Data Disk files, or ask your instructor or technical support person for assistance.

Course Labs

The Excel Level I tutorials feature an interactive Course Lab to help you understand spreadsheet concepts. There are Lab Assignments at the end of Tutorial 1 that relate to this Lab.

To start a Lab, click the **Start** button on the Windows taskbar, point to **Programs**, point to **Course Labs**, point to **New Perspectives Course Labs**, and click the name of the Lab you want to use.

Using Your Own Computer

If you are going to work through this book using your own computer, you need:

- **Computer System** Microsoft Windows 95, 98, NT, or higher must be installed on your computer. This book assumes a typical installation of Microsoft Excel.
- **Data Disk** You will not be able to complete the tutorials or exercises in this book using your own computer until you have your Data Disks.
- **Course Labs** See your instructor or technical support person to obtain the Course Lab software for use on your own computer.

Visit Our World Wide Web Site

Additional materials designed especially for you are available on the World Wide Web. Go to http://www.course.com.

To the Instructor

The Data files and Course Labs are available on the Instructor's Resource Kit for this title. Follow the instructions in the Help file on the CD-ROM to install the programs to your network or standalone computer. For information on creating Data Disks or the Course Labs, see the "To the Student" section above.

You are granted a license to copy the Data Files and Course Labs to any computer or computer network used by students who have purchased this book.

OBJECTIVES

In this tutorial you will:

- Start and exit Excel
- Discover how Excel is used in business
- Identify the major components of the Excel window
- Navigate an Excel workbook and worksheet
- Open, save, print, and close a worksheet
- Enter text, numbers, formulas, and functions
- Correct mistakes
- Perform what-if analyses
- Clear contents of cells
- Use the Excel Help system

LABS

Spreadsheets

USING WORKSHEETS TO MAKE BUSINESS DECISIONS

Evaluating Sites for an Inwood Design Group Golf Course

CASE

Inwood Design Group

Golf is big business in Japan. Spurred by the Japanese passion for the sport, golf enjoys unprecedented popularity in Japan. But because the country is small and mountainous, the 12 million golfers have fewer than 2,000 courses from which to choose. Fees for 18 holes on a public course average between $200 and $300; golf club memberships are bought and sold like stock shares. The market potential is phenomenal, but building a golf course in Japan is expensive because of inflated property values, difficult terrain, and strict environmental regulations.

Inwood Design Group plans to build a world-class golf course, and one of the four sites under consideration is Chiba Prefecture, Japan. Other possible sites are Kauai, Hawaii; Edmonton, Canada; and Scottsdale, Arizona. You and Mike Nagochi are members of the site selection team for Inwood. The team is responsible for collecting information on the sites, evaluating that information, and recommending the best site for the new golf course.

Your team identified five factors likely to determine the success of a golf course: Climate, Competition, Market Size, Topography, and Transportation. The team has already collected information on these factors for three of the four potential golf course sites. Mike has just returned from visiting the last site in Scottsdale, Arizona.

Using Microsoft Excel 2000 for Windows, Mike has created a worksheet that the team can use to evaluate the four sites. He needs to complete the worksheet by entering the data for the Scottsdale site. He then plans to bring the worksheet to the group's next meeting so that the team can analyze the information and recommend a site to management.

In this tutorial you will learn how to use Excel as you work with Mike to complete the Inwood site selection worksheet and with the Inwood team to select the best site for the golf course.

SESSION 1.1

In this session you will learn what a spreadsheet is and how it is used in business. You will learn what Excel is and about the Excel window and its elements, how to move around a worksheet using the keyboard and the mouse, and how to open a workbook.

What Is Excel?

Spreadsheets

Excel is a computerized spreadsheet. A **spreadsheet** is an important business tool that helps you analyze and evaluate information. Spreadsheets are often used for cash flow analysis, budgeting, decision making, cost estimating, inventory management, and financial reporting. For example, an accountant might use a spreadsheet like the one in Figure 1-1 for a budget.

Figure 1-1 BUDGET SPREADSHEET

Cash Budget Forecast

	January Estimated	*January Actual*
Cash in Bank (Start of Month)	$1,400.00	$1,400.00
Cash in Register (Start of Month)	100.00	100.00
Total Cash	$1,500.00	$1,500.00
Expected Cash Sales	$1,200.00	$1,420.00
Expected Collections	400.00	380.00
Other Money Expected	100.00	52.00
Total Income	$1,700.00	$1,852.00
Total Cash and Income	$3,200.00	$3,352.00
All Expenses (for Month)	$1,200.00	$1,192.00
Cash Balance at End of Month	$2,000.00	$2,160.00

To produce the spreadsheet in Figure 1-1, you could manually calculate the totals and then type your results, or you could use a computer and spreadsheet program to perform the calculations and print the results. Spreadsheet programs are also referred to as electronic spreadsheets, computerized spreadsheets, or just spreadsheets.

In Excel 2000, the document you create is called a **workbook**. Each workbook is made up of individual **worksheets**, or **sheets**, just as a spiral-bound notebook is made up of sheets of paper. You will learn more about using multiple sheets later in this tutorial. For now, just keep in mind that the terms *worksheet* and *sheet* are often used interchangeably.

Starting Excel

Mike arrives at his office early because he needs to work with you to finish the worksheet and get ready for your meeting with the design team.

Start Excel and complete the worksheet that Mike will use to help the design team decide about the golf course site.

To start Microsoft Excel:

1. Make sure Windows is running on your computer and the Windows desktop appears on your screen.
2. Click the **Start** button on the taskbar to display the Start menu, and then point to **Programs** to display the Programs menu.
3. Point to **Microsoft Excel** on the Programs menu. See Figure 1-2.

Figure 1-2 STARTING MICROSOFT EXCEL

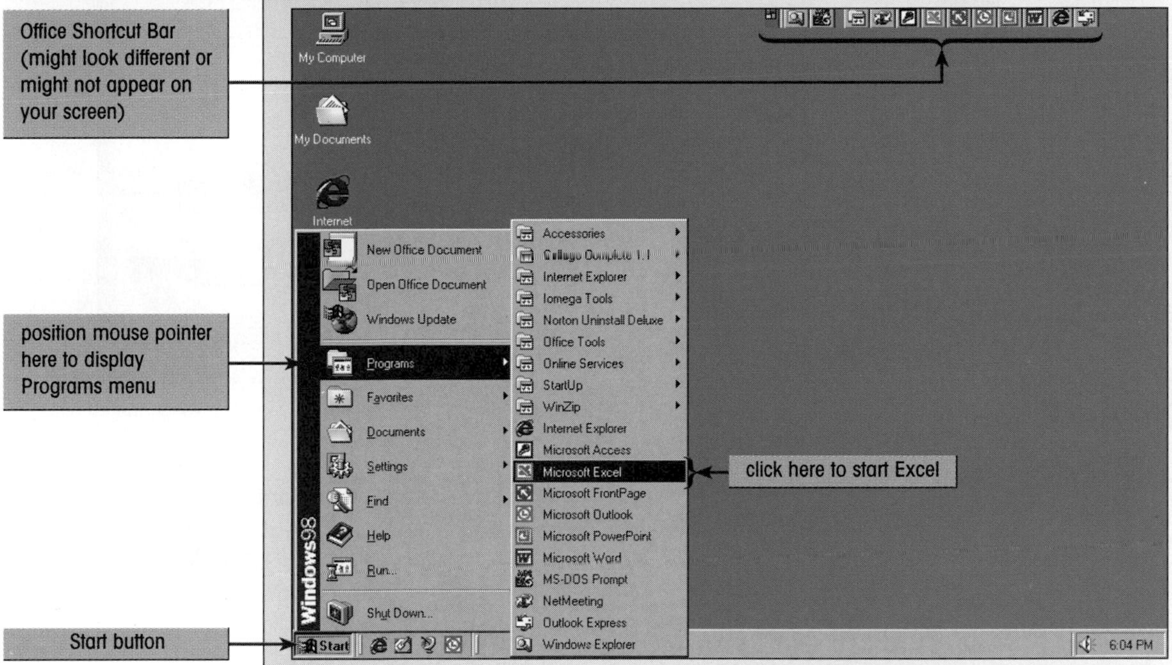

TROUBLE? Don't worry if your screen differs slightly. Although figures in this book were created while running Windows 98 in its default setting, these operating systems share the same basic user interface and Microsoft Excel runs equally well using Windows 95, Windows 98 in Web style, Windows NT, and Windows 2000.

TROUBLE? If the Office Shortcut Bar, which appears along the top border of the desktop in Figure 1-2, looks different on your screen or does not appear at all, your system may be set up differently. The steps in these tutorials do not require that you use the Office Shortcut Bar; therefore, the remaining figures do not display it.

4. Click **Microsoft Excel**. After a short pause, the Microsoft Excel copyright information appears in a message box and remains on the screen until the Excel program window and a blank worksheet appear. See Figure 1-3.

   TROUBLE? If the Office Assistant (see Figure 1-3) window opens when you start Excel, click Help on the menu bar then click Hide the Office Assistant. You'll learn more about the Office Assistant later in this tutorial.

Figure 1-3 EXCEL PROGRAM WINDOW WITH BLANK WORKSHEET

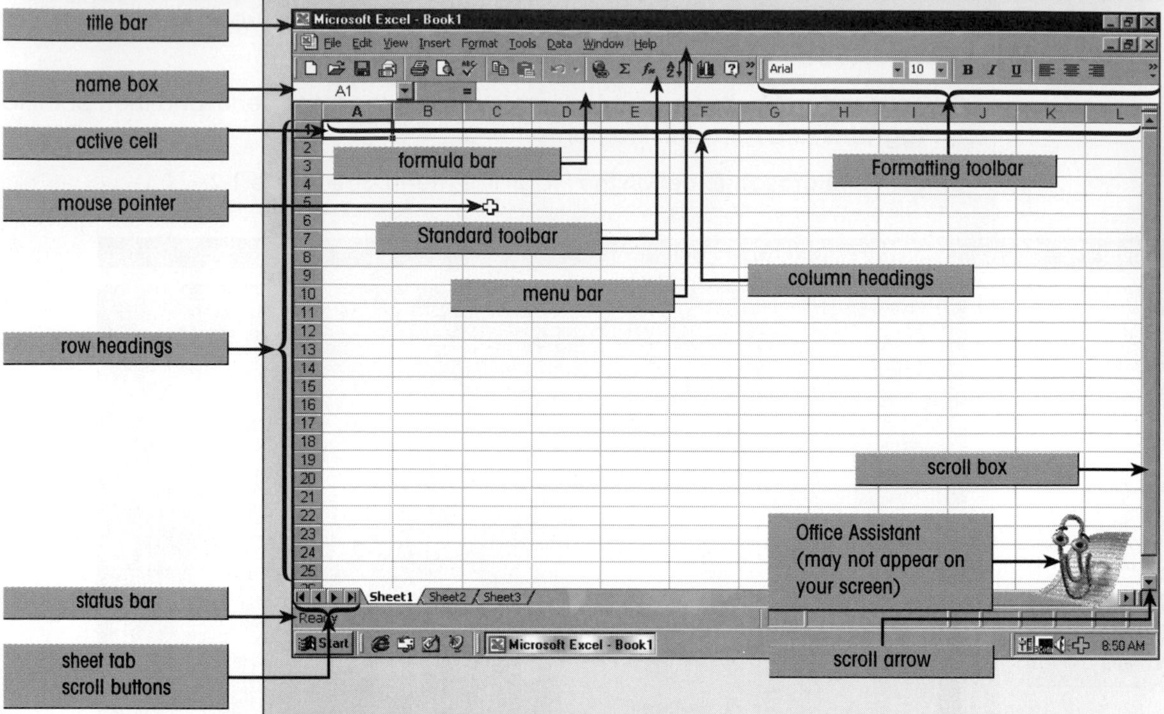

5. If the Microsoft Excel program window does not fill the entire screen as in Figure 1-3, click the **Maximize** button in the upper-right corner of the program window. If the Book1 window is not maximized, click in the upper-right corner of the Book1 window. Your screen should now resemble Figure 1-3.

The Excel Window

The Excel window layout is consistent with the layout of other Windows programs. It contains many common features, such as the title bar, menu bar, scroll bars, and taskbar. Figure 1-3 shows these elements as well as the main components of the Excel window. Take a look at each of these Excel components so you are familiar with their location and purpose.

Toolbars

Toolbars allow you to organize the commands in Excel. The menu bar is a special toolbar at the top of the window that contains menus such as File, Edit, and View. The Standard toolbar and the Formatting toolbar are located below the menu bar. The **Standard** toolbar contains buttons corresponding to the most frequently used commands in Excel. The **Formatting** toolbar contains buttons corresponding to the commands most frequently used to improve the appearance of a worksheet.

Formula Bar

The **formula bar**, located immediately below the toolbars, displays the contents of the active cell. A **cell's contents** is the text, numbers, and formulas you enter into it. As you type or edit data, the changes appear in the formula bar. The **name box** appears at the left end of the formula bar. This area displays the cell reference for the active cell.

Workbook Window

The document window, usually called the **workbook window** or **worksheet window**, contains the sheet you are creating, editing, or using. Each worksheet consists of a series of columns identified by lettered column headings and a series of rows identified by numbered row headings. Columns are assigned alphabetic labels from A to IV (256 columns). Rows are assigned numeric labels from 1 to 65,536 (65,536 rows).

A **cell** is the rectangular area where a column and a row intersect. Each cell is identified by a **cell reference**, which is its column and row location. For example, the cell reference B6 indicates the cell where column B and row 6 intersect. The column letter is always first in the cell reference. B6 is a correct cell reference; 6B is not. The **active cell** is the cell in which you are currently working. Excel identifies the active cell with a dark border that outlines one cell. In Figure 1-3, cell A1 is the active cell. Notice that the cell reference for the active cell appears in the name box of the formula bar. You can change the active cell when you want to work elsewhere in the worksheet.

Pointer

The **pointer** is the indicator that moves on your screen as you move your mouse. The pointer changes shape to reflect the type of task you can perform at a particular location. When you click a mouse button, something happens at the pointer's location. In Figure 1-3, the pointer looks like a white plus sign ✚.

Sheet Tabs

Each worksheet has a **sheet tab** that identifies the name of the worksheet. The name on the tab of the active sheet is bold. The sheet tabs let you move quickly between the sheets in a workbook; you can simply check the sheet tab of the sheet you want to move to. By default, a new workbook consists of three worksheets. If your workbook contains many worksheets, you can use the **sheet tab scroll buttons** to scroll through the sheet tabs that are not currently visible to find the sheet you want.

Moving Around a Worksheet

Before entering or editing the contents of a cell, you need to select that cell to make it the active cell. You can select a cell using either the keyboard or the mouse.

Using the Mouse

Using the mouse, you can quickly select a cell by placing the mouse pointer on the cell and clicking the mouse button. If you need to move to a cell that's not currently on the screen, use the vertical and horizontal scroll bars to display the area of the worksheet containing the cell you are interested in, and then select the cell.

Using the Keyboard

In addition to the mouse, Excel provides you with many keyboard options for moving to different cell locations within your worksheet. Figure 1-4 shows some of the keys you can use to select a cell within your worksheet.

Figure 1-4 KEYS TO MOVE AROUND THE WORKSHEET

KEYSTROKE	ACTION
↑, ↓, ←, →	Moves up, down, left, or right one cell
PgUp	Moves the active cell up one full screen
PgDn	Moves the active cell down one full screen
Home	Moves the active cell to column A of the current row
Ctrl + Home	Moves the active cell to cell A1
F5 (function key)	Opens Go To dialog box, in which you enter cell address of cell you want to make active cell

Now, try moving around the worksheet using your keyboard and mouse.

To move around the worksheet:

1. Position the mouse pointer ✚ over cell E8, then click the **left mouse** button to make it the active cell. Notice that the cell is surrounded by a black border to indicate that it is the active cell and that the name box on the formula bar displays E8.
2. Click cell **B4** to make it the active cell.
3. Press the → key to make cell C4 the active cell.
4. Press the ↓ key to make cell C5 the active cell. See Figure 1-5.

Figure 1-5 CELL C5 AS ACTIVE CELL

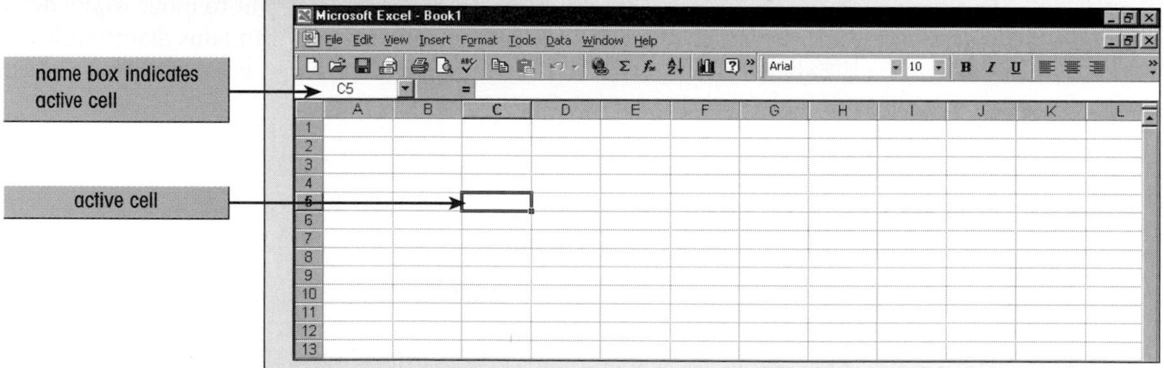

5. Press the **Home** key to move to cell A5, the first cell in the current row.
6. Press **Ctrl + Home** to make cell A1 the active cell. The shortcut key Ctrl + Home can be used at any time to move to the beginning of the worksheet. Normally this is cell A1.

So far you've moved around the portion of the worksheet you can see. Many worksheets can't be viewed entirely on one screen. Next, you'll use the keyboard and mouse to bring other parts of the worksheet into view.

To bring other parts of the worksheet into view:

1. Press the **Page Down** key to move the display down one screen. The active cell is now cell A26 (the active cell on your screen may be different). Notice that the row numbers on the left side of the worksheet indicate you have moved to a different area of the worksheet. See Figure 1-6.

Figure 1-6 WORKSHEET SCREEN AFTER MOVING TO DIFFERENT AREA OF WORKSHEET

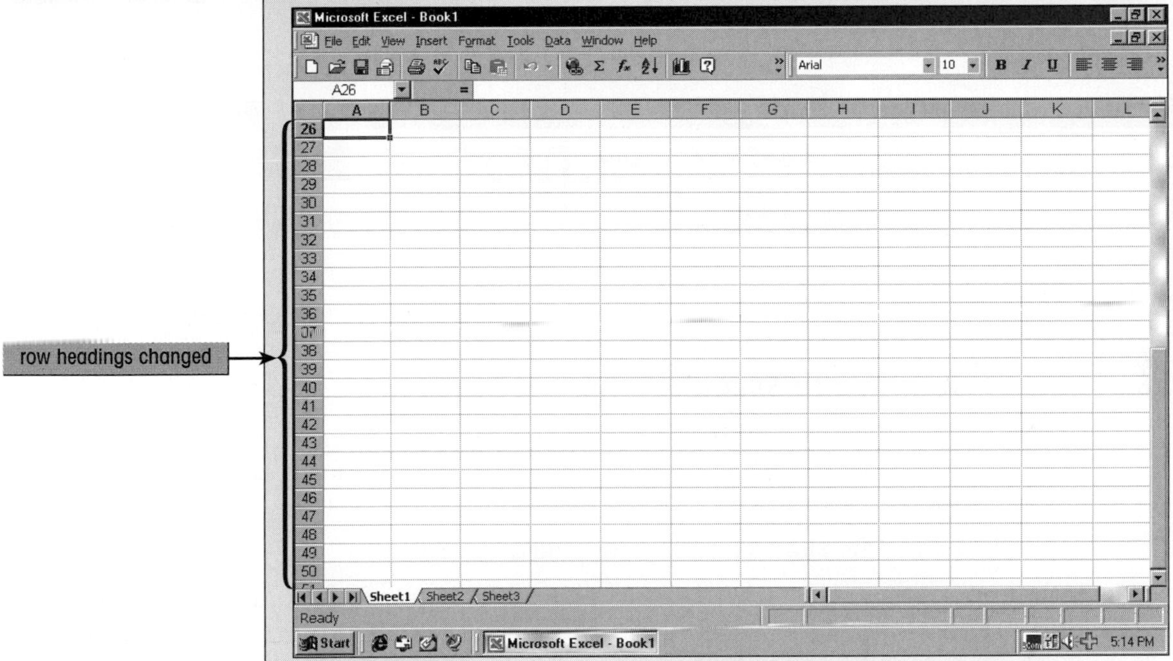

2. Press the **Page Down** key again to move the display down one screen. Notice that the row numbers indicate that you have moved to a different area of the worksheet.
3. Press the **Page Up** key to move the display up one screen. The active cell is now cell A26 (the active cell on your screen may be different).
4. Click the **vertical scroll bar up arrow** button until row 12 is visible. Notice that the active cell is still A26 (the active cell on your screen may be different). Using the scroll bar changes the portion of the screen you can view without changing the active cell.
5. Click cell **C12** to make it the active cell.
6. Click the blank area above the vertical scroll box to move up a full screen.
7. Click the blank area below the vertical scroll box to move down a full screen.
8. Click the **scroll box** and drag it to the top of the scroll area to again change the area of the screen you're viewing. Notice that the ScrollTip appears telling you the current row location.
9. Press **F5** to open the Go To dialog box.
10. Type **K55** in the Reference box and then click **OK**. Cell K55 is now the active cell.
11. Press **Ctrl + Home** to make cell A1 the active cell. Now click cell **E6**.

As you know, a workbook can consist of one or more worksheets. Excel makes it easy to switch between them. Next, try moving from worksheet to worksheet.

Navigating in a Workbook

The sheet tabs let you move quickly among the different sheets in a workbook. If you can see the tab of the sheet you want, click the tab to activate the worksheet. You can also use the sheet tab scroll buttons to see sheet tabs hidden from view. Figure 1-7 describes the four tab scrolling buttons and their effects.

Figure 1-7 SHEET TAB SCROLLING BUTTONS

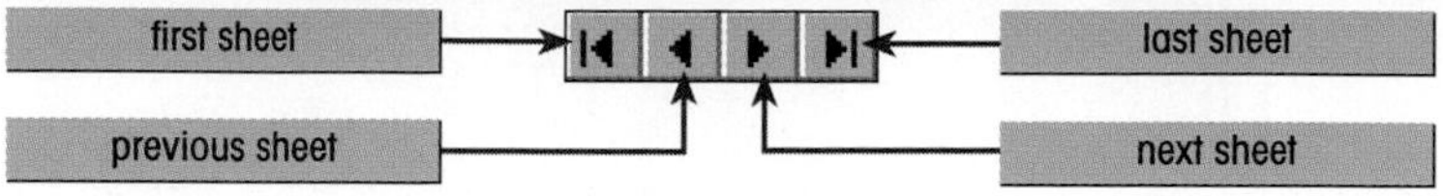

Next, try moving to a new sheet.

To move to Sheet2:

1. Click the **Sheet2** tab. Sheet2, which is blank, appears in the worksheet window. Notice that the Sheet2 sheet tab is white and the name is bold, which means that Sheet2 is now the active sheet. Cell A1 is the active cell in Sheet2.
2. Click the **Sheet3** tab to make it the active sheet.
3. Click the **Sheet1** tab to make it the active sheet. Notice that cell E6 is still the active cell.

Now that you have some basic skills navigating a worksheet and workbook, you can begin working with Mike to complete the golf site selection worksheet.

Opening a Workbook

When you want to use a workbook that you previously created, you must first open it. Opening a workbook transfers a copy of the workbook file from the hard drive or 3½-inch disk to the random access memory (RAM) of your computer and displays it on your screen. When the workbook is open, the file is both in RAM and on the disk.

After you open a workbook, you can view, edit, print, or save it again on your disk.

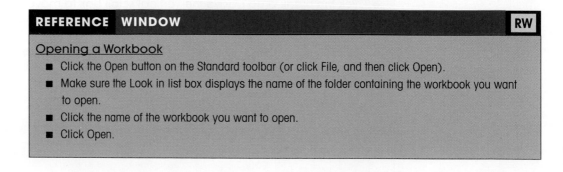

REFERENCE WINDOW RW

Opening a Workbook

- Click the Open button on the Standard toolbar (or click File, and then click Open).
- Make sure the Look in list box displays the name of the folder containing the workbook you want to open.
- Click the name of the workbook you want to open.
- Click Open.

Mike created a workbook to help the site selection team evaluate the four potential locations for the golf course. The workbook, Inwood, is on your Data Disk.

To open an existing workbook:

1. Place your Excel Data Disk in the appropriate drive.

TROUBLE? If you don't have a Data Disk, you need to get one before you can proceed. Your instructor or technical support person will either give you one or ask you to make your own by following the instructions on the "Read This Before You Begin" page before this tutorial. See your instructor or technical support person for information.

2. Click the **Open** button on the Standard toolbar. The Open dialog box opens. See Figure 1-8.

Figure 1-8 OPEN DIALOG BOX

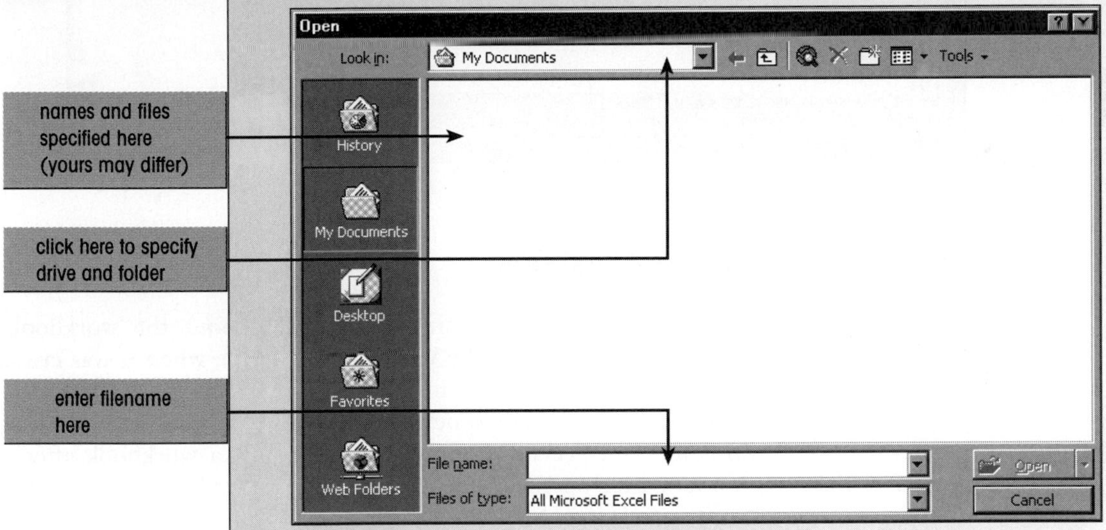

3. Click the **Look in** list arrow to display the list of available drives. Locate the drive containing your Data Disk. In this text, we assume your Data Disk is a 3½-inch disk in drive A.

4. Click the drive that contains your Data Disk. A list of documents and folders on your Data Disk appears in the list box.

5. In the list of document and folder names, double-click **Tutorial.01,** double-click **Tutorial** to display that folder in the Look in list box, then click **Inwood**.

6. Click the **Open** button. (You could also double-click the filename to open the file.) The Inwood workbook opens and the first sheet in the workbook, Documentation, appears. See Figure 1-9. Notice the filename, Inwood, appears on the title bar at the top of your screen.

Figure 1-9 DOCUMENTATION SHEET IN INWOOD WORKBOOK

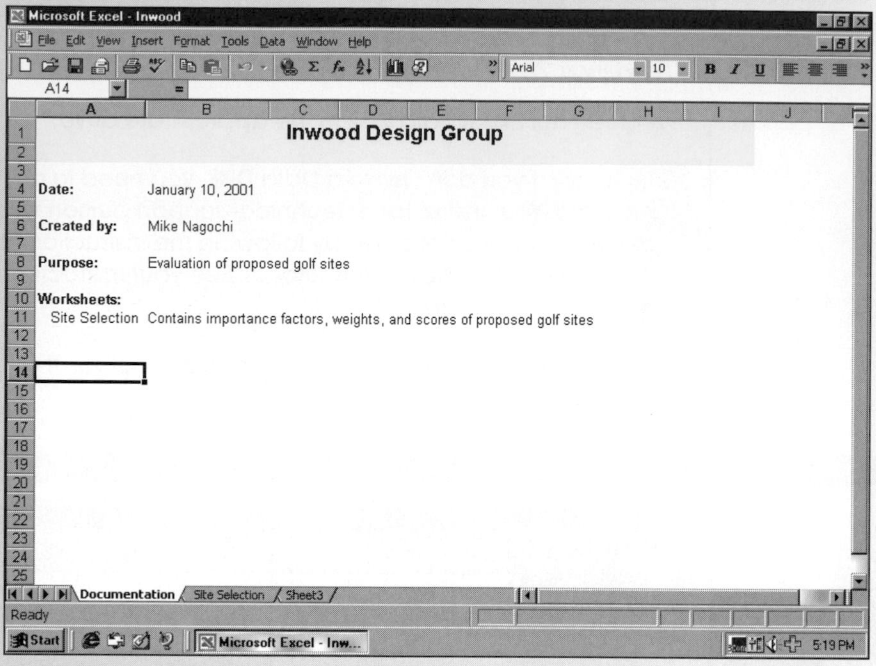

Layout of the Inwood Workbook

The first worksheet, Documentation, contains information about the workbook. The Documentation sheet shows who created the workbook, the date when it was created, its purpose, and a brief description of each sheet in the workbook.

Mike explains that whenever he creates a new workbook he makes sure he documents it carefully. This information is especially useful if he returns to a workbook after a long period of time (or if a new user opens it) because it provides a quick review of the workbook's purpose.

After reviewing the Documentation sheet, Mike moves to the Site Selection worksheet.

To move to the Site Selection worksheet:

1. Click the **Site Selection** sheet tab to display the worksheet Mike is preparing for the site selection team. See Figure 1-10.

Figure 1-10 SITE SELECTION WORKSHEET

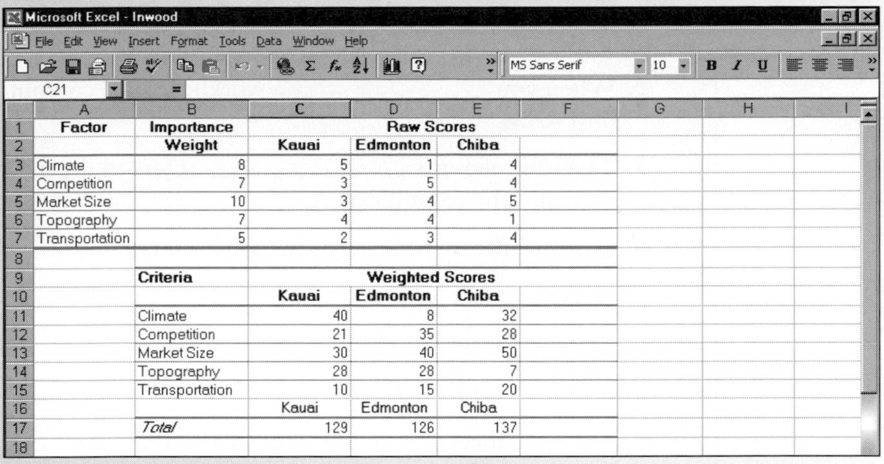

	A	B	C	D	E
1	Factor	Importance		Raw Scores	
2		Weight	Kauai	Edmonton	Chiba
3	Climate	8	5	1	4
4	Competition	7	3	5	4
5	Market Size	10	3	4	5
6	Topography	7	4	4	1
7	Transportation	5	2	3	4
8					
9		Criteria		Weighted Scores	
10			Kauai	Edmonton	Chiba
11		Climate	40	8	32
12		Competition	21	35	28
13		Market Size	30	40	50
14		Topography	28	28	7
15		Transportation	10	15	20
16			Kauai	Edmonton	Chiba
17		*Total*	129	126	137
18					

Mike explains the general layout of the Site Selection worksheet to you. He reminds you that to this point he has only entered data for three of the four sites. He will provide the missing Scottsdale information to you. Cells C2 through E2 list three of the four sites for which he has data. Cells A3 through A7 contain the five factors on which the team's decision will be based: Climate, Competition, Market Size, Topography, and Transportation. They assign scores for Climate, Competition, Market Size, Topography, and Transportation to each location. The team uses a scale of 1 to 5 to assign a raw score for each factor. Higher raw scores indicate strength; lower raw scores indicate weakness. Cells C3 through E7 contain the raw scores for the first three locations. For example, the raw score for Kauai's Climate is 5; the two other locations have scores of 1 and 4, so Kauai, with its warm, sunny days all year, has the best climate for the golf course of the three sites visited so far. Edmonton, on the other hand, has cold weather and only received a Climate raw score of 1.

The raw scores, however, do not provide enough information for the team to make a decision. Some factors are more important to the success of the golf course than others. The team members assigned an *importance weight* to each factor according to their knowledge of what factors contribute most to the success of a golf course. The importance weights are on a scale from 1 to 10, with 10 being most important. Mike entered the weights in cells B3 through B7. Market size, weighted 10, is the most important factor. The team believes the least important factor is Transportation, so Transportation is assigned a lower weight. Climate is important but the team considers Market Size most important. They do not use the raw scores to make a final decision; instead, they multiply each raw score by its importance weight to produce a weighted score. Which of the three sites already visited has the highest weighted score for any factor? If you look at the scores in cells C11 through E15, you see that Chiba's score of 50 for Market Size is the highest weighted score for any factor.

Cells C17 through E17 contain the total weighted scores for the three locations. With the current weighted and raw scores, Chiba is the most promising site, with a total score of 137.

Session 1.1 Quick Check

1. A(n) ______________ is the rectangular area where a column and a row intersect.
2. When you ______________ a workbook, the computer copies it from your disk into RAM.
3. The cell reference ______________ refers to the intersection of the fourth column and the second row.
4. To move the worksheet to the right one column:
   a. press the Enter key
   b. click the right arrow on the horizontal scroll bar
   c. press the Esc key
   d. press Ctrl + Home
5. To make Sheet2 the active worksheet, you would ______________.
6. What key or keys do you press to make cell A1 the active cell?

You have now reviewed the layout of the worksheet. Now, Mike wants you to enter the data on Scottsdale. Based on his meeting with local investors and a visit to the Scottsdale site, he has assigned the following raw scores: Climate 5, Competition 2, Market Size 4, Topography 3, and Transportation 3. To complete the worksheet, you must enter the raw scores he has assigned to the Scottsdale site. You will do this in the next session.

SESSION 1.2

In this session you will learn how to enter text, values, formulas, and functions into a worksheet. You will use this data to perform what-if analyses using a worksheet. You'll also correct mistakes and use the online Help system to determine how to clear the contents of cells. Finally, you'll learn how to print a worksheet and how to close a worksheet and exit Excel.

Text, Values, Formulas, and Functions

As you have now observed, an Excel workbook can hold one or more worksheets, each containing a grid of 256 columns and 65,536 rows. The rectangular areas at the intersections of each column and row are called cells. A cell can contain a value, text, or a formula. To understand how the spreadsheet program works, you need to understand how Excel manipulates text, values, formulas, and functions.

Text

Text entries include any combination of letters, symbols, numbers, and spaces. Although text is sometimes used as data, it is more often used to describe the data contained in a worksheet. Text is often used to label columns and rows in a worksheet. For example, a projected monthly income statement contains the months of the year as column headings and income and expense categories as row labels. To enter text in a worksheet, you select the cell in which you want to enter the text by clicking the cell to select it, then typing the text. Excel automatically aligns the text on the left in a cell.

Mike's Site Selection worksheet contains a number of column heading labels. You need to enter the label for Scottsdale in the Raw Scores and Weighted Scores sections of the worksheet.

To enter a text label:

1. If you took a break after the last session, make sure Excel is running and make sure the Site Selection worksheet of the Inwood workbook is showing.
2. Click cell **F2** to make it the active cell.
3. Type **Scottsdale**, then press the **Enter** key.

   TROUBLE? If you make a mistake while typing, you can correct the error with the Backspace key. If you realize you made an error after you press the Enter key, retype the entry by repeating Steps 2 and 3.

4. Click cell **F10** and type **S**. Excel completes the entry for you based on the entries already in the column. If your data involves repetitious text, this feature, known as **AutoComplete**, can make your data entry go more quickly.
5. Press the **Enter** key to complete the entry.
6. Click cell **F16**, type **S**, and press the **Enter** key to accept Scottsdale as the entry in the cell. See Figure 1-11. Next, you need to enter the raw scores Mike assigned to Scottsdale.

Figure 1-11 WORKSHEET AFTER TEXT HAS BEEN ENTERED

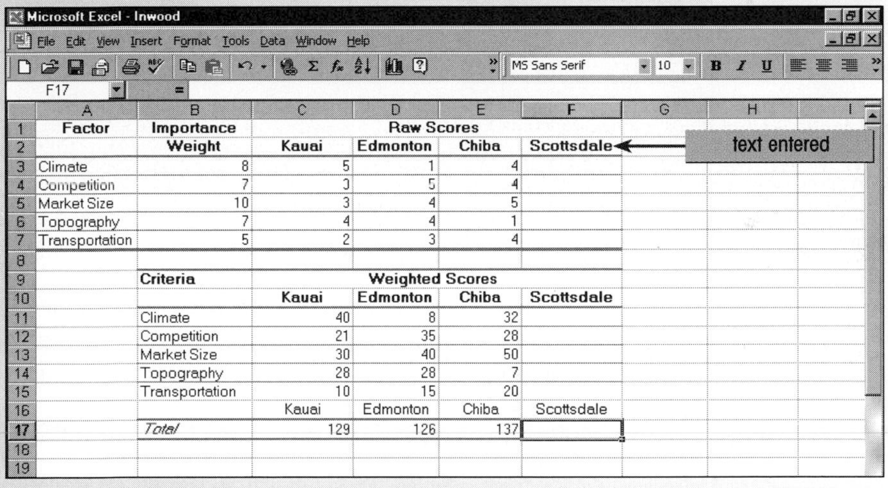

	A	B	C	D	E	F
1	Factor	Importance		Raw Scores		
2		Weight	Kauai	Edmonton	Chiba	Scottsdale
3	Climate	8	5	1	4	
4	Competition	7	3	5	4	
5	Market Size	10	3	4	5	
6	Topography	7	4	4	1	
7	Transportation	5	2	3	4	
8						
9		Criteria		Weighted Scores		
10			Kauai	Edmonton	Chiba	Scottsdale
11		Climate	40	8	32	
12		Competition	21	35	28	
13		Market Size	30	40	50	
14		Topography	28	28	7	
15		Transportation	10	15	20	
16			Kauai	Edmonton	Chiba	Scottsdale
17		*Total*	129	126	137	
18						
19						

Values

Values are numbers that represent a quantity of some type: the number of units in inventory, stock price, an exam score, and so on. Examples of values are 378, 25.275, and -55. Values can also be dates (11/29/99) and times (4:40:31). As you type information in a cell, Excel determines whether the characters you're typing can be used as values. For example, if you type 456, Excel recognizes it as a value and it is right-justified in the cell. On the other hand, Excel treats some data commonly referred to as "numbers" as text. For example, Excel treats a telephone number (1-800-227-1240) or a Social Security number (372-70-9654) as text that cannot be used for calculations.

You need to enter the raw scores for Scottsdale.

To enter a value:

1. If necessary, click the scroll arrow so row 2 is visible. Click cell **F3**, type **5** and then press the **Enter** key. The active cell is now cell F4.
2. With cell F4 as the active cell, type **2** and press the **Enter** key.
3. Enter the value **4** for Market Size in cell F5, the value **3** for Topography in cell F6, and the value **3** for Transportation in cell F7. See Figure 1-12.

Figure 1-12 WORKSHEET AFTER NUMBERS HAVE BEEN ENTERED

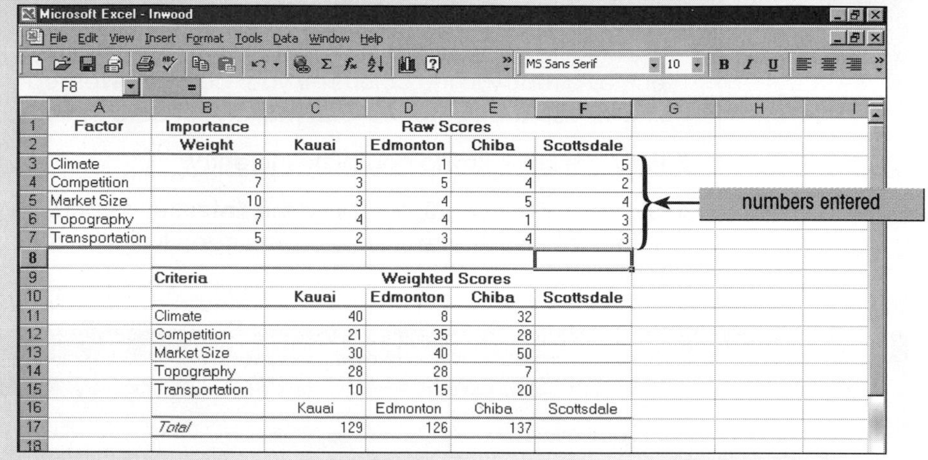

	A	B	C	D	E	F
1	Factor	Importance		Raw Scores		
2		Weight	Kauai	Edmonton	Chiba	Scottsdale
3	Climate	8	5	1	4	5
4	Competition	7	3	5	4	2
5	Market Size	10	3	4	5	4
6	Topography	7	4	4	1	3
7	Transportation	5	2	3	4	3
8						
9		Criteria		Weighted Scores		
10			Kauai	Edmonton	Chiba	Scottsdale
11		Climate	40	8	32	
12		Competition	21	35	28	
13		Market Size	30	40	50	
14		Topography	28	28	7	
15		Transportation	10	15	20	
16			Kauai	Edmonton	Chiba	Scottsdale
17		*Total*	129	126	137	
18						

Next, you enter the formulas to calculate Scottsdale's weighted score in each category.

Formulas

When you need to perform a calculation in Excel you use a formula. A **formula** is the arithmetic used to calculate values appearing in a worksheet. You can take advantage of the power of Excel by using formulas in worksheets. If you change one number in a worksheet, Excel recalculates any formula affected by the change.

An Excel formula always begins with an equal sign (=). Formulas are created by combining numbers, cell references, arithmetic operators, and/or functions. An **arithmetic operator** indicates the desired arithmetic operations. Figure 1-13 shows the arithmetic operators used in Excel.

Figure 1-13 ARITHMETIC OPERATORS USED IN FORMULAS

ARITHMETIC OPERATIONS	ARITHMETIC OPERATOR	EXAMPLE	DESCRIPTION
Addition	+	=10+A5 =B1+B2+B3	Adds 10 to value in cell A5 Adds the values of cells B1, B2, and B3
Subtraction	–	=C9–B2 =1–D2	Subtracts the value in cell B2 from the value in cell C9 Subtracts the value in cell D2 from 1
Multiplication	*	=C9*B9 =E5*.06	Multiplies the value in cell C9 by the value in cell B9 Multiplies the value in E5 by the constant .06
Division	/	=C9/B9 =D15/12	Divides the value in cell C9 by the value in cell B9 Divides the value in cell D15 by 12
Exponentiation	^	=B5^3 =3^B5	Raises the value stored in cell B5 to 3 Raises 3 to the value stored in cell B5

The result of the formula appears in the cell where you entered the formula. To view the formula that has been entered in a cell, you must first select the cell, then look at the formula bar.

REFERENCE WINDOW RW

Entering a Formula

- Click the cell where you want the result to appear.
- Type = and then type the rest of the formula.
- For formulas that include cell references, such as B2 or D78, you can type the cell reference or you can use the mouse or arrow keys to select each cell.
- When the formula is complete, press the Enter key.

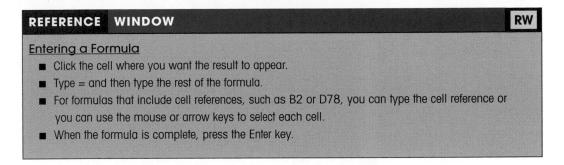

You need to enter the formulas to compute the weighted scores for the Scottsdale site. The formula multiples the raw score for a factor by the importance weight assigned to the factor. Figure 1-14 displays the formulas you need to enter into the worksheet.

Figure 1-14 FORMULAS TO CALCULATE SCOTTSDALE'S WEIGHTED SCORES

CELL	FORMULA	EXPLANATION
F11	=B3*F3	Multiplies importance weight by raw score for Climate
F12	=B4*F4	Multiplies importance weight by raw score for Competition
F13	=B5*F5	Multiplies importance weight by raw score for Market Size
F14	=B6*F6	Multiplies importance weight by raw score for Topography
F15	=B7*F7	Multiplies importance weight by raw score for Transportation

To enter the formulas to calculate each weighted score for the Scottsdale site:

1. Click cell **F11** to make it the active cell. Type **=B3*F3** to multiply the weight assigned to the Climate category by the raw score assigned to Scottsdale for the Climate category. Press the **Enter** key. The value 40 appears in cell F11.

   TROUBLE? If you make a mistake while typing, you can correct the error with the Backspace key. If you realize you made an error after you press the Enter key, repeat Step 1 to retype the entry.

2. Click cell **F11** to make it the active cell again. See Figure 1-15. Notice, the results of the formula appear in the cell, but the formula you entered appears on the formula bar.

Figure 1-15 WORKSHEET DISPLAYS VALUE IN CELL AND FORMULA IN FORMULA BAR

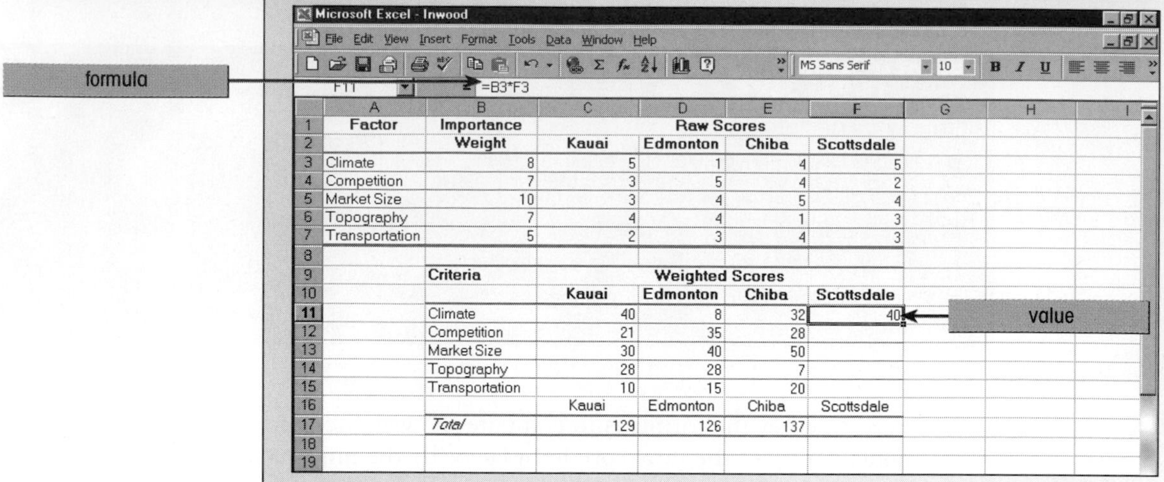

	A	B	C	D	E	F
1	Factor	Importance		Raw Scores		
2		Weight	Kauai	Edmonton	Chiba	Scottsdale
3	Climate	8	5	1	4	5
4	Competition	7	3	5	4	2
5	Market Size	10	3	4	5	4
6	Topography	7	4	4	1	3
7	Transportation	5	2	3	4	3
8						
9		Criteria		Weighted Scores		
10			Kauai	Edmonton	Chiba	Scottsdale
11		Climate	40	8	32	40
12		Competition	21	35	28	
13		Market Size	30	40	50	
14		Topography	28	28	7	
15		Transportation	10	15	20	
16			Kauai	Edmonton	Chiba	Scottsdale
17		*Total*	129	126	137	
18						
19						

3. Click cell **F12**, type **=B4*F4**, and then press the **Enter** key. This formula multiplies the weight assigned to Competition (the contents of cell B4) by Scottsdale's raw score for Competition (cell F4). The value 14 appears in cell F12.

4. Enter the remaining formulas from Figure 1-14 into cells F13, F14, and F15. When completed, your worksheet will contain the values 40, 14, 40, 21, and 15 in cells F11 to F15.

TROUBLE? If any value in cells F11 through F15 differs, retype the formula for that cell.

You now have to enter the formula to calculate the total weighted score for Scottsdale into the worksheet. You can use the formula *=F11+F12+F13+F14+F15* to calculate the total score for the Scottsdale site. As an alternative, you can use a function to streamline this long formula.

Functions

A **function** is a predefined or built-in formula that's a shortcut for commonly used calculations. For example, the SUM function is a shortcut for entering formulas that total values in rows or columns. You can use the SUM function to create the formula =SUM(F11:F15) instead of typing the longer *=F11+F12+F13+F14+F15*. The SUM function in this example adds the range F11 through F15. A **range** is a group of cells, either a single cell or a rectangular block of cells. The range reference F11:F15 in the function SUM(F11:F15) refers to the rectangular block of cells beginning in the upper-left corner (F11) and ending in the lower-right corner (F15) of the range. The colon separates the upper-left corner and lower-right corner of the range. Figure 1-16 shows several examples of ranges.

Figure 1-16 EXAMPLES OF RANGES

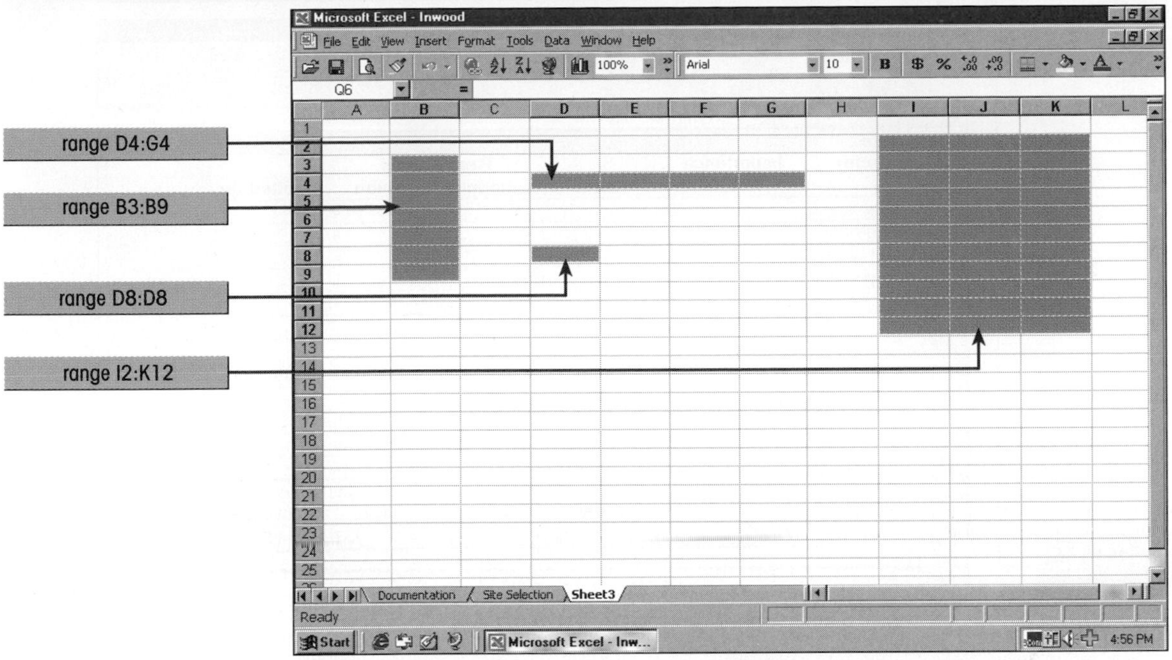

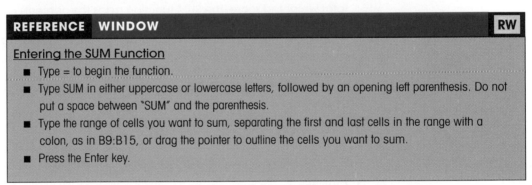

REFERENCE WINDOW RW

Entering the SUM Function

- Type = to begin the function.
- Type SUM in either uppercase or lowercase letters, followed by an opening left parenthesis. Do not put a space between "SUM" and the parenthesis.
- Type the range of cells you want to sum, separating the first and last cells in the range with a colon, as in B9:B15, or drag the pointer to outline the cells you want to sum.
- Press the Enter key.

You use the SUM function to compute the total score for the Scottsdale site.

To enter the formula using a function:

1. Click cell **F17** to make it the active cell.
2. Type **=SUM(F11:F15)**. Notice that the formula appears in the cell and the formula bar as you enter it. See Figure 1-17.

Figure 1-17 **VIEWING THE SUM FUNCTION BEFORE COMPLETING THE ENTRY**

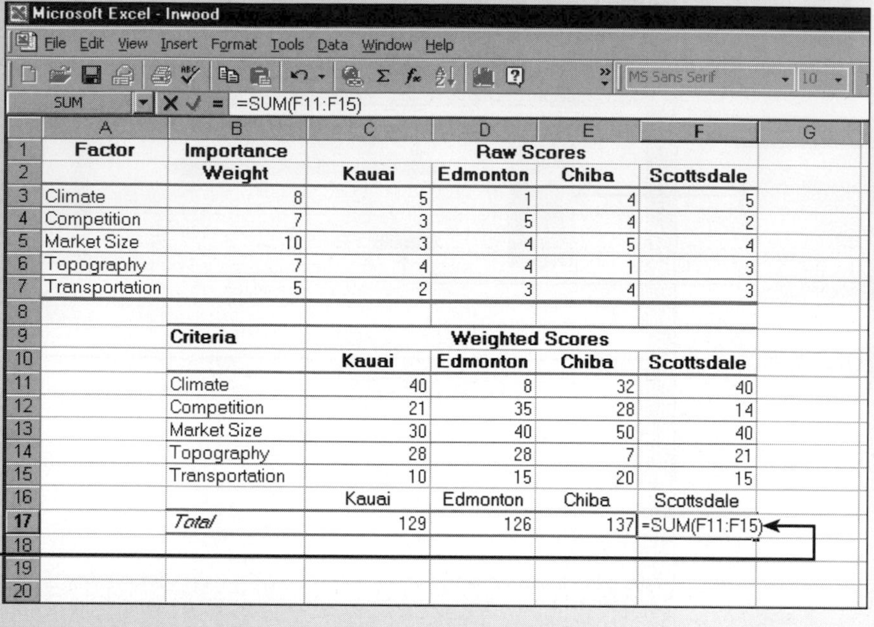

	A	B	C	D	E	F	G
1	**Factor**	**Importance**		**Raw Scores**			
2		**Weight**	**Kauai**	**Edmonton**	**Chiba**	**Scottsdale**	
3	Climate	8	5	1	4	5	
4	Competition	7	3	5	4	2	
5	Market Size	10	3	4	5	4	
6	Topography	7	4	4	1	3	
7	Transportation	5	2	3	4	3	
8							
9		**Criteria**		**Weighted Scores**			
10			**Kauai**	**Edmonton**	**Chiba**	**Scottsdale**	
11		Climate	40	8	32	40	
12		Competition	21	35	28	14	
13		Market Size	30	40	50	40	
14		Topography	28	28	7	21	
15		Transportation	10	15	20	15	
16			Kauai	Edmonton	Chiba	Scottsdale	
17		*Total*	129	126	137	=SUM(F11:F15)	
18							
19							
20							

SUM function appears in cell as you type

3. Press the **Enter** key to complete the formula entry and display 130, Scottsdale's total weighted score. The SUM function adds the contents of cells F11 through F15.

TROUBLE? If 130 is not displayed in cell F17, return to Step 1 and retype formula.

The Site Selection worksheet is now complete. Mike's worksheet contains columns of information about the site selection and a chart displaying the weighted scores for each potential site. To see the chart, you must scroll the worksheet.

To scroll the worksheet to view the chart:

1. Click the **scroll arrow** button on the vertical scroll bar until the section of the worksheet containing the chart appears. See Figure 1-18.

Figure 1-18 **SCROLLING THE WORKSHEET TO VIEW THE CHART**

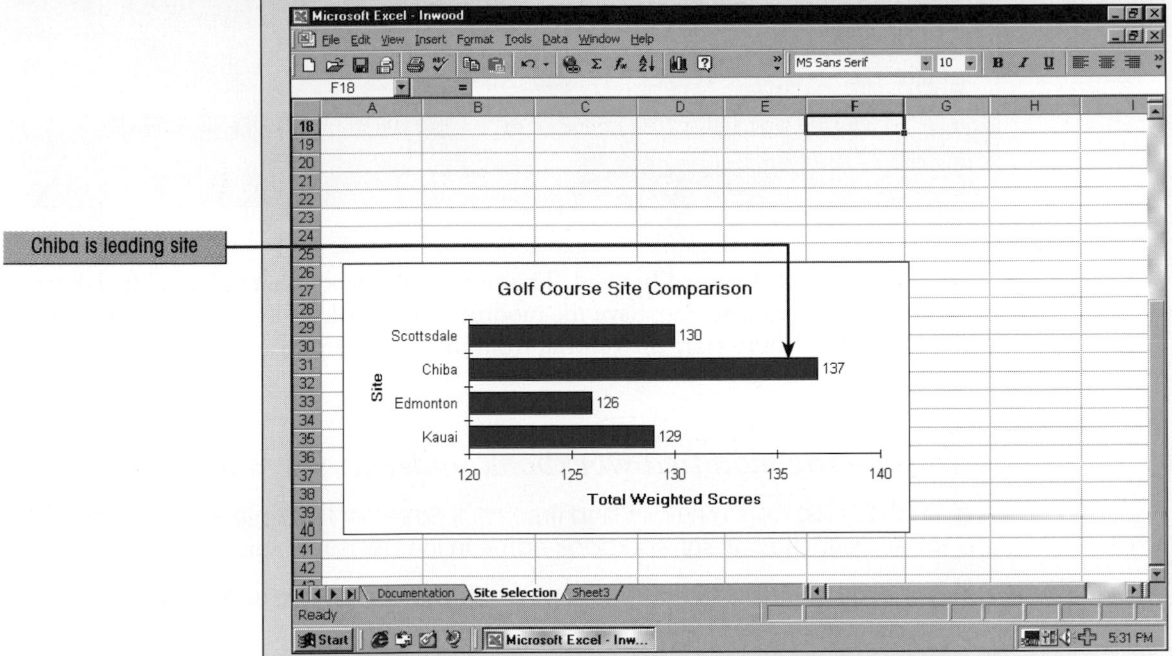

2. After you look at the chart, click and drag the **scroll box** to the top of the vertical scroll bar.

You have completed the worksheet; Mike decides to save it before showing it to the site selection team.

Saving the Workbook

To store a workbook permanently so you can use it again without having to reenter the data and formulas, you must save it as a file on a disk. When you save a workbook, you copy it from RAM onto your disk. You'll use either the Save or the Save As command. The Save command copies the workbook onto a disk using its current filename. If a version of the file already exists, the new version replaces the old one. The Save As command asks for a filename before copying the workbook onto a disk. When you enter a new filename, you save the current file under that new name. The previous version of the file remains on the disk under its original name.

As a general rule, use the Save As command the first time you save a file or whenever you modify a file and want to save both the old and new versions. Use the Save command when you modify a file and want to save only the current version.

It is a good idea to save your file often. That way, if the power goes out or the computer stops working, you're less likely to lose your work. Because you use the Save command frequently, the Standard toolbar has a Save button, a single mouse-click shortcut for saving your workbook.

REFERENCE WINDOW RW

Saving a Workbook with a New Filename

- Click File and then click Save As.
- Change the workbook name as necessary.
- Make sure the Save in box displays the folder in which you want to save your workbook.
- Click the Save button.

Mike's workbook is named Inwood. The version of Inwood that you modified during this work session is on your screen. Save the modified workbook under the new name Inwood 2. This way if you want to start the tutorial from the beginning, you can open the Inwood file and start over.

To save the modified workbook under a new name:

1. Click **File** on the menu bar, and then click **Save As**. The Save As dialog box opens with the current workbook name in the File name text box.
2. Click at the end of the current workbook name, press the **spacebar**, and then type **2**. (Do not press the Enter key.)

   Before you proceed, check the other dialog box specifications to ensure that you save the workbook on your Data Disk.
3. If necessary, click the **Save in** list arrow to display the list of available drives and folders. Click the Tutorial folder in **Tutorial.01**.
4. Confirm that the Save as type text box specifies "Microsoft Excel Workbook."
5. As the number of saved worksheets begins to accumulate, you can create new folders or subfolders to store related files. You can create a new folder by clicking the New Folder button. See Figure 1-19.
6. If you need to save an Excel file in an earlier Excel format, or another format such as Lotus 1-2-3, click the drop-down area next to the Save as type box and then select the file type from the list shown.
7. When your Save As dialog box looks like the one in Figure 1-19, click the **Save** button to close the dialog box and save the workbook. Notice that the new workbook name, Inwood 2, now appears in the title bar.

Figure 1-19 SAVING THE WORKSHEET WITH A NEW FILENAME

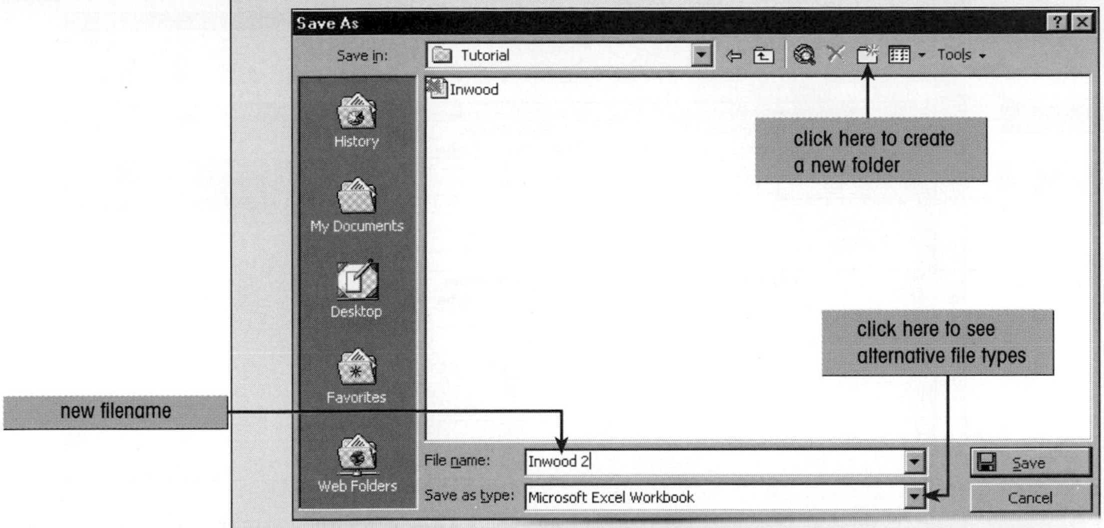

You now have two versions of the workbook: the original file—Inwood—and the modified workbook—Inwood 2.

What-if Analysis

The worksheet for site selection is now complete. Mike is ready to show it to the group. As the team examines the worksheet, you ask if the raw scores take into account recent news that a competing design group has announced plans to build a $325-million golf resort just 10 miles away from Inwood's proposed site in Chiba. Mike admits that he assigned the values before the announcement, so the raw scores do not reflect the increased competition in the Chiba market. You suggest revising the raw score for the Competition factor to reflect this market change in Chiba.

When you change a value in a worksheet, Excel automatically recalculates the worksheet and displays updated results. The recalculation feature makes Excel an extremely useful decision-making tool because it lets you quickly and easily factor in changing conditions. When you revise the contents of one or more cells in a worksheet and observe the effect this change has on all the other cells, you are performing a **what-if analysis**. In effect, you are saying, what if I change the value assigned to this factor? What effect will it have on the outcomes in the worksheet?

Because another development group has announced plans to construct a new golf course in the Chiba area, the team decides to lower Chiba's Competition raw score from 4 to 2.

To change Chiba's Competition raw score from 4 to 2:

1. Click cell **E4**. The black border around cell E4 indicates that it is the active cell. The current value of cell E4 is 4.
2. Type **2**. Notice that 2 appears in the cell and in the formula bar, along with a formula palette of three new buttons. The buttons shown in Figure 1-20—the Cancel button, the Enter button, and the Edit Formula button offer alternatives for canceling, entering, and editing data and formulas.

Figure 1-20 **CHANGING A CELL'S CONTENTS**

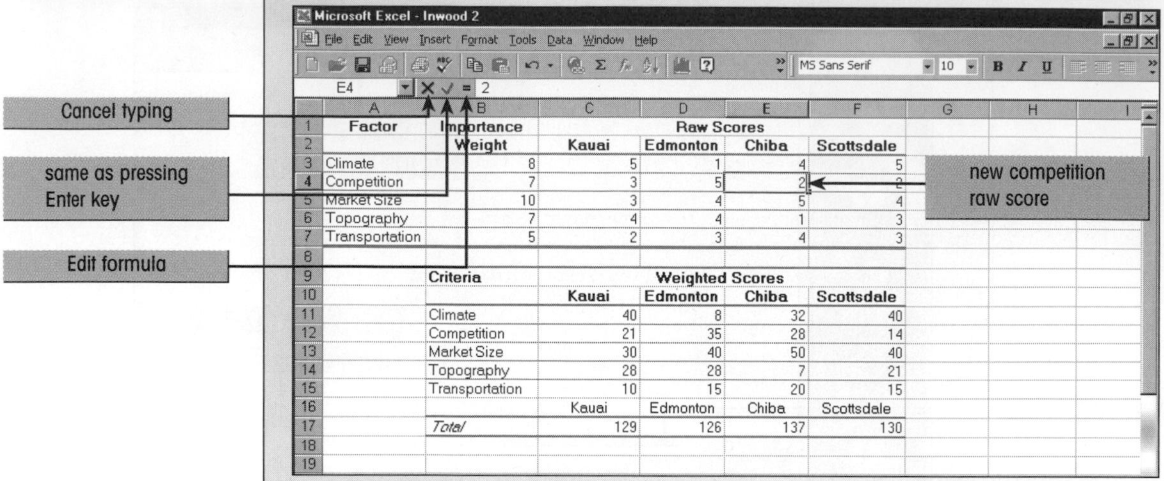

3. Click the **Enter** button. Excel recalculates Chiba's weighted score for the Competition factor (cell E12) and the total score for Chiba (cell E17). If necessary, click the **vertical scroll** arrow until row 17 is visible on your screen. The recalculated values are 14 and 123. See Figure 1-21.

Figure 1-21 **WORKSHEET AFTER FORMULAS ARE RECALCULATED**

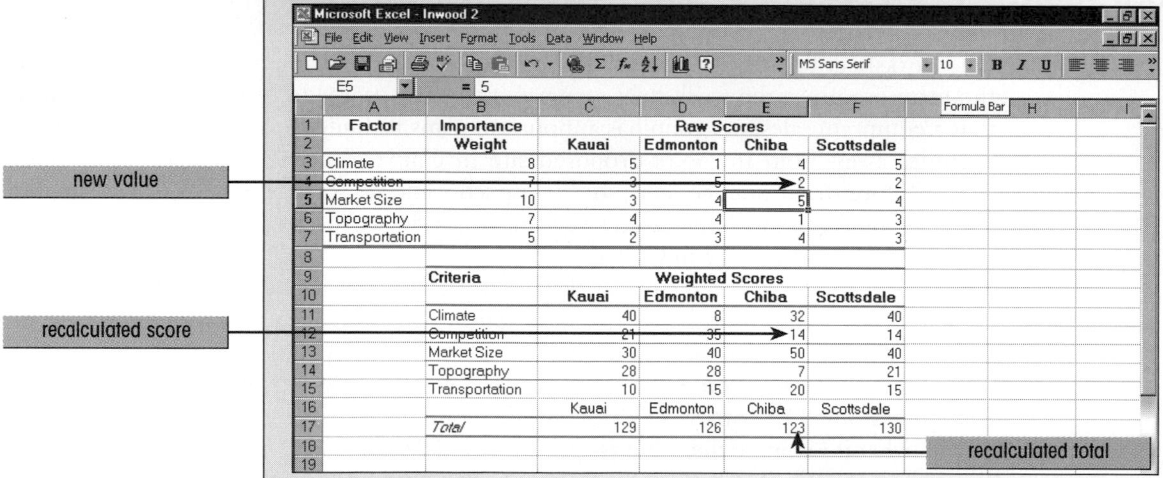

The team takes another look at the total weighted scores in row 17. Scottsdale is now the top-ranking site, with a total weighted score of 130, compared to Chiba's total weighted score of 123.

As the team continues to discuss the worksheet, several members express concern over the importance weight used for Transportation. In the current worksheet, Transportation is weighted 5 (cell B7). You remember that the group agreed to use an importance weight of 2 at a previous meeting. You ask Mike to change the importance weight for Transportation.

To change the importance weight for Transportation:

1. Click cell **B7** to make it the active cell.

2. Type **2** and press the **Enter** key. Cell B7 now contains the value 2 instead of 5. Cell B8 becomes the active cell. See Figure 1-22. Notice that the weighted scores for Transportation (row 15) and the total weighted scores for each site (row 17) have all changed.

Figure 1-22 WORKSHEET AFTER CHANGE MADE TO THE TRANSPORTATION IMPORTANCE WEIGHT

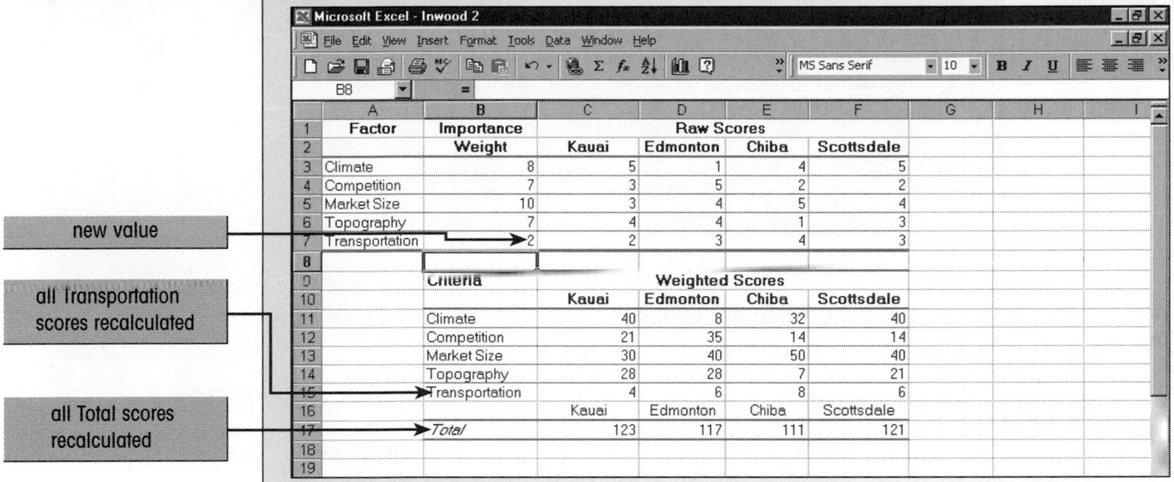

The change in the Transportation importance weight puts Kauai ahead as the most favorable site, with a total weighted score of 123.

As you enter and edit a worksheet, there are many data entry errors that can occur. The most commonly made mistake on a worksheet is a typing error. Typing mistakes are easy to correct.

Correcting Mistakes

It is easy to correct a mistake as you are typing information in a cell, before you press the Enter key. If you need to correct a mistake as you are typing information in a cell, press the Backspace key to back up and delete one or more characters. If you want to start over, press the Esc key to cancel all changes. When you are typing information in a cell, *don't* use the cursor arrow keys to edit because they move the cell pointer to another cell. One of the team members suggests changing the label "Criteria" in cell B9 to "Factors." The team members agree and you make the change to the cell.

To correct a mistake as you type:

1. Click cell **B9** to make it the active cell.

2. Type **Fak**, intentionally making an error, but don't press the Enter key.

3. Press the **Backspace** key to delete "k".

4. Type **ctors** and press the **Enter** key.

Now the word "Factors" is in cell B9. Mike suggests changing "Factors" to "Factor." The team agrees. To change a cell's contents after you press the Enter key, you use a different method. You can either retype the contents of a cell, or enter Edit mode to change the contents of a cell on the formula bar. Double-clicking a cell or pressing the F2 key puts Excel into **Edit** mode, which lets you use the Home, End, Delete, Backspace keys and the ← and → keys, and the mouse to change the text in the formula bar.

REFERENCE WINDOW RW

Correcting Mistakes Using Edit Mode

- Double-click the cell you want to edit to begin Edit mode. The contents of the cell appear directly in the cell as well as the formula bar (or click the cell you want to edit, then press F2).
- Use Home, End, Delete, Backspace, ←, → or the mouse to edit the cell's contents either in the cell or in the formula bar.
- Press the Enter key when you finish editing.

You use Edit mode to change "Factors" to "Factor" in cell B9.

To change the word "Factors" to "Factor" in cell B9:

1. Double-click cell **B9** to begin Edit mode. Note that "Edit" appears in the status bar, reminding you that Excel is currently in Edit mode.
2. Press the **End** key if necessary to move the cursor to the right of the word "Factors," then press the **Backspace** key to delete the "s".
3. Press the **Enter** key to complete the edit.

You ask if the team is ready to recommend a site. Mike believes that, based on the best information they have, Kauai should be the recommended site and Scottsdale the alternative site. You ask for a vote, and the team unanimously agrees with Mike's recommendation.

Mike wants to have complete documentation to accompany the team's written recommendation to management, so he wants to print the worksheet.

As he reviews the worksheet one last time, he thinks that the labels in cells C16 through F16 (Kauai, Edmonton, Chiba, Scottsdale) are unnecessary and decides he wants you to delete them before printing the worksheet. You ask how to delete the contents of a cell or a group of cells. Mike is not sure, so he suggests using the Excel Help system to find the answer.

Getting Help

If you don't know how to perform a task or forget how to carry out a particular task, Excel provides an extensive on-screen help. The Excel Help system provides the same options as the Help system in other Office programs—asking help from the Office Assistant, getting help from the Help menu, and obtaining help information from Microsoft's web site. If you are not connected to the Web, you only have access to the Help files stored on your computer.

One way to get help is to use the Office Assistant, which you may have seen on your screen when you first started Excel, and which you closed earlier in this tutorial. The Office Assistant, an animated object, pops up on the screen when you click the Microsoft Excel

Help button on the Standard toolbar. The Office Assistant answers questions, offers tips, and provides help for a variety of Excel features. In addition to the Office Assistant, Figure 1-23 identifies several other ways you can get Help.

Figure 1-23 ALTERNATIVE WAYS TO USE MICROSOFT EXCEL HELP

ACTION*	RESULTS IN
A. Right-click Office Assistant, click Options from short-cut menu and then click Use the Office Assistant checkbox to remove check	Office Assistant no longer in use
B. On Help menu, click Microsoft Excel Help, then click Contents tab	Displays an outline of topics and subtopics on which you can get information
C. On Help menu, click Microsoft Excel Help, then click Index tab	Displays alphabetical listing of topics; enter words or phrases to scroll to an entry
D. On Help menu, click Microsoft Excel Help, then click Answer Wizard tab	Displays a Help window where a question can be entered. After clicking Search button, Excel displays a selected list of Help topics
E. Press F1	Displays Microsoft Excel Help window
F. Press Shift + F1	Pointer changes to What's This which you click when positioned over any object or menu option on the screen to see a description of the object or option

*(Alternatives B–F assume that alternative A has been implemented.)

REFERENCE WINDOW RW

Using the Office Assistant

- Click the Microsoft Excel Help button on the Standard toolbar (or choose Microsoft Excel Help from the Help menu) to display the Office Assistant.
- Click Options to change the Office Assistant features you want to use.

or

- Type an English-language question on a topic where you need help, and then click Search.
- Click the suggested Help topic.
- To hide the Office Assistant, right-click the Office Assistant, then click Hide.

Use the Office Assistant to get information on how to clear the contents of cells.

To get Help using the Office Assistant:

1. Click **Help** from the menu bar, then click **Show the Office Assistant** to display an animated object. If necessary, click the **Office Assistant** to display the Information Box next to the Office Assistant. See Figure 1-24.

Figure 1-24 OFFICE ASSISTANT WITH INFORMATION BOX

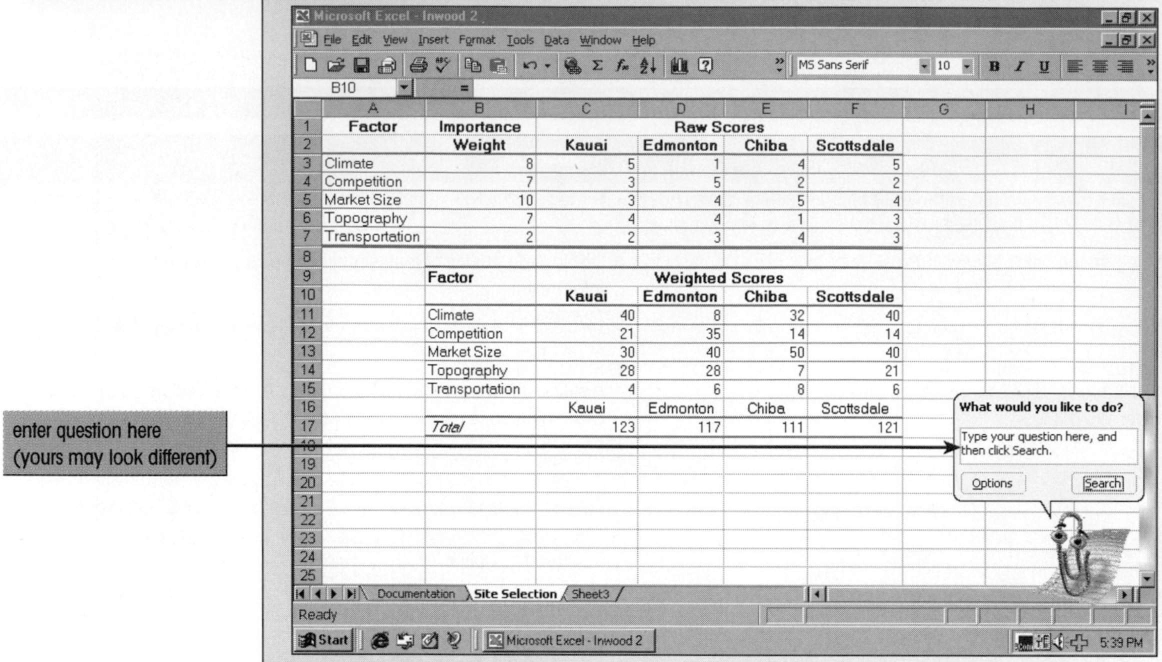

The Office Assistant can respond to an English-language question.

2. Type **how do I clear cells** in the box for your question, then click **Search** to display several possible Help topics. See Figure 1-25.

Figure 1-25 OFFICE ASSISTANT WITH SEVERAL SUGGESTED HELP TOPICS

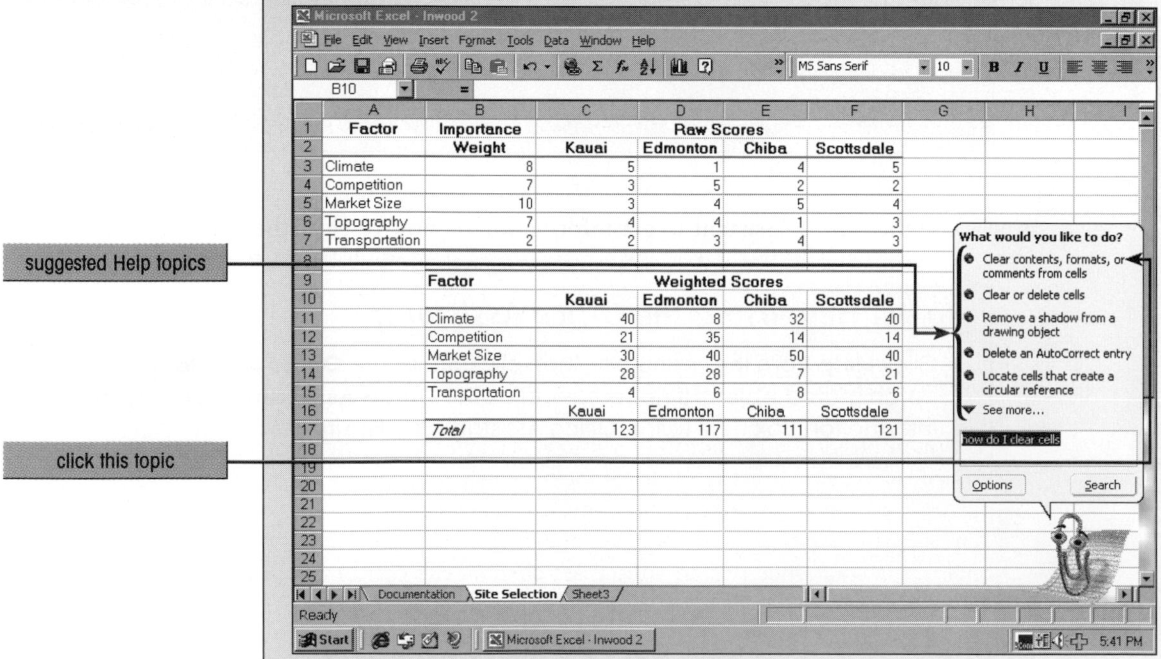

3. Click **Clear contents, formats, or comments from cells**, to display information on this topic. See Figure 1-26.

Figure 1-26 EXCEL HELP DISPLAYS INFORMATION ON CLEARING CELL CONTENTS

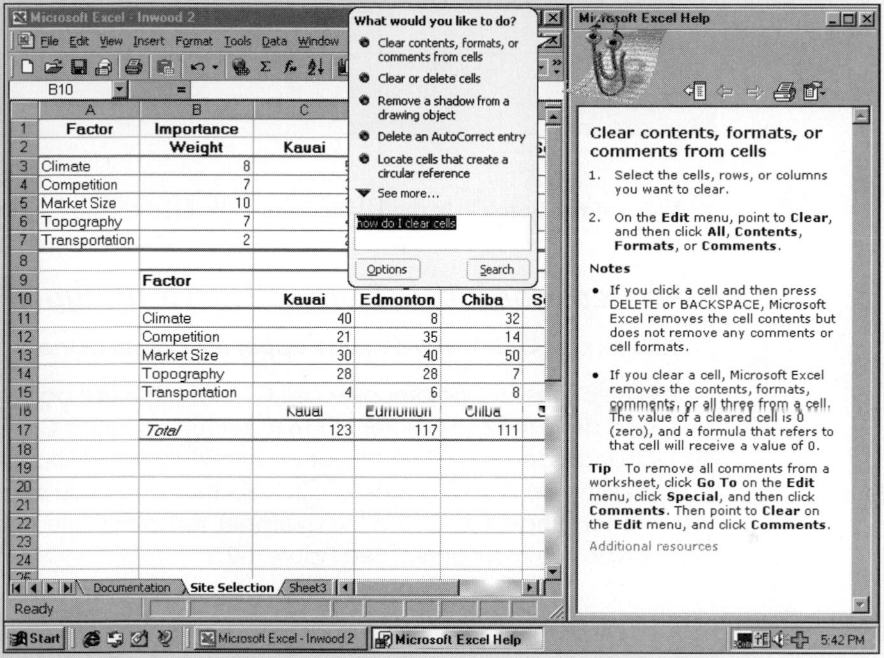

You can print the information on the topic, or you can keep the window on the screen where you can refer to it as you go through each step.

4. After reviewing the information, click the **Close** button on the Microsoft Excel Help window.

Hide the Office Assistant.

5. Move the mouse pointer over the Office Assistant, right-click the **mouse pointer**, then click **Hide**.

After reviewing the information from the Office Assistant, you are ready to remove the labels from the worksheet.

Clearing Cell Contents

As you are building or modifying your worksheet, you may occasionally find that you have entered a label, number, or formula in a cell that you want to be empty. To erase the contents of a cell, you use either the Delete key or the Clear command on the Edit menu. Removing the contents of a cell is known as clearing a cell. Do not press the spacebar to enter a blank character in an attempt to clear a cell's contents. Excel treats a blank character as text, so even though the cell appears to be empty, it is not.

REFERENCE WINDOW RW

Clearing Cell Contents

- Click the cell you want to clear, or select a range of cells you want to clear.
- Press the Delete key.

or

- Click Edit, point to Clear, and then click Contents to erase only the contents of a cell, or click All to completely clear the cell contents, formatting, and notes.

You are ready to clear the labels from cells C16 through F16.

To clear the labels from cells C16 through F16:

1. Click cell **C16**. This will be the upper-left corner of the range to clear.

2. Position the cell pointer over cell C16. With the cell pointer the shape of ✚, click and drag the cell pointer to F16 to select the range C16:F16. If your pointer changes to a crosshair +, or an arrow, do not drag the cell pointer to F16 until the pointer changes to ✚. Note that when you select a range, the first cell in that range, cell C16 in this example, remains white and the other cells in the range are highlighted. See Figure 1-27.

Figure 1-27 SELECTED RANGE

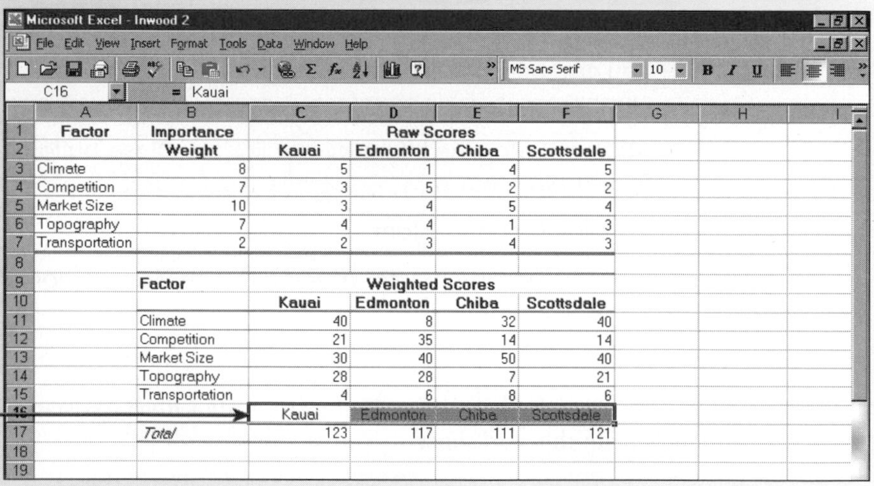

	A	B	C	D	E	F
1	Factor	Importance		Raw Scores		
2		Weight	Kauai	Edmonton	Chiba	Scottsdale
3	Climate	8	5	1	4	5
4	Competition	7	3	5	2	2
5	Market Size	10	3	4	5	4
6	Topography	7	4	4	1	3
7	Transportation	2	2	3	4	3
8						
9		Factor		Weighted Scores		
10			Kauai	Edmonton	Chiba	Scottsdale
11		Climate	40	8	32	40
12		Competition	21	35	14	14
13		Market Size	30	40	50	40
14		Topography	28	28	7	21
15		Transportation	4	6	8	6
16			Kauai	Edmonton	Chiba	Scottsdale
17		*Total*	123	117	111	121
18						
19						

selected range C16:F16

3. Press the **Delete** key to clear the contents of the cells.

4. Click any cell to deselect the range.

Now that you have cleared the unwanted labels from the cells, Mike wants you to print the Site Selection worksheet.

Printing the Worksheet

You can print an Excel worksheet using either the Print command on the File menu, the Print button on the Standard toolbar, or the Print Preview command on the File menu. If you use the Print command, Excel displays a dialog box where you can specify which worksheet pages you want to print, the number of copies you want to print, and the print quality (resolution). If you use the Print button, you do not have these options; Excel prints one copy of the entire worksheet using the current print settings. If you use the Print Preview command, you can see a preview of your printout before printing the worksheet.

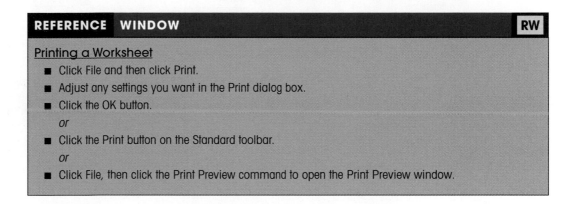

REFERENCE WINDOW RW

Printing a Worksheet

- Click File and then click Print.
- Adjust any settings you want in the Print dialog box.
- Click the OK button.

or

- Click the Print button on the Standard toolbar.

or

- Click File, then click the Print Preview command to open the Print Preview window.

If you are printing to a shared printer, many other people may be printing documents there as well. To avoid confusion finding your printed output in an office or computer lab environment, you should first set up a method to know which document is yours. You will enter your name as the person who prepared the work in a cell on the worksheet.

To enter your name as the person who prepared the Site Selection worksheet:

1. Click **Edit**, then click **Go To** to open the Go To dialog box. If necessary, click » to display Go To on the menu.
2. Type **A40** in the Reference box and click **OK**. The active cell is now A40.
3. Type **Prepared by *(enter your name here)***.
4. Press **Ctrl** + **Home** to return to cell A1.

Mike wants a printout of the entire Site Selection worksheet. You decide to select the Print command from the File menu instead of using the Print button so you can check the Print dialog box settings.

To check the print settings and then print the worksheet:

1. Make sure your printer is turned on and contains paper.

2. Click **File** on the menu bar, and then click **Print** to open the Print dialog box. See Figure 1-28.

Figure 1-28 PRINT DIALOG BOX

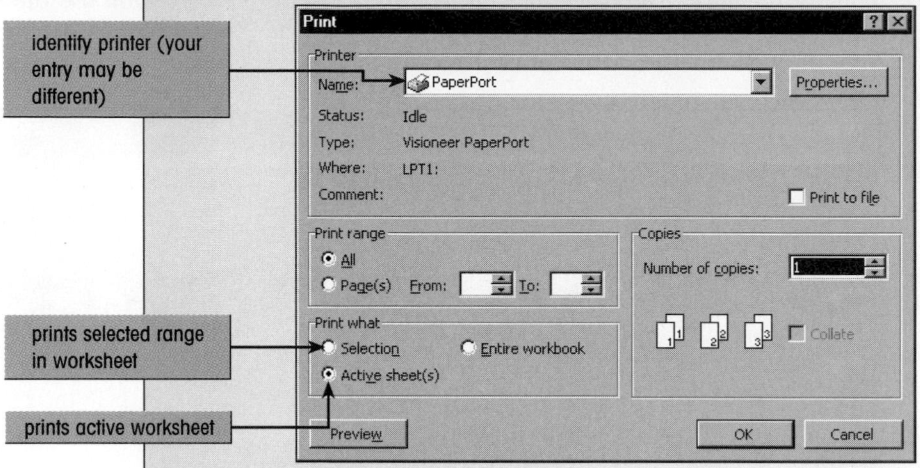

Now you need to select what to print. You could print the complete workbook, which would be the Documentation sheet and the Site Selection sheet. To do this, you would click the Entire workbook option button. You could also choose to print just a portion of a worksheet. For example, to print only the weighted scores data of the Site Selection worksheet, first select this range with your mouse pointer, and then select the Selection option button in the Print dialog box. In this case, Mike needs just the Site Selection worksheet.

3. If necessary, click the **Active sheet(s)** option button in the Print what section of the dialog box to print just the Site Selection worksheet, and not the Documentation sheet.

4. Make sure "1" appears in the Number of copies text box, as Mike only needs to print one copy of the worksheet.

5. Click the **OK** button to print the worksheet. See Figure 1-29.

TROUBLE? If the worksheet does not print, see your instructor or technical support person for help.

Figure 1-29 PRINTED WORKSHEET

Factor	Importance Weight	Raw Scores Kauai	Edmonton	Chiba	Scottsdale
Climate	8	5	1	4	5
Competition	7	3	5	2	2
Market Size	10	3	4	5	4
Topography	7	4	4	1	3
Transportation	2	2	3	4	3

Factor	Weighted Scores Kauai	Edmonton	Chiba	Scottsdale
Climate	40	8	32	40
Competition	21	35	14	14
Market Size	30	40	50	40
Topography	28	28	7	21
Transportation	4	6	8	6
Total	123	117	111	121

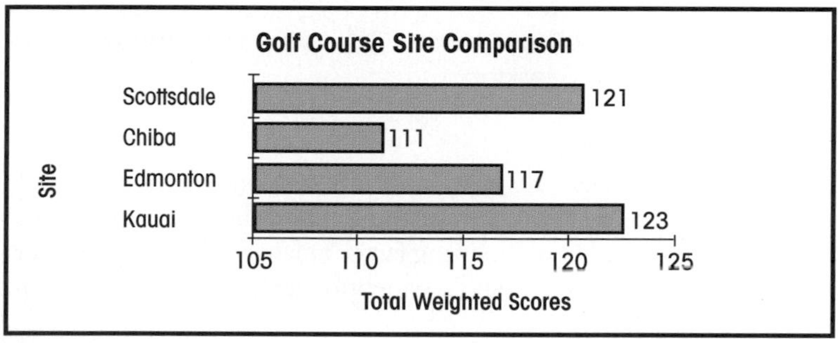

Prepared by Mike Nagochi

Mike volunteers to put together the report with the team's final recommendation, and the meeting adjourns. You and Mike are finished working with the worksheet and are ready to close the workbook.

Closing the Workbook

Closing a workbook removes it from the screen. If a workbook contains changes that have not been saved, Excel asks if you want to save your modified worksheet before closing the workbook. You can now close the workbook.

To close the Inwood 2 workbook:

1. Click **File** on the menu bar, and then click **Close**. A dialog box displays the message "Do you want to save the changes you made to 'Inwood 2.xls'?" Click Yes, if you want to save the changes you made since last saving the workbook. Click No, if you do not want to keep the changes you've made to the workbook.
2. Click **Yes** to save the Inwood 2 workbook before closing it.

The Excel window stays open so you can open or create another workbook. You do not want to, so your next step is to exit Excel.

Exiting Excel

To exit Excel, you can click the Close button on the title bar, or you can use the Exit command on the File menu.

To exit Excel:

1. Click the **Close** button on the title bar. Excel closes and you return to the Windows desktop.

The Inwood site selection team has completed its work. Mike's worksheet helped the team analyze the data and recommend Kauai as the best site for Inwood's next golf course. Although the Japanese market was a strong factor in favor of locating the course in Japan's Chiba Prefecture, the mountainous terrain and competition from nearby courses reduced the site's desirability.

Session 1.2 Quick Check

1. Indicate whether Excel treats the following cell entries as a value, text, or a formula:
   - **a.** 11/09/2001
   - **b.** Net Income
   - **c.** 321
   - **d.** =C11*225
   - **e.** 200-19-1121
   - **f.** D1-D9
   - **g.** 44 Evans Avenue
2. You type a character and Excel finishes the entry based on entries already in the column. This feature is known as ____________.
3. The formula =SUM(C3:I3) adds how many cells? Write an equivalent formula without using the SUM function.
4. What cells are included in the range D5:G7?
5. Why do you need to save a worksheet? What command do you use to save the worksheet?
6. Explain the term *what-if analysis*.
7. You can get Excel Help in any of the following ways except:
   - **a.** clicking Help on the menu bar
   - **b.** clicking the Help button on the Standard toolbar
   - **c.** closing the program window
   - **d.** pressing the F1 key

8. What key do you press to clear the contents of an active cell?

9. To print a copy of your worksheet, you use the ______________ command on the ______________ menu.

REVIEW ASSIGNMENTS

The other company that had planned a golf course in Chiba, Japan, has run into financial difficulties. Rumors are that the project may be canceled. A copy of the final Inwood Design Group workbook is on your Data Disk. Do the Tutorial Assignments to change this worksheet to show how the cancellation of the other project will affect your site selection.

1. If necessary, start Excel and make sure your Data Disk is in the appropriate disk drive. Open the **Inwood 3** file in the Review folder for Tutorial.01 on your Data Disk.
2. Use the Save As command to save the workbook as **Inwood 4** in the Review folder for Tutorial 1. That way you won't change the original workbook.
3. In the Site Selection worksheet, change the competition raw score for Chiba from 2 to 4. What site is ranked first?
4. The label "Topography" in cell A8 was entered incorrectly as "Topogriphy." Use Edit mode to change the "i" to "a".
5. Enter the text "Scores if the competing project in Chiba, Japan, is canceled" in cell A1.
6. Remove the raw scores for Chiba, cells E5 through E9.
7. Type your name in cell A42, then save the worksheet.
8. Print the worksheet.
9. Print the worksheet data without the chart. (*Hint*: Select the worksheet data before checking out the options in the Print dialog box.)
10. Use the What's This button [?]. Learn more about the following Excel window components:
    a. Name box
    b. Sheet tabs
    c. Tab scrolling button (*Hint*: Click [?], then click each item with the Help pointer.)
11. Use the Office Assistant to learn how to delete a sheet from a workbook. Write the steps to delete a sheet. Delete Sheet3.
12. In addition to the Office Assistant, Excel offers a Help window with three sections of Help: Contents, Index, and Answer Wizard. Use the Contents tab from Microsoft Excel Help window to learn how to insert an additional worksheet into your workbook. (*Hint*: Choose Working in workbooks.) Write the steps to insert a worksheet.
13. Close the workbook and exit Excel without saving the changes.

CASE PROBLEMS

Case 1. Enrollments in the University You work 10 hours a week in the provost's office at your college. The assistant to the provost has a number of meetings today and has asked you to complete a worksheet she needs for a meeting with college deans this afternoon.

1. Open the workbook **Enroll** in the Cases folder for Tutorial.01 on your Data Disk.
2. Use the Save As command to save the workbook as **Enrollment**.
3. Complete the workbook by performing the following tasks:
   a. Enter the title "Enrollment Data for University" in cell A1.
   b. Enter the label "Total" in cell A9.
   c. Calculate the total enrollment in the University for 2001 in cell B9.
   d. Calculate the total enrollment in the University for 2000 in cell C9.
   e. Calculate the change in enrollments from 2000 to 2001. Place the results in column D. Label the column heading "Change" and use the following formula:

      Change = 2001 enrollment – 2000 enrollment
4. Type "Prepared by [your name]" in cell A12.
5. Save the workbook.
6. Print the worksheet.

Case 2. Cash Budgeting at Halpern's Appliances Fran Valence, the business manager for Halpern's Appliances, a retail appliance store, is preparing a cash budget for January. The store has a loan that must be paid the first week in February. Fran wants to determine whether the business will have enough cash to make the loan payment to the bank.

Fran sketches the projected budget so that it will have the format shown in Figure 1-30.

Figure 1-30

Halpern's Appliances Cash Budget		
Projected Cash Receipts and Disbursements		
January 1, 2001		
Cash balance, January 1, 2001		XXXX
Projected receipts during January:		
Cash sales during month	XXXX	
Collections from credit sales	XXXX	
Total cash receipts		XXXX
Projected disbursements during January:		
Payments for goods purchased	XXXX	
Salaries	XXXX	
Rent	XXXX	
Utilities	XXXX	
Total cash disbursements		XXXX
Cash balance, January 31, 2001		XXXX

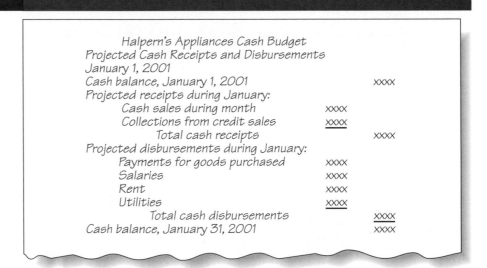

1. Open the workbook **Budget** in the Cases folder for Tutorial.01. Save as **BudgetSol**.
2. Enter the following formulas in cells C8, C14, and C15 of your worksheet:
   a. Total cash receipts = Cash receipts during month + Collections from credit sales
   b. Total cash disbursements = Payments for goods purchased + Salaries + Rent + Utilities
   c. Cash Balance, January 31, 2001 = Cash Balance, January 1, 2001 + Total cash receipts – Total cash disbursements
3. Enter the data in Figure 1-31 into the worksheet.
4. Type "Prepared by [your name]" in a cell two rows below the last line of the budget.

Figure 1-31

BUDGET ITEM	AMOUNT	BUDGET ITEM	AMOUNT
Cash balance at beginning of month	32000	Salaries	4800
Cash receipts during month	9000	Rent	1500
Collection from credit sales	17500	Utilities	800
Payments for goods purchased	15000		

5. Save the worksheet.
6. Print the projected cash budget.
7. After printing the budget, Fran remembers that in January the monthly rent increases by $150. Modify the projected cash budget. Print the revised cash budget.

Case 3. Selecting a Hospital Laboratory Computer System for Bridgeport Medical Center David Choi is on the Laboratory Computer Selection Committee for the Bridgeport Medical Center. After an extensive search, the committee has identified three vendors whose products appear to meet its needs. The Selection Committee has prepared an Excel worksheet to help evaluate the strengths and weaknesses of the three potential vendors. The formulas and raw scores for two of the vendors, LabStar and Health Systems, have already been entered. Now the formulas and raw scores must be entered for the third vendor, MedTech. Which vendor's system is best for the Bridgeport Medical Center? Complete these steps to find out which system is best.

1. Open the workbook **Medical** in the Cases folder for Tutorial.01.
2. Use the Save As command to save the workbook as **Medical 2** in the Cases folder for Tutorial 1. That way you won't change the original workbook for this case.
3. Examine the LAB worksheet, and type the following raw scores for MedTech: Cost = 6, Compatibility = 5, Vendor Reliability = 5, Size of Installed Base = 4, User Satisfaction = 5, Critical Functionality = 9, Additional Functionality = 8.
4. Enter the formulas to compute the weighted scores for MedTech in cells E17 to E23. See Figure 1-32.

Figure 1-32

CELL	FORMULA	CELL	FORMULA	CELL	FORMULA
E17	=B6*E6	E20	=B9*E9	E22	=B11*E11
E18	=B7*E7	E21	=B10*E10	E23	=B12*E12
E19	=B8*E8				

5. Enter the formula to compute MedTech's total weighted score.
6. In cell A2 type "Prepared by [your name]".
7. Activate the Documentation worksheet and enter information such as the name of the case, your name, date created, and purposes on this sheet.
8. Use the Save command to save the modified worksheet.
9. Print the worksheet and Documentation sheet.
10. Based on the data in the worksheet, which vendor would you recommend? Why?

11. Assume you can adjust the value for only one importance weight (cells B6 through B12). Which factor would you change and what would its new weight be in order for LabStar to have the highest weighted score? (*Hint*: Remember that the value assigned to any importance weight cannot be higher than 10.)
12. Print the modified worksheet. Close the workbook without saving it.

Case 4. Cash Counting Calculator Rob Stuben works at a local town beach in Narragansett where a fee is collected for parking. At the end of each day, the parking attendants turn in the cash they have collected, with a statement of the daily total. Rob is responsible for receiving the daily cash from each attendant, checking the accuracy of the total, and making the cash deposit to the bank.

Rob wants to set up a simple cash counter using Excel, so that he can insert the number of bills of each denomination into a worksheet and have the total cash automatically computed. By using this method he only has to count and enter the number of one-dollar bills, the number of fives, and so on.

1. Set up this worksheet for Rob. First, list all currency denominations (1, 2, 5, 10, 20, 50, 100) in the first column of your worksheet. The next column will be used to enter the count of the number of bills of each denomination (initially blank). In the third column, enter formulas to calculate totals for each denomination. That is, the number of bills multiplied by the denomination of the bill. Below this total column, enter a formula to calculate the grand total received.

   Next, you want to compare the grand total with the amount reported by an attendant. In the row below the grand total, enter the cash reported by the attendant.

   Finally, below the cash reported amount, enter the formula to calculate the difference between the grand total (calculated amount) and the cash reported by the attendant. The difference should equal zero.
2. On a separate worksheet, create a Documentation sheet. Include the title of the case, your name, date created, and the purpose of the worksheet.
3. On Rob's first day using the worksheet, the cash reported by an attendant was $1,560. Rob counted the bills and entered the following: five 50s, twenty-three 20s, forty-one 10s, sixty-five 5s, and one hundred and twenty 1s. Enter these amounts in your worksheet.
4. Type "Prepared by [your name]" in a cell two rows below the cash calculator worksheet.
5. Save the workbook in the Cases folder of Tutorial.01 using the name **CashCounter**.
6. Print the worksheet.
7. On the second day, the cash reported by an attendant was $1,395. Rob counted the bills and entered the following: two 100s, four 50s, seventeen 20s, thirty-four 10s, forty-five 5s, and ninety 1s. Delete the previous day's count and replace it with the new data.
8. Print the worksheet using the data for the second day.
9. Print the Documentation sheet.
10. Close the workbook without saving changes.

LAB ASSIGNMENTS

Spreadsheets

The New Perspectives Labs are designed to help you master some of the key computer concepts and skills presented in each chapter of the text. If you are using your school's lab computers, your instructor or technical support person should have installed the Labs software for you. If you want to use the Labs on your home computer, ask your instructor for the appropriate software. See the Read This Before You Begin page for more information on installing and starting the Lab.

Each Lab has two parts: Steps and Explore. Use Steps first to learn and review concepts. Read the information on each page and do the numbered steps. As you work through the Lab, you will be asked to answer Quick Check questions about what you have learned. At the end of the Lab, you will see a Summary Report of your answers to the Quick Checks. If your instructor wants you to turn in this Summary Report, click the Print button on the Summary Report screen.

When you have completed Steps, you can click the Explore button to complete the Lab Assignments. You can also use Explore to practice the skills you learned and to explore concepts on your own.

SPREADSHEETS Spreadsheet software is used extensively in business, education, science, and humanities to simplify tasks that involve calculations. In this Lab you will learn how spreadsheet software works. You will use spreadsheet software to examine and modify worksheets, as well as to create your own worksheets.

1. Click the Steps button to learn how spreadsheet software works. As you proceed through the Steps, answer all of the Quick Check questions that appear. After you complete the Steps, you will see a Quick Check Summary Report. Follow the instructions on the screen to print this report.

2. Click the Explore button to begin this assignment. Click OK to display a new worksheet. Click File, then click Open to display the Open dialog box. Click the file **Income.xls**, then press the Enter key to open the **Income and Expense Summary** worksheet. Notice that the worksheet contains labels and values for income from consulting and training. It also contains labels and values for expenses such as rent and salaries. The worksheet does not, however, contain formulas to calculate Total Income, Total Expenses, or Profit. Do the following:
   a. Calculate the Total Income by entering the formula =sum(C4:C5) in cell C6.
   b. Calculate the Total Expenses by entering the formula =sum(C9:C12) in C13.
   c. Calculate Profit by entering the formula =C6-C13 in cell C15.
   d. Manually check the results to make sure you entered the formulas correctly.
   e. Print your completed worksheet showing your results.

3. You can use a spreadsheet to keep track of your grade in a class. In Explore, click File, then click Open to display the Open dialog box. Click the file **Grades.xls** to open the Grades worksheet. This worksheet contains the labels and formulas necessary to calculate your grade based on four test scores. You receive a score of 88 out of 100 on the first test. On the second test, you score 42 out of 48. On the third test, you score 92 out of 100. You have not taken the fourth test yet. Enter the appropriate data in the **Grades.xls** worksheet to determine your grade after taking three tests. Print out your worksheet.

4. Worksheets are handy for answering "what if" questions. Suppose you decide to open a lemonade stand. You're interested in how much profit you can make each day. What if you sell 20 cups of lemonade? What if you sell 100? What if the cost of lemons increases?

   In Explore, open the file **Lemons.xls** and use the worksheet to answer questions a through d, then print the worksheet for question e:
   a. What is your profit if you sell 20 cups a day?
   b. What is your profit if you sell 100 cups a day?
   c. What is your profit if the price of lemons increases to $.07 and you sell 100 cups?
   d. What is your profit if you raise the price of a cup of lemonade to $.30? (Lemons still cost $.07 and assume you sell 100 cups.)
   e. Suppose your competitor boasts that she sold 50 cups of lemonade in one day and made exactly $12.00. On your worksheet adjust the cost of cups, water, lemons, and sugar, and the price per cup to show a profit of exactly $12.00 for 50 cups sold. Print this worksheet.

5. It is important to make sure the formulas in your worksheet are accurate. An easy way to test this is to enter 1's for all the values on your worksheet, then check the calculations manually. In Explore, open the worksheet **Receipt.xls**, which calculates sales receipts. Enter 1 as the value for Item 1, Item 2, Item 3, and Sales Tax %. Now, manually calculate what you would pay for three items that cost $1.00 each in a state where sales tax is 1% (.01). Do your manual calculations match those of the worksheet? If not, correct the formulas in the worksheet and print out a *formula report* of your revised worksheet.
6. In Explore, create your own worksheet showing your household budget for one month. You may make up numbers. Put a title on the worksheet. Use formulas to calculate your total income and expenses for the month. Add another formula to calculate how much money you were able to save. Print a formula report of your worksheet. Also, print your worksheet showing realistic values for one month.

INTERNET ASSIGNMENTS

The purpose of the Internet Assignments is to challenge you to find information on the Internet that you can use to create effective documents. The actual assignments are updated and maintained on the Course Technology Web site. Log on to the Internet and use your Web browser to go to the Student Online Companion to accompany this text at **www.course.com/NewPerspectives/office2000**. Click the Excel link, and then click the link for Tutorial 1.

QUICK CHECK ANSWERS

Session 1.1

1. cell
2. open
3. D2
4. b
5. click the "Sheet2" sheet tab
6. press Ctrl + Home

Session 1.2

1. **a.** value
b. text
c. value
d. formula
e. text
f. text
g. text
2. AutoComplete
3. 7; C3+D3+E3+F3+G3+H3+I3
4. D5,D6,D7,E5,E6,E7,G5,G6,G7
5. When you exit Excel, the workbook is erased from RAM. So if you want to use the workbook again, you need to save it to disk. Click File, then click Save As.
6. revising the contents of one or more cells in a worksheet and observing the effect this change has on all other cells in the worksheet
7. c
8. press the Delete key; click Edit, point to Clear, and then click Contents; click Edit, point to Clear, and then click All.
9. Print, File

OBJECTIVES

In this tutorial you will:

- Plan, build, test, document, preview, and print a worksheet
- Enter labels, values, and formulas
- Calculate a total using the AutoSum button
- Copy formulas using the fill handle and Clipboard
- Learn about relative, absolute, and mixed references
- Use the AVERAGE, MAX, and MIN functions to calculate values in the worksheet
- Spell check the worksheet
- Insert a row
- Reverse an action using the Undo button
- Move a range of cells
- Format the worksheet using AutoFormat
- Center printouts on a page
- Customize worksheet headers

CREATING A WORKSHEET

Producing a Sales Comparison Report for MSI

CASE

Motorcycle Specialties Incorporated

Motorcycle Specialties Incorporated (MSI), a motorcycle helmet and accessories company, provides a wide range of specialty items to motorcycle enthusiasts throughout the world. MSI has its headquarters in Atlanta, Georgia, but it markets products in North America, South America, Australia, and Europe.

The company's marketing and sales director, Sally Caneval, meets regularly with the regional sales managers who oversee global sales in each of the four regions in which MSI does business. This month, Sally intends to review overall sales in each region for the last two fiscal years and present her findings at her next meeting with the regional sales managers. She has asked you to help her put together a report that summarizes this sales information.

Specifically, Sally wants the report to show total sales for each region of the world for the two most recent fiscal years. Additionally, she wants to see the percentage change between the two years. She also wants the report to include the percentage each region contributed to the total sales of the company in 2001. Finally, she wants to include summary statistics on the average, maximum, and minimum sales for 2001.

SESSION 2.1

In this session you will learn how to plan and build a worksheet; enter labels, numbers, and formulas; and copy formulas to other cells.

Developing Worksheets

Effective worksheets are well planned and carefully designed. A well-designed worksheet should clearly identify its overall goal. It should present information in a clear, well-organized format and include all the data necessary to produce results that address the goal of the application. The process of developing a good worksheet includes the following planning and execution steps:

- determine the worksheet's purpose, what it will include, and how it will be organized
- enter the data and formulas into the worksheet
- test the worksheet
- edit the worksheet to correct any errors or make modifications
- document the worksheet
- improve the appearance of the worksheet
- save and print the completed worksheet

Planning the Worksheet

Sally begins to develop a worksheet that compares global sales by region over two years by creating a planning analysis sheet. Her planning analysis sheet helps her answer the following questions:

1. What is the goal of the worksheet? This helps to define the problem to solve.
2. What are the desired results? This information describes the output—the information required to help solve the problem.
3. What data is needed to calculate the results you want to see? This information is the input—data that must be entered.
4. What calculations are needed to produce the desired output? These calculations specify the formulas used in the worksheet.

Sally's completed planning analysis sheet is shown in Figure 2-1.

Figure 2-1 PLANNING ANALYSIS SHEET

Planning Analysis Sheet

My Goal:
To develop a worksheet to compare annual sales in each region for the last two fiscal years

What results do you want to see?
Sales by region for 2001, 2000
Total Sales for 2001, 2000
Average sales for 2001, 2000
Maximum sales for 2001, 2000
Minimum sales for 2001,2000
Percentage change for each region
Percentage of 2001 sales for each region

What information do I need?
Sales for each region in 2001
Sales for each region in 2000

What calculations do I perform?
Percentage change = (Sales in 2001 – Sales in 2000)/ Sales in 2000
Percentage of 2001 sales = Sales in a region for 2001/Total sales 2001
Total sales for year = Sum of sales for each region
Average sales in 2001
Maximum sales in 2001
Minimum sales in 2001

Next Sally makes a rough sketch of her design, including titles, column headings, row labels, and where data values and totals should be placed. Figure 2-2 shows Sally's sketch. With these two planning tools, Sally is now ready to enter the data into Excel and build the worksheet.

Figure 2-2 **SKETCH OF WORKSHEET**

Motorcycle Specialties Incorporated
Sales Comparison 2001 with 2000

Region	*Year 2001*	*Year 2000*	*% Change*	*% of 2001 Sales*
North America	365000	314330	0.16	0.28
South America	354250	292120	0.21	0.28
Australia	251140	262000	-0.04	0.19
Europe	310440	279996	0.11	0.24
Total	1280830	1148446	0.12	

Average	320207.5
Maximum	365000
Minimum	251140

Building the Worksheet

You use Sally's planning analysis sheet, Figure 2-1, and the rough sketch shown in Figure 2-2 to guide you in preparing the sales comparison worksheet. You begin by establishing the layout of the worksheet by entering titles and column headings. Next you work on inputting the data and formulas that will calculate the results Sally needs.

To start Excel and organize your desktop:

1. Start Excel as usual.
2. Make sure your Data Disk is in the appropriate disk drive.
3. Make sure the Microsoft Excel and Book1 windows are maximized.

Entering Labels

When you build a worksheet, it's a good practice to enter the labels before entering any other data. These labels help you identify the cells where you will enter data and formulas in your worksheet. As you type a label in a cell, Excel aligns the label at the left side of the cell. Labels that are too long to fit in a cell spill over into the cell or cells to the right, if those cells are empty. If the cells to the right are not empty, Excel displays only as much of the label as fits in the cell. Begin creating the sales comparison worksheet for Sally by entering the two-line title.

To enter the worksheet title:

1. If necessary, click cell **A1** to make it the active cell.
2. Type **Motorcycle Specialties Incorporated**, and then press the **Enter** key. Since cell A1 is empty, the title appears in cell A1 and spills over into cells B1, C1, and D1. Cell A2 is now the active cell.

TROUBLE? If you make a mistake while typing, remember that you can correct errors with the Backspace key. If you notice the error only after you have pressed the Enter key, then double-click the cell to activate Edit mode, and use the edit keys on your keyboard to correct the error.

3. In cell A2 type **Sales Comparison 2001 with 2000**, and then press the **Enter** key.

Next you enter the column headings defined on the worksheet sketch in Figure 2-2.

To enter labels for the column headings:

1. If necessary, click cell **A3** to make it the active cell.
2. Type **Region** and then press the **Tab** key to complete the entry. Cell B3 is the active cell.
3. Type **Year 2001** in cell B3, and then press the **Tab** key.

   Sally's sketch shows that three more column heads are needed for the worksheet. Enter those next.

4. Enter the remaining column heads as follows:

   Cell C3: **Year 2000**

   Cell D3: **% Change**

   Cell E3: **% of 2001 Sales**

   See Figure 2-3.

   TROUBLE? If any cell does not contain the correct label, either edit the cell or retype the entry.

Figure 2-3 WORKSHEET AFTER TITLES AND COLUMN HEADINGS HAVE BEEN ENTERED

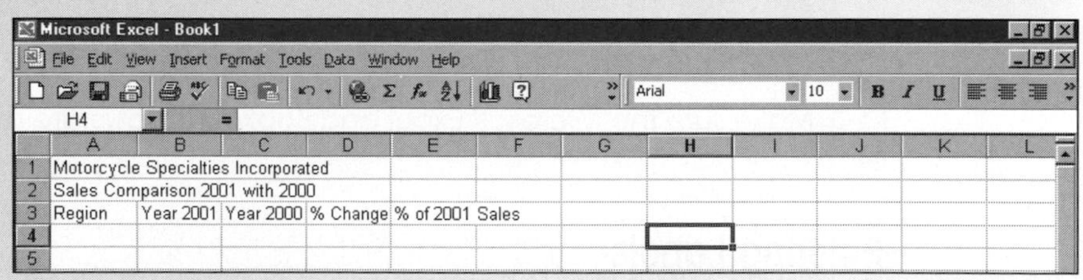

Recall that MSI conducts business in four different regions of the world, and the spreadsheet needs to track the sales information for each region. So Sally wants labels reflecting the regions entered into the worksheet. Enter these labels next.

To enter the regions:

1. Click cell **A4**, type **North America**, and then press the **Enter** key.
2. In cell **A5** type **South America**, and then press the **Enter** key.
3. Type **Australia** in cell A6, and then **Europe** in cell A7.

The last set of labels entered identifies the summary information that will be included in the report.

To enter the summary labels:

1. In cell A8 type **Total**, and then press the **Enter** key.
2. Type the following labels into the specified cells:

   Cell A9: **Average**

   Cell A10: **Maximum**

   Cell A11: **Minimum**

   See Figure 2-4.

Figure 2-4 WORKSHEET AFTER ALL LABELS HAVE BEEN ENTERED

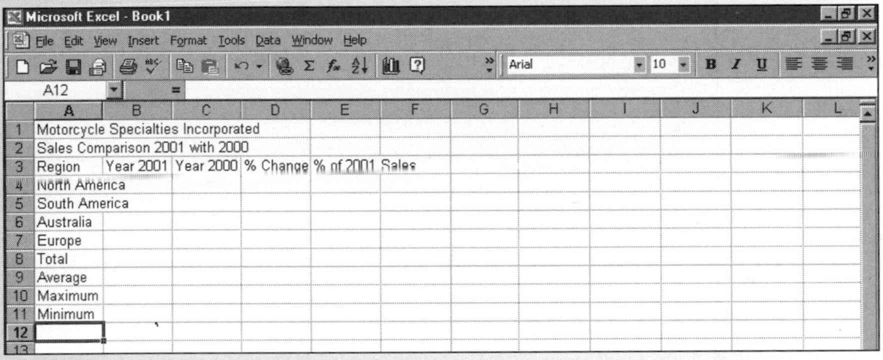

The labels that you just entered into the worksheet will help to identify where the data and formulas need to be placed.

Entering Data

Recall that values can be numbers, formulas, or functions. The next step in building the worksheet is to enter the data, which in this case are the numbers representing sales in each region during 2000 and 2001.

To enter the sales values for 2000 and 2001:

1. Click cell **B4** to make it the active cell. Type **365000** and then press the **Enter** key. See Figure 2-5. Notice that the region name, North America, is no longer completely visible in cell A4 because cell B4 is no longer empty. Later in the tutorial you will learn how to increase the width of a column in order to display the entire contents of cells.

Figure 2-5 WORKSHEET WITH LABEL TRUNCATED IN CELL

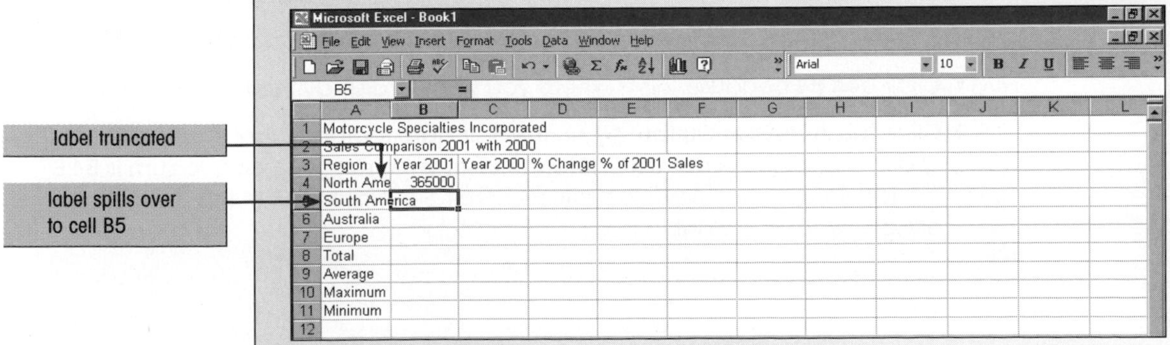

2. In cell B5 type **354250**, and then press the **Enter** key.

3. Enter the values for cells B6, **251140**, and B7, **310440**.

   Next, type the values for sales during 2000.

4. Click cell **C4**, type **314330**, and then press the **Enter** key.

5. Enter the remaining values in the specified cells as follows:

   Cell C5: **292120**

   Cell C6: **262000**

   Cell C7: **279996**

   Your screen should now look like Figure 2-6.

Figure 2-6 WORKSHEET AFTER SALES FOR 2001 AND 2000 HAVE BEEN ENTERED

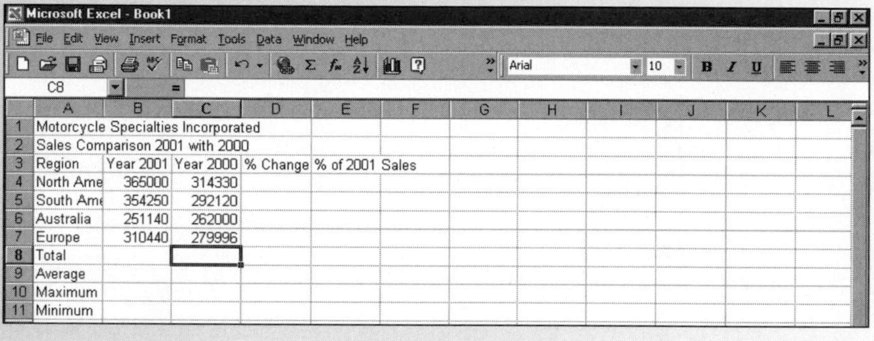

Now that you have entered the labels and data, you need to enter the formulas that will calculate the data to produce the output, or the results. The first calculation Sally wants to see is the total sales for each year. To determine total sales for 2001, you would simply sum the sales from each region for that year. In the previous tutorial you used the SUM function to calculate the weighted total score for the Scottsdale golf site by typing that function into the cell. Similarly, you can use the SUM function to calculate total sales for each year for MSI's comparison report.

Using the AutoSum Button

Since the SUM function is used more often than any other function, Excel includes the AutoSum button on the Standard toolbar. This button automatically creates a formula that contains the SUM function. To do this, Excel looks at the cells adjacent to the active cell, makes an assumption as to which cells you want to sum, and displays a formula based on its best determination about the range you want to sum. You can press the Enter key to accept the formula, or you can select a different range of cells to change the range in the formula. You want to use the AutoSum button to calculate the total sales for each year.

To calculate total sales in 2001 using the AutoSum button:

1. Click cell **B8** because this is where you want to display the total sales for 2001.

2. Click the **AutoSum** button Σ on the Standard toolbar. Excel enters a SUM function in the selected cell and determines that the range of cells to sum is B4:B7, the range directly above the selected cell. See Figure 2-7. In this case, that's exactly what you want to do.

Figure 2-7 **USING THE AUTOSUM TOOL**

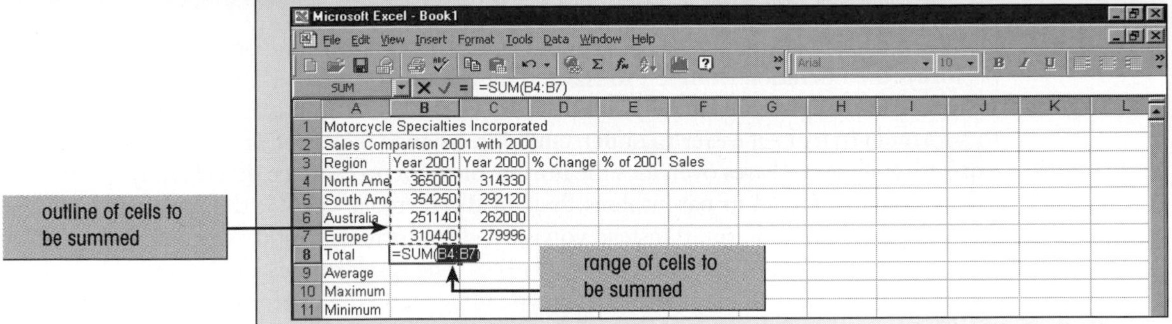

3. Press the **Enter** key to complete the formula. The result, 1280830, appears in cell B8.

Now use the same approach to calculate the total sales for 2000.

To calculate total sales in 2000 using the AutoSum button:

1. Click cell **C8** to make it the active cell.
2. Click the **AutoSum** Σ button on the Standard toolbar.
3. Press the **Enter** key to complete the formula. The result, 1148446, appears in cell C8.

Next you need to enter the formula to calculate the percentage change in sales for North America between 2001 and 2000.

Entering Formulas

Recall that a formula is an equation that performs calculations in a cell. By entering an equal sign (=) as the first entry in the cell, you are telling Excel that the numbers or symbols that follow constitute a formula, not just data. Reviewing Sally's worksheet plan, you note that you need to calculate the percentage change in sales in North America. The formula is:
Percentage change in sales for North America = (2001 sales in North America - 2000 sales in North America)/2000 sales in North America

So in looking at the worksheet, the formula in Excel would be:
=(B4-C4)/C4

If a formula contains more than one arithmetic operator, Excel performs the calculations in the standard order of precedence of operators, shown in Figure 2-8. The **order of precedence** is a set of predefined rules that Excel uses to unambiguously calculate a formula by determining which part of the formula to calculate first, which part second, and so on.

Figure 2-8 **ORDER OF PRECEDENCE FOR ARITHMETIC OPERATIONS**

ORDER	OPERATOR	DESCRIPTION
First	^	Exponentiation
Second	* or /	Multiplication or division
Third	+ or -	Addition or subtraction

Exponentiation is the operation with the highest precedence, followed by multiplication and division, and finally addition and subtraction. For example, because multiplication has precedence over addition, the result of the formula =3+4*5 is 23.

When a formula contains more than one operator with the same order of precedence, Excel performs the operation from left to right. Thus, in the formula =4*10/8, Excel multiplies 4 by 10 before dividing the product by 8. The result of the calculation is 5. You can add parentheses to a formula to make it easier to understand or to change the order of operations. Enclosing an expression in parentheses overrides the normal order of precedence. Excel always performs any calculations contained in parentheses first. In the formula =3+4*5, the multiplication is performed before the addition. If instead you wanted the formula to add 3+4 and then multiply the sum by 5, you would enter the formula =(3+4)*5. The result of the calculation is 35. Figure 2-9 shows examples of formulas that will help you understand the order of precedence rules.

Figure 2-9 EXAMPLES ILLUSTRATING ORDER OF PRECEDENCE RULES

FORMULA VALUE A1=10, B1=20, C1=3	ORDER OF PRECEDENCE RULE	RESULT
=A1+B1*C1	Multiplication before addition	70
=(A1+B1)*C1	Expression inside parentheses executed before expression outside	90
=A1/B1+C1	Division before addition	3.5
=A1/(B1+C1)	Expression inside parentheses executed before expression outside	.435
=A1/B1*C1	Two operators at same precedence level, leftmost operator evaluated first	1.5
=A1/(B1*C1)	Expression inside parentheses executed before expression outside	.166667

Now enter the percentage change formula as specified in Sally's planning sheet.

To enter the formula for the percentage change in sales for North America:

1. Click cell **D4** to make it the active cell.
2. Type **=(B4-C4)/C4** and then press the **Enter** key. Excel performs the calculations and displays the value 0.1612 in cell D4. The formula is no longer visible in the cell. If you select the cell, the result of the formula appears in the cell, and the formula you entered appears in the formula bar.

Next you need to enter the percentage change formulas for the other regions, as well as the percentage change for the total company sales. You could type the formula =(B5-C5)/C5 in cell D5, the formula =(B6-C6)/C6 in cell D6, the formula =(B7-C7)/C7 in cell D7, and the formula =(B8-C8)/C8 in cell D8. However, this approach is time consuming and error prone. Instead, you can copy the formula you entered in cell C4 (percentage change in North American sales) into cells D5, D6, D7, and D8. Copying duplicates the cell's underlying formula into other cells, automatically adjusting cell references to reflect the new cell address. Copying formulas from one cell to another saves time and reduces the chances of entering incorrect formulas when building worksheets.

Copying a Formula Using the Fill Handle

You can copy formulas using menu commands, toolbar buttons, or the fill handle. The **fill handle** is a small black square located in the lower-right corner of the selected cell, as shown in Figure 2-10. In this section you will use the fill handle to copy the formulas. In other situations you can also use the fill handle for copying values and labels from one cell or a group of cells.

Figure 2-10 **FILL HANDLE**

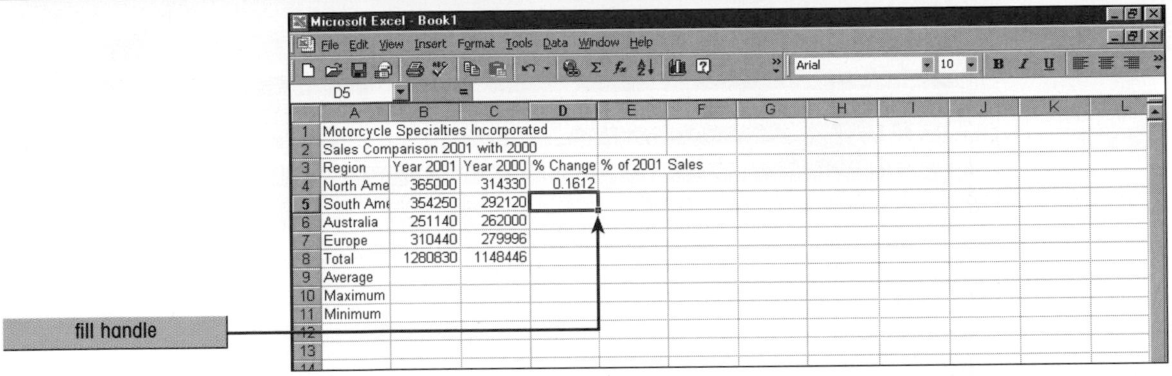

REFERENCE WINDOW — RW

Copying Cell Contents with the Fill Handle

- Click the cell that contains the label, value, or formula you want to copy. If you want to copy the contents of more than one cell, select the range of cells you want to copy.
- To copy to adjacent cells, click and drag the fill handle to outline the cells where you want the copy or copies to appear, and then release the mouse button.

You want to copy the formula from cell D4 to cells D5, D6, D7, and D8.

To copy the formula from cell D4 to cells D5, D6, D7, and D8:

1. Click cell **D4** to make it the active cell.
2. Position the pointer over the fill handle (in the lower-right corner of cell D4) until the pointer changes to +.
3. Click and drag the pointer down the worksheet to outline cells **D5** through **D8**. See Figure 2-11.

Figure 2-11 **COPYING A FORMULA**

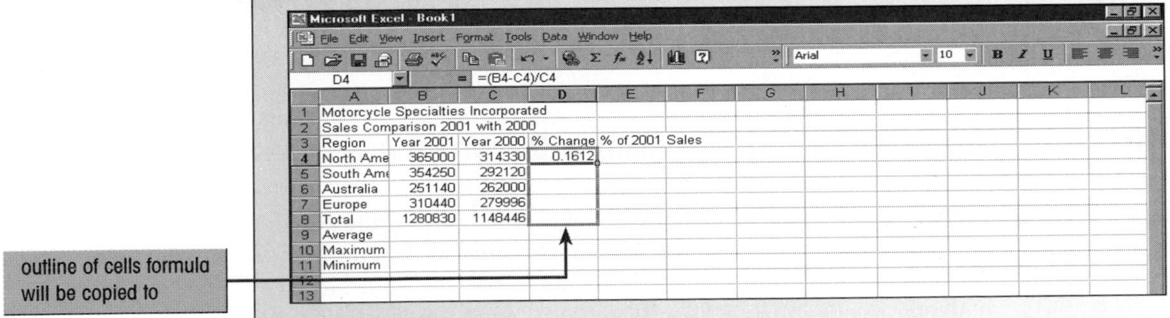

4. Release the mouse button. Excel copies the formula from D4 to cells D5 to D8. Values now appear in cells D5 through D8.

5. Click any cell to deselect the range. See Figure 2-12.

Figure 2-12 **WORKSHEET AFTER FORMULA HAS BEEN COPIED**

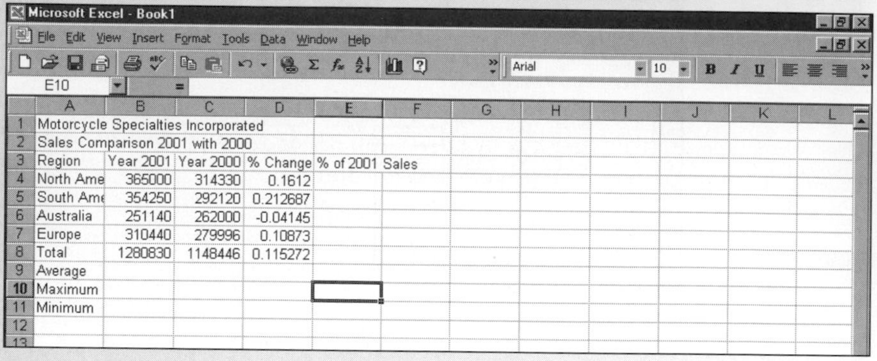

Notice that Excel didn't copy the formula =(B4-C4)/C4 exactly. It automatically adjusted the cell references for each new formula location. Why did that happen?

Copying a Formula Using Relative References

When you copy a formula that contains cell references, Excel automatically adjusts the cell references for the new locations. For example, when Excel copied the formula from cell D4, =(B4-C4)/C4, it automatically changed the cell references in the formula to reflect the formula's new position in the worksheet. So in cell D5 the cell references adjust to =(B5-C5)/C5. Cell references that change when copied are called **relative cell references**.

Take a moment to look at the formulas in cells D5, D6, D7, and D8.

To examine the formulas in cells D5, D6, D7, and D8:

1. Click cell **D5**. The formula =(B5-C5)/C5 appears in the formula bar.

   When Excel copied the formula from cell D4 to cell D5, the cell references changed. The formula =(B4-C4)/C4 became =(B5-C5)/C5 when Excel copied the formula down one row to row 5.

2. Examine the formulas in cells D6, D7, and D8. Notice that the cell references were adjusted for the new locations.

Copying a Formula Using an Absolute Reference

According to Sally's plan, the worksheet should display the percentage that each region contributed to the total sales in 2001. For example, if the company's total sales were $100,000 and sales in North America were $25,000, then sales in North America would be 25% of total sales. To complete this calculation for each region, you need to divide each region's sales by the total company sales, as shown in the following formulas:

Contribution by North America	=B4/B8
Contribution by South America	=B5/B8
Contribution by Australia	=B6/B8
Contribution by Europe	=B7/B8

First enter the formula to calculate the percentage North America contributed to total sales.

To calculate North America's percentage of total 2001 sales:

1. Click cell **E4** to make it the active cell.
2. Type **=B4/B8** and then press the **Enter** key to display the value .284971 in cell E4.

Cell E4 displays the correct result. Sales in North America for 2001 were 365,000, which is approximately .28 of the 1,280,830 in total sales in 2001. Next, you decide to copy the formula in cell E4 to cells E5, E6, and E7.

To copy the percentage formula in cell E4 to cells E5 through E7:

1. Click cell **E4**, and then move the pointer over the fill handle in cell E4 until it changes to +.
2. Click and drag the pointer to cell **E7** and release the mouse button.
3. Click any blank cell to deselect the range. The error value "#DIV/0!" appears in cells E5 through E7. See Figure 2-13.

Figure 2-13 ERROR VALUE IN WORKSHEET AFTER COPYING FORMULA

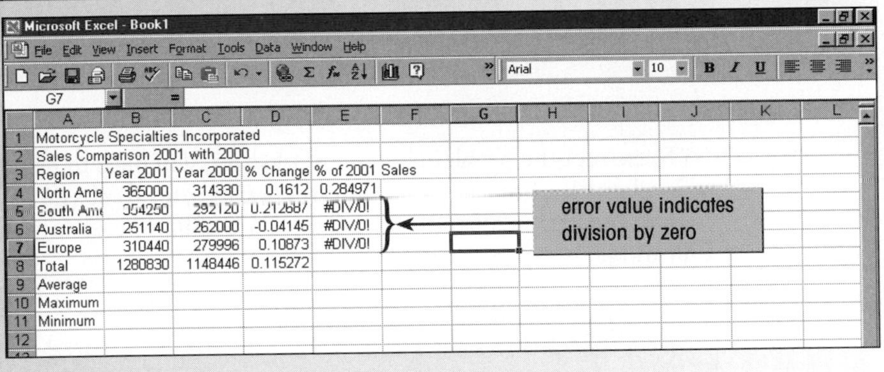

Something is wrong. Cells E5 through E7 display "#DIV/0!" a special constant, called an **error value.** Excel displays an error value constant when it cannot resolve the formula **#DIV/0!**, one of seven error value constants means that Excel was instructed to divide by zero. Take a moment to look at the formulas you copied into cells E5, E6, and E7.

To examine the formulas in cells E5 through E7:

1. Click cell **E5** and then look at the formula appearing in the formula bar, =B5/B9. The first cell reference changed from B4 in the original formula to B5 in the copied formula. That's correct because the sales data for South America is entered in cell B5. The second cell reference changed from B8 in the original formula to B9, which is not correct. The correct formula should be =B5/B8 because the total sales are in cell B8, not cell B9.
2. Look at the formulas in cells E6 and E7 and see how the cell references changed in each formula.

As you observed, the cell reference to total company sales (B8) in the original formula was changed to B9, B10, and B11 in the copied formulas. The problem with the copied formulas is that Excel adjusted *all* the cell references relative to their new location.

Absolute Versus Relative References

Sometimes when you copy a formula, you don't want Excel to change all cell references automatically to reflect their new positions in the worksheet. If you want a cell reference to point to the same location in the worksheet when you copy it, you must use an **absolute reference**. An absolute reference is a cell reference in a formula that does not change when copied to another cell.

To create an absolute reference, you insert a dollar sign ($) before the column and row of the cell reference. For example, the cell reference $B$8 is an absolute reference, whereas the cell reference B8 is a relative reference. If you copy a formula that contains the absolute reference $B$8 to another cell, the cell reference to $B$8 does not change. On the other hand, if you copy a formula containing the relative reference B8 to another cell, the reference to B8 changes. In some situations, a cell might have a **mixed reference**, such as $B8; in this case, when the formula is copied, the row number changes but the column letter does not.

To include an absolute reference in a formula, you can type a dollar sign when you type the cell reference, or you can use the F4 key to change the cell reference type while in Edit mode.

REFERENCE WINDOW RW

Changing Absolute, Mixed, and Relative References

- Double-click the cell that contains the formula you want to edit.
- Use the arrow keys to move the insertion point to the part of the cell reference you want to change.
- Press the F4 key until the reference is correct. Press the Enter key to complete the edit.

To correct the problem in your worksheet, you need to use an absolute reference, instead of a relative reference, to indicate the location of total sales in 2001. That is, you need to change the formula from =B4/B8 to =B4/$B$8. The easiest way to make this change is in Edit mode.

To change a cell reference to an absolute reference:

1. Click cell **E4** to move to the cell that contains the formula you want to edit.
2. Double-click the mouse button to edit the formula in the cell. Notice that each cell reference in the formula in cell E4 appears in a different color and the corresponding cells referred to in the formula are outlined in the same color. This feature is called **Range Finder** and is designed to make it easier for you to check the accuracy of your formula.
3. Make sure the insertion point is to the right of the division (/) operator, anywhere in the cell reference B8.
4. Press the **F4** key to change the reference to $B$8.

   TROUBLE? If your reference shows the **mixed reference** B$8 or $B8, continue to press the F4 key until you see $B$8.

5. Press the **Enter** key to update the formula in cell E4.

Cell E4 still displays .284971, which is the formula's correct result. But remember, the problem in your original formula did not surface until you copied it to cells E5 through E7. To correct the error, you need to copy the revised formula and then check the results. Although you can again use the fill handle to copy the formula, you can also copy the formula using the Clipboard and the Copy and Paste buttons on the Standard toolbar.

Copying **Cell Contents Using the Copy-and-Paste Method**

You can duplicate the contents of a cell or range by making a copy of the cell or range and then pasting the copy into one or more locations in the same worksheet, another worksheet, or another workbook.

When you copy a cell or range of cells, the copied material is placed on the Clipboard. You can copy labels, numbers, dates, or formulas.

REFERENCE WINDOW RW

Copying and Pasting a Cell or Range of Cells

- Select the cell or range of cells to be copied.
- Click the Copy button on the Standard toolbar.
- Select the range into which you want to copy the formula.
- Click the Paste button on the Standard toolbar.
- Press the Enter key.

You need to copy the formula in cell E4 to the Clipboard and then paste that formula into cells E5 through E7.

To copy the revised formula from cell E4 to cells E5 through E7:

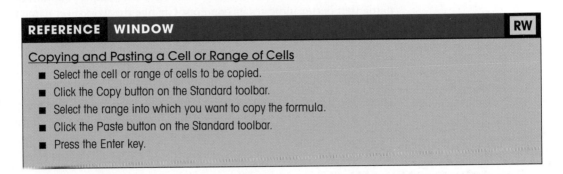

1. Click cell **E4** because it contains the revised formula that you want to copy.
2. Click the **Copy** button on the Standard toolbar. A moving dashed line surrounds cell E4, indicating that the formula has been copied and is available to be pasted into other cells.
3. Click and drag to select cells **E5** through **E7**.
4. Click the **Paste** button on the Standard toolbar. Excel adjusts the formula and pastes it into cells E5 through E7.
5. Click any cell to deselect the range and view the formulas' results. Press the **Escape** key to clear the Clipboard and remove the dashed line surrounding cell E4. See Figure 2-14.

Figure 2-14 RESULTS OF COPYING THE FORMULA WITH AN ABSOLUTE REFERENCE

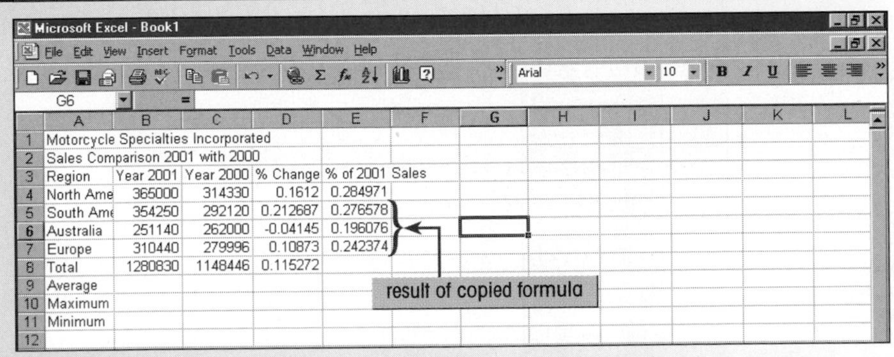

Copying this formula worked. When you pasted the formula from cell E4 into the range E5:E7, Excel automatically adjusted the relative reference (B4), while using the cell reference ($B$8) for all absolute references. You have now implemented most of the design as specified in the planning analysis sheet. Now rename the worksheet to accurately describe its contents, then save the workbook on your Data Disk before entering the formulas to compute the summary statistics.

Renaming the Worksheet

Before saving the workbook, look at the sheet tab in the lower-left corner of the worksheet window: the sheet is currently named Sheet1—the name Excel automatically uses when it opens a new workbook. Now that your worksheet is taking shape, you want to give it a more descriptive name that better indicates its contents. Change the worksheet name to Sales Comparison.

To change a worksheet name:

1. Double-click the **Sheet1** sheet tab to select it.
2. Type the new name, **Sales Comparison**, over the current name, Sheet1, and then click any cell in the worksheet. The sheet tab displays the name "Sales Comparison."

Saving the New Workbook

Now you want to save the workbook. Because this is the first time you have saved this workbook, you use the Save As command and name the file MSI Sales Report.

To save the workbook as MSI Sales Report:

1. Click **File** on the menu bar, and then click **Save As** to open the Save As dialog box.
2. In the File name text box, type **MSI Sales Report** but don't press the Enter key yet. You still need to check some other settings.
3. Click the **Save in** list arrow, and then click the drive containing your Data Disk.
4. In the folder list, select the **Tutorial** folder for **Tutorial.02**, into which you want to save the workbook. Your Save As dialog box should look like the dialog box in Figure 2-15.

Figure 2-15 SAVING THE WORKBOOK AS MSI SALES REPORT

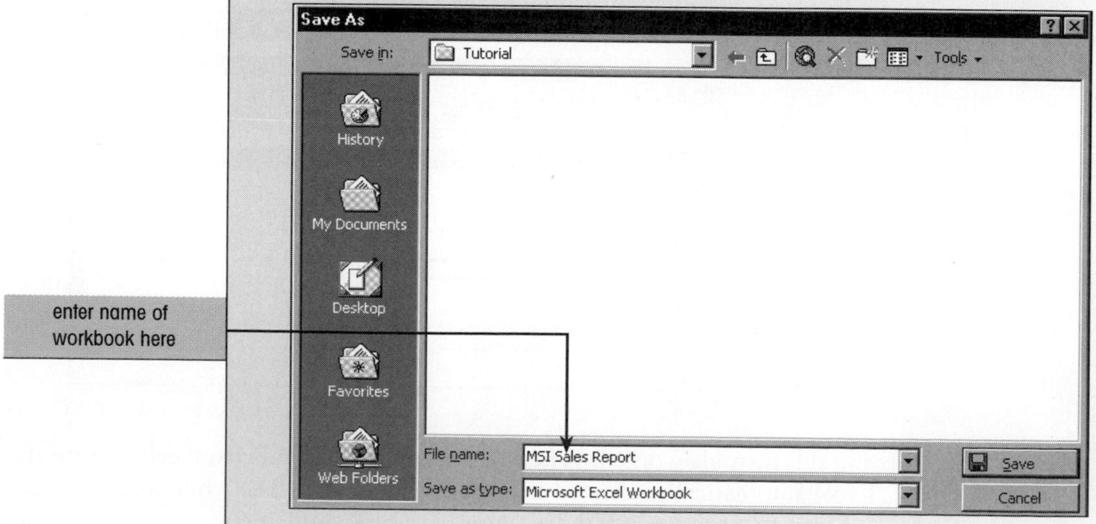

5. Click the **Save** button to save the workbook.

TROUBLE? If you see the message "Replace Existing MSI Sales Report," Excel found a file with the same name on the current folder. Click the Yes button to replace the file on the folder with the current version.

Session 2.1 QUICK CHECK

1. List the steps to follow to create a worksheet.
2. Describe how AutoSum works.
3. In cell D3 you have the formula =B3-C3. After you copy this formula to cell D4, the formula in cell D4 would appear in the formula bar as __________.
4. The __________ is a small black square located in the lower-right corner of a selected cell.
5. In the formula =D10*C10, D10 and C10 are examples of __________ references.
6. In the formula =A8+(1+$C$1), $C$1 is an example of a(n) __________.
7. When you copy a formula using the Copy and Paste buttons on the Standard toolbar, Excel uses the __________ to temporarily store the formula.
8. Describe the steps you take to change the name of the sheet tab.
9. What is meant by order of precedence?

Now that you have planned and built the Sales Comparison worksheet by entering labels, values, and formulas, you need to complete the worksheet by entering some functions and formatting the worksheet. You will do this in Session 2.2.

SESSION 2.2

In this session you will finish the worksheet. As you do this you will learn how to enter several statistical functions, increase the column width, insert a row between the titles and column headings, move the contents of a range to another location, and apply one of the Excel predefined formats to the report. You will also spell check the worksheet, preview, and print it.

Excel Functions

According to Sally's planning analysis sheet, you still need to enter the formulas for the summary statistics. To enter these statistics you'll use three Excel functions, AVERAGE, MAX, and MIN. The many Excel functions help you enter formulas for calculations and other specialized tasks, even if you don't know the mathematical details of the calculations. As you recall, a function is a calculation tool that performs a predefined operation. You are already familiar with the SUM function, which adds the values in a range of cells. Excel provides hundreds of functions, including a function to calculate the average of a list of numbers, a function to find a number's square root, a function to calculate loan payments, and a function to calculate the number of days between two dates.

Each function has a **syntax**, which specifies the order in which you must type the parts of the function and where to put commas, parentheses, and other punctuation. The general syntax of an Excel function is:

FUNCTION NAME(*argument1*,*argument2*,...)

The syntax of most functions requires you to type the function name followed by one or more arguments in parentheses. The name of the function, such as SUM or AVERAGE, describes the operation the function performs. Function **arguments** specify the values the function must use in the calculation, or the cell references that Excel must include in the calculation. For example, in the function SUM(A1:A20) the function name is SUM and the argument is A1:A20, which is the range of cells you want to total.

You can use a function in a simple formula such as =SUM(A1:A20), or a more complex formula such as =SUM(A1:A20)*52. As with all formulas, you enter the formula that contains a function in the cell where you want to display the results. The easiest way to enter a function in a cell is to use the Paste Function button on the Standard toolbar, which leads you step-by-step through the process of entering a formula containing a function.

If you prefer, you can type the function directly into the cell. Although the function name is always shown in uppercase, you can type it in either uppercase or lowercase. Also, even though parentheses enclose the arguments, you need not type the closing parenthesis if the function ends the formula. Excel automatically adds the closing parenthesis when you press the Enter key to complete the formula.

Figure 2-16 shows a few of the functions available in Excel organized by category. To learn more about functions, use the Paste Function button on the Standard toolbar or use the Help system. According to Sally's planning analysis sheet, the next step is to calculate the average regional sales for 2001.

Figure 2-16 SELECTED EXCEL FUNCTIONS

CATEGORY	FUNCTION NAME	SYNTAX	DEFINITION
Finance	PMT	PMT(rate,nper,pv,fv,type)	Calculates the payment for a loan based on constant payments and a constant interest rate
	FV	FV(rate,nper,pmt,pv,type)	Returns the future value of an investment based on periodic, constant payments and a constant interest rate
Math	ROUND	ROUND(number,num_digits)	Rounds a number to a specified number of digits
	RAND	RAND( )	Returns an evenly distributed random number greater than or equal to 0 and less than 1
Logical	IF	IF(logical_test,value_if_true, value_if_false)	Returns one value if a condition you specify evaluates to TRUE and another value if it evaluates to FALSE
	AND	AND(logical1,logical2, ...)	Returns TRUE if all its arguments are TRUE; returns FALSE if one or more arguments is FALSE
Lookup and Reference	VLOOKUP	VLOOKUP(lookup_value, table_array,col_index_num, range_lookup)	Searches for a value in the leftmost column of a table, and then returns a value in the same row from a column you specify in the table
	INDIRECT	INDIRECT(ref_text,a1)	Returns the reference specified by a text string–references are immediately evaluated to display their contents
Text	CONCATENATE	CONCATENATE (text1,text2,...)	Joins several text strings into one text string
	LEFT	LEFT(text,num_chars)	Returns the first (or leftmost) character or characters in a text string
Date and Time	TODAY	TODAY( )	Returns the serial number of the current date
	YEAR	YEAR(serial_number)	Returns the year corresponding to serial number–the year is given as an integer in the range 1900-9999
Statistical	COUNT	COUNT(value1,value2, ...)	Counts the number of cells that contain numbers and numbers within the list of arguments
	STDEV	STDEV(number1,number2,...)	Estimates standard deviation based on a sample

AVERAGE Function

AVERAGE is a statistical function that calculates the average, or the arithmetic mean. The syntax for the AVERAGE function is:

AVERAGE(*number1,number2,...*)

Generally, when you use the AVERAGE function, *number* is a range of cells. To calculate the average of a range of cells, Excel sums the values in the range, then divides by the number of non-blank cells in the range.

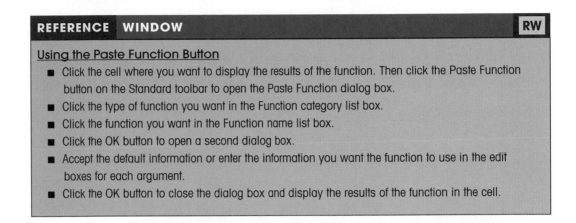

REFERENCE WINDOW RW

Using the Paste Function Button

- Click the cell where you want to display the results of the function. Then click the Paste Function button on the Standard toolbar to open the Paste Function dialog box.
- Click the type of function you want in the Function category list box.
- Click the function you want in the Function name list box.
- Click the OK button to open a second dialog box.
- Accept the default information or enter the information you want the function to use in the edit boxes for each argument.
- Click the OK button to close the dialog box and display the results of the function in the cell.

Sally wants you to calculate the average sales in 2001. You'll use the Paste Function button to enter the AVERAGE function, which is one of the statistical functions.

To enter the AVERAGE function using the Paste Function button:

1. If you took a break after the last session, make sure Excel is running and the MSI Sales worksheet is open. Click cell **B9** to select the cell where you want to enter the AVERAGE function.
2. Click the **Paste Function** button on the Standard toolbar to open the Paste Function dialog box.

   TROUBLE? If the Office Assistant opens and offers help on this feature, click the No option button.

3. Click **Statistical** in the Function category list box.
4. Click **AVERAGE** in the Function name list box. See Figure 2-17. The syntax for the AVERAGE function, AVERAGE(number1,number2,...), appears beneath the Function category box.

Figure 2-17 PASTE FUNCTION DIALOG BOX

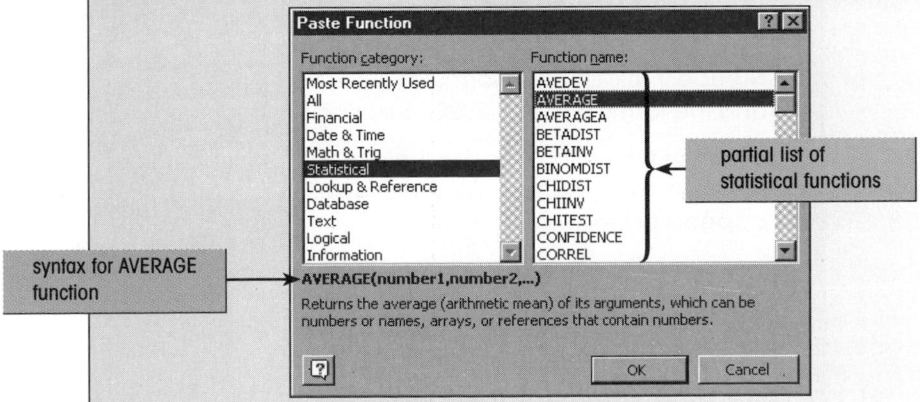

5. Click the **OK** button to open the formula palette for the Average function. The **formula palette** displays the name of the function, a text box for each argument of the function you selected, a description of the function and each argument, the current values of the arguments, the current results of the function, and the current results of the entire formula. Notice that the range B4:B8 appears in the Number1 edit box, and =AVERAGE(B4:B8) appears in the formula bar. See Figure 2-18.

Figure 2-18 AVERAGE FORMULA PALETTE

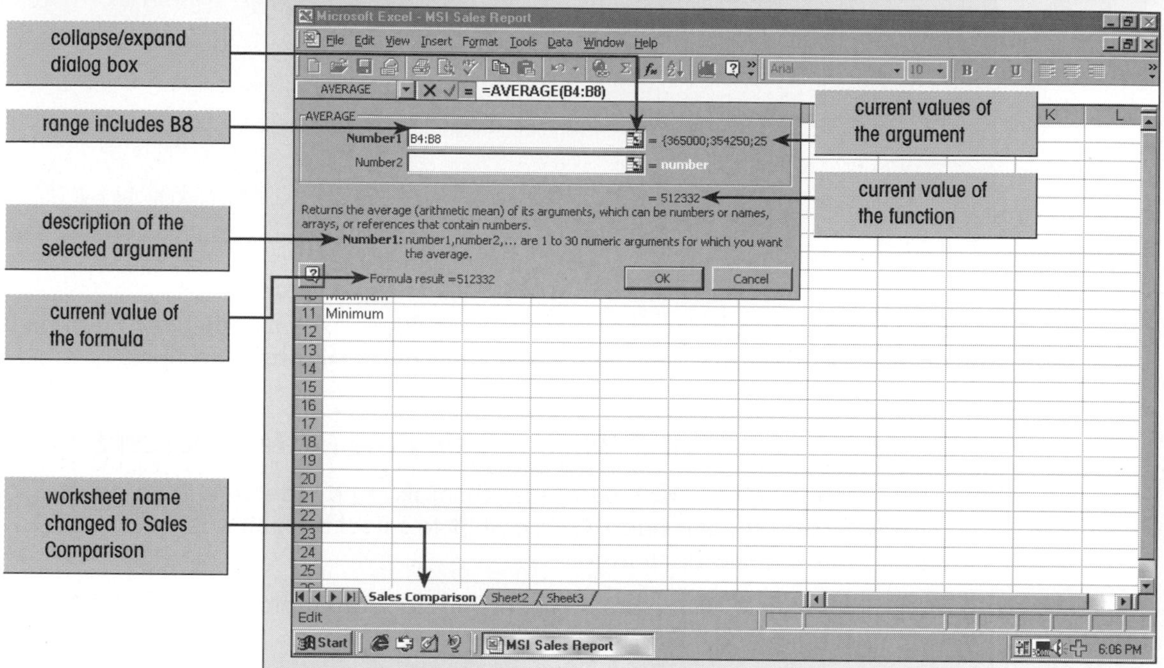

Excel has incorrectly included the total sales for 2001 (cell B8) in the range to calculate the average. The correct range is B4:B7.

6. Click the **Collapse** dialog box button to the right of the Number1 text box to collapse the dialog box to the size of one row. This makes it easier for you to identify and select the correct range.

7. Position the cell pointer over cell **B4**, and then click and drag to select the range **B4:B7**. As you drag the mouse over the range, notice that the message "4Rx1C" appears in a ScreenTip, informing you that four rows and one column have been selected, and then click the **Expand Dialog Box** button. The collapsed dialog box is restored and the correct range, B4:B7, appears in the Number1 text box. The formula =AVERAGE(B4:B7) appears in the formula bar and the formula result 320207.5 appears in the bottom of the formula palette.

8. Click the **OK** button to close the dialog box and return to the worksheet. The average, 320207.5, now appears in cell B9 and the completed function appears in the formula bar.

According to your plan, you need to enter a formula to find the largest regional sales amount in 2001. To do this, you'll use the MAX function.

MAX Function

MAX is a statistical function that finds the largest number. The syntax of the MAX function is:
MAX(*number1*,*number2*,...)

In the MAX function, *number* can be a constant number such as 345, a cell reference such as B6, or a range of cells such as B5:B16. You can use the MAX function to simply display the largest number or to use the largest number in a calculation. Although you can use the Paste Function to enter the MAX function, this time you'll type the MAX function directly into cell B10.

To enter the MAX function by typing directly into a cell:

1. If necessary, click cell **B10** to select it as the cell into which you want to type the formula that uses the MAX function.
2. Type **=MAX(B4:B7)** and then press the **Enter** key. Cell B10 displays 365000, the largest regional sales amount in 2001.

Next you need to find the smallest regional sales amount in 2001. For that, you'll use the MIN function.

MIN Function

MIN is a statistical function that finds the smallest number. The syntax of the MIN function is:
MIN(*number1*,*number2*,...)

You can use the MIN function to display the smallest number or to use the smallest number in a calculation.

You'll enter the MIN function directly into cell B11 using the pointing method.

Building Formulas by Pointing

Excel provides several ways to enter cell references into a formula. One is to type the cell references directly, as you have done so far in all the formulas you've entered. Another way to put a cell reference in a formula is to point to the cell reference you want to include while creating the formula. To use the **pointing method** to enter the formula, you click the cell or range of cells whose cell references you want to include in the formula. You may prefer to use this method to enter formulas because it minimizes typing errors.

Now use the pointing method to enter the formula to calculate the minimum sales.

To enter the MIN function using the pointing method:

1. If necessary, click cell **B11** to move to the cell where you want to enter the formula that uses the MIN function.
2. Type **=MIN(** to begin the formula.
3. Position the cell pointer in cell **B4**, and then click and drag to select cells **B4** through **B7**. As you drag the mouse over the range, notice that the message "4Rx1C" appears in a ScreenTip, informing you that four rows and one column have been selected. See Figure 2-19.

Figure 2-19 WORKSHEET IN PROCESS OF ENTERING FORMULA USING POINTING METHOD

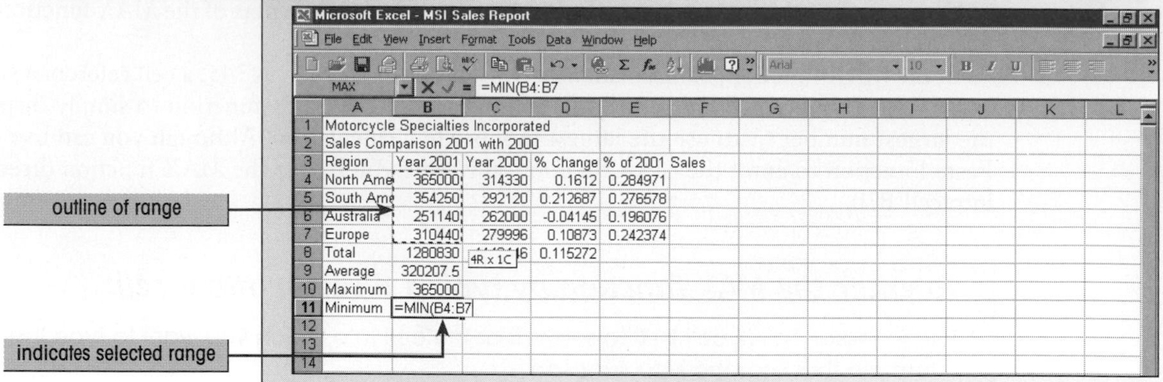

4. Release the mouse button, and then press the **Enter** key. Cell B11 displays 251140, the smallest regional sales amount for 2001.

Now that the worksheet labels, values, formulas, and functions have been entered, Sally reviews the worksheet.

Testing the Worksheet

Before trusting a worksheet and its results, you should test it to make sure you entered the correct formulas. You want the worksheet to produce accurate results.

Beginners often expect their Excel worksheets to work correctly the first time. Sometimes they do work correctly the first time, but even well-planned and well-designed worksheets can contain errors. It's best to assume that a worksheet has errors and test it to make sure it is correct. While there are no rules for testing a worksheet, here are some approaches:

- Entering **test values**, numbers that generate a known result, to determine whether your worksheet formulas are accurate. For example, try entering a 1 into each cell. After you enter the test values, you compare the results in your worksheet with the known results. If the results on your worksheet don't match the known results, you probably made an error.
- Entering **extreme values**, such as very large or very small numbers, and observing their effect on cells with formulas.
- Working out the numbers ahead of time with pencil, paper, and calculator, and comparing these results with the output from the computer.

Sally used the third approach to test her worksheet. She had calculated her results using a calculator (Figure 2-2) and then compared them with the results on the screen (Figure 2-19). The numbers agree, so she feels confident that the worksheet she created contains accurate results.

Spell Checking the Worksheet

You can use the Excel spell check feature to help identify and correct spelling and typing errors. Excel compares the words in your worksheet to the words in its dictionary. If Excel finds a word in your worksheet not in its dictionary, it shows you the word and some suggested corrections, and you decide whether to correct it or leave it as is.

REFERENCE WINDOW RW

Checking the Spelling in a Worksheet

- Click cell A1 to begin the spell check from the top of the worksheet.
- Click the Spelling button on the Standard toolbar.
- Change the spelling or ignore the spell check's suggestion for each identified word.
- Click the OK button when the spell check is complete.

You have tested your numbers and formulas for accuracy. Now you can check the spelling of all text entries in the worksheet.

To check the spelling in a worksheet:

1. Click cell **A1** to begin spell checking in the first cell of the worksheet.
2. Click the **Spelling** button on the Standard toolbar to check the spelling of the text in the worksheet. A message box indicates that Excel has finished spell checking the entire worksheet. No errors were found.

   TROUBLE? If the spell check does find a spelling error in your worksheet, use the Spelling dialog box options to correct the spelling mistake and continue checking the worksheet.

Improving the Worksheet Layout

Although the numbers are correct, Sally wants to present a more polished-looking worksheet. She feels that there are a number of simple changes you can make to the worksheet that will improve its layout and make the data more readable. Specifically, she asks you to increase the width of column A so that the entire region names are visible, insert a blank row between the titles and column headings, move the summary statistics down three rows from their current location, and apply one of the predefined Excel formats to the worksheet.

Changing Column Width

Changing the column width is one way to improve the appearance of the worksheet, making it easier to read and interpret data. In Sally's worksheet, you need to increase the width of column A so that all of the labels for North America and South America appear in their cells.

Excel provides several methods for changing column width. For example, you can click a column heading or click and drag the pointer to select a series of column headings and then use the Format menu. You can also use the dividing line between column headings in the column header row. When you move the pointer over the dividing line between two column headings, the pointer changes to ✢. You can then use the pointer to drag the dividing line to a new location. You can also double-click the dividing line to make the column as wide as the longest text label or number in the column.

REFERENCE WINDOW RW

Changing Column Width

- Click the column heading(s) whose width you want to change.
- Click Format, point to Column, and then click Width.
- In the Column Width dialog box, enter the new column width (or click AutoFit Selection to make the column(s) as wide as the longest text label or number in the column(s)).

or

- Drag the column heading dividing line to the right to increase column width or to the left to decrease column width.

or

- Double-click the column heading dividing line to make the column as wide as the longest text label or number in the column.

Sally has asked you to change the width of column A so that the complete region name is visible.

To change the width of column A:

1. Position the pointer ✜ on the A in the column heading area.
2. Move the pointer to the right edge of the column heading dividing columns A and B. Notice that the pointer changes to the resize arrow ✛.
3. Click and drag the resize arrow to the right, increasing the column width 12 characters or more, as indicated in the ScreenTip that pops up on the screen.
4. Release the mouse button. See Figure 2-20.

Figure 2-20 **WORKSHEET AFTER WIDTH OF COLUMN A INCREASED**

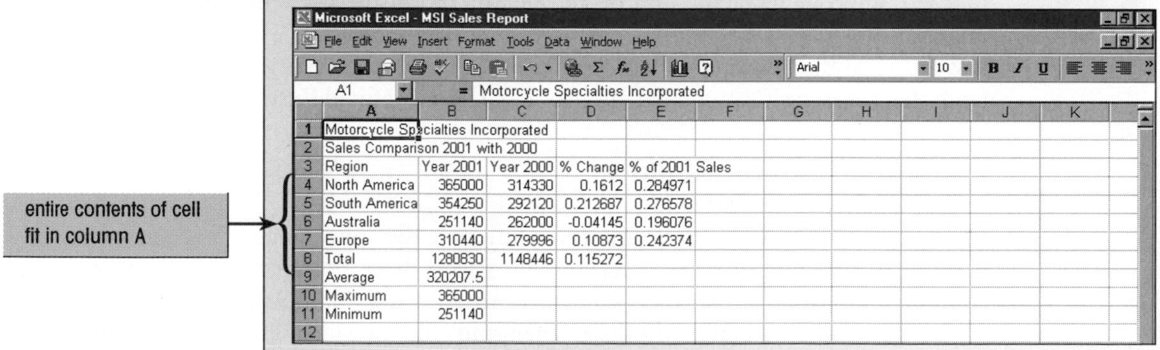

Next you need to insert a row between the title and the column heading.

Inserting a Row into a Worksheet

At times you may need to add one or more rows or columns to a worksheet to make room for new data or to make the worksheet easier to read. The process of inserting columns and rows is similar; you select the number of columns or rows you want to insert and then use the Insert command to insert them. When you insert rows or columns, Excel repositions other rows and columns in the worksheet and automatically adjusts cell references in formulas to reflect the new location of values used in calculations.

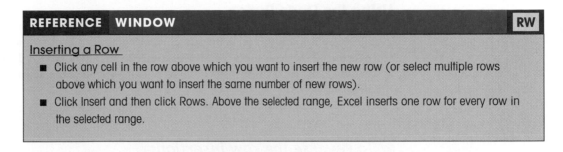

REFERENCE WINDOW RW

Inserting a Row

- Click any cell in the row above which you want to insert the new row (or select multiple rows above which you want to insert the same number of new rows).
- Click Insert and then click Rows. Above the selected range, Excel inserts one row for every row in the selected range.

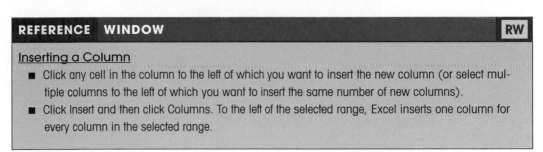

REFERENCE WINDOW RW

Inserting a Column

- Click any cell in the column to the left of which you want to insert the new column (or select multiple columns to the left of which you want to insert the same number of new columns).
- Click Insert and then click Columns. To the left of the selected range, Excel inserts one column for every column in the selected range.

Sally wants one blank row between the titles and column headings in her worksheet.

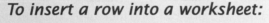

To insert a row into a worksheet:

1. Click cell **A2**.
2. Click **Insert** on the menu bar, and then click **Rows**. Excel inserts a blank row above the original row 2. All other rows shift down one row. Click any cell. See Figure 2-21.

Figure 2-21 WORKSHEET AFTER ONE ROW INSERTED ABOVE ORIGINAL ROW 2

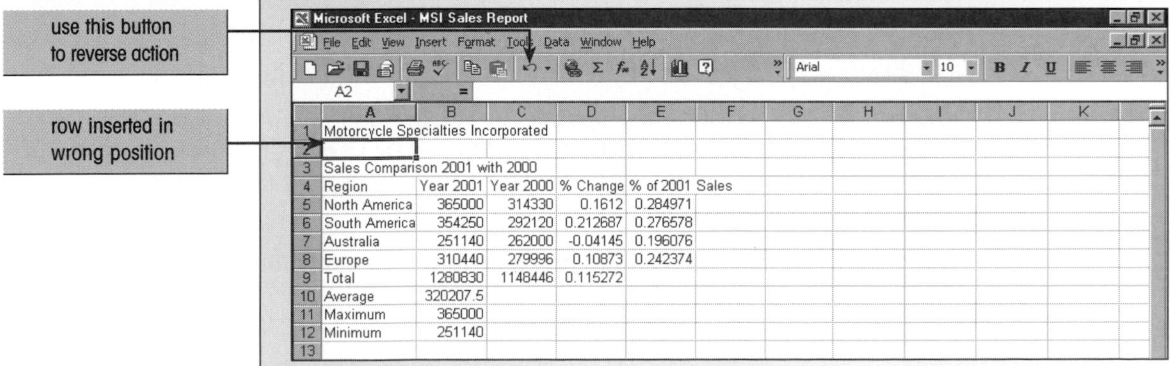

The blank row isn't really where you wanted it. You inserted a row between the two lines of the title instead of between the title and the column heading. To correct this error you can either delete the row or use the Undo button. If you need to delete a row or column, select the row(s) or column(s) you want to delete, then click Delete on the Edit menu, or press the Delete key on your keyboard. You use the Undo button because it is a feature you find valuable in many situations.

Using the Undo Button

The Excel Undo button lets you cancel recent actions one at a time. Click the Undo button to reverse the last command or delete the last entry you typed. To reverse more than one action, click the arrow next to the Undo button and click the action you want to undo from the drop-down list.

Now use the Undo button to reverse the row insertion.

To reverse the row insertion:

1. Click the **Undo** button on the Standard toolbar to restore the worksheet to its status before the row was inserted.

Now you can insert the blank row in the correct place—between the second line of the worksheet title and the column heads.

To insert a row into a worksheet:

1. Click cell **A3** because you want to insert one row above row 3. If you wanted to insert several rows, you would select as many rows as you wanted to insert immediately below where you want the new rows inserted before using the Insert command.
2. Click **Insert** on the menu bar, and then click **Rows**. Excel inserts a blank row above the original row 3. All other rows shift down one row.

Adding a row changed the location of the data in the worksheet. For example, the percentage change in North American sales, originally in cell D4, is now in cell D5. Did Excel adjust the formulas to compensate for the new row? Check cell D5 and any other cells you want to view to verify that the cell references were adjusted.

To examine the formula in cell D5 and other cells:

1. Click cell **D5**. The formula =(B5-C5)/C5 appears in the formula bar. You originally entered the formula =(B4-C4)/C4 in cell D4 to calculate percentage change in North America. Excel automatically adjusted the cell reference to reflect the new location of the data.
2. Inspect other cells below row 3 to verify that their cell references were automatically adjusted when the new row was inserted.

Sally has also suggested moving the summary statistics down three rows from their present location to make the report easier to read. So you will need to move the range of cells containing the average, minimum, and maximum sales to a different location in the worksheet.

Moving a Range Using the Mouse

To place the summary statistics three rows below the other data in the report, you could use the Insert command to insert three blank rows between the total and average sales. Alternatively, you could use the mouse to move the summary statistics to a new location. Because you already know how to insert a row, try using the mouse to move the summary statistics to a new location. This technique is called drag and drop. You simply select the cell range you want to move and use the pointer to drag the cells' contents to the desired location.

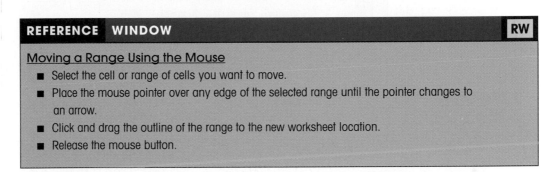

REFERENCE WINDOW RW

Moving a Range Using the Mouse

- Select the cell or range of cells you want to move.
- Place the mouse pointer over any edge of the selected range until the pointer changes to an arrow.
- Click and drag the outline of the range to the new worksheet location.
- Release the mouse button.

Sally has asked you to move the range A10 through B12 to the new destination area A13 through B15.

To move a range of cells using the drag-and-drop technique:

1. Select the range of cells **A10:B12,** which contains the sales summary statistics you want to move.
2. Place the mouse pointer over any edge of the selected range until the pointer changes to an arrow. See Figure 2-22.

Figure 2-22 RANGE TO BE MOVED

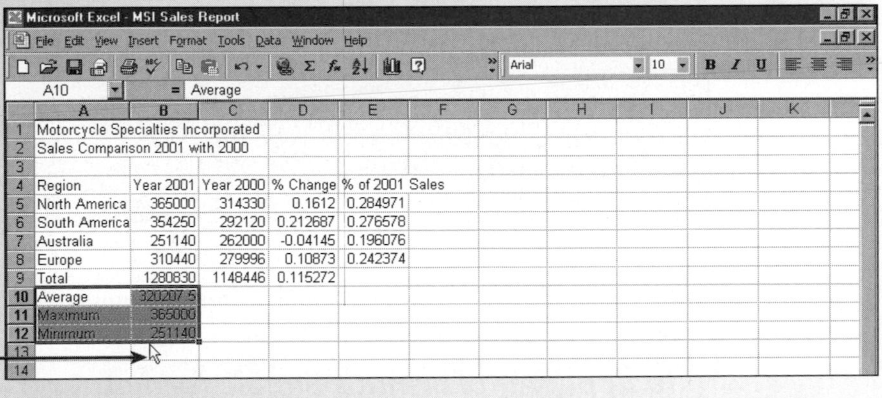

pointer shape indicates selected range can be moved

3. Click the mouse button and then hold the button down as you move (drag) the outline of the three rows down to range A13:B15. Notice how Excel displays a gray outline and a box with a range address that shows the destination of the cells.
4. Release the mouse button. Excel moves the selected cells to the designated location, A13:B15.

5. Click any cell to deselect the range. See Figure 2-23.

Figure 2-23 WORKSHEET AFTER RANGE MOVED

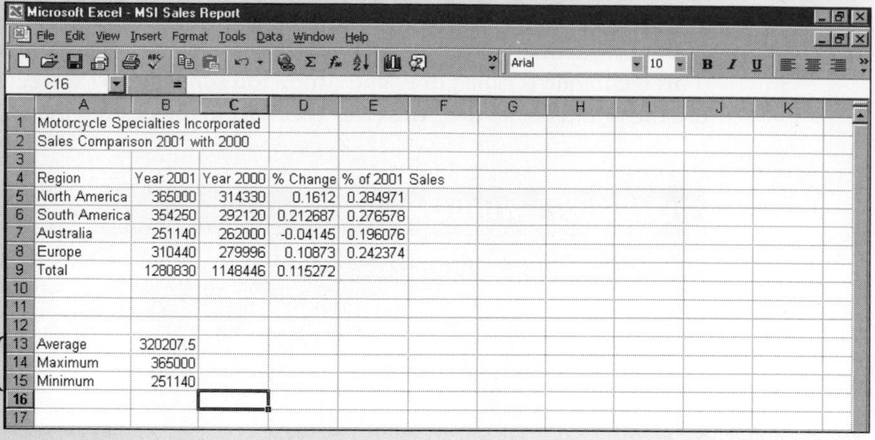

new location for summary statistics

Next Sally wants you to use the Excel AutoFormat feature to improve the worksheet's appearance by emphasizing the titles and aligning numbers in cells.

Using AutoFormat

The AutoFormat feature lets you change the appearance of your worksheet by selecting from a collection of predefined worksheet formats. Each worksheet format in the AutoFormat collection gives your worksheet a more professional appearance by applying attractive fonts, borders, colors, and shading to a range of data. AutoFormat also adjusts column widths, row heights, and the alignment of text in cells to improve the appearance of the worksheet.

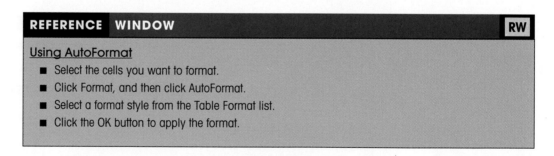

REFERENCE WINDOW RW

Using AutoFormat

- Select the cells you want to format.
- Click Format, and then click AutoFormat.
- Select a format style from the Table Format list.
- Click the OK button to apply the format.

Now you'll use AutoFormat's Simple format to improve the worksheet's appearance.

To apply AutoFormat's Simple format:

1. Select cells **A1:E9** as the range you want to format using AutoFormat.

2. Click **Format** on the menu bar, and then click **AutoFormat**. The AutoFormat dialog box opens. See Figure 2-24.

Figure 2-24 AUTOFORMAT DIALOG BOX

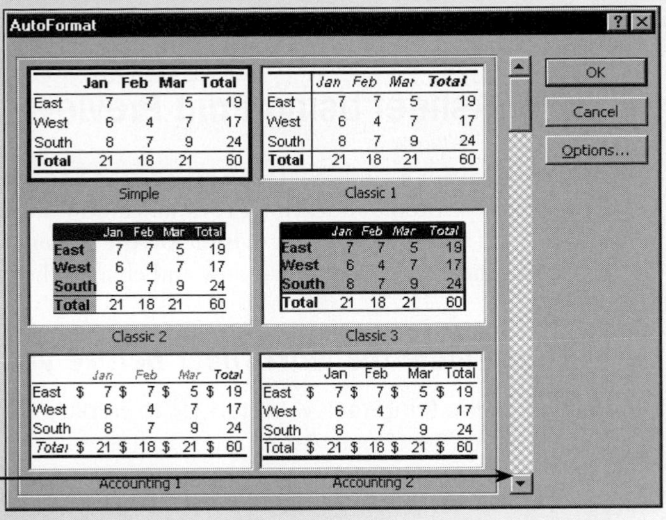

3. The dialog box displays a preview of how each format will appear when applied to a worksheet. Notice the dark border around the Simple format indicating it is the selected format.

4. Click the **OK** button to apply the Simple format.

5. Click any cell to deselect the range. Figure 2-25 shows the newly formatted worksheet.

Figure 2-25 WORKSHEET AFTER USING THE SIMPLE AUTOFORMAT

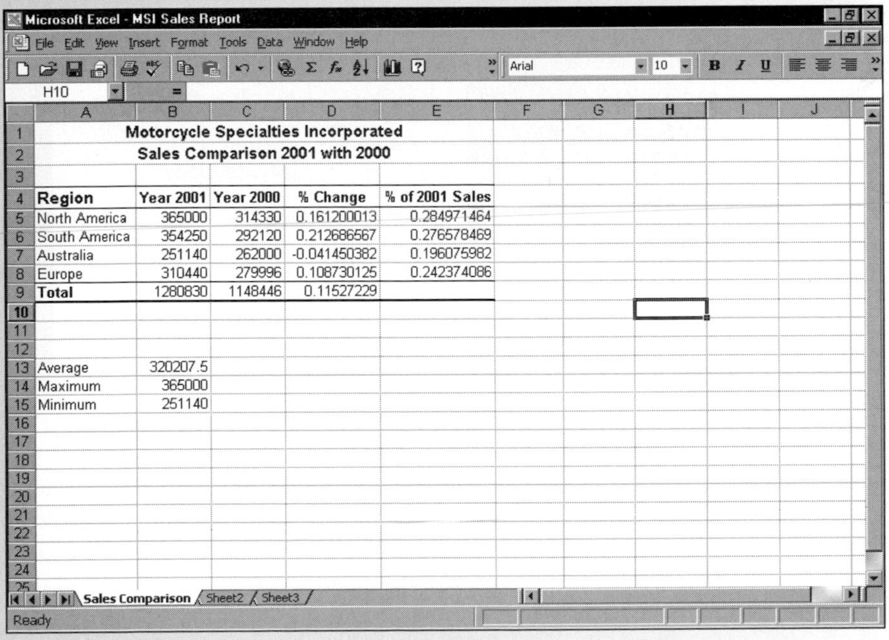

You show the worksheet to Sally. She's impressed with the improved appearance and decides to hand it out to the regional sales managers at their next meeting. She asks you to print it so she can make copies.

Previewing the Worksheet Using Print Preview

Before you print a worksheet, you can use the Excel Print Preview window to see how it will look when printed. The Print Preview window shows you margins, page breaks, headers, and footers that are not always visible on the screen. If the preview isn't what you want, you can close the Print Preview window and change the worksheet before printing it.

To preview the worksheet before you print it:

1. Click the Print Preview button to display the worksheet in the Print Preview window. See Figure 2-26.

TROUBLE? If you do not see the Print Preview button on the Standard toolbar, click More Buttons to display the Print Preview button.

Figure 2-26 PRINT PREVIEW OF SALES COMPARISON WORKSHEET

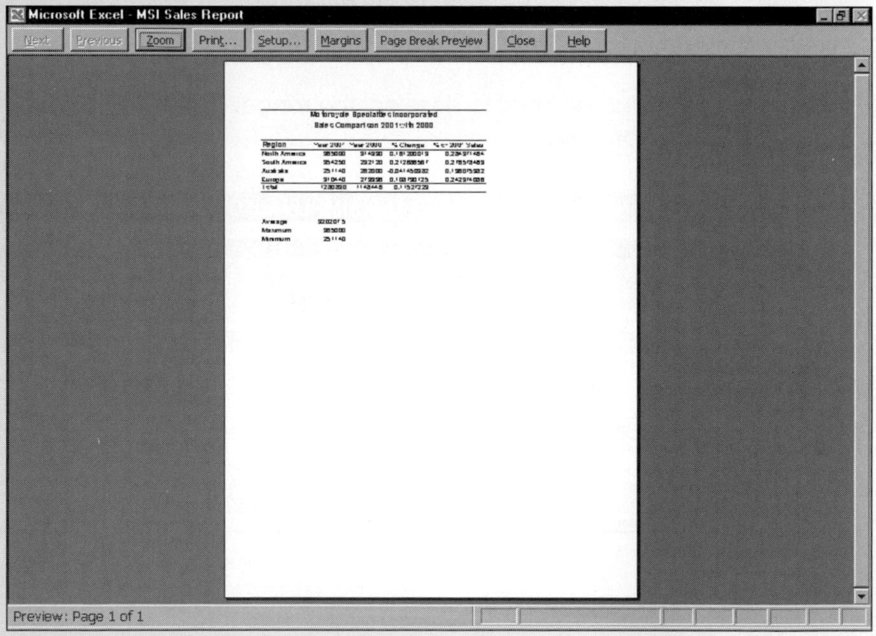

When Excel displays a full page in the Print Preview window, you might have difficulty seeing the text of the worksheet because it is so small. Don't worry if the preview isn't completely readable. One purpose of the Print Preview window is to see the overall layout of the worksheet and how it will fit on the printed page. If you want a better view of the text, you can use the Zoom button.

To display an enlarged section of the Print Preview window:

1. Click the **Zoom** button to display an enlarged section of the Print Preview.
2. Click the **Zoom** button again to return to the full-page view.

Notice that the Print Preview window contains several other buttons. Figure 2-27 describes each of these buttons.

Figure 2-27 DESCRIPTION OF PRINT PREVIEW BUTTONS

CLICKING THIS BUTTON	RESULTS IN
Next	Moving forward one page
Previous	Moving backward one page
Zoom	Magnifying the Print Preview screen to zoom in on any portion of the page; click again to return to full-page preview
Print	Printing the document
Setup	Displaying the Page Setup dialog box
Margins	Changing the width of margins, columns in the worksheet and the position of headers and footers
Page Break Preview	Showing where page breaks occur in the worksheet and which area of the worksheet will be printed; you can adjust where data will print by inserting or moving page breaks
Close	Closing the Print Preview window
Help	Activating Help

Looking at the worksheet in Print Preview, you observe that it is not centered on the page. By default, Excel prints a worksheet at the upper left of the page's print area. You can specify that the worksheet be centered vertically, horizontally, or both.

Centering the Printout

Worksheet printouts generally look more professional centered on the printed page. You decide that Sally would want you to center the sales comparison worksheet both horizontally and vertically on the printed page.

To center the printout:

1. In Print Preview, click the **Setup** button to open the Page Setup dialog box.
2. Click the **Margins** tab. See Figure 2-28. Notice that the preview box displays a worksheet positioned at the upper-left edge of the page.

Figure 2-28 MARGINS TAB OF PAGE SETUP DIALOG BOX

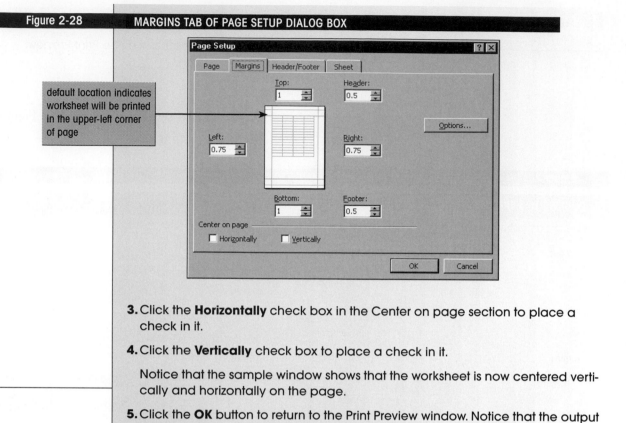

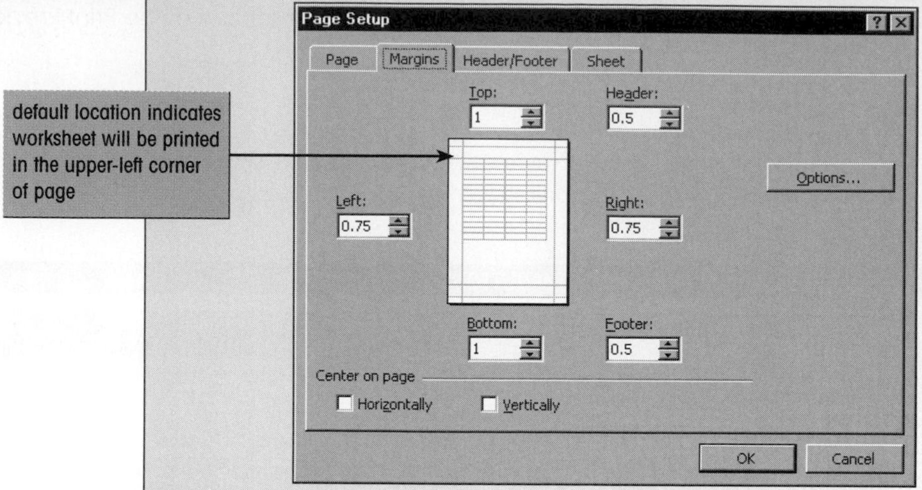

3. Click the **Horizontally** check box in the Center on page section to place a check in it.

4. Click the **Vertically** check box to place a check in it.

   Notice that the sample window shows that the worksheet is now centered vertically and horizontally on the page.

5. Click the **OK** button to return to the Print Preview window. Notice that the output in the Print Preview window is centered vertically and horizontally.

   TROUBLE? If you see only the worksheet name, click the Zoom button to view the entire page.

Adding Headers and Footers

Headers and footers can provide useful documentation on your printed worksheet, such as the name of the person who created the worksheet, the date it was printed, and its filename. The **header** is text printed in the top margin of every worksheet page. A **footer** is text printed in the bottom margin of every page. Headers and footers are not displayed in the worksheet window. To see them, you must preview or print the worksheet.

Excel uses formatting codes in headers and footers to represent the items you want to print. Formatting codes produce dates, times, and filenames that you might want a header or footer to include. Using formatting codes instead of typing the date, time, filename and so on provides flexibility. For example, if you use a formatting code for date, the current date appears on the printout whenever the worksheet is printed. You can type these codes, or you can click a formatting code button to insert the code. Figure 2-29 shows the formatting codes and the buttons for inserting them.

Figure 2-29 HEADER AND FOOTER FORMATTING BUTTONS

BUTTON	BUTTON NAME	FORMATTING CODE	ACTION
	Font	none	Sets font, text style, and font size
	Page number	&[Page]	Inserts page number
	Total pages	&[Pages]	Inserts total number of pages
	Date	&[Date]	Inserts current date
	Time	&[Time]	Inserts current time
	Filename	&[File]	Inserts filename
	Sheet name	&[Tab]	Inserts name of active worksheet

Sally asks you to add a custom header that includes the filename and today's date. She also wants you to add a custom footer that displays the preparer's name.

To add a header and a footer to your worksheet:

1. In the Print Preview window, click the **Setup** button to open the Page Setup dialog box, and then click the **Header/Footer** tab.
2. Click the **Custom Header** button to open the Header dialog box.
3. With the insertion point in the Left section box, click the **Filename** button. The code &(File) appears in the Left section box.

   TROUBLE? If you clicked the wrong code, double-click the code, press the Delete key, then repeat Steps 2 and 3.

4. Click the **Right section** box to move the insertion point to the Right section box.
5. Click the **Date** button. The code &(Date) appears in the Right section box. See Figure 2-30.

Figure 2-30 INSERTING FORMATTING CODES INTO THE HEADER DIALOG BOX

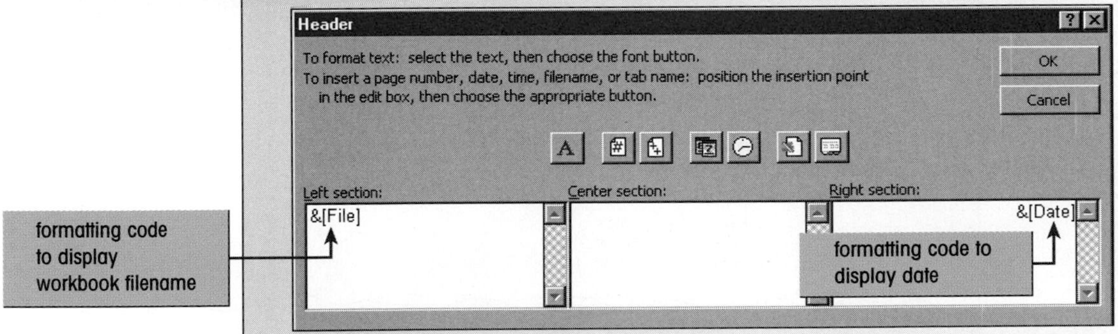

TROUBLE? If you clicked the wrong code, double-click the code, press the Delete key, and then repeat Step 5.

6. Click the **OK** button to complete the header and return to the Page Setup dialog box. Notice that the header shows the filename on the left and the date on the right.
7. Click the **Custom Footer** button to open the Footer dialog box.
8. Click the **Center section** box to move the insertion point to the Center section box.
9. Type **Prepared by (*enter your name here*).**
10. Click the **OK** button to complete the footer and return to the Page Setup dialog box. Notice that the footer shows your name in the bottom, center of the page.
11. Click the **OK** button to return to the Print Preview window. The new header and footer appear in the Print Preview window.
12. Click the **Close** button to exit the Print Preview window and return to the worksheet.

You'll use the Print button on the Standard toolbar to print one copy of the worksheet with the current settings. First, save the worksheet before printing it.

To save your page setup settings with the worksheet and print the worksheet:

1. Click the **Save** button on the Standard toolbar.
2. Click the **Print** button on the Standard toolbar. See Figure 2-31.

TROUBLE? If you see a message that indicates that you have a printer problem, click the Cancel button to cancel printing. Check your printer to make sure it is turned on and is online; also make sure it has paper. Then go back and try Step 2 again. If you have no printer available, click the Cancel button.

Figure 2-31 PRINTED WORKSHEET

Motorcycle Specialties Incorporated
Sales Comparison 2001 with 2000

Region	Year 2001	Year 2000	% Change	% of 2001 Sales
North America	365000	314330	0.161200013	0.284971464
South America	354250	292120	0.212686567	0.276578469
Australia	251140	262000	-0.041450382	0.196075982
Europe	310440	279996	0.108730125	0.242374086
Total	1280830	1148446	0.11527229	

Average	320207.5
Maximum	365000
Minimum	251140

Sally reviews the printed worksheet and is satisfied with its appearance. Now she asks for a second printout without the average, minimum, and maximum statistics.

Setting the Print Area

By default, Excel prints the entire worksheet. There are situations in which you are interested in printing a portion of the worksheet. To do this, you first select the area you want to print, and then use the Set Print Area command to define the print area.

To print a portion of the worksheet:

1. Select the range **A1:E9**.
2. Click **File**, point to Print Area, and then click **Set Print Area**.
3. Click the **Print Preview** button. Notice the average, minimum and maximum values are not included in the print preview window.
4. Click **Close** to return to the worksheet.
5. Click any cell outside the highlighted range. Notice the range A1: E9 is surrounded with a dashed line indicating the current print area for the worksheet.

If you want to print the entire worksheet once a print area has been set, you need to remove the current print area. Select File, point to Print Area, and click the Clear Print Area to remove the print area. Now the entire worksheet will print.

Documenting the Workbook

Documenting the workbook provides valuable information to those using the workbook. Documentation includes external documentation as well as notes and instructions within the workbook. This information could be as basic as who created the worksheet and the date it was created, or it could be more detailed, including formulas, summaries, and layout information.

Depending on the use of the workbook, the required amount of documentation varies. Sally's planning analysis sheet and sketch for the sales comparison worksheet are one form of external documentation. This information can be useful to someone who would need to modify the worksheet in any way because it states the goals, required input, output, and the calculations used.

One source of internal documentation would be a worksheet placed as the first worksheet in the workbook, such as the Documentation worksheet in Tutorial 1 to determine the best location for the new Inwood golf course. In more complex workbooks, this sheet may also include an index of all worksheets in the workbook, instructions on how to use the worksheets, where to enter data, how to save the workbook, and how to print reports. This documentation method is useful because the information is contained directly in the workbook and can easily be viewed upon opening the workbook, or printed if necessary. Another source of internal documentation is the **Property** dialog box. This dialog box enables you to electronically capture information such as the name of the workbook's creator, the creation date, the number of revisions, and other information related to the workbook.

If you prefer, you can include documentation on each sheet of the workbook. One way is to attach notes to cells by using the Comments command to explain complex formulas, list assumptions, and enter reminders.

The worksheet itself can be used as documentation. Once a worksheet is completed, it is a good practice to print and file a hardcopy of your work as documentation. This hardcopy file should include a printout of each worksheet displaying the values and another printout of the worksheet displaying the cell formulas.

Sally asks you to include a note in the worksheet that will remind her that the sales in Europe do not include an acquisition that was approved in December. You suggest inserting a cell comment.

Adding **Cell Comments**

Cell comments can help users remember assumptions, explain complex formulas, or place reminders related to the contents of a specific cell.

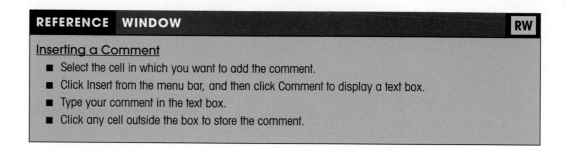

REFERENCE WINDOW RW

Inserting a Comment

- Select the cell in which you want to add the comment.
- Click Insert from the menu bar, and then click Comment to display a text box.
- Type your comment in the text box.
- Click any cell outside the box to store the comment.

Use the cell comment to insert the note for Sally.

To add a comment to a cell:

1. Click cell **B8**.
2. Click **Insert** and then click **Comment** to display a text box.

   TROUBLE? If the Comment item does not appear on the Insert menu, click [button] to view additional items on the Insert menu.

   Now enter your comment in the text box.
3. Type **Does not include sales from company acquired in December**. See Figure 2-32.

Figure 2-32 INSERTING A CELL COMMENT

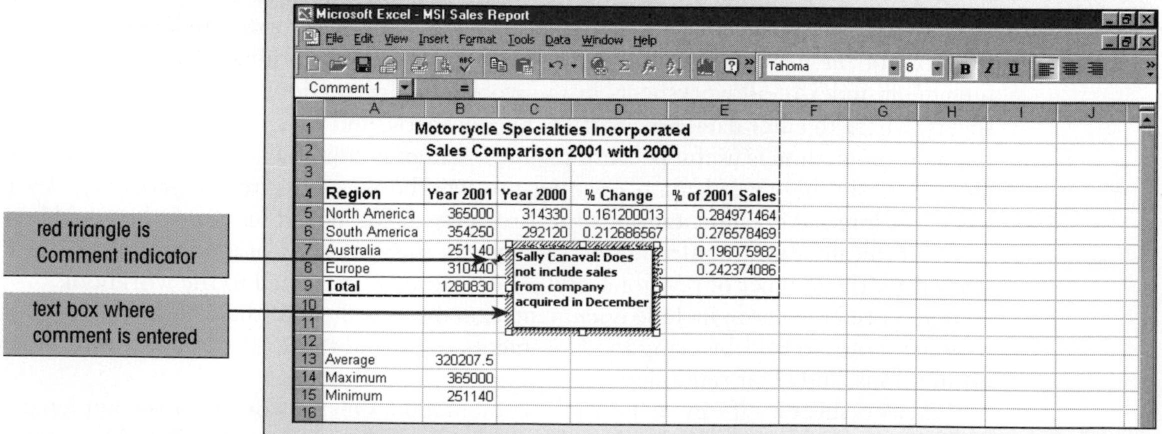

4. Click any cell outside the text box. The comment disappears. Notice, the **Comment indicator**, a tiny red triangle, appears in the upper-right corner of the cell indicating the cell contains a comment.

   Now view the comment.

   TROUBLE? If the comment remains on the screen, click View, then click Comments.

5. Move the mouse pointer over cell **B8**. The Comment appears, preceded by the name of the user who made the comment.
6. Move the mouse pointer to another cell. The comment disappears.
7. Save the workbook.

Once a comment is inserted, you can edit or delete the comment by right-clicking the cell and selecting Edit Comment or Delete Comment from the shortcut menu.

Now Sally asks for a printout of the worksheet formulas for her file.

Displaying and Printing Worksheet Formulas

You can document the formulas you entered in a worksheet by displaying and printing them. When you display formulas, Excel shows the formulas you entered in each cell instead of showing the results of the calculations. You want a printout of the formulas in your worksheet for documentation.

To display worksheet formulas:

1. Click **Tools** on the menu bar, and then click **Options** to open the Options dialog box.
2. Click the **View** tab, and then click the **Formulas** check box in the Window options section to select it.
3. Click the **OK** button to return to the worksheet. The width of each column nearly doubles to accommodate the underlying formulas. See Figure 2-33.

Figure 2-33 DISPLAYING FORMULAS IN A WORKSHEET

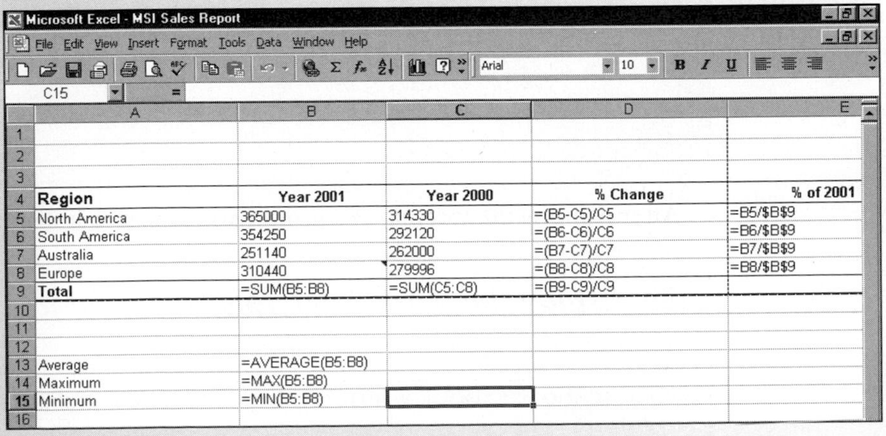

You may find the keyboard shortcut, Ctrl + ` (` is found next to the 1 in the upper-left area of the keyboard) easier to use when displaying formulas. Press the shortcut key once to display formulas and again to display results.

Now print the worksheet displaying the formulas. Before printing the formulas, you need to change the appropriate settings in the Page Setup dialog box to show the gridlines and the row/column headings, center the worksheet on the page, and fit the printout on a single page.

To adjust the print setups to display formulas:

1. Click **File** on the menu bar, and then click **Page Setup** to open the Page Setup dialog box.
2. Click the **Sheet** tab to view the sheet options, and then click the **Row and Column Headings** check box in the Print section to print the row numbers and column letters along with the worksheet results.
3. Click the **Gridlines** check box to select that option.
4. Click the **Page** tab and then click the **Landscape** option button. This option prints the worksheet with the paper positioned so it is wider than it is tall.
5. Click the **Fit to** option button in the Scaling section of the Page tab. This option reduces the worksheet when you print it, so it fits on the specific number of pages in the Fit to check box. The default is 1.
6. Click the **Print Preview** button to open the Print Preview window.
7. Click the **Print** button. See Figure 2-34. Notice that your printout does not include the formulas for average, minimum and maximum because the print area is still set for the range A1:E9.

Figure 2-34 PRINTOUT OF WORKSHEET FORMULAS

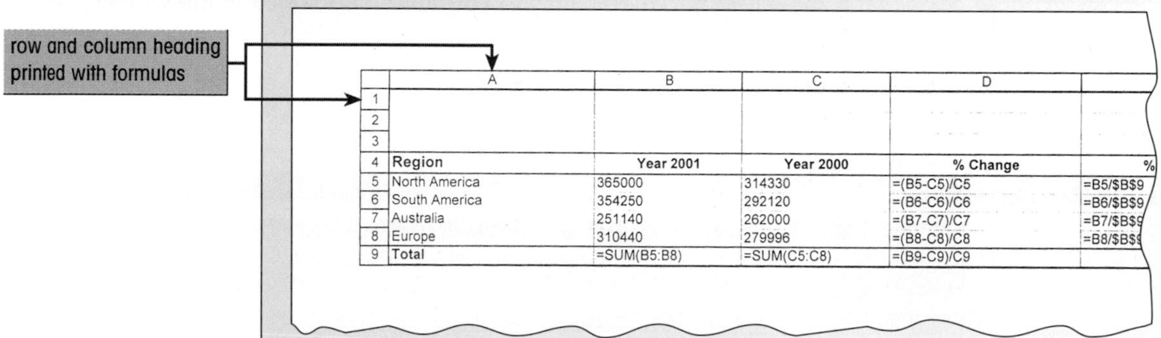

	A	B	C	D	
1					
2					
3					
4	Region	Year 2001	Year 2000	% Change	%
5	North America	365000	314330	=(B5-C5)/C5	=B5/$B$9
6	South America	354250	292120	=(B6-C6)/C6	=B6/$B$9
7	Australia	251140	262000	=(B7-C7)/C7	=B7/B
8	Europe	310440	279996	=(B8-C8)/C8	=B8/B
9	Total	=SUM(B5:B8)	=SUM(C5:C8)	=(B9-C9)/C9	

After printing the formulas, return the worksheet so it displays the worksheet values.

To display the worksheet values:

1. Press **Ctrl +** ` to display the worksheet values.
2. Close the workbook without saving it, and then exit Excel.

Session 2.2 QUICK CHECK

1. What is meant by syntax?
2. In the function MAX(A1:A8), identify the function name. Identify the argument(s).
3. Describe how you use the pointing method to create a formula that includes the SUM function.
4. Describe how to insert a row or a column.
5. To reverse your most recent action, which button should you click?
   a. 
   b. 
   c. 
6. To move a range of cells, you must ____________ the range first.
7. ____________ is a command that lets you change your worksheet's appearance by selecting a collection of predefined worksheet formats.
8. A ____________ is text that is printed in the top margin of every worksheet page.
9. A ____________ is a tiny red triangle in the upper-right corner of a cell that indicates the cell contains a ____________.
10. To display formulas instead of values in your worksheet, what command should you choose?
11. If your worksheet has too many columns to fit on one printed page, you should try ____________ orientation.

You have planned, built, formatted, and documented Sally's sales comparison worksheet. It is ready for her to present to the regional sales managers at their next meeting.

REVIEW ASSIGNMENTS

After Sally meets with the regional sales managers for MSI, she decides it would be a good idea to provide the managers with their own copy of the sales comparison worksheet, so they can update the report with next year's sales data and also modify it to use for their own sales tracking purposes. Before passing it on to them, she wants to provide more documentation and add some additional information that the managers thought would be useful to them. Complete the following for Sally:

1. Start Windows and Excel, if necessary. Insert your Data Disk into the appropriate disk drive. Make sure the Excel and Book1 windows are maximized.
2. Open the workbook **MSI 1** in the Review folder for Tutorial 2 on your Data Disk.
3. Save your workbook as **MSI Sales Report 2** in the Review folder for Tutorial 2 on your Data Disk.
4. Make Sheet2 the active sheet. Use Sheet2 to include information about the workbook. Insert the information in Figure 2-35 into Sheet2. Increase the width of column A as necessary.

Figure 2-35

CELL	TEXT ENTRY
A1	Motorcycle Specialties Incorporated
A3	Created by:
A4	Date Created:
A6	Purpose:
B3	enter your name
B4	enter today's date
B6	Sales report comparing sales by region 2001 with 2000

5. Change the name of the worksheet from **Sheet2** to **Documentation** and print the Documentation sheet.

Explore

6. Move the Documentation sheet so it is the first sheet in the workbook.
7. Make Sales Comparison the active sheet.
8. Insert a row between Australia and Europe. Add the following data (Africa, 125000, 100000) in columns A, B, and C. Copy the formulas for % Change and % of 2001 Sales into the row containing the data for Africa.
9. Open the Office Assistant and then enter the search phrase "Insert a column" to obtain instructions on inserting a new column into a worksheet. Insert a new column between columns C and D.
10. In cell D4, enter the heading "Change".
11. In cell D5, enter the formula to calculate the change in sales for North America from 2000 to 2001. (*Hint*: Check that the figure in cell D5 is 50670.)
12. Copy the formula in D5 to the other regions and total (D6 through D10) using the fill handle.
13. Calculate summary statistics for the year 2000. In cell C14 display the average sales, in cell C15 display the maximum, and in cell C16 display the minimum.
14. Save the workbook.
15. Print the sales comparison worksheet.
16. a. Insert the following comment into cell F4: "Divide 2001 sales in each region by total sales in 2001".
    b. Use the Office Assistant to learn how to print comments to a cell. List the steps.
17. a. Insert a new sheet into the workbook using the Worksheet command from the Insert menu. Activate the **Sales Comparison** sheet and select the range A1:E10. Copy the selected range to the Clipboard. Activate Sheet1 and paste the selected range to the corresponding cells in Sheet1. Apply a different AutoFormat to this range. Print Sheet1. *Note:* If the Office Clipboard toolbar appears, you can use the Office Assistant to learn "About collecting and pasting multiple items" in the Office Clipboard.
    b. Use the Delete Sheet command from the Edit menu to delete Sheet1.
    c. Save the workbook.

CASE PROBLEMS

Case 1. Annual Stockholders' Meeting at MJ Inc. Jeanne Phelp, chief financial officer (CFO) of MJ Incorporated is responsible for preparing the annual financial reports and mailing them to stockholders before the annual stockholder's meeting. She has completed some of the work for the annual meeting and is now in the process of finishing a report comparing the changes in net income between the current year and last year. Now you can help her complete this report.

1. Use columns A through D to enter the title, labels, and constants from Figure 2-36 into a worksheet.

Figure 2-36 MJ INCORPORATED INCOME STATEMENT

	2001	2000	PERCENTAGE CHANGE
Net Sales	1818500	1750500	
Cost of Goods Sold	1005500	996000	
Gross Profit			
Selling and Administrative expenses	506000	479000	
Income from Operations			
Interest expense	18000	19000	
Income before taxes			
Income tax expense	86700	77000	
Net Income			
Outstanding shares	20000	20000	
Earnings Per Share			

2. Complete the income statement for 2001 and 2000 by entering the following formulas for each year:
   - Gross profit = Net sales – Cost of goods sold
   - Income from operations = Gross profit – Selling and administrative expenses
   - Income before taxes = Income from operations – Interest expense
   - Net income = Income before taxes – Income tax expense
3. Compute the percentage change between the two years for each item in the income statement.
4. Compute earnings per share (net income / outstanding shares).
5. In cell B4 add the cell comment "Unaudited results".
6. Select an AutoFormat to improve the appearance of your worksheet.
7. Prepare a Documentation sheet, and then place it as the first sheet in the workbook.
8. Save the workbook as **MJ Income** in the Cases folder for Tutorial 2 on your Data Disk. *Note:* The workbook should open so the user can see the contents of the Documentation sheet. (*Hint:* Make the Documentation sheet the active sheet before you save the workbook.)

9. Add your name and date in the custom footer, then print the worksheet, centered horizontally and vertically.
10. Print the Documentation sheet.
11. Save the worksheet, and then print the formulas for the worksheet. Include row and column headings in the output. Do not save the workbook after printing the formulas.

Case 2. Compiling Data on the U.S. Airline Industry The editor of *Aviation Week and Space Technology* has asked you to research the current status of the U.S. airline industry. You collect information on the revenue-miles and passenger-miles for each major U.S. airline (Figure 2-37).

Figure 2-37 REVENUE-MILES AND PASSENGER MILES FOR MAJOR U.S. AIRLINES

AIRLINE	REVENUE-MILES (IN 1000S OF MILES)	PASSENGER-MILES (IN 1000S OF MILES)
American	26000	2210000
Continental	9300	620500
Delta	21500	1860000
Northwest	20800	1900500
US Airways	9850	1540000
United	35175	3675000

You want to calculate the following summary information to use in the article:

- total revenue-miles for the U.S. airline industry
- total passenger-miles for the U.S. airline industry
- each airline's share of the total revenue-miles
- each airline's share of the total passenger-miles
- average revenue-miles for U.S. airlines
- average passenger-miles for U.S. airlines

In order to provide the editor with your researched information, complete these steps:

1. Open a new workbook and then enter the title, column and row labels, and data from Figure 2-37.
2. Enter the formulas to compute the total and average revenue-miles and passenger-miles. Use the SUM and AVERAGE functions where appropriate. Remember to include row labels to describe each statistic.
3. Add a column to display each airline's share of the total revenue-miles. Remember to include a column heading. You decide the appropriate location for this data.
4. Add a column to display each airline's share of the total passenger-miles. Remember to include a column heading. You decide the appropriate location for this data.
5. In a cell two rows after the row of data you entered, insert a line reading : "Compiled by: *XXXX*", where *XXXX* is your name.
6. Rename the worksheet tab Mileage Data.
7. Save the worksheet as **Airline** in the Cases folder for Tutorial 2.

8. Print the worksheet. Make sure you center the report, do not include gridlines, and place the date in the upper-right corner of the header.
9. Select an AutoFormat to improve the appearance of your output.
10. Save your workbook.
11. Print the worksheet, centered on the page.
12. Save the worksheet and then print the formulas for the worksheet. Include row and column headings in the printout.

Case 3. Fresh Air Sales Incentive Program Carl Stambaugh is assistant sales manager at Fresh Air Inc., a manufacturer of outdoors and expedition clothing. Fresh Air sales representatives contact retail chains and individual retail outlets to sell the Fresh Air line.

This year, to stimulate sales, Carl has decided to run a sales incentive program for sales representatives. Each sales representative has been assigned a sales goal 12% higher than his or her total sales last year. All sales representatives who reach this new goal will be awarded an all-expenses-paid trip for two to Cozumel, Mexico.

Carl wants to track the results of the sales incentive program with an Excel worksheet. He has asked you to complete the worksheet by adding the formulas to compute:

- actual sales in 2001 for each sales representative
- sales goal in 2001 for each sales representative
- percentage of goal reached for each sales representative

He also wants a printout before he presents the worksheet at the next sales meeting. Complete these steps:

1. Open the workbook **Fresh** in the Cases folder for Tutorial 2 on your Data Disk. Maximize the worksheet window and then save the workbook as **Fresh Air Sales Incentives** in the Cases folder for Tutorial 2.
2. Complete the worksheet by adding the following formulas:
   a. 2001 actual for each employee = Sum of actual sales for each quarter
   b. Goal 2001 for each employee = 2000 Sales X (1 + Goal % increase)
   c. % goal reached for each employee = 2001 actual / 2001 goal

   (*Hint:* Use the Copy command. Review relative versus absolute references.)
3. At the bottom of the worksheet (three rows after the last sales rep), add the average, maximum, and minimum statistics for columns C through I.
4. Make formatting changes using an Autoformat to improve the appearance of the worksheet. Begin the formatting in row 6.
5. In cell C4, insert the cell comment "entered sales goal values between 10 and 15 percent".
6. Save the workbook.
7. Print the worksheet. Make sure you center the worksheet horizontally, add an appropriate header, and place your name, course, and date in the footer. Print the worksheet so it fits on one page.
8. Add a Documentation sheet. Save the workbook and then print the Documentation worksheet.
9. Change the sales goal to 14 percent. Print the worksheet.

Explore

10. As you scroll down the worksheet, the column headings no longer appear on the screen, making it difficult to know what each column represents. Use the Office Assistant to look up "Keep column labels visible." Implement this feature in your worksheet. Save the workbook. Explain the steps you take to keep the columns visible.

11. Print the formulas in columns H, I, and J. The printout should include row and column headings. Use the Set Print Area command so you only print the formulas in these three columns. Do not save the workbook after you complete this step.

Case 4. Stock Portfolio for Juan Cortez Your close friend, Juan Cortez, works as an accountant at a local manufacturing company. While in college, with a double major in accounting and finance, Juan dabbled in the stock market and expressed an interest in becoming a financial planner and running his own firm. To that end, he has continued his professional studies in the evenings with the aim of becoming a certified financial planner. He has already begun to provide financial planning services to a few clients. Because of his hectic schedule as a full-time accountant, part-time student, and part-time financial planner, Juan finds it difficult to keep up with the data-processing needs for his clients. You have offered to assist him.

Juan asks you to set up a worksheet to keep track of a stock portfolio for one of his clients.

Open a new workbook and do the following:

1. Figure 2-38 shows the data you will enter into the workbook. For each stock, you will enter the name, number of shares purchased, and purchase price. Periodically, you will also enter the current price of each stock so Juan can review the changes with his clients.

Figure 2-38

STOCK	NO. OF SHARES	PURCHASE PRICE	COST	CURRENT PRICE	CURRENT VALUE	GAINS/LOSSES
Excite	100	67.30		55.50		
Yahoo	250	121		90.625		
Netscape	50	24.50		26.375		
Microsoft	100	89.875		105.375		
Intel	50	69		83		

2. In addition to entering the data, you need to make the following calculations:
   a. Cost = No. of shares * Purchase price
   b. Current value = No. of shares * Current price
   c. Gains/Losses = Current value minus cost
   d. Totals for cost, Current value, and Gains/Losses

Enter the formulas to calculate the cost, current value, gains/losses, and totals.

3. In the cell where you enter the label for Current Price, insert the cell comment "As of 9/1/2001".

4. Apply an AutoFormat that improves the appearance of the worksheet.

5. Add a Documentation sheet to the workbook.

6. Save the workbook as **Portfolio** in the Cases folder for Tutorial 2.

7. Print the worksheet. Make sure you center the worksheet horizontally and add an appropriate header and footer.
8. Print the Documentation sheet.
9. Clear the prices in the Current Price column of the worksheet.
10. Enter the following prices:

Excite	57.250
Yahoo	86.625
Netscape	30.75
Microsoft	102.375
Intel	84.375

Print the worksheet.

11. Print the formulas for the worksheet. Make sure you include row and column headings in the printed output.
12. From the financial section of your newspaper, look up the current price of each stock (all these stocks are listed on the NASDAQ Stock Exchange). Enter these prices in the worksheet. Print the worksheet.

INTERNET ASSIGNMENTS

The purpose of the Internet Assignments is to challenge you to find information on the Internet that you can use to create effective documents. The actual assignments are updated and maintained on the Course Technology Web site. Log on to the Internet and use your Web browser and go to the Student Online Companion to accompany this text at **www.course.com/NewPerspectives/office2000**. Click the Excel link, and then click the link for Tutorial 2.

QUICK CHECK ANSWERS

Session 2.1

1. Determine the purpose of the worksheet, enter the data and formulas, test the worksheet; correct errors, improve the appearance, document the worksheet, save and print.
2. Select the cell where you want the sum to appear. Click the AutoSum button. Excel suggests a formula that includes the SUM function. To accept the formula press the Enter key.
3. =B4-C4
4. fill handle
5. Cell references; if you were to copy the formula to other cells, these cells are relative references.
6. absolute reference
7. Windows clipboard
8. Double-click the sheet tab, then type the new name, and then press the Enter key or click any cell in the worksheet to accept the entry.
9. Order of precedence is a set of predefined rules that Excel uses to unambiguously calculate a formula by determining which part of the formula to calculate first, which part second, and so on.

Session 2.2

1. Syntax specifies the set of rules that determine the order and punctuation of formulas and functions in Excel.
2. MAX is the function name; A1:A8 is the argument.
3. Assuming you are entering a formula with a function, first select the cell where you want to place a formula, type =, the function name and a left parenthesis, and then click and drag over the range of cells to be used in the formula. Press the Enter key.
4. Click any cell in the row above which you want to insert a row. Click Insert, then click Rows.
5. c
6. select
7. AutoFormat
8. header
9. comment indicator, comment
10. Click Tools, click Options, and then in the View tab, click the Formula check box.
11. landscape

OBJECTIVES

In this tutorial you will:

- Format data using the Number, Currency, Accounting, and Percentage formats
- Align cell contents
- Center text across columns
- Change fonts, font style, and font size
- Clear formatting from cells
- Delete cells from a worksheet
- Use borders and color for emphasis
- Add text box and graphics to a worksheet using the Drawing toolbar
- Remove gridlines from the worksheet
- Print in landscape orientation
- Hide and unhide rows and columns

DEVELOPING A PROFESSIONAL-LOOKING WORKSHEET

Producing a Projected Sales Report for the Pronto Salsa Company

CASE

Pronto Salsa Company

Anne Castelar owns the Pronto Salsa Company, a successful business located in the heart of Tex-Mex country. She is working on a plan to add a new product, de Chili Guero Four-Alarm Red Hot, to Pronto's gourmet salsa line.

Anne wants to take out a bank loan to purchase additional food-processing equipment to handle the requirements of the increased salsa production. She has an appointment with her loan officer at 2:00 p.m. today. To prepare for the meeting, Anne creates a worksheet to show the projected sales of the new salsa and the expected effect on profits. Although the numbers and formulas are in place on the worksheet, Anne has no time to format the worksheet to create the greatest impact. She planned to do that now, but an unexpected problem with today's produce shipment requires her to leave the office for a few hours. Anne asks you to complete the worksheet. She shows you a printout of the unformatted worksheet and explains that she wants the finished worksheet to look very professional—like those you see in business magazines. She also asks you to make sure that the worksheet emphasizes the profits expected from sales of the new salsa.

SESSION 3.1

In this session you will learn how to make your worksheets easier to understand through various formatting techniques. You will format values using Currency, Number, and Percentage formats. You will also change font styles and font sizes, and change the alignment of data within cells and across columns. As you perform all these tasks, you'll find the Format Painter button an extremely useful tool.

Opening the Workbook

After Anne leaves, you develop the worksheet plan in Figure 3-1 and the worksheet format plan in Figure 3-2.

Figure 3-1 PLANNING ANALYSIS WORKSHEET

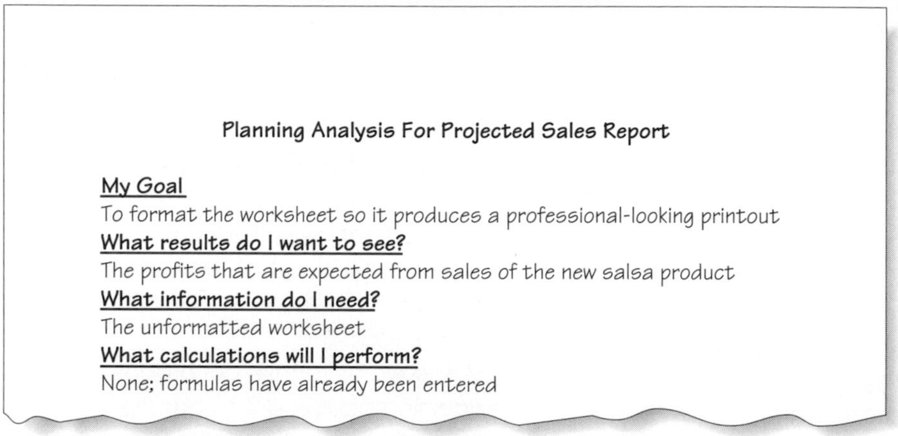

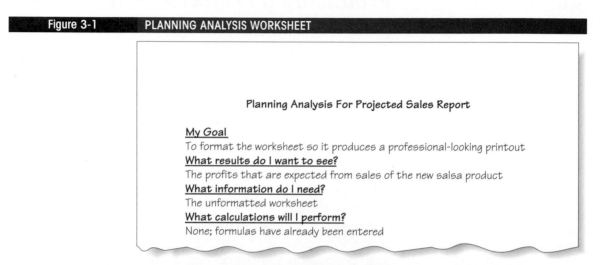

Planning Analysis For Projected Sales Report

My Goal
To format the worksheet so it produces a professional-looking printout
What results do I want to see?
The profits that are expected from sales of the new salsa product
What information do I need?
The unformatted worksheet
What calculations will I perform?
None; formulas have already been entered

Figure 3-2 FORMAT PLAN

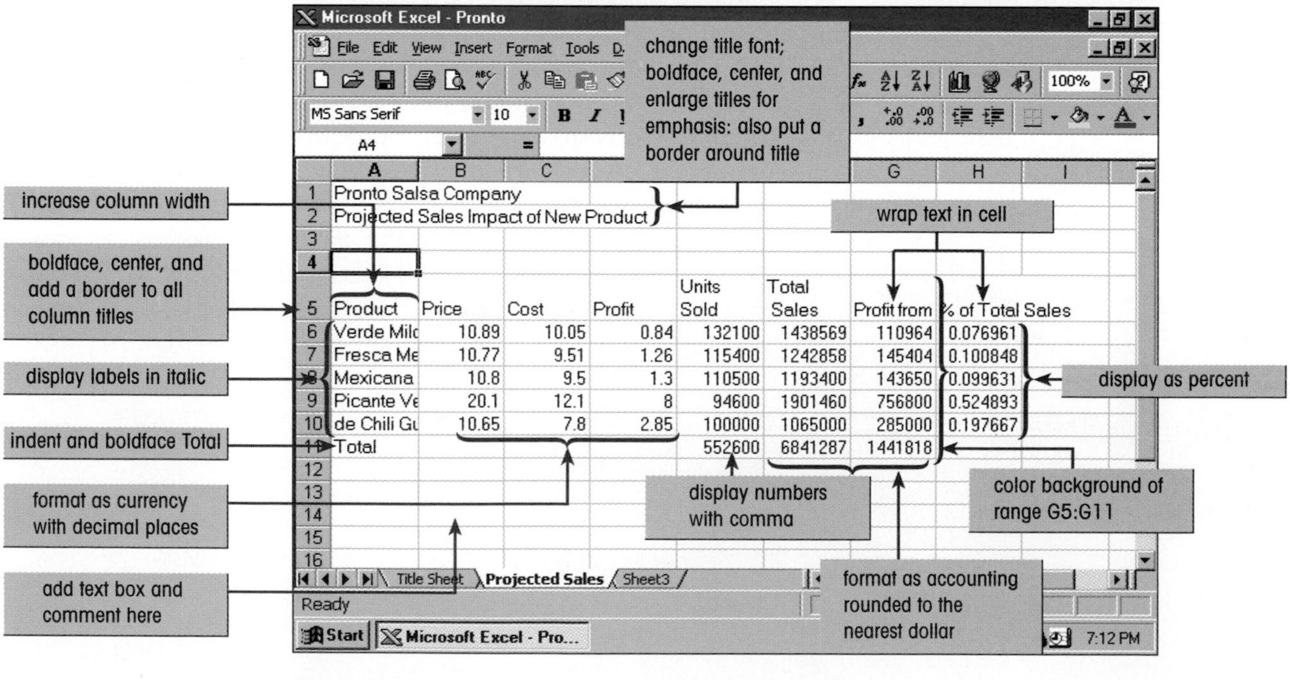

Anne has already entered all the formulas, numbers, and labels. Your main task is to format this information so it is easy to read and understand, and appears professional. This can be accomplished on two levels—by formatting the detailed data in the worksheet and by enhancing the appearance of the worksheet as a whole.

On the data level, you decide that the numbers should be formatted according to their use. For example, the product prices need to appear as dollar values, the column and row labels need to fit within their cells, and the labels need to stand out more. To enhance the worksheet as a whole, you need to structure it so that related information is visually grouped together using lines and borders. Anne also wants certain areas of the worksheet containing key information to stand out, color may be a useful tool for this.

With all that needs to be done before Anne's 2:00 p.m. meeting, you decide that the best place to begin is with formatting the data within the worksheet. Once that is done, you will work to improve the worksheet's overall organization and appearance.

Now that the planning is done, you are ready to start Excel and open the workbook of unformatted data that Anne created.

To start Excel and organize your desktop:

1. Start Excel as usual.
2. Make sure your Data Disk is in the appropriate disk drive.
3. Make sure the Microsoft Excel and Book1 windows are maximized.

Now you need to open Anne's file and begin formatting the worksheet. Anne stored the workbook as Pronto, but before you begin to change the workbook, save it using the filename Pronto Salsa Company. This way, the original workbook, Pronto, remains unchanged in case you want to work through this tutorial again.

To open the Pronto workbook and save the workbook as Pronto Salsa Company:

1. Click the **Open** button on the Standard toolbar to open the Open dialog box.
2. Open the Pronto workbook in the Tutorial folder for Tutorial 3 on your Data Disk.
3. Click **File** on the menu bar, and then click **Save As** to open the Save As dialog box.
4. In the File name text box, change the filename to **Pronto Salsa Company**.
5. Click the **Save** button to save the workbook under the new filename. The new filename, Pronto Salsa Company, appears in the title bar.

   TROUBLE? If you see the message "Replace existing file?", click the Yes button to replace the old version of Pronto Salsa Company with your new version.

6. Click the **Projected Sales** sheet tab. See Figure 3-3.

Figure 3-3 PRONTO SALSA COMPANY WORKSHEET

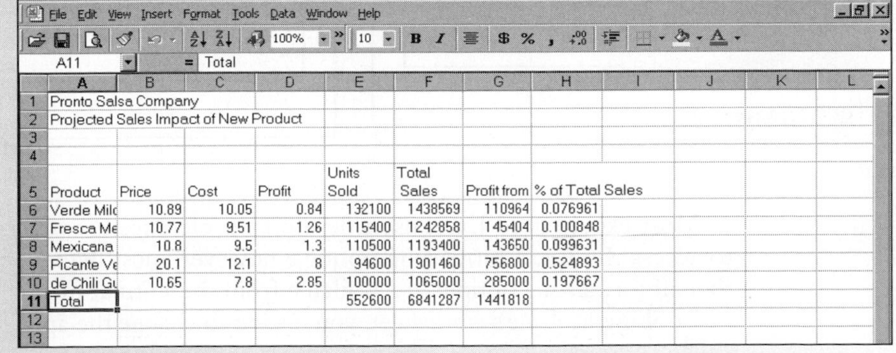

	A	B	C	D	E	F	G	H
1	Pronto Salsa Company							
2	Projected Sales Impact of New Product							
3								
4								
5	Product	Price	Cost	Profit	Units Sold	Total Sales	Profit from	% of Total Sales
6	Verde Milc	10.89	10.05	0.84	132100	1438569	110964	0.076961
7	Fresca Me	10.77	9.51	1.26	115400	1242858	145404	0.100848
8	Mexicana	10.8	9.5	1.3	110500	1193400	143650	0.099631
9	Picante Ve	20.1	12.1	8	94600	1901460	756800	0.524893
10	de Chili Gu	10.65	7.8	2.85	100000	1065000	285000	0.197667
11	Total				552600	6841287	1441818	
12								
13								

Studying the worksheet, you notice that the numbers are difficult to read. You decide to improve the appearance of the numbers in worksheet cells first.

Formatting Worksheet Data

Formatting is the process of changing the appearance of the data in worksheet cells. Formatting can make your worksheets easier to understand, and draw attention to important points.

In the previous tutorial you used AutoFormat to improve the appearance of your worksheet. AutoFormat applies a predefined format to a selected range in a worksheet. AutoFormat is easy to use, but its predefined format might not suit every application. If you decide to customize a worksheet's format, you can use the extensive Excel formatting options. When you select your own formats, you can format an individual cell or a range of cells.

Formatting changes only the appearance of the worksheet; it does not change the text or numbers stored in the cells. For example, if you format the number .123653 using a Percentage format that displays only one decimal place, the number appears in the worksheet as 12.4%; however, the original number, .123653, remains stored in the cell. When you enter data into cells, Excel applies an automatic format, referred to as the General format. The **General format** aligns numbers at the right side of the cell, uses a minus sign for negative values, and displays numbers without trailing zeros to the right of the decimal point. You can change the General format by using AutoFormat, the Format menu, the Shortcut menu, or toolbar buttons.

There are many ways to access the Excel formatting options. The Format menu provides access to all formatting commands.

The Shortcut menu provides quick access to the Format dialog box. To display the Shortcut menu, make sure the pointer is positioned within the range you have selected to format, and then click the right mouse button.

The Formatting toolbar contains formatting buttons, including the style and alignment buttons, and the Font Style and Font Size boxes, as shown in Figure 3-4.

Figure 3-4 FORMATTING TOOLBAR

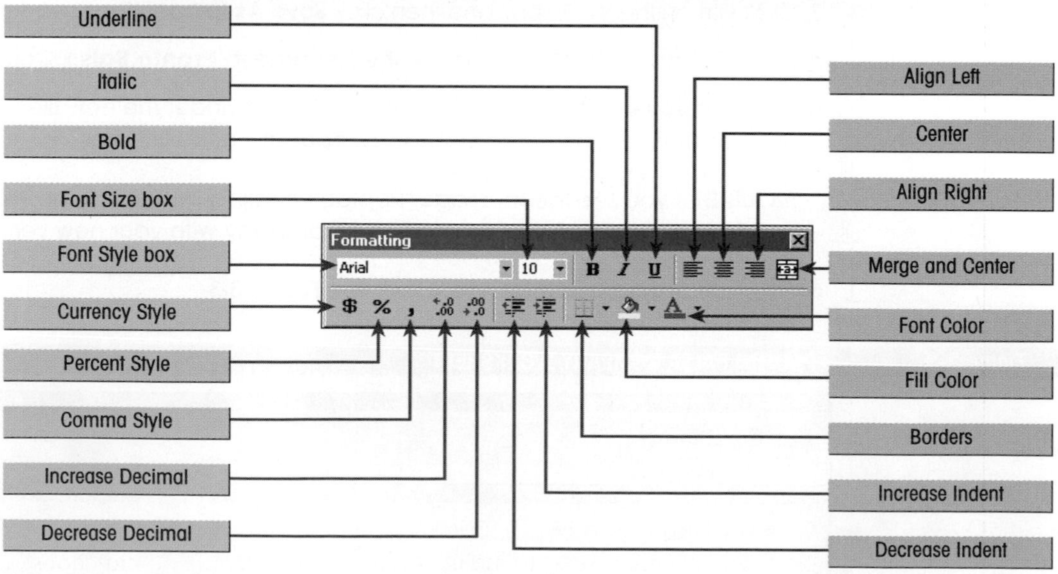

Most experienced Excel users develop a preference for which menu or buttons they use to access the Excel formatting options; however, most beginners find it easy to remember that all formatting options are available from the Format menu.

Looking at Anne's worksheet, you decide to change the appearance of the numbers first.

Changing the Appearance of Numbers

When the data in the worksheet appears as numbers, you want each number to appear in a style appropriate for what it is representing. The Excel default General format is often not the most appropriate style. For example, dollar values may require the dollar symbol ($) and thousand separators, and these can be applied to numerical data simply by changing the data's format. You can also use formatting to standardize the number of decimal places appearing in a cell. Excel has a variety of predefined number formats. Figure 3-5 describes some of the most commonly used formats.

Figure 3-5 COMMONLY USED NUMBER FORMATS

CATEGORY	DISPLAY OPTION
General	Excel default Number format; displays numbers without dollar signs, commas, or trailing decimal places
Number	Sets decimal places, negative number display, and comma separator
Currency	Sets decimal places and negative number display, and inserts dollar signs and comma separators
Accounting	Specialized monetary value format used to align dollar signs, decimal places, and comma separators
Date	Sets date or date and time display
Percentage	Inserts percent sign to the right of a number with a set number of decimal places

REFERENCE WINDOW RW

Formatting Numbers

- Select the cells in which you want the new format applied.
- Click Format, click Cells, and then click the Numbers tab in the Format Cells dialog box.
- Select a format category from the Category list box.
- Select the desired options for the selected format.
- Click the OK button.

To change the number formatting, you select the cell or range of cells to be reformatted, and then use the Format Cells command or the Formatting toolbar buttons to apply a different format.

Currency and Accounting Formats

In reviewing Anne's unformatted worksheet, you recognize that there are several columns of data that represent currency. You decide to apply the Currency format to the Price, Cost, and Profit columns.

You have several options when formatting values as currency. You need to decide the number of decimal places you want visible; whether or not you want to see the dollar sign; and how you want negative numbers to look. Keep in mind that if you want the currency symbols and decimal places to line up within a column, you should choose the Accounting format rather than the Currency format.

In the Pronto Salsa Company worksheet, you want to apply the Currency format to the values in columns B, C, and D. The numbers will be formatted to include a dollar sign with two decimal places. You also decide to put parentheses around negative numbers in the worksheet.

To format columns B, C, and D using the Currency format:

1. Select the range **B6:D10**.
2. Click **Format** on the menu bar, and then click **Cells** to open the Format Cells dialog box.
3. If necessary, click the **Number** tab. See Figure 3-6.

Figure 3-6 NUMBER TAB OF FORMAT CELLS DIALOG BOX

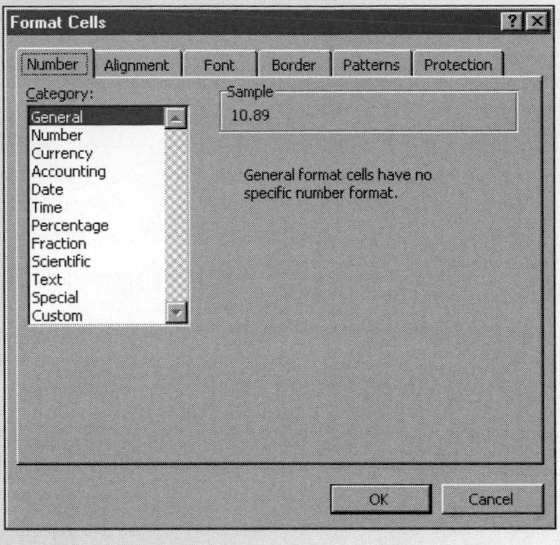

4. Click **Currency** in the Category list box. The Number tab changes to display the Currency formatting options, as shown in Figure 3-7. Notice that a sample of the selected format appears near the top of the dialog box. As you make further selections, the sample automatically changes to reflect your choices.

Figure 3-7 SELECTING A CURRENCY FORMAT

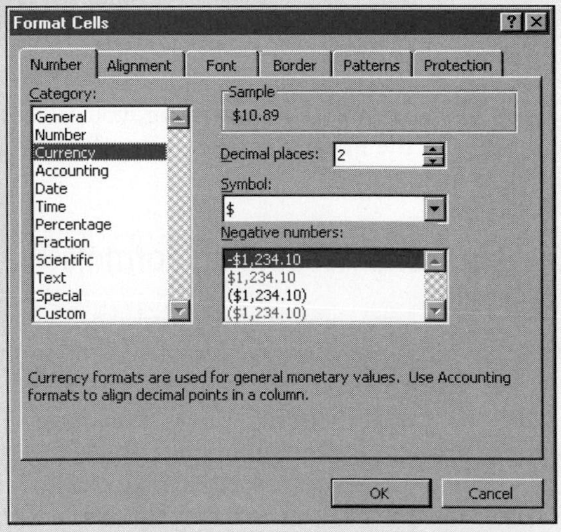

Notice that 2 decimal places is the default setting. A dollar sign ($) appears in the Symbol list box, indicating that the dollar sign will appear. If you are using a different currency, click the down arrow in the Symbol list box to select the currency symbol you want to use. Given the current options selected, you only need to select a format for negative numbers.

5. Click the third option **($1,234.10)** in the Negative numbers list box.

6. Click the **OK** button to format the selected range.

7. Click any cell to deselect the range and view the new formatting. See Figure 3-8.

Figure 3-8 CURRENCY FORMATS IN COLUMNS B, C, AND D

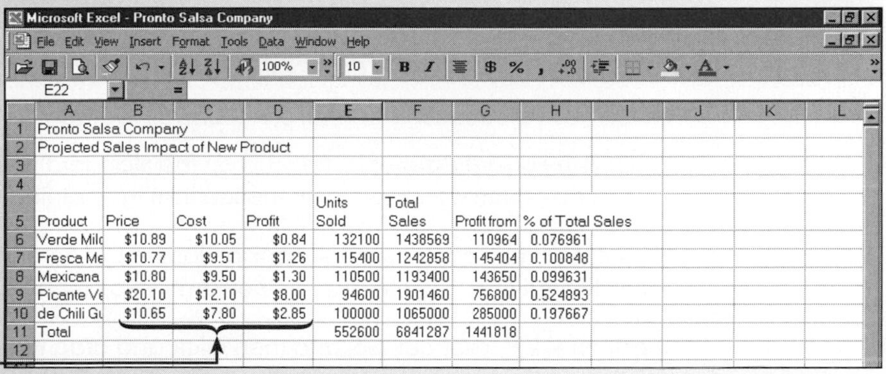

amounts displayed as currency with two decimal places

When your worksheet has large dollar amounts, you might want to use a Currency or Accounting format that does not display any decimal places. To do this you use the Decrease Decimal button on the Formatting toolbar, or change the decimal places setting in the Format Cells dialog box. Currency values appearing with no decimal places are rounded to the nearest dollar: $15,612.56 becomes $15,613; $16,507.49 becomes $16,507; and so on.

You decide to format the Total Sales column as using the Accounting style format rounded to the nearest dollar. The Accounting style format lines up the currency symbol and decimal points in a column.

To format cells F6 through F11 using the Accounting style format rounded to the nearest dollar:

1. Select the range **F6:F11**.

2. Click **Format** on the menu bar, and then click **Cells** to open the Format Cells dialog box.

3. If necessary, click the **Number** tab.

4. Click **Accounting** in the Category list box.

5. Click the **Decimal places** spin box down arrow twice to change the setting to 0 decimal places. Notice that the sample format changes to reflect the new settings.

6. Click the **OK** button to apply the format. Notice that Excel automatically increased the column width to accommodate the formatted numbers.

7. Click any cell to deselect the range.

After formatting the Total Sales figures in column F, you realize you should have used the same format for the numbers in column G. To save time, you simply copy the formatting from column F to column G.

The Format Painter Button

The Format Painter button on the Standard toolbar lets you copy formats quickly from one cell or range to another. You simply click a cell containing the formats you want to copy, click the Format Painter button, and then use the click-and-drag technique to select the range to which you want to apply the copied formats.

To copy the format from cell F6:

1. Click cell **F6** because it contains the format you want to copy.
2. Click the **Format Painter** button on the Standard toolbar. As you move the pointer over the worksheet cells, notice that the pointer turns to .

   TROUBLE? If you do not see the Format Painter button on the Standard toolbar, click More Buttons to display the Format Painter button.

3. Position over cell G6, and then click and drag to select cells **G6:G11**. When you release the mouse button, you notice that cells G6:G11 contain number symbols (######) instead of values. This is because the formatting change has caused the data to exceed the width of the cell.
4. Click any cell to deselect the range and view the formatted Profit from Sales column. See Figure 3-9.

Figure 3-9 WORKSHEET AFTER FORMAT PAINTER USED TO COPY FORMATS

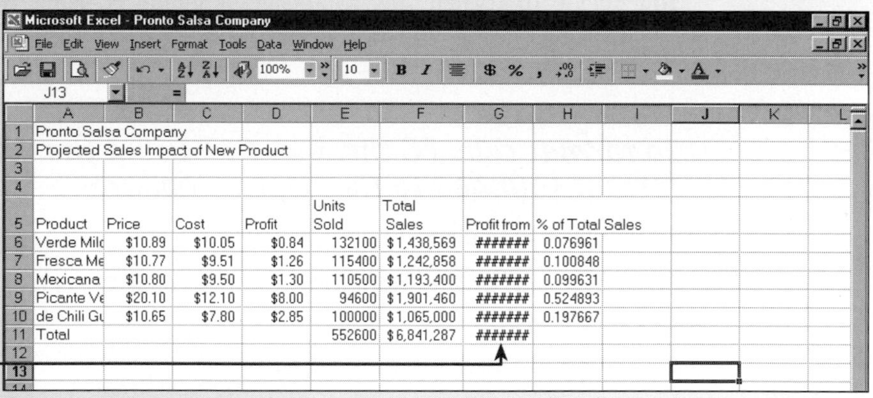

number symbols indicate column width needs to increase

As you review the changes on the screen, you notice that cells G6:G11 contain number symbols (######) instead of values. This is because the formatting change has caused the data to exceed the width of the cell.

Number Symbol (###) Replacement

If a number is too long to fit within a cell's boundaries, Excel displays a series of number symbols (###) in the cell. The number symbols indicate that the number of digits in the value exceeds the cell's width. The number or formula is still stored in the cell, but the current cell width is not large enough to display the value. To display the value, you just need to increase the column width. One way you can do this is to use the Shortcut menu.

To replace the number symbols by increasing the column width:

1. Position the mouse pointer over the column heading for column G, and then right-click to display the Shortcut menu.
2. Click **Column Width** to open the Column Width dialog box.
3. Type **11** in the Column Width box.
4. Click the **OK** button to view the total sales.
5. Click any cell to view the formatted data. See Figure 3-10.

Figure 3-10 WORKSHEET AFTER COLUMN WIDTH INCREASED TO DISPLAY FORMATTED NUMBERS

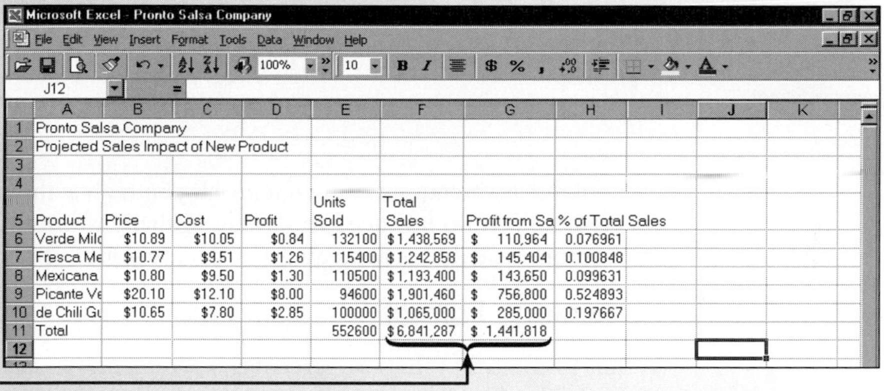

amounts displayed using Accounting style format

Now the cells containing price, cost, profit, total sales, and profit from sales are formatted using the currency and accounting styles. Next you want to apply formats to the numbers in columns E and H so they are easier to read.

Number Formats

Like Currency formats, the Excel Number formats offer many options. You can select Number formats to specify

- the number of decimal places that are visible
- whether to display a comma to delimit thousands, millions, and billions
- whether to display negative numbers with a minus sign, parentheses, or red numerals

To access all Excel Number formats, you can use the Number tab in the Format Cells dialog box. You can also use the Comma Style button, the Increase Decimal button, and the Decrease Decimal button on the Formatting toolbar to select some Number formats.

Looking at your planning sheet and sketch, you can see that the numbers in column E need to be made easier to read by changing the format to include commas.

To format the contents in column E with a comma and no decimal places:

1. Select the range **E6:E11**.
2. Click the **Comma Style** button on the Formatting toolbar to apply the Comma Style. The default for the Comma Style is to display numbers with two places to the right of the decimal. Click the **Decrease Decimal** button on the Formatting toolbar to decrease the number of decimal places to zero.

   TROUBLE? If you do not see the Comma Style button on the Standard toolbar, click More Buttons to display the Comma Style button.

3. Click any cell to deselect the range and view the formatted Units Sold column. See Figure 3-11.

Figure 3-11 **CELLS FORMATTED WITH NUMBER FORMAT**

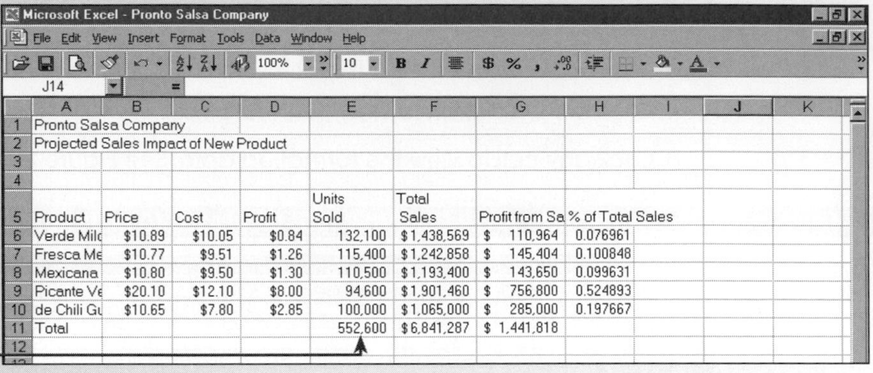

Looking at the numbers in column H, you realize that they are difficult to interpret and decide that you do not need to display so many decimal places. These numbers would be much more readable as percentages; what are your options for displaying percentages?

Percentage Format

When formatting values as percentages, you need to select how many decimal places you want visible. The Percentage format with no decimal places displays the number 0.18037 as 18%. The Percentage format with two decimal places displays the same number as 18.04%. If you want to use the Percentage format with two decimal places, you select this option using the Number tab in the Format Cells dialog box. You can also use the Percent Style button on the Formatting toolbar, and then click the Increase Decimal button twice to add two decimal places.

Your format plan (see Figure 3-2) specifies a Percentage format with no decimal places for the values in column H. You could use the Number tab to choose this format, but it's faster to use the Percent Style button on the Formatting toolbar.

To format the values in column H as percentages with no decimal places:

1. Select the range **H6:H10**.

2. Click the **Percent Style** button on the Formatting toolbar.

3. Click any cell to deselect the range and view the Percent Style. See Figure 3-12.

Figure 3-12 **PERCENTAGE OF TOTAL SALES FORMATTED WITH PERCENT STYLE**

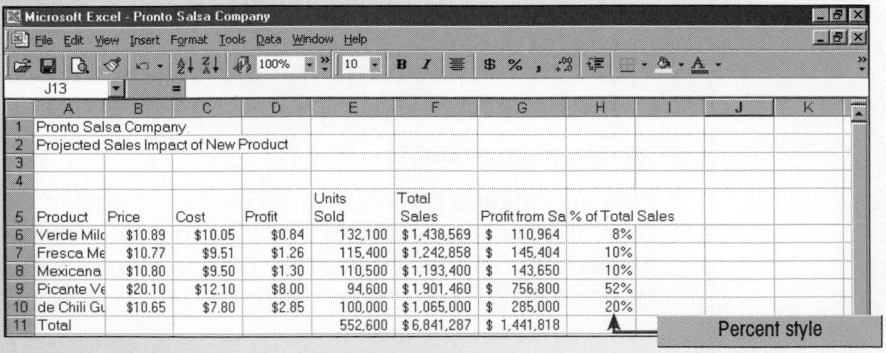

4. Click the **Save** button on the Standard toolbar to save your work.

You review the worksheet. You have now formatted all the numbers in the worksheet appropriately. The next step in formatting Anne's worksheet is to improve the alignment of the data in the cells.

Aligning Cell Contents

The **alignment** of data in a cell is the position of the data relative to the right and left edges of the cell. Cell contents can be aligned on the left or right side of the cell, or centered in the cell. When you enter numbers and formulas, Excel automatically aligns them on the cell's right side. Excel automatically aligns text entries on the cell's left side. The default Excel alignment does not always create the most readable worksheet. As a general rule, you should center column titles, format columns of numbers so that the decimal places are in line, and leave columns of text aligned on the left. You can change the alignment of cell data using the four alignment tools on the Formatting toolbar, or you can access additional alignment options by selecting the Alignment tab in the Format Cells dialog box.

To center the column titles within a cell:

1. Select the range **A5:H5**.
2. Click the **Center** button on the Formatting toolbar to center the cell contents.
3. Click any cell to deselect the range and view the centered titles. See Figure 3-13.

Figure 3-13 WORKSHEET WITH CENTERED COLUMN TITLES

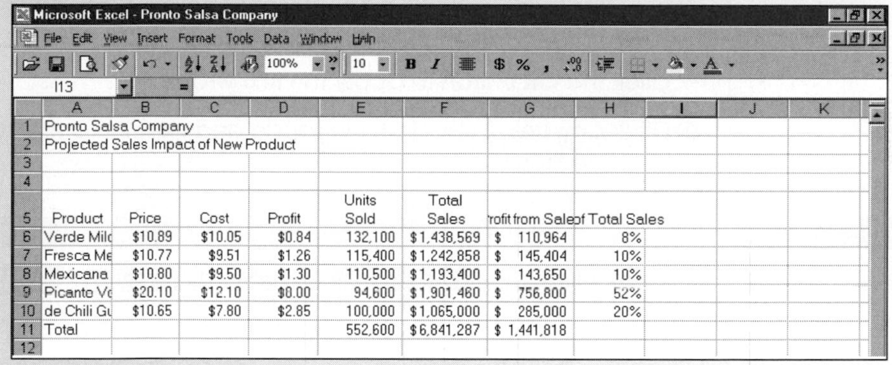

	A	B	C	D	E	F	G	H	I	J	K
1	Pronto Salsa Company										
2	Projected Sales Impact of New Product										
3											
4											
5	Product	Price	Cost	Profit	Units Sold	Total Sales	rofit from Sale	of Total Sales			
6	Verde Milc	$10.89	$10.05	$0.84	132,100	$1,438,569	$ 110,964	8%			
7	Fresca Me	$10.77	$9.51	$1.26	115,400	$1,242,858	$ 145,404	10%			
8	Mexicana	$10.80	$9.50	$1.30	110,500	$1,193,400	$ 143,650	10%			
9	Picanto Vc	$20.10	$12.10	$8.00	94,600	$1,901,460	$ 756,800	52%			
10	de Chili Gu	$10.65	$7.80	$2.85	100,000	$1,065,000	$ 285,000	20%			
11	Total				552,600	$6,841,287	$ 1,441,818				
12											

Notice that the column titles in columns G and H are not fully visible. Although you could widen the column widths of these two columns to display the entire text, the Excel Wrap Text option enables you to display a label within a cell's existing width.

Wrapping Text in a Cell

As you know, if you enter a label that's too wide for the active cell, Excel extends the label past the cell border and into the adjacent cells—provided those cells are empty. If you select the Wrap Text option, Excel will display your label entirely within the active cell. To accommodate the label, the height of the row in which the cell is located is increased, and the text is "wrapped" onto the additional lines.

Now wrap the column titles in columns G and H.

To wrap text within a cell:

1. Select the range **G5:H5**.
2. Click **Format** on the menu bar, and then click **Cells** to open the Format Cells dialog box.
3. Click the **Alignment** tab. See Figure 3-14.

Figure 3-14 ALIGNMENT TAB OF FORMAT CELLS DIALOG BOX

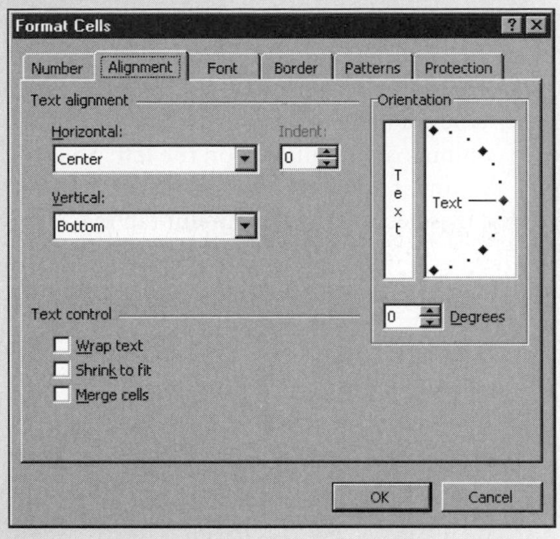

4. Click the **Wrap text** check box in the Text control area to select that option.
5. Click the **OK** button to apply the text wrapping.
6. Click any cell to deselect the range and view the entire text displayed in the cell. See Figure 3-15.

Figure 3-15 WRAPPING TEXT IN A CELL

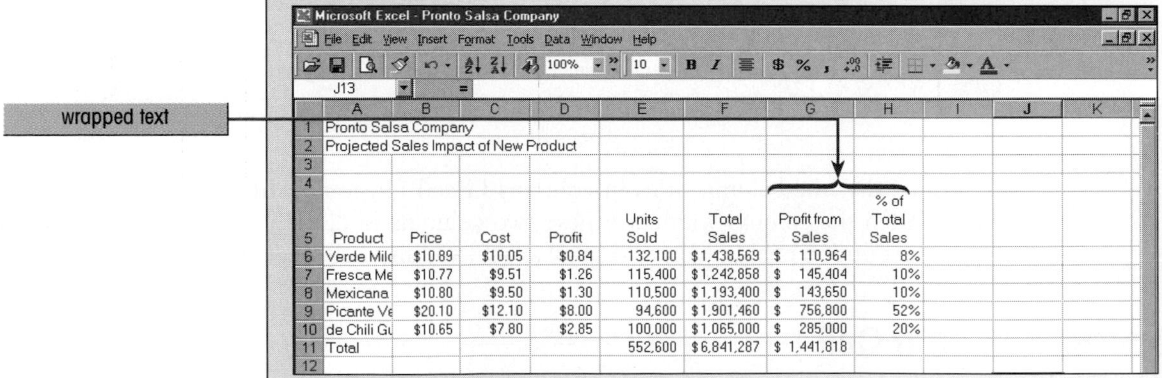

Now you are ready to center the main worksheet titles.

Centering Text Across Cells

Sometimes you might want to center the contents from one cell across more than one column. This is particularly useful for centering a title at the top of a worksheet. Now you use the Center Across Selection option in the Alignment tab from the Format Cells dialog box to center the worksheet titles in cells A1 and A2 across columns A through H.

To center the worksheet titles across columns A through H:

1. Select the range **A1:H2**.
2. Click **Format**, click **Cells**, and then, if necessary, click the **Alignment** tab in the Format Cells dialog box.
3. Click the arrow next to the **Horizontal** text alignment list box to display the horizontal text alignment options.
4. Click the **Center Across Selection** option to center the title lines across columns A through H.
5. Click the **OK** button.
6. Click any cell to deselect the range. See Figure 3-16.

Figure 3-16 WORKSHEET WITH TITLES CENTERED ACROSS SEVERAL COLUMNS

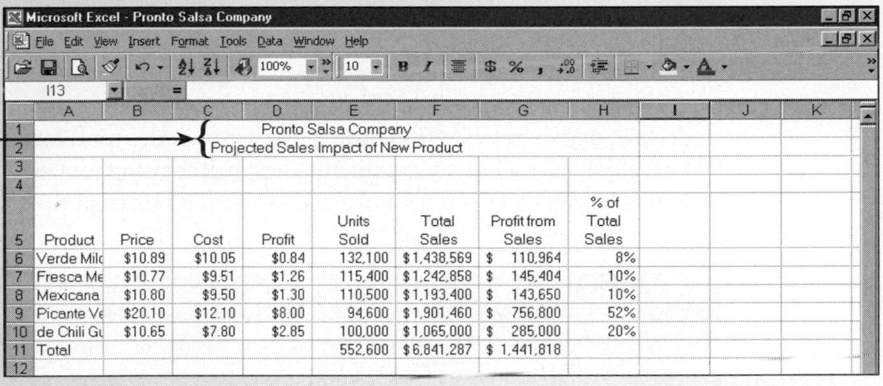

	A	B	C	D	E	F	G	H
5	Product	Price	Cost	Profit	Units Sold	Total Sales	Profit from Sales	% of Total Sales
6	Verde Milc	$10.89	$10.05	$0.84	132,100	$1,438,569	$ 110,964	8%
7	Fresca Me	$10.77	$9.51	$1.26	115,400	$1,242,858	$ 145,404	10%
8	Mexicana	$10.80	$9.50	$1.30	110,500	$1,193,400	$ 143,650	10%
9	Picante Ve	$20.10	$12.10	$8.00	94,600	$1,901,460	$ 756,800	52%
10	de Chili Gu	$10.65	$7.80	$2.85	100,000	$1,065,000	$ 285,000	20%
11	Total				552,600	$6,841,287	$ 1,441,818	

cell contents centered across columns A through H

Indenting Text Within a Cell

When you type text in a cell it is left-aligned. You can indent text from the left edge by using the Increase Indent button on the Formatting toolbar or the Index spinner button in the Alignment tab of the Format Cells dialog box. You decide to indent the word "Total" to provide a visual cue of the change from detail to summary information.

To indent text within a cell:

1. Click cell **A11** to make it the active cell.
2. Click the **Increase Indent** button on the Formatting toolbar to indent the word "Total" within the cell.
3. Click the **Save** button on the Standard toolbar to save the worksheet.

You check your plan and confirm that you selected formats for all worksheet cells containing data and that the data within the cells is aligned properly. The formatting of the worksheet contents is almost complete. Your next task is to improve the appearance of the labels by changing the font style of the title and the column headings.

You decide to use the Bold button on the Formatting toolbar to change some titles in the worksheet to boldface.

Changing the Font, Font Style, and Font Size

A font is a set of letters, numbers, punctuation marks, and symbols with a specific size and design. Figure 3-17 shows some examples. A font can have one or more of the following font styles: regular, italic, bold, and bold italic.

Figure 3-17 SELECTED FONTS

FONT	REGULAR STYLE	ITALIC STYLE	BOLD STYLE	BOLD ITALIC STYLE
Times	AaBbCc	*AaBbCc*	**AaBbCc**	***AaBbCc***
Courier	AaBbCc	*AaBbCc*	**AaBbCc**	***AaBbCc***
Garamond	AaBbCc	*AaBbCc*	**AaBbCc**	***AaBbCc***
Helvetica Condensed	AaBbCc	*AaBbCc*	**AaBbCc**	***AaBbCc***

Most fonts are available in many sizes, and you can also select font effects, such as strikeout, underline, and color. The Formatting toolbar provides tools for changing font style by applying boldface, italics, underline, and increasing or decreasing font size. To access and preview other font effects, you can open the Format Cells dialog box from the Format menu.

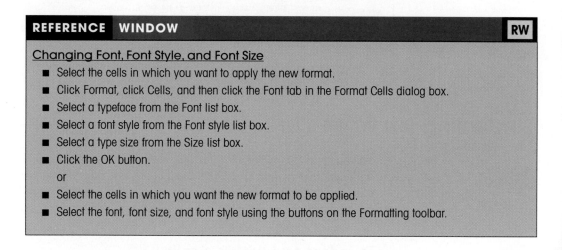

REFERENCE WINDOW RW

Changing Font, Font Style, and Font Size

- Select the cells in which you want to apply the new format.
- Click Format, click Cells, and then click the Font tab in the Format Cells dialog box.
- Select a typeface from the Font list box.
- Select a font style from the Font style list box.
- Select a type size from the Size list box.
- Click the OK button.

or

- Select the cells in which you want the new format to be applied.
- Select the font, font size, and font style using the buttons on the Formatting toolbar.

You begin by formatting the word "Total" in cell A11 in boldface letters.

To apply the boldface font style:

1. If necessary, click cell **A11**.
2. Click the **Bold** button B on the Formatting toolbar to set the font style to boldface. Notice that when a style like bold is applied to a cell's content, the toolbar button appears depressed to indicate that the style is applied to the active cell.

You also want to display the column titles in boldface. To do this, first select the range you want to format, and then click the Bold button to apply the format.

To display the column titles in boldface:

1. Select the range **A5:H5**.
2. Click the **Bold** button on the Formatting toolbar to apply the boldface font style.
3. Click any cell to deselect the range.

Next you want to change the font and size of the worksheet titles for emphasis. You use the Font dialog box (instead of the toolbar) so you can preview your changes. Remember, although the worksheet titles appear to be in columns A through F, they are just spilling over from column A. To format the titles, you need to select only cells A1 and A2—the cells where the titles were originally entered.

To change the font and font size of the worksheet titles:

1. Select the range **A1:A2**. Although the title is centered within the range A1:H2, the values are stored in cells A1 and A2.
2. Click **Format** on the menu bar, and then click **Cells** to open the Format Cells dialog box.
3. Click the **Font** tab. See Figure 3-18.

Figure 3-18 FONT TAB IN FORMAT CELLS DIALOG BOX

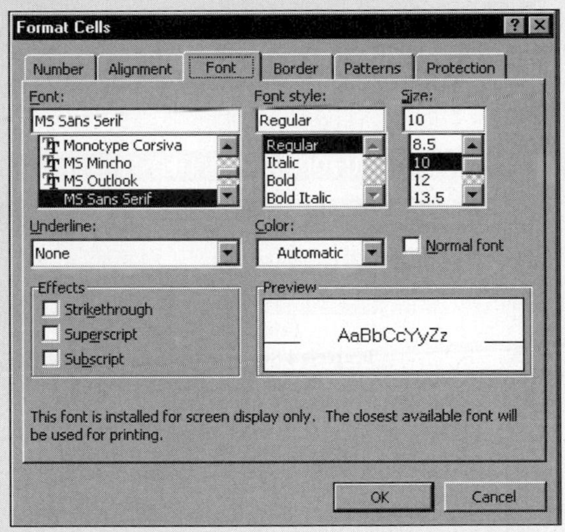

4. Use the Font box scroll bar to find the Times New Roman font. Click the **Times New Roman** font to select it.
5. Click **Bold** in the Font style list box.
6. Click **14** in the Size list box. A sample of the font appears in the Preview box.
7. Click the **OK** button to apply the new font, font style, and font size to the worksheet titles.
8. Click any cell to deselect the titles. See Figure 3-19.

Figure 3-19 TITLES AFTER NEW FONT, FONT STYLE, AND FONT SIZE APPLIED

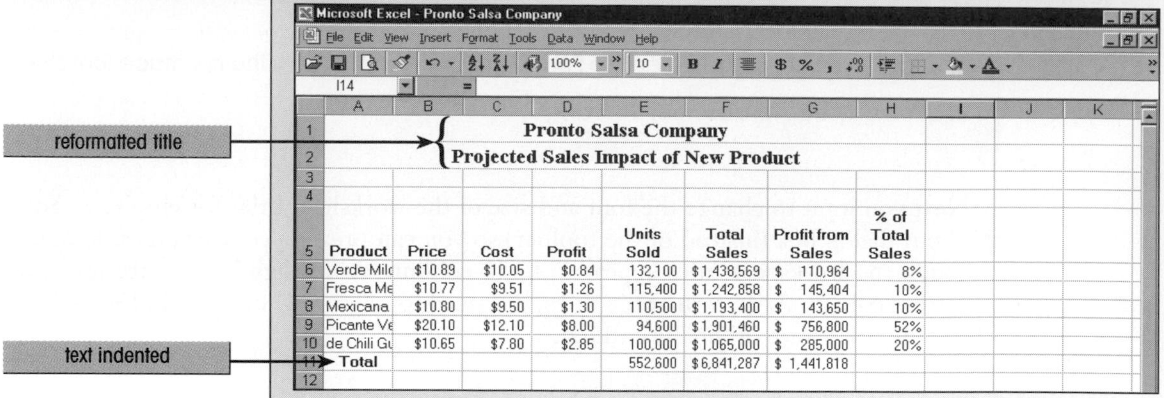

Product	Price	Cost	Profit	Units Sold	Total Sales	Profit from Sales	% of Total Sales
Verde Milc	$10.89	$10.05	$0.84	132,100	$1,438,569	$ 110,964	8%
Fresca Me	$10.77	$9.51	$1.26	115,400	$1,242,858	$ 145,404	10%
Mexicana	$10.80	$9.50	$1.30	110,500	$1,193,400	$ 143,650	10%
Picante Ve	$20.10	$12.10	$8.00	94,600	$1,901,460	$ 756,800	52%
de Chili Gu	$10.65	$7.80	$2.85	100,000	$1,065,000	$ 285,000	20%
Total				552,600	$6,841,287	$ 1,441,818	

9. Click the **Save** button on the Standard toolbar to save the worksheet.

Next you decide to display the products names in italics.

To italicize the row labels:

1. Select the range **A6:A10**.
2. Click the **Italic** button on the Formatting toolbar to apply the italic font style.
3. Click any cell to deselect the range and view the formatting you have done so far. See Figure 3-20.

Figure 3-20 BOLD AND ITALIC FORMATS APPLIED

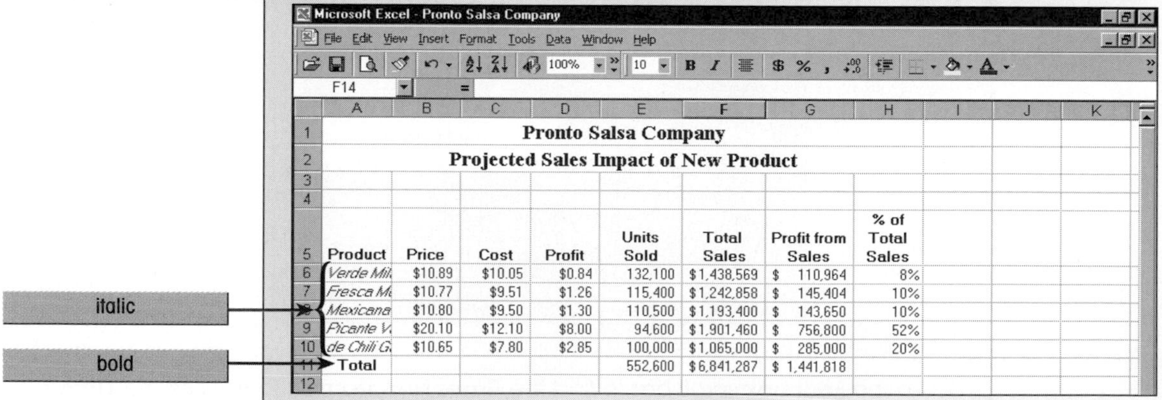

Product	Price	Cost	Profit	Units Sold	Total Sales	Profit from Sales	% of Total Sales
Verde Mil	$10.89	$10.05	$0.84	132,100	$1,438,569	$ 110,964	8%
Fresca M	$10.77	$9.51	$1.26	115,400	$1,242,858	$ 145,404	10%
Mexicana	$10.80	$9.50	$1.30	110,500	$1,193,400	$ 143,650	10%
Picante V	$20.10	$12.10	$8.00	94,600	$1,901,460	$ 756,800	52%
de Chili G	$10.65	$7.80	$2.85	100,000	$1,065,000	$ 285,000	20%
Total				552,600	$6,841,287	$ 1,441,818	

You hope Anne will approve of the Times New Roman font—it looks like the font on the Pronto salsa jar labels and would like to use it to create a style that can be applied to other worksheets.

Using Styles

A **style** is a saved collection of formatting, such as font, font size, pattern, and alignment that you combine, name and save as a group. A style can include from one to six attributes—Number, font, Alignment, Border, Pattern, and Protection. Once you have saved a style, you can apply it to a cell or range to achieve consistency in formatting. Excel has six predefined styles—Comma, Comma[0], Currency, currency[0], Normal, and Percent. By default, every cell in a worksheet is automatically formatted with the Normal style, which you use whenever you start typing in a new worksheet.

You can create a style in two ways: by using an example of the cell that has the formats you want associated with the style; or manually, by choosing formats from the Style dialog box and selecting the format you want associated with the style.

Although you won't create a style in this tutorial, you can follow the steps in the reference window if you want to create a style.

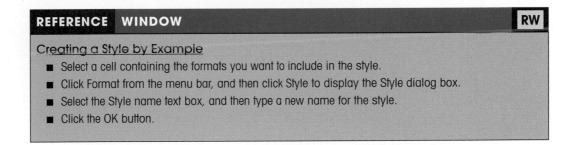

REFERENCE WINDOW RW

Creating a Style by Example

- Select a cell containing the formats you want to include in the style.
- Click Format from the menu bar, and then click Style to display the Style dialog box.
- Select the Style name text box, and then type a new name for the style.
- Click the OK button.

Clearing Formats from Cells

Anne reviews the worksheet and decides the italics format applied to the product names is not necessary. She asks you to remove the formatting from cells A6:A10. Although you could use Undo to remove the last step, you'll use the Edit, Clear command which erases formatting while leaving the cell's content intact. This command can be issued at any time to clear formatting from a cell.

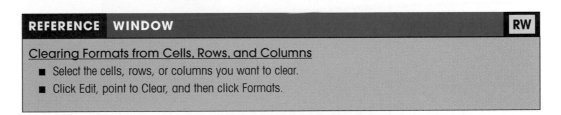

REFERENCE WINDOW RW

Clearing Formats from Cells, Rows, and Columns

- Select the cells, rows, or columns you want to clear.
- Click Edit, point to Clear, and then click Formats.

To clear the formatting of a cell:

1. Select cells A6:A10, the cells whose format you want to clear.
2. Click **Edit**, point to **Clear** and then click **Formats** to return the cell to its default (General) format. Notice the contents of the cells have not been erased.
3. Click any cell to deselect and view the product names in Regular style.

Deleting Cells from a Worksheet

Anne again reviews the worksheet and decides to remove the Cost data, range C5:C11, from the worksheet. You will use the Delete command from the Edit menu to remove these cells from the worksheet. When you delete one or more cells from a worksheet, you remove the space occupied by these cells and must specify if you want the cells beneath the deleted cells to shift up or the cells to the right of the deleted cells to shift to the left.

REFERENCE WINDOW RW

Deleting Cells, Rows, or Columns

- Select the cells, rows, or columns you want to delete.
- Click Edit, then click Delete to open the Delete dialog box.
- Select the direction in which you want the remaining cells to move:
  - Select Shift cells left to move cells to the right of deleted cells to the left.
  - Select Shift cells up to move cells below the deleted cell up to fill space previously occupied by deleted cells.
  - If you want to delete the entire row or column:
  - Select Entire Row to delete each row containing a selected cell.
  - Select Entire column to delete each column containing a selected cell.
- Click OK.

To delete cells from the worksheet

1. Select the range **C5:C11**, the cells to be deleted from the worksheet.
2. Click **Edit**, click **Delete** to open the Delete dialog box .See Figure 3-21.

Figure 3-21 DELETE DIALOG BOX

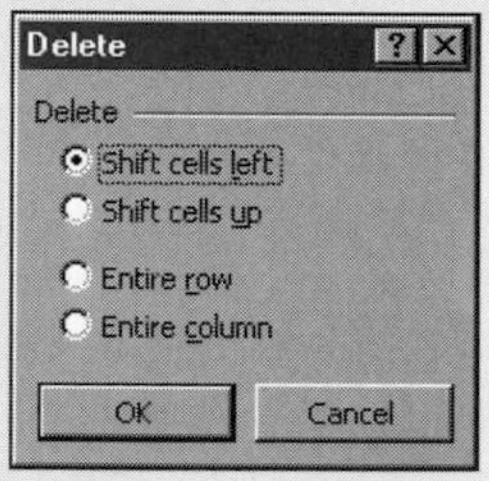

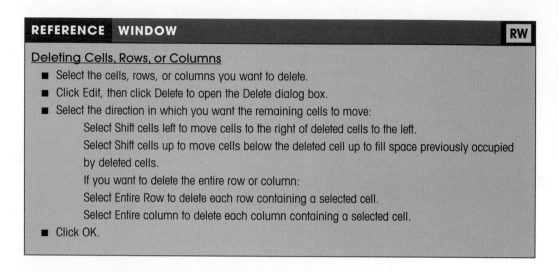

3. If necessary, click the **Shift cells left** option button.
4. Click OK. Notice all the cells from D5:H6 shift left one column.
5. Click any cell to observe that the Cost data no longer appears in the worksheet. See Figure 3-22. Save the worksheet.

Figure 3-22 WORKSHEET AFTER COST CELLS DELETED

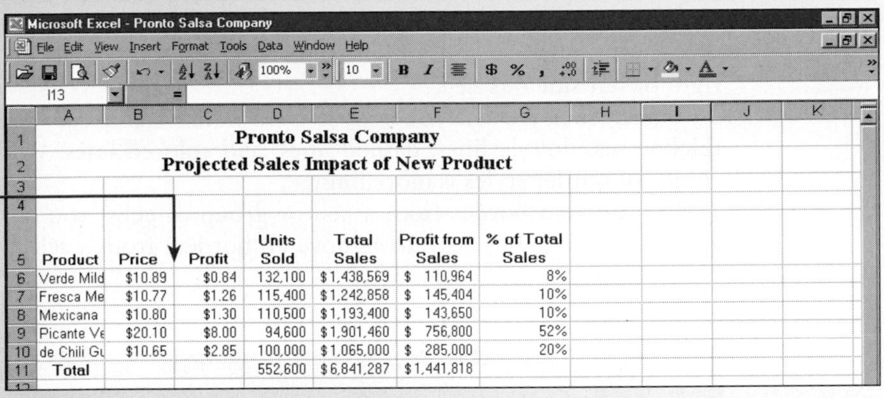

Product	Price	Profit	Units Sold	Total Sales	Profit from Sales	% of Total Sales
Verde Mild	$10.89	$0.84	132,100	$1,438,569	$ 110,964	8%
Fresca Me	$10.77	$1.26	115,400	$1,242,858	$ 145,404	10%
Mexicana	$10.80	$1.30	110,500	$1,193,400	$ 143,650	10%
Picante Ve	$20.10	$8.00	94,600	$1,901,460	$ 756,800	52%
de Chili Gu	$10.65	$2.85	100,000	$1,065,000	$ 285,000	20%
Total			552,600	$6,841,287	$1,441,818	

Session 3.1 QUICK CHECK

1. List three ways you can access formatting commands, options, and tools.
2. If the number .05765 is in a cell, what will Excel display if you:
   a. format the number using the Percentage format with one decimal place?
   b. format the number using the Currency format with 2 decimal places and the dollar sign?
3. The ____________ copies formats quickly from one cell or range to another.
4. A series of ####### in a cell indicates ____________.
5. Explain two ways to completely display a label that currently is not entirely displayed.
6. Explain why Excel might display 3,045.39 in a cell, but 3045.38672 in the formula bar.
7. What are the general rules you should follow for aligning column headings, numbers, and text labels?
8. List the options available on the Formatting toolbar for aligning data.

Now that you have finished formatting the data in the worksheet, you need to enhance the worksheet's appearance and readability as a whole. You will do this in Session 3.2 by applying borders, colors, and a text box.

SESSION 3.2

In this session you will learn how to enhance a worksheet's overall appearance by adding borders and color. You will use the Drawing toolbar to add a text box and graphic to the worksheet and use landscape orientation to print the worksheet.

Adding and Removing Borders

A worksheet is often divided into zones that visually group related information. Lines, called **borders**, can help to distinguish different zones of the worksheet and add visual interest.

You can create lines and borders using either the Borders button on the Formatting toolbar or the Border tab in the Format Cells dialog box. You can place a border around a single cell or a group of cells using the Outline option. To create a horizontal line, you place a border at the top or bottom of a cell. To create a vertical line, you place a border on the right or left side of a cell.

The Border tab lets you choose from numerous border styles, including different line thicknesses, double lines, dashed lines, and colored lines. With the Borders button, your choice of border styles is more limited.

To remove a border from a cell or group of cells, you can use the Border tab in the Format Cells dialog box. To remove all borders from a selected range of cells, select the None button in the Presets area.

REFERENCE WINDOW RW

Adding a Border

- Select the cell to which you want to add the border.
- Click Format, click Cells, and then click the Border tab.
- Click the line style you want to apply.
- Click the appropriate button to indicate the border placement you want.
- Click the OK button.

or

- Select the cell to which you want to add the border.
- Click the Borders button list arrow on the Formatting toolbar, and then click the type of border you want.

You decide that a thick line under all column titles will separate them from the data in the columns. To do this, you use the Borders button on the Formatting toolbar.

To underline column titles:

1. If you took a break after the last session, make sure Excel is running and the Projected Sales worksheet of the Pronto Salsa Company workbook is open.
2. Select the range **A5:G5**.
3. Click the **Borders** button list arrow on the Formatting toolbar. The Borders palette appears. See Figure 3-23.

Figure 3-23 BORDERS PALETTE

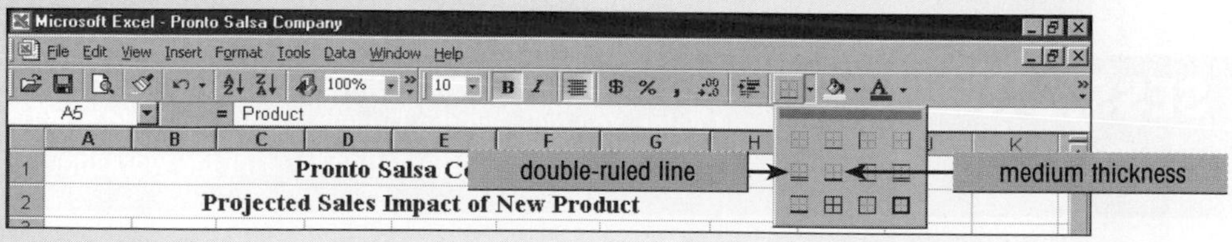

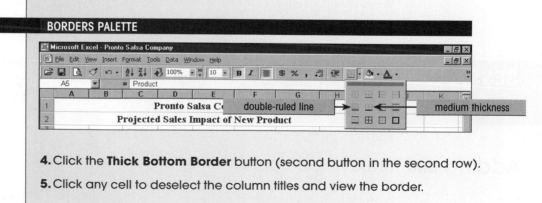

4. Click the **Thick Bottom Border** button (second button in the second row).
5. Click any cell to deselect the column titles and view the border.

You also want a line to separate the data from the totals in row 11, and a double-ruled line below the totals for added emphasis. This time you use the Border tab in the Format Cells dialog box to apply borders to cells.

To add a line separating the data and the totals and a double-ruled line below the totals:

1. Select the range **A11:G11**.
2. Click **Format** on the menu bar, click **Cells**, and then click the **Border** tab in the Format Cells dialog box. See Figure 3-24

Figure 3-24 BORDER TAB IN FORMAT CELLS DIALOG BOX

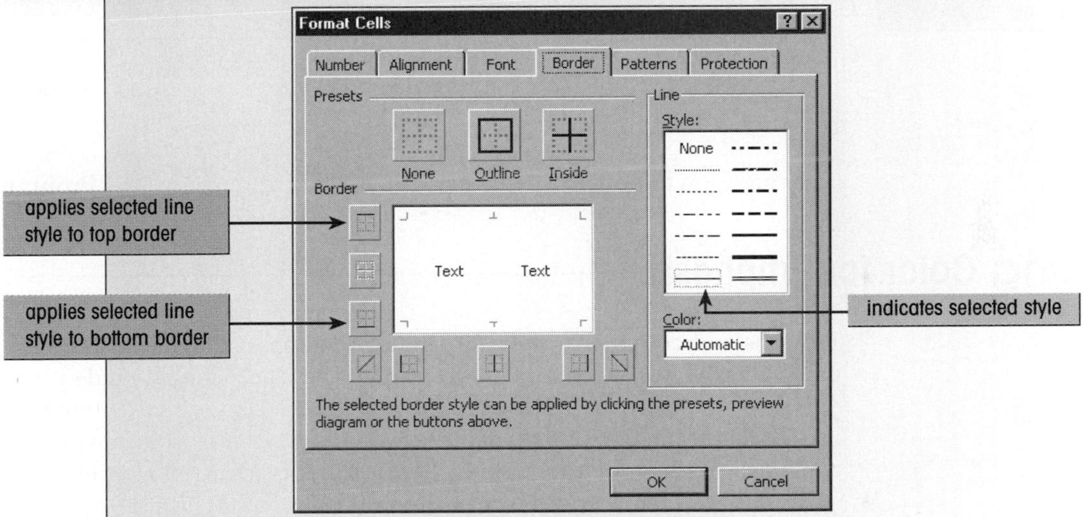

3. Click the **medium thick line** in the Line Style box (third from the bottom in the second column).
4. Click the **top border** button. A thick line appears at the top of the Border preview window.
5. Click the **double-ruled line** in the Line Style box.
6. Click the **bottom border** button. A double-ruled line appears at the bottom of the Border preview window.
7. Click the **OK** button to apply the borders.
8. Click any cell to deselect the range and view the borders. See Figure 3-25.

Figure 3-25 BORDERS APPLIED TO WORKSHEET

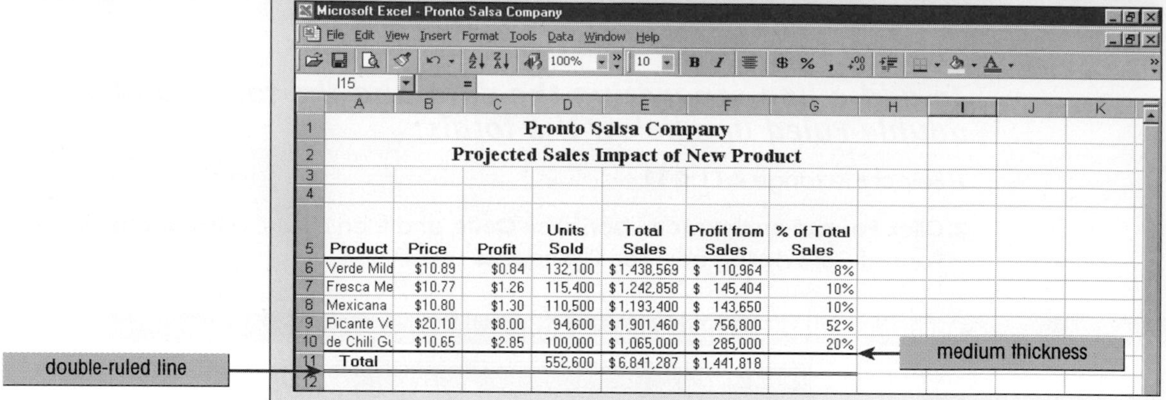

	A	B	C	D	E	F	G
1				Pronto Salsa Company			
2				Projected Sales Impact of New Product			
3							
4							
5	Product	Price	Profit	Units Sold	Total Sales	Profit from Sales	% of Total Sales
6	Verde Mild	$10.89	$0.84	132,100	$1,438,569	$ 110,964	8%
7	Fresca Me	$10.77	$1.26	115,400	$1,242,858	$ 145,404	10%
8	Mexicana	$10.80	$1.30	110,500	$1,193,400	$ 143,650	10%
9	Picante Ve	$20.10	$8.00	94,600	$1,901,460	$ 756,800	52%
10	de Chili Gu	$10.65	$2.85	100,000	$1,065,000	$ 285,000	20%
11	Total			552,600	$6,841,287	$1,441,818	
12							

9. Click the **Save** button on the Standard toolbar to save the worksheet.

In addition to borders, you want to add color to emphasize the Profit from Sales column.

Using Color for Emphasis

Patterns and colors provide visual interest, emphasize worksheet zones, or indicate data-entry areas. The way you intend to use the worksheet should guide your use of patterns or colors. If you print the worksheet in color and distribute a hard copy of it, or if you plan to use a color projection device to display your worksheet on screen, you can take advantage of the Excel color formatting options. If you do not have a color printer, you can use patterns because it is difficult to predict how colors you see on your screen will translate into gray shades on your printout.

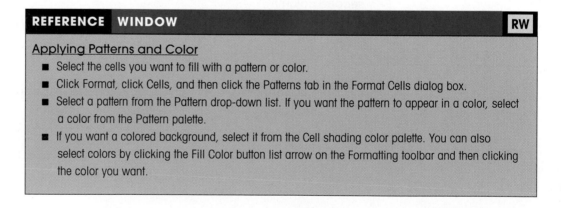

REFERENCE WINDOW RW

Applying Patterns and Color

- Select the cells you want to fill with a pattern or color.
- Click Format, click Cells, and then click the Patterns tab in the Format Cells dialog box.
- Select a pattern from the Pattern drop-down list. If you want the pattern to appear in a color, select a color from the Pattern palette.
- If you want a colored background, select it from the Cell shading color palette. You can also select colors by clicking the Fill Color button list arrow on the Formatting toolbar and then clicking the color you want.

You want your worksheet to look good when you print it in black and white on the office laser printer, but you also want it to look good on the screen when you show it to Anne. You decide that a yellow background will enable the Profit from Sales column to stand out and looks fairly good both on the screen and the printout. You apply this format using the Patterns tab in the Format Cells dialog box.

To apply a color to the Profit from Sales column:

1. Select the range **F5:F11**.
2. Click **Format** on the menu bar, click **Cells**, and then click the **Patterns** tab in the Format Cells dialog box. See Figure 3-26. A color palette appears.

Figure 3-26 COLOR PALETTE IN PATTERNS TAB OF FORMAT CELLS DIALOG BOX

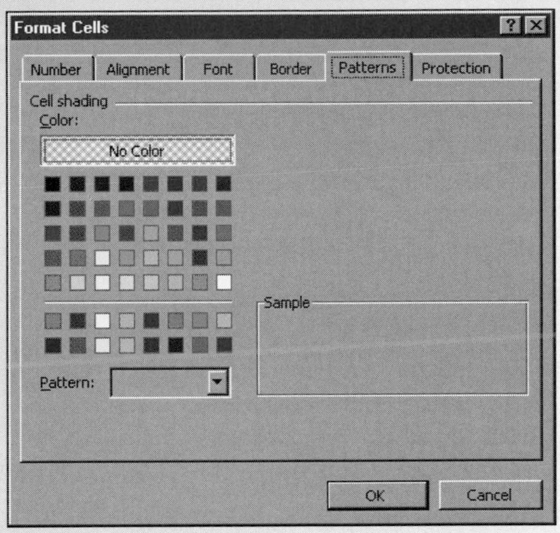

3. Click the **yellow square** in the fourth row (third square from the left) of the Cell shading Color palette.
4. Click the **OK** button to apply the color.
5. Click any cell to deselect the range and view the color in the Profit from Sales column. See Figure 3-27.

Figure 3-27 WORKSHEET AFTER APPLYING COLOR TO A COLUMN

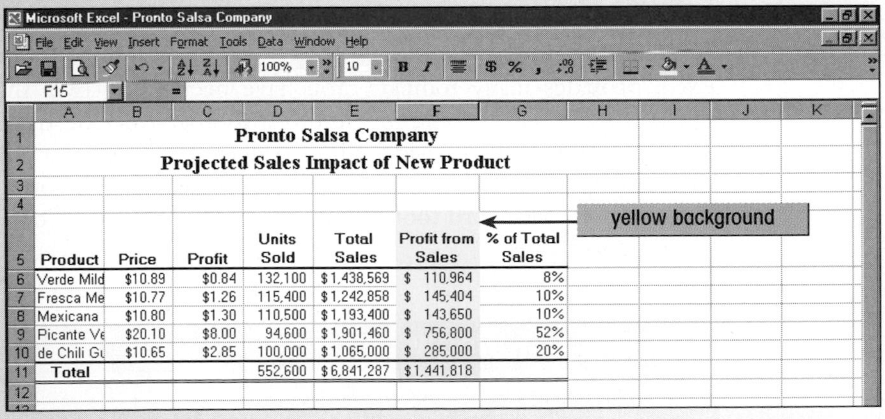

You can also use buttons on the Formatting toolbar to change the color for the cell background (Fill Color button) and text in a cell (Text Color button).

Now that you have finished formatting labels and values, you can change the width of column A to best display the information in that column. To do this, you use Excel's Automatic Adjustment feature to change the width of a column to fit the widest entry in a cell.

To change the column width to fit the contents of a column:

1. Position the pointer over the column boundary between column A and column B. The pointer changes to ✛.
2. Double-click the boundary. The column width automatically adjusts to accommodate the widest entry in column A. See Figure 3-28.

Figure 3-28 RESULTS OF CHANGING COLUMN WIDTH

column width increased

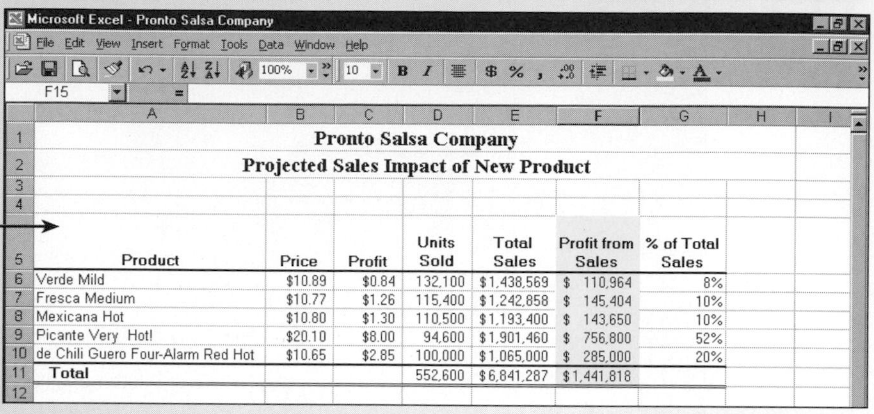

Pronto Salsa Company

Projected Sales Impact of New Product

Product	Price	Profit	Units Sold	Total Sales	Profit from Sales	% of Total Sales
Verde Mild	$10.89	$0.84	132,100	$1,438,569	$ 110,964	8%
Fresca Medium	$10.77	$1.26	115,400	$1,242,858	$ 145,404	10%
Mexicana Hot	$10.80	$1.30	110,500	$1,193,400	$ 143,650	10%
Picante Very Hot!	$20.10	$8.00	94,600	$1,901,460	$ 756,800	52%
de Chili Guero Four-Alarm Red Hot	$10.65	$2.85	100,000	$1,065,000	$ 285,000	20%
Total			552,600	$6,841,287	$1,441,818	

3. Click the **Save** button on the Standard toolbar to save the worksheet.

Using the Drawing Toolbar for Emphasis

The Excel Text Box feature lets you display notes, comments, and headings in a worksheet. A **text box** is like an electronic Post-it note that appears on top of the worksheet cells.

To add a text box you use the Text Box button, which is located on the Drawing toolbar, and type the note in the text box.

Activating the Drawing Toolbar

Excel provides many toolbars. You have been using two: the Standard toolbar and the Formatting toolbar. Some of the other toolbars include the Chart toolbar, the Drawing toolbar, and the Visual Basic toolbar. To activate a toolbar, it's usually easiest to use the toolbar Shortcut menu, but to activate the Drawing toolbar, you can simply click the Drawing button on the Standard toolbar. When you finish using a toolbar, you can easily remove it from the worksheet.

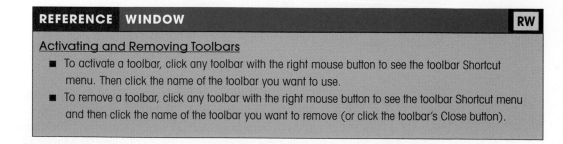

REFERENCE WINDOW RW

Activating and Removing Toolbars

- To activate a toolbar, click any toolbar with the right mouse button to see the toolbar Shortcut menu. Then click the name of the toolbar you want to use.
- To remove a toolbar, click any toolbar with the right mouse button to see the toolbar Shortcut menu and then click the name of the toolbar you want to remove (or click the toolbar's Close button).

You need the Drawing toolbar to accomplish your next formatting task. (If your Drawing toolbar is already active, skip the following step.)

To display the Drawing toolbar:

1. Click the **Drawing** button on the Standard toolbar.

The toolbar might appear in any location in the worksheet window; this is called a **floating** toolbar. You don't want the toolbar obstructing your view of the worksheet, so drag it to the bottom of the worksheet window to **anchor** it there. (If your toolbar is already anchored at the bottom of the worksheet window, or at the top, skip the next set of steps.)

To anchor the Drawing toolbar to the bottom of the worksheet window:

1. Position the pointer on the title bar of the Drawing toolbar.
2. Click and drag the toolbar to the bottom of the screen.
3. Release the mouse button to attach the Drawing toolbar to the bottom of the worksheet window. See Figure 3-29.

Figure 3-29 DRAWING TOOLBAR ATTACHED TO BOTTOM OF WINDOW

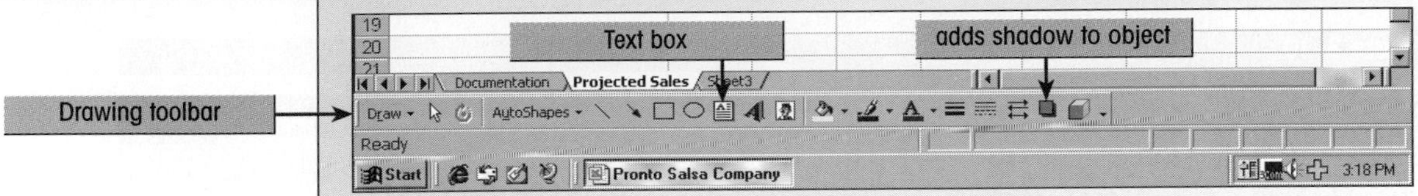

Now that the Drawing toolbar is where you want it, you proceed with your plan to add a comment to the worksheet.

Adding a Text Box

A **text box** is a drawing tool that contains text. It sits on top of the cells in a worksheet and is useful for drawing attention to important points in a worksheet or chart. With Excel you can use a variety of drawing tools, such as boxes, lines, circles, arrows, and text boxes to add graphic objects to your worksheet. To move, modify, or delete a graphic object, you first select it by moving the pointer over the object, then click it. Small square handles indicate that the object is selected. Use these handles to adjust the object's size, change its location, or delete it.

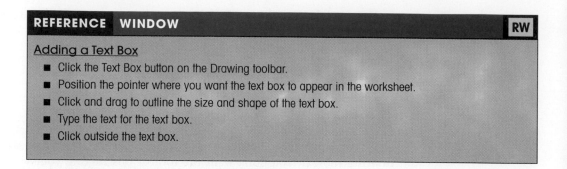

REFERENCE WINDOW RW

Adding a Text Box

- Click the Text Box button on the Drawing toolbar.
- Position the pointer where you want the text box to appear in the worksheet.
- Click and drag to outline the size and shape of the text box.
- Type the text for the text box.
- Click outside the text box.

You want to draw attention to the low price and high profit margin of the new salsa product. To do this, you plan to add a text box to the bottom of the worksheet that contains a note about expected profits.

To add a text box:

1. Click the **Text Box** button on the Drawing toolbar. As you move the pointer inside the worksheet area, the pointer changes to ↓. Position the crosshair of the pointer at the top of cell **A13** to mark the upper-left corner of the text box.
2. Click and drag + to cell **C18**, and then release the mouse button to mark the lower-right corner of the text box. See Figure 3-30.

   You are ready to type the text into the text box.

Figure 3-30 ADDING A TEXT BOX

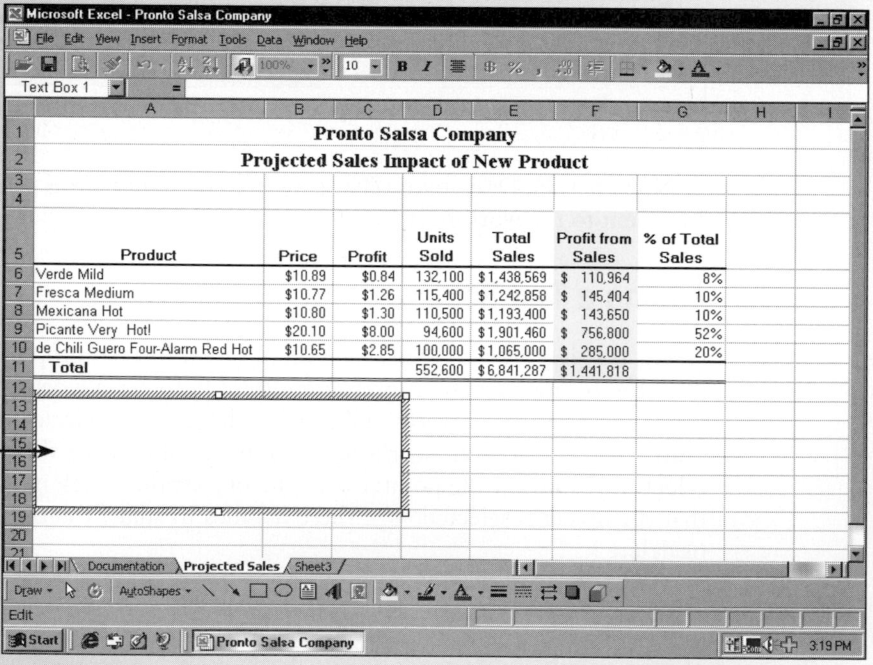

text box

3. Make sure the insertion point is in the text box and then type **Notice the high profit margin of the de Chili Guero Four-Alarm Red Hot. It has the second highest profit per unit.**

You want to use a different font style to emphasize the name of the new salsa product in the text box.

To italicize the name of the new salsa product:

1. Position I in the text box just before the word "de Chili."
2. Click and drag I to the end of the word "Hot," and then release the mouse button.

   TROUBLE? If the size of your text box differs slightly from the one in the figure, the lines of text might break differently. So don't worry if the text in your text box is not arranged exactly like the text in the figure.

3. Click the **Italic** button on the Formatting toolbar.
4. Click any cell to deselect the product name, which now appears italicized.

You decide to change the text box size so that there is no empty space at the bottom.

To change the text box size:

1. Click the **text box** to select it and display the patterned border with handles.
2. Position the pointer on the center handle at the bottom of the text box. The pointer changes to ↕.
3. Click and drag ↕ up to shorten the box, and then release the mouse button.

You want to change the text box a bit more by adding a drop shadow to it.

To add a shadow to the text box:

1. Make sure the text box is still selected. (Look for the patterned border and handles.)
2. Click the **Shadow** button on the Drawing toolbar to display the gallery of Shadow options. See Figure 3-31.

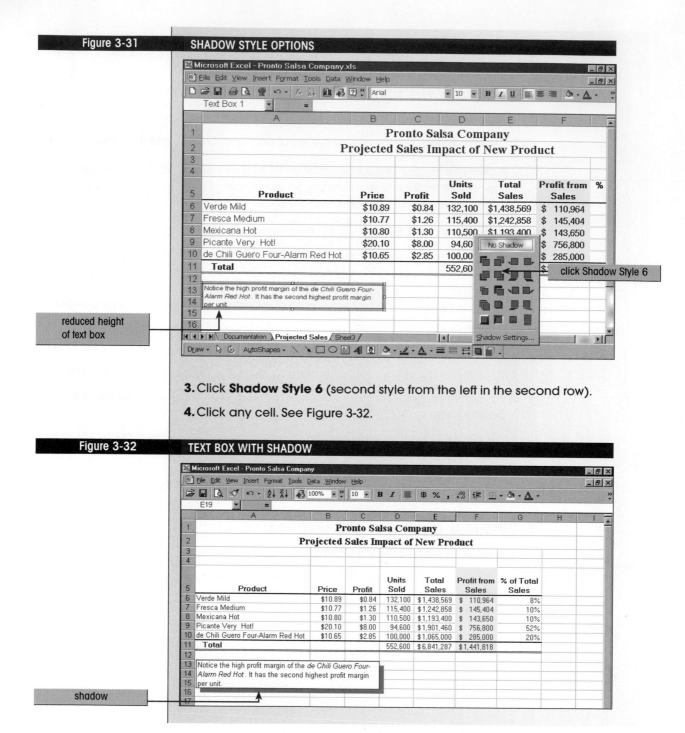

Figure 3-31 SHADOW STYLE OPTIONS

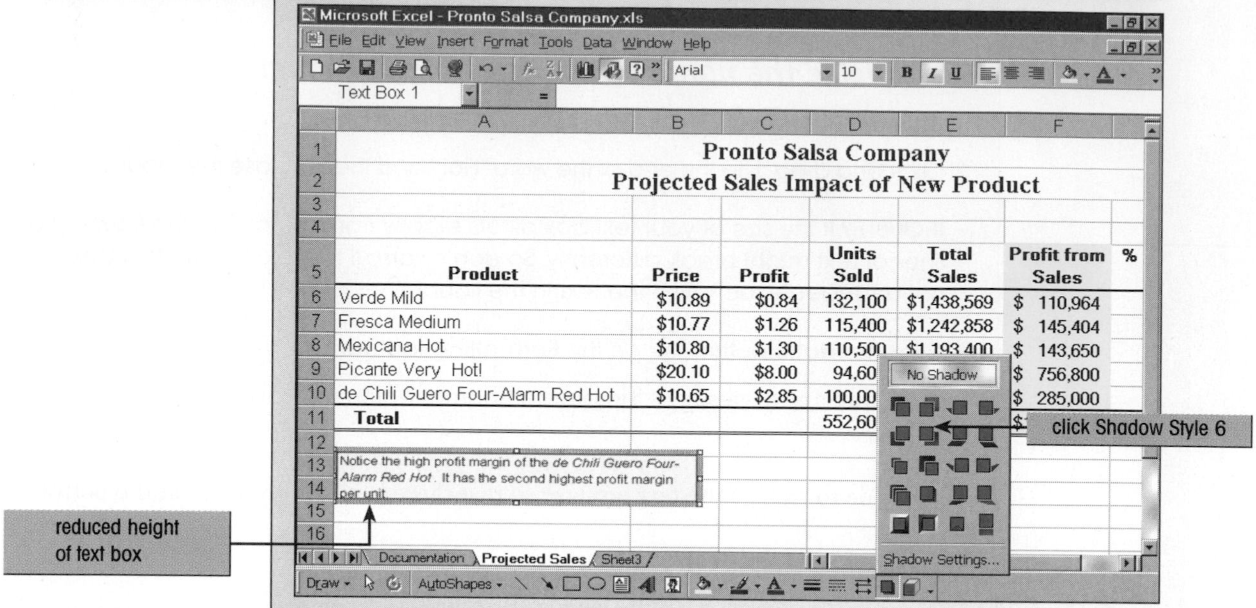

3. Click **Shadow Style 6** (second style from the left in the second row).

4. Click any cell. See Figure 3-32.

Figure 3-32 TEXT BOX WITH SHADOW

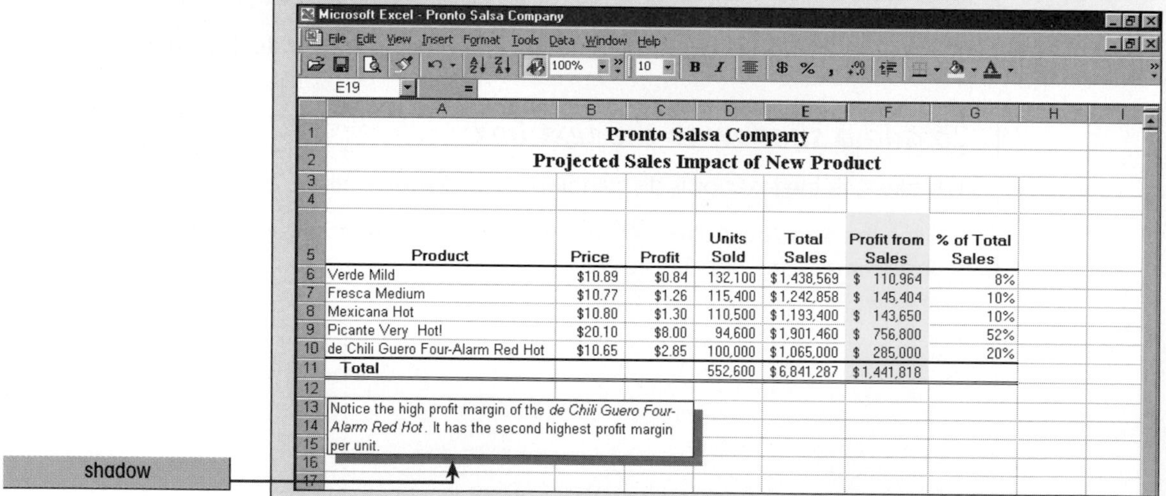

Adding an Arrow

You decide to add an arrow pointing from the text box to the row with information on the new salsa.

To add an arrow:

1. Click the **Arrow** button on the Drawing toolbar. As you move the mouse pointer inside the worksheet, the pointer changes to +.
2. Position + on the top edge of the text box in cell **B12**. To ensure a straight line, press and hold the **Shift** key as you drag to cell **B10**, and then release the mouse button.
3. Click any cell to deselect the arrow. See Figure 3-33.

Figure 3-33 ADDING AN ARROW

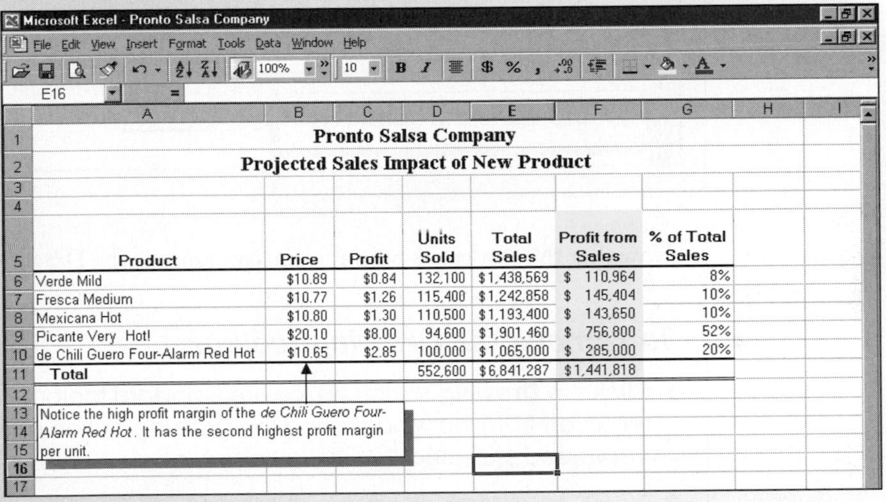

Product	Price	Profit	Units Sold	Total Sales	Profit from Sales	% of Total Sales
Verde Mild	$10.89	$0.84	132,100	$1,438,569	$ 110,964	8%
Fresca Medium	$10.77	$1.26	115,400	$1,242,858	$ 145,404	10%
Mexicana Hot	$10.80	$1.30	110,500	$1,193,400	$ 143,650	10%
Picante Very Hot!	$20.10	$8.00	94,600	$1,901,460	$ 756,800	52%
de Chili Guero Four-Alarm Red Hot	$10.65	$2.85	100,000	$1,065,000	$ 285,000	20%
Total			552,600	$6,841,287	$1,441,818	

You want the arrow to point to cell C10 instead of B10, so you need to reposition it.

Like a text box, an arrow is an Excel object. To modify the arrow object, you must select it. When you do so, two small square handles appear on it. You can reposition either end of the arrow by dragging one of the handles.

To reposition the arrow:

1. Move the pointer over the arrow object until the pointer changes to .
2. Click the **arrow**. Handles appear at each end of the arrow.
3. Move the pointer to the top handle on the arrowhead until the pointer changes to .
4. Click and drag + to cell **C10**, and then release the mouse button.
5. Click any cell to deselect the arrow object. See Figure 3-34.

Figure 3-34 MOVING AN ARROW

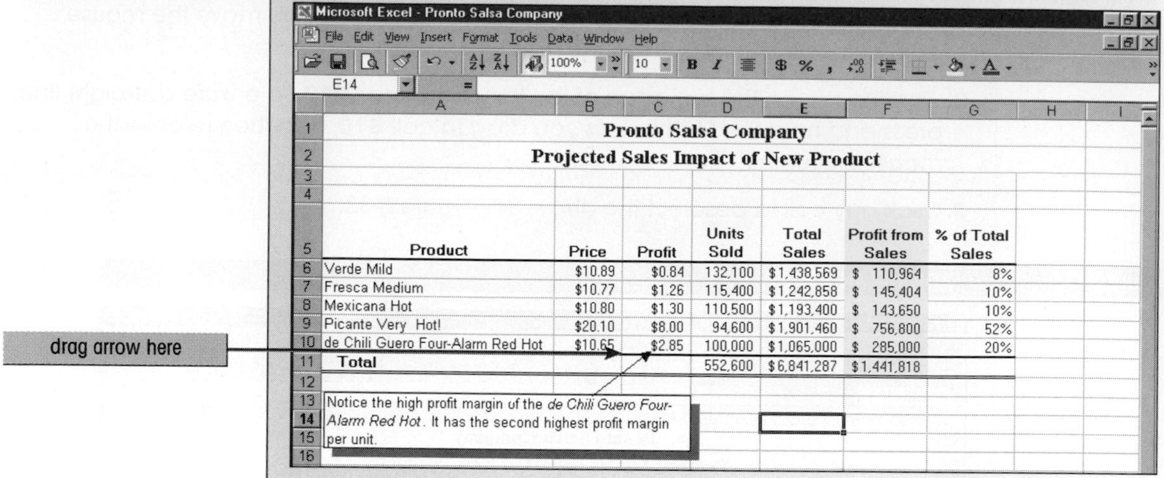

Now that the text box is finished, you can remove the Drawing toolbar from the worksheet.

To remove the Drawing toolbar:

1. Click the **Drawing** button on the Standard toolbar. The Drawing toolbar is removed from the window, and the Drawing button no longer appears depressed (selected).
2. Press **Ctrl + Home** to make cell A1 the active cell.
3. Click the **Save** button on the Standard toolbar to save your work.

You have now made all the formatting changes and enhancements to Anne's worksheet. She has just returned to the office, and you show her the completed worksheet. She is very pleased with how professional the worksheet looks, but she thinks of one more way to improve the appearance of the worksheet. She asks you to remove the gridlines from the worksheet display.

Controlling the Display of Gridlines

Although normally the boundaries of each cell are outlined in black, Anne has decided the worksheet will have more of a professional appearance if you remove the gridlines. To remove the gridline display, you deselect the Gridlines option in the View tab of the Options dialog box.

To remove the display of gridlines in the worksheet:

1. Click **Tools** on the menu bar, click **Options**, and if necessary, then click the **View** tab in the Options dialog box.
2. Click the **Gridlines** check box in the Window option to remove the check and deselect the option.

3. Click the **OK** button to display the worksheet without gridlines. See Figure 3-35.

Figure 3-35 WORKSHEET WITHOUT GRIDLINES

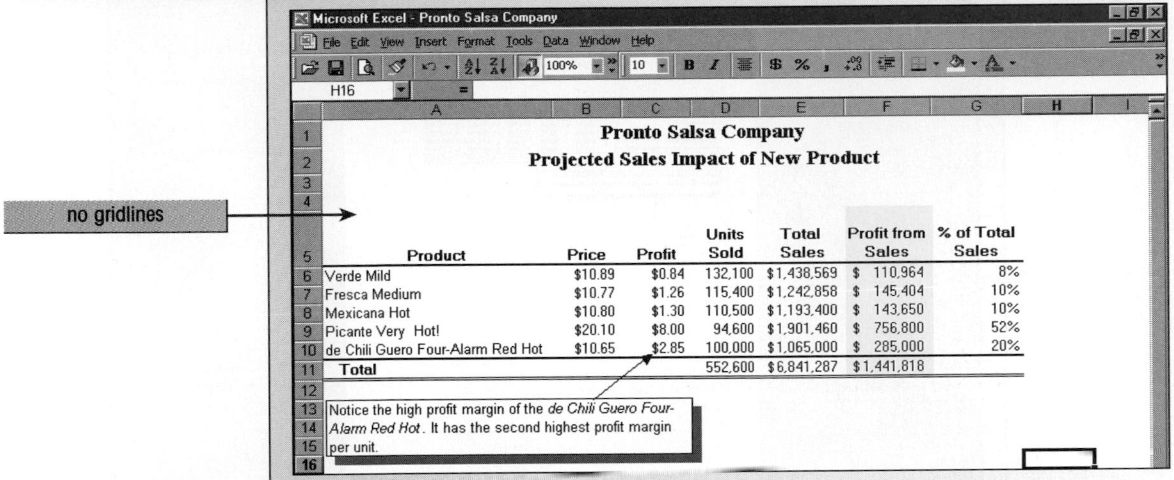

Now you are ready to print the worksheet.

Printing the Worksheet

Before you print a worksheet, you can use the Excel Print Preview window to see how it will look when printed. Recall that the Print Preview window shows you margins, page breaks, headers, and footers that arc not always visible on the screen.

To preview the worksheet before you print it:

1. Click the **Print Preview** button on the Standard toolbar to display the first worksheet page in the Print Preview window. See Figure 3-36.

Figure 3-36 PRINT PREVIEW

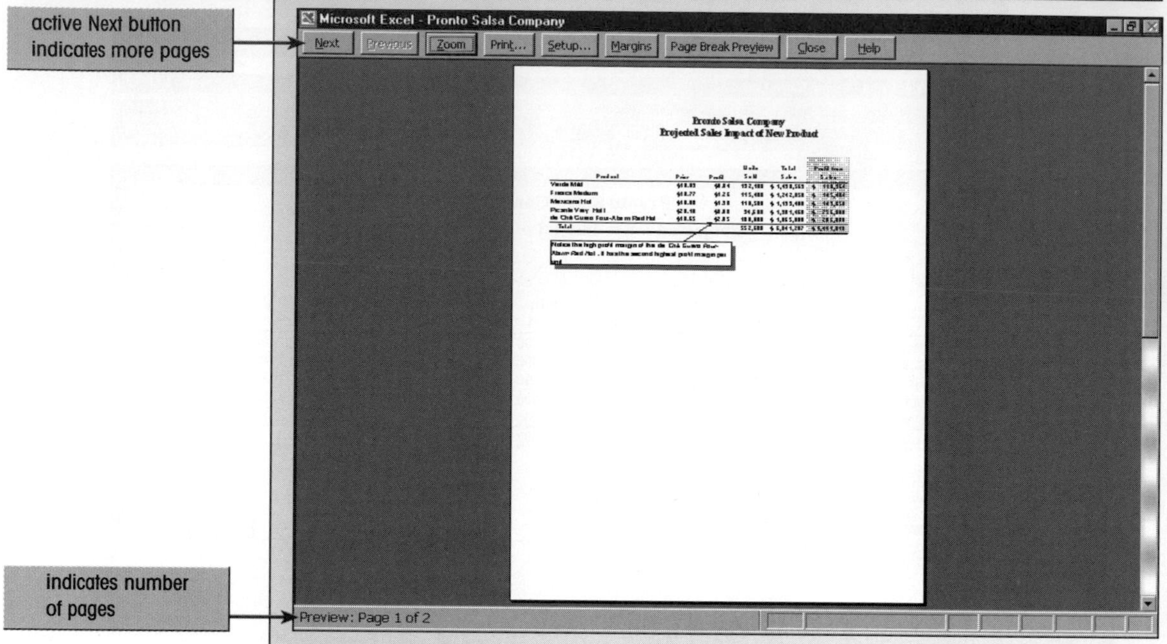

2. Click the **Next** button to preview the second worksheet page. Only one column appears on this page.

3. Click the **Previous** button to preview the first page again.

Looking at the Print Preview, you see that the worksheet is too wide to fit on a single page. You realize that if you print the worksheet horizontally (lengthwise), it will fit on a single sheet of paper.

Portrait and Landscape Orientations

Excel provides two print orientations, **portrait** and **landscape**. Portrait orientation prints the worksheet with the paper positioned so it is taller than it is wide. Landscape orientation prints the worksheet with the paper positioned so it is wider than it is tall. Because some worksheets are wider than they are tall, landscape orientation is very useful.

You can specify print orientation using the Page Setup command on the File menu or using the Setup button in the Print Preview window. Use the landscape orientation for the Projected Sales worksheet.

To change the print orientation to landscape:

1. In the Print Preview window, click the **Setup** button to open the Page Setup dialog box. If necessary, click the **Page** tab.
2. Click the **Landscape** option button in the Orientation section to select this option.
3. Click the **OK** button to return to the Print Preview window. See Figure 3-37. Notice the landscape orientation; that is, the page is wider than it is tall. The worksheet will now print on one page.

Figure 3-37 LANDSCAPE ORIENTATION

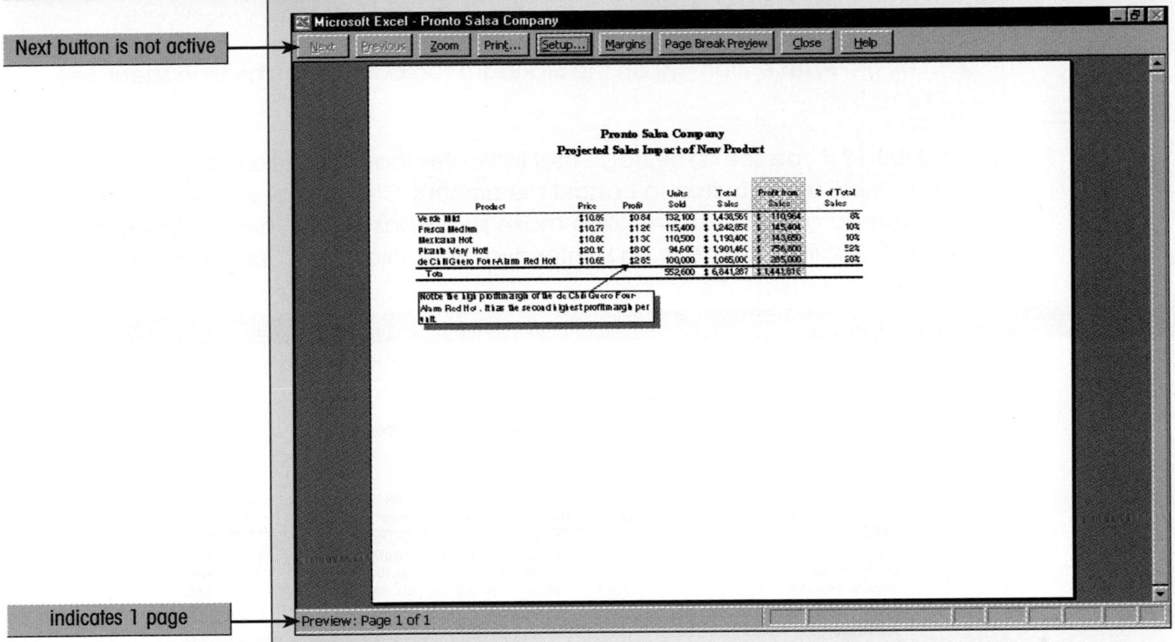

Before printing the worksheet, center the output on the page, and use the header/footer tab to document the printed worksheet.

To center the printed output:

1. Click the **Setup** button to open the Page Setup dialog box. Click the **Margins** tab.
2. Click the **Center on page Horizontally** check box to place a check in it and select that option.

Next modify the printed footer by adding your name in the center section.

To insert a custom footer for the worksheet:

1. Click the **Header/Footer** tab, and then click the **Custom footer** to open the Footer dialog box.
2. In the **Center section** box, type **Prepared by (enter your name here)**.
3. Click the **OK** button to complete the footer and return to the Page Setup dialog box.
4. Click the **OK** button to return to the Print Preview window.
5. Click the **Close** button to return to the worksheet.

The worksheet is ready to print, but you should always save your work before printing.

To save your Page Setup settings and print the worksheet:

1. Click the **Save** button on the Standard toolbar.
2. Click the **Print** button on the Standard toolbar to print the worksheet. See Figure 3-38.

   TROUBLE? If you see a message that indicates that you have a printer problem, click the Cancel button to cancel the printout. Check your printer to make sure it is turned on and is online; also make sure it has paper. Then go back and try Step 2 again. If you have no printer available, click the Cancel button.

Figure 3-38 PRINTED WORKSHEET

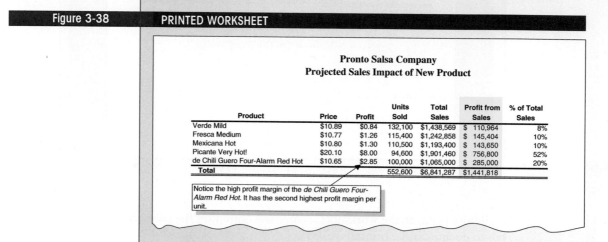

Pronto Salsa Company
Projected Sales Impact of New Product

Product	Price	Profit	Units Sold	Total Sales	Profit from Sales	% of Total Sales
Verde Mild	$10.89	$0.84	132,100	$1,438,569	$ 110,964	8%
Fresca Medium	$10.77	$1.26	115,400	$1,242,858	$ 145,404	10%
Mexicana Hot	$10.80	$1.30	110,500	$1,193,400	$ 143,650	10%
Picante Very Hot!	$20.10	$8.00	94,600	$1,901,460	$ 756,800	52%
de Chili Guero Four-Alarm Red Hot	$10.65	$2.85	100,000	$1,065,000	$ 285,000	20%
Total			552,600	$6,841,287	$1,441,818	

Notice the high profit margin of the *de Chili Guero Four-Alarm Red Hot*. It has the second highest profit margin per unit.

TROUBLE? If the title for the last two columns didn't print completely, you need to increase the row height for row 5. Select row 5, drag the border below row 5 until the row height is 42.75 or greater (check the reference area of the formula bar), and then click the Print button.

Hiding and Unhiding Rows and Columns

Anne asks for one more printout, this one omitting the Units Sold column. The printout will include the product name, price, profit, total sales, profit from sales and % of total sales.

Hiding rows and columns is useful if you don't want to display certain information when the worksheet is open, or don't want to print certain information in the worksheet.

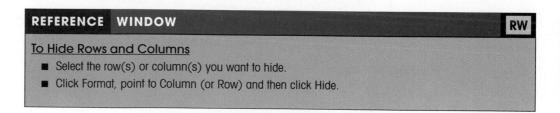

REFERENCE WINDOW RW

To Hide Rows and Columns

- Select the row(s) or column(s) you want to hide.
- Click Format, point to Column (or Row) and then click Hide.

To hide the Units Sold column:

1. Click the column header in column D. Notice the entire column is selected.
2. Click **Format**, point to **Column** and then click **Hide**.
3. Click any cell to observe that column D is hidden. See Figure 3-39.

Figure 3-39 WORKSHEET WITH COLUMN HIDDEN

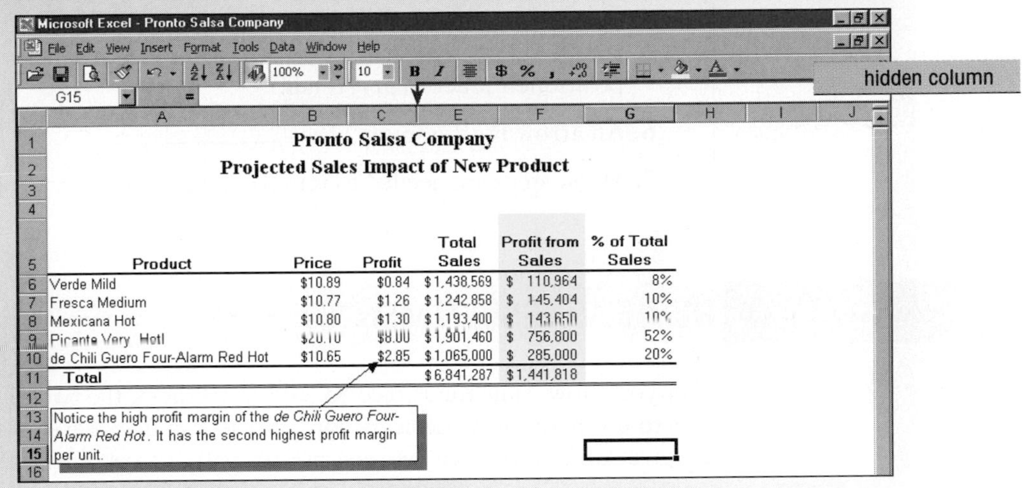

4. Print the report.

Before saving the workbook, unhide the hidden column.

To unhide the hidden column:

1. Position the pointer over the column header in column C.
2. Click and drag the pointer to the column header in column E. Notice that columns C and E are highlighted.
3. Click **Format**, point to **Column**, and then click **Unhide**. Column D is no longer hidden.
4. Click any cell to view column D.

   Now that you are done formatting the worksheet, close the workbook and exit Excel.
5. Save, then Close the workbook and exit Excel.

You have completed formatting the Projected Sales worksheet and are ready to give it to Anne to check over before she presents it at her meeting with the bank loan officer.

Session 3.2 QUICK CHECK

1. List two ways you can place a double-ruled line at the bottom of a range of cells.
2. Describe how to activate the Drawing toolbar.
3. To move, modify, or delete an object, you must ______________ it first.
4. A ______________ is a block of text that is placed in the worksheet.
5. ______________ orientation prints the worksheet with the paper positioned so it is taller than it is wide, and ______________ orientation prints so the paper is positioned wider than it is tall.
6. An arrow is an example of a ______________.
7. What steps are needed to remove the gridlines from the worksheet display?

REVIEW ASSIGNMENTS

After you show Anne the Projected Sales worksheet, the two of you discuss alternative ways to improve the worksheet's appearance. You decide to make some of these changes and give Anne the choice between two formatted worksheets. Do the following:

1. Start Windows and Excel, if necessary. Insert your Data Disk into the appropriate disk drive. Make sure the Excel and Book1 windows are maximized. Open the workbook **Pronto2** in the Review folder for Tutorial 3, and then save it as **Pronto3**.
2. Right-align the column heading in the Projected Sales worksheet.
3. Make the contents of cells A10:G10 bold to emphasize the new product. Make any necessary column-width adjustments.
4. Apply a yellow color to the range A1:G2.
5. Right-align the label in cell A11.
6. ***Explore*** Draw borders around the data in A1:G10 so it appears in a grid.
7. Replace the name currently in the footer with your name so that it appears on the printout of the worksheet. Make sure the footer also prints the date and filename. Place the sheet name in the center section of the custom header.
8. Make sure the Page Setup menu settings are set for centered horizontally and vertically.
9. Preview the printout to make sure it fits on one page. Save and print the worksheet.
10. ***Explore*** Fill the text box with the color yellow so that it appears as a "yellow sticky note." (*Hint:* select the text box by clicking on one of the selection handles. Use the Fill Color button on the Drawing toolbar.)
11. Change the color of the two-line title to blue (the text, not the background color).
12. In Step 4 you applied the color yellow to the cells A1 through G2. Remove the yellow color so that the background is the same as the rest of your worksheet.
13. If you've completed Steps 10, 11, or 12, save the worksheet as **Pronto4**.

Explore

14. a. Study the worksheet shown in Figure 3-40. Then open the Office Assistant and inquire about rotating data and merging cells.

Figure 3-40

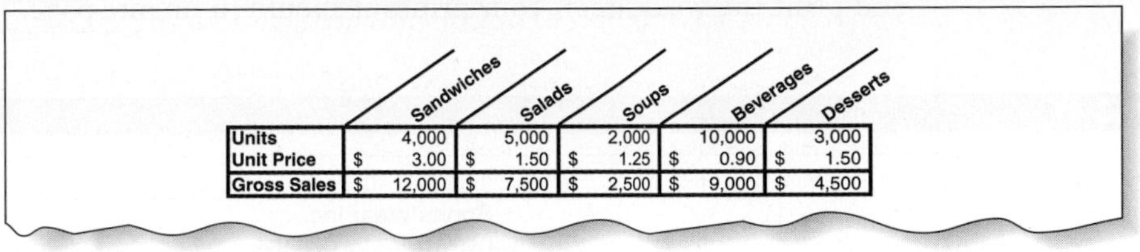

	Sandwiches	Salads	Soups	Beverages	Desserts
Units	4,000	5,000	2,000	10,000	3,000
Unit Price	$ 3.00	$ 1.50	$ 1.25	$ 0.90	$ 1.50
Gross Sales	$ 12,000	$ 7,500	$ 2,500	$ 9,000	$ 4,500

b. Open the workbook **Explore3** in the Tutorial 3 Review folder and then save it as **Explore3 Solution** in the same folder.

c. Use the Rotate Text formatting feature to change the worksheet so it is similar to Figure 3-40. Make any other changes to make the worksheet as similar as possible to the one shown in Figure 3-40.

d. Save and then print the worksheet.

CASE PROBLEMS

Case 1. ***Jenson Sports Wear Quarterly Sales*** Carol Roberts is the national sales manager for Jenson Sports Wear, a company that sells sportswear to major department stores. She has been using an Excel worksheet to track the results of her staff's sales incentive program. She has asked you to format the worksheet so it looks professional. She also wants a printout before she presents the worksheet at the next sales meeting. Complete these steps to format and print the worksheet:

1. Start Windows and Excel, if necessary. Insert your Data Disk into the appropriate disk drive. Make sure the Excel and Book1 windows are maximized. Open the workbook **Running** in the Cases folder for Tutorial 3 on your Data Disk. Maximize the worksheet window and then save the workbook as **Running2**.

2. Complete the worksheet by doing the following:
   a. Calculating totals for each product
   b. Calculating quarterly subtotals for the Shoes and Shirts departments
   c. Calculating totals for each quarter and an overall total

3. Modify the worksheet so it is formatted as shown in Figure 3-41.

4. Use the Page Setup dialog box to center the output both horizontally and vertically.

5. Add the filename, your name, and the date in the custom footer and delete both the formatting code &[File] from the Center section of the header.

6. Save the workbook.

7. Preview the worksheet and adjust the page setup as necessary for the printed results you want.

8. Print the worksheet. Your printout should fit on one page.

Explore

9. Place the note "Leading product" in a text box. Remove the border from the text box. (*Hint*: Use the Format Textbox dialog box—Colors and Lines Tab.) Draw an oval object around the text box. (*Hint*: Use the Oval tool on the Drawing toolbar and right-click to determine which command sends the oval object to the back.) Draw an arrow from the edge of the oval to the number in the worksheet representing the leading product. Save and print the worksheet. Your printout should fit on one page.

Figure 3-41

Sports Wear Inc.
Quarterly Sales by Product

Shoes	Qtr 1	Qtr 2	Qtr 3	Qtr 4	Total
Running	2,250	2,550	2,650	2,800	10,250
Tennis	2,800	1,500	2,300	2,450	9,050
Basketball	1,250	1,400	1,550	1,550	5,750
Subtotal	$ 6,300	$ 5,450	$ 6,500	$ 6,800	$ 25,050
Shirts	Qtr 1	Qtr 2	Qtr 3	Qtr 4	Total
Tee	1,000	1,150	1,250	1,150	4,550
Polo	2,100	2,200	2,300	2,400	9,000
Sweat	250	250	275	300	1,075
Subtotal	$ 3,350	$ 3,600	$ 3,825	$ 3,850	$ 14,625
Grand Total	**$ 9,650**	**$ 9,050**	**$ 10,325**	**$ 10,650**	**$ 39,675**

Case 2. State Recycling Campaign Fred Birnbaum is working as an intern in the state's Waste Disposal Department. They have a pilot project on recycling for three counties (Seacoast, Metro, and Pioneer Valley). You have been asked to complete the worksheet, summarizing the results of the pilot program and formatting it for presentation to their board of directors.

1. Start Windows and Excel, if necessary. Insert your Data Disk into the appropriate disk drive. Make sure the Excel and Book1 windows are maximized. Open the workbook **Recycle** in the Cases folder for Tutorial 3 on your Data Disk, and then save it as **Recycle2**.
2. Add two columns to calculate yearly totals for tons and a dollar value for each material in each county.
3. Insert three rows at the top of the worksheet to include:
   State Recycling Project
   Material Reclamation 1999
   <blank row>
4. Format the worksheet until you feel confident that the board of directors will be impressed with the appearance of the report.
5. Rename the worksheet **Recycle Data**.
6. Save the worksheet.
7. Print the worksheet centered horizontally and vertically on the page using landscape orientation. Include your name in the custom footer.

8. Remove the gridlines from the display. Use the Border tab of the Format Cells dialog box to place the recycle data in a grid. Save the workbook as **Recycle3**.

Explore

9. Change the magnification of the sheet so you can view the recycle data on the screen without having to scroll. (*Hint*: Use the Zoom control on the Standard toolbar.)

Case 3. State Government Expenditures Ken Dry, an assistant to the governor, has started an Excel worksheet summarizing current and proposed expenditures for all the state agencies. Ken has been called away on an emergency and asked you to complete the worksheet. He left the following note:

The column headings and agency and division names have been entered in the worksheet. Column A includes Divisions, which appear as the rows with no expenditure data in columns B and C. Agencies are those rows that include expenditure data in columns B and C. For example, the first division is General Government and the first agency within this division is Administration; the next division is Human Services and its first agency is Children and Families, and so on. See Figure 3-42.

You need to modify the worksheet by:

Figure 3-42

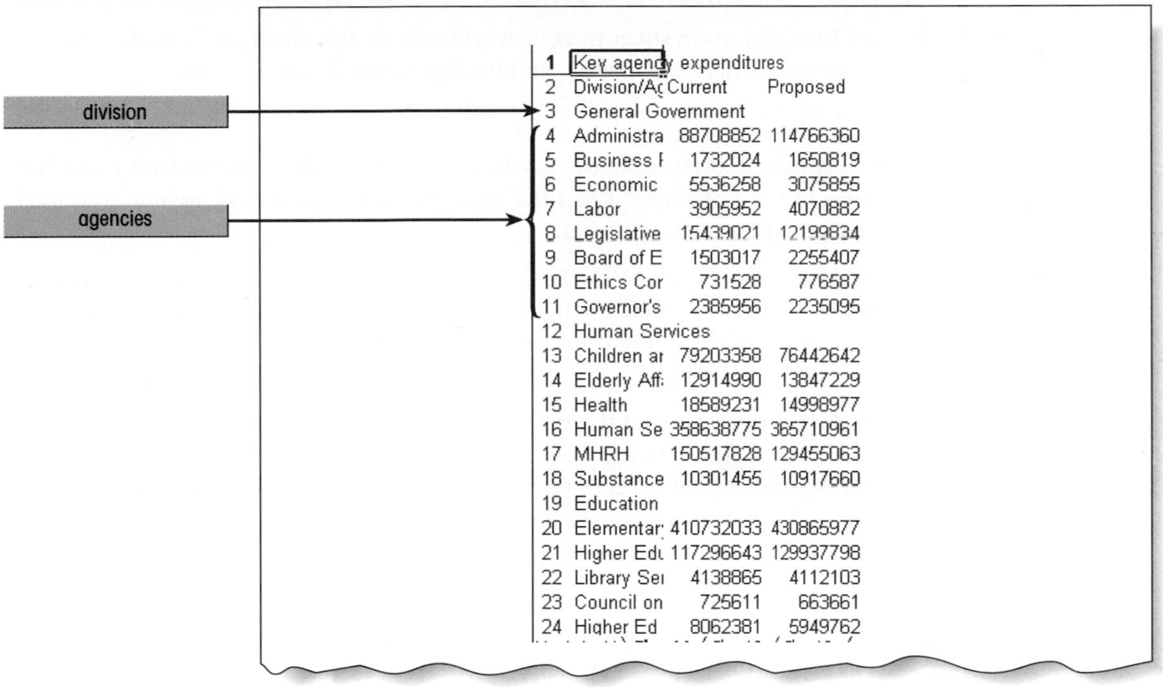

1	Key agency expenditures		
2	Division/Ag	Current	Proposed
3	General Government		
4	Administra	88708852	114766360
5	Business F	1732024	1650819
6	Economic	5536258	3075855
7	Labor	3905952	4070882
8	Legislative	15439021	12199834
9	Board of E	1503017	2255407
10	Ethics Cor	731528	776587
11	Governor's	2385956	2235095
12	Human Services		
13	Children ar	79203358	76442642
14	Elderly Aff:	12914990	13847229
15	Health	18589231	14998977
16	Human Se	358638775	365710961
17	MHRH	150517828	129455063
18	Substance	10301455	10917660
19	Education		
20	Elementar	410732033	430865977
21	Higher Edu	117296643	129937798
22	Library Ser	4138865	4112103
23	Council on	725611	663661
24	Higher Ed	8062381	5949762

- Calculating overall government totals (for all agencies) for both current and proposed expenditures
- Calculating totals for each division. Remember that the agencies in a division follow in the rows below the division name (if necessary, you can insert rows to provide room for totals).

- Add the following calculations in columns D, E, and F:
  a. percentage change between current and proposed (next year's) expenditures (column D)
  b. for proposed expenditures-percentage of agency's expenditures in a division to total expenditures in that division; for example, Administration is 81.4% of the General Government division expenditures and Children and Families is 12.4% of Health and Services (column E)
  c. for proposed expenditures-percentage of agency's expenditures to total government expenditures; for example, Administration is 7.5% of overall government expenditures, while Business Regulation is .1% of overall government expenditures (column F)

Do the following:

1. Open the workbook **StateGov.xls** in the Cases folder for Tutorial 3, and then save it as **State Government**.
2. Use the note left by Ken to complete the worksheet.
3. Your output will be handed out at a press conference, so you need to improve the appearance of the worksheet so it will look more professional.
4. Assign a descriptive sheet name to Sheet1.
5. Print your report on one page. Include your name, class, and date in the print footer and the sheet name as part of the print header.
6. Include a Documentation sheet in your workbook. In this sheet, include the title of the project, your name, date completed, and brief purpose. Print this sheet.
7. Save the workbook.
8. Print the formulas that underlie the worksheet. Save the worksheet before you display the formulas in the worksheet. Print the formulas on one page and include row and column headings as part of the printout.

Case 4. Ortiz Marine Services Vince DiOrio is an information systems major at a local college. He works three days a week at a nearby marina, Ortiz Marine Services, to help pay for his tuition. Vince works in the business office, and his responsibilities range from making coffee to keeping the company's books.

Recently, Jim Ortiz, the owner of the marina, asked Vince if he could help computerize the payroll for their employees. He explained that the employees work a different number of hours each week for different rates of pay. Jim does the payroll manually now and finds it time-consuming. Moreover, whenever he makes an error, he is embarrassed and annoyed at having to take the additional time to correct it. Jim was hoping Vince could help him.

Vince immediately agrees to help. He tells Jim that he knows how to use Excel and that he can build a worksheet that will save him time and reduce errors. Jim and Vince meet. They review the present payroll process and discuss the desired outcomes of the payroll spreadsheet. Figure 3-43 is a sketch of the output Jim wants to get.

Figure 3-43

Ortiz Marine Service Payroll
Week Ending

Employee	Hours	Pay Rate	Gross Pay	Federal Withholding	State Withholding	Total Deductions	Net Pay
Bramble	16	6					
Juarez	25	6.25					
Smith	30	8					
DiOrio	25	7.75					
Smiken	10	5.90					
Cortez	30	7					
Fulton	20	6					
Total							

Do the following:

1. Create the worksheet sketched in Figure 3-43.
2. Use the following formulas in your workbook to calculate total hours, gross pay, federal withholding, state withholding, total deductions and net pay for the company:
   a. Gross pay is hours times pay rate.
   b. Federal withholding is 15% of gross pay.
   c. State withholding is 4% of gross pay.
   d. Total deductions is the sum of federal and state withholding.
   e. Net pay is the difference between gross pay and total deductions.
3. Apply the formatting techniques learned in this tutorial to create a professional-looking workbook.
4. Assign a descriptive sheet name.
5. Create a Documentation sheet.
6. Save the workbook as **Payroll** in the Cases folder for Tutorial 3.
7. Print the worksheet, including appropriate headers and footers.
8. Remove the hours for the seven employees.
9. Enter the following hours: 18 for Bramble, 25 for Juarez, 35 for Smith, and 20 for DiOrio, 15 for Smiken, 35 for Cortez, and 22 for Fulton.
10. Print the new worksheet.
11. Print the formulas on one page. Include row and column headers in the printed output.

INTERNET ASSIGNMENTS

The purpose of the Internet Assignments is to challenge you to find information on the Internet that you can use to create effective spreadsheets. The actual assignments are updated and maintained on the Course Technology Web site. Log on to the Internet and use your Web browser to go to the Student Online Companion to accompany this text at **www.course.com/NewPerspectives/Office2000**. Click the Excel link, and then click the link for Tutorial 3.

QUICK CHECK ANSWERS

Session 3.1

1. click Format, click Cells; right-click mouse in cell you want to format; use buttons on the Formatting toolbar
2. **a.** 5.8% **b.** $0.06
3. Format Painter button
4. The column width of a cell is not wide enough to display the numbers, and you need to increase the column width.
5. Position the mouse pointer over the column header, right-click the mouse and click Column Width. Enter the new column width in the Column Width dialog box. Position the mouse pointer over the right edge of the column you want to modify, and then click and drag to increase the column width.
6. The data in the cell is formatted with the Comma style using two decimal places.
7. center column headings, right-align numbers, and left-align text
8. Left align button, Center button, Right align button, and Merge and Center button

Session 3.2

1. use the Borders tab on the Format Cells dialog box, or the Borders button on the Formatting toolbar
2. click the Drawing button on the Standard toolbar
3. select
4. text box
5. Portrait; landscape
6. drawing object
7. click Tools, click Options, click View tab, and then remove the check from the Gridlines check box

OBJECTIVES

In this tutorial you will:

- Identify the elements of an Excel chart
- Learn which type of chart will represent your data most effectively
- Create an embedded chart
- Move and resize a chart
- Edit a chart
- Change the appearance of a chart
- Place a chart in a chart sheet
- Select nonadjacent ranges
- Work with three-dimensional chart types
- Add a picture to a chart

CREATING CHARTS

Charting Sales Information for Cast Iron Concepts

CASE

Cast Iron Concepts

Andrea Puest, the regional sales manager of Cast Iron Concepts (CIC), a distributor of cast iron stoves, is required to present information concerning sales of the company's products within her territory. Andrea sells in the New England region, which currently includes Massachusetts, Maine, and Vermont. She sells four major models—Star Windsor, Box Windsor, West Windsor, and Circle Windsor. The Circle Windsor is CIC's latest entry in the cast iron stove market. Due to production problems, it was only available for sale the last four months of the year.

Andrea will make a presentation before the director of sales for CIC and the other regional managers next week when the entire group meets at corporate headquarters. Andrea gives you the basic data on sales in her territory for the past year. She must report on both total regional sales and total state sales for each model in her territory. She knows that this kind of information is often understood best when it is presented in graphical form. So she thinks she would like to show this information in a column chart as well as in a pie chart. You help her prepare for her presentation by creating the charts she needs.

SESSION 4.1

In this session you will learn about the variety of Excel chart types and how to identify the elements of a chart. You will learn how to create a column chart and a number of techniques for improving your chart, including moving and resizing it, adding and editing chart text, enhancing a chart title by adding a border, and using color for emphasis.

Excel Charts

Andrea's sales data is saved in a workbook named Concepts. You generate the charts from the data in this workbook.

To start Excel, open the Concepts workbook, and rename it:

1. Start Excel as usual.
2. Open the Concepts workbook in the Tutorial folder for Tutorial 4 on your Data Disk.

   The Documentation sheet appears as the first sheet in the workbook.
3. Type your name and the current date in the appropriate cells in the Documentation sheet.
4. Save the workbook as **Cast Iron Concepts**. After you do so, the new filename appears in the title bar.
5. Click the **Sales Data** tab to move to that sheet. See Figure 4-1.

Figure 4-1 SALES DATA WORKSHEET IN CAST IRON CONCEPTS WORKBOOK

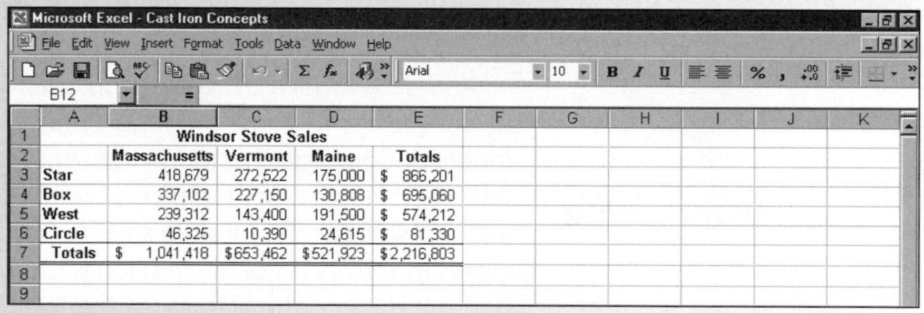

	A	B	C	D	E
1		Windsor Stove Sales			
2		Massachusetts	Vermont	Maine	Totals
3	Star	418,679	272,522	175,000	$ 866,201
4	Box	337,102	227,150	130,808	$ 695,060
5	West	239,312	143,400	191,500	$ 574,212
6	Circle	46,325	10,390	24,615	$ 81,330
7	Totals	$ 1,041,418	$653,462	$521,923	$2,216,803
8					
9					

The worksheet shows the annual sales in dollars for each Windsor stove model by state. The total sales during the year for each model are in column E, and the total sales for each state appear in row 7.

It is easy to visually represent this kind of worksheet data. You might think of these graphical representations as "graphs;" however, in Excel they are referred to as **charts**. Figure 4-2 shows the 14 chart types that you can use to represent worksheet data in Excel.

Each chart type has two or more subtypes that provide various alternative chart formats for the selected chart type. For example, the column chart type has seven subtypes, as shown in Figure 4-3.

Figure 4-2 EXCEL CHART TYPES

ICON	CHART TYPE	PURPOSE
	Area	Shows magnitude of change over a period of time
	Column	Shows comparisons between the data represented by each column
	Bar	Shows comparisons between the data represented by each bar
	Line	Shows trends or changes over time
	Pie	Shows the proportion of parts to a whole
	XY (Scatter)	Shows the pattern or relationship between sets of (x,y) data points
	Radar	Shows change in data relative to a center point
	Surface	Shows the interrelationships between large amounts of data
	Bubble	A special type of XY (Scatter) that shows the pattern or relationship between sets of data points; compares three sets of data
	Stock	Compares high, low, open, and close prices of a stock
	Cylinder	Shows comparisons between the data represented by each cylinder
	Cone	Shows comparisons between the data represented by each cone
	Pyramid	Shows comparisons between the data represented by each pyramid
	Doughnut	Shows the proportion of parts to a whole

Figure 4-3 CHART SUBTYPES FOR COLUMN CHART TYPE

CHART SUBTYPE ICON	DESCRIPTION
	Clustered column
	Stacked column
	100% stacked column
	Clustered column with 3-D visual effect
	Stacked column with 3-D visual effect
	100% stacked column with 3-D visual effect
	3-D column

Figure 4-4 shows the elements of a typical Excel chart. Understanding the Excel chart terminology is particularly important so you can successfully construct and edit charts.

Figure 4-4 EXCEL CHART ELEMENTS

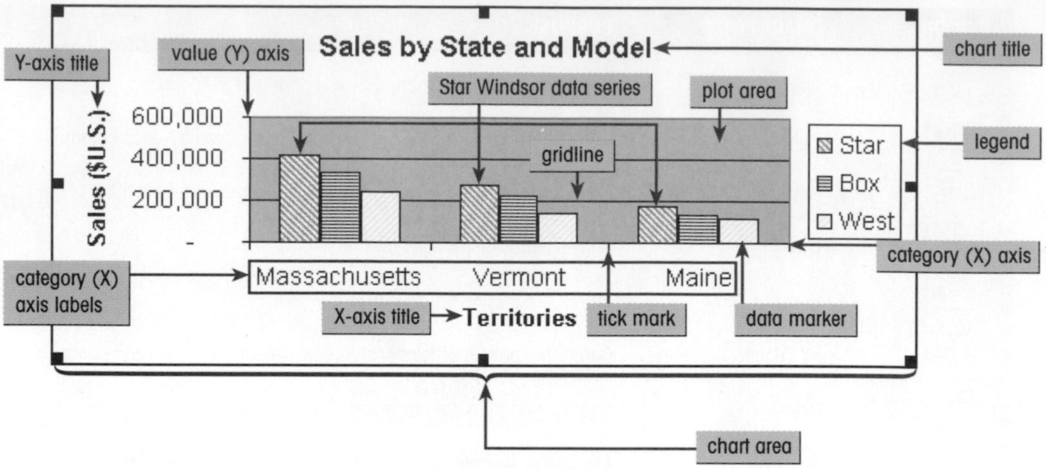

The entire chart and all its elements are contained in the **chart area**. The **plot area** is the rectangular area defined by the axes, with the Y-axis forming the left side and the X-axis forming the base; in Figure 4-4 the plot area is in gray. The **axis** is a line that borders one side of the plot area, providing a frame for measurement or comparison in a chart. Data values are plotted along the **value** or **Y-axis**, which is typically vertical. Categories are plotted along the **category** or **X-axis**, which is usually horizontal. Each axis in a chart can have a title that identifies the scale or categories of the chart data; in Figure 4-4 the **X-axis title** is "Territories" and the **Y-axis** title is "Sales ($U.S.)." The chart title identifies the chart.

A **tick mark label** identifies the categories, values, or series in the chart. **Tick marks** are small lines that intersect an axis, like divisions on a ruler, and represent the scale used for measuring values in the chart. Excel automatically generates this scale based on the values selected for the chart. **Gridlines** extend the tick marks on a chart axis to make it easier to see the values associated with the data markers. The **category names** or **category labels**, usually appearing on the X-axis, correspond to the labels you use for the worksheet data.

A **data point** is a single value originating from a worksheet cell. A **data marker** is a graphic representing a data point in a chart; depending on the type of chart, a data marker can be a bar, column, area, slice, or other symbol. For example, sales of the Star Windsor stove in Massachusetts (value 418,679 in cell B3 of the worksheet on your screen) is a data point. Each column in the chart in Figure 4-4 that shows the sales of Windsor stoves is a data marker. A **data series** is a group of related data points, such as the Star Windsor sales shown as red column markers in the chart.

When you have more than one data series, your chart will contain more than one set of data markers. For example, Figure 4-4 has three data series, one for each type of Windsor stove. When you show more than one data series in a chart, it is a good idea to use a **legend** to identify which data marker represents each data series.

Placement of Charts

Charts can be placed in the same worksheet as the data; this type of chart is called an **embedded chart** and enables you to place the chart next to the data so it can easily be reviewed and printed on one page. You can also place a chart in a separate sheet, called a **chart sheet**, which contains only one chart and doesn't have rows and columns. In this tutorial you create both an embedded chart and a chart that resides in a separate chart sheet.

Planning a Chart

Before you begin creating a chart you should plan it. Planning a chart includes the following steps:

- identifying the data points to be plotted, as well as the labels representing each data series and categories for the X-axis
- choosing an appropriate chart type
- sketching the chart, including data markers, axes, titles, labels, and legend
- deciding on the location of the chart within the workbook

Remember, Andrea wants to compare sales for each model in each state in which she sells. She thinks that a column chart is the best way to provide her audience with an accurate comparison of sales of Windsor stoves in her New England territory. She also needs to show sales of each stove model as a percentage of total sales. A pie chart is most effective when showing the size of each part as a percentage of a whole, so she will create a pie chart to use in her presentation as well.

Andrea sketched the column chart and pie chart shown in Figure 4-5.

Figure 4-5 SKETCH OF COLUMN AND PIE CHARTS

Sales Data

Windsor Stove Sales

	Massachusetts	Vermont	Maine	Totals
Star	418,679	272,522	175,000	$ 866,201
Box	337,102	227,150	130,808	$ 695,060
West	239,312	143,400	191,500	$ 574,212
Circle	46,325	10,390	24,615	$ 81,330
Totals	$ 1,041,418	$653,462	$521,923	$2,216,803

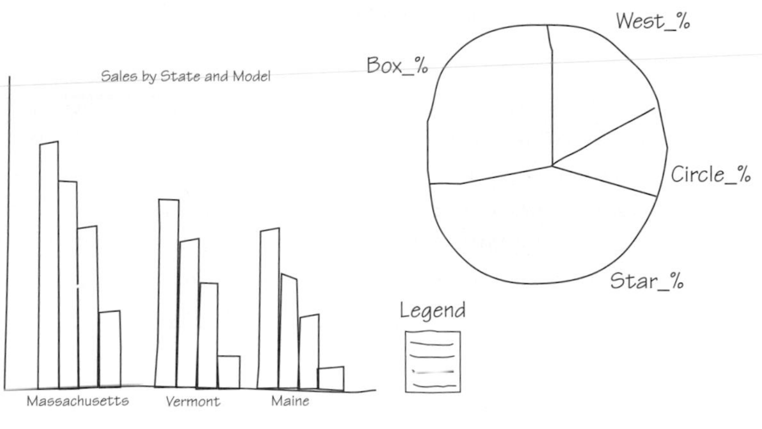

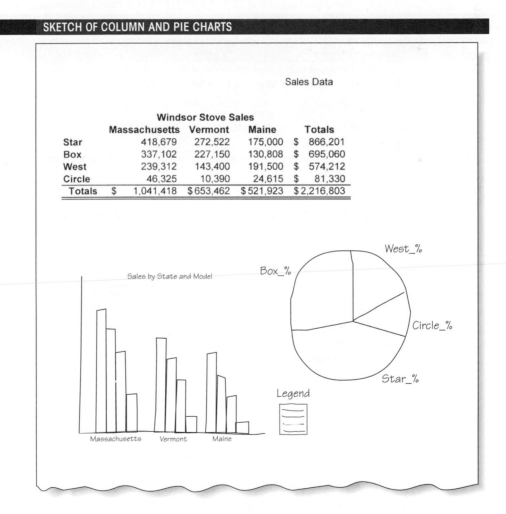

The sketches show roughly how Andrea wants the charts to look. It is difficult to envision exactly how a chart will look until you know how the data series looks when plotted; therefore, you don't need to incorporate every detail in the chart sketch. As you construct the charts, you can take advantage of Excel previewing capabilities to try different formatting options until your charts look just the way you want.

Create the column chart first. In looking at the sketch for this chart, note that Andrea wants to group the data by states; that is, the four models are shown for each of the three states. The names of the states in cells B2:D2 of the worksheet will be used as category labels. The names of each stove model, in cells A3:A6, will represent the legend text. The data series for the chart are in rows B3:D3, B4:D4, B5:D5, and B6:D6.

Creating a Column Chart

After studying Andrea's sketch for the column chart, you are ready to create it using the Sales Data worksheet. When you create a chart, you first select the cells that contain the data you want to appear in the chart and then you click the Chart Wizard button on the Standard toolbar. The Chart Wizard consists of four dialog boxes that guide you through the steps required to create a chart. Figure 4-6 identifies the tasks you perform in each of the Chart Wizard dialog boxes.

Figure 4-6 TASKS PERFORMED IN EACH STEP OF THE CHART WIZARD

DIALOG BOX	TASKS PERFORMED
Chart Type	Select the type of chart you want to create—lists the chart types available in Excel; for each chart type, presents you with several chart subtypes from which you can choose
Chart Source Data	Specify the worksheet cells that contain the data and labels that will appear in the chart
Chart Options	Change the look of the chart by changing options that affect the titles, axes, gridlines, legends, data labels, and data tables
Chart Location	Specify where to place the chart: embedded in a worksheet along with the worksheet data, or in a separate sheet called a chart sheet

You know that Andrea intends to create a handout of the worksheet and chart, so you want to embed the column chart in the same worksheet as the sales data, making it easier for her to create a one-page handout.

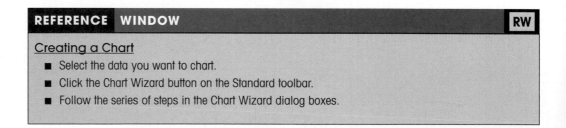

REFERENCE WINDOW RW

Creating a Chart
- Select the data you want to chart.
- Click the Chart Wizard button on the Standard toolbar.
- Follow the series of steps in the Chart Wizard dialog boxes.

Before activating the Chart Wizard, you need to select the cells containing the data the chart will depict. If you want the column and row labels to appear in the chart, include the cells that contain them in your selection as well. For this chart, select the range A2 through D6, which includes the sales of each Windsor stove model in the three states as well as names of the stove models and states.

To create the column chart using the Chart Wizard:

1. Select cells **A2:D6**, making sure no cells are highlighted in column E or row 7. Notice the totals are not included in the range. To include the totals along with the data points that make up totals in the same chart would make the comparison more difficult and might result in a misinterpretation of the data.

   Now that you have selected the chart range, you use the Chart Wizard to create the column chart.

2. Click the **Chart Wizard** button on the Standard toolbar to open the Chart Wizard - Step 1 of 4 - Chart Type dialog box. See Figure 4-7.

   TROUBLE? If the Office Assistant appears on your screen, click the button next to the message "No, don't provide help now" to close the Office Assistant.

   This first dialog box asks you to select the type of chart you want to create. The Chart type list box lists each of the 14 chart types available in Excel. The default chart type is the Column chart type. To the right of the Chart type list box is a gallery of chart subtypes for the selected chart. Select the chart type you want to create.

Figure 4-7 CHART WIZARD STEP 1 OF 4 - CHART TYPE DIALOG BOX

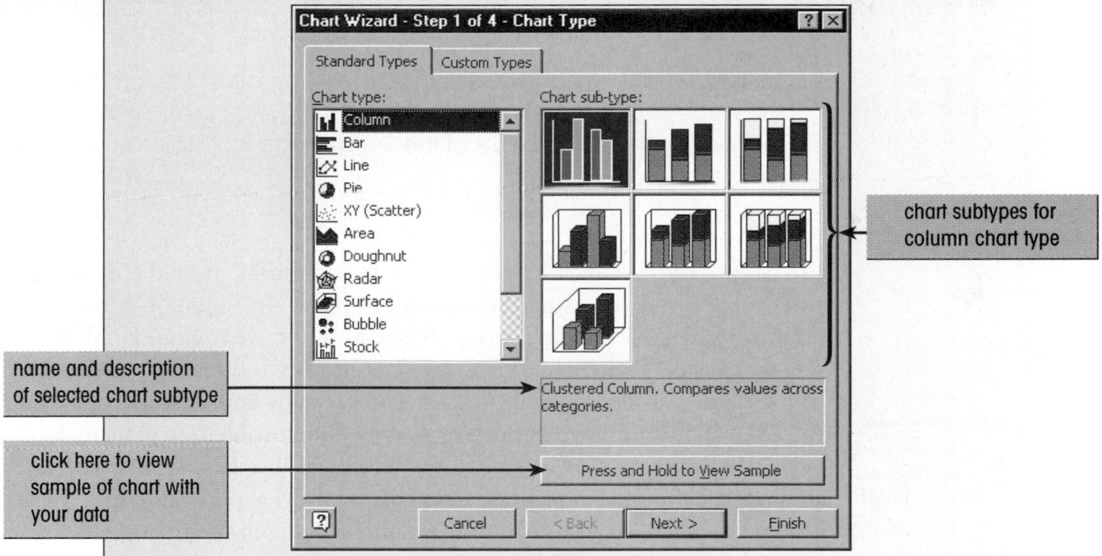

   You want to create a column chart.

3. If necessary, click the **Column** chart type (the default) to select it. Seven Column chart subtypes, preformatted chart designs for the column chart, appear. The Clustered Column chart subtype is the default subtype for the Column chart type. Click and hold the **Press and Hold to View Sample** button to see a preview of the Clustered Column chart subtype.

   To view any other Column chart subtype, select another subtype option and click the **Press and Hold to View Sample** button. If you select a different chart type, you will see a different set of subcharts.

   You decide to use the Clustered Column chart type, the default selection.

4. Click the **Next** button to open the Chart Wizard - Step 2 of 4 - Chart Source Data dialog box. See Figure 4-8. In this step you confirm or specify the worksheet cells that contain the data and labels to appear in the chart.

Figure 4-8 CHART WIZARD - STEP 2 OF 4 - CHART SOURCE DATA DIALOG BOX

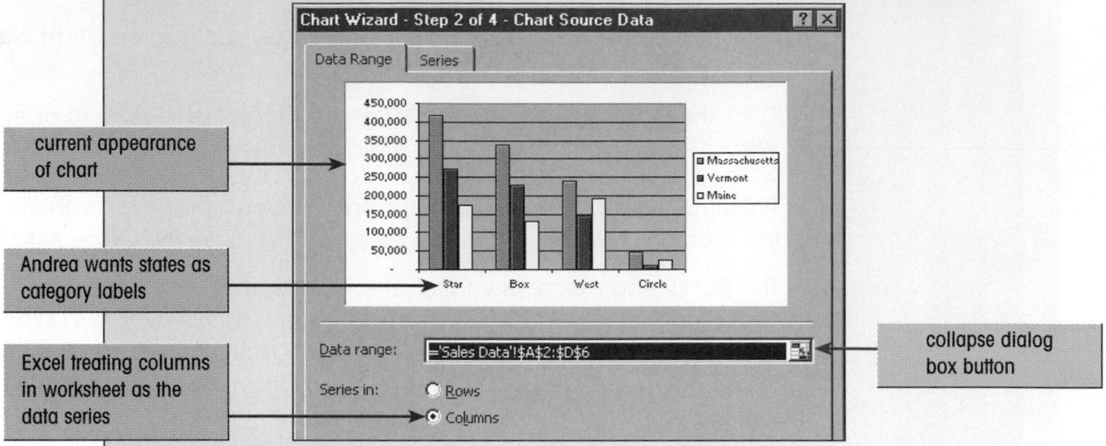

5. Make sure the Data range text box shows "='Sales Data'!$A$2:$D$6." This dialog box provides a preview of your chart.

TROUBLE? If the range shown on your screen is not ='Sales Data'!$A$2:$D$6, type the necessary corrections in the Data range text box, or click the Collapse dialog box button to the right of the Data range text box and select the correct range in the worksheet.

In Step 2 of the Chart Wizard, you can also modify how the data series is organized—by rows or by columns—using the **Series in** option. In Figure 4-8, the chart uses the columns in the worksheet as the data series. To see how the chart would look if the rows in the worksheet were used as the data series, you can modify the settings in this dialog box.

Does the sample chart shown on your screen and in Figure 4-8 look like the sketch Andrea prepared (Figure 4-5)? Not exactly. The problem is that the Chart Wizard assumes that if the range to plot has more rows than columns (which is true in this case), then the data in the columns (states) becomes the data series. Andrea wants the stove models (rows) as the data series, so you need to make this change in the dialog box.

To change the data series and continue the steps in the Chart Wizard:

1. Click the **Rows** option button in the Series in area of the dialog box. The sample chart now shows the stove models as the data series and the states as category labels. See Figure 4-9.

Figure 4-9 ROWS AS DATA SERIES

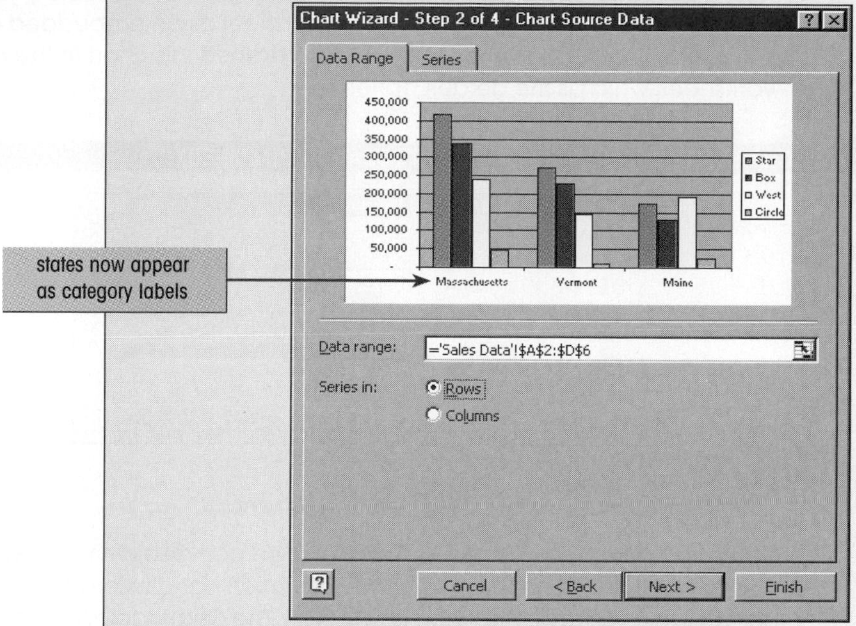

2. Click the **Next** button to open the Chart Wizard - Step 3 of 4 - Chart Options dialog box. See Figure 4-10. A preview area displays the current appearance of the chart. This tabbed dialog box enables you to change various chart options, such as titles, axes, gridlines, legends, data labels, and data tables. As you change these settings, check the preview chart in this dialog box to make sure you get the look you want.

Now add a title for the chart.

Figure 4-10 CHART WIZARD - STEP 3 OF 4 - CHART OPTIONS DIALOG BOX

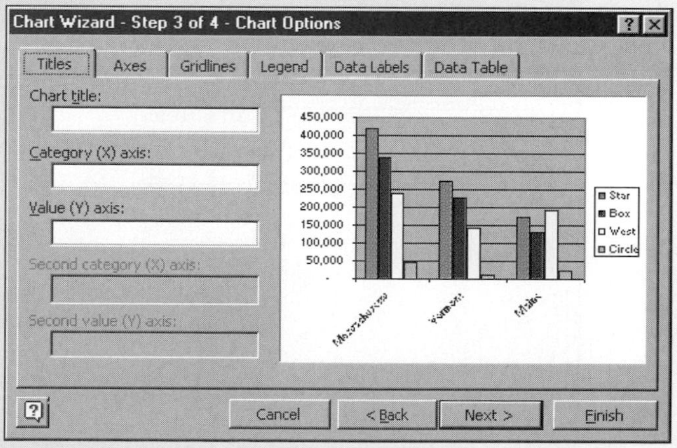

3. If necessary click the **Titles** tab, click the **Chart title** text box, and then type **Sales by State** for the chart title. Notice that the title appears in the preview area.

4. Click the **Next** button to display the Chart Wizard - Step 4 of 4 - Chart Location dialog box. See Figure 4-11. In this fourth dialog box, you decide where to place the chart. You can place a chart in a worksheet as an embedded chart, or place it in its own chart sheet. You want to embed this chart in the Sales Data worksheet, which is the default option.

Figure 4-11 CHART WIZARD - STEP 4 OF 4 - CHART LOCATION DIALOG BOX

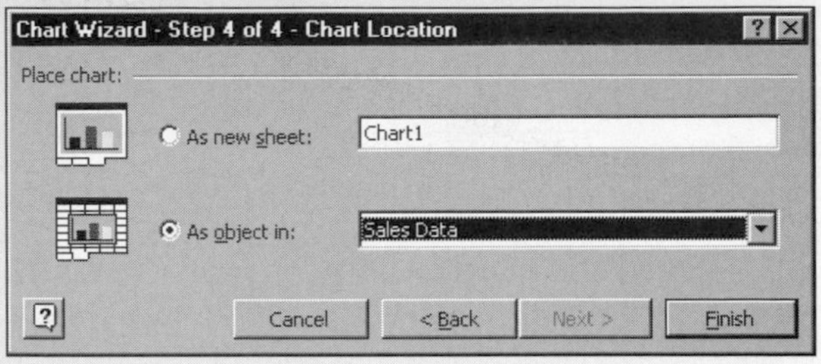

You have finished the steps in the Chart Wizard.

5. Click the **Finish** button to complete the chart and display it in the Sales Data worksheet. See Figure 4-12. Notice the selection handles around the chart; these handles indicate that the chart is selected. The Chart toolbar automatically appears when the chart is selected. Figure 4-13 describes each button on the chart toolbar. Also, notice that the data and labels for the chart are outlined in blue, green, and purple in the worksheet. This enables you to quickly see which cells make up the chart.

TROUBLE? If you don't see the Chart toolbar, click View on the menu bar, click Toolbars, and then click the Chart check box to select that option.

Figure 4-12 COMPLETED COLUMN CHART

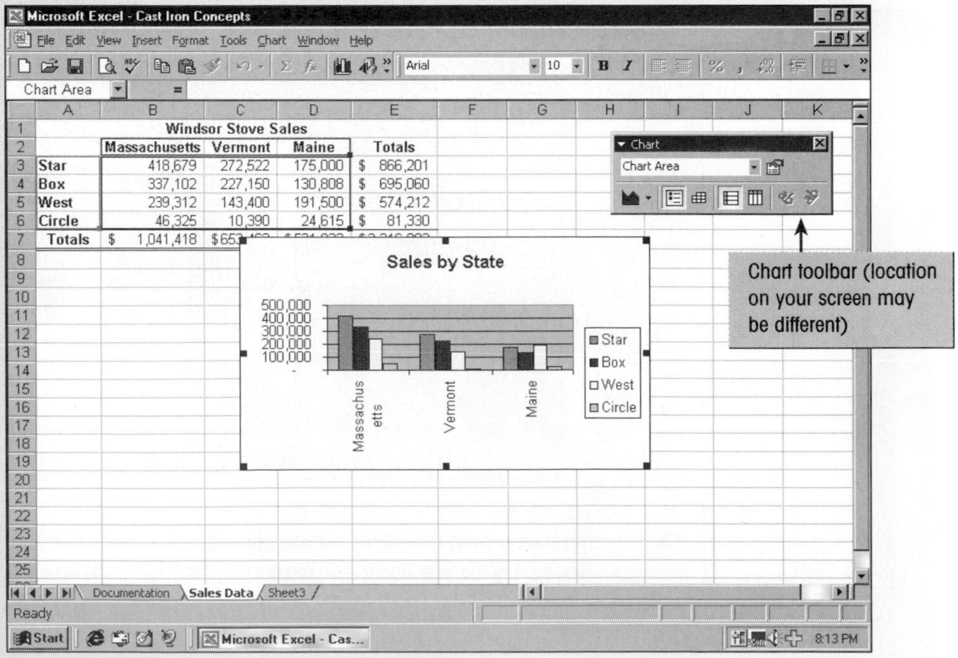

Figure 4-13 DESCRIPTION OF CHART TOOLBAR ELEMENTS

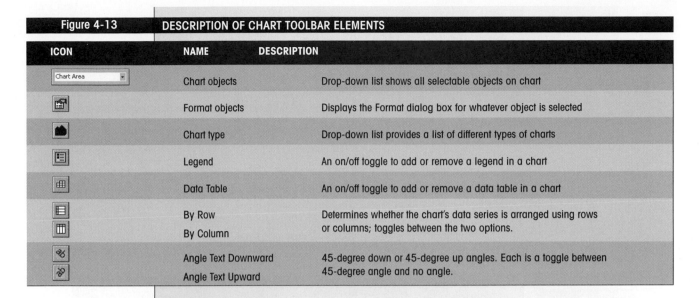

ICON	NAME	DESCRIPTION
Chart Area	Chart objects	Drop-down list shows all selectable objects on chart
	Format objects	Displays the Format dialog box for whatever object is selected
	Chart type	Drop-down list provides a list of different types of charts
	Legend	An on/off toggle to add or remove a legend in a chart
	Data Table	An on/off toggle to add or remove a data table in a chart
	By Row By Column	Determines whether the chart's data series is arranged using rows or columns; toggles between the two options.
	Angle Text Downward Angle Text Upward	45-degree down or 45-degree up angles. Each is a toggle between 45-degree angle and no angle.

6. Click anywhere outside the chart to deselect it. Notice that the selection handles no longer surround the chart, indicating that the chart is no longer selected, and the Chart toolbar is no longer visible. The Chart toolbar only appears when the chart is selected.

After reviewing the column chart, you think that the area outlined for the chart is too small to highlight the comparison between models. You also note that you need to move the chart so that it does not cover the worksheet data.

Moving and Resizing a Chart

When you use the Chart Wizard to create an embedded chart, Excel displays the chart in the worksheet. The size of the chart may not be large enough to accentuate relationships between data points or display the labels correctly. Because a chart is an object, you can move, resize, or copy it like any object in the Windows environment. However, before you can move, resize, or copy a chart, you must select, or **activate** it. You select a chart by clicking anywhere within the chart area. Small black squares, called **selection handles** or **sizing handles**, appear on the boundaries of the chart, indicating that it is selected. You will also notice that some of the items on the menu bar change to enable you to modify the chart instead of the worksheet.

You decide to move and resize the chart before showing it to Andrea.

To change the size and position of the chart:

1. Click anywhere within the white area of the chart border to select the chart. Selection handles appear on the chart border.

TROUBLE? If the Name box does not display the name "Chart Area," click the Chart Objects list box arrow on the Chart toolbar to display the list of chart objects. Select Chart Area.

TROUBLE? If the Chart toolbar is in the way, click and drag it to the bottom of the window to anchor it there.

2. Position the pointer anywhere on the chart border. Click and hold down the mouse button (the pointer changes to ✥) as you drag the chart down and to the left until you see the upper-left corner of the dashed outline in column A of row 8. Release the mouse button to view the chart in its new position.

   Now increase the height and width of the chart.

3. Position the pointer on the bottom, right selection handle. When the pointer changes to ↘, hold down the mouse button (note the pointer now changes to +) and drag the selection handle downward to the right until the chart outline reaches the right edge of column H and row 23. Release the mouse button to view the resized chart. See Figure 4-14.

Figure 4-14 **CHART AFTER BEING MOVED AND RESIZED**

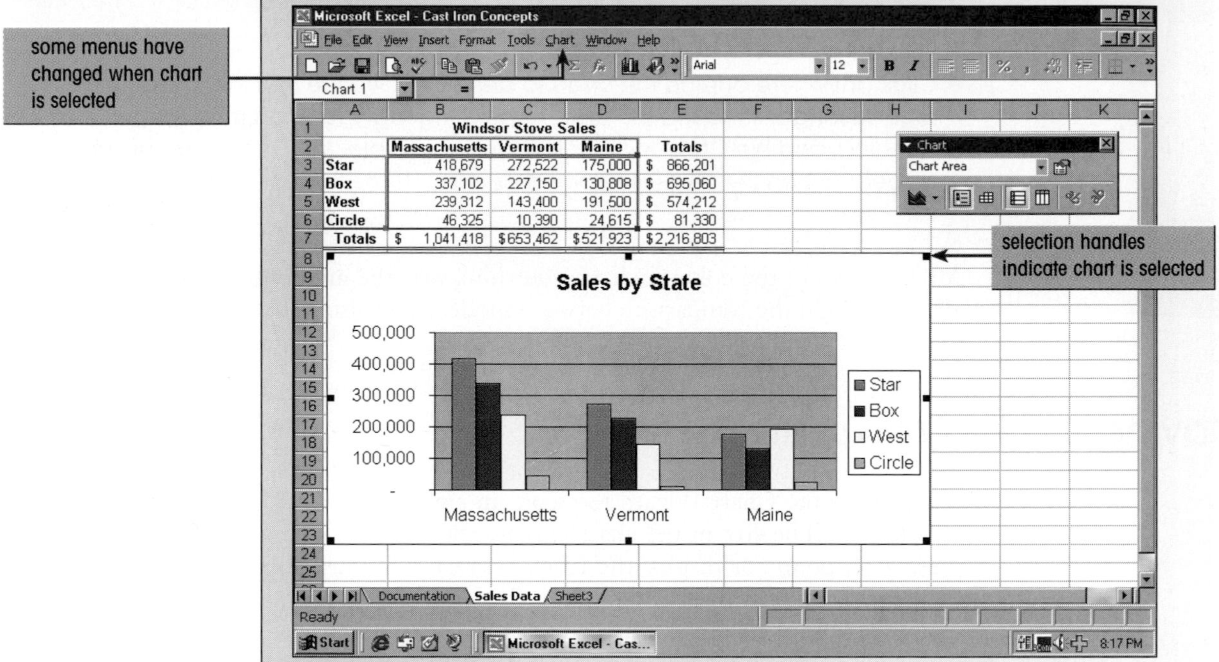

4. Click anywhere outside the chart border to deselect the chart. Notice that some of the menus on the menu bar change because the chart is no longer active.

The chart is repositioned and resized. You show Andrea the chart embedded in her Sales Data worksheet. As she reviews the chart, Andrea notices an error in the value entered for West Windsor stoves sold in Maine.

Updating a Chart

Every chart you create is linked to the worksheet data. As a result, if you change the data in a worksheet, Excel automatically updates the chart to reflect the new values. Andrea noticed that sales of West Windsor in Maine were entered incorrectly. She accidentally entered sales as 191,500, when the correct entry should have been 119,500. Correct this data entry error and observe how it changes the column chart.

To change the worksheet data and observe changes to the column chart:

1. Observe the height of the data marker for the West model in Maine (yellow data marker) in the column chart.
2. Click cell **D5**, type **119500**, and then press the **Enter** key. See Figure 4-15. The total West sales (cell E5) and total sales for Maine (cell D7) automatically change. In addition, Excel automatically updates the chart to reflect the new source value. Now the data marker for the West Windsor sales in Maine is shorter.

Figure 4-15 MODIFIED COLUMN CHART AFTER CHART'S SOURCE DATA CHANGED

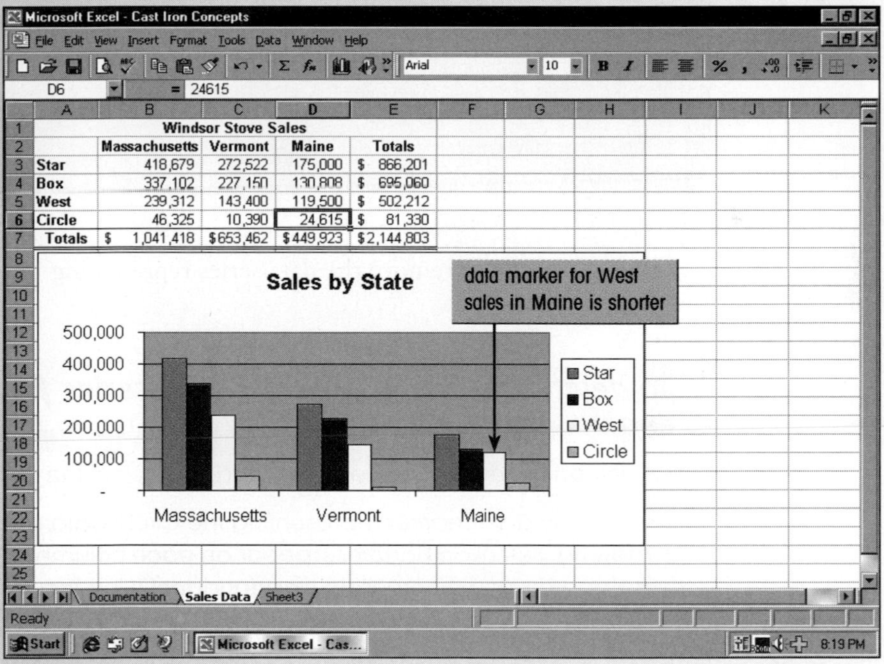

Now that the data for the West stove sales in Maine is corrected, you review the chart with Andrea for ways you can improve the presentation of the chart data.

Modifying an Excel Chart

You can make many modifications to a chart, including changing the type of chart, the text, the labels, the gridlines, and the titles. To make these modifications, you need to activate the chart. Selecting, or activating, a chart, as mentioned earlier, allows you to move and resize it. It also gives you access to the Chart commands on the menu bar and displays the Chart toolbar to use as you alter the chart.

After reviewing the column chart, Andrea believes that the Circle Windsor will distract the audience from the three products that were actually available during the entire period. Recall that the Circle Windsor was only on the market for four months and even then there were production problems. She wants to compare sales only for the three models sold during the entire year.

Revising the Chart Data Series

After you create a chart, you might discover that you specified the wrong data range, or you might decide that your chart should display a different data series. Whatever your reason, you do not need to start over in order to revise the chart's data series.

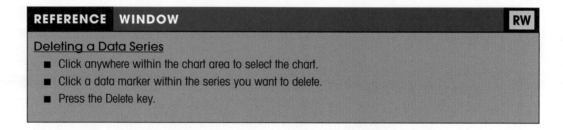

REFERENCE WINDOW RW

Deleting a Data Series

- Click anywhere within the chart area to select the chart.
- Click a data marker within the series you want to delete.
- Press the Delete key.

Andrea asks you to remove the data series representing the Circle Windsor model from the column chart.

To delete the Circle Windsor data series from the column chart:

1. Click anywhere within the chart border to select the chart.
2. Click any data marker representing the Circle data series (any light blue data marker). Selection handles appear on each column of the Circle Windsor data series and a ScreenTip appears identifying the selected chart item. See Figure 4-16.

Figure 4-16 CHART WITH CIRCLE DATA SERIES SELECTED

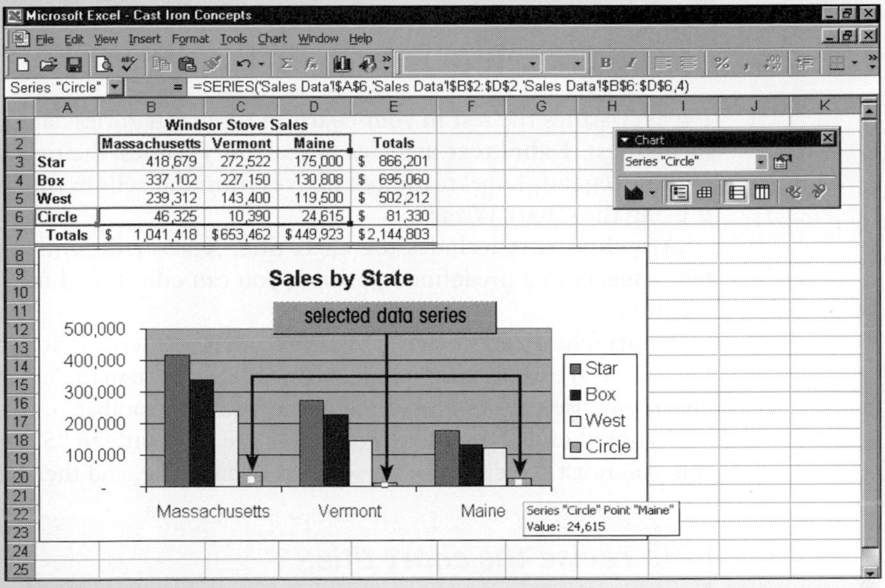

3. Press the **Delete** key. See Figure 4-17. Notice that the Circle Windsor data series disappears from the chart.

Figure 4-17 COLUMN CHART AFTER DATA SERIES REMOVED

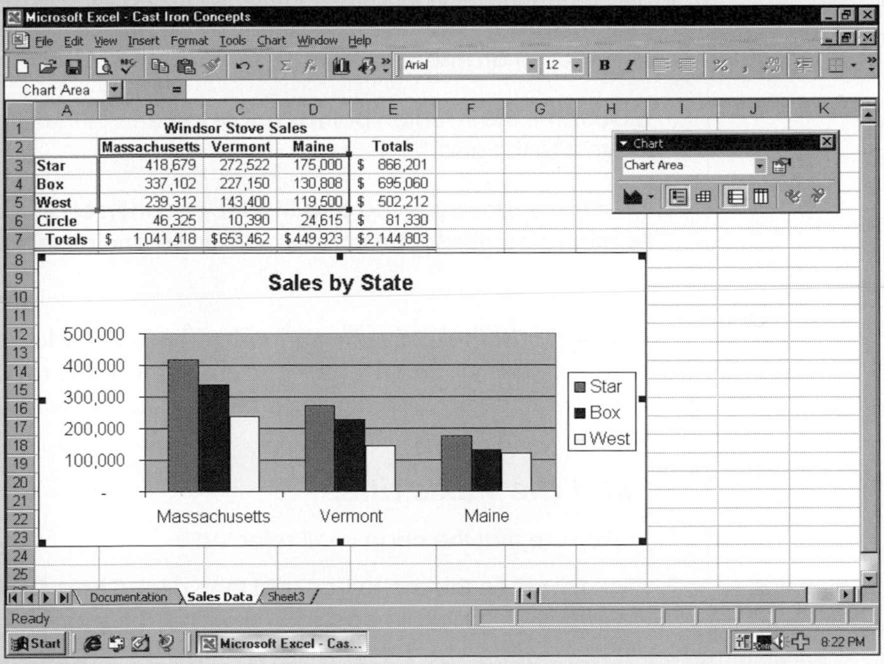

TROUBLE? If you deleted the wrong data series, click the Undo button and then repeat Steps 2 and 3.

Andrea reviews her sketch and notices that the chart title is incomplete; the intended title was "Sales by State and Model." She asks you to make this change to the chart.

Editing Chart Text

Excel classifies the text in your charts in three categories: label text, attached text, and unattached text. **Label text** includes the category names, the tick mark labels, the X-axis labels, and the legend. Label text often derives from the cells in the worksheet; you usually specify it using the Chart Wizard.

Attached text includes the chart title, X-axis title, and Y-axis title. Although attached text appears in a predefined position, you can edit it, and move it using the click-and-drag technique.

Unattached text includes text boxes or comments that you type in the chart after it is created. You can position unattached text anywhere in the chart. To add unattached text to a chart, you use the Text Box tool on the Drawing toolbar.

As noted earlier, you need to change the chart title to "Sales by State and Model." To do this you must select the chart, select the chart title, and then add "and Model" to the title.

To revise the chart title:

1. If the chart is not selected, click the **chart** to select it.
2. Click the **Chart Title** object to select it. Notice that the object name Chart Title appears in the Name box and as a ScreenTip; also, selection handles surround the Chart Title object.
3. Position the pointer in the Chart Title text box at the end of the title, and then click to remove the selection handles from the Chart Title object. The pointer changes to an insertion point I.

   TROUBLE? If the insertion point is not at the end of the title, press the End key to move it to the end.
4. Press the **spacebar**, type **and Model**, and then click anywhere within the chart border to complete the change in the title and deselect it.

Checking Andrea's sketch, you notice that the Y-axis title was not included. To help clarify what the data values in the chart represent, you decide to add "Sales ($U.S.)" as a Y-axis title. You use the Chart Option command on the Chart menu to add this title.

To add the Y-axis title:

1. Make sure that the chart is still selected.
2. Click **Chart** on the menu bar, and then click **Chart Options** to open the Chart Options dialog box. If necessary, click the **Titles** tab.
3. Click the **Value (Y) axis** text box, and then type **Sales ($U.S.)**.
4. Click the **OK** button to close the Chart Options dialog box.
5. Click anywhere within the chart border to deselect the Y-axis title. See Figure 4-18.

Figure 4-18 CHART AFTER TITLE MODIFIED AND VALUE AXIS LABEL INSERTED

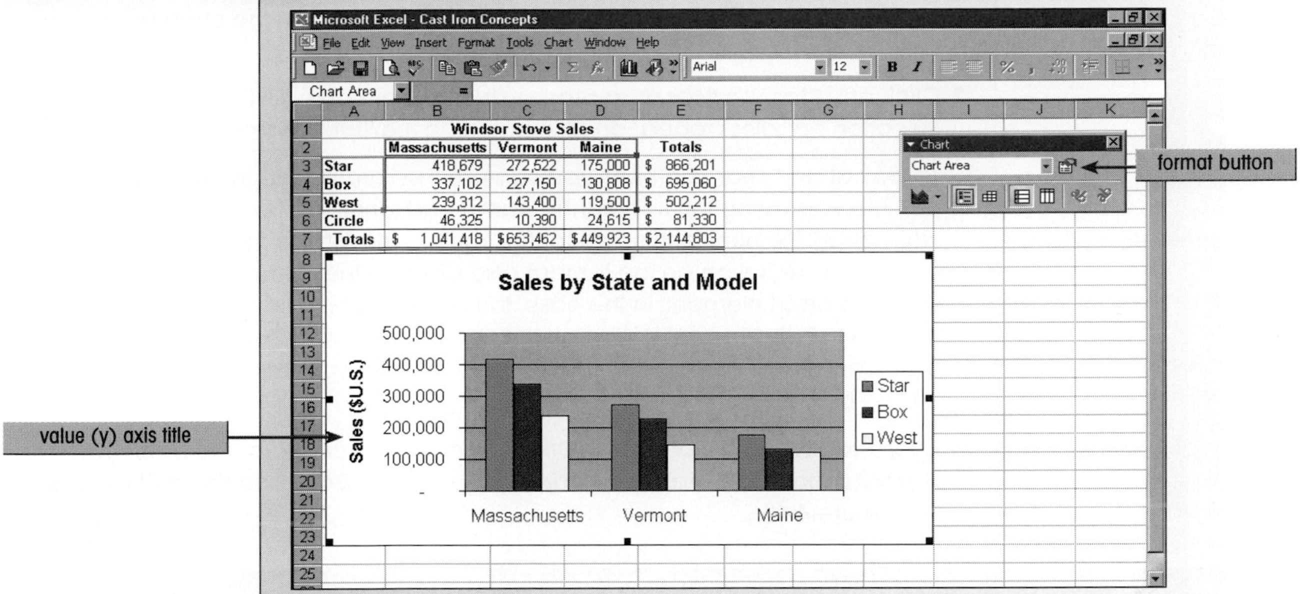

Now that the titles accurately describe the chart data, Andrea asks you to add data labels to show the exact values of the Star Windsor data series—CIC's leading model.

Adding Data Labels

A data label provides additional information about a data marker. Depending on the type of chart, data labels can show values, names of data series (or categories), or percentages. You can apply a label to a single data point, an entire data series, or all data markers in a chart.

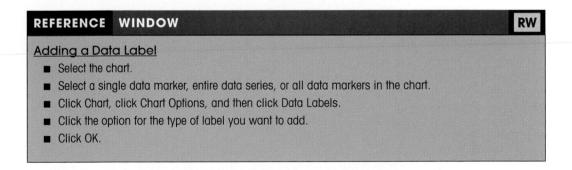

REFERENCE WINDOW **RW**

Adding a Data Label

- Select the chart.
- Select a single data marker, entire data series, or all data markers in the chart.
- Click Chart, click Chart Options, and then click Data Labels.
- Click the option for the type of label you want to add.
- Click OK.

In this case, Andrea wants to add data labels to the Star model data series.

To apply data labels to a data series:

1. If the column chart is not selected, click anywhere within the chart border to select it.
2. Click any **Star Windsor** data marker (blue data marker) within the chart. Selection handles appear on all columns in the Star Windsor data series.

   To format any chart element, you can use the Format button on the Chart toolbar. The Format button's ScreenTip name and function change depending on what chart element is selected for formatting. The list box that appears to the left of the Format button on the toolbar also displays the name of the currently selected chart element. In this case, the Star Windsor data series marker is selected, so the Format button on the Chart toolbar appears as the Format Data Series button, and when selected, opens the Format Data Series dialog box.
3. Click the **Format Data Series** button on the Chart toolbar to open the Format Data Series dialog box, and then click the **Data Labels** tab if necessary. See Figure 4-19.

Figure 4-19 DATA LABELS TAB IN FORMAT DATA SERIES DIALOG BOX

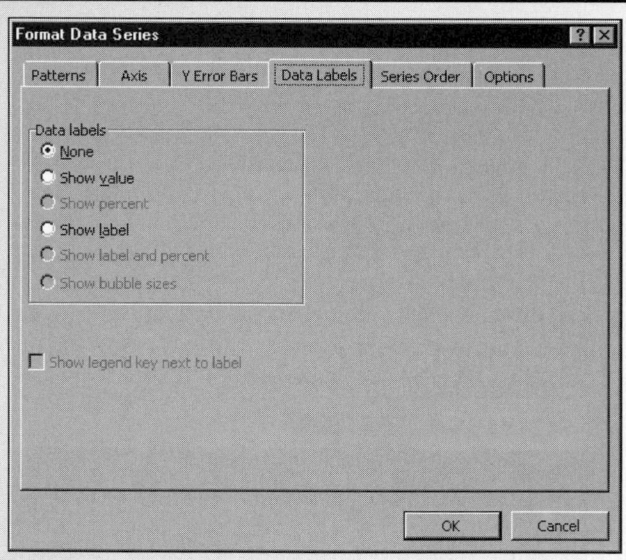

4. Click the **Show value** option button.
5. Click the **OK** button to display the column chart with data labels.
6. Click anywhere within the chart border to deselect the Star Windsor data series. See Figure 4-20.

Figure 4-20 CHART WITH DATA LABELS

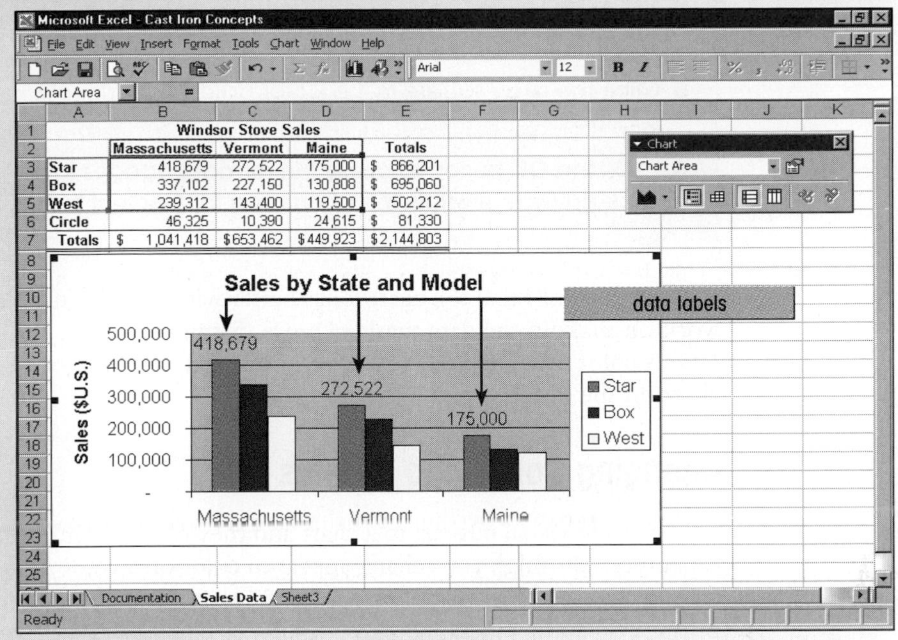

7. Save the worksheet.

Andrea is pleased with the changes in the chart. Now she wants to add visual interest to the chart, making it look more polished.

Enhancing the Appearance of the Chart

There are many ways to give charts a more professional look. The use of different font styles, types, and sizes can make chart labels and titles stand out. Using colors, borders, and patterns can also make a chart more interesting to view.

Andrea thinks that a border and some color could accentuate the title of the chart.

Emphasizing the Title with Border and Color

The chart title is an object that you can select and format using the menu options or the toolbar buttons. Now make the changes to the chart title.

To display the title with border and color:

1. Click the **Chart Title** to select it and display selection handles. Now that the chart title is selected, notice that the Format button on the Chart toolbar becomes the Format Chart Title button, and the Chart Objects list box displays "Chart Title."
2. Click the **Format Chart Title** button on the Chart toolbar to open the Format Chart Title dialog box, and then, if necessary, click the **Patterns** tab.

3. Click the **Weight** list arrow in the Border section to display a list of border weights.
4. Click the **second line** in the list.
5. Click the **gray** square in the Color palette (fourth row, last column) in the Area section.
6. Click the **OK** button to apply the format changes to the chart title, and then click anywhere within the chart area to deselect the title.

Andrea thinks that the chart looks better with its title emphasized. Now she wants you to work on making the data markers more distinctive. They certainly stand out on her computer's color monitor, but she is concerned that this will not be the case when she prints the chart on the office's black and white printer.

Changing Colors and Patterns

Patterns add visual interest to a chart and they can be useful when your printer has no color capability. Although your charts appear in color on a color monitor, if your printer does not have color capability, Excel translates colors to gray shades when printing. It's difficult to distinguish some colors, particularly darker ones, from one another when Excel translates them to gray shades and then prints them. To solve this potential problem, you can make your charts more readable by selecting a different pattern for each data marker.

To apply a different pattern to each data series you use the Patterns dialog box.

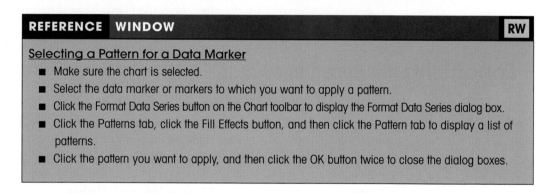

REFERENCE WINDOW RW

Selecting a Pattern for a Data Marker

- Make sure the chart is selected.
- Select the data marker or markers to which you want to apply a pattern.
- Click the Format Data Series button on the Chart toolbar to display the Format Data Series dialog box.
- Click the Patterns tab, click the Fill Effects button, and then click the Pattern tab to display a list of patterns.
- Click the pattern you want to apply, and then click the OK button twice to close the dialog boxes.

You want to apply a different pattern to each data series.

To apply a pattern to a data series:

1. Make sure the chart is selected.
2. Click any **data marker** for the Star data series (blue data marker) to display selection handles for all three data markers for that data series.
3. Click the **Format Data Series** button on the Chart toolbar to open the Format Data Series dialog box.

4. If necessary, click the **Patterns** tab, click the **Fill Effects** button to open the Fill Effects dialog box, and then click the **Pattern** tab to display the Pattern palette. See Figure 4-21.

Figure 4-21 PATTERN OPTIONS IN FILL EFFECTS DIALOG BOX

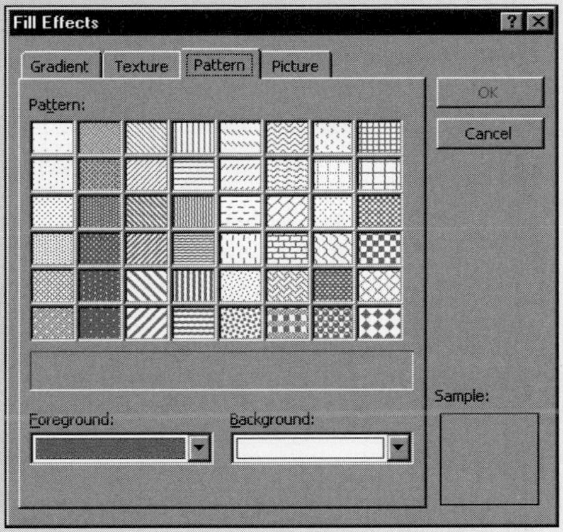

5. Click the **dark downward diagonal** pattern (third row, third column) to select it. Notice that the pattern you selected appears in the Sample box for you to preview.

6. Click the **OK** button to close the Fill Effects dialog box, and then click the **OK** button to close the Format Data Series dialog box and apply the pattern to the Star data series in the chart.

7. Repeat Steps 2 through 6 to select a **narrow horizontal** pattern (fourth row, fourth column) for the Box data series, and again to select a **dark upward diagonal** pattern (fourth row, third column) for the West data series. After you select patterns for the data series, your chart should look like Figure 4-22.

Figure 4-22 **PATTERN COLUMN CHART DATA MARKERS**

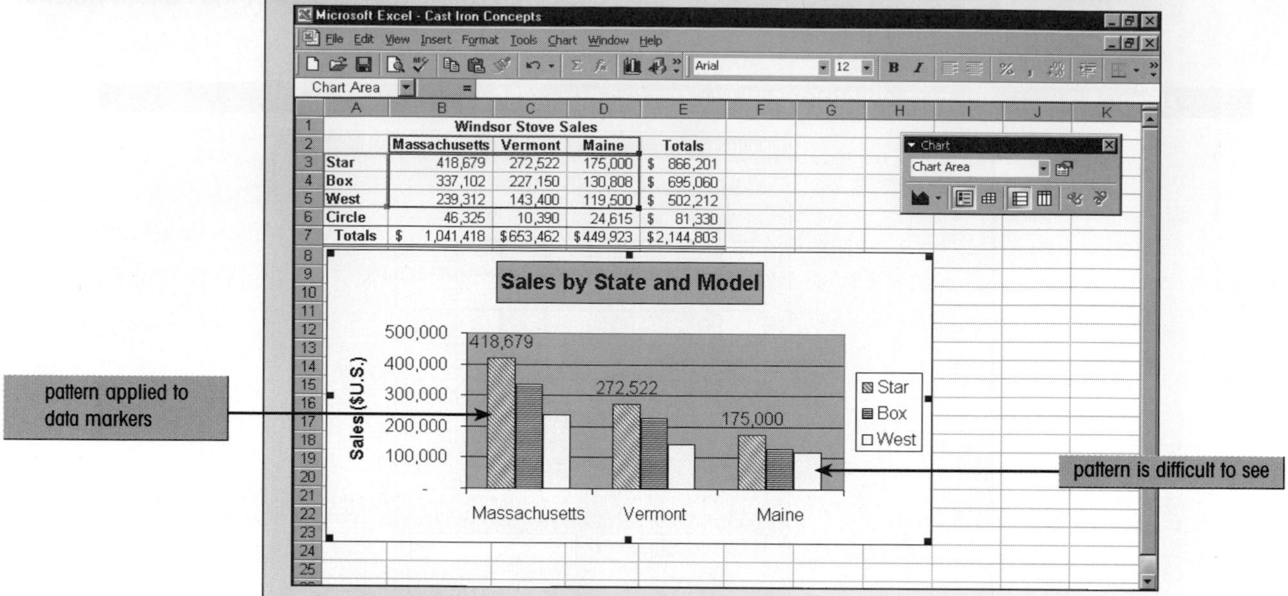

You notice that the West markers appear to have no pattern applied because the pattern is very difficult to see when applied against the yellow color. You decide to change the color of the West markers to a darker color—green, so the pattern will be more visible.

Instead of changing the color using the Chart toolbar or the Chart menu on the menu bar, you'll use Excel's shortcut menu. Many elements within a chart have a shortcut menu providing context-sensitive commands. To use the shortcut menu, right-click on the chart element and choose a command.

To change the color of data markers:

1. Position the mouse pointer over any West data marker and right-click the mouse button. A shortcut menu appears.
2. Click **Format Data Series** to open the Format Data Series dialog box.
3. If necessary, click the **Patterns** tab, click the **Fill Effects** button, and then click the **Pattern** tab in the Fill Effects dialog box to display the patterns palette.
4. In the Pattern tab, click the **Background** list arrow to display a color palette. Click the **green** square in the third row, third column, and then click the **OK** button to close the Fill Effects dialog box and return to the Format Data Series dialog box.
5. Click the **OK** button to close the Format Data Series dialog box, and then click anywhere outside the chart border to deselect the chart.

You show the chart to Andrea, and she decides that it is ready to be printed and duplicated for distribution at the meeting.

Previewing and Printing the Chart

Before you print you should preview the worksheet to see how it will appear on the printed page. Remember that Andrea wants the embedded chart and the worksheet data to print on one page that she can use as a handout at the meeting.

To save and print an embedded chart:

1. Click the **Save** button on the Standard toolbar to save the workbook.
2. Click the **Print Preview** button on the Standard toolbar to display the Print Preview window.
3. Add your name in the custom footer.
4. Click the **Print** button to open the Print dialog box, and then click the **OK** button. See Figure 4-23.

Figure 4-23 PRINTOUT OF WORKSHEET WITH EMBEDDED COLUMN CHART

Sales Data

Windsor Stove Sales

	Massachusetts	Vermont	Maine	Totals
Star	418,679	272,522	175,000	$ 866,201
Box	337,102	227,150	130,808	$ 695,060
West	239,312	143,400	119,500	$ 502,212
Circle	46,325	10,390	24,615	$ 81,330
Totals	$ 1,041,418	$653,462	$449,923	$2,144,803

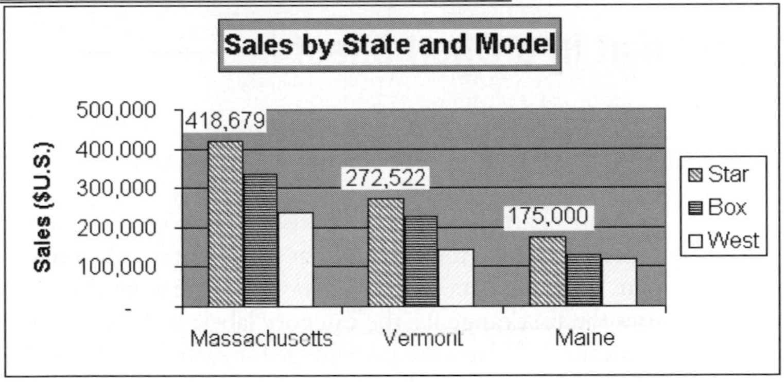

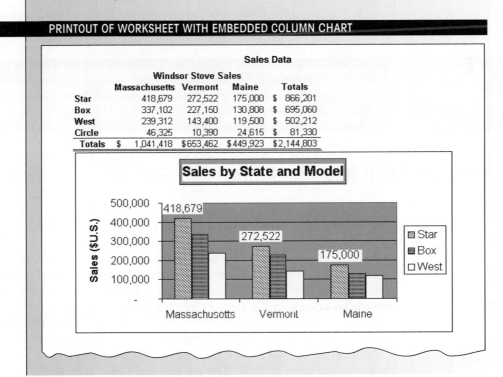

You have finished creating the column chart showing stove sales by state and model for Andrea. Next, you need to create the pie chart showing percentage of total stove sales by model. You will do this in Session 4.2.

Session 4.1 QUICK CHECK

1. A column chart is used to show ____________.
2. Explain the difference between a data point and a data marker.
3. What is the purpose of a legend?
4. Describe the action you're likely to take before beginning Step 1 of the Chart Wizard.
5. When you click an embedded chart, it is ____________.
6. How do you move an embedded chart to a new location using the mouse?
7. What happens when you change a value in a worksheet that is the source of data for a chart?
8. Explain how to revise a chart's data series.
9. Explain the difference between an embedded chart and a chart.

SESSION 4.2

In this session you will create a pie chart. You will also learn how to select nonadjacent ranges, how to change a two-dimensional pie chart to a three-dimensional pie chart, and how to "explode" a slice from a pie chart. You will also learn how to use chart sheets and how to add a border to a chart.

Creating a Chart in a Chart Sheet

Now Andrea wants to show the contribution of each Windsor model to the total stove sales. Recall from the planning sketch she did (Figure 4-5) that she wants to use a pie chart to show this relationship.

A pie chart shows the relationship, or proportions, of parts to a whole. The size of each slice is determined by the value of that data point in relation to the total of all values. A pie chart contains only one data series. When you create a pie chart, you generally specify two ranges. Excel uses the first range for the category labels and the second range for the data series. Excel automatically calculates the percentage for each slice, draws the slice to reflect the percentage of the whole, and gives you the option of displaying the percentage as a label in the completed chart.

Andrea's sketch (see Figure 4-5) shows estimates of each stove's contribution and how she wants the pie chart to look. The pie chart will have four slices, one for each stove model. She wants each slice labeled with the stove model's name and its percentage of total sales. Because she doesn't know the exact percentages until Excel calculates and displays them in the chart, she put "__%" on her sketch to show where she wants the percentages to appear.

Creating a Pie Chart

You begin creating a pie chart by selecting the data to be represented from the worksheet. You refer to your worksheet and note in the sketch that the data labels for the pie slices are in cells A3 through A6 and the data points representing the pie slices are in cells E3 through E6. You must select these two ranges to tell the Chart Wizard the data that you want to chart, but you realize that these ranges are not located next to each other in the worksheet. You know how to select a series of adjacent cells; now you need to learn how to select two separate ranges at once.

Selecting Nonadjacent Ranges

A nonadjacent range is a group of individual cells or ranges that are not next to each other. Selecting nonadjacent ranges is particularly useful when you construct charts because the cells that contain the data series and those that contain the data labels are often not side by side in the worksheet. When you select nonadjacent ranges, the selected cells in each range are highlighted. You can then format the cells, clear them, or use them to construct a chart.

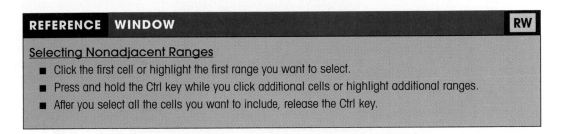

REFERENCE WINDOW RW

Selecting Nonadjacent Ranges

- Click the first cell or highlight the first range you want to select.
- Press and hold the Ctrl key while you click additional cells or highlight additional ranges.
- After you select all the cells you want to include, release the Ctrl key.

Now select the nonadjacent ranges to be used to create the pie chart.

To select range A3:A6 and range E3:E6 in the Sales Data sheet:

1. If you took a break after the last session, make sure that Excel is running, the Cast Iron Concepts workbook is open, and the Sales Data worksheet is open.
2. Click anywhere outside the chart border to make sure the chart is not activated. Press **Ctrl + Home** to make cell A1 the active cell.
3. Select cells **A3** through **A6**, and then release the mouse button.
4. Press and hold the **Ctrl** key while you select cells **E3** through **E6,** and then release the mouse and the Ctrl key. The two nonadjacent ranges are now selected: A3:A6 and E3:E6. See Figure 4-24.

   TROUBLE? If you didn't select the cells you want on your first try, click any cell to remove the highlighting, then go back to Step 2 and try again.

Figure 4-24 SELECTING NONADJACENT CELL RANGES

nonadjacent ranges selected

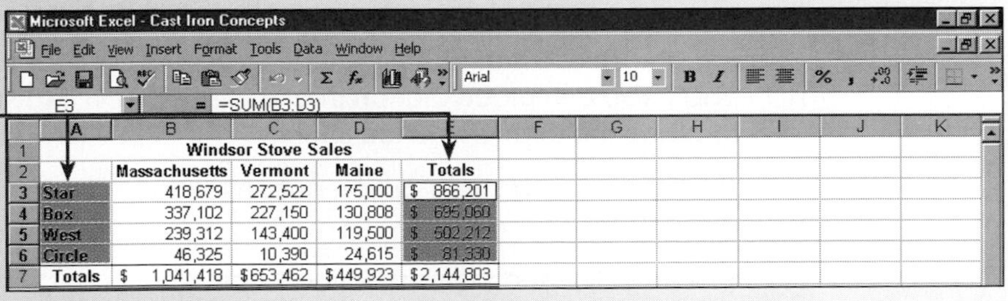

	A	B	C	D	E
1		Windsor Stove Sales			
2		Massachusetts	Vermont	Maine	Totals
3	Star	418,679	272,522	175,000	$ 866,201
4	Box	337,102	227,150	130,808	$ 695,060
5	West	239,312	143,400	119,500	$ 502,212
6	Circle	46,325	10,390	24,615	$ 81,330
7	Totals	$ 1,041,418	$653,462	$449,923	$2,144,803

This time you'll place your new chart in a chart sheet, a special sheet that contains only one chart. It does not have the rows and columns of a regular worksheet. If you have many charts to create, you may want to place each chart in a separate chart sheet to avoid cluttering the worksheet. This approach also makes it easier to locate a particular chart because you can change the name on the chart sheet tab.

To create a pie chart in a chart sheet:

1. Click the **Chart Wizard** button on the Standard toolbar to open the Chart Wizard - Step 1 of 4 - Chart Type dialog box.

   TROUBLE? If the Office Assistant appears on your screen, click the button next to the message "No, don't provide help now" to close the Office Assistant.

   You want to create a pie chart.

2. Click the **Pie** chart type to select it. Six Pie chart subtypes appear. The Two-dimensional Pie chart subtype is the default subtype for the Pie chart type. Click the **Press and hold to view sample** button to display a preview of the Pie chart type.

   You decide to use the default chart subtype.

3. Click the **Next** button to open the Chart Wizard - Step 2 of 4 - Chart Source Data dialog box. Make sure the Data range text box displays "='SalesData'!$A$3:$A$6, 'Sales Data'!$E$3:$E$6." This dialog box also displays a preview of your chart.

   TROUBLE? If the range shown on your screen is not "='Sales Data'!$A$3:$A$6, 'Sales Data'!$E$3:$E$6," type the necessary corrections in the Data range text box, or click the Collapse Dialog button located to the right of the Data range text box, and then select the correct range in the worksheet.

4. Click the **Next** button to open the Chart Wizard - Step 3 of 4 - Chart Options dialog box.

   Add a title for the chart.

5. If necessary, click the **Titles** tab, click the **Chart title** text box, and then type **Sales by Model** for the chart title. Notice that the title appears in the preview area.

6. Click the **Data Labels** tab, and then click the **Show label and percent** option button to place the label and percentage next to each slice.

   Now remove the legend because it is no longer needed.

7. Click the **Legend** tab, and then click the **Show legend** check box to remove the check and deselect that option.

8. Click the **Next** button to open the Chart Wizard - Step 4 of 4 - Chart Location dialog box. Recall that in the fourth dialog box you decide where to place the chart. You can place a chart in a worksheet or in its own chart sheet. You want to place this chart in a chart sheet.

9. Click the **As new sheet** option button to place the chart in the Chart1 chart sheet.

   You have finished the steps in the Chart Wizard.

10. Click the **Finish** button to complete the chart. The new chart, along with the Chart toolbar, appears in the chart sheet named Chart1. The chart sheet is inserted into the workbook before the worksheet on which it is based. See Figure 4-25.

Figure 4-25 PIE CHART IN A CHART SHEET

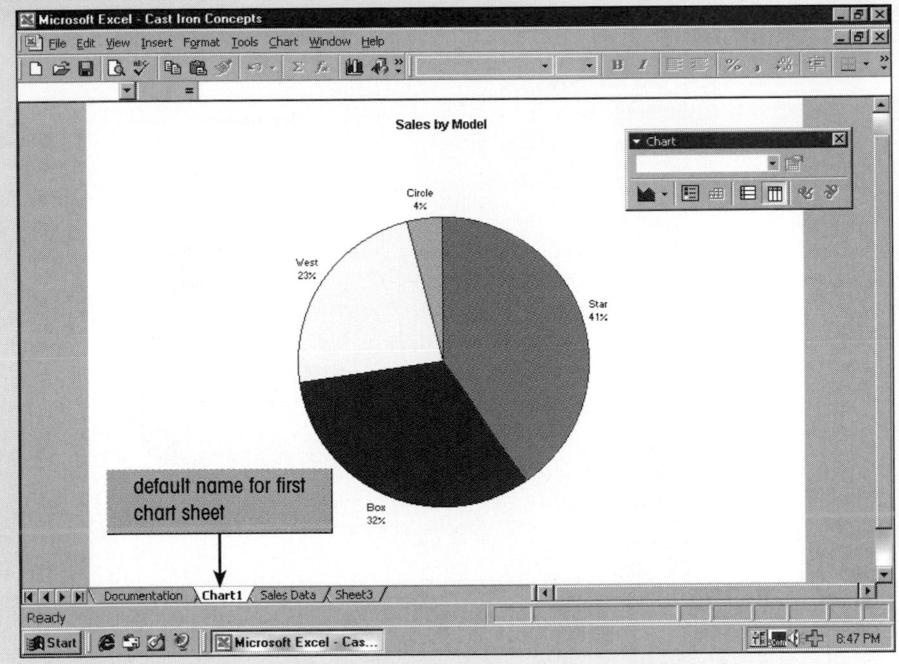

After reviewing the pie chart, Andrea asks you to change the current pie chart to a three-dimensional design to give the chart a more professional look.

Changing the Chart Type from Two-Dimensional to Three-Dimensional

As you recall, Excel provides 14 different chart types that you can choose from as you create a chart. You can also access these chart types after the chart is created and change from one type to another. To change the chart type, you can use the Chart Type command on the Chart menu or the Chart Type button on the Chart toolbar. You use the Chart toolbar to change this two-dimensional pie chart to a three-dimensional pie chart.

To change the pie chart to a three-dimensional pie chart:

1. Make sure the chart area is selected, and then click the **Chart Type** arrow on the Chart toolbar to display a palette of chart types. See Figure 4-26.

   TROUBLE? If the Chart toolbar does not appear on the screen, click View on the menu bar, point to Toolbars, and then click the Chart check box to display the Chart toolbar.

Figure 4-26 PALETTE OF CHART TYPES

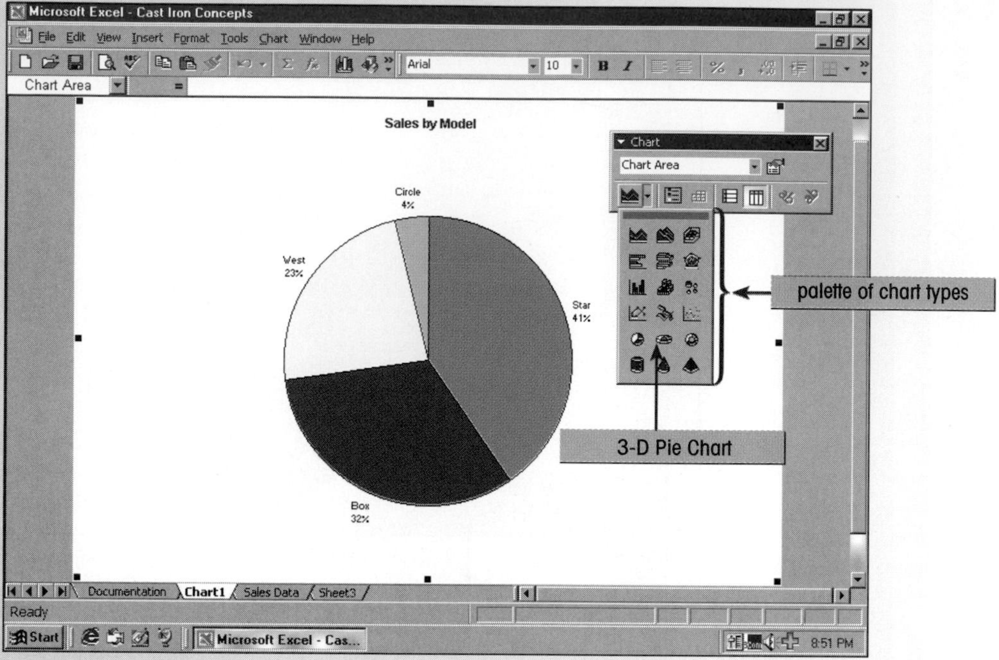

2. Click the **3-D Pie Chart** sample in the fifth row of the second column. The chart reappears as a three-dimensional pie chart. Notice that the Chart Type icon now reflects the new chart type. See Figure 4-27.

Figure 4-27 THREE-DIMENSIONAL PIE CHART

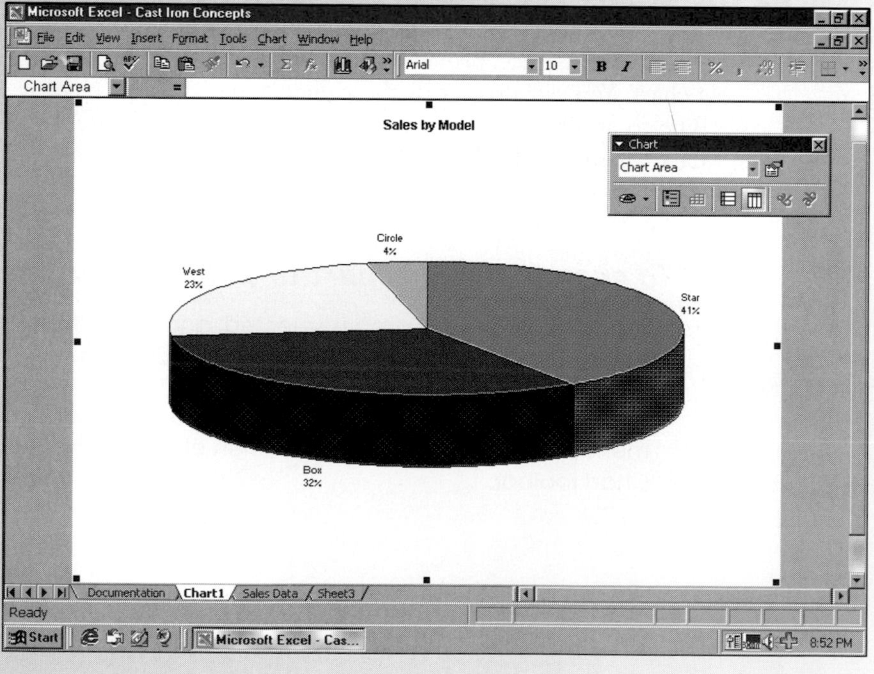

In her presentation, Andrea plans to emphasize the importance of the Star model because it is her best-selling model in the New England territory. She decides to "explode" the Star slice.

Exploding a Slice of a Pie Chart

When you create a pie chart, you may want to focus attention on a particular slice in the chart. You can present the data so a viewer can easily focus attention on one component, for example, which product sold the most. One method of emphasizing a particular slice over others is separating or "exploding" the slice from the rest of the pie. The *cut* slice is more distinct because it is not connected to the other slices. A pie chart with one or more slices separated from the whole is referred to as an exploded pie chart.

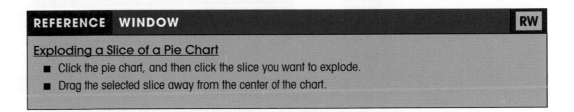

REFERENCE WINDOW RW

Exploding a Slice of a Pie Chart

- Click the pie chart, and then click the slice you want to explode.
- Drag the selected slice away from the center of the chart.

Andrea asks you to explode the slice that represents sales for the Star model.

To explode the slice that represents the Star model sales:

1. Click anywhere in the pie chart to select it. One selection handle appears on each pie slice and the Name box indicates that Series 1 is the selected chart object.
2. Now that you have selected the entire pie, you can select one part of it, the Star slice. Position the pointer over the slice that represents Star model sales. As you move the pointer over this slice, the ScreenTip "Series 1 Point: "Star" Value: $866,201 (41%)" appears. Click to select the slice. Selection handles now appear on only this slice.
3. With the pointer on the selected slice, click and hold down the mouse button while dragging the slice to the right, away from the center of the pie chart. As you drag the slice, an outline of the slice marks your progress.
4. Release the mouse button to leave the slice in the new position. See Figure 4-28.

Figure 4-28 PIE CHART WITH EXPLODED SLICE

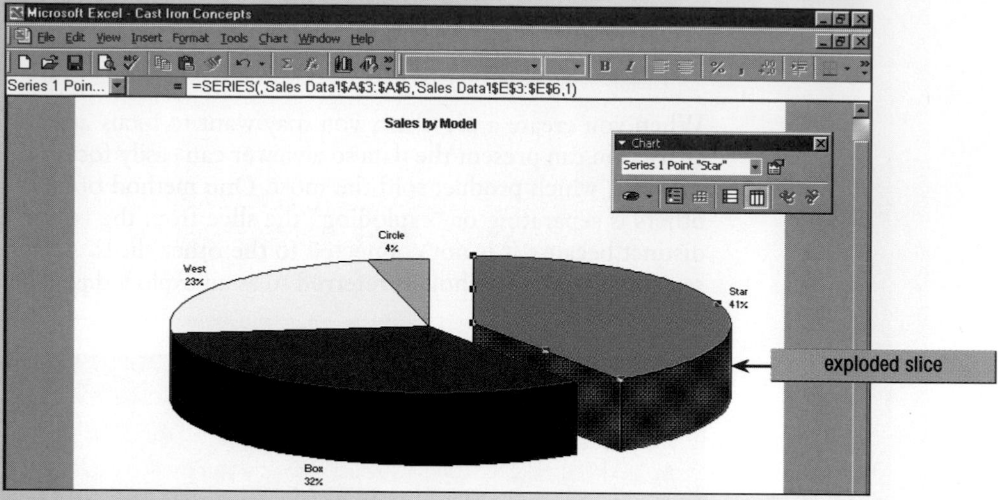

5. Click any white chart area of the pie chart to deselect the exploded slice.

The Star model now is exploded in the pie chart, but Andrea still isn't satisfied. You suggest moving the slice to the front of the pie.

Rotating a Three-Dimensional Chart

When working with a three-dimensional chart, you can modify the view of your chart to change its perspective, elevation, or rotation. You can change the elevation to look down on the chart or up from the bottom. You can also rotate the chart to adjust the placement of objects on the chart. Now rotate the chart so that the Star slice appears at the front of the chart.

To change the three-dimensional view of the chart:

1. Click **Chart** on the menu bar, and then click **3-D View** to open the 3-D View dialog box. See Figure 4-29.

Figure 4-29 3-D VIEW DIALOG BOX

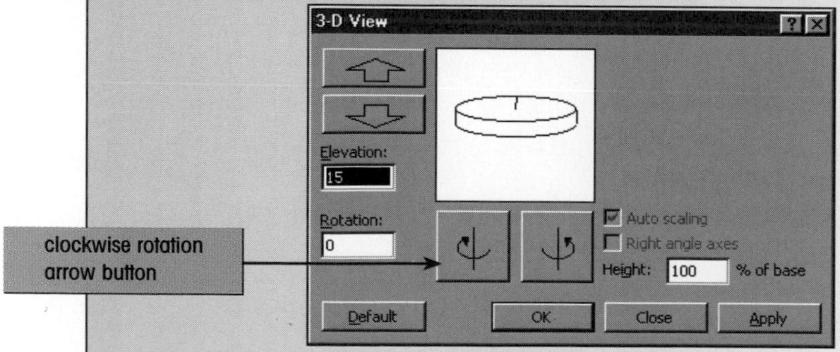

2. Click the **clockwise rotation arrow** button until the Rotation box shows **90**; as you do this, notice that the pie chart sketch in the dialog box rotates to show the new position.

3. Click the **OK** button to apply the changes.

4. Click anywhere in the white area of the chart. See Figure 4-30.

Figure 4-30 THREE-DIMENSIONAL PIE CHART AFTER VIEW ROTATED TO DISPLAY CUT SLICE

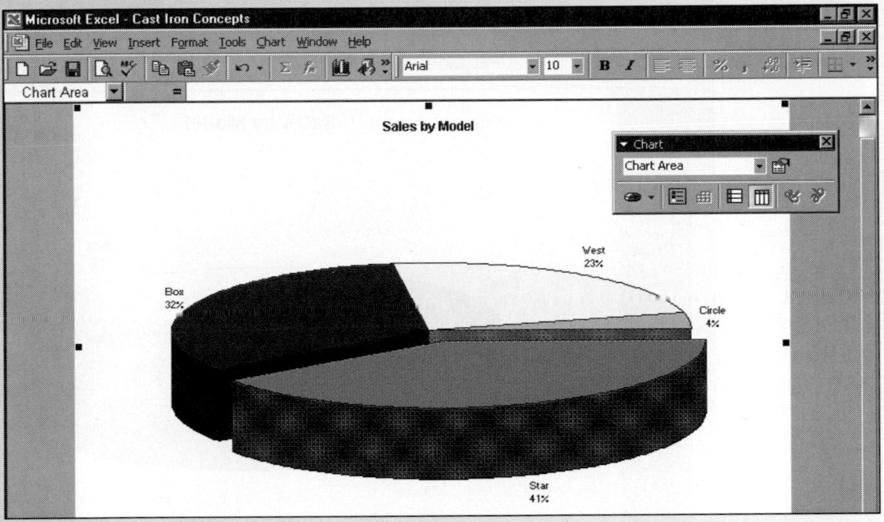

After looking over the chart, you decide to increase the size of the chart labels so that they are easier to read.

Formatting Chart Labels

You can change the font type, size, style, and the color of text in a chart using the Formatting toolbar buttons.

You look at the chart and decide that it will look better if you increase the size of the data labels from 10 to 14 points and apply a bold style to them.

To change the font size and style of the chart labels:

1. Click any one of the four data labels to select all the data labels. Selection handles appear around all four labels, and the Name box displays "Series 1 Data Labels."

2. Click the **Font Size** list arrow on the Formatting toolbar, and then click **14**.

3. Click the **Bold** button on the Formatting toolbar.

Now increase the font size of the title to 20 points.

To change the font size of the chart title:

1. Click the **chart title** to select it. Selection handles appear around the title.
2. Click the **Font Size** list arrow on the Formatting toolbar, and then click **20**.
3. Click any white area of the pie chart to deselect the title. See Figure 4-31.

Figure 4-31 THREE-DIMENSIONAL PIE CHART AFTER FONT SIZE OF DATA LABELS AND TITLE INCREASED

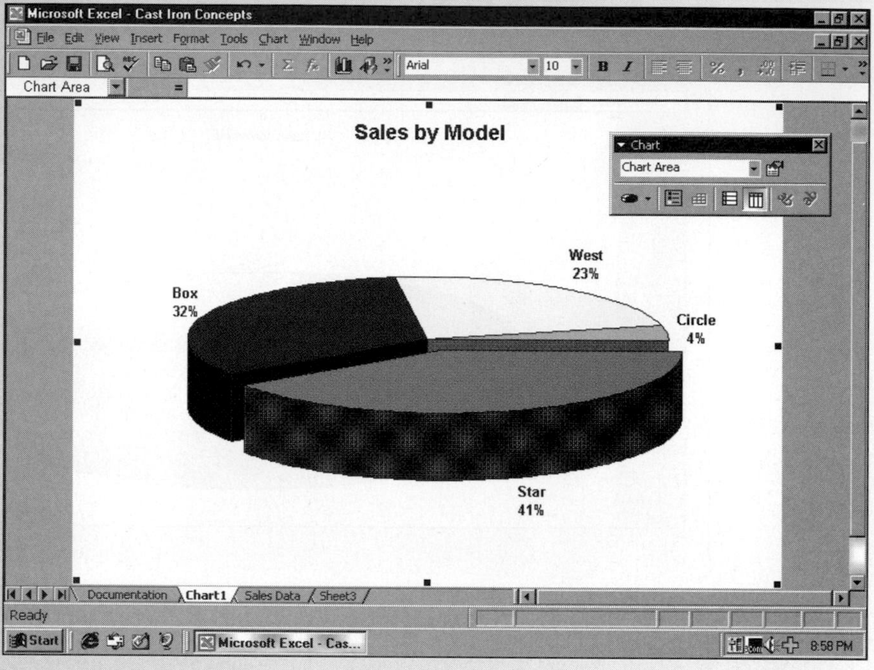

The pie chart looks good but Andrea has one last request. She asks you to apply a blue texture to the chart background.

Applying a Texture Fill Effect to the Chart Background

You can apply texture or gradient fill effects to chart walls, floors, bars, columns, and chart and plot background areas. These fill effects provide a professional look. You want to change the white chart area of the pie chart to a blue texture.

To apply a texture fill effect to the chart background:

1. Make sure the chart area is selected. If it is not, click the white area around the pie chart.
2. Click the **Format Chart Area** button on the Chart toolbar to open the Format Chart Area dialog box.
3. If necessary, click the **Patterns** tab, click the **Fill Effects** button to open the Fill Effects dialog box, and then click the **Texture** tab. See Figure 4-32.

Figure 4-32 TEXTURE OPTIONS IN FILL EFFECTS DIALOG BOX

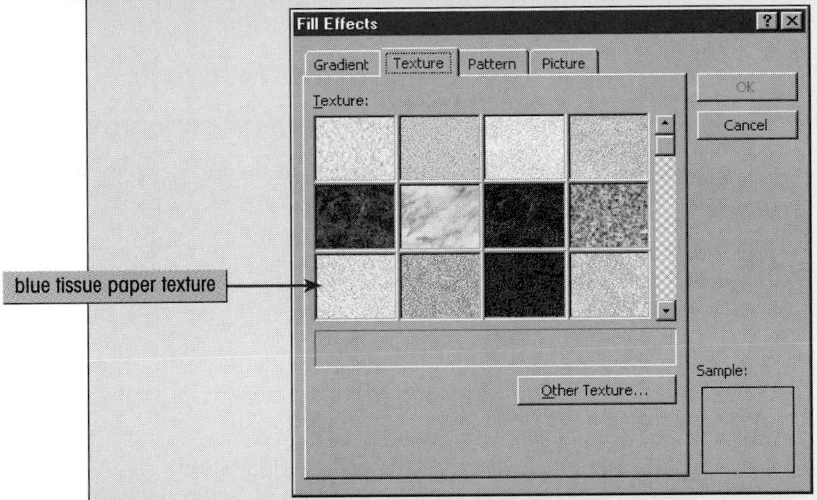

4. Click the **Blue tissue paper** texture box (third row, first column).

5. Click the **OK** button twice to apply the texture to the chart area. See Figure 4-33.

Figure 4-33 COMPLETED THREE-DIMENSIONAL PIE CHART

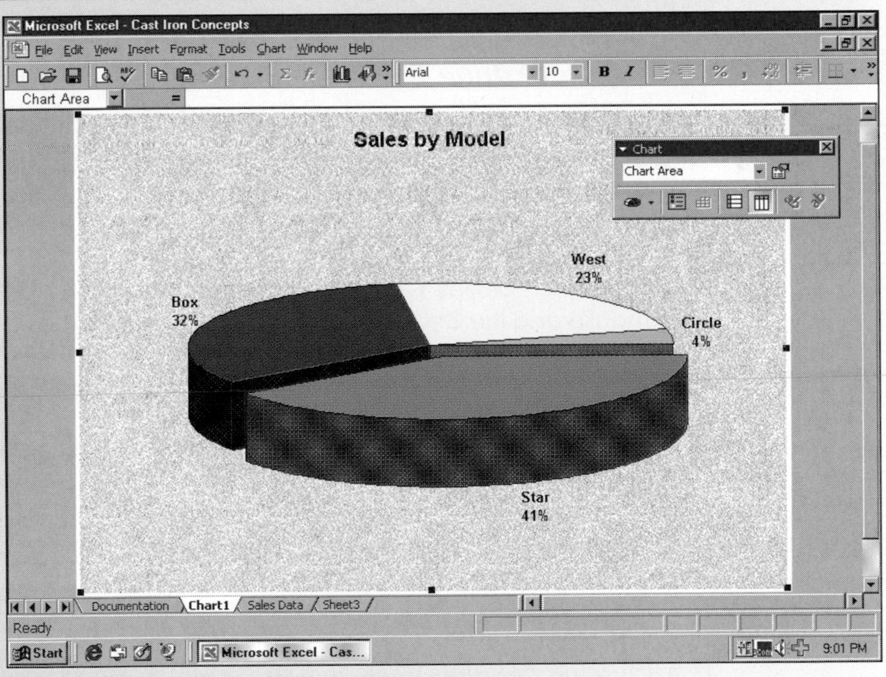

The chart is now complete. You decide to print it and show it to Andrea.

Printing the Chart from the Chart Sheet

When you create a chart in a separate sheet, you can print that sheet separately. If necessary, you can make page setup decisions for the chart sheet alone. In this case, the chart in the chart sheet is ready for printing. You don't need to change any setup options. Now that the three-dimensional pie chart is complete, save the workbook and print a copy of the chart.

To save the workbook and print the chart:

1. Click the **Save** button on the Standard toolbar to save the workbook.
2. Click the **Print** button on the Standard toolbar to print the chart.

Andrea is pleased with the printed chart and believes it will help her when she makes her presentation next week.

Creating a Bar Chart

Andrea decides to spend some time during her presentation reviewing sales of all stoves in each state in her territory. She recalls from one of her college classes that both the bar and column chart are useful for comparing data by categories. The bar chart may have an advantage if you have long labels, because the category labels in bar charts are easier to read. Andrea asks you to prepare a bar chart comparing sales of all stoves by state.

To prepare this chart, you first select the cells containing the categories and data needed to create the chart. For this chart, select the range B2 through D2 for the category axis (states) and B7 through D7 for the data series (total sales in each state).

To select range B2:D2 and range B7:D7 in the Sales Data sheet:

1. Click the **Sales Data** tab to activate the Sales Data worksheet, and then press **Ctrl + Home** to make cell A1 the active cell.
2. Select cells **B2:D2**, and then release the mouse button.
3. Press and hold the **Ctrl** key while you select cells **B7:D7**, and then release the mouse and the Ctrl key. The two nonadjacent ranges are now selected: B2:D2 and B7:D7.

   TROUBLE? If you didn't select the cells you want on your first try, click any cell to remove the highlighting, and then go back to Step 2 and try again.

Place the bar chart in a separate chart sheet so that Andrea can easily locate it.

To create a bar chart in a chart sheet:

1. Click the **Chart Wizard** button on the Standard toolbar to open the Chart Wizard - Step 1 of 4 - Chart Type dialog box.

   You want to create a bar chart.

2. Click the **Bar** chart type to select it. Six Bar chart subtypes appear. The Clustered Bar chart is the default subtype for the Bar chart. Click the **Press and Hold to View Sample** button to display a preview of the Clustered Bar chart subtype.

   You decide to use the Clustered Bar chart type.

3. Click the **Next** button to open the Chart Wizard - Step 2 of 4 - Chart Source Data dialog box. Make sure the Data range box displays "='Sales Data'!$B$2:$D$2, 'Sales Data'!$B$7:$D$7." This dialog box also displays a preview of your chart.

   TROUBLE? If the range shown on your screen is not "='Sales data'!$B$2:$D$2, 'Sales Data'!$B$7:$D$7," type the necessary corrections in the Data range text box, or click the Collapse Dialog button, and then select the correct range in the worksheet.

4. Click the **Next** button to open the Chart Wizard - Step 3 of 4 - Chart Options dialog box.

   Add a title for the chart.

5. If necessary, click the **Titles** tab, and click the **Chart title** text box. Type **Sales by State** for the chart title. Notice that the title appears in the preview area. Click the **Category (X) axis** box, and type **Territories**. Click the **Value (Y) axis** box, and then type **Sales ($U.S.)**.

   There is only one data series, so remove the legend.

6. Click the **Legend** tab and then click the **Show legend** check box to remove the check and deselect that option.

7. Click the **Next** button to open the Chart Wizard - Step 4 of 4 - Chart Location dialog box. You want this chart to be placed in a chart sheet.

8. Click the **As new sheet option** button to place this chart in a chart sheet, and then type **Bar Chart** in the As new sheet text box to rename the chart sheet.

   You have finished the steps in the Chart Wizard.

9. Click the **Finish** button to complete the chart. The new chart, along with the Chart toolbar, appears in the chart sheet named Bar Chart. The chart sheet is inserted into the workbook before the worksheet on which it is based. See Figure 4-34.

Figure 4-34 BAR CHART IN A CHART SHEET

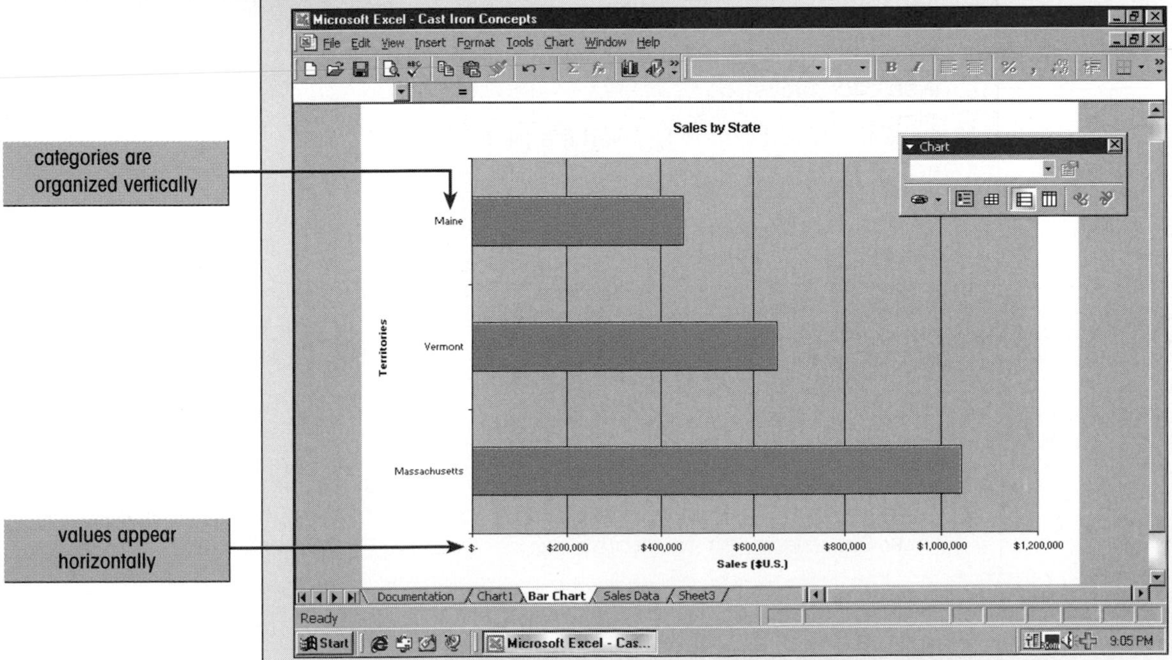

Andrea reviews the bar chart and believes it will focus the audience's attention on sales in each state.

Using Pictures in a Bar Chart

When making a presentation, an interesting way to enhance a bar or column chart is to replace the data markers with graphic images, thereby creating a picture chart. Any graphic image that can be copied to the Clipboard can serve as the basis for a picture chart. Andrea wants you to use a picture of the Windsor stove from CIC's latest catalog as the data marker in your bar chart.

REFERENCE WINDOW RW

Using a Picture in a Bar or Column Chart

- Create a bar or column chart using the Chart Wizard.
- Select all the bars or columns you want to replace with the picture.
- Click Insert, point to Picture, and then click From File to display the Insert Picture dialog box.
- Select the image file you want to use.
- Click Insert.

The graphic image of the Windsor stove is located in the Tutorial folder for Tutorial 4 on your Data Disk. The file is named Stove. To replace the plain bars with the graphic image, you need to select one bar or column of the chart and use the Picture command on the Insert menu.

To insert the picture into the bar chart:

1. Click any bar in the chart so that all three data markers are selected.
2. Click **Insert** on the menu bar, point to Picture, and then click **From File** to open the Insert Picture dialog box.
3. Make sure the Tutorial folder for Tutorial 4 is shown in the Look In list box, and then click **Stove**.
4. Click the **Insert** button to insert the picture into the chart. The three bars are each filled by the picture of the stove. See Figure 4-35. Notice that each picture is "stretched" to fit the bar it fills.

   TROUBLE? If a dialog box appears asking for the Import Graphic feature, please consult your instructor or technical support person.

Figure 4-35 **PICTURE CHART WITH STRETCHED GRAPHIC**

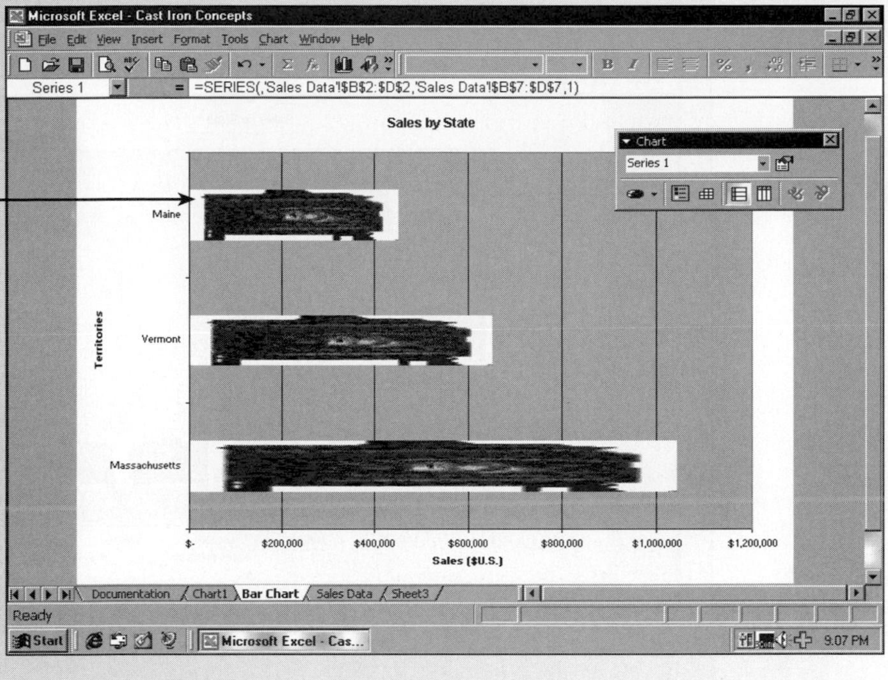

When you insert a picture into a bar or column chart, Excel automatically stretches the picture to fill the space formerly occupied by the marker. Some pictures stretch well, but others become distorted, and detract from, rather than add to, the chart's impact.

Stretching and Stacking Pictures

As an alternative to stretching a picture, you can stack the picture so that it appears repeatedly in the bar, reaching the height of the original bar in the chart. You'll stack the Windsor stove picture in your chart to improve its appearance.

The value axis has tick mark labels at $200,000; $400,000; $600,000; and so on. To match the axis labels, you'll stack one stove each 200,000 units.

To stack the picture:

1. If the handles have disappeared from the bars, click any bar in the chart to select all the bars.
2. Click **the Format Data Series** button on the Chart toolbar to open the Format Data Series dialog box, and if necessary, click the **Patterns** tab.
3. Click the **Fill Effects** button to open the Fill Effects dialog box, and then click the **Picture** tab if necessary.
4. Click the **Stack and scale to** option button. Accept the Units/Picture value in the format section.
5. Click the **OK** button to close the Fill Effects dialog box, and then click the **OK** button to close the Format Data Series dialog box and return to the chart sheet where the data markers now contain stacked stoves.
6. Click the white area of the chart to deselect the data markers. See Figure 4-36.

Figure 4-36 **PICTURE CHART WITH STACKED GRAPHIC**

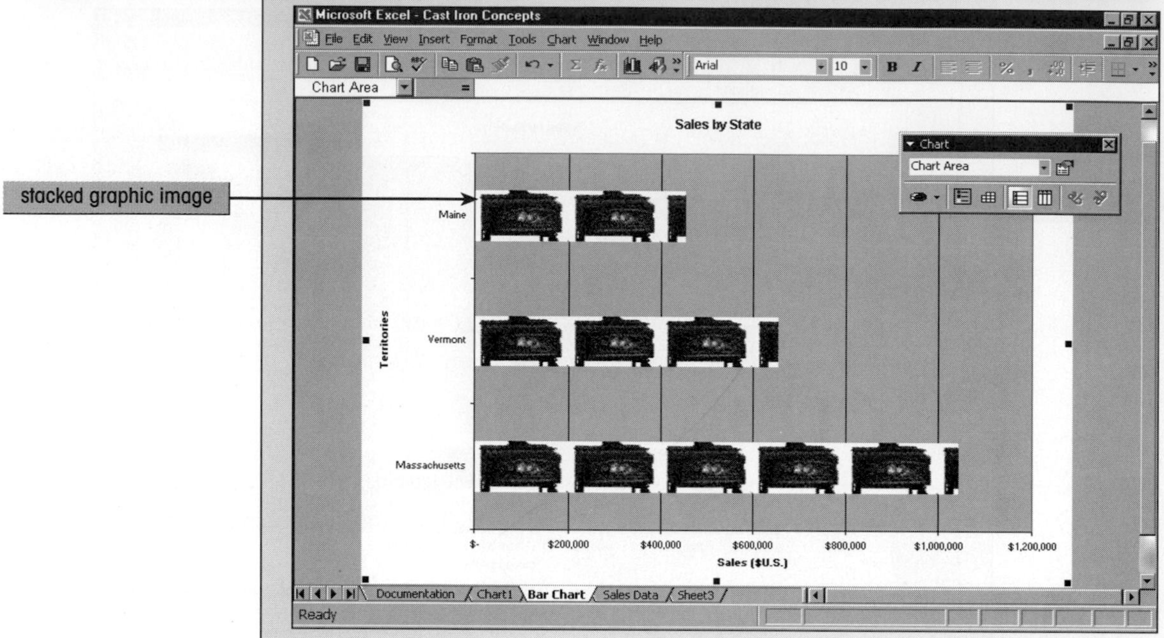

Andrea likes the picture chart but is not sure how her audience will react to it. She asks you to save the workbook with the picture chart included and will let you know whether to print the picture chart or return to the bar chart. If Andrea asks you to return to the original bars for the data markers, you will select the data series, click Edit, click Clear, and then click Formats.

Now save the workbook.

To save the workbook:

1. Click the **Documentation** tab to make it the active worksheet.
2. Click the **Save** button on the Standard toolbar.
3. Close the workbook and exit Excel.

You have finished creating the column chart, pie chart, and bar chart that Andrea needs.

Session 4.2 QUICK CHECK

1. What type of chart shows the proportion of parts to a whole?
2. Define the following terms in relation to a pie chart:
   a. data point **b.** data marker **c.** data series
3. When creating charts, why is it important to know how to select nonadjacent ranges?
4. Explain how to select cells A1, C5, and D10 at the same time.
5. When you change a two-dimensional pie chart to a three-dimensional pie chart, you change the ________________.
6. Explain how to explode a slice from a pie chart.
7. Explain how to rotate a three-dimensional pie chart.

REVIEW ASSIGNMENTS

Andrea comes to work the next morning and asks you to create one more chart for her presentation. Do the following:

1. Start Windows and Excel, if necessary. Insert your Data Disk into the disk drive. Make sure that the Excel and Book1 windows are maximized. Open the file **Concept2** in the Review folder for Tutorial 4.
2. Save the file under the new name **Cast Iron Concepts 2** in the Review folder.
3. Type your name and the current date in the Documentation sheet.
4. In the Sales Data sheet, select the range that contains the models (A3:D6).
5. Use the Chart Wizard to create a stacked column chart with three-dimensional visual effect.
6. Move the legend to the bottom and add "Total Stove Sales" as the chart title.
7. Place the completed chart in a chart sheet. Rename the chart sheet "Stacked Column".
8. ***Explore*** Put a box around the chart's title, using a thick line for a border. Add a drop shadow.
9. Save the workbook. Print the chart. Include your name, the filename, and the date in the footer.
10. ***Explore*** Select the Walls chart element and apply a one-color gradient fill effect. Select an appropriate color. Also apply a one-color gradient fill effect to the floor chart element. (*Hint:* Move the pointer over the different chart elements to identify the floor and wall elements.)
11. ***Explore*** Select the value axis and change its scale so that the major unit is 150000. (*Hint*: Format the value axis, Scale tab.)
12. Annotate the column chart with the note "Star model our best seller!" by adding a text box and arrow using the tools on the Drawing toolbar.
13. Save the workbook, and then print the stacked bar chart.
14. Open the workbook **ElectronicFilings** and save it as **Filing Solution**.
    a. Prepare an embedded line chart. Add the title "Electronic Filings at the IRS" and the value axis label "Number filed". Remove the legend.
    b. Move and resize the chart until you are satisfied with its appearance.
    c. Change the line weight to the thickest option.
    d. Add a square yellow data marker at each data point.
    e. Save and print the worksheet with the chart.

CASE PROBLEMS

Case 1. Illustrating Production Data at TekStar Electronics You are an executive assistant at TekStar Electronics, a manufacturer of consumer electronics. You are compiling the yearly manufacturing reports and have collected production totals for each of TekStar's four manufacturing plants. The workbook TekStar contains these totals. You need to create a three-dimensional pie chart showing the relative percentage of CD players each plant produced.

1. Open the workbook **Tekstar** in the Cases folder for Tutorial 4 and add information to the Documentation sheet to create a summary of the workbook. Save the workbook as **TekStar Electronics** in the Cases folder for Tutorial 4.
2. Activate the Units Sold sheet. Use the Chart Wizard to create a three-dimensional pie chart in a chart sheet that shows the percentage of CD players produced at each plant location. Use the Pie with three-dimensional visual effect subtype.
3. Enter "Production of CD Players" as the chart title. Show "Label" and "Percent" as the data labels. Remove the legend.

4. Pull out the slice representing the Chicago plant's CD player production.
5. Increase the font size of the title and data labels so that they are easier to read.
6. Name the chart sheet "3D Pie Chart".
7. Preview and print the chart sheet. Save your work.
8. Create an embedded chart comparing sales of all the products by city. Select the appropriate range and then use the Chart Wizard to create a clustered bar chart. Use the products as the data series and the cities as the X-axis (category) labels. Enter "Production by Product and Plant Location" as the title.
9. Move the bar chart under the table, and then enhance the chart in any way you think appropriate.
10. Preview and print the embedded bar chart, and then save your work.
11. Create a clustered column chart with three-dimensional visual effect comparing the production of VCRs by city. Remove the legend, and then place the chart in a chart sheet named "VCRs".
    a. Add a data table (a grid in a chart that contains the numeric data used to create the chart) to the chart. (*Hint*: Use the Office Assistant to find out how to add a data table to a chart.)
    b. Save the workbook, and then print the chart.

Case 2. Dow Jones Charting You work for a stock analyst who plans to publish a weekly newsletter. One component of the newsletter will be a 15-week chart tracking the Dow Jones average. Create the chart to be used for the newsletter.

1. Open the workbook **DowJones** in the Cases folder for Tutorial 4. Save the workbook as **Dow Jones Chart** in the Cases folder for Tutorial 4.
2. Use the Chart Wizard to create an embedded line chart (Line subtype) in the Dow Jones worksheet. Specify "Dow Jones Average" as the chart title and "Index" as the title for the Y-axis. Do not add a legend or X-axis title.
3. Place the chart to the right of the present worksheet data and resize it until you are satisfied.
4. Edit the chart as follows:
    a. Change the line marker to a thick line.
    b. Apply a texture fill effect to the chart area. You decide the texture.
    c. Change the color of the plot area. You decide the color.
    Explore
    d. Angle the text upward for the dates on the category axis. (*Hint*: Select the category axis and review the buttons on the chart toolbar.)
    e. Change the scale of the Y-axis so the minimum value is 7000.
5. Add your name to a custom footer, and then print the data and the chart.
6. Add the text box with the note "Market roars back to new high" and then insert an arrow pointing from the text box to anywhere between 11/27/98 and 12/11/98.
7. Save your workbook. Print only the chart.
8. The Dow Jones average for the week ending 12/18/98 was 8600.
    a. Insert this data in the row before the 12/11/98 entry.
    Explore
    b. Modify the chart by plotting the 15-week period beginning 9/11/98 and ending 12/18/98. (*Hint*: Modify the source data range.)
    Explore
    c. Change the location of the chart to a chart sheet. (*Hint*: Check out the Location command on the Chart menu.)
    d. Save the workbook as **Dow Jones 2**, preview your work, and then print the chart.

Case 3. California Chronicle You work as an intern for Gerry Sindle, business economist, of the *California Chronicle*. The paper plans to publish an economic profile of regions in the state, and you are assisting.

1. Open the workbook **California** in the Cases folder for Tutorial 4. Save the workbook as **California Economic Data**. Create three charts, each in its own chart sheet.

2. Create a pie chart that compares the population of the five geographic areas in the study. Title the chart and enhance it as you think appropriate. Rename the chart sheet to reflect the chart it contains.
3. Create a column chart that compares the number of establishments in retail and services by the five geographic areas. Place the type of establishment on the category axis; each geographic area is a data series. Title the chart and enhance it as you think appropriate. Rename the chart sheet to reflect the chart it contains.
4. Create a bar chart comparing Retail sales and Service receipts by geographic area (categorize by geographic area; the data series is sales and receipts). Title the chart and enhance it as you think appropriate. Rename the chart sheet to reflect the chart it contains.
5. Add a documentation sheet that includes your name, date created, purpose, and a brief description of each sheet in the workbook.
6. Save the workbook.
7. Print the entire workbook (documentation, data worksheet, and the three chart sheets).

Case 4. Association of Realtors Each year the Association of Realtors collects data on the number of homes sold and the median prices of those sales. Figure 4-37 shows data compiled by the Association since 1987. To better inform the community about occurrences in the home sales market over a ten-year period, the Association wants to release information to the press. Because charts show the data in a more understandable format, the Association has hired you as a part-time analyst to create charts.

Figure 4-37

	Houses Sold	Median Price
1988	4344	$118,500
1989	4294	$127,500
1990	4224	$129,900
1991	3728	$126,000
1992	3477	$123,000
1993	4352	$117,000
1994	4784	$115,300
1995	5081	$115,000
1996	4567	$115,000
1997	5115	$117,000
1998	5199	$117,500

1. Prepare a worksheet using the data from Figure 4-37. (*Hint*: Enter the year as text by typing an apostrophe (') in front of the year.)
2. Create an embedded chart showing the trend in house sales between 1988 and 1998. Title the chart and enhance it as you think appropriate.
3. Create an embedded chart showing the trend in median prices for houses between 1988 and 1998. Title the chart and enhance it as you think appropriate. Print the worksheet including the embedded charts.

Explore

4. Create a chart showing the trend in house sales and median price between 1988 and 1998 (one chart). Place this chart in a chart sheet. Title the chart and enhance it as you think appropriate. (*Hint*: Look up Secondary Value Axis in Help.)
5. The Association of Realtors touted the home sales figures as "shattering all records." Do you agree? Modify the chart in Step 4 by inserting annotated comments supporting or disagreeing with the Association. Print the chart.
6. Save the workbook as **RealtorCharts** in the Cases folder for Tutorial 4.

INTERNET ASSIGNMENTS

The purpose of the Internet Assignments is to challenge you to find information on the Internet that you can use to create effective spreadsheets. The actual assignments are updated and maintained on the Course Technology Web site. Log on to the Internet and use your Web browser to go to the Student Online Companion to accompany this text at **www.course.com/NewPerspectives/office2000**. Click the Excel link, and then click the link for Tutorial 4.

QUICK CHECK ANSWERS

Session 4.1

1. comparison among items or changes in data over a period of time
2. A data point is a value in the worksheet, whereas the data marker is the symbol (pie slice, column, bar, and so on) that represents the data point in a chart.
3. identifies the pattern or colors assigned to the data series in a chart
4. select the range of cells to be used as the source of data for the chart
5. selected; also referred to as activated
6. select the chart, move the pointer over the chart area until the pointer changes to an arrow, and then click and drag to another location on the worksheet
7. The data marker that represents that data point will change to reflect the new value.
8. Select the appropriate chart, click Chart menu, and then Source Data. Click the Collapse dialog box button, select values to be included in the chart, press the Enter key, and then click the OK button.
9. An embedded chart is a chart object placed in a worksheet and saved with the worksheet when the workbook is saved; a chart sheet is a sheet in a workbook that contains only a chart.

Session 4.2

1. pie chart
2. **a.** a value that originates from a worksheet cell
   b. a slice in a pie chart that represents a single point
   c. a group of related data points plotted in a pie chart that originate from rows or columns in a worksheet
3. often, the data you want to plot is not in adjacent cells
4. select cell A1, press and hold Ctrl key, and then select cells C5 and D10
5. chart type
6. select the slice you want to "explode," and then click and drag the slice away from the center
7. select the pie chart you want to rotate, click Chart on the Menu bar, click 3-D View to open the 3-D View dialog box, and then click one of the rotate buttons to rotate the chart

New Perspectives on

MICROSOFT® EXCEL 2000

Read This Before You Begin

To the Student

Data Disks

To complete the Level II tutorials, Review Assignments, and Case Problems in this book, you need four Data Disks. Your instructor will either provide you with Data Disks or ask you to make your own.

If you are making your own Data Disks, you will need five blank, formatted high-density disks. You will need to copy a set of folders from a file server, standalone computer, or the Web onto your disks. Your instructor will tell you which computer, drive letter, and folders contain the files you need. You could also download the files by going to www.course.com, clicking Data Disk Files, and following the instructions on the screen.

The following shows you which folders go on each of your disks, so that you will have enough disk space to complete all of the Tutorials, Review Assignments, and Case Problems:

Data Disk 1

Write this on the disk label:
Data Disk 1: Level II Tutorial 5

Put these folders on the disk:
Tutorial.05

Data Disk 2

Write this on the disk label:
Data Disk 2: Level II Tutorial 6

Put these folders on the disk:
Tutorial.06

Data Disk 3

Write this on the disk label:
Data Disk 3: Level II Tutorial 7

Put these folders on the disk:
Tutorial.07

Data Disk 4

Write this on the disk label:
Data Disk 4: Level II Tutorial 8

Put these folders on the disk:
Tutorial.08

Data Disk 5

Write this on the disk label:
Data Disk 5: Level II Appendix 1

Put these folders on the disk:
Appendix.01

When you begin each tutorial, be sure you are using the correct Data Disk. See the inside front or inside back cover of this book for more information on Data Disk files, or ask your instructor or technical support person for assistance.

Using Your Own Computer

If you are going to work through this book using your own computer, you need:

- **Computer System** Microsoft Excel 2000 and Windows 95 or higher must be installed on your computer. This book assumes a complete installation of Excel 2000.
- **Data Disks** You will not be able to complete the tutorials or exercises in this book using your own computer until you have Data Disks.

Visit Our World Wide Web Site

Additional materials designed especially for you are available on the World Wide Web.
Go to http://www.course.com.

To the Instructor

The Data files are available on the Instructor's Resource Kit for this title. Follow the instructions in the Help file on the CD-ROM to install the programs to your network or standalone computer. For information on creating Data Disks, see "To the Student" section above.

You are granted a license to copy the Student Files to any computer or computer network used by students who have purchased this book.

OBJECTIVES

In this tutorial you will:

- Identify the elements of an Excel list
- Freeze rows and columns
- Find and Replace values in a worksheet
- Change Zoom settings to display a worksheet
- Sort data in a list
- Enter, search for, edit, and delete records using a data form
- Filter data in a list using AutoFilters
- Apply conditional formatting to a range
- Use worksheet labels in formulas
- Insert subtotals into a list and change the subtotals outline view
- Insert page breaks using Page Break Preview
- Summarize a list using pivot tables and create a pivot chart

WORKING WITH EXCEL LISTS

Managing Faculty Data at North State University

CASE

North State University

Janice Long is the dean of the College of Business Administration at North State University (NSU). The College of Business Administration has three academic departments: management, marketing, and accounting. Each faculty member holds an academic rank, such as professor or associate professor. Most faculty members are hired as instructors or assistant professors, and then after a period of time, might be promoted to associate professor and then to full professor. Faculty salaries usually reflect the faculty member's rank and length of service in the department.

The dean frequently asks you to locate and summarize information about the College of Business Administration faculty. This week, she has several important budget and staffing meetings to attend in which she will need to produce detailed and specific information regarding her faculty. She asks for your help to compile the necessary data. She has provided an Excel worksheet that contains the name, academic rank, department, hire date, salary, and sex of each faculty member in the College of Business Administration (CBA). She asks you to use the worksheet to create several reports that will organize the information to produce the specific output she requires for each meeting.

SESSION 5.1

You already know how to use Excel to perform calculations using numeric data or values you enter into worksheet cells. In this session you will learn how to use Excel to manage lists of data. You will learn how to increase the amount of a worksheet that appears on the screen at one time and how to find and replace values in a large worksheet. You will discover how easy it is to sort the information in a worksheet, to add and delete data, and to search for specific information.

Introduction to Lists

One of the more common uses of a worksheet is to manage lists of data, such as client lists, phone lists, and transaction lists. Excel provides you with the tools to manage such tasks. Using Excel, you can store and update data, sort data, search for and retrieve data, summarize and compare data, and create reports.

In Excel a **list** is a collection of similar data stored in a structured manner, in rows and columns. Figure 5-1 shows a portion of the College of Business Administration faculty list. Within an Excel list, each column represents a **field** that describes some attribute or characteristic of an object, person, place, or thing. In this situation, a faculty member's last name, the department in which the faculty member works, and the faculty member's annual salary are all examples of fields. When related fields are grouped together in a row, they form a **record**, a collection of fields that describes a person, place, or thing. For example, the data for each faculty member—first name, last name, department, rank, year hired, sex, and salary—represents a record. A collection of related records makes up an Excel list.

Figure 5-1 PORTION OF FACULTY LIST

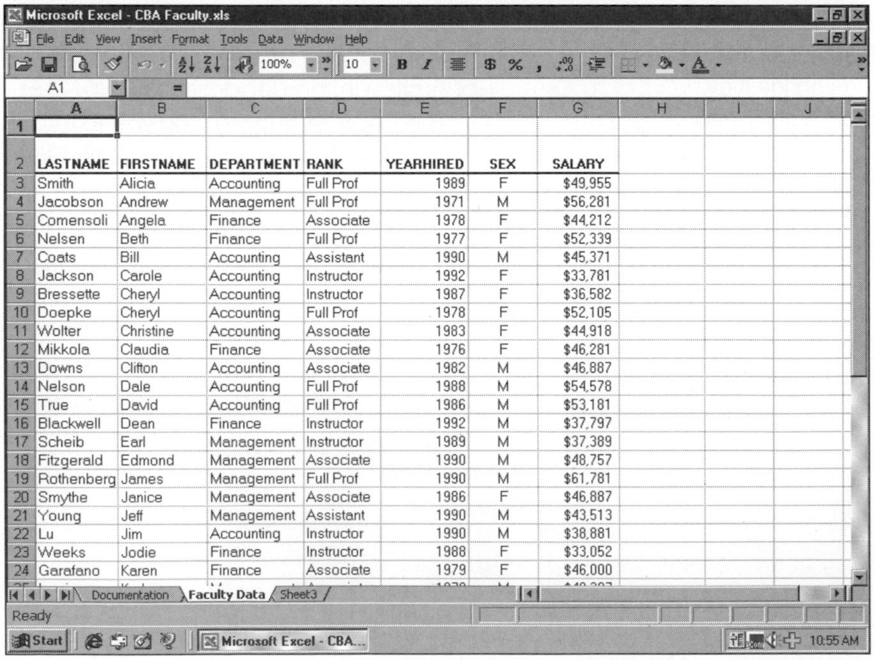

LASTNAME	FIRSTNAME	DEPARTMENT	RANK	YEARHIRED	SEX	SALARY
Smith	Alicia	Accounting	Full Prof	1989	F	$49,955
Jacobson	Andrew	Management	Full Prof	1971	M	$56,281
Comensoli	Angela	Finance	Associate	1978	F	$44,212
Nelsen	Beth	Finance	Full Prof	1977	F	$52,339
Coats	Bill	Accounting	Assistant	1990	M	$45,371
Jackson	Carole	Accounting	Instructor	1992	F	$33,781
Bressette	Cheryl	Accounting	Instructor	1987	F	$36,582
Doepke	Cheryl	Accounting	Full Prof	1978	F	$52,105
Wolter	Christine	Accounting	Associate	1983	F	$44,918
Mikkola	Claudia	Finance	Associate	1976	F	$46,281
Downs	Clifton	Accounting	Associate	1982	M	$46,887
Nelson	Dale	Accounting	Full Prof	1988	M	$54,578
True	David	Accounting	Full Prof	1986	M	$53,181
Blackwell	Dean	Finance	Instructor	1992	M	$37,797
Scheib	Earl	Management	Instructor	1989	M	$37,389
Fitzgerald	Edmond	Management	Associate	1990	M	$48,757
Rothenberg	James	Management	Full Prof	1990	M	$61,781
Smythe	Janice	Management	Associate	1986	F	$46,887
Young	Jeff	Management	Assistant	1990	M	$43,513
Lu	Jim	Accounting	Instructor	1990	M	$38,881
Weeks	Jodie	Finance	Instructor	1988	F	$33,052
Garafano	Karen	Finance	Associate	1979	F	$46,000

If you have worked with spreadsheets before, you may associate the term *database* with what Excel now calls a list. Since the introduction of Excel Version 5, Microsoft refers to database tables in Excel worksheets as lists. The term **database** refers to files created using database management software, such as dBASE, Access, and Paradox. In this tutorial we focus on Excel lists.

Planning and Creating a List

Before you create a list, you will want to do some planning. As you spend time thinking about how you will use the list, consider the types of reports, queries, and searches you may need. This process should help you determine the kind of information to include for each record and the contents of each field. As with most projects, the planning you do will help you avoid redesigning the list later.

To create the faculty list, the dean first determined her information requirements. As a way of documenting the information requirements of the faculty list, she developed a **data definition table** that describes the fields she plans to maintain for each faculty member at the College of Business Administration. Figure 5-2 shows the data definition table the dean developed to define her data requirements. She used this as a guide in creating the faculty list.

Figure 5-2 DATA DEFINITION TABLE FOR FACULTY LIST

FIELD NAME	DESCRIPTION
LASTNAME	Faculty member's last name
FIRSTNAME	Faculty member's first name
DEPARTMENT	Name of department (accounting, finance, and management)
RANK	Faculty rank (instructor, assistant, associate, and full)
YEARHIRED	Year in which faculty member was hired
SEX	Female (F) or male (M)
SALARY	Annual salary

Once you determine the design of your list, you can create the list in a worksheet. You can use a blank worksheet or one that already contains data.

When creating a list in Excel, use the following guidelines:

- The top row of the list should contain a **field name**, a unique label describing the contents of the data in the rows below it. This row of field names is sometimes referred to as the **field header row**.
- Field names can contain up to 255 characters. Usually a short name is easier to understand and remember. Short field names also enable you to display more fields on the screen at one time.
- You should boldface the field names, change the font, or use a different color to make it easier for Excel to distinguish between the data in the list and the field names.
- Each column should contain the same kind of information for each row in the list.

The list should be separated from any other information in the same worksheet by at least one blank row and one blank column because Excel automatically determines the range of the list by identifying blank rows and columns. For the same reason, you should avoid blank rows and columns within the list.

Now open the workbook the dean created to help you maintain the data on faculty at NSU's College of Business Administration.

To open the Faculty workbook:

1. Start Excel. Make sure your Data Disk is in the appropriate drive, and then open the workbook **Faculty** in the Tutorial folder for Tutorial .05 on your Data Disk, and immediately save it as **CBA Faculty**.

2. Switch to the **Faculty Data** worksheet to display the faculty list. See Figure 5-3. The dean's worksheet contains the list of faculty at the College of Business Administration. Currently there are 41 faculty. Each faculty record is stored as a separate row (rows 3 through 43). There are seven fields for each faculty record (columns A through G). Notice that the field names are boldfaced to make it easier for Excel to distinguish the field names from the data in the list.

Figure 5-3 **FACULTY LIST**

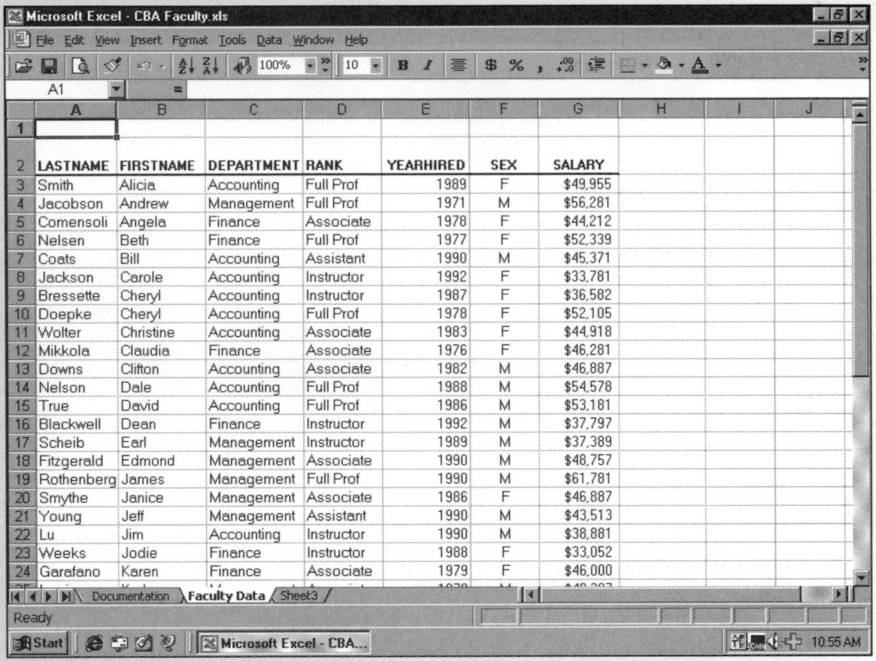

	LASTNAME	FIRSTNAME	DEPARTMENT	RANK	YEARHIRED	SEX	SALARY
3	Smith	Alicia	Accounting	Full Prof	1989	F	$49,955
4	Jacobson	Andrew	Management	Full Prof	1971	M	$56,281
5	Comensoli	Angela	Finance	Associate	1978	F	$44,212
6	Nelsen	Beth	Finance	Full Prof	1977	F	$52,339
7	Coats	Bill	Accounting	Assistant	1990	M	$45,371
8	Jackson	Carole	Accounting	Instructor	1992	F	$33,781
9	Bressette	Cheryl	Accounting	Instructor	1987	F	$36,582
10	Doepke	Cheryl	Accounting	Full Prof	1978	F	$52,105
11	Wolter	Christine	Accounting	Associate	1983	F	$44,918
12	Mikkola	Claudia	Finance	Associate	1976	F	$46,281
13	Downs	Clifton	Accounting	Associate	1982	M	$46,887
14	Nelson	Dale	Accounting	Full Prof	1988	M	$54,578
15	True	David	Accounting	Full Prof	1986	M	$53,181
16	Blackwell	Dean	Finance	Instructor	1992	M	$37,797
17	Scheib	Earl	Management	Instructor	1989	M	$37,389
18	Fitzgerald	Edmond	Management	Associate	1990	M	$48,757
19	Rothenberg	James	Management	Full Prof	1990	M	$61,781
20	Smythe	Janice	Management	Associate	1986	F	$46,887
21	Young	Jeff	Management	Assistant	1990	M	$43,513
22	Lu	Jim	Accounting	Instructor	1990	M	$38,881
23	Weeks	Jodie	Finance	Instructor	1988	F	$33,052
24	Garafano	Karen	Finance	Associate	1979	F	$46,000

To become familiar with the data, you decide to scroll the faculty list.

3. Click the **vertical scroll bar down arrow** to scroll to the bottom of the list (row 43). As you scroll, notice that the column headings are no longer visible.

4. After viewing the last record in the faculty list, press **Ctrl + Home** to return to cell A1.

You want to keep the column headings on the screen as you scroll the faculty list because not being able to see the column headings makes it difficult to know what the data in each column represents.

Freezing Rows and Columns

You can freeze rows and columns so they will not scroll off the screen as you move around the worksheet. This lets you keep headings on the screen as you work with the data in a large worksheet.

REFERENCE WINDOW RW

Freezing Rows And Columns

- Select the cell below and to the right of row(s) and column(s) you want to freeze.
- Click Window, and then click Freeze Panes.

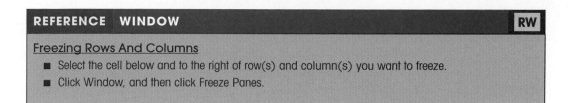

You decide to freeze the row with the column headings and the LASTNAME column so that they remain on the screen as you scroll the list.

To freeze rows and columns:

1. Click cell **B3** to make it the active cell.
2. Click **Window** on the menu bar, and then click **Freeze Panes** to freeze the rows above row 3 and the columns to the left of column B. Excel displays dark horizontal and vertical lines to indicate which rows and columns are frozen.

   Now scroll the list.
3. Click the **vertical scroll bar down arrow** to scroll down to the bottom of the list (row 43). As you scroll, notice that the column headings remain visible. See Figure 5-4.

Figure 5-4 FACULTY LIST WITH COLUMN LABELS VISIBLE AS YOU SCROLL

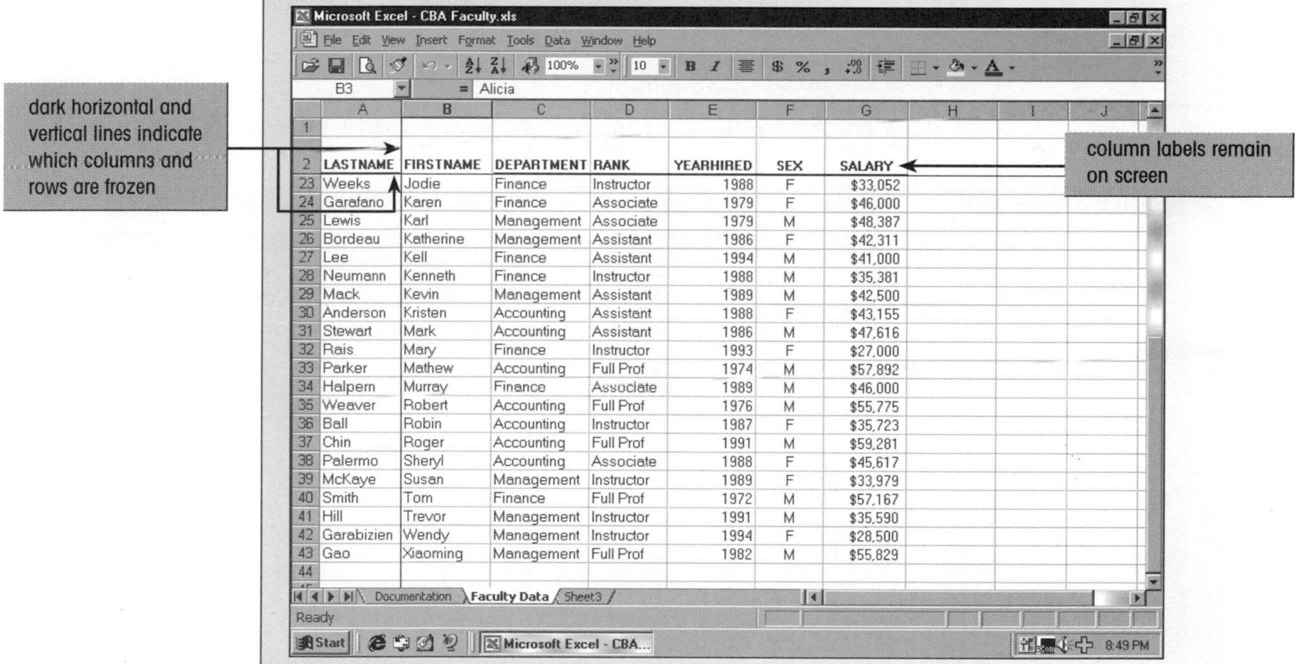

4. Click the **horizontal scroll bar right arrow**. As you scroll to the right, notice that column A, LASTNAME, remains visible.
5. Press **Ctrl + Home** to return to cell B3. Notice that Ctrl + Home no longer returns you to cell A1—instead it returns you to the cell directly below and to the right of the frozen row and column.

To unfreeze the rows and columns, select Unfreeze Panes from the Window menu, but for now, keep the frozen settings.

Changing the Zoom Setting of a Worksheet

Normally, a worksheet appears at 100% magnification. The Zoom command on the View menu (or the Zoom box on the Standard toolbar) enables you to reduce the Zoom percentage so you can see more of the worksheet on a screen (zooming out) or magnify a portion of the worksheet by increasing the Zoom percentage (zooming in) so you can make it easier to read the worksheet.

You want to see how the Zoom command will effect the display of the faculty list.

To change the zoom setting of the Faculty worksheet:

1. Click **View**, click **Zoom** to open the Zoom dialog box. See Figure 5-5.

Figure 5-5 ZOOM DIALOG BOX

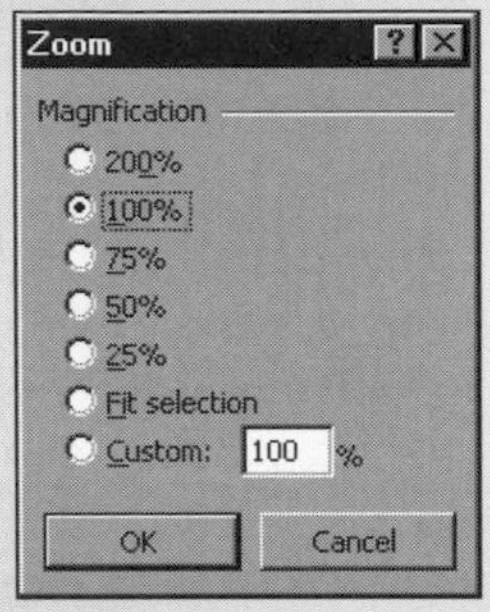

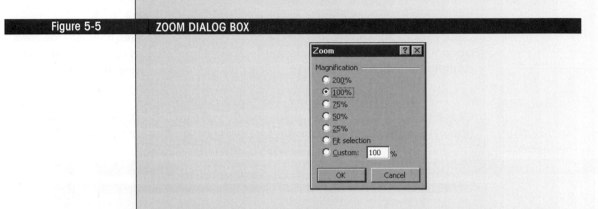

2. Click the **50%** option button.

3. Click **OK**. See Figure 5-6. Notice that you can see all the rows in the faculty list.

Figure 5-6 ZOOM OUT TO SEE MORE OF WORKSHEET

Zoom box

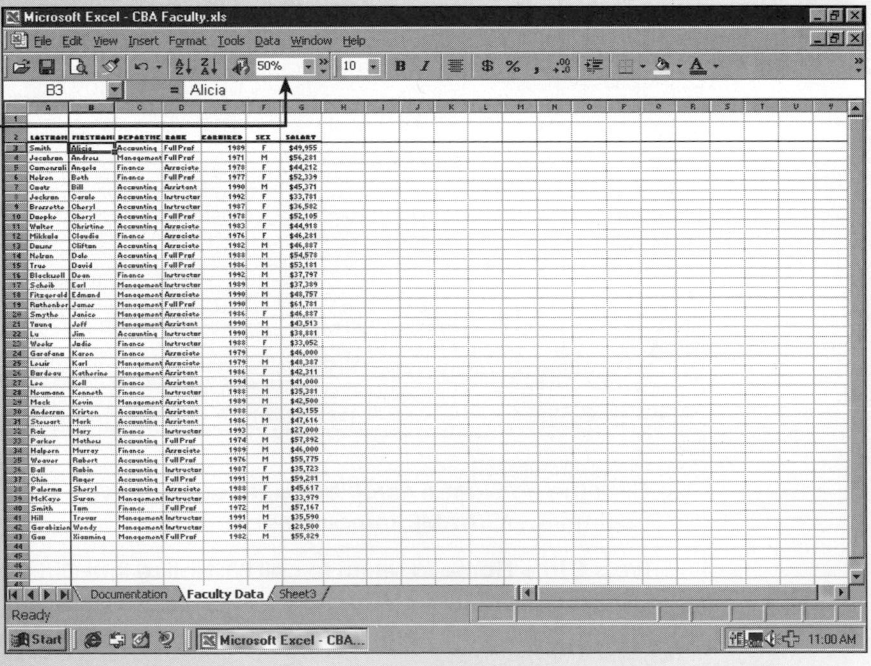

The values are small and too hard to read, so you decide to return to the normal zoom setting—100%. Although you can use the Zoom command to make this change, you'll use the Zoom box on the Standard toolbar instead.

To return the zoom setting to 100% size using the Zoom box:

1. Click the **Zoom** control drop-down list arrow on the standard toolbar to display a list of magnifications.
2. Click **100%**. Notice the worksheet returns to normal view.

As you review the worksheet with the dean, the dean observes the value "Full Prof" in the Rank column of the Faculty list. She asks you to change the code to "Full" instead of "Full Prof" before any reports are prepared.

Using Find and Replace

To find every occurrence of a character string or value in a large worksheet, you can use the Find and Replace commands. The Find command locates a value or character string, and the Replace command overwrites values or character strings.

Now, change every faculty rank containing "Full Prof" to "Full".

To replace the value Full Prof with Full in the Rank column:

1. Select the cells **D3:D43**, the rank column.
2. Click **Edit**, then click **Replace** to open the Replace dialog box. See Figure 5-7.

Figure 5-7 REPLACE DIALOG BOX

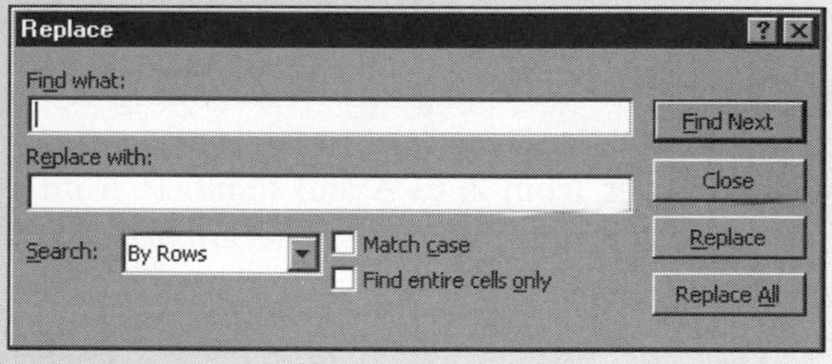

3. Type **Full Prof** in the Find what box.
4. Type **Full** in the Replace with box.
5. Click the **Find entire cells only** check box to specify that the text in the Find what box must match the entire cell contents.
6. Click the **Replace All** button to replace all matches. See Figure 5-8. Notice the "Full Prof" entries have all changed to "Full".

Figure 5-8 FACULTY LIST AFTER THE RANK CODE FOR FULL PROFESSORS CHANGED

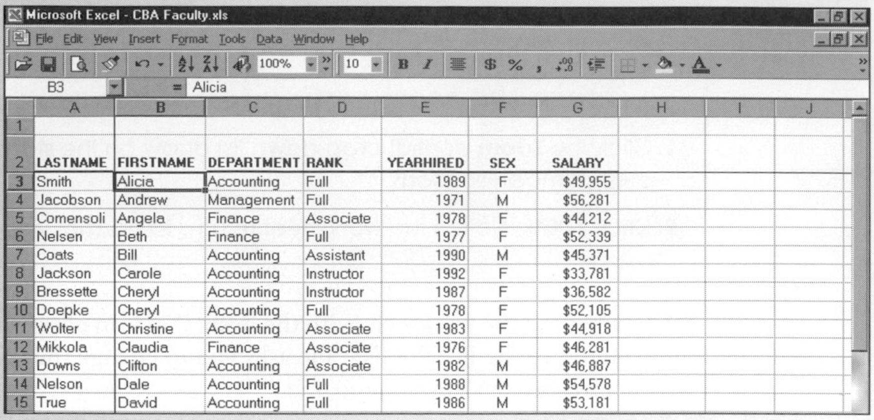

LASTNAME	FIRSTNAME	DEPARTMENT	RANK	YEARHIRED	SEX	SALARY
Smith	Alicia	Accounting	Full	1989	F	$49,955
Jacobson	Andrew	Management	Full	1971	M	$56,281
Comensoli	Angela	Finance	Associate	1978	F	$44,212
Nelsen	Beth	Finance	Full	1977	F	$52,339
Coats	Bill	Accounting	Assistant	1990	M	$45,371
Jackson	Carole	Accounting	Instructor	1992	F	$33,781
Bressette	Cheryl	Accounting	Instructor	1987	F	$36,582
Doepke	Cheryl	Accounting	Full	1978	F	$52,105
Wolter	Christine	Accounting	Associate	1983	F	$44,918
Mikkola	Claudia	Finance	Associate	1976	F	$46,281
Downs	Clifton	Accounting	Associate	1982	M	$46,887
Nelson	Dale	Accounting	Full	1988	M	$54,578
True	David	Accounting	Full	1986	M	$53,181

7. Press **Ctrl + Home**.

Sorting Data

In preparation for her meetings this week, the dean wants a list of faculty members sorted by last name so she can have quick access to faculty data when not near a computer. She asks you to prepare a list of all faculty, alphabetized by last name.

When you initially enter records into a list, each new record is placed at the bottom of the list. To rearrange records in a list, you sort based on the data in one or more of the fields (columns). The fields you use to order your data are called **sort fields** or **sort keys**.

For example, to sort the faculty list alphabetically by last name, you order the data using the values in the LASTNAME field. LASTNAME becomes the sort field. Because LASTNAME is the first sort field, and in this case the only sort field, it is the **primary sort field**.

Before you complete the sort, you will need to decide whether you want to put the list in ascending or descending order. **Ascending order** arranges labels alphabetically from A to Z and numbers from smallest to largest. **Descending order** arranges labels in reverse alphabetical order from Z to A and numbers from largest to smallest. In both ascending and descending order, any blank fields are placed at the bottom of the list. For the quick reference list of faculty, the dean wants to sort the list by last name in ascending order.

Sorting a List Using One Sort Field

To sort data in an Excel worksheet, you can use the Sort Ascending and Sort Descending buttons on the Standard toolbar, or you can use the Sort command on the Data menu. The easiest way to sort data when there is only one sort key is to use the Sort Ascending or Sort Descending buttons. If you are sorting using more than one sort key, you should use the Sort command to specify the columns on which you want to sort.

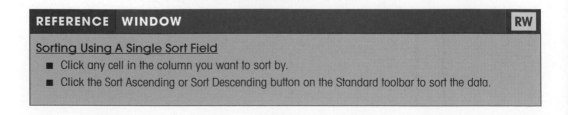

REFERENCE WINDOW RW

Sorting Using A Single Sort Field

- Click any cell in the column you want to sort by.
- Click the Sort Ascending or Sort Descending button on the Standard toolbar to sort the data.

Produce the dean's alphabetized list by sorting the faculty list using LASTNAME as the sort field.

To sort a list using a single sort field:

1. Click any cell in the LASTNAME column. Notice that you do not select the entire faculty list, range A2:G43. Excel automatically determines the range of the faculty list when you click any cell inside the list.

2. Click the **Sort Ascending button** on the Standard toolbar. The data is sorted in ascending order by last name. See Figure 5-9.

   TROUBLE? If you selected the wrong column before sorting the list, and your data is sorted in the wrong order, you can undo it. To undo a sort, click the Undo button on the Standard toolbar.

Figure 5-9 FACULTY LIST SORTED BY LAST NAME

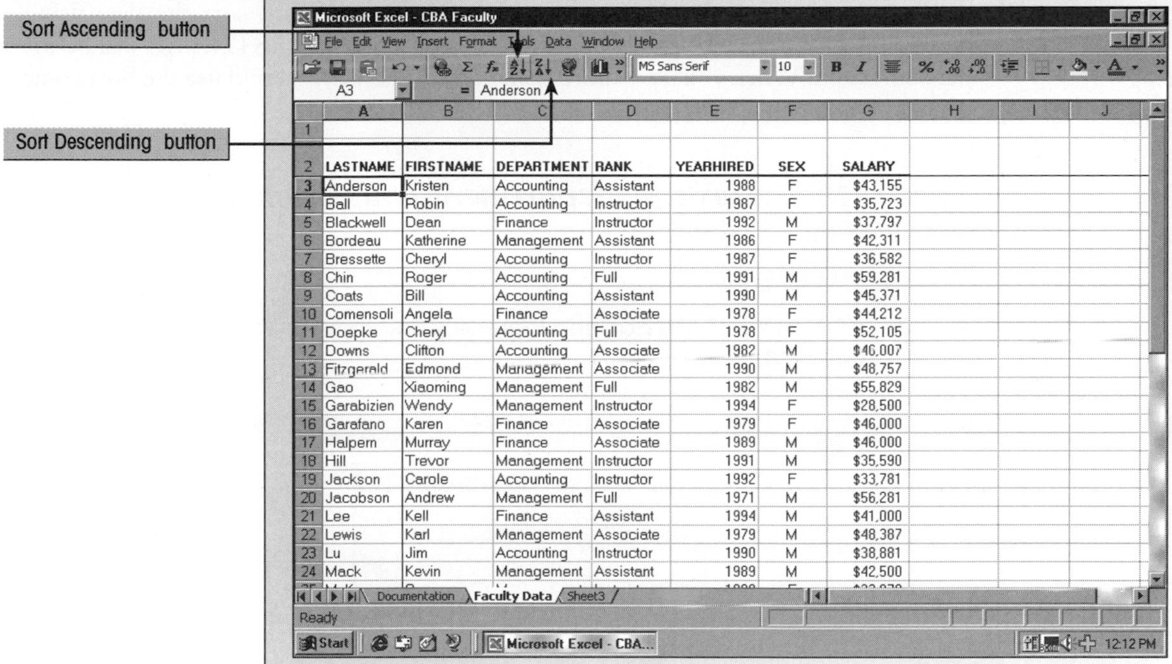

When sorting, do not highlight the entire sort key column. If you do, Excel will only sort the values in the selected column rather than sort the entire record.

The dean also requests a list of faculty sorted alphabetically by department, and within each department, by last name.

Sorting a List Using More than One Sort Field

Sometimes sorting by one sort field results in ties. A **tie** occurs when more than one record has the same value for a field. For example, if you sort the faculty list on the DEPARTMENT field, all employees with the same department name would be grouped together. To break a tie you can sort the list on multiple fields. For example, you can sort the faculty list by department, and then by last name within each department. In this case, you specify the DEPARTMENT field as the primary sort field and the LASTNAME field as the **secondary sort field**.

REFERENCE WINDOW **RW**

Sorting A List Using More Than One Sort Field

- Click any cell in the list.
- Click Data on the menu bar, and then click Sort to open the Sort dialog box.
- Click the Sort By list arrow to display a list of column headings. Select the column you want to use as the primary sort field. Click the appropriate option button to specify sort order.
- Click the first Then By list box and use the list arrow to select the desired column heading for the secondary sort field. Click the appropriate option button to specify sort order.
- If you want to sort out a third column, click the second Then By list box and select the desired column heading. Click the appropriate option button to specify sort order.
- Click the OK button to sort the list.

The dean asked you to sort by department and then alphabetically by last name within each department. To prepare this second list, you will need to sort the data using two columns: DEPARTMENT will be the primary sort field and LASTNAME will be the secondary sort field. When you have more than one sort key, you should use the Sort command on the Data menu to specify the columns you want to sort.

To sort the records by department and within department by last name:

1. Click any cell in the list.
2. Click **Data** on the menu bar, and then click **Sort** to open the Sort dialog box. See Figure 5-10.

Figure 5-10 **SORT DIALOG BOX**

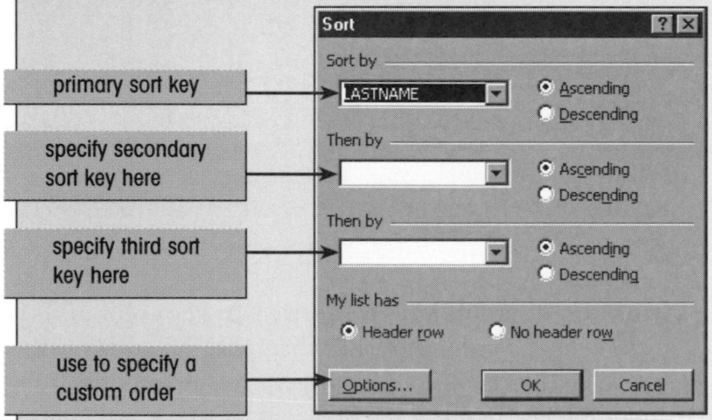

3. Click the **Sort By** list arrow to display the list of column headings, and then click **DEPARTMENT**.
4. If necessary, click the **Ascending** option button to specify that you want to sort the DEPARTMENT field in ascending order.

   Now specify the secondary sort field.
5. Click the first **Then By** list arrow to display the list of column headings, and then click **LASTNAME**.

6. Make sure the Ascending option button is selected.

7. Click the **OK** button. See Figure 5-11.

Figure 5-11 FACULTY LIST SORTED BY DEPARTMENT AND WITHIN DEPARTMENT BY LAST NAME

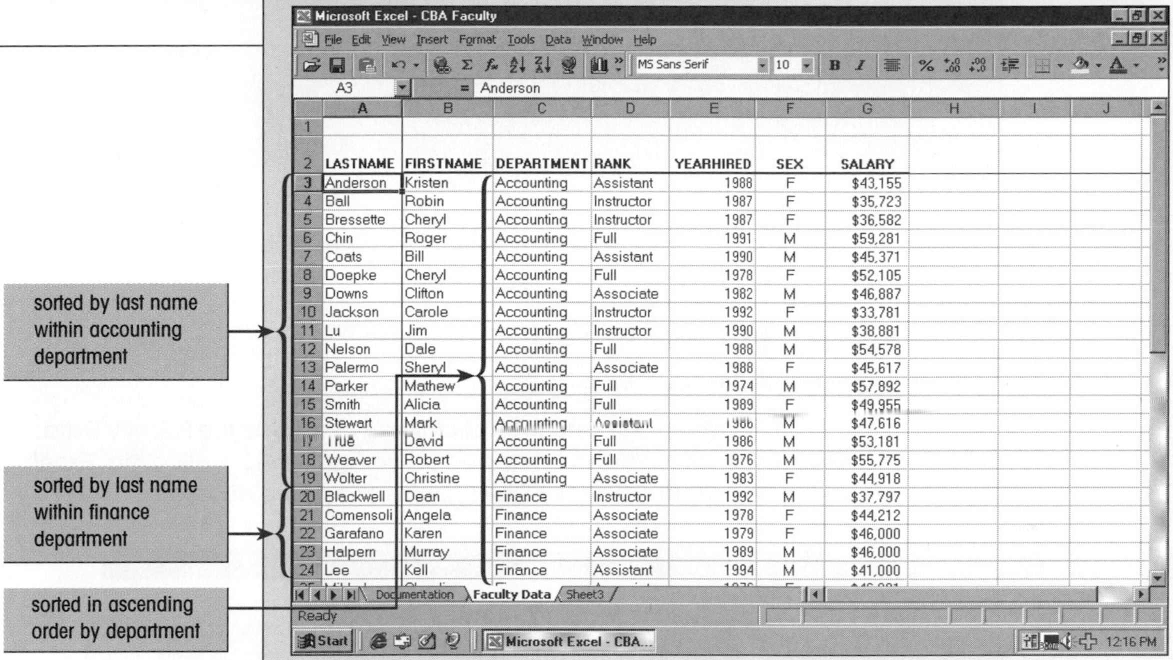

	A	B	C	D	E	F	G
1							
2	LASTNAME	FIRSTNAME	DEPARTMENT	RANK	YEARHIRED	SEX	SALARY
3	Anderson	Kristen	Accounting	Assistant	1988	F	$43,155
4	Ball	Robin	Accounting	Instructor	1987	F	$35,723
5	Bressette	Cheryl	Accounting	Instructor	1987	F	$36,582
6	Chin	Roger	Accounting	Full	1991	M	$59,281
7	Coats	Bill	Accounting	Assistant	1990	M	$45,371
8	Doepke	Cheryl	Accounting	Full	1978	F	$52,105
9	Downs	Clifton	Accounting	Associate	1982	M	$46,887
10	Jackson	Carole	Accounting	Instructor	1992	F	$33,781
11	Lu	Jim	Accounting	Instructor	1990	M	$38,881
12	Nelson	Dale	Accounting	Full	1988	M	$54,578
13	Palermo	Sheryl	Accounting	Associate	1988	F	$45,617
14	Parker	Mathew	Accounting	Full	1974	M	$57,892
15	Smith	Alicia	Accounting	Full	1989	F	$49,955
16	Stewart	Mark	Accounting	Assistant	1986	M	$47,616
17	True	David	Accounting	Full	1986	M	$53,181
18	Weaver	Robert	Accounting	Full	1976	M	$55,775
19	Wolter	Christine	Accounting	Associate	1983	F	$44,918
20	Blackwell	Dean	Finance	Instructor	1992	M	$37,797
21	Comensoli	Angela	Finance	Associate	1978	F	$44,212
22	Garafano	Karen	Finance	Associate	1979	F	$46,000
23	Halpern	Murray	Finance	Associate	1989	M	$46,000
24	Lee	Kell	Finance	Assistant	1994	M	$41,000

8. Scroll the list to view the data sorted by department and within department by last name.

9. Save the workbook.

Now the dean has a list of faculty members sorted by department and then by last name. This will make finding information about faculty members much easier.

Maintaining a List Using a Data Form

The dean has several changes regarding the faculty status that need to be reflected in the faculty list. First, the accounting department has hired an instructor, Mary Hutch, to teach the introductory accounting courses. Her record needs to be added to the faculty list. Second, Kevin Mack just received official confirmation on his promotion to associate professor. Kevin's record must be updated to reflect his change in rank and new salary of $45,000. Finally, Wendy Garabizien retired at the end of the term; her record needs to be deleted from the faculty list. The dean asks you to update the faculty list to reflect these changes.

One of the easiest ways to maintain a list in Excel is to use a data form. A **data form** is a dialog box in which you can add, find, edit, and delete records in a list. A data form displays one record at a time, as opposed to the table of rows and columns you see in the worksheet. Although you can use the worksheet to make changes directly to the list, using the data form can help prevent mistakes that can occur if you accidentally enter data in the wrong column or row.

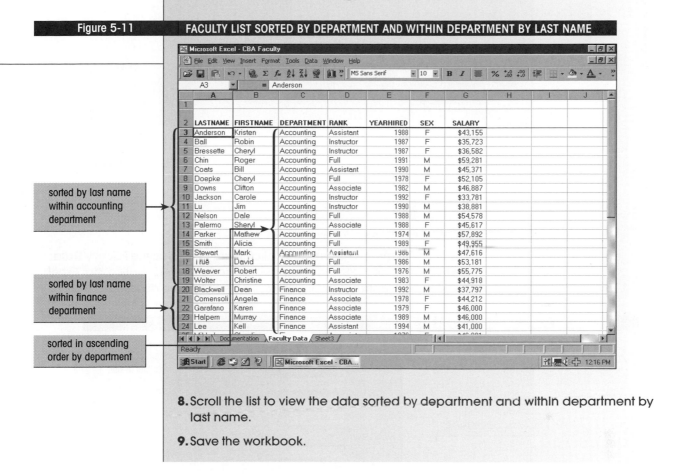

REFERENCE WINDOW RW

Adding A Record Using A Data Form

- Click any cell in the list.
- Click Data, and then click Form to display a data form.
- Click the New button to display a blank form.
- Type the values for the new record, pressing the Tab key to move from field to field.
- Press the Enter key to add the record.
- When finished adding records, click the Close button.

Begin updating the faculty list by adding Mary Hutch's data, using the data form.

To add a new record using the data form:

1. Click any cell in the list.
2. Click **Data** on the menu bar, and then click **Form** to display the Faculty Data data form. The first record in the list appears. See Figure 5-12. Notice that Excel uses the worksheet name, "Faculty Data", as the title of the data form.

Figure 5-12 FACULTY DATA DATA FORM

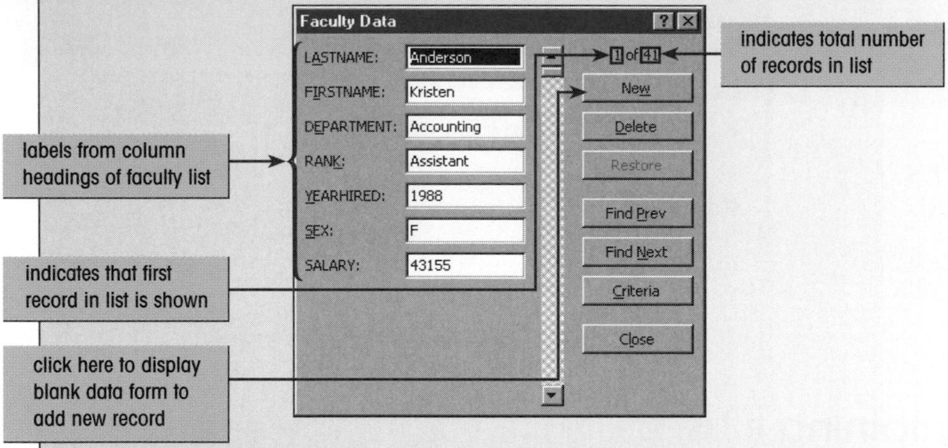

The names that appear on the left side of the data form are taken from the header row of the faculty list.

In the upper-right corner of the form, there is information on how many records are in the list and which row is currently selected.

Now add the new record.

3. Click the **New** button to display a blank data form. Notice that the label "New Record" appears in the upper-right corner of the data form. Enter the values for the record in the text boxes next to each field name.
4. Type **Hutch** in the LASTNAME text box, and then press the Tab key to move to the FIRSTNAME text box.

TROUBLE? If you pressed the Enter key instead of the Tab key, a blank data form appears. Click the Find Prev button to return to the previous record, the record you were entering, and continue entering the data.

5. Type **Mary** in the FIRSTNAME text box, and then press the **Tab** key to move to the DEPARTMENT text box.

6. Type **Accounting** in the DEPARTMENT text box, and then press the Tab key to move to the RANK text box. Continue entering the remaining data. Remember to press the Tab key after you complete each entry.

   RANK: **Instructor** YEARHIRED: **2001** SEX: **F** SALARY: **28000**

7. Press the **Enter** key to add the record to the bottom of the list.

   The data form is blank again, ready for you to add a new record. But since you don't have any new records to add now, return to the worksheet.

8. Click the **Close** button to close the data form and return to the worksheet.

   Confirm that the new record has been added to the faculty list. It should appear at the bottom of the list.

9. Press **Ctrl + Home** to return to cell B3.

10. Press **End + (Down Arrow)** to move to the last record in the list, in cell B44. Verify that the last record contains the data for Mary Hutch.

11. Press **Ctrl + Home** to return to cell B3.

Now you can make the other updates to the faculty list. You still need to complete two tasks: change Kevin Mack's rank and salary, and delete Wendy Garabizien's record. Although you can manually scroll through the list to find a specific record, with larger lists of data this method is slow and prone to error. The quicker and more accurate way to find a record is to use the data form's search capabilities. You will use this method to make Kevin Mack's changes and delete Wendy Garabizien's record.

Using the Data Form to Search for Records

You can use the data form to search for a specific record or group of records. When you initiate a search, you specify the search criteria, or instructions for the search. Excel starts from the current record and moves through the list, searching for any records that match the search criteria. If Excel finds more than one record that matches the search criteria, it displays the first record that matches the criteria. You can use the Find Next button in the data form to display the next record that matches the search criteria.

You need to find Kevin Mack's record to change his salary. Use the data form to find this record.

To search for a record in a list using the data form:

1. Make sure the active cell is inside the faculty list.

2. Click **Data** on the menu bar, and then click **Form** to display the Faculty Data data form.

3. Click the **Criteria** button to display a blank data form. The label "Criteria" in the upper-right corner of the data form indicates that the form is ready to accept search criteria.

Enter the search criterion in the appropriate field.

4. Click the **LASTNAME** text box, and then type **Mack**.

If necessary, you can enter multiple criteria. If you enter multiple criteria, all criteria must be met for Excel to find a match.

5. Click the **Find Next** button to display the next record in the list that meets the specified criterion—LASTNAME equal to Mack. See Figure 5-13.

Figure 5-13 DATA FORM AFTER FINDING KEVIN MACK'S RECORD

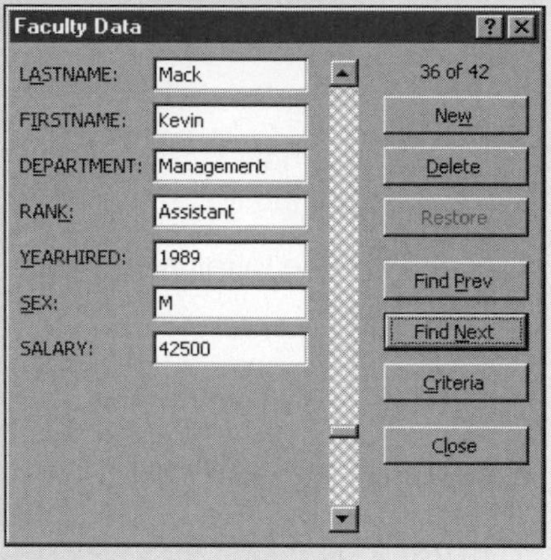

Kevin Mack is the record you're looking for. However, if more than one employee were named Mack and this was not the record you were interested in, you could click the Find Next button again and the next record meeting the search criterion would appear.

If no records meet the search criterion, no message appears. Instead, the data form simply displays the current record.

Now update his record.

6. Double-click the **RANK** text box, and then type **Associate**.

7. Double-click the **Salary** text box, and then type **45000**.

8. Click the **Close** button to return to the faculty list. The rank and salary for Kevin Mack have been updated.

9. Scroll the list to verify that Kevin Mack's salary is now $45,000, and then press **Ctrl + Home** to return to cell B3.

Now complete the final update to the list, deleting Wendy Garabizien's record.

Using the Data Form to Delete a Record

To delete Wendy Garabizien's record, you will again use a search criterion to find the record. If you enter the full name as the search criterion, the spelling must be absolutely correct; otherwise there will be no match and Wendy Garabizien's record won't be found.

As an alternative, the data form allows you to use wildcard characters when you enter search criteria. A **wildcard character** is a symbol that stands for one or more characters. Excel recognizes two wildcards: the question mark (?) and the asterisk (*).

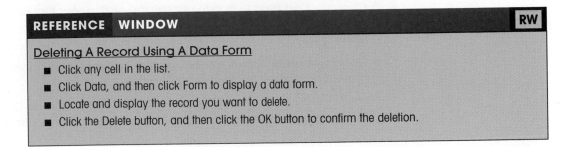

REFERENCE WINDOW RW

Deleting A Record Using A Data Form

- Click any cell in the list.
- Click Data, and then click Form to display a data form.
- Locate and display the record you want to delete.
- Click the Delete button, and then click the OK button to confirm the deletion.

You use the asterisk (*) wildcard to represent any group of characters. For example, if you use "Gar*" as the search criterion for LASTNAME, Excel will find all the records with a last name that begins with Gar, no matter what letters follow. You use the question mark (?) to substitute for a single character. For example, if you enter "Richm?n" as the search criterion, and you might find Richman, Richmen, or Richmon.

To avoid entering Wendy Garabizien's name incorrectly, use the asterisk wildcard character to help find her record.

To search for a record using a wildcard character:

1. Click any cell in the list, click **Data** on the menu bar, and then click **Form** to display the Faculty Data data form.
2. Click the **Criteria** button to begin entering the search criterion.

   Specify the new search criterion.
3. Click the **LASTNAME** text box, and then type **Gar***. See Figure 5-14.

Figure 5-14 SEARCHING FOR FACULTY MEMBERS USING WILDCARD CHARACTER

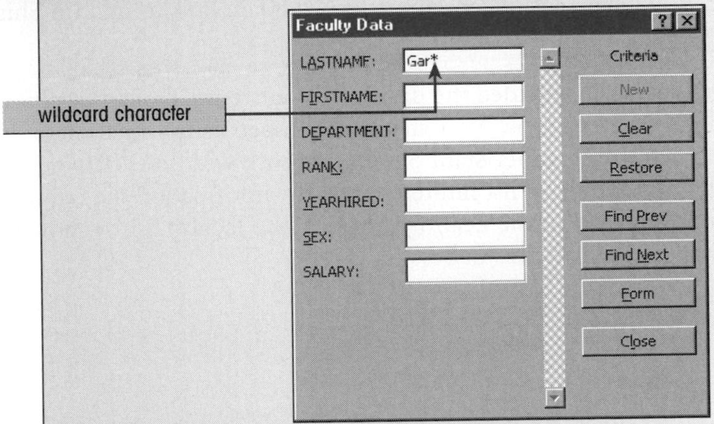

4. Click the **Find Next** button to display the first record in the list that contains the letters Gar as first three letters of the last name. Karen Garafano is not the record you want to delete.

TROUBLE? If you did not retrieve Karen Garafano's record, click the Close button, click Data on the menu bar, and then click Form before repeating Steps 1 through 4.

5. Click the **Find Next** button to display the next record that contains the letters Gar at the beginning of the name. Wendy Garabizien is the record you're looking for.
6. Click the **Delete** button. A message box appears warning you that the displayed record will be permanently deleted from the list.
7. Click the **OK** button to confirm the record deletion. Wendy Garabizien's record has been deleted from the list, and the next record in the list appears in the data form.
8. Click the **Close** button to close the data form and return to the worksheet.

Session 5.1 Quick Check

1. A row within a data list is often called a ______________.
2. A column within a data list is often called a ______________.
3. In Excel, a ______________ is a collection of similar data stored in a structured manner.
4. Explain how to order a student list so that all students in the same major appear together in alphabetical order by the student's last name.
5. A ______________ sort key is a field used to arrange records in a list.
6. If you sort the faculty list from the most recent start date to the earliest start date, you have sorted the faculty in ______________ order.
7. The ______________ button in the Data Form is used to add a record to a list.
8. You have a list of 250 employees. Explain how to find Jin Shinu's record using the data form.

You have now provided the dean with a current list of all faculty members, sorted alphabetically by department. Now she requires specific information on only some of the faculty at different levels on her staff. She could work with the complete list to find this information, but a customized list limited to just the information she requires would be more useful to her. You can help the dean by filtering the faculty list to show just the information she requires. You will do this in Session 5.2.

SESSION 5.2

In this session you will learn to filter a list to display only specific information using AutoFilters, and you will learn how to customize filters to meet more complex criteria. You will use conditional formatting to highlight data in the list. You will also expand the list to include a new field using natural language formulas, and insert subtotals to display summary information in the list. Finally, you will use Page Break Preview to insert custom page breaks for printing the list.

Filtering a List Using AutoFilters

Now that the dean has the full list of faculty organized for easy reference, she is ready to use the list to prepare the reports she needs for her upcoming meetings. The first scheduled meeting is with the other deans at NSU—their task is to form a university-wide accreditation committee comprising faculty representatives from each of the individual colleges and departments at the university. The dean needs to select a faculty member from the College of Business Administration to serve on the committee. She wants to select a senior faculty member and asks you for a list of full professors.

To get a list of faculty members who are full professors, you could scan the entire faculty list. However, locating the data you need within large lists can be difficult and time-consuming. Sorting can help you group the data; however, you're still working with the entire list. You could use a data form, but if you use a data form to find records that meet specified criteria, you will only display one record at a time. A better solution is to have Excel find the specific records you want, displaying only these records in the worksheet. This process of "hiding" certain records and viewing the ones you want is called **filtering** your data. All records that do not meet your criteria are temporarily hidden from view.

REFERENCE WINDOW RW

Filtering A List With AutoFilter

- Click any cell in the list.
- Click Data, point to Filter, and then click AutoFilter to insert list arrows next to each column label in your list.
- Click the list arrow in the column that contains the data you want to filter.
- Click the criteria you want to filter.

The Excel AutoFilter feature allows you to filter your data so you view only the records you want. You will use this feature to create a list of full professors in the College of Business Administration.

To filter a list using the AutoFilter command:

1. If you took a break after the last session, make sure Excel is running, the CBA Faculty workbook is open, and the Faculty Data worksheet is active. Make sure the active cell is within the faculty list.
2. Click **Data** on the menu bar, point to **Filter**, and then click **AutoFilter**. List arrows appear next to each column label in the list. To see a list of filtering criteria for a specific column, click the list arrow next to the column heading.

3. Click the **RANK column** list arrow in cell D2 to display a list of criteria you can use to filter the data. See Figure 5-15. In addition to the unique values—Assistant, Associate, Full, and Instructor in the RANK column, three other choices appear that apply to every column. Figure 5-16 describes these three options.

Figure 5-15 FILTERING OPTIONS FOR RANK FIELD

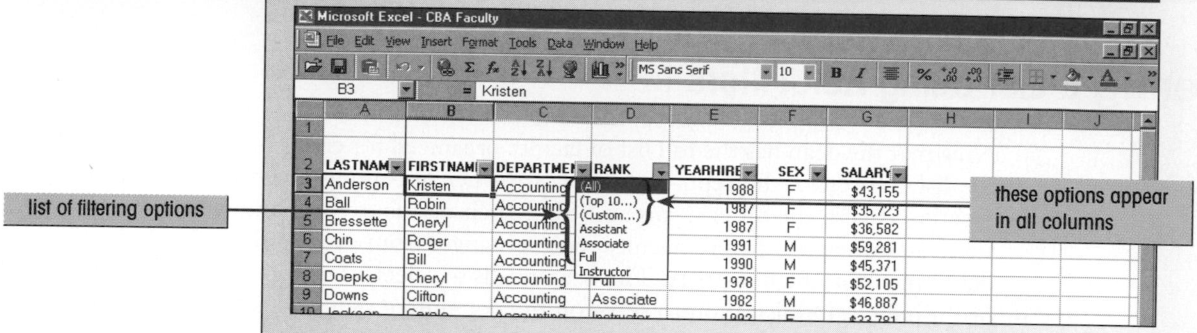

Figure 5-16 DEFAULT FILTERING OPTIONS

OPTION	DESCRIPTION
All	Displays all items in the column and removes filtering for the column
Top 10	Displays the top or bottom *n* items in the list
Custom	Specifies more complex criteria

Now select your criterion for filtering the data.

4. Click **Full** to display only full professors. See Figure 5-17. In the status bar, Excel displays the number of records found out of the total records in the list. Review the list to verify that only records with a value equal to Full in the RANK column are visible. Excel hides all rows (records) that do not have the value Full in this column.

Figure 5-17 FACULTY LIST DISPLAYING ONLY FULL PROFESSORS

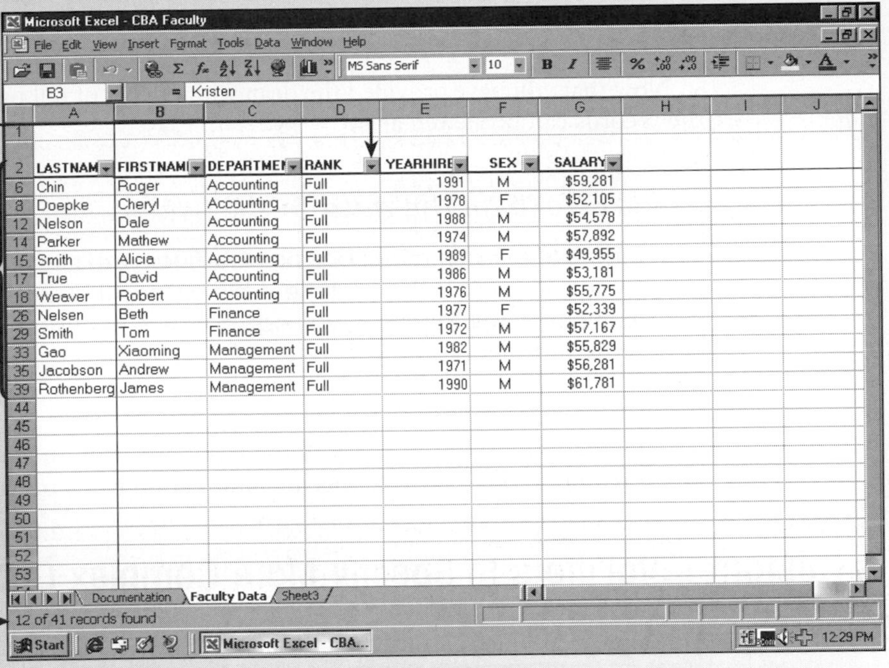

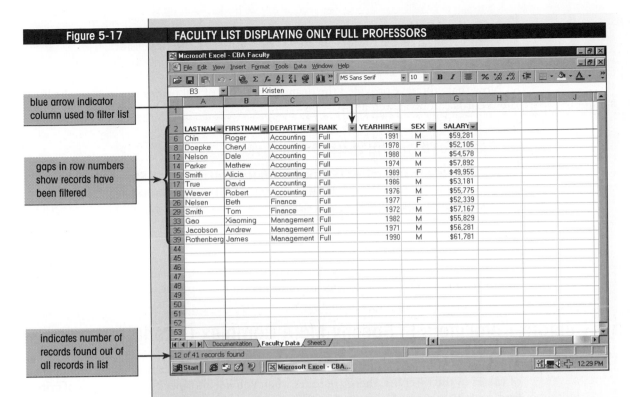

blue arrow indicator column used to filter list

gaps in row numbers show records have been filtered

indicates number of records found out of all records in list

Notice the gaps in the row numbers in the worksheet, and the blue color of the row numbers of the filtered records. In addition the color of the list arrow next to the RANK column changes to blue to let you know that this column has been used to filter the list. The dean will find this useful in making her recommendation for faculty to serve on the accreditation committee.

If you need to, you can further restrict the records that appear in the filtered list by selecting entries from another drop-down list. For instance, if the dean wanted to select from a pool of female faculty with a rank of full professor, you could simply click the SEX column and then click F.

To filter by more than one criterion:

1. Click the **SEX** column list arrow in cell F2, and then click **F** to display the female full professors. See Figure 5-18.

Figure 5-18 FACULTY LIST SHOWING FEMALE FULL PROFESSORS

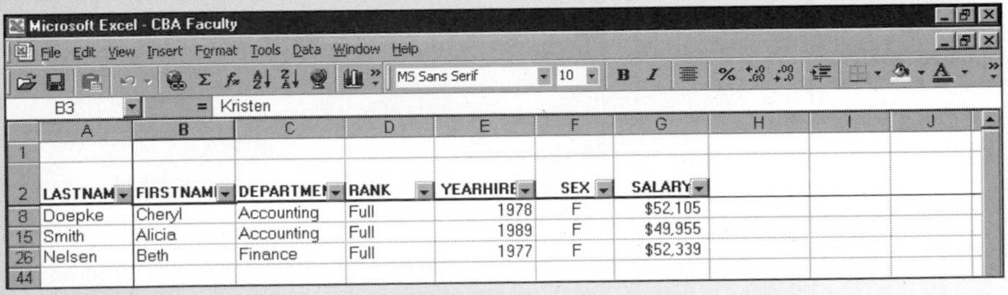

Now remove the filter from the SEX field.

2. Click the **SEX** column list arrow, and then click **All** to remove the filter from this field. Notice all full professors, males and females, are now listed.

Now that you have provided the dean with the list of full professors, restore the list so all the records can be viewed again.

To restore all the data to the list:

1. Click **Data** on the menu bar, point to **Filter**, and then click **Show All**. All the records appear in the worksheet, but all the list arrows remain next to the column headings. Therefore, you can continue to customize the list by filtering it to show certain data.

Now that the list again shows all the faculty records, the dean has a more complex task, which requires you to provide specific information based on customized criteria.

Using Custom AutoFilters to Specify More Complex Criteria

Although you can often find the information you need by selecting a single item from a list of values in the filter list, there are times when you need to specify a custom set of criteria to find certain records. **Custom AutoFilters** allow you to specify relationships other than "equal to" to filter records. For instance, the dean will be meeting with the university's budget director, Bin Chi, later this week to review the College of Business Administration's budget needs for the next fiscal cycle. She received a memo today from the budget office asking for a list of faculty who earn over $50,000 a year and were hired during the 1980s. The dean asks you to print this information. You can develop a custom set of criteria using the Custom option in the AutoFilter list to retrieve these records for the dean.

To use a custom AutoFilter to filter a list:

1. Click the **YEARHIRED** list arrow, and then click **Custom** to open the Custom AutoFilter dialog box. See Figure 5-19.

Figure 5-19 CUSTOM AUTOFILTER DIALOG BOX

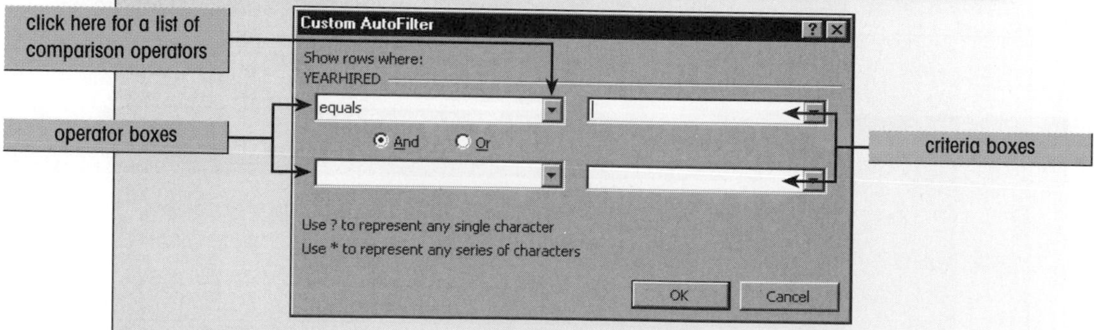

The operator list box, the first list box in the Show rows where section of the dialog box, lets you specify a comparison operator by selecting an item from a list.

The criteria list box, the list box to the right of the operator list box, lets you specify the field value by typing a value or selecting an item from a list.

The And and Or option buttons are used if you want to display rows that meet two conditions for the field. You select And to display rows that meet both criteria. You select Or to display rows that meet either criterion.

2. Click the first operator list arrow, and then click **is greater than or equal to**.
3. Click the first criteria list box, and then type **1980** in the list box.
4. If necessary, click the **And** option button.
5. Click the second operator list arrow, and then click **is less than**.
6. Click the second criteria list box, and then type **1990**. See Figure 5-20.

Figure 5-20 CUSTOM AUTOFILTER DIALOG BOX SHOWING CUSTOM CRITERIA

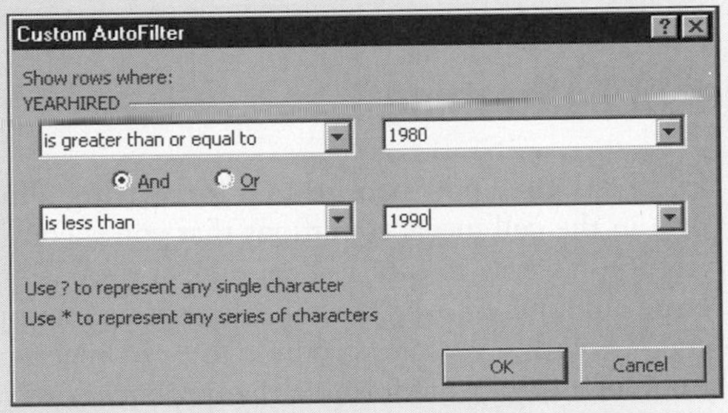

7. Click the **OK** button to display the filtered list consisting of all faculty hired between 1980 and 1989. Notice the status bar indicates 19 of 41 records found.

   You have only some of the information the dean requires, however, because she also needs to know all the faculty hired during the 1980s who earn more than $50,000. So you need to further restrict the filtered list to those faculty earning more than $50,000.

8. Click the **SALARY** list arrow, and then click **Custom** to open the Custom AutoFilter dialog box.
9. Click the first operator list arrow, click **is greater than** from the list of operators, click the **first criteria** list box, and then type **50000**.
10. Click the **OK** button to view the filtered list showing faculty hired between 1980 and 1989 and who earn more than $50,000. See Figure 5-21.

Figure 5-21 FILTERED LIST OF FACULTY HIRED 1980 – 1989 EARNING MORE THAN $50,000

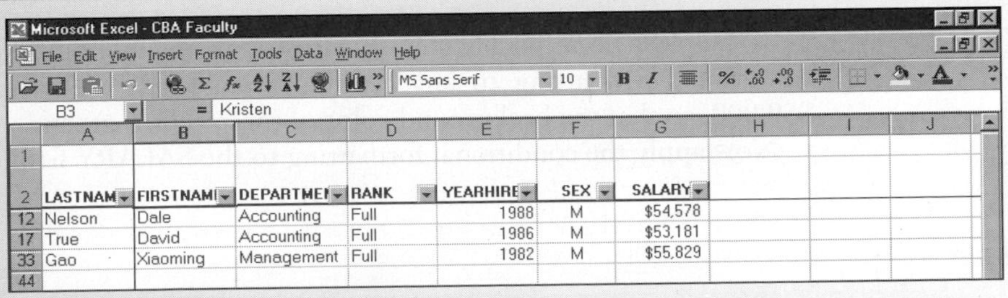

You show the list to the dean. She asks you to sort the list in descending order by salary.

To sort the filtered list, and then restore all the records to the list:

1. Click any field in the SALARY column.
2. Click the **Sort Descending** button on the Standard toolbar to sort the filtered list in descending order by salary.

   You can now remove all the filters to return to the original complete faculty list.
3. Click **Data** on the menu bar, point to **Filter**, and then click **AutoFilter** to remove all the filters. All the records are listed and the list arrows no longer appear in the column headings.

   The dean wants to be able to quickly identify faculty earning more than $50,000 and asks you to apply the new Excel conditional formatting feature to the SALARY field.

Using Conditional Formatting

Excel lets you apply **conditional formatting**—formatting that appears in a cell only when data in the cell meets conditions that you specify or are the result of a formula. Using this feature, it's easy to spot critical highs or lows in a report. For example, cells representing large amounts of overtime, or sales not meeting projections can be formatted in bold font style or with a red background. You can specify up to three conditions that apply to the value of a cell or the formula that produces the value in that cell. For each condition, you specify the formatting (font, font style, font color, border, etc.) that will be applied to the cell if the condition is true.

REFERENCE WINDOW RW

Apply Conditional Formats To Cells

- Select the cells you want to format.
- Click Format on the menu bar, then click Conditional Formatting to open the Conditional Formatting dialog box.
- Specify the condition on which to apply formatting.
- Click the Format button to open the Format Cells dialog box.
- Select the font style, font color, underlining, borders, shading, or patterns you want to apply, then click the OK button to return to the Conditional Formatting dialog box.
- Click the OK button to apply conditional formats to cells.

To help the dean quickly identify faculty earning more than $50,000, you decide to apply conditional formatting to any cell in the SALARY field containing a value exceeding $50,000, so that the background color of these cells is green.

Now apply the conditional formatting to the SALARY field.

To apply conditional formatting to the SALARY field:

1. Select the range **G3:G43**.
2. Click **Format** on the menu bar, and then click **Conditional Formatting** to open the Conditional Formatting dialog box. See Figure 5-22. First, specify the condition that will be applied to the salary range.

   TROUBLE? If the Office Assistant appears, select the option "No, don't provide help now."

Figure 5-22 CONDITIONAL FORMATTING DIALOG BOX

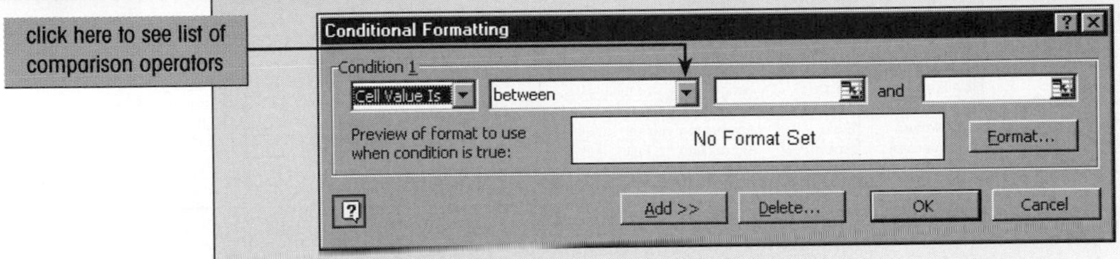

3. Because the contents of the cells in the SALARY field are values, as opposed to formulas or text, make sure Cell Value Is appears in the Condition 1 list box.

   Next, choose the comparison operator to compare with the cell value.
4. Click the list arrow in the second list box to display a list of comparison operators, and then click **greater than**. Notice the number of boxes in the dialog box changes to reflect the comparison operator you selected.

   Now enter the value.
5. Click the third list box for Condition 1, and type **50000**. The condition has been defined. If you needed to, you could specify two additional conditions by clicking the **Add>>** button in the Conditional Formatting dialog box.

   Now define the formatting to be applied to the cell or range if the condition is true.
6. Click the **Format** button in the Conditional Formatting dialog box to open the Format Cells dialog box.
7. Click the **Patterns** tab, and then click the color **green** from the Cell Shading palette (fourth row, fourth column).
8. Click the **OK** button to return to the Conditional Formatting dialog box. Notice that green shading appears in the Preview box.
9. Click the **OK** button to apply the conditional formatting to the selected cells.

   If you had additional conditions to specify, three can be entered, click the **Add>>** button and return to Step 3. To remove a conditional format, click the Delete button and select the condition to delete.
10. Click any cell to deselect the range. See Figure 5-23. Notice that the background color of several cells in the range is now green.

Figure 5-23 **FACULTY LIST AFTER CONDITIONAL FORMATTING APPLIED**

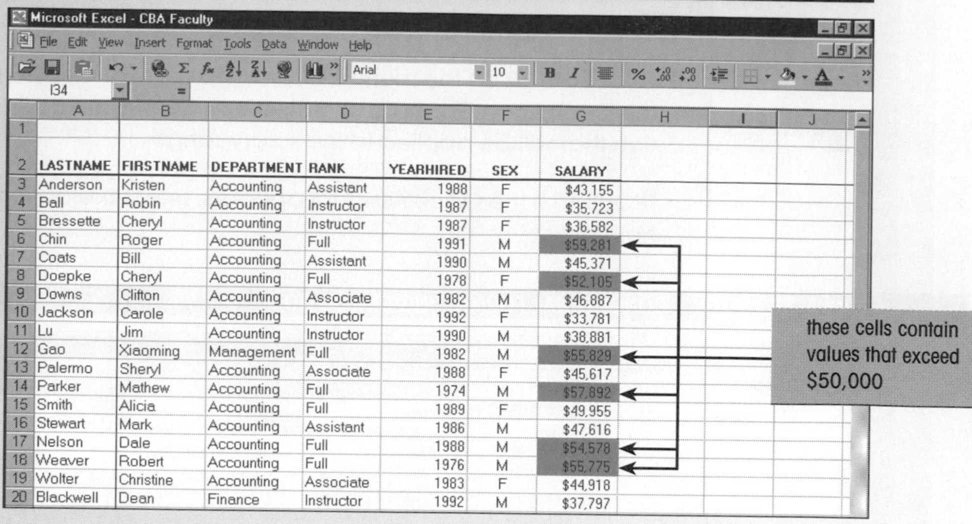

	A	B	C	D	E	F	G
1							
2	LASTNAME	FIRSTNAME	DEPARTMENT	RANK	YEARHIRED	SEX	SALARY
3	Anderson	Kristen	Accounting	Assistant	1988	F	$43,155
4	Ball	Robin	Accounting	Instructor	1987	F	$35,723
5	Bressette	Cheryl	Accounting	Instructor	1987	F	$36,582
6	Chin	Roger	Accounting	Full	1991	M	$59,281
7	Coats	Bill	Accounting	Assistant	1990	M	$45,371
8	Doepke	Cheryl	Accounting	Full	1978	F	$52,105
9	Downs	Clifton	Accounting	Associate	1982	M	$46,887
10	Jackson	Carole	Accounting	Instructor	1992	F	$33,781
11	Lu	Jim	Accounting	Instructor	1990	M	$38,881
12	Gao	Xiaoming	Management	Full	1982	M	$55,829
13	Palermo	Sheryl	Accounting	Associate	1988	F	$45,617
14	Parker	Mathew	Accounting	Full	1974	M	$57,892
15	Smith	Alicia	Accounting	Full	1989	F	$49,955
16	Stewart	Mark	Accounting	Assistant	1986	M	$47,616
17	Nelson	Dale	Accounting	Full	1988	M	$54,578
18	Weaver	Robert	Accounting	Full	1976	M	$55,775
19	Wolter	Christine	Accounting	Associate	1983	F	$44,918
20	Blackwell	Dean	Finance	Instructor	1992	M	$37,797

Note that if the value of the cell changes and no longer meets the specified condition(s), Excel temporarily suppresses the formats associated with that cell. However, the conditional formats remain applied to the cells until you remove them, even when none of the conditions are met and the specified cell formats do not appear.

The dean has a request for information she needs for her meeting with the budget director, and she meets with you to discuss how the faculty list can be used in this task.

Using Worksheet Labels in Formulas

Bin, the budget director, is getting ready to start the next budget cycle. He asks each college dean to provide him with a list of faculty and their proposed salary for next year. Currently, the plan is to increase each faculty member's salary by 3% to keep pace with inflation. The report requested by Bin should list each faculty member by department and should include a departmental subtotal for the PROPOSED SALARY field.

You will need to add a new field to the faculty list—PROPOSED SALARY. This is a calculated field equal to each faculty member's current salary times 1.03.

Although you can use cell references to build this formula, Excel 2000 has a feature that enables you to refer to related data within worksheet formulas by using labels at the top of each column and to the left of each row. For example, in Figure 5-24 you have two labels, Sales and Expenses, which identify the values in cells B1 and B2. These labels can be used to build the formula to compute net income. Instead of entering the formula =B1-B2, the formula =Sales - Expenses uses row labels to calculate net income.

Excel doesn't automatically recognize column and row labels used in formulas. First you must turn this feature on.

To turn the Accept Labels in Formula feature on:

1. Click **Tools**, then click **Options** to display the Options dialog box.
2. Click the **Calculation** tab.

3. In the worksheet options section, click the **Accept Labels in Formula** check box to turn this feature on.

4. Click **OK**.

Figure 5-24 EXAMPLE OF A FORMULA USING WORKSHEET LABELS

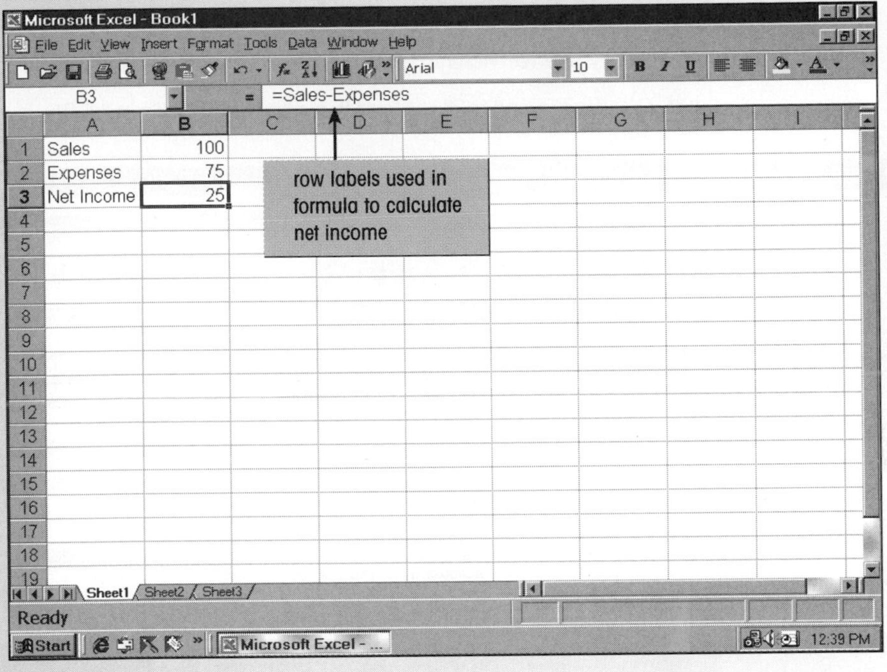

Now, add the PROPOSED SALARY field to the faculty list using the worksheet label to create the formula.

To enter and format the column heading for proposed salary:

1. Click cell **H2**, and then type **PROPOSED SALARY**.
2. Click cell **G2**, click the **Format Painter** button on the Standard toolbar, and then click cell **H2** to copy the format in cell G2 to cell H2.
3. Click **Format** on the menu bar, and then click **Cells** to open the Format Cells dialog box.
4. Click the **Alignment** tab, click the **Wrap Text** check box, and then click the **OK** button to apply text wrapping to cell H2.

Now enter the formula to calculate the proposed salary.

To use a worksheet label to create a formula:

1. In cell H3, type **=salary*1.03**, and then press the **Enter** key. "Salary" in the formula is the column heading. Excel uses the corresponding cell in the SALARY column (G3) to multiply times 1.03.

TROUBLE? If the #NAME? error value appears in the cell, you need to turn the Accept Labels in Formula feature on and then reenter the formula. Return to the steps labeled "To turn the Accept Labels in Formula feature on."

Apply the format used in the SALARY field to the PROPOSED SALARY field.

2. Click cell G3, click the **Format Painter** button and then click cell H3 to copy the formatting.

3. Copy the formula in cell H3 to the range H4:H43. Scroll to the top of the list.

4. Click any cell to deselect the range. See Figure 5-25.

Figure 5-25 **FACULTY LIST WITH NEW FIELD**

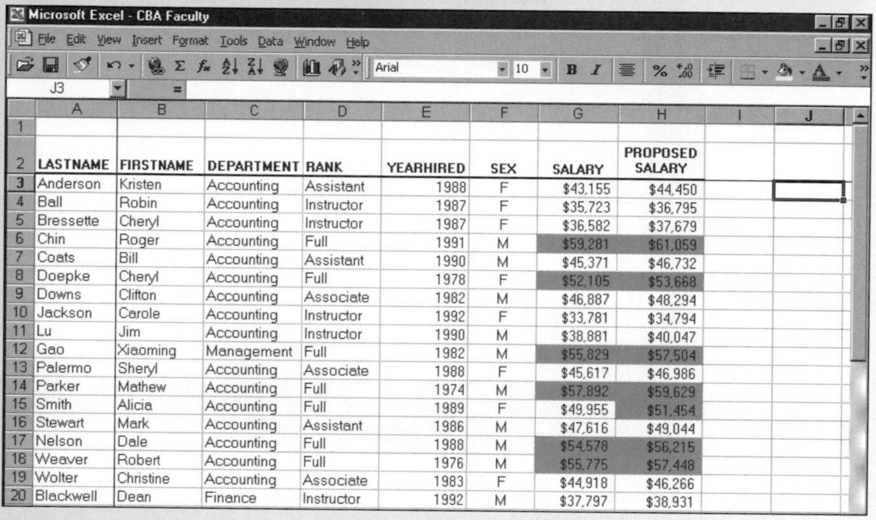

	A	B	C	D	E	F	G	H
1								
2	LASTNAME	FIRSTNAME	DEPARTMENT	RANK	YEARHIRED	SEX	SALARY	PROPOSED SALARY
3	Anderson	Kristen	Accounting	Assistant	1988	F	$43,155	$44,450
4	Ball	Robin	Accounting	Instructor	1987	F	$35,723	$36,795
5	Bressette	Cheryl	Accounting	Instructor	1987	F	$36,582	$37,679
6	Chin	Roger	Accounting	Full	1991	M	$59,281	$61,059
7	Coats	Bill	Accounting	Assistant	1990	M	$45,371	$46,732
8	Doepke	Cheryl	Accounting	Full	1978	F	$52,105	$53,668
9	Downs	Clifton	Accounting	Associate	1982	M	$46,887	$48,294
10	Jackson	Carole	Accounting	Instructor	1992	F	$33,781	$34,794
11	Lu	Jim	Accounting	Instructor	1990	M	$38,881	$40,047
12	Gao	Xiaoming	Management	Full	1982	M	$55,829	$57,504
13	Palermo	Sheryl	Accounting	Associate	1988	F	$45,617	$46,986
14	Parker	Mathew	Accounting	Full	1974	M	$57,892	$59,629
15	Smith	Alicia	Accounting	Full	1989	F	$49,955	$51,454
16	Stewart	Mark	Accounting	Assistant	1986	M	$47,616	$49,044
17	Nelson	Dale	Accounting	Full	1988	M	$54,578	$56,215
18	Weaver	Robert	Accounting	Full	1976	M	$55,775	$57,448
19	Wolter	Christine	Accounting	Associate	1983	F	$44,918	$46,266
20	Blackwell	Dean	Finance	Instructor	1992	M	$37,797	$38,931

Now that the PROPOSED SALARY field has been added to the list, you can prepare the information for the dean. Remember, this report will list the faculty by department, followed by totals for each department.

Inserting Subtotals into a List

Excel can summarize data in a list by inserting subtotals. The Subtotals command offers many kinds of summary information, including counts, sums, averages, minimums, and maximums. The Subtotals command automatically inserts a subtotal line into the list for each group of data. A grand total line is also added to the bottom of the list. Because Excel inserts subtotals whenever the value in a specified field changes, you need to sort the list so records with the same value in a specified field are grouped together before you can use the subtotals command.

REFERENCE WINDOW RW

Calculating Subtotals In A List

- Sort the list by the column for which you want a subtotal.
- Click a cell in the list.
- Click Data, and then click Subtotals to open the Subtotal dialog box.
- In the At each change in list box, select the column containing the group you want to subtotal.
- In the Use function list box, select the function you want to use to summarize the data.
- In the Add subtotal to list box, select the column containing the values you want to summarize.
- Click the OK button.

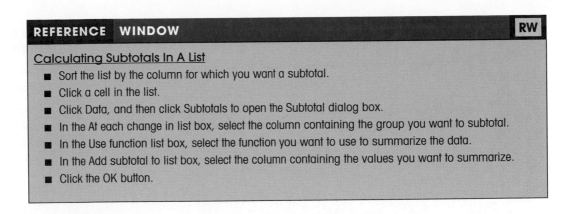

To supply Bin with the information he requested, you will develop a list of faculty, sorted by department, with subtotals calculated for the PROPOSED SALARY field. Each subtotal will be inserted after each departmental grouping.

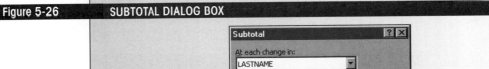

To calculate subtotals by department:

1. If the list is not sorted by department, click any cell in the DEPARTMENT column, and then click the **Sort Ascending** button on the Standard toolbar. The list is sorted by department.

   Now calculate the subtotals in the list.

2. Click **Data** on the menu bar, and then click **Subtotals** to open the Subtotal dialog box. See Figure 5-26.

Figure 5-26 SUBTOTAL DIALOG BOX

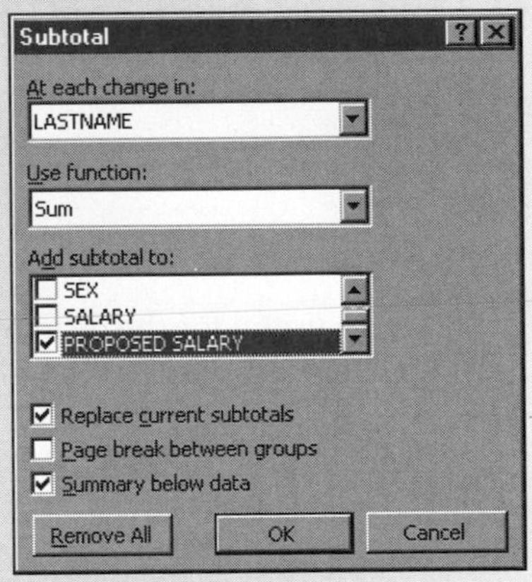

3. Click the **At each change in** list arrow, and then click **DEPARTMENT** to select the column containing the field for which you want subtotals.

4. If necessary, click the **Use function** list arrow, and then click **Sum** to select the function you want to use to summarize the data.

   You want departmental subtotals for the PROPOSED SALARY field.

5. In the Add subtotal to list box, scroll the list and, if necessary, remove any check marks in the category check boxes, and then click the **PROPOSED SALARY** check box, the column containing the field you want to summarize.

6. Make sure the Replace current subtotals and the Summary below data check boxes are checked so that the subtotals appear below the related data.
7. Click the **OK** button to insert subtotals into the list. Subtotals are added to the PROPOSED SALARY column, showing the total salaries for each department.
8. Scroll through the list to be sure you can see all the subtotals and the grand total at the bottom. If necessary, increase the column width so you can view the subtotal values. See Figure 5-27. Notice the Outline buttons to the left of the worksheet, which show the levels of detail possible while the Subtotals command is active.

Figure 5-27 **FACULTY LIST WITH SUBTOTALS**

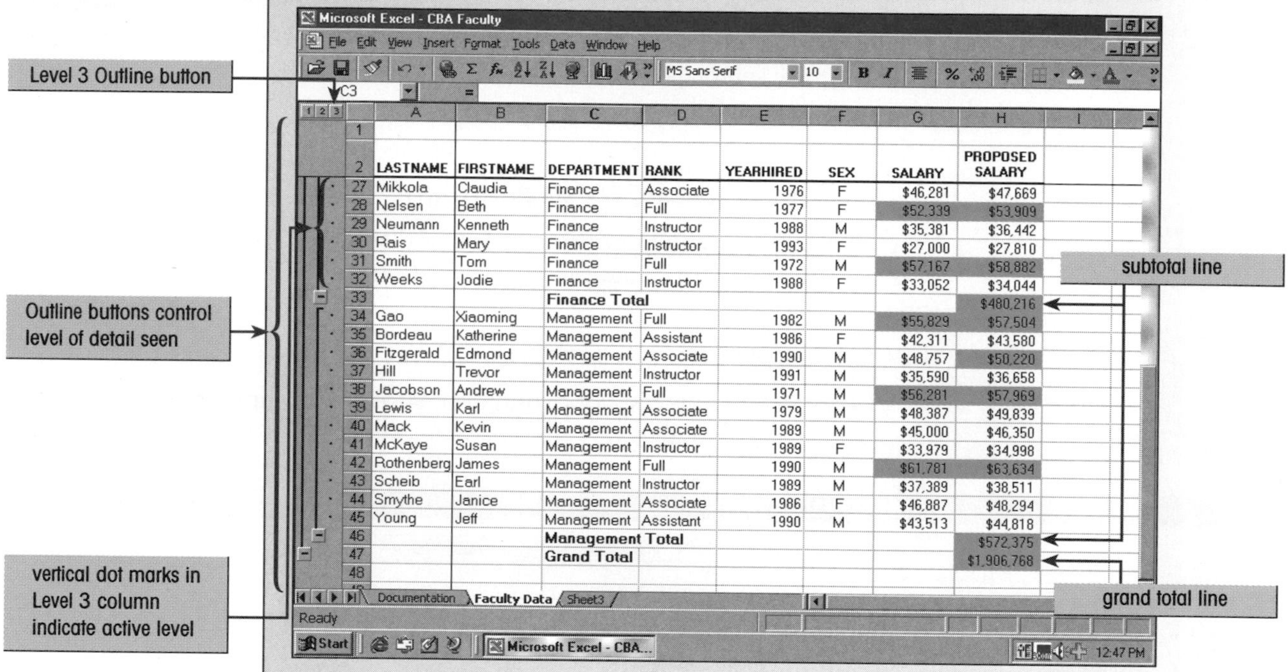

The subtotals are useful for the dean to see, but she asks if there is a way to isolate the different subtotal sections so that she can focus on them individually.

Using **the Subtotals Outline View**

In addition to displaying subtotals, the Subtotals command "outlines" your worksheet so you can control the level of detail that is displayed. The three Outline buttons at the top of the outline area in Figure 5-27 allow you to show or hide different levels of detail in your worksheet. By default, the highest level is active, in this case Level 3. Level 3 displays the most detail—the individual faculty records, the subtotals, and the grand total. If you click the Level 2 Outline button, only the subtotals and the grand total appear but not the individual records. If you click the Level 1 Outline button, only the grand total appears. Now, use the Outline buttons to prepare a report that includes only subtotals and the grand total.

To use the Outline buttons to hide the detail:

1. Press **Ctrl + Home** to make cell B3 the active cell.
2. Click the **Level 2** Outline button. See Figure 5-28. Notice that the worksheet hides the individual faculty records and shows only the subtotals for each department and the grand total.

Figure 5-28 SUBTOTALS AFTER LEVEL 2 OUTLINE BUTTON SELECTED

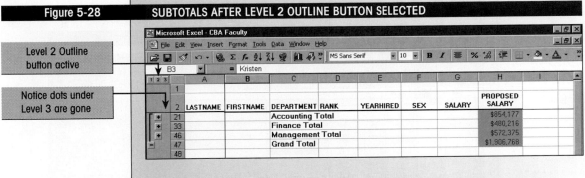

Level 2 Outline button active

Notice dots under Level 3 are gone

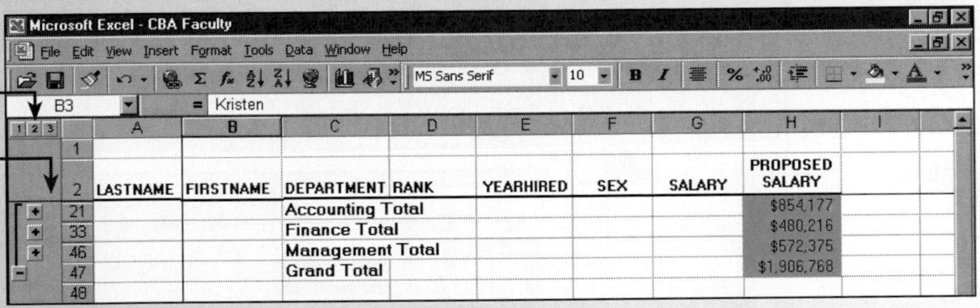

3. Include your name in a custom footer and then print the worksheet.
4. Click the **Level 3** Outline button to show all the records again.

Now that you have prepared the list with subtotals, you can remove the subtotals from the list.

To remove the subtotals from the list:

1. Click any cell in the list, click **Data** on the menu bar, and then click **Subtotals** to open the Subtotal dialog box.
2. Click the **Remove All** button to remove the subtotals from the list.
3. If necessary, click **Ctrl + Home** to return to the top of the list.
4. Save the worksheet.

The dean is very pleased with the way you have manipulated the faculty list to provide her with the data she needs. She now needs printouts she can hand out to the various department heads.

Printing the List Using Page Breaks

When you printed the faculty list, it printed on one page. The dean has asked that the data for each department be printed on a separate page so copies can be shared with each department head as well as the budget director. You can use the Page Break Preview button from the Print Preview window to view where Excel breaks pages in your worksheet and to change either a horizontal or a vertical page break. Alternatively, you can also activate Page Break Preview by clicking View from the menu bar and then clicking Page Break Preview.

To insert a page break to start a new page:

1. Click the **Print Preview** button on the Standard toolbar to display the faculty list. Notice that only one page is needed to print the list.

2. Click the **Page Break Preview** button to view a version of the worksheet that shows the entire print area with page breaks and page numbers superimposed on it. Excel is now in Page Break Preview view. See Figure 5-29.

   TROUBLE? If the Message, "Welcome to Page Break View. You can adjust where the page breaks are by clicking and dragging them with your mouse" appears, click the check box, and then click the OK button, so the message does not appear again.

Figure 5-29 PAGE BREAK PREVIEW VIEW

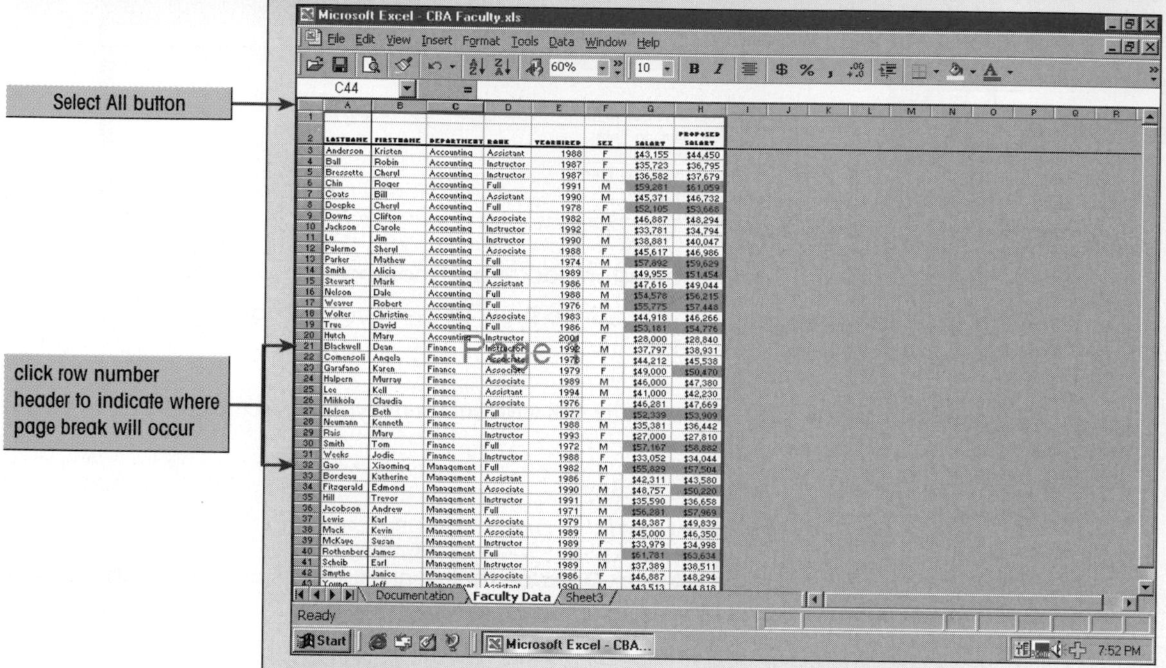

Page Break Preview is different from Print Preview in that you can make some modifications to the worksheet in this mode.

3. Click the **row number header** to the left of column A at row 21, the row where you want to start a new page.
4. Click **Insert** on the menu bar, and then click **Page Break**.
5. Repeat Steps 3 and 4 to insert a page break at row 32. Notice that after you insert the page break, a thick blue line appears to indicate where the break is located.
6. Click the **Print** button on the Standard toolbar to print the faculty list on separate pages for each department.

Printing Row and Column Titles on Every Page

As you review the printouts, you notice the column headings only appear on the first page. By default, the row and column titles just print on the first page. If you want to repeat the row and column titles printed on every page, use the Rows to Repeat At Top and Column To Repeat at Left text boxes on the Sheet tab of the Page Setup dialog box to specify the rows and columns you want to repeat. Although you won't step through this task in the tutorial, you can try it in the Review Assignments by following the steps in the reference window below.

REFERENCE WINDOW RW

Printing Row And Column Titles On Every Page

- Click File, then click Page Setup to open the Page Setup dialog box.
- Click the Sheet tab.
- In the Print titles section, click the Collapse dialog box button of the Rows to repeat at top or Columns to repeat at left text boxes, and then select the row or column titles to repeat on each page.
- Click the Collapse dialog box button again to restore the Page Setup dialog box.
- Click OK.

Removing Page Breaks

Because you will not need these page breaks for future printouts of the faculty list, remove them now.

To remove page breaks from the worksheet:

1. Click the **Select All** button located at the intersection of the row and column headings of your worksheet (if necessary, refer to Figure 5-29), click **Insert** on the menu bar, and then click **Reset All Page Breaks**.

   Now return to normal view.

2. Click **View** on the menu bar, and then click **Normal**. The worksheet returns to normal view.
3. Click any cell, and save the workbook.

Session 5.2 QUICK CHECK

1. If you have a list of 300 students in the College of Business Administration and wanted to print only finance majors, you would use the ______________ commands from the menu.
2. Explain how you can display a list of marketing majors with a GPA of 3.0 or greater from a list of 300 students.
3. ______________ enables formatting to appear only when the data in a cell meets a condition you specify.
4. If you had a worksheet with the column headings Shares and Cost Per Share, and entered the formula =*Shares * Cost Per Share* to compute Total Cost, you used ______________ in the formula.
5. Explain the relationship between the Sort and Subtotals commands.
6. Once subtotals are visible, you can use the ______________ button to control the level of detail displayed.
7. If you have a list of students sorted by major and you wanted to print the students in each major on a separate page, you would use the ______________.

You have supplied the dean with the information she needs for her meeting with the budget director to review financial plans for the next fiscal cycle. Now the dean needs to generate some information for a meeting with the affirmative action task force. You will work with the CBA faculty list in the next session to gather the information she needs for that meeting.

SESSION 5.3

In this session you will learn to summarize data from an Excel list in different formats using the PivotTable and PivotChart Wizard.

Creating and Using Pivot Tables to Summarize a List

An Excel list can contain a wealth of information, but because of the large amounts of detailed data, it is often difficult to form a clear, overall view of the information. You can use a pivot table to help organize the information. A **pivot table** is an interactive table that enables you to group and summarize an Excel list into a concise, tabular format for easier reporting and analysis. A pivot table summarizes data in different categories using functions such as COUNT, SUM, AVERAGE, MAX, and MIN.

All pivot tables have similar elements. These include **column fields**, **row fields**, and **page fields**. Typically, the values in category fields, such as department, rank, year hired, and sex, appear in pivot tables as rows, columns, or pages. In creating a pivot table, you also specify which fields you want to summarize. Salaries, sales, and costs are examples of fields that you usually summarize. In pivot table terminology, these are known as **data fields**.

One advantage of pivot tables is that you can easily rearrange, hide, and display different categories in the pivot table to provide alternative views of the data. This ability to "pivot" your table—for example, change column headings to row positions and vice versa—gives the pivot table its name and makes it a powerful analytical tool.

The dean now wants some tabulated information for an affirmative action report. She first reviewed the data within the faculty list to try to get a feel for whether men and women in comparable positions are making comparable salaries. She became overwhelmed and asked you to set up a pivot table.

You consider the information that the dean wants and create a pivot table plan (Figure 5-30) and a pivot table sketch (Figure 5-31). Your plan and sketch will help you work with the PivotTable and PivotChart Wizard to produce the pivot table you want.

Figure 5-30 PIVOT TABLE PLAN FOR CALCULATING AVERAGE SALARIES

Pivot Table Plan

My Goal:
Create a table that compares female and male average salary for each academic rank

What results do I want to see?
Average female salary for each rank
Average male salary for each rank
Overall average female salary
Overall average male salary
The average salary at each rank for males and females combined

What information do I need?
The table rows will show the data for each rank
The table columns will show the data for each sex
The table will summarize salary data

What calculation method will I use?
The salary data will be averaged for each rank and sex

Figure 5-31 SKETCH OF TABLE TO COMPARE AVERAGE SALARIES

Average Salaries by Rank for Females and Males

Rank	Females	Males	Totals
Instructor	xx	xx	xx
Assistant	xx	xx	xx
Associate	xx	xx	xx
Full	xx	xx	xx
Totals	xx	xx	xx

Now you are ready to create a pivot table summarizing average faculty salaries of men and women by rank.

Creating a Pivot Table

To create the pivot table for the dean, you use the Excel PivotTable and PivotChart Wizard to guide you through a three-step process. Although the PivotTable and PivotChart Wizard will prompt you for the information necessary to create the table, the preliminary plan and sketch you created will be helpful in achieving the layout the dean wants.

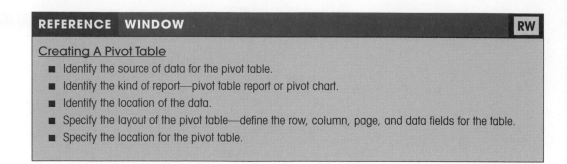

REFERENCE WINDOW RW

Creating A Pivot Table

- Identify the source of data for the pivot table.
- Identify the kind of report—pivot table report or pivot chart.
- Identify the location of the data.
- Specify the layout of the pivot table—define the row, column, page, and data fields for the table.
- Specify the location for the pivot table.

Most often when creating a pivot table, you begin with a list stored in a worksheet. In this case, you will use the faculty list in the Faculty Data worksheet to create the pivot table.

To create a pivot table:

1. If you took a break after the last session, make sure the CBA Faculty workbook is open and the Faculty Data worksheet is active. Click any cell in the list, click **Data** on the menu bar, and then click **PivotTable and PivotChart Report** to open the PivotTable and PivotChart Wizard - Step 1 of 3 dialog box. See Figure 5-32. In this dialog box, you specify the source of the data that is to be used to create the pivot table. You can select from an Excel list; an external data source, such as a dBase or Access file; multiple consolidation ranges; or another pivot table. To develop the average salaries pivot table, you use the Excel list in the Faculty Data worksheet. In this step you also specify the kind of report to create: a pivot table only or a pivot chart along with a pivot table.

   TROUBLE? If the Office Assistant appears, select the option "No, don't provide help now."

Figure 5-32 PIVOTTABLE AND PIVOTCHART WIZARD - STEP 1 OF 3 DIALOG BOX

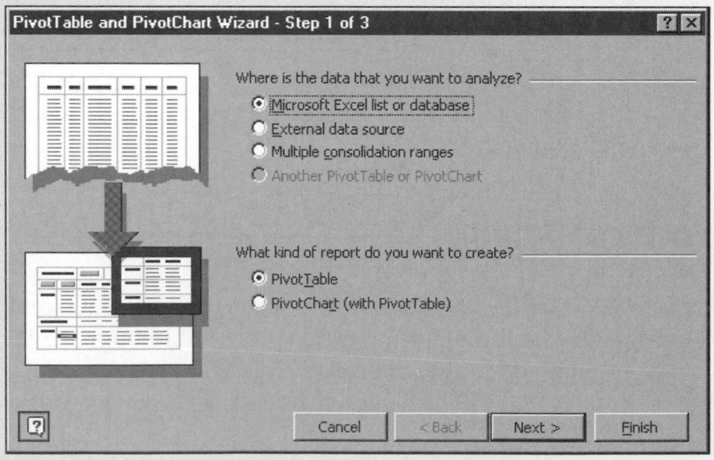

2. Make sure the Microsoft Excel list or database option is selected as the source of data and the PivotTable option is selected as the kind of report. Then, click the **Next** button to open the PivotTable and PivotChart Wizard - Step 2 of 3 dialog box. See Figure 5-33.

Figure 5-33 PIVOTTABLE AND PIVOTCHART WIZARD - STEP 2 OF 3 DIALOG BOX

At this point, you need to identify the location of the data you are going to summarize in the pivot table.

Because the active cell is located within the range of the Excel list, the Wizard automatically selects the range of the faculty list, 'Faculty Data'!$A$2:$H$43, as the source of data for the pivot table.

TROUBLE? If the Range box in the PivotTable and PivotChart Wizard - Step 2 of 3 displays "Database" instead of $A$2:$H$43 as the source of the data, click the Next button to go to Step 3 of the PivotTable and PivotChart Wizard. If an error message appears when you click the Next button, click OK, click the Collapse Dialog box button and select the range A2:H43, then click the Collapse Dialog box button again, and then continue to Step 3.

3. Click the **Next** button to open the PivotTable and PivotChart Wizard - Step 3 of 3 dialog box. See Figure 5-34.

In this step you decide where to place the pivot table—either in a new worksheet or in an existing worksheet. You also have the opportunity to complete the layout of the pivot table within the Wizard by selecting the Layout button, otherwise you can complete the pivot table directly on the worksheet.

You will place the pivot table in a new worksheet and complete the pivot table directly in the worksheet.

Figure 5-34 PIVOTTABLE AND PIVOTCHART WIZARD - STEP 3 OF 3 DIALOG BOX

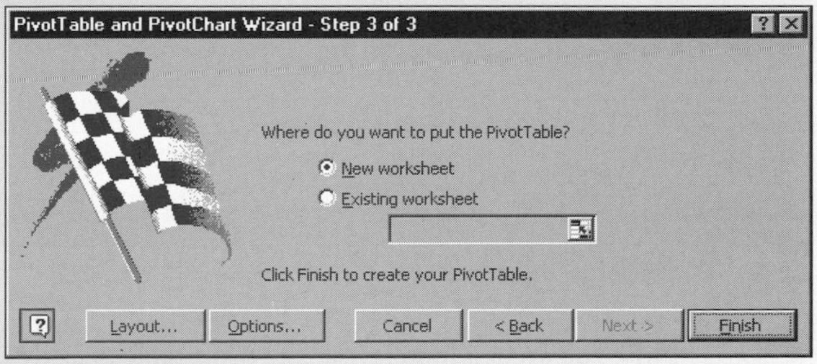

4. Make sure the **New worksheet** option button is selected, and then click the **Finish** button to create the pivot table report framework. See Figure 5-35. A new worksheet, Sheet1, appears to the left of the Faculty Data sheet. This sheet contains a PivotTable report framework, a diagram containing blue outlined drop areas, which will assist you in completing the pivot table. Additionally, the PivotTable toolbar appears. Figure 5-36 describes the tools available on this toolbar.

TROUBLE? If you don't see the field buttons on the toolbar, make sure the toolbar is undocked, click within the PivotTable diagram and make sure the Display Fields button on the toolbar is pressed in.

Figure 5-35 PIVOT TABLE REPORT FRAMEWORK

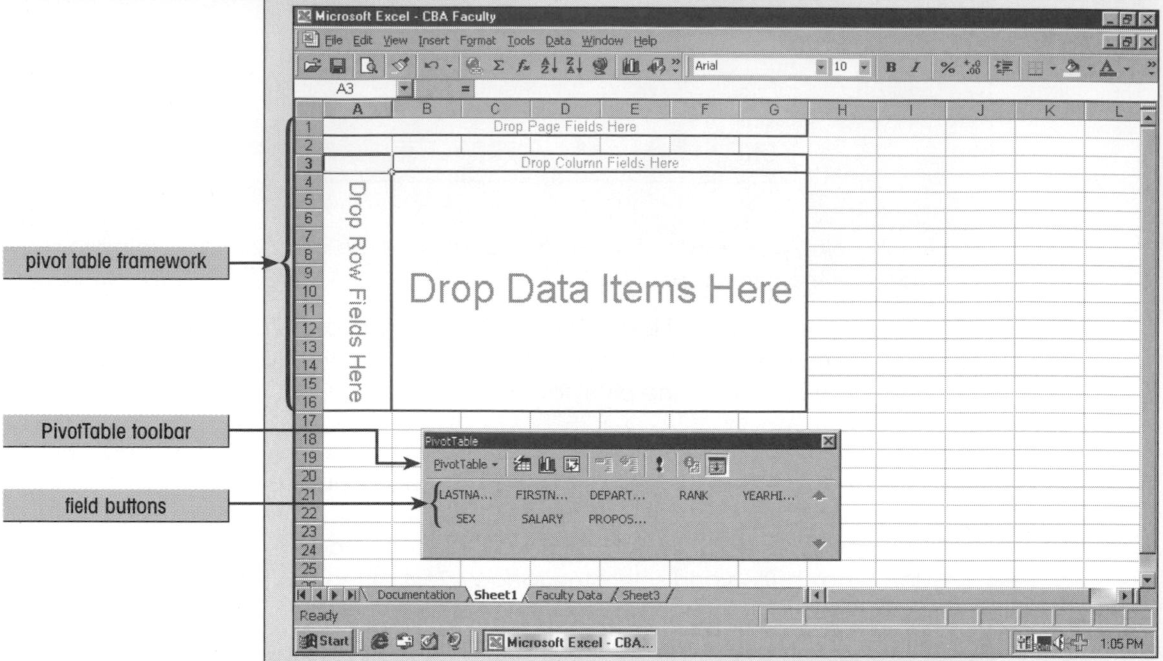

Figure 5-36 TOOLS AVAILABLE ON PIVOTTABLE TOOLBAR

BUTTON	NAME	FUNCTION
PivotTable ▾	PivotTable	Shortcut menu of all pivot table commands
	Format Report	Displays a list of preformatted styles for pivot table reports
	Chart Wizard	Creates a chart of the pivot table report in a chart sheet
	PivotTable Wizard	Accesses the PivotTable wizard so you can modify the pivot table
	Hide Detail	Hides Detail lines for a selected field in a pivot table
	Show Detail	Shows Detail lines from a selected field in a pivot table
	Refresh Data	Updates the contents of a pivot table based on changes made to the source data
	Field settings	Opens the PivotTable Field dialog box so you can modify the options for the selected field
	Hide fields	Displays field buttons on toolbar if they are not visible, hides field buttons if they are visible

Now you are ready to layout the pivot table directly on the worksheet.

Laying Out the Pivot Table Directly on the Worksheet

In the PivotTable report framework, you specify which fields will appear as column, row, and page headings in the pivot table and which fields contain the data you want to summarize. In this step the fields are represented by a set of field buttons found on the PivotTable toolbar. You create the layout by dragging the field buttons from the toolbar to any of the four areas of the pivot table diagram: Drop Rows Fields Here, Drop Column Fields Here, Drop Page Fields Here, or Drop Data Items Here.

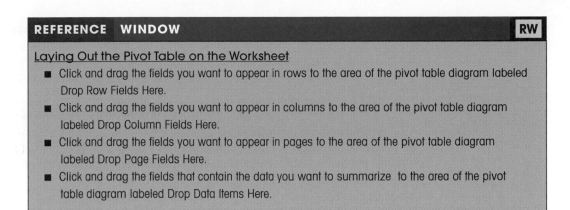

REFERENCE WINDOW RW

Laying Out the Pivot Table on the Worksheet

- Click and drag the fields you want to appear in rows to the area of the pivot table diagram labeled Drop Row Fields Here.
- Click and drag the fields you want to appear in columns to the area of the pivot table diagram labeled Drop Column Fields Here.
- Click and drag the fields you want to appear in pages to the area of the pivot table diagram labeled Drop Page Fields Here.
- Click and drag the fields that contain the data you want to summarize to the area of the pivot table diagram labeled Drop Data Items Here.

In the pivot table you are creating, you will compute average salaries for males and females for each rank and sex. The values in the RANK field will appear as row labels, the values in the SEX field will appear as column headings, and the SALARY field will be the data that is summarized.

Now layout the pivot table in the worksheet.

To layout a pivot table on the worksheet:

1. From the group of field buttons on the toolbar, click and drag the **RANK** field button to the area on the PivotTable diagram labeled Drop Row Fields Here. When you release the mouse button, the RANK button appears in the pivot table report framework. See Figure 5-37. When the pivot table is complete the report will contain a row label for each unique value in the RANK field.

Figure 5-37 PIVOTTABLE DIAGRAM WITH RANK FIELD ADDED

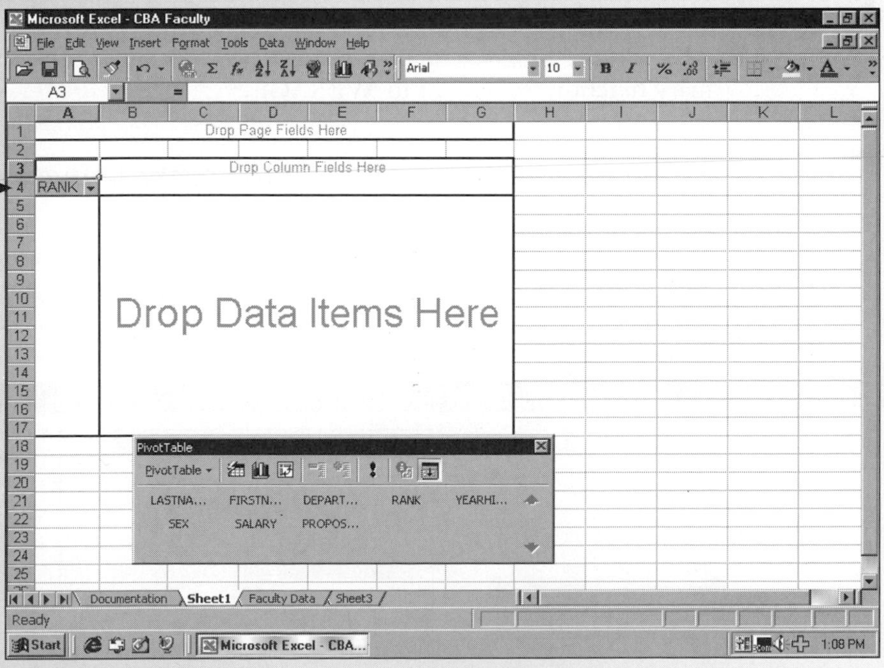

RANK field button dragged to row area

TROUBLE? If you moved the wrong field into the pivot table diagram, you can remove it by dragging it anywhere outside the diagram or clicking the Undo button.

2. Click and drag the **SEX** field button from the PivotTable toolbar to the area of the diagram labeled Drop Column Fields Here. When you release the mouse button, the SEX button appears in the report framework. When the pivot table is complete, the report will contain a column label for each unique value in the SEX field.

3. Click and drag the **SALARY** field button from the PivotTable toolbar to the area of the diagram labeled Drop Data Items Here. When you release the mouse button, the pivot table appears. See Figure 5-38. The Sum of Salary button on the report indicates the type of summary; the report contains total salaries for men and women for each rank.

Figure 5-38 PIVOT TABLE COMPARING TOTAL SALARIES FOR MALES AND FEMALES BY RANK

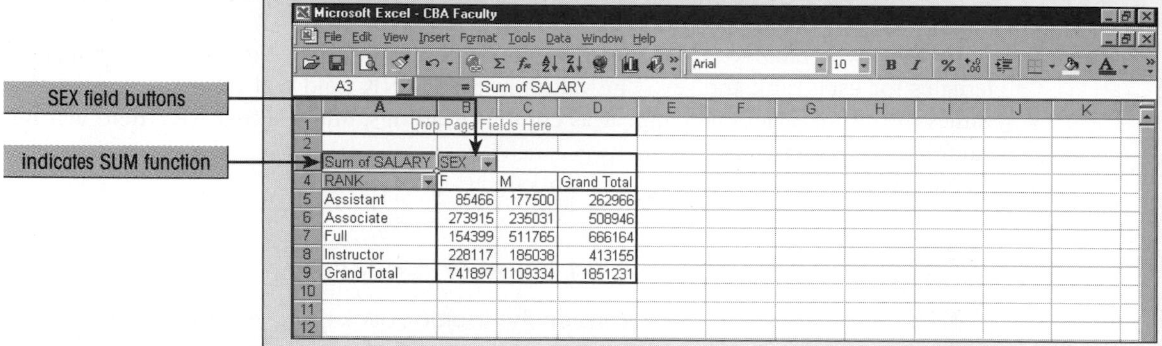

By default, Excel uses the SUM function for calculations involving numeric values placed in the Drop Data Items Here area, and the COUNT function for nonnumeric values. If you want to use a different summary function, such as AVERAGE, MAX, or MIN, you can click the Field Settings button in the PivotTable toolbar and select the summary function from a list of available functions in the PivotTable Field Settings box.

The dean wants to compare average salary by rank and sex. You need to change the summary function from SUM to AVERAGE.

To change the pivot table to compute average salaries by sex and rank:

1. Make sure a value inside the pivot table is selected, then click the **Field Settings** button on the PivotTable toolbar to open the PivotTable Field dialog box. See Figure 5-39.

Figure 5-39 PIVOTTABLE FIELD SETTINGS DIALOG BOX

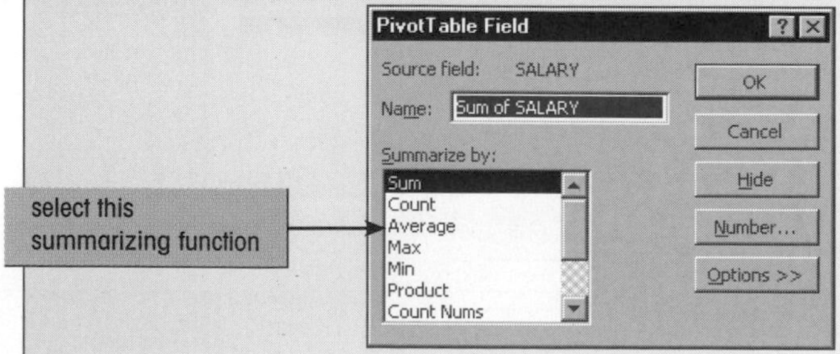

2. Click **Average** in the Summarize by list box, and then click the **OK** button to return to the pivot table report. See Figure 5-40. Notice that the summary button indicates Average of SALARY and the data in the pivot table represents average salaries by rank and sex.

Figure 5-40 PIVOT TABLE SHOWING AVERAGE SALARIES FOR MALES AND FEMALES BY RANK

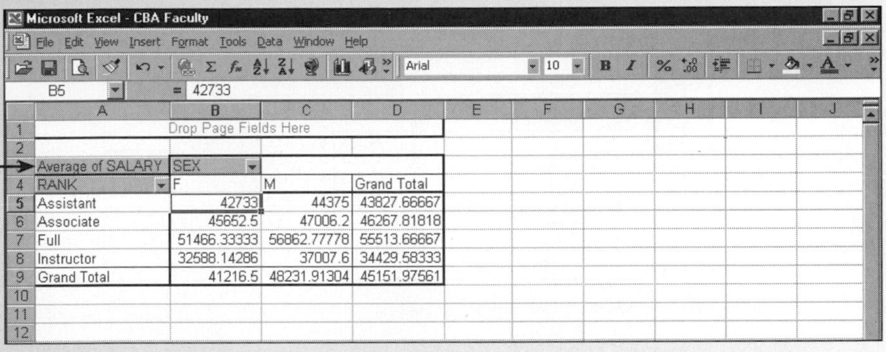

Average of SALARY	SEX		
RANK	F	M	Grand Total
Assistant	42733	44375	43827.66667
Associate	45652.5	47006.2	46267.81818
Full	51466.33333	56862.77778	55513.66667
Instructor	32588.14286	37007.6	34429.58333
Grand Total	41216.5	48231.91304	45151.97561

indicates Average summary function

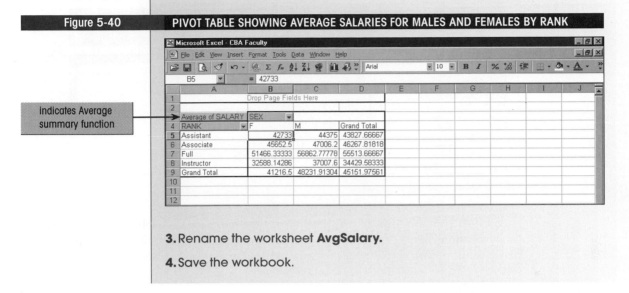

3. Rename the worksheet **AvgSalary.**

4. Save the workbook.

The pivot table in Figure 5-40 shows the average salaries paid to male and female faculty members in each rank. Although the data in a pivot table may look like data in any other worksheet, you cannot directly enter or change data in the DATA area of the pivot table, because the pivot table is linked to the source data. Any changes that affect the pivot table must first be made to the Excel list. Later in the tutorial, you will update a faculty member's salary and learn how to reflect that change in the pivot table.

Changing the Layout of a Pivot Table

Although you cannot change the values inside the pivot table, there are many ways you can change the layout, formatting, and computational options of a pivot table. For example, once the pivot table is created, you have numerous ways of rearranging, adding, and removing fields.

Formatting Numbers in the Pivot Table

As the dean runs off to a meeting, she mentions to you that the numbers in the pivot table are difficult to read. You can apply number formats to the cells in the pivot table just as you would format any cell in a worksheet. You will format the average salary using the Currency style.

To specify the currency style format for pivot table values:

1. Select the range **B5:D9**.

2. Click the **Currency Style** button on the Formatting toolbar. Click the **Decrease Decimal** button on the Formatting toolbar twice to reduce the number of decimal places to zero. If necessary, increase the column width so the formatted average salary values can fit in the cell.

3. Click any cell to deselect the range and view the newly formatted pivot table. See Figure 5-41.

Figure 5-41 PIVOT TABLE AFTER FORMATTING

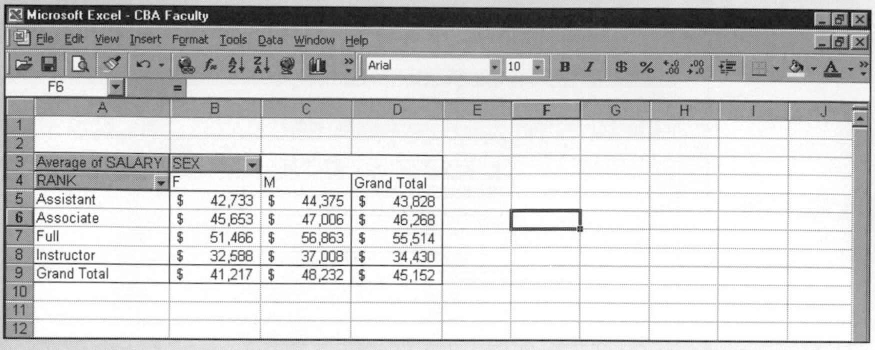

	A	B	C	D
3	Average of SALARY	SEX		
4	RANK	F	M	Grand Total
5	Assistant	$ 42,733	$ 44,375	$ 43,828
6	Associate	$ 45,653	$ 47,006	$ 46,268
7	Full	$ 51,466	$ 56,863	$ 55,514
8	Instructor	$ 32,588	$ 37,008	$ 34,430
9	Grand Total	$ 41,217	$ 48,232	$ 45,152

With the numbers formatted, the data in the pivot table is much easier to interpret. You can also apply Excel's AutoFormats to format a pivot table. Select the range you want to format, click the Format menu and select the format you want to apply.

Repositioning a Field in the Pivot Table

Recall that the benefit of a pivot table is that it summarizes large amounts of data into a readable format. Once you have created the table, you can also choose to view the same data from different angles. At the top of the pivot table's ROW and COLUMN areas are field buttons that enable you to change, or pivot, the view of the data by dragging these buttons to different locations in the pivot table.

The dean reviews the tabular format of the pivot table you have created and decides it might be more useful if it displayed males and females as row classifications under rank. Reposition the column headings for the SEX field as row labels.

To move a column field to a row field in the pivot table:

1. Click and drag the **SEX** field button below the RANK field button. See Figure 5-42. Notice that when you place the mouse over the SEX field button, your mouse pointer changes to ✥. As you click and drag below the RANK field button, the mouse pointer changes to [pointer icon].

Figure 5-42 REPOSITIONING SEX FIELD BUTTON IN PIVOT TABLE

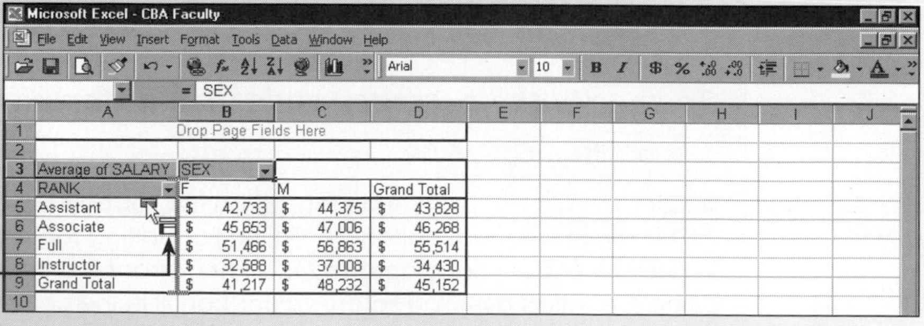

	A	B	C	D
3	Average of SALARY	SEX		
4	RANK	F	M	Grand Total
5	Assistant	$ 42,733	$ 44,375	$ 43,828
6	Associate	$ 45,653	$ 47,006	$ 46,268
7	Full	$ 51,466	$ 56,863	$ 55,514
8	Instructor	$ 32,588	$ 37,008	$ 34,430
9	Grand Total	$ 41,217	$ 48,232	$ 45,152

indicates field button is being moved

2. Release the mouse button. See Figure 5-43. The pivot table is reordered so that the SEX field is treated as a row field instead of a column field.

TROUBLE? If the SEX field appears to the left of the RANK field, click the Undo button on the Standard toolbar to undo the last step and then repeat Step 1. When you drag the SEX field button, just drag the button into the blank area under the RANK button. If you drag the button much farther to the left, you will change the order of the fields.

Figure 5-43 **REARRANGED PIVOT TABLE**

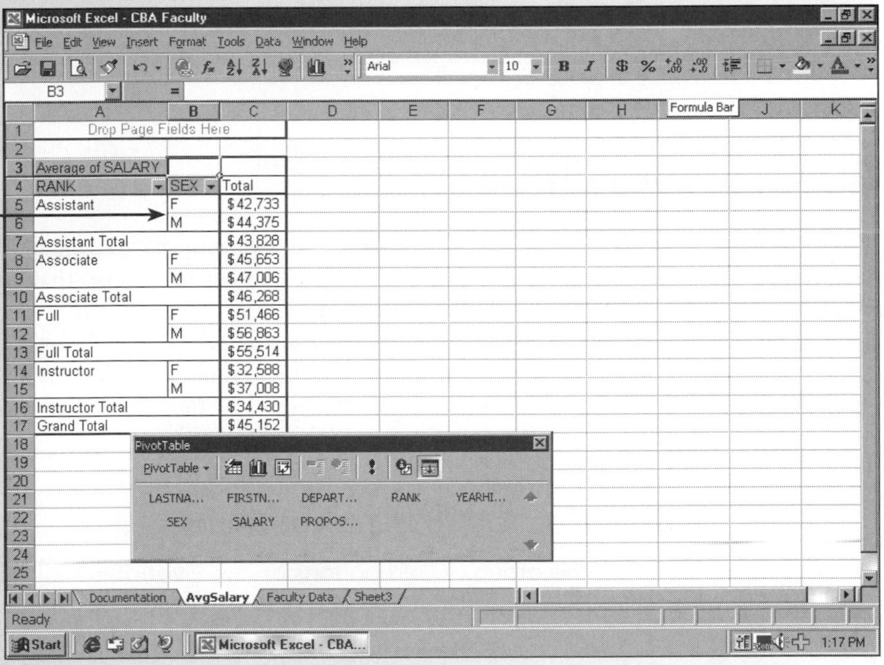

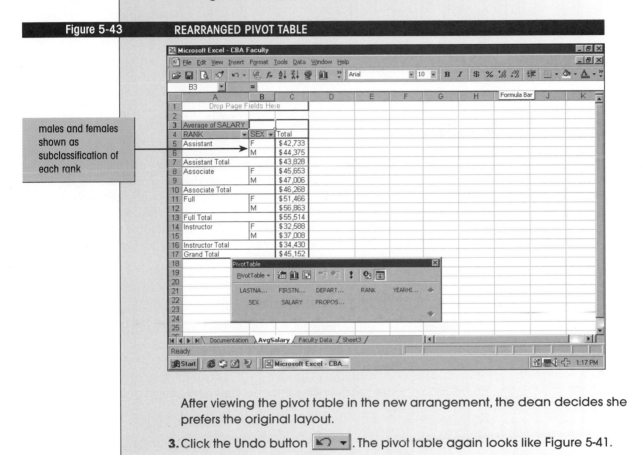

males and females shown as subclassification of each rank

After viewing the pivot table in the new arrangement, the dean decides she prefers the original layout.

3. Click the Undo button. The pivot table again looks like Figure 5-41.

Sorting Items Within the Pivot Table

After reviewing the pivot table, the dean asks you to rearrange it so that it displays the rank with the highest average salary first. To complete this task, you can sort the data in the pivot table.

To sort a pivot table:

1. Click cell **D5** to place the cell pointer in the cell that contains the field you want to sort.

2. Click the **Sort Descending** button on the Standard toolbar. See Figure 5-44. The full professor rank is now the first rank in the pivot table.

Figure 5-44 PIVOT TABLE AFTER VALUES SORTED

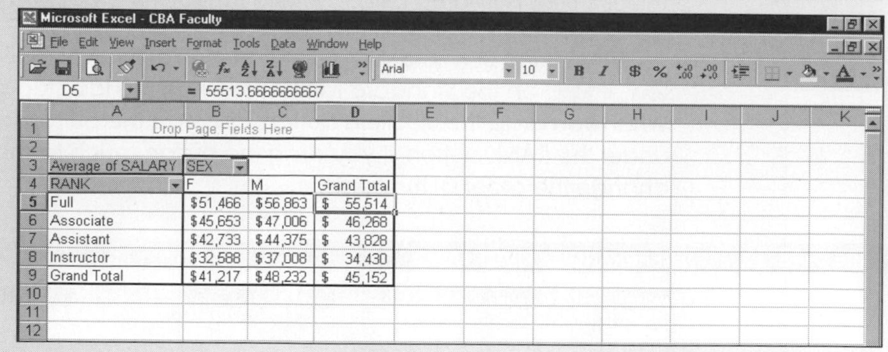

Average of SALARY	SEX		
RANK	F	M	Grand Total
Full	$51,466	$56,863	$ 55,514
Associate	$45,653	$47,006	$ 46,268
Assistant	$42,733	$44,375	$ 43,828
Instructor	$32,588	$37,008	$ 34,430
Grand Total	$41,217	$48,232	$ 45,152

Adding a Field to a Pivot Table

You can expand a pivot table by adding columns, rows, page fields, and data fields; this creates a more informative table. For example, the dean believes that a more accurate comparison of average salaries would include the DEPARTMENT field. Adding this field to the pivot table enables you to calculate average salaries based on an additional breakdown—one that categorizes faculty in each rank into departmental classifications as well as by sex. The dean thinks the additional information will be useful in her discussion with the affirmative action task force, and she asks you to add it to the pivot table.

To add a field to the pivot table:

1. From the group of field buttons on the PivotTable toolbar, click and drag the **DEPARTMENT** field button immediately below the arrow of the RANK field button, and release the mouse button. Excel adds the DEPARTMENT field button and redisplays the pivot table. See Figure 5-45. The pivot table now displays department subcategories (accounting, finance, and management) for each rank.

   TROUBLE? If the DEPARTMENT field button appears to the left of the RANK field button, click and drag the RANK button over the DEPARTMENT button and release the mouse button.

   TROUBLE? If the PivotTable toolbar is in the way, drag it to a different location on your screen.

Figure 5-45 PIVOT TABLE AFTER DEPARTMENT FIELD ADDED

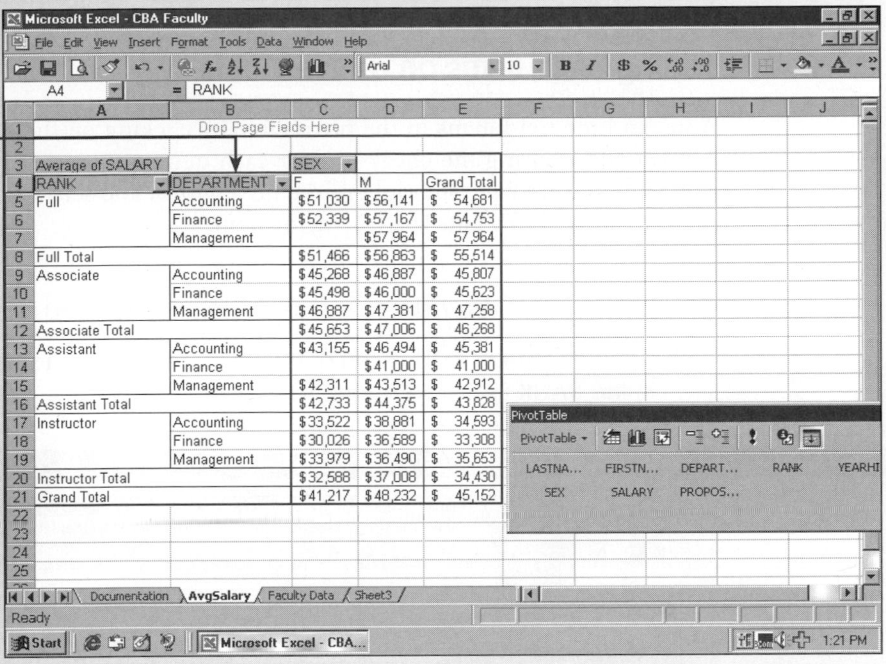

Removing a Field from the Pivot Table

If you decide you want to remove a field from the pivot table, just drag the field button outside the pivot table. The dean reviews the pivot table showing the data arranged by rank, department, and sex. While she thinks this is important information, she feels the additional breakdown is not needed to show the difference in average salaries between men and women. She asks you to remove the DEPARTMENT field from the pivot table.

To remove a field from the pivot table:

1. Click and drag the **DEPARTMENT** field button outside the pivot table range. When the field button is outside the pivot table, it changes to ![cursor]. See Figure 5-46.

Figure 5-46 DEPARTMENT FIELD BUTTON OUTSIDE PIVOT TABLE RANGE

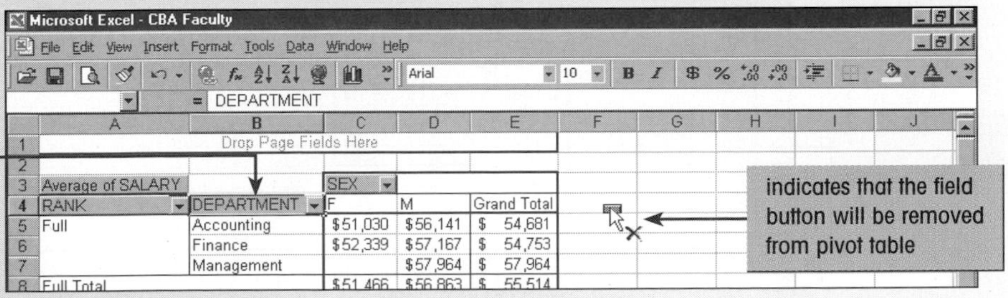

2. Release the mouse button. The DEPARTMENT field is removed from the pivot table. Removing a field from the pivot table has no effect on the underlying list; the DEPARTMENT field is still in the faculty list.

The Dean wants to focus the analysis on the faculty ranks eligible for tenure—assistant, associate and full professors. She asks you to remove the instructors from the report.

Hiding Field Items on a Pivot Table

You can hide field items in the pivot table by clicking on the arrow at the right of the field button and clearing the check box for each item you want to hide. To show hidden items, you click the arrow to the right of the field button and select the check box for the item you want to show. Now hide the Instructor item.

To hide the Instructor item from the pivot table:

1. Click the **arrow** to the right of the RANK field button to display a list of each item in the RANK field. See Figure 5-47.

Figure 5-47 LIST OF FIELD ITEMS FOR RANK FIELD

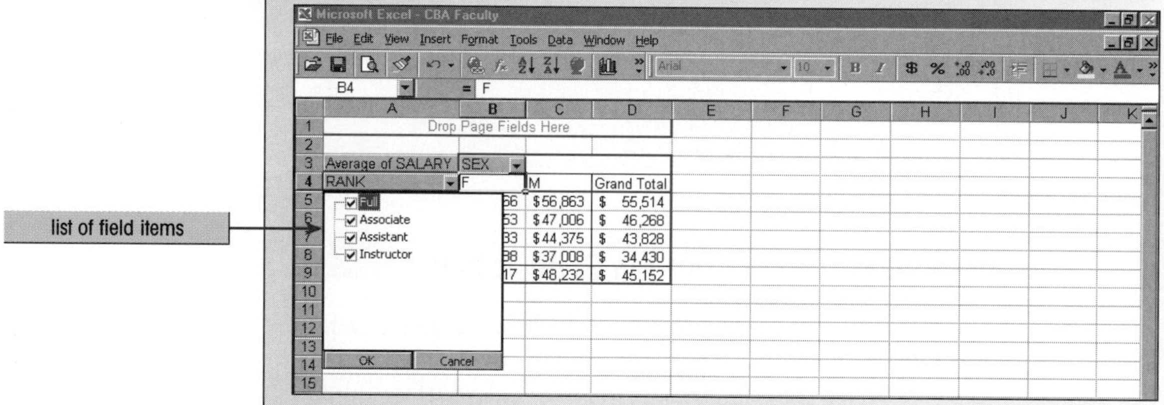

2. Click the **check box** next to Instructor to clear the check.

3. Click **OK** to display the pivot table with the Instructor row hidden. See Figure 5-48.

Figure 5-48 PIVOT TABLE WITH INSTRUCTOR ITEM HIDDEN

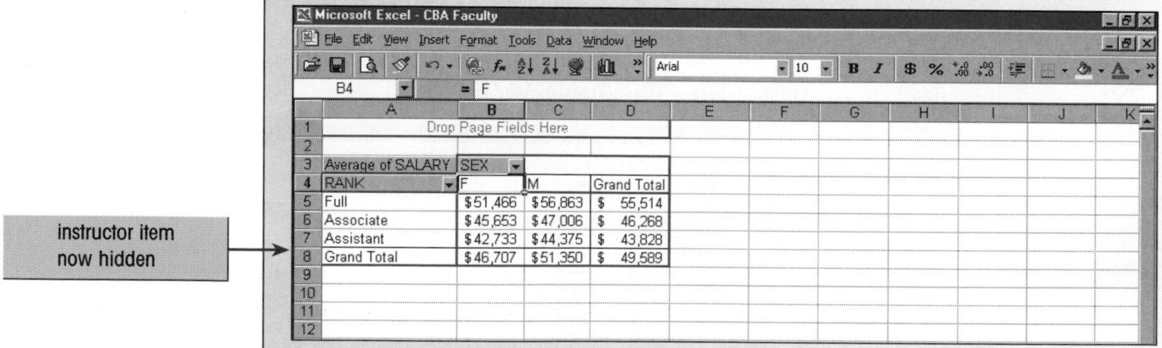

Now, the report contains the faculty ranks the dean wants to review. Before making copies of the pivot table for her meeting, the dean asks you to include Karen Garafano's $3,000 salary increase into the pivot table report.

Refreshing a Pivot Table

Recall that you cannot directly change the data in the pivot table; in order to change the data in the pivot table, you must first make the changes to the original Excel list; you can then update the pivot table. To update a pivot table so it reflects the current state of the faculty list, you update, or "refresh," the pivot table using the Refresh command.

You receive a memo from the dean informing you that Karen Garafano, a faculty member in the finance department, will receive an additional $3,000 in salary because her merit increase was approved. Her new salary is $49,000. Update her record in the faculty list and see how this affects the pivot table. (Make a note at this point that the average salary for female associate professors is $45,653.) Observe whether there is any change in the pivot table after you update Karen Garafano's salary in the Excel list.

To update Karen Garafano's salary:

1. Activate the **Faculty Data** worksheet, and then click any cell in the list.
2. Click **Data** on the menu bar, and then click **Form** to open the Faculty Data data form dialog box.
3. Click the **Criteria** button to display a blank data form.

   Enter the search criterion in the appropriate field.

4. If necessary, click the **LASTNAME** text box, and then type **Garafano.**
5. Click the **Find Next** button to display the next record in the list that meets the specified criterion—LASTNAME equal to Garafano.
6. Change Karen Garafanos' salary to **$49,000.**
7. Click the **Close** button. The salary for Karen Garafano has been updated in the Faculty list.

   Now return to the pivot table to observe whether there is any change in the average salary for female associate professors.

8. Switch to the **AvgSalary** worksheet. Notice that the average salary for female associate professors remains at $45,653.

Because the pivot table is not automatically updated when data in the source list is updated, the pivot table must be "refreshed."

To refresh a pivot table:

1. Select any cell inside the pivot table.
2. Click the **Refresh Data** button on the PivotTable toolbar to update the pivot table. See Figure 5-49. The new average salary for female associate professors is $46,153.

Figure 5-49 PIVOT TABLE AFTER BEING REFRESHED

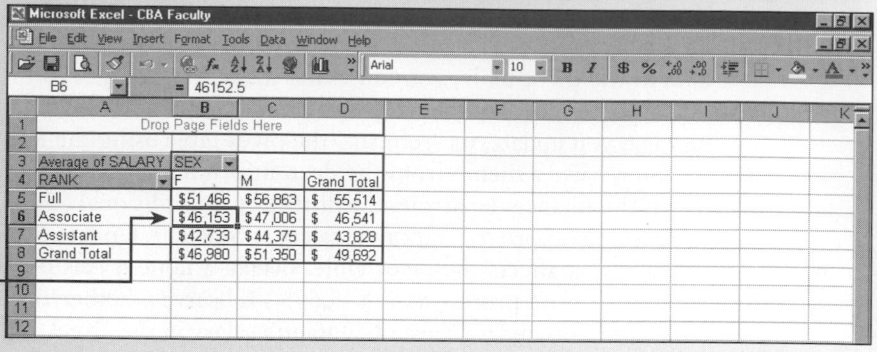

this average has changed

Making a Chart from a Pivot Table

The dean thinks a chart can more effectively convey the summary information of the pivot table. She asks you to create a Clustered column chart. Creating a pivot chart linked directly to a pivot table takes a single mouse click.

To link a chart to a pivot table:

1. Click the **Chart Wizard** button on the PivotTable toolbar. A Stacked column chart and Chart toolbar appear in a new chart sheet, Chart1. See Figure 5-50.

Figure 5-50 STACKED COLUMN CHART LINKED TO PIVOT TABLE

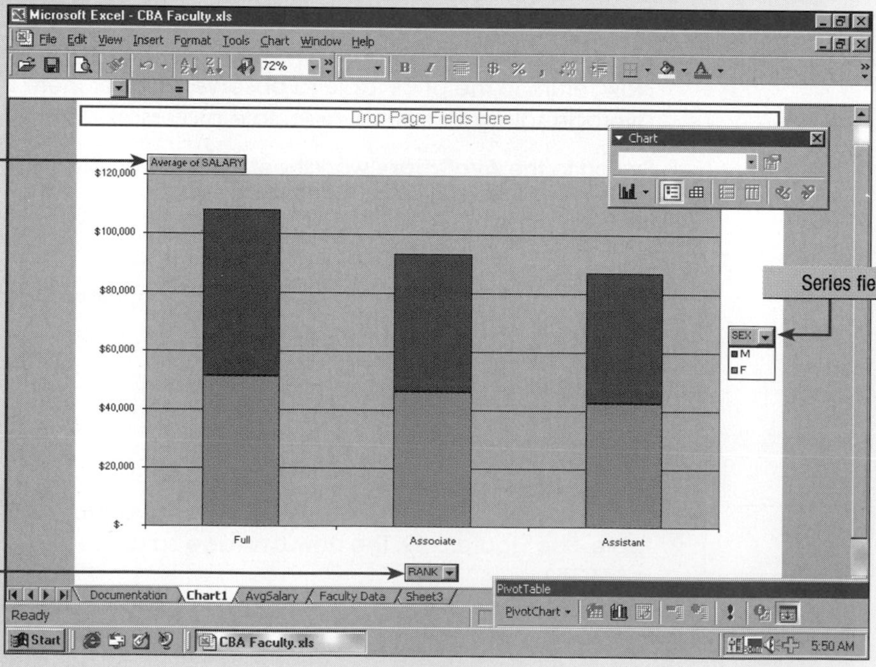

Data field button

Series field button

Category field button

Convert the chart to a Clustered column chart.

2. Click [icon]. The Chart Wizard-Step 1 of 4-Chart Type dialog box opens.
3. Click the **Clustered column** chart sub-type (first sub-type option).
4. Click **Next** to open the Chart Wizard-Step 3 of 4-Chart Options dialog box.
5. Click the **Chart title** box and type **Average Salary by Rank and Sex**.
6. Click **Finish** to display the Clustered column chart. See Figure 5-51.

Figure 5-51 CLUSTERED COLUMN CHART LINKED TO PIVOT TABLE

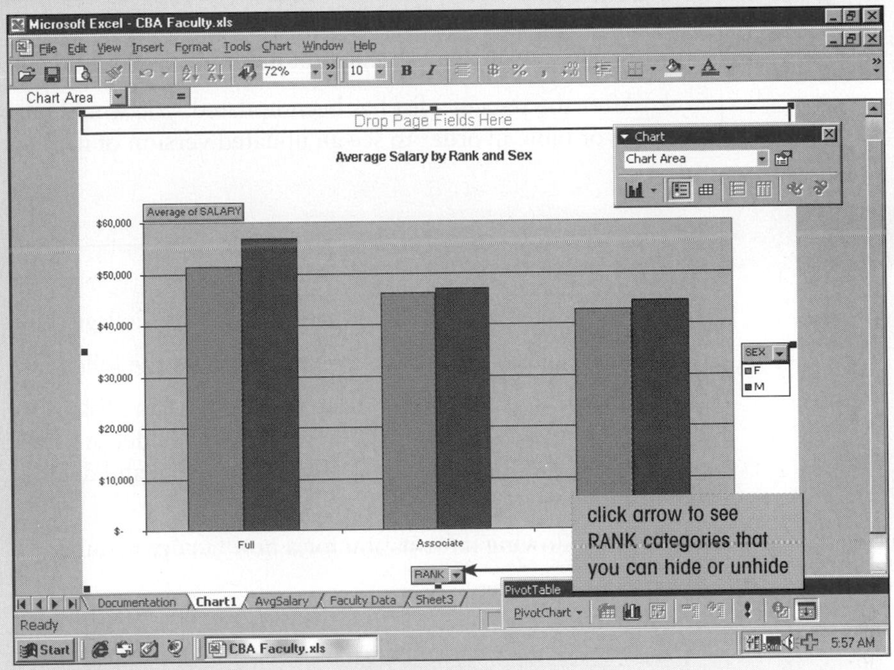

7. Click the **Documentation** sheet tab and save the workbook.
8. Preview and print the pivot table and pivot chart.
9. Close the workbook and exit Excel.

The dean is pleased with the appearance of the pivot table and chart. Both the table and chart show that the average salary paid to females is lower in every rank than the average salary paid to males.

You have modified and added data to an Excel list. You have also filtered the data in the list in numerous ways to highlight certain budget information that the dean of the College of Business Administration needs for her meeting with the university's budget director. Finally, you have created a pivot table and pivot chart from the list to further organize the information into specialized reports that the dean can use in her upcoming meetings with the affirmative action task force.

Session 5.3 QUICK CHECK

1. Assume that you have a list of students; the list includes codes for males and females and a field identifying the student major. Which tool, AutoFilter or pivot table, would you use in each of the following situations:
   a. You want a list of all females majoring in history.
   b. You want a count of the number of males and females in each major at your institution.
2. Fields such as region, state, country, and zip code are most likely to appear as ____________ in a pivot table.
3. What is the default calculation method for numeric data in a pivot table?
4. After the data in a list has been updated, you would have to ____________ the pivot table in order to see an updated version of it.

REVIEW ASSIGNMENTS

The dean has asked for more information about the College of Business Administration faculty. To provide the answers she asks you to complete the following:

1. If necessary, start Excel and make sure your Data Disk is in the appropriate disk drive. Open the workbook **Faculty2** in the Review folder in Tutorial.05 on your Data Disk, and save it as **CBA Faculty 2**. Type your name and date in the Documentation sheet, then move to the Faculty Data sheet.
2. Add the following information for a new faculty member.
   Last name = Gerety
   First name = Estelle
   Department = Management
   Rank = Assistant
   Year hired = 2001
   Sex = F
   Salary = 42500
3. Use the data form to determine how many faculty members hold the rank of full professor. Explain the steps you followed to get your answer.
4. Sort the faculty list by sex, within sex by rank, and within rank by salary. Arrange the salaries in descending order. Include your name in the custom footer, then print the sorted list so that males and females print on separate pages.
5. Use the Subtotals command to count how many males and how many females are on the faculty. Print the faculty list with the subtotals.
6. Use the AutoFilter command to display a list of all females in the accounting department. Sort by last name. Print the filtered list.
7. Further refine the list from Question 6 so you list all female accounting faculty hired after 1990. Print the list.
8. Use the AVERAGE function to determine the average faculty salary. Based on this information, print a list of all faculty earning above the average salary.
9. Use conditional formatting to boldface the YEARHIRED field for faculty hired before 1980. Print the faculty list.
10. Use the Subtotals command to compute the average salary paid by department.

11. Based on Question 10, use the appropriate Outline button to display only the subtotals and the grand total. Print the result.

12. Create a pivot table to show the maximum salary by rank and sex. Place your pivot table in a blank worksheet. Format your pivot table to produce an attractive printout. Add an appropriate title. Rename the pivot table sheet using an appropriate name. Include your name in the custom footer, then print the pivot table.

Explore 13. Modify the pivot table in Question 12 to also display the minimum salary by rank and sex. (*Hint*: Use the Office Assistant to learn about "Using more than one summary function for a PivotTable data field.") Print the modified pivot table.

Explore 14. Use AutoFilters to produce and then print the faculty with the top five salaries in descending order. (*Hint*: Check out the Top 10 option in the list of available AutoFilters.)

Explore 15. Print a list of faculty sorted by department and within department by last name. Include only the last name, department, year hired, and gender in the output. (*Hint*: Use the Office Assistant to learn to "hide a column".) After printing the report, unhide the columns.

Explore 16. When you used the Page Break command in the tutorial to print each department's faculty on a separate page, you may have noticed that the column headings appeared only on the first page. Use the Print Area and Print Title sections of the Page Setup dialog box (Sheet tab), along with the Page Break command, to print the column headings on each page.

17. In column H, create a new calculated field using a worksheet label to create a formula reflecting an alternative Proposed Salary of a 4 1/2% increase.

18. Save and close the workbook.

CASE PROBLEMS

Case 1. Inventory at OfficeMart Business Supplies You are an assistant buyer at OfficeMart Business Supplies, a retail business supply store. Your boss, Ellen Kerrigan, created an Excel workbook with product and pricing information for inventory items purchased from each primary vendor. Ellen is preparing her monthly order for EB Wholesale Office Supplies, one of OfficeMart's suppliers. She wants you to print a list of all back-ordered EB Wholesale products to include in the order. She also wants a list of all discontinued items so you can remove them from the catalog. Do the following:

1. If necessary, start Excel and make sure your Data Disk is in the appropriate disk drive. Open the workbook **Office** in the Cases folder for Tutorial.05 on your Data Disk and save it as **Office Supplies**.

2. Freeze the panes so the column headings and the Part number row labels remain on the screen as you scroll the office supplies list.

3. Print the items in each status category on a separate page.

4. Display only the records for back-ordered items (Status = B). Sort the back-ordered items by part description. Print the records for back-ordered items.

5. Apply conditional formatting to all discontinued products (Status = D) so that the status code appears in red for each discontinued product.

6. Add a new field to the list. Name the field "Retail Value" and format it appropriately. For each inventory item, calculate the value at retail (quantity on hand multiplied by retail) using a worksheet label to create the formula. Format the numbers in the new field. Print the list so it prints on one page.

7. Use the Subtotals command to compute the total retail value of the inventory by status category (B, D, and S). Print the list with subtotals.
8. Prepare the same list with subtotals as in Question 7, but exclude all records whose retail value is zero.
9. Prepare a pivot table to summarize the retail value of inventory by status category. For each status category, include a count of the number of different items (this is not the sum of the quantity on hand), the total retail value, and the average retail value. (*Hint:* This pivot table uses one variable to summarize data concerning the retail value of the inventory.) Place the pivot table in a new sheet. Assign a descriptive name to the sheet. Print the pivot table.
10. Display only the discontinued items (Status = D). Copy these records to a blank worksheet. Rename the worksheet **Discontinued**. Print the list of discontinued items.
11. Save and close the workbook.

Case 2. Sales Analysis at Medical Technology, Inc. Medical Technology, Inc. distributes supplies to hospitals, medical laboratories, and pharmacies. Records of all customer and accounts receivable data are available to department managers on the company's mainframe computer. Tom Benson, the manager of credit and collections, noticed that the outstanding balances of several customers in Rhode Island and Massachusetts appeared to be higher than the average customer balances. He thinks the average customer balance is approximately $4,000. He wants to study these accounts in more detail in order to create a plan to bring them closer to the average balance.

Tom was able to download the necessary data from the company's mainframe, and he set up an Excel list. Do the following:

1. If necessary, start Excel and make sure your Data Disk is in the appropriate disk drive. Open the workbook **Medical** in the Cases folder for Tutorial.05, and then save it as **Med Tech**.
2. Sort the list by state (ascending) and within state by Type customer (ascending) and within type by year-to-date (YTD) sales (descending). Remember to insert your name in a custom footer before printing the sorted list.
3. Insert subtotals (SUM) on Balanced Owed by type of customer. Print the list with only subtotals and the grand total included. After printing, remove the subtotals.
4. Use conditional formatting to display all customers with YTD sales above $55,000 in blue text, and apply boldface.
5. Display all customers with a balance owed above $25,000 from Rhode Island. Sort the list in descending order by balance owed. How many customers are in this list? Which customer owes the most? Print the list.
6. Print a list of customers that have the word "lab" anywhere in the customer name. Explain how you got your results.
7. Prepare and format a pivot table summarizing total YTD sales by sales rep. Include your name in a custom footer and then print it. Name the pivot table sheet Sales Rep.

Explore

8. Use the Format Report button on the PivotTable toolbar to select an autoformat for the pivot table you prepared in Question 7. Sort total YTD sales in descending order. Print the modified pivot table.
9. There appears to be a problem in the collection of money (balance) owed for one state and one type of customer. Identify the state and customer type that has the highest average outstanding balance. Print a report that supports your observation.
10. Save and close the workbook.

Case 3. Revenue at the Tea House Arnold Tealover, sales manager for Tea House Distributors, is getting ready for a semiannual meeting at the company headquarters, at which plans to present summary data on his product line. The data he has accumulated consists of revenues by product, by month, and by region for the last six months. Help him summarize and analyze the data. Do the following:

1. If necessary, start Excel and make sure your Data Disk is in the appropriate drive. Open the workbook **Teahouse** in the Cases folder for Tutorial.05 on your Data Disk, and save it as **Teahouse Revenue**.
2. Improve the formatting of the revenue field.
3. Freeze the column headings so they remain on the screen as you scroll the worksheet.
4. Revenue for Duke Gray Tea for June in the West region was $53,420. Use the data form to enter "Duke Gray Tea", "June", "West", "53420".
5. Sort the tea list by product and within product by month. Insert subtotals by product and also by month for each product. Remember to include your name in a custom footer, then print the information for each product on a separate page.
6. Use conditional formatting to display revenue below $25,000.
7. Use the Subtotals command to display total sales by product. Print the list with subtotals.
8. Use the Outline buttons to display only the subtotals and grand total. Print this information.

Explore

9. Sort the data by month and within month by region. The months should appear in January through December sequence. (*Hint*: Click the Options button in the sort dialog box to customize your sort options.) Print the list.
10. Determine which product was the company's best seller during May or June in the West region. Print the list that supports your answer.
11. You want to determine which month had the highest sales and which region had the lowest sales. Prepare one pivot table to provide you with information to use for the answer to both questions. Use a text box to place the answer in the sheet with the pivot table. Name the sheet with the pivot table MaxMin. Print the pivot table.

Explore

12. Summarize each product's revenue using a pivot table. Use the Chart Wizard button on the PivotTable toolbar to create a column chart of total revenue by product. Improve the appearance of the chart. Print the pivot table and pie chart. Assign descriptive names to all new sheets.
13. Sort the list by region. Print the data for each region on a separate page. Use Page Break Preview to drag the automatic page breaks to the appropriate locations. (*Hint*: You may also need to insert additional page breaks manually.)

Explore

14. Sort the data by region. The region should appear in the following sequence: North, South, East, West. Print the list. (*Hint*: Use online Help to search on customizing, sort order.)
15. Save and close the workbook.

Case 4. NBA Player Salaries Sharon Durfee is a summer intern at the National Basketball Association (NBA) headquarters in New York City. Every day the NBA office receives requests for information from sportswriters, TV and radio announcers, team owners, and agents. Sharon's assignment is to set up a database of player salaries to help the NBA staff provide accurate information quickly.

1. If necessary, start Excel and make sure your Data Disk is in the appropriate drive. Open the workbook **NBA** in the Cases folder for Tutorial.05 on your Data Disk, and save it as **NBA Salaries**.
2. Freeze the column headings and first and last name row labels.
3. Use the data form to find Antoine Walker's record. Change the salary to "$2,000,000."

4. Sort the data by team and within team by position and within position by salary (highest to lowest salary). Remember to include your name in a custom footer, then print the list.
5. Apply conditional formatting so the salary field of players earning below $500,000 appear with a red background and players earning more than $5,000,000 but less than $10,000,000 appear with a blue background.
6. Print all players earning less than $1,000,000, sorted by team.
7. Prepare a pivot table report to summarize the average salaries by team and by position. Rename the sheet tab with a more descriptive name. Print the pivot table report.
8. Save the workbook.

Explore

9. Prepare a pivot chart showing the total salaries by team. Print the chart.

Explore

10. Modify the pivot table created in Step 7 so TeamID is presented as a Page field instead of a Row field. Print the sheet.

QUICK CHECK ANSWERS

Session 5.1

1. record
2. field
3. list
4. Sort by major and within major by last name
5. primary; alternative answer might be sort field or sort key
6. descending
7. new
8. Assuming you have the fields FirstName and LastName as part of the employee list, you would click the Criteria button in the Data Form dialog box. In the FirstName field text box type "Jin"; in the LastName field text box type "Shinu". Click the Find Next button to display the record in the data form.

Session 5.2

1. Data, AutoFilter
2. Use the AutoFilter feature. Click the Major field filter arrow and then click Marketing. For the GPA field, click Custom from the list of filtering options, enter the comparison operator > and the constant 3.0 to form the condition GPA greater than 3.0.
3. Conditional formatting
4. natural language
5. In order for Excel to calculate subtotals correctly, you must first sort the data because the subtotals are inserted whenever the value in the specified field changes
6. Outline
7. Page Break Preview view

Session 5.3

1. **a.** AutoFilter **b.** Pivot table
2. row, columns, or pages
3. Sums the field or SUM
4. refresh

OBJECTIVES

In this tutorial you will:

- Learn about Object Linking and Embedding (OLE)
- Paste a graphic object into an Excel worksheet
- Embed a WordArt object in Excel
- Link an Excel worksheet to a Word document
- Update linked documents
- Embed an Excel chart into a Word document
- Complete a mail merge using an Excel list and a Word document
- View, preview and print a mail-merged document
- Create hyperlinks to connect files
- Convert worksheet data to HTML format

INTEGRATING EXCEL WITH OTHER WINDOWS PROGRAMS AND THE WORLD WIDE WEB

Creating Integrated Documents for Basket Weavers

CASE

Basket Weavers

Nearly fifteen years ago, Karen Sanicola began selling gift baskets for all occasions. At the urging of her customers, she opened a small shop in her garage. Today, Karen's business, Basket Weavers, has grown to include three shops, located in Brooklyn, New York; Montvale, New Jersey; and the newest one in Greenwich, Connecticut.

The customer base has grown from townspeople and neighbors to include companies throughout the Northeast. This year, Basket Weavers has received the much-prized recognition as the largest corporate gift house in the Northeast, an award established by the Northeast Premiums Association (NPA).

Karen wants to display a flyer at the checkout counter at each store announcing the new baskets for the year. In addition to inserting the company logo, she can use WordArt, a shared program that comes with all Microsoft Office 2000 programs, to dress up the new products flyer. Karen also has drafted the body of a letter to her customers, highlighting the company's recent award from NPA, and previewing five new gift baskets that will be available this holiday season. To present this information in an easy-to-understand format, she plans to include a table listing the five new gift baskets. In addition, she wants the letter to include a chart that NPA has supplied depicting the company's status as the top company in the region. She will then merge an Excel list containing her customer addresses to the list.

Lastly, Karen wants her customers who use the Internet and the World Wide Web to have access to the new gift basket information online. She will create a Web page showing this information.

You'll complete the flyer, the letter, and the Web page for Karen using the integration features of Excel, which allow you to easily incorporate information from documents created in other programs.

SESSION 6.1

In this session you will learn about the different methods of integrating information between Windows programs to create compound documents. You will paste a logo into an Excel worksheet, create a WordArt object, link an Excel workbook to a Word document, and embed an Excel chart into a Word document.

Methods of Integration

Like Karen, you may occasionally need to copy data between two or more programs to produce the type of document you require. This type of document is referred to as a **compound document**—a document made up of parts created in more than one program. For example, you may want to incorporate data from a worksheet, a graphic design, or a chart, and insert it into a word-processed report.

Excel is part of a suite of programs called Microsoft Office 2000. In addition to Excel, the Office programs consist of Word, a word-processing program; Access, a database program; PowerPoint, a program used for creating presentations; and Outlook, a personal information manager. Microsoft Office also contains some shared programs, such as WordArt, that allow you to customize your documents even further. All of these programs can share information, which saves time and ensures consistency.

There are essentially three ways to copy data between Windows programs: you can use pasting, linking, or embedding. Regardless of the method used, a copy of the data appears in the compound document. Figure 6-1 provides a description of each of these methods, and examples of when each method would be appropriate.

Figure 6-1 COMPARISON OF METHODS OF INTEGRATING INFORMATION

METHOD OF SHARING	DESCRIPTION	USE WHEN
Copying and Pasting	Places a copy of the information in a document	You will be exchanging the data between the two documents only once, and it doesn't matter if the data changes.
Linking	Displays an object in the destination document but doesn't store it there—only the location of the source document is stored in the destination document	You want to use the same data in more than one document, and you need to ensure that the data will be current and identical in each document. Any changes you make to the source document will be reflected in the destination document(s).
Embedding	Displays and stores an object in the destination document	You want the source data to become a permanent part of the destination document, or the source data will no longer be available to the destination document. Any changes you make to either the destination document or the source document will not affect the other.

Pasting Data

You can **paste** an object, such as a range of cells or a chart, from one program to another using copy-and-paste operations. This creates a static copy of the data. For example, you can paste a range of cells from an Excel worksheet into a Word document and use it as part of your Word document.

Once you paste an object from one program into another, that data is now part of the new document. The pasted data has no connection to the source document and can only be altered in that new document's program. For example, if you paste a range of cells from

Excel into a Word document, you can only edit or change that data using the Word commands and features. The pasted data becomes a table of text and numbers, just as if you had entered it directly from the keyboard. There is no connection to the Excel worksheet. Once you have pasted the range of cells, you need to repeat the copy-and-paste operation if you want any subsequent changes in the worksheet to appear in the Word document. Pasting is used when you need to perform a one-time exchange of information between programs.

Object Linking and Embedding

There are situations when copying and pasting information into a document is not the best solution. Excel supports a technology called **Object Linking and Embedding** (OLE, pronounced "oh-lay"). This technology enables you to copy and paste objects—a graphic file, a worksheet range, a chart, or a sound file—in such a way that the data is associated with its source. For example, using OLE you can insert a worksheet or chart into a Word document as either a linked object or an embedded object.

OLE involves the exchange of information between two programs, called the **source** or **server program** and the **destination** or **client program**. The source is the program in which the data was created. The destination is the program that receives the data. For example, if you insert an Excel pivot table into a Word document, Excel is the source program and Word is the destination program.

Using OLE, you can share data (objects) between programs by creating a **link** between files. Linking files lets information created in one file be displayed in another file. When an object is linked, the data is stored in the original source file. For example, you can link a chart from a worksheet to a Word document. Although the chart appears in the Word document, it actually exists as a separate file. The destination document simply displays the object. In effect, the destination document stores a **reference** or link (location and name of the source file) to the object in the source file. Thus, only one copy of the original, or source, object exists. If you make changes to the original object, changes also appear in the destination document. With only one version of the object, every document containing a link to the source object uses the same copy of the object.

Embedding lets you store data from multiple programs—for example, a worksheet, chart, graphic image or sound file—directly in the destination document. The information is totally contained in one file. The copied object, which is embedded, exists as a separate object within the destination document. To make changes to the embedded object, you edit the embedded object directly from within the destination document. The embedded object has no link to the original source document, which means that changes to the embedded object do not alter the original object. This also means that the changes you make to the original source data do not appear in the document that contains the embedded object.

The main differences between linked and embedded objects are where the data is stored and how it is updated after you place it in the destination document. Figure 6-2 illustrates the differences between linking and embedding.

Figure 6-2 EMBEDDING CONTRASTED WITH LINKING

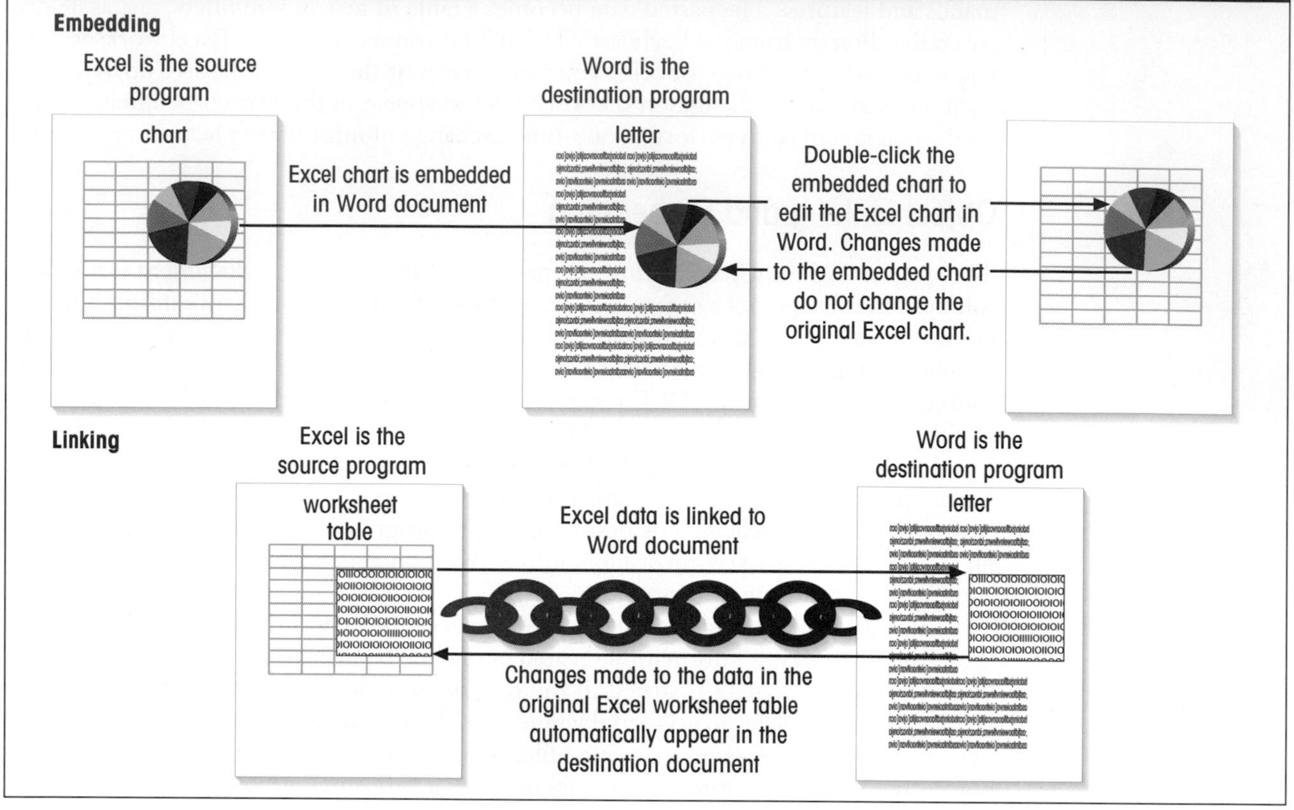

Planning the Integration

Recall that Karen has two documents she wants to create: a flyer and a customer letter. The flyer will describe the five new baskets being offered. The table of new baskets and their prices is contained in an Excel file, Baskets. To create the flyer, Karen needs to paste the company logo at the top, which she can do using Excel's Insert command, as this will be a one-time exchange of data. Then she will use WordArt to insert a visually pleasing title above the new baskets table.

In the case of the customer letter, Karen has already created the body of the letter in Word. However, the Excel new baskets table will be linked to the Word document because the prices of some of the baskets might change, and both customer letter and product worksheet will need to show the latest prices. The NPA pie chart depicting Basket Weavers as the leading area seller needs to be integrated into the customer letter as well. Karen knows the data in the chart will not change, but she might need to modify the chart's size and appearance once it is integrated into the letter. To do this, Karen will want to use the Excel commands for modifying a chart; therefore she decides to embed the chart. Figure 6-3 shows Karen's plan for integrating these pieces to create the flyer and the customer letter.

Figure 6-3 KAREN'S INTEGRATION PLANS FOR THE FLYER AND CUSTOMER LETTER

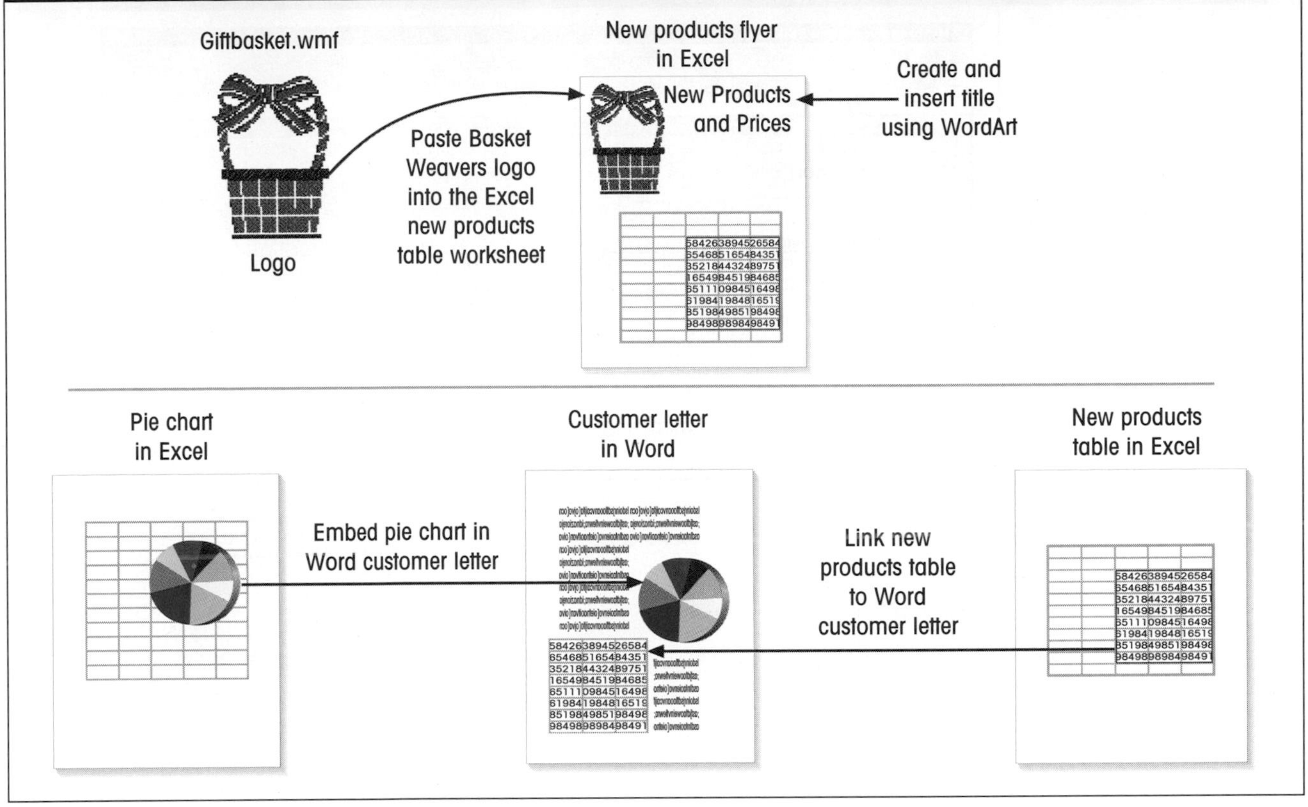

Creating the New Products Flyer

Karen wants to complete the flyer first. To create this document, she needs to insert the Basket Weavers logo, a graphic file, into the Excel worksheet, which contains the table of new baskets. She also needs to create and then insert a WordArt image in the Excel worksheet.

To open the Baskets workbook:

1. Start Excel as usual. Make sure your Data Disk is in the appropriate disk drive.
2. Open the Excel workbook named **Baskets** in the Tutorial folder for Tutorial.06 on your Data Disk. Use the Save As command to save the file as **New Baskets**.
3. Activate the **New Products** sheet. See Figure 6-4.

Figure 6-4 NEW PRODUCTS WORKSHEET

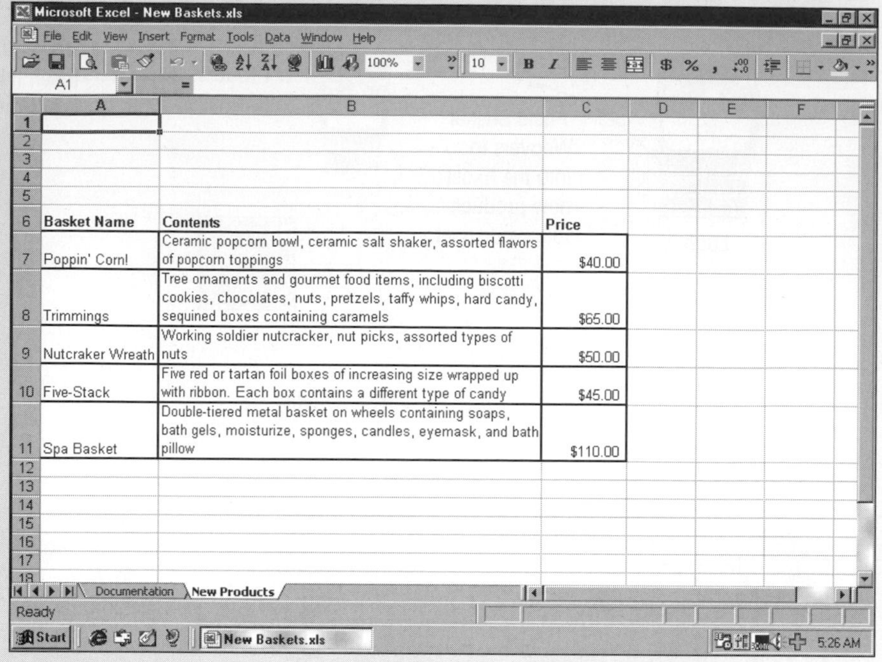

You are now ready to insert the Basket Weavers logo at the top of the new products table.

To insert the company logo into the worksheet:

1. Make sure cell A1 is selected.
2. Click **Insert** on the menu bar, point to **Picture**, and then click **From File** to open the Insert Picture dialog box.
3. Make sure the Look in list box displays the Tutorial folder for Tutorial.06, click **GiftBasket** in the list of available files, and then click the **Insert** button to paste the company logo into the worksheet.
4. Move the pointer over the lower-right selection handle until the pointer shape changes to ↖↘.
5. Click and drag up and to the left to the bottom of cell A5. Release the mouse button. See Figure 6-5. Notice that the Picture toolbar appears on the screen while the graphic object is selected. The Picture toolbar contains tools you can use to change the characteristics of a graphic image. For example, you can crop the image, or adjust its brightness.

Figure 6-5 **WORKSHEET AFTER COMPANY LOGO INSERTED**

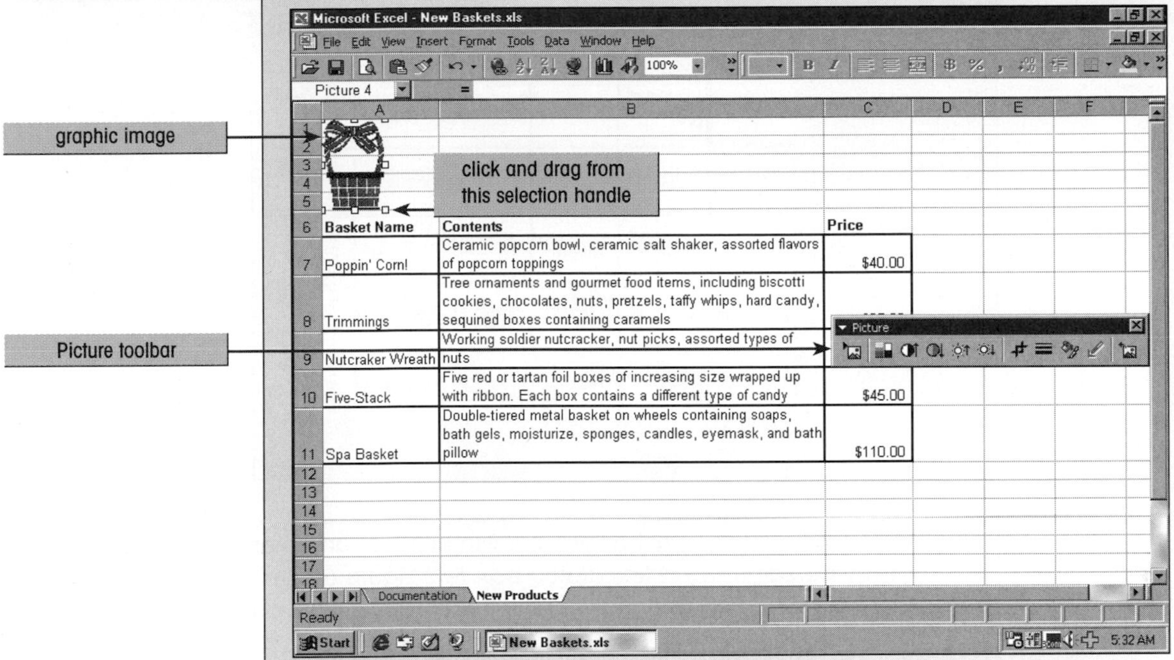

Copy the graphic image to the right side of the table.

6. Right-click the graphic image to display the shortcut menu. Click **Copy**.
7. Click cell **C1**. Click **Edit**, then click **Paste** to display a copy of the company logo in column C.
8. Click outside the logo to deselect it. The Picture toolbar closes when the logo is no longer selected.

Karen still needs to add a title to the new baskets table.

Inserting **WordArt into an Excel Worksheet**

When Karen reviews her work so far, she knows that her table shows the basic data but it does nothing to attract her customers' attention. To add some pizzazz, she would like you to use WordArt, a shared application available to all Office programs. WordArt enables you to add special graphic effects to your documents. You can bend, rotate, and stretch the text, and insert the graphic object into other documents, such as an Excel worksheet.

To prepare Karen's flyer, you will start WordArt while in Excel, create the graphic object, and then return to Excel to insert the object into the Excel worksheet.

To create a WordArt graphic object:

1. If necessary, click the **Drawing** button on the Standard toolbar to display the Drawing toolbar. You can access the WordArt program from the Drawing toolbar.
2. Click the **Insert WordArt** button on the Drawing toolbar to display a gallery of WordArt special effects styles. See Figure 6-6.

Figure 6-6 WORDART STYLES

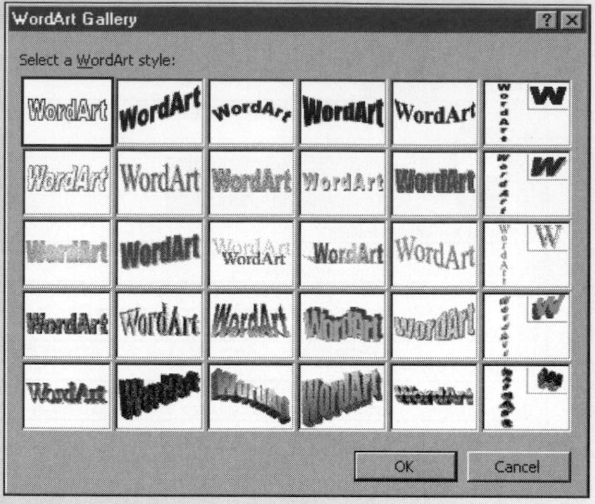

3. Click the WordArt style in the third row, fifth column, and then click the **OK** button to open the Edit WordArt Text dialog box. See Figure 6-7. In this dialog box, you specify the text you want to appear in the WordArt style you selected. If you want, you can also change the font, font size, and font style in the dialog box. For now, just type the text you want as the title of the worksheet. You will adjust the font size and style as necessary after you see how it appears in the worksheet.

Figure 6-7 EDIT WORDART TEXT DIALOG BOX

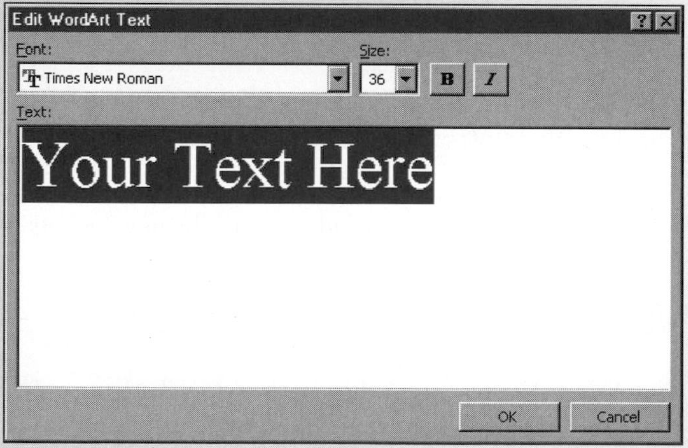

4. Type **New Products from Basket Weavers** and then click the **OK** button to place the WordArt graphic on your worksheet. See Figure 6-8. Notice that the WordArt toolbar appears on the screen while the WordArt object is selected. Figure 6-9 describes each button on the WordArt toolbar.

TROUBLE? If the WordArt toolbar does not appear on your screen, click View on the menu bar, point to Toolbars, and then click WordArt to place a check next to this option and display the WordArt toolbar on your screen.

Figure 6-8 WORDART GRAPHIC IN WORKSHEET

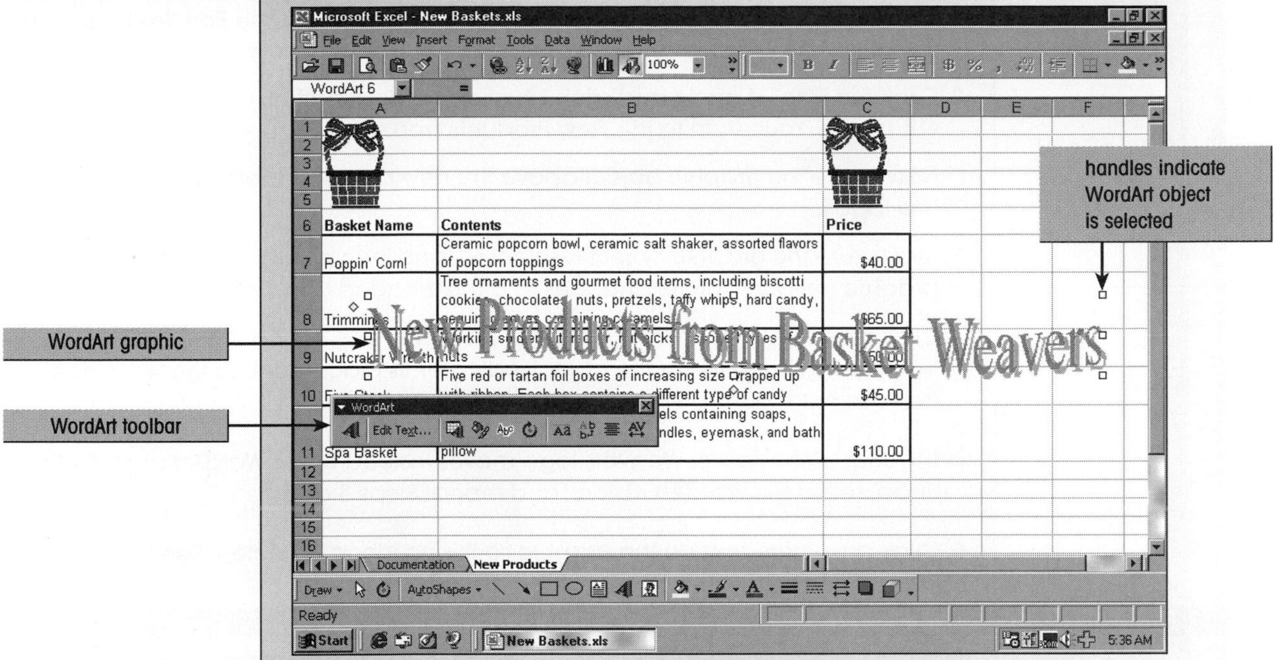

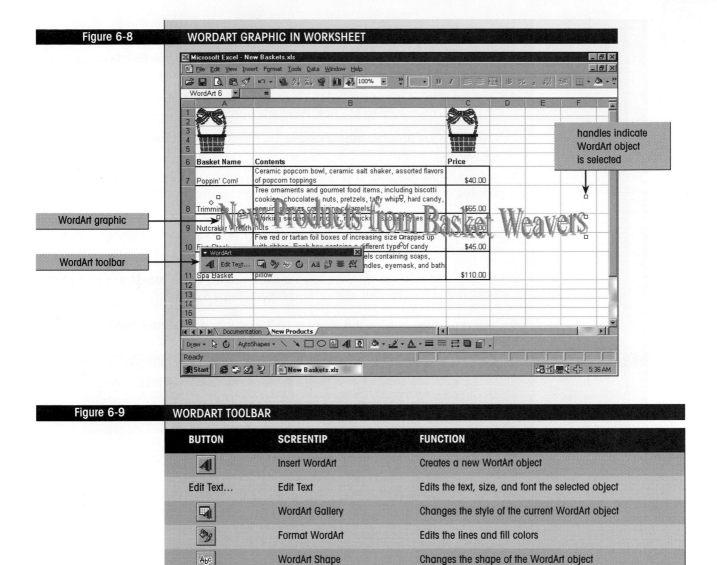

Figure 6-9 WORDART TOOLBAR

BUTTON	SCREENTIP	FUNCTION
	Insert WordArt	Creates a new WortArt object
Edit Text...	Edit Text	Edits the text, size, and font the selected object
	WordArt Gallery	Changes the style of the current WordArt object
	Format WordArt	Edits the lines and fill colors
	WordArt Shape	Changes the shape of the WordArt object
	Free Rotate	Rotates the WordArt object
	WordArt Same Letter Heights	Makes all the letters the same height
	WordArt Vertical Text	Changes between vertical and horizontal text orientation
	WordArt Alignment	Changes the text alignment
	WordArt Character Spacing	Changes the spacing between letters

As you review the WordArt graphic object, you decide that the graphic is too large. You decide to change the point size from 36 to 16 points and apply a bold style to make the graphic stand out. To make these changes, you need to return to the WordArt program because when you insert WordArt into an Excel worksheet, the object is embedded. This means that in order to modify the object, you need access to the commands and features of its source program.

To change the font point size and style of the WordArt object:

1. Make sure the graphic object is selected, and then click the **Edit Text** button on the WordArt toolbar to return to the Edit WordArt Text dialog box.

2. Click the **Size** list arrow and click **16**, click the **Bold** button, and then click the **OK** button. You return to the New Products worksheet.

   Now move the graphic object above the new products table, and between the two logos.

3. Make sure the graphic object is selected, and then position the pointer over the graphic until the pointer changes to a four-headed arrow ✥.

4. Click and drag the WordArt object to the top of row 2 in column B. As you drag the object, an outline of the object indicates its placement on the worksheet. Release the mouse button.

   TROUBLE? If the Basket Weavers logo moves instead of the WordArt object, click Undo, select the WordArt object, and repeat Steps 3 and 4.

5. Click anywhere outside the graphic so it is no longer selected. See Figure 6-10.

Figure 6-10 WORDART GRAPHIC AFTER BEING MOVED AND EDITED

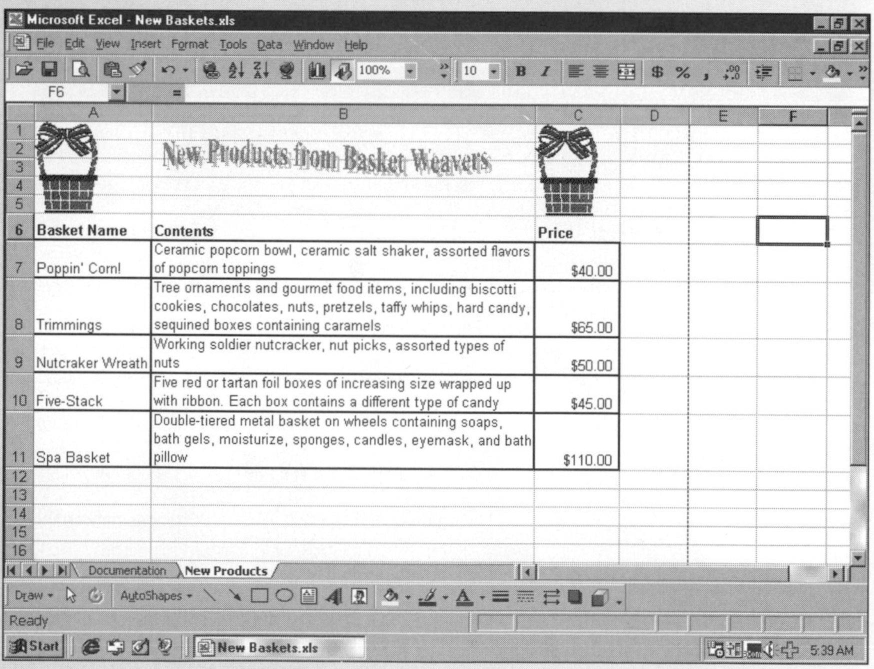

6. Save the worksheet.

7. Preview and print the worksheet for Karen.

8. Click the **Drawing** button on the Standard toolbar to remove the Drawing toolbar.

Karen wants to show Michael Flynn, the business manager for Basket Weavers, the flyer she designed. She attaches the flyer in an e-mail message she sends to him.

Mail a Workbook as an Attachment

Karen decided to take advantage of Excel's built-in features to use electronic mail. As long as Excel 2000 and one of the following e-mail programs: Outlook, Outlook Express, Microsoft Exchange Client, or Lotus cc:Mail is present, you can send or route workbooks or worksheets as attachments in e-mail messages.

REFERENCE WINDOW RW

Mail a Workbook or Worksheet as an Attachment

- In Microsoft Excel, open the workbook or worksheet you want to send as an attachment.
- Click File on the menu bar, point to Send To, and then click Mail Recipient (as Attachment).
- In the To and Cc boxes, enter recipient names, separated by semicolons.
- Set the options you want for the message.
- Click Send.

If your computer has a mail program, you can use the Send To Recipient (as attachment) command to automatically attach a copy of the current workbook to an e-mail message. When the message is received, the recipient double-clicks the Excel icon in the mail message to open the workbook.

In his reply, Michael Flynn comments on the professional look that the company logo and WordArt lends to the worksheet. Karen is ready to print copies of the table, and distribute them as flyers at each store.

Linking an Excel Worksheet to a Word Document

Now Karen needs to link the new products table created in Excel and the customer letter created in Word. As you know, Karen maintains her new product and pricing information in an Excel workbook. She wants to include the new products table in a letter to her customers. Because the product and pricing information is always subject to change, the copy-and-paste method is not the appropriate method to integrate these documents. Recall that pasting only allows you to change or modify the pasted object in the destination program. Karen wants the most current pricing information to appear both in the original source file (the new products worksheet) and the destination document (the customer letter). Therefore, a better solution is to create a link between the data copied from Excel to Word. By creating a link, if the data changes in the source document, these changes automatically appear in the destination document. For example, Karen believes that the price of gift baskets will most likely change when she receives a signed quote from her supplier of baskets. It's possible that she won't receive this quote until right before she plans to send out the letter. Therefore, you'll link the table from the New Products worksheet to the Customer Letter document so that you can make changes to the Excel new products table and have these changes automatically reflected in the Word document.

REFERENCE WINDOW RW

Linking an Object

- Start the source program, open the file containing the object to be linked, select the object or information you want to link to the destination program, and then click the Copy button on the Standard toolbar.
- Start the destination program, open the file that will contain the link to the copied object, position the insertion point where you want the linked object to appear, click Edit, and then click Paste Special.
- Click the Paste link option button, select the option you want in the As list box, and then click the OK button.

Karen has given you the Word file containing her letter. You need to link the new products table to the customer letter. First you need to select the new products table, which is the Excel object to be linked.

To link the new products table to the customer letter:

1. Make sure the New Products worksheet is the active sheet. Select the range of cells **A6:C11** to select the new products table.
2. Click the **Copy** button on the Standard toolbar to copy the data to the Clipboard.

Now, you need to start Word, and then open the customer letter document.

To start Word and open the customer letter document:

1. Make sure your Data Disk is in the appropriate disk drive. Click the **Start** button on the taskbar, point to **Programs**, and then click **Microsoft Word** to start this program.
2. Open the **Letter** document, which is located in the Tutorial folder for Tutorial.06 on your Data Disk. Karen's letter to the Basket Weavers' customers appears in the document window in print layout view. See Figure 6-11.

   TROUBLE? If your document does not show the nonprinting characters, click the Show/Hide button ¶ on the Standard toolbar.

   Next you'll save the file with a new name. That way, the original letter remains intact on your Data Disk, in case you want to start the tutorial again.

Figure 6-11 BEGINNING OF CUSTOMER LETTER

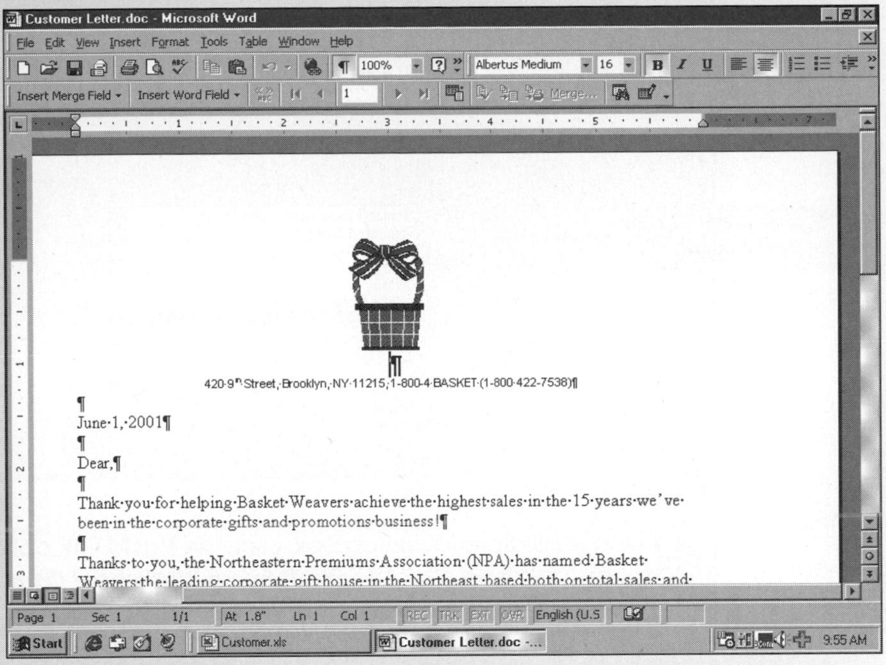

3. Use the **Save As** command to save the file as **Customer Letter** in the Tutorial folder for Tutorial.06 on your Data Disk.

   Now link the Excel new products table to the customer letter.

4. Scroll the document and position the insertion point to the left of the paragraph mark above the paragraph that begins, "You will receive..." This is where you want the product and pricing data to appear. See Figure 6-12.

Figure 6-12 PLACEMENT OF NEW PRODUCTS TABLE IN CUSTOMER LETTER

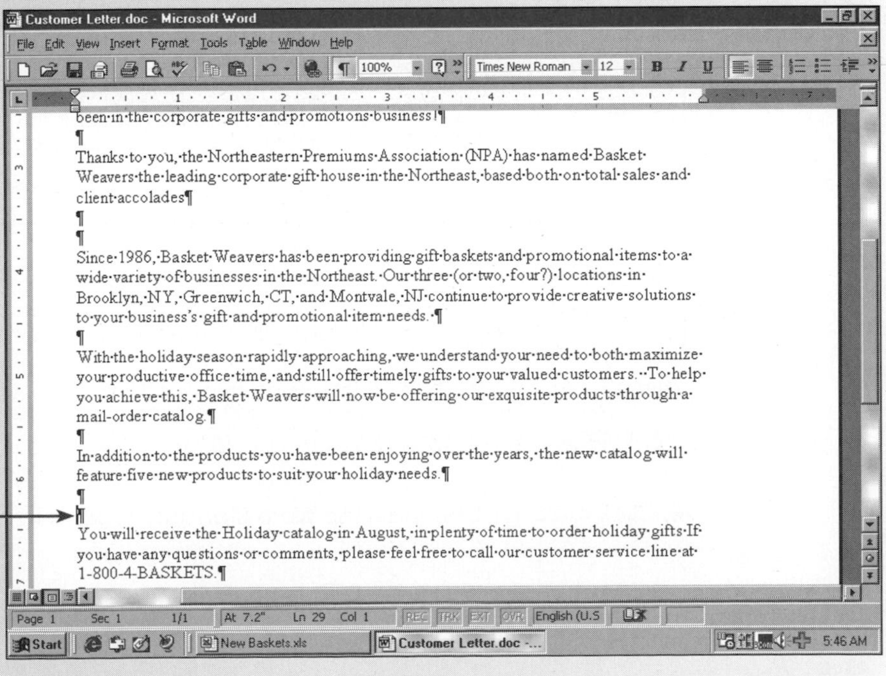

insert here

5. Click **Edit** on the menu bar, and then click **Paste Special**. The Paste Special dialog box opens. See Figure 6-13.

Figure 6-13 PASTE SPECIAL DIALOG BOX

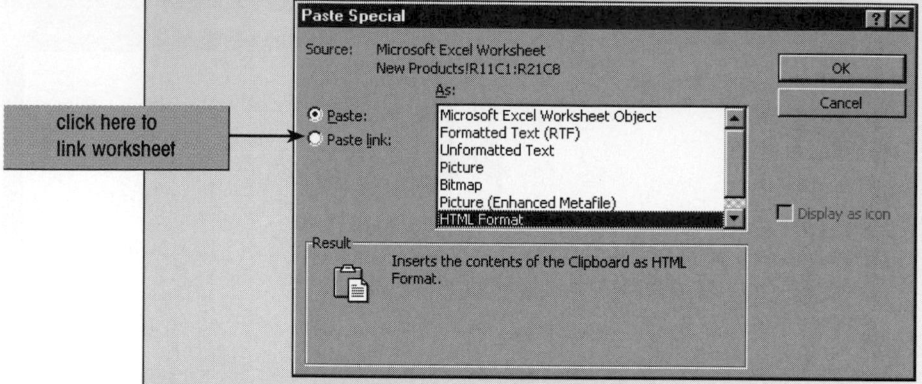

6. In the Paste Special dialog box, click the **Paste link** option button to select this option, and then click **Microsoft Excel Worksheet Object** in the As list box.

   The Paste link option specifies that the table will be linked.

7. Click the **OK** button to close the Paste Special dialog box and link the Excel worksheet to the customer letter. See Figure 6-14.

Figure 6-14 NEW PRODUCTS TABLE IN WORD DOCUMENT

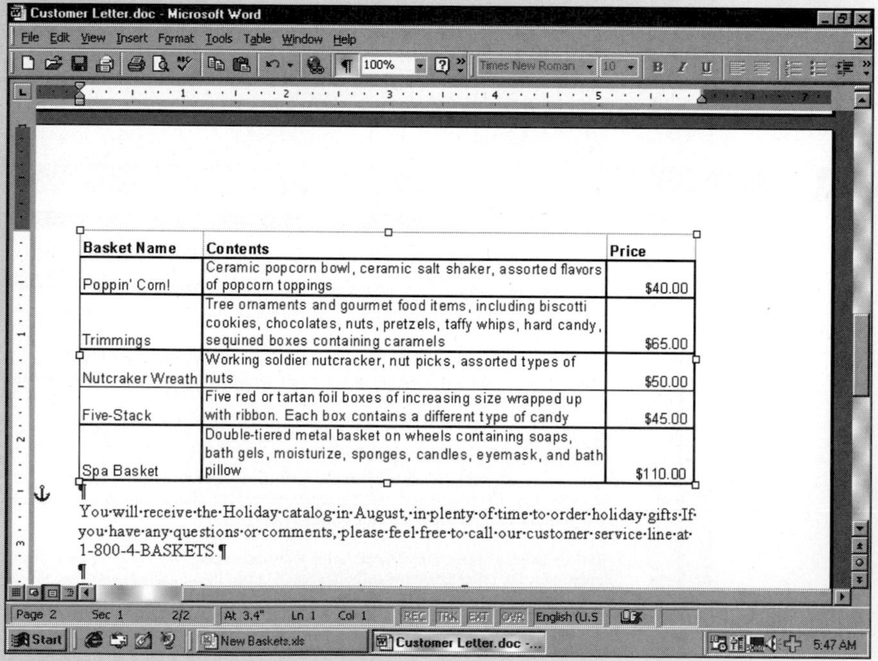

8. Click the **Save** button on the Word Standard toolbar to save the customer letter.

Karen has just received the signed quote from her basket supplier. As she expected, some of the prices have changed. She would now like you to update the new products table.

Updating Linked Objects

Now that you have linked the new products table from Excel to the customer letter, when you make changes to the source document, the Excel new products table, the changes will automatically be reflected in the destination file. When making changes, you can have one or both files open.

To update the new products table in Excel:

1. Click the **Microsoft Excel** button on the taskbar to switch to the New Baskets workbook. Make sure the New Products sheet is the active sheet.
2. Click any cell to deselect the table and press the **Esc** key to remove the data from the Clipboard.

   The price of Trimmings basket has changed from $65.00 to $70.00 each.
3. Enter **70** in cell C8.

   Now check to see if this change is reflected in the customer letter.
4. Click the **Microsoft Word** button on the taskbar to switch to the customer letter and view the price of Trimmings basket. Because you linked the table from Excel to Word, the change you just made to the price of Trimmings basket also appears in the destination document. See Figure 6-15.

Figure 6-15 CUSTOMER LETTER WITH UPDATED PRICE

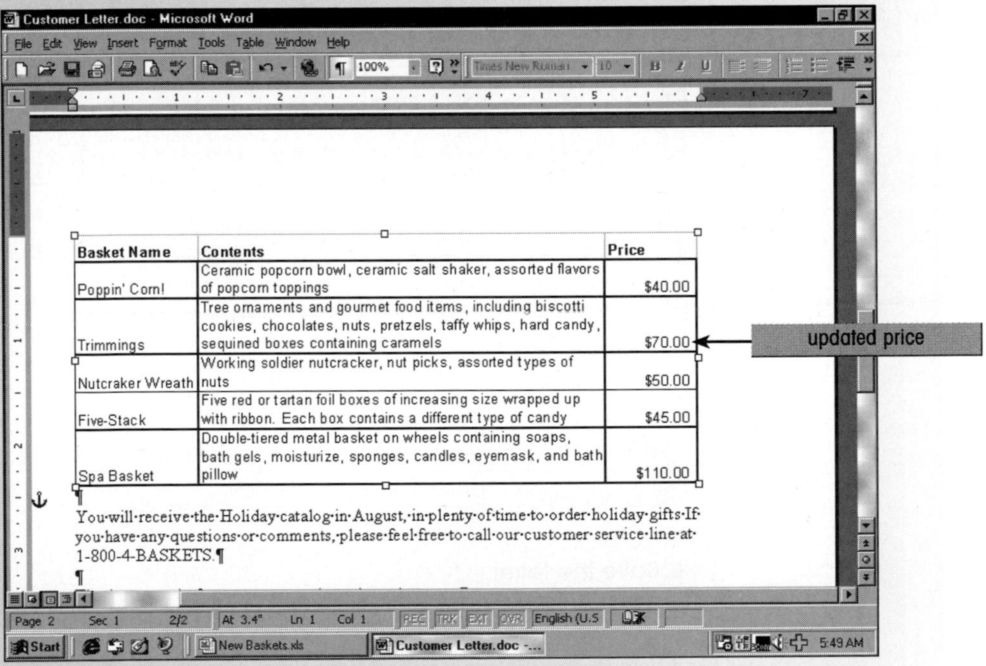

Basket Name	Contents	Price
Poppin' Corn!	Ceramic popcorn bowl, ceramic salt shaker, assorted flavors of popcorn toppings	$40.00
Trimmings	Tree ornaments and gourmet food items, including biscotti cookies, chocolates, nuts, pretzels, taffy whips, hard candy, sequined boxes containing caramels	$70.00
Nutcracker Wreath	Working soldier nutcracker, nut picks, assorted types of nuts	$50.00
Five-Stack	Five red or tartan foil boxes of increasing size wrapped up with ribbon. Each box contains a different type of candy	$45.00
Spa Basket	Double-tiered metal basket on wheels containing soaps, bath gels, moisturize, sponges, candles, eyemask, and bath pillow	$110.00

You will receive the Holiday catalog in August, in plenty of time to order holiday gifts. If you have any questions or comments, please feel free to call our customer service line at 1-800-4-BASKETS.

5. Click the **Save** button on the Word Standard toolbar to save the customer letter.

What would happen if you were working on the new products table in Excel without the Word document open? Would the information still be updated in the customer letter? To find out, make the remaining changes to the prices for gift baskets with the customer letter closed. You can then reopen the customer letter to ensure that the changes appear there as well.

To change the linked object with the Word document closed:

1. Click **File** on the Word menu bar, and then click **Close** to close the Customer Letter document.
2. Click the **Microsoft Excel** button on the taskbar to switch to the New Baskets workbook.
3. Enter **53** in cell C9, and then enter **47** in cell C10.
4. Click the **Save** button on the Excel Standard toolbar.
5. Close the Excel workbook.

   Now reopen the customer letter to confirm that the prices have been updated in the linked new baskets table.

6. Click the **Microsoft Word** button on the taskbar. Click **File** on the menu bar, and then open the **Customer Letter** file.
7. Scroll the document to view the linked table. Notice that the new basket prices appear in the linked table in Word. See Figure 6-16.

Figure 6-16 LINKED TABLE AFTER ALL PRICES UPDATED

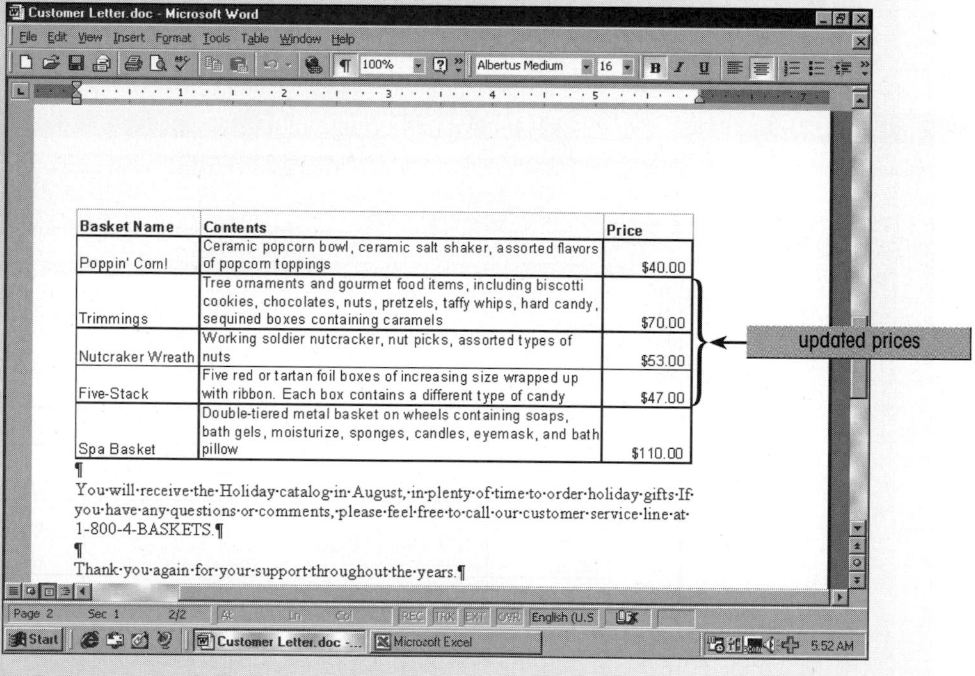

8. Save the letter.

The customer letter is almost complete. Now Karen just needs you to add the NPA pie chart.

Embedding an Excel Chart in a Word Document

Karen wants her letter to include the pie chart from the NPA workbook showing Basket Weavers as the top seller in the area. Karen knows the data for the chart will not change, so there is no need for her to link the pie chart in her Word letter to the source file. Therefore, she decides to embed it. That way, if the pie chart needs to be resized or moved once it is in the customer letter, she can make these changes using Excel chart commands. (Recall that when you embed an object, you automatically have access to the commands and features of the source program to manipulate it in the destination program.)

REFERENCE WINDOW RW

Embedding an Object

- Start the source program, open the file containing the object to be embedded, select the object or information you want to embed in the destination program, and then click the Copy button on the Standard toolbar.
- Start the destination program, open the file that will contain the embedded object, position the insertion point where you want to place the object, click Edit, and then click Paste Special.
- Click the Paste option button, select the option you want in the As list box, and then click the OK button.

Now you can embed the pie chart in the customer letter.

To embed the Excel chart in the Word document:

1. Click the **Microsoft Excel** button on the taskbar to switch to Excel. Open the **NPA** workbook, which is located in the Tutorial folder for Tutorial.06 on your Data Disk. The workbook appears in the worksheet window. See Figure 6-17.

Figure 6-17 NPA PIE CHART

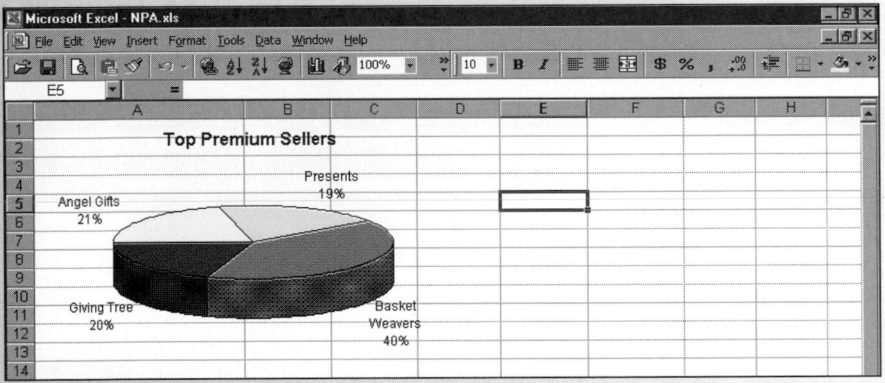

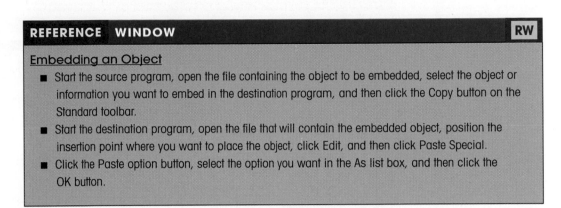

2. If necessary, click the **chart area** (the white area around the pie) to select the chart. When the chart is selected, handles appear on the chart area.
3. Click **Edit** on the menu bar, then click **Copy** to copy the chart to the Clipboard. The chart now appears with a rotating dashed line around its frame, indicating that it has been copied.
4. Click the **Microsoft Word** button on the taskbar to return to the Customer Letter document.

5. Scroll to page 1 of the Customer Letter document, and then click to the left of the paragraph mark immediately above the paragraph that begins "Since 1986, Basket Weavers..." to position the insertion point where you need to embed the pie chart. See Figure 6-18.

Figure 6-18 PLACEMENT OF PIE CHART IN CUSTOMER LETTER

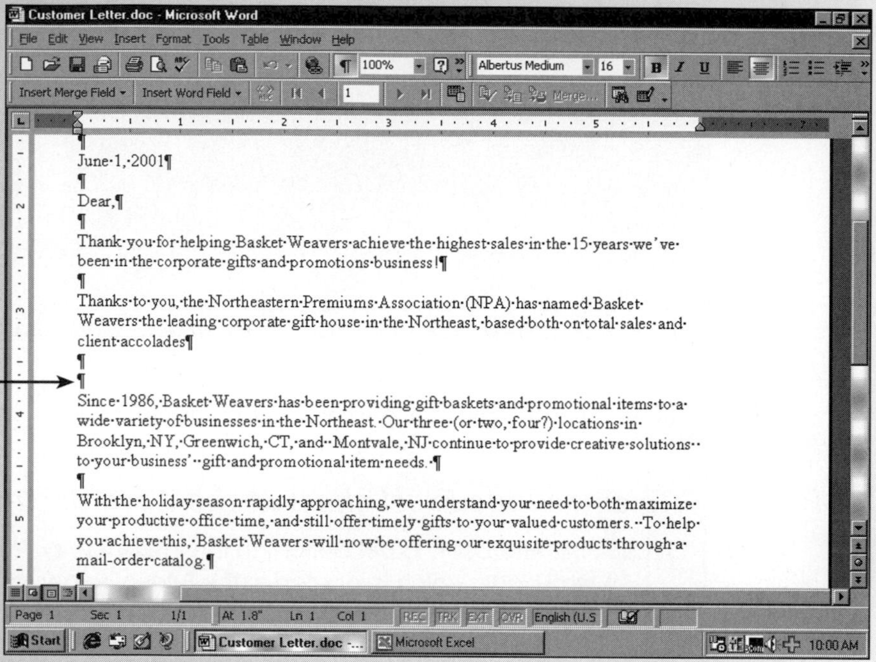

position insertion point here

6. Click **Edit**, and then click **Paste Special**. The Paste Special dialog box opens. See Figure 6-19.

Figure 6-19 PASTE SPECIAL DIALOG BOX WITH SETTING FOR PASTE

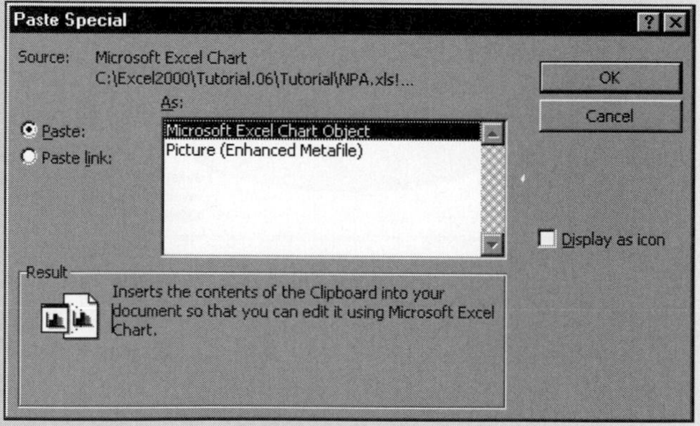

7. Make sure the Paste option button is selected. This option will embed the chart.

8. In the As list box, make sure Microsoft Excel Chart Object is selected as the object to be embedded.

TROUBLE? If the Microsoft Excel Chart Object option does not appear in the As list box, you might not have selected and copied the chart correctly. Click the Cancel button, and then repeat Steps 1 through 8, making sure that when you select the chart, handles appear around the chart area, and that when you copy the chart, a rotating dashed line appears around the chart area.

9. Click the **OK** button. The Paste Special dialog box closes, and the Excel pie chart appears embedded in the letter. See Figure 6-20.

Figure 6-20 CUSTOMER LETTER WITH EMBEDDED PIE CHART

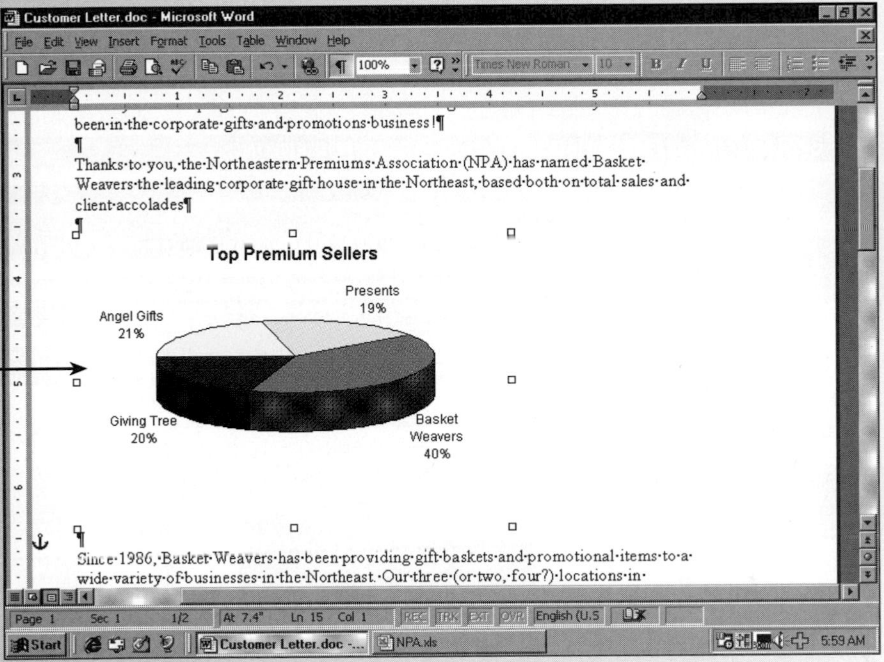

embedded pie chart

10. Click the **Save** button on the Word Standard toolbar to save the letter with the embedded chart.

11. Click the **Microsoft Excel** button on the taskbar, click any cell outside of the chart area to deselect the chart, and then close the NPA workbook.

TROUBLE? If a dialog box opens asking if you would like to save changes to the file before closing it, click the No button.

After reviewing the letter with the embedded pie chart, Karen decides that the Basket Weavers slice should be "exploded" and rotated to the front so the reader's attention is drawn to the fact that Basket Weavers' percentage of the market is the greatest among the competitors. Because you embedded the chart (as opposed to just copying and pasting it), you can use Excel chart commands from within the Word document to modify the chart.

Modifying an Embedded Object

When you make changes to an embedded object within the destination program, the changes are made to the embedded object only; the original object in the source program is not affected. When you select an embedded object, the menu commands on the menu bar of the destination program change to include the menu commands of the embedded object's source program. You can then use these commands to modify the embedded object.

Now that you have embedded the pie chart in Word, you can modify it by exploding the Basket Weavers pie slice.

To edit the pie chart from within Word:

1. Click the **Microsoft Word** button on the taskbar.
2. Double-click the **chart** to select it. After a moment, a thick border appears around the chart, and the Excel chart menu appears at the top of the Word window. See Figure 6-21. Notice that the embedded object appears within the Excel worksheet borders. You can now edit this object in place using Excel commands. Thus, you have access to all of the Excel features while you are in Word.

Figure 6-21 EMBEDDED OBJECT SELECTED FOR EDITING

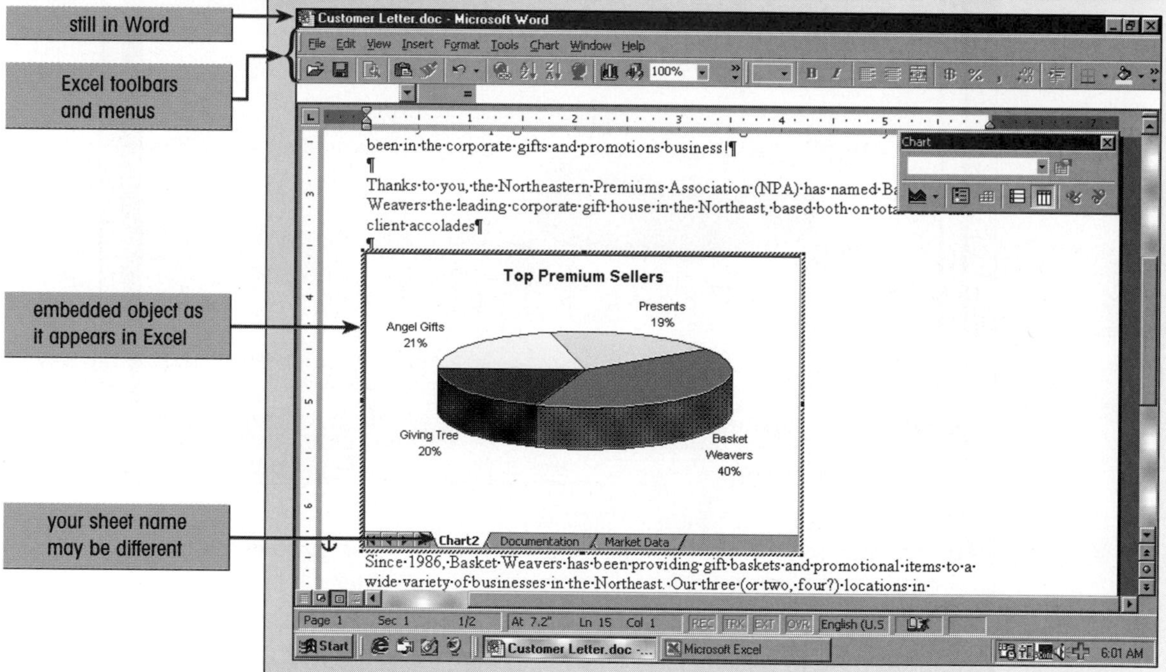

Now you can modify the chart.

3. Click anywhere within the **chart** to select it, and then click the **Basket Weavers slice** to select it. Selection handles now appear on only this slice.

   TROUBLE? If the floating Chart toolbar appears, click its Close button to close it.

4. With the pointer on the selected slice, click and drag the Basket Weavers slice down and to the right, and then release the mouse button. The Basket Weavers slice is exploded.
5. Click **Chart** on the menu bar, and then click **3-D View** to open the 3-D View dialog box.
6. Click the **clockwise rotation arrow** button until the Rotation box shows 75, then click **OK**.

7. Click outside of the chart area to deselect the chart and return the window to the display of Word commands and features only. See Figure 6-22.

Figure 6-22 PIE CHART IN WORD DOCUMENT AFTER SLICE EXPLODED AND ROTATED

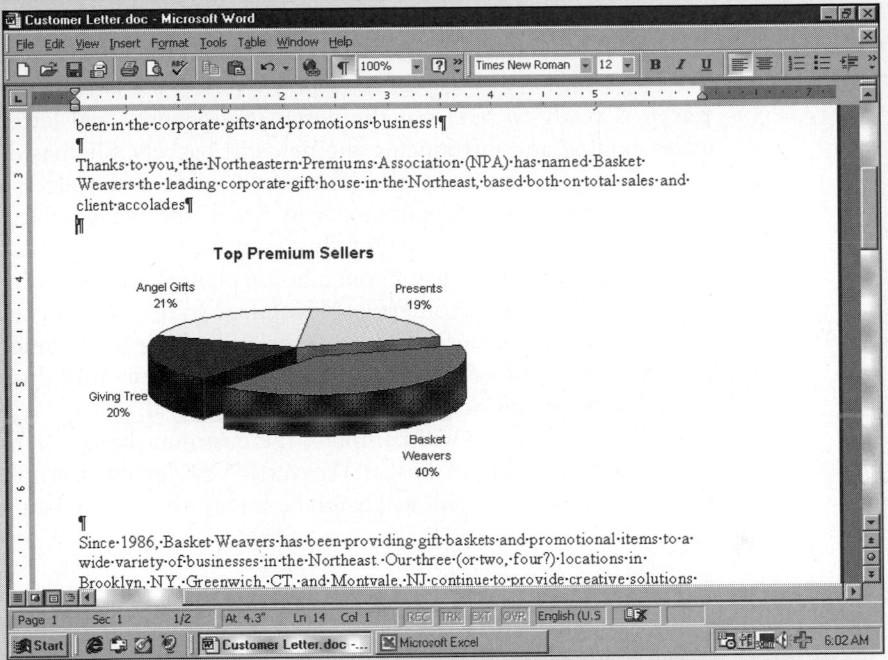

8. Click the **Save** button on the Word Standard toolbar to save the Customer Letter document.

Session 6.1 QUICK CHECK

1. OLE stands for ______________.
2. If two documents are ______________ using OLE, changing the source document will automatically change the destination document.
3. Updating an embedded object (does, does not) affect the original source object.
4. When you ______________ an object, that object is now part of the new document, and can only be altered from within that document's program.
5. You should ______________ an object if you plan to use the same data in several documents and need to ensure that the data will be identical in each document.
6. You can create special text effects using ______________.
7. When linking objects, you use the ______________ command on the Edit menu.
8. You have embedded a range of cells in a Word document. Describe what happens when you double-click the embedded object.

Now that you have completed the body of the customer letter, Karen is ready for you to send it to her New Jersey customers. You can do this through a mail merge. You will do this in Session 6.2.

SESSION 6.2

In this session you will plan and complete a mail merge by inserting merge fields into a form letter that links to data in an Excel list.

Customizing a Form Letter Using an Excel List

Karen is ready to send out the completed promotional letter announcing the new mail-order catalog and introducing the new gift baskets. She has decided to customize the customer letter by inserting the customer's name and address into each letter. Using her customer list, which is maintained in Excel, she plans separate mailings to coincide with promotional events at each of her company's three stores. For instance, the store in Montvalle, New Jersey has an open house planned next month, and Karen wants to send the letter to only those customers in New Jersey so that they receive the letter in advance of the open house. Later, she will do a separate mailing for Connecticut customers to coincide with a winter festival, and then a mailing to New York customers to coincide with the Brooklyn store's participation in a holiday carnival.

In this section you will complete the customer letter for Karen by merging it with the names and addresses of Basket Weavers' New Jersey customers. This data is stored as an Excel list. Therefore, you will again be integrating Excel data with a Word document.

Planning the Form Letter

Karen plans to use the Mail Merge feature of Word to send the customer letter you completed in the previous session to each Basket Weavers customer in New Jersey. She will be sending the same letter, a form letter, to each customer; only the name and address will change. A **form letter** is a Word document that contains standard paragraphs of text and a minimum of variable text, usually just the names and addresses of the letter recipients. The **main document** of a form letter contains the text that stays the same in each letter, as well as the **merge fields** that tell Word where to insert the variable information into each letter. The variable information, the information that changes from letter to letter, is contained in a **data source**, which can be another Word document, an Excel list, an Access database, or some other source. The main document and the data source work together—when you merge the main document with the data source, Word replaces the merge fields with the corresponding field values from the data source. The process of merging the main document with the data source is called a **mail merge**.

In this case, Karen's customer letter will be the main document, and a customer list maintained in Excel containing the names and addresses of Basket Weavers customers will be the data source. Figure 6-23 shows Karen's plan for the form letter.

Figure 6-23 KAREN'S PLAN FOR THE FORM LETTER

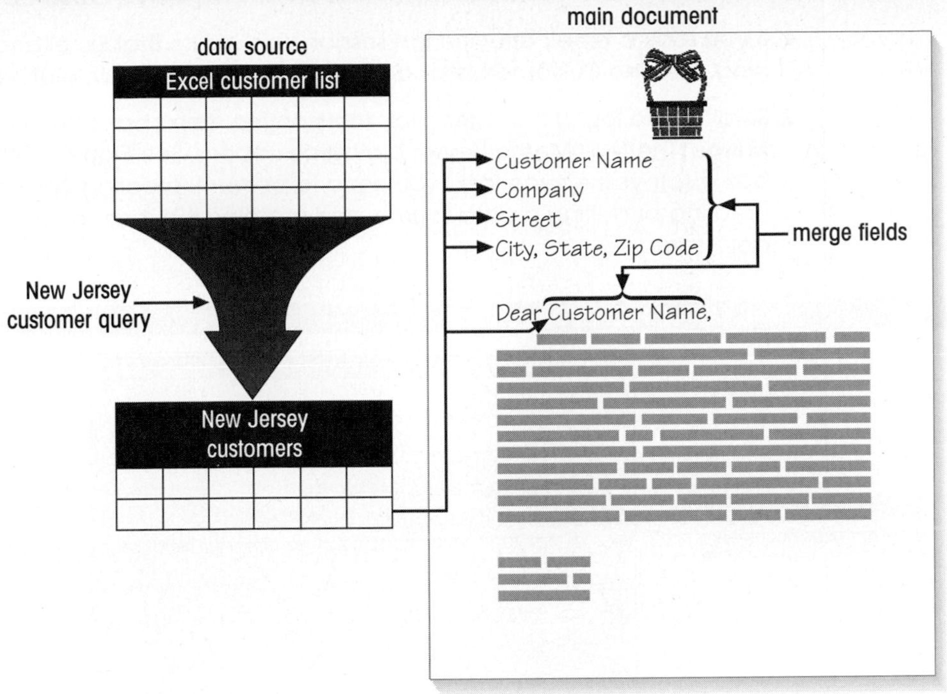

Note that the data source contains all Basket Weavers customers. Karen first wants to send the letter to only the New Jersey customers.

REFERENCE WINDOW RW

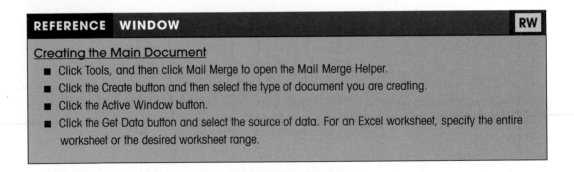

Creating the Main Document

- Click Tools, and then click Mail Merge to open the Mail Merge Helper.
- Click the Create button and then select the type of document you are creating.
- Click the Active Window button.
- Click the Get Data button and select the source of data. For an Excel worksheet, specify the entire worksheet or the desired worksheet range.

To help simplify the mail-merge process, you will use the Word Mail Merge Helper, which guides you through the steps of the mail merge.

Specifying a Main Document and a Data Source

A mail-merged main document can be a new or existing Word document. In this case, the main document is Karen's customer letter.

Now you need to specify the customer letter as the main document and the Excel customer list as the data source.

To specify the main document and the data source:

1. If you took a break after the last session, make sure that Excel and Word are running, and the Customer Letter document is open and visible on your screen.
2. Scroll to the top of the letter, click **Tools** on the menu bar, and then click **Mail Merge**. The Mail Merge Helper dialog box opens. See Figure 6-24. The dialog box displays the three tasks you need to perform: creating the main document, creating or getting a data source, and merging the main document with the data source.

Figure 6-24 MAIL MERGE HELPER DIALOG BOX

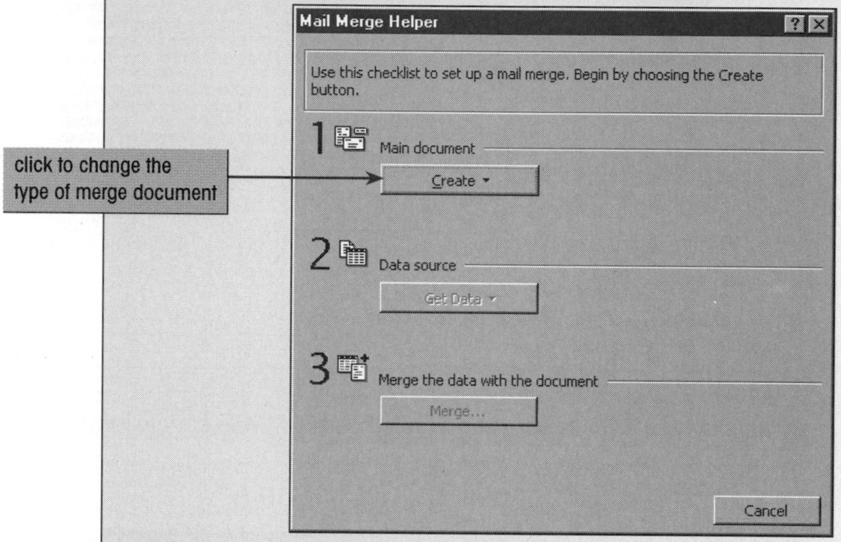

The type of merge document you need to create is a form letter.

3. Click the **Create** button in the Main document section to display the list of main document types. Click **Form Letters**. A message box appears asking whether you want to use the active window as the main document or create a new main document. In this case, you want to use the open document, Customer Letter, as the main document.
4. Click the **Active Window** button. The area below the Create button now indicates the type of mail merge (Form Letters) and the file path (drive and folder) and name of the main document (Customer Letter).

   You have now established Customer Letter as the main document. Next you need to specify the data source, the source of the variable information that will be inserted into the main document during the merge process. The data source is an Excel workbook named Customers.
5. Click the **Get Data** button in the Data source section of the Mail Merge Helper dialog box, and then click **Open Data Source**. The Open Data Source dialog box opens.

   The Customers workbook is located in the Tutorial folder for Tutorial.06 on your Data Disk.
6. Make sure that the Tutorial folder appears in the Look in list box.

Because the dialog box currently shows only the Word documents in the selected folder, you need to change the entry in the Files of type list box to show the Excel files.

7. Click the **Files of type** list arrow, and then click **MS Excel Worksheets**. The dialog box now shows a list of all the Excel files in the Tutorial.06 folder on your Data Disk.

8. Click **Customer** and then click the **Open** button. A Microsoft Excel dialog box opens, in which you can choose the data source—either the entire spreadsheet or the range containing the customer list. In this case, you need to specify the range Customers. See Figure 6-25.

Figure 6-25 CHOOSE DATA SOURCE

click this data source

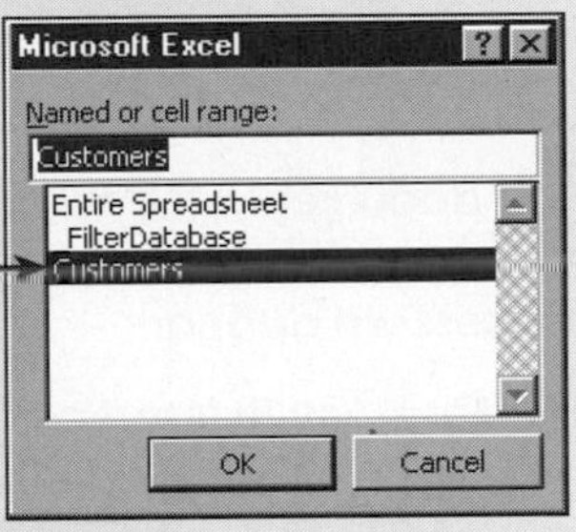

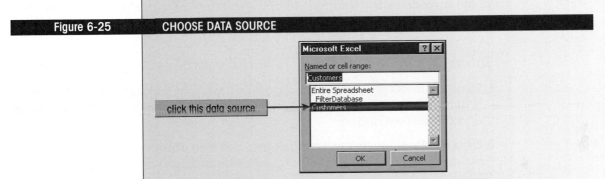

9. Click **Customers** in the list box, and then click the **OK** button. A message box appears indicating that your main document does not contain merge fields.

Your next step will be to insert the merge fields into the main document, the customer letter, so you need to edit the main document.

10. Click the **Edit Main Document** button. The Mail Merge Helper dialog box closes and the Mail Merge toolbar appears on the screen. See Figure 6-26.

Figure 6-26 TOP OF MAIN DOCUMENT

Mail Merge toolbar

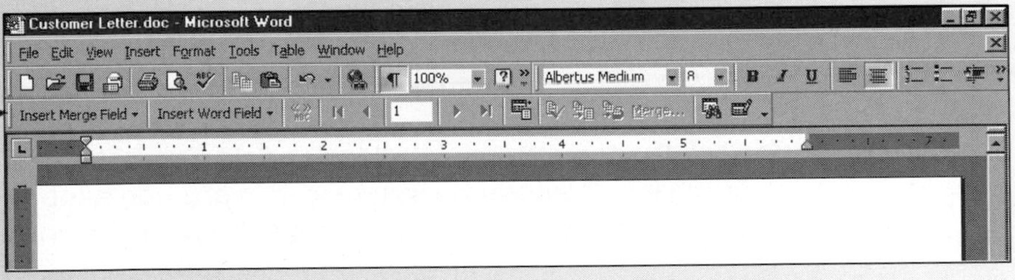

Inserting the Merge Fields

Because you now have a data source to use with the main document, you can go back to the main document and identify which fields in the Excel list to pull into the document as well as where to place each field. This process is called **inserting merge fields**. As noted earlier, a merge field is a special instruction that tells Word where to insert the variable information from the data source into a form letter.

REFERENCE WINDOW RW

Inserting Merge Fields into a Main Document

- Position the insertion point where you want the merge field to appear in the main document.
- Click the Insert Merge Field button on the Mail Merge toolbar.
- Click the name of the field you want to insert.

To complete Karen's form letter, you need to insert seven merge fields, one for each of the following pieces of information: customer name, company name (if any), street, city, state, and zip code—all for the inside address—and customer name again in the salutation of the letter.

To insert the merge fields into the customer letter document:

1. Scroll the document window and position the insertion point in the blank paragraph directly above the salutation ("Dear,"). This is where the customer's name and address will appear.
2. Press the **Enter** key to insert a blank line, and then click the **Insert Merge Field** button on the Mail Merge toolbar. A list of the available merge fields appears. See Figure 6-27.

Figure 6-27 INSERTING MERGE FIELDS INTO MAIN DOCUMENT

available fields from customer list

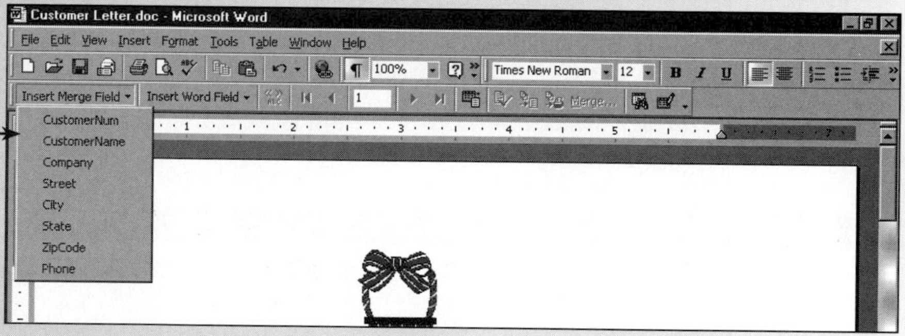

3. Click **CustomerName** to select this field. See Figure 6-28. Word inserts the field name into the document, enclosed in chevron symbols (<< >>). The chevrons distinguish the merge fields from the rest of the text in the main document.

Figure 6-28 MAIN DOCUMENT AFTER ONE MERGE FIELD INSERTED

merge field

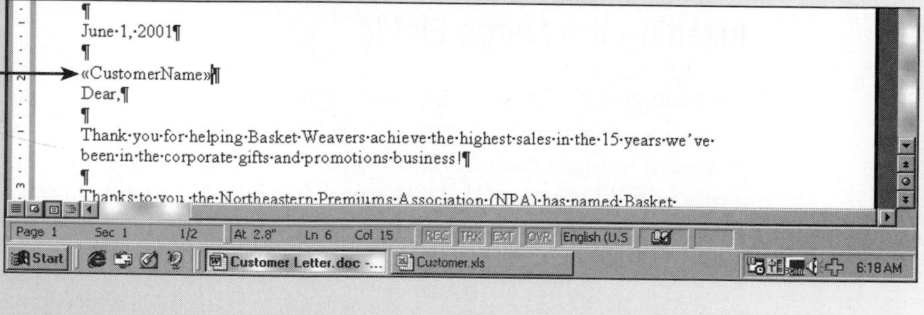

The company name (if any) should appear on the line below the customer name.

4. Press the **Enter** key to move the insertion point to the next line, click the **Insert Merge Field** button on the Mail Merge toolbar, and then click **Company**. The Company merge field is now in the document.

5. Repeat Step 4 to insert the **Street** field on the third line of the inside address.

6. Repeat Step 4 to insert the **City** field on the fourth line of the inside address.

   The State and ZipCode fields must appear on the same line as the City field, with a comma and a space separating the city and state, and a space separating the state and zip code.

7. Type **,** (a comma), press the **Spacebar**, click the **Insert Merge Field** button on the Mail Merge toolbar, and then click **State**.

8. Press the **Spacebar**, click the **Insert Merge Field** button on the Mail Merge toolbar, and then click **ZipCode**.

9. Press the **Enter** key to insert a blank line between the inside address and the salutation. The final merge field you need to insert is the CustomerName field again, after the word "Dear" in the salutation of the letter.

10. Position the insertion point between the "r" in the word "Dear" and the comma following it, press the **Spacebar**, click the **Insert Merge Field** button on the Mail Merge toolbar, and then click **CustomerName**. The merge fields are now complete. See Figure 6-29.

Figure 6-29 ALL MERGE FIELDS INSERTED INTO MAIN DOCUMENT

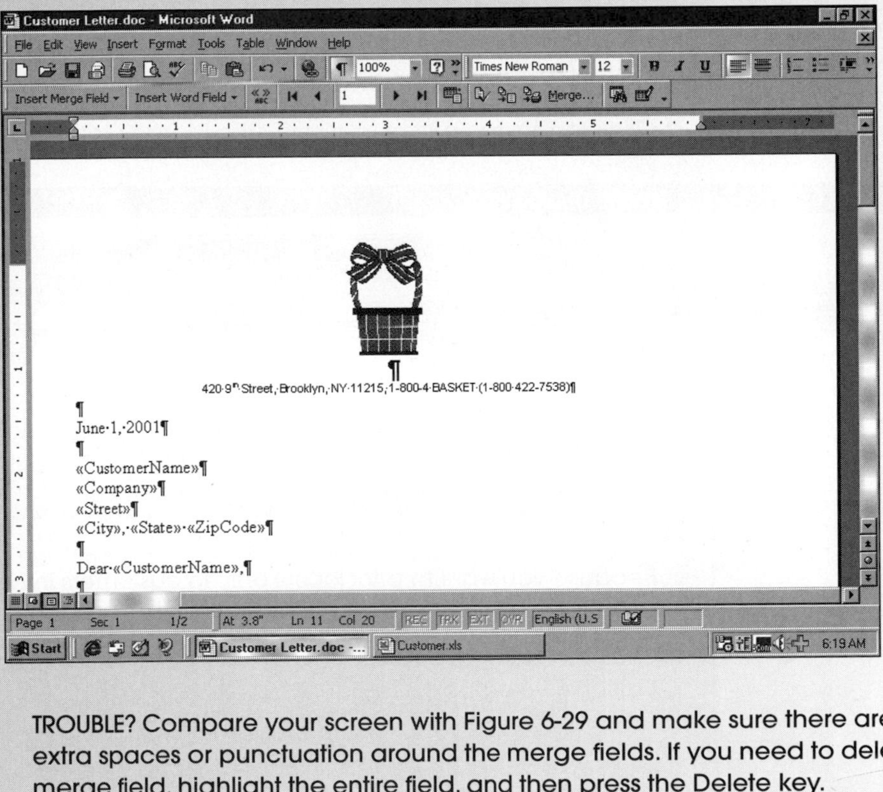

TROUBLE? Compare your screen with Figure 6-29 and make sure there are no extra spaces or punctuation around the merge fields. If you need to delete a merge field, highlight the entire field, and then press the Delete key.

11. Click the **Save** button on the Word Standard toolbar to save the letter.

Performing the Mail Merge

With the main document and merge fields in place, you're ready to merge the main document with the data source—the Excel customer list—to produce the customized letter.

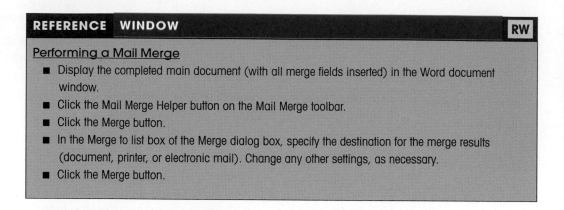

REFERENCE WINDOW RW

Performing a Mail Merge

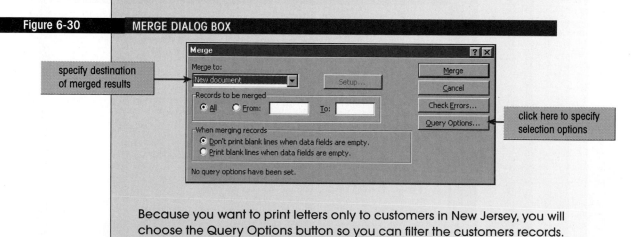

- Display the completed main document (with all merge fields inserted) in the Word document window.
- Click the Mail Merge Helper button on the Mail Merge toolbar.
- Click the Merge button.
- In the Merge to list box of the Merge dialog box, specify the destination for the merge results (document, printer, or electronic mail). Change any other settings, as necessary.
- Click the Merge button.

In this case, Karen wants the merge results placed in a new document, so that she can check the merged form letters before printing them. First she needs to specify the records that are to be included in the mail merge—customers in New Jersey.

To specify selection criteria for records to retrieve from the data source:

1. Click the **Mail Merge Helper** button on the Mail Merge toolbar. The Mail Merge Helper dialog box opens.
2. Click the **Merge** button to display the Merge dialog box. See Figure 6-30.

Figure 6-30 MERGE DIALOG BOX

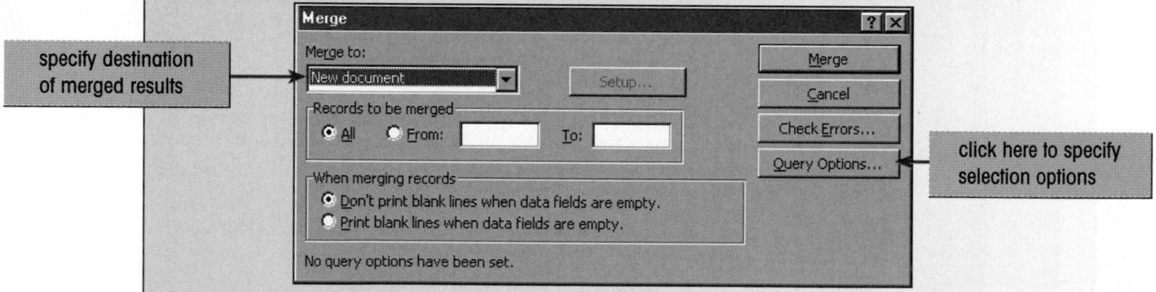

Because you want to print letters only to customers in New Jersey, you will choose the Query Options button so you can filter the customers records.

3. Click the **Query Options** button to display the Filter Records tab in the Query Options dialog box. See Figure 6-31.

Figure 6-31 QUERY OPTIONS DIALOG BOX

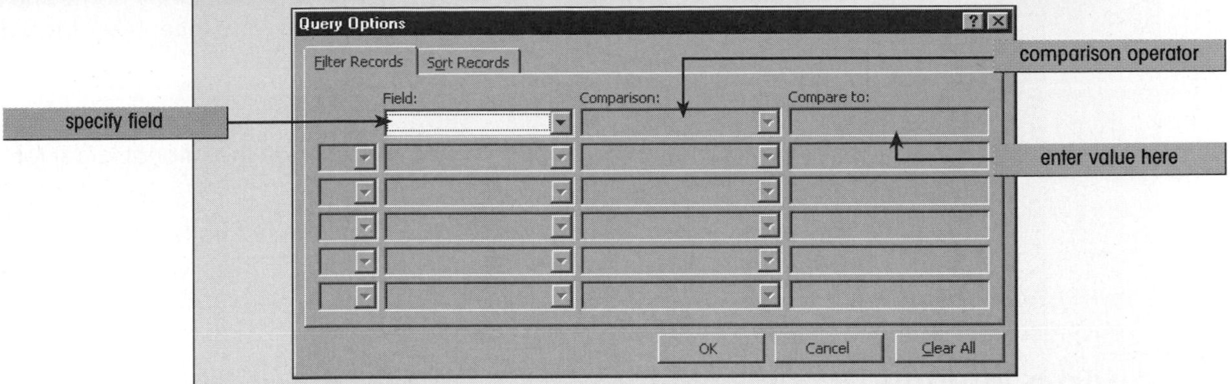

4. Click the **Field** list arrow to display the list of fields from the customer list. Scroll the list until the State field appears. Click **State** to select the field on which you want to base your selection. Notice that the Comparison operator box now displays the default operator—Equal to. Accept the default comparison operator and enter a value to compare to the State field.

5. Make sure the insertion point is in the Compare to text box and then type **NJ**.

6. Click the **OK** button to return to the Merge dialog box.

   You are now ready to merge the data with the letter. You can merge the data to a new document, or merge directly to the printer, electronic mail, or fax. Karen wants to check the merged document before printing, so you will merge to a new document.

7. Click the **Merge** button. The Excel data is merged with the Word form letter and placed in a new document named Form Letters1 (the default name supplied by Word). The form letter for each of the five New Jersey customers is contained in the merged document, each separated by a section break.

8. Scroll the document until you can see the first merged address. Word replaced each merge field with the appropriate Excel data. See Figure 6-32.

Figure 6-32 MERGED RESULTS IN NEW DOCUMENT

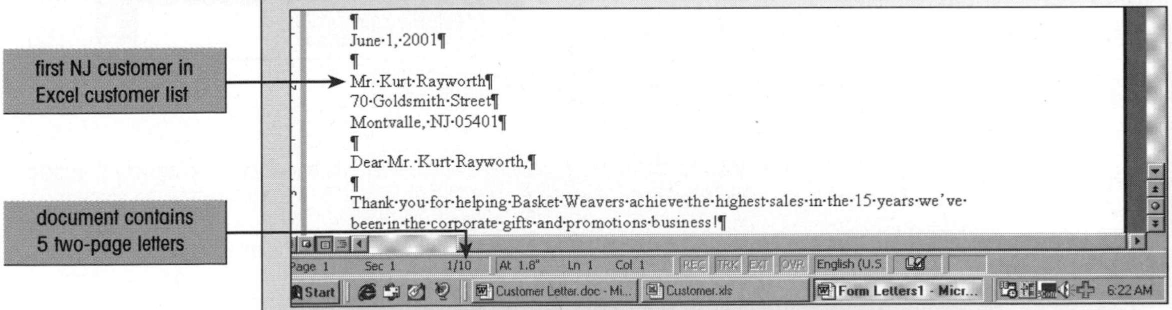

Notice that the merged document contains 10 pages. Each letter is two pages long, and there are five letters in all.

9. Use the buttons in the vertical scroll bar to page through the merged document. Notice that in addresses that do not include a company name, the blank line is suppressed. Also, notice that each two-page form letter is separated from the others by a section break.

   Now you'll save the merged document and then close it.

10. Save the document as **Merged Customer Letters** in the Tutorial folder for Tutorial.06 on your Data Disk.

11. Close the Merged Customer Letters document. You return to the main document, the customer letter.

Viewing **Merged Documents**

When you're working with mail-merge documents, you don't have to open the document containing the merge results in order to view them. You can view the merged documents right from the main document.

The View Merged Data button on the Mail Merge toolbar lets you check the merge results quickly. When you click this button, information from the first data record appears in place of the merge fields. You can then use the navigation buttons on the Mail Merge toolbar to view the results for other data records. You'll practice using the navigation buttons to view the merge results.

To view the merge results from the main document:

1. Click the **View Merged Data** button on the Mail Merge toolbar. See Figure 6-33. The information from the first merged letter appears in place of the merge fields.

Figure 6-33 VIEWING MERGED RESULTS FROM MAIN DOCUMENT

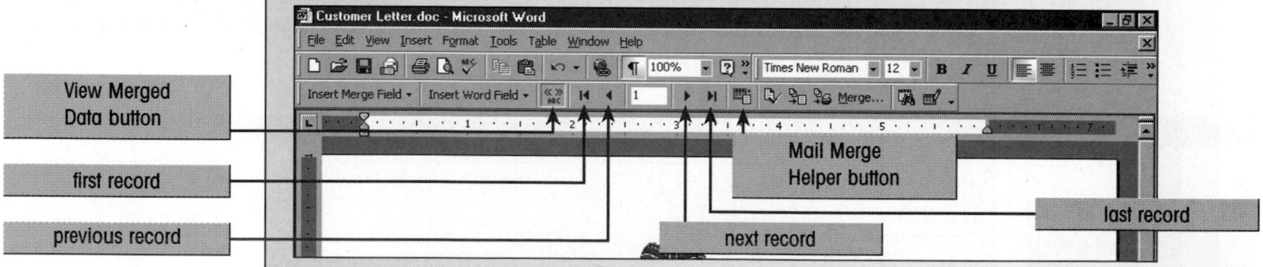

2. Click the **Next Record** button on the Mail Merge toolbar to display the second form letter (for Steve Donovan).

3. Click the **Last Record** button on the Mail Merge toolbar to display the last form letter (the fifth letter, which is for KuMan Ranjan).

4. Click the **First Record** button on the Mail Merge toolbar to redisplay the first form letter.

5. Click the **View Merged Data** button again. The merge fields appear in the main document again.

Karen has just learned that one of her customers, Wilson Gift Store, has moved to a different location. She asks you to enter the new address for this customer in Excel and then re-merge the Word document with the data.

To change the address and then re-merge the document:

1. Click the **Microsoft Excel** button on the taskbar to switch to Excel.
2. Use the data form to locate Wilson Gift Store (customer number 192) and change the Street entry to **10 Main Street**.
3. Click the **Microsoft Word** button on the taskbar to switch back to Word.
4. Click the **View Merged Data** button on the Mail Merge toolbar. The information from the first merged letter appears.

   The record for Wilson Gift Store is the second record (in the mail merge).
5. Click the **Next Record** button on the Mail Merge toolbar to select the next record. The record for Wilson Gift Store appears. Note that the data has been updated to show the new street address (10 Main Street).

   Although the main document now shows the updated record data, the document containing the merge results—Merged Customer Letters—still contains the old address, because it contains only the results of the previous merge. In order to update the Merged Customer Letters document, you need to re-merge the main document with the data source and then save the updated merge results.
6. Click the **Mail Merge Helper** button on the Mail Merge toolbar. The Mail Merge Helper dialog box opens.
7. Click the **Merge** button to open the Merge dialog box, and then click the **Merge** button. The mail merge results appear in a new document window.
8. Scroll through the results until you find the address for Wilson Gift Store. Note that it now includes the updated street data.

   Now you need to save the merge results as Merged Customer Letters to overwrite the existing document.
9. Use the Save As command to save the document containing the merge results as **Merged Customer Letters**, answer **Yes** to the prompt for replacing the existing file, and then close the Merged Customer Letters document. You return to the main document, which still displays the data for Wilson Gift Store.

After viewing the merged documents, Karen decides to print just one of the letters to check its appearance and layout before printing all the letters.

Previewing and Printing a Merged Document

You can preview and print a merged document in the same way that you do any Word document—using the Print Preview and Print buttons on the Standard toolbar. For the sample letter Karen wants to print, she decides that it would be best to print one that includes a company name in the address. This will allow her to make sure that the additional line for the company name does not cause a bad page break across the two pages of the letter. Because the main document already displays the data for Wilson Gift Store, which includes the company name, you can preview and print this merged letter.

To preview and print the merged letter for Wilson Gift Store:

1. Click the **Print Preview** button on the Standard toolbar. Both pages of the letter appear in Print Preview. See Figure 6-34.

Figure 6-34 MERGED LETTER FOR WILSON GIFT STORE IN PRINT PREVIEW

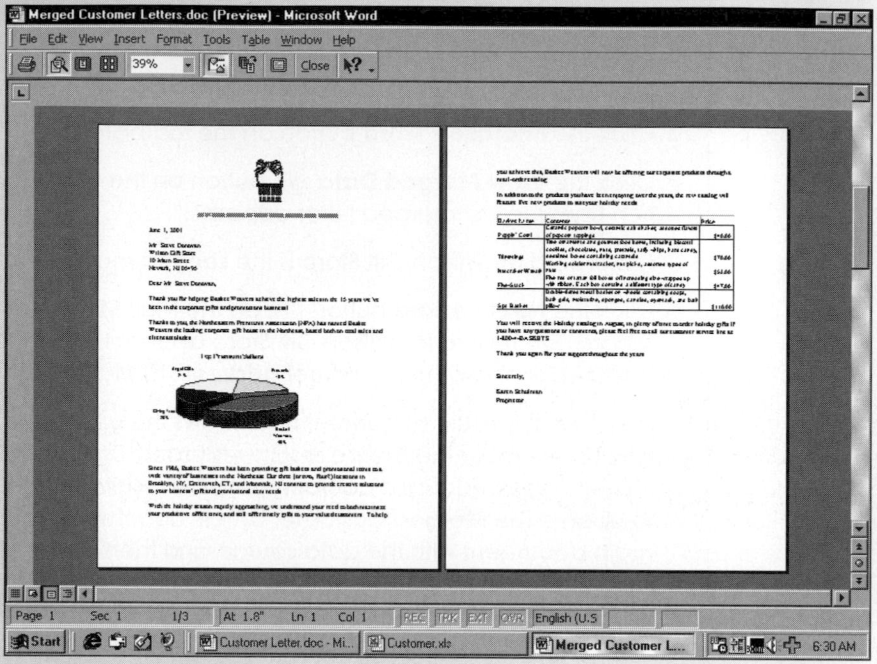

TROUBLE? If only one page appears, click the Multiple Pages button on the Print Preview toolbar, and then drag to select 1 x 2 pages.

Karen approves of the layout and pagination of the letter, and she asks you to print one copy of it and then close it.

2. Click the **Print** button on the Standard toolbar. One copy of the current merged letter (for Wilson Gift Store) prints.
3. Click the **Close** button on the Print Preview toolbar to return to the main document. Before saving and closing the document, you need to redisplay the merge fields so that they will appear instead of the address data the next time the main letter document is opened.
4. Click the **View Merged Data** button on the Mail Merge toolbar to redisplay the merge fields.
5. Save and close the customer letter. The Customers workbook automatically closes. Click the **Yes** button to save the changes you made to the Customers workbook.
6. Exit Word.

Karen plans on reviewing the printed letter with her assistants to make sure everyone approves of it before she prints and mails all the form letters.

Session 6.2 QUICK CHECK

1. The ______________ document of a form letter contains the text that stays the same, as well as the ______________.
2. A ______________ contains the variable information in a form letter.
3. How do you insert merge fields into a main document?
4. How do you view merged documents directly from the main document?
5. During the mail-merge process you updated the customer list in Excel. After re-merging, you observed the updated address in the merged customer letter. That process illustrates ______________.

Karen is pleased with her finished letter, which integrates her Excel data. She is confident that it will contribute to the successful promotion of Basket Weavers.

SESSION 6.3

In this session you will create hyperlinks between documents so that you can easily access other information from a single document. You will learn how to navigate a series of hyperlinks using the Web toolbar. You will also learn how to convert an Excel worksheet to HTML format so you can display Excel data as a Web document.

Creating Hyperlinks to Connect Files

In Sessions 6.1 and 6.2, you worked with several files from two different programs, Excel and Word, that contained related information. To do this, you opened each program and then navigated between the two using their program buttons on the taskbar. With Excel 2000, you can now insert links to documents created using Microsoft Office programs. These links allow you to easily navigate to different documents created in different programs, without having to launch each program first.

To link various documents, you can use a hyperlink. A **hyperlink** is an object (computer file pathname or address, text, or graphic) in a document that you can click to access information in other locations in that document or in other documents. This system of linked information is called **hypertext**. A hyperlink can be a filename, a word, a phrase, or a graphic that has been assigned an address to a file located elsewhere. If the hyperlink is a filename or text, the hyperlink will appear in color and as underlined text. If the hyperlink is a graphic, there is no visual cue until you position your mouse over the graphic. Then the mouse pointer changes to a pointing hand and displays the location of the link's destination. When you click a hyperlink, the destination document is brought into memory and appears on the screen. This hyperlink may reference

- a document created in Word, Excel, PowerPoint, or Access
- a section farther down in the same document
- a document on the World Wide Web

Hyperlinks offer a new way of making information available. Files containing hyperlinks are called **hyperlink documents**. Using the hyperlinks available to you in a hyperlink document, you are able to jump from one topic to the next in whatever order you want, regardless of where they reside.

As more hyperlinks are added between and within various documents, a structure emerges that you can navigate, traveling from hyperlink to hyperlink, following a path of information and ideas. You have already worked with such a structure when you accessed the Excel online Help system. By clicking a keyword or phrase, you were able to access additional information on the topic you were interested in. The Excel online Help system is an example of a series of hyperlink documents.

Inserting a Hyperlink

Karen asks you to place a hyperlink in the New Baskets workbook to the Merged Customer Letters (Word file) and to the Customers workbook (Excel file). With the files connected, she can easily jump to the other files if she wants to recall specific information. For instance, by including links to the customer list and the merged customer letter, she can check a customer's name or make sure she sent a letter to an important new client while working in the New Baskets workbook.

REFERENCE WINDOW RW

Inserting a Hyperlink

- Select the text, graphic, or cell in which you want to insert the hyperlink, and then click the Insert Hyperlink button on the Standard toolbar to open the Insert Hyperlink dialog box.
- Type the address of the Web page or file you want to jump to. If you are not sure of the filename, click the Browse button to display the Link to File dialog box. Find and select the file you want to link to.
- If you want to jump to a particular location within the file, enter the location in the Named location in file text box.
- Click the Use relative path for hyperlink check box if you want the Excel destination's relative file address.

To insert a hyperlink into an Excel worksheet:

1. If you took a break after the last session, make sure Excel is running and your Data Disk is in the appropriate disk drive.
2. Open the **New Baskets** workbook located in the Tutorial folder for Tutorial.06 on your Data Disk.
3. Make sure the Documentation sheet is active, and then click cell **A10**. The Documentation sheet is where you want to insert the hyperlinks to the other files Karen works with when using this workbook.
4. Type **Cross-Reference to Related Documents**, and then press the **Enter** key.
5. Click cell **A10**, and then click the **Bold** button on the Formatting toolbar.

   Enter the text you want to use as a reference.
6. Click cell **A11**, type **Merged Customer Letters**, and press the **Enter** key.
7. In cell A12, type **Customer List**, and then press the **Enter** key.

   Now you need to specify the location of the destination file for each hyperlink. You do this using the Insert Hyperlink button on the Standard toolbar.
8. Click cell **A11** and then click the **Insert Hyperlink** button on the Standard toolbar to open the Insert Hyperlink dialog box. See Figure 6-35.

TROUBLE? If the message "You should save this document before creating a hyperlink..." appears, click the Yes button and save the document before inserting the link.

Figure 6-35 INSERT HYPERLINK DIALOG BOX

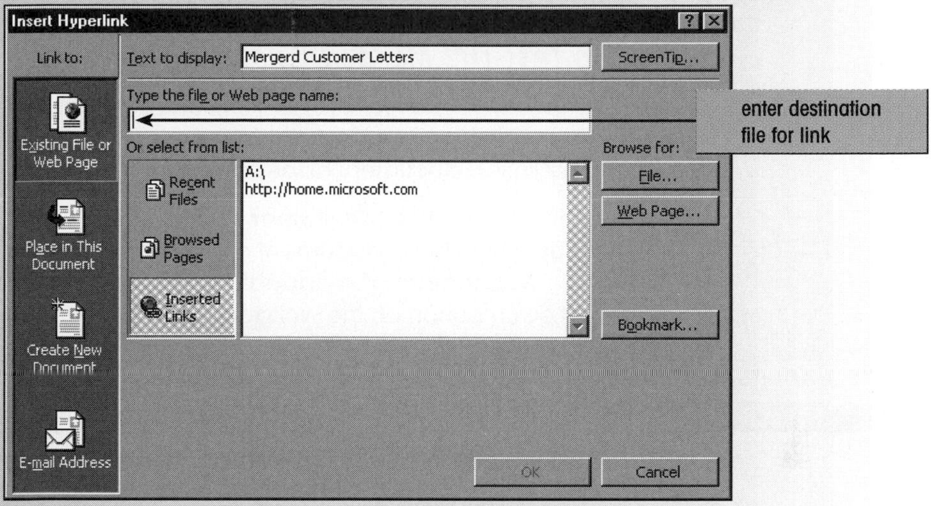

Enter the address of the merged customer letter, which is its filename.

9. Click the **File** button in the Browse for section to open the Link to File dialog box. Make sure your Data Disk is in the appropriate disk drive, and the Tutorial folder is specified in the Look in list box.

10. Click **Merged Customer Letters** and then click the **OK** button.

11. Click the **OK** button to close the dialog box. Notice that the hyperlink text is colored and underlined, which indicates the text is a hyperlink.

12. Click cell **A12** and repeat Steps 8–12 to create a hyperlink to the Customer workbook. See Figure 6-36.

Figure 6-36 HYPERLINKS INSERTED INTO DOCUMENTATION SHEET

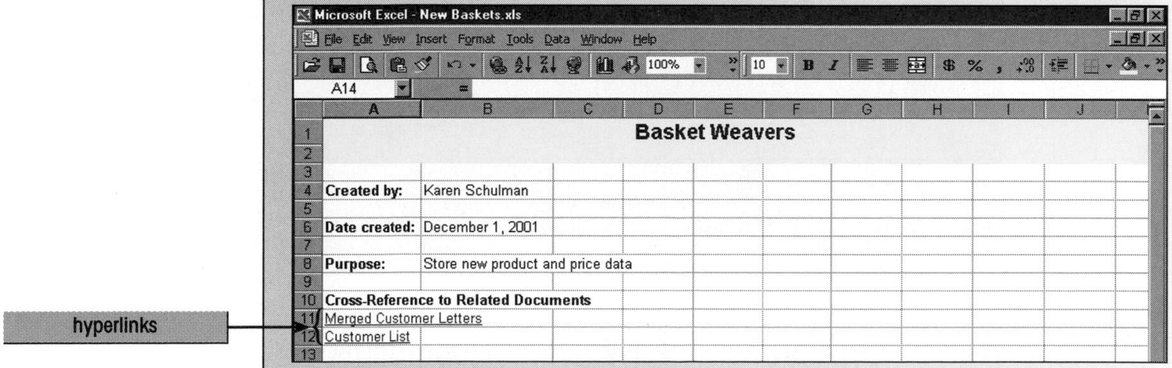

Now that you have created the hyperlinks, you should test them.

Testing Hyperlinks

Now that you have created the hyperlinks, you decide to test them to make sure each one links to the correct location. Recall that by clicking a hyperlink you jump to the referenced location. First, test the hyperlink to the merged customer letters.

To test the Merged Customer Letters hyperlink:

1. Position the pointer over the text **Merged Customer Letters** in cell A11. The pointer changes to a pointing hand, and a ScreenTip showing the address of the linked document appears.
2. Click the **Merged Customer Letters** hyperlink. Word launches and the Merged Customer Letters document opens on your screen. See Figure 6-37. Notice that the Web toolbar also appears on your screen. Figure 6-38 describes the function of each button on the Web toolbar in navigating between documents that contain hyperlinks.

Figure 6-37 MERGED CUSTOMER LETTERS DOCUMENT OPENED FROM HYPERLINK

Web toolbar

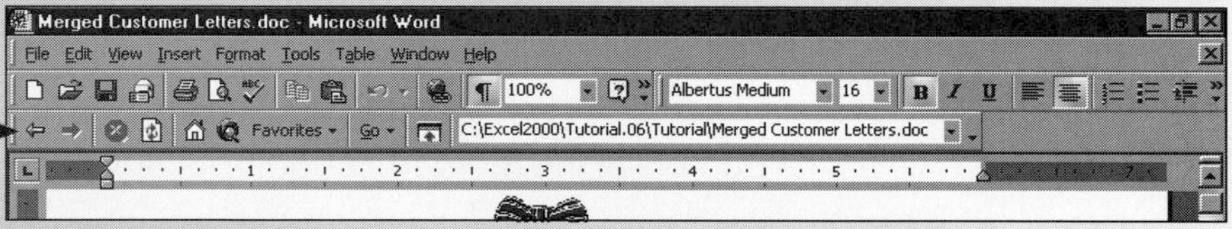

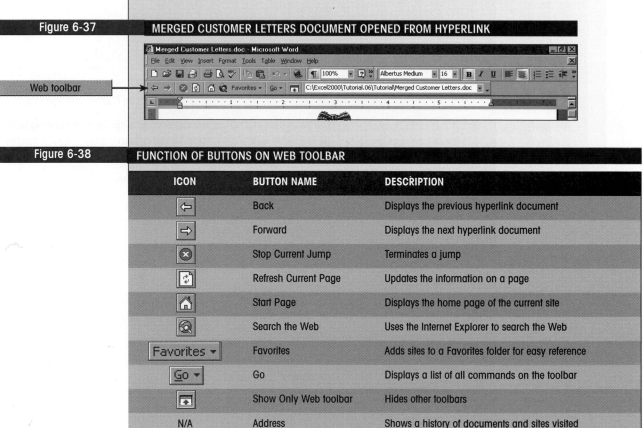

Figure 6-38 FUNCTION OF BUTTONS ON WEB TOOLBAR

ICON	BUTTON NAME	DESCRIPTION
	Back	Displays the previous hyperlink document
	Forward	Displays the next hyperlink document
	Stop Current Jump	Terminates a jump
	Refresh Current Page	Updates the information on a page
	Start Page	Displays the home page of the current site
	Search the Web	Uses the Internet Explorer to search the Web
Favorites	Favorites	Adds sites to a Favorites folder for easy reference
Go	Go	Displays a list of all commands on the toolbar
	Show Only Web toolbar	Hides other toolbars
N/A	Address	Shows a history of documents and sites visited

Navigating Between the Hyperlink Documents

After reviewing the letter, you are ready to return to Excel. Instead of using the program button on the taskbar use the navigational buttons on the Web toolbar to move forward and backward between the hyperlink documents.

To move forward and backward between hyperlink documents:

1. Click the **Back** button on the Web toolbar to return to the Documentation sheet for the New Baskets workbook. Notice that the hyperlink reference has changed color, indicating that you have used the hyperlink at least once to jump to the linked document.
2. Click the **Customer List** hyperlink. The Customers workbook opens.
3. Click the **Back** button on the Web toolbar to return to the New Baskets workbook.

   TROUBLE? If the Web toolbar does not appear, click View on the menu bar, click Toolbars, and then click Web. Repeat Step 3.
4. Click the **Forward** button on the Web toolbar to jump to the Customers workbook again.
5. Click the **Back** button on the Web toolbar to return to the New Baskets workbook.
6. Save the New Baskets workbook. Close the Customer workbook. Remove the Web toolbar.
7. Switch to Word, close the Word document without saving it, and then exit Word.

Karen is pleased to have the hyperlinks in place for navigating between these related Basket Weavers documents.

Publishing Excel Data on a Web Page

The **World Wide Web (WWW)**, commonly called the Web, is a structure of documents connected electronically over the **Internet**, which is a large computer network made up of smaller networks and computers all connected electronically. Each document on the Web is called a **Web document** or **Web page**. These documents store different types of information, including text, graphics, sound, animation, and video. A Web page often includes hypertext links to other Web documents. These hypertext links point to other Web pages and allow you to follow related information by jumping from computer to computer to retrieve the desired information. Each Web page or document has a specific address, called its **Uniform Resource Locator**, or more commonly, **URL**. The URL indicates where the Web document is stored on the Web.

As a progressive businessperson, Karen recognized early the potential marketing power of the Internet. Understanding this potential, she hired a small firm to develop her company's documents to be placed on the Web. This provides Karen with another means to inform her customers of new gift baskets and events, in addition to the customer letter and the in-store flyers.

Now, she plans to develop an additional Web page showing her new gift baskets list. Fortunately, Karen can use her existing New Products worksheet to create this Web page.

Saving Excel Data as a Web Page

When people access the World Wide Web, they use a software program, called a **Web browser**, that enables them to access, view, and navigate all the Web documents on the Web. Web browsers recognize files that are in the HTML format. Therefore, any document that's on the Web needs to be in this HTML format. **HTML**, short for **HyperText Markup Language**, is the language in which your data needs to be formatted in order to be accessible on the Web. In order to display your Excel data on the Web, you need to convert it to HTML format. Excel workbook data can easily be converted to HTML format. You can put text, numbers, PivotTable reports, charts, graphics, and other items from a worksheet on a Web page. By using the publishing and saving features in Excel 2000, you can save an Excel workbook or some part of it in HTML format and make it available as a Web page that users can access with a Web browser.

Excel data can be saved in either *interactive* or *noninteractive* format. In interactive format, a person using a Web browser can work with the data and make changes to it. For example, a mortgage calculation worksheet can be published in an interactive format so users can enter their own information and determine their monthly mortgage payments. When you save data in a noninteractive format, users can only view the data. No changes to worksheet values are possible. For example, if you want to report your company's financial condition for the past year and do not want or expect users to change the data in any way, then a noninteractive approach is appropriate.

REFERENCE WINDOW RW

Insert Noninteractive Excel Data into a Web Page

- Click **File** on the menu bar, click **Save as Web Page**.
- Click **Publish**.
- In the **Choose** list, click the type of data you want to publish, and in the box or list below that, specify the item you want.
- Make sure the **Add interactivity with** check box is cleared.
- To add a title to the published section, click **Change**, type the title you want, and then click **OK**.
- In the **File name** box, click **Browse**, and locate the drive, folder, Web folder, Web server, or FTP location where you want to save or publish your Web page.
- Click **Publish**.

Karen wants users accessing the New Baskets Web page to view the product and price list, but not edit it. Therefore, she asks you to put the product and price list worksheet data on a Web page in a noninteractive format.

First, Karen wants to see how the worksheet will look as a Web page before saving it in HTML format.

To preview the workbook as a Web page:

1. Make sure the New Baskets workbook is open and the New Products worksheet is selected. Click **File** on the menu bar, and then click **Web Page Preview** to open your Web browser. Excel opens the Internet Explorer (or the Web browser installed on your computer) and displays the workbook as a file. See Figure 6-39. Note, this preview shows all data in the workbook in noninteractive form.

Figure 6-39 PREVIEW OF WEB PAGE

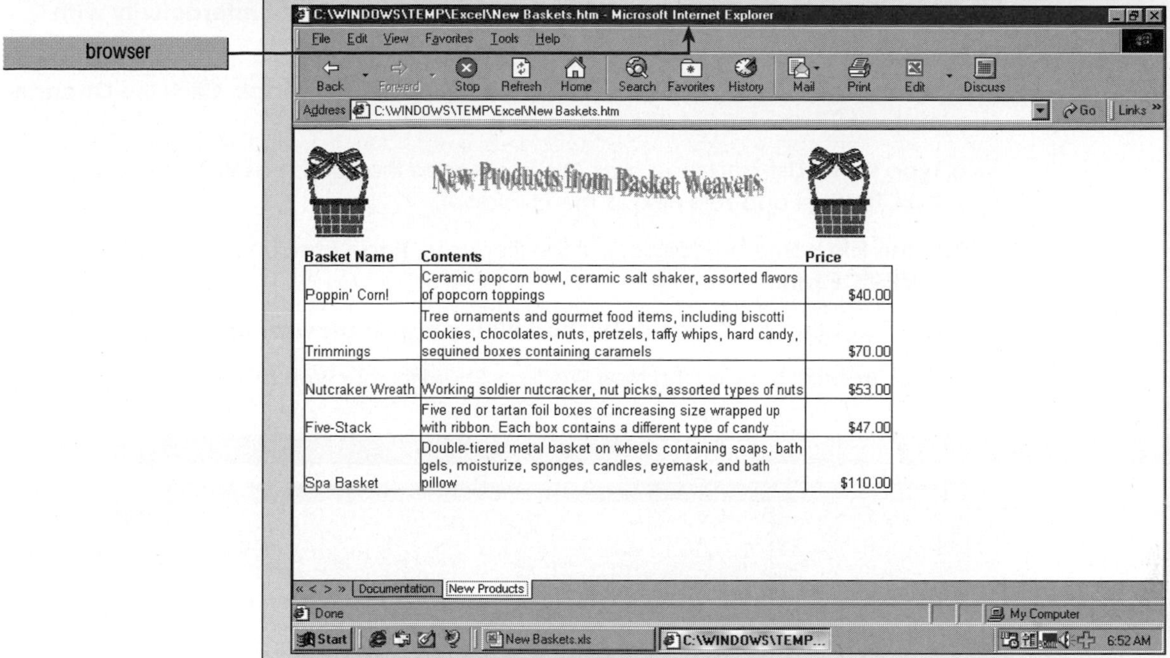

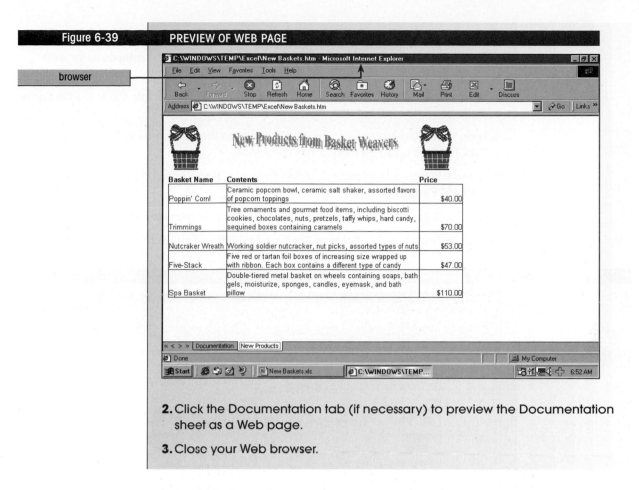

2. Click the Documentation tab (if necessary) to preview the Documentation sheet as a Web page.
3. Close your Web browser.

Karen likes the results and asks you to save only the New Products worksheet as a Web page.

To save a worksheet as a noninteractive Web page:

1. Click **File** on the menu bar, and then click **Save as Web Page** to open the Save As dialog box.
2. Click **Publish** to open the Publish as Web Page dialog box. See Figure 6-40.

Figure 6-40 PUBLISH AS WEB PAGE DIALOG BOX

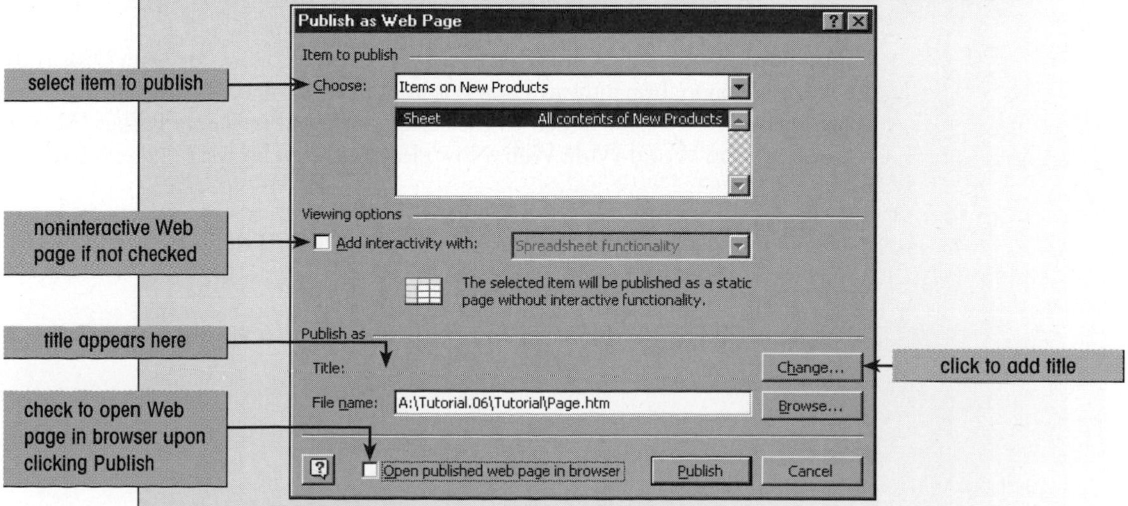

3. Make sure the Choose list displays Items on New Products.
4. To create a noninteractive Web page, make sure the **Add interactivity with** box is cleared.
5. Now you are ready to add a title to the top of the Web page. Click the **Change** button to open the Set Title dialog box.
6. Type **Price List**, and then click **OK** to return to the Publish as Web Page dialog box. The title appears next to the Title label.
7. In the File name box, select just the filename, **Page.htm**, and replace it with **BWPRICE.htm**.
8. Click to select the **Open published Web page in browser** check box.
9. Click **Publish** to open the New Products Sheet in your Web browser. See Figure 6-41.

Figure 6-41 WEB PAGE OPEN IN BROWSER

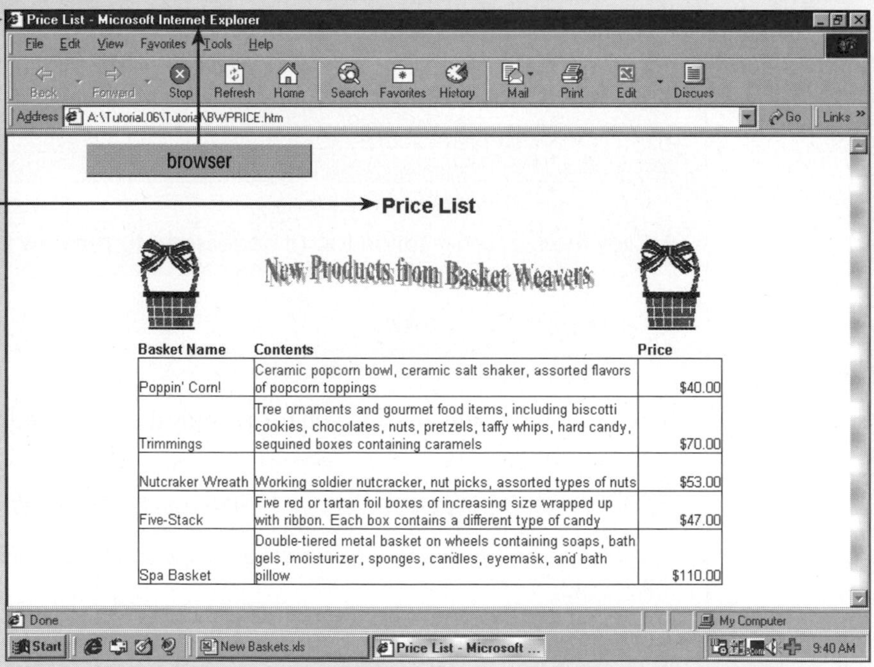

Karen is very pleased with the New Baskets Web page.

You have completed the Web page and it is now saved on your Data Disk as BWPRICE.htm. The file extension .htm indicates that it is in HTML format, and therefore readable using a Web browser. It is ready to be added to the series of Web documents Basket Weavers currently has available on the World Wide Web. Now close the Web browser and exit Excel.

To close the Web browser and exit Excel.

1. Click the **Close** button on the Web browser.
2. Click any cell to deselect the range. Press **Ctrl + Home** to make cell A1 the active cell.
3. Save the workbook.
4. Exit Excel.

Karen is very pleased to have informed her customers of the new baskets using a variety of methods—distributing flyers, mailing customized letters, and creating a Web document to be viewed on the World Wide Web.

Session 6.3 QUICK CHECK

1. A hyperlink can be a ____________, ____________, or ____________.
2. You can jump to a document by clicking a ____________.
3. The ____________ button on the Standard toolbar is used to insert a hyperlink.
4. You use the ____________ and the ____________ buttons on the ____________ toolbar to move forward and backward between hyperlink documents.
5. A software program called a ____________ enables you to access Web documents.
6. ____________ is the language used to present documents on the World Wide Web.
7. To convert Excel data to HTML format, you can use the ____________ command.
8. The file extension ____________ indicates that the file is in HTML format.

REVIEW ASSIGNMENTS

Karen is ready to send the merged customer letter to the Connecticut Basket Weavers customers. She also wants to add the NPA pie chart to a Web page to be viewable online. Finally, she needs to inform her advisory board, a group of local business professionals, about the company's new gift baskets and the NPA recognition. Help Karen with these tasks.

Do the following:

1. Start Word and open the document **CustLtr2** in the Review folder for Tutorial.06 and save it as **Customer Letter 2**.
2. Use the Merge Mail Helper to modify the selection criteria so only the Connecticut customers are selected. Merge the letter with the modified criteria. Close the Form Letters 1 document without saving it. (Note: The document Customer Letter 2 is still open.)
3. Print the letter for Ronald Kooienga.
4. Return to the customer list in Excel and change the street address of Ronald Kooienga (Customer Number 133) to 20 Freedom Trail. Print the revised letter. Save Customer Letter 2 and exit Word.
5. Open the workbook **NPA** in the Review folder for Tutorial.06. This workbook contains a pie chart comparing sales of the top premium sellers in the Northeast. Karen wants to add this chart as a new page on her Web site. Save the chart as a Web page named **NPA.htm**. Open your Web browser and view the Web document. Print the Web page from your browser.

6. Open the workbook **NewBask2** and save it as **New Baskets 2**. Use this workbook to answer Questions 7 through 11.
7. Activate the **New Products** worksheet. Use WordArt to create your own graphic. The text of the graphic is "New Baskets & Prices." Place the graphic above the new baskets list. Experiment with some of the features on the WordArt and Drawing toolbar. Save the workbook. Print the worksheet with the graphic.
8. Activate the Documentation sheet and add a hyperlink to the NPA workbook in cell A14. Instead of using a word or phrase as the hyperlink, use the file address of the NPA workbook in the Review folder for Tutorial.06 as the hyperlink.

Explore

9. In cell A15, create a hyperlink to a Gift, Premiums, and Stationery home page on the WWW. Its URL is **http://www.tdc.org.hk/prodmag/gifts/gifts.htm**. The hyperlink text should be "Gifts, Premiums & Stationery."
10. In cells A17:A18, create a WordArt object with the text "Store Sales." Use the WordArt graphic as a hyperlink to the MonSales workbook (located in the Review folder for Tutorial.06).
11. Save the **New Baskets 2** workbook. Print the Documentation worksheet. Close the workbook.
12. Karen has written a letter to her advisory board telling them of the Basket Weavers new baskets and their sales. Open the letter **AdvLetr** in the Review folder for Tutorial.06 and save it as **Advisory Board Letter**. Open the workbook **MonSales** in the Review folder for Tutorial.06 and save it as **MonSales2**. Link the **MonSales2** worksheet to the Word document **Advisory Board Letter**. Print the letter.
13. Add the sales for Connecticut (Figure 6-42) to the worksheet and print the advisory board letter again. Save and close both the letter and the workbook.

Figure 6-42

PRODUCT	CT
Poppin' Corn!	300
Trimmings	200
Nutcracker Wreath	1000
Five-Stack	750
Spa Basket	400

14. Open the letter **AdvLetr** in the Review folder for Tutorial.06 and save it as **Advisory Board Letter2**. Open the workbook **MonSales** in the Review folder for Tutorial.06 and embed it in the **Advisory Board Letter2**. Add the sales for Connecticut (Figure 6-42) to the worksheet in the Word document. Save and print the letter. Close Word.
15. Use Windows Explorer to compare the file size of the two Word documents: Advisory Board Letter and Advisory Board Letter2 in the Review folder for Tutorial.06. What is the file size of each file in bytes? Explain the difference in file sizes.
16. Close all open windows.

CASE PROBLEMS

Case 1. Reporting Sales for Toy World Fred Galt, the manager of the local Toy World store, must report to the regional manager each week. He faxes a memo each week to the regional sales office indicating his recommendations regarding any special sales or promotions he feels will be needed, based on the summary sales information he includes in the report. Fred maintains a worksheet that summarizes sales in units and dollars for each day of the week. This sales summary is included in his weekly report, and on the company's Web page. Do the following:

1. If necessary, start Excel and make sure your Data Disk is in the appropriate drive. Open **ToyStore.xls** in the Cases folder for Tutorial.06. This is Fred's partially completed worksheet. Save it as **Toy Store Sales.**
2. Complete the worksheet by computing total sales in dollars for each day (including the formula for Saturday) by multiplying the number of units sold of each product by the price per unit (the price table is in the upper-right corner of the worksheet). Also, compute total sales for each product and the total sales for the store. (*Hint*: Check number for Monday through Friday: Total store sales = $87,654.20.)
3. Save the worksheet.
4. Start Word and open the document **ToyLtr** and save it as **Toy Memo.**
5. Link the worksheet range A1:F15 to the memo. Print the memo.
6. Saturday evening, Fred faxes the memo to the regional manager, indicating that sales are on target for the week and no special promotions are necessary at this time. Update store sales for Saturday using the following data: 20, 5, 19, 16. Save the workbook.
7. Print the memo.
8. Save the memo and exit Word.
9. Create a Web page named **ToySales.htm** which includes the range A7:F15. Open your Web browser and view the Web document. Print the page from your Web browser.
10. Use WordArt to replace the title "Store Analysis" with the title "Toy World Sales." Print the worksheet excluding the Product Price Table.
11. Save and close the workbook.

Case 2. Quarterly Sales at Happy Morning Farms Casandra Owens is product manager for a line of breakfast cereals at Happy Morning Farms. Casandra is waiting for one figure so that she can complete her Sales Report—Summarized by State for next week's Operations Management Team (OMT) meeting. As she is working on the report, she receives an urgent call from one of her sales representatives indicating that he needs Casandra in Denver immediately to deal with a customer problem that requires management attention. Casandra realizes that she will not be able to make the next OMT meeting, so she plans to complete her report on the road. She will get the last figure she needs, finish the report, and then fax it to John Styles, who will represent her at the meeting. Before she leaves the office, Casandra decides to embed her data in a memo. Do the following:

1. If necessary, start Excel and make sure your Data Disk is in the appropriate drive. Open the workbook **StSales** in the Cases folder for Tutorial.06.
2. Open the Word document **StMemo** in the Cases folder for Tutorial.06 and save it as **State Sales Memo.**

3. Embed the **StSales** worksheet in the Word document, **State Sales Memo**, which can be found in the Cases folder for Tutorial.06.
4. Save the Word document with the embedded worksheet.
5. Print the memo with the embedded worksheet.
6. After arriving in Denver, Casandra gets a call with the missing sales figure—sales in Iowa this quarter were $42. Update the Word document by entering the Iowa sales number in the embedded worksheet.
7. Save the Word document and print the memo again. Close the Word document.
8. Print the source worksheet, **StSales**. Comment on the sales data in the source worksheet versus the sales data in the Word document.
9. Now repeat the process using a different approach. Activate the workbook **StSales** in the Cases folder for Tutorial.06 and save it as **State Sales**.
10. Open the Word document **StMemo1** in the Cases folder for Tutorial.06 and save the document as **State Sales Memo1**.
11. Link cell D49 in the State Sales workbook to the end of the first sentence in the State Sales Memo1 Word document. (*Hint*: For the best placement of the linked object, use the Unformatted text option instead of Microsoft Excel Worksheet object when you link the object.) Save the document. Print the letter.
12. Update the **State Sales** workbook by entering the Iowa sales number ($42).
13. Save and print **State Sales Memo1**.
14. At the bottom of the State Sales Memo1 document, add the line "Details for Sales are in the State Sales workbook." Create a hyperlink in the Word document to the State Sales workbook. The hyperlink text should be "State Sales workbook." Save the Word document. Test the hyperlink.
15. Save and close any open documents.

Case 3. Horizons State Alumni Office Charlene Goodwin, director of alumni affairs, has been planning a marketing "blitz" in which she will use three methods to reach Horizons' alumni. For campus visitors, she will develop a flyer inviting friends of HSU to visit the campus store to view its new line of Horizons affinity products. For World Wide Web users, she plans to create a Web page highlighting these products. For all alumni, she plans a letter announcing the affinity products that alums can order using a mail-order form. Help her get these jobs completed. Do the following:

1. If necessary, start Excel and make sure your Data Disk is in the appropriate drive. Open the workbook **AlumProd** in the Cases folder for Tutorial.06, and save it as **Alumni Products**. This is the product list.
2. Open the Word document **Alumltr** in the Cases folder for Tutorial.06 and save it as **Alumni Letter**. Link the product list from the Alumni Products workbook beginning at the line [insert price list here]. Remember to remove the note [insert price list here]. Print the letter with the linked object.
3. You notice an error in the product list—the price of item 3 should be $80. Return to Excel and correct the error in the worksheet. Print the letter. Save and close the Word document.
4. Create a logo for Horizons State using WordArt. Insert it at the top of the product list in the Alumni Products workbook. Save the workbook and print the price list with your graphic.

5. Create a Web page for the product list in the Alumni Products workbook. Name the page **HorzPrc.htm**. View the page using your Web browser. Print the Web page using your Web browser.
6. Create a Documentation sheet with appropriate information to describe the workbook. Print the Documentation sheet.
7. In the Documentation sheet, insert a hyperlink to the Word document Alumni Letter.
8. In the Documentation sheet, insert a hyperlink to your institution's Web page.
9. Save and close any open files.

Case 4. Inwood Design Group of Japan Spurred by the Japanese passion for the sport, golf enjoys unprecedented popularity in Japan. Inwood Design Group plans to build a world-class golf course, and one of the four sites under consideration is Chiba Prefecture, Japan. Other possible sites are Kauai, Hawaii; Edmonton, Canada; and Scottsdale, Arizona. You and Mike Nagochi are members of the site selection team for Inwood Design Group. The team is responsible for collecting information on the sites, evaluating that information, and recommending the best site for the new golf course.

Your team identified five factors likely to determine the success of a golf course: climate, competition, market size, topography, and transportation. The team has collected information on these factors for all of the four potential golf course sites.

Mike created a worksheet that the team can use to evaluate the four sites. He brought the completed worksheet to the group's meeting so that the team could analyze the information and recommend a site to management.

Prepare a memo to the site selection committee with your team's findings. Do the following:

1. If necessary, start Excel and make sure your Data Disk is in the appropriate drive. Open the workbook **Inwood** in the Cases folder for Tutorial.06. Save the workbook as **Inwood 1**. Review the worksheet.
2. Open Word and write a brief memo to the site selection committee. State your recommendation for a site selection and reason(s). Support your narrative by referencing the Weighted Score section of the Inwood worksheet. Paste the Weighted Score section of the worksheet into your memo.
3. Save the Word document as **Inwood Memo** in the Cases folder for Tutorial.06.
4. Print the memo. Close Word.
5. Explain why pasting rather than linking or embedding is appropriate in this situation.
6. In the Inwood 1 workbook, activate the Documentation sheet and insert a hyperlink to the Inwood Memo. Test the hyperlink.
7. Use your Web browser to access one of the following sites: **www.yahoo.com**, or **www.excite.com**. Use the information at these Web sites to locate an interesting golf-related Web site. In the Inwood 1 workbook, below the hyperlink to the Inwood Memo, insert a hyperlink to this site.
8. Replace the Inwood Design Group title in the Documentation sheet with a WordArt image with the same text.
9. Save the **Inwood 1** workbook, print the Documentation sheet, then close and exit the workbook.

INTERNET ASSIGNMENTS

The purpose of the Internet Assignments is to challenge you to find information on the Internet that you can use to create effective spreadsheets. The actual assignments are updated and maintained on the Course Technology Web site. Log on to the Internet and use your Web browser to go to the Student Online Companion to accompany this text at **www.course.com/NewPerspectives/office2000**. Click the Excel link, and then click the link for Tutorial 6.

QUICK CHECK ANSWERS

Session 6.1

1. Object Linking and Embedding
2. linked
3. does not
4. embed
5. link
6. WordArt
7. Paste Special
8. The Excel menus and toolbars replace the menus and toolbar in the Word window. The embedded object now has column and row headings and the sheet tabs appear. Excel becomes the active program.

Session 6.2

1. main, merge fields
2. merge field
3. Position the insertion point where you want the merge field; click the Insert Merge Field button, and then click the name of the field you want to insert.
4. Click the View Merged data button on the Mail Merge toolbar
5. linking

Session 6.3

1. file address, text, graphic image
2. hyperlink
3. Insert Hyperlink
4. Forward, Back, Web
5. Web browser
6. HTML or Hypertext Markup Language
7. Save As Web Page
8. .htm

OBJECTIVES

In this tutorial you will:

- Arrange a worksheet in sections
- Assign data validation rules to a cell
- Assign and use range names
- Use IF and FV functions in formulas
- Create a series using AutoFill
- Protect worksheets
- Delete unnecessary sheets from a workbook
- Plan and record Excel macros
- Run a macro using menu commands, a shortcut key, and a button object
- View Visual Basic for Applications code

DEVELOPING AN EXCEL APPLICATION

Employee 401(k) Planning at CableScan

CASE

CableScan

CableScan intends to implement a 401(k) plan this year, and Mary Kincaid, benefits administrator, will travel to the company's three sites to present the plan and its features to all of the employees. A 401(k) plan is a retirement savings program that allows employees to deduct funds from their monthly pay, before taxes, provided that they invest them directly into various options within the 401(k) plan.

To introduce the 401(k) plan, Mary will hold formal meetings at each company location. At the meetings, she will give employees an audio-visual presentation that includes an overview of the plan, the administrative procedures, and the investment options. Currently, no other retirement plans are available to the employees other than personal savings, and the company wants to be sure that there is high participation in the 401(k) plan. Management has set a goal of 80% participation in the plan for all eligible employees. To help ensure this high rate of participation, the company will match, dollar for dollar, whatever the employee contributes, up to 4% of the employee's salary. Additionally, employees can contribute up to a total of 20% of their salaries.

Mary has asked you to work with individual employees after each of the formal presentations by answering any questions they may have. She also wants to provide an Excel workbook that can be used by employees to determine the appropriate amount they can contribute to the plan, and see how different contribution amounts will affect their retirement savings over the next five to 30 years. Employees can use this workbook to conduct their own what-if analyses on their retirement plans.

SESSION 7.1

In this tutorial you will develop a more complex workbook than you have in any previous tutorial. You'll build it in three sessions. In this session you will start the process by dividing your worksheet into separate sections for input and calculations. You'll use the Excel data validation feature to specify the type of data that a cell can store. You'll assign names to cells and use these names instead of cell addresses to build the formulas in your worksheet. Finally, you'll use the IF function to build formulas where the value you store in a cell depends on the result of a condition.

Planning the 401(k) Workbook Application

You have been asked to develop a simple investment model that will allow each CableScan employee to see the effect (dollar accumulation) of investing a percentage of his or her current salary each year at an annual return on investment over a 30-year period. You can use Excel to create a workbook that the employees can use to make these calculations and plan their retirement funding.

You realize that many of the employees at CableScan are familiar with Excel and will have no trouble using a 401(k) planning workbook. However, there are others who will require assistance in using the workbook, and you will be working on a one-on-one basis with those employees after Mary presents the plan. Because the CableScan employees using the workbook will have varying amounts of experience with Excel and computers in general, you want the workbook to be as easy to use as possible. It needs to produce valuable information clearly, while being nearly foolproof to use.

Figures 7-1 and 7-2 show the planning analysis sheet and the sketch that Mary has created to assist you in completing the workbook. You can see from the planning analysis sheet that the formulas to be used in the workbook are somewhat complex. Fortunately, Excel provides a few means of simplifying complex formulas. Mary also wants you to build the worksheet so that employees enter only valid data in the correct cells in the worksheet. Note in the sketch in Figure 7-2 that the worksheet will be divided into manageable sections—sections where the employee provides (inputs) information and sections containing information produced from calculating the input to produce output. Also note that the workbook allows the employee to view and analyze the information numerically and graphically, by including a line chart.

Figure 7-1 PLANNING ANALYSIS SHEET

Planning Analysis Sheet

My Goal
To develop a simple investment planing worksheet

What information do I need?
Name of Employee
Current salary
Percent of salary invested—enter a percent of salary. NOTE: The maximum percent an employee can contribute is 20 percent.
Annual rate of return—enter as a percent

What calculations do I need to perform?
Employee contributions— monthly = current salary* percent of salary invested/12
Employer contributions— monthly = monthly employee contribution
NOTE: Remember that for every dollar employee contribution, employer invests a dollar, up to 4% of employee's salary: employer invests nothing above 4% of employee's salary
Total monthly contributions = monthly employee contribution + monthly employer contribution
Value of investment at 5, 10, 15, 20, 25, and 30 years. NOTE: use =FV(monthly rate of return, number of periods, total monthly contribution) to compute future value of investment

What output do I want to see?
Table showing future of investment at 5, 10, 15, 20, 25, and 30 years
Line chart displaying future value of investment

Figure 7-2 SKETCH OF WORKSHEET PLAN

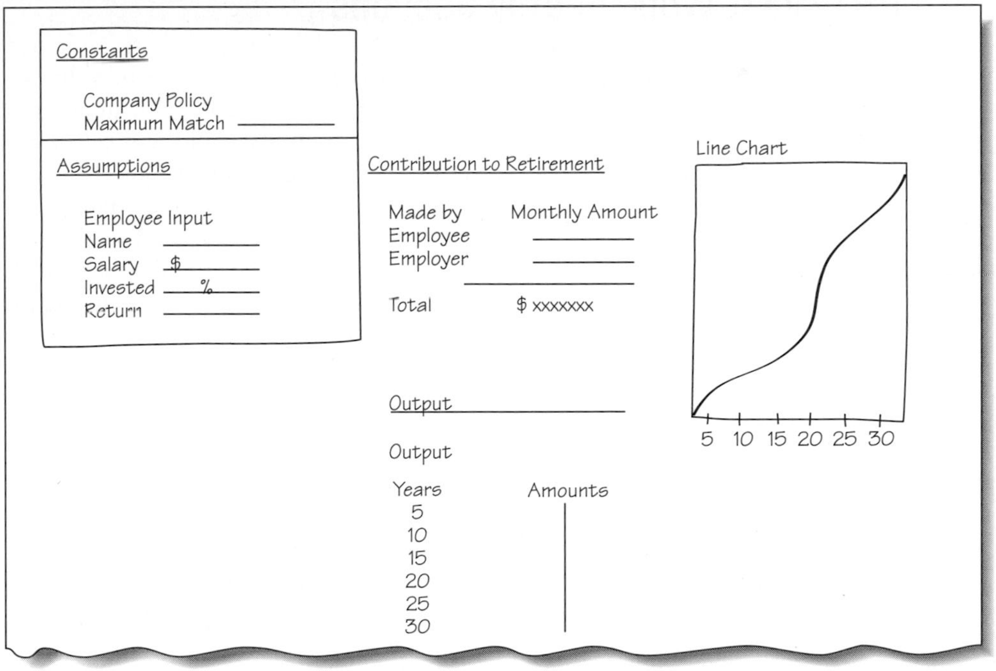

Use these planning documents to build the worksheet for Mary. She has already started to create the workbook.

Open the 401k file and examine the work Mary has done so far.

To open the 401k workbook and save the workbook as 401kPlan:

1. Start Excel. Make sure your Data Disk is in the appropriate disk drive, open the workbook 401k in the Tutorial folder for Tutorial.07 on your Data Disk, and immediately save it as **401kPlan**.
2. Click the **401kPlan** sheet tab. In the 401kPlan worksheet, the labels and column headings have already been entered. See Figure 7-3.

Figure 7-3 INITIAL 401KPLAN WORKSHEET

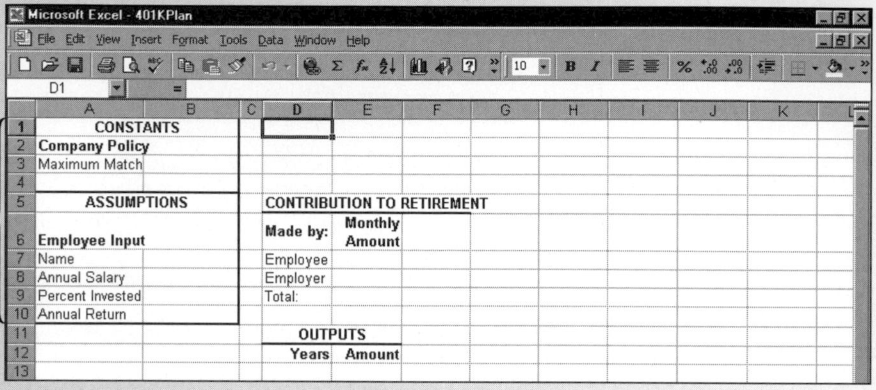

input section

Arranging a Worksheet in Sections

Because many people will be using the worksheet, and will want to change assumptions such as current salary, percentage of salary invested, and annual return on investment, Mary has divided her worksheet into two sections: input and calculation/output. The input section contains the data values used in formulas. Sometimes the input section is said to contain the worksheet's initial conditions and assumptions because the results of the worksheet are based on the values in the input section. A second section, the calculation/output section, performs the calculations and displays the results of the model. The formulas in this section do not contain constants; instead they reference cells in the input section. For example, the formula to calculate the monthly employee contribution to the 401(k) plan (cell E7) will reference cells B8 and B9 in the input section, which contain values for the employee's salary and the percentage of salary the employee invests in the 401(k) plan, rather than constants, such as 30000 and .05.

Dividing the worksheet into sections has the following benefits:

- The user knows exactly where to enter and change values—in the input area. Changes to the worksheet are made only to values in the input area.
- The user clearly sees what factors affect the results of the worksheet.
- The user doesn't have to change specific values in formulas to reflect new assumptions.

Entering Initial Values

Now that you have examined the current status of the workbook, it's time for you to continue creating the 401(k) application. Because the labels and headings have already been entered, you'll begin by entering and formatting the values shown in Figure 7-4.

Figure 7-4 INITIAL ASSUMPTIONS

CELL	VALUE	FORMATTING
B3	.04	Percent style
B7	Mike Tobey	
B8	30000	Currency style, no decimal place
B9	.05	Percent style
B10	.08	Percent style

To enter and format the input values:

1. Click cell **B3**, type **.04**, and press the **Enter** key. Return to cell B3 and click the **Percent style** button on the Formatting toolbar.
2. Click cell **B7** and enter the remaining values and formatting shown in Figure 7-4. When you're finished entering the data, your input section of the worksheet should look like Figure 7-5.

Figure 7-5 INPUT SECTION AFTER VALUES ENTERED

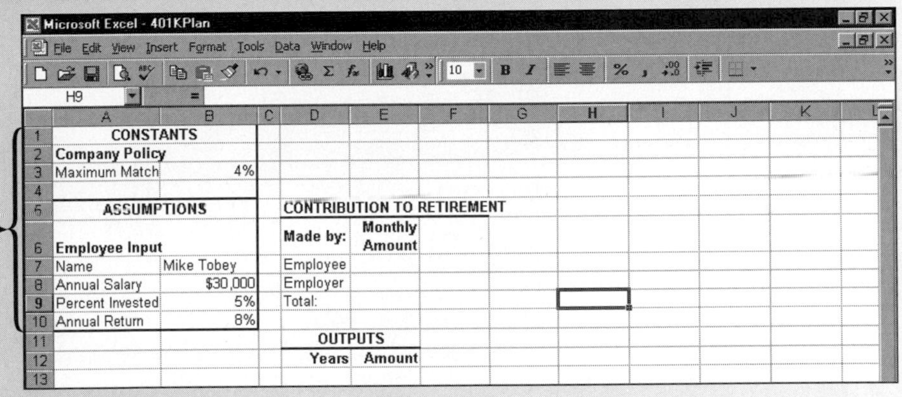

Input section

Mary is concerned that an employee may accidentally enter invalid data into the worksheet, which will result in output that is not correct. For example, employees are not allowed to invest more than 20% of their salary in the 401(k) plan. If an employee entered a value greater than 20% of his or her salary, the value of future investments would be inaccurate, because the plan does not allow for this level of investment.

You can use the Excel data validation feature to prevent a user from entering an invalid value. This will allow you to minimize errors introduced by the workbook user.

Validating Data Entry

One way to make sure the correct data is entered in a cell or range is to use the Excel data validation feature to restrict the information being entered in the worksheet. For instance, you can specify the type of data (whole numbers, dates, time, or text) allowed in a cell, as well as the range of acceptable values (for example, numbers between 1 and 100). If you wish, you can display an input message that appears when a user enters data in a given cell, reminding the user of valid entries for this cell. You can also display an error message when the user enters an invalid entry. Because the maximum percentage of salary an employee can invest is 20, Mary asks you to establish a validation rule so that a user cannot exceed this limit.

Specifying Data Type and Acceptable Values

The first step in using the data validation feature is to specify the type of data as well as the acceptable values allowed in a cell or range of cells. You need to specify that in cell B9 only decimal values less than or equal to .2 (or 20%) are permitted.

To specify a data type and acceptable values:

1. Click cell **B9**, the cell where you want to apply data validation.
2. Click **Data** on the menu bar, and then click **Validation** to open the Data Validation dialog box. See Figure 7-6. This dialog box allows you to specify the parameters for the validation, the message that appears as the user inputs a value, and an error alert message that appears if the user enters an invalid value.

Figure 7-6 SETTINGS TAB OF DATA VALIDATION DIALOG BOX

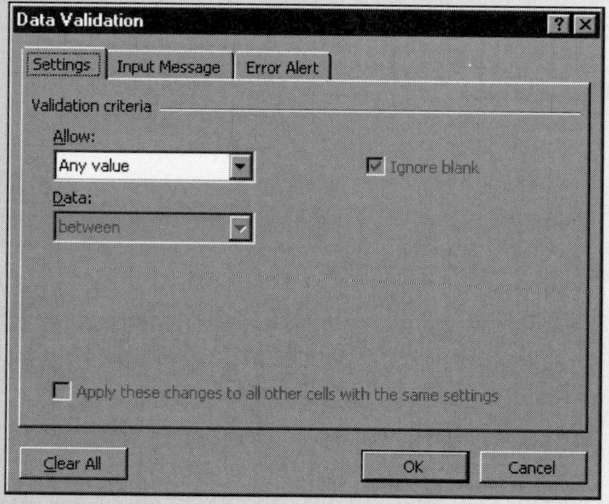

3. Make sure the **Settings** tab is selected, click the **Allow** list arrow, and then click **Decimal** from the list of allowable data types. Notice the number of text boxes in the dialog box changed to reflect the selection you made in the Allow list box.

   Next, specify the range of values you will allow.

4. Click the **Data** list arrow, and then click **less than or equal to**. Notice that when you select this data operator, the number of text boxes in the dialog box change so that you can further specify the appropriate criteria for validation.
5. In the Maximum text box, type **.2**. The data validation rule of a value of less than or equal to 20% is now specified.

   TROUBLE? If you accidentally pressed the Enter key or clicked the OK button and the Data Validation dialog box closed, you can reopen the dialog box by clicking Data on the menu bar, and then clicking Validation.

Next, establish a prompt that will appear when users select that cell, indicating the type of data they can enter into the cell.

Specifying an Input Message

Now create an input prompt that informs the user what kind of data is allowed in the selected cell. The message will appear as a ScreenTip beside the cell when the user selects it. Although the input message is optional, Mary asks you to include the input message—"Percent of salary invested by employee cannot exceed 20%," as an aid to the user during data entry.

To enter a data validation input message:

1. In the Data Validation dialog box, click the **Input Message** tab. See Figure 7-7.

Figure 7-7 INPUT MESSAGE TAB OF DATA VALIDATION DIALOG BOX

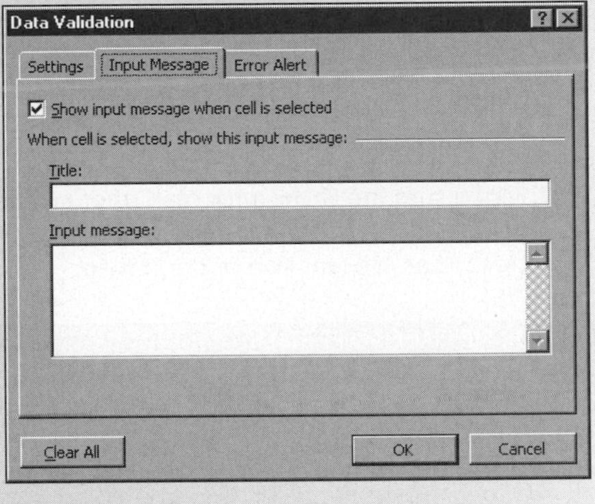

2. Make sure the Show input message when cell is selected check box is checked. This will ensure that the message will appear when the user selects the cell.
3. Click the **Title** text box, and then type **Valid Data**. This title will be at the top of the input message when it appears.
4. Click the **Input message** text box, and then type **Percent of salary invested by employee cannot exceed 20%**. This message will appear as a ScreenTip whenever the user selects cell B9.

The input message that you have entered will help minimize the chances of employees entering an invalid percentage of salary value. However, if users still enter a value above 20%, then you want them to be prompted to reenter a correct percentage.

Specifying an Error Alert Style and Message

You can also use the Data Validation dialog box to establish an error alert message, which is a message that appears if an invalid entry is typed in the cell. This message should inform the user of the error and identify a means to correct the error and enter a valid value.

Now create an appropriate error alert message for this cell.

To enter the error alert message:

1. In the Data Validation dialog box, click the **Error Alert** tab. See Figure 7-8.

Figure 7-8 ERROR ALERT TAB OF DATA VALIDATION DIALOG BOX

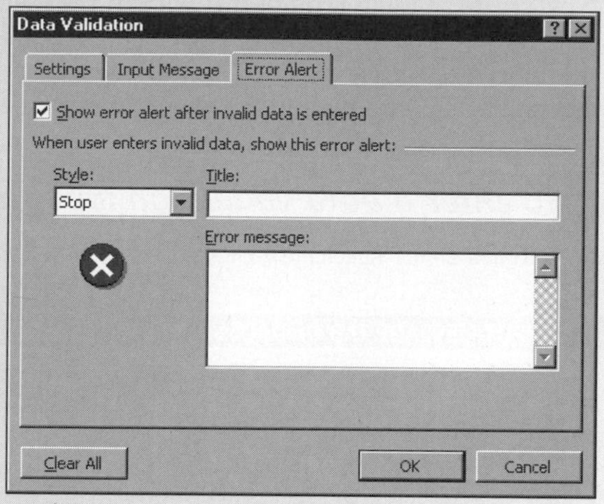

2. Make sure the Show error alert after invalid data is entered check box is checked. Now select the message style: Stop, Warning, or Information. Figure 7-9 describes the function of each style.

Figure 7-9 ERROR MESSAGE ALERT STYLE

ICON	TYPE OF ALERT	LABEL ON BUTTON	ACTION IF BUTTON CLICKED
	Warning	Continue Yes Continue No Cancel	Value entered in cell; processing continues. Value entered in cell; Excel stops, waiting for you to enter another value. Value not entered in cell.
	Information	OK Cancel	Value entered in cell; processing continues. Value not entered in cell.
	Stop	Retry Cancel	Value remains in cell; Excel stops, waiting for you to enter another value. Value not entered in cell.

You decide to use the Stop style, because you don't want to continue data entry until the percentage invested is 20% or less.

3. If necessary, click the **Style** list arrow, and then click **Stop**.

Now specify the error alert message.

4. In the Title text box, type **Invalid Data**.

5. In the Error message text box, type **You entered a value above 20%. A valid percentage is 20% or less.**

6. Click the **OK** button to close the Data Validation dialog box.

The data validation rule is complete. Now test the validation rule to make sure it is working correctly when invalid data is entered in the cell.

To test data validation:

1. If necessary, click cell **B9**. The input message for Valid Data appears. See Figure 7-10.

Figure 7-10 DISPLAY OF INPUT MESSAGE

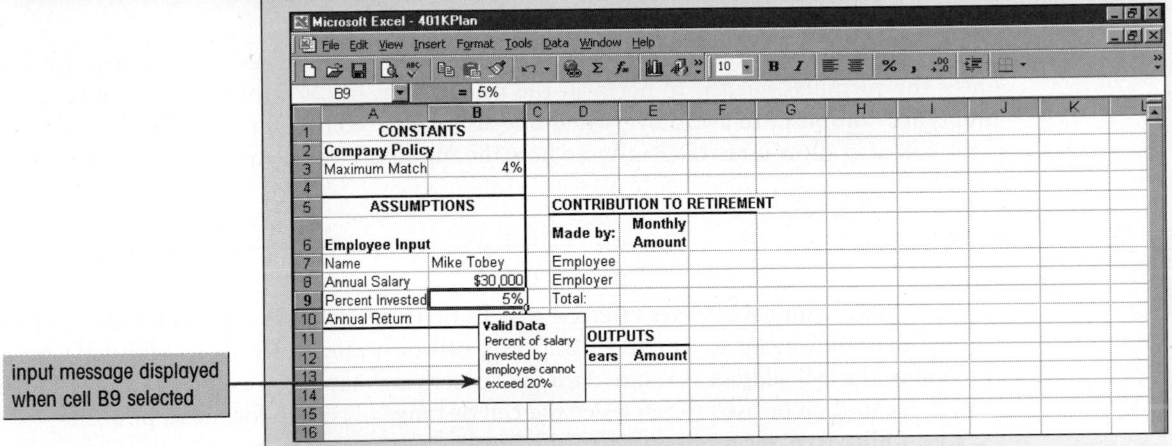

Now attempt to enter an invalid value.

2. Type **.25** and press the **Enter** key. The error alert message for Invalid Data appears. See Figure 7-11. Your choices are to click Retry to correct the value or click Cancel. You decide to correct the value.

Figure 7-11 DISPLAY OF ERROR ALERT MESSAGE

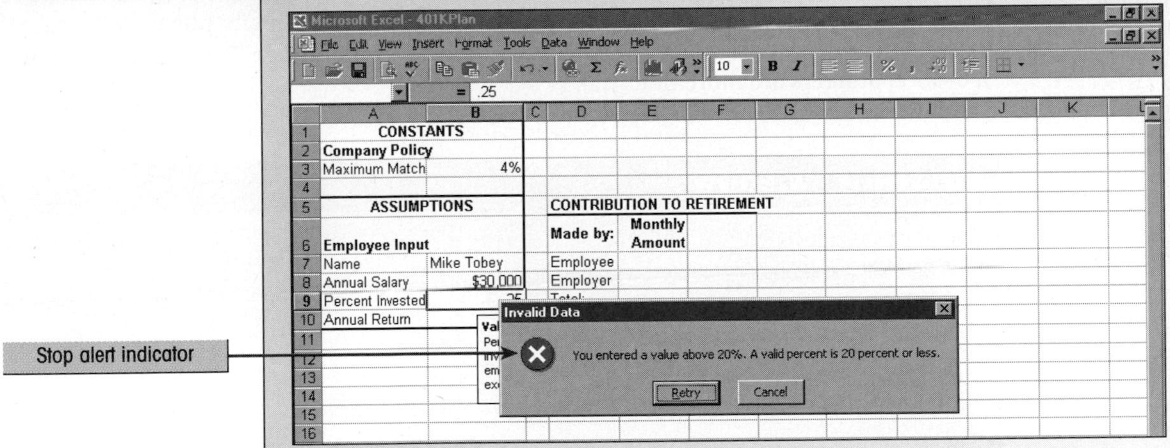

3. Click the **Retry** button. Cell B9 is highlighted, and you can now enter a corrected value.

4. Type **.05** and press the **Enter** key. This entry is valid, so the cell pointer moves to the next cell, cell B10.

Now that you have made the data entry process easier and less error-prone for users, enter the formulas needed to perform the calculations in the workbook. Some of the formulas are complex. To avoid overwhelming users, you want to simplify the formulas a bit. This will also allow users to clearly see how the inputs are calculated to produce the output.

Using Range Names

So far in Excel you have always referred to cells by their addresses. Excel provides a valuable feature that allows you to assign a name to a cell or a range of cells so you don't have to remember the cell address. A **range name** is a descriptive name you assign to a cell or range of cells that can then be used to reference the cell or range of cells in formulas, print ranges, etc.

The ability to name a cell or range allows

- easier formula construction and entry
- improved documentation and clarification of the meaning of formulas
- navigation of large worksheets simply by using the Go To command to move the pointer to a named range
- specification of a print range

Range names must begin with a letter or the underscore character (_). After the first letter, any character, letter, number, or special symbol—except hyphens and spaces—is acceptable. You can assign names of up to 255 characters, although short, meaningful names of 5-15 characters are more practical.

REFERENCE WINDOW RW

Naming a Cell or Range of Cells

- Select the cell or range of cells you want to name.
- Click Insert, point to Name, and then click Define to open the Define Name dialog box.
- Type the range name in the Names in workbook text box.
- Click Add to add the name to the Names in workbook list.
- Click the OK button to return to the worksheet.

Defining a Range Name

You decide to assign range names to several cells in the input area. This will make it easier for you when you create the formulas to be used to calculate the output. Use the range name MaxMatch in cell B3, Salary in cell B8, Invested in cell B9, and Return in cell B10.

To define a range name:

1. Click cell **B8**, the cell for which you want to assign a range name.
2. Click **Insert** on the menu bar, point to Name, and then click **Define** to open the Define Name dialog box. See Figure 7-12. Notice that the name Annual_Salary already appears in the Names in workbook text box with the text label in the cell to the left of the selected cell. You can keep that name or change it by typing a new name in the text box. In this case, shorten the name to Salary.

Figure 7-12 DEFINE NAME DIALOG BOX

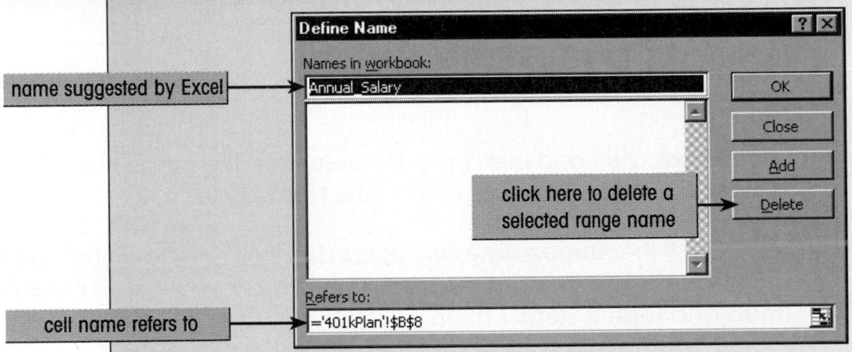

3. Type **Salary** in the Names in workbook text box, and then click the **OK** button to close the dialog box. Notice that the range name of the cell appears in the Name box to the left of the formula bar.
4. Repeat Steps 2 and 3 to name cell B9 **Invested** and cell B10 **Return**.

As you have noticed, the range name of the selected cell appears in the Name box to the left of the formula bar. This Name box allows you to work with named ranges more easily.

Using the Name Box to Define a Range Name

You can also use the Name box as another means of assigning names to cells. You can use this Name box to define a range or to select and move to an already defined range. Assign the name MaxMatch to cell B3 using the Name box.

To assign a range name using the Name box:

1. Click cell **B3**, the cell you want to name.
2. Click the **Name** box to the left of the formula bar. See Figure 7-13.

Figure 7-13 USING THE NAME BOX TO ASSIGN A RANGE NAME

Name box

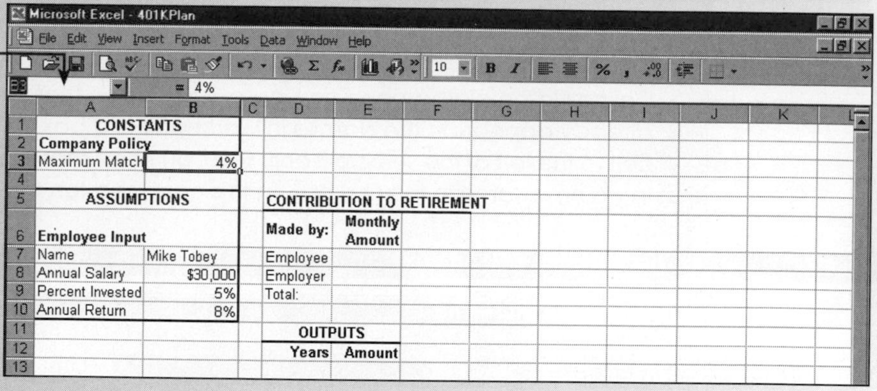

3. Type **MaxMatch** and then press the **Enter** key. The range name has been assigned to cell B3 and appears in the Name box.

TROUBLE? If the range name appears in the cell instead of the Name box, press Esc if you haven't pressed the Enter key. If you have pressed the Enter key, click Undo and repeat Steps 1 through 3.

Now that you have assigned names to the input cells, you can use them as you create the formulas for the 401(k) investment model. First, calculate the amount the employee plans to invest each month.

Using a Range Name in a Formula

You can use the name of a cell or range in a formula instead of cell addresses as you enter your formulas into the worksheet. Rather than using the formula =B8*B9/12 to compute the amount the employee plans to invest each month, you can enter the formula using the range names =Salary*Invested/12. Now enter the formula to compute the monthly employee contribution.

To enter a formula using a range name:

1. Click cell **E7**, the cell where you calculate the monthly amount the employee contributes to the retirement plan.
2. Type **= Salary*Invested/12** and press the **Enter** key. Excel performs the calculations and displays the value 125.
3. Click cell **E7** and examine the formula in the formula bar. Notice that the range names appear in the formula instead of the cell addresses. See Figure 7-14.

Figure 7-14 RANGE NAMES APPEAR IN FORMULA BAR

formula bar displays range name

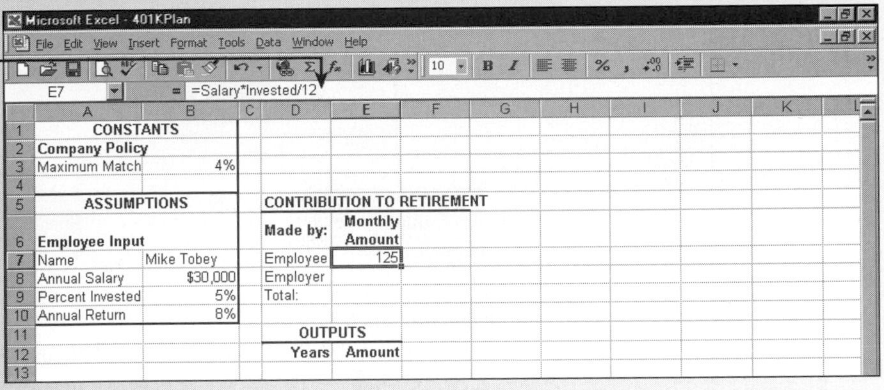

To delete a range name, you click Insert, point to Name and then click Define. Select the range name you want to remove, click the Delete button, and then click OK.

Next you need to enter a formula to calculate the amount of money the employer will contribute to the employee's 401(k) investment. The formula to calculate the employer's contribution is not as straightforward as the one for the employee's contribution. The amount the employer contributes depends on the percentage of salary the employee invests in the 401(k) plan. Recall that the company policy is to match dollar for dollar up to 4% of the employee's salary and nothing above 4% of the employee's salary. This calculation requires that you determine whether the employee is contributing more than 4%. If the employee is investing more than 4% of his or her salary, then the employer will only match 4% of the salary. On the other hand, if the employee is investing 4% or less, the employer will contribute an amount equal to the employee contribution.

Building a Conditional Formula Using the IF Function

There are many situations in which the value you store in a cell depends on certain conditions. For example:

- An employee's gross pay may depend on whether that employee worked overtime.
- A taxpayer's tax rate depends on his or her taxable income.
- A customer's charge depends on whether the size of the order entitles that customer to a discount.

In Excel, the IF function allows you to evaluate a specified condition, performing one action if the condition is true and another action if the condition is false. The IF function has the following format:

IF(logical_test, value_if_true, value_if_false)

where

- A logical_test evaluates a logical expression (condition) as either True or False.
- A value_if_true is the value returned if the logical_test is True.
- A value_if_false is the value returned if the logical_test is False.

An example may help illustrate how the IF function works. Suppose you need to determine whether an employee earns overtime pay, that is, whether he or she worked more than 40 hours in a week. Figure 7-15 illustrates the logic of this function.

Figure 7-15 FLOWCHART OF THE IF FUNCTION

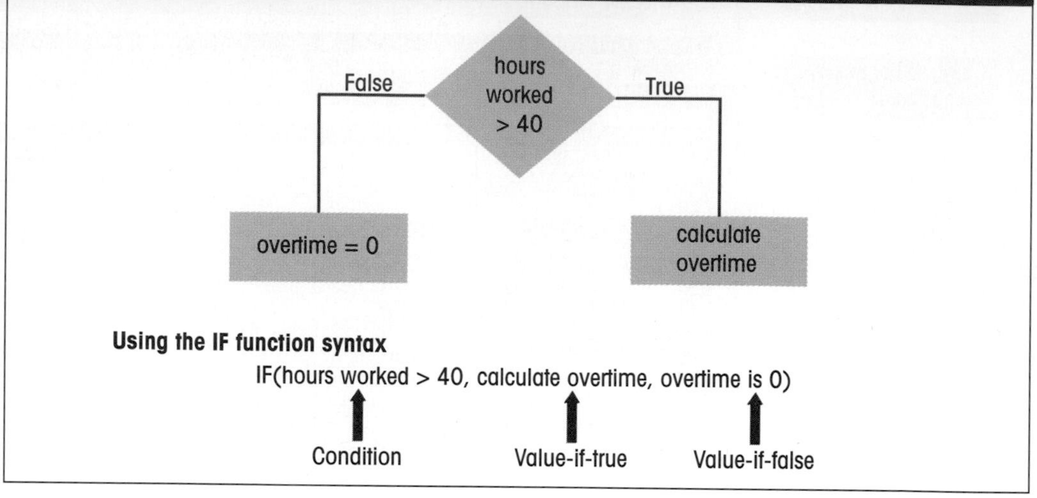

In this example, the condition is the comparison between the hours an employee works and 40 hours. The value_if_true is returned if an employee works more than 40 hours; then the condition is true and overtime pay is calculated. The value_if_false is returned if an employee works 40 hours or less; then the condition is false and overtime pay is 0.

The most common condition, a simple condition, is a comparison between two expressions. An **expression** may be a cell or range, a number, a label, a formula, or another function that represents a single value. For example, B5, B6*B7, and "West" are expressions. In addition to expressions, a condition contains a comparison operator. A **comparison operator** indicates a mathematical comparison, such as less than or greater than. Figure 7-16 shows the comparison operators allowed in Excel.

Figure 7-16 COMPARISON OPERATORS

TYPE OF COMPARISON	COMPARISON OPERATOR SYMBOL
Less than	<
Greater than	>
Less than or equal to	<=
Greater than or equal to	>=
Equal to	=
Not equal to	<>

A comparison operator is combined with an expression to form a condition. For example, say the hours worked value is stored in D10; then the condition "the number of hours worked is greater than 40" would be expressed in Excel as IF(D10>40…). Figure 7-17 illustrates several examples of conditional situations and how they can be expressed in Excel.

Figure 7-17 EXAMPLES OF CONDITIONAL SITUATIONS

CONDITIONAL SITUATION	EXCEL FORMULA
IF salesperson's sales are > 5000 THEN return .1 (10% bonus) ELSE return 0.05 (5% bonus)	=IF(B24>5000,0.10,0.05) NOTE: cell B24 stores salesperson's sales
IF company's region code equals 3 THEN return the label East ELSE return the label Other	=IF(N7=3,"East","Other") NOTE: cell N7 stores code for region
IF person's age is 65 or less THEN amount X 65 or under rate ELSE amount X over 65 rate	=IF(A21<=65,B21*C21,B21*D21) NOTE: cell A21 stores person's age; cell B21 stores amount; cell C21 stores 65 or under rate; and cell D21 stores over 65 rate

Mary developed a flowchart to establish the logic behind the formula needed to calculate the employer's matching contribution to the 401(k) plan. See Figure 7-18.

Figure 7-18 FLOWCHART OF EMPLOYER'S MONTHLY MATCHING CONTRIBUTION

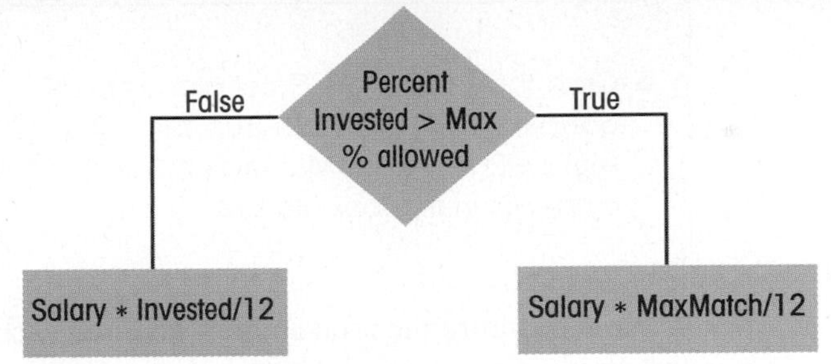

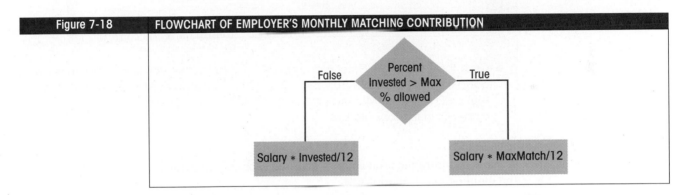

Now enter the IF function needed to calculate the employer's monthly matching contribution to the 401(k) plan.

To enter the IF function:

1. Click cell **E8** to select the cell where you want to enter the IF function.
2. Click the **Paste Function** button on the Standard toolbar to open the Paste Function dialog box. Click **Logical** in the Function category list box, click **IF** in the Function name list box, and then click the **OK** button to open the IF function dialog box.

   TROUBLE? If the Office Assistant opens and offers Help on this feature, click the No button.

   Now enter the condition.
3. In the Logical_test text box, type **Invested>MaxMatch**.
4. Click the **Value_if_true** text box, and then type **Salary*MaxMatch/12**, the value to be returned if the condition is true. Because you're already in cell E8, you do not have to reference the cell again (do not enter E8= Salary* MaxMatch/12).

5. Click the **Value_if_false** text box, and then type **Salary*Invested/12**, the value to be returned if the condition is false. See Figure 7-19. Note again that you do not have to reference cell E8.

Figure 7-19 IF FUNCTION DIALOG BOX AFTER ARGUMENTS ENTERED

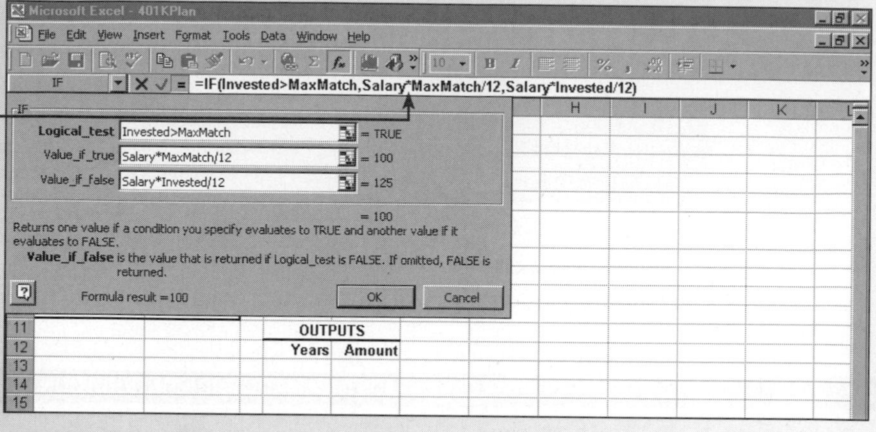

formula developed by Excel based on your entries in the IF function dialog box

6. Click the **OK** button. Excel places the IF function in the worksheet. Because the condition in this case is True, the value 100 appears in cell E8. Notice that the formula =IF(Invested>MaxMatch,Salary*MaxMatch/12,Salary*Invested/12) appears in the formula bar.

Now compute the total amount invested each month, which is the sum of the employee and employer contributions.

To calculate the total contribution:

1. Click cell **E9**, click the **AutoSum** button Σ, and press the **Enter** key. The total amount invested is 225.

   Now name cell E9 TotContribution.

2. Return to cell **E9**, click the **Name** box, type **TotContribution**, and press the **Enter** key.

   TROUBLE? If the label TotContribution appears in cell E9, click the Undo button on the Standard toolbar, and then click the Name box, type TotContribution, and press the Enter key.

3. Format the range E7:E9 using the Currency style and zero decimal places.
4. Click any cell to deselect the range.
5. Save the workbook.

Session 7.1 QUICK CHECK

1. During data validation, the error alert message appears ______________.
2. When you restrict the information being placed in a particular cell, you are applying ______________.
3. During data validation, the input message appears when you ______________.
4. Which of the following are invalid range names?
   a. Annual_Total
   b. 3rdQtr
   c. Qtr3
   d. Annual total
5. When you select a named cell or range, the name appears in the ______________.
6. Rather than enter constants in formulas, you should reference values from a separate section of your worksheet referred to as the ______________.
7. When the value you store in a cell depends on certain conditions, you should consider using a(n) ______________ in your formula.
8. The symbol <= is an example of a ______________.

You have completed the input section of the 401kPlan worksheet. By applying data validation rules, defining range names, and using range names and IF functions to create formulas, you have made the worksheet both easier for you to develop and for the numerous CableScan employees to use. In Session 7.2 you will complete the worksheet's calculation/output section.

SESSION 7.2

In this session you will finish the 401(k) planning workbook by entering the remaining formulas using the Excel AutoFill feature and FV function, creating a line chart, and protecting worksheet cells.

Computing the Retirement Fund

The last set of calculations will determine the dollars accumulated over time, or the total retirement fund, often called the "retirement nest egg." The values 5, 10, 15, 20, 25, 30—representing the years left until retirement—need to be entered in the first column, range D13:D18. Although you can type these numbers, there is an easier approach you can use when the values represent a series.

Creating a Series Using AutoFill

When working in Excel, you sometimes need to enter a series of data. If you enter one or two initial values in a series of numbers, dates, or text, the **AutoFill** feature of Excel completes the series for you. Figure 7-20 shows several series that AutoFill recognizes and automatically completes. You can quickly enter the series of data with the assistance of the fill handle. Enter the series 5, 10, 15, 20, 25, and 30 to represent the number of years left until retirement.

Figure 7-20 EXAMPLES OF SERIES COMPLETED USING AUTOFILL

INITIAL VALUE	REMAINING SERIES
Sunday	Monday, Tuesday, Wednesday, ...
1/10/2001	1/11/01, 1/12/01, 1/13/01
Qtr1	Qtr2, Qtr3, Qtr4
January	February, March, April, May, ...

To generate a series using AutoFill:

1. If you took a break after the last session, make sure Excel is running, the 401kPlan workbook is open, and the 401kPlan sheet is active.
2. In cell D13, enter **'5**. In cell D14, enter **'10**. Notice the values are left-aligned and stored as text, as a result of typing the apostrophe ahead of the value.
3. Select the range **D13:D14**.
4. Click and drag the fill handle in cell D14 through cells **D15:D18**. Notice that a ScreenTip displays each number in the series as you drag the mouse pointer. Release the mouse button. Excel has created the series, using the specified interval (5) between the two selected values.
5. Click any cell to deselect the range. See Figure 7-21.

Figure 7-21 SERIES CREATED USING AUTOFILL

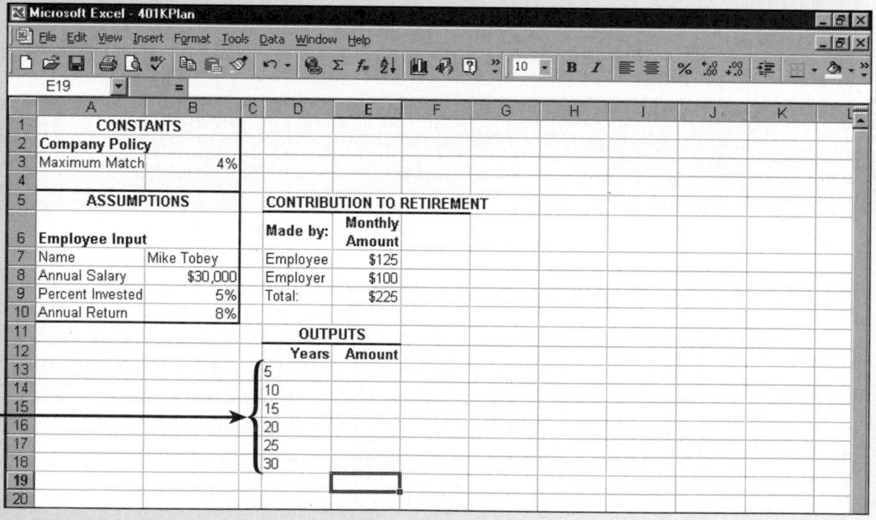

values are left-aligned and stored as text

Inserting the FV Function

Now enter the formula to calculate the future value of the investment, the retirement nest egg. The future value of an investment is its value at some future date based on a series of payments of equal amounts made over a number of periods earning a constant interest rate. You will use the financial function FV to compute the future value of the investment. The FV function has the following format:

FV(*rate*, *nper*, *pmt*)

where

- *rate* is the interest rate per period
- *nper* is the number of periods in which payments will be made
- *pmt* is the payments made each period. It cannot change over the life of the investment

This is one of several financial functions available in Excel. Figure 7-22 lists some of the other Excel financial functions.

Figure 7-22 SELECTED FINANCIAL FUNCTIONS

FUNCTION NAME	DESCRIPTION
PV	Computes the present value of a series of equal payments
PMT	Computes the periodic payment required to amortize a loan over a specified number of periods
RATE	Computes the rate of return of an investment that generates a series of equal periodic payments
DDB	Computes an asset's depreciation using the double-declining balance method
IRR	Computes an internal rate of return for a series of periodic cash flows

Now enter the future value formula, using the Paste Function button on the Standard toolbar.

To enter the future value formula:

1. Click cell **E13** to select the cell where you want to enter the FV function.
2. Click the **Paste Function** button on the Standard toolbar to open the Paste Function dialog box. Click **Financial** in the Function category list box, click **FV** in the Function name list box, and then click the **OK** button to open the FV function dialog box. See Figure 7-23.

   TROUBLE? If the Office Assistant opens offering Help on this feature, click the No button.

Figure 7-23 **FV FUNCTION DIALOG BOX**

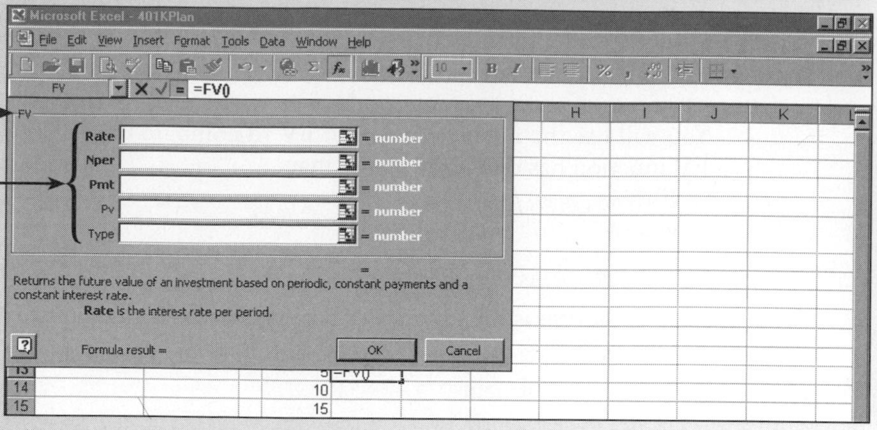

Now enter the arguments for this function. First, calculate the monthly return on the investment by dividing the annual return by 12.

3. In the **Rate** text box, type **Return/12**. Notice that the monthly return of .006666667 appears to the right of the Rate text box.

   Next, calculate the number of monthly payments during the life of the investment.

4. In the **Nper** (number of periods) text box, type **D13*12**. Notice that 60, the number of months in five years, appears to the right of the Nper text box.

   Now, enter the total amount invested each month.

5. In the **Pmt** text box, type **TotContribution** and press the **Enter** key. The value ($16,532.29) appears as a red negative value in cell E13. See Figure 7-24. This value, ($16,532.29), means that if an investment of $225 is made each month for 60 months and earns interest at a rate of 0.67% per month, you will have accumulated $16,532.29 in five years. By default, Excel shows this value as a negative number (in parentheses). You think the employees will be confused if they see the value of their investment as a negative number, so edit the formula and place a minus sign in front of the function name in order to display the future value as a positive number.

Figure 7-24 FUTURE VALUE COMPUTATION FOR FIVE YEARS

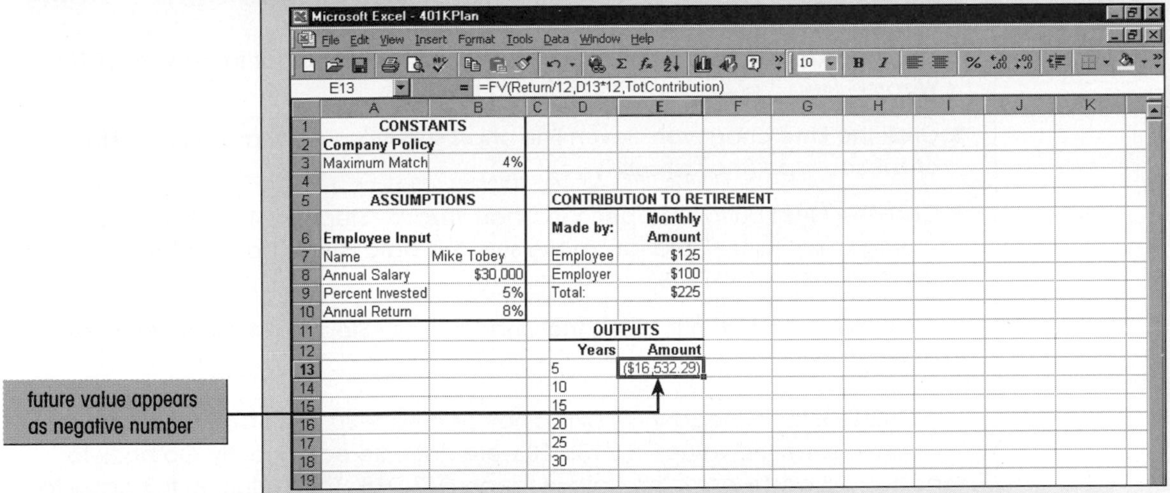

6. Double-click cell **E13**. Position the insertion point to the right of the equal sign (=) and type **-** (negative), and then press the **Enter** key. The value appears as a positive number.

7. Copy the formula in cell E13 to cells **E14:E18**.

   TROUBLE? If the width of column E is too narrow, increase the column width to display the value.

8. Click any cell to deselect the range. See Figure 7-25.

Figure 7-25 FUTURE VALUE COMPUTATION OVER 30-YEAR PERIOD IN FIVE-YEAR INCREMENTS

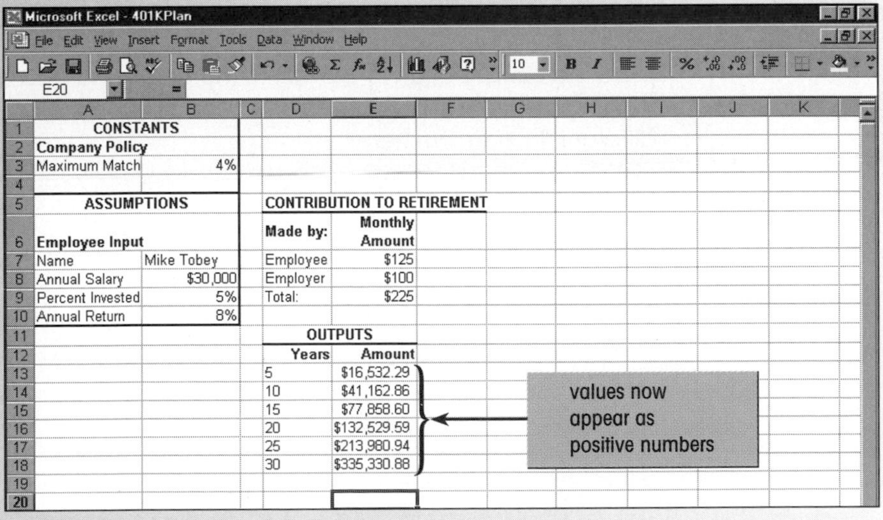

The output table showing the dollars accumulated over 30 years is complete. Now display this information as a line chart showing the accumulation of dollars over the 30-year period.

To create the line chart:

1. Select the range **D13:E18**.
2. Click the **Chart Wizard** button on the Standard toolbar to open the Chart Wizard - Step 1 of 4 - Chart Type dialog box.
3. Click the **Line** chart type. Seven line chart sub-types appear. Click the **Line chart** sub-type (the first sub-type).
4. Click the **Next** button to open the Chart Wizard - Step 2 of 4 - Chart Source Data dialog box. On the Data tab, make sure the Data range box displays ='401kPlan'!$D$13:$E$18.
5. Click the **Next** button to open the Chart Wizard - Step 3 of 4 - Chart Options dialog box.

   TROUBLE? If the Category (X) axis is not labeled 5–30, click **Cancel** to exit the Chart Wizard. The values in D13:D18 were not entered correctly. Go back to page 7.18 and reenter the data in range D13:D18. Then return to this page to check the line chart.

   Next, add a title to the chart.
6. If necessary, click the **Titles** tab, click the **Chart title** text box, and type **Retirement Nest Egg** for the chart title. Click the **Category (X) axis** title box, and then type **Years in future**. Click the **Value (Y) axis** title box, and then type **Dollars**.

   Because there is only one data series, remove the legend; it is not needed.
7. Click the **Legend** tab and then click the **Show Legend** check box to remove the check and deselect that option.
8. Click the **Next** button to open the Chart Wizard - Step 4 of 4 - Chart Location dialog box. Embed the chart in the 401kPlan worksheet (the default option).
9. Click the **Finish** button to complete the chart and display it in the 401kPlan worksheet. See Figure 7-26. Note that the scale on your y-axis may appear different than shown here.

Figure 7-26 COMPLETED LINE CHART

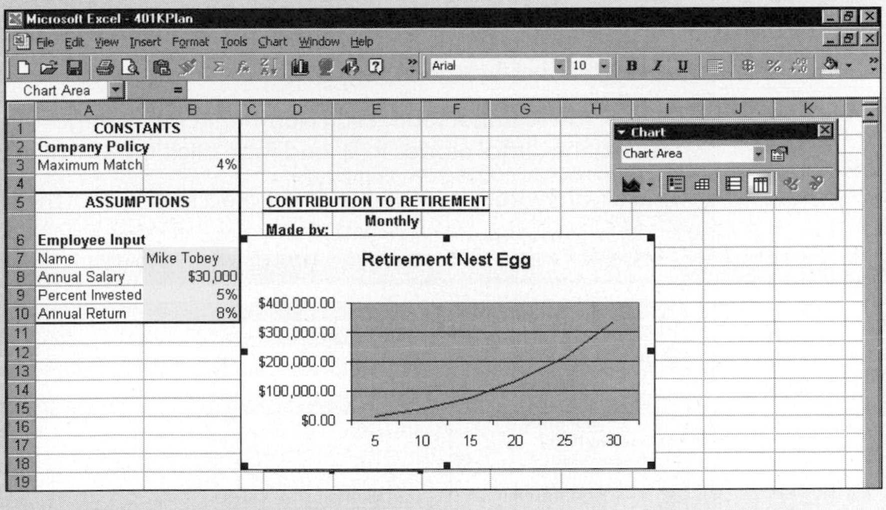

You need to move and resize the chart to improve its appearance.

To change the size and position of the chart:

1. Move and resize the chart object so it appears in the range **F6:K18**. See Figure 7-27.

Figure 7-27 LINE CHART AFTER BEING MOVED AND RESIZED

floating Chart toolbar may appear in a different location of your screen

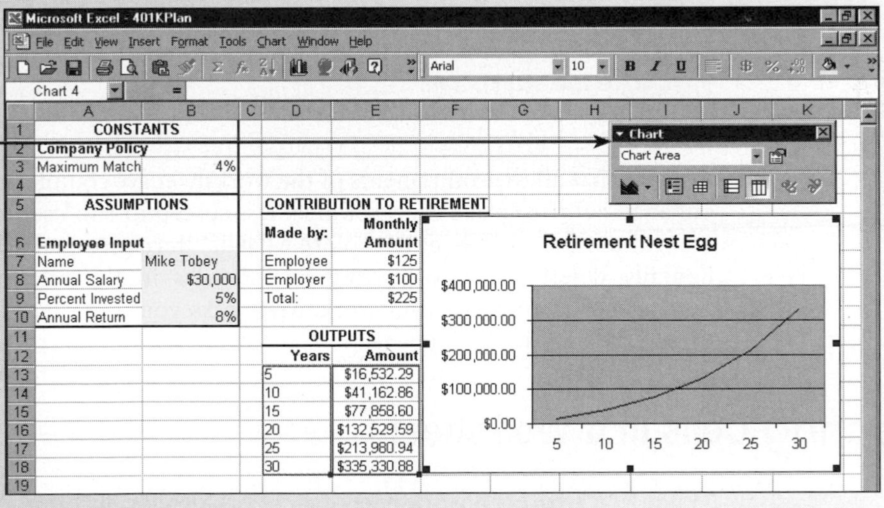

Now enhance the chart's appearance.

To improve the appearance of the chart:

1. Double-click the **Series 1** (Line object) to open the Format Data Series dialog box. On the Patterns tab, click the **Weight** list arrow, select the **thickest** line weight, and then click the **OK** button.
2. Click the **Numbers** tab, click Number in the Category list and change the number of decimal places to **0**, and then click the **OK** button.
3. Click anywhere outside the chart area to deselect the chart. See Figure 7-28.

Figure 7-28 FINAL VERSION OF LINE CHART

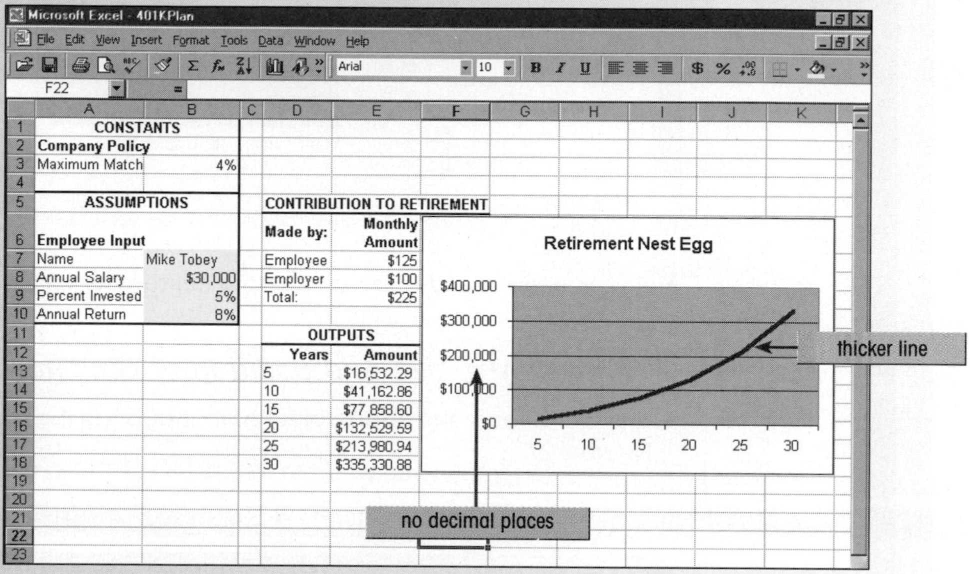

4. Save the workbook.

Now that all the components of the worksheet are complete, you still need to make a few enhancements to make the worksheet less susceptible to user error. Mary realizes that others will use the worksheet to explore what-if alternatives, and she worries about a user accidentally deleting the formatting or formulas in the calculation/output section of the worksheet. To preserve your work, Mary asks you to protect all the cells in the worksheet except the cells in the input section.

Protecting Cells in a Worksheet

When you **protect** a worksheet, data in protected cells cannot be changed. Once you have protected worksheet cells, the data in these cells can be viewed, but not edited or modified. Once you protect a worksheet, you cannot enter data, insert or delete rows, or change cell formats or column widths. Only the values in unprotected cells can be changed.

Unlocking Individual Cells

Most of the time you will not want to lock every cell in a worksheet. For example, in a worksheet that you share with others, you might want to protect the formulas and formatting, but leave particular cells unprotected so that necessary data may be entered. When you want to protect some but not all worksheet cells, you implement protection by following a two-step process. By default all cells in a worksheet have the locked property turned on, which means the cell is capable of being protected. First you need to identify the cells you want unprotected and turn off the "lock" associated with each of these cells. Once you have "unlocked" the selected cells, you activate the protection command to "turn on" protection for the remaining cells. Figure 7-29 illustrates this process.

Figure 7-29 PROCESS OF PROTECTING WORKSHEET CELLS

Default Status

By default, every cell in the worksheet has a locked property turned on, which means each cell has the capability of being protected, but at this step no cell is protected. You can enter data in any cell.

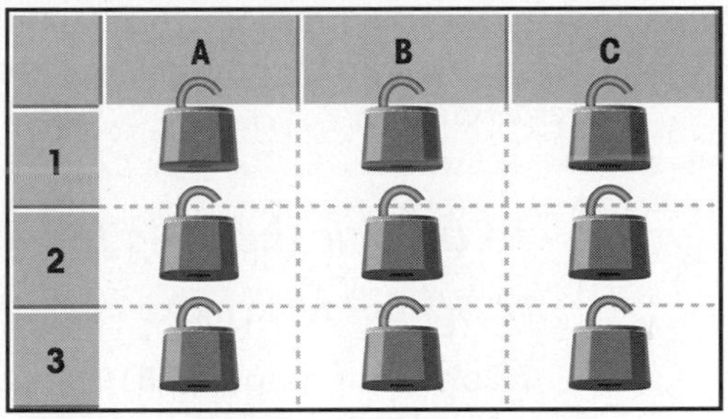

Step 1

The worksheet after some cells have their locks removed (locked property turned off). At this step no cell is protected. You can enter data in any cell.

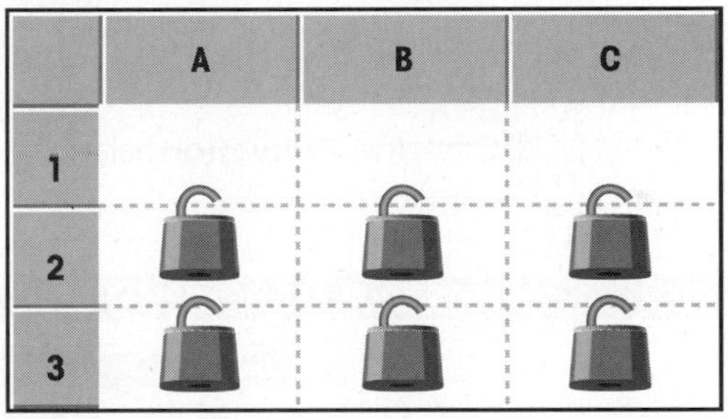

Step 2

The worksheet after the Protect Sheet command has been activated. The cells in the bottom two rows are protected– no data may be entered in these cells. You can still enter data in the first row.

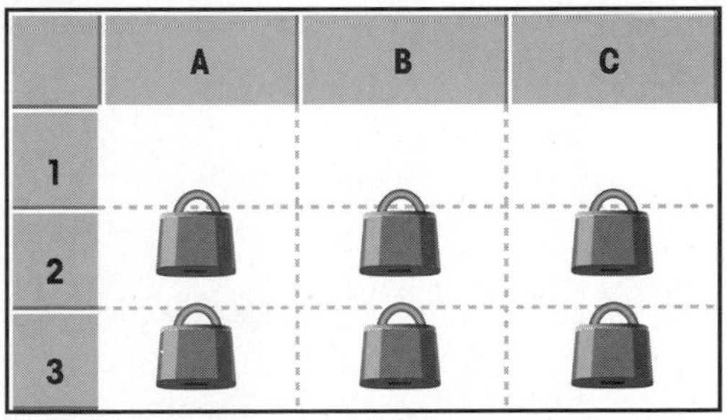

REFERENCE WINDOW RW

Protecting Cells

- Select the cells you want to remain unprotected.
- Click Format, and then click Cells to open the Format Cells dialog box.
- In the Format Cells dialog box, click the Protection tab.
- Remove the check from the Locked check box, and then click the OK button.
- Click Tools, point to Protection, and then click Protect Sheet to open the Protect Sheet dialog box.
- If desired, enter a password in the Protect Sheet dialog box, and then reenter the password in the Confirm Password dialog box.

You start by unlocking the range of cells where the user can enter data, which in this case would be the input area of the 401kPlan worksheet. Then activate the protection for the rest of the worksheet, which will protect the data and formulas you do not want the employees to change.

To unlock the cells for data entry:

1. Click cell **A5** to make it the active cell, so you can view the input section.
2. Select the range **B7:B10**, the cells the user can change and therefore do not require protection.
3. Click **Format** on the menu bar, and then click **Cells** to open the Format Cells dialog box.
4. Click the **Protection** tab. By default, the Locked check box contains a check. See Figure 7-30.

Figure 7-30 PROTECTION TAB OF FORMAT CELLS DIALOG BOX

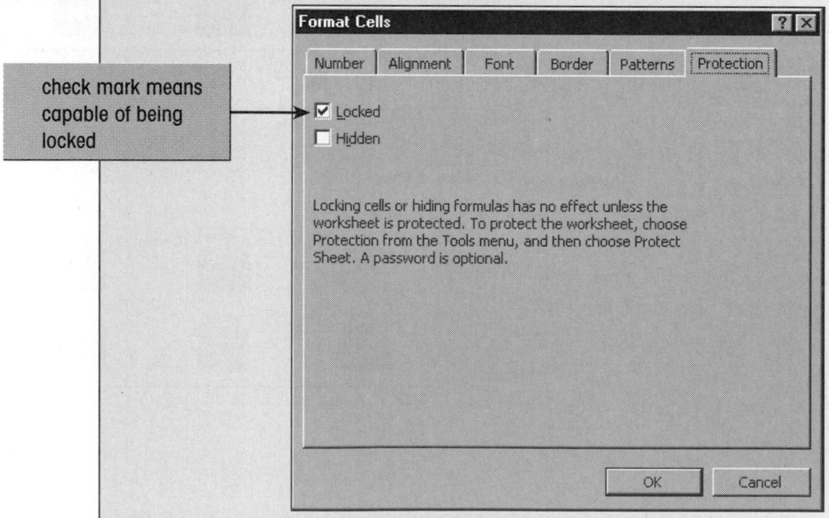

5. Click the **Locked** check box to remove the check.
6. Click the **OK** button. Nothing visible happens to the worksheet to show that cells are unlocked.

Because Excel does not provide any on-screen indication of the protection status of individual cells, you decide to change the background color of the unlocked cells to distinguish them from the protected cells. This will be a nice visual cue for the employees using the worksheet, indicating which cells they should use to input their investment information.

To change the fill color of unprotected cells:

1. If necessary, select cells **B7:B10**.
2. Click the **Fill** color button list arrow on the Formatting toolbar to display the Color palette.
3. Click **Yellow** in the fourth row, third column of the Color palette.
4. Click any cell to view the yellow color applied to the unprotected cells.

Protecting the Worksheet

Now that you have unlocked the cells for data entry, you will turn on protection for the entire worksheet to protect every cell that you didn't unlock.

When you protect the worksheet, Excel lets you enter a password that must be used to unprotect the worksheet. If you specify a password, you must make sure to remember it so you can unprotect the worksheet in the future. Unless you are working on confidential material, it's probably easier not to use a password at all.

To turn protection on:

1. Click **Tools** on the menu bar, point to Protection, and then click **Protect Sheet** to open the Protect Sheet dialog box. See Figure 7-31. The Password text box lets you enter a password of your choice. The Contents check box locks the cells in the sheet. The Objects check box prevents changes to charts or graphical objects, and the Scenarios check box locks any scenario you've created.

Figure 7-31 OPTIONS FOR PROTECTING A WORKSHEET

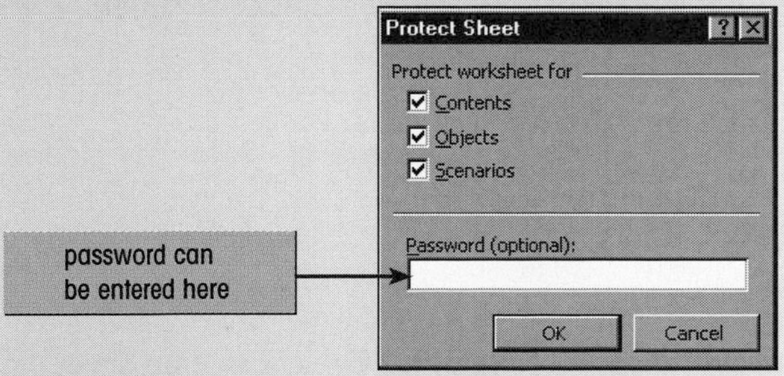

2. Click the **OK** button. If you had entered a password, a Confirm Password dialog box would open and you would be asked to retype the same password to make sure you remember it and that you entered it correctly the first time.

Testing Cell Protection

After protection is enabled, you cannot change a locked cell. Before you distribute the workbook to the employees to use, you decide to test the worksheet to assure yourself that protection has been implemented successfully.

To test worksheet protection:

1. Click cell **E13**, and then try typing **40000**. A message indicating that this cell is locked and cannot be changed appears. See Figure 7-32.

Figure 7-32 MESSAGE DISPLAYED WHEN YOU ATTEMPT TO CHANGE A PROTECTED CELL

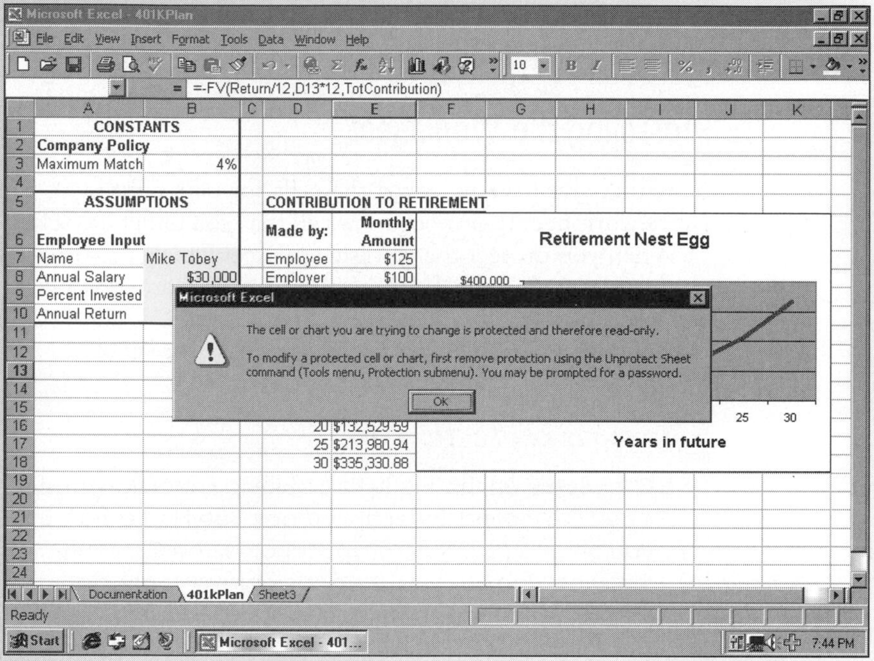

2. Click the **OK** button to continue.

   Now enter a value in a cell that is unlocked.

3. Click cell **B8**, type **40000**, and press the **Enter** key. Notice that the calculation and outputs changed.

Now that you are done creating the workbook, and have customized it so it is user friendly and appropriate for use by all CableScan employees, you give it to Mary to review. She is very pleased with the finished workbook. Her only suggestion is to further simplify the workbook by removing any unnecessary sheets. She thinks this will eliminate any possibility of people trying to enter data in the wrong area of the workbook.

Deleting Unnecessary Worksheets

If you want to remove an empty worksheet or a worksheet you no longer need, you can delete it. You decide to delete Sheet3 because it is not used in the 401(k) application.

To delete a worksheet:

1. Click the **Sheet3** tab to activate the Sheet3 worksheet.
2. Click **Edit**, and then click **Delete Sheet**. A message appears letting you know that the selected sheet will be permanently deleted.
3. Click the **OK** button. Notice that Sheet3 has been deleted from the workbook.
4. Save the workbook.

Session 7.2 Quick Check

1. You can use the Excel ______________ feature to complete a series of numbers, dates, or text values.
2. The FV function stands for ______________. This function is found in the ______________ category.
3. How does cell protection differ from data validation?
4. What happens when you try to enter a value in a protected cell?
5. Protecting a worksheet is a two-step process. You ______________ and then you ______________.
6. Why were the unprotected cells filled with color?

You have now completed the worksheet. In this next section you will create two macros that will simplify some of the tasks a user performs when using this workbook.

SESSION 7.3

In this session you will learn what macros are and how they can be used to automate tasks in a workbook for the user. You will also plan and create two macros using the Excel macro recorder.

Automating Tasks Using Macros

Typically macros are used to automate repetitive tasks. A **macro** is a series of commands and functions that you can initiate whenever you want to perform a particular task. That is, you create them to automatically perform a series of Excel operations, such as menu selections, dialog box selections, range selections, or keystrokes. They carry out repetitive tasks more quickly than you can yourself, making your work more productive and helping you make fewer errors. For example, you can create macros to automate the following tasks:

- move through a large worksheet quickly
- add a date and time stamp to a cell in the current worksheet

- extract data from an Excel list and create a chart
- print several reports from a worksheet, each with different print specifications
- apply a common set of formats to any sheet in a workbook

Macros simplify the use of workbooks for both experienced and novice users. In reviewing the 401kPlan workbook with Mary, you realize that macros would be useful to include. You know that all users will need to clear the input section after completing the worksheet so the next user doesn't see confidential financial information. You also know that people will most likely want to have a hard copy of some or all of the worksheet. Therefore, printing is another task that would be good to simplify.

Creating Macros

You can create a macro in two ways: you can use the macro recorder to record your keystrokes and mouse actions as you perform them (recording the selection of ranges, menu commands, dialog box options, etc.), or you can write your own macros by entering a series of commands in the **Visual Basic for Applications (VBA)** programming language, which tells Excel how to do a particular task.

The easiest way to create a macro in Excel is to use the macro recorder. When you record a macro, your keystrokes and mouse actions are automatically translated into Visual Basic instructions (code) that you can play back, or run, whenever you want to repeat those particular keystrokes and tasks. Your actions are recorded and then translated into a series of instructions in VBA. When you run the macro, the instructions are read and executed in sequence, thereby duplicating the actions you performed when you recorded the macro.

In this section you will create two macros using the macro recorder. The first will be a ClearInputs macro that will automate the task of clearing values from the input section of the workbook, so the user can enter new data. The second macro you will create will be a Print macro, which will simplify the printing process.

Planning Macros

As with most complex projects, you need to plan your macro. Decide what you want to accomplish and the best way to go about doing it. Once you know the purpose of the macro, you should carry out the keystrokes or mouse actions before you actually record them. Going through each step before recording a macro might seem like extra work, but it reduces the chances of error when you actually create the macro.

Mary realizes that many different employees will use the worksheet and will enter different sets of input assumptions. She wants you to create a macro that will automatically clear the values in the input section and place the cell pointer in cell B7—ready for the user to enter a new set of data.

She sits down at her computer and goes through the steps to include in the macro before you actually record them. This way you will be familiar with the steps to include in the macro, and the chances for errors in the macro are fewer. Figure 7-33 lists the steps Mary plans to include in the macro.

Figure 7-33 PLANNING THE CLEARINPUTS MACRO

ACTION	RESULT
Select the range B7:B10	Highlights the range you want to clear of data
Press the Delete key	Clears the contents of the selected range
Click cell B7	Makes cell B7 the active cell

Recording the ClearInputs Macro

After planning the macro, you are ready to record it. There are several actions you need to take before actually recording the macro. First, you want to decide on an appropriate name for the macro. For example, the first macro Mary asked you to create is for clearing the input section of any values, so a good name for this macro would be ClearInputs. A macro name can be up to 255 characters long; it must begin with a letter, and it can contain only letters, numbers, and the underscore character. No spaces or other punctuation marks are permitted. For multiple-word macros such as Clear Inputs, you can use initial caps (ClearInputs) or the underscore (Clear_Inputs).

When you record a macro, every keystroke and mouse click is stored by Excel. Therefore, your second task before you can record the macro is to specify where you want the macro stored. The macro is stored in the form of a VBA program, and its storage location plays a part in how you will be able to access and use the macro once it is created. There are three possible locations you can choose to store the macro. By default, the recorded macro is stored as part of the current workbook—in a hidden module that is part of the workbook. Macros stored in a workbook are available only when the workbook is open. If a workbook is closed, the macros stored within the workbook can't be used. Use this storage option to store macros that you plan to use only within this workbook.

If you use some macros on a regular basis, you may want to make them available at all times. In that case, you would choose to store the macros in the Personal Macro workbook. With this option, the macro is stored in a special workbook file named Personal Macro. When you start Excel, this workbook is opened and hidden automatically, making the macros in it available to any open workbook.

You can also store the macro in a new workbook file. In this case, another workbook opens to store the recorded macro. To use macros stored in another workbook, you need to open both the workbook with the macros as well as the workbook containing the application.

In addition to considering where you want to store your macro, before you record a macro you also need to make sure your worksheet is set up exactly as you want it to exist at the time you play back the recorded macro. This may involve opening a specific workbook, activating a specific sheet in which you want the macro to run, and moving to the location where you want to start recording. Otherwise the macro may not work as planned, and you may have to record it again.

REFERENCE WINDOW RW

Recording a Macro

- Click Tools, point to Macro, and then click Record New Macro to open the Record Macro dialog box.
- In the Macro name text box, type a name for the macro.
- If you want to run the macro by pressing a keyboard shortcut key, enter a letter in the Shortcut key text box.
- In the Store macro in list box, click the location where you want to store the macro.
- In the Description text box, type a description of the macro.
- Click the OK button. The macro recorder starts recording.
- Perform the tasks you want the macro to automate.
- Click the Stop Recording button on the Stop Recording toolbar (or click Tools, point to Macro, and then click Stop Recording to stop the recording process).

When you record a macro, you name and describe it. You can also set up a shortcut key to run the macro, and specify the workbook in which to store the macro.

To record a macro to clear a range of cells:

1. If you took a break after the last session, make sure Excel is running, the 401kPlan workbook is open, and the 401kPlan sheet is active. If necessary, press **Ctrl + Home** to make cell A1 the active cell.

   Now start the macro recorder.

2. Click **Tools** on the menu bar, point to Macro, and then click **Record New Macro** to open the Record Macro dialog box. See Figure 7-34.

Figure 7-34 RECORD MACRO DIALOG BOX

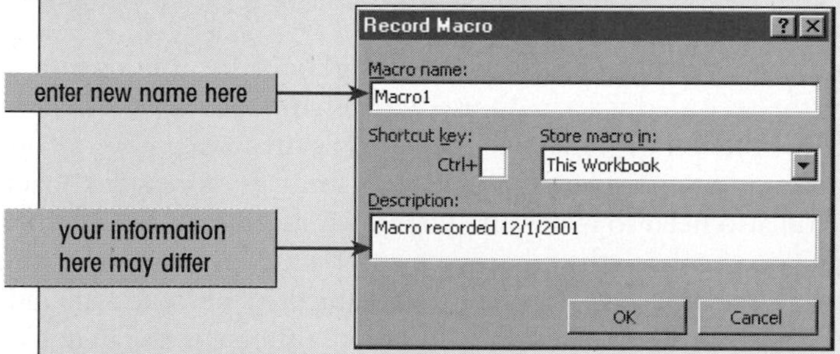

   Excel proposes a default name for the macro. This default macro name consists of the word "Macro" and a number corresponding to the number of macros you have recorded in the workbook in the current work session. You should change the macro name to a name more descriptive of what the macro will do. Name the macro ClearInputs.

3. Type **ClearInputs** in the Macro name text box.

Now specify the location of your macro. You want the macro to be accessible only to this workbook, and when this workbook is open. Therefore, you want to store the macro as part of this workbook.

4. Make sure the option This Workbook is selected in the Store macro in list box.

Notice the brief description indicating the date the macro is being recorded. You can add additional comments to explain the purpose of the macro.

5. Click anywhere within the **Description** text box. If the insertion point is not at the end of the default description, move it there. Press the **Enter** key to start a new line. Type **Clear the values from the input section**. See Figure 7-35.

Figure 7-35 COMPLETED RECORD MACRO DIALOG BOX

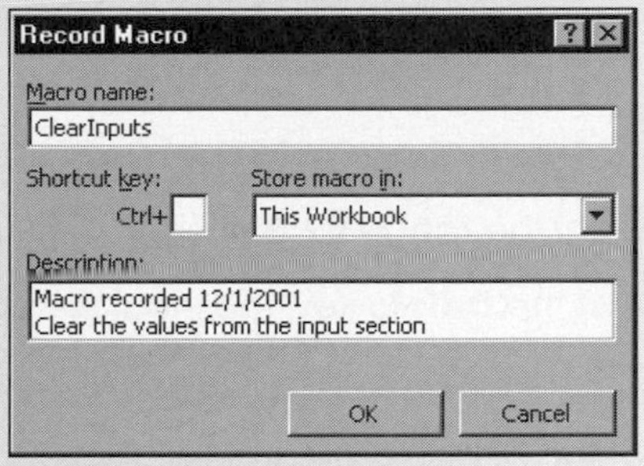

6. Click the **OK** button to start recording the macro. See Figure 7-36. Excel returns to the worksheet and the message "Recording" appears in the status bar at the bottom of the screen. You are now in Record mode and all keystrokes and mouse clicks will be recorded until you stop the macro recorder.

Figure 7-36 STOP RECORDING TOOLBAR

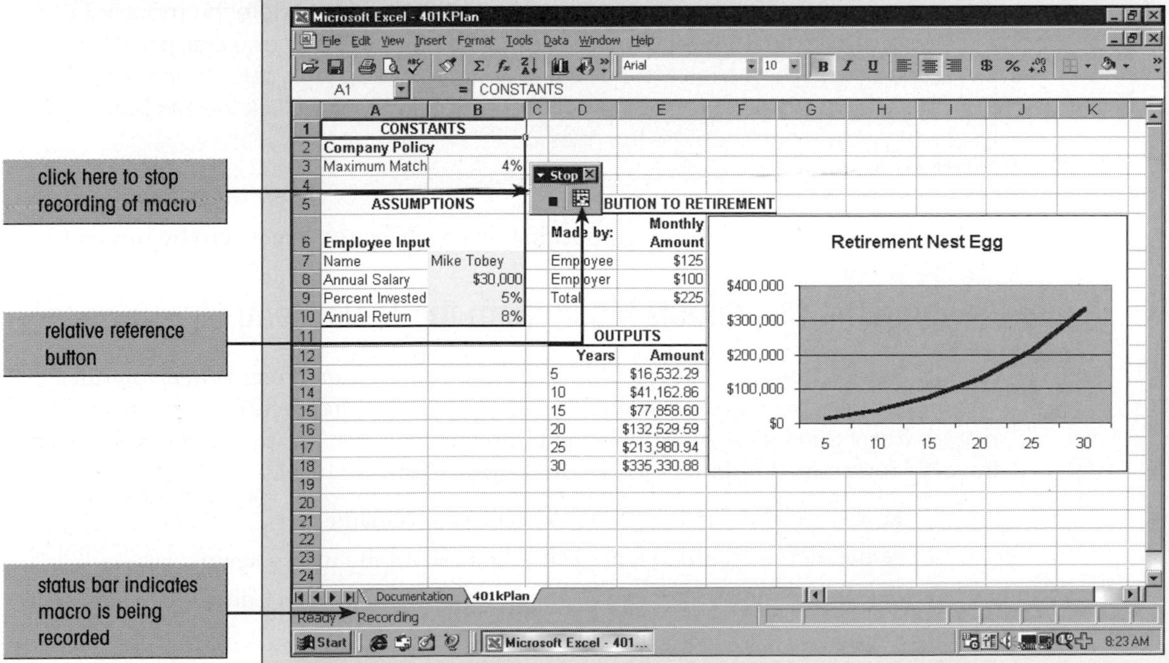

Notice that the Stop Recording toolbar also appears. This toolbar contains two buttons, the Stop Recording button and the Relative Reference button. By default Excel uses absolute references while recording macros. If you wanted a macro to select cells regardless of the position of the cell pointer in the worksheet when you run the macro, then you would click the Relative Reference button to record macros using relative references. When you have finished entering all tasks, you can use the Stop Recording button to stop the macro recorder.

TROUBLE? If a warning message appears indicating that the macro name already exists, click the Yes button and proceed to record the tasks in your macro. The existing macro is replaced with whatever you now record.

Now perform the tasks you want recorded.

To perform the steps to be recorded:

1. Select the range **B7:B10**.
2. Press the **Delete** key. The input section is now cleared.
3. Click cell **B7** to make it the active cell.

   You have completed the actions that you want recorded. Next, you will stop the macro recorder.

4. Click the **Stop Recording** button ■ on the Stop Recording toolbar or click **Tools**, point to Macro, and then click **Stop Recording** to stop the recording process. Notice that the message "Recording" no longer appears in the status bar and the Stop Recording toolbar disappears.

   TROUBLE? If you forget to turn off the macro recorder, it continues to record all of your actions. If this happens to you, you may need to delete the macro and record it again. To delete the macro, click Tools on the menu bar, point to Macro, and then click Macros in the Macros dialog box, select ClearInputs in the Macro Name list, and then click the Delete button. Click the Yes button to verify you want to delete the macro.

You have completed recording your first macro. Now test the macro by running it.

Running the ClearInputs Macro from the Tools Menu

After recording a macro, you can play it back, or run it, at any time. When you run a macro, you are telling Excel to execute the previously recorded instructions contained within the macro. It is a good idea to run the macro directly after you create it as a test to ensure that it works correctly. If it doesn't work correctly, you can:

- re-record the macro using the same macro name
- delete the recorded macro and then record the macro again
- edit the incorrect macro by opening the Visual Basic Editor

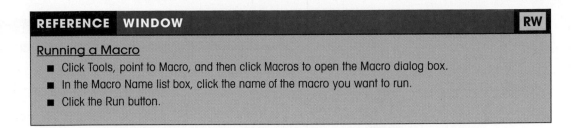

REFERENCE WINDOW RW

Running a Macro

- Click Tools, point to Macro, and then click Macros to open the Macro dialog box.
- In the Macro Name list box, click the name of the macro you want to run.
- Click the Run button.

The first time you run the macro, you are testing it to determine whether it works as expected. Run the macro you just created to see if it automatically clears the values from the input section. To do this, you need to first enter values in the section so they can be cleared.

To run a macro using the Macro command on the Tools menu:

1. Enter a new set of input values in cells B7:B10. Enter **Mary Higgins, 45000, .02, .06**.
2. Press **Ctrl + Home** to move to cell A1.

   Now save the workbook before running the macro for the first time in case anything goes wrong while running it.
3. Click the **Save** button on the Standard toolbar to save the workbook.
4. Use the ClearInputs macro to erase the input values.
5. Click **Tools** on the menu bar, point to Macro, and then click **Macros** to open the Macro dialog box. See Figure 7-37. A list of all macros found in all open workbooks appears in the Macro Name list box.

Figure 7-37 MACRO DIALOG BOX

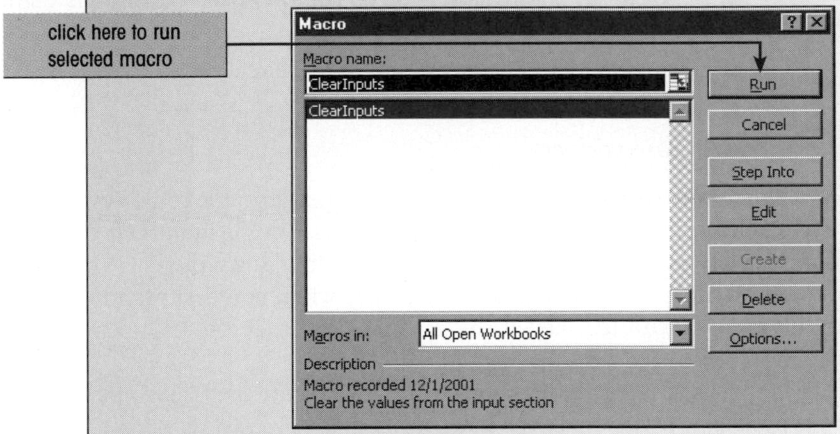

   Select the name of the macro you want to run.
6. If necessary, click **ClearInputs** to display ClearInputs in the Macro name text box, and then click the **Run** button. The ClearInputs macro runs and clears the values in cells B7:B10. See Figure 7-38.

Figure 7-38 WORKSHEET AFTER MACRO RUN

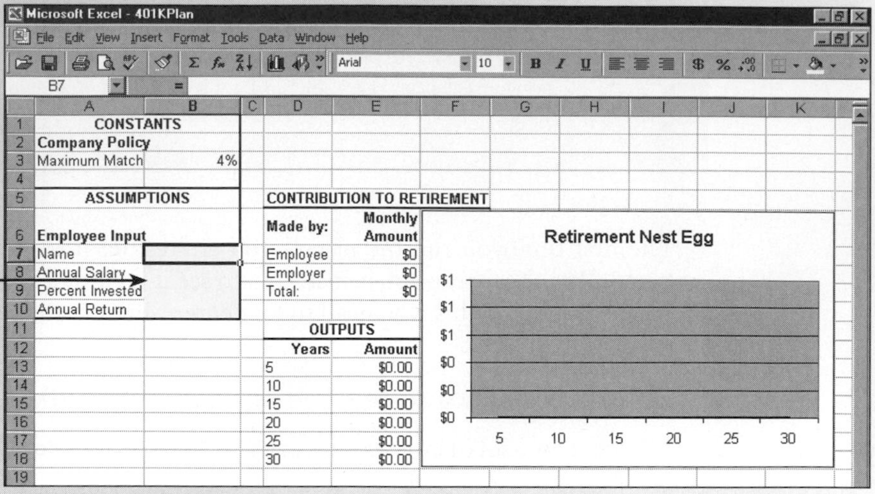

input values cleared

The macro ran successfully. Now that you know the macro works, you want to make it easy for users to run. There are several ways to do this.

Creating a Macro Shortcut Key

You can use the Macro command on the Tools menu to run macros that you execute infrequently, but this approach is inconvenient if you need to run the macro often. There are several ways to make it easier to run a macro. You can assign the macro to a:

- shortcut key that enables you to run the macro by using a combination of the Ctrl key and a letter key
- command that appears on one of the Excel menus
- button on a toolbar
- drawing object

A quick way to run a macro is to assign it to a shortcut key, a key you press along with the Ctrl key to run the macro. The shortcut key is a single uppercase or lowercase letter. If you use this option, you can run the macro by holding down the Ctrl key and pressing the shortcut key. Normally you assign a shortcut key when you first record a macro; however, if you didn't create a shortcut key at the time you recorded the macro, you can still assign one to the macro.

Mary asks you to create a shortcut key to execute the ClearInputs macro. She wants users to type Ctrl + c to execute the macro.

To assign a shortcut key to the macro:

1. Click **Tools** on the menu bar, point to Macro, and then click **Macros** to open the Macro dialog box.
2. If necessary, click **ClearInputs**, and then click the **Options** button to open the Macro Options dialog box. See Figure 7-39.

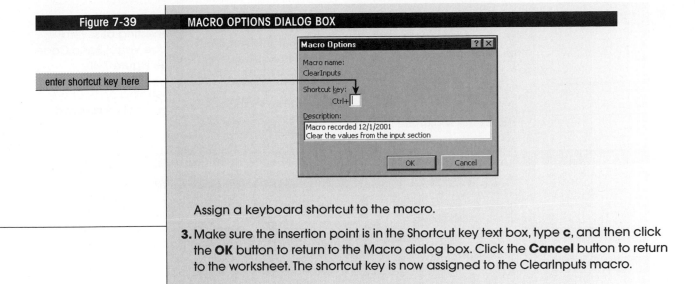

Figure 7-39 MACRO OPTIONS DIALOG BOX

enter shortcut key here

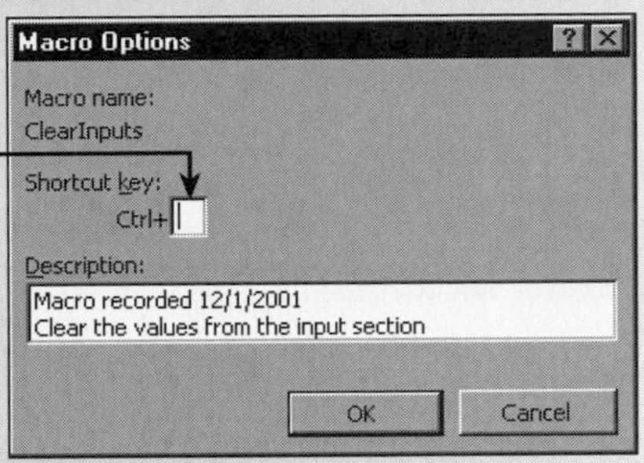

Assign a keyboard shortcut to the macro.

3. Make sure the insertion point is in the Shortcut key text box, type **c**, and then click the **OK** button to return to the Macro dialog box. Click the **Cancel** button to return to the worksheet. The shortcut key is now assigned to the ClearInputs macro.

Now test the shortcut key to see if the macro runs when Ctrl + c is pressed.

To test the shortcut key:

1. In cells B7:B10, enter **FJ Miles, 50000, .05, .05**, to enter a new set of input values.
2. Press **Ctrl + c** to run the macro. The input values are erased and B7 is the active cell.

   Note that shortcut keys are case-sensitive, so if a user types Ctrl + Shift C, the shortcut will not run the ClearInputs macro.

The shortcut key successfully ran the macro. Now let's take a look at the code behind the ClearInputs macro.

Viewing the ClearInputs Macro Code

As you may have realized, you can successfully record and run a macro without looking at or understanding the instructions underlying it. For simple macros this approach is fine. There will be times, however, when you may welcome the greater flexibility that comes from understanding the commands underlying the recorded macro.

As Excel records your actions, it translates them into a series of instructions in the Visual Basic for Applications programming language. To view or edit the macro, you need to open the **Visual Basic Editor**, a separate application that works with Excel.

To view the Visual Basic code:

1. Click **Tools** on the Menu bar, point to Macro, and then click **Macros** to open the Macro dialog box.

2. Click **ClearInputs** in the Macro name list box, and then click the **Edit** button. The Visual Basic Editor opens as a separate application consisting of several windows. One of the windows, the Code window, contains the Visual Basic Code generated while your ClearInputs macro was recorded. See Figure 7-40.

   TROUBLE? The number of windows that open may vary depending on your system. We will focus on the Code window. If the Code window is not maximized, click the Maximize button.

Figure 7-40 VISUAL BASIC EDITOR DISPLAYS VISUAL BASIC CODE FOR CLEARINPUTS MACRO

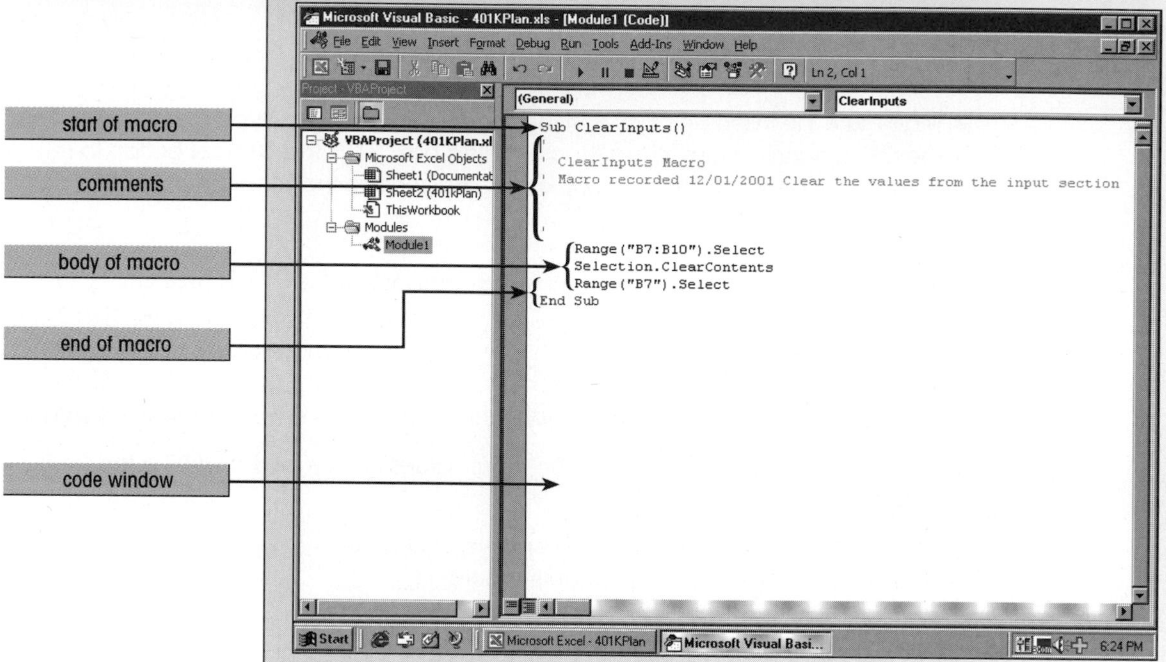

Visual Basic for Applications Code

The Visual Basic for Applications code shown in Figure 7-40 has the following components: **Sub/End Sub** are keywords that mark the beginning and end of a macro. The keyword Sub in the statement

Sub ClearInputs()

signals the start of the macro. It is followed by the macro name ClearInputs and then by left and right parentheses. The keywords End Sub signal the end of the macro. **Comments** are statements that explain or document what is happening in the macro. Any line of the code that is preceded by an apostrophe is a comment and is ignored when the macro is run. In Figure 7-40, the comments are the macro name, the date recorded, and the description you entered in the Record Macro dialog box.

The **body of the macro** is the series of statements between Sub and End Sub representing the VBA translation of the actions you performed while recording the macro. In Figure 7-40 the statement

Range("B7:B10").Select

is the VBA equivalent of selecting the range B7:B10.

The next statement

Selection.ClearContents

is the VBA equivalent of pressing the Delete key to clear the contents of the selected range. The last statement

Range("B7").Select

is the VBA equivalent of clicking B7 to make it the active cell.

Now that you have viewed the code behind the macro, you're ready to create your next macro, a macro to print a portion of the 401kPlan worksheet. First, close the Visual Basic Editor.

To close the Visual Basic Editor:

1. Click **File** on Visual Basic Editor menu bar, and then click **Close and Return to Microsoft Excel**. The Visual Basic Editor closes and the 401kPlan worksheet appears.

Recording the Print401k Macro

Because your worksheets may be large, containing input sections, data, tables, reports, charts, etc., you may want to use a macro to help you simplify the steps for printing different parts of a worksheet. Also, the addition of one or more print macros will make the printing process much easier for other users.

After an employee has made changes to certain input values and viewed the revised table and chart, Mary wants the employee to be able to print a hard copy of the worksheet for his or her records. Some employees may only want to print the table and chart from the 401k worksheet. Instead of the user having to establish print settings to get the output of just the table and chart, for example, you could create a macro to print just these sections of the worksheet. You would need to specify the print area for the portion of the worksheet you are printing. Mary also wants the user's output to automatically have informative headers and footers. Before printing, the user should also be able to view the output in the Print Preview window. Figure 7-41 shows the planning for this macro. Using this planning sheet, record the macro for Mary. Mary suggests that you name the macro Print401k and that it be stored just in this workbook. Now, set up the worksheet just the way you want it before you begin the macro recorder.

Figure 7-41 PLANNING THE PRINT401K MACRO

ACTION	RESULT
Click File, click Page Setup	Opens the Page Setup dialog box
Click the Sheet tab, click Print area, type D5:L18	Defines print area
Click Margins, click Horizontally check box	Horizontally centers output
Click Header/Footer tab, click Custom Header, click the Tab Name button, click OK	Defines custom header
Click Custom Footer, type Prepared by [enter your name], click OK	Defines custom footer
Click Print Preview	Displays output in Print Preview window
Click Close	Closes Print Preview window
Click cell A5	Makes cell A5 the active cell

To record the Print401k macro:

1. Enter **Tammy Beach, 25000, .04, .10** in the appropriate cells in range B7:B10 to input new values. Click cell **A1**.

   Now start the macro recorder.

2. Click **Tools** on the menu bar, point to Macro, and then click **Record New Macro** to open the Record Macro dialog box.

   The name Macro2 automatically appears because this is the second macro you have recorded during this work session. Change the name of the macro to Print401k.

3. Type **Print401k** in the Macro name text box.

   Now add a shortcut key.

4. Click the **Shortcut key** text box, and then type **p**.

   Add an additional comment to explain the purpose of the macro.

5. Place the insertion point at the end of the default description. Press the **Enter** key and type **Print preview output table and chart**.

6. Click the **OK** button to start the macro recorder.

7. Click **File** on the menu bar, and then click **Page Setup** to open the Page Setup dialog box.

   By default, the entire worksheet prints. To print only a part of the worksheet, you must specify the part you want.

8. Click the **Sheet** tab of the Page Setup dialog box, click the **Print area** text box, and then type **D5:K18**.

   Now specify the print settings so the output is centered horizontally.

9. Click the **Margins** tab, and then check the **Horizontally** check box to select it.

10. Click the **Header/Footer** tab, and then click the **Custom Header** button. In the center section, click the **Tab Name** button (last button), and then click the **OK** button.

11. Click the **Custom Footer** button, type **Prepared by (enter your name)** in the Right section, and then click the **OK** button.

    Review the output in the Print Preview window.

12. Click the **Print Preview** button on the right side of the dialog box to preview the output. See Figure 7-42.

Figure 7-42 PRINT PREVIEW AS A RESULT OF RECORDING THE MACRO

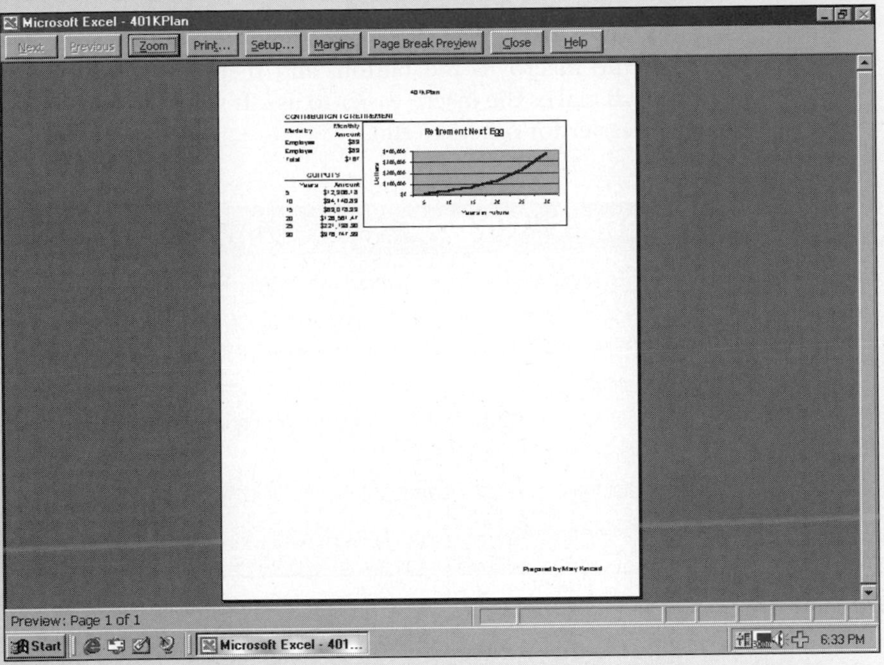

13. Click the **Close** button to close the Print Preview window and return to the 401kPlan sheet. Note that you cannot stop the macro until you leave the Print Preview window.

14. Click cell **A5** to make it the active cell.

You have completed the tasks for the macro; now turn off the macro recorder.

15. Click the **Stop Recording** button on the Stop Recording toolbar to stop recording the macro.

Now test the Print401k macro using the shortcut key.

To test the macro using the shortcut key:

1. Save the workbook.
2. Press **Ctrl + p** to run the macro. The output table and chart appear in the Print Preview window.
3. If you want a hard copy, click the **Print** button on the Print Preview toolbar, and then click the **OK** button in the Print dialog box; otherwise click the **Close** button.

The shortcut key successfully ran the print macro. However, Mary thinks it may be easier for a user to run the print macro by clicking a button placed on the worksheet. Mary asks you to create this button.

Assigning the Print401k Macro to a Button on the Worksheet

Another way to run a macro is to assign it to a button. You place the button on a worksheet, assign the macro to the button, and then run the macro by clicking the button. This approach makes the macro easier to use. It will speed up your own work, as well as make the macro easier for others to run.

REFERENCE WINDOW RW

Assigning a Macro to a Button on a Worksheet

- Click the Button button on the Forms toolbar.
- Position the mouse pointer where you want the button, and then click and drag the mouse pointer until the button is the size and shape you want.
- Release the mouse button. The button appears on the worksheet with a label, and the Assign Macro dialog box opens.
- Select the name of the macro that you want to assign to the button from the Macro Name list box.
- Click the OK button.

Because the workbook is still protected, you need to turn protection off in order to make any changes to the worksheet (except in unlocked cells), such as placing a button on the worksheet.

To turn protection off:

1. Click **Tools** on the menu bar, point to Protection, and then click **Unprotect Sheet**. The worksheet is unprotected. If you had password-protected the worksheet, the Unprotect Sheet dialog box would open so that you could enter the password.

Now place a button on the worksheet.

To place a button on the worksheet and assign a macro to the button:

1. Click cell **D2**.

   Next, display the Forms toolbar, which contains the tools you need to place the button on the worksheet.

2. Click **View** on the menu bar, point to Toolbars, and then click **Forms** to display the Forms toolbar. If necessary, drag the Forms toolbar out of the way. See Figure 7-43.

Figure 7-43 FORMS TOOLBAR DISPLAY IN WORKSHEET WINDOW

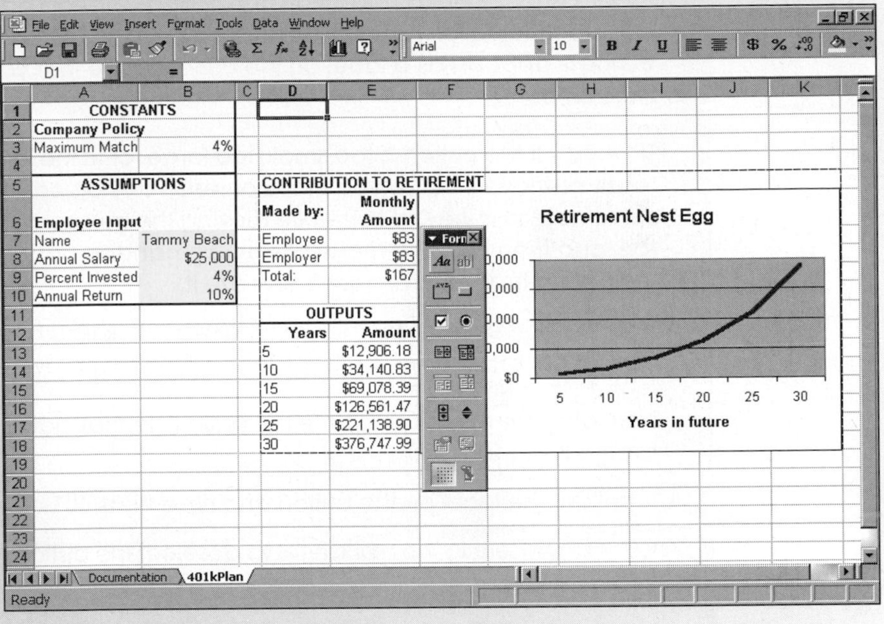

3. Click the **Button** button on the Forms toolbar. Now position the mouse pointer in the worksheet where you want the button to appear.

4. Position the mouse pointer in the upper-left corner of cell D2. The pointer shape changes to +. Click and drag the mouse pointer until the box covers the range **D2:E3**. When you release the mouse button, the Assign Macro dialog box opens. See Figure 7-44. Here you select the macro that will be run when the user clicks this button. This is referred to as assigning a macro to a button.

Figure 7-44 BUTTON AND ASSIGN MACRO DIALOG BOX

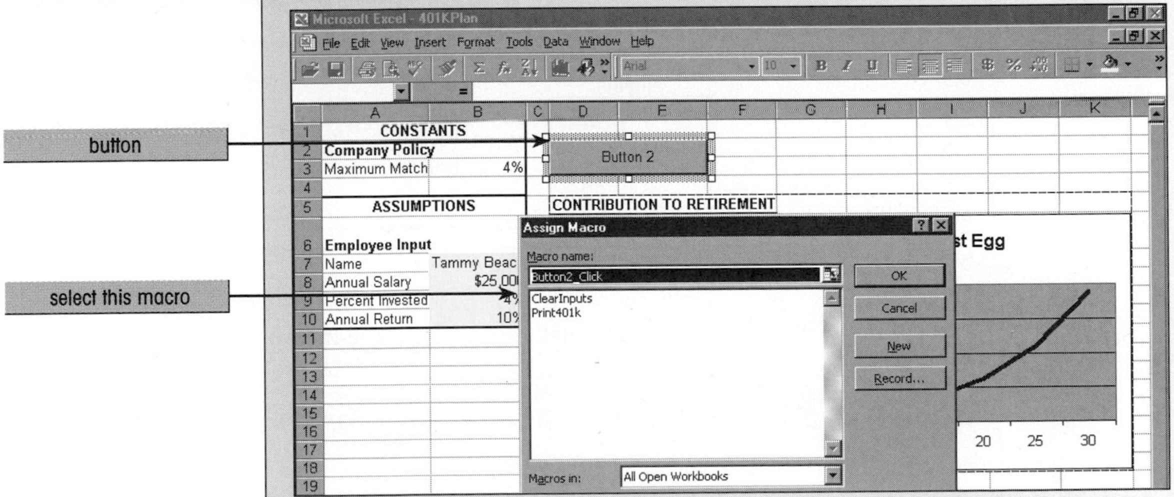

5. Click **Print401k** in the Macro Name list box, and then click the **OK** button. The macro is assigned to the button. The button appears on the worksheet. It is selected (selection handles appear around the button), and the default name Button 2 appears as a label on the button. Note that your button number may differ.

TROUBLE? If the button is too small, too large, or in the wrong location, you can resize or move it just as you move or resize any object. If the button is not selected, press the Ctrl key while moving the mouse pointer on top of the button, and then click the mouse. Selection handles appear around the button, indicating that you can move or resize it.

TROUBLE? If the Forms toolbar is in the way, click and drag it to move it out of the way, or click the Forms toolbar Close button to remove it from the screen.

Now change the name on the button to one that indicates the function of the macro assigned to it.

6. Highlight the label on the button and type **Print 401k Report**.
7. Click anywhere in the worksheet to deselect the button.
8. If you haven't already removed the Forms toolbar, click its **Close** button to remove it now. See Figure 7-45.

Figure 7-45 BUTTON TO RUN PRINT401K MACRO

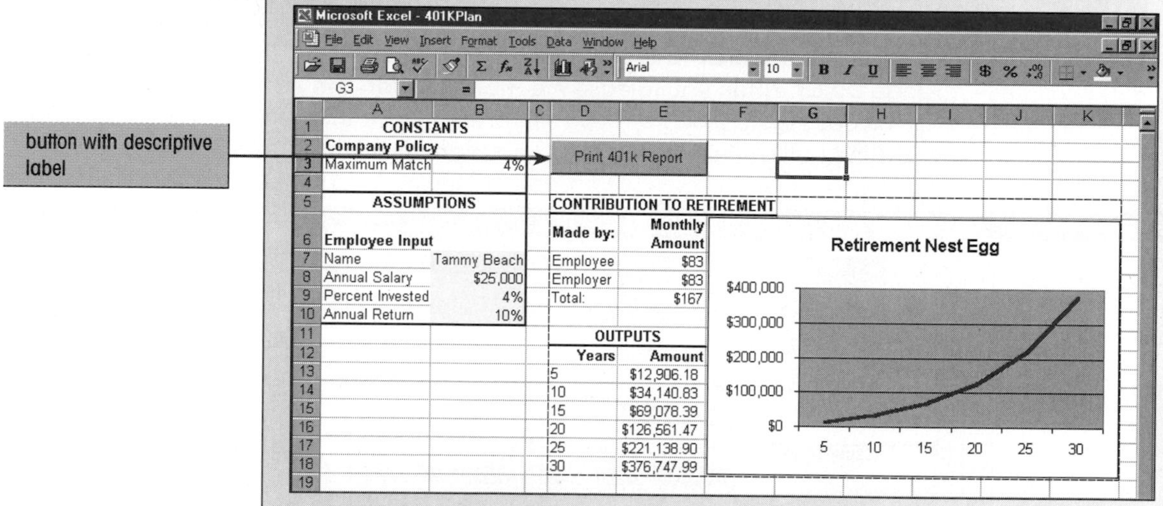

Now test the command button to make sure it runs the macro.

To test the Print401k macro using the command button:

1. Type **.08** in cell B10 and press the **Enter** key.
2. Click the **Print 401k Report** button. The output and chart appears in the Print Preview window.
3. If you want a hard copy, click the **Print** button and then click the **OK** button in the Print dialog box; otherwise click the **Close** button.

Your Print401k macro worked successfully using the button. Now protect the worksheet again.

4. Click **Tools**, point to **Protection**, click **Protect Sheet**, and then click **OK**.

5. Save the workbook, and then close it and exit Excel.

You have created a workbook for the CableScan employees that will allow them to easily and efficiently plan and establish 401(k) plans.

Session 7.3 Quick Check

1. A ______________ automates repetitive tasks.
2. You can create a macro by ______________ or ______________.
3. A recorded macro stores instructions in the ______________ programming language.
4. Print Chart is a valid macro name. (True/False)
5. Macros are stored in a(n) ______________, ______________, or ______________.
6. To stop recording a macro, you ______________.
7. Name three ways to run a macro.
8. What is the purpose of a shortcut key?

REVIEW ASSIGNMENTS

After the presentation at the first CableScan site, you received feedback from the employees on how to improve the usability of the 401kPlan workbook. Do the following:

1. If necessary, start Excel and make sure your Data Disk is in the appropriate disk drive. Open the workbook **401kPlan2** in the Review folder for Tutorial.07 and save it as **401kPlan3**. A message appears informing you that this workbook contains macros. Click the Enable Macros button to continue.
2. Remove cell protection from 401kPlan3 worksheet.
3. Specify a data validation rule for the Salary value, cell B8. You want to allow integer values between 5000 and 150000.
4. Test the data validation. Enter a salary of 200000. What happens?
5. Modify the data validation you just assigned in cell B8 to include an input message. The message should state "Valid salary values are between 5000 and 150000" and have the title Valid Data.
6. Modify the data validation you assigned in cell B8 to include an error alert message. The error message should have the title Invalid Data, and the message should state "You entered a value less than $5000 or greater than $150,000." Use the Warning style in defining the error alert.

7. Test the data validation again. Enter a value of 200000. What happens?
8. Change the error alert style to Information. Enter 200000 as the current salary. What happens?
9. Assign the name Contributions to the range E7:E8. Replace the formula in cell E9 with the formula =Sum(Contributions). What value appears in E9?
10. The FV function in cell E13 assumes that payments are made at the end of the month. A more realistic assumption is that payments are made at the beginning of the month. Use the Paste Function button on the Standard toolbar to modify the FV function in cell E13 by placing a 1 in the Type argument. Copy the modified formula to the other cells in the output table. Use the Print 401k Report button to print the worksheet.

Explore

11. Modify the IF function in cell E8 so the condition is expressed Invested <=MaxMatch instead of Invested > MaxMatch. Modify the other arguments of the IF function so you get the same results as in the tutorial. What formula did you enter in cell E8?
12. Plan and create a macro to print preview the entire worksheet except the range A1:B4. Name the macro PrintWorksheet. Include the label "CableScan 401k Plan" as a custom header in the center setting and change the page orientation to Landscape. Assign a shortcut key to the macro. Place a button on the worksheet next to the Print 401k Report button. Label the button Print Worksheet. Test your macro twice, using the Print Worksheet button and the shortcut key. (Note: By default, the macro button does not print.)
13. Delete Sheet3 from the workbook, and then save and close the workbook.

Explore

14. Open a new workbook and use AutoFill to create the series
    a. Q197,Q297,Q397,Q497,Q198,Q298,...,Q199,...,Q499. Print the series.
    b. What values must be entered in the worksheet in order for Excel to recognize the pattern and create this series?
    c. What value appears after Q499?
    d. Save the workbook as **AutoFill Exercise** in the Review folder for Tutorial.07 on your Data Disk.

Explore

15. Open a new workbook and create two macros that are identical, except that in the first case you'll record the macro using absolute references and in the second, you'll record the macro using relative references. Both macros enter a company's name and address into three worksheet cells. Figure 7-46 describes the steps required for each macro.

Figure 7-46

<u>**Name of Macro:**</u> NameAddress1 Shortcut key: x Description: using absolute references
Click cell A1
Type Adobe Development Corporation
In cell A2, type 101 Terra Way
In cell A3, type Tucson, AZ

<u>**Name of Macro:**</u> NameAddress2 Shortcut key: y Description: using relative references
Click Relative Reference button
Click cell A1
Type Adobe Development Corporation
In cell A2, type 101 Terra Way
In cell A3, type Tucson, AZ
Click Relative Reference button

Do the following:

a. Record the NameAddress1 macro, as described in Figure 7-46.

b. Before you record the second macro, clear the contents of cells A1:A3, and then make A3 the active cell.
c. Record the Name Address2 macro described in Figure 7-46.
d. Activate Sheet2.
e. Click cell D5 and run the NameAddress1 macro using the shortcut key.
f. Click cell D12 and run the NameAddress2 macro using the shortcut key.
g. Activate Sheet3.
h. Click cell D5 and run the NameAddress1 macro.
i. Click cell D12 and run the NameAddress2 macro.
j. Save the workbook as **Relative vs. Absolute** in the Review folder for Tutorial.07. Close the workbook.

Comment on the differences between the two macros.

CASE PROBLEMS

Case 1. Travel Expense Worksheet for Tax Purposes Jack Conners, an accountant for a manufacturing company, has been preparing tax returns on weekends for several years to earn extra income. Although Jack uses a commercial tax package to prepare tax returns, he has discovered that it doesn't provide assistance in determining the portion of a business trip that is tax deductible. Jack has asked you to develop a worksheet to determine deductible travel expenses that he can use with a client who travels on business.

The IRS rules state that a taxpayer can deduct travel expenses incurred while pursuing a business purpose. Those travel expenses include transportation, lodging, incidentals, and 50% of meals. Incidentals are items such as local transportation, laundry, and similar small items that are necessary while traveling. Sometimes a trip may involve both business and personal activities. If fewer than 50% of the travel days are devoted to business, none of the transportation expenses are deductible; otherwise the transportation expenses are fully deductible. The costs for lodging, meals, and incidentals are deductible to the extent that they are related specifically to business activities. Only 50% of meals associated with business travel, are deductible.

Figure 7-47 incorporates the information you need to complete the travel expense worksheet.

Figure 7-47

Inputs

Name of taxpayer
Dates of travel
Destination
Purpose
Number of business travel days
Number of personal travel days
Transportation (total cost)
Lodging (cost per day)
Meals (cost per day)
Incidentals (cost per day)

Calculations

```
Transportation = IF Number of business travel days is greater than Number of personal travel days THEN
                     Transportation = (total cost)
                 ELSE
                     Transportation = 0
                 END IF
Lodging = Number of business travel days × Lodging (cost per day)
Meals = Number of business travel days × Meals (cost per day) x 50%
Incidentals = Number of business travel days × Incidentals (cost per day)
Total deductible travel expense = Transportation + Lodging + Meals + Incidentals
```

Do the following:

1. If necessary, start Excel and make sure your Data Disk is in the appropriate disk drive.
2. Prepare a travel expense worksheet based on the information in Figure 7-47. Name the sheet **Travel**.
3. Divide the worksheet into two sections: input and calculation/output. As you develop the input section, assign range names to each cell.
4. The IRS guideline limits the deduction for meals to $75 per day, unless the taxpayer has receipts to justify a higher expense. Set up a data validation rule in the input section to comply with this guideline. You should include an input message and determine appropriate text for the message. Also, include an error alert message using the Warning style. You determine the text of the error alert message. Test the data validation.
5. Use the range names to build the formulas in the calculation section of your worksheet.
6. Improve the appearance of the worksheet, so you have a professional-looking report you can output.
7. Print the worksheet using Taxpayer 1 data from Figure 7-48.

Figure 7-48

INPUT FIELD	TAXPAYER 1	TAXPAYER 2
Name of taxpayer	Ken Tuner	Ellen Wymer
Dates of travel	Jan 5-12	April 21-28
Destination	Austin, Tx	San Antonio, Tx
Purpose	Sales call	Consulting
Number of business travel days	3	5
Number of personal travel days	5	3
Transportation (total cost)	300	375
Lodging (cost per day)	125	110
Meals (cost per day)	60	70
Incidentals (cost per day)	20	15

8. Save the worksheet as **Travel Expense** in the Cases folder for Tutorial.07 on your Data Disk.
9. Print the formulas for the worksheet. Include row and column headers. Output the formulas on one page.
10. Create macros to clear the input section and print the worksheet. Assign each macro to a button. Use Taxpayer 2 data from Figure 7-48 to test your macros.
11. Apply cell protection to all cells in the worksheet except cells in the input section. Test the cell protection. Assign a color to identify the range that is unprotected.
12. Delete any unused worksheets in the workbook, then save and close the workbook.

    (Note: If you get a Runtime error message box when testing a macro, click the End button to return to the worksheet. Review the steps in your macro and re-record the macro using the same name.)

Case 2. Sales Agreement Application for Desert Dreams Desert Dreams, a self-contained community, is being developed in New Mexico by Adobe Sun Corporation as an environment to appeal to people of all ages. Desert Dreams offers lifestyle features such as an 18-hole golf course, state-of-the-art fitness center, swimming and tennis center, and hiking and bike paths. In addition, the floor plans for the houses in the development are winners of numerous architectural awards.

Interest in the community has been abundant. To assist the sales associates, you have been asked to develop a Sales Agreement worksheet to use with potential home buyers as they finalize the sale of a home.

The worksheet should summarize the total purchase price, which consists of the cost of the lot, the base price of the home, and the cost of extras (options). In addition, the worksheet should lay out the payment schedule for two alternative financing schedules: a cash plan and a mortgage payment plan. Figure 7-49 shows the information you need to include in your worksheet.

Do the following:

1. If necessary, start Excel and make sure your Data Disk is in the appropriate disk drive.
2. Design the worksheet with the two users in mind. Make it useful to sales associates as they enter data but also attractive and easy to follow for home buyers, who will receive a copy of the sales agreement. Consider dividing the worksheet into input and calculation/output sections. In your calculation/output section include a payment schedule for both the mortgage and cash financing plans. Use the information in Figure 7-49 as you build your worksheet. Name the sheet **Sales Agreement**.

Figure 7-49

Input

- Name of buyer
- Lot cost
- Base price of home
- Cost of options

Calculations

- Purchase Price = Lot cost + Base price of home + Cost of options

Financing Plan – Mortgage payment

1	Deposit at signing sales agreement	$7500
2	Down payment at start of construction	18% × purchase price
3	Final payment at closing	Purchase price less (down payment + deposit)
4	Total cash paid out	Sum of 3 payments

Financing Plan – Cash payments

1	Deposit at signing sales agreement	$15000
2	Down payment at start of construction	30% × purchase price
3	Payment at start of framing	35% × purchase price
4	Final payment at closing	Purchase price less (sum of 3 payments + cash discount)
5	Cash discount	2.5% of base price
6	Total cash paid out	Sum of payments (1 – 4)

3. Apply the following data validation rules:
   - Base price of home does not exceed $300,000.
   - Lot prices are between $20,000 and $100,000.
   - For each rule you should include an appropriate input and error alert message.

4. Create and use range names as you build formulas and in any other way you see fit. (*Hint:* Values in the input section and selected calculations are the most useful choices for range names.)
5. Format an attractive sales agreement worksheet, using features you have learned throughout the tutorials.
6. Save your workbook as **Sales Agreement** in the Cases folder for Tutorial.07 on your Data Disk.
7. Enter the data in Figure 7-50, and then print the worksheet.

Figure 7-50

Name of buyer	Helen Chomas
Lot cost	30000
Base price	160000
Options	12500

8. Develop macros to:
   a. clear input values from your input section. Name this macro ClearInputs and assign it to a button.
   b. print the portion of the worksheet that includes inputs and costs of both financing plans. Name this macro PrintData, and assign it to a button.
9. Helen Chomas has just selected some additional options which increased the options cost to $15,000. Make this change to the input section of your worksheet and use your PrintData macro to print a new output of the financing plans.
10. Create a Documentation sheet. Print the Documentation sheet.

Explore

11. Use the Index tab in the Help dialog box to learn how to "paste" range names and their associated addresses into your worksheet. Create a section in your Documentation sheet to include all range name information in your worksheet. Print the modified Documentation sheet.
12. Protect all cells in your worksheet except the cells where a user enters input values.
13. Save your worksheet, and then print the worksheet formulas. Remember to include row and column headers in your output.

Explore

14. Modify the Financing Plan - Mortgage to include a line for the monthly mortgage payment. Assume 8% annual interest, 25 years, and amount borrowed (use final payment at closing). Read Appendix 1 or use the Office Assistant to learn about the PMT function. Use your print macro to output the Sales Agreement worksheet.
15. Save and close the workbook.

Case 3. Customer Billing for Apex Auto Rental

Apex Auto Rental is the only car rental company in a midwest city. The company has been in business for two years. John Prescott, president and founder of Apex, has asked you to help him computerize the bills he gives to his customers.

Apex rents two types of cars: compact and luxury. The current rental rates are shown in Figure 7-51.

Figure 7-51

TYPE	CHARGE/DAY	CHARGE/MILE
Compact	$40	$0.25
Luxury	$50	$0.35

1. If necessary, start Excel and make sure your Data Disk is in the appropriate disk drive.
2. Develop a worksheet that calculates and prints customer bills. Divide your workbook into the following sheets:
   - A Documentation sheet that includes a title, your name, date developed, filename, and purpose.
   - A worksheet for the customer bill. Name the worksheet **Customer Bill**. The customer bill should include the information shown in Figure 7-52. Divide your worksheet into input, calculation, and output sections. Use the layout in Figure 7-53 to design your output section. As you create your input and calculation sections, assign range names to these cells.

Figure 7-52

Assumptions
Rental rate information (Figure 7-51)

Rental Inputs
Customer name
Type of car (compact or luxury)
Number of days rented
Number of miles driven

Calculations
Charge per day (depends on type of car rented, which is entered in input section. Get charge from rental rate information)

Charge per mile (depends on type of car rented, which is entered in input section. Get charge from rental rate information)

Amount due = (days driven × charge per day) + (miles driven × charge per mile)

Figure 7-53

Apex Car Rental
Customer Bill

Customer Name: xxxxxxxxxxxxxxxx

Type of Car: xxxxxxxxxxx

Days Driven: x Charge/Day: xx

Miles Driven: xxxx Charge/Mile: xx

Amount Due: $ x,xxx.xx

Explore

3. Apply the data validation rules from Figure 7-54 to the input section. You decide on appropriate input and error alert messages.

Figure 7-54

FIELD	RULE
Number of Days	<30
Number of miles	<5000
Type of car	List (use values from rental rate information)

4. Use the range names as you build the formulas for the customer bill.
5. Improve the appearance of your worksheet.
6. Save your worksheet as **Apex Rental** in the Cases folder for Tutorial.07.
7. Enter the Customer 1 data from Figure 7-55 into the input section of your worksheet. Print the entire worksheet.

Figure 7-55

INPUT FIELD	CUSTOMER 1	CUSTOMER 2
Customer name	Marisa Flowers	Henry Bibbs
Type of car	Compact	Luxury
Days driven	3	8
Miles driven	225	1150

8. Create macros to:
   a. clear the rental input section. Name this macro ClearInputs and assign the macro to a button.
   b. print only the customer bill. Name this macro PrintBill and assign it to a button.
   c. use the Customer 2 data from Figure 7-55 to test your macros.
9. Print the formulas (include row and column headers).
10. Apply cell protection to the worksheet cells, while permitting the user to enter data in the input section. Use color or shading to identify the unprotected area.

Case 4. Aging Invoices at Duchess Pools MaryAnn Kodakci works in the accounting department of Duchess Pools. She has several reports to prepare for the monthly meeting and plans to use Excel to analyze the data. She's downloaded data on outstanding sales invoices and asks you to do the following:

1 Start Excel, open the file **Invoices** in the Tutorial folder for Tutorial.07 and save it as **Sales Invoices**.

2. Freeze the pane so the column headings and Invoice No field don't scroll off the screen as you navigate the sales Invoice list.

3. Compute the Number of days outstanding for each invoice.

   a. Place the label "Age as of" in cell A1 and "10/1/99" in cell B1. Assign the range name "AsOfDate" to cell B1.

   b. Subtract the Invoice date for each invoice from the Age as of date (cell B1) and place the result in the Days Outstanding column. (Note: when you subtract dates the displayed values may appear in a dd/mm/yy format. If this occurs, format the values using the General format so the values appear as numbers.)

4. Assign the Amount Owed to one of four columns (30 days or less, 31–60 days, 61–90 days, and Over 90 days.) Use the Days Outstanding, computed in Question 3, to determine which column to assign the Amount Owed to.

   (*Hint:* The amount owed for each invoice can only appear in one of the four columns; the other three should be equal to zero. You may want to read Appendix 1 or use Office Assistant to learn about the AND function.)

5. Prepare a macro to sort the Invoice list by Customer number and within customer number by Invoice date (earliest date first). Name the macro CustSort. Assign the macro to a button and place the button in rows 2 to 3 above the Cust No field in the Invoice list. Change the label on the button to read "Sort by customer". Test the macro.

Explore

6. Prepare a macro that goes to the last record in the list. Name the macro LastRecord (cell A100). Assign the macro to a button and place the button in rows 2 to 3. Change the label on the button to "Last Record". Test the macro.

7. Prepare a macro that goes to first record in the list. Name the macro FirstRecord (cell A5). Assign the macro to a button and place the button in rows 2 to 3. Change the label on the button to "First Record". Test the macro.

8. Prepare a macro that previews (Print Preview) invoices that have an Amount Owed greater than zero. This report should sort so the largest amount owed appears first. The page setup for the output should include a custom header with the sheet name and a custom footer with your name; landscape orientation, scaled to fit 1 page wide, and centered horizontally on the page. Name the macro AmtOwed. Assign the macro to a button on the worksheet and place the button in rows 2 to 3 above the Amount Owed field name in the Invoice list. Change the label on the button to read "Who Owes". Tasks on this macro include (1) filtering records, (2) sorting the filtered records, (3) setting Page Setup, (4) print previewing the filtered list, and (5) removing the filter arrows after closing the Print Preview window. Test the AmtOwed macro. Print the AmtOwed report.

   (*Note:* If you get a Runtime error Message box when you attempt to run the macro, click the End button to return to the worksheet. Review the steps in the macro and re-record the macro using the same name to replace the current macro.)

9. Save the workbook.

INTERNET ASSIGNMENTS

The purpose of the Internet Assignments is to challenge you to find information on the Internet that you can use to create effective spreadsheets. The actual assignments are updated and maintained on the Course Technology Web site. Log on to the Internet and use your Web browser to go to the Student Online Companion to accompany this text at **www.course.com/NewPerspectives/office2000**. Click the Excel link, and then click the link for Tutorial 7.

QUICK CHECK ANSWERS

Session 7.1

1. if you enter a value that violates the validation rule
2. data validation
3. click on a cell
4. b and d
5. Name box
6. input section
7. IF Function
8. comparison operator

Session 7.2

1. AutoFill
2. Future Value; Financial
3. Cell protection prevents you from entering any data in a protected cell. Assuming a cell is unprotected, data validation allows you to specify what values users are allowed to enter in the cell.
4. A message box appears informing you that the cell is protected.
5. remove the Locked property from cells you want to be able to enter into, activate the Protect Sheet command
6. To help users identify them

Session 7.3

1. macro
2. recording, or entering Visual Basic code
3. Visual Basic for Applications or VBA
4. False. Macro names cannot contain spaces. Use an underscore.
5. current workbook, another workbook, or Personal Macro workbook
6. Click the Stop Recording button
7. Shortcut key (Ctrl + letter), command button object, Run button from Macro dialog box
8. provides a quick way to run a macro

OBJECTIVES

In this tutorial you will:

- Insert, name, and move worksheets
- Create worksheet groups
- Edit multiple worksheets at the same time
- Consolidate information from multiple worksheets and workbooks
- Create a workbook template
- Learn how to store templates
- Create a lookup table and use Excel's lookup function
- Create and use an Excel workspace

WORKING WITH MULTIPLE WORKSHEETS AND WORKBOOKS

Creating Grading Sheets at MidWest University

CASE

MidWest University

Professor Karen White teaches calculus in the mathematics department at MidWest University, a liberal arts school that draws students from the Midwest and from across the United States. Her Calculus 223 course is one of the most popular courses in the department. Because her calculus course is required for computer science, as well as several other majors at the university, Professor White's lecture is filled with over 200 students each semester. Students attend Professor White's weekly lecture, as well as smaller biweekly discussion sections with a teaching assistant (TA) to receive extra instruction, discuss special topics, and work on problems. In addition to leading discussion sections, the four TAs assigned to Professor White's lecture are responsible for grading all the homework assignments, midterm exams, and final exams of the students in their sections. Professor White's TAs teach three discussion sections, each with about 20 students per section.

In the past, Professor White and her TAs have used handwritten grading sheets to keep track of homework and exam scores and to calculate final grades. Professor White feels that the accuracy and efficiency of record-keeping for her calculus course could be greatly improved if the TAs used Microsoft Excel 2000 for these tasks instead of the grading sheets currently used. She also thinks automating the record-keeping process would save time for her TAs, who carry full course loads in addition to their assistantships.

Professor White has asked you to use Excel to create a grading workbook that her TAs can use to both record the progress of their students and to give her an overall picture of how well all the classes, and each of her assistants, is doing. For each TA's sections, the workbook must be able to calculate the average of the homework and exam results, weigh each one according to the values determined by Professor White, and automatically assign a final letter grade. Professor White would also like to be able to combine the results from each TA's workbook into a single summary workbook, so she can combine and compare the information to evaluate TA performance. In addition, she would like to use Excel to automatically assign grades based on students' numeric scores.

As you plan a spreadsheet solution that meets Professor White's needs, you review her requirements. You know that you will need a worksheet that can display both the detail and summary information clearly, that can be readily distributed to the TAs, and that will have a consistent format so you can easily combine the results. To meet these goals, you explore the possibility of using multiple worksheets with Excel.

SESSION 8.1

In this session you will learn how to work with multiple worksheets, including inserting and moving worksheets. You'll learn how to work with groups of worksheets at the same time. Finally, you'll be introduced to 3-D cell references that allow you to summarize data from several worksheets.

Why Use Multiple Worksheets?

One of the most useful ways to organize information in your workbooks is to use multiple worksheets. Using multiple worksheets makes it easier for you to group your information. For example, a company with branches located in different regions could place sales information for each region on a separate worksheet. Users could then view regional sales information by clicking a sheet in the workbook, rather than scrolling through a large and complicated worksheet.

By using multiple worksheets, you can also more easily hide information that might not be of interest to all users. For example, if your director is only interested in the bottom line, the first worksheet could contain your conclusions and summary data, with more detailed information available on separate worksheets.

You can also use separate worksheets to organize your reports, because it is easier to print a single worksheet than it is to select and define a print area within a large worksheet and then print it.

Finally, if individual worksheets in a single workbook contain the same type of data and formatting (which is often true of documents like regional sales reports), Excel allows you to edit several worksheets simultaneously and to easily combine the results of several worksheets, saving you time.

Whenever you use multiple worksheets, it's important to plan the content and organization carefully.

Planning a Multiple-Sheet Workbook

Before creating a workbook with multiple worksheets, you should consider how you will organize the sheets to create a coherent and easy-to-use document. Proper organization is particularly important if other people will be using your workbook. One way of organizing your workbook is to create a Documentation sheet, data sheets, and a summary sheet.

As you know, a **Documentation sheet** describes the content, structure, and purpose of the workbook. Sometimes called a **Title sheet**, it is usually the first worksheet in a workbook. The Documentation sheet should include any information that you think would help other people who might use your workbook. It should list the source of the data, the assumptions you used in creating the workbook, and any conclusions you've derived from analyzing the workbook data. The Documentation sheet should enable anyone who opens your workbook to use it without additional assistance from you. Although the Excel File Properties dialog box and cell notes are useful tools for documenting worksheets, every well-designed workbook also should contain a Documentation sheet.

After the Documentation sheet, use a separate worksheet for each group you plan on including in the worksheet. These **data sheets** could contain data on different sales regions, departments, or areas of production. They can contain both data and charts.

Finally, if the information from each of the data sheets can be summarized, you should place this information in a **summary worksheet**. In the sales example, the summary worksheet could contain total sales figures for all the individual regions. You can place the summary sheet either at the start of the workbook after the Documentation sheet, or at the end. If you, or the people who will use the workbook, are more interested in the overall picture than in the details, place the summary worksheet at the beginning of the workbook. On the other hand, if you want your workbook to tell a "story" to the user, where the details are just as important as the final product, place the summary worksheet at the end of the workbook.

Professor White has sketched out the workbook structure she envisions, shown in Figure 8-1. The workbook will have a Documentation sheet that will include the TA's name, contact information, office hours, and class times for each of his or her sections. You'll place grades for each section on a separate worksheet. Because you know Professor White is as interested in the details as in the summary information, you'll place a summary of the discussion section grades on a summary sheet at the end of the workbook. Later on, you'll summarize the information on these summary sheets from each TA's workbook into a single workbook for Professor White to use.

Figure 8-1 PROPOSED STRUCTURE OF THE GRADING WORKBOOK EACH TA WILL USE

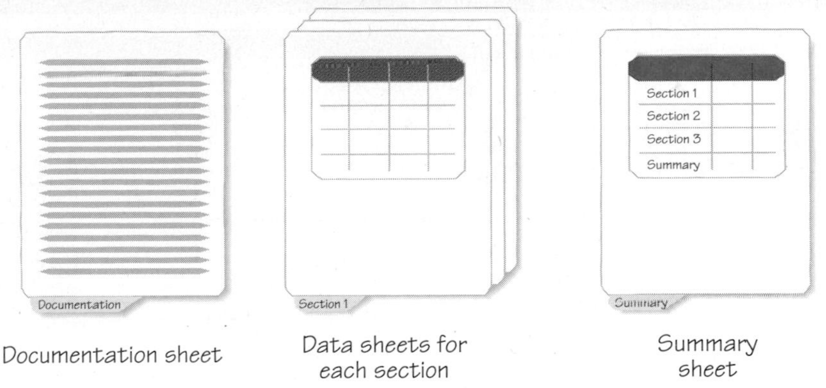

Inserting a Worksheet

To create Professor White's grading workbook, you begin by starting Excel, saving the new workbook, and creating a Documentation sheet and separate sheets for each of the sections. Because you are the author of this workbook and the person who will be responsible for maintaining it, you will also add your name and the date that the workbook was created.

REFERENCE WINDOW RW

Inserting A Worksheet

- Right-click the Sheet tab of a worksheet in the current workbook.
- Click Insert on the Shortcut menu.
- Click the Worksheet icon on the General tab of the Insert dialog box, and then click the OK button.

First you'll create a new workbook and practice adding a new sheet to that workbook.

To create the new workbook and insert a new worksheet:

1. Start Excel as usual, and make sure your Data Disk is in the appropriate drive.
2. Open a new workbook and save as **Grades** in the Tutorial folder in Tutorial.08 folder on your Data Disk.
3. Right-click the **Sheet1** sheet tab, and then click **Insert** on the Shortcut menu to open the Insert dialog box.

   You could also have modified one of the blank sheets, turning it into the Documentation sheet. This approach however gives you a chance to practice inserting new sheets into your workbook.
4. Click the **Worksheet** icon, as shown in Figure 8-2, and then click the **OK** button.

Figure 8-2 INSERT DIALOG BOX

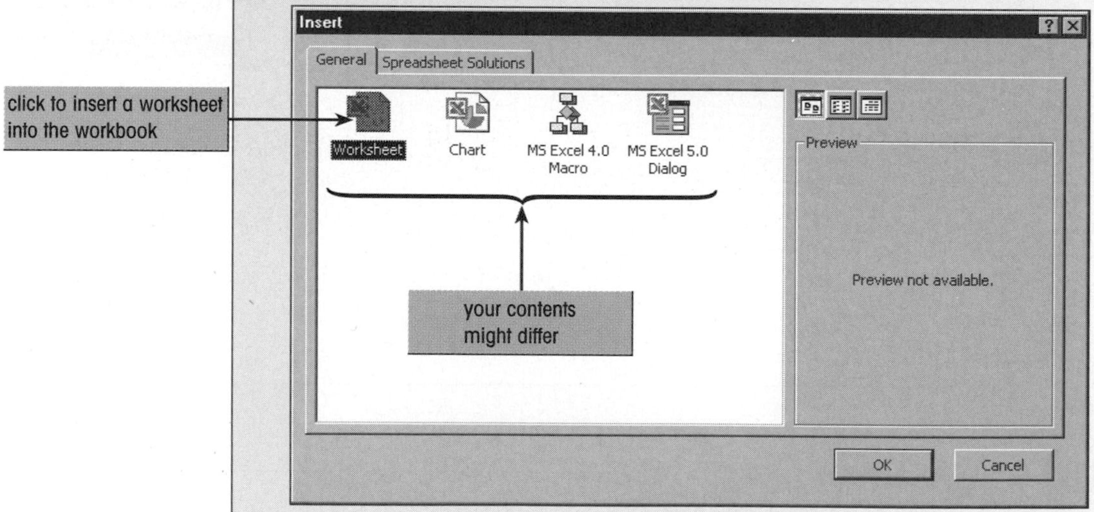

5. Double-click the new worksheet's sheet tab, type **Documentation**, and then press the **Enter** key.

Next, you'll enter Documentation sheet information.

To set up the Documentation sheet:

1. Enter the following titles in the Documentation worksheet:

Cell A1: **TA Name**
Cell A2: **Office**
Cell A3: **Phone #**
Cell A4: **Office Hours**
Cell A6: **Section 1**
Cell A7: **Section 2**
Cell A8: **Section 3**
Cell A10: **Purpose:**
Cell A13: **Workbook:**
Cell A14: **Created by:**
Cell A15: **Date Created:**
Cell B5: **Section Times**
Cell C5: **Location**

Now enter the purpose of the worksheet.

2. Click cell **B10**, type **To record the grades for Section 1 - Section 3** and then press the **Enter** key.

3. In cell B11, enter the following text: **discussion groups of Prof. White's Calculus 223 lecture**.

4. Type **Grades** in cell B13.

5. Enter [***Your Name***] and the date in cells B14 and B15, respectively.

6. Apply the boldface style to the ranges A1:A15 and B5:C5. Adjust the width of column A to make the column fit its content, resize columns B and C to 25 characters, and then press **Ctrl + Home** to return to cell A1. See Figure 8-3.

Figure 8-3 COMPLETED DOCUMENTATION SHEET

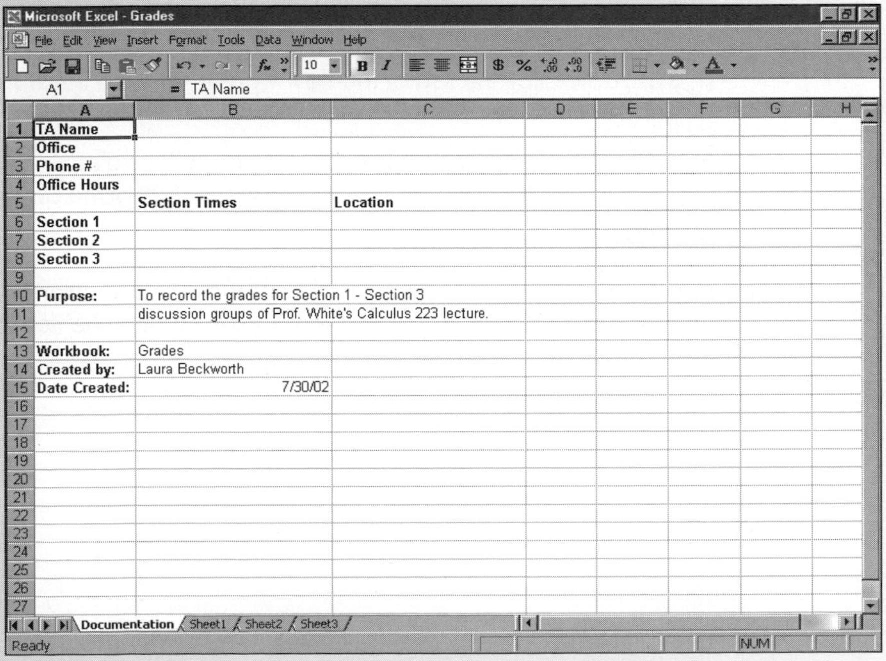

You'll leave the rest of the Documentation sheet to be completed by the TAs when they start using your workbook. Next you'll set up the individual grading sheets.

Moving Worksheets

Now that you have created a Documentation sheet, you'll create the grading sheet for each discussion section. Each of Professor White's four TAs teaches three discussion sections, so you'll be inserting three grading sheets into the workbook.

As you saw when you created the Documentation sheet, Excel places new worksheets directly to the left of the currently selected sheet. You want the Documentation sheet to be the first sheet in the workbook, so you'll have to move the new grading sheet directly to the right of the Documentation sheet. You can do this using drag and drop.

REFERENCE WINDOW RW

Moving or Copying A Worksheet

- Click the tab of the worksheet you want to move.
- Drag the sheet tab along the row of sheet tabs until the small arrow is in the desired location.
- Release the mouse button.
- To create a copy of the worksheet, hold down the Ctrl key as you drag the sheet tab to the desired location.

Try moving the first grading sheet now.

To insert and move the first grading sheet:

1. Right-click the **Documentation** sheet tab, and then click **Insert** on the Shortcut menu.
2. Make sure the Worksheet icon is selected, and then click the **OK** button.
3. Double-click the tab of the new worksheet, type **Section 1**, and then press the **Enter** key.
4. Click the **Section 1** tab, and then hold down the mouse button so that your pointer changes to , and drag it directly to the right of the Documentation sheet.
5. Release the mouse button.
6. Repeat the technique from Steps 1 through 5 to insert two additional worksheets named **Section 2** and **Section 3**, placed after the Section 1 worksheet. See Figure 8-4.

Figure 8-4 GRADES WORKBOOK WITH THREE GRADING SHEETS

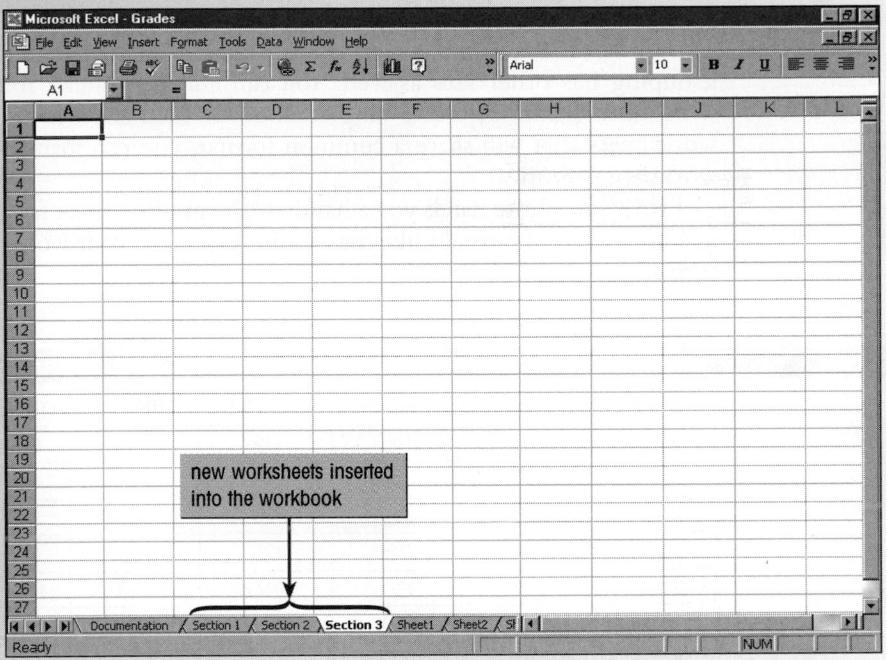

Your workbook now contains the Documentation sheet and the grading sheets you need. Next you'll remove the extra worksheets from the workbook, which you can do in one step by creating a worksheet group.

Working with Worksheet Groups

When you start the Excel program, it opens a new workbook with three blank worksheets (although your version of Excel might be set up to display a different number of worksheets). You don't need these additional sheets in Professor White's workbook, so you can delete them. You could delete the sheets one at a time, but it's more efficient to select the entire group of worksheets and delete them all at once.

To group and delete the worksheets:

1. Click the **Sheet1** sheet tab.
2. Press and hold down the **Shift** key and click the rightmost worksheet in the workbook (you might have to click the Last Worksheet button to see it.) All three sheet tabs become white, indicating that they are selected.
3. Right-click any one of the selected sheets, and then click **Delete** on the Shortcut menu.
4. Click the **OK** button to confirm the deletion. The blank worksheets are deleted from your workbook.

Your workbook is now set up according to Professor White's sketch. Next you'll add column titles to the Section 1 grading worksheet, which you can then copy to the other worksheets.

Copying Information Across Worksheets

The process you used to select multiple worksheets for deletion is called **grouping**. Grouping the blank worksheets in the Grading workbook made it easy to delete them, but grouping has other uses as well. You can enter formulas, format and copy values into a worksheet group, or create range names for each sheet in the group. If you have several worksheets that will share a common format, you can format them all at once by using a worksheet group.

Professor White hands you a handwritten grading sheet from a previous semester, shown in Figure 8-5. She would like the grading sheets in your workbook to have the same structure as this sheet.

Figure 8-5 PROFESSOR WHITE'S GRADING SHEET

Student ID	Homework 1	Homework 2	Homework 3	Homework 4	Exam 1	Exam 2	Final	Overall	Grade
1001	90	95	92	88	96	89	91	90	A
1002	81	88	85	70	88	72	80	81	B
1003	85	85	90	95	86	92	95	93	A
1004	81	78	65	75	80	72	76	75	BC
1005	99	65	100	99	100	100	95	95	A
1006	81	90	92	85	88	85	86	86	AB
1007	70	100	72	75	75	70	71	74	BC
1008	95	95	95	90	91	92	88	88	AB
1009	94	100	100	81	100	91	93	96	A
1010	100	95	81	96	96	84	89	88	AB
1011	100	100	100	100	100	100	98	98	A
1012	95	94	92	96	95	93	97	97	A
1013	100	100	92	96	100	91	94	98	A
1014	70	75	70	72	76	69	78	77	BC
1015	85	92	81	88	91	84	87	86	B
1016	81	68	75	60	81	65	71	70	C
1017	88	92	84	87	90	65	85	87	AB
1018	75	72	71	75	73	81	71	70	C
1019	92	81	84	85	87	65	87	86	B
1020	94	96	93	90	95	84	91	90	AB

Professor White scores homework and exams on a 100-point scale. She then calculates an overall average of each student's scores and assigns a letter grade based on the average. Professor White uses the traditional ABC grading system with grades of AB and BC assigned to intermediate grades. Because she gives the same assignments and tests for every section, you can create column titles for the Section 1 grading sheet and then copy them to the Section 2 and Section 3 worksheets.

To add column titles to the Section 1 worksheet:

1. Click the **Section 1** sheet tab.
2. Type **ID** in cell A1, and then press the **Tab** key.
3. Type **Home1** in cell B1, and then press the **Tab** key.

4. Continue entering the following column titles in the first row of the worksheet: **Home2**, **Home3**, **Home4**, **Exam1**, **Exam2**, and **Final**. See Figure 8-6.

Figure 8-6 COLUMN TITLES FOR THE SECTION 1 GRADING WORKSHEET

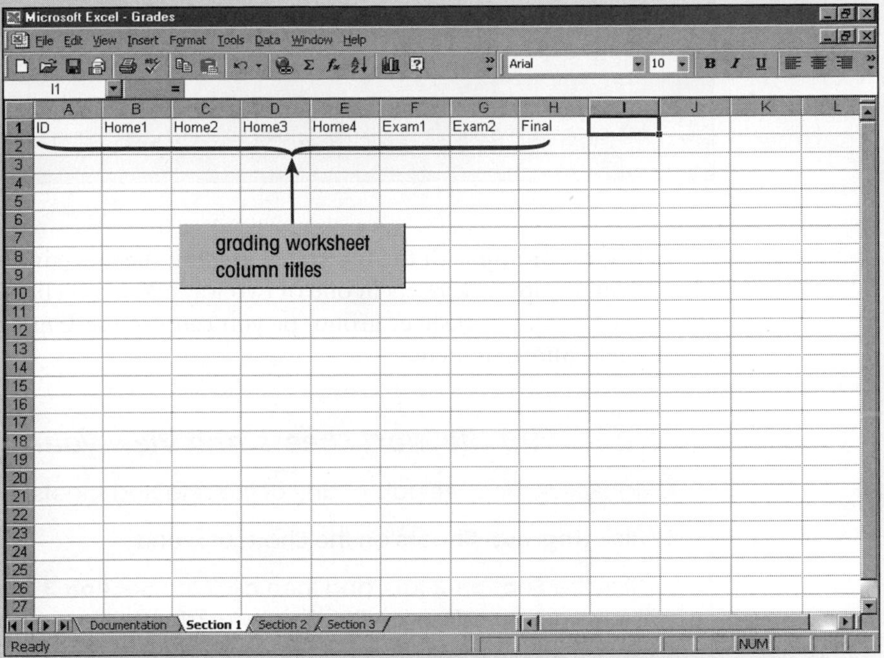

With the column titles in place, you'll group the worksheets and use the Excel Fill Across Worksheets command to copy the titles to the other two grading sheets.

To copy the Section 1 column titles:

1. Select the range **A1:H1**.
2. Press and hold down the **Shift** key and click the **Section 3** tab, and then release the **Shift** key.
3. Click **Edit** on the menu bar, point to **Fill**, and then click **Across Worksheets**.
4. Click the **All** option button, and then click the **OK** button.

The Fill Across Worksheets command only copies the cells that you've selected. When you use the Fill Across Worksheets command, you can copy the contents of the selected cells only, the formats, or both. In the preceding steps, you copied both the cell contents and formats.

REFERENCE WINDOW RW

Grouping And Ungrouping Worksheets

- Click the sheet tab of the first worksheet in the group, press and hold down the Shift key, and then click the sheet tab of the last sheet in the group.
- To select non-consecutive worksheets, press and hold down the Ctrl key, and then click the sheet tab of each worksheet you want to include.
- To ungroup worksheets, either click the sheet tab of a worksheet not in the group, or right-click the tab of one of the sheets in the group, and select Ungroup Sheets on the Shortcut menu.

To begin working with the individual grading sheets again, you must first ungroup them. You can ungroup worksheets in one of two ways: You can click a sheet in the workbook that is not part of the worksheet group, or you can use the Ungroup Sheets command on the worksheet's Shortcut menu.

To ungroup the worksheets and view your changes:

1. Right-click the sheet tab of any of the selected sheets.
2. Click **Ungroup Sheets** on the Shortcut menu.
3. Click the **Section 2** tab, and then click the **Section 3** tab. You can see that the titles you entered on the Section 1 worksheet are copied into both the Section 2 and Section 3 worksheets.

   With the basic structure of the grading sheets in place, your next task will be to enter formulas that summarize the students' test scores. This information is available in another workbook.
4. Click the **Documentation** sheet tab, and then press **Ctrl + Home** to return to cell A1.
5. Save and close the Grades workbook, leaving Excel running.

You're now ready to work with some sample data.

Entering Text and Formulas into a Worksheet Group

Professor White has given you the scores of former students in her class from a previous semester. This data has been placed in the Grades2 workbook. Open and view this workbook now.

To view Professor White's workbook of previous grades:

1. Open the **Grades2** workbook in the Tutorial folder for Tutorial.08 on your Data Disk and save the workbook as **Grades3**.
2. Enter **Grades3** in cell B13 of the Documentation sheet along with (***Your Name***) and the data in cells B14:B15.
3. Click the **Section 1** sheet tab. The Section 1 worksheet displays scores for all the homework assignments, exams, and the final exam for each of 20 students. See Figure 8-7.

Figure 8-7 SAMPLE STUDENT SCORES IN THE SECTION 1 WORKSHEET

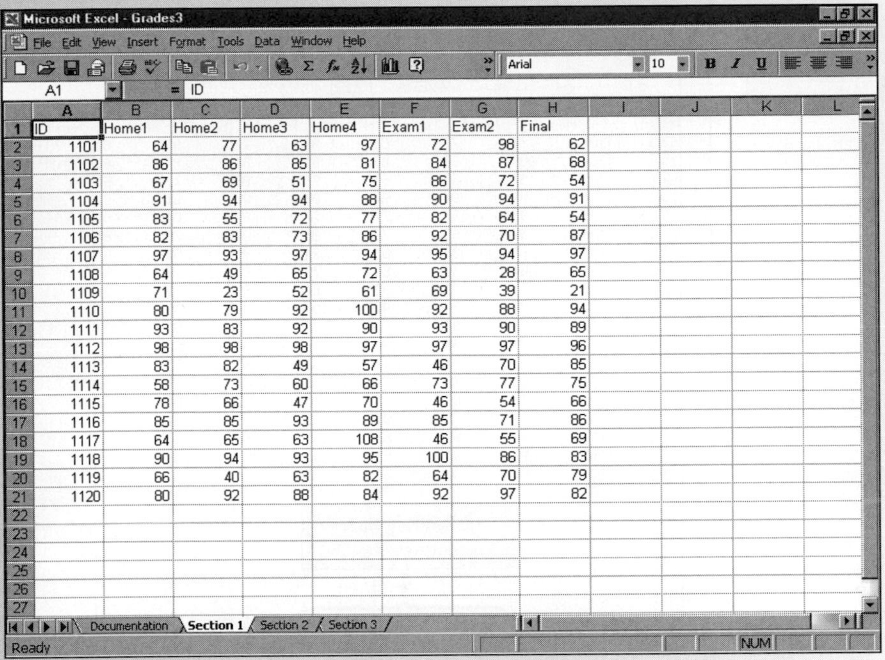

ID	Home1	Home2	Home3	Home4	Exam1	Exam2	Final
1101	64	77	63	97	72	98	62
1102	86	86	85	81	84	87	68
1103	67	69	51	75	86	72	54
1104	91	94	94	88	90	94	91
1105	83	55	72	77	82	64	54
1106	82	83	73	86	92	70	87
1107	97	93	97	94	95	94	97
1108	64	49	65	72	63	28	65
1109	71	23	52	61	69	39	21
1110	80	79	92	100	92	88	94
1111	93	83	92	90	93	90	89
1112	98	98	98	97	97	97	96
1113	83	82	49	57	46	70	85
1114	58	73	60	66	73	77	75
1115	78	66	47	70	46	54	66
1116	85	85	93	89	85	71	86
1117	64	65	63	108	46	55	69
1118	90	94	93	95	100	86	83
1119	66	40	63	82	64	70	79
1120	80	92	88	84	92	97	82

4. Look at the Section 2 and Section 3 worksheets, and verify that they also contain sample scores, and then return to the Section 1 worksheet.

As you look over the grading sheets, you realize that you still have to create a column for each student's overall score. In Professor White's grading system, the average homework grade is worth 20%, the average of the two midterm exams is worth 40%, and the final exam counts for 40% of the final grade. To create this column for all three grading sheets, you could add a column to the Section 1 grading sheet that calculates this weighted average and then use the Fill Across Worksheets command to transfer the formula to the remaining sheets. Another option, which will save you a step, is to group the three grading sheets together and enter the formula simultaneously in all three sheets. You'll try this method now.

To add the weighted average to all grading sheets:

1. With the Section 1 tab still selected, press and hold down the **Shift** key and click the **Section 3** tab to group the worksheets. Notice that the word "(Group)" appears in the title bar, indicating that a group is selected.
2. Click cell **I1**, type **Overall**, and then press the **Enter** key. Now you'll enter the formula for the weighted averages.
3. In cell I2, type **=20%*AVERAGE(B2:E2)+40%*AVERAGE(F2:G2)+40%*H2** and then press the **Enter** key. The first student's average score of 73.85 appears in cell I2, this being the sum of the weighted averages of the student's grades (20%), midterm exams (40%), and final exam (40%.) Now you'll copy the formula to calculate the averages for the rest of the students.
4. Click cell **I2** and then click and drag the fill handle down to cell **I21**.

The weighted average scores for the Section 1 worksheet are shown in Figure 8-8.

Figure 8-8 **WEIGHTED AVERAGES FOR SAMPLE STUDENT SCORES IN SECTION 1**

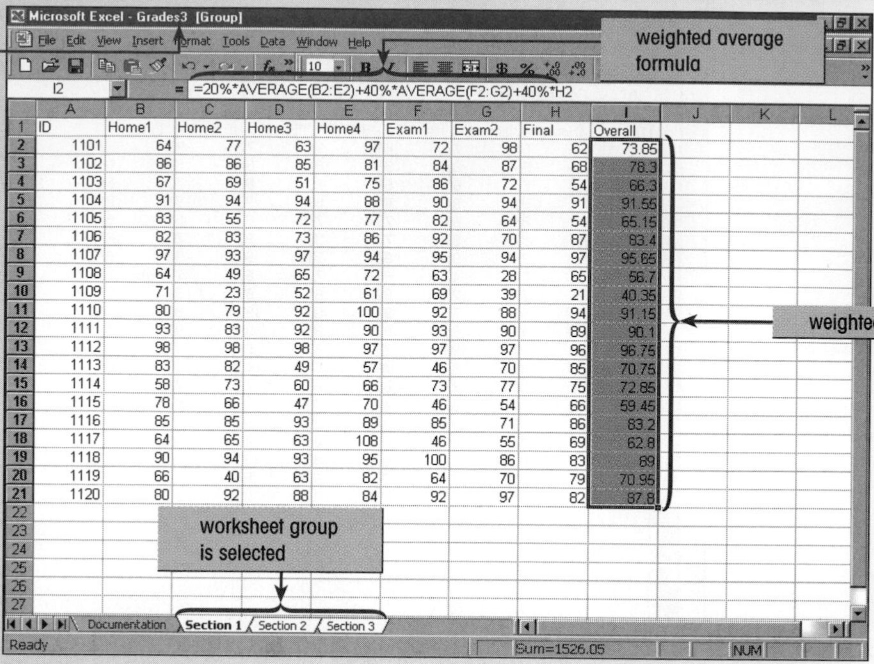

ID	Home1	Home2	Home3	Home4	Exam1	Exam2	Final	Overall
1101	64	77	63	97	72	98	62	73.85
1102	86	86	85	81	84	87	68	78.3
1103	67	69	51	75	86	72	54	66.3
1104	91	94	94	88	90	94	91	91.55
1105	83	55	72	77	82	64	54	65.15
1106	82	83	73	86	92	70	87	83.4
1107	97	93	97	94	95	94	97	95.65
1108	64	49	65	72	63	28	65	56.7
1109	71	23	52	61	69	39	21	40.35
1110	80	79	92	100	92	88	94	91.15
1111	93	83	92	90	93	90	89	90.1
1112	98	98	98	97	97	97	96	96.75
1113	83	82	49	57	46	70	85	70.75
1114	58	73	60	66	73	77	75	72.85
1115	78	66	47	70	46	54	66	59.45
1116	85	85	93	89	85	71	86	83.2
1117	64	65	63	108	46	55	69	62.8
1118	90	94	93	95	100	86	83	89
1119	66	40	63	82	64	70	79	70.95
1120	80	92	88	84	92	97	82	87.8

Because you have grouped the worksheets, the formulas you entered in the Section 1 worksheet should also have been entered in the corresponding cells on the other worksheets in the group.

5. Click the **Section 2** sheet tab. The worksheet displays the new column of weighted averages shown in Figure 8-9.

Figure 8-9 **WEIGHTED AVERAGES FOR SAMPLE STUDENT SCORES IN SECTION 2**

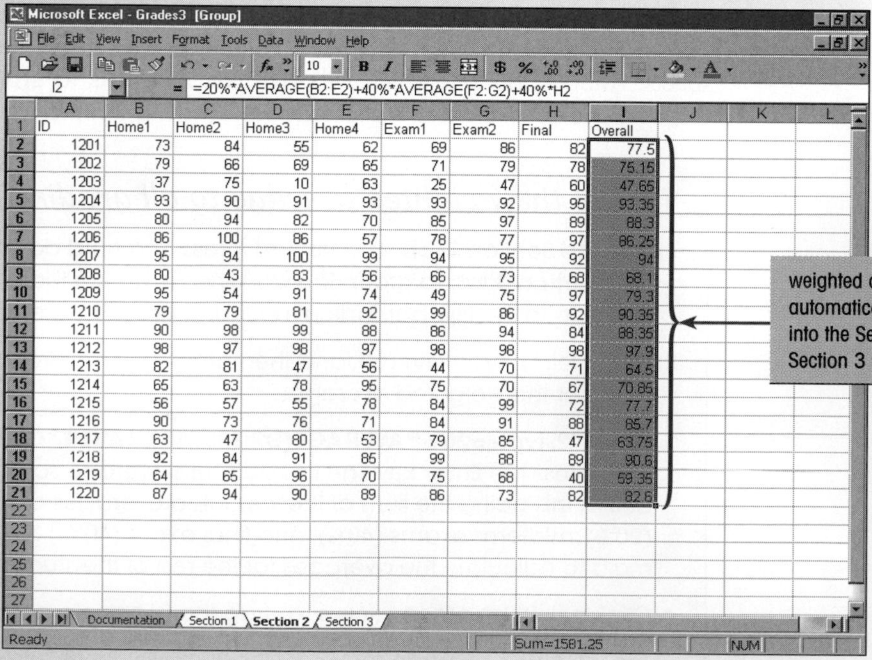

ID	Home1	Home2	Home3	Home4	Exam1	Exam2	Final	Overall
1201	73	84	55	62	69	86	82	77.5
1202	79	66	69	65	71	79	78	75.15
1203	37	75	10	63	25	47	60	47.65
1204	93	90	91	93	93	92	95	93.35
1205	80	94	82	70	85	97	89	88.3
1206	86	100	86	57	78	77	97	86.25
1207	95	94	100	99	94	95	92	94
1208	80	43	83	56	66	73	68	68.1
1209	95	54	91	74	49	75	97	79.3
1210	79	79	81	92	99	86	92	90.35
1211	90	98	99	88	86	94	84	88.35
1212	98	97	98	97	98	98	98	97.9
1213	82	81	47	56	44	70	71	64.5
1214	65	63	78	95	75	70	67	70.85
1215	56	57	55	78	84	99	72	77.7
1216	90	73	76	71	84	91	88	85.7
1217	63	47	80	53	79	85	47	63.75
1218	92	84	91	85	99	88	89	90.6
1219	64	65	96	70	75	68	40	59.35
1220	87	94	90	89	86	73	82	82.6

6. View the sample scores for the Section 3 worksheet, and then return to the Section 1 worksheet, leaving the sheets grouped.

Although Professor White's grading sheet from last semester included only the individual scores for each test and the weighted average for each student, it would probably be helpful for her and her TAs to see the section average for each homework assignment and exam. Then they could quickly see how the whole section scored on an exam or homework assignment. To create section averages, you will add an additional row to each grading sheet that averages the scores entered into the columns.

To insert a formula calculating homework and exam averages:

1. Click cell A22, type **Average**, and then press the **Tab** key.
2. In cell B22, type **=AVERAGE(B2:B21)** and then press the **Tab** key. The value 79 appears in cell B22.
3. Click cell **B22** and then drag the fill handle to cell **I22**.

   Figure 8-10 displays the Section 1 averages for homework assignments and exams.

Figure 8-10 **SECTION 1 AVERAGES FOR HOMEWORK ASSIGNMENTS AND EXAMS**

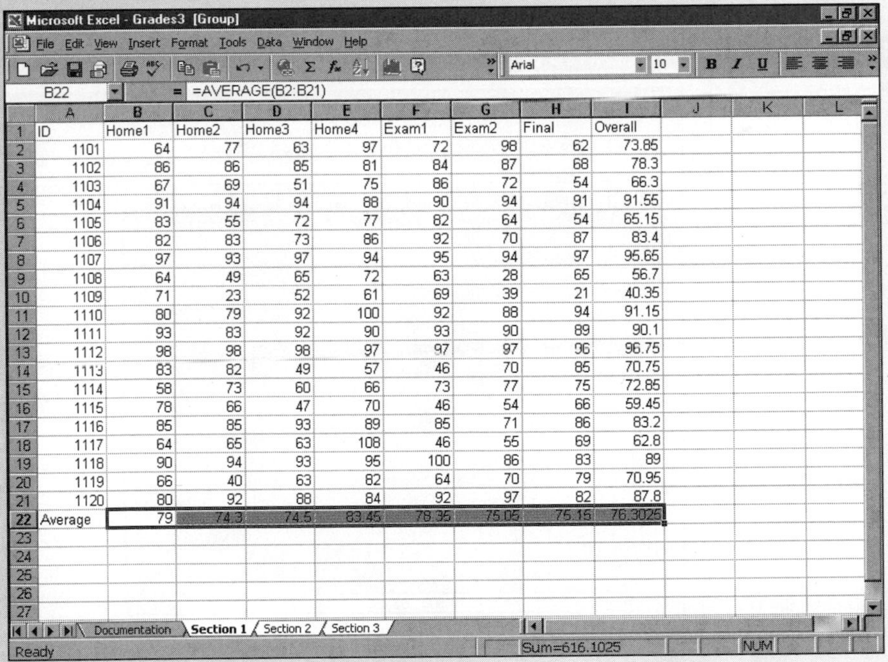

ID	Home1	Home2	Home3	Home4	Exam1	Exam2	Final	Overall
1101	64	77	63	97	72	98	62	73.85
1102	86	86	85	81	84	87	68	78.3
1103	67	69	51	75	86	72	54	66.3
1104	91	94	94	88	90	94	91	91.55
1105	83	55	72	77	82	64	54	65.15
1106	82	83	73	86	92	70	87	83.4
1107	97	93	97	94	95	94	97	95.65
1108	64	49	65	72	63	28	65	56.7
1109	71	23	52	61	69	39	21	40.35
1110	80	79	92	100	92	88	94	91.15
1111	93	83	92	90	93	90	89	90.1
1112	98	98	98	97	97	97	96	96.75
1113	83	82	49	57	46	70	85	70.75
1114	58	73	60	66	73	77	75	72.85
1115	78	66	47	70	46	54	66	59.45
1116	85	85	93	89	85	71	86	83.2
1117	64	65	63	108	46	55	69	62.8
1118	90	94	93	95	100	86	83	89
1119	66	40	63	82	64	70	79	70.95
1120	80	92	88	84	92	97	82	87.8
Average	79	74.3	74.5	83.45	78.35	75.05	75.15	76.3025

Because the three grading sheets are still grouped together, the formulas in the Section 1 worksheet are also entered into the Section 2 and Section 3 worksheets.

Now that you have entered the formulas that will calculate the section averages Professor White and her TAs need, you'll format the worksheet to make it attractive and readable.

Formatting a Worksheet Group

You have used worksheet groups to insert formulas and text into more than one worksheet at once. You can also use groups to simultaneously format the appearance of multiple worksheets. You decide to format the test scores, and use one of the Excel built-in worksheet designs to format the column titles.

To format the column averages, totals, and scores:

1. Make sure the Section 1 worksheet is selected, and that the three section worksheets are still grouped.
2. Select the range **I2:I21**, and then click the **Increase Decimal** button on the Excel toolbar.
3. Select the range **B22:I22**, and then click three times.

   Now both the overall totals and averages appear to three decimal place accuracy. Next you'll format the appearance of the values.
4. Select the range **A1:I22**, click **Format** on the menu bar, and then click **AutoFormat**.
5. Click **Classic 3** from the Table format list, and then click the **OK** button.
6. Press **Ctrl + Home** to return to cell A1.
7. The worksheet is now formatted with the Classic 3 AutoFormat. See Figure 8-11.

Figure 8-11 FORMATTED SECTION 1 WORKSHEET

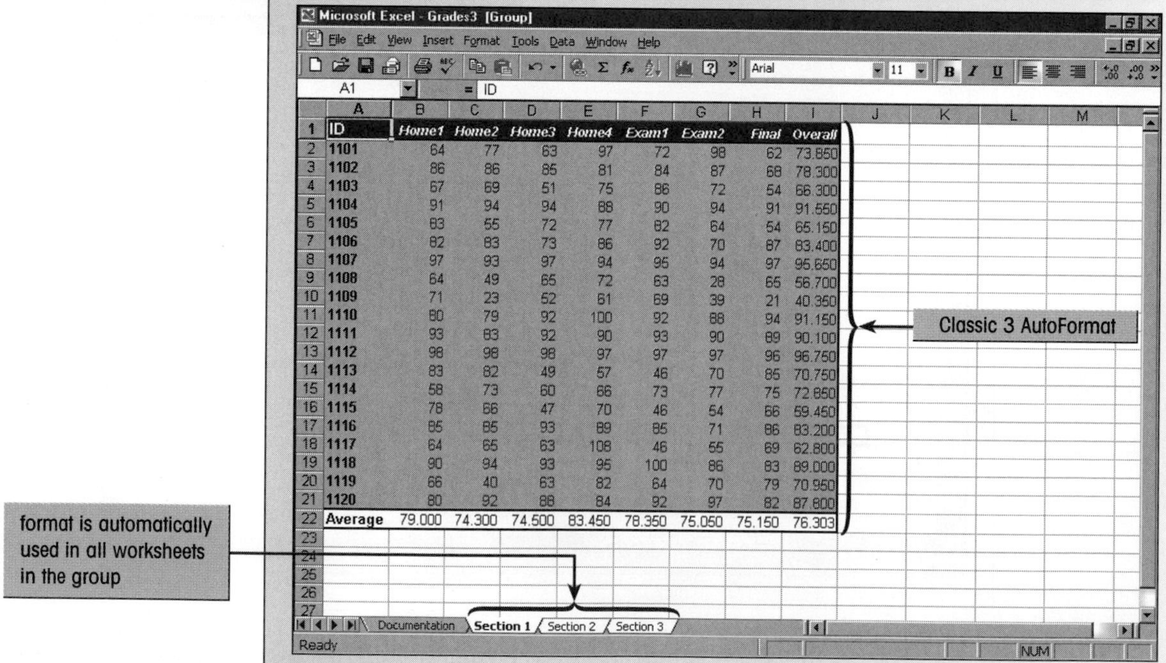

	A	B	C	D	E	F	G	H	I
1	ID	Home1	Home2	Home3	Home4	Exam1	Exam2	Final	Overall
2	1101	64	77	63	97	72	98	62	73.850
3	1102	86	86	85	81	84	87	68	78.300
4	1103	67	69	51	75	86	72	54	66.300
5	1104	91	94	94	88	90	94	91	91.550
6	1105	83	55	72	77	82	64	54	65.150
7	1106	82	83	73	86	92	70	87	83.400
8	1107	97	93	97	94	95	94	97	95.650
9	1108	64	49	65	72	63	28	65	56.700
10	1109	71	23	52	61	69	39	21	40.350
11	1110	80	79	92	100	92	88	94	91.150
12	1111	93	83	92	90	93	90	89	90.100
13	1112	98	98	98	97	97	97	96	96.750
14	1113	83	82	49	57	46	70	85	70.750
15	1114	58	73	60	66	73	77	75	72.850
16	1115	78	66	47	70	46	54	66	59.450
17	1116	85	85	93	89	85	71	86	83.200
18	1117	64	65	63	108	46	55	69	62.800
19	1118	90	94	93	95	100	86	83	89.000
20	1119	66	40	63	82	64	70	79	70.950
21	1120	80	92	88	84	92	97	82	87.800
22	Average	79.000	74.300	74.500	83.450	78.350	75.050	75.150	76.303

8. View the Section 2 and Section 3 worksheets to verify that the format has been applied to all three sheets, then click the **Section 1** sheet tab.
9. Right-click the **Section 1** tab, and then click **Ungroup Sheets** on the Shortcut menu to ungroup the worksheets.

Creating a Summary Worksheet

Now that you have used sample scores in your workbook to calculate student and section averages and formatted the worksheets, you'll summarize the data from the three sections into a single worksheet. Using the summary worksheet, the TAs can get a quick comparison of the different sections.

First, you'll create the summary worksheet, then you can use the techniques you've learned so far to copy the format of the grading sheets into the new summary worksheet.

To create and format the summary sheet:

1. Insert a blank worksheet at the end of the workbook named **Summary**.
2. Group together the Section 3 and Summary worksheets.

   TROUBLE? If you have not ungrouped the Section 1 - Section 3 sheets, you should do so now.

3. Select the cell range **A1:I22** on the Section 3 worksheet.
4. Click **Edit** on the menu bar, point to **Fill**, and then click **Across Worksheets**.

   The Fill Across Worksheets dialog box opens, asking if you want to fill the contents, formats, or both.

5. Click the **Formats** option button, and then click the **OK** button.

   Now, you'll copy the column titles to the Summary worksheet.

6. Select the cell range **A1:I1**, click **Edit** on the menu bar, point to **Fill**, and then click **Across Worksheets**.
7. Click the **Contents** option button, and then click the **OK** button.

The grading sheet that you used to create the Summary sheet contains information for 20 students. Because the Summary sheet will summarize the results from only three sections, you'll have to remove the unnecessary rows from the table.

To complete the Summary worksheet:

1. Ungroup the worksheets and then select the Summary sheet.
2. Select the cell range **A5:I21**, click **Edit** on the menu bar, and then click **Delete**.
3. Click the **Shift cells up** option button, and then click the **OK** button.
4. Click cell **A1**, type **Section**, and then press the **Enter** key.
5. Enter the following in column A:

   Cell A2: **1**
   Cell A3: **2**
   Cell A4: **3**
   Cell A5: **All**

6. Press **Ctrl + Home** to return to cell A1.

   Figure 8-12 shows the final layout of the Summary sheet.

Figure 8-12 SUMMARY WORKSHEET

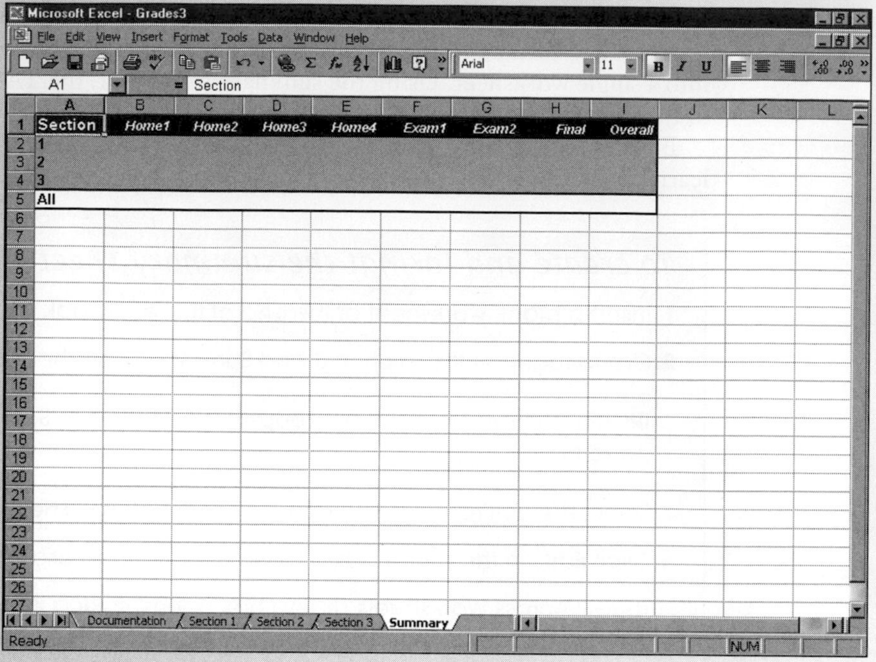

Having set up the Summary sheet, you are ready to start consolidating the information from the individual sections.

Consolidating Data with 3-D References

When you consolidate worksheet data, you use formulas that summarize the results contained in several worksheets (or workbooks) into a single cell. For example, consolidation formulas can total sales figures from several regional sales worksheets, or simply report the values from several regions, in one easy-to-read table. In your grading workbook, you want the Summary worksheet to consolidate grading information from the individual sections, showing the section averages for each homework assignment and exam. You'll then use this information to calculate an overall average, pooling information from all the sections that the TA is teaching. Figure 8-13 shows a diagram of the consolidation you'll be creating.

Figure 8-13 CONSOLIDATING THE SECTION WORKSHEETS

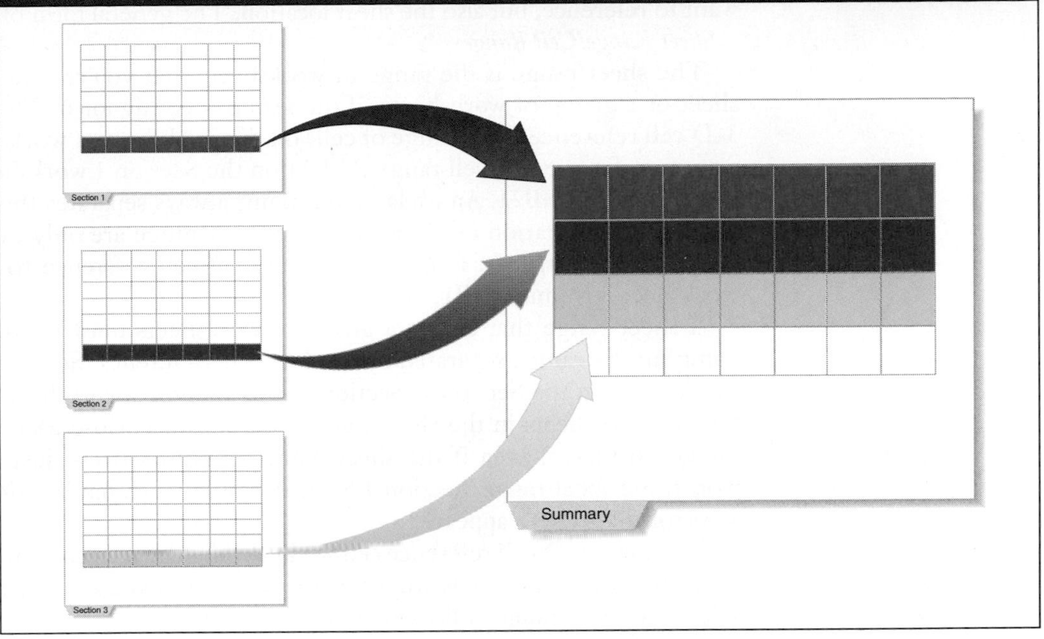

To consolidate data in a workbook, you need to know some of the basic rules for referencing cells in other worksheets. Cell references that specify cells in other worksheets are called 3-D cell references. As shown in Figure 8-14, you can consider the rows and columns as representing two dimensions. The worksheets themselves comprise the third dimension.

Figure 8-14 THE THREE DIMENSIONS OF A WORKBOOK

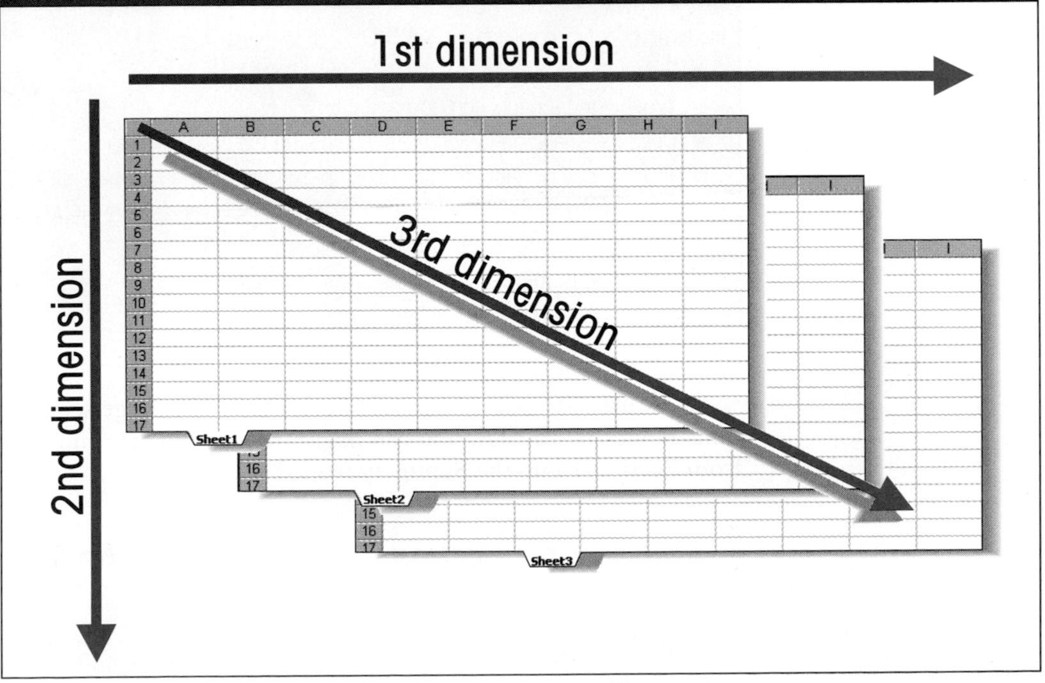

A 3-D cell reference must include not only the rows and columns that contain the data you want to reference, but also the sheet location. The general form of a 3-D cell reference is:

Sheet Range!Cell Range

The sheet range is the range of worksheets that you're referencing. It can be a single sheet or a group of worksheets (if the group is contiguous). The cell range portion of the 3-D cell reference is the range of cells on the worksheet or worksheets. For example, if you want to reference the cell range B2:B21 on the Section 1 worksheet, the 3-D cell reference is 'Section 1'!B2:B21. An exclamation point always separates the sheet range from the cell range. The quotation marks around the sheet range are only necessary if the sheet name contains blank spaces. For example, the 3-D cell reference to cell B1 on the Summary worksheet is Summary!B1, not 'Summary'!B1.

A sheet range that covers a group of worksheets must include the first and last sheet names in the range, separated by a colon. The reference 'Section 1:Section 3'!A1, refers to the A1 cells in the Section 1, Section 2, and Section 3 worksheets. When you are including several worksheets in the sheet range, you do not enclose each worksheet name in single quotation marks, even if the sheet name contains spaces—just the sheet range. In other words, the sheet range 'Section 1:Section 3' is correct, but 'Section 1':'Section 3' will cause an error message to appear.

You enter 3-D cell references either by typing the reference or by selecting the appropriate cells with the mouse as you enter the formula. If you are using the mouse, you must first select the sheet range, followed by the cell range.

A note of caution: Calculations or charts based on data on a worksheet might become inaccurate if you move the worksheet. Similarly, if you move a new worksheet into the middle of a sheet range referred to elsewhere by a 3-D formula reference, the data on the new worksheet might be included in the calculation. It's generally a good idea NOT to move worksheets around in your workbook if they contain 3-D cell references.

REFERENCE WINDOW RW

Inserting A Formula Using A 3-D Cell Reference

- Select the cell where you want the formula to appear.
- Type = and the function name, if any.
- Click the sheet tab for the sheet containing the cell (or cells) that you want to reference.
- To reference a range of worksheets, press and hold down the Shift key, and then click the tab of the last sheet in the range.
- Click the cell range you want to reference.
- Finish the formula and then press the Enter key.

You'll use 3-D cell references to calculate the average scores from each of the three sections taught by the TA. You can begin by consolidating the exam and homework averages from Section 1 into the Summary worksheet.

To insert the Section 1 averages into the Summary worksheet:

1. Click cell **B2** on the Summary worksheet.
2. Type =

3. Click the **Section 1** sheet tab (you might have to scroll through the sheet tabs to see it.)

4. Click cell **B22** and then press the **Enter** key.

The value 79 appears in the Summary sheet in cell B2. Now go back and view the formula.

5. Click cell **B2** and see that the formula ='Section 1'!B22 appears in the formula bar. Now that you know the formula is correct, you'll copy it to the other summary cells for Section 1.

6. Drag the fill handle from cell B2 to cell **I2** and release the mouse button.

Each exam and homework average score for Section 1 now appears in the range B2:I2. See Figure 8-15.

Figure 8-15 SUMMARY SCORES FOR SECTION 1

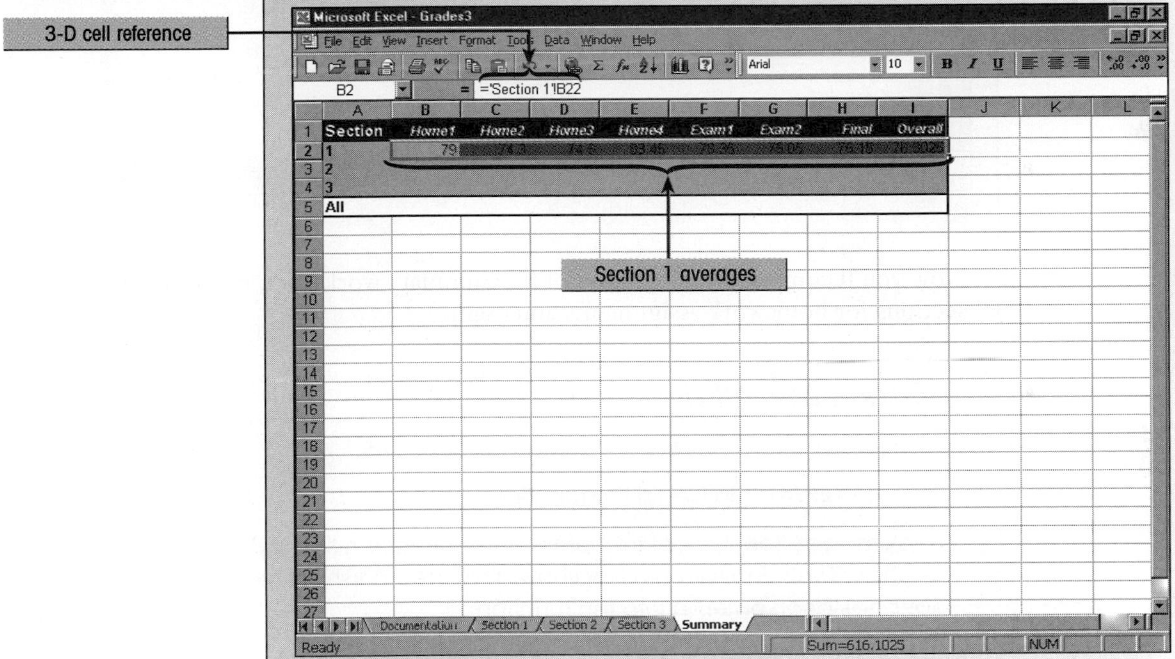

7. Repeat this technique to create references to the exam and homework averages in the range B3:I3 for Section 2 and in the range B4:I4 for Section 3.

8. Figure 8-16 shows the Summary sheet with average scores from each section.

Figure 8-16 **SUMMARY SCORES FOR ALL SECTIONS**

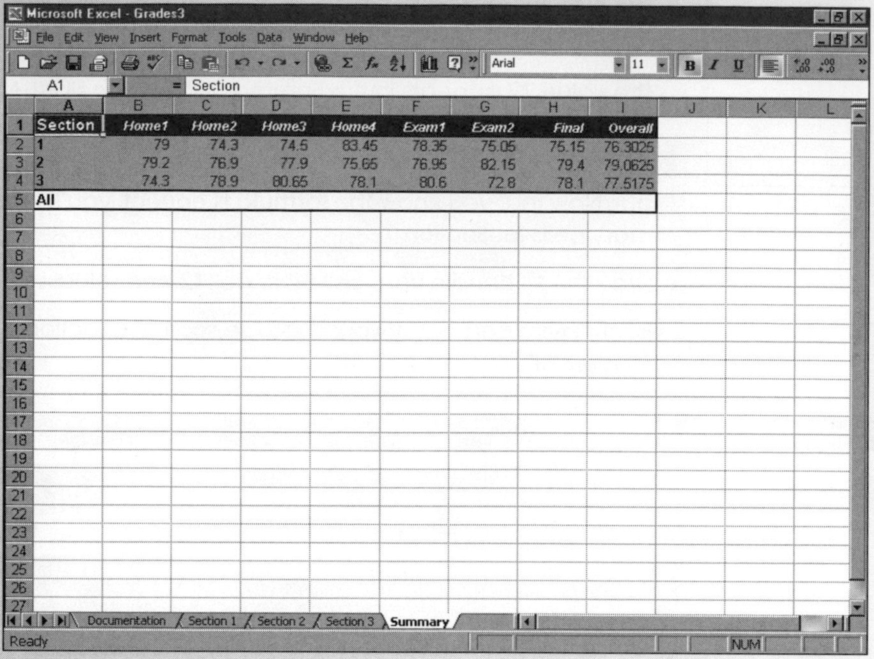

Now you'll complete the final part of the Summary worksheet, the average scores across all sections for homework assignments and exams.

To insert overall averages:

1. With the Summary sheet still selected, click cell **B5**.
2. Type **=AVERAGE(** to begin the function.
3. Click the **Section 1** sheet tab, press and hold down the **Shift** key and click the **Section 3** tab. The formula bar shows that the worksheet range for the three sections has been entered into the function.
4. Click cell **B22**, type **)** (a closing parenthesis), and then press the **Enter** key.

   Excel inserts the formula, "=AVERAGE('Section 1:Section 3'!B22)" into cell B5, displaying the value 77.500.
5. Click **B5** and drag the fill handle to cell **I5**. The overall averages for all tests for all sections appear in the All row.
6. Select the range **B2:I5** and then click the **Increase Decimal** button on the Formatting toolbar three times. All the numbers in the table should now appear with three decimal place accuracy.
7. Press **Ctrl + Home** to return to cell A1.

   Figure 8-17 shows the completed Summary sheet.

Figure 8-17 **COMPLETED SUMMARY WORKSHEET**

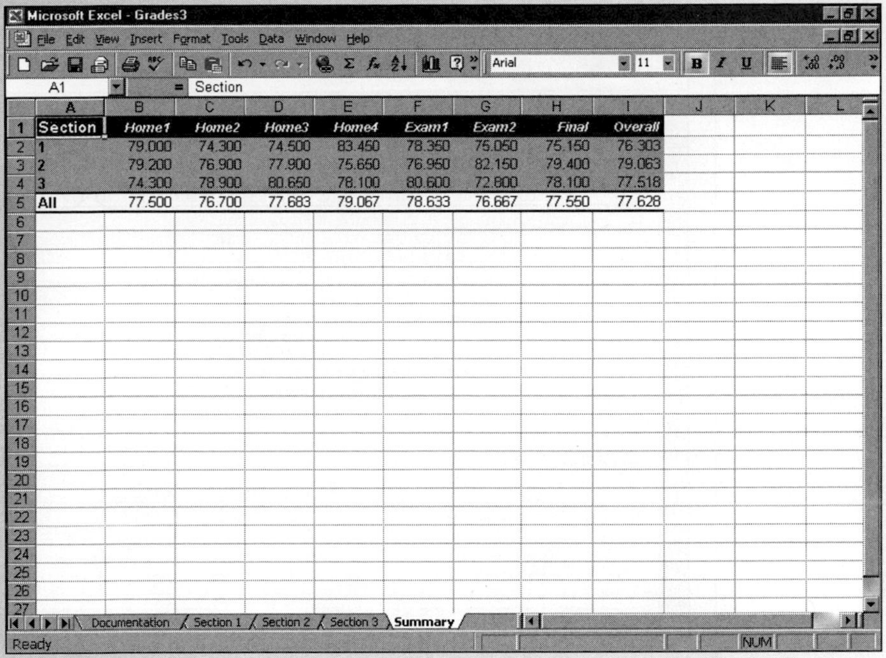

Section	Home1	Home2	Home3	Home4	Exam1	Exam2	Final	Overall
1	79.000	74.300	74.500	83.450	78.350	75.050	75.150	76.303
2	79.200	76.900	77.900	75.650	76.950	82.150	79.400	79.063
3	74.300	78.900	80.650	78.100	80.600	72.800	78.100	77.518
All	77.500	76.700	77.683	79.067	78.633	76.667	77.550	77.628

The summary table you've just created will be automatically updated whenever sample scores in the individual grading sheets are added or changed. To test this feature, you decide to change one of the sample scores in the Section 1 worksheet. First, notice that the current overall average for Section 1 is 76.303 and the average across all three sections is 77.628.

To change one of the values in the Section 1 worksheet:

1. Click the **Section 1** sheet tab.
2. Click cell **H2**, type **92**, and then press the **Enter** key.
3. Click the **Summary** sheet tab.

   Figure 8-18 shows the revised values in the Summary worksheet.

Figure 8-18 REVISED SUMMARY WORKSHEET

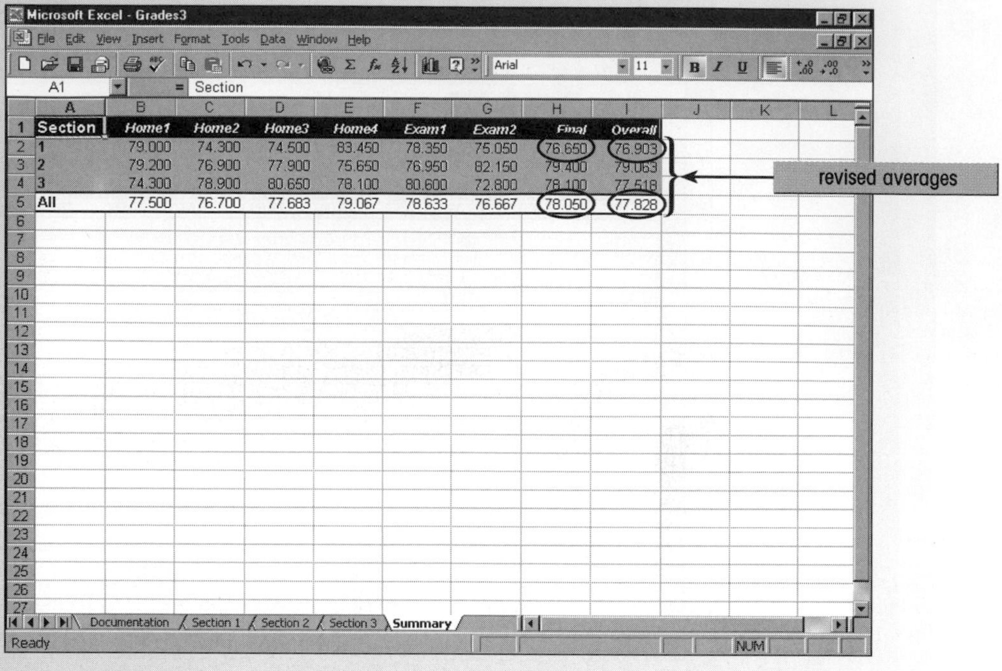

By changing the value of the score in cell H2 of the Section 1 worksheet from 62 to 92, the overall average for Section 1 is increased from 76.303 to 76.903 and the overall average for all sections is automatically increased from 77.628 to 77.828.

Now that you've completed your grading worksheets, you can print them using worksheet groups.

Printing Worksheet Groups

Now that you've completed the grading workbook, you decide to print it, but first you'll set up the pages. You can set up your pages individually, or you can quickly format all the worksheets by using the Page Setup command to apply to all the worksheets in the group. You decide to print the grading sheets and the Summary sheet centered on the page both vertically and horizontally, with the worksheet name in the page header and the workbook name in the page footer.

To print the grading sheets and the Summary sheet:

1. Group the range of worksheets from Section 1 to Summary.
2. Click **File** on the menu bar, and then click **Page Setup**.
3. Click the **Margins** tab and then select the **Center on page Horizontally** and **Vertically** check boxes.
4. Click the **Header/Footer** tab, click **Section 1** in the Header list box and then click **Grades3** in the Footer list box to place the worksheet name in the header and the workbook name in the footer for all the worksheets in the group.

TROUBLE? If Section 1 does not appear in your list box but Summary does, this just means you clicked the Summary tab first when you selected the range. Click Cancel, reselect the group, then reopen the dialog box and continue. If you see "Grades3.xls" instead of "Grades3" in the footer list box, use that instead.

5. Click the **Print Preview** button and verify that the same page setup has been used for all sheets in the worksheet group, using the Next and Previous buttons at the top of the Preview window to view each sheet. Figure 8-19 displays the Section 1 worksheet in Print Preview.

Figure 8-19 PRINT PREVIEW OF THE SECTION 1 WORKSHEET

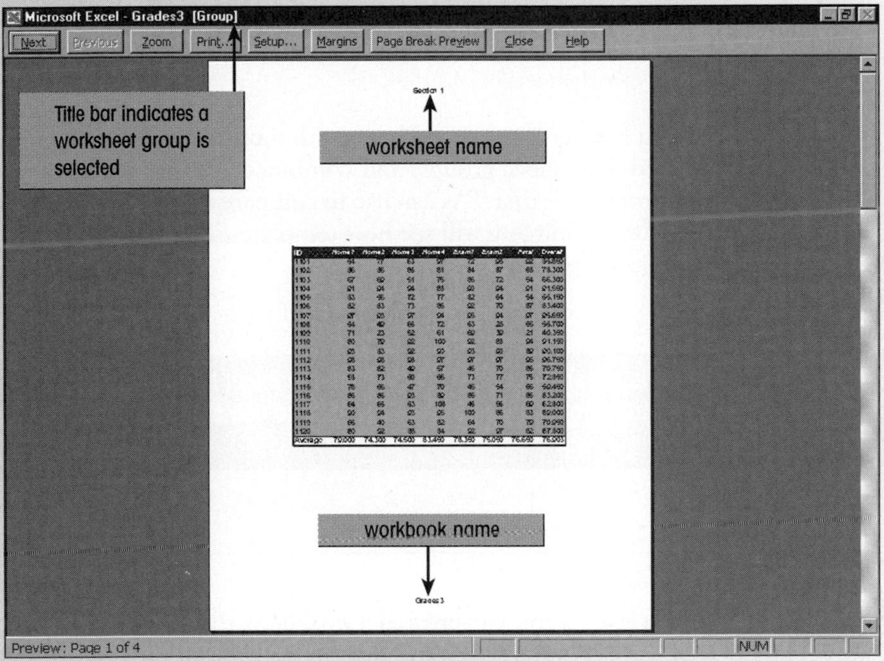

6. Click the **Print** button on the Print Preview toolbar, and then click the **OK** button to print the selected worksheets.
7. Click the **Documentation** tab so that the next time this worksheet is opened, the user sees the Documentation sheet.
8. Save and close the **Grades3** workbook.

Using a worksheet group has made it possible to format and print all the grading worksheets at the same time.

Session 8.1 QUICK CHECK

1. Explain how to insert a new worksheet directly to the right of the active sheet.
2. What is a worksheet group?
3. How do you select and deselect a worksheet group?
4. How do you copy text and formulas from one worksheet into a range of worksheets?
5. What are the two parts of a 3-D cell reference?
6. What is the 3-D cell reference to cells A1:A10 in the Section 1 worksheet?
7. What is the 3-D cell reference to cells A1:A10 in the Sheet1 through Sheet10 worksheets?

You have created a workbook with multiple worksheets, inserted and moved worksheets, created worksheet groups, and combined data from separate worksheets into a consolidation worksheet that TAs can use to compare the performance of their discussion sections. In the next session you will see how templates can help Professor White and the TAs share the workbook you have created.

SESSION 8.2

In this session you will create and use Excel templates. You'll learn how Excel organizes templates on your computer and how to use some of the built-in templates Excel provides.

Using Templates

In the last session you created a workbook that the TAs in Professor White's calculus lecture will use to maintain grading records for their discussion sections. But how should you make the new workbook available to them? One possibility is to simply give a copy of the workbook to each user. However, there is a potential problem with this approach: Once the file leaves your hands, you have no way of controlling the changes the TAs will make to it. You would like to have a single workbook file that will be available to them but that will always retain the format you created. One way of doing this is to create a template.

A **template** is an Excel document that contains specific content and formatting that you can use as a model for Excel workbooks. A template can include standardized text such as page headers and row and column labels, as well as formulas, macros, and customized menus and toolbars. When you open a template, Excel opens a blank workbook with content and formatting identical to the template. You then add data to the blank workbook and save it as an Excel file with any name you choose. The original template will retain its original design and formats for the next time you or another user need to create another workbook based on it. This is very useful if you want several users to maintain a workbook containing the same types of information. The original workbook design will always be available to them because they will only save files based on the template. The template itself will remain unchanged.

Excel has several templates that are automatically installed on your hard disk when you install the program. In fact, whenever you start Excel and see the blank workbook called Book1, you are actually using a workbook that's based on a template known as the **default template**. Excel also includes several specialized templates that you can use for specific tasks, such as creating an accounting ledger or sales worksheet.

Opening a Workbook Based on a Template

To see how templates work, you'll create a new workbook based on one of the built-in Excel templates.

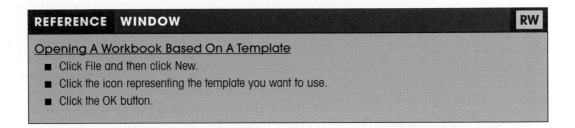

REFERENCE WINDOW RW

Opening A Workbook Based On A Template

- Click File and then click New.
- Click the icon representing the template you want to use.
- Click the OK button.

You'll open an Excel Invoice template, so you can get an idea of how the grading template you'll create for Professor White will look when the TAs open it.

To open a built-in template:

1. If you took a break at the end of the last session, make sure Excel is running.
2. Click **File** on the menu bar, and then click **New**. The New dialog box opens.

   TROUBLE? If a new, blank workbook opened instead of the New dialog box, you probably clicked the New button on the Standard toolbar. In order to open a template, you must use the New command from the File menu, not the New button on the toolbar.

3. Click the **Spreadsheet Solutions** tab.

   The tab displays icons representing templates, shown in Figure 8-20.

Figure 8-20 BUILT-IN TEMPLATES PROVIDED BY EXCEL

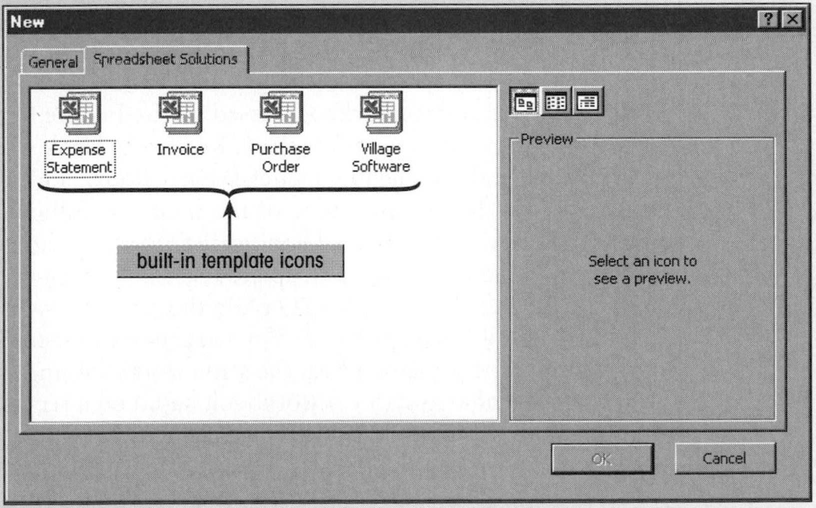

TROUBLE? Depending upon how Office 2000 or Excel 2000 was installed on your system, you might see different workbook templates. If you don't see the Invoice template, open any other template.

Next, you'll open a blank workbook based on the Invoice template.

4. Click the **Invoice** icon and then click the **OK** button.

TROUBLE? You may be asked to insert the Office 2000 CD to use this feature. If so, insert the CD if you have it, and follow the instructions to install the Invoice template. If the CD is not available or if you have other problems, talk to your instructor.

5. Click the **Enable Macros** option button to enable the macros that are included with the Invoice template.

Excel opens the workbook shown in Figure 8-21.

Figure 8-21 THE INVOICE TEMPLATE

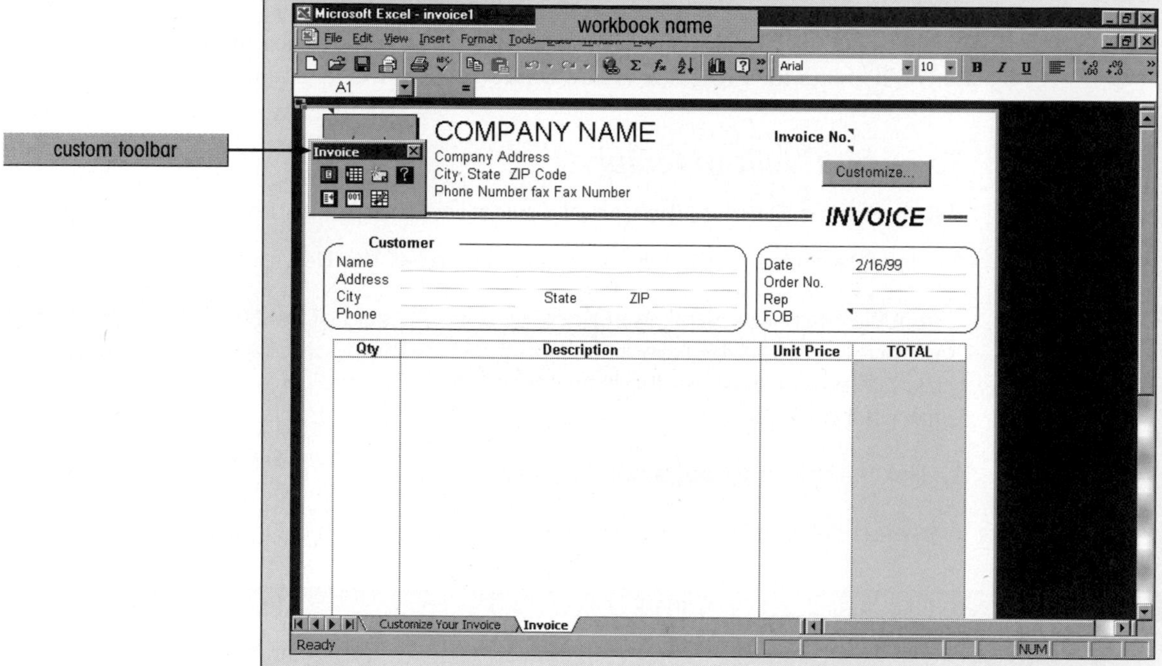

Figure 8-21 displays a workbook based on the Invoice template. Notice that the name in the title bar is not Invoice but Invoice1. Just as the blank workbooks you see when you first open Excel have the sequential names Book1, Book2 and so forth, a workbook based on a template always displays the name of the template, followed by a sequential number. Any additions you make to this workbook will only affect the new document you are creating and will not affect the Invoice template itself. However if you want to save your changes, you would save the Invoice1 workbook in the same way you save the Book1 workbook that you see when you first start Excel. The next time you create a new workbook based on this template, you'll be presented with the same workbook and workbook features.

Having seen how to create a workbook based on a template, you can close the Invoice1 workbook. You do not need to save your changes.

To close the Invoice1 workbook:

1. Click **File** on the menu bar, and then click **Close**.
2. Click the **No** button when prompted to save your changes.

Now that you've seen how to access a template, you can see how useful a template would be for Professor White's TAs. You can make your grading sheet into a template, make it available to the TAs, and they can create grading sheet documents based on your template. At regular intervals, they can submit their sheets to you or Professor White, who can easily consolidate the information because it will have the same structure and format on all the worksheets.

Next you'll learn how to save your workbook as a template and learn about storing templates in the correct folder, so it is available to those who need it.

Creating and Storing a Workbook Template

To create a template, you simply save an Excel workbook as a template file using the Save As command. Excel will then automatically convert the workbook to a template file. You decide to try this with the grading workbook you created in the last session.

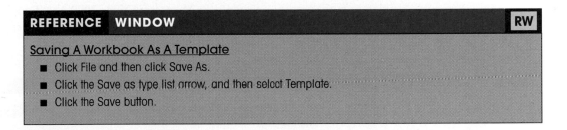

REFERENCE WINDOW RW

Saving A Workbook As A Template

- Click File and then click Save As.
- Click the Save as type list arrow, and then select Template.
- Click the Save button.

The Grades4 workbook in the Tutorial folder for Tutorial.08 on your Data Disk contains many of the same formulas and formats that you created in the last session. The main difference is that the sample data has been removed to allow teachers to enter fresh data. You'll open the Grades4 workbook and save it as a template file now.

To save the Grades4 workbook as a template file:

1. Open the **Grades4** workbook in the Tutorial folder for Tutorial.08 on your Data Disk. Notice that it has the same structure as the previous workbook. Now you'll save it as a template.
2. Click **File** on the menu bar, and then click **Save As** to open the Save As dialog box.
3. Type **Grading Sheet** in the File name text box, and then press the **Tab** key.
4. Click the **Save as type** list arrow, and click **Template** in the Save as Type list box.
5. In the Save in list box, locate the Tutorial folder for Tutorial.08 on your Data Disk.

   TROUBLE? When you select the Template file type, Excel automatically opens a folder named "Template." As you'll see, Excel is preset to put all template files in this folder. But because you might not have access to your computer network's Template folder, you should save the template file to your Data Disk.

6. Click the **Save** button. Excel saves the Grades4 workbook as a template file named "Grading Sheet" on your Data Disk.

7. Close the Grading Sheet template.

Once you've converted a workbook to a template, you have to make the template accessible to other users. To do this, you have to understand how Excel stores templates.

Using the Templates Folder

To use a template file like the one you just created, the template must be placed in the Templates folder that is in the Microsoft Office folder on your computer or network. You cannot create a workbook based on your template unless it's in the Templates folder. As you've seen, Excel will try to save any template files you create to that folder by default.

Depending on your computer environment, you might not be able to modify the contents of your Templates folder. If Excel and Microsoft Office are installed on a computer network, it may be that only a limited group of people has access to the folder. For that reason, the material that follows is provided for you to review, but you might not be able to perform the steps on your system. If you would like to work with the Templates folder yourself but are not sure if you have access to it, ask your instructor or the technical support person in your computer lab.

The exact location of the Templates folder depends on how Microsoft Office was installed on your computer. For example, in Microsoft Office 2000, the Templates folder is located in the C:\WINDOWS\Application Data\Microsoft\Templates folder. Figure 8-22 shows the location of the Templates folder as shown in Windows Explorer.

Figure 8-22 SAMPLE CONTENTS OF THE TEMPLATES FOLDER

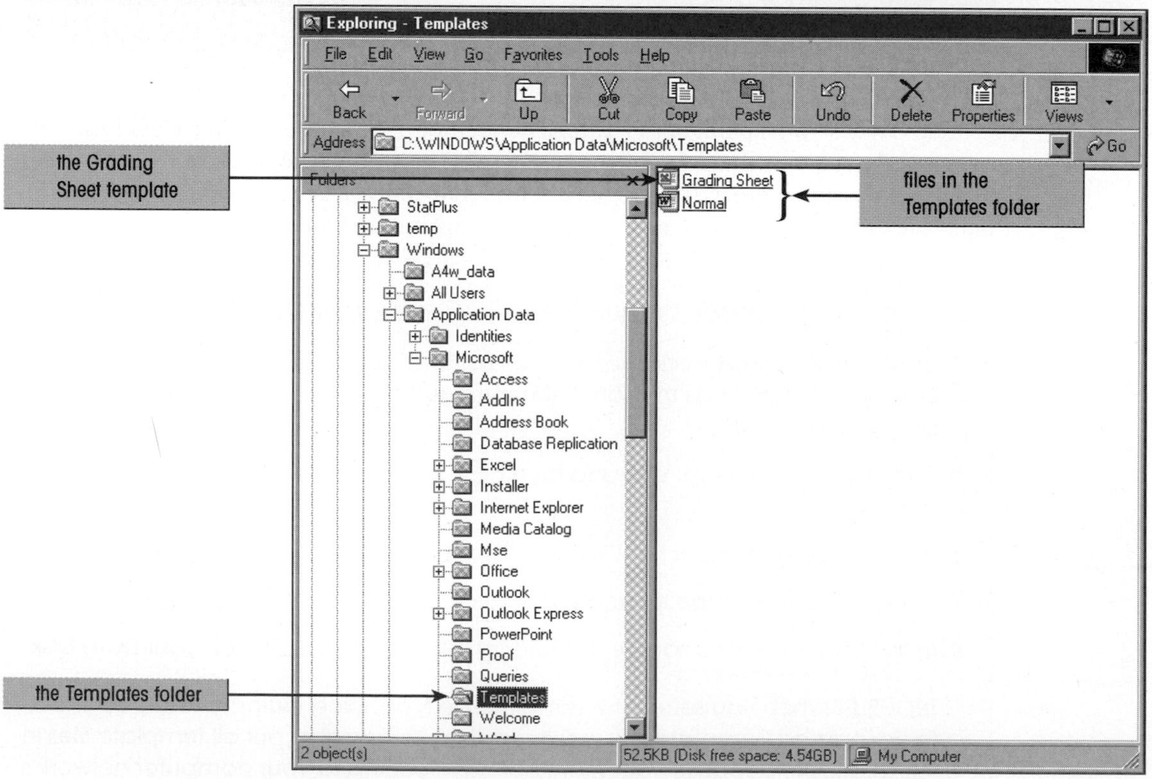

If you did have access to the Templates directory, the Grading Sheet template would be stored as shown in Figure 8-22. Excel workbooks are shown with a icon and Excel templates with a icon. Template files created in other Office 2000 applications (in this case, Word) appear in this folder as well.

When a template is placed in the Templates folder, its icon will appear on the General tab in the New dialog box. Figure 8-23 shows the Excel New dialog box that corresponds to the Templates folder from Figure 8-22. It displays your Grading Sheet template but not other Office 2000 template files because you are viewing it from within Excel.

Figure 8-23 NEW DIALOG BOX CONTAINING THE GRADING SHEET TEMPLATE

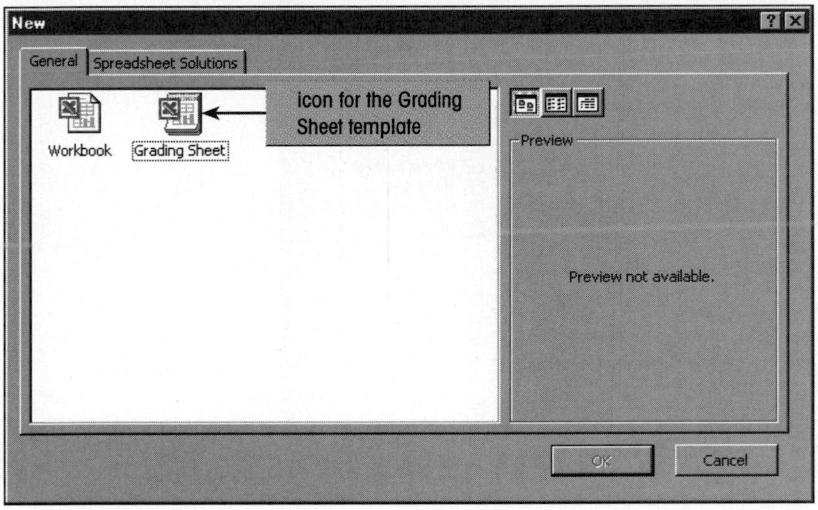

The Templates folder can include subfolders used to organize your different Office 2000 template files. The Templates folder shown in Figure 8-24 contains a single subfolder named "Classroom" into which the Grading sheet template has been placed.

Figure 8-24 CLASSROOM SUBFOLDER OF THE TEMPLATES FOLDER

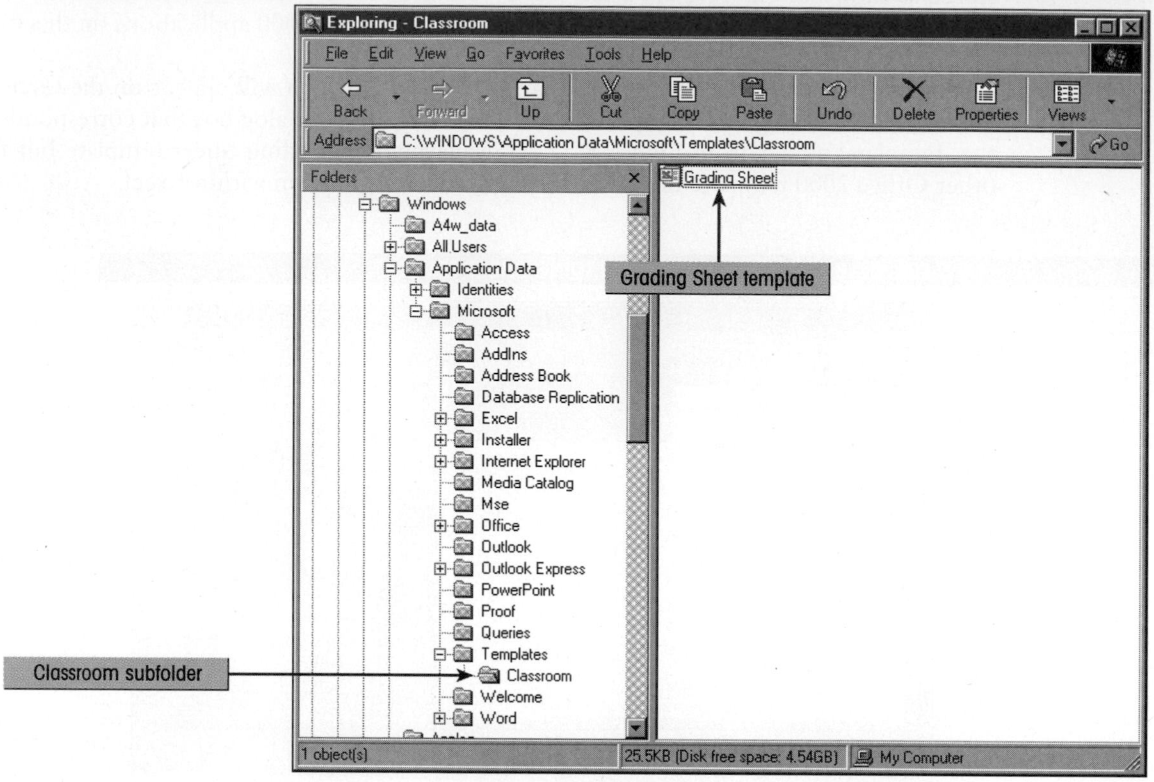

Subfolders containing Excel template files will then appear as dialog tabs in Excel's New dialog box. For example, the Classroom subfolder from Figure 8-24 appears as the Classroom dialog tab shown in Figure 8-25.

Figure 8-25 CLASSROOM TAB IN THE NEW DIALOG BOX

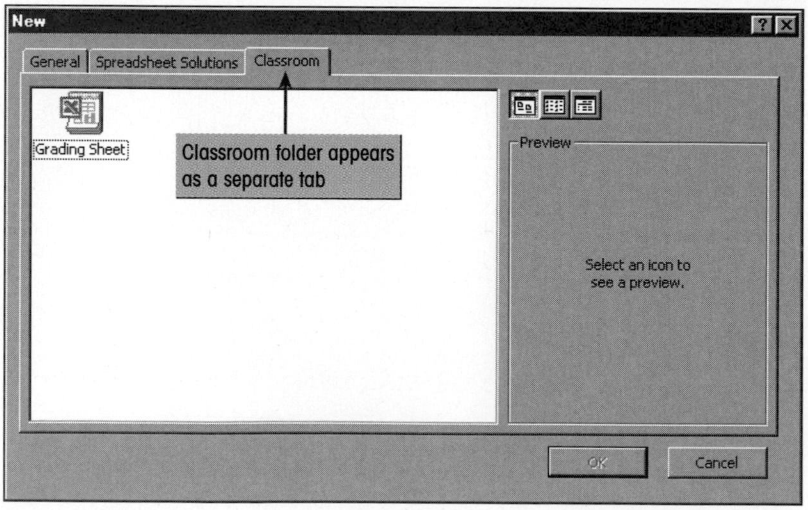

Because MidWest University has installed Office 2000 on the campus network, your Grading Sheet template would be readily available to Professor White's four TAs, as shown in Figure 8-26. If you decide to make changes to the template, you can place the updated template file on the network. The TAs could then easily create new workbooks based on your revised template.

Figure 8-26 ACCESSING THE GRADING SHEET TEMPLATE

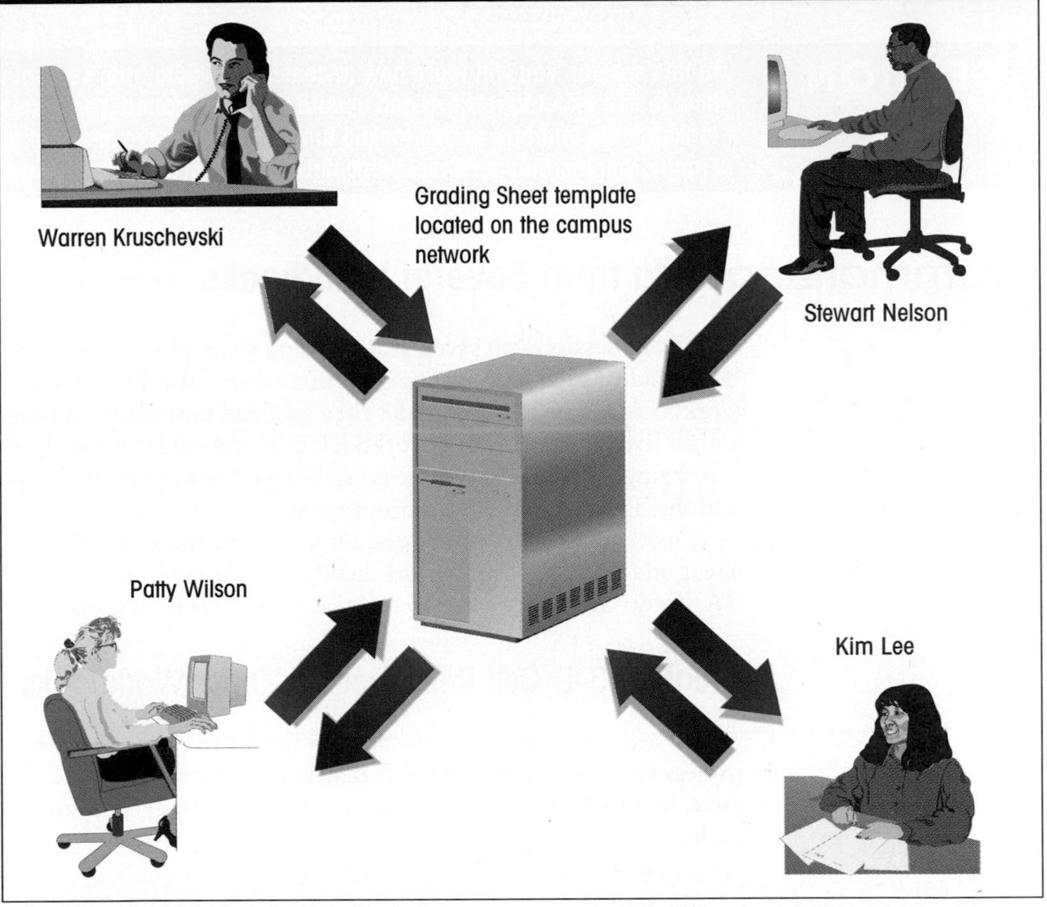

If your template was indeed placed on the university network, TAs would then use it to create their grading workbooks, which they would then turn in to you or Professor White. You'll use their workbooks created from your template to help you design the next version of the Grading Sheet workbook.

Session 8.2 Quick Check

1. What is a template?
2. What are two advantages of using a template instead of simply distributing a workbook file?
3. What is the default workbook template?
4. How do you save a file as a template?
5. Where must you store your templates?
6. How would you place a template into its own tab in the New dialog box?

You have created the grading workbook template and learned about the Template folder. In the next session you will learn how to consolidate information from the TAs' completed workbooks into a single workbook that Professor White will use to evaluate all the sections of her Calculus 223 course.

SESSION 8.3

In this session you will learn how to consolidate data from several workbooks. You'll learn how to use Excel to retrieve and update that information. You'll also learn how to create a lookup table and how to use lookup functions to retrieve information from the table. Finally, you'll create an Excel workspace file to access several workbooks at once.

Summarizing Data from Several Workbooks

In the last session you saved your grading sheet as a template. Since then, the template has been made available to Professor White's four TAs. They have used the template to create a workbook containing the grades they assigned to students in their sections. Professor White would like you to create a workbook that consolidates the data from the TAs' workbooks into a single file. She'll use the consolidated file to monitor the performance of the students and the TAs as the semester progresses.

A workbook has been created for you, with the name "White." It has a Documentation sheet and a consolidation worksheet in which you'll place the summary grades from each TA. To do this, you'll have to create a 3-D cell reference to each TA's workbook.

Creating 3-D Cell References to Other Workbooks

A 3-D cell reference to a workbook is similar to the 3-D cell references you created earlier in Session 8.1. The difference is that you'll include the name of the workbook in the reference, in addition to the name of a worksheet. The general form of a 3-D cell reference that includes the workbook is:

Location[*Workbook name*]*Sheet Range*!*Cell Range*

The location is the drive and folder that contains the workbook to which you are creating the reference. For example, assume you want to create a reference to the cell range B5:E5 on the "Summary Info" worksheet of the Sales.xls workbook, and the workbook is located in the Business folder on drive E of your computer. In this case, the 3-D cell reference is:

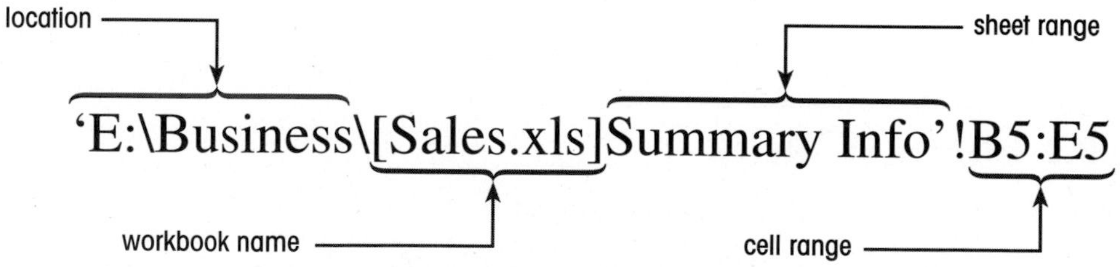

As you did earlier when you used sheet references with the sample data, you enclose the Location[Workbook name]Sheet Range portion of the 3-D cell reference in single quotation marks if there are any blank spaces in the location, workbook, or worksheet names. For example, 'E:\Business\[Sales.xls]Summary Info' needs quotation marks, but E:\Business\[Sales.xls]Summary does not.

If you are referring to workbooks located in the same folder as the active workbook, you do not need to include the location information in your cell reference. Excel will assume that if you do not specify a location, you want to use workbooks located in the folder of the active workbook, and it will add the location information for you automatically.

The four TAs assigned to Professor White's lecture have stored their grading sheets in the following files: TA1, TA2, TA3, and TA4. Because each TA has created his or her workbook from the template you created earlier, you know where the relevant information has been stored. For example, you know that the name of each TA should be entered on the Documentation sheet of each workbook in cell B1 (recall Figure 8-3). With that in mind, you can create a reference to that cell in Professor White's Summary Grades workbook.

To open the workbook and add a reference to each TA's name:

1. If you took a break after the last session, restart Excel.
2. Open the **White** workbook in the Tutorial folder for Tutorial.08 of your Data Disk.
3. Enter [***Your Name***] and the date in cells B14 and B15. Enter **Summary Grades** in cell B13.
4. Save the workbook as **Summary Grades**.
5. Click the **Summary** tab.

   Now you'll enter the 3-D cell reference that will enter the name of the first TA in cell A2.
6. Click cell **A2** and type **=[TA1]Documentation!B1** and then press the **Enter** key. The name "Stewart Nelson" appears in cell A2.
7. Click the **A2** cell again and notice that Excel has automatically inserted the path indicating the location of the TA1 workbook file into the cell reference.

Next you'll continue entering the references to the remaining TA names. You'll use a reference to the TA2 workbook to enter Patty Wilson's name in cell A3, TA3 to enter Kim Lee's name in A4, and TA4 to enter Warren Kruschevski's in A5.

To complete the column of TA names:

1. Click cell **A3**.
2. Type **=[TA2]Documentation!B1** and then press the **Enter** key. Patty Wilson's name appears in cell A3.
3. In cell A4, enter **=[TA3]Documentation!B1**. Kim Lee's name appears.
4. In cell A5 enter **=[TA4]Documentation!B1**. Warren Kruschevski's name appears.

   Figure 8-27 displays the completed column of TA names.

Figure 8-27 **TA NAMES PULLED FROM THE GRADING SHEET WORKBOOKS**

TA names taken from the TA1, TA2, TA3, and TA4 workbooks

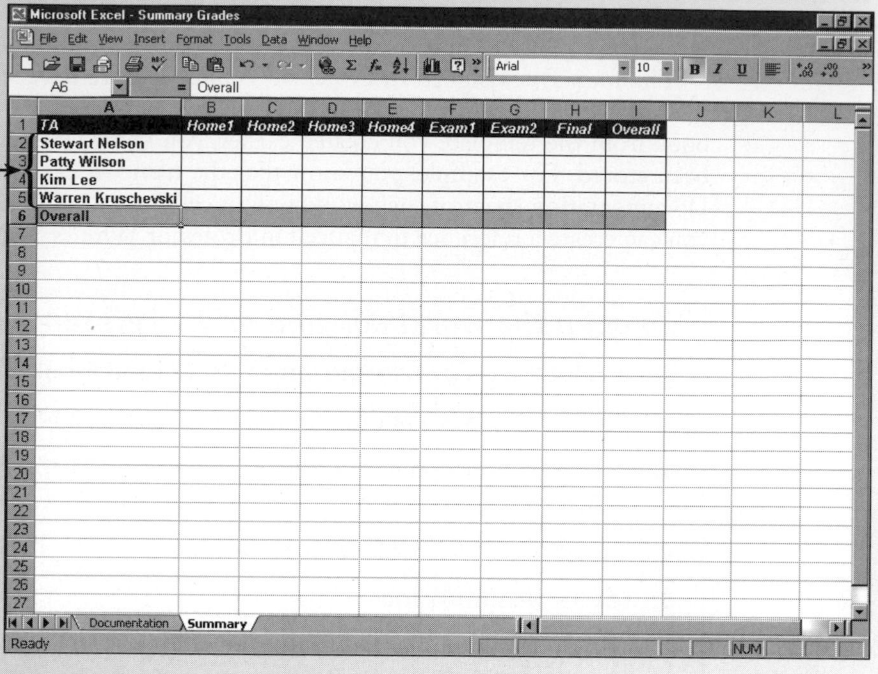

Next you'll need to reference the average scores that are recorded on the Summary sheet of each TA's workbook in cells B5:I5 (see Figure 8-17). As with the column of TA names, you can create columns of homework and exam averages, but here you can use the Fill Right command because the structure of the Summary sheet from Figure 8-17 is identical to the Summary sheet in the Summary Grades workbook. Start with the grades for Stewart Nelson's discussion sections row 2 drawn from the TA1 workbook.

To create a reference to Stewart Nelson's grading averages:

1. Click cell **B2** and type **=[TA1]Summary!B5** and then press the **Enter** key. The value 77.50 appears in cell B2.
2. Click cell **B2** and drag the fill handle to **I2** and release the mouse button.
3. Click cell **A1**.

   As shown in Figure 8-28, Excel has filled in the average scores for homework and exams for Stewart Nelson's discussion sections from the TA1 workbook. See Figure 8-28.

Figure 8-28 **SUMMARY SCORES FROM THE TA1 WORKBOOK**

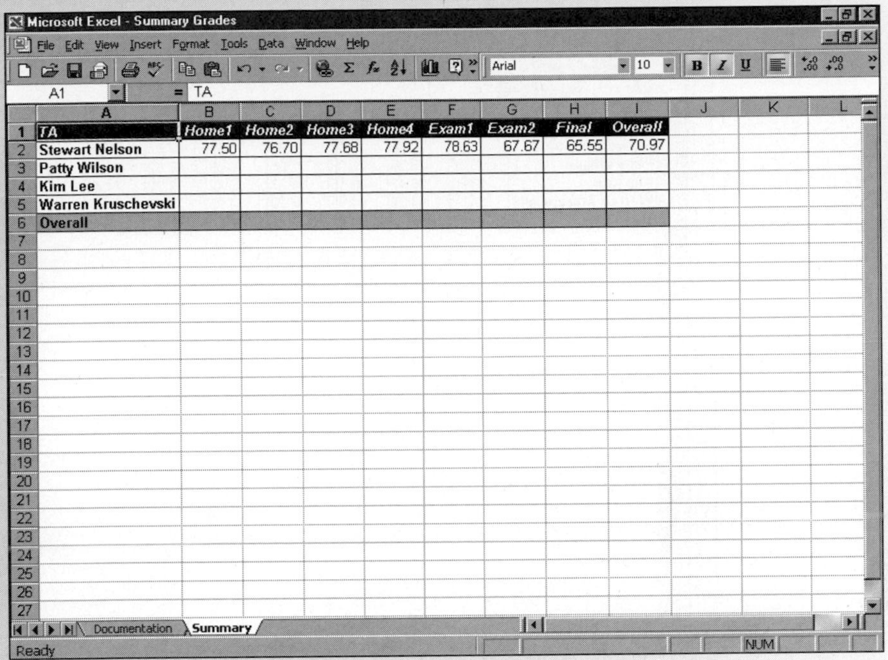

Next you'll fill in the scores for the other TAs. Patty Wilson's scores are in the TA2 workbook, Kim Lee's are in TA3, and Warren Kruschevski's are in TA4.

To add references to the rest of the TA workbooks:

1. Click cell **B3** and type **=[TA2]Summary!B5**, and then press the **Enter** key. The value 79.07 appears in cell B3.
2. Type **=[TA3]Summary!B5** in cell B4.
3. Type **=[TA4]Summary!B5** in cell B5.
4. Select the range **B3:B5** and drag the fill handle to the range **I3:I5**.

   Note that you can use the keyboard shortcut Ctrl + R in place of the Edit, Fill, and Right commands.
5. Click **A1**.

   Your screen should display all the average scores for each TA, as shown in Figure 8-29.

Figure 8-29 SUMMARY SCORES FROM THE TA1–TA4 WORKBOOKS

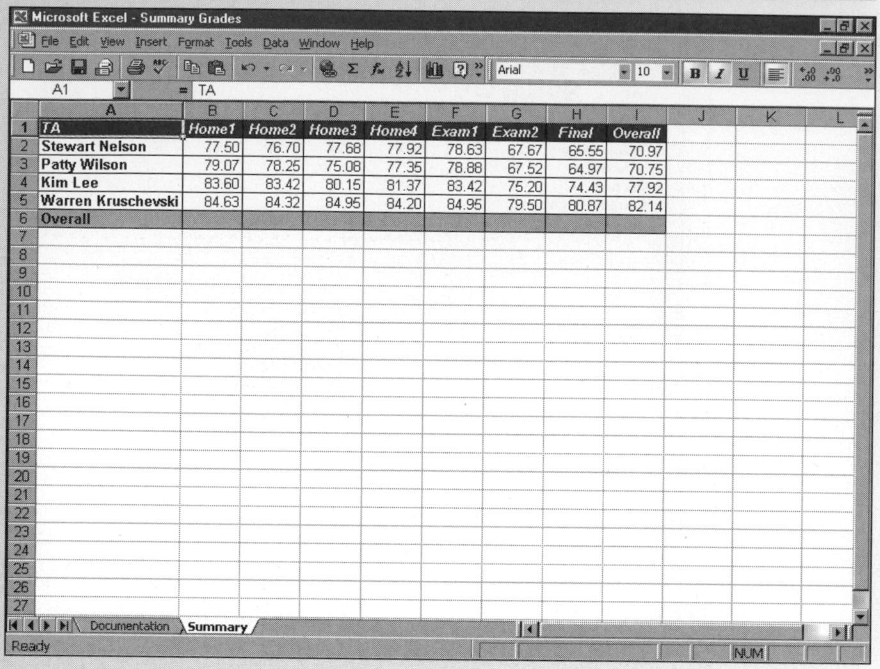

Finally, Professor White would like you to calculate the overall average scores for the four TAs. You can place these values in row 6.

To calculate the average of the TA grades:

1. Click cell **B6** and type the formula **=AVERAGE(B2:B5)**. The value 81.20 appears in cell B6.
2. Click cell **B6** and drag the fill handle to cell **I6**.
3. Click cell **A1**.

   The average scores for each TA appear in row 6 of the Summary worksheet. See Figure 8-30.

Figure 8-30 COMPLETED SUMMARY WORKSHEET

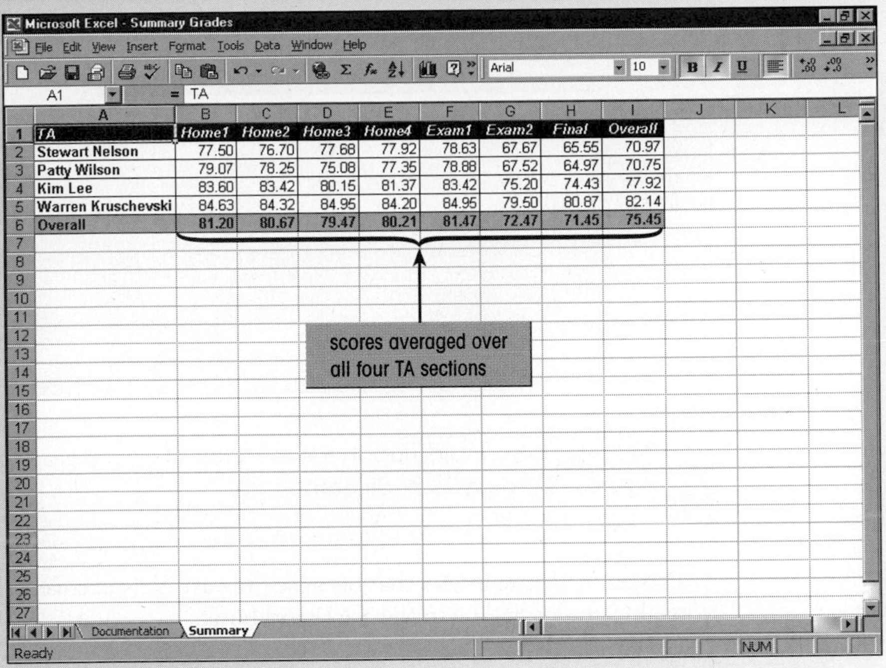

From your Summary sheet, Professor White will be able to see that two of the TAs, Stewart Nelson and Patty Wilson, have section averages well below the other two. She will most likely want to look into the reasons for this.

When you created the 3-D references in Professor White's Summary Grades workbook, you actually created a link between the Summary workbook and the four TA workbooks. You'll learn how to examine these links in the next section.

Working with Linked Workbooks

When you create a 3-D cell reference to another workbook, you are also creating a link, or a "live" connection, between workbooks. Because the workbooks are linked (recall the earlier discussion of linked files in Tutorial 6), changing a score in one TA's workbook causes a change in the Summary workbook. You've already seen this principle in action within a workbook when a changed value in one of the worksheets resulted in a changed value in a summary worksheet.

Professor White has talked to a student who feels that an answer was incorrectly marked wrong on her final exam. After reviewing the problem, Professor White decides that the student is right, which will increase her final exam score from 85 to 95. The student's ID number is 1107, and she is in Stewart Nelson's first discussion section. If Professor White wants to update the grading sheet, how will she know which workbook to access? She can view the list of linked workbooks.

To view the list of links:

1. Click **Edit** on the menu bar, and then click **Links**.

   Figure 8-31 shows the list of workbooks linked to the Summary Grades workbook.

Figure 8-31 **FILES LINKED TO THE SUMMARY GRADES WORKBOOK**

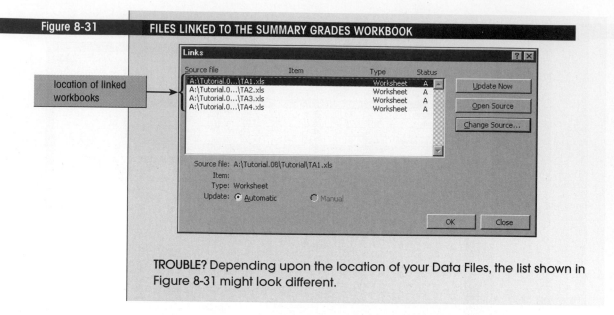

location of linked workbooks

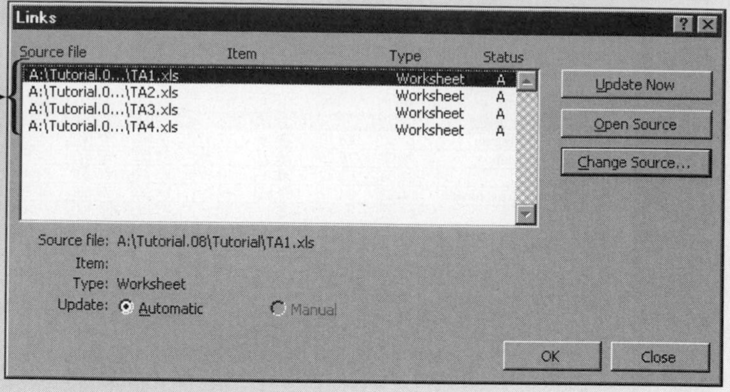

TROUBLE? Depending upon the location of your Data Files, the list shown in Figure 8-31 might look different.

Professor White knows that because Stewart Nelson covers the first set of discussion sections, his grades will be in the TA1 workbook.

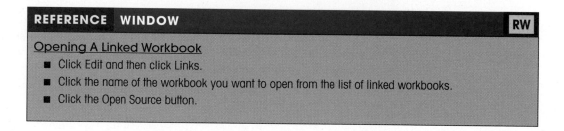

REFERENCE WINDOW RW

Opening A Linked Workbook

- Click Edit and then click Links.
- Click the name of the workbook you want to open from the list of linked workbooks.
- Click the Open Source button.

Professor White can open Stewart Nelson's workbook through the Links dialog box. Try this now.

To open the TA1 workbook:

1. Click **TA1.xls** in the Source file list box.
2. Click the **Open Source** button.

   Excel opens the TA1 workbook.
3. Click the **Section 1** tab, type **95** in cell H8, and then press the **Enter** key. Figure 8-32 shows the new values.

Figure 8-32 **REVISED SCORE IN THE SECTION 1 WORKSHEET OF THE TA1 WORKBOOK**

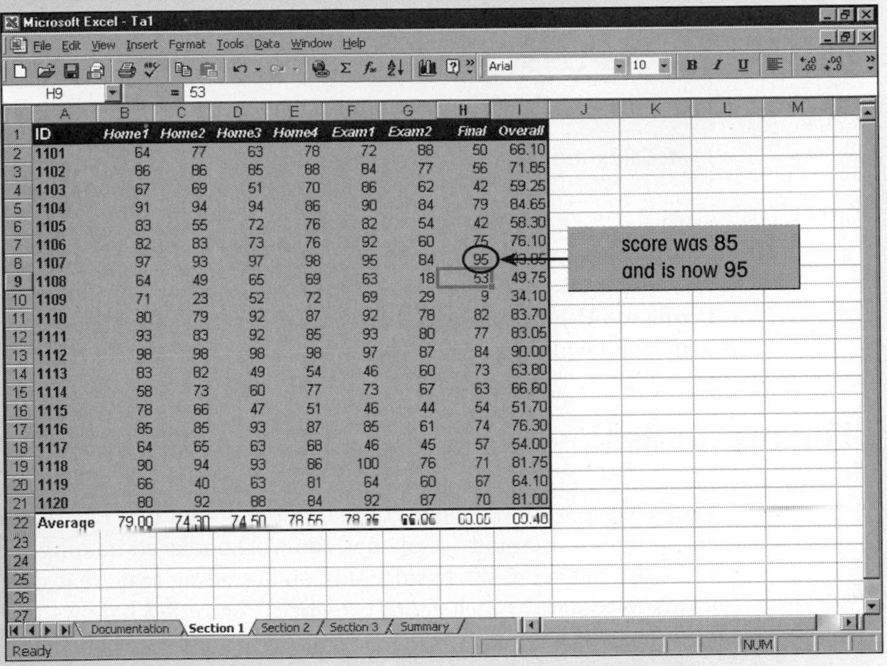

ID	Home1	Home2	Home3	Home4	Exam1	Exam2	Final	Overall
1101	64	77	63	78	72	88	50	66.10
1102	86	86	85	88	84	77	56	71.85
1103	67	69	51	70	86	62	42	59.25
1104	91	94	94	86	90	84	79	84.65
1105	83	55	72	76	82	54	42	58.30
1106	82	83	73	76	92	60	75	76.10
1107	97	93	97	98	95	84	95	[illegible]
1108	64	49	65	69	63	18	53	49.75
1109	71	23	52	72	69	29	9	34.10
1110	80	79	92	87	92	78	82	83.70
1111	93	83	92	85	93	80	77	83.05
1112	98	98	98	98	97	87	84	90.00
1113	83	82	49	54	46	60	73	63.80
1114	58	73	60	77	73	67	63	66.60
1115	78	66	47	51	46	44	54	51.70
1116	85	85	93	87	85	61	74	76.30
1117	64	65	63	68	46	45	57	54.00
1118	90	94	93	86	100	76	71	81.75
1119	66	40	63	81	64	60	67	64.10
1120	80	92	88	84	92	87	70	81.00
Average	79.00	74.30	74.50	78.55	78.35	66.06	[illegible]	[illegible]

4. Save and close the TA1 workbook.

After changing the student's final exam grade, the average final exam grade in Stewart Nelson's discussion sections, in cell H2 of the Summary worksheet, has increased from 65.55 to 65.72 and the average of his overall scores in cell I2 has increased from 70.97 to 71.04.

Opening and changing a source file in this way will automatically update the formulas to which it is linked in the workbook. If the Summary workbook is closed when you change the source, when you reopen it Excel will ask you if you want to update links to other files. If you click the Yes button, Excel retrieves any new or updated data. This guarantees that the workbook contains accurate and timely information.

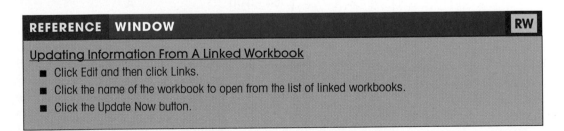

REFERENCE WINDOW **RW**

Updating Information From A Linked Workbook

- Click Edit and then click Links.
- Click the name of the workbook to open from the list of linked workbooks.
- Click the Update Now button.

Professor White would like to know what would happen if one of her TAs makes changes to the linked file while she is working on the Summary Grades workbook. You explain that when this happens, she can manually update the link to that workbook. For example, what if, while she was changing the grade of the student in Stewart Nelson's discussion section, Kim Lee was making changes in her grading sheet workbook? In that case, Professor White could retrieve the new information from Kim's source file by manually updating the link. You show her how to update the link to Kim Lee's grading sheet, located in the TA3 workbook.

To update information from the TA3 workbook:

1. Click **Edit** on the menu bar, and then click **Links**.
2. Click **TA3.xls** in the Source file list box.
3. Click the **Update Now** button.
4. Click the **OK** button to close the Links dialog box.

Any changes that Kim may have saved to her TA3.xls workbook will now be incorporated into the Summary Grades workbook. Because the end of the semester is approaching, Professor White turns her attention to assigning final letter grades to each of her students, which she will do by using lookup tables.

Using Lookup Tables

Professor White has reviewed each of the grades her TAs recorded. She has noted the overall average scores and has opened the workbooks containing the individual scores. Based on what she has seen, she has decided on a grading scale that determines the letter grades she wants to assign to each score category. Figure 8-33 shows the grading scale and the letter grades she has created.

Figure 8-33 PROFESSOR WHITE'S GRADING SCALE

compare values →

OVERALL SCORE	GRADE	GRADE POINT
0 - < 30	F	0.0
30 - < 50	D	1.0
50 - < 60	C	2.0
60 - < 70	BC	2.5
70 - < 77	B	3.0
77 - < 84	AB	3.5
84 - 100	A	4.0

Professor White could just give this table to her TAs and have them manually enter each student's letter grade, but it would be much more efficient to have the letter grades automatically entered into the grading sheet workbooks using a lookup table. A **lookup table** consists of rows and columns of information organized into separate categories. For example, the table in Figure 8-33 displays seven different categories in the overall score column. If you knew what a student's score was, you could determine the student's letter grade or grade point from the table by finding the appropriate row in the table and then looking in the letter grade or grade point column. You'll enter Professor White's grading scale as an Excel lookup table.

The categories for the lookup table are usually located in the table's first row or column and are called **compare values**, because an individual student's score is compared to each category to determine the grade. The value that is sent to the table is called the **lookup value**. In Figure 8-33, the first column contains compare values and each student's score is the lookup value.

A lookup table can have many different columns or rows to incorporate more pieces of information. Professor White's grading table displays both the letter grade and the corresponding grade point. To use this lookup table, you have to specify both the lookup value (the student's test score) and whether you're interested in retrieving the student's grade or grade point. See Figure 8-34.

Figure 8-34 USING A LOOKUP TABLE

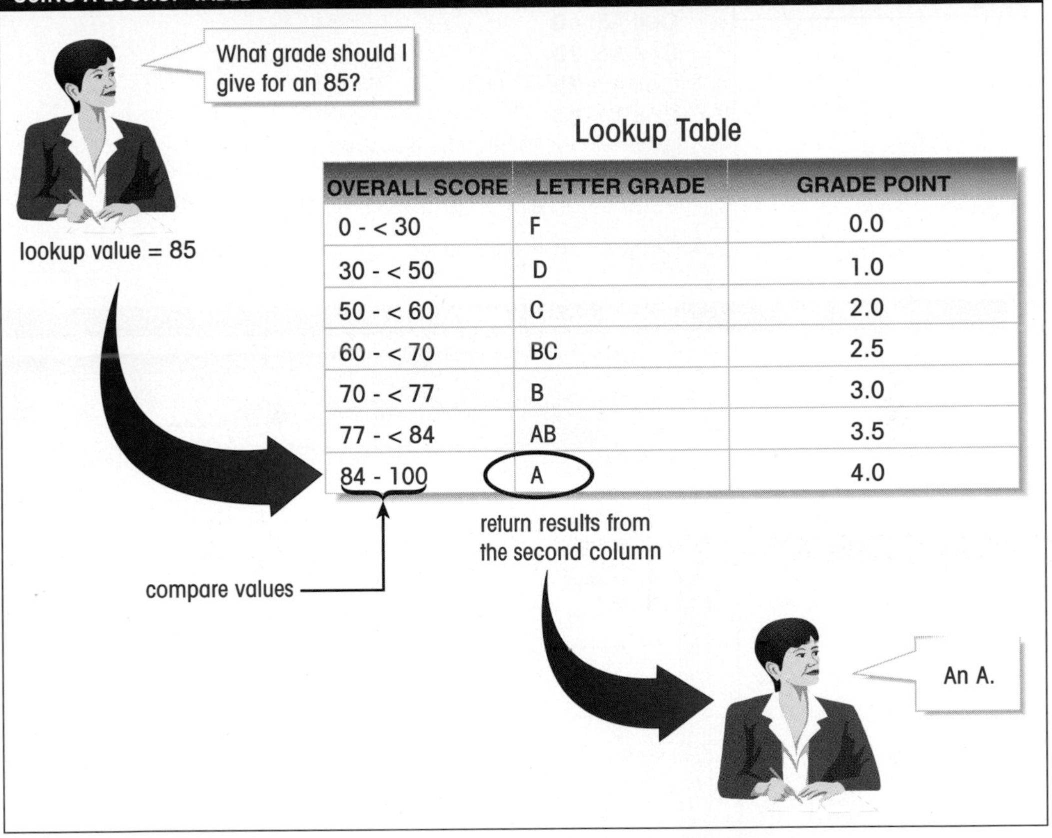

OVERALL SCORE	LETTER GRADE	GRADE POINT
0 - < 30	F	0.0
30 - < 50	D	1.0
50 - < 60	C	2.0
60 - < 70	BC	2.5
70 - < 77	B	3.0
77 - < 84	AB	3.5
84 - 100	A	4.0

Professor White wants you to enter the values from Figure 8-33 into the Summary Grades workbook. Because of the way Excel works with lookup tables, you'll only insert the lowest value that a student needs to receive a particular letter grade in the compare values column of the table. For example, in the lookup table you'll type the value "84" rather than "84 – 100" for As; or "70" rather than "70 – < 77" for Bs. This point will become clearer when you learn about lookup functions later in the tutorial.

To create the lookup table:

1. Insert a worksheet named **Grading Scale** to the right of the Summary sheet.

2. Enter the following values on the Grading Scale worksheet:

Cell A1: **Score**
Cell B1: **Grade**
Cell C1: **Grade Point**
Cell A2: **0**
Cell A3: **30**
Cell A4: **50**
Cell A5: **60**
Cell A6: **70**
Cell A7: **77**
Cell A8: **84**

3. Enter the remaining grades and grade points from the table in Figure 8-33 to columns B and C in the Grading scale worksheet.

4. Click **A1**. The final table is shown in Figure 8-35.

Figure 8-35 GRADING SCALE LOOKUP TABLE

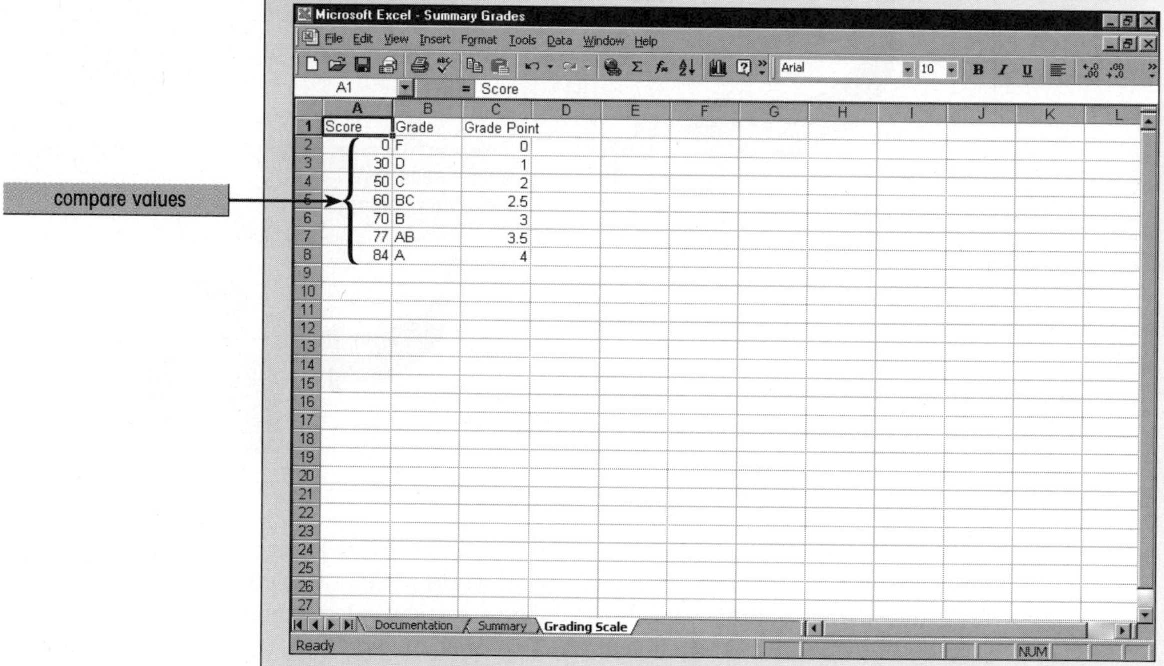

Finally, you should give a range name to your lookup table. Although this is not necessary in creating a lookup table, a range name will make it easier for functions to refer to values in the table, because the function would only have to include the range name and not the cell reference.

To name the lookup table:

1. Select the range **A1:C8**.

2. Click **Insert** on the menu bar, point to **Name**, and then click **Define**.

3. Type **Grade_Scale** in the Names in workbook text box, and click the **OK** button.

4. Save your changes and close the Summary Grades workbook.

Now that you've created the lookup table, you'll see how Professor White's TAs can use it to calculate letter grades for each of their students.

Using **Lookup Functions**

To retrieve a value, in this case a letter grade, from a lookup table, you'll use one of Excel's lookup functions. In a lookup function, you specify the location of the lookup table, the lookup value, and the column or row that contains the values you want retrieved from the table. Excel has two lookup functions: the VLOOKUP function and the HLOOKUP function. The VLOOKUP (or vertical lookup) function is used for lookup tables in which the compare values are placed into the first column of the table, and the HLOOKUP (or horizontal lookup) function assumes that the compare values are located in the table's first row. With the lookup table you created in Professor White's workbook, you'll use the VLOOKUP function because the compare values (the scores) were placed in the table's first column. The form of the VLOOKUP function is:

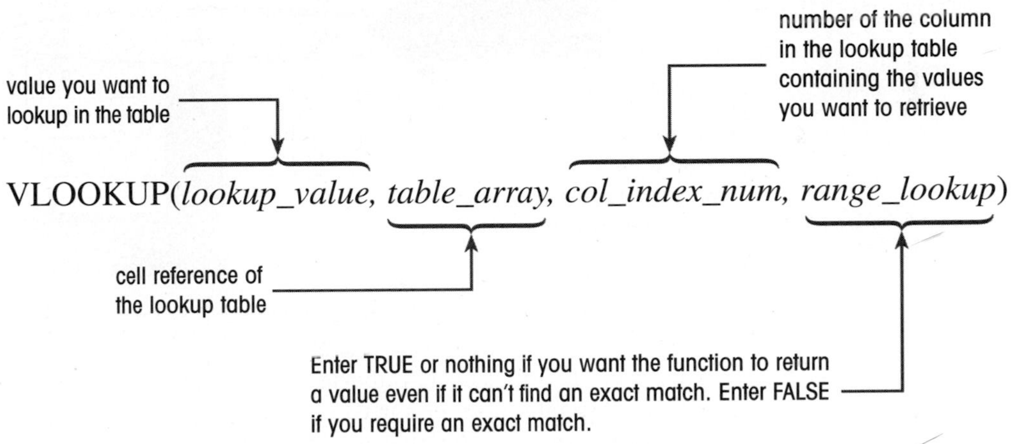
value you want to lookup in the table
number of the column in the lookup table containing the values you want to retrieve
VLOOKUP(lookup_value, table_array, col_index_num, range_lookup)
cell reference of the lookup table
Enter TRUE or nothing if you want the function to return a value even if it can't find an exact match. Enter FALSE if you require an exact match.

The VLOOKUP formula can look imposing, but once you examine each piece of the function, you'll find it easier to understand. The first argument in the function is the **lookup value**, this is the value you want to compare with other values in the table. For example, the lookup value shown in the example from Figure 8-34 is 85. For your VLOOKUP function, you'll enter references to the cells that contain the student scores rather than the scores themselves. The second argument is the **table_array**, which is the cell reference that specifies the location of the lookup table. In the lookup table you just created, the table_array would be '[Summary Grades]Grading Scale'!A1:C8, or if you use the range name you created, '[Summary Grades]'!Grade_Scale (note that you don't need to specify the worksheet name if you use a range name.) The **col_index_num** is the column number that contains the information you want to retrieve. For example, a col_index_num of 1 returns the value in the first column of the lookup table, a col_index_num of 2 returns the value from the second column and so forth. You'll want your VLOOKUP function to look at column 2, the letter grade column, and retrieve the appropriate grade.

The **range_lookup** is a logical value that can be either TRUE or FALSE. It tells VLOOKUP how to match the compare values in the first column of the table with your lookup value. If the range_lookup value is FALSE, the function will look for only exact matches to your lookup value. For example, if you are trying to retrieve values for a particular student, you would want an exact match to that student's ID number. If the VLOOKUP function fails to find an exact match, an #N/A error value is generated.

If the range_lookup value is TRUE or omitted, the situation is a little more complicated. In this case, Excel uses the largest compare value that is less than the lookup value. To see how this works examine Figure 8-36. Recall that when you created the lookup table, you entered the lower end of the range for each letter grade in the compare values column. Now you'll see why. If you want to see what letter grade is given for a score of 65, the VLOOKUP function moves down the Score column until it locates the highest score value that is less than 65. In this case that is 60, and the function returns a letter grade of BC. Based on the table, you can determine that any score greater than or equal to 60 and less than 70 will return a grade of BC, which is what you want based on the table shown from Figure 8-34.

Figure 8-36 RETURNING A VALUE WITH THE RANGE_ LOOKUP VALUE SET TO TRUE

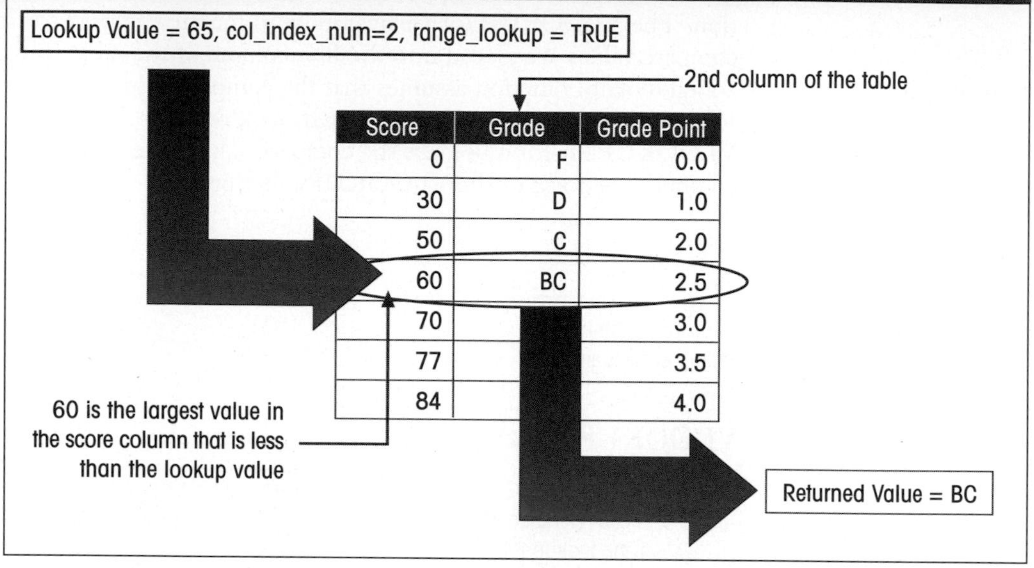

Score	Grade	Grade Point
0	F	0.0
30	D	1.0
50	C	2.0
60	BC	2.5
70		3.0
77		3.5
84		4.0

This example brings up an important point. If the range_lookup value is TRUE or omitted, the lookup table *must* be sorted in ascending order of the compare values. If it isn't, the VLOOKUP function will either return an incorrect value or an error.

Because the VLOOKUP function seems to be just what you need to automatically generate letter grades, you'll add the function to Stewart Nelson's grading sheet in the TA1 workbook. In this tutorial, you'll only add the function to TA1; you can add it to TA2, TA3, and TA4 at another time.

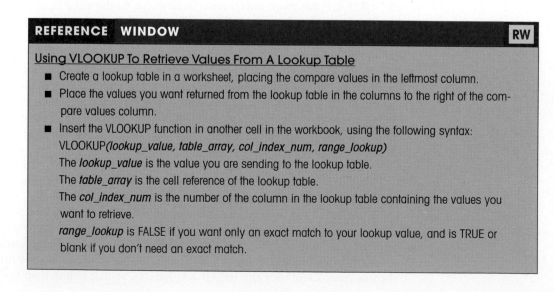

REFERENCE WINDOW RW

Using VLOOKUP To Retrieve Values From A Lookup Table

- Create a lookup table in a worksheet, placing the compare values in the leftmost column.
- Place the values you want returned from the lookup table in the columns to the right of the compare values column.
- Insert the VLOOKUP function in another cell in the workbook, using the following syntax:
  VLOOKUP(*lookup_value, table_array, col_index_num, range_lookup)*
  The ***lookup_value*** is the value you are sending to the lookup table.
  The ***table_array*** is the cell reference of the lookup table.
  The ***col_index_num*** is the number of the column in the lookup table containing the values you want to retrieve.
  range_lookup is FALSE if you want only an exact match to your lookup value, and is TRUE or blank if you don't need an exact match.

You'll begin by opening the TA1 workbook and entering the lookup function in a new Grades column that you'll add to each of the section worksheets.

To add a column of final grades to the worksheet:

1. Open the **TA1** workbook from the Tutorial folder for Tutorial.08 on your Data Disk.
2. Enter (***Your Name***) and the date in cells B14:B15 of the Documentation worksheet. Type **TA1Lookup** in cell B13.
3. Save the workbook as **TA1Lookup**.
4. Group the Section 1 through Section 3 worksheets. Click the **Section 1** worksheet tab.
5. In cell J2, type **=VLOOKUP(I2,'Summary Grades'!Grade_Scale,2)** and then press **Enter**.

   You have instructed Excel to use the value in cell I2 to retrieve the corresponding letter grade located in the second column of the lookup table named "Grade_Scale" in the Summary Grades workbook.

   TROUBLE? If you receive an error message stating that Excel cannot find the Summary Grades workbook, verify that you've typed the name of the file correctly. The Summary Grades workbook should be in the same folder as the current workbook you're editing.

6. Click cell **J2** and drag the fill handle down to cell **J21**.
7. Click cell **A1**.

   Figure 8-37 shows the final version of the table. Because you've grouped the three grading sheets, the VLOOKUP formula and cell formats have been added to all three worksheets. A quick glance at the grades assigned to the students indicates a fairly even mix of letter grades.

Figure 8-37 GRADES FOR THE STUDENTS IN THE TA1 WORKBOOK

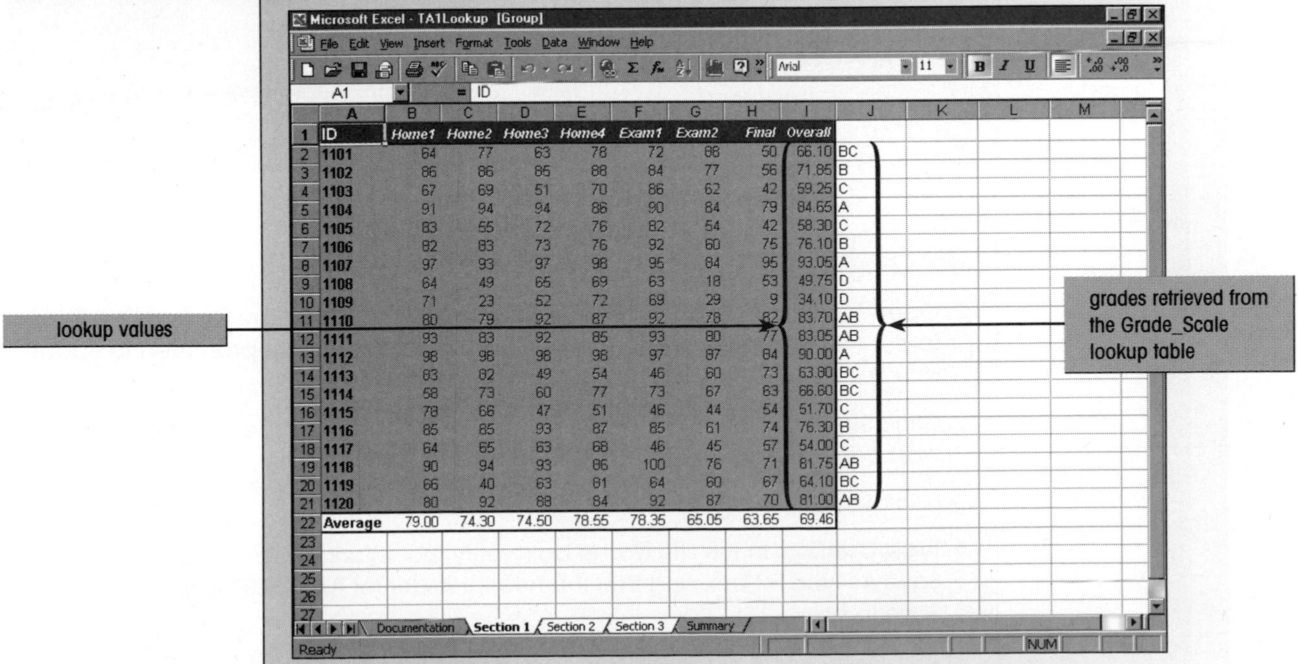

ID	Home1	Home2	Home3	Home4	Exam1	Exam2	Final	Overall	
1101	64	77	63	78	72	88	50	66.10	BC
1102	86	86	85	88	84	77	56	71.85	B
1103	67	69	51	70	86	62	42	59.25	C
1104	91	94	94	86	90	84	79	84.65	A
1105	83	55	72	76	82	54	42	58.30	C
1106	82	83	73	76	92	60	75	76.10	B
1107	97	93	97	98	95	84	95	93.05	A
1108	64	49	65	69	63	18	53	49.75	D
1109	71	23	52	72	69	29	9	34.10	D
1110	80	79	92	87	92	78	82	83.70	AB
1111	93	83	92	85	93	80	77	83.05	AB
1112	98	98	98	98	97	87	84	90.00	A
1113	83	82	49	54	46	60	73	63.80	BC
1114	58	73	60	77	73	67	63	66.60	BC
1115	78	66	47	51	46	44	54	51.70	C
1116	85	85	93	87	85	61	74	76.30	B
1117	64	65	63	68	46	45	57	54.00	C
1118	90	94	93	86	100	76	71	81.75	AB
1119	66	40	63	81	64	60	67	64.10	BC
1120	80	92	88	84	92	87	70	81.00	AB
Average	79.00	74.30	74.50	78.55	78.35	65.05	63.65	69.46	

8. Check to see if appropriate letter grades have been entered into the Section 2 and Section 3 worksheets.

9. Select the Documentation sheet and then save and close your workbook.

With the lookup table in place, if Stewart makes a change in one of his student's homework or exam scores, or if Professor White revises her grading scale, the grades in column J can be automatically updated. This is much more accurate and efficient than simply entering the grades by hand. In the future, you can use this technique in all of the TA workbooks.

Creating an Excel Workspace

Professor White now has five different workbooks to keep track of grades in her course: the four TA workbooks and the Summary Grades workbook. Most of the time, she'll need to access only one workbook at a time, but there will be those occasions (such as at the end of the term) when she'll have all five opened simultaneously. It would be a great help for Professor White if she could open all those workbooks at once. For one thing, it would save time; but more importantly, it would save her the trouble of remembering all those filenames and their folder locations.

To do this, you'll create a workspace. A **workspace** is an Excel file that saves information about all of the currently opened workbooks, such as their locations, their window sizes, and screen positions. The workspace does not contain the workbooks themselves—only information about them. That is enough however. You can open all of the workbooks for the Calculus 223 lecture and then create the workspace file based on those workbooks. To open that set of workbooks again, Professor White can simply open the workspace file and the five workbooks will be opened as well.

REFERENCE WINDOW RW

Creating And Using An Excel Workspace

- Open only those workbooks you want to include in the workspace.
- Click Save Workspace from the File menu.
- Assign a name for your workspace file and click the Save button.
- To access the workspace later, open the workspace file from the Open command in the File menu. All workbooks related to your workspace will be automatically opened.

To create the Calculus223 workspace file:

1. Open the **TA1**, **TA2**, **TA3**, **TA4** and **Summary Grades** workbooks from the Tutorial folder for Tutorial.08 on your Data Disk. Click **Yes** if you are prompted to update any links.
2. Click **Summary Grades** from the Windows menu so that the Summary Grades workbook appears in the document window.
3. Click **Save Workspace** from the File menu.
4. Type **Calc223** in the File Name box, verify that "Workspaces" is selected in the Save As Type list box and that the Tutorial folder for Tutorial.08 appears in the Save In box.

5. Click the **Save** button.

The Calc223 workspace file is created on your Data Disk.

TROUBLE? If Excel prompts you to save changes to one of your workbooks, click the Yes button.

Now that you've created the workspace file, your next step is to open it to confirm that it opens all five of Professor White's grading workbooks.

To test the Calc223 workspace:

1. Close all five of the grading workbooks contained in the Calc223 workspace.
2. Click **Open** from the File menu.
3. Select **Calc223** from the Tutorial folder for Tutorial.08 and click the **Open** button. See Figure 8-38. Click **Yes** if you are prompted to update any links.

Figure 8-38 OPENING THE CALC223 WORKSPACE FILE

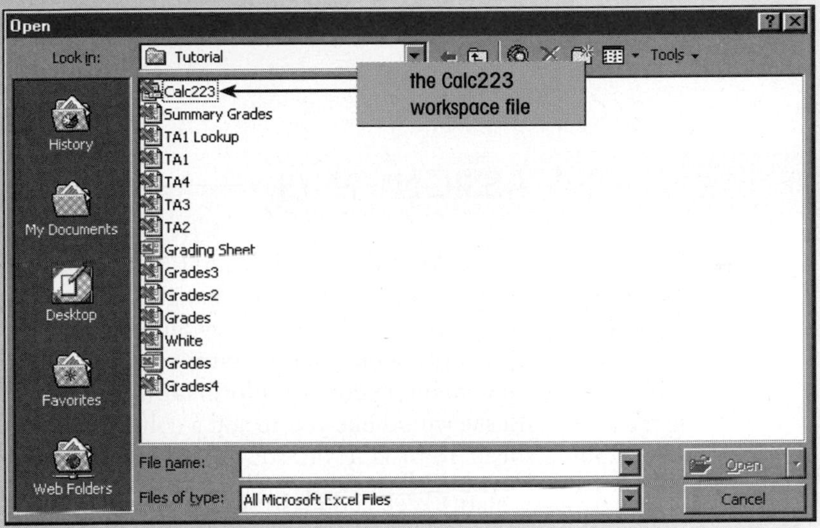

The five workbooks in the Calc223 workspace are open.

4. Close all of the Calc223 workbooks. You don't need to save any changes because you haven't modified the document.
5. Exit Excel.

You display the workspace file to Professor White. She's very happy with it and realizes that she can create a separate workspace file for each of her courses. She teaches several classes, and a workspace is an excellent way of organizing all of those workbooks. That's a job for the future, for now you've completed your work for Professor White.

Session 8.3 Quick Check

1. What is the 3-D cell reference for the A1:A10 cell range on the Sales Info worksheet in the Product Report workbook located in the Reports folder on drive D?
2. How does a 3-D cell reference to a workbook differ from a 3-D reference to a worksheet?
3. How would you view a list of links to other workbooks in your current workbook?
4. Define lookup table, lookup value, and compare value.
5. What are two of the functions that Excel uses to retrieve values from a lookup table?
6. What is the range_lookup value? What does a value of TRUE mean for the range_lookup value?
7. What is a workspace file? Explain how workspace files can help you organize your work.

In this tutorial, you have worked with multiple worksheets and workbooks, learned about templates, and used the Excel VLOOKUP function. Professor White is pleased with the grading sheets you've created. She'll look over your work and let you know if she has any changes.

REVIEW ASSIGNMENTS

Professor White has looked over the grading workbooks you've created. Based on her suggestions, you've made some formatting changes to the documents. She has a couple of items that she wants you to add to her new Summary Grades workbook and to each of her TA's grading sheet workbooks. In her Summary Grades workbook, she would like you to add a worksheet containing contact information for each TA retrieved from the TA1–TA4 workbooks, and she would like you to add a column with the student's grade point to each TA's grading sheet. To make Professor White's modifications, do the following:

1. If necessary, start Excel, and make sure your Data Disk is in the appropriate drive. Open the **Calc223** workbook in the Review folder for Tutorial.08, and save it as **Calc223 Grades**. When you are asked if you want to update links, click the Yes button.
2. On the Documentation worksheet, enter the new workbook name, [**Your Name**], and the date in cells B13:B15.
3. Insert a new worksheet between the Documentation sheet and the Summary worksheet, and name it **TA Info**.
4. Enter the following column titles:

Cell A1:	"Sections 1-3"
Cell B1:	"Sections 4-6"
Cell C1:	"Sections 7-9"
Cell D1:	"Sections 10-12"

5. Increase the size of columns A through D to 20 characters.
6. Type a 3-D cell reference in cell A2 referring to cell B1 in the Documentation sheet of the TA1 workbook.

7. Drag the fill handle from cell A2 to A5 to fill in the complete TA information for Sections 1–3.

8. Repeat the last two steps on columns B through D, referencing the TA information for Patty Wilson, Kim Lee, and Warren Kruschevski located in the TA2, TA3, and TA4 workbooks.

9. Save your changes to the workbook. Print the TA Info worksheet and then close the document.

10. Open the **TA1** workbook from the Review folder for Tutorial.08, and then save it as **SNelson**.

11. On the Documentation sheet, enter the new workbook name, your name and the date in cells B13:B15.

12. Group the three section grading sheets, select the cells in the table, and copy the format from the Section 1 worksheet into the Section 2 and Section 3 worksheets.

13. In column J, use the VLOOKUP function to add the grade point for each student to each of the three grading sheets using the grading table found in the Calc223 Grades workbook. (*Hint*: The lookup table in the Calc223 Grades workbook has the range name, Grade_Scale. Grade point values are located in the third column of the table.)

14. Calculate the average grade point for the three sections in the SNelson workbook. What are the three grade point averages?

15. Print the three grouped grading sheets with a common page setup format: Center the table of scores and grades on the page, place your name in the page header and the date in the page footer.

16. Ungroup the worksheets and save your changes.

17. Reopen the **Calc223 Grades** workbook you created in previous steps and close all other workbooks aside from it and the SNelson workbook. Create a workspace file named **Calc223 Workbooks** that contains information about these two documents.

CASE PROBLEMS

Case 1. Consolidating Copier Sales at DOC-Centric DOC-Centric makes six brands of copiers. They track sales information from four sales regions—North, South, East and West—in a sales workbook. You've been asked by your supervisor, Peter Mitchell, to format the workbook and to create a summary worksheet that will sum up the sales information from all four regions. To do this, you'll use the Excel worksheet grouping feature and 3-D cell references. Do the following:

1. If necessary, start Excel, and make sure your Data Disk is in the appropriate drive. Open the Copiers workbook in the Cases folder for Tutorial.08, and save it as Copier Sales.

2. Enter the workbook name, [**Your Name**], and the date in cells B5, B6 and B7 of the Documentation sheet worksheet.

3. Insert a new sheet in the workbook titled **Total Sales** at the end of the workbook.

4. Using the Edit, Fill Across Sheets command, copy the row titles and column titles from the East worksheet into the Total Sales worksheet.

5. In cells B3:F9 of the Total Sales worksheet, insert the sum of the sales in the corresponding cells in the North–East worksheets. (Be sure to ungroup the worksheets first.)

6. Format the numbers in the North–Total Sales worksheets with the Comma style, reducing the number of decimal places shown to 0.
7. Format the tables in the North–Total Sales worksheets using the Classic 2 AutoFormat table style.
8. Ungroup the worksheets and print the Total Sales worksheet.
9. Save your changes.
10. Remove the sales data, but not any summary formulas, from the four region sales worksheets and remove the workbook name, your name and the date from the Documentation sheet.
11. Save the empty workbook as a template with the name **Copier Sales Form** in the Cases folder for Tutorial.08 on your Data Disk.
12. Print the template and close the template file.

Case 2. Examining Sales Information at Kitchen WareHouse Jaya Torres tracks the sales of kitchen appliances at Kitchen WareHouse. Kitchen WareHouse has stores in five regions. Jaya has recorded the monthly sales of refrigerators, microwaves, ovens, and dishwashers for each region in a workbook titled Kitchen located in the Cases folder for Tutorial.08 on your Data Disk. Jaya would like to include a worksheet that consolidates the sales information from the five regions. She would also like to take advantage of the Excel lookup feature to allow users to quickly retrieve the total sales of a particular product in a specific month.

Jaya has already placed an empty worksheet in her workbook that will be the summary sheet. The worksheet's title is All Regions. She wants you to add formulas to the table that sum the sales for each product in each month across the five sales regions.

She has also included a worksheet entitled Sales Results, in which she wants you to use the VLOOKUP function to allow a user to enter the month number and the product ID code, and have the total sales appear in a cell labeled Units Sold.

Do the following:

1. If necessary, start Excel, open the **Kitchen** workbook in the Cases folder for Tutorial.08 on your Data Disk, and then save it as **Kitchen WareHouse**.
2. Enter the new workbook name, your name, and the date in cells B3, B4, and B5 of the Documentation sheet.
3. In cells B4:N8 of the Summary worksheet, enter a formula that sums the values in the corresponding cells from the Region 1 to Region 5 worksheets.
4. Print the Summary worksheet.
5. Assign the range name Total_Sales to cells A3:N8 in the Summary worksheet. This will be the lookup table used in the following step.

Explore

6. In cell B5 of the Sales Results worksheet, create a lookup formula with the VLOOKUP function that will display sales figures based on the Month Number entered into cell B3 and the Product Number entered into cell B4 (*Hint*: Use the Product Number as your lookup value. Retrieve sales figures from the column in the lookup table corresponding to the Month Number plus one. The function should only look for exact matches.)
7. Test the lookup function by using it to answer the following questions:
   a. How many refrigerators were sold in all regions in January?
   b. How many dishwashers were sold in all regions over the entire year?
   c. How many appliances were sold in all regions in March?
   d. How many ovens were sold in all regions in June?
8. Print and save the final version of the Kitchen WareHouse workbook.

Case 3. Using the MATCH Function to Create a Stock Index Reporter Kelly Watkins is an investment counselor at Davis and Burns. Some of the many kinds of information that she refers to in her job are the daily stock indices on the New York Stock Exchange (NYSE). The indices are measures of changes in the market value of NYSE common stocks, adjusted to eliminate the effects of new stock listings and deleted stock listings. There are four subgroup indices—Industrial, Transportation, Utility, and Finance—and a Composite index combining the values of the other four. Kelly is constructing a workbook that contains long-term historical data on the NYSE. Kelly would like to be able to find the closing value of any of these subgroups on any particular day from her historical data. As a starting point in constructing her historical workbook, she has some raw data for the 1990 NYSE. She would like you to help her create a simple workbook in which she would only need to enter the date from that year and the name of the subgroup and have Excel tell her the closing value. In the future, she'll build on this simple model to include more years and more stock information.

Do the following:

1. Open the **Index** workbook in the Cases folder for Tutorial.08 of your Data Disk, and save it as **NYSE Index**.
2. Enter your name, the date, and the workbook name in the Documentation sheet.
3. In the Index Data worksheet, name the range A1:F254 "Closing_Values".
4. In the Reporter worksheet, insert a VLOOKUP in cell C6 that displays the closing value based on the date entered into cell C4 and an Index number entered into cell C5 (*Hint*: The date is your lookup value, the Index number represents the column from the Closing Values table—2 = Composite, 3 = Industrial, 4 = Transport, 5 = Utility and 6 = Finance. Use only exact matches to the date.)
5. Test your function with the following set of dates and index values:
   a. Date = 10/4/90, Index = 2
   b. Date = 10/4/90, Index = 3
   c. Date = 3/14/90, Index = 4
6. Print the Reporter sheet with the results of the last lookup and save your changes to the NYSE Index workbook.

   Kelly has viewed the workbook. She wants this "index reporter" to be friendly and easy to use because she plans on sharing it with other people who might not be experienced computer users. So she wants you to remove the code numbers for each stock index and instead allow users to type in the name of the index itself.

   You'll use the MATCH function to solve this problem. The MATCH function operates like the lookup functions, except that it indicates the location of matching values in a list of values. For example, in matching the word *Utility* to the list—Date, Composite, Industrial, Transport, Utility, Finance—the MATCH function would return the value "5" because Utility is the fifth item in the list. You can use the MATCH function in place of the index number in the VLOOKUP function. Instead of having the user indicate the column number from a lookup table, the user can enter the index name and have the MATCH function determine the column number. The syntax of the MATCH function is

   MATCH(*lookup_value*,*lookup_array*,*match_type*)

   where *lookup_value* is the value you want to find, *lookup_array* is the column or row containing the values, and *match_type* is a variable that determines the type of match you want. Set match_type to 0 for exact matches. For more information, see the Excel Office

Assistant Help file on the MATCH function. Now that you've seen how the MATCH function works, you can modify your VLOOKUP function to take advantage of it.

7. Return to the Documentation sheet of the NYSE Index workbook and enter "NYSE Index 2" into cell C3. Save the workbook as **NYSE Index 2** in the Cases folder for Tutorial.08.
8. In the Index Data worksheet, name the range A1:F1 as "Index_Groups".

Explore

9. Go to the Reporter worksheet. Edit the VLOOKUP function in cell C6, replacing the column index parameter (which currently is the cell reference, C5) with the following formula: "MATCH(C5,Index_Groups,0)".
10. Test your new function using the following parameters:
    a. Date = 10/4/90, Index = Composite
    b. Date = 10/4/90, Index = Industrial
    c. Date = 3/14/90, Index = Transport
11. Print the Reporter sheet with the results of the last lookup, and then save and close the NYSE Index 2 workbook.

Case 4. Projected Income Statement for the Bread Bakery Your supervisor, David Keyes, has asked you to prepare the annual projected income statement for The Bread Bakery—a company specializing in fine baked breads. You've been given workbooks from three regions in the country. Each workbook has quarterly projected income statements for three of the company's products: French baguettes, sourdough wheat bread, and sourdough white bread. David wants you to summarize each workbook for him, reporting the annual totals for Earnings Before Tax in a new worksheet. Once you have added this information to each workbook, he wants you to consolidate the information from the three regional workbooks, reporting in a single workbook, the same information for the entire company.

Do the following:

1. Open each regional sales workbook, R1–R3, in the Cases folder for Tutorial.08 of your Data Disk and save **R1** as **North**, **R2** as **South** and **R3** as **Southwest**.
2. In each regional sales workbook, enter your name, the name of the workbook, and the date on the Documentation sheet.
3. Place a worksheet named **Summary** near the beginning of each regional sales workbook, right after the Documentation sheet. The Summary sheet should total all the Earnings Before Tax figures for each of the products for each of the four quarters. Also include summary values for the Earnings Before Tax figures across all four quarters and for all products.
4. Format the Summary sheet using any format you choose.
5. Create a new workbook named **Bread Bakery Report** in the Cases folder for Tutorial.08 of your Data Disk.
6. Create a documentation sheet in the Bread Bakery Report workbook containing the workbook name, [**Your Name**], and the date.
7. Create a summary worksheet in the Bread Bakery Report workbook. The sheet should contain the Earnings Before Tax values summarized over region, product, and quarter. Include summary totals over these ranges.
8. The format and design of the Bread Bakery Report workbook is up to you.
9. Print the Summary sheets from the four workbooks you've created.
10. Create a workspace named **Bread Bakery** for the four workbooks you created in this assignment.

INTERNET ASSIGNMENTS

The purpose of the Internet Assignments is to challenge you to find information on the Internet that you can use to create effective spreadsheets. The actual assignments are updated and maintained on the Course Technology Web site. Log on to the Internet and use your Web browser to go to the Student Online Companion to accompany this text at **www.course.com/NewPerspectives/office2000**. Click the Excel link, and then click the link for Tutorial 8.

QUICK CHECK ANSWERS

Session 8.1

1. Right-click the sheet tab of the active sheet, click Insert on the Shortcut menu, click the worksheet icon in the Insert dialog box, then click the OK button; click the sheet tab of the newly created worksheet, then drag it to the right of the previously active sheet.
2. A worksheet group is a collection of worksheets that have all been selected for editing and formatting.
3. Select the worksheet group by either pressing and holding down the Ctrl key and clicking the sheet tab of each worksheet in the grouping or if the worksheets occupy a contiguous range in the workbook, by clicking the first sheet tab in the range, pressing and holding down the Shift key, and clicking the sheet tab of the last sheet in the range. Deselect a worksheet group by either clicking the sheet tab of a worksheet not in the group or right-clicking one of the sheet tabs in the group and clicking Ungroup Sheets on the Shortcut menu.
4. Create a worksheet group consisting of the range of worksheets. In the first worksheet in the group, select the text and formulas you want to copy and click Edit, click Fill , then click Across Worksheets. Select whether you want to copy the contents, formulas, or both, then click the OK button.
5. the sheet range and the cell range
6. 'Section1'!A1:A10
7. Sheet 1:Sheet10!A1:A10

Session 8.2

1. A template is a workbook that contains specific content and formatting that you can use as a model for other similar workbooks.
2. A user can modify the contents of a workbook based on a template without changing the template file itself. The next time a workbook is created based on a template, it is opened with all the original properties intact.
3. the template used in creating the blank workbook you first see when starting a new Excel session
4. click File, Save As, click Template in the Save as type list box, then click the Save button
5. Templates folder (a subfolder of the Microsoft Office folder)
6. create a subfolder in the Templates folder, then move the template file into it

Section 8.3

1. 'D:\Reports\[Product Report]Sales Info'!A1:A10
2. It includes both the location and the name of the workbook.
3. click Edit, then click Links
4. A lookup table is a table in which rows and columns of information are organized into separate categories. The lookup value is the value that indicates the category in which you are looking. The categories for the lookup table are usually located in the table's first row or column and are called compare values.
5. VLOOKUP and HLOOKUP
6. The range_lookup value is a parameter in the VLOOKUP and HLOOKUP functions that tell Excel where to look for an exact match in a lookup table. A value of TRUE means that Excel does not have to find an exact match.
7. A workspace file is a file containing information about all of the currently opened workbooks, including their locations, window sizes, and screen positions. By opening a workspace file, you open all related workbooks. This helps you organize projects that may involve several workbooks because you don't have to keep a list of those filenames.

LEVEL III

New Perspectives on

MICROSOFT® EXCEL 2000

Read This Before You Begin

To the Student

Data Disks

To complete the Level III tutorials, Review Assignments, and Case Problems in this book, you need seven Data Disks. Your instructor will either provide you with Data Disks or ask you to make your own.

If you are making your own Data Disks, you will need seven blank, formatted high-density disks. You will need to copy a set of folders from a file server or standalone computer or the Web onto your disks. Your instructor will tell you which computer, drive letter, and folders contain the files you need. You could also download the files by going to **www.course.com**, clicking Data Disk Files, and following the instructions on the screen.

The following list shows you which folders go on each of your disks, so that you will have enough disk space to complete all the Tutorials, Review Assignments, and Cases:

Data Disk 1

Write this on the disk label:
Data Disk 1: Level III Tutorial 9

Put these folders on the disk:
Tutorial.09

Data Disk 2

Write this on the disk label:
Data Disk 2: Level III Tutorial 10

Put these folders on the disk:
Tutorial.10

Data Disk 3

Write this on the disk label:
Data Disk 3: Level III Tutorial 11

Put these folders on the disk:
Tutor11

Data Disk 4

Write this on the disk label:
Data Disk 4: Level III Tutorial 12

Put these folders on the disk:
Tutorial.12

Data Disk 5

Write this on the disk label:
Data Disk 5: Level III TutAd

Put these folders on the disk:
TutAd

Data Disk 6

Write this on the disk label:
Data Disk 6: Level III Appendix 2 and 3

Put these folders on the disk:
Appendix.02
Appendix.03

Data Disk 7

Write this on the disk label:
Data Disk 7: Level III Appendix 4

Put these folders on the disk:
Appendix.04

When you begin each tutorial, be sure you are using the correct Data Disk. See the inside front or inside back cover of this book for more information on Data Disk files, or ask your instructor or technical support person for assistance.

Course Lab

The Level III tutorials in this book feature one interactive Course Lab to help you understand Database concepts. There are Lab Assignments at the end of Tutorial 11 that relate to this Lab.

To start a Lab, click the Start button on the Windows taskbar, point to Programs, point to Course Labs, point to New Perspectives Applications, and click Databases.

Using Your Own Computer

If you are going to work through this book using your own computer, you need:

- **Computer System** Microsoft Excel 2000 and Windows 95 or higher must be installed on your computer. This book assumes a complete installation of Excel 2000.
- **Data Disks** You will not be able to complete the tutorials or exercises in this book using your own computer until you have Data Disks.

Visit Our World Wide Web Site

Additional materials designed especially for you are available on the World Wide Web. Go to **http://www.course.com**.

To the Instructor

The Data files and Lab are available on the Instructor's Resource Kit for this title. Follow the instructions in the Help file on the CD-ROM to install the programs to your network or standalone computer. For information on creating Data Disks, see the "To the Student" section above.

You are granted a license to copy the Data Files and Lab to any computer or computer network used by students who have purchased this book.

OBJECTIVES

In this tutorial you will:

- Examine cost-volume-profit relationships
- Learn the principles of multiple what-if analyses
- Use one-variable data tables to perform a what-if analysis
- Use two-variable data tables to perform a what-if analysis
- Create scenarios to perform what-if analyses
- Create a scenario summary report to save your conclusions

DATA TABLES AND SCENARIO MANAGEMENT

Perform Cost-Volume-Profit Analysis for Davis Blades

CASE

Davis Blades

Davis Blades is a manufacturer of in-line skates in Madison, Wisconsin and has retail outlets across the Central and Midwestern regions of the country. Davis Blades has been in business for four years, and sales have increased each year due to the increasing popularity of rollerblading as a sport and as a form of exercise across all age groups. The company carries six models of in-line skates at various prices. One of its most popular products is the Professional model, a high-quality in-line skate that is popular with men and women who participate in roller hockey leagues.

Although the company sales figures have increased each year, the sales manager of the North Central region, Anne Costello, regularly monitors manufacturing costs, overhead expenses, and pricing policies to make sure Davis Blades remains profitable in the rapidly changing business environment. She asks you to create a report describing the profitability of the Professional model for her region. She gives you information detailing the expenses involved in creating the Professional model, as well as its retail price per unit. She wants you to use this information to calculate monthly operating income generated by the Professional model, using several assumptions regarding sales price and sales volume. With this information, she will be able to make sound business decisions to keep the product profitable.

SESSION 9.1

In this session you'll examine the basic principles of cost-volume-profit analysis. You'll learn about data tables and how they can help you describe the relationship between cost, volume, and profits under different sets of circumstances. You'll learn about one- and two-variable data tables and how to create and display them.

Principle of Cost-Volume-Profit Relationships

One of Anne's major tasks at Davis Blades is to quantify the different factors that affect the company's profitability. For example, if the company sells an additional 10,000 pairs of in-line skates a month, how much additional income will that generate? How much additional expense would be incurred? How many pairs does the company need to sell each month in order to break even?

You can find answers to questions like these by using cost-volume-profit analysis. **Cost-Volume-Profit (CVP) analysis** expresses the relationship among a product's expenses (cost), its volume (units sold), and the resulting profit. CVP analysis is an important business decision-making tool because it helps managers quickly and easily predict the effects of cutting overhead or raising prices on profit. Although volume and profit are straightforward terms, you should understand the types of expenses that are part of CVP calculations.

Types of Expenses

The first component of CVP analysis is cost, or expense. A business like Davis Blades has three types of expenses. **Variable expenses** change in direct proportion to the number of units produced. For example, Davis Blades must purchase raw materials to create its in-line skates, such as leather and bearings. As it increases the number of units it produces, it must spend more money on raw materials. So raw material is a variable expense for Davis Blades, because the expense increases with higher quantities produced. To give you an idea how much expenses increase, Anne tells you that one pair of Professionals costs the company $50 in raw materials and $30 in manufacturing expenses. The graph in Figure 9-1 displays the company's variable expenses. As the number of units increases (shown on the horizontal x-axis), so does the cost of material (shown on the vertical y-axis). If Davis Blades produces 500 units, its variable expenses are $40,000. If it produces no in-line skates, its variable expenses are zero.

Figure 9-1 GRAPH OF VARIABLE EXPENSES

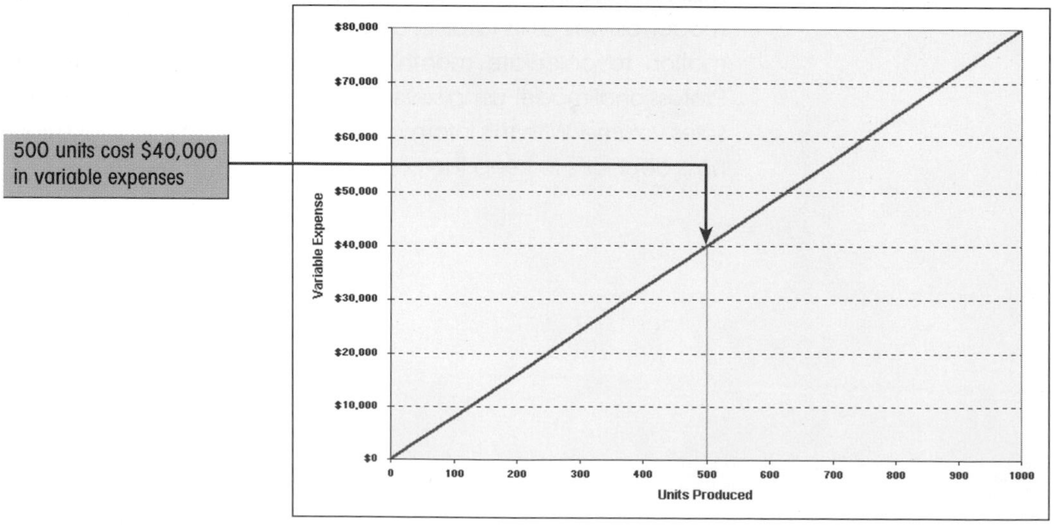

Anne tells you that Davis Blades sells the Professional for a unit price of $198 a pair. If you deduct the variable expenses ($80) from the unit price, it might seem like the company earns a profit of almost $120 from each unit. It doesn't, however, because it also has to pay for a second type of expense, **fixed expense**. A fixed expense is an expense that Davis Blades must pay regardless of the number of units it sells. For example, machinery leasing or office rental does not change with an increase or decrease in production. Davis Blades spends about $120,000 a month on fixed expenses, even if it doesn't sell any units of the Professional.

Mixed expenses are part variable and part fixed. Salaries are sometimes a mixed expense. For example, Davis Blades has some employment expenses regardless of how many units it produces, such as the salaries of the office manager and the marketing staff. But salary costs will increase if the company decides to hire new manufacturing employees to accommodate an increase in production.

By adding its variable, fixed, and mixed expenses, Davis Blades can predict how much it costs to produce a specific number of Professionals. Figure 9-2 displays the company's monthly expenses—variable, fixed, and mixed—as they relate to the number of in-line skates produced.

Figure 9-2 GRAPH OF TOTAL MONTHLY EXPENSES

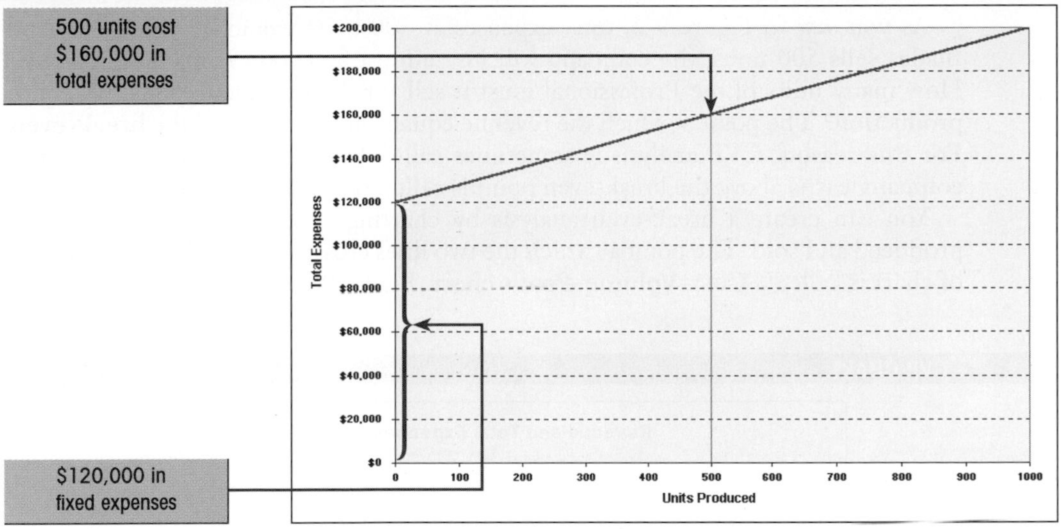

This chart more accurately represents Davis Blades' expenses. If Davis Blades produces no in-line skates, it would still have $120,000 in total expenses. If it produces 500 units, its total expenses would total $160,000 ($40,000 in variable expenses and $120,000 in fixed expenses.) With a better picture of Davis Blades' expenses, you can calculate another important component of CVP analysis: the break-even point.

The Break-Even Point

As Davis Blades increases the volume of in-line skates it sells, it increases its revenue, as shown in Figure 9-3. Because a pair of Professional in-line skates sells for $198, its revenue for 500 pairs would be almost $100,000.

Figure 9-3 GRAPH OF REVENUE PER NUMBER OF UNITS SOLD

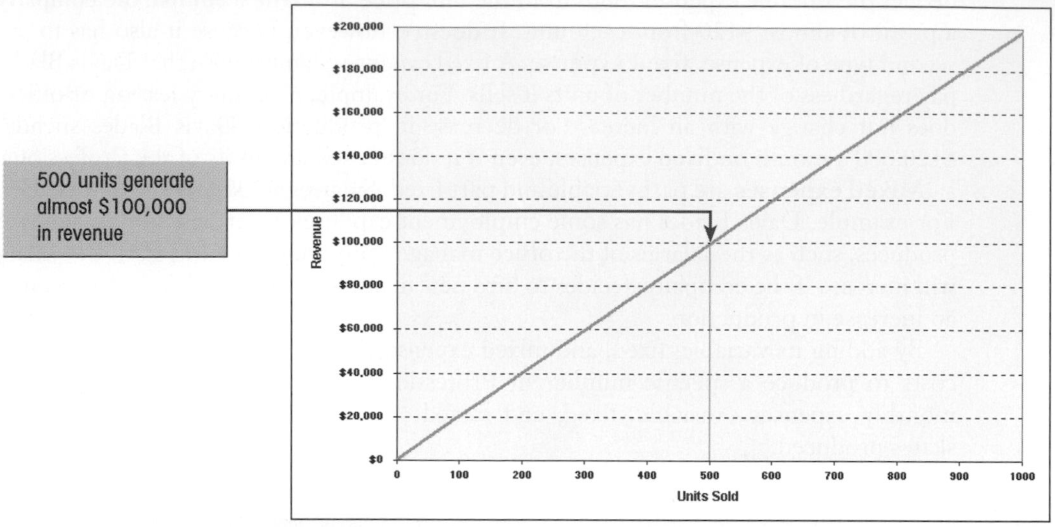

As you saw in Figure 9-2, total expenses at 500 units would be $160,000. So if Davis Blades sells 500 units, the company will lose almost $60,000 ($160,000 minus $100,000). How many units of the Professional must it sell for the revenue to equal the total cost of production? The point at which the revenue equals the cost is called the **break-even point**. For this reason, CVP analysis is sometimes called **break-even analysis**. Any money the company earns above the break-even point is called **operating income**, or **profit**.

You can create a break-even analysis by charting revenue and expenses versus units produced and sold. The point at which the two lines cross is the break-even point. This type of chart is called a **Cost-Volume-Profit chart**. Figure 9-4 shows a typical CVP chart.

Figure 9-4 CVP CHART

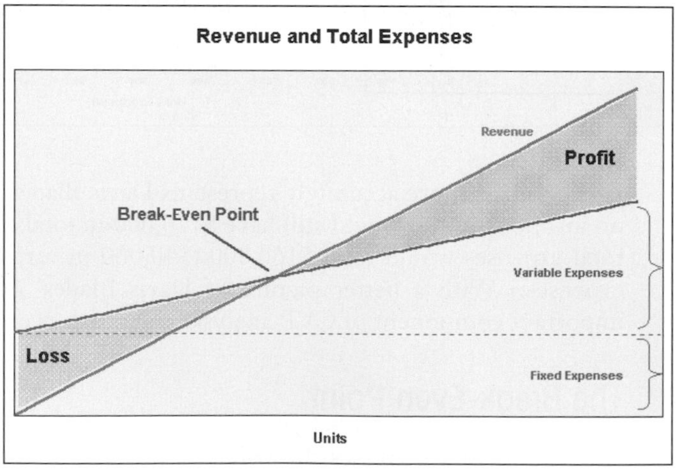

Using a chart like this, you can quickly determine the unit sales volume necessary for a company to show a profit from a particular product.

Planning Income and Expenses at Davis Blades

Anne wants to determine the number of units Davis Blades has to sell to break even and then produce a profit. She also wants to see the cost-volume-profit picture at Davis Blades, so she can make sure its prices reflect the cost of doing business. To help you obtain this information, she has given you a worksheet containing income and expense figures for the Professional in-line skates for a typical month. You will use these figures as the basis for a CVP analysis using Excel. The workbook is stored as Davis on your Data Disk.

To open the Davis workbook and view the datasheet:

1. Start Excel as usual, insert your Data Disk in the appropriate drive, open the file **Davis** from the Tutorial folder for Tutorial.09 on your Data Disk then save the file as **Break-even Analysis**.
2. Type **Break-even Analysis** in cell B3, type (**Your Name**) in cell B4, and type the (**Date**) in cell B5.
3. Click the **CVP Data** sheet tab. Figure 9-5 shows Anne's sales and expense figures.

Figure 9-5 CVP TABLE FOR THE PROFESSIONAL MODEL

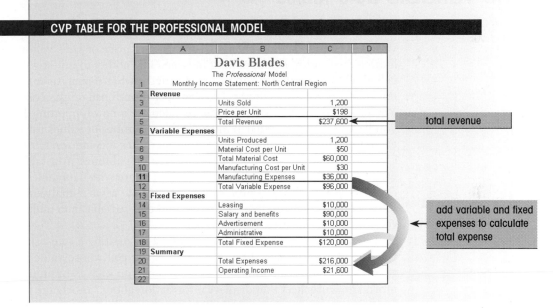

	A	B	C	D
1	Davis Blades The *Professional* Model Monthly Income Statement: North Central Region			
2	**Revenue**			
3		Units Sold	1,200	
4		Price per Unit	$198	
5		Total Revenue	$237,600	
6	**Variable Expenses**			
7		Units Produced	1,200	
8		Material Cost per Unit	$50	
9		Total Material Cost	$60,000	
10		Manufacturing Cost per Unit	$30	
11		Manufacturing Expenses	$36,000	
12		Total Variable Expense	$96,000	
13	**Fixed Expenses**			
14		Leasing	$10,000	
15		Salary and benefits	$90,000	
16		Advertisement	$10,000	
17		Administrative	$10,000	
18		Total Fixed Expense	$120,000	
19	**Summary**			
20		Total Expenses	$216,000	
21		Operating Income	$21,600	
22				

total revenue

add variable and fixed expenses to calculate total expense

The CVP Data sheet contains an Income Statement, showing the Professional's price per unit and anticipated sales volume for a one-month period. It also shows the variable and fixed expenses Davis Blades incurs by producing that quantity of the Professional model in-line skates. No mixed expenses are reported. As you can see in Figure 9-5, each pair of Professionals sells for $198. The total material cost per unit ($50) and manufacturing cost per unit ($30) is $80. If Davis Blades sells 1200 units of the Professional, variable costs for manufacturing and materials will total $96,000. The total fixed expenses for each month are $120,000. The formula in cell C21 calculates the operating income by subtracting total expenses from total revenue. If the North Central region of Davis Blades can produce and sell 1200 units, they can cover their variable and fixed expenses and show an operating income or profit of $21,600 each month.

Anne would like to know what would happen to monthly operating income if the region's monthly sales of the Professional increased to 1300 units.

To calculate income for sales of 1300 units:

1. Click cell **C3**.
2. Type **1300** and press the **Enter** key. The monthly operating income for Davis Blades for sales of the Professional model increases to $33,400, as shown in cell C21.
3. Enter **1200** in cell C3 to return the Break-even Analysis workbook back to its original state.

You call Anne and give her the new profit figure. Anne decides that she would like to have operating income calculations for sales levels ranging from 800 to 1500 units per month. To do this, you could enter each sales figure individually in cell C3 and record the results as you go, but it would be much easier to have Excel do the work for you. You can use Excel to create a data table that will calculate the operating income for any sales level you specify.

One-Variable **Data Tables**

One of the advantages of spreadsheets is that they allow you to quickly see how changing variables (items that can change), such as sales price or sales volume, can affect the value of a calculated figure like operating income. The ability to investigate different possibilities is called **what-if analysis**. You just performed a what-if analysis for Anne by determining the effect that increasing sales by 100 units per month had on the company's operating income. You changed the Units Sold value to calculate a new Operating Income value. Sometimes you'll want to create what-if analyses for a number of values for a particular variable. For example, Anne wants you to examine operating income for sales from 800 to 1500 units. Organizing and presenting these different possibilities in a table makes the information easier to view and use. Excel provides this feature with data tables. **Data tables** are a way of organizing and displaying the results of multiple what-if analyses. Excel supports two kinds of data tables: one-variable data tables and two-variable data tables. You'll examine the one-variable data table first.

There are two important cells involved in creating a one-variable data table: the input cell and the result cell. The **input cell** is the cell whose value you want to change. The **result cell** is the cell containing the outcome you want to examine. For example, consider a mortgage worksheet that displays information about a mortgage with a monthly payment of $840.85 at an interest rate of 9.50%. Figure 9-6 illustrates these conditions.

Figure 9-6 INPUT AND RESULT CELLS

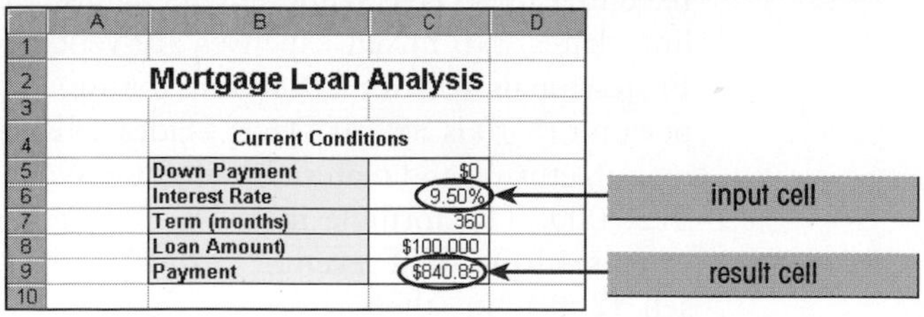

You're wondering what will happen to the monthly payment if you refinance the loan at a different interest rate. The value you want to change is the interest rate, cell C6. So cell C6 is the input cell. The outcome you want to examine is the monthly payment, cell C9—the result cell.

You'd like to calculate monthly payments for a whole set of possible interest rates. Those possible interest rates are called **input values**; they are variations of the value entered into the input cell. The input cell C6 currently has the value 9.50%. You'd like to try input values of 8.75%, 9.00%, 9.25%, and so on. Based on those input values, you want to produce result values that are the outcome of each input value you use. For example, if you use an input value of 8.75%, your result value is a monthly payment of $786.70. Figure 9-7 displays the relationship between input values and result values.

Figure 9-7 SUBSTITUTING INPUT VALUES FOR THE INPUT CELL TO ARRIVE AT RESULT VALUES

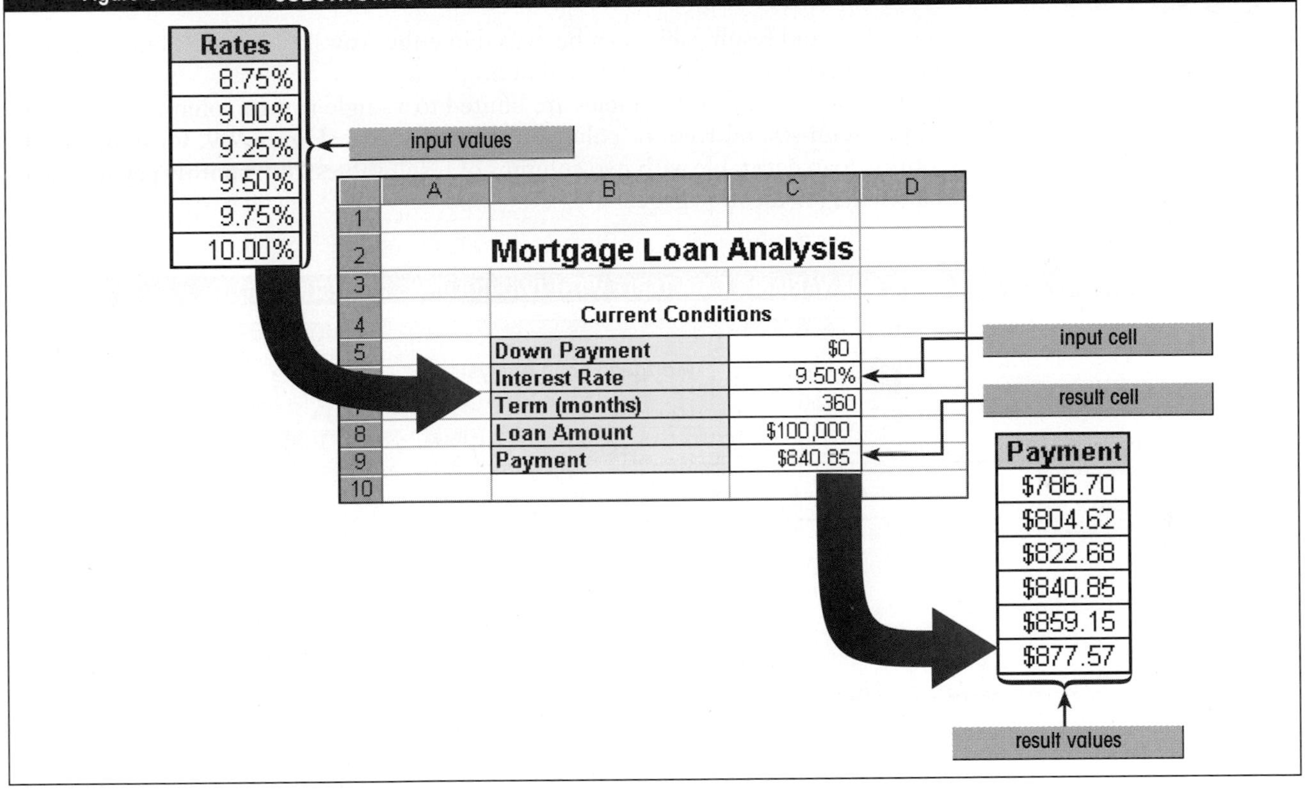

A **one-variable data table** is a table containing input values and their corresponding result values. Figure 9-8 shows a one-variable data table with current conditions for the loan on the left and the data table on the right. The data table lists the input values (the possible interest rates) in the left column and the result values (the corresponding monthly payment for each interest rate) in the right column.

Figure 9-8 A SAMPLE ONE-VARIABLE DATA TABLE

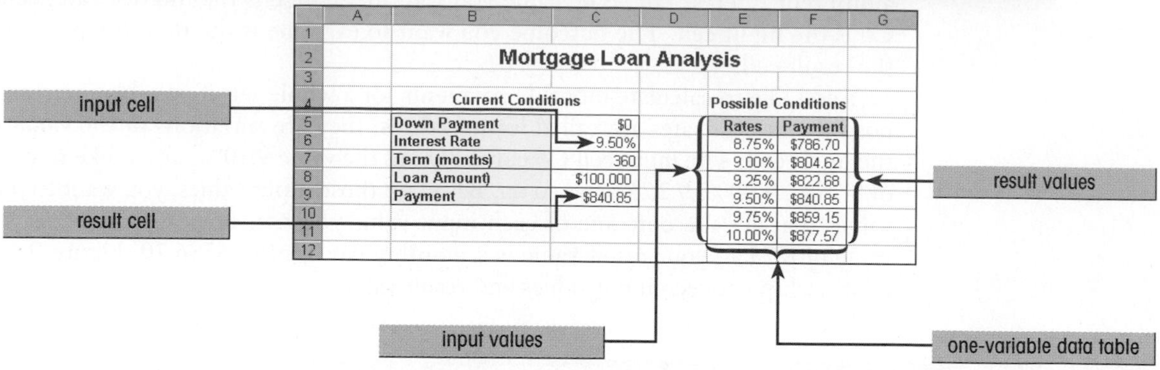

Input values and result values can be placed in either rows or columns, but the input values must be placed in the *first* row or column.

Although one-variable input tables are limited to a single row or column of input values, they can contain several rows or columns of result values. Figure 9-9, for example, shows the monthly loan data table with two columns of result values: the monthly payment and the total payments for the mortgage.

Figure 9-9 A SAMPLE ONE-VARIABLE DATA TABLE WITH TWO COLUMNS OF RESULT VALUES

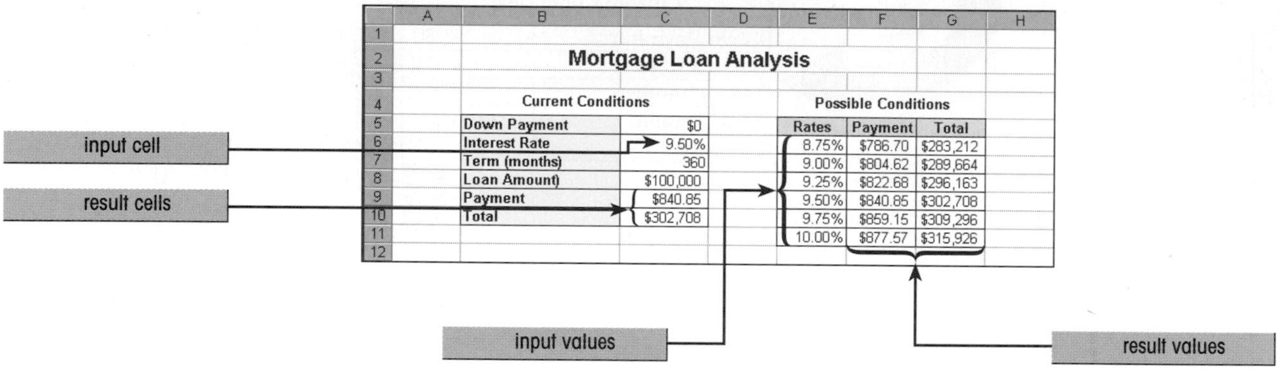

Now that you have seen what a one-variable data table looks like, you are ready to create your own in the Break-even Analysis workbook.

Creating a One-Variable Data Table

To supply the information Anne needs, you'll create a one-variable data table that allows you to evaluate the financial situation when varying quantities of Professional in-line skates are sold. The input cell is cell C3, the number of units sold and the input values range from 800 to 1500 units in increments of 100. The result cells are the total revenue (cell C5), total expenses (cell C20) and income (cell C21.) Thus, this data table will have four columns—one for the input values and one for each of the three results values. Figure 9-10 shows the areas of the worksheet you'll work with.

Figure 9-10 PLANNING THE ONE-VARIABLE DATA TABLE FOR DAVIS BLADES

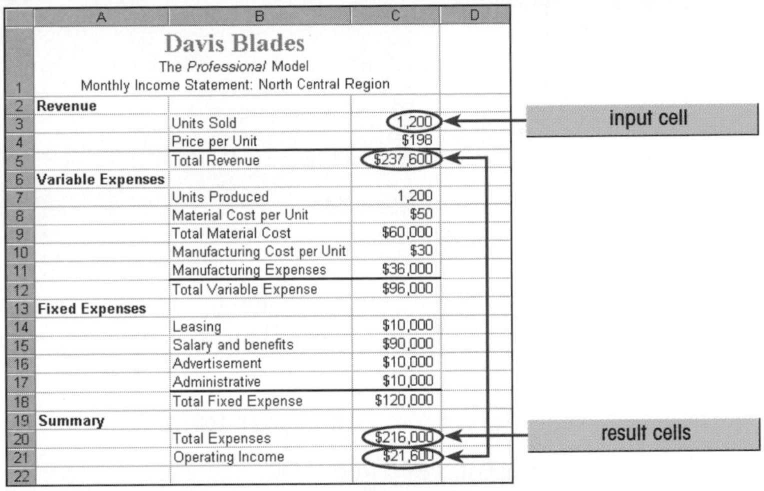

	A	B	C	D
1	Davis Blades The *Professional* Model Monthly Income Statement: North Central Region			
2	**Revenue**			
3		Units Sold	1,200	
4		Price per Unit	$198	
5		Total Revenue	$237,600	
6	**Variable Expenses**			
7		Units Produced	1,200	
8		Material Cost per Unit	$50	
9		Total Material Cost	$60,000	
10		Manufacturing Cost per Unit	$30	
11		Manufacturing Expenses	$36,000	
12		Total Variable Expense	$96,000	
13	**Fixed Expenses**			
14		Leasing	$10,000	
15		Salary and benefits	$90,000	
16		Advertisement	$10,000	
17		Administrative	$10,000	
18		Total Fixed Expense	$120,000	
19	**Summary**			
20		Total Expenses	$216,000	
21		Operating Income	$21,600	
22				

REFERENCE WINDOW RW

Creating a One-Variable Data Table

- Determine whether you want values for the input cell to appear in the first row or first column of the table.
- Insert a reference to the input cell in the upper-left cell of the table.
- If you want input values in the first row, insert input values in the first row of the table. If you want input values in the first column, insert input values in the first column of the table.
- If you want input values in the first row, insert references to result cells in the first column of the table beneath the reference to the input cell. If you want input values in the first column, insert references to result cells in the first row of the table to the right of the reference to the input cell.
- Select the table, click Data, and then click Table.
- Enter the cell reference for the input cell in the Row input cell box when input values are in the first row, or in the Column input cell box when input values are in the first column, and then click the OK button.

You're ready to create the data table to address Anne's sales concerns. You'll place the table in the cell range E2:H11 of the CVP Data worksheet.

To start creating the one-variable data table:

1. Enter **Units** in cell E2. Enter the remaining labels as follows:

   in cell F2: **Revenue**

   in cell G2: **Expenses**

   in cell H2: **Income**

2. Now enter references to the Units Sold, Revenue, Expenses, and Income cells. These are the current values of these cells in the worksheet.

in cell E3: **=C3**

in cell F3: **=C5**

in cell G3: **=C20**

in cell H3: **=C21**

With the column headings and formulas entered for the data table, you'll now enter a column of input values. This will be placed in the first column, cell range E4:E11.

To enter the input values:

1. Enter **800** in cell E4.

2. Enter **900** in cell E5.

3. Select the range **E4:E5**, and then drag the fill handle to extend the range to cell **E11**.

After you release the mouse button, Excel fills the range with the units sold values ranging from 800 to 1500 in increments of 100. See Figure 9-11.

Figure 9-11 ENTERING INPUT VALUES

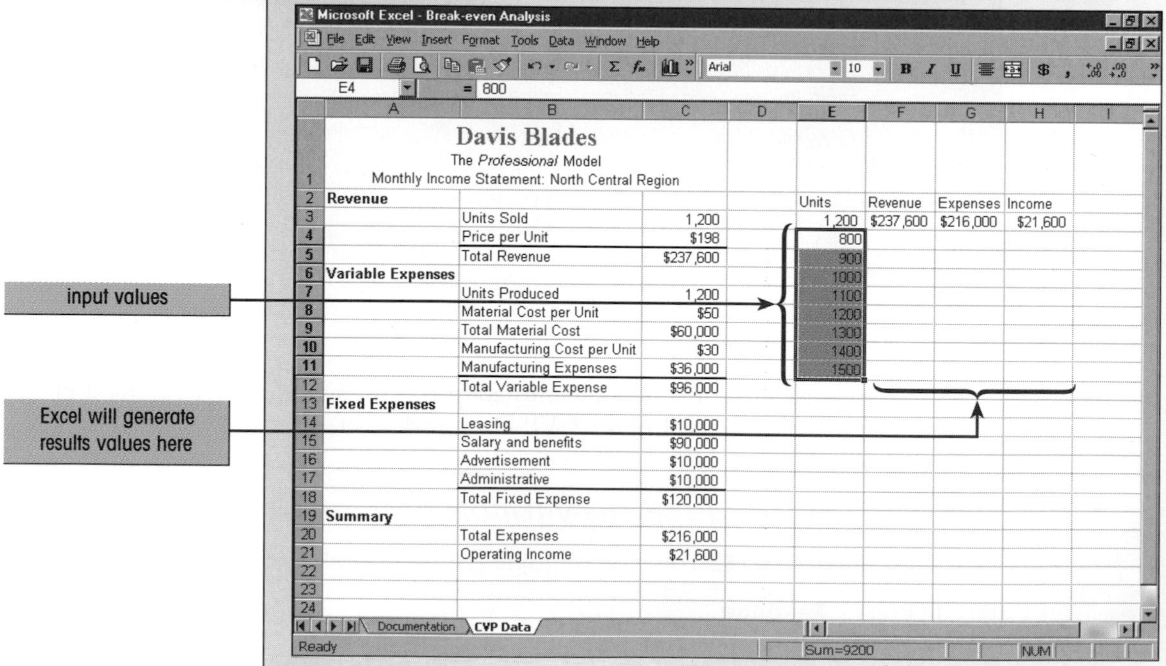

The final step in creating the one-variable data table is to instruct Excel to fill the table with the result values. To do this, you select the range of the data table (excluding the column headings you created) and run Excel's Data Table command. You will then need to designate the input cell and indicate whether the input values are in column or row format. Because your input values are in a column, you will use the Column input cell option. If you had oriented the table so that the input values were in a single row, you would use the Row input cell option.

To complete the one-variable data table:

1. Select the range **E3:H11**, click **Data** on the menu bar, and then click **Table**. The Table dialog box opens. Now you'll specify that the input cell is cell C3 and that it is in column format.

2. Type **C3** in the Column input cell box to reference the cell containing the units sold. See Figure 9-12.

Figure 9-12 ENTERING THE LOCATION OF THE INPUT CELL

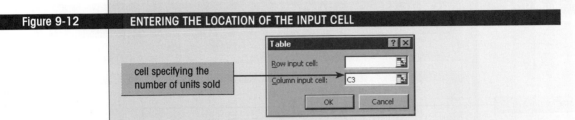

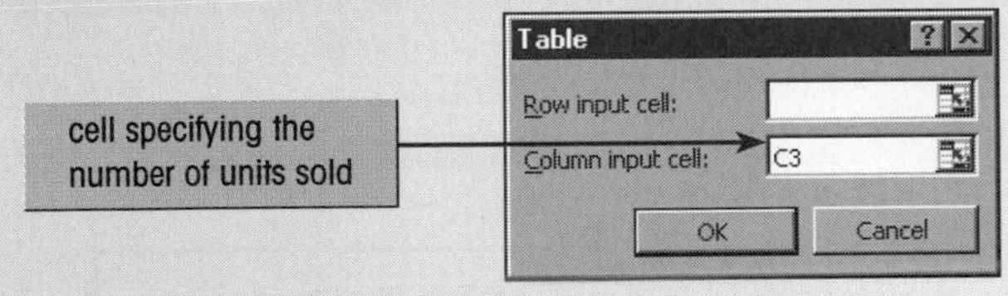

3. Click the **OK** button. Excel places the result values into the data table, as shown in Figure 9-13.

Figure 9-13 THE RESULT VALUES FOR REVENUE, TOTAL EXPENSES, AND INCOME

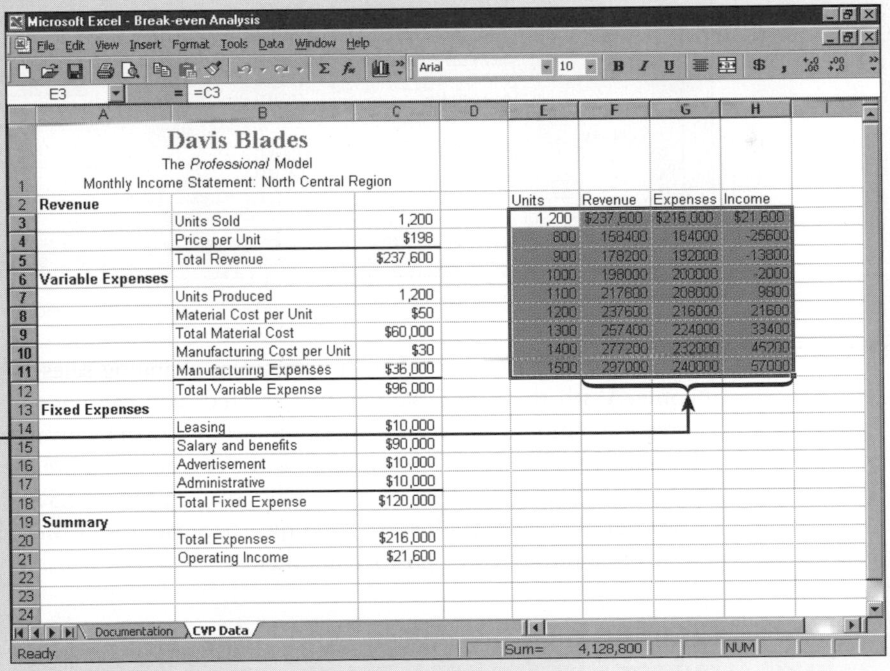

result values

It'll be easier to interpret the table if you reformat the values. You can do this quickly using the Format Painter tool on the toolbar. Recall that the Format Painter allows you to copy the format used in one range of cells and insert that format into another cell range.

To format the values in the table:

1. Select the range **E3:H3** and click the **Format Painter** button on the Standard toolbar. (You might have to click the More Buttons button on the toolbar.) Now you'll apply the format of the range you selected to the rest of the values in the table.
2. Select the range **E4:H11** to apply the formats.
3. Click cell **E2** to deselect the range. Figure 9-14 displays the one-variable data table with the values nicely formatted.

Figure 9-14 THE FINAL, FORMATTED DATA TABLE

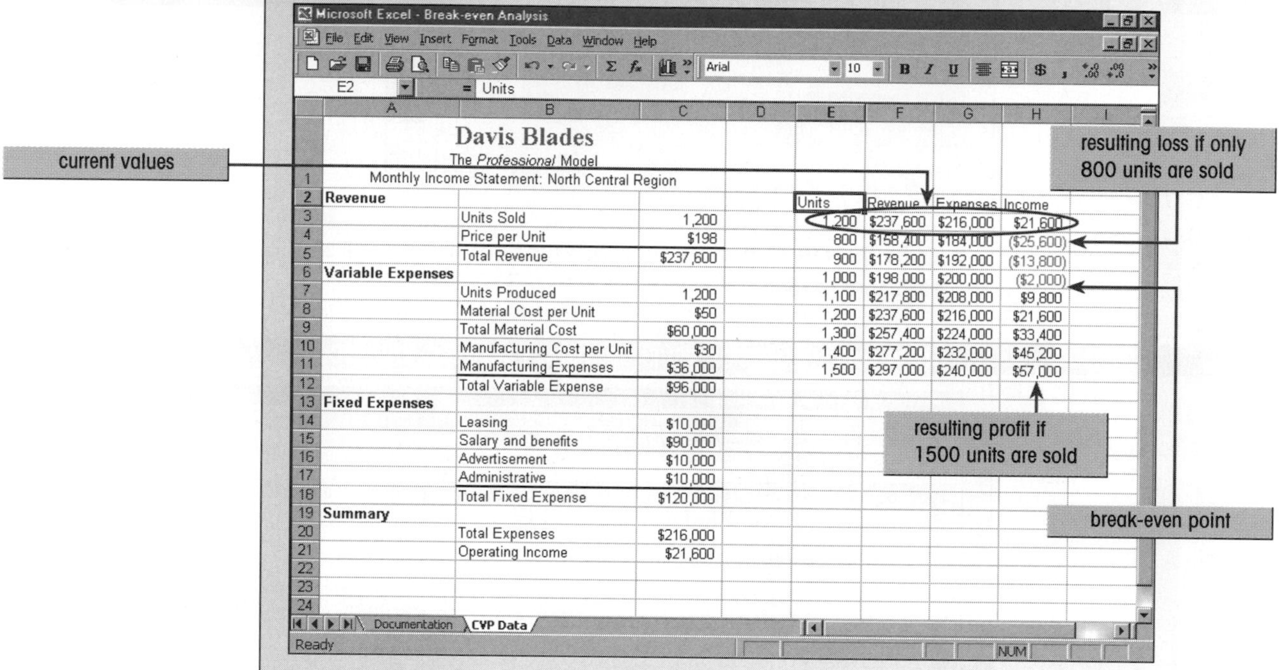

Anne wanted to know what the impact of changing sales volume would be on operating income. With the data table you just created, you can answer her question. If sales of the Professional model fall to 800 units a month in North Central region, Anne will be reporting a loss of $25,000. On the other hand, if the region can increase monthly sales to 1500 units, she will be able to report an operating income or profit of $57,000. The break-even point lies somewhere between 1000 and 1100 units, because it is at these levels that operating income goes from a negative to a positive number.

Charting a One-Variable Data Table

You could give Anne a copy of the data table you have created, but the results will be much clearer if you include a CVP chart along with the table. The chart will give her a better picture of the relationship among the three variables. To create the chart, you'll need figures for the number of units sold, revenue, and expenses, which are all in the one-variable data table you've created.

To create the CVP chart:

1. Select the range **E2:G11**, click **Insert** on the menu bar, and then click **Chart**.

TROUBLE? If the Office Assistant appears, click the "No, don't provide help now button."

2. Click **XY (Scatter)** in the Chart type list box, click the **Scatter with data points connected by lines without markers** chart sub-type as shown in Figure 9-15, and then click the **Next** button twice.

Figure 9-15 CREATING A CVP SCATTER CHART

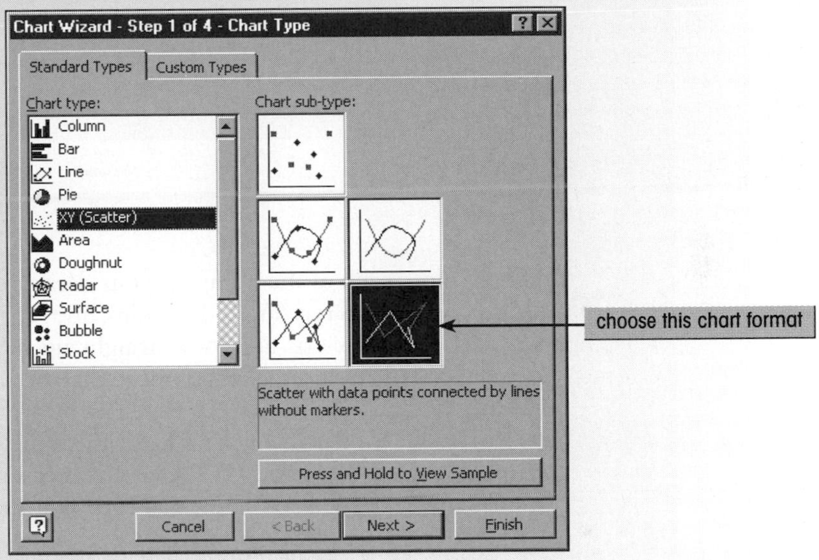

Now you'll label the chart and the horizontal axis so that others will know how to interpret the chart.

3. Type **Cost-Volume-Profit** in the Chart title box, and press the **Tab** key.

4. Type **Units Sold** in the Value (X) Axis box, and click the **Next** button. Now you'll specify that you want the chart placed on a separate sheet.

5. Click the **As new sheet** option button, and type **CVP Chart** in the As new sheet text box.

6. Click the **Finish** button. Figure 9-16 displays the completed chart.

Figure 9-16 THE COMPLETED CVP CHART

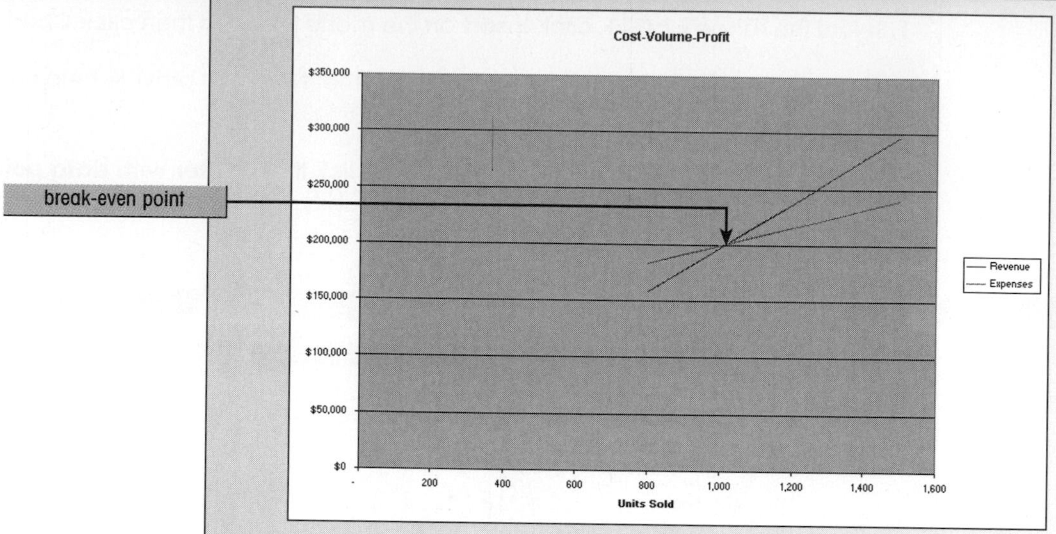

Excel plots each of the points in your data table, connecting them with a line. The dark blue line represents revenue and the pink line represents expenses. If you locate the 800 units sold mark on the x-axis and look straight up to the lines, you'll see that expenses exceed revenue—in other words, a loss of more than $25,000. If you locate 1400 units on the x-axis, you can see that revenue exceeds expenses by around $45,000. These loss and profit figures agree with the ones in the data table for the same levels of units sold.

With the data table and CVP chart, you can give Anne a comprehensive picture of the impact of sales levels upon both total expenses and revenue.

Two-Variable **Data Tables**

Anne has reviewed your figures and incorporated them into her plans. Currently, competitive conditions have changed. A rival company, Street-Wise, is selling an in-line skate model that competes with the Professional. The model sells for $20 less. Anne wants to know what kind of cost-volume-profit results she would see if Davis Blades reduced the price of the Professional by $20.

Because data tables are dynamic, changes in the worksheet are automatically reflected in the data table. To see the effect of changing the unit price in the data table, you'll change the value in cell C4 from $198 to $178.

To view the effect of changing the sales price:

1. Click the **CVP Data** sheet tab to return to the sales worksheet.
2. Enter **178** in cell C4. Figure 9-17 shows the updated worksheet and data table. Note that the monthly operating income (assuming 1200 units sold) is now an operating loss of $2,400, as shown in cell C21.

Figure 9-17 THE EFFECT OF REDUCING THE PRICE PER UNIT FROM $198 TO $178

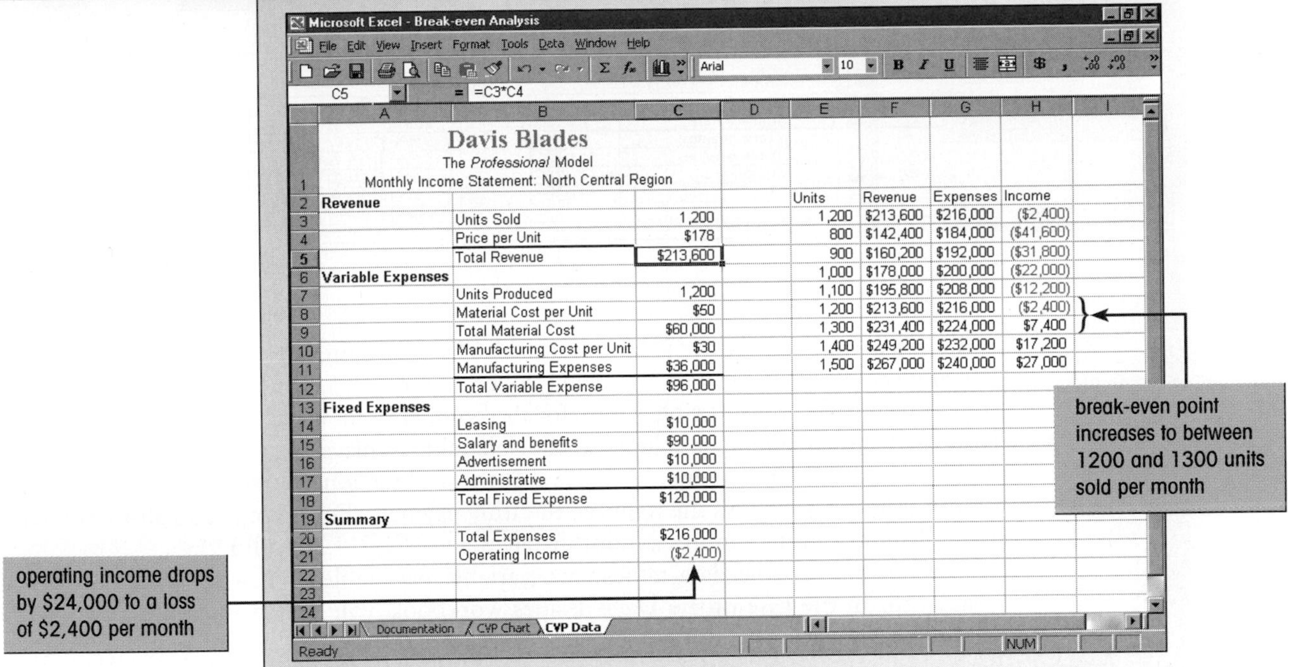

3. View the CVP Chart sheet. The break-even point, where the Revenue and Expenses lines intersect, has moved to the right, indicating that Davis Blades would have to sell more units at this lower price to break even. Now return the price to its original level.

4. Return to the CVP Data worksheet, and enter **198** in cell C4. The one-variable data table and the rest of the worksheet now display their prior values.

Based on the information from Figure 9-17, the region would have to sell somewhere between 1200 and 1300 units of its Professional model per month to break even at a unit price of $178. Moreover, the region would have to sell between 1400 and 1500 units per month to generate the same profit margin it had by selling 1200 units of the Professional a month for $198.

When she learns these results, Anne decides that she would like to see how other prices for this model affect her region's monthly operating income, in conjunction with the varying levels of units sold. She asks you to give her the operating income for unit prices of $176, $180, $184, $188, $192 and $196, and for monthly sales volumes of 800 to 1500 units, in increments of 100 units. This means you now have to analyze the effects of two variables on operating income: price and sales volume.

You can analyze the effect of these two variables with a two-variable data table. As the name implies, a two-variable data table uses two input cells representing two components that can change to create its result values. Figure 9-18 shows an example of a two-variable data table that calculates mortgage costs.

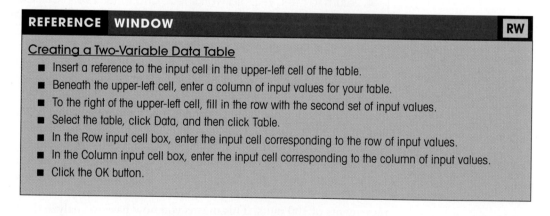

Figure 9-18 A SAMPLE TWO-VARIABLE DATA TABLE

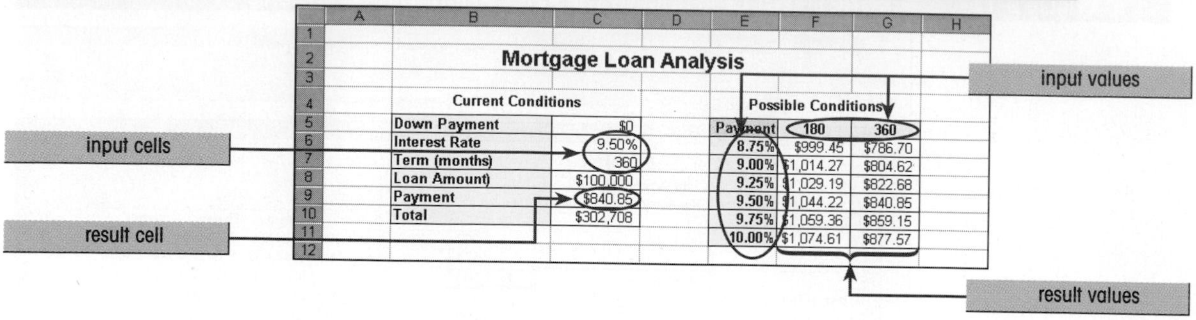

In this example, there are two input cells: cell C6, the interest rate, and cell C7, the number of months before the loan is repaid (180 or 360 months). Notice that the first row of the data table displays two possible values for the number of months before the loan is paid (180 and 360 months). The first column of the data table displays different possible interest rates (8.75% to 10%, in increments of 0.25%). At the intersection of each interest rate and length of term, the table displays the required monthly payment. For example, a 180-month term at a 9.50% interest rate requires a monthly payment of $1,044.22 (cell F9).

Unlike one-variable data tables, two-variable data tables can work with only a single result cell. In the case of the Davis Blades workbook, you decide to create a two-variable data table that uses operating income as its result cell.

Creating a Two-Variable Table

Operating income is displayed in cell C21 of the CVP Data worksheet. The two input cells are Units Sold, located in cell C3, and Price per Unit, found in C4.

REFERENCE WINDOW RW

<u>Creating a Two-Variable Data Table</u>

- Insert a reference to the input cell in the upper-left cell of the table.
- Beneath the upper-left cell, enter a column of input values for your table.
- To the right of the upper-left cell, fill in the row with the second set of input values.
- Select the table, click Data, and then click Table.
- In the Row input cell box, enter the input cell corresponding to the row of input values.
- In the Column input cell box, enter the input cell corresponding to the column of input values.
- Click the OK button.

You'll place the two-variable data table below the one-variable data table you just created. First start by creating the input values for the table.

To start creating the two-variable data table:

1. In the CVP Data worksheet, type **$176** in cell F14 as the first possible price for the Professional and press **Tab**.
2. Type **$180** in cell G14. Now you'll complete the row in price increments of $4.

3. Select the range **F14:G14**, and then drag the fill handle to extend the range to **K14**. After you release the mouse button, Excel fills the range with unit prices ranging from $176 to $196, in increments of $4. See Figure 9-19.

Figure 9-19 POSSIBLE PRICES FOR THE PROFESSIONAL MODEL

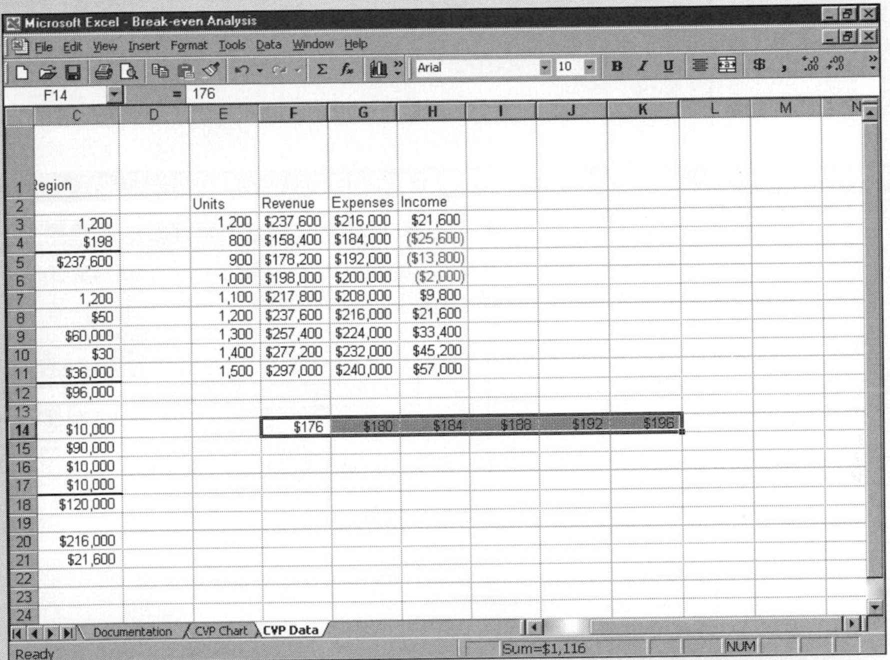

To save time, copy the input values from the one-variable table.

4. Copy the input values in the range **E4:E11** and paste to the range **E15:E22**.

In two-variable tables, you must always place a reference to the result cell in the upper-left corner of the table at the intersection of the row input values and the column input values. This means that you'll place a formula referencing the operating income in cell E14.

Because placing that value in this location on your table might prove confusing to some, you'll format the cell to hide the actual value. Instead of displaying the reference, the format you'll choose will display "Units Sold", a title describing the values in the first column of the table.

To insert a reference to the result cell in the two-variable table:

1. Click cell **E14**, type **=C21**, and press the **Enter** key. The current operating income appears. Now you'll format the cell to hide the actual value and instead display a title for the Units Sold column.

2. Right-click cell **E14** and click **Format Cells** on the shortcut menu. The Format Cells dialog box opens. Normally, you use this dialog box to assign standard formats to cell values. In this case, however, you'll use the Custom format to display a label in cell E14.
3. Click the **Number** tab and click **Custom** in the Category list box. Now you'll replace the default format code with a label.
4. Delete the format code appearing in the Type box.
5. Type "**Units Sold**" (include the quotation marks) in the Type box. See Figure 9-20.

Figure 9-20 SPECIFYING THE FORMAT FOR CELL E14

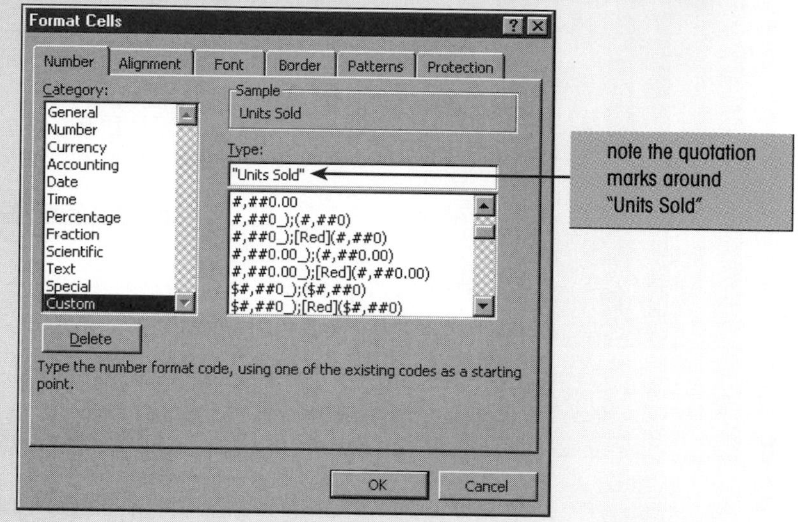

6. Click the **OK** button.

The label "Units Sold" appears in cell E14. The underlying formula entered in that cell, however, remains intact even if it is not visible.

TROUBLE? If the Units Sold text that appears in your cell E14 appears incorrect, you may have forgotten to include the quotation marks. Go back and insert them now and then press the Enter key.

Now you'll enter some descriptive text above the column of possible unit prices.

7. Type **Price per Unit** in cell F13.
8. Select the range **F13:K13** and click the **Merge and Center** button on the Formatting toolbar. (You might need to click the More Buttons button on the toolbar.) The text is now centered above the range of possible prices.
9. Click cell **E14**. Your two-variable table should now look like Figure 9-21.

Figure 9-21 STRUCTURE OF THE TWO-VARIABLE DATA TABLE FOR DAVIS BLADES

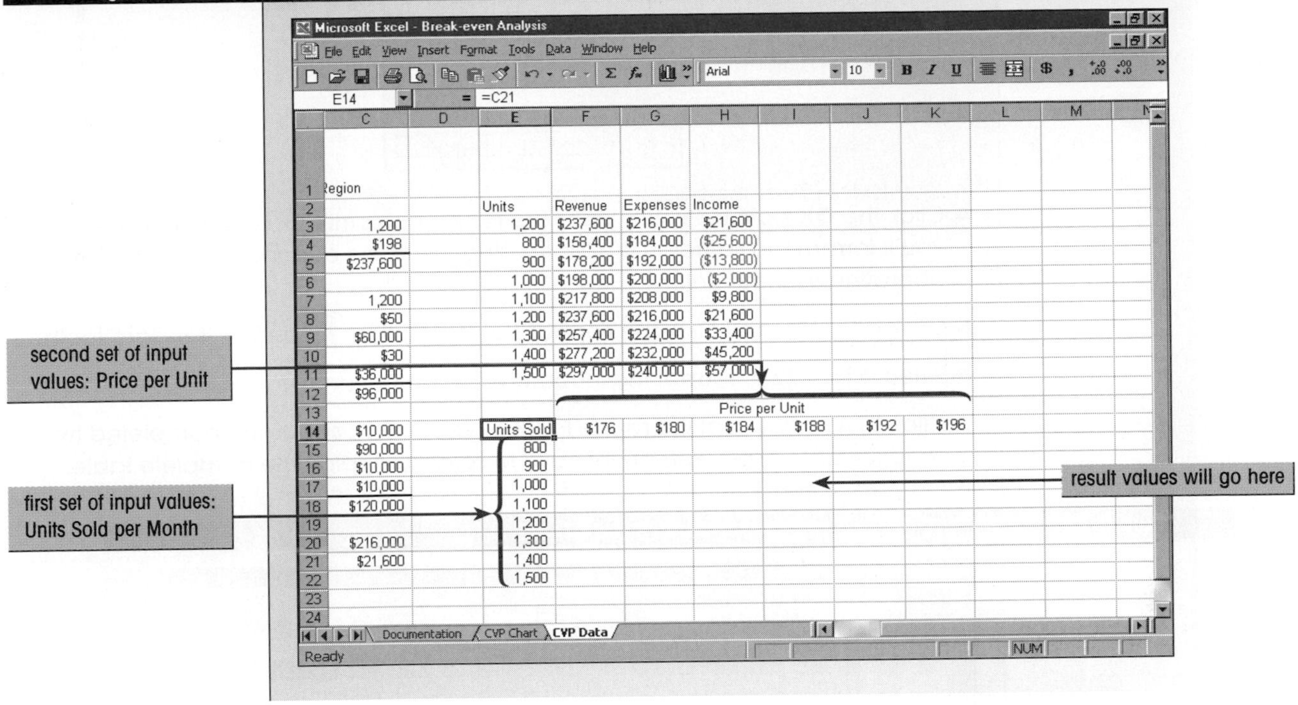

Now that you've set up the table, you can use Excel's Data Table command to calculate and display operating income for each combination of units sold and unit price. When creating a two-variable data table, you must identify the row input cell and the column input cell. The **row input cell** is the cell whose input values are placed in the first row of the table. The first row of your data table contains unit prices, so the row input cell is C4—the cell containing unit price data for the Professional model. Similarly, the **column input cell** is the cell whose input values are placed in the first column of the data table. In this case, that would be C3, the number of units sold per month.

To complete the two-variable table:

1. Select the range **E14:K22**, click **Data** on the menu bar, and then click **Table**. The Table dialog box opens.
2. Type **C4** in the Row input cell box to refer to the cell containing the unit price, and press the **Tab** key.
3. Type **C3** in the Column input cell box to refer to the cell containing the number of units sold. See Figure 9-22.

Figure 9-22 DESIGNATING INPUT CELLS FOR A TWO-VARIABLE DATA TABLE

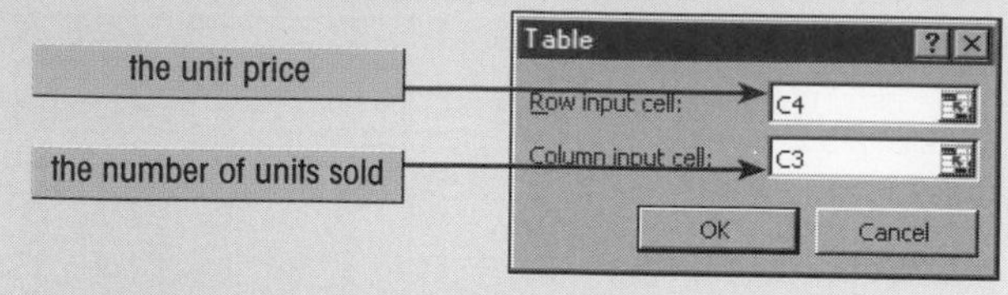

4. Click the **OK** button. Excel places the result values into the data table. Next you'll format the values in the table using the same currency format as the operating income cell.
5. Click cell **C21** and click the **Format Painter** button on the Standard toolbar.
6. Select **F15:K22** to format the income values in currency format.
7. Click **E14** to deselect the range F15:K22. Figure 9-23 shows the completed two-variable data table. You might have to scroll to display the complete table.

Figure 9-23 THE COMPLETED TWO-VARIABLE DATA TABLE

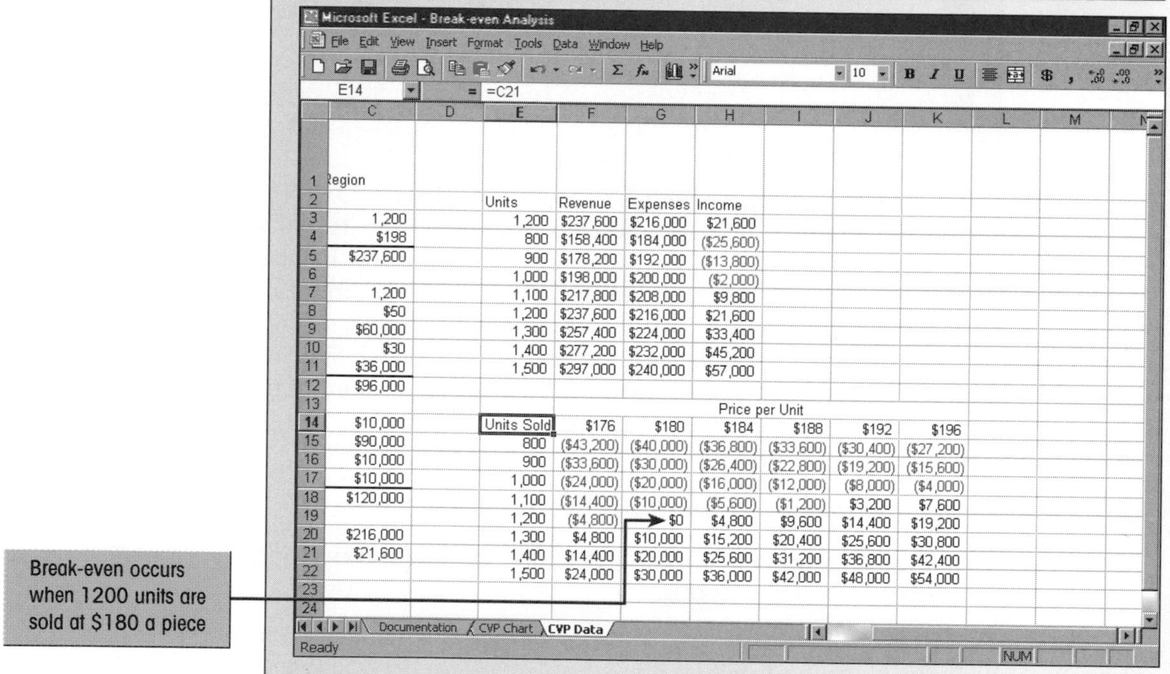

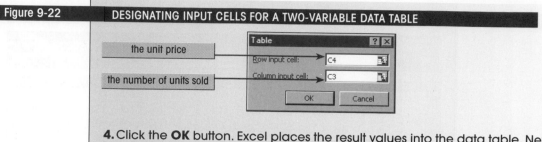

Based on the results shown in Figure 9-23, you tell Anne that if Davis Blades reduces the price of the Professional to $180 to compete with the price offered by Street-Wise, the region will break even at the current sales volume of 1200 units per month. However, if sales drop by 100 units to 1100 units per month, the region will show a loss of $10,000. The region could show a profit at that sales volume only if the unit price is kept at around $192 or more.

Charting a Two-Variable Data Table

There are so many possible combinations of price and sales volume to consider. Perhaps making a chart of these different combinations will simplify matters.

To begin creating the CVP chart:

1. Select the range **E15:K22**, click **Insert** on the menu bar, and then click **Chart**.
2. Click **XY (Scatter)** in the Chart type list box, click the **Scatter with data points connected by lines without markers** box, and then click the **Next** button.

   Because of the structure of the two-variable table, you must manually insert the unit prices into the chart's legend. You can do this by entering the names for each series.
3. Click the **Series** tab and click the **Name** text box.
4. Click the **Collapse dialog box** button, click cell **F14** on the CVP Data worksheet, and then press the **Enter** key. The address for cell F14 appears in the Name box. See Figure 9-24.

Figure 9-24 SETTING UP THE CVP CHART

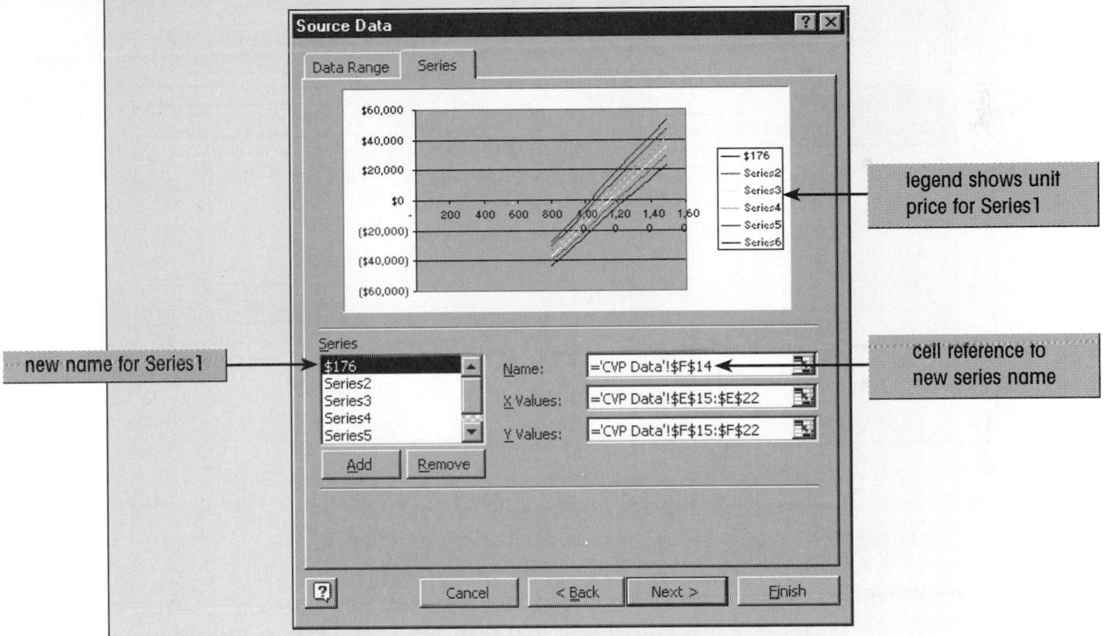

The Series list box displays the value "$176" in the legend for Series1 and the Name box shows the reference "='CVP Data'!$F$14". You could have typed the actual value into the Name box, but by using the reference, you can change input values in the data table, and then both the chart and the chart legend will update automatically.

To replace each series name with the unit price:

1. Click **Series2** in the Series list box, click the **Name** text box, click the **Collapse dialog box** button, click cell **G14**, and then press the **Enter** key.

   Using the same technique:
2. Replace the name for Series3 with the cell reference to **H14**.
3. Replace the Series4 name with the cell reference to **I14**.

4. Replace the Series5 name with the **J14** cell reference.
5. Replace the Series6 name with the **K14** cell reference.
6. Each series name should now have been replaced by the six different unit prices. See Figure 9-25.

Figure 9-25 CVP CHART WITH NEW LEGEND TEXT

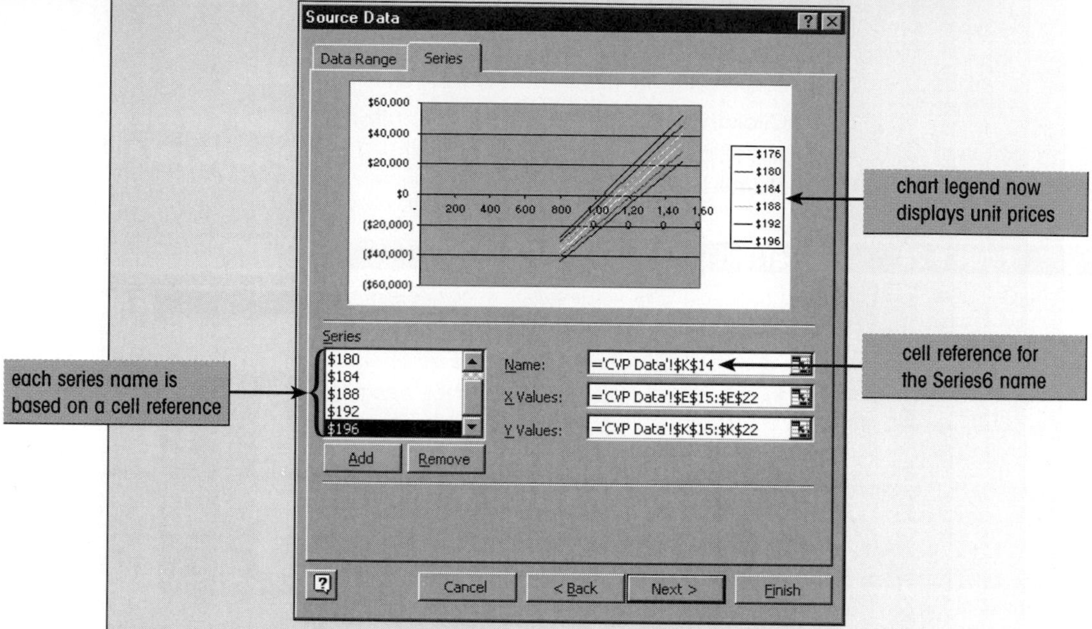

7. Click the **Next** button.

Use the Chart Wizard to complete the chart by adding titles for the chart and axes.

To complete the chart of two-variable table values:

1. Click the **Chart title** text box, type **Operating Income vs. Sales Volume** and then press the **Tab** key.
2. In the Value (X) Axis text box, type **Units Sold** and then press the **Tab** key.
3. In the Value (Y) Axis text box, type **Operating Income** and click the **Next** button.
4. Click the **As new sheet** button, type **Profit vs. Sales Volume**, and click the **Finish** button. Figure 9-26 displays the completed chart of operating income.

Figure 9-26 **REVENUE UNDER DIFFERENT SALES AND PRICE COMBINATIONS**

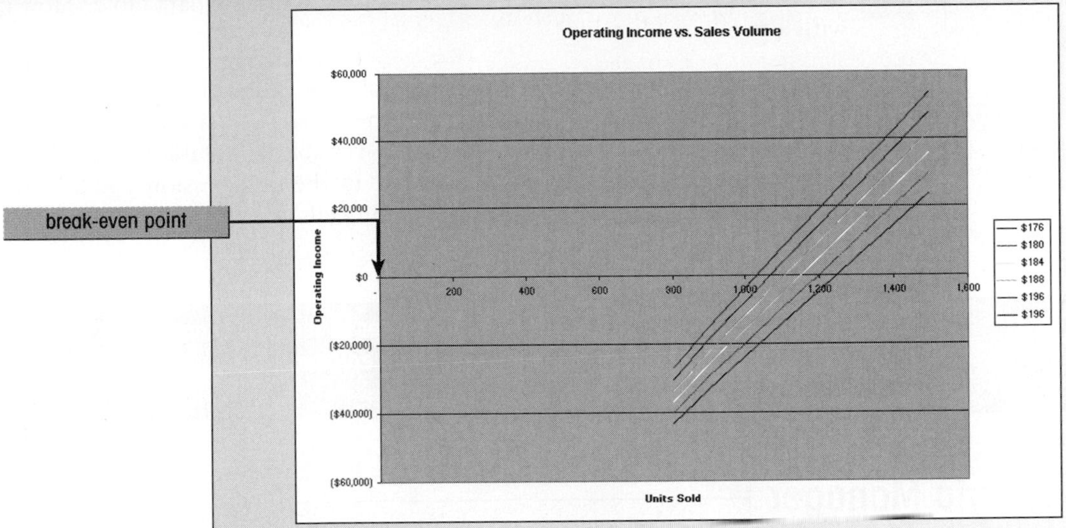

By viewing the chart, Anne can quickly see how different prices for the Professional will affect the relationship between operating income and units sold. At the lowest price of $176, the region will break even only if more than 1200 units are sold each month. At the highest price of $196, the break-even point is just above a monthly sales volume of 1000 units. The graph also makes it clear that at a level of 1500 units, a difference of $20 in the price of the Professional results in a difference in profit of $30,000 per month.

This information will help Anne plan her marketing strategy for the Professional to effectively compete with Street-Wise. Anne will take these figures and study them for a while. For now your job is finished. Save your changes to the Break-even Analysis workbook and print your work.

To complete your work:

1. Click the **Documentation** sheet tab so the next user sees the Documentation sheet when this workbook is opened.
2. Save your changes, print the workbook, and close the workbook.

Anne thanks you for supplying her with the information she needs.

Session 9.1 QUICK CHECK

1. Define CVP analysis.
2. What is the difference between variable, fixed, and mixed expenses?
3. What is the break-even point?
4. What is a data table?
5. What is an input cell? What is a result cell?
6. What is a one-variable data table?

7. What is a two-variable data table?
8. How many result cells can you show with a one-variable data table? How many with a two-variable table?

In this session you learned about the principles of cost-volume-profit relationships, including the break-even point. You created a one-variable data table that calculates the results of changing the price variable, and a two-variable data table to see the results of changing both the price and units sold variables. In the next session you'll learn how to analyze outcomes when more than one or two input cells vary.

SESSION 9.2

In this session you'll use the Excel Scenario Manager to see how changing several input cells affects several result cells. You'll learn how to edit and save your scenarios and to print scenario reports.

Using Scenario Manager

Anne has looked over your figures and discussed them with the regional managers. They would like to look at several different options for reducing cost and/or increasing sales to deal with the new competition from Street-Wise. They have settled on four pricing and expense options and have estimated what they believe to be reasonable sales figures under each option. Figure 9-27 displays the current situation and three other options.

Figure 9-27 FOUR PRICE AND EXPENSE OPTIONS

OPTION	CONDITIONS
Status Quo	■ Units sold = 900 ■ Unit price = $198 ■ Material cost per unit = $50 ■ Advertisement expense = $10,000 ■ Administrative expense = $10,000
Low Cost	■ Units sold = 1400 ■ Unit price = $170 ■ Material cost per unit = $44 ■ Advertisement expense = $10,000 ■ Administrative expense = $5,000
Competitive	■ Units sold = 1300 ■ Unit price = $180 ■ Material cost per unit = $44 ■ Advertisement expense = $16,000 ■ Administrative expense = $5,000
High Cost	■ Units sold = 1000 ■ Unit price = $190 ■ Material cost per unit = $44 ■ Advertisement expense = $10,000 ■ Administrative expense = $5,000

The *Status Quo* option would keep things as they are at Davis Blades. Management feels that sales could drop from 1200 units per month to 900 units, given the increased competition from Street-Wise. Under the ***Low Cost*** option, Davis Blades would reduce the price of the Professional from $198 to $170—$8 less than the Street-Wise price. At the same time, the company would try to reduce its per unit cost of materials from $50 to $44, and would cut administrative overhead (a part of fixed costs) from $10,000 a month to $5,000. The managers feel that reducing the price of the Professional would cause an increase in sales to 1400 units per month.

Under the *Competitive* option, Davis Blades would reduce the cost of the Professional to $180 to compete directly with the Street-Wise price of $178. Davis Blades would try to reduce the per-unit cost of materials from $50 to $44 per unit, and would increase the advertising budget from $10,000 per month to $16,000. At the same time, it would reduce administrative costs to $5,000. Under this option, the company assumes that sales would increase to 1300 units per month.

Finally, the *High Cost* option assumes that Davis Blades would reduce the cost of the Professional to $190 while reducing administrative overhead to $5,000. The company would try to reduce the per-unit cost of materials to $44. This option assumes a decrease in sales from 1200 to 1000 units per month.

Anne wants you to use Excel to evaluate all of these options and create a report summarizing them. She is interested in knowing the revenue that would be generated, the total monthly expenses, and the region's monthly operating income from sales of the Professional under each option.

You quickly see that you can't generate such a report using a data table because Anne has asked you to work with more than two input cells. To deal with problems with more than two input cells, you have to create scenarios. A **scenario** is a set of values entered into a worksheet that describes different situations, like the options that Davis Blades created in Figure 9-27. Instead of creating workbooks for each possible situation, or entering values every time you want to perform a what if analysis, you set up these situations as scenarios using Excel's Scenario Manager. Once you have saved the scenarios, you can view them and work with them any time you want. You'll use Scenario Manager to create the four scenarios that Anne has outlined for you.

First though, open the Davis workbook and save it as Scenario Report.

To open the workbook and display the data:

1. If you took a break after the last session, make sure that Excel is running, and make sure your Data Disk is in the appropriate drive.
2. Open the workbook named **Davis** in the Tutorial folder for Tutorial.09 on your Data Disk, and save it as **Scenario Report.**
3. Enter **Scenario Report** in cell B3, **(Your Name)** in cell B4, and the **(Date)** in cell B5.
4. Go to the **CVP Data** worksheet.

Naming Input and Result Cells

Before using Scenario Manager, you should assign range names to all the input and result cells that you intend to use in your scenarios. As you'll see later, the range names will automatically appear in Scenario Manager's dialog boxes and reports. Though not a requirement, range names make it easier for you to work with your scenarios and for other people to understand your scenario reports.

You can quickly create range names for the values in the Davis Blades workbook using the Excel Create Names feature. This feature allows you to automatically assign names from the cells' labels to cells containing values. The Monthly Income Statement contains labels on the left in column B and values on the right in column C. The Create Names feature will assign, for example, the range name Units_Sold to cell C3, because that is the entry to its left. Use this feature to assign range names to the values in column C based on the corresponding text in column B.

To create range names for the values in the table:

1. Select the range **B3:C21**.
2. Click **Insert** on the menu bar, point to **Name**, and click **Create**.
3. Make sure the Left column check box is the only check box selected, and then click the **OK** button.
4. Click cell **A2** to deselect the range.

Now that you have entered the range names in the workbook, you are ready to start defining the scenarios using Scenario Manager.

Defining Scenarios

To create the first scenario, you start Scenario Manager and enter a name for the scenario.

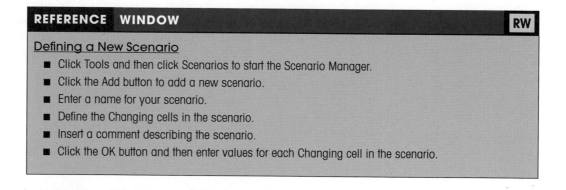

REFERENCE WINDOW RW

Defining a New Scenario

- Click Tools and then click Scenarios to start the Scenario Manager.
- Click the Add button to add a new scenario.
- Enter a name for your scenario.
- Define the Changing cells in the scenario.
- Insert a comment describing the scenario.
- Click the OK button and then enter values for each Changing cell in the scenario.

You'll enter the Status Quo scenario first.

To start Scenario Manager and add a new scenario:

1. Click **Tools** on the menu bar, and then click **Scenarios**. The Scenario Manager dialog box opens. See Figure 9-28.

Figure 9-28 SCENARIO MANAGER OPENING DIALOG BOX

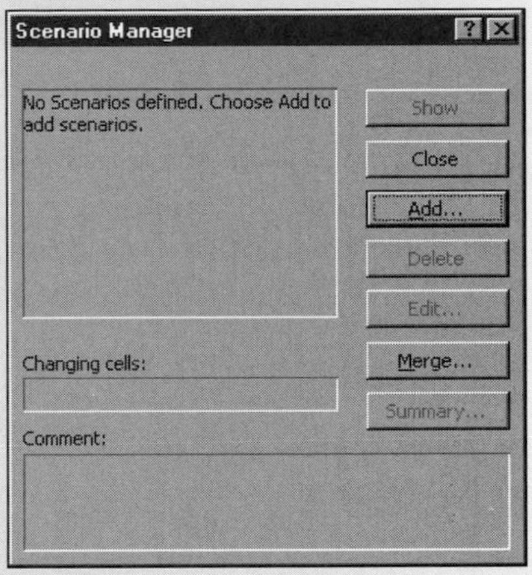

2. Click the **Add** button to add a new scenario to the workbook. The Add Scenario dialog box opens.

3. To name the first scenario you'll create, type **Status Quo** in the Scenario name box, and then press the **Tab** key.

Next you'll specify the input cells you want to use for this scenario. Scenario Manager refers to input cells as **changing cells** because these are the worksheet cells whose values you want to change. Changing cells can be located anywhere on the worksheet. You can type in the names or locations of changing cells, but it's usually easier to select them with the mouse. To select nonadjacent changing cells, hold down the Ctrl key as you click each cell. In each scenario shown earlier in Figure 9-27, the values that will change are:

- C3: Units Sold
- C4: Price per Unit
- C8: Material Cost per Unit
- C16: Advertisement Expense
- C17: Administrative Expense

To specify the changing cells in a scenario:

1. With the Changing cells box selected, click the **Collapse dialog box** button, and select the range **C3:C4** on the worksheet.

2. Press and hold down the **Ctrl** key and click cell **C8**, the Material Cost per Unit.

3. With the Ctrl key still pressed, select the range **C16:C17**, the fixed costs.

4. Release the Ctrl key and press the **Enter** key. The cell range, $C$3:$C$4,$C$8,$C$16:$C$17, should appear in the Changing cells box. Now that you have entered the changing cells, you'll document the scenario with the assumptions that apply to it. That way, other users will know how this scenario relates to the current situation.

5. Press the **Tab** key and type **Projected profit assuming current prices and a drop in monthly sales**. in the Comment box. See Figure 9-29.

Figure 9-29 **SPECIFYING CHANGING CELLS FOR THE STATUS QUO SCENARIO**

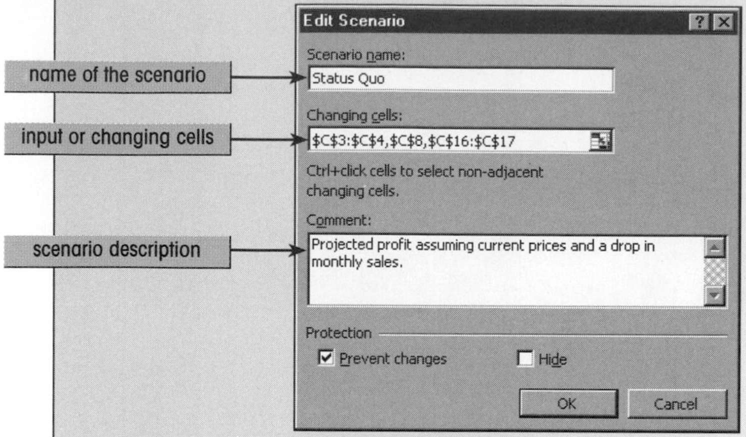

If you want to protect your scenarios from being changed by unauthorized users or hide your scenarios from others, you can select the Prevent Changes and Hide check boxes. Both options require you to protect the worksheet from further changes. See Tutorial 12 for more information about protecting your worksheet and workbook.

6. Click the **OK** button. The Scenario Values dialog box opens.

So far you've specified the location of the changing cells. Now you need to enter the values you want to test under this scenario. With the Status Quo scenario, most of the values will be unchanged from the current workbook, except that management anticipates a decline in monthly sales from 1200 units to 900 units.

To specify values for the changing cells in the scenario:

1. In the Units_Sold box, type **900**. The rest of the values in the Scenarios Values dialog box remain the same. See Figure 9-30.

Figure 9-30 **SPECIFYING VALUES FOR THE CHANGING CELLS OF THE STATUS QUO SCENARIO**

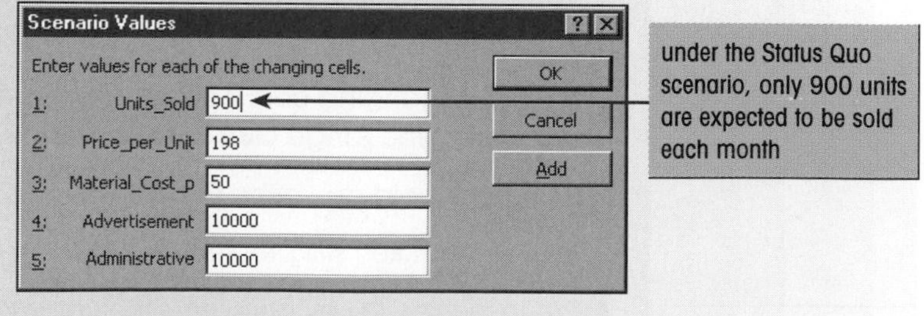

2. Click the **Add** button. Excel adds the scenario you've specified to its list of scenarios, and opens the Add Scenario dialog box.

In Figure 9-30, note that Excel uses the range names you've created to identify each input cell in the Scenario Values dialog box. This makes it easier for you to correctly enter scenario information. Note also that because you clicked the Add button rather than the OK button, you are returned to the Add Scenario dialog box and can proceed to add Anne's remaining scenarios.

To add the three remaining scenarios:

1. Type **Low Cost** in the Scenario name box, and then press the **Tab** key twice.
2. Type **Projected profit assuming $170 price and a rise in sales.** and click the **OK** button.

   Enter the following Low Cost values in the Scenarios Values dialog box:

   1400 in the Units_Sold box
   170 in the Price_per_Unit box
   44 in the Material_cost box
   10000 in the Advertisement box
   5000 in the Administrative box
3. Click the **Add** button, type **Competitive** in the Scenario name box, type **Projected profit assuming $180 price and a slight rise in sales.** in the Comment box.
4. Click the **OK** button and enter the following values for the Competitive scenario:

   Units Sold: **1300**
   Price per Unit: **180**
   Material Cost: **44**
   Advertisement: **16000**
   Administrative: **5000**
5. Click the **Add** button, create the next scenario with the name, **High Cost**, and the description, **Projected profit assuming $190 price and a slight decline in sales.**
6. Click the **OK** button and enter the High Cost scenario values:

   Units Sold: **1000**
   Price per Unit: **190**
   Material Cost: **44**
   Advertisement: **10000**
   Administrative: **5000**
7. Click the **OK** button. Figure 9-31 shows all four scenarios listed in the Scenario Manager dialog box.

Figure 9-31 THE FOUR SCENARIOS IN THE DAVIS BLADES WORKBOOK

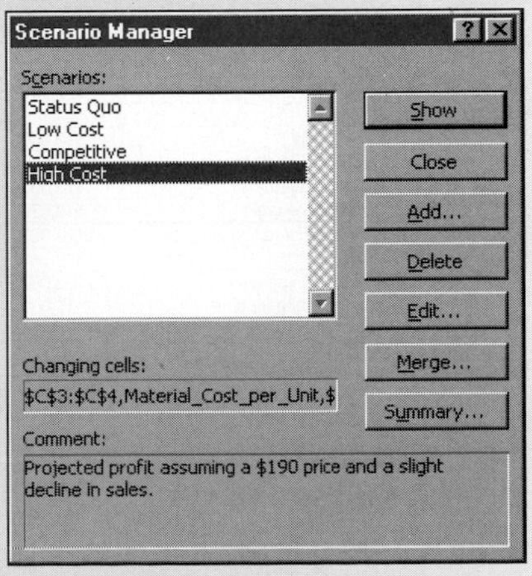

Your scenarios are entered, and you are ready to view the effect of each scenario.

Viewing Scenarios

Now that you have entered the four scenarios, you can view the impact each scenario has on operating income by selecting the scenario and clicking the Show button or by double-clicking the scenario name.

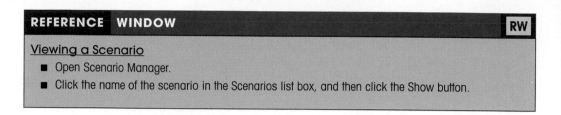

REFERENCE WINDOW RW

Viewing a Scenario

- Open Scenario Manager.
- Click the name of the scenario in the Scenarios list box, and then click the Show button.

You'll preview the effect of each scenario on the region's monthly profit.

To view each scenario:

1. Click **Status Quo** in the Scenarios list box.
2. Click the **Show** button.
3. If necessary, move the Scenario Manager dialog box to allow you to view the values in the CVP Data worksheet. See Figure 9-32.

Figure 9-32 OUTCOME OF THE STATUS QUO SCENARIO

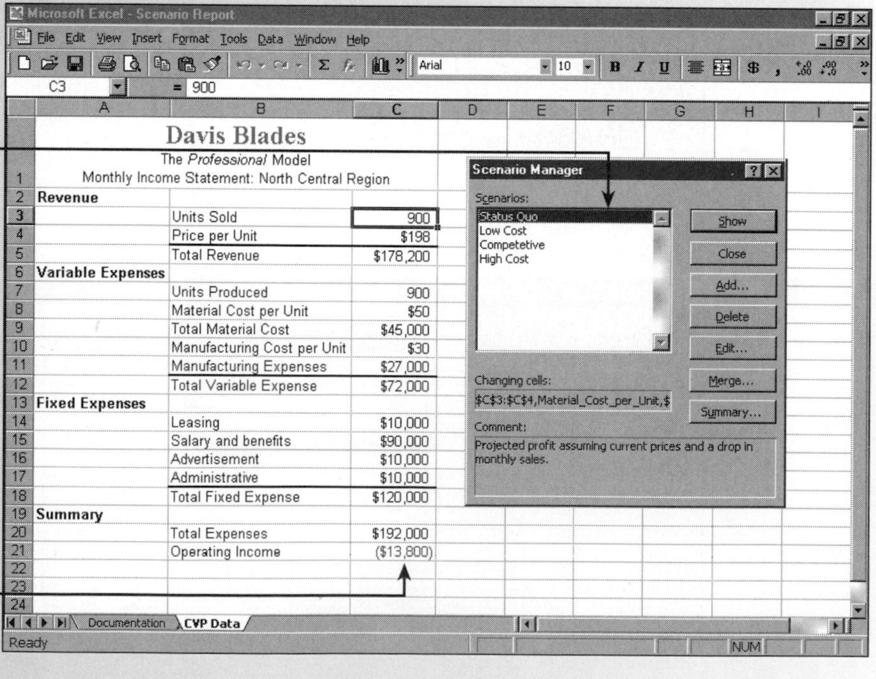

the current scenario

Status Quo scenario results in a loss of $13,800 per month

Excel has automatically changed the first input cell, Units Sold to 900. The operating income is recalculated in the scenario to be an operating loss of $13,800, as you can see in cell C21. See how this compares with the other scenarios.

To view the remaining scenarios:

1. Double-click **Low Cost** from the list of scenarios.
2. Double-click **Competitive**.
3. Double-click **High Cost**.
4. Figure 9-33 shows the resulting values for the three remaining scenarios.

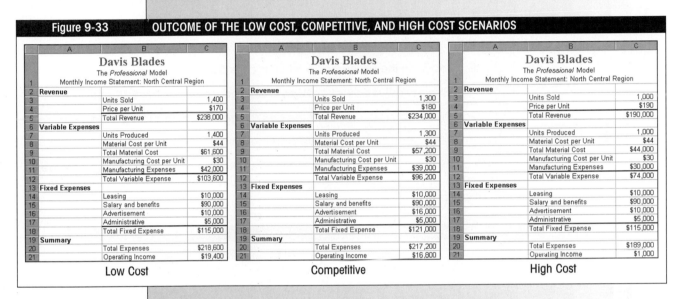

Figure 9-33 OUTCOME OF THE LOW COST, COMPETITIVE, AND HIGH COST SCENARIOS

Low Cost

	A	B	C
1		**Davis Blades** The *Professional* Model Monthly Income Statement: North Central Region	
2	**Revenue**		
3		Units Sold	1,400
4		Price per Unit	$170
5		Total Revenue	$238,000
6	**Variable Expenses**		
7		Units Produced	1,400
8		Material Cost per Unit	$44
9		Total Material Cost	$61,600
10		Manufacturing Cost per Unit	$30
11		Manufacturing Expenses	$42,000
12		Total Variable Expense	$103,600
13	**Fixed Expenses**		
14		Leasing	$10,000
15		Salary and benefits	$90,000
16		Advertisement	$10,000
17		Administrative	$5,000
18		Total Fixed Expense	$115,000
19	**Summary**		
20		Total Expenses	$218,600
21		Operating Income	$19,400

Competitive

	A	B	C
1		**Davis Blades** The *Professional* Model Monthly Income Statement: North Central Region	
2	**Revenue**		
3		Units Sold	1,300
4		Price per Unit	$180
5		Total Revenue	$234,000
6	**Variable Expenses**		
7		Units Produced	1,300
8		Material Cost per Unit	$44
9		Total Material Cost	$57,200
10		Manufacturing Cost per Unit	$30
11		Manufacturing Expenses	$39,000
12		Total Variable Expense	$96,200
13	**Fixed Expenses**		
14		Leasing	$10,000
15		Salary and benefits	$90,000
16		Advertisement	$16,000
17		Administrative	$5,000
18		Total Fixed Expense	$121,000
19	**Summary**		
20		Total Expenses	$217,200
21		Operating Income	$16,800

High Cost

	A	B	C
1		**Davis Blades** The *Professional* Model Monthly Income Statement: North Central Region	
2	**Revenue**		
3		Units Sold	1,000
4		Price per Unit	$190
5		Total Revenue	$190,000
6	**Variable Expenses**		
7		Units Produced	1,000
8		Material Cost per Unit	$44
9		Total Material Cost	$44,000
10		Manufacturing Cost per Unit	$30
11		Manufacturing Expenses	$30,000
12		Total Variable Expense	$74,000
13	**Fixed Expenses**		
14		Leasing	$10,000
15		Salary and benefits	$90,000
16		Advertisement	$10,000
17		Administrative	$5,000
18		Total Fixed Expense	$115,000
19	**Summary**		
20		Total Expenses	$189,000
21		Operating Income	$1,000

5. Click the **Close** button to close the Scenario Manager dialog box.

As you look over the four scenarios, you can draw several conclusions. The Status Quo scenario assumes a sales volume drop to 900 units per month and produces an operating loss of $13,800. However, the Low Cost scenario indicates that by lowering prices, reducing overhead, and increasing sales, the region's monthly operating income could be a positive $19,400. This is close to the operating income of $16,800 shown in the Competitive scenario. Finally, the monthly operating income in the High Cost scenario is only $1,000. At this point, the most attractive scenarios seem to be the ones in which Davis Blades drops prices and increases sales. Of course, these scenarios assume that the sales will increase and that Davis Blades will be able to successfully control its overhead. If sales do not increase, this could result in a huge loss for the company.

You present the scenario results to Anne, who evaluates the impact of each strategy on monthly operating income. After some thought, she decides she would like you to modify the High Cost scenario, this time assuming that sales will fall to only 1100 units per month in her region. To do this, you'll edit the scenario.

Editing Scenarios

Once you have created a scenario, it's easy to make changes so you can examine variations of given sets of assumptions. The scenario results will automatically update to reflect the new information.

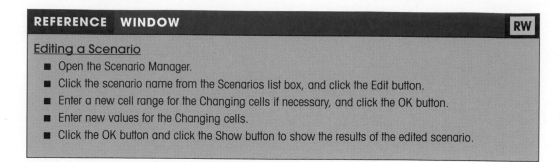

REFERENCE WINDOW RW

Editing a Scenario
- Open the Scenario Manager.
- Click the scenario name from the Scenarios list box, and click the Edit button.
- Enter a new cell range for the Changing cells if necessary, and click the OK button.
- Enter new values for the Changing cells.
- Click the OK button and click the Show button to show the results of the edited scenario.

You return to the worksheet to modify the Units Sold value in the High Cost scenario.

To edit the High Cost scenario:

1. Click **Tools** on the menu bar, and then click **Scenarios.**
2. In the Scenarios list box, click **High Cost** and then click the **Edit** button.
3. Click the **OK** button to accept the cell range for the changing cells.
4. In the Units_Sold box, type **1100** and then click the **OK** button.
5. Click the **Show** button and then click the **Close** button. The Income Statement showing the values for the High Cost scenario with the new Units Sold value appears. See Figure 9-34.

Figure 9-34 NEW HIGH COST SCENARIO VALUES

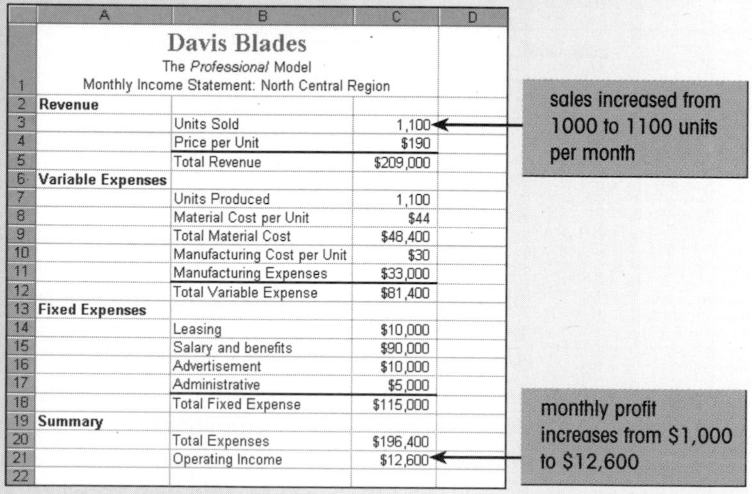

	A	B	C	D
1	Davis Blades The *Professional* Model Monthly Income Statement: North Central Region			
2	**Revenue**			
3		Units Sold	1,100	
4		Price per Unit	$190	
5		Total Revenue	$209,000	
6	**Variable Expenses**			
7		Units Produced	1,100	
8		Material Cost per Unit	$44	
9		Total Material Cost	$48,400	
10		Manufacturing Cost per Unit	$30	
11		Manufacturing Expenses	$33,000	
12		Total Variable Expense	$81,400	
13	**Fixed Expenses**			
14		Leasing	$10,000	
15		Salary and benefits	$90,000	
16		Advertisement	$10,000	
17		Administrative	$5,000	
18		Total Fixed Expense	$115,000	
19	**Summary**			
20		Total Expenses	$196,400	
21		Operating Income	$12,600	
22				

Monthly operating income from sales of the Professional rises to $12,600 under this revised scenario. So the High Cost scenario might be more attractive to Anne if she were confident that they could sell more units.

While the scenarios help you make important business decisions, it can be time consuming to compare the results of each scenario. Anne still will want to have a table of scenario values that she can hold in her hand and show to others. You could type the results of each scenario into a table for Anne, or you can save yourself time by having Scenario Manager generate a formatted report automatically.

Creating a Scenario Summary Report

A scenario summary report is a useful tool for making business decisions based on scenario results. Rather than listing all the cells on the Income Statement, the summary report lists only the changing cells, or input values, and the result cells for each scenario. The report's tabular layout makes it easy to compare the results of each scenario, and the automatic formatting makes it useful for reports and meetings.

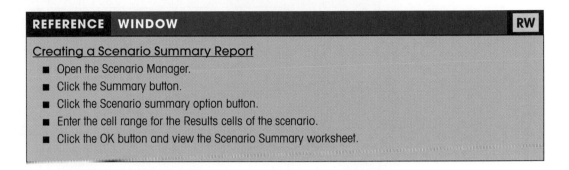

REFERENCE WINDOW RW

Creating a Scenario Summary Report

- Open the Scenario Manager.
- Click the Summary button.
- Click the Scenario summary option button.
- Enter the cell range for the Results cells of the scenario.
- Click the OK button and view the Scenario Summary worksheet.

In creating the report, you can identify which cells are the result cells. Anne is most interested in the following values:

- C5: Total Revenue
- C20: Total Expense
- C21: Operating Income

Put these values along with the values of the changing cells into your report.

To create the scenario summary report:

1. Click **Tools** on the menu bar, and then click **Scenarios**.
2. Click the **Summary** button. The Scenario Summary dialog box opens, allowing you to create a scenario summary or a scenario pivot table.
3. Verify that the Scenario summary option button is selected. Now enter the result cells representing revenue, expenses, and operating income.
4. Type **C5,C20:C21** in the Result cells box. See Figure 9-35.

Figure 9-35 PREPARING A SCENARIO SUMMARY REPORT

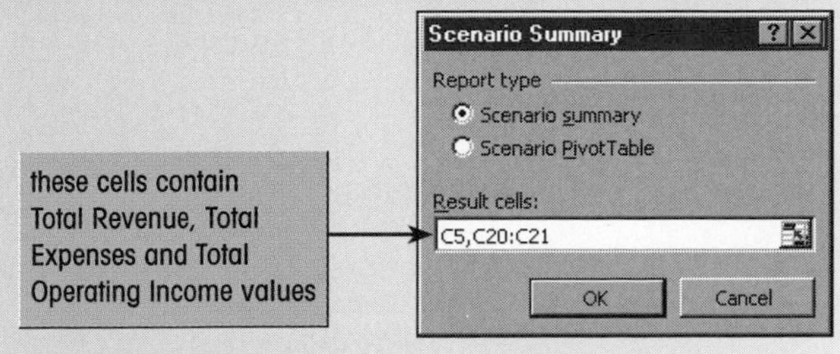

5. Click the **OK** button. Excel creates the Scenario Summary worksheet shown in Figure 9-36. You might have to scroll to see the entire report.

Figure 9-36 THE COMPLETED SCENARIO SUMMARY REPORT

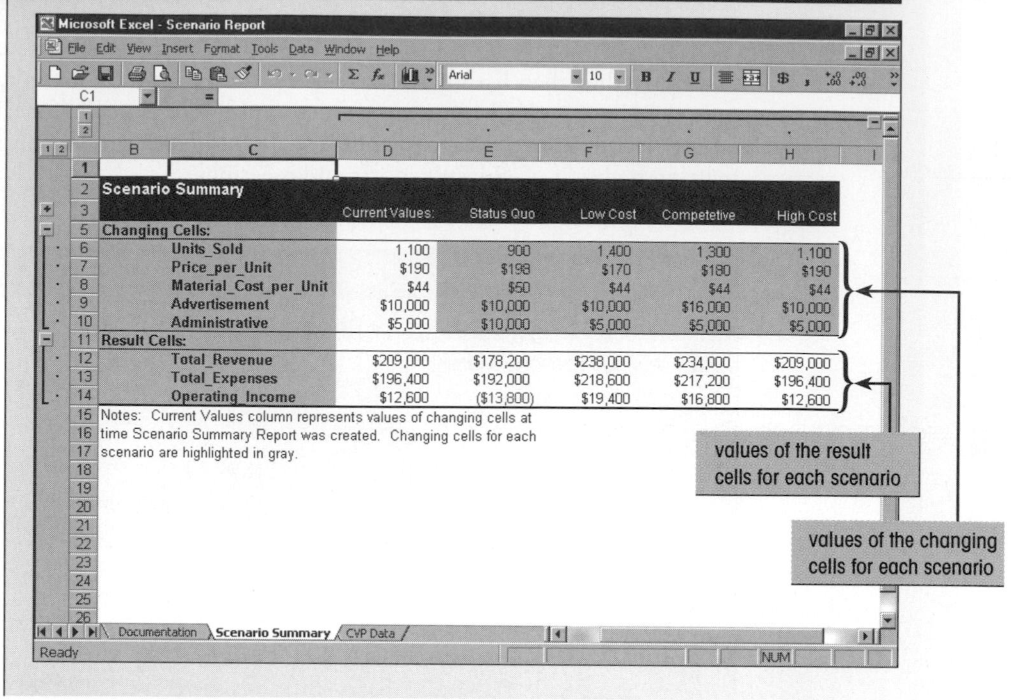

The Scenario Summary worksheet displays the values for the changing cells and result cells for each scenario. Each scenario is listed by name, and the current worksheet values are also shown. As it did with the individual scenarios, Scenario Manager has labeled each cell using the range names you defined earlier. By creating range names, you've made the report easier for Anne to interpret. Note that the report also includes a column showing the current values in the worksheet, regardless of whether those values belong to a particular scenario or not.

Using the Report Manager

Another way of easily printing out the results of your different scenarios without having to rerun each scenario in your list is to use the Report Manager. The **Report Manager** is an Excel add-in that allows you to store various reports and views of your workbook. **Add-ins** are special programs that "add to" the capabilities of Excel. The Report Manager adds the capability of creating and organizing reports about your workbook. For example, you can create a report that displays the results of all of your scenarios. Once the report is created, you can use the Report Manager to quickly and easily print out the report results. Try this now, creating a report based on the four scenarios in your workbook.

To create a report using Report Manager:

1. Click **View** and **Report Manager** on the Excel menu.

   The list of reports in your workbook appears. Because you probably haven't created any reports yet, the list should be empty.

TROUBLE? If you don't see Report Manager, click the Tools menu, click Add-Ins, and then click Report Manager to select it. It will then appear on the View menu.

TROUBLE? If Excel prompts you for your installation disk, it means that you have not installed Report Manager yet. If you are working on your own machine, locate your Office 2000 disk and install it now. If you are working on a network computer, talk to your instructor or technical support person about installing the add-in.

2. Click the **Add** button to create a new report.

3. Type **Scenario Results** in the Name box of the Add Report dialog box. See Figure 9-37.

Figure 9-37 CREATING A REPORT IN THE REPORT MANAGER

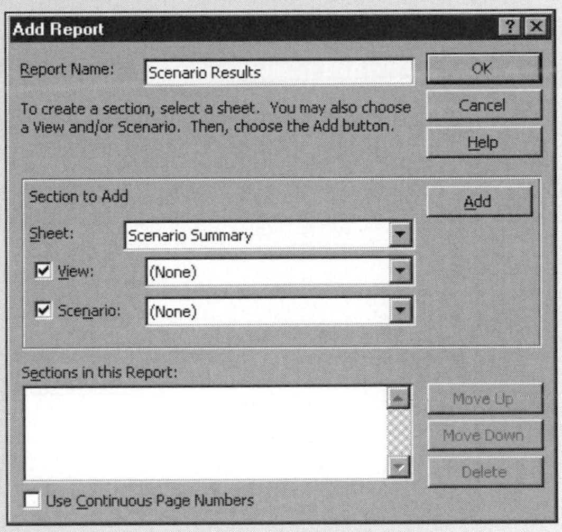

The first thing you'll do in designing the Scenario Results report is to add the various report sections.

Adding Report Sections

A report is comprised of sections, where a **section** is a sheet in your workbook. You can further define each section by specifying which scenario in that worksheet you want to print. If you have views defined on that worksheet, you also specify which view you want to use in your printout. A **view** is a set of display and print settings you can name and apply to a workbook. You can create more than one view for each workbook. You can learn more about views in Excel's online Help.

In your workbook, you have four scenarios available on the CVP Data worksheet; but you don't have any user-defined views. You'll therefore create four sections in your report, one for each of your scenarios. You'll also add a fifth section based on the Documentation worksheet. Add this section now.

To add the section for the Documentation worksheet:

1. Select **Documentation** from the Sheet drop-down list box.

2. Click the **Add** button.

The Documentation sheet appears in the list of sections in the report.

Now add sections for each of the scenarios. Because these scenarios exist on the CVP Data worksheet, you must first select this worksheet from the Sheet list and then select each scenario from the Scenario list.

To add sections for each of your scenarios:

1. Select **CVP Data** from the drop-down Sheet list.
2. Select **Status Quo** from the drop-down Scenario list.
3. Click the **Add** button.
4. Select **Low Cost** from the drop-down Scenario list and click the **Add** button.
5. Add the **Competitive** scenario to the list of sections.
6. Add the **High Cost** scenario to the sections list.
7. Figure 9-38 displays the complete list of sections in the Scenario Results report.

Figure 9-38 ADDING SECTIONS TO THE SCENARIO RESULTS REPORT

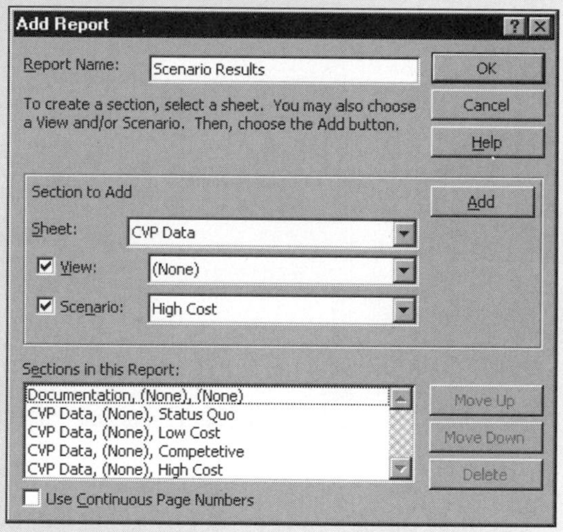

8. Click the **OK** button to close the Add Report dialog box.

Printing a Report

Now that you've completed the report, you can use the Report Manager to print it.

To print the Scenario Results report:

1. Within the Report Manager dialog box, verify that Scenario Results is the selected report in the list of reports.
2. Click the **Print** button.
3. Enter the number of copies to print and then click the **OK** button.

You've completed your work for Anne, so save your results and close the Scenario Report workbook.

To save your work and close Excel:

1. Click the **Documentation** sheet tab to return to the Documentation sheet.
2. Save the workbook and close Excel.

You hand in your report. Anne will look it over, discuss it with other managers, and get back to you if she needs any additional scenario results. Based on your findings, it is clear that Davis Blades will have to change some of its operating practices in the North Central region. It will probably have to cut the price of the Professional model and find ways to reduce expenses.

Session 9.2 QUICK CHECK

1. What is an advantage of scenarios over data tables?
2. What should you do before starting Scenario Manager in order to make the reports you generate easier to interpret?
3. What are changing cells?
4. What are result cells? Where do you define result cells in Scenario Manager?
5. How do you display a scenario?
6. How do you create a scenario summary report?

In this tutorial you have created one- and two-variable data tables. You've seen how to use Excel to easily investigate different scenarios for Davis Blades and how to report those results using a scenario summary report and the Report Manager. Davis Blades will use these results to try and remain competitive in a changing marketplace.

REVIEW ASSIGNMENTS

Anne is considering using the Low Cost scenario you analyzed for her. She would like some more information before recommending that course of action. She would like to know what would happen to the region's operating income if the price per unit remained at $170 and the monthly sales of the Professional were 1000, 1100, 1200, 1300, 1400, or 1500 units. She would like you to place this information in a one-variable data table.

She would also like you to create a two-variable data table that includes the values from the one-variable data table and reports the operating income for unit prices of $170 through $178. Finally, she is not sure that the region can cut the material cost per unit to $44 or monthly administrative expenses to $5,000. She would like you to report on a new scenario, called "Low Cost 2" where:

- Units Sold = 1400
- Unit Price = $174
- Material Cost per Unit = $48
- Advertising expense = $10,000
- Administrative expense = $8,000

To report on Anne's scenarios:

1. If necessary, start Excel and make sure your Data Disk is in the appropriate drive. Open the **LowCost** workbook in the Review folder for Tutorial.09 and save it as **Low Cost Scenario 2**.
2. On the Documentation Sheet worksheet, enter your name, the date, and the new workbook name.
3. Go to the CVP Data worksheet and in cell E4, enter a formula referencing the value in cell C3 ("Units Sold") and in cell F4, a formula referencing the value in cell C21 ("Operating Income").
4. In cells E5:E10, enter the values "1000," "1100," "1200," "1300," "1400," and "1500."
5. Create a one-variable data table in the range E4:F10 based on units sold. Add descriptive labels to the data table and format the values in the table. Can the region still show a profit from the Professional if the monthly sales volume is 1200 units?
6. Create a chart sheet titled **Profit Chart**, and chart operating income against units sold. Label the axes appropriately.
7. Copy the unit sales values in the range E5:E10 to the range E14:E19. Enter the unit price values $170 through $178 in two-dollar increments in the range F13:J13.
8. In cell E13, type a formula referencing the Operating Income value in cell C21.
9. Select the range E13:J19 and create a two-variable data table. Format cell E13 to display the text "Units Sold." Add the label "Price Per Unit" across the cells F12 to J12 and format the values in the table. What combination of units sold and unit price will result in an operating income of $2,600 per month?
10. Using the Name Create command, create names for values in column C based on the labels in column B.
11. Using Scenario Manager, create a scenario titled "Low Cost 2" using the Low Cost 2 values shown earlier.
12. Create a scenario summary report displaying the Total Revenue, Total Expenses, and Operating Income.
13. Print the Scenario Summary report and the worksheet containing the one-variable and two-variable data tables.
14. Using the Report Manager, create a report named "New Scenario" displaying the Documentation sheet and the Low Cost 2 scenario. (*Hint*: You may have to use page setup to control how each page prints *before* using the Report Manager.)
15. Save your workbook on your Data Disk.

CASE PROBLEMS

Case 1. ***Calculating the Break-Even Point for HomeEd Videos*** You can calculate the break-even point for cost-volume-profit relationships if you know the total fixed expense and the profit per unit. The break-even point is calculated as:

Break-even Point = Total Fixed Expenses /(Price per Unit – Unit Variable Expense)

You work at HomeEd Videos, a company that makes educational videos for home instruction. Cindy Webber, the sales manager for HomeEd Videos, wants you to look at how changing the price per unit will affect the company's break-even point. To perform a CVP analysis, do the following:

1. If necessary, start Excel and make sure your Data Disk is in the appropriate drive. Open the **HomeEd** workbook in the Cases folder for Tutorial.09 and save it as **HomeEd Analysis**.
2. Enter the new workbook name, your name, and the date on the Documentation worksheet.
3. In cell C20 of the Sales worksheet, enter the break-even formula. How many units per month must HomeEd videos sell to break even?
4. In range E2:F14, create a one-variable data table that will use the unit price value as the input cell and the break-even value as the result cell, applying the following: Enter the text "Unit Price" in cell E2 and "Break Even" in cell F2. Enter references to the current values in cells E3:F3. Use unit prices of \$20 to \$30 in increments of \$1 as the input values in your data table.
5. Format the values in F4:F14 with the format found in C20.
6. Create a chart sheet named "Break-Even," and chart unit price against the break-even point. Label the axes appropriately.
7. Among the unit prices in the one-variable data table, what price should HomeEd Videos set if it wants to sell less than 1300 units and still break even?

Cindy asks you to repeat the analysis, this time with a two-variable data table, assuming that the cost of producing each video is \$4, \$5, \$6, or \$7 per unit.

8. In cell E16, enter a formula referencing the break-even value in C20.
9. Copy the Unit Price values from the range E4:E14 into the range E17:E27.
10. Enter the Unit Expense values \$4, \$5, \$6, and \$7 into the range F16:I16.
11. Select the range E16:I27 and create a two-variable data table using the Unit Price as the Column Input cell and the Unit Expense as the Row Input cell.
12. Format the values in the range F17:I27 with the format found in C20.
13. Format cell E16 to display the label "Break-Even."
14. If the number of units produced each month by HomeEd video is about 1300, what combinations of unit price and unit cost will result in the company breaking even? In general, how great of a markup over the unit cost of each video must the company use in order to break even?
15. Print the worksheet containing the one-and two-variable data tables.
16. Save your changes and close the **HomeEd Analysis** workbook.

Case 2. Sales Mix at Fine Prints Inc. When a company sells more than one product, it must produce and sell the right combination of products in order to maximize its profits. This combination is called the "sales mix," and is an important factor in determining CVP relationships. At Fine Prints Inc., the manager, Mark Davis, is selling posters for the upcoming Summer Olympic games. He has three styles of posters: regular, fine, and matted.

Mark wants you to determine how sales mix affects the cost-volume-profit relationship. At present, Mark produces and sells about 500 copies of the Olympics prints in the following proportions: regular – 40%, fine – 30%, and matted – 30%. Mark wants you to explore what would happen to the operating income and the break-even point if the sales mix were as follows:

- Current Units Sold=500, Regular = 40%, Fine = 30%, Matted = 30%
- Even Units Sold=500, Regular = 33.3%, Fine = 33.3%, Matted = 33.3%
- Regular Units Sold=500, Regular = 50%, Fine = 25%, Matted = 25%
- Fine Units Sold=500, Regular = 25%, Fine = 50%, Matted = 25%
- Matted Units Sold=500, Regular = 25%, Fine = 25%, Matted = 50%

Do the following:

1. Open the **Prints** workbook in the Cases folder for Tutorial.09 and save it as **Sales Mix**.
2. Enter the new workbook name, your name, and the date in the Documentation worksheet.
3. In the Sales worksheet, name the Total Prints Sold value in cell C4, "Units_Sold." Use the Create Names command to create names for the Percentage of Sales values found in the D6:F6 range of the Sales worksheet.
4. Using Scenario Manager, create the five scenarios previously described. The changing cells in each scenario are the percentage of sales values found in the D6:F6 range and the Units Sold value found in cell C4. Add a description of each scenario.
5. Use the Names Create command to create names for the outcome values in the range C20:C21.
6. Create a Scenario Summary for the five scenarios. Include the operating income and the break-even point in the scenario summary report.
7. Print the scenario summary report in landscape orientation.
8. Analyze the report. Which sales mix results in the highest operating income and the lowest break-even point? Based on this, which of the three print types is the most profitable to the company?

Explore

9. Use the Scenario manager to create a Scenario pivot table. Format the pivot table so that it only displays the Fine, Regular and Matted scenarios.
10. Create a report named "Sales Mixes" that includes all five of the scenarios you created.
11. Save your changes and close the **Sales Mix** workbook.

Case 3. Calculating the Present Value of an Investment When companies plan expenditures for upgrading equipment or adding new products, they hope that the expenditure will produce additional revenue and profit. Given that they could invest their money elsewhere, companies need to determine if the income generated by capital improvements gives them a desirable rate of return on the investment. One way to do this is to calculate the **present value** of the expenditure based on its anticipated earnings in the future. The present value expresses the worth of the investment in today's dollars. If the present value is greater than the initial investment, the investment is profitable. If not, the company may want to consider investing in other vehicles that are more likely to produce the desired rate of return.

You work with Allan Williams, owner of the Bread House bakery. Allan has $50,000 to invest and is considering using it to upgrade the bakery's kitchen. The cost of the upgrade is $50,000. Allan expects that the new kitchen will result in increased efficiency and productivity, which will be worth about $15,000 a year for the next five years. Allan wants to know how this level of increased revenue compares to other investments which could yield returns of 10 to 16% a year. If the level is equal to or above the return rate of other investments, he will proceed with the renovation.

A workbook calculating the net present value of Allan's proposed kitchen upgrade has been placed in the Bakery workbook in the Cases folder for Tutorial.09 on your Data Disk. The workbook shows the present value of upgrading the equipment, based on the assumptions that (1) the renovation will increase revenue by $15,000 per year, and considering that (2) Allan would like to see at least a 12% return on his $50,000 investment.

Allan would like you to use this workbook to calculate the value of upgrading the bakery for return rates other than 12%, such as rates between 10% and 16%.

Allan is also not sure that the upgrade will generate the type of extra revenue he is expecting. He wants you to calculate the present value of his investment assuming that the bakery upgrade yields the revenue shown in the following scenarios:

Low Initial Income Desired Rate of Return = 12%

Year 1 = $5,000
Year 2 = $10,000
Year 3 = $15,000
Year 4 = $25,000
Year 5 = $35,000

Early Income Desired Rate of Return = 12%

Year 1 = $25,000
Year 2 = $20,000
Year 3 = $15,000
Year 4 = $10,000
Year 5 = $5,000

Steadily Growing Income Desired Rate of Return = 12%

Year 1 = $10,000
Year 2 = $12,000
Year 3 = $14,000
Year 4 = $16,000
Year 5 = $20,000

What is the present value of the purchase under each of these scenarios? To answer Allan's questions, do the following:

1. Open the **Bakery** workbook in the Cases folder for Tutorial.09 on your Data Disk, and save it as **Bakery Analysis**.
2. Enter the new workbook name, your name, and the date in the Documentation worksheet.
3. In the Present Value worksheet, create in the cell range F6:G13, a one-variable data table using the desired rate of return as the input cell and the net present value as the result cell. Use the following input values in the data table: 10%, 11%, 12%, 13%, 14%, 15%, and 16%.
4. Label the data table appropriately.

5. Analyze the table and determine the rate of return at which the investment in the equipment is no longer as profitable. In other words, under what conditions is the present value of the upgrade worth less than $50,000? If Allan can get a 16% yearly rate by investing his money elsewhere, should he do so?

6. Name the cells in the range B7:B11 based on the year. Name cells B4 and D14 as well.

7. Use the Scenario Manager to create the three scenarios that Allan has outlined for you. Do any of the scenarios show a negative net present value for the kitchen upgrade?

8. Create a scenario summary report based on your three scenarios displaying the net present value. What would you tell Allan regarding the value of the kitchen upgrade versus investing the $50,000 elsewhere? Are there some situations that Allan should watch out for given that he wants his upgrade to be financially successful?

9. Print out your scenario summary reports, data table, and analysis of the results. Save your work.

Case 4. Starting a New Business Ray and Debbie Chen are considering opening a new restaurant. Both are experienced in cooking and in restaurant management. The restaurant they intend to lease has a maximum of eight tables, each of which can seat four people. Debbie has drawn up the following expense estimates:

Variable Expense

Average cost of food, including preparation	$8 per meal

Fixed Expenses

Salaries and Benefits	$50,000 per year
Rent (property and equipment)	$30,000 per year
Cleaning and upkeep	$3,600 per year
Utilities	$9,600 per year
Phone	$2,400 per year
Advertising	$3,600 per year
Miscellaneous overhead	$1,800 per year

Debbie is trying to determine, on average, how much she should charge per meal and how many meals she should serve per night in order for the restaurant to show a profit. Debbie is assuming that the restaurant will be open 360 nights per year and that the average price charged per meal will range from $20 to $30. She assumes that the restaurant will serve an average of 10 to 30 people per night. Ray and Debbie believe that the restaurant should show an operating income of $80,000 per year in order for them to risk the venture. They would like your help in analyzing the situation.

Your analysis should include the following:

1. The **Chen** workbook that you create and save in the Cases folder for Tutorial.09 on your Data Disk.

2. A worksheet showing the operating income under the assumption that the price per meal is $25 and the number of meals served each night is 20 and the number of meals produced is equal to the number of meals served.

3. A one-variable data table showing the revenue, total expenses and operating income under the assumption that the price of each meal is $25 and that 10 to 30 people (in increments of 2) are served each night.

4. A CVP chart based on your one-variable data table.

5. An analysis of your results, answering the question "How many people should be served on average each night to show an operating income of at least $80,000 per year?"
6. A two-variable data table assuming that 10 to 30 people are served each night and that the average price per meal is $20, $22, $24, $26, $28 or $30.
7. An analysis that determines how many people on average must be served each night before the restaurant starts showing a profit based on the results of the two-variable data table.
8. The results of the following possible scenarios:

   Low Cost

   Price per meal = $22
   Cost of preparing meal = $7
   Average meals per day = 26
   Yearly salaries and benefits = $40,000

   Medium Cost

   Price per meal = $26
   Cost of preparing meal = $8
   Average meals per day = 24
   Yearly salaries and benefits = $45,000

   High Cost

   Price per meal = $28
   Cost of preparing meal = $9
   Average meals per day = 22
   Yearly salaries and benefits = $55,000

9. A scenario summary report for each of three scenarios displaying the total revenue, total expenses, and operating income under each scenario. Make sure that you create range names for the appropriate values.
10. When finished with these tasks, save your workbook, print the scenario summary reports in landscape orientation, as well as your worksheets.

INTERNET ASSIGNMENTS

The purpose of the Internet Assignments is to challenge you to find information on the Internet that you can use to create effective spreadsheets. The actual assignments are updated and maintained on the Course Technology Web site. Log on to the Internet and use your Web browser to go to the Student Online Companion to accompany this text at **www.course.com/NewPerspectives/office2000**. Click the Excel link, and then click the link for Tutorial 9.

QUICK CHECK ANSWERS

Session 9.1

1. CVP analysis expresses the relationship between a product's expenses (cost), its volume (units sold), and the resulting profit.
2. Variable expenses increase in direct relation to the number of units produced. Fixed expenses remain constant regardless of production. Mixed expenses are fixed expenses that are somewhat susceptible to increases in production, causing an increase in their value.
3. the point at which total expenses equal total revenue
4. a table that shows the results of several what-if analyses
5. An input cell is the cell in the table that contains the value you want to change. The result cell is the cell containing the results you're interested in viewing.
6. a data table with a single column or row of input values
7. a data table that uses two sets of input values, one in the first row of the table and the other in the first column
8. You can display an unlimited number of result values with the one-variable data table, but only one result value with the two-variable data table.

Session 9.2

1. Scenarios allow you to perform what-if analyses with more than one input cell.
2. assign range names to the cells
3. cells whose values you are changing in the scenario
4. Result cells display the output in which you are interested. You define result cells when creating scenario summary reports.
5. Click Tools, click Scenarios, then click the scenario name in the list of available scenarios, and click the Show button.
6. Click the summary button in the Scenario Manager dialog box, click the Scenario Summary option button, then click the OK button.

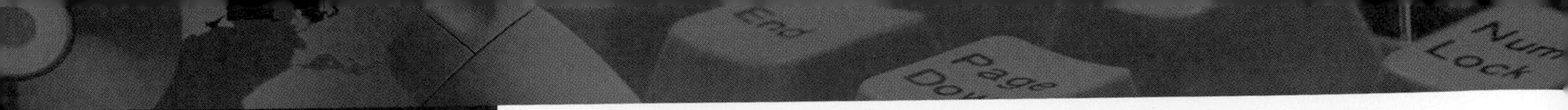

OBJECTIVES

In this tutorial you will:

- Formulate a problem
- Perform what-if analyses
- Try to solve a problem using trial and error
- Use Goal Seek to automate the trial-and-error process
- Use Solver to find the best solution
- Create an answer report

USING SOLVER FOR COMPLEX PROBLEMS

Determining the Most Profitable Product Mix for Appliance Mart Superstore, Inc.

CASE

Appliance Mart Superstore, Inc.

Jordan Maki is the general manager of the Appliance Mart Superstore in Boulder, Colorado. Appliance Mart has been in business for 25 years and is one of the biggest appliance dealers in Boulder County. The company specializes in laundry and kitchen appliances, including washers, dryers, dishwashers, refrigerators, stoves, and microwave ovens. Like all large appliance dealers, one of the managers' biggest problems is deciding how much inventory they should keep in their warehouse. They like to take advantage of special manufacturer price reductions, but they have a limited amount of warehouse space. They regularly must determine the most efficient and profitable combination of products (or "product mix") to keep on hand, given this limited amount of space.

One of Jordan's largest suppliers, GoldStar Corporation, just advertised special dealer pricing on selected models of GoldStar stoves, refrigerators, and microwave ovens. The Coldpoint, a refrigerator that usually costs $935 wholesale, is now on sale to dealers for $875. The Breakdale stove, which usually costs $450 wholesale, is $420. And the popular Quickcook microwave oven, which usually costs $220 wholesale, is now $195. Jordan thinks this looks like a great opportunity to stock up on some fast-moving merchandise and to increase profits.

Jordan asks you to recommend how many refrigerators they should order to take advantage of the special GoldStar pricing. You return to your desk to consider the problem and realize that you'll need more information in order to make a recommendation based on sound inventory-management principles. You begin to make a list of the information you need.

In this tutorial you'll plan and create the workbook that will calculate the best combination of appliances that Jordan should buy. You'll consider the dealer cost and customer price for each type of appliance, and enter cost and profit formulas. You'll use a trial-and-error process to try to determine how many refrigerators will produce the most profit. Then you'll use an Excel feature that automates the trial-and-error process. You'll move on to a more complex problem: finding the correct mix of refrigerators, stoves, and microwaves to order, given limits imposed by such factors as budget, warehouse space, and the number of orders Jordan has already received from customers. Finally, you'll use Excel to create a report that summarizes your analysis.

SESSION 10.1

In this session you will plan and create the refrigerator order workbook, perform a what-if analysis, seek a solution by trial and error, and use the Excel Goal Seek command. With the skills you learn in this session, you will be able to use Excel to find answers to questions by experimenting with different sets of circumstances.

Planning the Worksheet

Your first step is to assemble the information you have, and to determine what information you need. You know that the Coldpoint refrigerator usually costs Appliance Mart $935 wholesale and that it is now $875. However, you also need to know the retail price of the refrigerator to calculate the total profit Appliance Mart will make from selling the refrigerators from this order.

Next, you need to know if there are any customer orders for the Coldpoint refrigerator. If there are, you should recommend to Jordan that he order at least the number of refrigerators required to fill the customer orders.

You also need to know if there is a limitation on Appliance Mart's warehouse space that might affect the maximum number of refrigerators Jordan could order. If warehouse space is limited, you need to know the size of each refrigerator so you can determine how many would fit into the available space. Finally, you wonder if Jordan has placed a limit on the funds available for the GoldStar order. Although he did not mention a limit, you guess that he probably has one in mind.

You begin to gather the information you need. The sales manager tells you that each Coldpoint refrigerator has a retail price of $1,250 and that there are six existing customer orders. From the inventory manager, you learn that each of these apartment-sized Coldpoints requires 25 cubic feet of storage space.

You can't determine the warehouse space limitation yet because the warehouse manager is at lunch. In addition, you can't track down Jordan to ask him his spending limit for the GoldStar order. While you wait for this additional information, you start working on an Excel worksheet that could help you analyze inventory purchase decisions. You develop the worksheet plan shown in Figure 10-1. Then, you make the sketch for the order worksheet shown in Figure 10-2.

Figure 10-1 WORKSHEET PLAN

Worksheet Plan for GoldStar Order

My Goal:
Calculate how many Coldpoint refrigerators to order from GoldStar.

What results do I want to see?
The total cost of the order.
The total warehouse space required for the refrigerators.
The amount of profit from selling all the refrigerators on the order.

What information do I need?
The wholesale cost of each GoldStar refrigerator.
The retail price of each GoldStar refrigerator.
The number of customer orders for GoldStar refrigerators.
The amount of warehouse space available (in cubic feet).
The size (in cubic feet) of each GoldStar refrigerator.
The maximum amount of funds available for the order.

What calculations will I perform?
profit per unit = unit retail price – unit wholesale cost
total cost = unit wholesale cost * quantity to order
total profit = profit per unit * quantity to order
total cubic feet = cubic ft. per unit * quantity to order

Figure 10-2 WORKSHEET SKETCH

Appliance Mart Superstore
GoldStar Order Worksheet

	Refrigerators
Unit Wholesale Cost	$875.00
Unit Retail Price	$1,250.00
Profit per Unit	${profit per unit formula}
Cubic Ft. per Unit	###
Customer Orders	6
Quantity to Order	###
Total Cost	${total cost formula}
Total Profit	${total profit formula}
Total Cubic Feet	{total cubic feet formula}

Creating the Order Worksheet

Begin creating your worksheet by launching Excel.

To launch Excel and organize the desktop:

1. Start Excel as usual, make sure your Data Disk is in the appropriate disk drive, and make sure the Microsoft Excel and Book1 windows are maximized.

Start by entering information on the content and purpose of the workbook into the Documentation sheet.

2. Rename Sheet1 **Documentation**. Enter the information shown in Figure 10-3, with your name in cell B4 and the date in cell B5.

3. Format the titles as shown in Figure 10-3.

Figure 10-3 REFRIGERATOR ORDER DOCUMENTATION SHEET

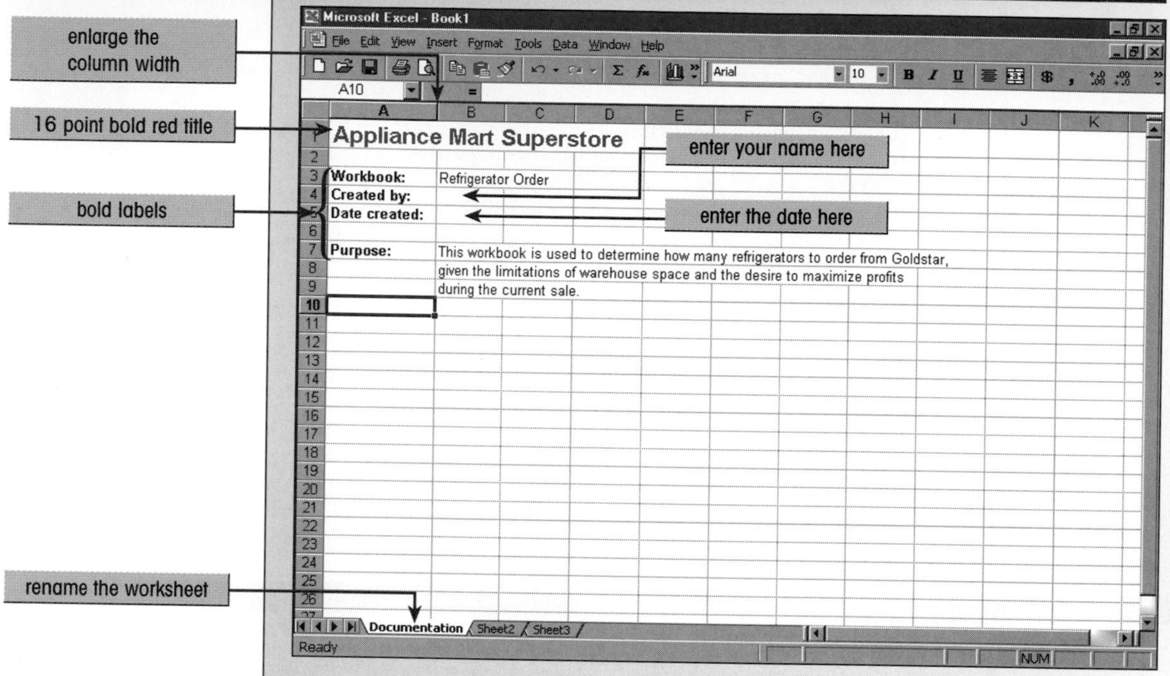

With the Documentation worksheet finished, you'll now enter titles and labels for the worksheet that you'll use to determine how many refrigerators to order.

To enter the worksheet titles and labels:

1. Click the **Sheet2** tab.

2. Enter the titles and formats in Figure 10-4.

3. Resize **column A** to accommodate the longest label (aside from the two title lines) in the worksheet.

4. Rename Sheet2 **Orders**.

5. Delete **Sheet3** from the workbook.

Figure 10-4 ORDER WORKSHEET

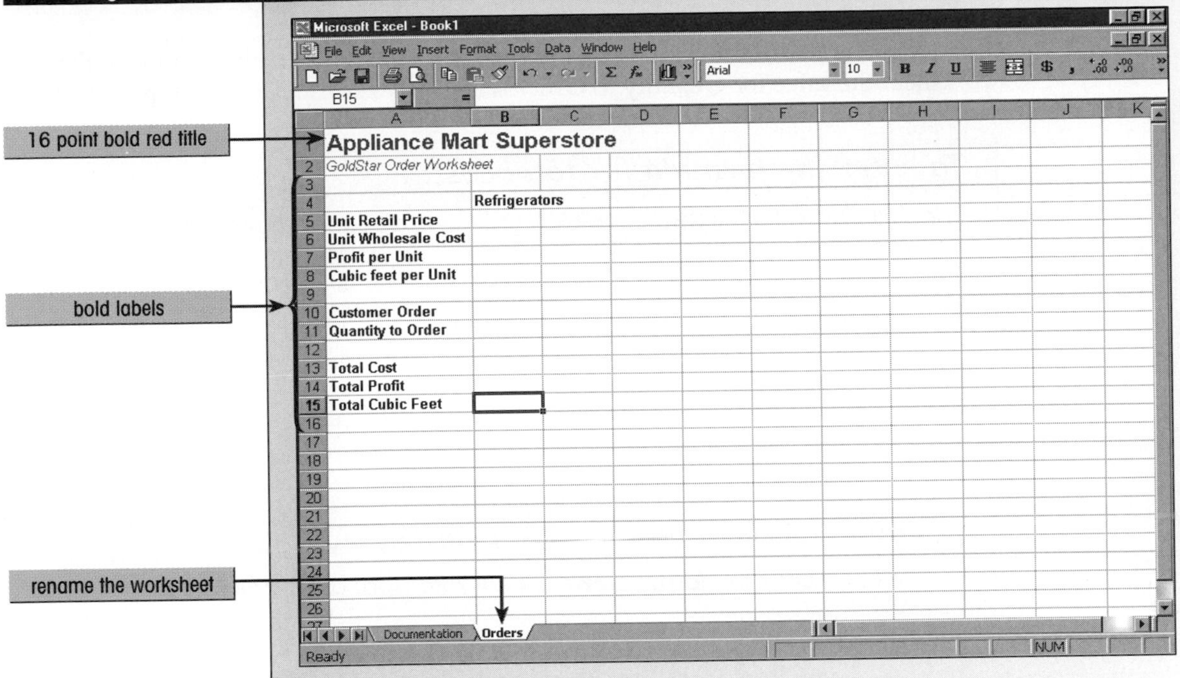

Next, enter the information you know about cost, price, size, and the number of customer orders on the worksheet.

To enter the values into the worksheet:

1. In cell B5, enter **1250** to specify the unit retail price.
2. In cell B6, enter **875** to specify the unit wholesale cost.
3. In cell B8, enter **25** to specify the cubic feet per unit.
4. In cell B10, enter **6** to specify the number of orders Appliance Mart has already received from customers for this model.

Now that you've entered descriptive information about the Coldpoint refrigerator, you are ready to enter the formulas you'll use in the worksheet. The first formula on your planning sheet calculates the profit per unit, that is, how much money Appliance Mart will make on each Coldpoint refrigerator. The profit on a refrigerator unit is the retail price minus the wholesale cost:

Profit per Unit = Unit Retail Price - Unit Wholesale Cost

On your worksheet, the unit retail price is in cell B5, and the unit wholesale cost from GoldStar is in cell B6. You'll enter this formula in cell B7.

To enter the formula for profit per unit:

1. In cell B7, enter the formula **=B5-B6**. The formula result, 375, appears in cell B7.

Next, in cell B13 you'll enter the formula to calculate the total cost of the order:

*Total Cost = Unit Wholesale Cost * Quantity to Order*

After you enter this formula, you expect to see a zero as the result, because on the current worksheet the value for Quantity to Order is blank, or zero, and 875 multiplied by 0 is 0.

To enter the formula for total cost:

1. In cell B13, enter the formula **=B6*B11**. A zero appears in cell B13.

The formula for total profit that you'll enter in cell B14 is:

*Total Profit =Profit per Unit * Quantity to Order*

You also expect this formula to display a zero as the result until you enter a value for quantity to order.

To enter the formula for total profit:

1. In cell B14, enter the formula **=B7*B11**. A zero appears in cell B14.

In cell B15, you'll enter the formula that calculates total cubic feet:

*Total Cubic Feet = Cubic Feet per Unit * Quantity to Order*

As with the results of the two previous formulas, you expect this formula to display a zero as the result until you enter a value other than zero for quantity to order.

To enter the formula for total cubic feet:

1. In cell B15, enter the formula **=B8*B11**. A zero appears in cell B15.

Finally, you'll format the values and formulas you've entered into the worksheet. Because the refrigerators are priced in whole dollar amounts, you'll use the currency format with no decimal places. You can format the currency cells by selecting nonadjacent ranges that contain currency amounts and then using the Format menu to apply the currency format.

To format the currency amounts and save the workbook:

1. Use the Format Cells dialog box to format the values in the range B5:B7 and in cells B13 and B14. Apply the currency style with no decimal places, and show negative numbers in black, without parentheses.

   Figure 10-5 shows the formatted data.

Figure 10-5 ORDERS WORKSHEET WITH VALUES, FORMULAS, AND FORMATS

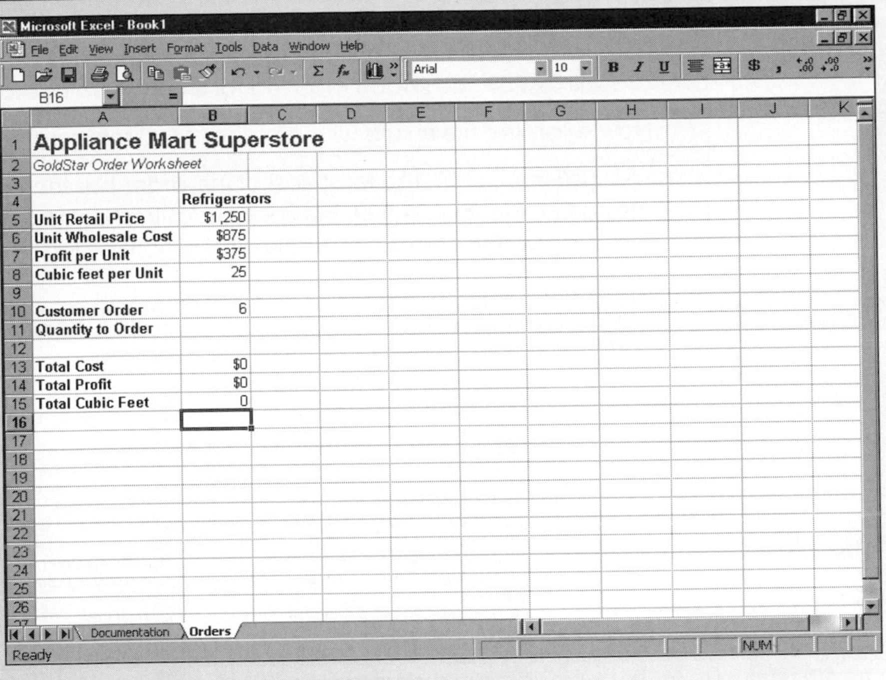

2. Save the workbook as **Refrigerator Order** in the Tutorial folder for Tutorial.10 on your Data Disk.

Now that you have set up the worksheet, you are ready to examine the problem and see how Excel can help you solve it.

Finding a Solution

You have completed the labels and formulas, but you have not yet received a call from the warehouse manager, so you don't know how much warehouse space is available. While waiting for the call, you enter some values for the quantity to order to see how much profit Appliance Mart could potentially make when it sells the GoldStar refrigerators. By inserting some hypothetical numbers into your worksheet, you'll start to get a feel for the cost of the purchase, as well as the impact on warehouse space, and potential profit for the company. Your goal is to balance the desire for high profits, the amount of money the company wants to invest in stock, and warehouse space limitations for the duration of the sale.

You know that there are customer orders for six GoldStar refrigerators, so you first want to determine the total cost, the total profit, and the total cubic feet for an order of six refrigerators. But you also know that Appliance Mart usually keeps at least 20 Coldpoint refrigerators in stock. So you want to know what the cost, profit, and space requirement would be for an order of 20 refrigerators as well. To see the results under both of these scenarios, enter order values of 6 and 20 into cell B11 of the Orders worksheet.

To calculate cost, profit, and cubic feet for 6 and 20 refrigerators:

1. Enter **6** in cell B11. The cost of ordering 6 refrigerators is $5,250 and the total profit is $2,250. The space required for storing 6 refrigerators is 150 cubic feet.

   Now examine the results with an order of 20 refrigerators.

2. Enter **20** in cell B11. The total cost of the order has increased to $17,500 that results in a profit of $7,500. The space requirements have grown to 500 cubic feet. Figure 10-6 compares the results for both orders.

Figure 10-6 **IMPACT OF ORDER QUANTITY ON COST, PROFIT, AND SPACE**

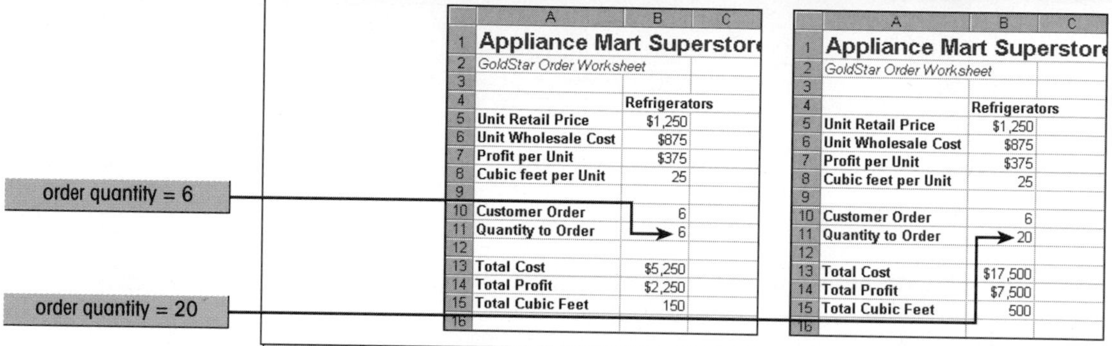

Although profits are obviously much higher with 20 refrigerators, you are not sure if Jordan will approve an order costing $17,500. You call him, and he says that he would like to keep the cost of the order down to about $15,000. Soon after you talk to Jordan, you receive a call from the warehouse manager who says that he has about 1,000 cubic feet of space for the refrigerators. Given these limitations, how many refrigerators should you order?

Finding Solutions by Trial and Error

When you used your worksheet for the what-if analyses, you were interested in the results for the total cost, the total profit, and the total cubic feet, but you were not concerned with any limits that might affect these results. Now you know that there are two limiting factors: Jordan does not want to spend more than $15,000 on the order, and the refrigerators on the order cannot take up more than 1,000 cubic feet of warehouse space. You decide to modify the worksheet plan's "goal" and "results" sections to reflect these limiting factors, as shown in Figure 10-7.

Figure 10-7 **REVISED WORKSHEET PLAN**

The revised worksheet plan

Worksheet Plan for GoldStar Order

<u>My Goal:</u>
Calculate how many Coldpoint refrigerators to order from GoldStar without exceeding cost and space limits.

<u>What results do I want to see?</u>
The total cost of the order does not exceed $15,000.
The total warehouse space required for the refrigerators does not exceed 1,000 cubic feet.
The amount of profit from selling all the refrigerators in this order.

<u>What information do I need?</u>
The wholesale cost of each GoldStar refrigerator.
The retail price of each GoldStar refrigerator.
The number of customer orders for GoldStar refrigerators.
The amount of warehouse space available (in cubic feet).
The size (in cubic feet) of each GoldStar refrigerator.
The maximum amount of funds available for the order.

<u>What calculations will I perform?</u>
profit per unit = unit retail price – unit wholesale cost
total cost = unit wholesale cost * quantity to order
total profit = profit per unit * quantity to order
total cubic feet = cubic ft. per unit * quantity to order

You now have a particular solution you are trying to reach. You want the value for the total cost in cell B13 to be as close to $15,000 as possible without exceeding that number, at the same time you must also make sure the value for total cubic feet in cell B15 does not exceed 1,000. You decide to adjust the value for quantity to order in cell B11 until the value for total cost in cell B13 is close to $15,000. This strategy is referred to as trial and error because you "try" different entries and they result in "errors" (solutions that are not optimal) until you enter the value that produces the result you want.

To determine the number of units by trial and error:

1. Enter **10** in cell B11. This order would cost $8,750 and take up 250 cubic feet of storage.

   It appears that you could order more than 10 units without exceeding the available funds and storage space. Now try a higher quantity.

2. Enter **15** in cell B11. Cell B13 displays $13,125.

   You could order more than 15 units and not exceed the two limitations.

3. Enter **17** in cell B11.

   The total cost for 17 units is $14,875.

With the total cost only $125 less than the $15,000 limit, you recognize that 17 is the maximum number of refrigerators Jordan can purchase with the available funds. Only 425 cubic feet are required for the 17 refrigerators, so the units will fit in the warehouse.

Just as you arrive at this solution, Jordan calls to tell you that GoldStar has announced an additional discount on Coldpoint refrigerators purchased for this sale. With this additional discount, the wholesale cost of each Coldpoint refrigerator is only $850. Jordan also tells you that because of this price reduction, he has decided to allocate a total of $18,000 for the refrigerator order. He asks you to determine the maximum number of units that he can purchase at the new price.

You begin by changing the value for unit wholesale cost in cell B6.

To enter the new refrigerator price:

1. Enter **850** in cell B6.

The value for total cost in cell B13 changes to $14,450, which is well below the new order limit of $18,000.

You could start the trial-and-error process again to determine the maximum amount of refrigerators to order, but there is an Excel feature called Goal Seek that will help you find a solution to the new problem much more quickly.

Finding Solutions with Goal Seek

The Excel **Goal Seek** command automates the trial-and-error process of changing one cell to make another cell display a specified result. Goal Seek uses a different approach from traditional what-if analysis, in which you change the *input values* in worksheet cells and Excel uses these values to calculate formula results. With Goal Seek, you specify the *results* you want a formula to display, and Excel changes the *input values* that the formula uses. Figure 10-8 illustrates the difference between a what-if analysis and a Goal Seek.

Figure 10-8 WHAT-IF ANALYSIS AND GOAL SEEK

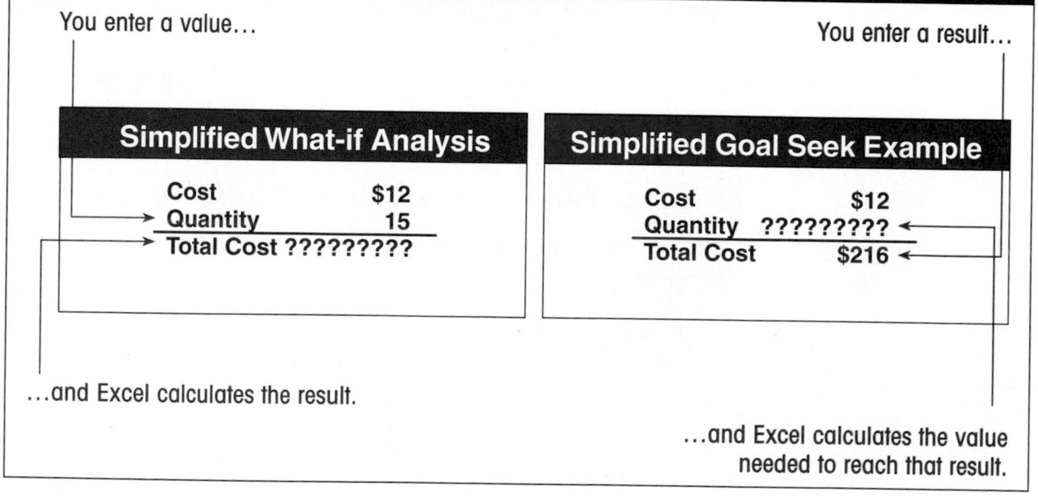

Suppose you want to purchase some audio CDs that cost $12 each. You can ask the what-if question, "*What* would it cost *if* I bought 15 CDs?" In Figure 10-8, the what-if analysis is shown on the left. If you were to place this data in Excel, you would quickly write a formula to calculate what it would cost you to purchase 15 CDs.

The Goal Seek example on the right in Figure 10-8 shows a different approach to the problem: If you have $216 to spend on CDs, how many can you purchase? You could use the Goal Seek capability to determine the answer, 18. Unlike traditional what-if analysis, Goal Seek starts with the end result (the formula) and determines what value you should use to reach a desired answer.

REFERENCE WINDOW RW

Using Goal Seek

- Set up the worksheet with labels, formulas, and values.
- Click Tools, and then click Goal Seek to open the Goal Seek dialog box.
- In the Set cell box, enter the location of the result cell.
- In the To value box, enter the value that you want to see in the result cell.
- In the By changing cell box, enter the location of the changing cell.
- Click the OK button.

You can use Goal Seek to solve your refrigerator problem. As you know, this problem has two limiting factors. First, the total cost of the order is limited to a maximum of $18,000. Second, the space required is limited to a maximum of 1,000 cubic feet. So, in fact, you have two goal-seeking questions: One is "How many refrigerators can I order with $18,000?" and the other is "How many refrigerators can I order to fill up a 1,000 cubic foot space?"

You can't do both goal-seeking problems at the same time. Therefore, you decide to first solve the goal-seeking problem for cost. By first observing the cost factor and then the space factor, you can determine which one is the limiting factor and specify the maximum number of refrigerators you can order, without spending too much money or overstocking the warehouse.

To set up the first Goal Seek, you first identify two cells in your worksheet: the result cell and the changing cell. The **result cell** is the cell containing your goal, which in this case is cell B13—the total cost of the order. The **changing cell** is the cell whose value is changed in order to reach your goal. In this case, the changing cell is B11, the number of refrigerators in the order.

What about the limitation on warehouse space? Excel will not consider this factor as it seeks a result for the problem. So after Excel solves the problem, you will need to manually confirm that the space limitation was not exceeded. You are ready to try the Goal Seek command.

To use Goal Seek to determine the number of refrigerators you can order for $18,000:

1. Click **Tools** on the menu bar, and then click **Goal Seek** to open the Goal Seek dialog box.
2. Enter **B13** in the Set cell box and press **Tab**.
3. Type **18000** in the To value box to indicate that the total cost in cell B13 cannot exceed $18,000 and press **Tab**.
4. Type **B11** in the By changing cell box to indicate that Goal Seek should change the order quantity in cell B11 to arrive at the result. The dialog box should look like Figure 10-9.

Figure 10-9 **COMPLETED GOAL SEEK DIALOG BOX**

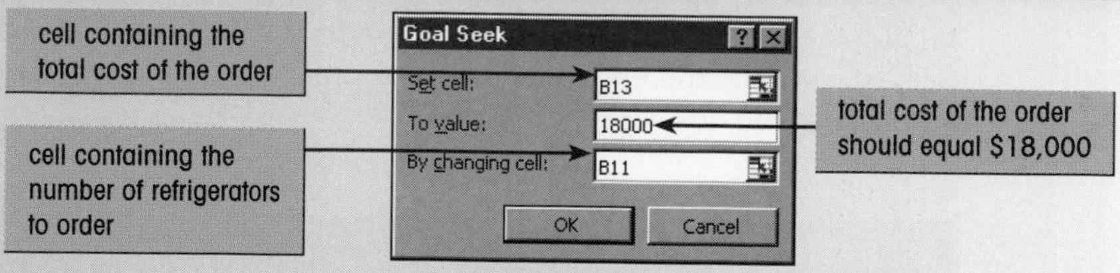

5. Click the **OK** button to seek the goal. The Goal Seek Status dialog box, shown in Figure 10-10, indicates that Goal Seek has found a solution.

Figure 10-10 **GOAL SEEK'S SOLUTION**

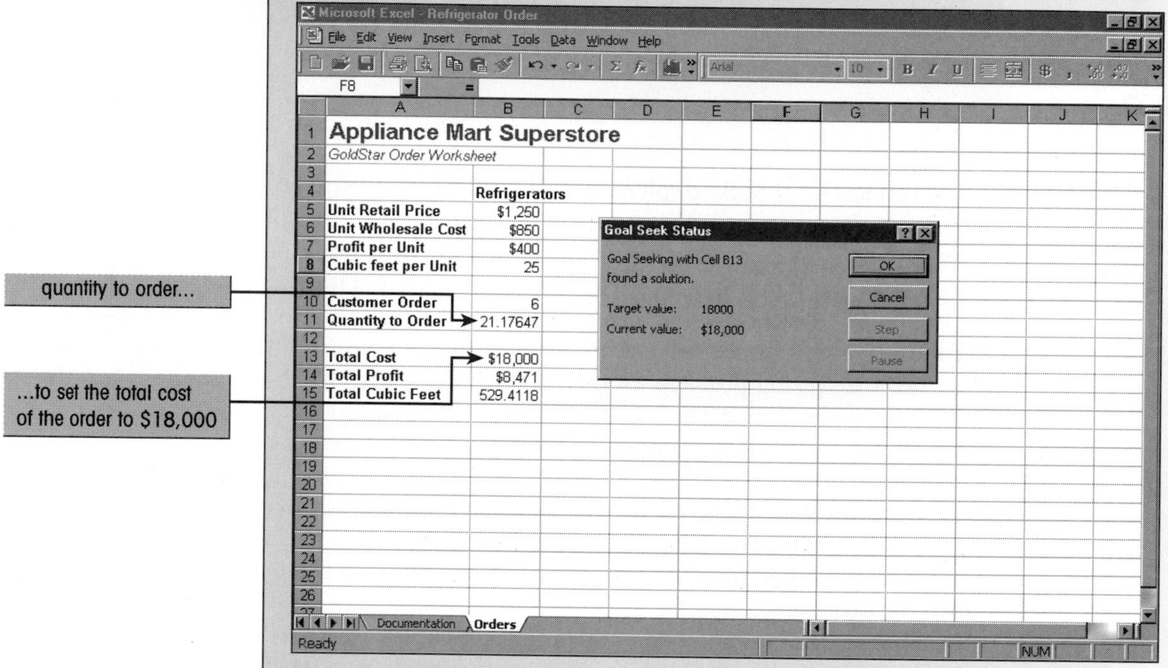

You'll close the dialog box and examine the solution Goal Seek has entered on the worksheet.

6. Click the **OK** button to continue.

Goal Seek determined that an order for 21.17647 refrigerators would use up the entire $18,000 that Jordan has allotted for the purchase. Because you cannot order a fraction of a refrigerator, you'll take the whole number part and manually change the order to 21 refrigerators in the worksheet.

To change the number of refrigerators in the order:

1. Enter **21** in cell B11, which contains the number of refrigerators to order.

Before going further, look at cell B15 to check the total cubic feet needed to store the 21 refrigerators. The total space required is 525 cubic feet, well below the 1,000 cubic feet available in the warehouse.

So you have some additional space in the warehouse. How many refrigerators can you order before filling up that space? Find out this answer by formulating the second goal-seeking problem.

To use Goal Seek to determine the number of refrigerators that will fit in a 1000 cubic foot space:

1. Click **Tools** on the menu bar, and then click **Goal Seek** to open the Goal Seek dialog box.
2. Enter **B15**, the cell containing the total cubic feet of space required by the order, in the Set cell box.
3. Type **1000** in the To value box, to specify that the total cubic feet should be set to 1000.
4. Type **B11**, the order quantity, in the By changing cell box.
5. Click the **OK** button. The Goal Seek Status dialog box indicates that Goal Seek has found a solution.
6. Click the **OK** button. Figure 10-11 shows that you can order 40 refrigerators to fill the 1000 cubic feet the warehouse allotted to you.

Figure 10-11 GOAL SEEK SOLUTION TO FILL UP WAREHOUSE SPACE

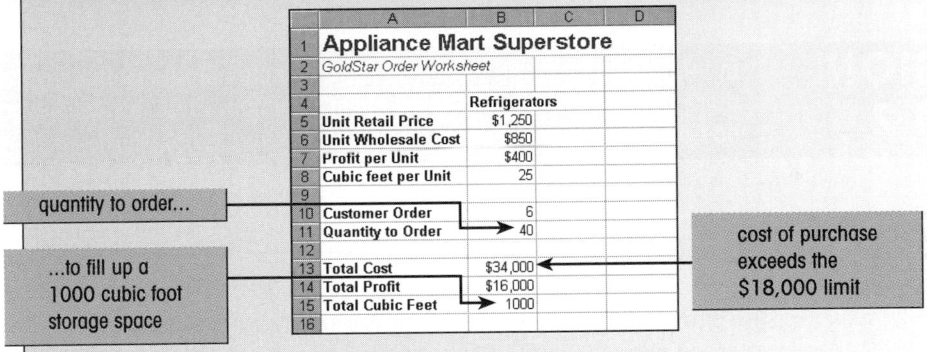

In looking over your results, you observe the cost of purchasing 40 refrigerators. The total cost, $34,000, almost doubles the amount Jordan said you could spend. You've found your limiting factor. In this case, it's not the space in the warehouse that will determine how many refrigerators you can buy; it's the total cost allowed for the purchase. Under the restriction set by Jordan, you can purchase up to 21 refrigerators, but no more. You'll enter 21 as the quantity to order in your workbook and then close the workbook and show Jordan your results.

To save, print, and close the Refrigerator Order workbook:

1. Enter **21** as the quantity to order in cell B11.
2. Print the worksheet.
3. Press **Ctrl + Home** to return to cell A1, and then click the **Documentation** sheet tab so that the next time the workbook is opened, this will be active worksheet.
4. Save and close the workbook.

Goal Seek has given you a solution to the ordering problem, and you expect that Jordan will be pleased when he learns how Appliance Mart can best benefit from the GoldStar sale.

Session 10.1 Quick Check

1. Describe the trial-and-error process.
2. What is a limitation of the trial-and-error process?
3. Describe the difference between a what-if analysis and a Goal Seek.
4. Identify a typical business problem that you could solve using Goal Seek.
5. Define the following terms:
   changing cell
   resulting cell
6. Name the three components of the Goal Seek command.

In this session, you planned and created a workbook that calculates the number of refrigerators that Appliance Mart should order, using both trial and error and Goal Seek. Although Goal Seek is a useful tool in solving problems like these, you'll need to learn to solve more complex inventory problems, which you'll do in the next session.

SESSION 10.2

In this session you will work with more complex problems that involve changing two or more parameters to arrive at the "best" solution. To do this you'll work with a useful Excel add-in called Solver.

Exploring More Complex Problems

Jordan stops by to see how you are doing, so you show him the worksheet. Jordan is so pleased with the work you have done that he asks you to take charge of the entire GoldStar order. He explains that GoldStar has great prices on Breakdale stoves and Quickcook microwave ovens, in addition to refrigerators. He wants you to determine the most profitable mix of refrigerators, stoves, and microwave ovens to order. He gives you a total budget of $50,000 for the order.

You check with the sales manager and learn that Appliance Mart has customer orders for 14 Breakdale stoves and 19 Quickcook microwave ovens. You realize that your solution must take into account the customer orders for 6 refrigerators, as well as the orders for the 14 stoves and 19 microwave ovens. Next, you call the warehouse and learn that the products for the entire order must fit in 1300 cubic feet of storage space. Your task is to find the best combination of refrigerators, stoves, and microwaves that will meet the purchasing budget and also fit within the warehouse space allotted to you. You'll find an answer to this complex problem using Excel.

A revised worksheet containing columns for stoves and microwaves is stored on your Data Disk as GoldStar. First, open and resave the file.

To open and resave the revised workbook:

1. If you took a break after the last session, make sure Excel is running, open the **GoldStar** workbook in the Tutorial folder for Tutorial.10 on your Data Disk, and save it as **Appliance Order**.
2. On the Documentation worksheet, type **Appliance Order** in cell B3.
3. Type (**Your Name**) in cell B4 and the (**Date**) in cell B5.
4. Click the **Orders** tab to display the worksheet showing price, cost, and order information for all three types of appliances. So far, only the number of appliances needed to meet customer orders has been entered. See Figure 10-12.

Figure 10-12 APPLIANCE ORDER WORKBOOK

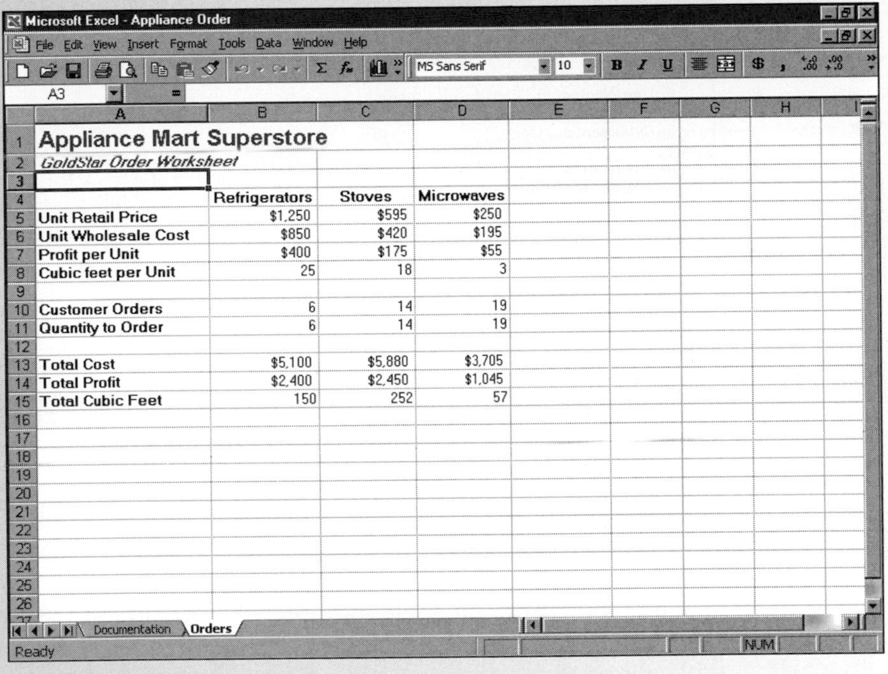

Notice that the worksheet has a column for stoves and a column for microwave ovens, each with the same format as the refrigerator column. There are also cells for the unit wholesale cost, the unit retail price, and the customer orders for each product.

You need to calculate the total order cost, the total order profit, and the total space required for all of the refrigerators, stoves, and microwave ovens on the order. To do this, you'll add a new column to the table that sums these values over all three appliances.

To add a column for total orders:

1. In cell E4, type **All Appliances**.
2. Select the range **E10:E11**, and then press and hold down the **Ctrl** key and select the range **E13:E15**.
3. Click the **AutoSum** button Σ on the Standard toolbar.

   Excel automatically sums the values in columns B through D and places the result in column E.

4. Select the range **D13:D15**.

5. Click the Format Painter button on the Standard toolbar, and click cell **E13**.

6. Apply the bold format to the contents of the range **E4:E15**.

7. Enlarge the width of column E to fit the column title.

8. Click cell **A3**. Figure 10-13 displays the revised Goldstar Order worksheet.

Figure 10-13 TOTALS FOR ALL APPLIANCES

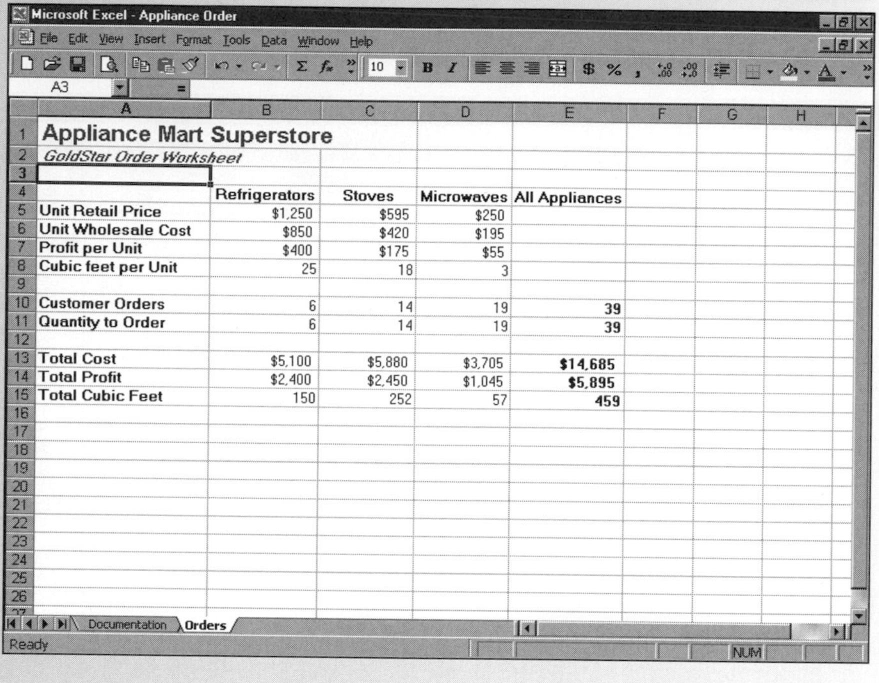

	A	B	C	D	E
1	Appliance Mart Superstore				
2	*GoldStar Order Worksheet*				
3					
4		Refrigerators	Stoves	Microwaves	All Appliances
5	Unit Retail Price	$1,250	$595	$250	
6	Unit Wholesale Cost	$850	$420	$195	
7	Profit per Unit	$400	$175	$55	
8	Cubic feet per Unit	25	18	3	
9					
10	Customer Orders	6	14	19	**39**
11	Quantity to Order	6	14	19	**39**
12					
13	Total Cost	$5,100	$5,880	$3,705	**$14,685**
14	Total Profit	$2,400	$2,450	$1,045	**$5,895**
15	Total Cubic Feet	150	252	57	**459**

The total cost of the GoldStar order that would just meet customer orders is $14,685, the total profit from all appliances is $5,895, and the space required to store the order is 459 cubic feet.

Formulating the Problem

You need to determine the mixture of refrigerators, stoves, and microwave ovens that will generate the greatest profit, assuming all units are sold. The total order cost cannot exceed $50,000, and the total space required cannot exceed 1300 cubic feet.

You might consider using Goal Seek to determine how many of each appliance you should order. However, Goal Seek is too limited for this task because it can change the contents of only one cell to find the solution. To determine how many of each appliance to order, three cells must change: cell B11, which contains the number of refrigerators to order; cell C11, which contains the number of stoves to order; and cell D11, which contains the number of microwave ovens to order. First you'll try solving the problem by trial and error.

Solving Complex Problems Using Trial and Error

Because it appears that Goal Seek won't work, you consider using trial and error to solve the problem manually. At first, this seems easy. Your worksheet currently shows the result of ordering 6 refrigerators, 14 stoves, and 19 microwave ovens. The cost of this order would be $14,685 and the appliances would take up 459 cubic feet of storage space. If you place this order, you would not use the entire $50,000 or fill the storage space, so you can order additional appliances. But should you order more stoves, refrigerators, or microwave ovens?

You can see from the values in cells B7, C7, and D7 that refrigerators generate the greatest profit, so you consider purchasing as many refrigerators as space and funds permit, and then purchase stoves and microwave ovens to use up the remaining money and storage space. Try to manually solve the problem of what product mix will provide the most profit, while still meeting the total order cost and space limitations. You start by ordering 50 refrigerators.

To solve the product mix problem by trial and error:

1. In cell B11, enter **50**. The total order cost is $52,085 and the total space required is 1,559.

   There is not enough money or storage space for 50 refrigerators, so you try a smaller number.

2. Enter **40** in cell B11. The total order cost is $43,585 and the total space required is 1309.

   There is not quite enough space to store 40 refrigerators, so again you try a smaller number.

3. Enter **39** in cell B11. The total order cost is $42,735 and the total space required is 1284.

   There is sufficient money and space to order 39 units. The total profit from selling the appliances on this order would be $19,095.

You see that there is quite a bit of money left, but only 16 cubic feet of storage space. Microwave ovens require 3 cubic feet of space, so you decide to purchase five more microwave ovens to use up the remaining space and some of the remaining money.

To add five more microwave ovens to the order:

1. Enter **24** in cell D11.

   The total order profit increases to $19,370 with a total order cost of $43,710 and a total space requirement of 1299 cubic feet.

You look at the worksheet and wonder if this is really the best answer. You used just about all of the available storage space but you still have over $6,000 left. What would happen if you had ordered more microwave ovens and fewer refrigerators?

Test the effect of ordering only 35 refrigerators and as many microwave ovens as you can purchase with the remaining money.

To test the effect of ordering more microwave ovens instead of refrigerators:

1. Reduce the number of refrigerators by entering **35** in cell B11.

   Next, increase the number of microwaves.

2. Enter **50** in cell D11. The total profit drops to $19,200, but the order would require only 1277 cubic feet, leaving 23 cubic feet of remaining space.
   Because each microwave requires 3 cubic feet of storage, there seems to be room for 7 more microwave ovens.
3. Enter **57** in cell D11.

   Total profit increases to $19,585.

This is the best solution yet. It yields a profit of $19,585, compared to $19,370 for the previous solution. But there are so many combinations. It could take hours or even days to try them all. You explain the problem to Jordan, who suggests that you try the Solver feature in Excel. He explains that Solver calculates solutions to what-if scenarios just like this one.

Solving **Complex Problems Using Solver**

Solver is an Excel add-in, or a program that you can install on your computer to add extra capabilities. Solver automatically calculates a maximum or minimum value of a cell by changing other cells that are "connected" to it by a formula.

When you use Solver, you must identify a target cell, the adjustable or changing cells, and the constraints that apply to your problem. A **target cell** is a cell that you want to maximize, minimize, or change to a specific value. One example is the total profit from the appliance order, a value you want to maximize. An **adjustable cell** is a cell that Excel changes to produce the desired result in the target cell. The number of refrigerators to order is an adjustable cell in this case. Finally, a **constraint** is a value that limits the way the problem is solved. One of your constraints is that you have to fit the appliance into the warehouse space allotted to you. You specify the target cell, changing cells, and constraints using the Solver Parameters dialog box. The settings you make in this dialog box are called the problem's **parameters**.

Setting Up Solver to Find a Solution

You examine the worksheet and determine that the target cell on your order worksheet is cell E14. This cell displays the total profit that will result from selling all the appliances on the order. You want Excel to produce a solution that maximizes the value in this cell.

The changing cells—the cells Excel can change to reach the solution—are cells B11, C11, and D11, the same cells that you changed when you tried to solve the problem manually. These cells contain the quantity to order for each appliance.

The two major constraints for this problem are the $50,000 spending limit and the 1300 cubic-foot space limit. Next you'll set up the parameters to solve this problem using Solver.

REFERENCE WINDOW **RW**

Using Solver

- Create a worksheet that contains the labels, values, and formulas for the problem you want to solve.
- Click Tools, and then click Solver to open the Solver parameters dialog box.
- The Set Target Cell box must contain the cell reference for the target cell, the cell you want to maximize, minimize, or set to a certain value.
- In the By Changing Cells box, list the cells that Excel can change to arrive at the solution.
- Use the Add button to add constraints that limit the changes Solver can make to the values in the cells.
- Click the Solve button to generate a solution.
- Click the OK button to return to the worksheet.

First, open the Solver Parameters dialog box, where you'll specify the target cell, changing cells, and constraints.

To set up the target cell and changing cells in Solver:

1. Click **Tools** on the menu bar, and then click **Solver**. Drag the Solver dialog box to display as much of the Orders worksheet as you can. See Figure 10-14.

Figure 10-14 SOLVER PARAMETERS DIALOG BOX

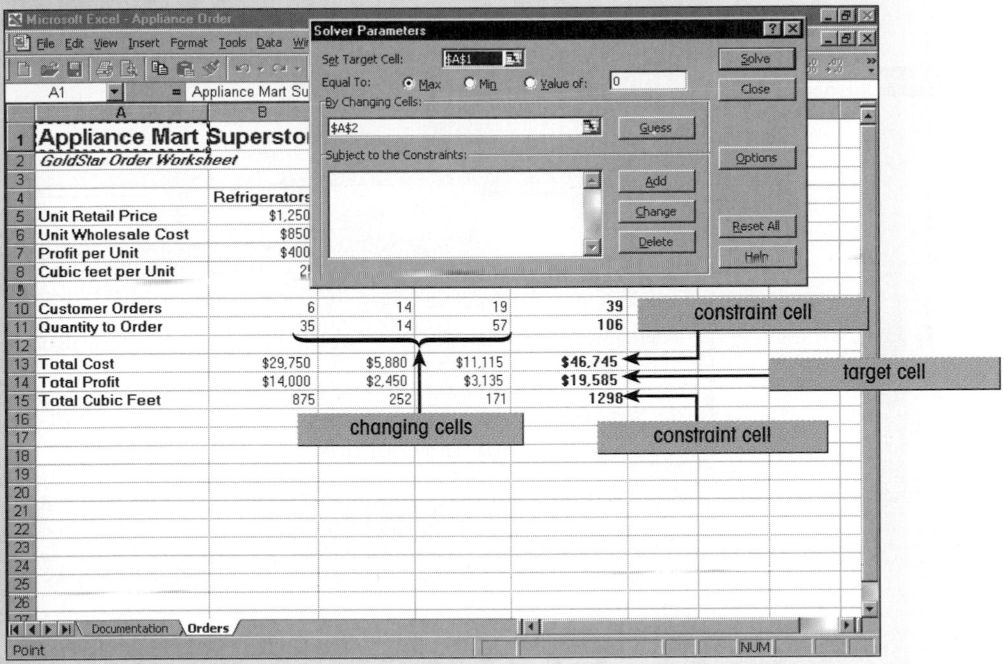

TROUBLE? If you don't see Solver on the Tools menu, or it doesn't appear when you click it, it might not be installed on your system. Click Tools on the menu bar, click Add-Ins, and select the Solver Add-In from the list. If you don't see the Solver Add-in listed, you will have to install it from the Excel installation disks or CD. Ask your instructor or technical support person for more information.

To specify the target cell, you'll reduce the dialog box and enter the cells you want to include, which is easier and more accurate than typing them.

2. Type **E14**, the cell containing the total profit of the order, in the Set Target Cell box.

3. Click the **Max** option button, if necessary, to indicate that you want Solver to maximize the total order profit.

4. In the By Changing Cells box, enter **B11:D11**, the cells containing the quantity to order for refrigerators, stoves, and microwaves.

Now that you have identified the target and changing cells, identify the other parameters for Solver by entering the two constraints. The first constraint is that the total order cost (in cell E13) must be less than or equal to $50,000, which can be expressed as E13 <= 50000. The second constraint is that the total space required (in cell E15) must be less than or equal to 1300 cubic feet, which can be expressed as E15<=1300. You can either type these equations or select the cell references with your mouse. Because these are just single-cell references, you'll type them in.

To enter the constraints in Solver:

1. Click the **Add** button to open the Add Constraint dialog box.
2. Type **E13**, the cell containing the total cost of all the appliances, in the Cell Reference box.
3. Click the **Constraint** list arrow in the middle of the Add Constraint dialog box, and then click the **<=** option from the list, if necessary.
4. Type **50000** in the Constraint box to set the maximum cost of the appliances at $50,000. See Figure 10-15.

Figure 10-15 ADD CONSTRAINT DIALOG BOX

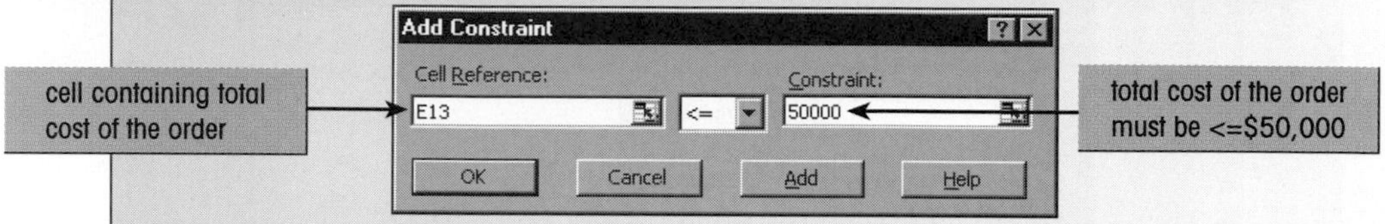

Next you need to add a second constraint, this time to limit the total cubic feet in cell E15 to 1300.

5. Click the **Add** button. Solver stores the first constraint, and clears the dialog box so you can add another one.
6. Type **E15**, the cell containing the total cubic feet required to store the appliances, in the Cell Reference box.
7. Make sure that the **<=** option is still selected from the comparison list.
8. Click the Constraint box, and then type **1300**, the maximum total cubic feet.
9. Click the **OK** button to return to the Solver Parameters dialog box. See Figure 10-16.

Figure 10-16 SETTING THE TARGET CELL, CHANGING CELLS, AND CONSTRAINTS

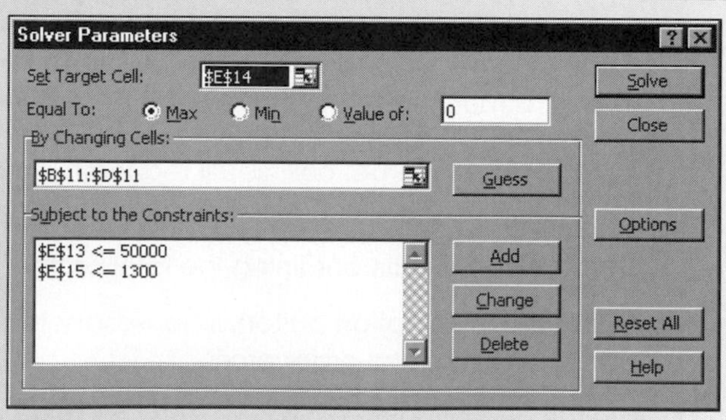

The two constraints you entered are listed in the Subject to the Constraints list.

TROUBLE? If the constraints on your screen are not the same as those in Figure 10-16, do one of the following: Select a constraint, click the Change button if you need to change the cell references in a constraint, click the Add button if you need to add a constraint; or click the Delete button if you need to delete a constraint.

Now that you have specified the target cell, changing cells, and constraints, you are ready to have Solver look for a solution to the problem.

To generate the solution using Solver:

1. Click the **Solve** button. In the status bar, you can see Solver rapidly "trying out" solutions. After a short time, the Solver Results dialog box opens and displays the message, "Solver has converged to the current solution. All constraints are satisfied." See Figure 10-17.

Figure 10-17 SOLVER RESULTS

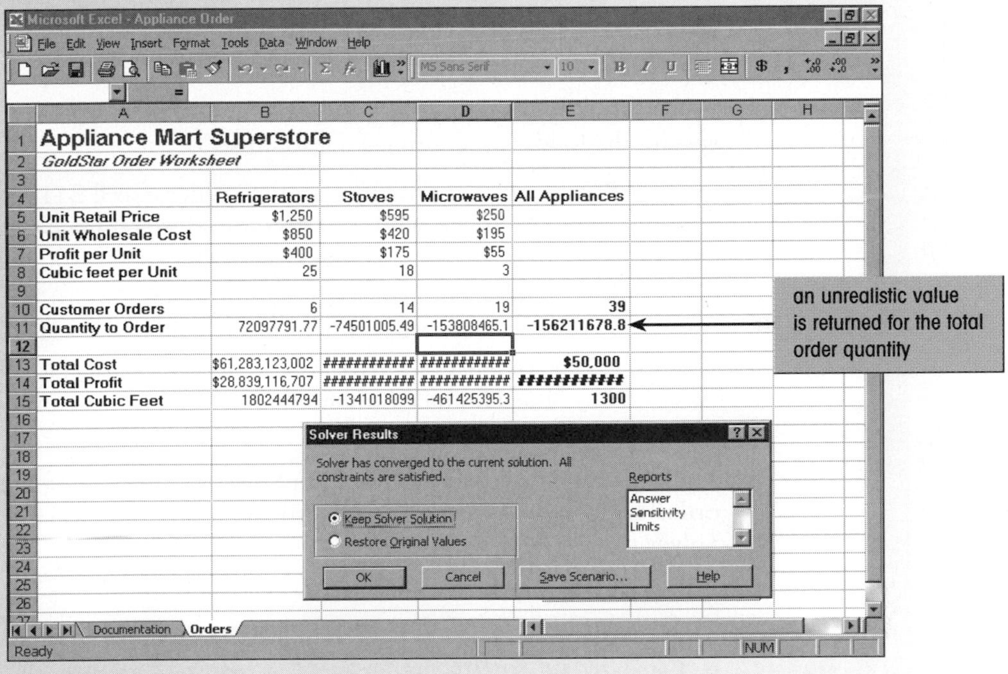

TROUBLE? If you see the message, "The Set Target Cell Values do not Converge" in the Show Trial Solutions dialog box, click the Stop button. When the Solver Results dialog box opens, continue with the following steps. If you see any other message in the Solver Results dialog box, simply continue with the steps.

2. If necessary, drag the dialog box out of the way to view the values Solver has produced so far as a solution to the problem.

You see that something is clearly wrong. In the current trial solution, Solver recommends ordering a very large number of refrigerators and large negative numbers of stoves and microwave ovens. Some of these values are so large that they don't fit within the cell width and Excel must instead display "#####" symbols. Ordering these large quantities results in an enormous profit for the company but, of course, you can't order a negative number of items. You can solve this problem by adding additional constraints.

Inserting Additional Constraints

You need additional constraints for your analysis to take into account the fact that you need to order at least enough refrigerators, stoves, and microwaves to cover customer demands. First, though, you need to remove the values Solver placed in the worksheet and add some additional constraints.

To remove the current values from the target cells:

1. Click the **Restore Original Values** option button in the Solver Results dialog box.
2. Click the **OK** button to close the Solver Results dialog box. Solver restores the original values to the worksheet.

To allow Solver to produce a realistic solution that reflects all the circumstances, you will specify the following additional constraints:

- The number of refrigerators to order in cell B11 must be greater than or equal to the customer orders for refrigerators in cell B10; in Solver terms, the constraint would be B11>=B10.
- The number of stoves to order in cell C11 must be greater than or equal to the customer orders for stoves in cell C10, or C11>=C10.
- The number of microwave ovens to order in cell D11 must be greater than or equal to the customer orders for microwave ovens in cell D10, or D11>=D10.

These constraints will also prevent Solver from ordering negative quantities because the order quantities are greater than zero. Now add these three additional constraints to the Solver parameters.

To add constraints requiring an order large enough to cover customer demand:

1. Click **Tools** on the menu bar, and then click **Solver** to start Solver.
2. Click the **Add** button.
3. Enter the constraint **B11 >= B10** in the Add Constraint dialog box to require the number of refrigerators to order to equal or exceed the size of the customer order.
4. Click the **Add** button.
5. Enter the constraint **C11 >= C10** to ensure that the stove order matches or exceeds the customer demand.
6. Click the **Add** button.
7. Enter the constraint **D11 >= D10** to ensure that the microwave order matches or exceeds the number of microwaves ordered by the customers.
8. Click the **OK** button.
9. The new constraints are shown in the Subject to the Constraints box displayed in Figure 10-18.

Figure 10-18 **ADDITIONAL CONSTRAINTS IN THE SOLVER PARAMETERS DIALOG BOX**

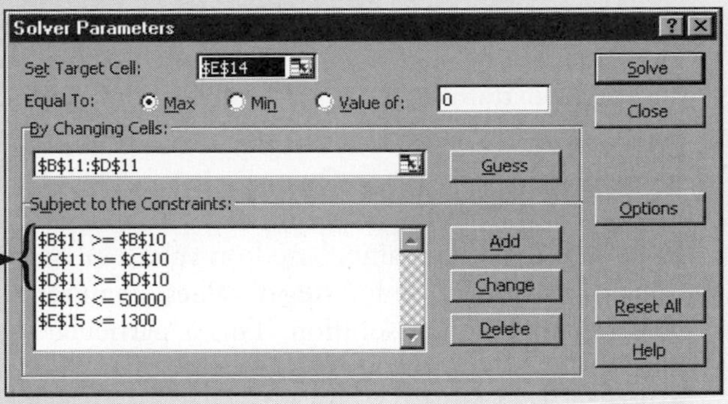

new constraints

TROUBLE? If the constraints on your screen are not the same as those in Figure 10-18, click a constraint, click the Change button if you need to change the cell references in a constraint, click the Add button if you need to add a constraint, or click the Delete button if you need to delete a constraint.

Now, have Solver try again to find a solution, this time using the new set of constraints.

To activate Solver:

1. Click the **Solve** button. This time the Solver dialog box message says, "Solver found a solution. All constraints and optimality conditions are satisfied."

   The solution is shown in Figure 10-19.

Figure 10-19 **SOLVER'S SECOND SOLUTION**

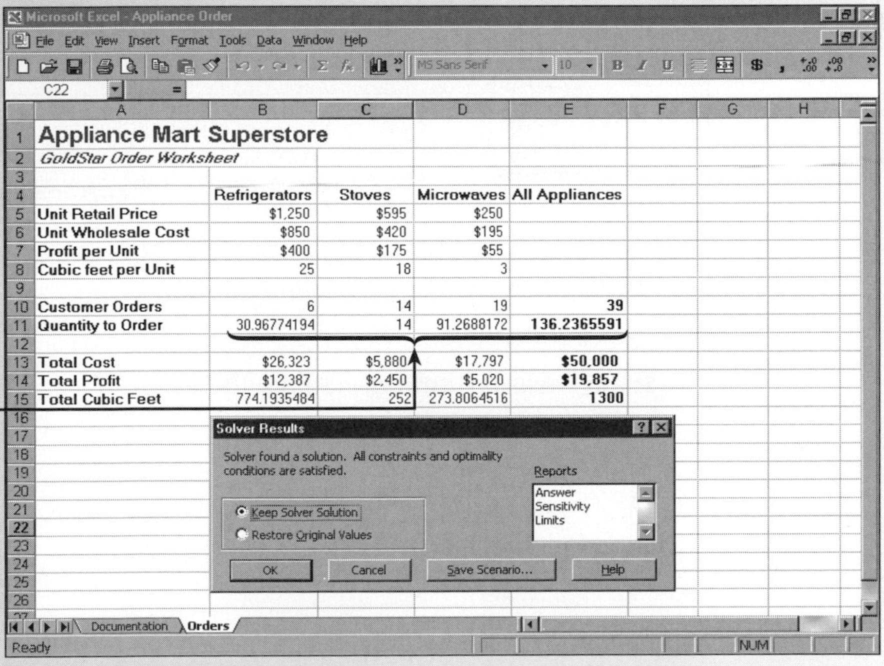

	Refrigerators	Stoves	Microwaves	All Appliances
Appliance Mart Superstore				
GoldStar Order Worksheet				
Unit Retail Price	$1,250	$595	$250	
Unit Wholesale Cost	$850	$420	$195	
Profit per Unit	$400	$175	$55	
Cubic feet per Unit	25	18	3	
Customer Orders	6	14	19	39
Quantity to Order	30.96774194	14	91.2688172	136.2365591
Total Cost	$26,323	$5,880	$17,797	$50,000
Total Profit	$12,387	$2,450	$5,020	$19,857
Total Cubic Feet	774.1935484	252	273.8064516	1300

order quantities are not integers

This solution is better. Solver did not order negative quantities, and you can see in row 11 that it did recommend ordering enough of each item to cover the customer orders shown in row 10. However, you notice yet another problem. Solver has ordered 30.96774194 refrigerators and 91.2688172 microwave ovens. Because you can only order whole units, you need another constraint to have Solver order nonfractional unit quantities: the integer constraint.

Inserting an Integer Constraint

In addition to constraints based on values or on the contents of other cells, you can have Solver recommend only integer values, commonly called "whole numbers," in the cells it changes to reach the solution. This is particularly important in a situation like your appliance order, where you can't order part of an appliance. You need to specify that adjustable cells B11, C11, and D11 must contain integer values.

To specify integers in cells B11, C11, and D11:

1. Click the **Restore Original Values** option button, and then click the **OK** button.
2. Restart Solver.
3. Click the **Add** button in the Solver Parameters dialog box.
4. Enter **B11:D11**, the cells containing order quantities for each appliance, in the Cell Reference box.
5. Click **int** from the Constraints list arrow. The word "integer" appears in the Constraint box, as shown in Figure 10-20.

Figure 10-20 ADDING AN INTEGER CONSTRAINT

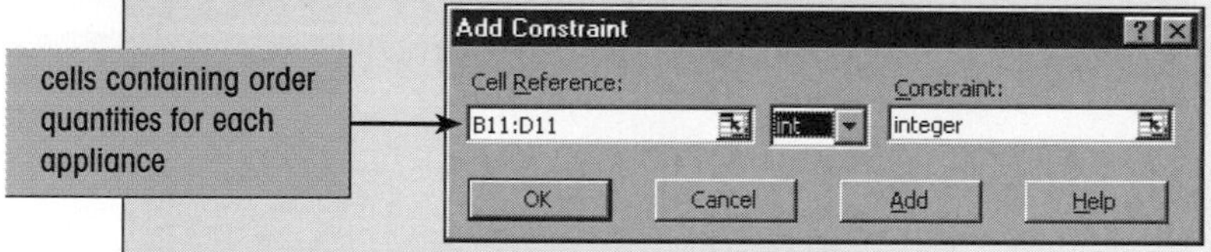

6. Click the **OK** button.

   Now run Solver with the new constraint.

7. Click the **Solve** button in the Solver Parameters dialog box. Solver returns a message stating that it has found a solution.
8. Click the **OK** button.

   Solver's solution is shown in Figure 10-21.

Figure 10-21 SOLVER'S THIRD SOLUTION

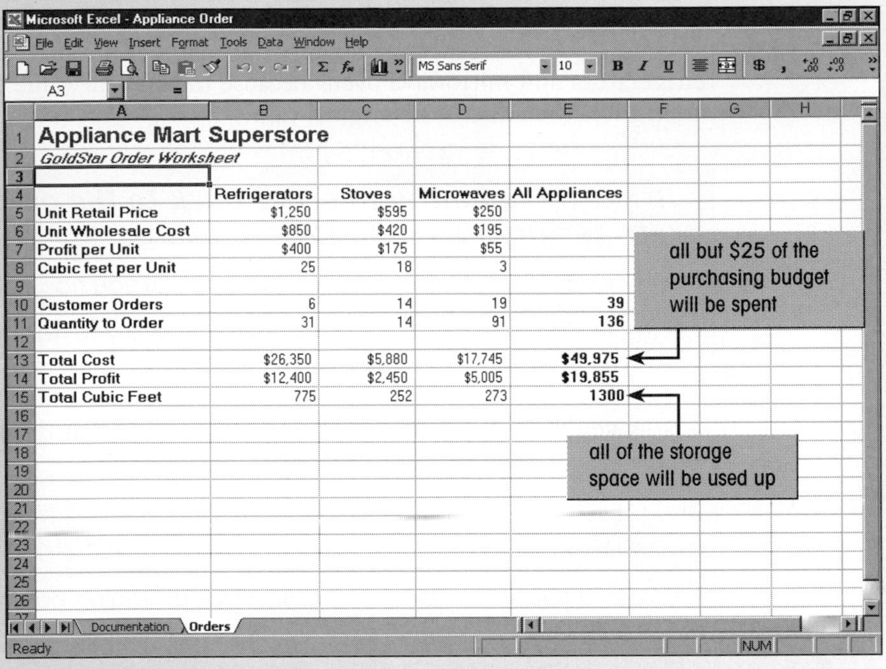

Solver indicates that you should order 31 refrigerators, 14 stoves, and 91 microwave ovens. This solution uses all but $25 of the available funds and all of the available storage space. It also generates a total profit of $19,855. Note that this might not be the ultimate solution because Solver tries a limited number of combinations in its search for a solution. There is a small chance that the best solution might not be found. However, with all storage space used and only $25 left, you are fairly certain that this solution must be very close to the optimal solution.

You've come up with an excellent solution to the problem of maximizing profits while staying within Jordan's budget and within the space allotted to you by the warehouse manager. You are ready to start preparing your report for Jordan. You can do this in Excel by creating an answer report.

Creating an Answer Report

How do you evaluate and report the solution that Solver produced? Solver can create three different reports—an answer report, a sensitivity report, and a limits report.

The **answer report** is the most useful of the three because it summarizes the results of a successful solution by displaying information about the target cell, changing cells, and constraints. This report includes the original and final values for the target and changing cells, as well as the constraint formulas.

The **sensitivity** and **limits reports** are used primarily in science and engineering environments when the user wants to investigate the mathematical aspects of the Solver solution. These reports allow you to quantify the reliability of the solution. However, you can't use these reports when your problem contains integer constraints, so you will create only an answer report for your inventory solution.

You decide to create an answer report as part of the final written report you'll give Jordan about your analysis.

An answer report provides information on the process used to go from the original values to the final solution. To make sure that the answer report includes information on the entire process, you'll set the quantities to order back to their original values, and then solve the problem again and generate the answer report. You only need to change the values for refrigerators and microwave ovens because the current value for the quantity of stoves to order, 14, is the same as the original value.

To set the quantity to order back to the original values for refrigerators and microwave ovens:

1. In cell B11, enter **6**, the original quantity that you had in this cell.
2. In cell D11, enter **19**, the original quantity that you had in this cell.

Now you'll use Solver to solve the problem again, but this time you'll create an answer report.

To solve the problem again and create an answer report:

1. Restart Solver. Your original parameters, changing cells, and constraints remain as you set them earlier.
2. Click the **Solve** button. After a few seconds the Solver Results dialog box opens.

   You can now create the answer report.
3. Click **Answer** in the Reports list box. Make sure the Keep Solver Solution option button is selected this time. See Figure 10-22.

Figure 10-22 CREATING AN ANSWER REPORT

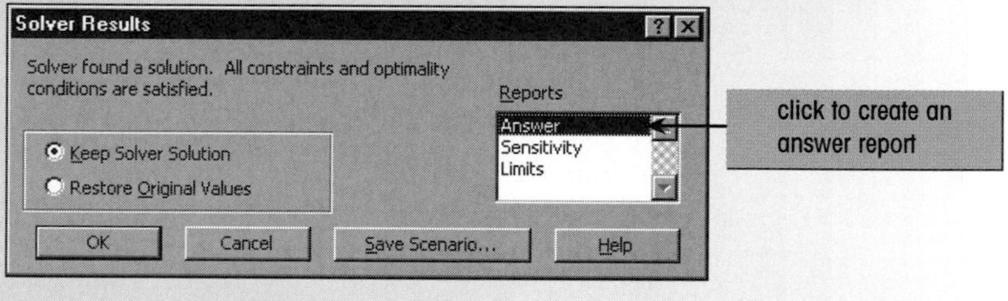

4. Click the **OK** button to save the answer report. Solver places the answer report in a separate sheet called "Answer Report 1."

The first time you create an answer report for a problem, Excel names it Answer Report 1. It calls the second report Answer Report 2, and so on. You decide to view the answer report.

To examine the answer report:

1. Click the **Answer Report 1** tab. Figure 10-23 shows the answer report for the solution Solver just produced.

Figure 10-23 SOLVER ANSWER REPORT

Target Cell (Max)

Cell	Name	Original Value	Final Value
$E$14	Total Profit All Appliances	$5,895	$19,855

section 2

Adjustable Cells

Cell	Name	Original Value	Final Value
$B$11	Quantity to Order Refrigerators	6	31
$C$11	Quantity to Order Stoves	14	14
$D$11	Quantity to Order Microwaves	19	91

section 3

Constraints

Cell	Name	Cell Value	Formula	Status	Slack
$E$13	Total Cost All Appliances	$49,975	$E$13<=50000	Not Binding	25
$E$15	Total Cubic Feet All Appliances	1300	$E$15<=1300	Binding	0
$B$11	Quantity to Order Refrigerators	31	$B$11>=$B$10	Not Binding	25
$C$11	Quantity to Order Stoves	14	$C$11>=$C$10	Binding	0
$D$11	Quantity to Order Microwaves	91	$D$11>=$D$10	Not Binding	72
$B$11	Quantity to Order Refrigerators	31	$B$11=integer	Binding	0
$C$11	Quantity to Order Stoves	14	$C$11=integer	Binding	0
$D$11	Quantity to Order Microwaves	91	$D$11=integer	Binding	0

section 4

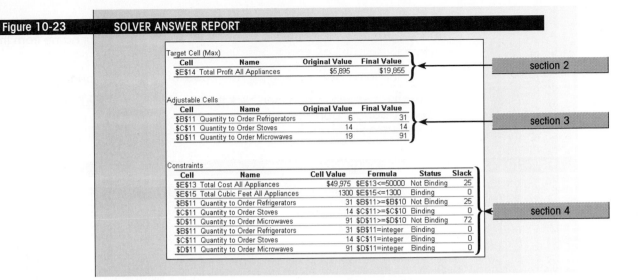

The answer report is divided into four sections. The first section includes titles, which indicate that this is an Excel answer report created from the Orders sheet in the Appliance Order workbook. The second section displays information about the target cell, in this case Total Profit, including its location, the cell label, and the cell's original value and final values.

The third section displays information about the changing cells, which the report calls Adjustable Cells. This section of the report shows the location, column and row label, the original value, and the final value of each cell. The column and row labels from the worksheet are joined to form the cell name in the answer report. For example, on the worksheet, Quantity to Order is the row label and Refrigerators is the column label, so cell B11 is called Quantity to Order Refrigerators in the answer report.

The fourth section of the report displays information about the constraints. In addition to the location, name, and value of each constraint, this section shows the constraint formulas. The second column from the right shows the status of each constraint. The status of Total Cost All Appliances, Quantity to Order Refrigerators, and Quantity to Order Microwaves is listed as "Not Binding." **Not Binding** means that these constraints were not limiting factors in the solution. The status of the other constraints is listed as "Binding." **Binding** means that the final value in these cells was equal to the constraint value. For example, the Total Cubic Feet All Appliances constraint was E15 <=1300. In the solution, cell E15 is 1300, which is at the maximum limit of the constraint, so this was a binding constraint in the solution.

The last column on the right shows the slack for each constraint. The **slack** is the difference between the value in the cell and the value at the limit of the constraint. For example, the constraint for the Total Cost All Appliances was $50,000. In the solution the total order cost was $49,975. The difference, or slack, between these two numbers is $25. Binding constraints show a slack of zero. Constraints listed as not binding show the difference between the constraint limit and the final value.

You decide to add a header as additional documentation and then print the answer report.

To add a header and print the answer report:

1. Click the **Print Preview** button on the Standard toolbar.
2. Click the **Setup** button to open the Page Setup dialog box, and then click the **Header/Footer** tab.
3. Click **Custom Header** to open the Header dialog box.

4. Delete any headers in the Left or Center Section, and then enter **(Your Name)** in the **Right Section** and press the **spacebar** to separate your name from the date.

5. Click the **Insert Date** button. The code for the date appears.

6. Press the **spacebar**, and then click the **File Name** button. The filename code appears. Don't be concerned if "&(File)" appears on a separate line. See Figure 10-24.

Figure 10-24 COMPLETED HEADER DIALOG BOX

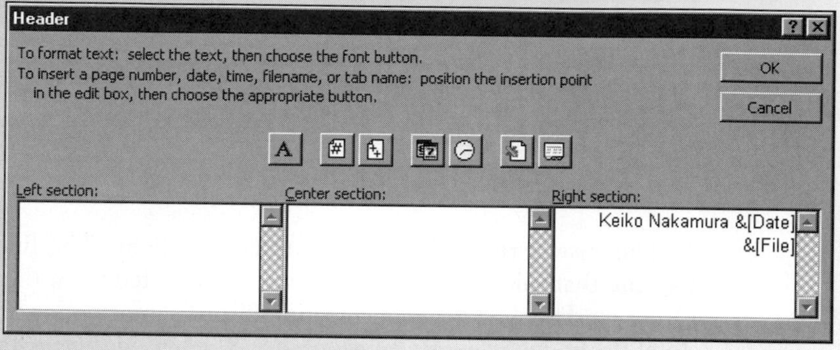

7. Click the **OK** button to return to the Page Setup dialog box.

8. Click the **OK** button to return to the Print Preview window.

9. Click the **Print** button on the Print Preview toolbar to open the Print dialog box.

10. Click the **OK** button to print the report.

Next, you'll print the Orders worksheet.

To save and print the Orders worksheet:

1. Click the **Orders** tab.

2. Click the **Print Preview** button on the Standard toolbar.

3. Click the **Setup** button and format the printout so that it prints in landscape mode on a single page, with the gridlines turned off. The header should be the same as the one used in the printout for the answer report.

4. Click the **OK** button to return to the Print Preview window.

5. Click the **Print** button and then click the **OK** button to print the worksheet. Your printout should look like Figure 10-25.

Figure 10-25 PRINTOUT OF ORDERS WORKSHEET

Keiko Nakamura 8/1/2001 Appliance Order

Appliance Mart Superstore
GoldStar Order Worksheet

	Refrigerators	Stoves	Microwaves	All Appliances
Unit Retail Price	$1,250	$595	$250	
Unit Wholesale Cost	$850	$420	$195	
Profit per Unit	$400	$175	$55	
Cubic feet per Unit	25	18	3	
Customer Orders	6	14	19	**39**
Quantity to Order	31	14	91	**136**
Total Cost	$26,350	$5,880	$17,745	**$49,975**
Total Profit	$12,400	$2,450	$5,005	**$19,855**
Total Cubic Feet	775	252	273	**1300**

Page 1

Examine the printed worksheet and answer report to make sure they contain the correct information.

6. Save and close the workbook, and exit Excel.

You can now take the printed reports to Jordan. He'll be pleased that you used one of Excel's more powerful features to determine how best to order appliances that fit your budget and space constraints.

Session 10.2 QUICK CHECK

1. Describe Excel Solver in your own words.
2. Under what circumstances would you use Solver rather than Goal Seek or trial and error?
3. Define the following terms:
   target cell
   constraint
4. What should you do if Solver returns an erroneous solution (such as negative product orders) to your problem?
5. What should you do if you do not want Solver to produce fractional numbers as the solution?
6. What is an answer report?
7. Define the following terms:
   Not Binding constraint
   Binding constraint
   slack
8. Why should you reset your worksheet back to its original values before generating an answer report?

In this tutorial you formulated problems that had several parameters and constraints, and attempted to solve them using trial and error, Goal Seek, and Solver. Solver proved to be the fastest and most effective way of solving more complex problems. Then you generated an answer report to help you evaluate the Solver solution to your inventory problem.

REVIEW ASSIGNMENTS

Jordan was impressed with your report that provided him with the best "mix" of product to buy. Now, in addition to refrigerators, stoves, and microwave ovens, GoldStar has offered Appliance Mart Superstore special pricing on dryers. GoldStar dryers are available wholesale for $215 and require 11 cubic feet of storage space; the retail price is $385. There are five orders for GoldStar dryers at this time, and the sales manager thinks they will sell very well. Given funds of $75,000 and a storage space limit of 1500 cubic feet for all the items on the order, Jordan would like you to perform a similar analysis to help him decide what mix of products he should order.

Do the following:

1. If necessary, start Excel, and open the **Dryers** workbook in the Review folder for Tutorial.10 and save it as **Dryer Order**.
2. Enter the new workbook name, "Dryer Order," in cell B4 of the Documentation sheet, and enter your name and the date in cells B5 and B6.
3. Go to the Orders worksheet, insert a new column between column D and column E and enter the heading "Dryers" in the new cell E4.
4. Enter the retail cost of a dryer in cell E5 and the wholesale unit price of a dryer in E6.
5. Enter the formula in cell E7 to calculate the profit for a dryer.

6. Enter the cubic feet of storage required for a dryer in cell E8.
7. Enter "5" for the customer orders and the quantity to order.
8. Copy the formulas from the range D13:D15 to the range E13:E15.
9. Activate Solver and adjust the changing cells to $B$11:$E$11.
10. Change the integer constraint so all of the units ordered must be integers.
11. Add a constraint so the quantity of dryers to order is greater than or equal to customer orders for dryers.
12. Change the constraint that limits the total order cost from $50,000 to $75,000.
13. Change the storage space constraint that limits total space required to 1500.
14. Use Solver to solve the problem and produce an answer report.
15. Replace the default headers on the worksheet and on the answer report so they contain your name, the date, and the filename.
16. Preview the worksheet and the answer report, and give it a professional appearance by using font styles, shaded fills, and/or other formatting features.
17. Save the modified workbook.
18. Print the worksheet and the answer report.
19. Print the formulas for the worksheet.

CASE PROBLEMS

Case 1. Ordering Products for a Furniture Sale at Home Furnishings WareHouse Bruce Hsu is the assistant manager at Home Furnishings WareHouse, a retail furniture outlet. One of Home Furnishings WareHouse's suppliers is having a sales promotion featuring special prices on couches and chairs. Bruce has been asked to determine the mix of products that will generate the greatest profit within the limits of the available funds and display space. Bruce can spend up to $60,000 on the order, and display space is limited to 1300 square feet. There are no customer orders for either couches or chairs, but the sales manager doesn't want Bruce to order more than 15 chairs.

Bruce has created a worksheet for this problem and has made several attempts to determine the solution manually. Bruce has asked you to help him use Solver to find the best solution. Do the following:

1. If necessary, start Excel, and then open the **Couches** workbook in the Cases folder for Tutorial.10 of your Data Disk. Save it in the same folder as **Furniture Order**. Enter the new workbook name, your name, and the date on the Documentation sheet.
2. Click the Orders tab, and then set up the Solver parameters for this problem using the following hints:
   a. The target cell contains the value for total order profit. Solver should attempt to maximize this cell.
   b. The changing cells contain the quantities of couches and chairs to order.
   c. The total order cost cannot exceed $60,000.
   d. The total space required must be less than or equal to 1300.
   e. You cannot order more than 15 chairs.
   f. You must order couches and chairs in whole units.
   g. You must order a positive number of couches and chairs.

3. Use Solver to produce a solution, and then create an answer report.
4. Format the Orders worksheet to give it a professional appearance.
5. Preview the worksheet and make any necessary formatting changes.
6. Save the workbook, and then preview and print its contents.

Case 2. Manufacturing Pontoon Boats at Robbins Pontoon Incorporated Mike Chignell is the assistant to the director of manufacturing at Robbins Pontoon Incorporated. Robbins manufactures four different models of pontoon boats: All Purpose, Camping, Utility, and Fishing. Each of the four models is built on the same boat frame. A topside assembly is attached to the frame to create each model.

Robbins currently has 135 boat frames in stock and a limited number of the four different topside assemblies. Mike wants you to determine the mix of models that will generate the greatest profit, given the available frames and topside assemblies. You'll have to make sure he manufactures enough of each model to fill the customer orders. Do the following:

1. If necessary, start Excel, open the **Pontoon** workbook in the Cases folder for Tutorial.10 on your Data Disk, and save it in the same folder as **Pontoon Boat Order**. Enter the new worksheet name, your name, and the date on the Documentation sheet.
2. Go to the Orders worksheet and then set up the Solver parameters for this problem using the following guidelines:
   a. You want to maximize the total profit from all models of pontoon boats by changing the quantity to make of each boat model.
   b. The optimal solution should include the following limits:
      - You cannot make more boats than you have available assemblies for each type.
      - You have to satisfy the customer orders for each boat type.
      - The total number of boats you make cannot exceed the total number of available frames.
      - Make only complete boats.
3. Use Solver to produce a solution and generate an answer report.
4. Modify the answer report worksheet so it contains your name, the date, and the filename.
5. Format the worksheet to give it a professional appearance.
6. Preview the printout and make any formatting changes necessary for a professional appearance.
7. Save the completed workbook, and then preview and print the completed worksheet.

Case 3. Scheduling Employees at Chipster's Pizza Lisa Avner is the assistant manager at Chipster's Pizza, a popular pizza place located in Cedar Falls, Iowa. Chipster's is open every day from 5:00 p.m. to 1:00 a.m. Friday and Saturday are the busiest nights; Sunday and Wednesday nights are moderately busy; Monday, Tuesday, and Thursday are the slowest nights.

Lisa is responsible for devising a schedule that provides enough employees to meet the usual demand, without scheduling more employees than are needed for each shift. All of Chipster's employees work five consecutive days and then have two days off. This means Lisa can schedule employees for seven different shifts—the Sunday through Thursday shift, the Monday through Friday shift, the Tuesday through Saturday shift, and so forth.

Lisa has created a worksheet showing the number of employees scheduled for each of the seven shifts, the total hours scheduled for each day, the hours needed for each day, and the difference between the hours scheduled and the hours needed. Lisa has asked you to help her find the schedule that will result in enough employee hours to meet the daily demand without scheduling excess hours.

Do the following:

1. If necessary, start Excel, and open the **Pizza** workbook in the Cases folder for Tutorial.10 of your Data Disk. Save it as **Chipster Employee Schedule** in the same folder. Enter the new workbook name, your name, and the date on the Documentation sheet.
2. Go to the **Schedule** worksheet. Cell B13 displays the current total of 560 scheduled hours. Cell B14 displays the current total of 448 needed hours. Cell B15 displays the current total of 112 excess scheduled hours.
3. Set up the Solver parameters to find a solution to the scheduling problem using the following parameters:
   a. Minimize the total difference between total hours worked and hours needed so that you don't over-schedule employees.
   b. Minimize the difference between hours worked and hours needed by modifying the number of shifts for each schedule.
   c. Use the following constraints:
      - You must have at least as many total hours worked over the entire schedule as total hours needed.
      - The number of workers for each shift must be greater than or equal to zero.
      - Workers must be scheduled for an entire shift.
      - You must schedule enough workers so the difference between the total hours worked each day and the total hours needed each day is greater than or equal to zero.
4. Use Solver to produce a solution and create an answer report.
5. Modify the headers on the worksheet and the answer report so they contain your name, the date, and the filename.
6. Save the workbook.
7. Preview and print the worksheet and the answer report.

Case 4. Furniture Purchasing at Southland Furniture Eve Bowman is the manager of Southland Furniture store, and she is planning a New Year's Day sale. The store has only 75 square feet of space available to display and stock this merchandise. During the sale, each folding table costs $5, retails for $11, and takes up 2 square feet of space. Each chair costs $4, retails for $9, and takes up 1 square foot of space. The maximum amount allocated for purchasing the tables and chairs for the sale is $280. Eve doesn't think she can sell more than 40 chairs, but the demand for tables is virtually unlimited. Eve has asked you to help her determine how many tables and chairs she should purchase in order to make the most profit. Complete the following:

1. What is the goal in this problem?
2. Which element of the problem would you specify for the changing cells if you used Solver to find a solution to this problem?
3. List the constraints for this problem.
4. Enter the information into a worksheet in Excel, including a Documentation sheet and data on total cost, total profit, and total space.

5. Save the workbook as **Southland Furniture** in the Cases folder for Tutorial.10 on your Student Disk.
6. Using Solver, determine how many folding tables and folding chairs should be purchased to maximize profits.
7. Create an answer report, detailing the parameters of the problem and the optimal solution.
8. Modify the headers on the worksheet and the answer report so they contain your name, the date, and the filename.
9. Save the workbook, and then preview and print the worksheet and the answer report.

QUICK CHECK ANSWERS

Session 10.1

1. a hit-and-miss strategy in which you try different values, attempting to find the optimal solution
2. With several variables to consider, you might never hit upon the best solution.
3. In a what-if analysis, you change the input cell to observe the value in the result cell. In a Goal Seek, you define a value you want to obtain for the result cell, and then determine what input value is required in the input cell.
4. One example is: "How should I change the price of my product to reach a desired level of profit?"
5. The changing cell is the cell in the Goal Seek that you want to modify. The result cell is the cell in a Goal Seek that contains the value you want to match.
6. the location of the changing cell, the location of the result cell, and the value you want to see in the result cell

Session 10.2

1. Solver is an Excel add-in that calculates solutions to what-if scenarios based on adjustable cells and constraints. Adjustable cells contain values that Solver can change to reach the optimal result; constraints are limits placed on Solver in changing the values of adjustable cells.
2. when you have too many variables in the worksheet that must be maximized, minimized, or that must reach a specific value in the result cell
3. The target cell is the cell that is maximized, minimized, or set to a specific value. A constraint is a limitation placed on a cell in the worksheet when Solver is run.
4. click the Restore Original Values option button to set the worksheet back to the state it was in before you ran solver
5. use an integer constraint on the target cell
6. An answer report includes information about the target cell, changing cell, and constraints. The report includes the original and final values for these cells.
7. A Not Binding constraint is a constraint that was not a limiting factor in the Solver solution. A Binding constraint was a limiting factor. Slack is the difference between the value of the constraining cell and the limiting value of the constraint.
8. so that the answer report will include information on the entire Solver process, from the original values through to its final solution

OBJECTIVES

In this tutorial you will:

- Import data from a text file into an Excel workbook
- Retrieve data from a database using the Query Wizard
- Retrieve data from multiple database tables
- Retrieve data from a database into a pivot table
- Retrieve stock market data from the World Wide Web
- Use hyperlinks to view information on the World Wide Web

IMPORTING DATA INTO EXCEL

Working with a Stock Portfolio for Davis & Larson

CASE

Davis & Larson

Davis & Larson is a brokerage firm based in Chicago. Founded by Charles Davis and Maria Larson, the company has provided financial planning and investment services to Chicago-area corporations and individuals for the last 15 years. As part of its investment services business, the company advises clients on its investment portfolios, so it needs to have a variety of stock market information available at all times. Like all brokerage firms, the company is connected to many financial and investment information services. The investment counselors at the company must have access to current financial data and reports, but they also must be able to examine information on long-term trends in the market.

Some of this information comes from Excel workbooks, but other information is stored in specialized financial packages and statistical programs. In addition, the company maintains a database with detailed financial information about a variety of stocks, bonds, and funds. Company employees also have access to the Internet to receive up-to-the-minute market reports. Because much of the information the counselors need comes from outside the company, they must retrieve information in order to analyze it and make decisions.

Kelly Watkins is an investment counselor at Davis & Larson. She wants you to help her manage the different types of data available to her as she works on the Sunrise Fund, one of the company's most important stock portfolios. Because Kelly prefers to work with financial data using Excel, she wants you to retrieve the data for her and place it into an Excel workbook.

SESSION 11.1

In this session, you'll use the Excel Text Import Wizard to retrieve data from a text file. You'll select columns of data for retrieval and specify the format of the incoming data. You'll learn about basic database concepts, and about how to retrieve information from a database using the Query Wizard. Finally, you'll learn how to create retrieval criteria so you can retrieve only the information you want.

Planning Data Needs at Davis & Larson

In her job as an investment counselor at Davis & Larson, Kelly needs to help her clients plan their investment strategies. To do her job well, Kelly needs to look at the market from a variety of angles. She needs to examine long-term trends to help her clients understand the benefits of creating a long-term investment strategy. She also needs to see market performance for recent months in order to analyze current trends. Finally, she needs to be able to assess the daily mood of the market by regularly viewing up-to-the-minute reports.

The information that Kelly needs to do her job comes from a variety of sources. As shown in Figure 11-1, long-term and historical stock information from the company's old record-keeping system has been retrieved from other financial software packages and placed in text files that are accessible to all counselors. The company stores its current market information in databases, which is where Kelly gets information on recent trends. Finally, Kelly can access current market reports electronically from the Internet.

Figure 11-1 KELLY'S DATA SOURCES

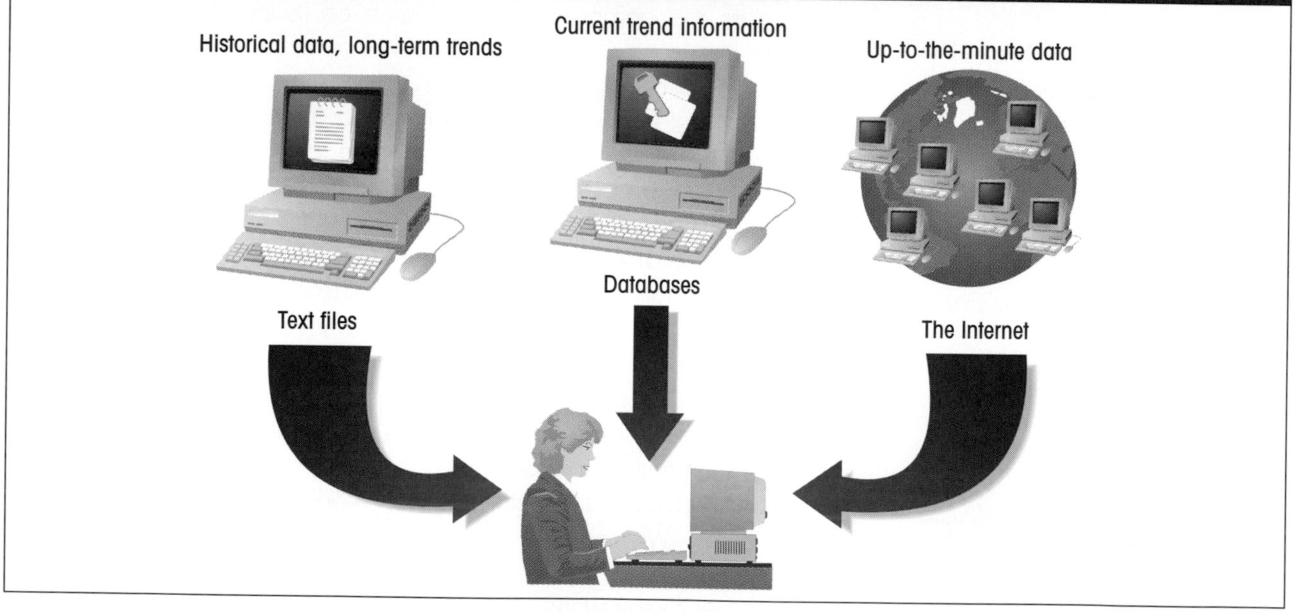

Kelly is responsible for tracking the performance of one of the company's investment vehicles called the Sunrise Fund. The Sunrise Fund is composed of 21 different stocks on the New York Stock Exchange (NYSE), and it is one of Davis & Larson's oldest and most successful funds. Kelly would like to have a single Excel workbook that summarizes essential information about the Sunrise Fund. She wants the workbook to include historical information describing: (1) how the fund has performed over the past few years; (2) more recent information on the fund's performance in the last year as well as the last few days; and (3) up-to-the-minute reports on the fund's current status.

Kelly has written up a layout for the workbook that she wants you to create, shown in Figure 11-2.

Figure 11-2 KELLY'S PLAN FOR THE SUNRISE FUND WORKBOOK

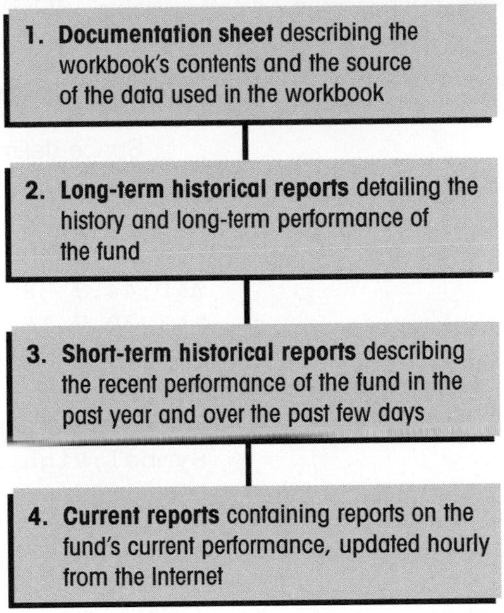
1. **Documentation sheet** describing the workbook's contents and the source of the data used in the workbook
2. **Long-term historical reports** detailing the history and long-term performance of the fund
3. **Short-term historical reports** describing the recent performance of the fund in the past year and over the past few days
4. **Current reports** containing reports on the fund's current performance, updated hourly from the Internet

Once she has these three types of information in her Excel workbook, Kelly will use Excel tools to analyze the data.

Locating and organizing the different types of data Kelly wants in the workbook will be challenging because you will have to bring in data from three different sources. You quickly see that you're going to have to master the techniques of retrieving information from each of them.

You'll begin by retrieving the first piece of information she needs, the Sunrise Fund's historical data. After talking with a few coworkers, you manage to locate a text file containing daily values for the fund over the last three years. You'll import this text file into Excel.

Working with Text Files

A **text file** contains only text and numbers, without any formulas, graphics, special fonts, or formatted text that you would find in a file saved in a spreadsheet program format. Text files are one of the simplest and most widely used methods of storing data because most software programs can both save and retrieve data in a text file format. For example, Excel can open a text file into a worksheet, where you can then format it as you would any data. Excel can also save a worksheet as a text file, preserving only the data, without any of the formats applied to it. In addition, many different types of computers can read text files. So although text files contain only raw, unformatted data, they are very useful in situations where you want to share data with others. There are several types of text file formats, which you'll learn about in the next section.

Text File Formats

Because a text file doesn't contain formatting codes to give it structure, there must be some other way of making it understandable to a program that will read it. If a text file contains only numbers, how will the importing program know where one column of numbers ends and another begins? When you import or create a text file, you have to know how that data is organized within the file. One way to structure text files is to use a **delimiter**, which is a symbol, usually a space, a comma, or a tab, that separates one column of data from another. The delimiter tells a program that retrieves the text file where columns begin and end. Text that is separated by delimiters is called **delimited text**. Figure 11-3 shows three examples of the same stock market data delimited by spaces, commas, and tabs.

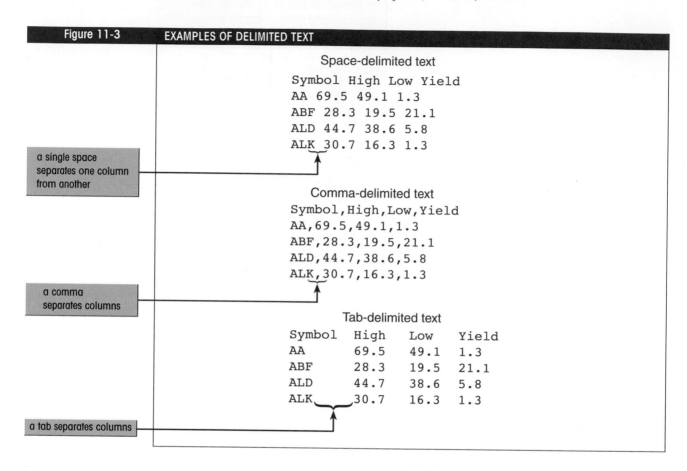

Figure 11-3 EXAMPLES OF DELIMITED TEXT

Space-delimited text

```
Symbol High Low Yield
AA 69.5 49.1 1.3
ABF 28.3 19.5 21.1
ALD 44.7 38.6 5.8
ALK 30.7 16.3 1.3
```

a single space separates one column from another

Comma-delimited text

```
Symbol,High,Low,Yield
AA,69.5,49.1,1.3
ABF,28.3,19.5,21.1
ALD,44.7,38.6,5.8
ALK,30.7,16.3,1.3
```

a comma separates columns

Tab-delimited text

```
Symbol	High	Low	Yield
AA	69.5	49.1	1.3
ABF	28.3	19.5	21.1
ALD	44.7	38.6	5.8
ALK	30.7	16.3	1.3
```

a tab separates columns

In each example, there are four columns of data: Symbol, High, Low, and Yield. In the first example, a space separates the columns. The second example shows the same data, except that a comma separates each data column. In the third example, a tab separates the columns. As you can see, columns in delimited text files are not always vertically aligned as they would be in a spreadsheet, but this is not a problem for a program that reads and recognizes the delimiter. A tab delimiter is often the best way of separating text columns, because tab-delimited text can include spaces or commas within each column.

In addition to delimited text, you can also organize data with a fixed width file. In a **fixed width** text file, each column will start at a same location in the file. For example, the first column would start at the first space in the file; the second column will start at the 10th space, and so forth. Figure 11-4 shows columns arranged in a fixed width format. As you can see, all the columns line up visually, because each entry in the columns start at the same location.

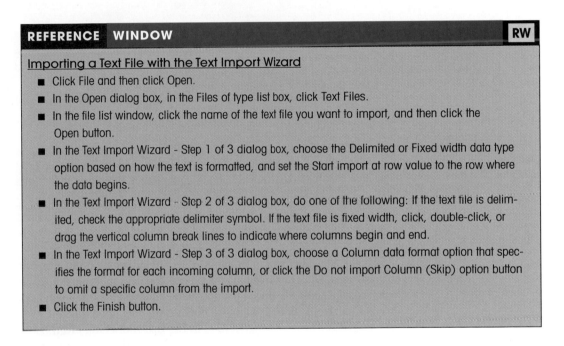

Figure 11-4 AN EXAMPLE OF FIXED WIDTH TEXT

```
Symbol  High   Low    Yield
AA      69.5   49.1   1.3
ABF     28.3   19.5   21.1
ALD     44.7   38.6   5.8
ALK     30.7   16.3   1.3
```

each column entry begins at the same point in the text file

When Excel starts to open a text file, it automatically starts the **Text Import Wizard** to determine whether the data is in a fixed width format or a delimited format—and if it's delimited, what delimiter is used. If necessary, you can also intervene and tell it how to interpret the text file.

REFERENCE WINDOW RW

Importing a Text File with the Text Import Wizard

- Click File and then click Open.
- In the Open dialog box, in the Files of type list box, click Text Files.
- In the file list window, click the name of the text file you want to import, and then click the Open button.
- In the Text Import Wizard - Step 1 of 3 dialog box, choose the Delimited or Fixed width data type option based on how the text is formatted, and set the Start import at row value to the row where the data begins.
- In the Text Import Wizard - Step 2 of 3 dialog box, do one of the following: If the text file is delimited, check the appropriate delimiter symbol. If the text file is fixed width, click, double-click, or drag the vertical column break lines to indicate where columns begin and end.
- In the Text Import Wizard - Step 3 of 3 dialog box, choose a Column data format option that specifies the format for each incoming column, or click the Do not import Column (Skip) option button to omit a specific column from the import.
- Click the Finish button.

Having seen some of the issues involved in using a text file, you are ready to import the file containing the Sunrise Fund's historical data.

Starting the Text Import Wizard

The text file that Kelly wants you to import into Excel is stored in the file named History.txt. The .txt filename extension identifies it as a text file. (Some other common text filename extensions are .dat, .prn, and .csv.) The person who gave you the text file didn't tell you anything about its structure, but you can easily determine the structure using the Text Import Wizard. You'll begin by opening the text file, which is similar to opening an Excel workbook, except that in the Open dialog box, you need to tell Excel to display text filenames in the file list. By default, Excel will display only Excel files unless you indicate you want to see other types of files.

To open the History text file:

1. Start Excel as usual, and make sure your Data Disk is in the appropriate drive.
2. Click **File** on the menu bar and then click **Open**.
3. In the Look in list box, locate the Tutorial folder for Tutor11 on your Data Disk.
4. Click the **Files of type** list arrow (near the bottom of the dialog box) and then click **Text Files**. The names of all text files in that folder now appear.
5. Click **History** in the File List window, and click the **Open** button. Excel starts the Text Import Wizard, as shown in Figure 11-5.

Figure 11-5 TEXT IMPORT WIZARD - STEP 1 OF 3

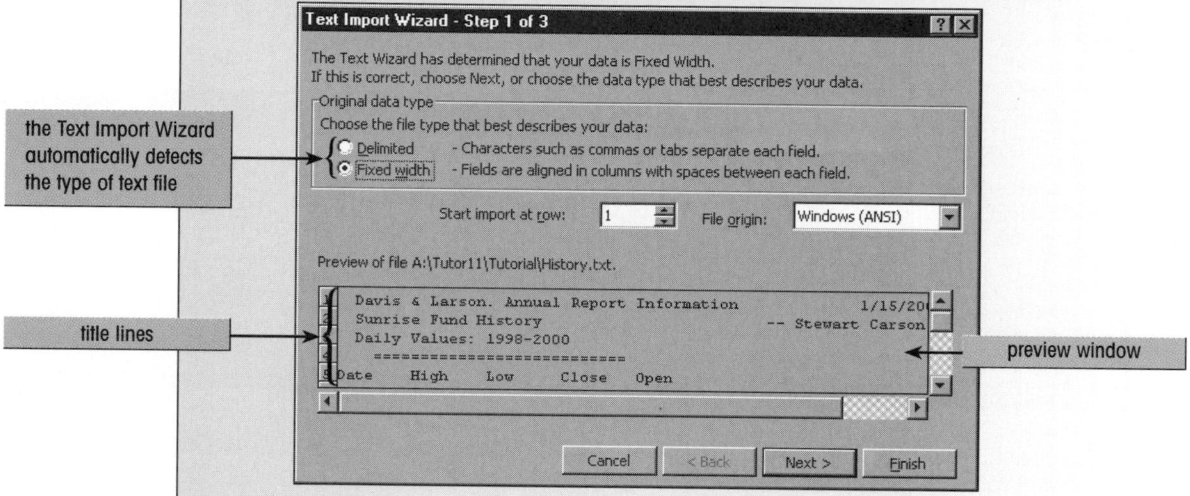

In the Original data type section, the Fixed width option button is already selected. This means that the Text Import Wizard has determined that the data is arranged in fixed width format. By scrolling down the Preview window, you can view the data in the text file. Note that the data list doesn't actually begin until row 6, or row 5 if you include the column titles.

There are five columns of data in the text file: Date, High, Low, Close, and Open, corresponding to the date, the fund's high and low values on that date, and the fund's opening and closing values. The Preview window also shows that the first four lines, or rows, of the text file contain titles and lines describing the contents of the file. You want to import only the data, not the title lines, so you'll indicate the row at which you want to begin the import process, called the starting row.

Specifying the Starting Row

By default, the Text Import Wizard will start importing text with the first row of the file. Because you're only interested in retrieving the data and not the title lines, you will have the Text Import Wizard skip the first three lines of the file. You do this by specifying a new starting row for the import. You want it to start with the fifth row, which contains the labels for each column of numbers.

To specify the starting row or line number of the text file:

1. Click the **Start import at row** spin up arrow to change the value to **5**. The Preview window now displays only the data from the text file, without the rows of descriptive text.

   TROUBLE? If the Preview window doesn't change quickly, don't be concerned, it might take a few seconds before the window updates.

2. Click the **Next** button to open the Text Import Wizard - Step 2 of 3 dialog box. See Figure 11-6.

Figure 11-6 TEXT IMPORT WIZARD - STEP 2 OF 3

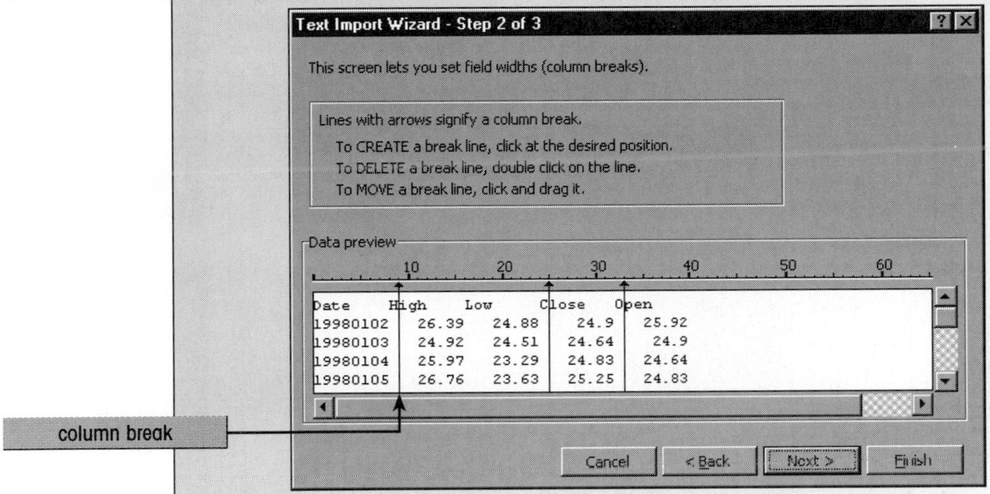

Having specified the starting row for the text file, you'll next indicate the starting and stopping points for each column.

Editing Column Breaks

In order for a fixed width text file to import correctly into Excel, there must be some way for the Text Import Wizard to know where each column begins and ends. The point at which one column ends and another begins is called a **column break**. In a delimited file, the delimiter automatically determines the column break. In a fixed width file, the Wizard tries to determine the location of the column breaks for you, and places vertical lines in the Data preview window at its best guess at column locations. Sometimes the Wizard's attempt to define the number and location of columns is not exactly right, so you should always check it, and edit the columns if necessary. Figure 11-6 shows the columns that the Wizard has proposed for your text file. Unfortunately, the Wizard has not inserted a column break between the High and the Low columns. In addition, some of the column breaks are in the wrong positions. The column break between the Date and High columns cuts the High column title in half, for example. Clearly, you'll have to revise the Text Import Wizard's choice of column breaks and their locations.

You insert a new column break by clicking the position in the Data preview window where you want the break to appear. If a break is in the wrong position, you click and drag it to a new location in the Data preview window. Finally, you can delete an extra column break by double-clicking it. You'll use these techniques to modify the column breaks for the History text file.

To edit the Text Import Wizard's column breaks:

1. Click the vertical line between the Date and High columns and drag it to the left so that it lies between the High column title and the values in the Date column.
2. Click the space between the High and Low columns to create a break there. Make sure the break does not intersect any values or text.
3. Drag the vertical line between the Low and Close columns to left, so as to not cross over any values or text in either column.
4. Drag the column break between the Close and Open columns to left. Make sure the vertical line does not intersect any values or text in either column. Figure 11-7 shows the Data preview window with the column breaks in the correct locations. When it imports this text file, Excel will now place each column into a separate column in the worksheet.

Figure 11-7 REVISED COLUMN BREAKS

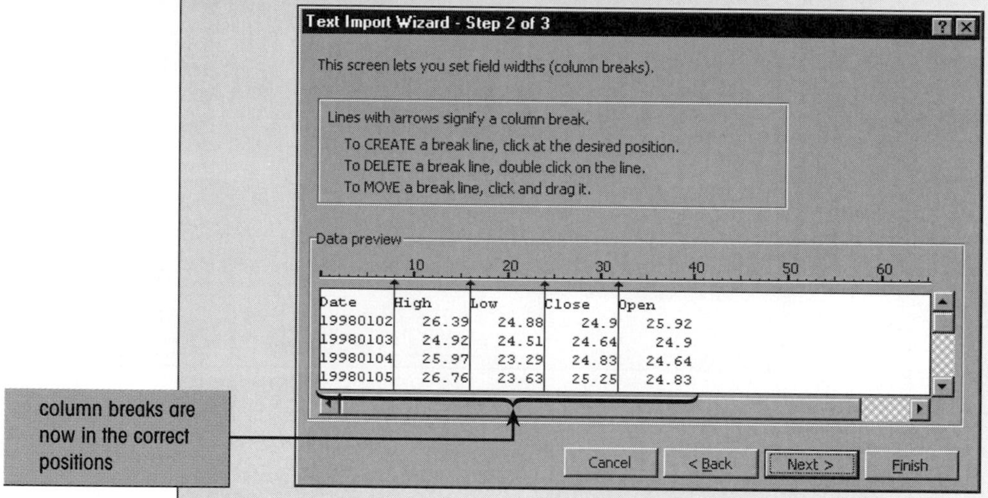

5. Click the **Next** button to open the Text Import Wizard - Step 3 of 3 dialog box. See Figure 11-8.

Figure 11-8 TEXT IMPORT WIZARD - STEP 3 OF 3

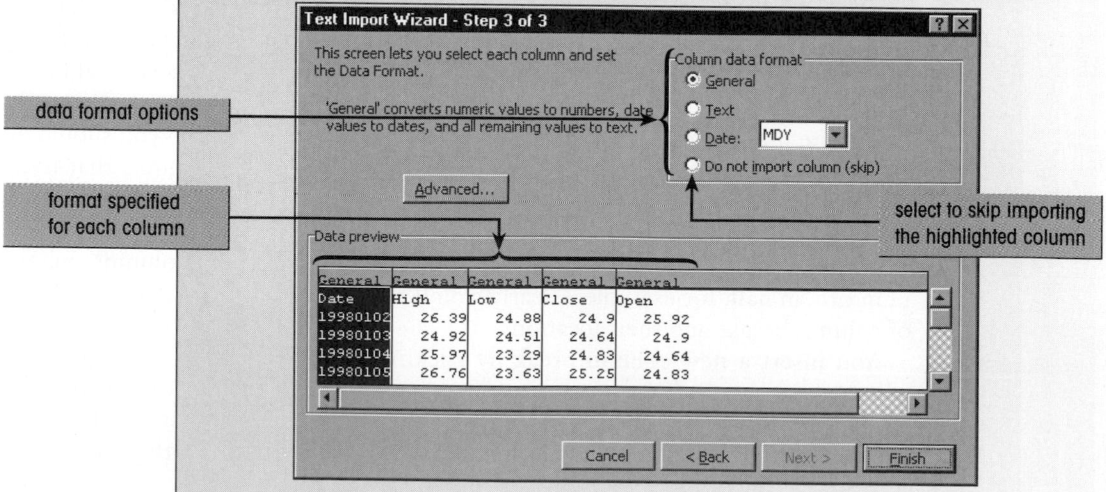

Now you'll tell Excel how you want to format each column of the incoming data.

Formatting and Trimming Incoming Data

The third and final step of the Text Import Wizard allows you to format the data in each column. Unless you specify a format, Excel will apply a General format to all columns, which means that the Import Wizard tries to determine which columns contain text, numbers, or dates.

If you're worried that the Import Wizard will misinterpret the format of a column, you can specify the format yourself in the Step 3 of 3 dialog box, before the column is imported. In addition to specifying the data format, you can also indicate which columns you do not want to import at all. Eliminating columns is useful when there are only a few items you want to import from a large text file containing many columns.

As you look over the Data preview window shown in Figure 11-8, you note that the Date column displays the year first, followed by the month and the day with no separators. This is an unusual date format, so you'll want to make sure that the Text Import Wizard correctly interprets these values by applying a date format to these values, rather than the General format.

In addition, to reduce the amount of data in the workbook, you decide not to import the daily opening value of the Sunrise Fund because it's the same as the closing value from the previous day. You'll therefore only import the date and the high, low, and close values of the fund for each day.

To specify a Date format and remove the Open column:

1. Make sure that the first column is selected in the Data preview window.

   Now you'll assign the correct date format.

2. In the Column data format section, click the **Date** option button.

3. Click the **Date** list arrow, and click **YMD** from the list of date formats. Although the data appears unchanged, the column heading changes from General to YMD, indicating that Excel will interpret the values in this column as dates formatted with the year first, followed by the month and day.

   Now you'll omit the Open column from the import.

4. In the Data preview window, click anywhere in the **Open** column to select it.

5. Click the **Do not import column (skip)** option button. The column format for the Open column changes to Skip Column, indicating that Excel will not import it.

6. Click the **Finish** button. Excel retrieves the data from the text file and places it into a new workbook.

7. Name the new worksheet **Fund History**.

8. Format the worksheet to show the high, low, and close values with two decimal places, and the column titles boldface and centered. See Figure 11-9.

Figure 11-9 **WORKSHEET IMPORTED INTO EXCEL**

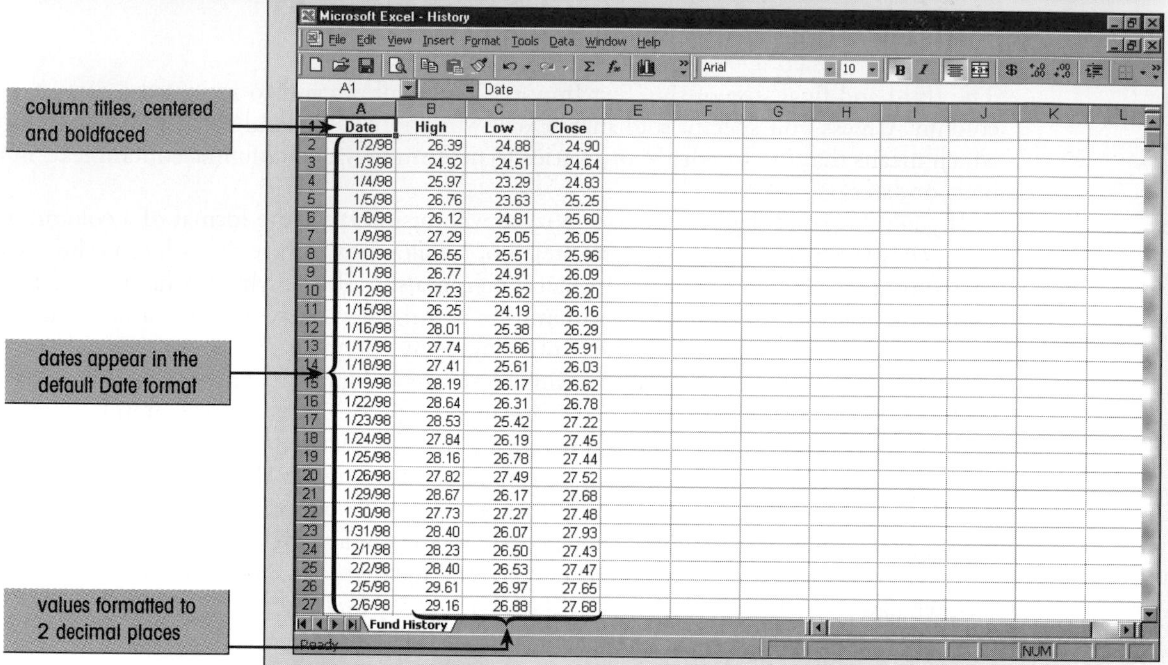

	A	B	C	D
1	Date	High	Low	Close
2	1/2/98	26.39	24.88	24.90
3	1/3/98	24.92	24.51	24.64
4	1/4/98	25.97	23.29	24.83
5	1/5/98	26.76	23.63	25.25
6	1/8/98	26.12	24.81	25.60
7	1/9/98	27.29	25.05	26.05
8	1/10/98	26.55	25.51	25.96
9	1/11/98	26.77	24.91	26.09
10	1/12/98	27.23	25.62	26.20
11	1/15/98	26.25	24.19	26.16
12	1/16/98	28.01	25.38	26.29
13	1/17/98	27.74	25.66	25.91
14	1/18/98	27.41	25.61	26.03
15	1/19/98	28.19	26.17	26.62
16	1/22/98	28.64	26.31	26.78
17	1/23/98	28.53	25.42	27.22
18	1/24/98	27.84	26.19	27.45
19	1/25/98	28.16	26.78	27.44
20	1/26/98	27.82	27.49	27.52
21	1/29/98	28.67	26.17	27.68
22	1/30/98	27.73	27.27	27.48
23	1/31/98	28.40	26.07	27.93
24	2/1/98	28.23	26.50	27.43
25	2/2/98	28.40	26.53	27.47
26	2/5/98	29.61	26.97	27.65
27	2/6/98	29.16	26.88	27.68

Excel displays the Date column in the default month/day/year format, and all the columns were imported except the Open column.

Now that you've imported the historical data on the Sunrise Fund, you can use an Excel custom chart to create a traditional high-low-close chart.

To create a high-low-close chart for the fund data:

1. Click cell **A1**, click **Insert** on the menu bar, and then click **Chart** to open the Chart Wizard - Step 1 of 4 - Chart Type dialog box.
2. Click **Stock** in the Chart type list box and click the **High-Low-Close** chart sub-type, if necessary, as shown in Figure 11-10.

Figure 11-10 CHOOSING ONE OF THE CUSTOM STOCK CHARTS

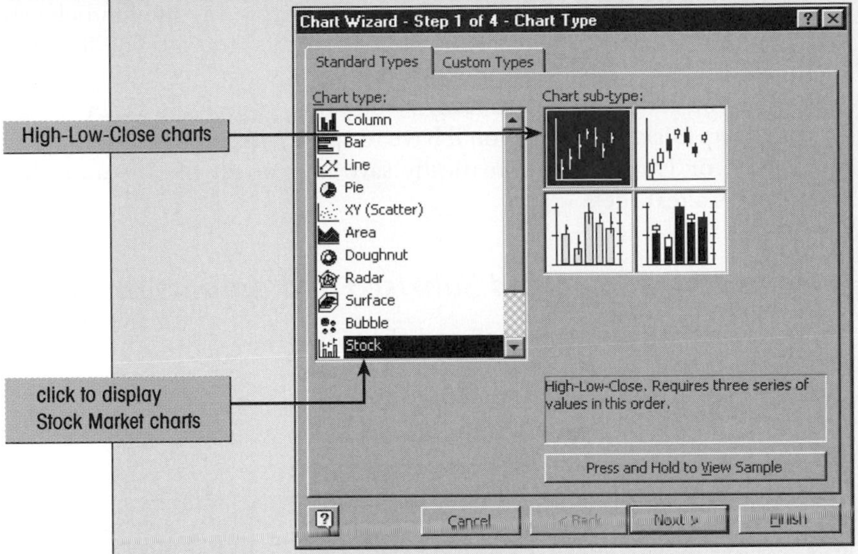

3. Click the **Next** button twice to open the Chart Wizard - Step 3 of 4 - Chart Options dialog box.

4. Click the **Titles** tab, if necessary, and enter the chart title **Sunrise Fund: 1998-2000**, the Category (X) axis title **Date**, and the Value (Y) axis title, **Fund Value**.

5. Click the **Legend** tab, click the **Show legend** check box to deselect this option and remove the legend from the chart, and then click the **Next** button to open the fourth and final Chart Wizard dialog box.

6. Place the chart on a new chart sheet named **History Chart**, and then click the **Finish** button. Figure 11-11 shows the Sunrise Fund value from 1998 through 2000.

Figure 11-11 CHART OF THE FUND'S PERFORMANCE FROM 1998–2000

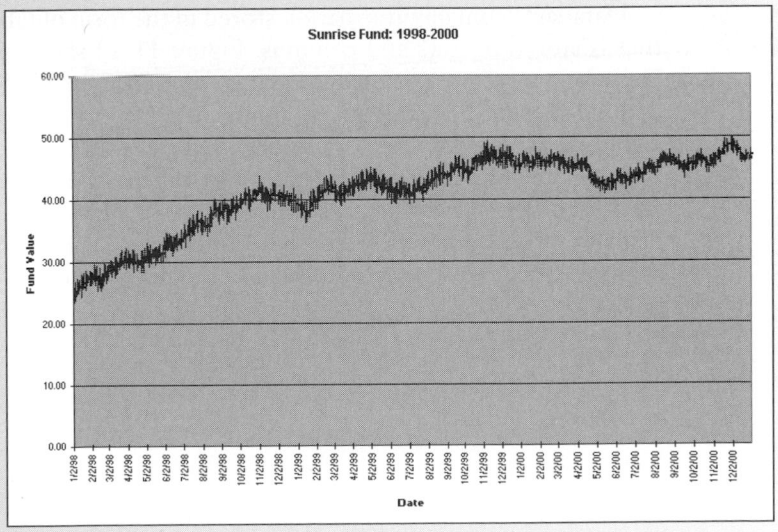

You've successfully imported the fixed width text file containing the Sunrise Fund's performance over the past three years into an Excel workbook and created a High-Low-Close stock chart. Kelly will find the chart useful in interpreting the fund's behavior over the past few years. In the Case Problems at the end of this tutorial, you'll learn how to import a delimited file using the Text Import Wizard.

Before you add more data to Kelly's workbook, you should save your file as Sunrise Fund to your Data Disk. However, you'll have to specify that you want to save the file as an Excel workbook, or Excel will automatically save it as a text file (because the original file you opened was a text file).

To save the imported Sunrise Fund data as an Excel workbook:

1. Click **File** on the menu bar, and click **Save As**.
2. Click the **Save as type** list arrow, and click **Microsoft Excel Workbook** if necessary.
3. Type **Sunrise Fund** in the File name text box.
4. Save the workbook in the Tutorial folder for Tutor11 on your Data Disk.

Kelly is pleased with the progress you've made in locating the text file and importing it into Excel. Now that she has the historical stock information she needs, she wants you to insert some current data from the company's databases.

Databases and Queries

As in many financial firms, much of the information Davis and Larson analysts work with is stored in databases. A **database** is a program that stores and retrieves large amounts of data and creates reports describing that data. There are many database programs available, including Microsoft Access, Borland dBASE, Borland Paradox, and Microsoft FoxPro. Excel can retrieve data from most database programs. At Davis & Larson, information on the stocks in the Sunrise Fund is stored in the Sunrise database.

Databases contain information stored in the form of tables. A **table** is a collection of data that is stored in rows and columns. Figure 11-12 shows an example of one database table Kelly wants you to work with. Each column of the table, called a **field**, stores information about a specific characteristic of a person, place, or thing. In this example, the middle field, called the Company field, stores the names of the companies whose stock is part of the Sunrise portfolio. Each row of the table, called a **record**, displays the collection of characteristics of a particular person, place, or thing. The first record in the table in Figure 11-12 displays stock information for the Aluminum Company of America, which has the ticker symbol AA, and belongs to the group of industrial stocks.

Figure 11-12 A DATABASE TABLE

row or record

Ticker Symbol	Company	Category
AA	Aluminum Company of America	INDUSTRIALS
ABF	Airborne Freight Corporation	TRANSPORTATION
AEP	American Electric Power Company, Inc.	UTILITIES
CRR	CONRAIL Inc.	TRANSPORTATION
CX	Centerior Energy Corporation	UTILITIES
ED	Consolidated Edison Company of New Y	UTILITIES
EK	Eastman Kodak Company	INDUSTRIALS
GM	General Motors Corporation	INDUSTRIALS
LUV	Southwest Airlines Co.	TRANSPORTATION
NMK	Niagara Mohawk Power Corporation	UTILITIES
R	Ryder System, Inc.	TRANSPORTATION
T	AT&T Corp.	INDUSTRIALS
TX	Texaco Inc.	INDUSTRIALS
UCM	Unicom Corporation	UTILITIES
UNP	Union Pacific Corporation	TRANSPORTATION

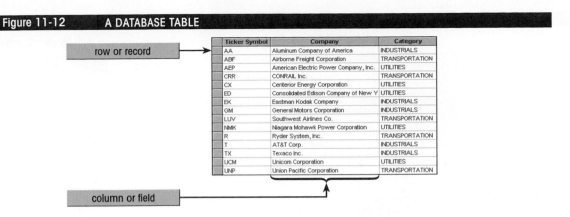

column or field

The Sunrise database has four such tables: Company, Long Term Performance, Recent Performance, and Stock Info. Figure 11-13 describes the contents of each table.

Figure 11-13 SUNRISE DATABASE TABLE NAMES AND DESCRIPTIONS

TABLE NAME	DESCRIPTION
Company	Data about each company in the fund and the percentage of the fund that is allocated to purchasing stocks for that company
Long-term performance	Summarizes the performance over the last 52 weeks for each stock, recording the high and low values over that period of time, and its volatility
Recent performance	Daily high, low, closing, and volume values for each stock in the portfolio over the last five days
Stock Info	Description of each stock including the yield, dividend amount and date, earnings per share, and the number of outstanding shares

With several tables in a database, you need some way of relating information in one table to information in another. You relate tables to one another by using **common fields**, which are the fields that are the same in each table. As shown in Figure 11-14, both the Company table and the Stock Info table contain the Ticker Symbol field, so Ticker Symbol is a common field in this database.

Figure 11-14 COMBINING TABLES BASED ON A COMMON FIELD

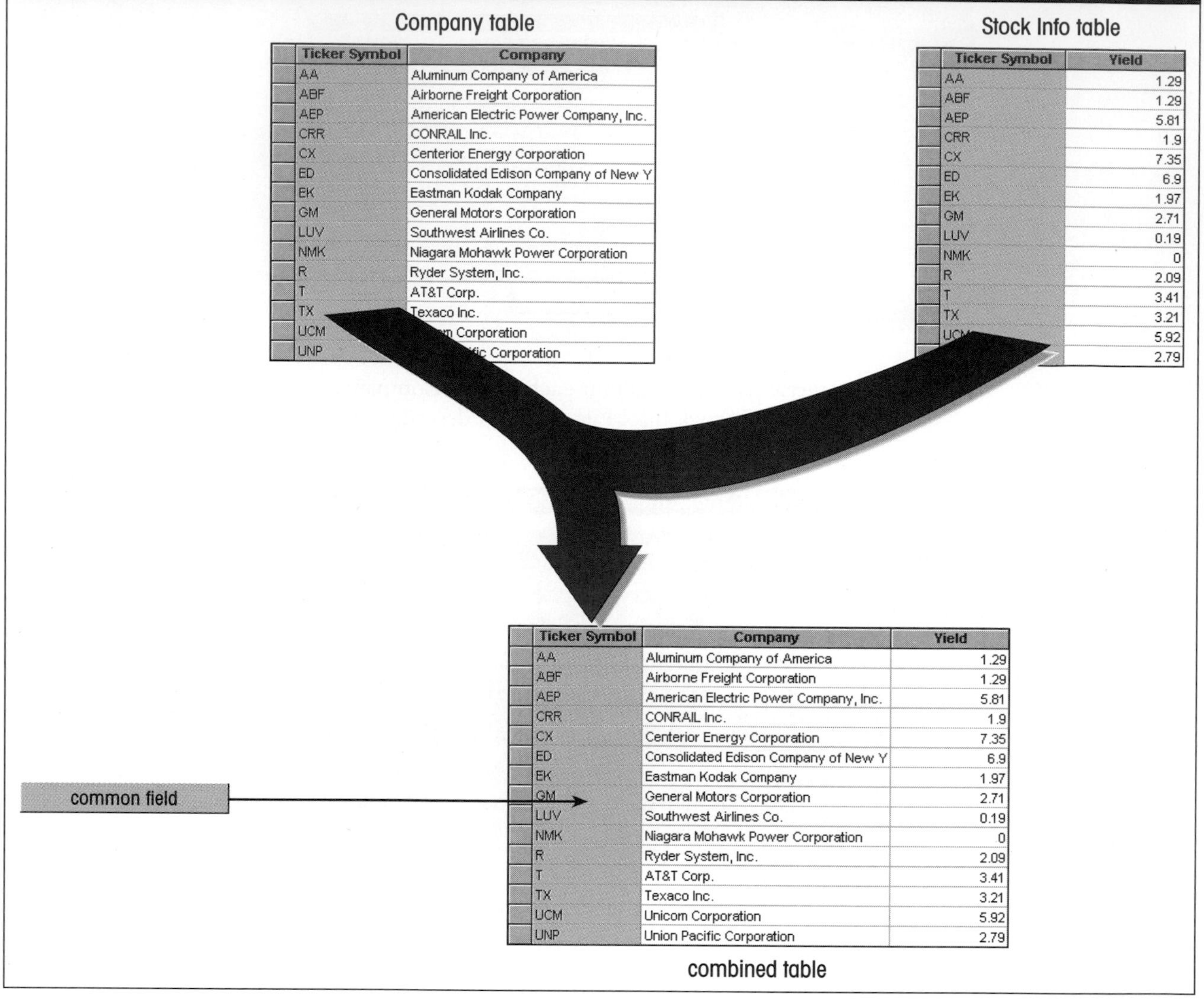

Company table

Ticker Symbol	Company
AA	Aluminum Company of America
ABF	Airborne Freight Corporation
AEP	American Electric Power Company, Inc.
CRR	CONRAIL Inc.
CX	Centerior Energy Corporation
ED	Consolidated Edison Company of New Y
EK	Eastman Kodak Company
GM	General Motors Corporation
LUV	Southwest Airlines Co.
NMK	Niagara Mohawk Power Corporation
R	Ryder System, Inc.
T	AT&T Corp.
TX	Texaco Inc.
UCM	[illegible] Corporation
UNP	[illegible] Corporation

Stock Info table

Ticker Symbol	Yield
AA	1.29
ABF	1.29
AEP	5.81
CRR	1.9
CX	7.35
ED	6.9
EK	1.97
GM	2.71
LUV	0.19
NMK	0
R	2.09
T	3.41
TX	3.21
UCM	5.92
[illegible]	2.79

combined table

Ticker Symbol	Company	Yield
AA	Aluminum Company of America	1.29
ABF	Airborne Freight Corporation	1.29
AEP	American Electric Power Company, Inc.	5.81
CRR	CONRAIL Inc.	1.9
CX	Centerior Energy Corporation	7.35
ED	Consolidated Edison Company of New Y	6.9
EK	Eastman Kodak Company	1.97
GM	General Motors Corporation	2.71
LUV	Southwest Airlines Co.	0.19
NMK	Niagara Mohawk Power Corporation	0
R	Ryder System, Inc.	2.09
T	AT&T Corp.	3.41
TX	Texaco Inc.	3.21
UCM	Unicom Corporation	5.92
UNP	Union Pacific Corporation	2.79

When you want to retrieve information from two tables, like the Company table and the Stock Info table, Excel matches the value of the ticker symbol in one table with the value of the ticker symbol in the other. Because the ticker symbol values match, you can create a new table that contains information about both the company and the stock itself. Without common fields, there would be no way of matching the company information from one table with the yield information from the other.

A large database can have many tables and each table can have several fields and thousands of records, so you need a way to choose only the information that you most want to see. When you want to look only at specific information from a database, you create a query. A **query** is a question you ask about the data in the database. In response to your query, the database finds the records and fields that meet the requirements of your question, and then **extracts**, or reads only that data and places it in a separate table. A query might ask something like, "What are the names of all the stocks in the portfolio, and what are their corresponding ticker symbols?" To answer this question, you would submit the query to the database in a form that the database can read. The database would then extract the relevant information and create a table of all the stocks and their symbols.

When you query a database, you might want to extract only selected records. In this case, your query would contain **criteria**, which are conditions you set to limit the number of records the database extracts. A criterion tells Excel to extract only those records that match certain conditions. For example, you might want to know the names and ticker symbols of only the top five performing stocks from the past three months. In submitting the query to the database, you would include this criterion to limit the information returned to only the top five performing stocks from that time period in the portfolio.

In a query, you can also specify how you want the data to appear. If you want the names and ticker symbols of the top five performing stocks arranged alphabetically by ticker symbol, you can include that in your query definition.

Extracting just the information you need from a database to answer a particular question might seem like a daunting task, but Excel provides the Query Wizard, which greatly simplifies the task of creating and running your queries. You'll use the Query Wizard to extract data from Davis & Larson's database, and to add the next set of worksheets to Kelly's Sunrise Fund workbook.

Using the Query Wizard

Kelly next wants you to add a worksheet to the workbook that lists the stocks in the Sunrise Fund and describes their performance in the last year. As you'll remember from the worksheet plan, you can get this current trend information from the company database called Sunrise. You'll start the process of retrieving this information with the Excel Get Data command. Before doing that, you'll have to insert a new worksheet into the workbook.

To start retrieving data from an external source:

1. Insert a new worksheet at the beginning of the workbook and name it **Portfolio**.

   Now you are ready to start the process of retrieving the stock information into this worksheet.

2. Click **Data** on the menu bar, point to **Get External Data**, and click **New Database Query**. The Choose Data Source dialog box opens, as shown in Figure 11-15. Your list might look different.

   TROUBLE? If the Get External Data or Create New Query commands are not available, you may have to install Microsoft Query from your installation disk. See online Help, your instructor, or technical support person for more information.

Figure 11-15 CHOOSE DATA SOURCE DIALOG BOX

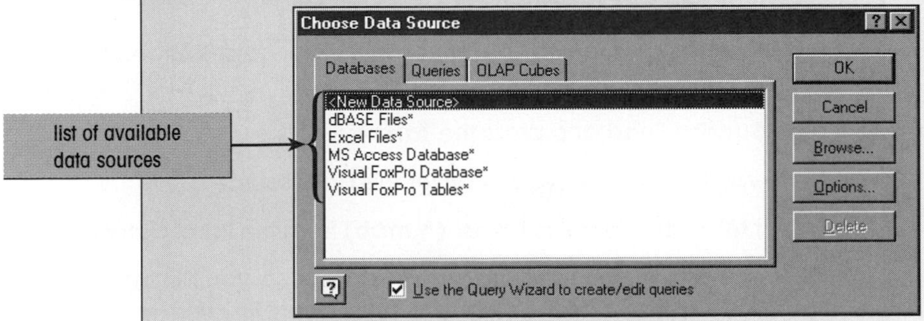

Notice that the list of database sources shown in Figure 11-15 includes some of the well-known database types such as Microsoft Access and dBase. You can also specify your own database source that points to a specific database. You'll create a new data source for the Sunrise Fund for this purpose.

Defining a Data Source

A **data source** is any file that contains the data that you want to retrieve. Data sources can be databases, text files, or other Excel workbooks.

When you define a data source you have to do three things: (1) You have to give the data source a name that will identify it to Excel, (2) You have to choose a driver for the data source. The **driver** translates information between the data source and Excel. Unless the data source is another Excel workbook, the source most likely stores data in a different way than Excel does. The function of the driver is to make sure that no data is lost in the retrieval. (3) Finally, you have to specify the location of the data source, whether it is on your disk, on your hard drive, or on the computer network. The location of the data is also part of the data source's definition.

In some situations, you might have to enter additional information in your data source's definition. For example, if your data source is a password-protected database, you may have to specify the password before you can use the data source.

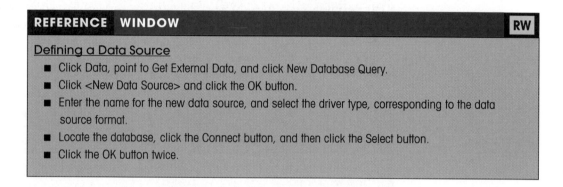

REFERENCE WINDOW RW

Defining a Data Source

- Click Data, point to Get External Data, and click New Database Query.
- Click <New Data Source> and click the OK button.
- Enter the name for the new data source, and select the driver type, corresponding to the data source format.
- Locate the database, click the Connect button, and then click the Select button.
- Click the OK button twice.

The company database from which you'll extract data is named Sunrise; it is located in the Tutorial folder for Tutorial.11 of your Data Disk. It's an Access database, so you'll use the Access driver when you define your data source.

To define a data source:

1. Make sure that **<New Data Source>** is selected on the Databases tab and that the **Use the Query Wizard to create/edit queries** check box is selected (if not, click it to select it), and then click the **OK** button.

   A dialog box asks you to give a name to your data source. You'll name it Sunrise Fund.

2. Type **Sunrise Fund** and press the **Tab** key.

   Next, you'll define the type of driver this data source uses.

3. Select **Microsoft Access Driver (*.mdb)** from the list of database drivers.

   Now that you've specified the type of database, you'll connect Excel to the specific Access database from which you want to retrieve data.

4. Click the **Connect** button. The ODBC Microsoft Access Setup dialog box opens.
5. Click the **Select** button to open the Select Database dialog box.
6. Locate the Tutorial folder for Tutor11 on your Data Disk in the Directories list box, click **Sunrise.mdb** in the Database Name list box, as shown in Figure 11-16, and then click the **OK** button.

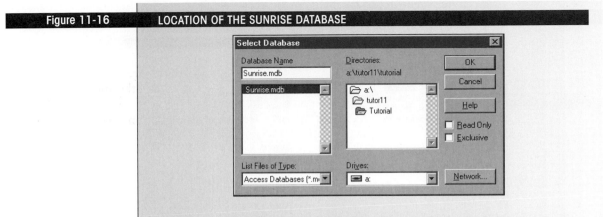

Figure 11-16 **LOCATION OF THE SUNRISE DATABASE**

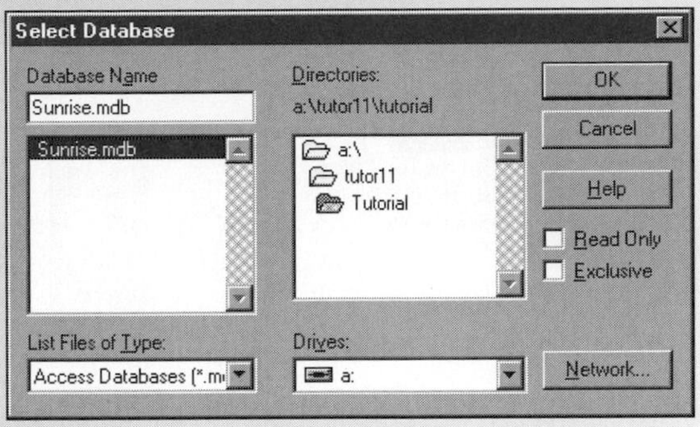

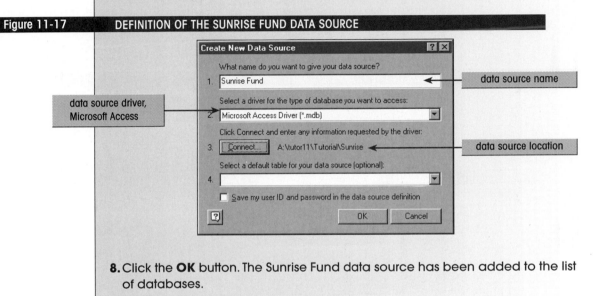

7. Click the **OK** button to close the ODBC Microsoft Access Setup dialog box. The completed Create New Data Source dialog box opens. See Figure 11-17.

Figure 11-17 **DEFINITION OF THE SUNRISE FUND DATA SOURCE**

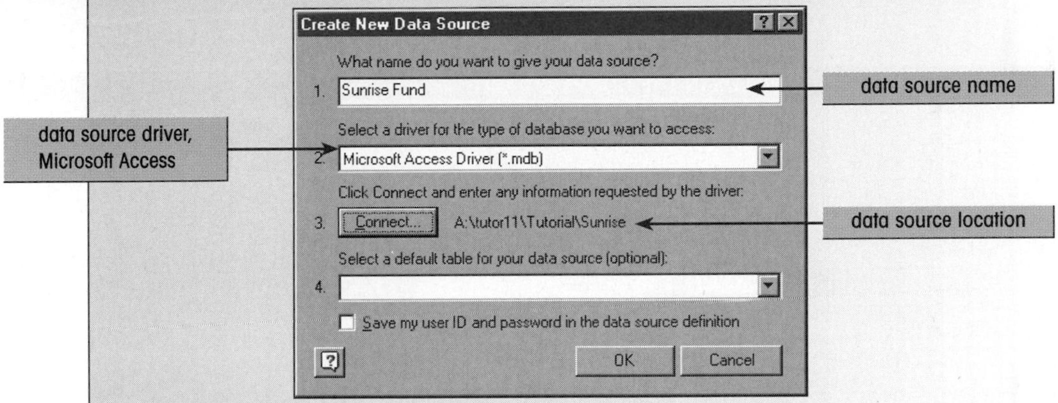

8. Click the **OK** button. The Sunrise Fund data source has been added to the list of databases.

Now that you have defined a data source, you are ready to create a query to extract data from it.

Choosing Tables and Columns

The next step in retrieving data from the Sunrise database is to choose the table and fields (columns) that you want to include in the query. The Query Wizard lets you "peek" inside the database so that you can preview the structure of the database and its contents.

To view a list of the tables and columns in the Sunrise database:

1. Make sure that the **Use the Query Wizard** check box at the bottom of the Choose Data Source dialog box is selected.

2. Click **Sunrise Fund** in the list of data sources if necessary, and then click the **OK** button. The Query Wizard starts and displays the four tables in the Sunrise database. See Figure 11-18.

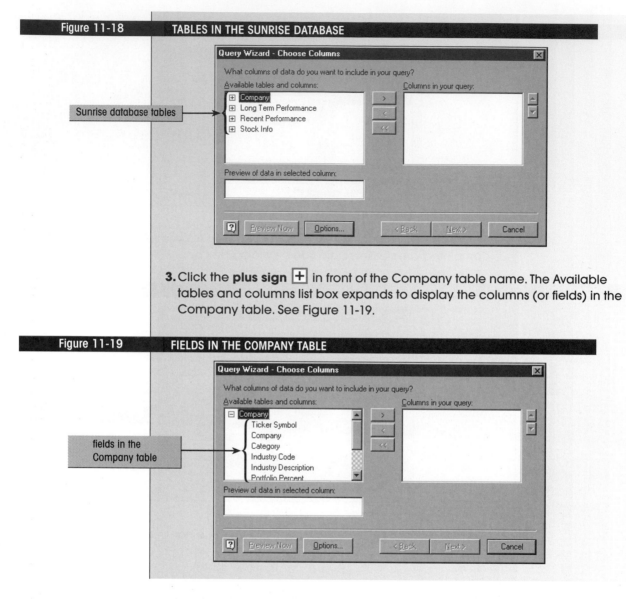

Figure 11-18 **TABLES IN THE SUNRISE DATABASE**

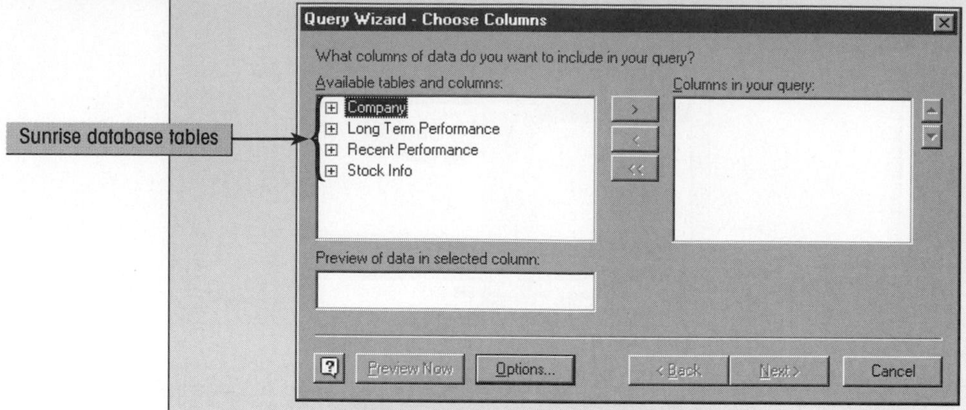

3. Click the **plus sign** ⊞ in front of the Company table name. The Available tables and columns list box expands to display the columns (or fields) in the Company table. See Figure 11-19.

Figure 11-19 **FIELDS IN THE COMPANY TABLE**

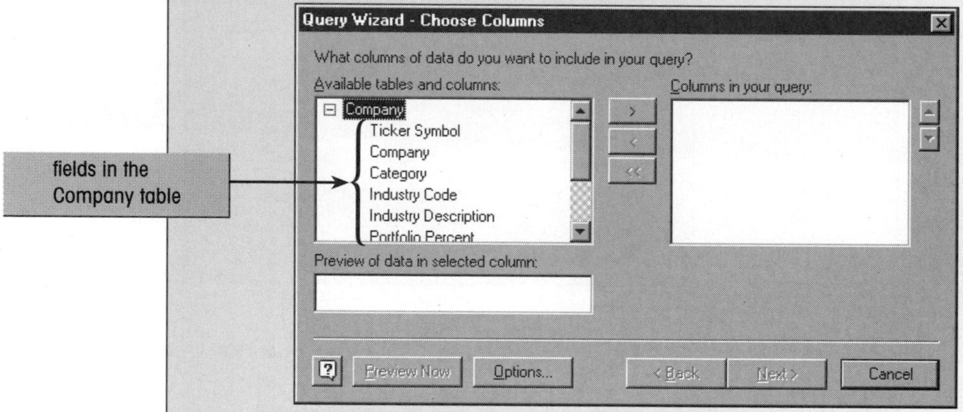

You're not sure which fields Kelly wants to place into the worksheet. You contact her and she indicates that she would like to include the Ticker Symbol, the Company, and the Portfolio Percent from the Company table. The Portfolio Percent, you learn, is the percentage of the portfolio that is invested in each particular stock. Kelly also wants the Year High and Year Low fields from the Long Term Performance table so that she can tell what the high and low points in the previous year have been for each stock in the portfolio. Because the two tables share Ticker Symbol as a common field, you'll select data from both tables with the Query Wizard.

REFERENCE WINDOW **RW**

Choosing Columns to Import Using the Query Wizard

- Choose a data source. Make sure that the Use Query Wizard check box is selected, and click the OK button.
- To select all the columns in a table, click the table name in the Available tables and columns list box, and click the Move button.
- To select only a few columns, click the plus sign in front of the tables containing data you want to retrieve to display the columns contained in the table, and double-click each column you want to retrieve.
- To remove a single column from a query, click the column name in the Columns in your query list box, and then click the Back button.
- To remove all of the columns, click the Remove all columns button.

To select fields, you can click the field name and click the Move button [>], or you can simply double-click the field name, and Excel will automatically move it to the list of selected columns in your query.

To select the columns you want to import into Excel:

1. Click **Ticker Symbol** in the Available tables and columns list box, and then click [>]. Ticker Symbol moves to the Columns in your query of the Query Wizard - Choose Columns dialog box, indicating that it will be included in your query.

   You'll continue selecting the remaining columns that Kelly wants to view by using the alternative method of double-clicking.

2. Double-click **Company**.
3. Double-click **Portfolio Percent**.

   Next you'll open the Long Term Performance table and select the other fields you need.

4. Scroll down and click the **plus sign** [+] in front of the Long Term Performance table name.
5. Double-click **Year High** and then double-click **Year Low**. The five fields that Kelly wants should now be selected. See Figure 11-20.

Figure 11-20 **FIELDS SELECTED FOR THE QUERY**

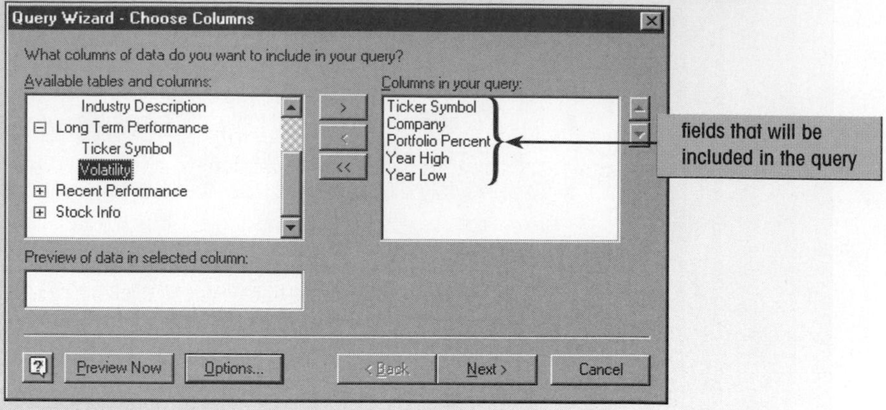

You can preview the contents of each field in the table by selecting it (either in the left pane or the right pane of the Choose Columns dialog box) and then clicking the Preview Now button. You decide to preview the contents of the Company field to get an idea of the types of entries it contains.

To preview the contents of the Company field:

1. Click **Company** in the Columns in your query list box.
2. Click the **Preview Now** button. Some of the values in this column appear in the Preview of data in selected column list box. See Figure 11-21.

Figure 11-21 **PREVIEW OF THE COMPANY FIELD**

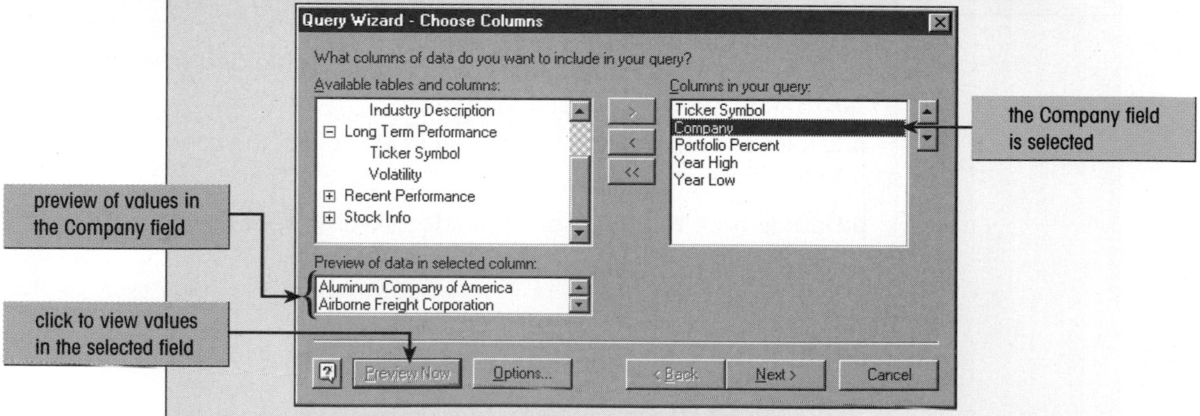

3. Click the **Next** button to open the Query Wizard - Filter Data dialog box.

Now that you have selected the five columns for your Portfolio worksheet, you next have to determine whether to retrieve all of the records in the database or only records that satisfy particular criteria.

Filtering and Sorting Data

In discussing the issue with Kelly, she indicates that she would like you to retrieve information on all the stocks. However, she thinks she will want you to filter the incoming data at selected times. You decide to examine the filtering capabilities of the Query Wizard to get familiar with them.

When you filter data, you specify which records you want to retrieve. In this query, you can filter the data to remove particular stocks or to retrieve only those stocks that perform at a certain level.

REFERENCE WINDOW RW

Filtering Data in a Query

- Start the Query Wizard, select the columns to include in your query, and click the Next button to open the Query Wizard Filter Data dialog box.
- In the Column to Filter list box, click a column you want to include in your filter.
- In the Only Include Rows Where list box, select a comparison type.
- Select a value for the comparison in the adjacent list box.
- Specify any additional comparisons for the selected column.

To see how the data filter works, you'll create a filter that will retrieve stock information only for stocks from the Eastman Kodak Company and the Unicom Corporation.

To create a filter:

1. Click **Company** in the Column to filter list box.

   On the right side of the Query Wizard - Filter Data dialog box, there are two columns of list boxes. The column on the left specifies the type of comparison you want to make in the filter, such as "equals," "greater than," or "less than." In the column on the right, you enter a value for the comparison. You'll use these two list boxes to have the query retrieve the Eastman Kodak stock.

2. Click the list arrow in the first row of the left column, and then click **equals**.
3. Click the list box in the first row of the right column, and then click **Eastman Kodak Company**.

   Next, you'll add a second set of conditions so that the query includes either the Eastman Kodak Company or the Unicom Corporation.

4. Click the **Or** option button.

   Now that you have completed the first row and indicated that you want to include another filter, the second row of list boxes becomes available.

5. Click the list arrow in the second row of the left column, and then click **equals**.
6. In the right column of the second row, click **Unicom Corporation** from the list box. Figure 11-22 shows the completed Filter Data dialog box.

Figure 11-22 ENTERING A DATA FILTER

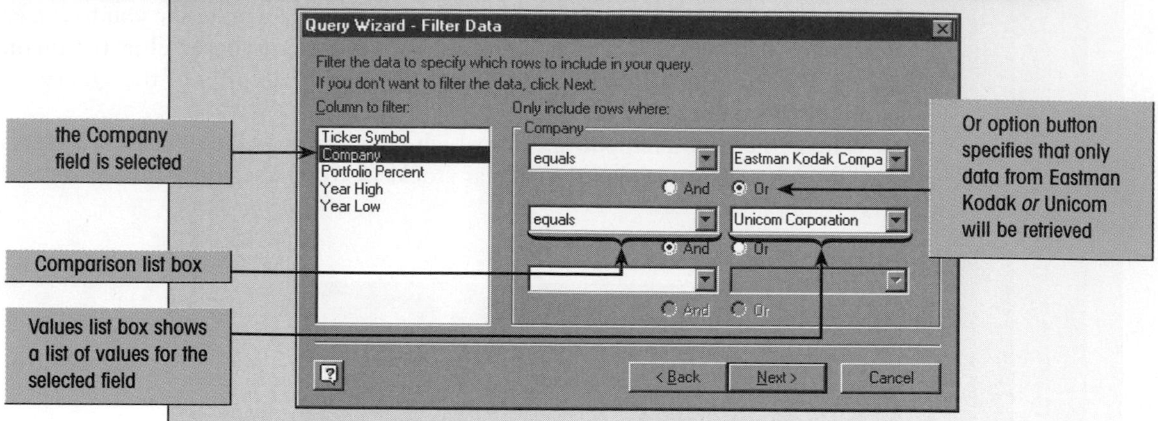

The filter you created will retrieve only those records for Eastman Kodak *or* for Unicom. The Query Wizard will not retrieve stock information for other companies in the Sunrise Fund. Only three rows of criteria are shown in the Filter Data dialog box; additional rows would be added if you inserted additional requirements to your filter. However, because Kelly wants information on all the companies in the portfolio, you'll now remove the data filters you just created.

To remove a filter:

1. Click the **Comparison** list box in the second row of the left column, and click the blank space at the top of the list (you may have to scroll up to see it).
2. Repeat for the comparison list box in the first row. The filters are removed from the query.

   You can proceed to the next step of the Query Wizard.
3. Click the **Next** button.

So far, you've identified the fields you want to retrieve, and you've had a chance to filter out any records. In the last part of creating your query, you specify whether you want the data sorted in a particular order.

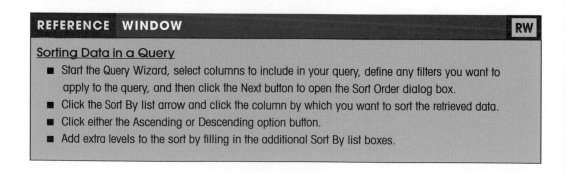

REFERENCE WINDOW RW

Sorting Data in a Query

- Start the Query Wizard, select columns to include in your query, define any filters you want to apply to the query, and then click the Next button to open the Sort Order dialog box.
- Click the Sort By list arrow and click the column by which you want to sort the retrieved data.
- Click either the Ascending or Descending option button.
- Add extra levels to the sort by filling in the additional Sort By list boxes.

Kelly has indicated that she would like to have the portfolio listed starting with the stocks in which the Sunrise Fund has the largest capital investment and proceeding down to the stocks with the smallest capital investment. The Portfolio Percent field tells you how much of the fund is invested in each stock, so you should sort the data by the values in that field in descending order (from highest percentage to lowest).

To sort the data by Portfolio Percent:

1. Click the **Sort By** list arrow, and click **Portfolio Percent**.
2. Click the **Descending** option button.
3. Click the **Next** button to open the final Query Wizard dialog box.

You have finished defining your query. You could run the query now and get the information that Kelly has requested, but you should first save your query.

Saving Your Queries

When you save a query, you are actually placing the query choices you've made into a file. You can open the file later and run the query, saving you the trouble of redefining it. You can also share the query with others who might want to extract the same type of information. Query files can be stored in any folder you choose. The default folder for queries is the Queries folder, which is located in the Windows/Application Data/Microsoft folder. Saving the query file to this folder has some advantages. If you are running Excel on a network, you can make the query file accessible to other network users. Also, query files in this folder will appear on the Queries tab of the Choose Data Source dialog box (see Figure 11-15), giving you quick and easy access to your saved queries. In this case, however, you'll save your query to your Data Disk, because you may not have access to your Queries folder. After saving a query as a file, you automatically return to the last dialog box of the Query Wizard, where you can then retrieve the data from the database into your workbook.

REFERENCE WINDOW RW

Saving a Query

- Run the Query Wizard, completing all the dialog boxes and proceeding to the final Query Wizard dialog box.
- Click the Save Query button.
- Select a location for your query.
- Enter a name for the query, and click the Save button.
- Return to the Query Wizard, and retrieve the data from the query.

You decide to save your query with the name "Sunrise Portfolio," because it lists stocks in the Sunrise Fund. Save this query to your Data Disk.

To save a query:

1. Click the **Save Query** button.
2. Open the Tutorial folder for Tutor11 on your Data Disk.
3. Enter **Sunrise Portfolio** in the File name text box. The file type for query files is (*.dqy), meaning that your saved query files will have the .dqy extension.
4. Click the **Save** button.

Now that you have saved your query, you have three options.

1. You can return (import) the data into your Excel workbook.
2. You can open the results of your query in Microsoft Query. Microsoft Query is a program included on your installation disk with several tools that allow you to create even more complex queries.
3. Create an OLAP cube. **OLAP** (**On-line Analytical Processing**) is a way to organize large business databases. An OLAP cube organizes data so that reports summarizing results of your query are easier to create. An OLAP cube allows you to work with larger data sets than you would otherwise be capable of in Excel. Data returned via an OLAP cube appears in the form of a PivotTable report, not as individual records.

You can learn more about these three options from Excel's online Help. Which one should you choose now? You don't need to refine the query at this point, so you don't need to open it in Microsoft Query. Moreover, you're interested in viewing individual records from the database and not a summary report, therefore, you won't be using this query to create an OLAP cube. Therefore, you'll choose the first option and simply import the data into the Sunrise Fund workbook.

To retrieve the data from the Sunrise database:

1. If necessary, click the **Return Data to Microsoft Excel** option button to select it.
2. Click the **Finish** button. A dialog box asks you where you want to place the imported data.
3. Click cell **A3** in the workbook to insert the retrieved data into the worksheet, starting at that cell.
4. Click the **OK** button. Excel retrieves the data from the Sunrise database and inserts it into the current worksheet. Excel also displays the External Data toolbar, which lets you perform several common tasks with your data; you'll use it in the next session. See Figure 11-23.

Figure 11-23 PORTFOLIO DATA RETRIEVED INTO THE SUNRISE FUND WORKBOOK

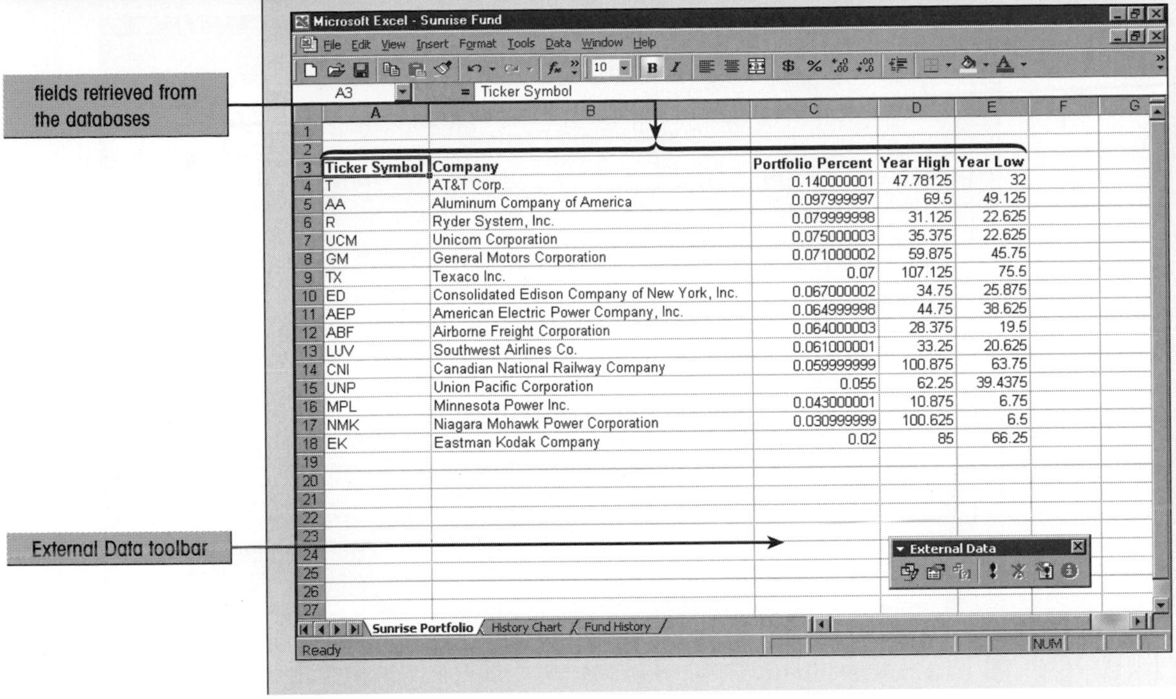

Before closing and saving your workbook, you should add a title and then format the portfolio information.

To format the Portfolio worksheet:

1. Type **Sunrise Fund Portfolio** in cell A1. Format it in 16-point boldface type, and center it across the first five columns of the worksheet.
2. Apply the Percent format to the values in the Portfolio Percent column, and display the percentages with two decimal places.
3. Change the name of the Portfolio Percent column to **Percent**, and reduce the column width to 7 characters (or slightly larger if necessary to display the entire text.)

   Now format the Year High and Year Low values to show fractional values instead of decimal values.

4. Select the range **D4:E18**, click **Format** on the menu bar, and then click **Cells**.
5. Click the **Number** tab if necessary, click **Fraction** in the list of format categories, and then click **Up to three digits (312/943)** in the type list. This is a format often used for data that appears as fractions.
6. Click the **OK** button, and if necessary widen the columns to 11 points to show all the values with fractions.
7. Press **Ctrl + Home**. Figure 11-24 shows the contents of the formatted Portfolio worksheet.

Figure 11-24 **FORMATTED PORTFOLIO WORKSHEET**

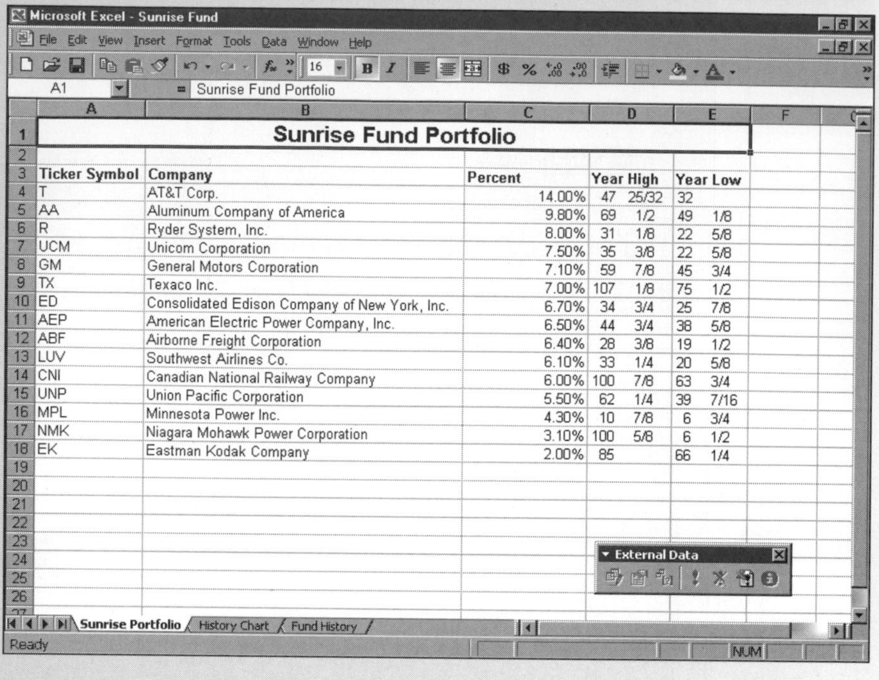

Sunrise Fund Portfolio

Ticker Symbol	Company	Percent	Year High	Year Low
T	AT&T Corp.	14.00%	47 25/32	32
AA	Aluminum Company of America	9.80%	69 1/2	49 1/8
R	Ryder System, Inc.	8.00%	31 1/8	22 5/8
UCM	Unicom Corporation	7.50%	35 3/8	22 5/8
GM	General Motors Corporation	7.10%	59 7/8	45 3/4
TX	Texaco Inc.	7.00%	107 1/8	75 1/2
ED	Consolidated Edison Company of New York, Inc.	6.70%	34 3/4	25 7/8
AEP	American Electric Power Company, Inc.	6.50%	44 3/4	38 5/8
ABF	Airborne Freight Corporation	6.40%	28 3/8	19 1/2
LUV	Southwest Airlines Co.	6.10%	33 1/4	20 5/8
CNI	Canadian National Railway Company	6.00%	100 7/8	63 3/4
UNP	Union Pacific Corporation	5.50%	62 1/4	39 7/16
MPL	Minnesota Power Inc.	4.30%	10 7/8	6 3/4
NMK	Niagara Mohawk Power Corporation	3.10%	100 5/8	6 1/2
EK	Eastman Kodak Company	2.00%	85	66 1/4

Looking at the contents of the portfolio, you can quickly see that 14% of the fund is invested in the AT&T Corporation and that the value of that stock has ranged from a high of 47 25/32 points to a low of 32 points. This worksheet will be very helpful to Kelly in working with the stocks in the Sunrise Fund portfolio.

Print the Portfolio worksheet, and then save and close your workbook.

To print and save the Sunrise Fund data:

1. Print the **Portfolio** worksheet (not the Fund History worksheet).
2. Save the workbook.

You'll show Kelly the progress you've made in importing the data from the company database. If she is satisfied with it, you'll move on to importing data from external databases.

Session 11.1 QUICK CHECK

1. What is the difference between a fixed width and a delimited text file?
2. Name three delimiters that can separate data in a delimited text file.
3. How do you insert column breaks when importing a text file using the Text Import Wizard?

4. Define the following terms:
   a. database
   b. table
   c. field
   d. record
   e. common field
5. What is a query?
6. What is a data source? What are three of the characteristics you specify when defining a data source?
7. Once you've finished creating your query, describe the three options Excel provides for using that query.

Kelly thanks you for your work. She will work with the newly imported Sunrise Fund Portfolio and see if it meets her needs. In the next session you'll add more current information about the Sunrise Fund stocks to your workbook. You'll learn how to refresh data, edit your queries, and how to control the way Excel retrieves data from its data sources. You'll then see how to import data into pivot tables.

SESSION 11.2

In this session you'll learn how to edit and rerun your queries to retrieve new data. You'll see how to modify the properties of your existing queries. Finally, you'll learn how to use pivot tables to summarize the data in your database.

Working with External Data and Queries

In the last session you learned two ways to bring data into Excel: by importing a text file and by importing data from a database. Importing data from a database has several advantages over importing from a text file. Using queries, you can control which records you import into your workbook. More importantly, by retrieving data from a database, you can easily refresh, or update, the data in your workbooks when the data source itself is updated.

Refreshing External Data

When you retrieved the portfolio data for Kelly in the last session, you did more than insert the data into the Excel workbook. By defining a data source, you also gave Excel information about where to go to find updated information for your workbook. Davis & Larson are constantly updating their databases, and it's important for Kelly to be able to view the most up-to-date information on the Sunrise Fund so that she can offer accurate and timely advice to her clients.

Excel allows you to keep your data current by refreshing the data in your queries. When you refresh a query, Excel retrieves the most current data from the data source, using the query definition you've already created.

REFERENCE WINDOW RW

Refreshing External Data

- Click a cell in the range containing the external data, and click the Refresh button on the External Data toolbar.

or

- If your workbook contains several external data ranges, click the Refresh All button on the External Data toolbar to refresh all the external data in the workbook.

You've explained the concept of refreshing data to Kelly. She wants you to show her how to refresh the information in the Sunrise Fund workbook so she can make sure she has the most current version of the database information. To refresh the imported data, you select a cell from the range containing the data and use the Refresh command.

To refresh the Portfolio data:

1. If you took a break at the end of the last session, make sure Excel is running, and open the **Sunrise Fund** workbook in the Tutorial folder for Tutor11 on your Data Disk.
2. Click cell **A3** in the Portfolio worksheet. Although you've selected cell A3 here, you can select any cell in the data range when you refresh your data.
3. Click the **Refresh Data** button ! on the External Data toolbar.

   TROUBLE? If the External Data toolbar is not visible, click View on the menu bar, point to Toolbars, and click External Data to display the toolbar.

   Excel goes to the Sunrise database and retrieves the current information from the database back into the workbook. The contents of this workbook don't change, because the Sunrise database has not been modified since you last saved the Sunrise Fund workbook.

Having seen how the refresh command works, Kelly wonders if there are any other ways to control how and when Excel refreshes external data.

Setting External Data Properties

Kelly likes the fact that she can refresh her external data so quickly and easily, but she has a couple of concerns. She worries that she may forget to refresh the data each time she opens her workbook, so she prefers to have Excel automatically refresh the data. On the other hand, there are times when she wants some of her workbooks to contain a "snapshot" of the data as it exists at a particular moment in time. In that case, her needs are just the opposite—she doesn't want the data refreshed at all.

You can meet both of these requirements by modifying the properties of the query. By modifying the query properties, you can:

- remove the underlying external data query, freezing the data so that it cannot be refreshed.
- require that the user enter a password before the data is refreshed, thus keeping other users from updating the data without permission.

- run the query in the background, so you can work on other portions of the workbook as you wait for the data to be retrieved; this is helpful if you are retrieving large amounts of data.
- refresh the data automatically whenever the workbook is reopened or at specific intervals when the workbook is in use.
- specify how new data from the external data source is added when the size of the external data range changes. You can insert new cells and delete unused cells, insert an entire row and clear unused cells, or replace existing cells with new data.
- automatically copy formulas into adjacent columns, preserving them as the size of the external data range expands into new columns after refreshing.

As you can see, Excel gives you a great deal of flexibility as to how and when you refresh your external data.

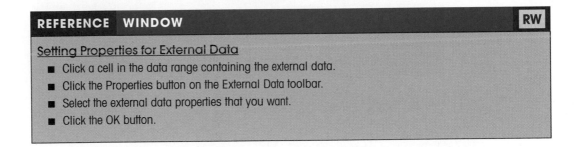

REFERENCE WINDOW RW

Setting Properties for External Data

- Click a cell in the data range containing the external data.
- Click the Properties button on the External Data toolbar.
- Select the external data properties that you want.
- Click the OK button.

Because she frequently consults her database files as she advises her clients on stock market trends, Kelly decides that she would like to have the query refreshed automatically whenever she opens the Sunrise Fund workbook.

To set properties for the Industrial Stocks external data:

1. Click the **Properties** button on the External Data toolbar.
2. Click the **Refresh data on file open** check box to select this option.

   Clicking this check box also makes the Remove external data from worksheet before saving check box appear. Clicking this option causes Excel to remove the data that you've retrieved from the workbook before closing the workbook. The advantage of using this option is that it makes the size of the workbook relatively small when it's not in use. Then, when you reopen the workbook, Excel automatically retrieves the data and puts it back in its proper place. You tell Kelly about this option, but she decides to keep the data in the workbook at all times because the amount of data being retrieved is not very large.

   You could also click the "Refresh every" check box in order to have the results of the query refreshed periodically when the workbook is opened. However, because this query retrieves historical data, it is unlikely that the database will be updated within the period of time that Kelly is working on it. So you'll leave this check box unselected.

   The completed External Data Range Properties dialog box should appear as shown in Figure 11-25.

Figure 11-25 PROPERTIES OF THE SUNRISE FUND QUERY

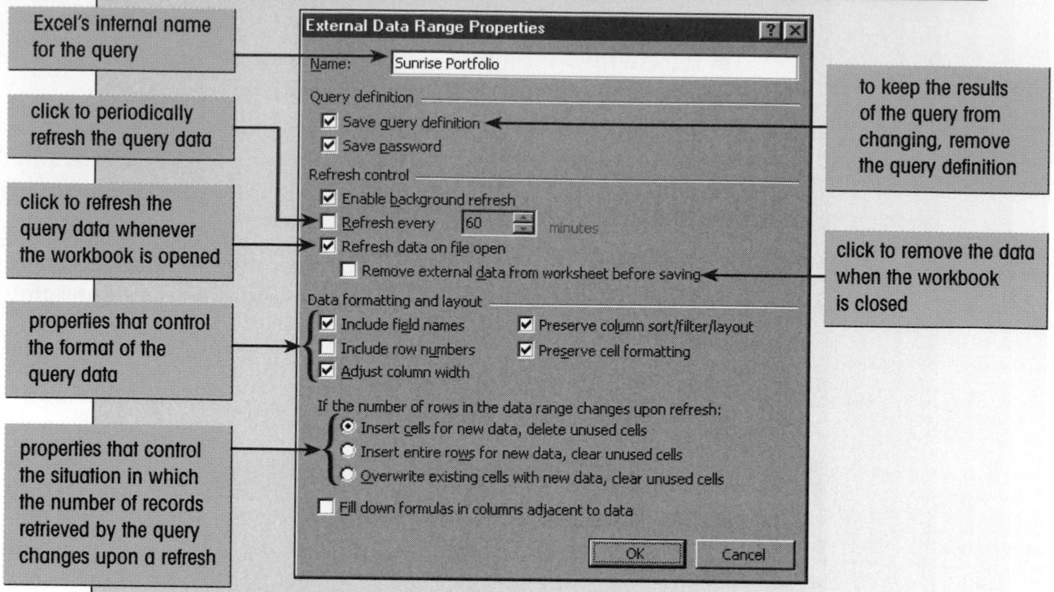

3. Click the **OK** button.

From now on, whenever Kelly opens this workbook, Excel will automatically refresh the data. Kelly now asks you how she can modify the query that you performed earlier, in case she needs to import additional information.

Editing a Query

Once you've created a query, you can go back and modify the query's definition using the Query Wizard. By editing the query, you can add new columns to your worksheet, change the sort order options, or specify a filter.

Kelly has reviewed the contents of the Portfolio worksheet. She would like you to include categories for each stock: industrials, transportation, and utilities. She would like to know how the fund is distributed over these kinds of classifications. She would also like to have the data sorted by stock category, and within each stock category by descending order of portfolio percentage. You can add the Category column to the Portfolio worksheet and modify the sort order by editing the query.

To edit the query:

1. Click the **Edit Query** button on the External Data toolbar. The Query Wizard starts and opens the Query Wizard - Choose Columns dialog box.

First, you'll add the Category column to the list of selected fields.

2. Click the **plus sign** in front of the Company table, and double-click **Category**. Category is added to the list of columns in the query. See Figure 11-26.

Figure 11-26 ADDING THE CATEGORY FIELD TO THE SUNRISE FUND QUERY

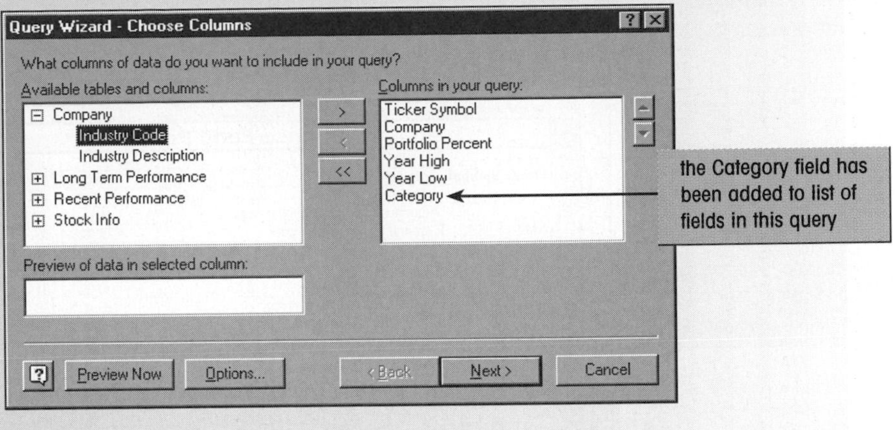

3. Click the **Next** button twice to go to the Query Wizard - Sort Order dialog box, where you'll enter the two sorting criteria.
4. Click **Category** in the Sort by list box, and then click the **Ascending** option button.
5. Click **Portfolio Percent** in the Then by list box, and then click the **Descending** option button.
6. Click the **Next** button and then click the **Finish** button to retrieve the data.

   By retrieving the data, you've overwritten the Percent column title because, by default, the Query field is set to retrieve names along with the data. But you can retype this title now.
7. Type **Percent** in cell C3, and reduce the column width to **7** characters (or a size that is sufficient to still display the text in cell C3.)

   Figure 11-27 displays the contents of the Portfolio worksheet with the newly added Category column and the sort order changed. Notice that the first Category listed is INDUSTRIALS and within INDUSTRIALS, the Percent column is ordered from highest to lowest.

Figure 11-27 REVISED PORTFOLIO WORKSHEET

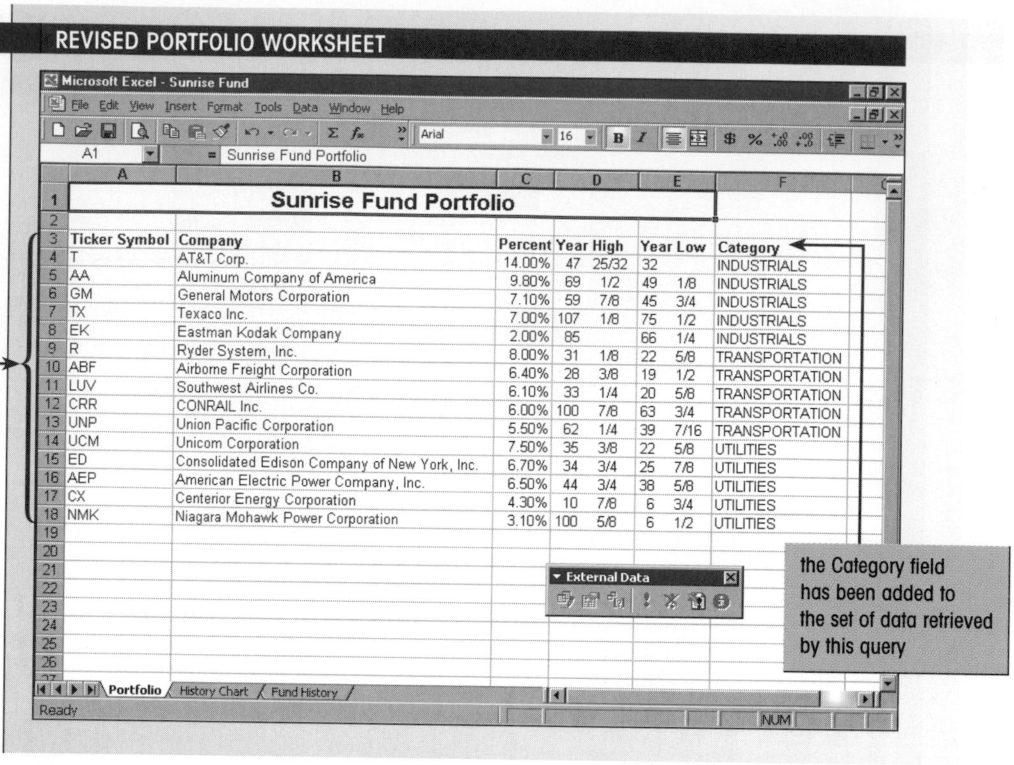

Ticker Symbol	Company	Percent	Year High	Year Low	Category
T	AT&T Corp.	14.00%	47 25/32	32	INDUSTRIALS
AA	Aluminum Company of America	9.80%	69 1/2	49 1/8	INDUSTRIALS
GM	General Motors Corporation	7.10%	59 7/8	45 3/4	INDUSTRIALS
TX	Texaco Inc.	7.00%	107 1/8	75 1/2	INDUSTRIALS
EK	Eastman Kodak Company	2.00%	85	66 1/4	INDUSTRIALS
R	Ryder System, Inc.	8.00%	31 1/8	22 5/8	TRANSPORTATION
ABF	Airborne Freight Corporation	6.40%	28 3/8	19 1/2	TRANSPORTATION
LUV	Southwest Airlines Co.	6.10%	33 1/4	20 5/8	TRANSPORTATION
CRR	CONRAIL Inc.	6.00%	100 7/8	63 3/4	TRANSPORTATION
UNP	Union Pacific Corporation	5.50%	62 1/4	39 7/16	TRANSPORTATION
UCM	Unicom Corporation	7.50%	35 3/8	22 5/8	UTILITIES
ED	Consolidated Edison Company of New York, Inc.	6.70%	34 3/4	25 7/8	UTILITIES
AEP	American Electric Power Company, Inc.	6.50%	44 3/4	38 5/8	UTILITIES
CX	Centerior Energy Corporation	4.30%	10 7/8	6 3/4	UTILITIES
NMK	Niagara Mohawk Power Corporation	3.10%	100 5/8	6 1/2	UTILITIES

the data is sorted by stock category and portfolio percentage

the Category field has been added to the set of data retrieved by this query

In reviewing the category values, you note that the fund is comprised of 15 stocks with 5 industrials, 5 transportation stocks, and 5 utilities. The fund is therefore well balanced across the three categories. Kelly is satisfied with the appearance of the Portfolio worksheet. The next thing she wants you to insert into the workbook is the most recent performance of the 15 stocks in the Sunrise Fund.

Creating a Pivot Table and Chart from External Data

Kelly and you discuss how the worksheet with the recent stock performance data should appear. She wants data for each stock to look like the sample table shown in Figure 11-28 for the Eastman Kodak stock. The table displays the high, low, and close figures for each day for the past five market days.

Figure 11-28 EASTMAN KODAK DATA FROM THE RECENT PERFORMANCE TABLE

Ticker Symbol	Date	Volume	High	Low	Closing
EK	02/04/2001	909900	89.875	86	89.75
EK	02/05/2001	1047200	89.75	87	87
EK	02/06/2001	558800	87.5	86	86.625
EK	02/07/2001	571000	89.375	87.25	89.125
EK	02/10/2001	803200	91	89.125	89.5

EK is the ticker symbol for Eastman Kodak

market date

volume of shares traded

stock values

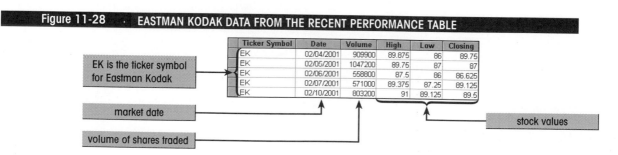

Kelly would also like the workbook to include the chart shown in Figure 11-29, so that she can visually track each stock's recent history.

Figure 11-29 EASTMAN KODAK CHART OF HIGH, LOW, AND CLOSING VALUES

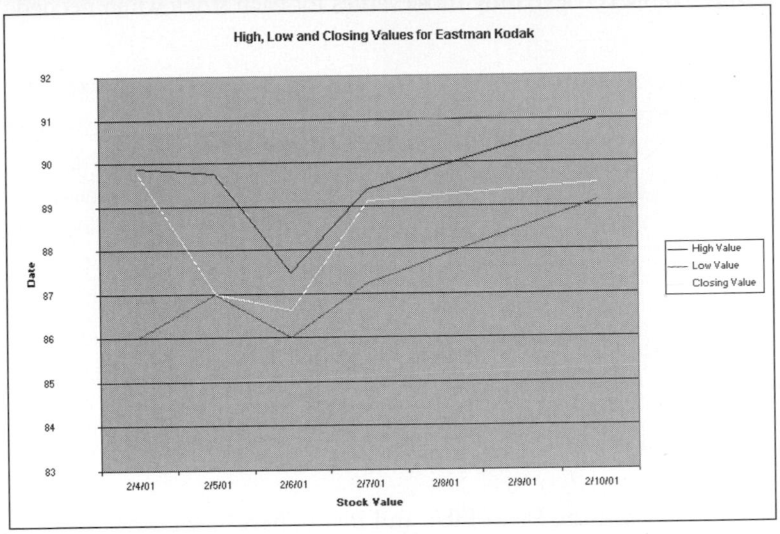

As you review the table, you wonder how best to display the results in the workbook. You could have 15 worksheets—one for each stock in the fund, displaying the table of values and an accompanying chart. Kelly vetoes the idea, thinking that it would be too cumbersome to navigate through 15 worksheet pages. Besides, she argues, at some point she wants to create similar workbooks for other funds that might have hundreds of stocks in their portfolios.

A second option occurs to you. You can create a pivot table and pivot chart that will display market values from the past five days. By using the page feature of pivot tables and charts, you can include a list box that Kelly can use to display the values for only the stock that she is interested in. As Kelly clicks a different stock from the page's list box, a new table and chart will be created. Figure 11-30 shows a preview of what you intend to create.

Figure 11-30 THE PIVOT TABLE AND CHART YOU PLAN TO CREATE

	A	B	C	D	E
1	Ticker Symbol	EK			
2					
3		Data			
4	Date	High Value	Low Value	Closing Value	
5	2/4/01	89 7/8	86	89 3/4	
6	2/5/01	89 3/4	87	87	
7	2/6/01	87 1/2	86	86 5/8	
8	2/7/01	89 3/8	87 1/4	89 1/8	
9	2/10/01	91	89 1/8	89 1/2	
10					

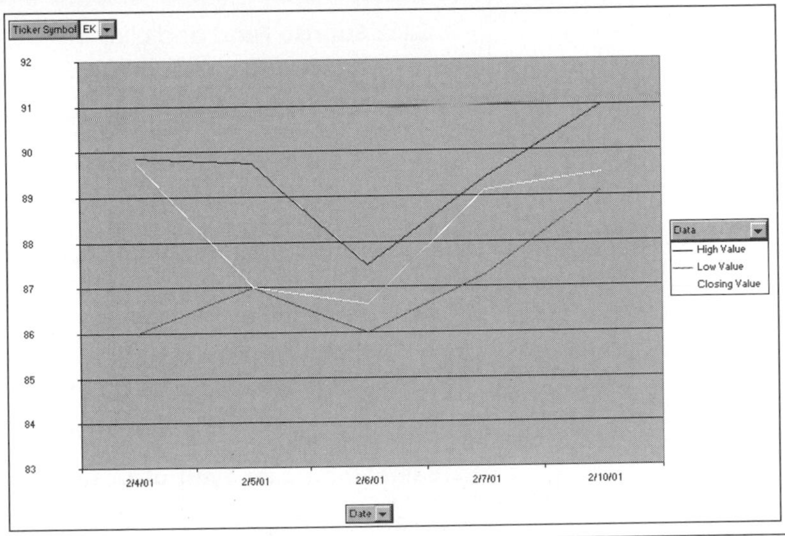

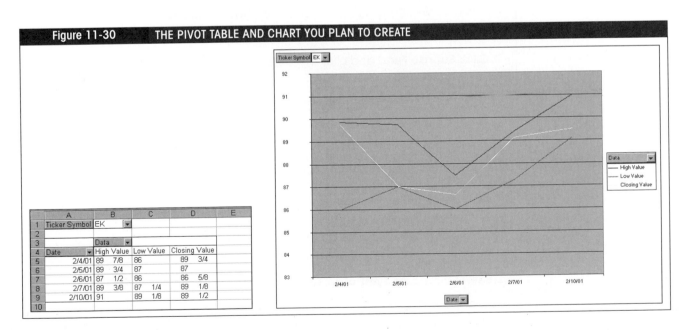

One advantage of this approach is that you can place the recent performance data on a single worksheet. A second advantage is that the pivot table can use data that's stored in databases or other external files. This means that you won't have to insert the entire contents of the Recent Performance table to display recent performance values. You can let the pivot table retrieve only those values for each stock when needed.

REFERENCE WINDOW RW

Retrieving External Data Into a Pivot Table and Chart

- Click Pivot Table and PivotChart Report from the Data menu.
- In the PivotTable and PivotChart Wizard - Step 1 of 4 dialog box, click the External Data Source option button, click Pivot Chart (with Pivot Table), and click the Next button to open the second dialog box.
- Click the Get Data button to access the external data source.
- Select a data source from the list of sources or create a new data source.
- Use the Query Wizard to define your query and retrieve the data into the pivot table and chart.
- Complete the PivotTable and PivotChart Wizard.

Start the PivotTable and PivotChart Wizard now.

To start creating the pivot table and pivot chart:

1. Insert a new sheet after the Portfolio worksheet and name it **Recent Results**.
2. Click **Data** on the menu bar, and click **PivotTable and PivotChart Report**.
3. In the first step of the PivotTable and PivotChart Wizard, click the **External data source** option button.
4. Click the **PivotChart(with PivotTable)** option button.
5. Click the **Next** button.
6. Click the **Get Data** button to open the Choose Data Source dialog box.

   Here you select the data source.
7. Click **Sunrise Fund** and click the **OK** button.

Now you indicate the columns that you want to include in the table. You want to retrieve the ticker symbol of each stock, the daily high and low of the stock, and the closing value. All these fields are located in the Recent Performance table. Once you've selected the columns for the table, you can go through the rest of the Query Wizard without specifying any filters or sorting. You're only interested in the complete and unfiltered recent performance data.

To enter the query for the pivot table:

1. Expand the **Recent Performance** table.
2. Select the **Ticker Symbol**, **Date**, **High**, **Low,** and **Closing** fields.
3. Click the **Next** button three times to reach the end of the Query Wizard.
4. Click the **Finish** button. You are returned to the PivotTable and PivotChart Wizard - Step 2 of 3 dialog box. The comment, "Data fields have been retrieved" now appears next to the Get Data button.

You're finished with the query and the PivotTable Wizard has retrieved the data. You'll next design the layout for your pivot table.

To design the pivot table's layout:

1. Click the **Next** button to display the third step of the PivotTable and PivotChart Wizard.
2. Verify that the **Existing worksheet** option button is selected. Click cell **A1** so that the pivot table will be inserted in a range starting at cell A1.
3. Click the **Layout** button.

   First, you'll place the Ticker Symbol field in the Page area of the pivot table diagram. This will create the list box you saw in Figure 11-30.
4. Drag the **Ticker Symbol** button to the Page area of the pivot table diagram.

   Next, place the Date field in the Row area of the pivot table.
5. Drag the **Date** button to the Row area of the sample pivot table.

   Finally, you'll place the stock values in the data section of the pivot table.
6. Drag the **High, Low,** and **Closing** buttons to the Data area of the table. Figure 11-31 displays the layout of the pivot table.

Figure 11-31 LAYOUT OF YOUR PIVOT TABLE

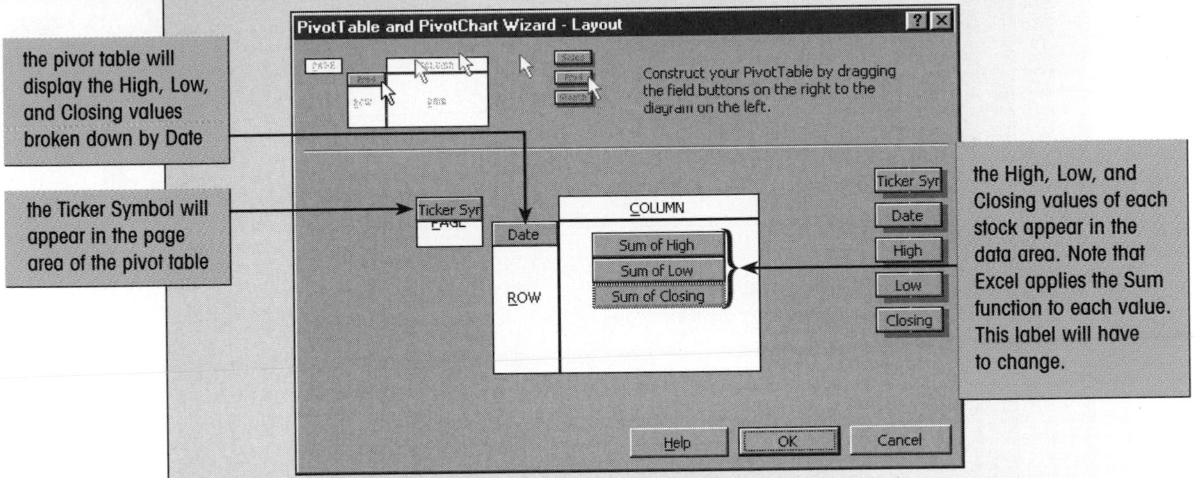

TROUBLE? If your layout does not match the one shown in Figure 11-31, drag the buttons until the positions match those shown in the figure.

Notice that the Data area labels say "Sum of" before the name of each field. This is a little misleading, because there is only one value of these items for each stock on each day, so the pivot table will show a "sum" of only one record. Although the table will display individual volume and stock values, you should change these labels to avoid confusing others who might interpret them as the sum of many such values. You can also specify the format for these values at this time.

To change the labels and enter the number format for the data values of the table:

1. Double-click the **Sum of High** button in the Data area of the pivot table to open the PivotTable Field dialog box.
2. Type **High Value** in the Name text box.
3. Click the **Number** button to open the Format Cells dialog box, click Fraction in the Category list box, and then select the **Up to three digits (312/943)** Fraction format.
4. Click the **OK** button twice to return to the PivotTable Wizard, and rename the two remaining data values **Low Value** and **Closing Value**. Format each with the three-digit Fraction format you used for the High Value field. See Figure 11-32 for the revised pivot table layout.

Figure 11-32 REVISED DATA NAMES FOR THE PIVOT TABLE

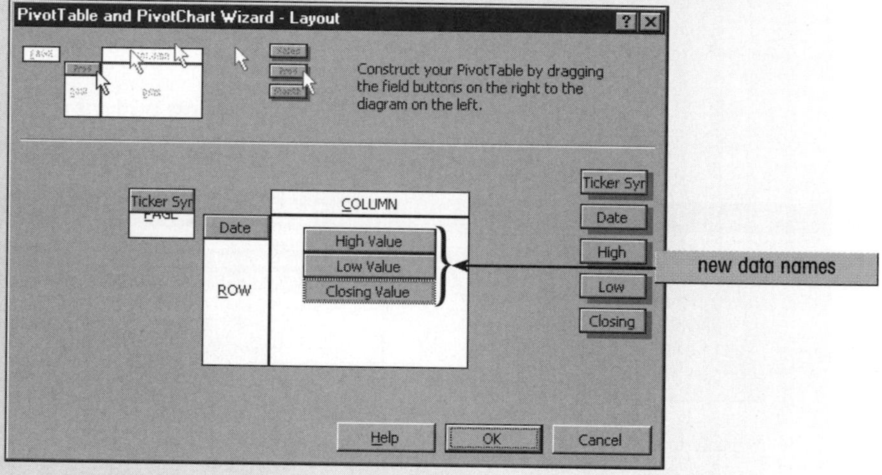

5. Click the **OK** button.

You're almost finished defining the pivot table. You still have to set some of the options for the behavior of the pivot table and chart.

To define pivot table and chart options:

1. Click the **Options** button.
2. Deselect the **Grand totals for columns** and **Grand totals for rows** check boxes so that the pivot table and chart do not include grand totals.
3. Click the **Refresh on open** check box so that Excel will refresh the pivot table and chart whenever the Sunrise Fund workbook is open, drawing the latest data from the company's database.
4. Click the **OK** button.
5. Click the **Finish** button. Excel creates the pivot chart and pivot table on separate sheets as shown in Figure 11-33.

   The chart and table don't look as you expected. This is because you have to make one minor change to the layout of the pivot table.

Figure 11-33 PIVOT TABLE AND PIVOT CHART

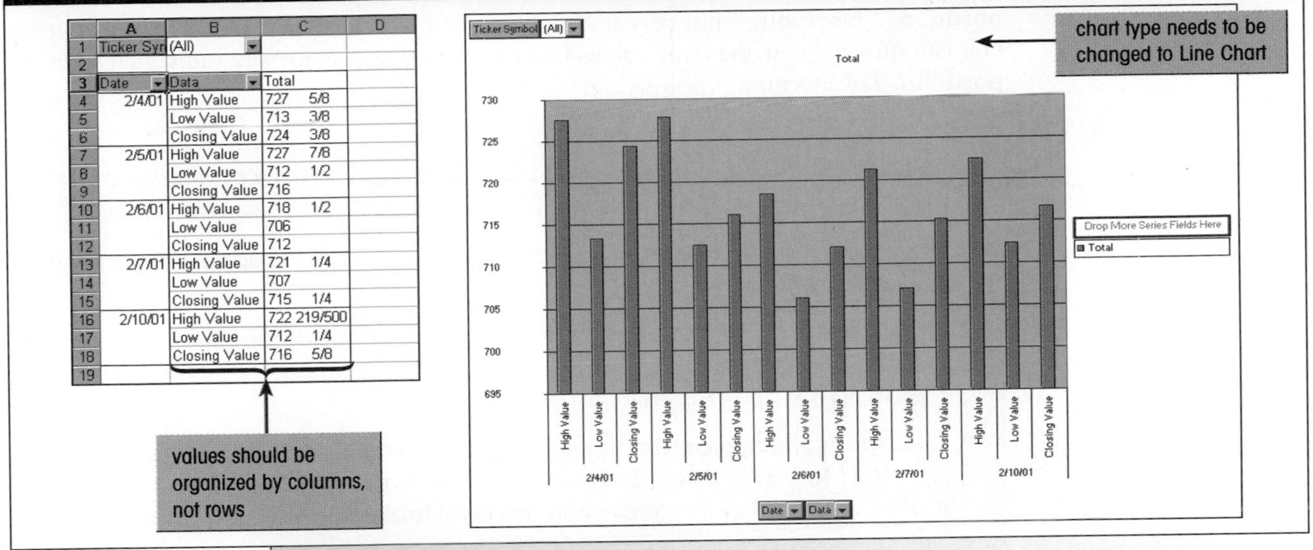

	A	B	C	D
1	Ticker Syr	(All)		
2				
3	Date	Data	Total	
4	2/4/01	High Value	727 5/8	
5		Low Value	713 3/8	
6		Closing Value	724 3/8	
7	2/5/01	High Value	727 7/8	
8		Low Value	712 1/2	
9		Closing Value	716	
10	2/6/01	High Value	718 1/2	
11		Low Value	706	
12		Closing Value	712	
13	2/7/01	High Value	721 1/4	
14		Low Value	707	
15		Closing Value	715 1/4	
16	2/10/01	High Value	722 219/500	
17		Low Value	712 1/4	
18		Closing Value	716 5/8	
19				

6. Click the **Recent Results** worksheet tab to view the pivot table.
7. Click the **Data** button in cell B3, drag the Data button over to cell **C3**, and then release the mouse button. By moving the Data button, you change the orientation of the data results from rows to columns.

   Now return to the pivot table chart sheet. You have to change the chart type from a column chart to a line chart.
8. Go to the pivot table chart and click the **Chart Type** list arrow from the Chart menu.
9. Click **Line Chart** from the Chart Type list box and then double-click the first Chart sub-type (labeled "Line. Displays trend over time or categories"). See Figure 11-34 for the final version of the pivot table and chart.

Figure 11-34 FINAL VERSION OF THE PIVOT TABLE AND PIVOT CHART

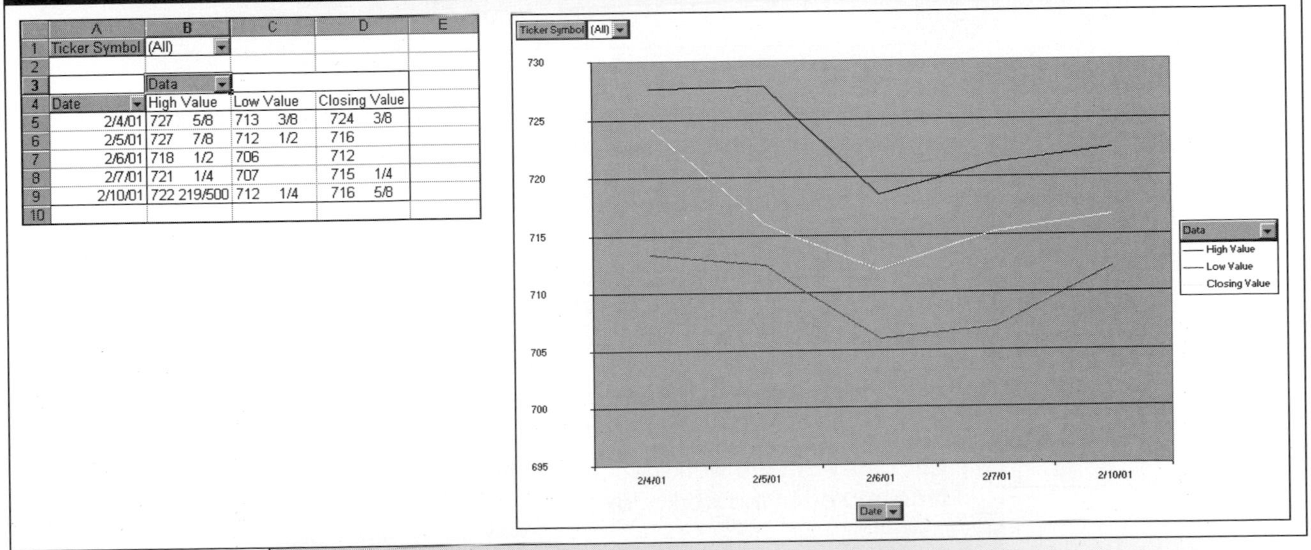

	A	B	C	D	E
1	Ticker Symbol	(All)			
2					
3		Data			
4	Date	High Value	Low Value	Closing Value	
5	2/4/01	727 5/8	713 3/8	724 3/8	
6	2/5/01	727 7/8	712 1/2	716	
7	2/6/01	718 1/2	706	712	
8	2/7/01	721 1/4	707	715 1/4	
9	2/10/01	722 219/500	712 1/4	716 5/8	
10					

10. Rename the pivot table chart sheet as **Recent Results Chart**.

The line chart gives you a quick view of each stock's low, high, and closing values. By default, the pivot table and chart show the sum of these values over all of the stocks in the portfolio. This, itself, is not very useful; however by clicking the Ticker Symbol list arrow, you can quickly view the daily values from the last five days for any individual stock in the portfolio. Try this now.

To use the pivot table to display five-day market values for a stock:

1. Click the **Ticker Symbol** drop-down list box located in the upper-left corner of the chart.
2. Click **AA** (Alcoa Aluminum) from the list of stock symbols and then click the **OK** button. The stock values for Alcoa Aluminum for the last five days appear, replacing the prior values in the pivot chart.
3. Click the **Ticker Symbol** list box again, and this time select **GM**. Values for the General Motors stock replace those for Aluminum Alcoa. See Figure 11-35. Note that as you change the pivot chart, the pivot table automatically changes with it.

Figure 11-35 STOCK VALUES FOR GM OVER THE PREVIOUS FIVE DAYS

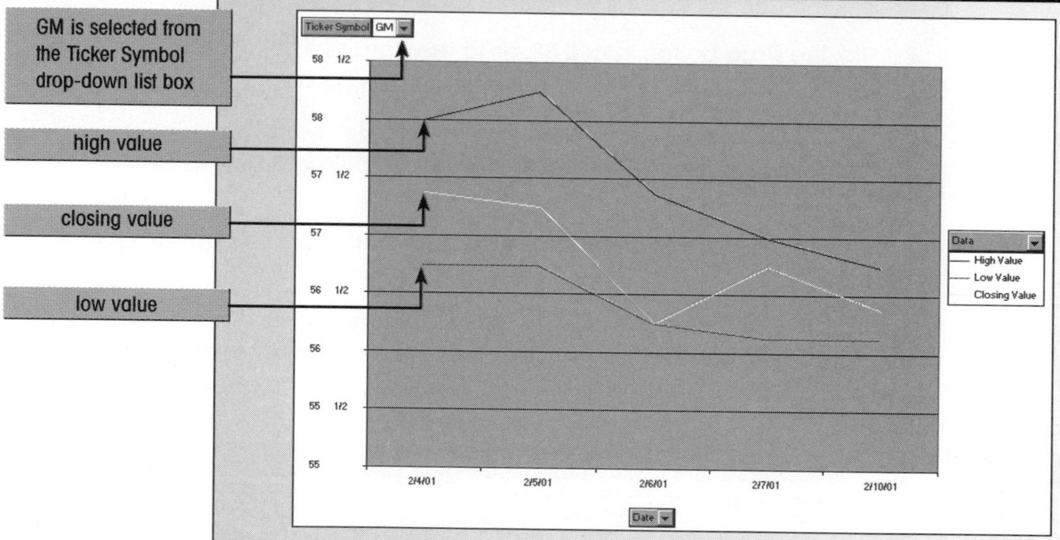

4. Click the **Recent Results** worksheet tab. The pivot table displays the values for General Motors that you saw reflected in the pivot chart.

You show Kelly the latest version of the Sunrise Fund workbook. She likes working with the pivot table and chart to retrieve values from the Sunrise database quickly and easily. Kelly will experiment with the workbook and get back to you later with any changes she wants you to make. For now you can close the workbook.

To save the Sunrise Fund workbook:

1. Click the **Portfolio** worksheet so that this is the first worksheet you'll see the next time you open the workbook.
2. Save and close the workbook.

Session 11.2 QUICK CHECK

1. How do you refresh external data and what does refreshing do?
2. How would you set up your external data so that it refreshes automatically whenever the workbook is opened?
3. How do you edit a query?
4. How do you format stock market data to display 3.25 as 3 1/4?
5. How do you create a pivot table and pivot chart based on an external data source?
6. What is the advantage of using external data in a pivot table rather than importing data into the workbook and creating a pivot table from the imported data?

In this session you've learned some techniques to increase the power and flexibility of your database queries. You've seen how to control the properties of your query and how to edit them. You've used queries to create pivot tables to summarize data from your database. In the next session you'll learn how to retrieve the most current data Kelly needs from the World Wide Web.

SESSION 11.3

In this session you'll learn how to use Web queries to retrieve data from the World Wide Web into your Excel workbook. You'll see how to use hyperlinks within your workbook to quickly access the Web. Finally, you'll create your own simple Web query to retrieve information from a Web page stored locally.

Web Queries

Although text files and databases contain a wealth of information that Kelly and her colleagues at Davis & Larson will be able to use in their everyday work, the Internet is also an important source of financial information. The **Internet** is a worldwide collection of interconnected computer networks. The computers on the Internet contain information on a variety of subjects, from sports and history to financial reports. The primary way users access materials on the Internet is through the World Wide Web. The **World Wide Web**, often called just the "Web," is a graphical interface to the Internet that allows users to access different information sources by clicking a button. These information sources are viewed in **Web pages**, which are documents containing text, graphics, video, sound, and other elements. Web pages can often be linked to databases to allow users quick and easy access to data online.

To use the World Wide Web, you need to have a computer that can access the Internet, either through a direct connection in a campus or business computer lab, or with a dial-up connection using your computer's modem and the phone lines. You also need a Web browser. A **Web browser** is a program that displays Web pages. Microsoft Office 2000 comes with the Internet Explorer Web browser, and this feature is also built into Windows. Netscape Navigator™ is another popular browser. If you're not sure whether your computer is capable of connecting to and retrieving information from the World Wide Web, ask your instructor or technical support person before proceeding with the steps in this session.

Once you have the hardware and software you need to use the World Wide Web, you can start retrieving data into your Excel workbooks using the Excel Web query feature. A **Web query** operates like the queries you created earlier in this tutorial: it connects to the World Wide Web, retrieves data requested by the user, and places it in the active workbook.

To help you access data from the Web, Excel has supplied four Web query files. These files are similar to the query file you created and saved on your Data Disk earlier in this tutorial, except that they define how to retrieve data from a page on the Web rather than from a database.

Kelly knows that there is a huge amount of stock information available on the Web, and she wants you to make sure her Sunrise Fund workbook is capable of retrieving current values on all of the stocks in the Sunrise portfolio.

Retrieving Multiple Stock Quotes

There are 15 stocks in the Sunrise Fund, and Kelly wants to be able to view current information on all of them. One of the Web query files Excel supplies is the Microsoft Investor Stock Quotes query. It allows you to enter up to 20 ticker symbols (abbreviations for the stock names used by the market), and then it retrieves current market values of those stocks and places the information into a table in the workbook. This seems to be just what Kelly wants, so you reopen the Sunrise Fund workbook and begin creating a worksheet with values imported from a Web query.

To open the Sunrise Fund workbook:

1. If you took a break after the last session, make sure Excel is running, and open the **Sunrise Fund** workbook in the Tutorial folder for Tutor11 on your Data Disk.
2. Insert a new worksheet directly to the right of the Portfolio worksheet and name it **Current Values**.
3. Click cell **A1** to make it the active cell.

You'll place the Web query results in this worksheet.

REFERENCE WINDOW RW

Running a Web Query

- Click Data, point to Get External Data, and click Run Saved Query.
- Click Web Queries from the Files of Type list box.
- Locate the folder containing your Web query file.
- Select the Web query you want to run and click the Get Data button.

With the worksheet created, you'll now run the Stock Quotes Web query.

To run the Stock Quotes Web query:

1. Click **Data** on the menu bar, point to **Get External Data**, and then click **Run Saved Query**.
2. Click **Web Queries** from the Files of Type list box. Excel displays the Web queries located in the Queries folder. See Figure 11-36.

   TROUBLE? Your list of Web queries may be different from the one shown in Figure 11-36.

Figure 11-36 LIST OF BUILT-IN WEB QUERIES

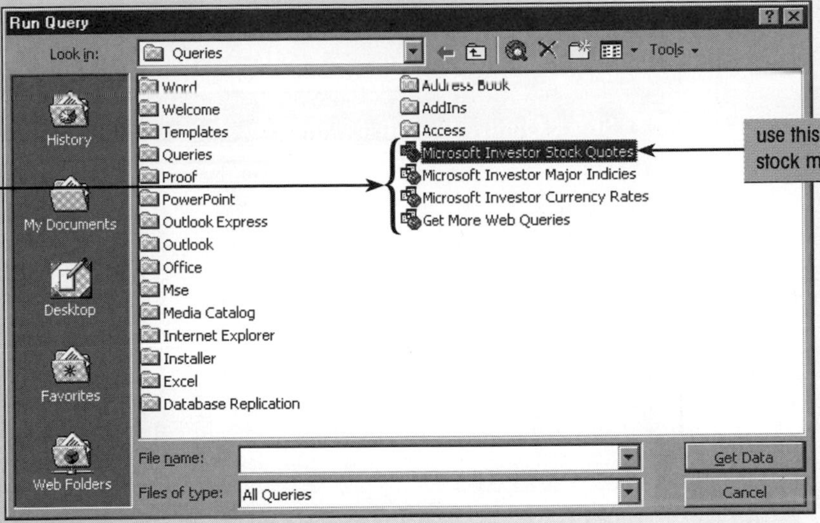

3. Click the **Microsoft Investor Stock Quotes** query and then click the **Get Data** button. Excel displays a dialog box in which you can specify the parameters for your query.

   If you click the OK button now, Excel will then prompt you for the ticker symbols of the stocks you want to see. You can also have Excel retrieve the ticker symbols from a cell range in the workbook. Because you've already retrieved this information and placed it in the Portfolio worksheet, you'll choose that option and save yourself some typing.

4. Click the **Parameters** button.

5. Click the **Get the value from the following cell** option button.

   Now you'll select the cell range containing the ticker symbols.

6. Click the **Collapse Dialog Box** button and select the range **A4:A18** on the Portfolio worksheet and press **Enter**.

7. Click the **OK** button twice to initiate your Web query. Depending on the speed of your Internet connection, it might take a few seconds or up to a minute to retrieve current stock quotes from the Web. Once you are connected and the query is processed, Excel displays the data in the table format shown in Figure 11-37.

Figure 11-37 STOCK QUOTES RETRIEVED FROM THE WEB

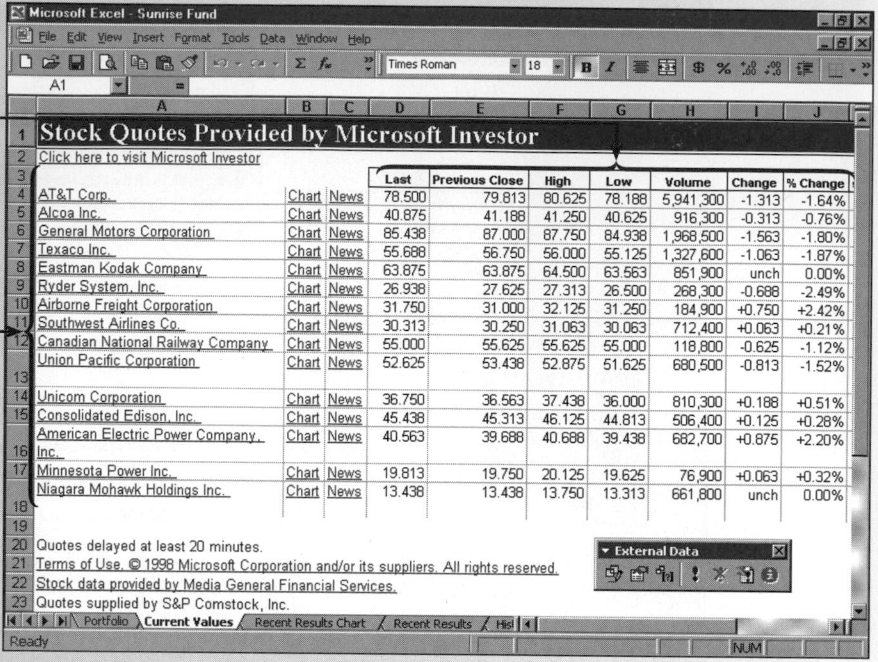

current stock values

blue, underlined text contain hyperlinks to documents on the Web

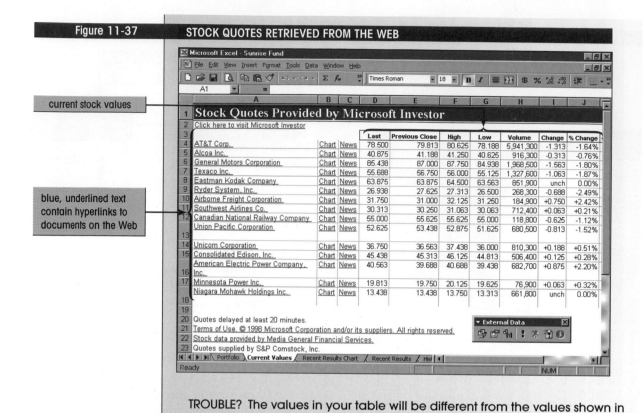

TROUBLE? The values in your table will be different from the values shown in Figure 11-37 because you are retrieving stock values at a different point in time.

You show the results of the Web query to Kelly. Based on this information, she has a good idea how the stocks of the Sunrise Fund are doing today. Kelly is happy that it is so easy to retrieve timely information from the Web into her Excel workbooks. You point out to her that the stock quotes returned from the Web query are 20 minutes old; paid subscribers to an investor service can receive up-to-the-minute stock information. She asks you how she would update stock quotes during a normal workday. You tell her she can refresh a Web query in much the same way she would refresh queries for data retrieved from the company's database.

Refreshing a Web Query

Kelly can easily refresh the information in her workbook at any time. When you direct Excel to refresh Web data, Excel reconnects to the Web page supplying the data. To show Kelly how this works, you decide to refresh the Multiple Stock Quotes query.

To refresh the Multiple Stock Quotes query:

1. Click the **Refresh Data** button on the External Data toolbar.
2. If necessary, you may have to reconnect to the Internet.

   Excel connects the Web site again and retrieves the latest information on the stocks.

Another way of ensuring current stock results is to have Excel periodically refresh the stock quotes for you. You can set up this procedure through the Properties dialog box for the Web query. You decide to set up the query so that it automatically retrieves stock information every 10 minutes when the workbook is open.

To set up Excel to periodically retrieve stock quotes:

1. Click the **Data Range Properties** button on the External Data toolbar.
2. Click the **Refresh data on file open** check box so that Excel will automatically retrieve stock information when the workbook is initially opened.
3. Click the **Refresh Every** check box and enter **10** in the minutes spin box. See Figure 11-38.

Figure 11-38 MODIFYING THE PROPERTIES OF THE WEB QUERY

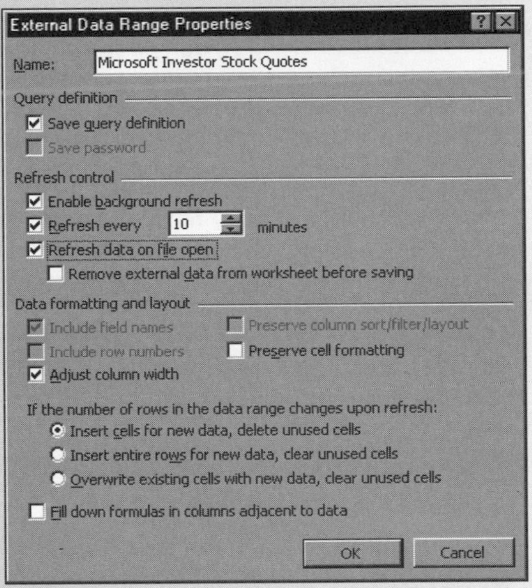

The workbook will now retrieve stock values every 10 minutes from the Microsoft Investor Web page. Please note however, that these stock values will be at least 20 minutes old. If you need to have real-time stock reports, you will have to pay for that service.

4. Click the **OK** button.

Using Hyperlinks

In looking over the results of the Web query in the Current Values worksheet, Kelly notices that some of the text is underlined in blue. Underlined blue text in Excel, and in many other programs, usually means that the text in the cell is hypertext. **Hypertext** consists of words that are connected to related information; when you click the text, the related information is retrieved and displayed. Hypertext shows you information not in a linear fashion, like a book that you would read straight from the front cover to the back cover, but rather through a set of associations linking common ideas and topics. Think of reading an encyclopedia in which an article on Einstein refers you to other articles on relativity and physics. With an encyclopedia, you still have to get up and manually locate the articles. But with hypertext, you simply click on a word, phrase, or picture, called a **link** or **hyperlink**, and the computer takes you directly to the related material. The Excel Help system is a hypertext document in which clicking symbols or underlined words "jumps" you to related material or displays a definition. The World Wide Web applies this principle to information on a larger scale involving information stored on thousands of computers around the world.

Clicking a hypertext entry in a worksheet will activate your computer's Web browser to display the Web page associated with that entry. Kelly will find this feature useful when she wants more detailed information about a particular stock in the Sunrise Fund. She can even use a hyperlink to access the Web page of each of the stocks in the portfolio. You decide to demonstrate this feature by activating the hyperlink associated with AT&T.

To activate a hyperlink:

1. Position your mouse pointer over the **AT&T** hyperlink in cell A4. The pointer changes to a .

   TROUBLE? If the AT&T hyperlink does not appear in your table, choose a different hyperlink and continue with the remaining steps.

2. Click the **mouse** button. Excel starts your default Web browser and displays the Web page shown in Figure 11-39.

   TROUBLE? Note: The first time you access this site, you'll see a Welcome page.

Figure 11-39 WEB PAGE FOR AT&T STOCK

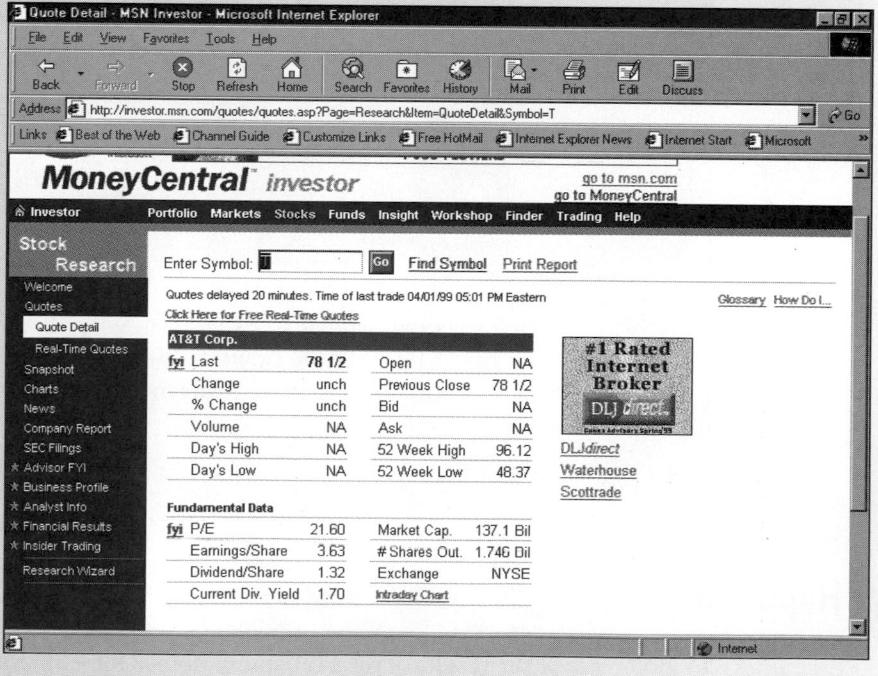

TROUBLE? The numeric values of the Web page you retrieve will be different from the ones shown in Figure 11-39 because the figures change rapidly over time. Also, if you are using a different Web browser, such as Netscape, you might notice some other differences as well. If you can't get the links to work, talk to your instructor or technical support person.

3. Click **File** on the menu bar, and click **Close** to close the Web browser.

TROUBLE? If you are using a browser other than Internet Explorer, you might have to click File on the menu bar and then click Exit to close the browser and return to your workbook.

The Web page you've linked to contains additional information about the stock along with links to other pages on the Web with even more information. Thus, the Sunrise Fund portfolio workbook contains important information in its own right, but it will also act as a gateway to additional data resources.

Creating a Web Query

Davis & Larson has a Web page containing descriptive information about the fund. Kelly asks if you could include this information as a separate worksheet in the workbook. A preview of the page is shown in Figure 11-40.

Figure 11-40 SUNRISE FUND INFORMATION PAGE

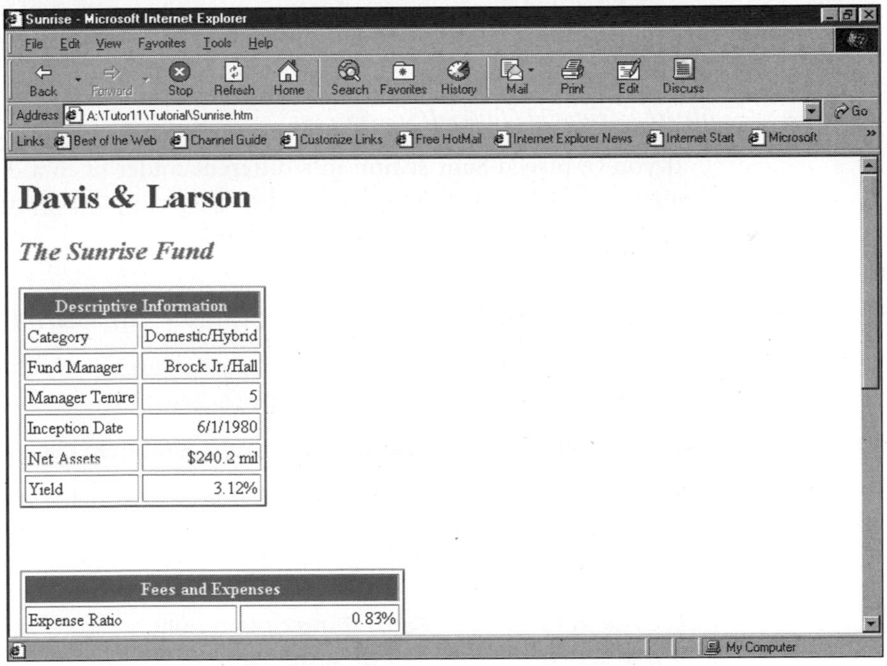

There are many ways to fulfill Kelly's request. You could copy and paste the data from the Web page into your workbook for example, but Kelly would like to have the data be automatically refreshed whenever she opens the file. The worksheet should be consistent with whatever information the company is putting out on its Web site. What you need is a Web query, but none of the prepackaged queries provided by Excel would work in this situation. You have to create your own from scratch.

To create your own Web query, you need to know the URL of the Web page you're accessing. The **URL (Uniform Resource Locator)** is the address of the page on the Web. Each page or document has a unique URL. You also need to know something about the structure of the Web page. If the page contains tables, you can create a query that will only retrieve the tables and the data they contain, or you can retrieve only specific tables from the page, ignoring all other information. On the other hand, you can retrieve all of the text in the page, in and outside of the tables.

The formatting used in the Web page is also an issue. You can have Excel ignore formatting when retrieving the page's text, or you can have Excel retrieve the text along with rich text formatting. **Rich text formatting** includes the text along with simple formatting (such as boldfacing, italics, and color), but not advanced formatting including hyperlinks or complicated table structures. Finally, you can have Excel apply Full HTML formatting. **Full HTML formatting** includes all simple and advanced HTML formatting features including hyperlinks. Although Full HTML formatting does include the most format information, it can often result in a worksheet that is unreadable. Determining which formatting option best fits a particular Web page can only be done by trial and error, and you may have to edit the Web page itself before it is ready to be retrieved in good form into your Excel workbook.

A copy of the Sunrise Fund's information Web page has been made available to you with the filename, Sunrise.htm. Rather than connecting to the Web, in this situation you'll access the file locally. This will give you a chance to test how well Excel retrieves the page into the Sunrise Fund workbook.

The URL for this Web page depends upon the location of your Data Disk. If your Data Disk is in drive A, and Sunrise.htm is located in the Tutorial folder for Tutor11, the URL will be:

file:///A:/Tutor11/Tutorial/Sunrise.htm

If you've placed Sunrise.htm in a different folder or in a different drive, you'll have to change the URL accordingly. You've also decided to retrieve the entire Web page and will apply Full HTML formatting in the retrieval.

To create a Web query to retrieve the Sunrise Web page:

1. Create a new worksheet named **Sunrise Fund** at the beginning of your workbook and click cell A1 if necessary.
2. Click **Data**, point to **Get External Data,** and then click **New Web Query**.
3. Type **file:///A:/Tutor11/Tutorial/Sunrise.htm** in the first text box of the New Web Query dialog box.
4. Click the **Entire Page** option button.
5. Click the **Full HTML Formatting** option button. Figure 11-41 displays the completed New Web Query dialog box.

Figure 11-41 CREATING A WEB QUERY FOR THE SUNRISE FUND INFORMATION PAGE

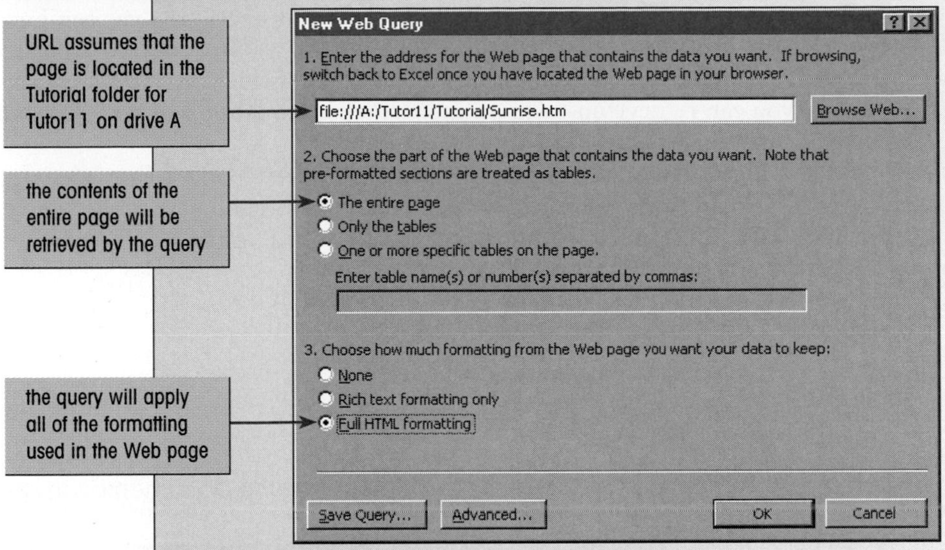

6. Click the **OK** button twice to start retrieving the Web page. Figure 11-42 shows the contents of the Sunrise Web page as it appears in your workbook.

Figure 11-42 THE SUNRISE FUND INFORMATION PAGE RETRIEVED INTO EXCEL

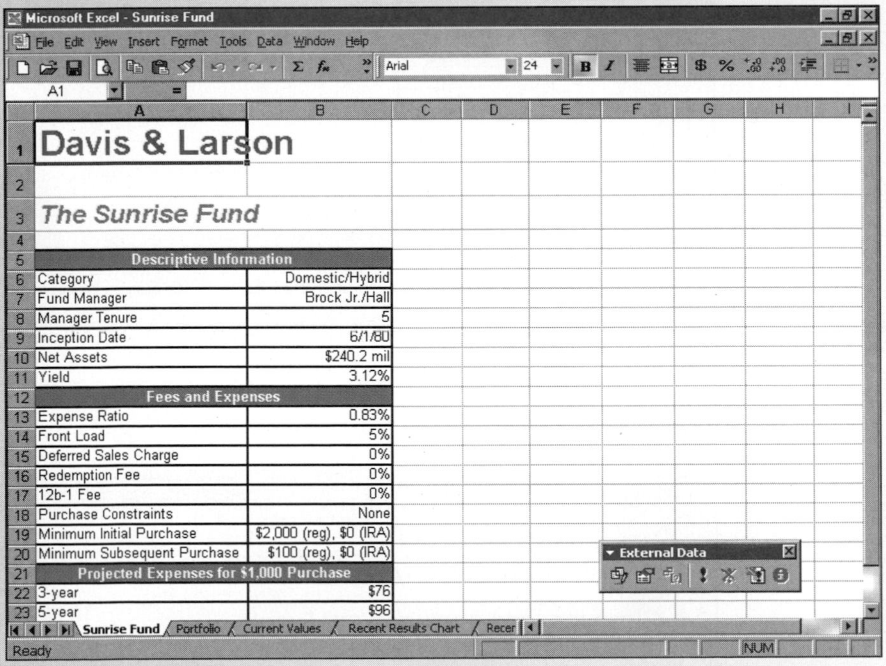

TROUBLE? If the query fails, you may have mistyped the URL for the page. Check the structure and syntax of the URL you entered against the example.

As you look over the Web page, you decide that the Web query has worked well in retrieving information from the page into the workbook. Kelly is pleased with the additional information that this query provides, and that the information can be updated from the Web page. Later on, you'll need to modify this query so that it points to the company's Web page on the World Wide Web.

You've completed your job of retrieving data into Excel. You've seen how easy it is to retrieve data from text files using the Text Import Wizard and how flexible the Query Wizard is in allowing you to choose the records and fields you want to display. Using Web queries, you can retrieve up-to-the-minute stock information and refresh that data any time you want.

To complete the Sunrise Fund workbook, you should add a Documentation sheet and save it. The Documentation sheet should include information about the source of all data in the workbook. This will help create an audit trail so that others who use your workbook can, if needed, go to the primary data sources.

To finish and save the workbook:

1. Insert a new worksheet named **Documentation** at the beginning of the workbook.

2. Enter the information shown in Figure 11-43 into the Documentation sheet.

Figure 11-43 DOCUMENTATION SHEET FOR THE SUNRISE FUND WORKBOOK

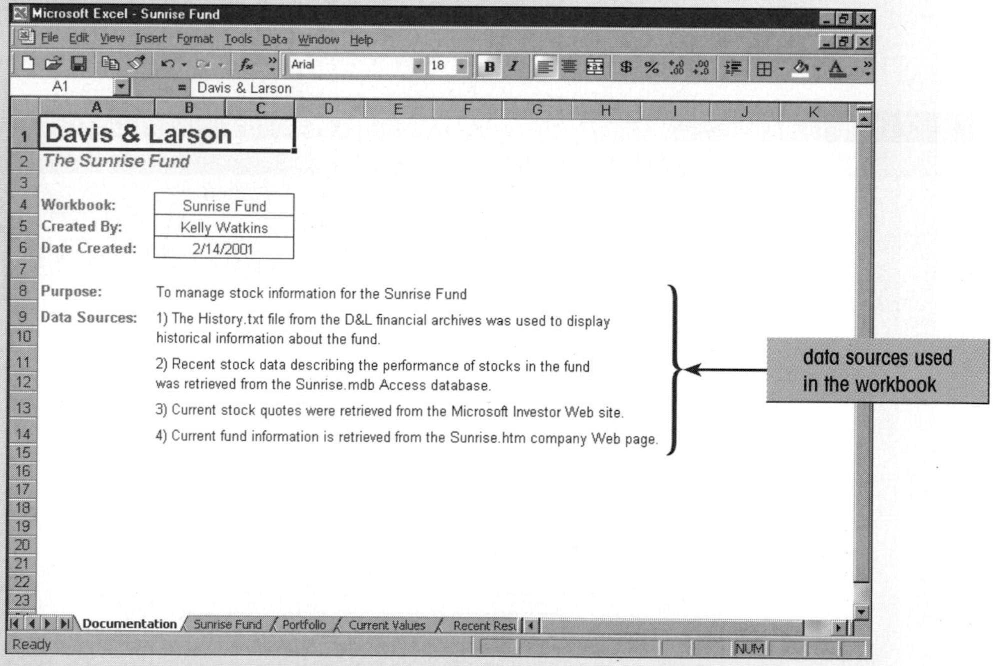

3. Save the completed workbook in the Tutorial folder for Tutor11 of your Data Disk.

4. Close the workbook and exit Excel.

You're finished with the Sunrise Fund workbook. Kelly appreciates the work you've done. By tapping into a variety of data sources, you've created a document for her that she can use to get current information on the fund as well as examine long-term and short-term data to look for important trends. She expects to find many ways to incorporate this wealth of new information into her daily work as an investment counselor at Davis & Larson.

Session 11.3 Quick Check

1. What are the Internet and the World Wide Web?
2. What is a Web query?
3. What is a Web browser?
4. What do you need to have before you run a Web query?
5. How do you update the data values in a Web query?
6. What is hypertext? What are hyperlinks?

In this tutorial you imported a text file and used the Query Wizard to import database information into Excel. You created a pivot table from an external database and used Web queries and hyperlinks to retrieve current stock information. Finally, you documented your workbook to help others who may use it in the future.

REVIEW ASSIGNMENTS

Kelly Watkins has had a chance to work with some of the data you've retrieved for her. She would like you to create a new workbook that analyzes the performance of the stocks in the Sunrise database by the three NYSE categories: the industrials, the transportation, and the utilities.

She has a text file that contains the daily indexes of these subgroups for the year 2000. First she wants you to import the text file into the Excel workbook. Then she would like you to create a table of yield and P/E ratio values for the stocks in the Sunrise database, sorted by category. Your next task will be to create a table and chart that displays the average closing values of the industrial, transportation, and utility stocks in the Sunrise Fund over the past five days. She wants the data in a pivot table in which she can click a Category list box and view the corresponding table and chart for that category (industrial, transportation, or utility). Finally, she would like a worksheet that displays a table of current Dow Jones Stock quote data retrieved from the Web.

To create Kelly's workbook, do the following:

1. If necessary, start Excel, and make sure your Data Disk is in the appropriate drive. Open the text file **NYA2000** in the Review folder for Tutor11.
2. Using the Text Import Wizard, choose the appropriate columns to import, ignoring the first three lines of the text file. Adjust column breaks as necessary.
3. Format the date column in YMD format. Do not import data from the Finance column into the workbook.
4. Save the workbook as **NYSE Index Analysis** in the Review folder for Tutor11. Be sure to save it in Excel format.
5. Insert a new sheet named **Yield and PE Values** into the workbook.
6. Use the Query Wizard to retrieve the following fields from the Sunrise Fund data source:

   Ticker Symbol and Category fields from the Company table
   Yield and P/E Ratios from the Stock Info table

7. Sort these values by the Category field in ascending order, and place them in the new worksheet.
8. Create a pivot table and chart displaying the average closing value for each stock category over the last five days. Organize the pivot table as follows:
   - In the Page area of the pivot table, display the Category field taken from the Company table.
   - In the Row area, display the Date field taken from the Recent Performance table.
   - In the Data area, insert the Average of the Closing value from the Recent Performance table.
   - Set up the query so that it refreshes when the workbook is opened.
   - Do not display grand totals for the columns or rows of the pivot table.
9. Format the pivot chart as a line chart.
10. Verify that your line chart changes as you change values in the Category list box.
11. Name the worksheet containing the pivot table **Recent Index Performance** and the pivot chart sheet **Recent Index Performance Chart**.
12. Add a new sheet to the workbook named **Dow Jones**.
13. Using the Web query, "Microsoft Investor Major Indices," retrieve stock and category data from the Web and insert it into the Dow Jones worksheet.

Explore

14. Insert a new worksheet named **Summary** at the beginning of your workbook. Create a Web query that accesses the Summary.htm file located in the Review folder for Tutor11 of your Data Disk. Set up the query so that it retrieves only the tables on the page and formats them using rich text formatting.
15. Add a Documentation sheet to the beginning of your workbook, describing the source of the data used in the workbook. Include your name, the workbook name, and the current date in the title sheet.

CASE PROBLEMS

Case 1. Retrieving Invoice Data for a Freelance Programmer Kevin Perkins is a freelance programmer who manages most of his financial data in a budget program. Occasionally though, Kevin needs to export his data into Excel to analyze his data and produce reports. His budget program does not allow him to save his data as an Excel workbook, but he can export it as a comma-delimited text file. Kevin has created a text file named Invoice.txt containing invoice records from the last month and a half, and he needs your help in retrieving the data and placing it into Excel. To help Kevin retrieve the data, do the following:

1. Open the **Invoice.txt** file in the Cases folder for Tutor11 from within Excel.

Explore

2. Open the text file using a comma-delimited format.
3. Specify the MDY Format for the Date column.
4. Do not import the Hours and the Hourly Rate columns.
5. Using the Pivot Table Wizard, create a pivot table on a new sheet, showing the total amount that Kevin has charged on his invoices, broken down by Project and then by Project Category.

6. Analyze the results. On which project has he made the most money in the recent months? Does he make more money with hourly-rate charges or with a flat fee?
7. Name the sheet containing the pivot table **Invoice Report**.
8. Print the **Invoice** worksheet and the **Invoice Report** worksheet.
9. Save your workbook in Excel format as **Invoice Data** in the Cases folder of Tutor11 on your Data Disk.

Case 2. Retrieving Parts Information at EZ Net Robert Crawford has just started working as the parts inventory manager at EZ Net, one of the leading suppliers of computer network cards and devices. He's responsible for managing the parts inventory. The company uses an Access database to store information on the parts that it uses and the vendors that supply the parts.

The database, named EZNet, contains three tables: Orders, Parts, and Vendors. The Orders table records information on the parts orders the company places with vendors. The Parts table contains descriptive information on each part. The Vendors table records descriptive information on each vendor. Common fields link each table with another.

EZ Net purchases its parts from many different vendors. Robert wants to retrieve the contents of the three tables into an Excel workbook so that he can examine which vendors are responsible for which parts. He also wants to create a table that will tabulate the number of parts broken down by part number and vendor. He's asked you to help him perform these tasks. To help Robert retrieve the table contents, do the following:

1. Open a blank workbook in Excel and create a data source to the EZNet database located in the Cases folder for Tutor11 on your Data Disk. Name the data source **EZNet**.
2. Using the Query Wizard, retrieve the contents of the Orders, Parts, and Vendors tables and place them in three separate worksheets in your workbooks.
3. Name the three worksheets **Orders**, **Parts**, and **Vendors**.
4. Add a fourth worksheet to your workbook named **Parts Summary**.
5. Using the Pivot Table Wizard, retrieve the following fields from the EZNet database into a pivot table on the Parts Summary worksheet:

   Quantity from the Orders table
   Description from the Parts table
   Name from the Vendors table
6. Place the name of the vendor in the row section, the description of the part in the column section, and the sum of quantity in the data section of the table.
7. Write a paragraph analyzing the table you created. Which vendor supplies most of the parts to EZNet? Which one supplies the least?
8. Modify each query in the workbook so that it refreshes automatically whenever the workbook is opened.
9. Print the four worksheets in the workbook.
10. Add a Documentation sheet describing the contents of the workbook and the source of the data. Include your name and the date in the sheet.
11. Save the workbook as **Inventory Data** in the Cases folder for Tutor11 on your Data Disk.

Case 3. Retrieving Sales Information at EuroArts EuroArts, located in Ste. Genevieve, Missouri, sells reproductions of European art to American interior design companies and to homeowners by mail order. Jeanne Domremy is the finance manager who prepares quarterly reports on the company's products and sales. The company is interested in increasing its sales to the home market, so she's particularly interested in information on sales and products intended for home use. She's asked you to help retrieve some product and sales information from the company database into an Excel workbook.

The company data is stored in an Access database named Arts. The database has five tables: Products, Customer, Orders, Item, and Staff. Each table shares a common field with at least one other table in the database. The Products table stores information about products in the company's catalog. The Customer table records personal information about people who have bought products from EuroArt. The Orders table contains information about each order, including the date, who placed the order, and who recorded the transaction. The Item table records the items purchased in each order. Finally, the Staff table contains information about the sales personnel who take the orders.

Jeanne wants the following information:

- What items in the current catalog are of interest to homeowners? She would like the list to include the catalog ID #, product brand, product location, product type, product description, and price. She wants the list sorted by descending order of price.
- How many units have been sold recently, of what kind, and where? She wants a pivot table that shows items sold by region versus product type.

To find the information Jeanne needs, do the following:

1. Open a blank workbook and create a new data source for the Arts database located in the Cases folder for Tutor11 on your Data Disk, and name it **EuroArts**.
2. Start the Query Wizard and start retrieving the necessary data from the Arts database.
3. Select all the fields in the Products table.

Explore

4. In the Query Wizard's Filter Data dialog box, limit the query to only those records whose Location value equals Home or Multiple.
5. Sort the query in descending order of Item Price and retrieve the data.
6. Set up the query so that it is refreshed whenever the workbook is opened.
7. Print the worksheet containing the products list, and then save the workbook as **Home Catalog** in the Cases folder for Tutor11 on your Data Disk.
8. Open a new blank workbook, and start the Pivot Table Wizard to create a pivot table.
9. Access the EuroArts data source and select the following fields from the following tables:
   Order_ID# and Region from the Orders table
   Item_ID# and Quantity from the Item table
   Type from the Products table
10. Do not add any criteria to the query, but return to the Pivot Table Wizard.
11. Place Region in the Column area of the table, Type in the Row area of the table, and Sum of Quantity in the Data area of the pivot table.
12. Set up the query so that it refreshes whenever the workbook is opened.
13. Add a Documentation sheet describing the contents of the workbook and the source of the data. Include your name and the date in the sheet.

14. Print the worksheet containing the resulting pivot table, and then save the workbook as **Regional Sales** in the Cases folder for Tutor11 on your Data Disk.

Case 4. Retrieving and Running a Web Query at Brooks & Beckman Henry Sanchez is a financial consultant at Brooks & Beckman. He would like to use the Excel Web query feature to retrieve timely financial data. Unfortunately, he's not interested in the market queries supplied with Excel. Instead, he would like to retrieve current information on Pacific currency exchange rates and place them into his Excel workbooks.

Fortunately, Excel includes a Web query to retrieve additional Web queries. He asks you to help him find a Web query to retrieve Pacific currency exchange rates, and then to run that Web query to create a workbook containing exchange rate information. To retrieve the currency data that Henry needs, do the following:

1. If necessary, start Excel, and make sure your Data Disk is in the appropriate drive. Open a blank workbook and run the Web query titled **Get More Web Queries**.
2. Save the results of your query into a workbook named **Web Query Data**. Insert a Documentation sheet at the beginning of the workbook containing the workbook name, your name, and the date. Save the workbook in the Cases folder for Tutor11 on your Data Disk

Explore

3. Use the hyperlinks in the worksheet to retrieve the Pacific Exchange Rates from the Pacific Commerce company.
4. Save the Web query on your Data Disk, in the Cases folder.
5. Use the Pacific Exchange Rates query to retrieve the latest currency information, and place that information on a new sheet named "Currency Data" in your Web Query Data workbook.
6. Edit the query so that it refreshes when the workbook is opened and every 10 minutes while the workbook is in use.
7. Save the query on your Data Disk, and print the Currency Data worksheet.

INTERNET ASSIGNMENTS

The purpose of the Internet Assignments is to challenge you to find information on the Internet that you can use to create effective spreadsheets. The actual assignments are updated and maintained on the Course Technology Web site. Log on to the Internet and use your Web browser to go to the Student Online Companion to accompany this text at **www.course.com/NewPerspectives/office2000**. Click the Excel link, and then click the link for Tutorial 11.

QUICK CHECK ANSWERS

Session 11.1

1. A fixed width text file places all columns in the same location in the file; a delimited text file uses a special character to separate columns.
2. space, comma, tab
3. click the location in the Data preview window of the Text Import Wizard where you want the column break to appear

4. a. program that stores and retrieves large amounts of data and creates reports describing that data
   b. collection of data that is stored in rows and columns
   c. stores information about a specific characteristic for a person, place, or thing
   d. a row of the table that displays the collection of characteristics for a particular person, place, or thing
   e. a field that is shared by two or more tables and is used to combine information from those tables
5. a question asked about the data in a database
6. A data source is any file that contains the data that you want to retrieve. Data sources can be databases, text files, or other Excel workbooks. To define a data source, you must specify the name of the data source, its location, and the type of driver to use in accessing data from it.
7. return (import) the data into an Excel workbook; open the results in Microsoft Query, or create an OLAP cube

Session 11.2

1. Click the Refresh Data button on the External Data toolbar. Refreshing data causes Excel to go back to the data source and retrieve the data using the query you created.
2. with a cell selected in the data range containing the external data, click the Data Range Properties button on the External Data toolbar, and click the Refresh data on file open check box
3. click the Edit Query button on the External Data toolbar
4. format the data by selecting the Fraction format category in the Format Cells dialog box and specifying one of the format types in that category
5. start the PivotTable and PivotChart Wizard and click the External Data Source option button in the first step
6. It reduces the size of the workbook.

Session 11.3

1. The Internet is a worldwide collection of interconnected computer networks. The World Wide Web is a graphical interface to the Internet that allows users to access different information sources by clicking a button or link.
2. a query that retrieves data from the Internet, placing it in your Excel workbook
3. a program that retrieves and displays Web pages from the World Wide Web
4. an Internet connection, a Web browser, and a Web Query file
5. click the Refresh Data button on the External Data toolbar
6. Hypertext is text that is linked to related material so that when the text is clicked or otherwise activated, the linked material is retrieved and displayed. A hyperlink is a word, phrase, or image that when clicked or activated, "jumps" the user to another document or information source.

OBJECTIVES

In this tutorial you will:

- Create macros using the Macro Recorder
- Assign a macro to a button
- View macro code in the Visual Basic Editor
- Learn about the features of the Visual Basic Editor
- Write a macro with the Visual Basic Editor
- Learn basic concepts and principles of the Visual Basic programming language
- Write an interactive macro that asks the user for input
- Modify a macro so it responds to different user input
- Customize Excel's Menu and Toolbars
- Change the properties of your Excel workbook

LABS

ENHANCING EXCEL WITH VISUAL BASIC

Creating a Customized Application for the Imageon Shareholders' Convention

CASE

Imageon Inc.

Imageon, Inc. is a mid-sized manufacturer of high-quality computer imaging products, including scanners, copiers, and laser printers. Located in Seattle, Washington, Imageon was founded in 1989. The company has grown rapidly since then and is now a leader in the computer imaging market.

The company is planning to hold its annual shareholders' conference next month, and you're assisting the convention coordinator, Steve Howard, in preparing materials for the convention. The materials will focus on building shareholders' confidence in Imageon by emphasizing the company's success over the last several years. Steve feels that past shareholder conventions have given attendees more printed information than necessary. This year he wants to set up an information center called a kiosk in the convention hall lobby, with computers that shareholders can use to display company information. Specifically, he wants the shareholders to be able to display and view financial tables and charts describing the company's performance over the last few fiscal years. Most of the tables and charts are in Excel workbooks. Steve cautions you that many of the shareholders are not experienced Excel users, so he wants you to make it as easy as possible for them to work with the various Excel files.

You are already familiar with some basic Excel macros, and you know that Excel includes a programming language called Visual Basic, a very powerful and easy-to-use tool that helps you create more complex macros. You suggest adding user-friendly macros to the workbooks to help the shareholders view tables and charts easily and quickly. These more sophisticated macros can help you customize the way users interact with a workbook. You can even have a workbook perform alternate tasks based on different user responses. You decide to explore how you can use Visual Basic to create an easy-to-use system for the convention kiosk. The conference is next month, so you don't have much time to prepare.

SESSION 12.1

In this session you'll review how to create a macro using the Excel Macro Recorder and how to assign that macro to a button in the workbook. After creating the macro, you'll view the macro code in the Visual Basic Editor. You'll learn about some of the features of the editor, and you'll use it to create a second macro based on the first one you recorded.

Planning Your Macros

You sit down with Steve to review the contents of one of the workbooks he wants to place on the computer in the kiosk. The Imageon workbook, shown in Figure 12-1, includes reports that show the financial performance of the company over the past four years.

Figure 12-1 CONTENTS OF THE IMAGEON WORKBOOK

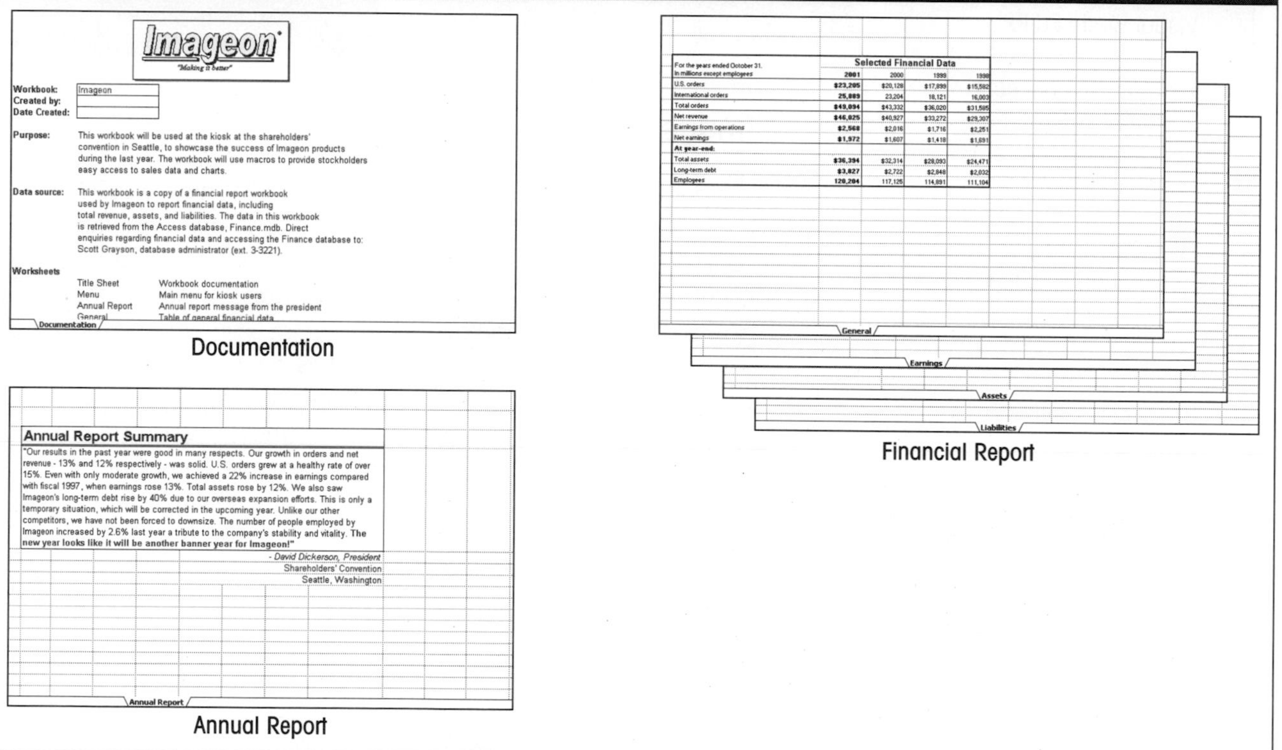

There are six worksheets: a Documentation sheet, a sheet containing a message from the company president, and four sheets of financial reports. Steve doesn't want the shareholders to have to click each tab in the workbook to locate the report they want to view. Because users might not know Excel, it would be ideal if they only had to click self-explanatory buttons on the screen that would immediately display a particular sheet. Steve wants you to use Excel to create an application that would make this possible.

You look into the matter and discover that you can create what Steve needs by creating a customized application, a program that uses Excel macros written in the Visual Basic programming language to perform a specific task. You learn that creating a customized application is a six-step planning process:

1. **Define your needs.**
   Write a short statement describing what tasks you want your customized application to perform. Can you perform any of the tasks using built-in Excel features instead? If so, what limitations of these features are you trying to overcome?

2. **Decide on the application's appearance.**
   How will the application appear to the end user? Will you ask the user to supply information in response to a dialog box? If so, what type of message will the dialog box display? What limitations, if any, will you put on what the user enters?

3. **Use the Macro Recorder.**
   If some of the tasks can be performed using standard Excel commands, consider using the Macro Recorder to record them as macros. You can then use the macro that the recorder creates as a building block to help form a larger application, and as a springboard to better understand Visual Basic.

4. **Modify the macros.**
   Once you've created the foundation of your macros with the Macro Recorder, edit the code to meet your needs. You can take advantage of the Visual Basic online Help feature as you enter new code and modify existing statements. You can use Visual Basic to create dialog boxes to make your workbook more flexible and easier to use.

5. **Finalize the appearance of the application.**
   Evaluate the appearance of the workbook containing your application. What elements of the Excel document window will you keep, which ones will you remove, and which will you modify? Will you want screen elements like sheet tabs, or row and column headers visible to the user? What do you want the menu bar to look like? Will you create a customized toolbar?

6. **Protect the application.**
   Add a password and modify other properties of the workbook in order to prevent other users from changing your application.

You decide to apply the planning process to Steve's proposal. By defining Steve's needs, you know that the application he has in mind is a simple one. He wants users to easily access certain worksheets from the workbook by clicking self-explanatory buttons. Although you can, of course, display an Excel worksheet by clicking its tab, Steve sees a couple of limitations in this method. First, shareholders who have never used Excel might not know about this method for displaying worksheets. Secondly, even if they do know it, there are several worksheets in the workbook, and not all of the worksheet tabs would be immediately visible. Users could easily overlook some of the worksheets. In this situation, a macro would be very useful in helping shareholders find all the information they need quickly and easily.

How should this customized application appear to the user? Imageon sales representatives will staff the kiosk, but they will be busy talking with shareholders and won't have much time to help attendees use the computers. So the **interface**, the way the program communicates to the user, needs to be self-explanatory. It should not overwhelm the user with choices, but it should concisely display the available options. Steve thinks the shareholders will want to view either the Annual Report Summary or one of the financial worksheets. He sketches out a diagram like the one shown in Figure 12-2 showing how he wants the application to appear.

Figure 12-2 **THE CUSTOM APPLICATION THAT STEVE IS PLANNING**

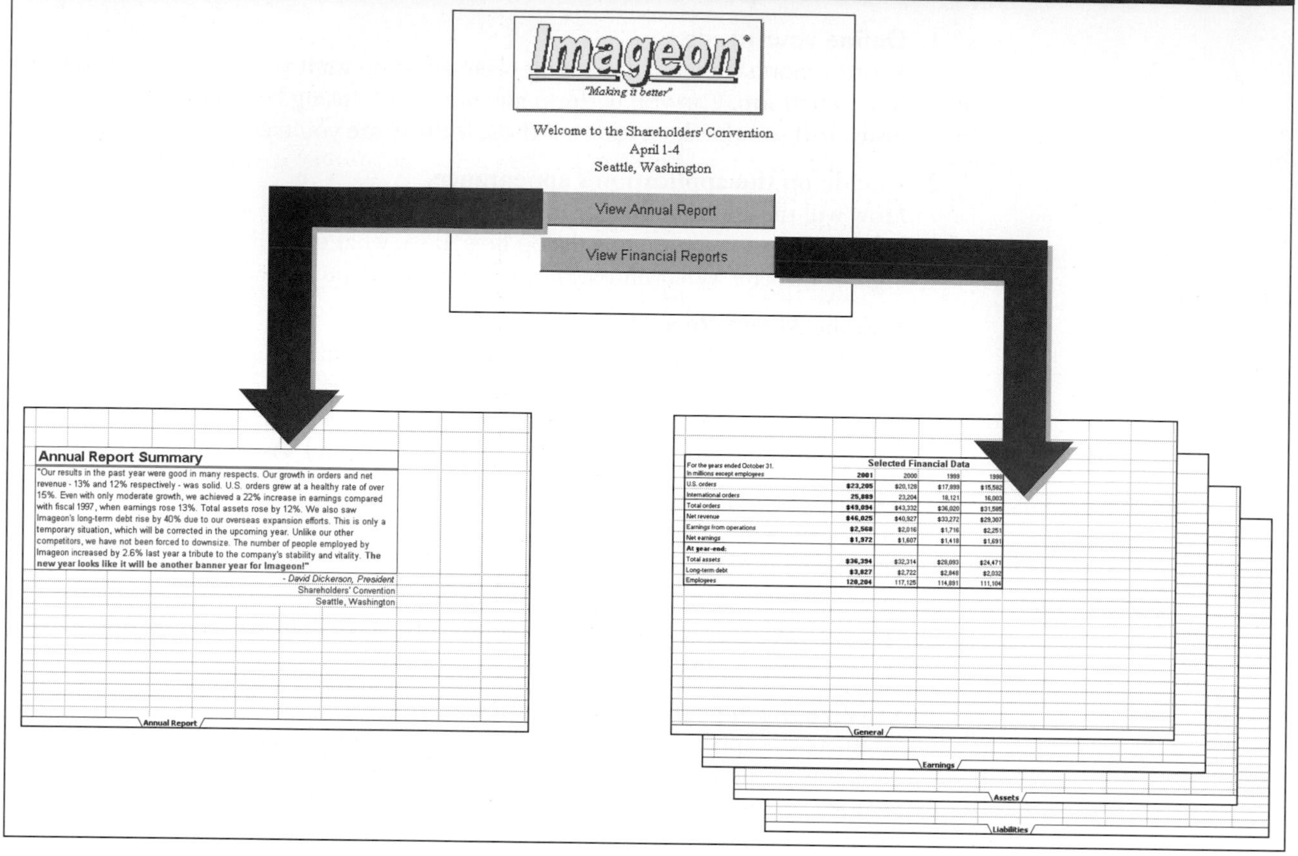

Now that you know what tasks you want the application to perform and how you want the interface to look, you are ready to start using the macro recorder to lay the foundation for your customized application. The Imageon workbook that contains the Annual Report Summary and the financial reports that Steve wants displayed have been stored on your Data Disk. You'll open the workbook now.

To open the Imageon workbook:

1. Start Excel as usual, and make sure your Data Disk is in the appropriate drive. Open the **Imageon** workbook in the Tutorial folder for Tutorial.12 of your Data Disk and save it as **Kiosk 1**.
2. On the Documentation sheet, enter **Kiosk 1** in the Workbook box in cell B7; enter your name and date in the proper cells as well.

Take a moment to become familiar with the contents of the workbook. Steve has added a new worksheet named Menu that contains the Imageon logo and a welcome message that the convention goers will see. On this worksheet, you'll add the buttons they'll click to display the Annual Report and the financial reports. After the Menu worksheet, the Annual Report worksheet contains a message from company president, David Dickerson, summarizing the company's Annual Report. After the Annual Report worksheet, four financial worksheets give information on the company's general fiscal state as well as its earnings, assets, and liabilities for the last four years. Once you know what the workbook contains, you're ready to start programming your macros.

Creating and Running a Simple Macro

The fastest way to create macros is to use the Excel Macro Recorder. As you saw earlier, you record a macro by turning on the recorder, performing a set of tasks, and then turning off the recorder when you're finished. The recorder saves the steps you performed, and users can rerun the macro any time to perform the same tasks. Then, because users need an easy way to run your macro, you can assign it to a button, so that whenever the user clicks the button, your macro will run.

You'll record a macro that takes users to the Annual Report worksheet. Then you'll create a button with the text "View Annual Report Summary" that users can click to display the Annual Report worksheet.

Using the Macro Recorder

The macro you'll record will be a simple one: It will display the Annual Report worksheet and then select cell A1, to make sure that the entire Annual Report Summary appears in the document window. You'll name this macro "Annual_Report."

To start recording the Annual_Report macro:

1. Click **Tools** on the menu bar, point to **Macro**, and click **Record New Macro**.

   Now you'll name the macro, using a name with an underscore character because macro names cannot contain spaces.

2. Type **Annual_Report** in the Macro name text box. Make sure that This Workbook is selected in the Store macro in list box because this macro will only be used in the current workbook.

   Now add a description of the macro.

3. In the Description text box, replace the existing text with the following: **This macro displays the Annual Report worksheet.** See Figure 12-3 for the completed Record Macro dialog box.

Figure 12-3 RECORD MACRO DIALOG BOX

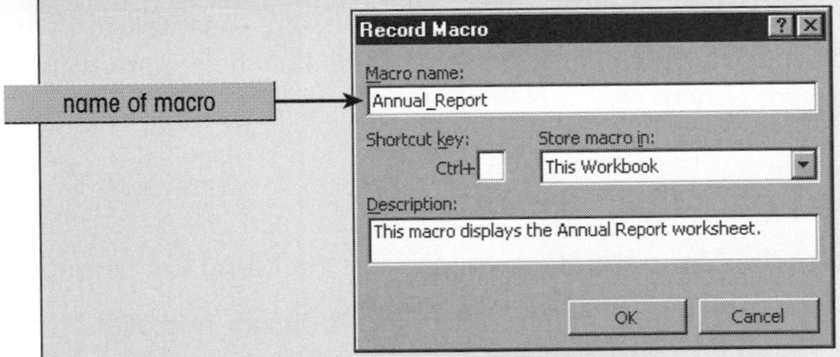

4. Click the **OK** button. The Macro Recorder toolbar appears on the screen. Excel is now in Record mode, so you should not perform any tasks other than those specified in the following steps.

With the Macro Recorder active, you'll go through the steps of selecting the Annual Report worksheet, clicking cell A1, and then turning off the recorder when you're finished.

To record the Annual_Report macro:

1. Click the **Annual Report** worksheet tab.
2. Click cell **A1**.
3. Click the **Stop Recording** button ■.

Before going further with the macro, you should run it and verify that it works correctly.

To test the Annual_Report macro:

1. Click the **Menu** sheet tab.
2. Click **Tools** on the menu bar, point to **Macro**, and click **Macros** to open the Macro dialog box.
3. Click **Annual_Report** in the Macro Name list box, and click the **Run** button. The Annual Report worksheet appears in the document window with cell A1 selected.

   TROUBLE? If the Annual_Report macro does not display the Annual Report worksheet, go back to the Macro name list box, and click the Delete button to delete it. Then use the Macro Recorder to record the macro again.

Now you know the macro runs correctly. Because you don't want users to have to use the Tools menu to run your macro, you'll place a button on the Menu worksheet and assign the button to the macro you created. Then you'll place the text "View Annual Report Summary" on the button so users know they can simply click the button to view the Annual Report worksheet.

Assigning a Macro to a Button

To create a button on the worksheet and assign a macro to it, you first display the Forms toolbar. This toolbar contains several tools that help you create the interface that makes your macros easy to use.

To display the Forms toolbar:

1. Click the **Menu** sheet tab to return to the Menu worksheet.
2. Click **View** on the menu bar, point to **Toolbars**, and click **Forms**. The Forms toolbar appears. See Figure 12-4.

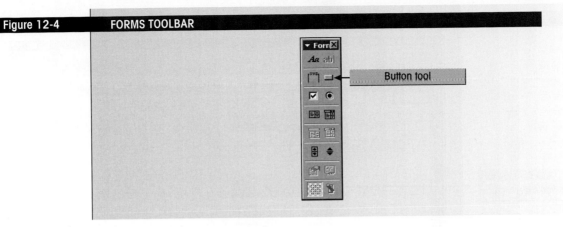

Figure 12-4 FORMS TOOLBAR

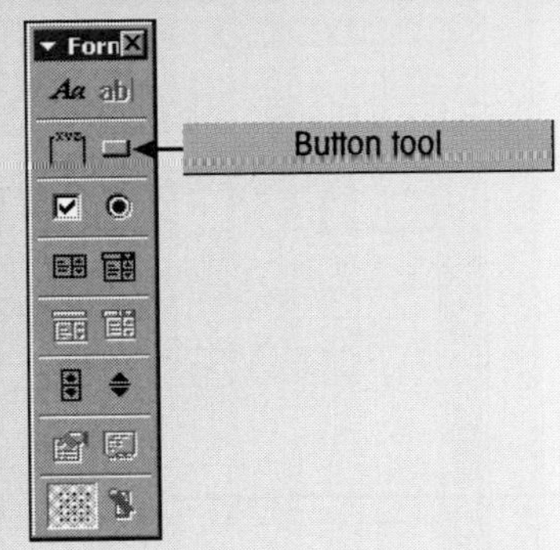

Now you'll use the Button tool to place a button on the worksheet. After you create the button, Excel will automatically ask you for a macro to assign to it. You'll specify the Annual_Report macro that you just created with the Macro Recorder.

To create the View Annual Report button:

1. Click the **Command Button** tool on the Forms toolbar. When you move the pointer over the worksheet, the pointer changes to +.
2. Drag the pointer over the range **D10:F11**, and then release the mouse button. A button appears, and you are asked to name the macro you want to assign to it.
3. Click **Annual_Report** from the list of macros, and then click the **OK** button.

   Now you'll enter the text that will appear on the button.
4. Type **View Annual Report Summary** into the new button and click cell **A1** to deselect it.

   TROUBLE? If you accidentally deselected the button before typing the caption, you can reselect it again by right-clicking the button and then pressing the **Esc** key to hide the pop-up menu.
5. Click the **Close** box on the Forms toolbar to close it. The Menu worksheet appears with the new button. See Figure 12-5.

Figure 12-5 MENU WORKSHEET WITH THE VIEW ANNUAL REPORT BUTTON

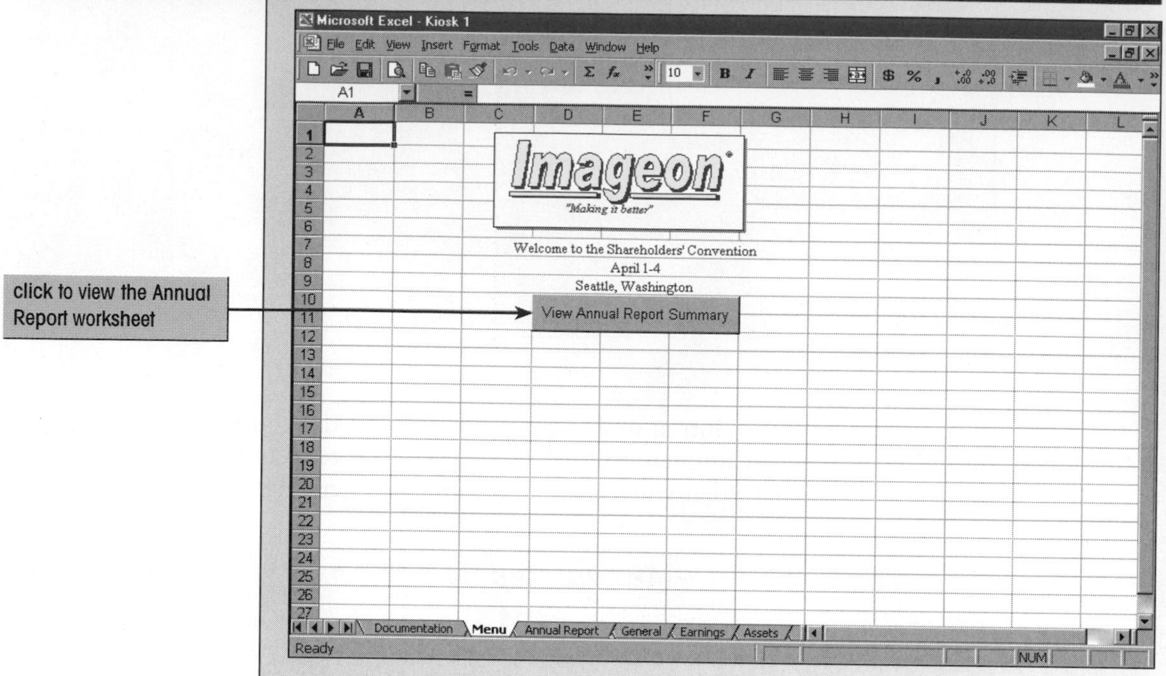

To make sure that the button and macro work properly, you should test them.

To test the View Annual Report Summary button:

1. Move the mouse pointer over the button so that the pointer changes to a ☝ and then click the mouse button. The Annual Report worksheet appears with cell A1 selected.

Having created and tested your first macro in this workbook, you are ready to examine the macro code to see how it works. By examining the code, you can learn some of the techniques you'll need to create new and more sophisticated macros. To look at the code, you'll use the Visual Basic Editor.

Starting the Visual Basic Editor

All Office 2000 macros are written in a programming language called Visual Basic (or Visual Basic for Applications, also called VBA). When you master the art of writing macros in Excel, you have a firm foundation for writing macros in the other Office products.

To edit the macros you've created with the Macro Recorder, you need to use the Visual Basic Editor. The editor is an application that allows you to edit your macros, create customized dialog boxes, and modify the contents of your Excel workbook. You use the same Visual Basic Editor whether you are creating macros in Excel, Word, Access, or PowerPoint.

REFERENCE WINDOW RW

Starting the Visual Basic Editor

- Click Tools and point to Macro.
- Click Visual Basic Editor to start

or

- Click Macros to open the Macro dialog box, select the name of the macro you want to edit, and then click the Edit button

or

- Press Alt+F11 from your keyboard.

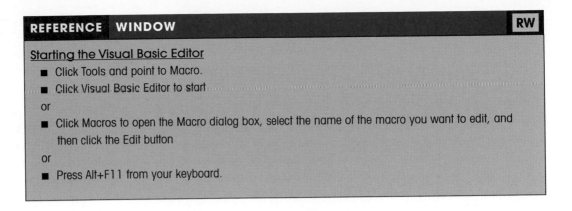

You can open the Visual Basic Editor directly, or by editing a macro you've created using the Macro Recorder. You'll open the Annual_Report macro, which will automatically open the Visual Basic editor.

To start the Visual Basic Editor:

1. Click **Tools** on the menu bar, point to **Macro**, and click **Macros**.
2. Click **Annual_Report** in the Macro Name list box, and click the **Edit** button. The Visual Basic Editor opens. See Figure 12-6.

Figure 12-6 VISUAL BASIC EDITOR

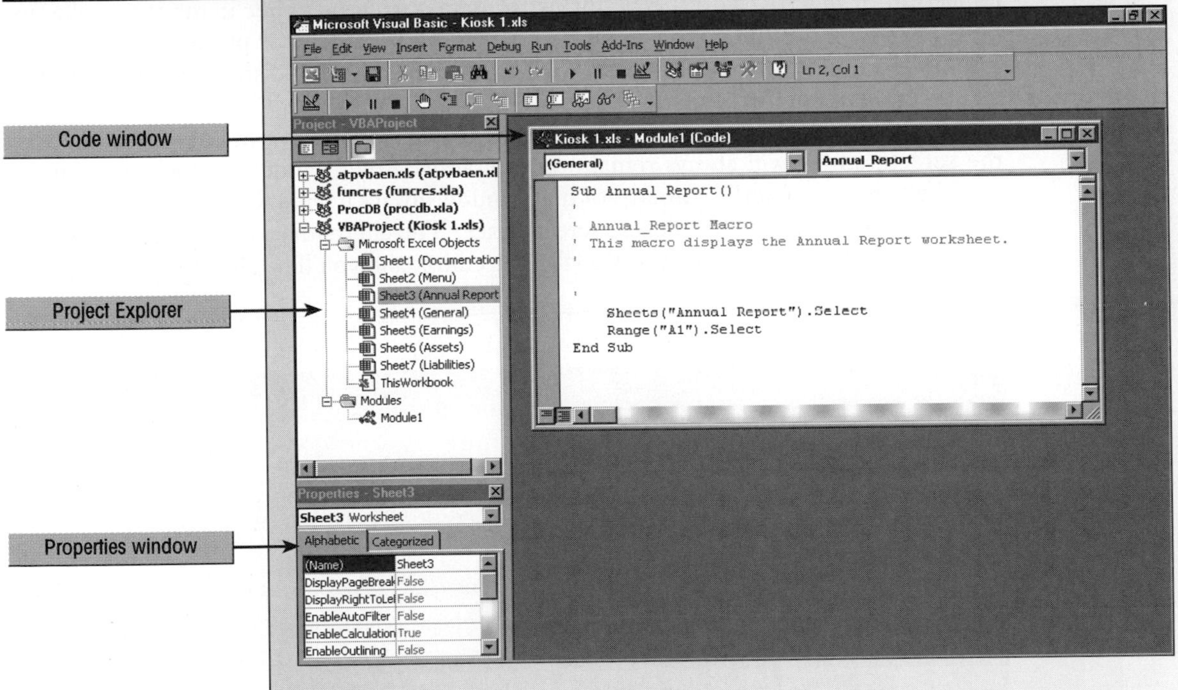

TROUBLE? If your Visual Basic Editor screen does not look like the one shown in Figure 12-6, don't worry. It might be set up differently on your system. You'll change the appearance of the editor shortly.

Before you begin studying the code of the Annual_Report macro, take a moment to become familiar with the main features of Visual Basic Editor.

Elements of the Visual Basic Editor

When the Visual Basic Editor opens, it displays three windows: the Project Explorer, the Properties window, and the Code window. You can use these windows to look at the structure and content of your workbooks, as well as any macros you've created. You might see other windows, depending on how the editor was installed on your system. To start learning about the different features of the editor, you'll begin with a clean slate by closing these windows and reopening them one at a time.

To clear the Visual Basic Editor window:

1. Click the Close box ☒ on each window in Visual Basic Editor window. The Visual Basic Editor window is now clear.

Now you are ready to examine some of the important elements of the Visual Basic Editor. You'll start with the Project Explorer.

The Project Explorer

One important use of the Visual Basic Editor is to manage your projects. A **project** is a collection of macros, worksheets, forms for data entry, and other items that make up the customized application you're trying to create. You manage your projects with the Project Explorer. The **Project Explorer** is a window in the editor that displays a hierarchical list of all currently opened projects and their contents.

The Project Explorer window is **dockable**, meaning that you can drag it to the edge of the screen, and it will always remain on top, above other windows. Docking a window is useful when you want the contents of that window always in view, but this can be a drawback if the window is taking up valuable screen space. The alternative is to not dock the window, and then it'll float free within the Visual Basic editor, and you'll be able to resize or minimize it as you would other windows.

REFERENCE WINDOW RW

Viewing Windows in the Visual Basic Editor

- Click View and click the name of the window you want to view.
- To make a window undockable, right-click the window's title bar, and deselect Dockable from the shortcut menu.
- To make a window dockable again, click Tools and click Options. In the Options dialog box, click the Docking tab, and click to select the check box corresponding to the window you want to dock.

To begin working with your Visual Basic project, you'll display the contents of the Project Explorer. You'll also make the window undockable to make it easier to view the other windows that you'll soon open.

To view and undock the Project Explorer:

1. Click **View** on the menu bar, and then click **Project Explorer**. The Project Explorer window opens, with Project - VBAProject in its title bar.
2. Right-click the title bar of the Project Explorer window, and deselect **Dockable** from the pop-up menu. Figure 12-7 shows the contents of the undocked Project Explorer window.

   TROUBLE? If you don't see a shortcut menu when you right-click the title bar, Project Explorer is already undocked, and you can continue with the tutorial.

   TROUBLE? Depending on what other workbooks or Excel add-ins you might have open, your Project Explorer window might look different from the one shown in Figure 12-7.

Figure 12-7 THE UNDOCKED PROJECT EXPLORER WINDOW

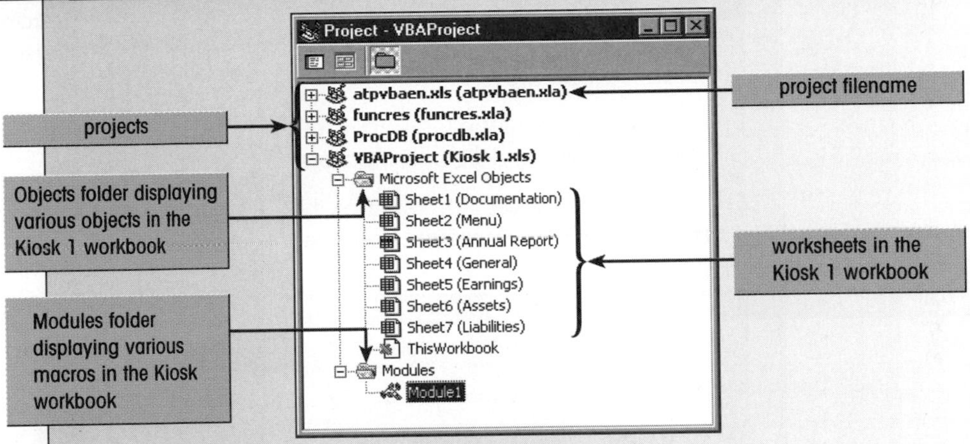

Like Windows Explorer, the Project Explorer arranges your project components hierarchically. At the top of the hierarchy is the project itself. In Figure 12-7, there are four projects listed (you may have other projects depending on how Excel is configured on your system.) Each project is identified by the icon followed by the project name and the filename in parenthesis. One of these is the "VBAProject" for the Kiosk 1 workbook. VBAProject is the default name the editor assigns to new projects. What are the other projects? They're Excel add-ins such as Solver or the Report Manager which appear as projects within the Project Explorer window. Within each project are various items called objects. An **object** is an element of a custom application, such as a worksheet, a macro or the workbook. In Visual Basic, just about anything can be an object, including a project. As you can see in Figure 12-7, some of the objects listed for the Kiosk 1 workbook include each of the worksheets and an object called "ThisWorkbook," which actually refers to the Kiosk 1 workbook itself.

REFERENCE WINDOW RW

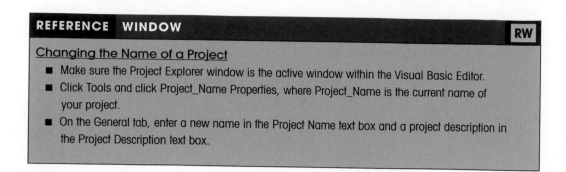

Changing the Name of a Project

- Make sure the Project Explorer window is the active window within the Visual Basic Editor.
- Click Tools and click Project_Name Properties, where Project_Name is the current name of your project.
- On the General tab, enter a new name in the Project Name text box and a project description in the Project Description text box.

The default name for your project, "VBAProject" isn't very descriptive, so you'll change it to something more informative for future users of the workbook. You can change the name and enter a description of the project in the Project Properties dialog box.

To change the name of your project:

1. Click the title bar of the Project Explorer window to make it the active window if necessary.
2. Click **Tools** on the menu bar, and then click **VBAProject Properties**. Because project names cannot include spaces, you'll use an underscore to separate the words in the name.
3. If necessary, select the General tab, type **Shareholders_Convention** in the Project Name text box, and then press the **Tab** key.
4. In the Project Description text box, type **A custom application for the Imageon Shareholders' convention.** See Figure 12-8.

Figure 12-8 COMPLETED VBAPROJECT - PROJECT PROPERTIES DIALOG BOX

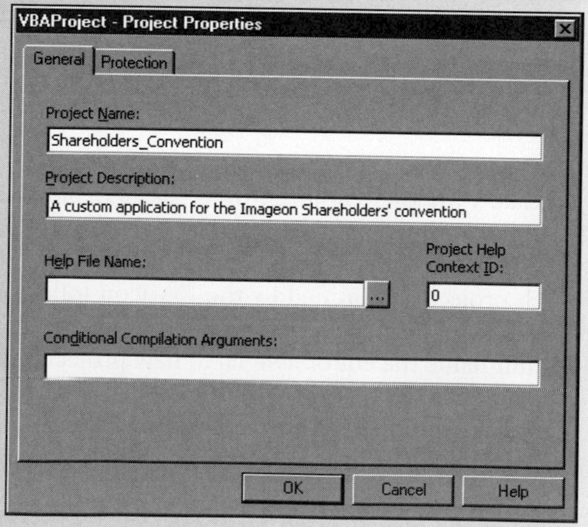

5. Click the **OK** button.
6. The Project Explorer window displays the new project name. See Figure 12-9.

Figure 12-9 THE REVISED PROJECT EXPLORER WINDOW

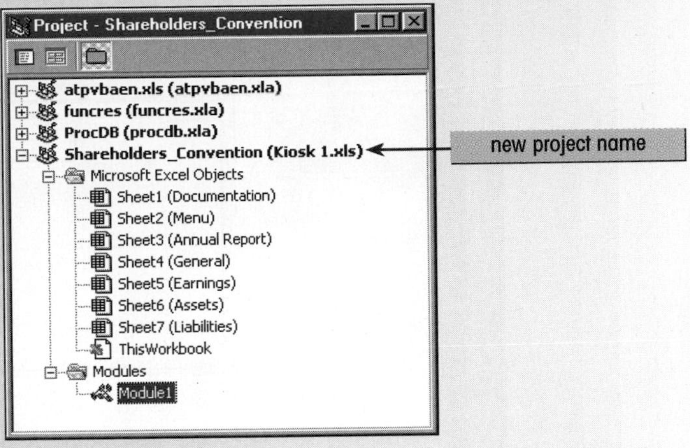

You've changed the name and description of your project, but if you want to change characteristics of other objects, you'll have to learn about the Properties window.

The Properties Window

When you entered the name and description of your project, you were actually modifying two of its properties. A **property** is an attribute of an object that defines one of its characteristics, such as its name, size, color, or location on the screen. All objects have properties. You can view a list of properties for any object in the **Properties window**. Try displaying the Properties window now for the Shareholders_Convention project.

To view the Properties window:

1. Click **Shareholders_Convention** from the Project Explorer.
2. Click **View** on the menu bar, and then click **Properties Window**. The Properties window opens.
3. If the window is docked, right-click the title bar of the Properties window, and deselect **Dockable** from the shortcut menu. The Properties window undocks from the menu bar and appears as a window in the Visual Basic Editor display area. See Figure 12-10.

Figure 12-10 PROPERTIES WINDOW FOR THE SHAREHOLDERS_CONVENTION PROJECT

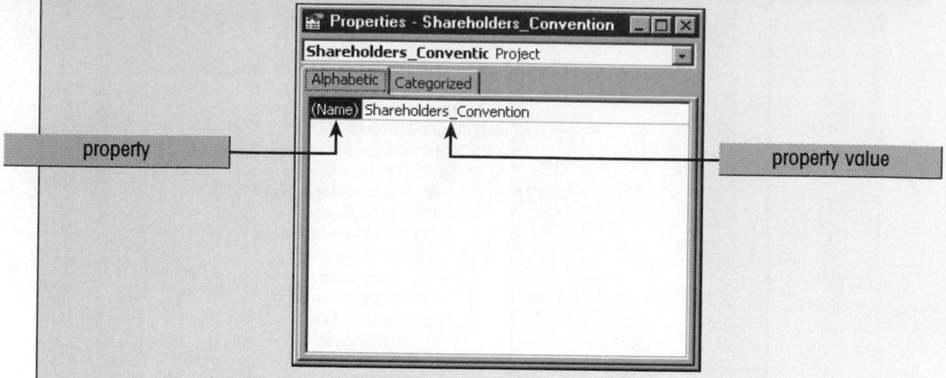

TROUBLE? If you don't see a shortcut menu when you right-click the title bar, the Properties window is already undocked, and you can continue with the tutorial.

The Properties window displays each property in the left column and the property's value in the right column. You can view the list of properties alphabetically and by category by clicking the Alphabetic and Categorized tabs at the top. In Figure 12-10, there is only one property listed, the Name property, which has the value "Shareholders_Convention."

To see how the Properties window works for objects other than projects, you decide to change the name of the Menu worksheet in the Kiosk 1 workbook to "Main Menu." True, you could do this from within Excel, but changing it here will give you some practice with the Project Explorer and the Properties window.

To change the name of the Menu worksheet:

1. Click **Sheet2 (Menu)** in the Project Explorer.

   The contents of the Properties window immediately change to show a list of properties for the Menu worksheet.

2. Click the Alphabetic tab in the Properties window, if necessary.

3. If necessary, scroll down to the bottom of the window until you see the Name property (listed before the ScrollArea property) and then select the property value, **Menu**.

4. Type **Main Menu** and press the **Enter** key.

   The name of the worksheet appearing in the Project Explorer window changes to Main Menu. See Figure 12-11. The next time you return to the Kiosk 1 workbook, you will find that the worksheet name has been changed there as well.

Figure 12-11 USING THE PROPERTIES WINDOW TO CHANGE A WORKSHEET NAME

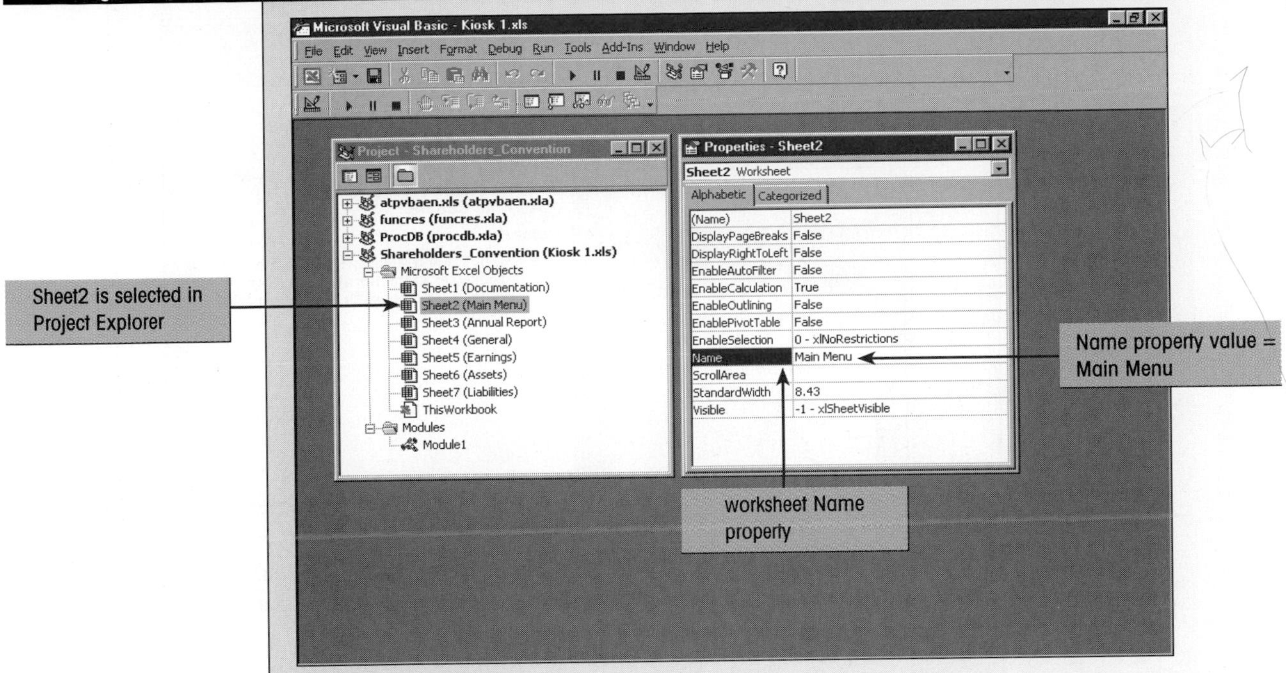

There can be many properties listed in the Properties window. The meaning of some of them will be very clear (such as the Name property), while others will not be as readily understandable. If you need more information about a particular property in the Property window, you can use Visual Basic online Help. You'll use online Help now to learn more about one of the properties of the Main Menu worksheet.

To view information on a property:

1. Click **StandardWidth** in the list of properties.
2. Press the **F1** key. The Help window shown in Figure 12-12 appears with the information that the StandardWidth property returns or sets the standard (default) width of all the columns in the worksheet. So if you want to change the default width of the columns in the Main Menu worksheet, you would change the value for this property.

Figure 12-12 HELP FILE ON THE STANDARDWIDTH PROPERTY

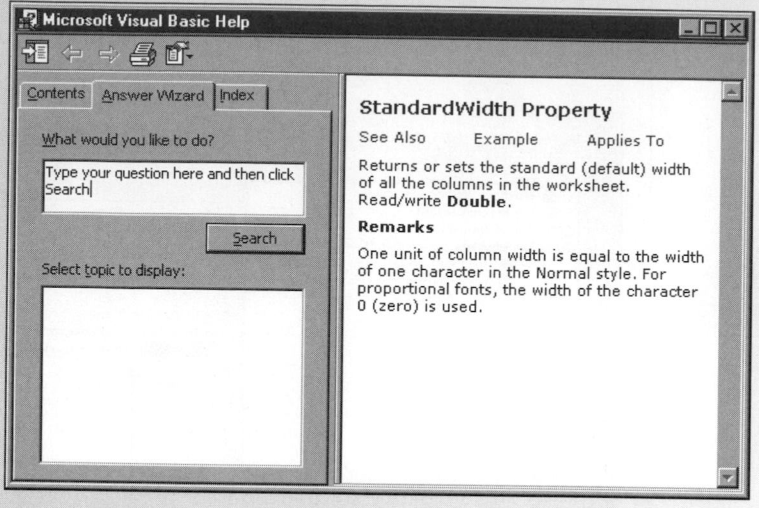

TROUBLE? If the Visual Basic Editor fails to display the Help topic, the Visual Basic Help files might not be installed. See your instructor or technical support person.

3. Click the **Close** box ☒ to close the Visual Basic Help window.

In the Visual Basic Editor, if you are not sure what a button, command, or object does, you can get information on it by selecting it and pressing the F1 key. You can display online Help either when you are in the Properties window or when you're writing and viewing Visual Basic code.

Now that you're familiar with the Project Explorer and Properties windows, you'll learn about modules, one of the most important parts of the Project Explorer.

Modules

When you viewed your project in the Project Explorer, you might have noticed the folder at the bottom of the object list called Modules. A module is a collection of macros. You might use several modules in a single project to group macros according to the type of tasks they perform. For example, you might group all the macros that handle printing tasks in one module, and the macros that format worksheets in another. When you recorded the Annual_Report macro, the Visual Basic Editor created a module and assigned it the default name "Module1".

You can give your module a name that better describes the type of macros it will contain. You decide to change the name of Module1 to "Report_Macros."

To change the name of a macro module:

1. Click **Module1** in the Project Explorer window.
2. Click the Properties window title bar to make the window active, and then double-click **Module1** in the (Name) row, type **Report_Macros**, and press the **Enter** key. The name of the module in the Project Explorer window and the Properties window changes to Report_Macros. See Figure 12-13.

Figure 12-13 CHANGING THE NAME OF A PROJECT MODULE

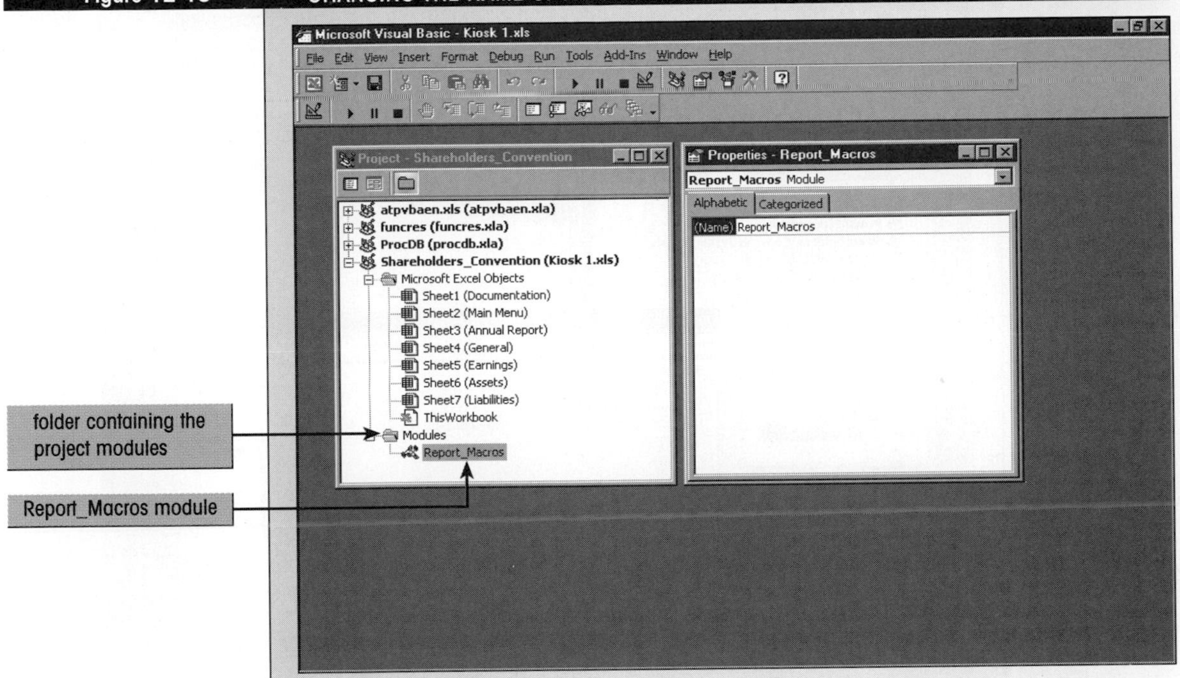

Having seen a little of the structure of your project and how to modify its properties, you're ready to start looking at the macro you created for your Shareholders_Convention project. You'll view the macro in the Code window.

The Code Window

When you want to view the contents of the macros in your project modules, you use the Code window. The **Code window** displays the Visual Basic macro code associated with any item in the Project Explorer. You saw the Code window when you first opened the Visual Basic Editor. You'll reopen it now.

To view the Code window:

1. Click **View** on the menu bar, and click **Code**. Figure 12-14 shows the contents of the Code window for the Report_Macros module. The Code window contains lines of Visual Basic code that make up your Annual_Report macro.

Figure 12-14 VIEWING THE CODE WINDOW

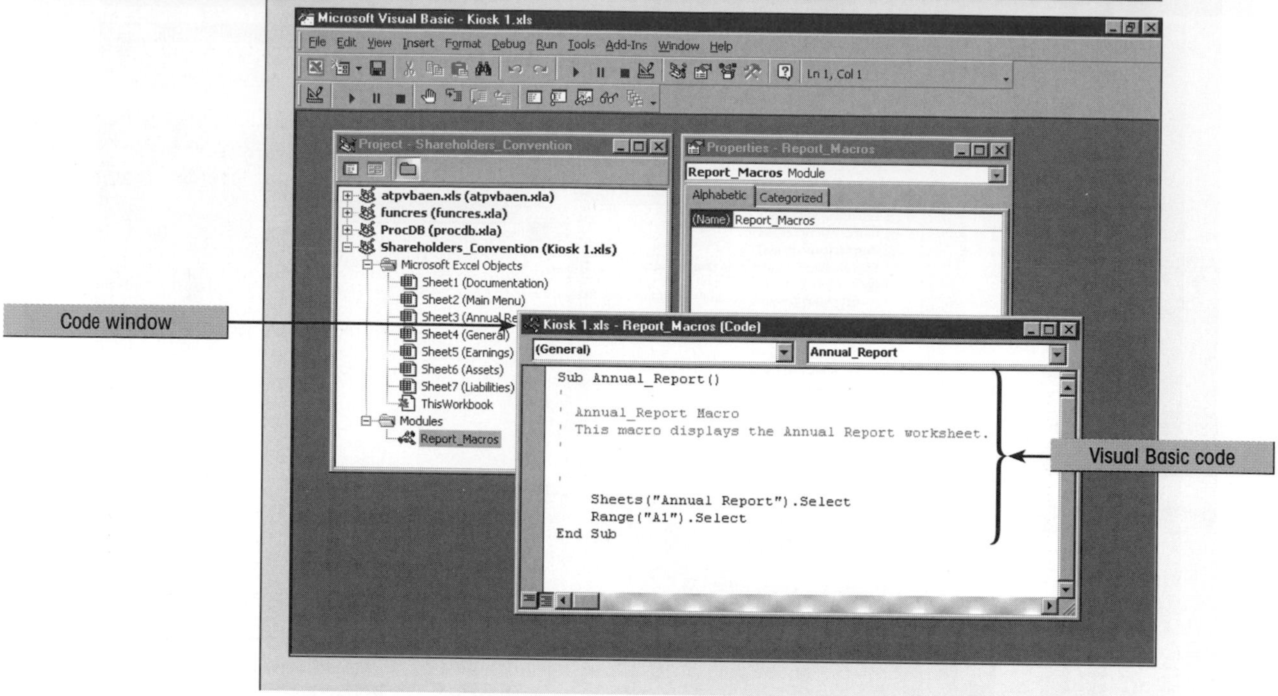

Now that you've viewed the Code window, you can use it to look closely at the contents of your macro. To understand the code, you'll first need to learn about Visual Basic procedures.

Working with Visual Basic Sub Procedures

A macro in Visual Basic is called a **procedure**. Visual Basic supports three kinds of procedures: sub procedures, function procedures, and property procedures. A **sub procedure** performs an action on your project or workbook, such as formatting a cell or displaying a chart. A **function procedure** returns a value. You would use a function procedure if you wanted to create a customized function to use in your worksheets. A **property procedure** is a more advanced subject used when you want to create customized properties for the objects in your project.

Because your project deals with displaying different worksheets within the Kiosk workbook, which are all actions, you'll be creating only sub procedures.

Introducing Sub Procedures

In order to write a sub procedure, you'll have to know a few basic rules of Visual Basic syntax. Syntax refers to the set of rules specifying how you must enter certain commands so that Visual Basic will interpret them correctly, much like grammatical syntax rules make our sentences understandable to others. If you use improper syntax, Excel will not be able to run your macro, or it might run it incorrectly. The general syntax for a Visual Basic sub procedure is:

```
Sub Procedure_Name( )
     <Visual Basic commands and comments>
End Sub
```

Here, *Procedure_Name* is the name of the sub procedure or macro, such as Annual_Report. The parentheses after the procedure name can contain any information passed to the procedure that will control its operation. Many of the procedures you'll write in this tutorial will not require any information in the parentheses, but the parentheses are required anyway.

After the Sub Procedure_Name( ) line, you enter either commands that perform certain tasks or comments that document the procedure's use. The *End Sub* command is always the last line in a sub procedure and tells Visual Basic to stop running the procedure. To see an example of a sub procedure, look at the Annual_Report macro you created earlier.

Figure 12-15 ANNUAL_REPORT SUB PROCEDURE

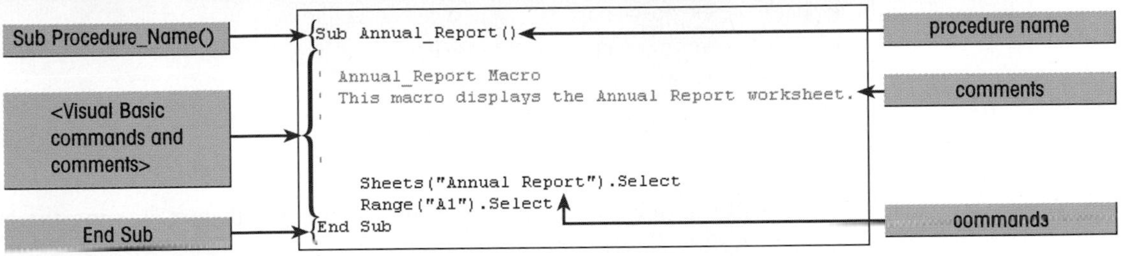

Figure 12-15 shows the Visual Basic code for the Annual_Report macro. The name of the macro, Annual_Report, is also the name of the procedure, and appears in the Sub Procedure_Name( ) line. Below that, the sub procedure displays the comments you entered in the Macro Recorder dialog box (see Figure 12-3.) **Comments** are statements that describe the behavior of the procedure, they begin with an apostrophe and usually appear in green type. After the comments, the procedure lists the Visual Basic commands needed to first select and display the Annual Report worksheet, and then to select cell A1 on that worksheet. The End Sub line signals the end of the Annual_Report sub procedure.

If you want more information about sub procedures or about any of the commands in the Annual_Report macro, you can open online Help the same way you did earlier in the Properties window.

To view additional information about sub procedures:

1. Select the word **Sub** in the first line of the Annual_Report macro.
2. Press the **F1** key. The Visual Basic Editor displays a Help window with additional information on sub procedures and the Sub statement.
3. Click the **Close** box to close the Visual Basic Help window.

You can use the F1 key to get Help on most of the commands and statements you'll see in the Code window.

Now that you are familiar with the structure of your Annual_Report macro, you'll create another, similar macro by copying and pasting that code.

Creating a Sub Procedure Using Copy and Paste

The Annual_Report macro you created displays the Annual Report worksheet. But once they use your macro, they will need another sub procedure that will take them back to the Main Menu worksheet where all of your command buttons will be placed. This code will be very similar to the Annual_Report sub procedure. Without learning the details of Visual Basic commands in the Annual_Report macro (you'll do that in the next session), you can copy the macro lines and adapt them to create the new macro. You'll begin by adding a new sub procedure to the Report_Macros module, and then copying and pasting the code from the Annual_Report sub procedure into it. You'll then edit that macro, replacing the occurrences of the text, "Annual Report" with "Main Menu."

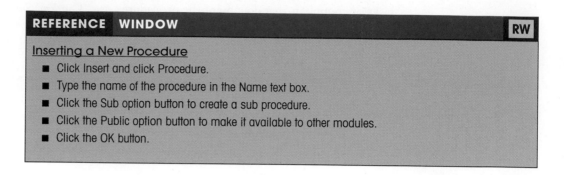

REFERENCE WINDOW RW

Inserting a New Procedure

- Click Insert and click Procedure.
- Type the name of the procedure in the Name text box.
- Click the Sub option button to create a sub procedure.
- Click the Public option button to make it available to other modules.
- Click the OK button.

You'll call the new sub procedure Main_Menu. You'll start creating the new sub procedure by using the Insert Procedure command.

To insert a new procedure into the Code window:

1. If necessary, click the title bar of the Code window to activate it.
2. Click **Insert** on the menu bar, and then click **Procedure**. The Add Procedure dialog box opens, where you'll enter the name and type of procedure you're creating.
3. Type **Main_Menu** in the Name text box to assign a title to the macro. See Figure 12-16.

Figure 12-16 INSERTING A NEW PROCEDURE INTO A MODULE

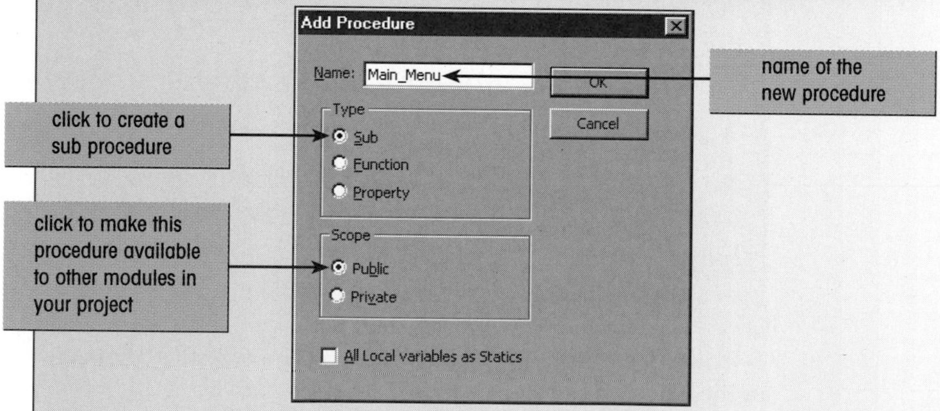

4. Make sure that the Sub and Public option buttons are selected, to indicate that you want a sub procedure that will be available to all modules in this project.
5. Click the **OK** button.

Figure 12-17 THE NEW MAIN_MENU SUB PROCEDURE

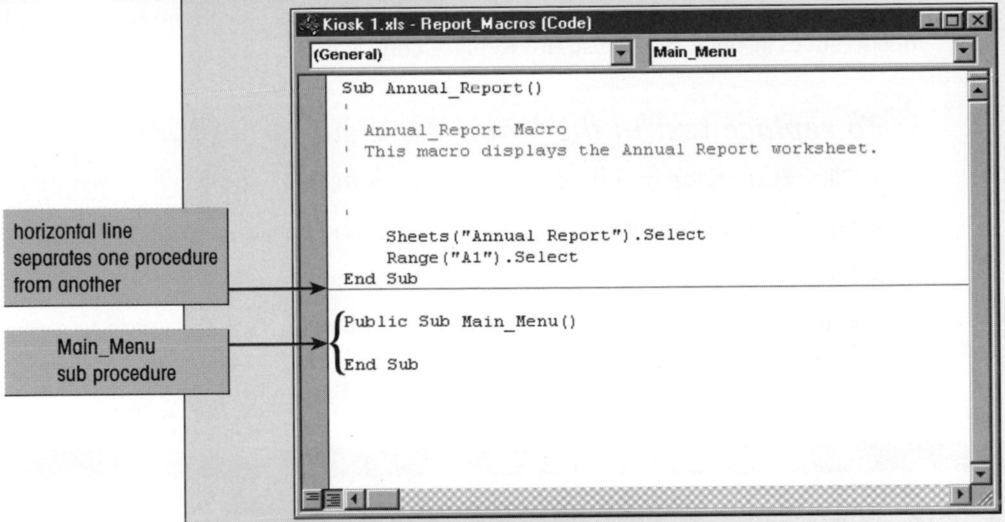

The Code window displays the beginning and ending lines of the new sub procedure. A horizontal line separates the new procedure from the first one. See Figure 12-17.

The first line of code indicates that the macro is public, and then shows the name you gave the macro in the Add Procedure dialog box. The Annual_Report procedure is also public, even though the text, "Public" is not shown. All procedures are considered public unless prefixed with the term, "Private."

With the new procedure created, you are ready to copy the Visual Basic code from the Annual_Report sub procedure into the Main_Menu sub procedure. You add, delete, and replace text in the Code window the same way you do in a word processor.

To copy and paste the Visual Basic code:

1. Scroll up the Code window until you can see the entire Annual_Report macro.
2. Select the code between the line that says "Sub Annual_Report()" and the line that says "End Sub."
3. Click the **Copy** button on the toolbar.
4. Scroll down and click the blank line in the middle of the Main_Menu sub procedure.
5. Click the **Paste** button. The Visual Basic code is pasted into the Main_Menu sub procedure.

   TROUBLE? You might want to enlarge the Code window to make it easier to copy, paste, and view your Visual Basic code.

Your next task is to replace the occurrences of "Annual Report" and "Annual_Report" with "Main Menu" and "Main_Menu". You can do this by selecting the old text and typing over it with the new text, or you can use the editor's Replace command to replace all the occurrences at once. You'll use the Replace command.

To replace text in the Main_Menu sub procedure:

1. Click **Edit** on the menu bar, and then click **Replace**.
2. Type **Annual Report** in the Find What text box, and then press the **Tab** key.
3. Type **Main Menu** in the Replace With text box.
4. In the Search section, click the **Current Procedure** option button to replace only the occurrences of the words "Annual Report" in the current procedure (not in the entire module or project). See Figure 12-18.

Figure 12-18 COMPLETED REPLACE DIALOG BOX

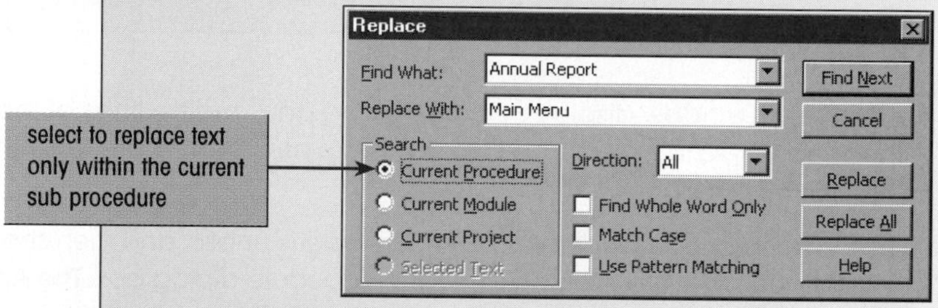

5. Click the **Replace All** button. Excel indicates that two occurrences of the text, "Annual Report" have been replaced.

   TROUBLE? If the message says that four occurrences have been replaced, you have accidentally changed all the occurrences in the module. To restore the changed occurrences, click the Undo button.

6. Click the **OK** button.

   Now replace the occurrences of the word "Annual_Report" with "Main_Menu."

7. Type **Annual_Report** in the Find What text box, press the **Tab** key, and then type **Main_Menu** in the Replace With text box.
8. Verify that the **Current Procedure** option button is selected and click the **Replace All** button. One occurrence of the word "Annual_Report" is replaced.
9. Click the **OK** button, and then click the **Cancel** button to close the Replace dialog box. Figure 12-19 displays the Main_Menu sub procedure after the text replacement.

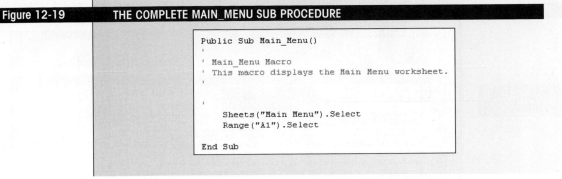

Figure 12-19 **THE COMPLETE MAIN_MENU SUB PROCEDURE**

```
Public Sub Main_Menu()
'
' Main_Menu Macro
' This macro displays the Main Menu worksheet.
'

'
    Sheets("Main Menu").Select
    Range("A1").Select

End Sub
```

Using copy, paste, find, and replace, you've created a new procedure in the Shareholders_ Convention project. Because you've replaced the name "Annual Report" with "Main Menu," this new procedure should display the contents of the Main Menu worksheet when you run it. You decide to return to Excel and test the new macro. In Excel, you'll assign this procedure to a button on the Annual Report worksheet, and run the macro by clicking the button.

To close the Visual Basic Editor and return to Excel:

1. Click **File** on the menu bar, and then click **Close and Return to Microsoft Excel**. The Visual Basic Editor closes, and the Annual Report worksheet appears. Notice that the second worksheet in the workbook has been changed from "Menu" to "Main Menu," a change you instituted earlier from the Project Explorer window of the Visual Basic Editor.

Now using the techniques you used earlier, you'll add a button to the Annual Report worksheet and assign the newly created Main_Menu macro to it.

To create the Main Menu button:

1. If necessary, click the **Annual Report** worksheet tab to display the worksheet. You should also redisplay the Forms toolbar.
2. Click the **Command Button** tool  on the Forms toolbar, and drag the pointer over the range **E1:G2**, and then release the mouse button.
3. Click **Main_Menu** in the Macro Name list box, and click the **OK** button.

   Now you'll enter the text that will appear on the button.
4. Type **Return to the Main Menu** and click cell **A1**.

   The "Return to the Main Menu" button appears on the Annual Report sheet. See Figure 12-20.

Figure 12-20 THE RETURN TO THE MAIN MENU BUTTON PLACED ON THE WORKSHEET

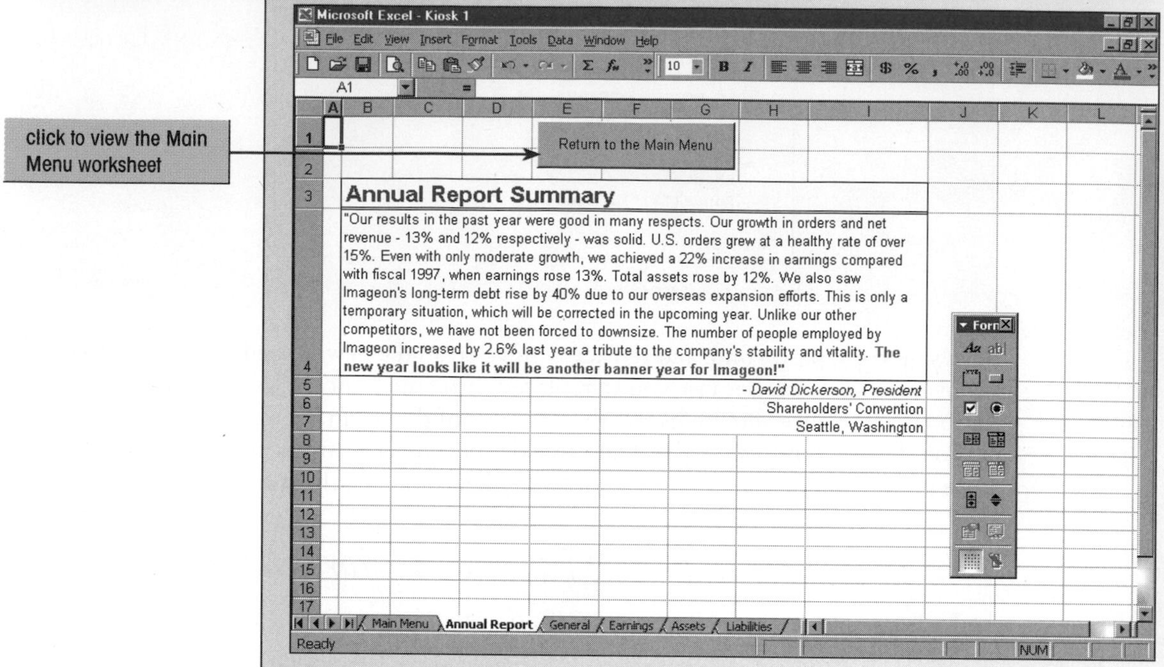

5. Close the **Forms** toolbar.

6. Click the **Return to the Main Menu** button to confirm that it displays the Main Menu worksheet, with cell A1 selected.

So far, you've added two macros to the Kiosk workbook: one using the Macro Recorder and the other using the Visual Basic Editor. You can use the Visual Basic Editor to add other procedures to the workbook to display the remaining worksheets. Before proceeding though, you decide to save the workbook and show it to Steve to discuss your progress and get his comments.

To save your changes:

1. Return to the **Documentation** sheet so that the next time you open this worksheet, this sheet appears.

2. Press **Ctrl + Home** to return to cell A1, and save and close the workbook.

Session 12.1 Quick Check

1. What are five basic steps you should follow in planning and creating your customized application?
2. Describe what each of the following is used for:
   a. Project Explorer
   b. Properties window
   c. Code window
3. Define the following terms:
   a. project
   b. object
   c. property
   d. module
   e. syntax
4. How would you get Help on a particular property listed in the Properties window?
5. What are the three types of procedures in Visual Basic?
6. Describe the syntax of a sub procedure.
7. Why would a project contain several modules?

You have begun to create the workbook that will make it easy for Imageon stockholders to view company financial information at the annual shareholders' conference. You have created a simple macro using the Macro Recorder and attached the macro to a button you placed on a worksheet. You've opened the Visual Basic Editor and learned about some of the editor's features. You've also been introduced to the Visual Basic programming language and have created your first Visual Basic sub procedure by copying and pasting code from one procedure into another. In the next session you'll learn more about the Visual Basic programming language. You'll see how the Visual Basic Editor helps you write your own procedures, and you'll learn how to create a sub procedure that asks the user for information.

SESSION 12.2

In this session you'll learn about the fundamentals of the Visual Basic programming language. You'll learn how the Visual Basic Editor can help enter Visual Basic code without errors. Finally, you'll learn how to create a macro that prompts the user for input and uses that information to determine what tasks the macro will perform.

Introducing **Visual Basic**

You've completed the first stage of the Kiosk workbook application, in which users can easily move back and forth between the Main Menu and Annual Report sheets. To unlock the power of Visual Basic and the Visual Basic Editor, you'll learn more about the elements and structure of the Visual Basic language. There are four terms you should know to understand Visual Basic: objects, properties, methods, and variables. After you learn the meaning of each term, you'll apply this knowledge to the Visual Basic commands you created in the Annual_Report macro. Then you'll use it as a basis for creating more sophisticated procedures.

Objects

Visual Basic is an **object-oriented programming language**, which means that it performs tasks by manipulating objects. An object can be almost anything in Excel, from a single cell or worksheet to the Excel application itself. Each object has an **object name**. Figure 12-21 lists some of the objects often used in writing Visual Basic programs.

Figure 12-21 OBJECTS AND THEIR VISUAL BASIC OBJECT NAMES

OBJECT	VISUAL BASIC OBJECT NAME
A cell in a worksheet	Range
A worksheet in a workbook	Worksheet
A workbook	Workbook
The Microsoft Excel Application	Application
A chart in the workbook	Chart
A Visual Basic project	VBProject

Objects are commonly grouped into collections, which are themselves objects, called **collection objects**. For example, a sheet in your workbook is an object, as is the collection of all the sheets in the workbook. Some of the object collections and their object names that you'll use frequently in your Visual Basic programs are shown in Figure 12-22.

Figure 12-22 OBJECT COLLECTIONS

OBJECT COLLECTION	VISUAL BASIC OBJECT NAME
The chart sheets in the workbook	Charts
The worksheets in the workbook	Worksheets
Sheets of any kind in the workbook	Sheets
Currently open workbooks	Workbooks
Currently open projects	VBProjects

When you want to refer to a particular object in a collection, you use either the name of the object or its position in the collection. For example, in the Kiosk 1 workbook, the second worksheet is the Main Menu worksheet. If you wrote a Visual Basic program that modified that object, you could refer to it as Sheets("Main Menu"), which refers to the name of the object within the collection of worksheets (see Figure 12-19 for example.) Or you could call it Sheets(2), where 2 refers to its position as the second sheet in the collection of worksheets.

Most of your Visual Basic programs modify objects. You modify objects by either changing the object's properties or by applying a method to the object; you'll learn more about properties and methods in the next sections.

Properties

Properties are the attributes that distinguish an object, such as its name, and whether it's active, visible, or selected. In the last session, you used the Project Explorer and the Properties window to change the value of some of the properties in your project. For example, you changed the Name property of the Menu worksheet object to "Main_Menu." Figure 12-23 displays some Visual Basic objects and the properties associated with them.

Figure 12-23 OBJECTS AND THEIR PROPERTIES

OBJECT	PROPERTIES	DESCRIPTION
Range	Formula Name Value	The formula entered into a cell The name assigned to the cell range The value entered into a cell
Worksheet	Name Visible	The name of the worksheet Whether the worksheet is hidden or not
Workbook	HasPassword Name Saved	Whether the workbook is password protected The name of the workbook Whether the workbook has been saved
Sheets	Count	The number of sheets of any kind in the workbook
Application	ActiveCell ActiveSheet ActiveWorkbook Selection	The cell that is active in the worksheet The sheet currently active in the workbook The workbook that is currently active within Excel The selected object

This list is only a small sample of the vast number of objects and properties available to you in Visual Basic programs.

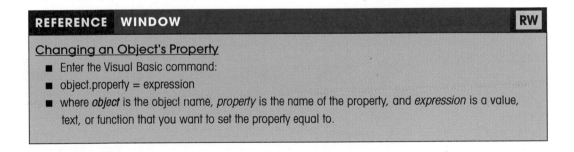

REFERENCE WINDOW RW

Changing an Object's Property

- Enter the Visual Basic command:
- object.property = expression
- where *object* is the object name, *property* is the name of the property, and *expression* is a value, text, or function that you want to set the property equal to.

To change the property of an object, you use the following syntax, or structure, in your Visual Basic command:

```
object.property = expression
```

In this case, *object* is the object name, *property* is the name of the property, and *expression* is a value that you want to assign to the property. Figure 12-24 shows three examples of Visual Basic statements that use this syntax. Note that text values and formulas must always be enclosed within double quotes.

Figure 12-24 EXAMPLES OF "OBJECT.PROPERTY = EXPRESSION" COMMANDS

CODE	INTERPRETATION
Worksheets("Menu").Name = "Main Menu"	Change the Name property of the "Menu" worksheet to "Main Menu," renaming the worksheet.
Range("A1").Value = 23	Change the Value property of cell A1 to 23
Range("A5").Formula = "=SUM(A1:A4)"	Change the Formula property of cell A5, to calculate the sum of cells A1:A4.

Note that the first example from Figure 12-24 changes the Name property of the Menu worksheet object to "Main Menu." You did this in the last session when you changed the name of the worksheet using the Properties window. This is how you would write the command to do the same thing in Visual Basic.

You can also use an object property statement to turn a property on or off, as in the following Visual Basic command:

```
Sheets("Documentation").Visible = False
```

This command hides the Documentation worksheet from the user by making the Visible property "False" (that is, hidden). To make the worksheet visible again, you would use this command:

```
Sheets("Documentation").Visible = True
```

Properties are one way to control objects; another way is with methods.

Methods

A **method** is an action that can be performed on an object. For example, one of the things you can do to a workbook is close it, so "Close" is a method that goes with the Workbook object. Figure 12-25 shows some of the objects and methods used in Visual Basic.

Figure 12-25 OBJECTS AND THEIR METHODS

OBJECT	METHODS	DESCRIPTION
Range	Clear Copy Merge	Clears all formulas and values in the range Copies values of the range into the Clipboard Merges the cells in the range
Worksheet	Delete Select	Deletes the worksheet Selects (and displays) the worksheet
Workbook	Close Protect Save	Closes the workbook Protects the workbook Saves the workbook
Chart	Copy Select Delete	Copies the chart Selects the chart Deletes the chart
Charts	Select	Selects chart sheets in the workbook
Worksheets	Select	Selects worksheets in the workbook

REFERENCE WINDOW RW

Applying a Method to an Object

- Enter the Visual Basic command:

  `object.method`

  where *object* is the object name and *method* is the method you want to apply to the object

The syntax for applying a method to an object is:

```
object.method
```

Here, *object* is the name of the object, and *method* is the method that you want to apply. Figure 12-26 shows three examples of methods applied to objects:

Figure 12-26 EXAMPLES OF "OBJECT.METHOD" COMMANDS

CODE	INTERPRETATION
Sheets("Main Menu").Delete	Apply the Delete method to the "Main Menu" worksheet, removing the worksheet.
Range("A1:B10").Clear	Apply the Clear method, clearing values from cells A1:B10
Workbooks("Kiosk 1").Save	Apply the Save method to the "Kiosk 1" workbook, saving the workbook file.

Some methods require a **parameter**, a piece of information that controls how the method is applied. For example, to apply the SaveAs method in order to save a workbook, you need to supply the workbook's name. The value that the user enters for the parameter is the **parameter value**. Some methods require more than one parameter value. The syntax for methods that require parameters is:

```
object.method(parameter values)
```

Figure 12-27 shows some examples of methods that require parameter values:

Figure 12-27 EXAMPLES OF "OBJECT.METHOD(PARAMETER VALUES)" COMMANDS

CODE	INTERPRETATION
Workbooks("Kiosk 1").SaveAs("Kiosk 2")	Apply the SaveAs method to the Kiosk 1 workbook, saving it as "Kiosk 2."
Range("A1").AddComment("Total Assets")	Apply the AddComment method to cell A1, adding the comment, "Total Assets" to the cell.
Workbooks("Kiosk 1").Protect("Glencoe")	Apply the Protect method to the Kiosk 1 workbook, protecting the contents of the workbook with the password "Glencoe."

With what you've learned about how Visual Basic works with objects, properties, and methods, you can interpret the Annual_Report sub procedure you created in the last session. See Figure 12-28.

Figure 12-28 INTERPRETING THE ANNUAL_REPORT MACRO

CODE	INTERPRETATION
Sheets("Annual Report").Select	Apply the Select method to the Annual Report worksheet in order to display the worksheet.
Range("A1").Select	Apply the Select method to cell A1.

Now that you've been introduced to objects, properties, and methods, the last major area you'll explore is variables.

Variables

Occasionally you will want your Visual Basic procedures to retrieve and store information. You do this with variables. A **variable** is a named storage location containing data that you can retrieve and modify while the program is running. Every variable is identified by a **variable name**. For example, you could create a variable named "Workforce" and use it to store the total number of people employed by Imageon. You could create a variable named "Company" and use it to store the company's name. You could also create a variable named "Wbook" and use it to store the name of the currently open workbook. All of these items are considered variables because they can change, or assume different values, over time.

The Visual Basic syntax for storing data in a variable is:

```
variable = expression
```

Here, *variable* is the name of the variable that will store the information and *expression* is a value, text, a function, or a property. Figure 12-29 shows a few sample Visual Basic statements that use variables.

Figure 12-29 EXAMPLES OF VISUAL BASIC COMMANDS THAT ASSIGN VALUES TO VARIABLES

CODE	INTERPRETATION
Workforce = 927	Set the value of the Workforce variable to 927.
Sheetname = "Main Menu"	Set the value of the Sheetname variable to "Main Menu".
Assets = Range("B22").Value	Set the value of the Assets variable to whatever value is stored in cell B22.

Once you've created a variable and given it a value, you can assign that value to an object's property. This is one of the more common tasks in a Visual Basic program. Earlier you changed the name of the Menu worksheet to "Main Menu." You could also do this using a variable, as shown in the following set of Visual Basic steps:

```
Sheetname = "Main Menu"
Sheets("Menu").Name = Sheetname
```

The first line stores the text "Main Menu" in the variable Sheetname, and the second line changes the Name property of the Menu worksheet to equal the value of Sheetname. The end result is that the name of the Menu worksheet is changed to "Main Menu".

You've finished reviewing some of the basic concepts of the Visual Basic programming language. Now you'll put these principles to work by enhancing the macros in the Kiosk 1 workbook.

Retrieving Information from the User

Steve has looked over your first version of the Kiosk workbook. He's pleased with what he's seen so far. In this version of the workbook, he wants you to provide a button that will let users display one of the workbook's financial worksheets. The four financial worksheets in the Kiosk workbook are described in Figure 12-30.

Figure 12-30 FINANCIAL REPORTS IN THE KIOSK 2 WORKBOOK

WORKSHEET NAME	DESCRIPTION
General	Table of general financial data
Earnings	Table of earnings and net revenue
Assets	Table of current and long-term company assets
Liabilities	Table of liabilities and long-term debts

Steve hopes to add more financial reports and charts to the workbook before the convention, and he doesn't want to clutter the main menu with buttons for each worksheet. So he wants you to create a single button that prompts the user for the name of the worksheet, and then acting on that information displays the appropriate sheet. Steve's plan for the macro is shown in Figure 12-31.

Figure 12-31 STEVE'S PLAN FOR THE FINANCIAL_REPORTS MACRO

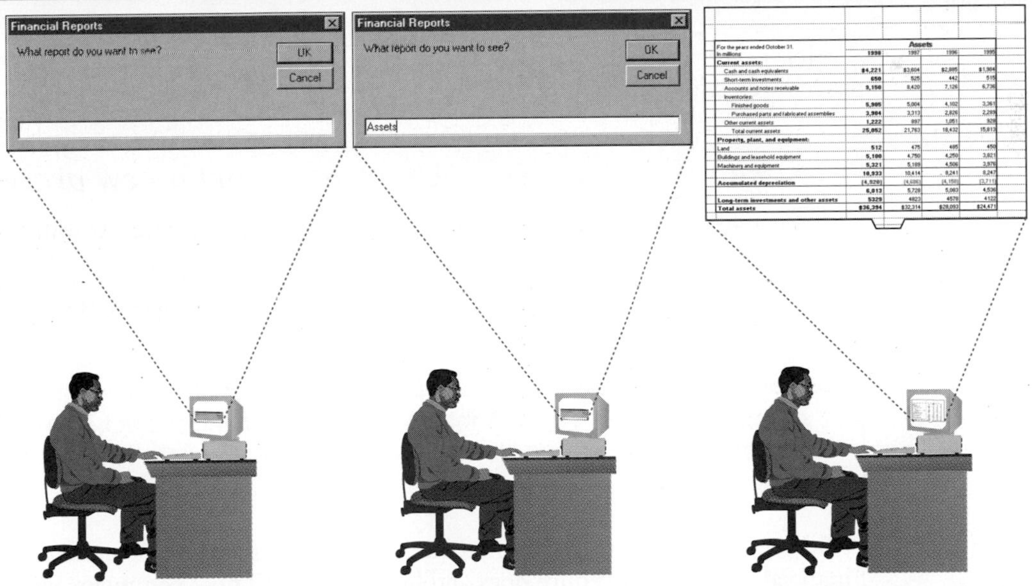

1) User is prompted for the name of a financial report.

2) User enters the report name.

3) Report appears on the computer monitor.

To create a procedure like this, you'll need a Visual Basic command that prompts users for information and stores the information they type in a variable for later use in the program.

To practice what you've learned about Visual Basic, you'll create that procedure from scratch, using only the Code window in the Visual Basic Editor. This will also give you a chance to see how the Visual Basic Editor helps you write error-free code.

First, you'll open the Kiosk 1 workbook. In other tutorials in this book, you revised previously saved versions of a workbook using the same workbook name. When you're working with Visual Basic, however, it's a good idea to save later versions of your workbook under a new name. Then you can easily repeat a session, without having to redo all the steps in the tutorial. Also, if you make a mistake, it's easier to go back to a version of your program that was error-free. Here, you'll resave the Kiosk 1 workbook from the last session as Kiosk 2.

To open and save the Kiosk 1 workbook:

1. If you took a break after the last session, make sure Excel is running. Open the **Kiosk 1** workbook from the Tutorial folder for Tutorial.12 of your Data Disk.
2. If you are reopening the workbook, and you see a dialog box about macros, click the **Enable Macros** button.

   TROUBLE? Some viruses work within macros and attack Excel workbooks. The Enable Macros message informs you of the existence of these kinds of viruses. If you open a workbook that you are sure does not contain macros, but you see this message anyway, the file may have been infected with a macro virus. If this happens, you should avoid opening the workbook and contact either the person who sent you the workbook or your technical support person for ways of removing the virus. If your worksheet does contain macros, and it has come to you from a trustworthy source, click the Enable Macros button.

3. Save the workbook as **Kiosk 2**.
4. Enter **Kiosk 2** in the Workbook box in cell B7 of the Documentation worksheet.

First you'll create a new procedure called Financial_Reports, and then document the procedure using comment lines.

To open the Visual Basic Editor and start a new procedure:

1. Press **Alt+F11** on your keyboard. The Visual Basic Editor opens with the same windows you worked with at the end of Session 1.
2. Click the Code window title bar to activate it, click **Insert** on the menu bar, and click **Procedure**.
3. Type **Financial_Reports** in the Name text box. Because you want to create a sub procedure that will be available to all modules in this project, make sure that the Sub and Public option buttons are selected, and then click the **OK** button.

Before attempting to write any code, you should first enter comments about what the Financial_Reports procedure does and how to use it. These comments will document your application so anyone else modifying it can easily learn its purpose. The Macro Recorder did this for you automatically in the last session.

To add comments to the Financial_Reports macro:

1. Click the **Maximize** box to maximize the Code window in the Visual Basic Editor display area.
2. If it is not already selected, click the blank line between the Public Sub statement and the End Sub statement.

3. Type **'Financial_Reports Macro** and press the **Enter** key. Like all comment lines, the comment text appears in green type.

   TROUBLE? If you do not start the line with an apostrophe, Visual Basic will not interpret the line as a comment. Do not type an apostrophe at the end of the line. If you get an error message that Visual Basic expected a particular statement, you most likely forgot to type the starting apostrophe.

4. Continue entering the following comment lines in the Code window. Notice that the first and the fourth lines contain only apostrophes, which create blank lines in your comments.

```
'
'This macro prompts the user to enter a worksheet name.
'The macro then opens the worksheet with that name in
'the workbook.
'
'For use at the Shareholders' Convention.
```

5. Press the **Enter** key after the last comment line.

   Figure 12-32 shows the Financial_Reports macro with the comments you have entered.

Figure 12-32 COMMENTS IN THE FINANCIAL_REPORTS SUB PROCEDURE

```
Public Sub Financial_Reports()
'Financial_Reports Macro
'
'This macro prompts the user to enter a worksheet name.
'The macro then opens the worksheet with that name in
'the workbook.
'
'For use at the Shareholders' Convention.

End Sub
```

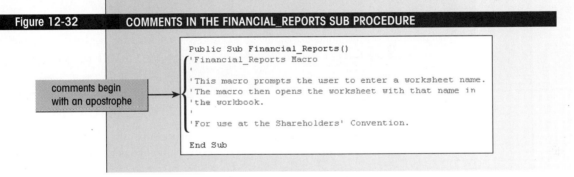

comments begin with an apostrophe

Now that you have entered the comments, you are ready to enter a command that opens a dialog box, prompting the user for information, and storing that information in a variable. To do this, you'll need to use the InputBox function.

Entering the InputBox Function

As part of your macro, you want the Imageon stockholders to see a dialog box that asks them to type in the name of the financial statement that they want to see. When you want an easy way to prompt the user for information, you can create an input box by inserting the InputBox function into your Visual Basic program. A function in Visual Basic has the same syntax and purpose as a function you enter in a worksheet cell. The syntax for the InputBox function is:

```
variable = InputBox(Prompt,Title)
```

Here, *variable* is a variable whose value is set based on whatever the user enters into the input box, *Prompt* is the message you want to appear in the input box, *Title* is the text that appears in the title bar of the input box. Figure 12-33 displays the relationship between the InputBox function and the input box that Visual Basic will display to the user.

Figure 12-33 THE INPUTBOX FUNCTION

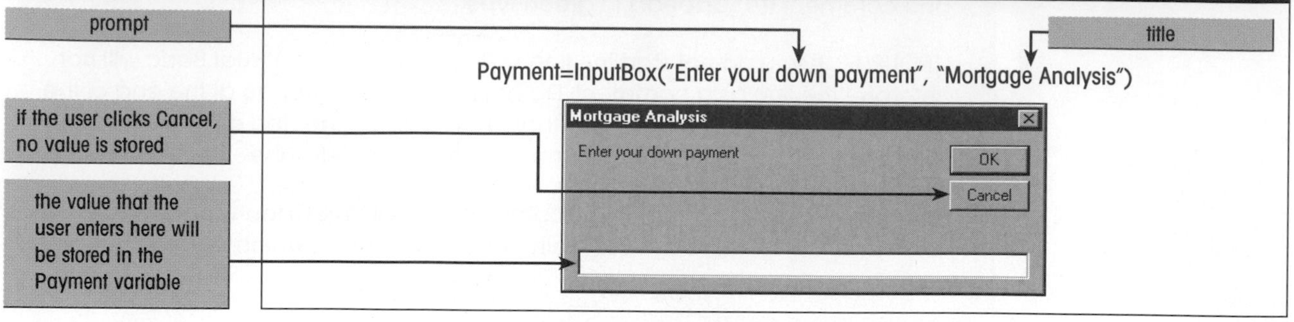
prompt
title
Payment=InputBox("Enter your down payment", "Mortgage Analysis")
Mortgage Analysis
Enter your down payment
OK
Cancel
if the user clicks Cancel, no value is stored
the value that the user enters here will be stored in the Payment variable

In this example that concerns mortgage payments, the results from the input box will be stored in a variable named "Payment." In your Financial_Reports sub procedure, you'll create an input box and store the value the user enters in a variable named "Sheetname."

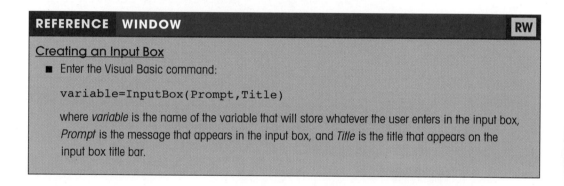

REFERENCE WINDOW RW

Creating an Input Box

- Enter the Visual Basic command:

  `variable=InputBox(Prompt,Title)`

  where *variable* is the name of the variable that will store whatever the user enters in the input box, *Prompt* is the message that appears in the input box, and *Title* is the title that appears on the input box title bar.

Try entering the InputBox function into your procedure now. When you do, you'll see how the Visual Basic Editor helps you use the correct syntax as you type.

To enter the InputBox function:

1. Type **Sheetname=InputBox(** but do *not* press the Enter key.

   As soon as you type the opening parenthesis, the editor displays the syntax of the InputBox function. See Figure 12-34.

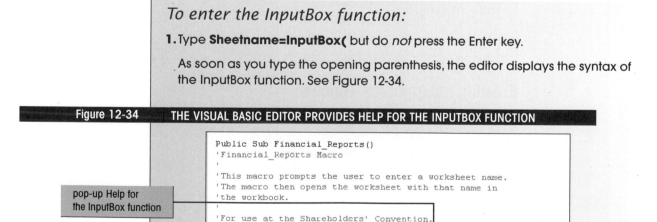

Figure 12-34 THE VISUAL BASIC EDITOR PROVIDES HELP FOR THE INPUTBOX FUNCTION

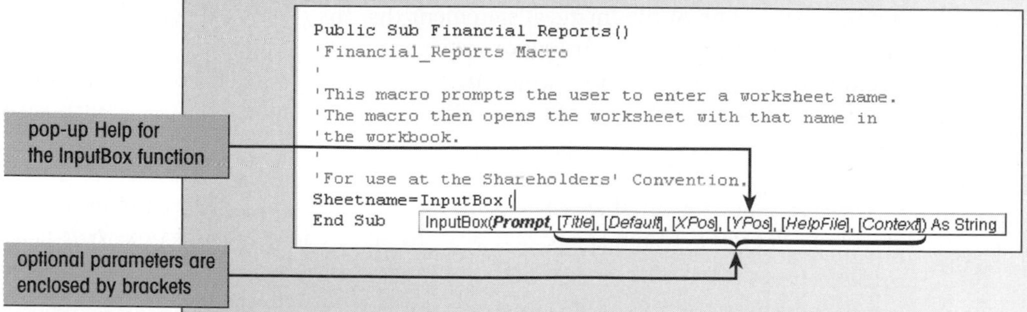
Public Sub Financial_Reports()
'Financial_Reports Macro
'
'This macro prompts the user to enter a worksheet name.
'The macro then opens the worksheet with that name in
'the workbook.
'
'For use at the Shareholders' Convention.
Sheetname=InputBox(
End Sub
InputBox(Prompt, [Title], [Default], [XPos], [YPos], [HelpFile], [Context]) As String
pop-up Help for the InputBox function
optional parameters are enclosed by brackets

If you can't remember the exact syntax of the function, the editor tells you which parameters to enter, and in what order. The parameter the editor expects you to enter next is in bold type; in this case, it expects you to enter the prompt. The editor displays optional parameters, such as the location of the input box in the document window, in brackets. You won't be using the location parameter in your InputBox function.

Continue entering the InputBox function, starting with the Prompt parameter enclosed in quotation marks. Your prompt will contain the names of the four worksheets; you want the user to type one of these names.

2. Type **"Type General, Earnings, Assets, or Liabilities"** but do *not* press the Enter key. As you finish entering the prompt in the input box, the Visual Basic Editor bolds the next parameter it is expecting, the Title parameter. This parameter is enclosed in brackets, so it's an optional parameter.

   You'll enter a title anyway to provide extra information to the user.

3. Press the **Spacebar**, type **"Name of Report")** and then press the **Enter** key to complete the line.

   TROUBLE? If you receive an error message and the line appears in red after you press the Enter key, you made a typing mistake in entering the command. Review the line you typed and compare it to the preceding instructions; verify that you typed everything correctly, including the quotation marks and the ending parenthesis.

So far, you have entered the InputBox function into your procedure, including a variable called Sheetname that will store the information the user types. Now you are ready to finish the macro. In the next line, you'll insert a command to select the worksheet specified in the Sheetname variable. To do this, you will use the Select method with a Sheets object. The Visual Basic Editor will again help you with the syntax.

To enter the Visual Basic line that selects a worksheet:

1. Type **Sheets(**. The editor recognizes that you've entered the name for an object collection and displays information indicating that it's now expecting a value such as the name of a worksheet or a number indicating its place in the order of sheets (1, 2, 3, etc.).

   You'll enter the sheet name, using the Sheetname variable.

2. Type **Sheetname). Select** and then press the **Enter** key.

   TROUBLE? If you get a message that reads "Compile Error: Expected: End of statement," you might have forgotten to type the period before "Select." Check your typing carefully.

Finally, enter the line telling Excel to select cell A1 in the worksheet. Once again, be prepared to take advantage of some of the editor's helpful hints.

To select the A1 cell:

1. Type **Range(**. The editor displays a pop-up box, indicating that it expects you to enter a cell reference.
2. Type **"A1")**.
3. After you type the period at the end of the statement, the editor displays a list of all of the properties or methods associated with a Range object. Properties are identified by the icon, and methods are indicated with the icon.

   You can select the property or method directly from the pop-up list box to enter it into your program.
4. Press the **S** key to display the Select method. See Figure 12-35.

Figure 12-35 PROPERTIES AND METHODS ASSOCIATED WITH RANGE OBJECTS

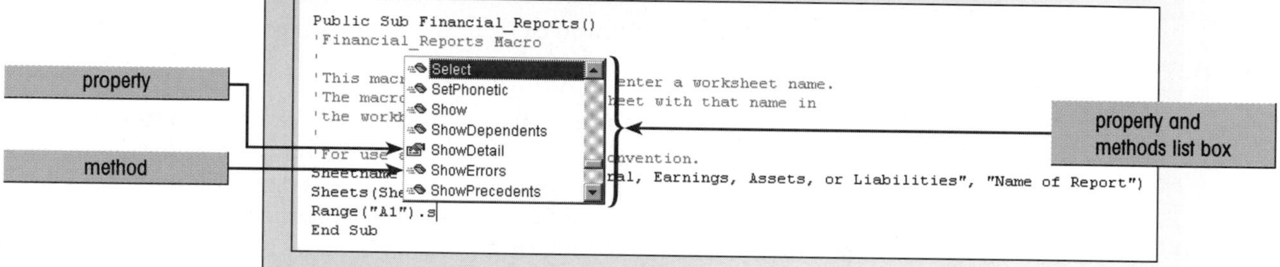

5. Double-click the **Select** method.

   The Select method is automatically appended to the Range object you entered.
6. Press the **Down Arrow** key to complete the line.

   Figure 12-36 shows the completed Financial_Reports sub procedure.

Figure 12-36 PROPERTIES AND METHODS ASSOCIATED WITH RANGE OBJECTS

```
Public Sub Financial_Reports()
'Financial_Reports Macro
'
'This macro prompts the user to enter a worksheet name.
'The macro then opens the worksheet with that name in
'the workbook.
'
'For use at the Shareholders' Convention.
Sheetname = InputBox("Type General, Earnings, Assets, or Liabilities", "Name of Report")
Sheets(Sheetname).Select
Range("A1").Select
End Sub
```

You've finished entering the Financial_Reports macro, including selecting the sheet that the user enters, and selecting cell A1 on that sheet. Now you'll create a button that will activate the macro, and then test your macro and input box by using them in the worksheet.

Using the Input Box

To test your new macro, you'll return to the Kiosk 2 workbook and add a new button to the Main Menu worksheet that activates the Financial_Reports sub procedure.

To create the View Financial Reports button:

1. Click **File** on the menu bar, and click **Close and Return to Microsoft Excel**.
2. Click the **Main Menu** sheet tab.

   Now you'll add the button that will activate your macro.
3. Display the **Forms** toolbar and use it to create a button in range of **D12:F13**. The button should be assigned to the **Financial_Reports** macro and contain the text, **View Financial Reports**.
4. Close the Forms toolbar and click cell **A1**. See Figure 12-37.

Figure 12-37 THE VIEW FINANCIAL REPORTS BUTTON

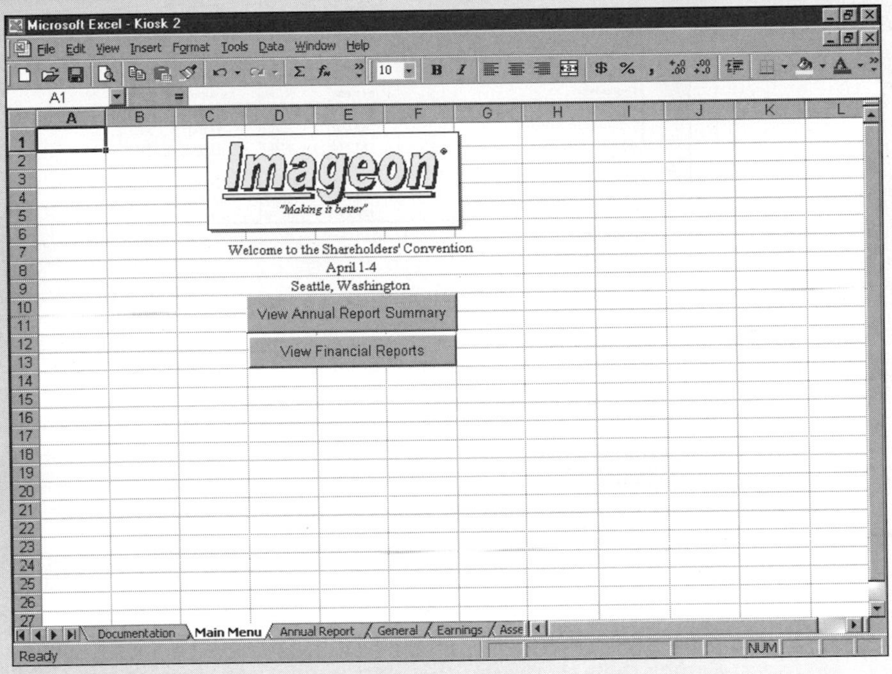

Now you'll test your macro by using it to display Imageon general financial data from the past few years.

To display the General worksheet:

1. Click the **View Financial Reports** button on the Main Menu worksheet. The dialog box you created in your macro opens, asking you to enter the name of the sheet you want to see.
2. Type **General** in the Name of Report input box. See Figure 12-38.

Figure 12-38 THE VIEW FINANCIAL REPORTS INPUT BOX

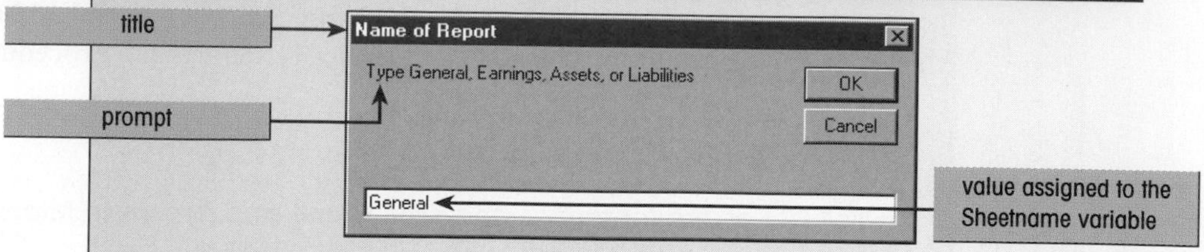

3. Click the **OK** button. Excel displays the General worksheet. See Figure 12-39.

Figure 12-39 GENERAL WORKSHEET WITH CELL A1 SELECTED

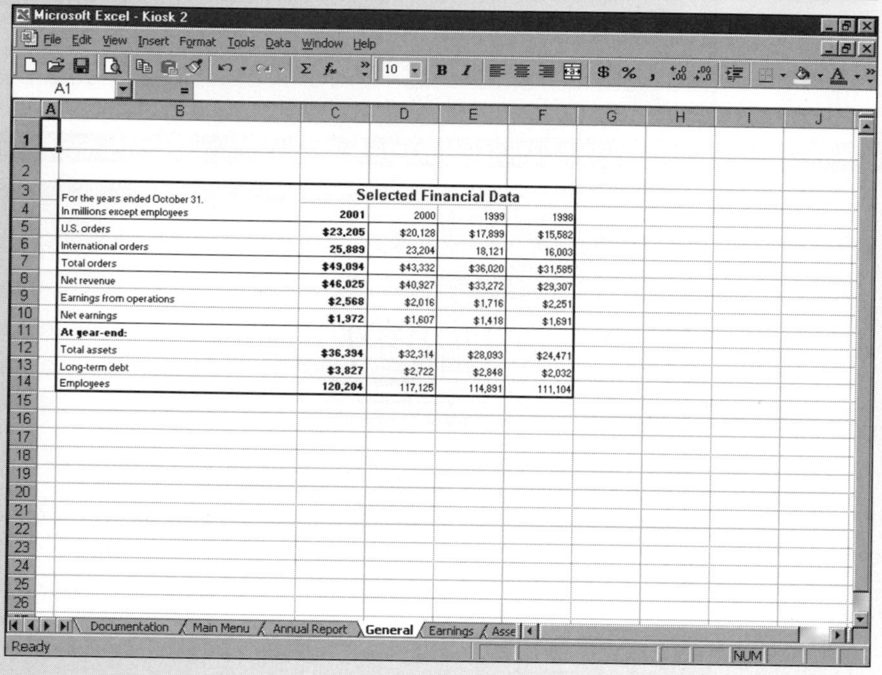

The macro works as you hoped it would. By entering the name of one of the four reports, the user can view the worksheet for that report. Your final task is to create buttons on each of the financial report worksheets that will take the user back to the Main Menu worksheet. Rather than recreating that button, you can copy and paste the button you created in the last session. Copying a button not only copies the button's image, but also copies the macro assigned to it. You'll try this now by pasting the "Return to Main Menu" button on the General worksheet and then on the remaining worksheets.

To copy and paste the Return to Main Menu button:

1. Click the **Annual Report** sheet tab.
2. Right-click the **Return to Main Menu** button.
3. Click **Copy** from the shortcut menu.
4. Click cell **A1** to deselect the button.
5. Click the **General** sheet tab and click cell **A1** if necessary to select it.

6. Click the **Paste** button and click cell **A1** again to deselect the button.
7. Click the **Return to the Main Menu** button to test it. The Main Menu worksheet should appear.
8. Paste the button into the other three financial report worksheets. Because you've already copied the button image, you do not have to recopy it. Each time you paste the button, deselect the pasted button by clicking cell **A1**.
9. Test your macro buttons by verifying that you can open each of the financial worksheets and return to the Main Menu from each one.

TROUBLE? If you type the name of one of the financial worksheets incorrectly, or click Cancel and receive a Runtime error or Subscript Out of Range error when trying to run the Financial_Reports macro, click the End button in the dialog box. You'll learn how to deal with problems of this kind in the next session.

You're finished working on the Financial_Reports macro for now. Save the Kiosk 2 workbook.

To save your changes:

1. Return to the **Documentation** sheet and click cell **A1**.
2. Save the workbook.

You'll show Steve what you've accomplished and then get his recommendations on what to do next.

Session 12.2 Quick Check

1. Define the following terms:
   a. object-oriented programming language
   b. collection object
   c. method
   d. parameter
   e. variable
2. What Visual Basic command would you enter to change the name of the Assets worksheet to "Assets Table"? (*Hint*: The object name is Sheets("Assets") and the name of the worksheet is contained in the Name property.)
3. What Visual Basic command would you enter to select the Assets worksheet?
4. What Visual Basic command would you enter to store the name of the Assets worksheet in a variable named "Sheetname"?
5. How do you enter comments into your Visual Basic procedures?
6. What are optional parameters and how are they displayed in the Visual Basic Editor's pop-up help?
7. What Visual Basic command would you enter to display an input box containing the prompt "Enter your last name", the text "Log In" in the title bar, and then save whatever the user entered into a variable named "Lastname"?

You've learned some of the fundamentals of Visual Basic and how to work with selected objects, properties, and methods. You've learned about variables and how to use them in your Visual Basic programs. You've created an input box that convention attendees will use to display the financial worksheets. In the next session you'll learn how to create procedures called control structures that "make decisions" based on the type of information the attendees enter. Finally, you'll learn how to create message boxes that will give attendees information describing what they should enter.

SESSION 12.3

In this session you'll learn about control structures that cause your macros to operate differently under different conditions. You'll learn how to create message boxes that provide directions for your users. Finally, you'll learn how to modify the toolbars and menus used by Excel and how to protect your workbook from unauthorized changes.

Introducing **Control Structures**

You've shown Steve the Kiosk 2 workbook that you completed in the last session. He was very impressed. He clicked on the View Financial Reports button and was able to quickly bring up the General financial report table. In response to the input box you created, he entered "Assets" and was able to view the Assets table. Unfortunately, when he tried to view the Liabilities table, he mistyped it as 'Libelities" and was confronted with the dialog box shown in Figure 12-40.

Figure 12-40 THE ERROR MESSAGE STEVE SEES AFTER HIS TYPING MISTAKE

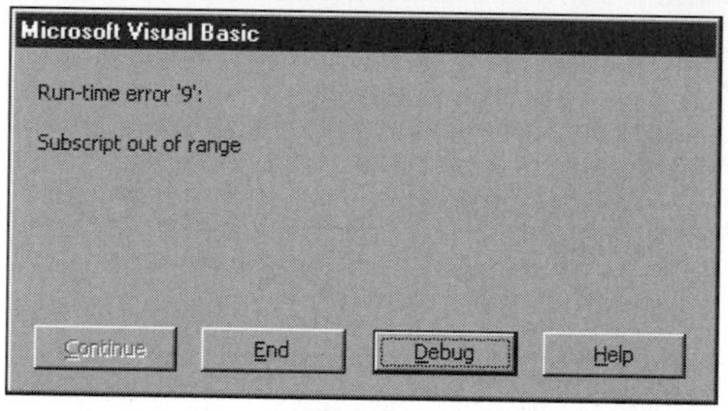

What happened? There's no worksheet named "Libelities" in the Kiosk 2 workbook, and when the Financial_Reports macro tried to select that worksheet, it failed to find it, which caused Visual Basic to display an error message. This is the last thing Steve wants to see happen at the shareholders' convention. He asks you if you can revise the macro so that it checks the user-entered value to make sure it is one of the four financial worksheets in the Kiosk workbook.

To do this, you have to create a **control structure**. A control structure is a series of commands that evaluates conditions in your program, and then directs the program to perform certain actions based on the status of those conditions. Figure 12-41 shows the kind of control structure that Steve has in mind for the Financial_Reports macro.

Figure 12-41 DIFFERENT CONDITIONS THAT MIGHT ARISE WHEN RUNNING THE FINANCIAL_REPORTS MACRO

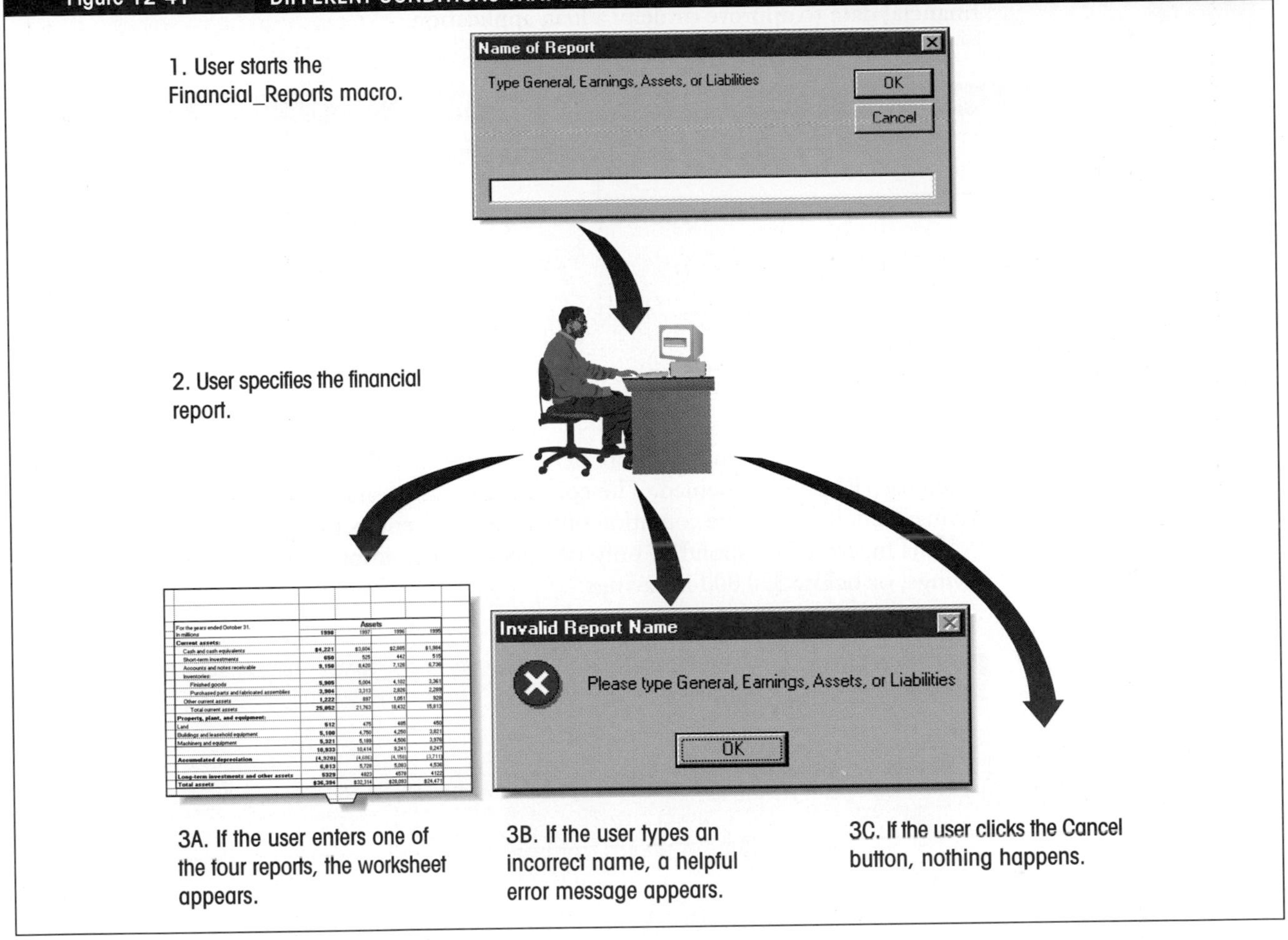
1. User starts the Financial_Reports macro.
Name of Report
Type General, Earnings, Assets, or Liabilities
OK
Cancel
2. User specifies the financial report.
Invalid Report Name
Please type General, Earnings, Assets, or Liabilities
OK
3A. If the user enters one of the four reports, the worksheet appears.
3B. If the user types an incorrect name, a helpful error message appears.
3C. If the user clicks the Cancel button, nothing happens.

In this control structure, the user will start the Financial_Reports macro by clicking the View Financial Reports button on the Main Menu worksheet of the Imageon workbook. The procedure will first ask for the name of the financial report, and then evaluate whatever the user enters. If the user enters one of the four worksheet names containing financial data, the program selects and displays that worksheet. However, if the user does not enter one of the four worksheet names, the program displays a message, telling the user what the acceptable entries are. If the user clicks the Cancel button instead of entering the name of a report, the input box closes and redisplays the Main Menu worksheet.

To adjust your macro to handle all three of these situations, you'll need to create a Visual Basic If-Then-Else control structure.

Using the If-Then-Else Control Structure

The most commonly used control structure in Visual Basic is the If-Then-Else control structure. In this structure, Visual Basic evaluates some conditions. IF those conditions are true, THEN Visual Basic runs a set of commands, or ELSE it will run a different set of commands. The syntax for an If-Then-Else control structure is:

```
If <Condition> Then
        <Visual Basic statements>
Else
        <Visual Basic statements>
End If
```

Figure 12-42 shows an example of an If-Then-Else control structure that evaluates financial data to approve or deny a loan application.

Figure 12-42 AN EXAMPLE OF AN IF-THEN-ELSE CONTROL STRUCTURE

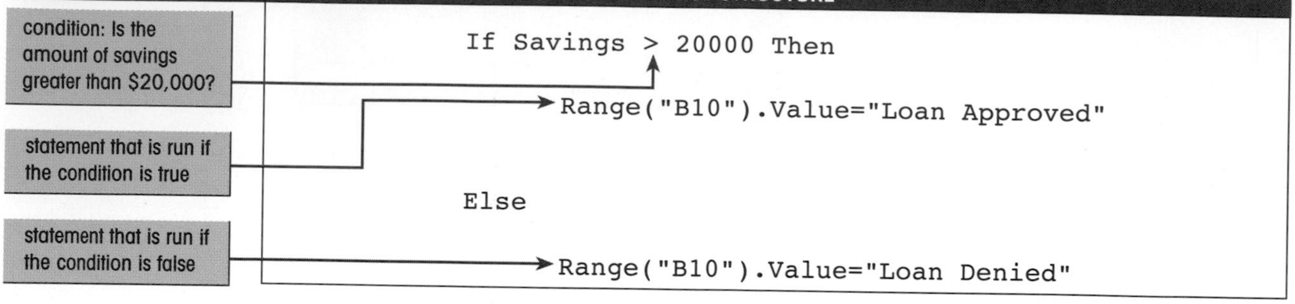
condition: Is the amount of savings greater than $20,000?
statement that is run if the condition is true
statement that is run if the condition is false
If Savings > 20000 Then
Range("B10").Value="Loan Approved"
Else
Range("B10").Value="Loan Denied"

IF the user enters a savings figure that is greater than $20,000, THEN the loan is approved, otherwise (ELSE) it is denied. The control structure evaluates the value of a variable named Savings and, based on the condition of that variable, enters the appropriate text in cell B10.

This macro can respond to only two possible conditions: the user has above $20,000 in savings, or below $20,000 in savings.

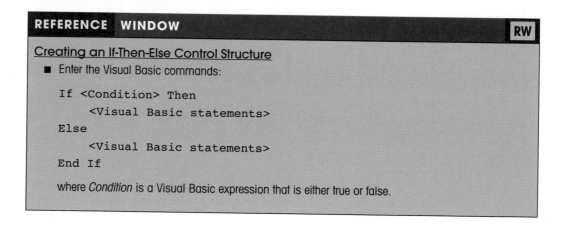

REFERENCE WINDOW RW

<u>Creating an If-Then-Else Control Structure</u>

- Enter the Visual Basic commands:

```
If <Condition> Then
     <Visual Basic statements>
Else
     <Visual Basic statements>
End If
```

where *Condition* is a Visual Basic expression that is either true or false.

If your control structure has more than two conditions, you may want to use an If-Then-ElseIf control structure. The syntax for this control structure in Visual Basic is:

```
If <Condition> Then
       <Visual Basic statements>
ElseIf <condition 2> Then
       <Visual Basic statements>
ElseIf <condition 3> Then
       <Visual Basic statements>
Else
       <Visual Basic statements>
End If
```

In order to cover all possible conditions, control structures can have an unlimited number of conditions. Figure 12-43 shows an example of Visual Basic code using multiple conditions in a control structure that evaluates whether or not a user qualifies for a loan. In this example, there are three conditions. The person applying for the loan could have more than $20,000 in savings, or she could have more than $15,000, or she could have less than $15,000. There are three conditions, and based on which of these conditions is true, the text “Loan Approved”, “Loan Pending”, or “Loan Denied” is entered into cell B10.

Figure 12-43 AN EXAMPLE OF AN IF-THEN-ELSEIF CONTROL STRUCTURE

```
If Savings > 20000 Then

        Range("B10").Value="Loan Approved"

ElseIf Savings > 15000 Then

        Range("B10").Value="Loan Pending"

Else

        Range("B10").Value="Loan Denied"

End If
```

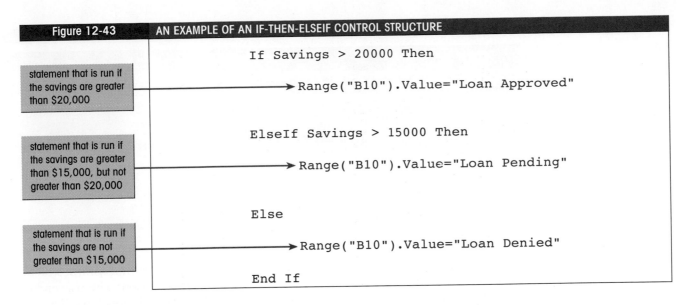

- statement that is run if the savings are greater than $20,000 → Range("B10").Value="Loan Approved"
- statement that is run if the savings are greater than $15,000, but not greater than $20,000 → Range("B10").Value="Loan Pending"
- statement that is run if the savings are not greater than $15,000 → Range("B10").Value="Loan Denied"

The first If-Then statement and the last Else statement are the same as the ones in Figure 12-42. The second statement handles the second possible condition, where the user has more than $15,000 but not more than $20,000 in savings.

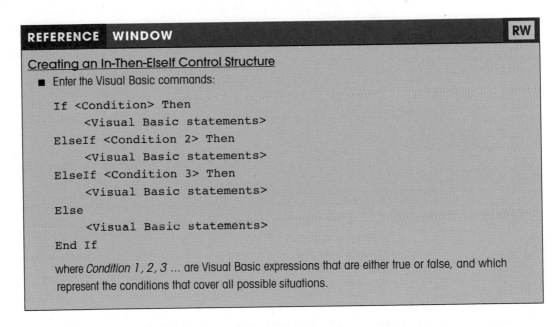

REFERENCE WINDOW RW

Creating an In-Then-ElseIf Control Structure

- Enter the Visual Basic commands:

```
If <Condition> Then
    <Visual Basic statements>
ElseIf <Condition 2> Then
    <Visual Basic statements>
ElseIf <Condition 3> Then
    <Visual Basic statements>
Else
    <Visual Basic statements>
End If
```

where *Condition 1, 2, 3* ... are Visual Basic expressions that are either true or false, and which represent the conditions that cover all possible situations.

When control structures evaluate conditions, they determine how a value compares to another value. To do this, the condition statement uses comparison and logical operators.

Comparison and Logical Operators

When you enter conditions in your Visual Basic control structure, you will usually be comparing one value to another. You saw an example of this in Figure 12-43 where the value of the Savings variable was compared to the values $20,000 and $15,000. The > symbol used in that example is a comparison operator, because you use it to compare values or expressions within a condition. If the comparison is true, then Visual Basic performs the tasks in the lines that follow. If the comparison is not true, then it performs another task. Figure 12-44 shows some of the comparison operators you'll frequently use in your Visual Basic control structures.

Figure 12-44 COMPARISON OPERATORS

COMPARISON OPERATOR	DESCRIPTION
>	Greater than
<	Less than
>=	Greater than or equal to
<=	Less than or equal to
=	Equal to
<>	Not equal to
is	Compares whether one object is the same as another

Another type of operator that you'll use in writing conditions for your control structures are logical operators. Logical operators are used to combine expressions within a condition. The most commonly used logical operators are the AND and OR operators. The AND operator requires both expressions to be true before the procedure acts upon them, whereas the OR operator requires only one of the conditions to be true. Figure 12-45 shows an example of a condition that uses the AND logical operator.

Figure 12-45 AN EXAMPLE OF A CONDITION USING THE AND LOGICAL OPERATOR

logical operator

condition: Is the amount of savings greater than $20,000? and is the credit rating "Good"?

```
If Savings > 20000 and Credit="Good" Then
    Range("B10").Value="Loan Approved"
Else
    Range("B10").Value="Loan Denied"
End If
```

In this example, the text "Loan Approved" will be placed in cell B10 only if the Savings variable has a value greater than 20,000 AND the Credit variable has the value "Good". Otherwise, the value placed in cell B10 is "Loan Denied". Figure 12-46 shows an example of a condition that uses the OR logical operator.

Figure 12-46 AN EXAMPLE OF A CONDITION USING THE OR LOGICAL OPERATOR

logical operator

condition: Is the amount of savings greater than $20,000 or is the equity greater than $10,000?

```
If Savings > 20000 or Equity > 10000 Then
    Range("B10").Value="Loan Approved"
Else
    Range("B10").Value="Loan Denied"
End If
```

In this example, the loan is approved if either the Savings variable is greater than 20,000 or the value of the equity in a home mortgage is greater than 10,000.

As you continue to learn Visual Basic, you'll discover that it supports other control structures. These include the For-Next control structure, which allows you to repeat a series of commands a set number of times, and the Do-While control structure, which repeats a series of commands as long as a particular condition is true. For the Financial_Reports macro, however, you will need only the If-Then-ElseIf control structure.

Writing an If-Then-ElseIf Control Structure

You are ready to write the If-Then-ElseIf control structure needed to make the Financial_Reports macro work under all possible conditions. You should first save the Kiosk 2 workbook as Kiosk 3.

To open the Kiosk 2 workbook:

1. If you took a break after the last session, make sure Excel is running, and that the **Kiosk 2** workbook is open.
2. If you are reopening the workbook, click the **Enable Macros** button when prompted by Excel.
3. Save the workbook as **Kiosk 3** in the Tutorial folder for Tutorial.12 of your Data Disk, and update the workbook name on the Documentation sheet.

Before you start revising the Financial Reports sub procedure, review the various conditions that you have to account for in the macro. When the dialog box asks the user to enter a report name, there are three possible outcomes. These are:

1. The user enters a valid financial report name.
2. The user enters an invalid financial report name.
3. The user clicks the Cancel button.

Because you have three conditions to account for, you will have to include an If-Then-ElseIf control structure. Also, you'll have to account for the fact that the first condition (that the user enters a valid name for the report) has four possible answers, and therefore that condition will need to contain several expressions. You will have to link the four possibilities with an OR logical operator, so that if the user enters any one of the four allowed report names, the procedure will then display the appropriate worksheet.

Now that you understand the conditions your macro needs to account for, you are ready to start editing the Financial_Reports macro.

To edit the Financial_Reports macro:

1. Click **Tools** on the menu bar, point to **Macro**, and click **Macros**.
2. Click **Financial_Reports** in the Macro name list box, and click the **Edit** button. The Visual Basic Editor opens with the Code window still maximized and displaying the Financial_Reports sub procedure.

The first line you'll add to the macro will include the IF statements that test the condition of whether the user has entered one of the four valid report names.

To enter the first condition in the If-Then-ElseIf control structure:

1. Click the beginning of the line "Sheets(Sheetname).Select" and press the **Enter** key to place a blank line above it.
2. Press the **Up Arrow** key to move the insertion point into the new blank line.
3. Type **If Sheetname=“General” or Sheetname=“Earnings” or Sheetname=“Assets” or Sheetname=“Liabilities” Then**
4. Press the **Down Arrow** key twice to go the end of the line that selects cell A1.

After the IF statement that you just entered, the macro selects the worksheet the user typed, which was stored in the Sheetname variable and then selects cell A1. So if the user has entered one of the four correct names, the program will then select and display one of the four financial report worksheets, and select cell A1 on that sheet.

In the next part of the control structure, you'll account for the two remaining possibilities: the user has entered the wrong name in the input box, or by clicking the Cancel box has not entered any value. You'll first determine whether a value was entered into the input box, and if so, display an error message that an incorrect name was entered.

To enter the second condition in the If-Then-ElseIf control structure:

1. Press the **Enter** key to insert a new blank line before the End Sub line.

   Now you'll enter a condition using the "not equal to" operator, <>.

2. Type **ElseIf Sheetname <>“” Then** and press the **Enter** key. This is the second condition. It tests whether the Sheetname variable is "not equal to" nothing. In other words, as long as something was entered into the input box, this condition will be true.

   TROUBLE? If you see a Compile error after you press the Enter key, click the OK button and check to make sure you have typed spaces in the correct places in the statement, and that you have capitalized the words correctly.

3. Type **‘Display an error message** and press the **Enter** key. This is a comment that you'll be replacing later on with Visual Basic code that displays an error message.

So far you've accounted for two conditions. The first condition tests if the user has entered one of the four correct report names. Assuming this is not the case, the second condition tests whether the user entered anything at all, because if they did it must be wrong (because we have already eliminated the possibility that they entered one of the four correct names.) The only remaining possibility is that the user has entered nothing at all, which would occur if the Cancel button on the input box had been clicked. If this happens, you want the procedure to end without doing anything, so you simply end the If-Then-ElseIf structure and the Financial_Reports sub procedure. This will close the input box without performing any task in the workbook.

To finish If-Then-ElseIf control structure:

1. Type **End If** and press the **Down Arrow** key.
2. To make the program code easier to read, indent the lines between the If, ElseIf and End If statements by pressing the **Tab** key at the beginning of those lines. Figure 12-47 displays the Financial_Reports macro at this point in time.

Figure 12-47 THE IF-THEN-ELSEIF CONTROL STRUCTURE FOR THE FINANCIAL_REPORTS MACRO

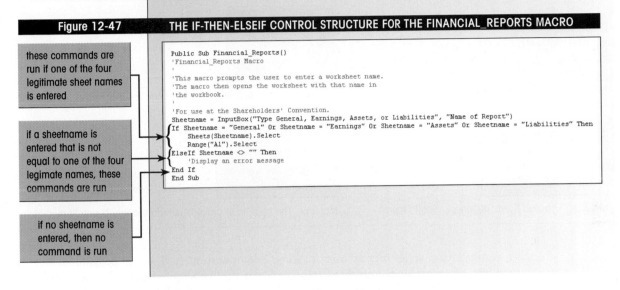

```
Public Sub Financial_Reports()
'Financial_Reports Macro
'
'This macro prompts the user to enter a worksheet name.
'The macro then opens the worksheet with that name in
'the workbook.
'
'For use at the Shareholders' Convention.
Sheetname = InputBox("Type General, Earnings, Assets, or Liabilities", "Name of Report")
If Sheetname = "General" Or Sheetname = "Earnings" Or Sheetname = "Assets" Or Sheetname = "Liabilities" Then
    Sheets(Sheetname).Select
    Range("A1").Select
ElseIf Sheetname <> "" Then
    'Display an error message
End If
End Sub
```

these commands are run if one of the four legitimate sheet names is entered

if a sheetname is entered that is not equal to one of the four legimate names, these commands are run

if no sheetname is entered, then no command is run

If you study Figure 12-47, you'll see how the value of the Sheetname variable controls which commands are run by the macro. If the user enters a sheet name equal to "General", "Earnings", "Assets", or "Liabilities", then these commands are run:

```
Sheets(Sheetname).Select
Range("A1").Select
```

and the macro selects cell A1 in the appropriate worksheet. On the other hand, if the user enters *something* that is *not* equal to one of the four worksheet names (in other words, enters a *wrong* value), then this command is run:

```
'Display an error message
```

which will soon be replaced by a Visual Basic command to display a message box. Finally, if neither of these conditions is true, then the macro ends without doing anything.

Your next step is to replace the error message comment with a command that displays an error message in a dialog box when the user enters an incorrect name. To do this, you'll use the MsgBox (message box) function.

Creating a Message Box

To create a message box, you use the MsgBox function, which is similar to the InputBox function you used in the last session, except that it does not contain a text box for the user to enter values. You would use a message box for situations where you simply want to inform the user and have them click the OK button. The user does not type in any text. The syntax for the MsgBox function is:

```
MsgBox Prompt, Buttons, Title
```

As in the InputBox function, *Prompt* is the message in the dialog box, and *Title* is the text that appears in the title bar. The *Buttons* parameter specifies the kind of buttons that appear in the message box, as well as the style of the message box itself. There are several options you can choose for the Buttons parameter, a few of which are shown in Figure 12-48.

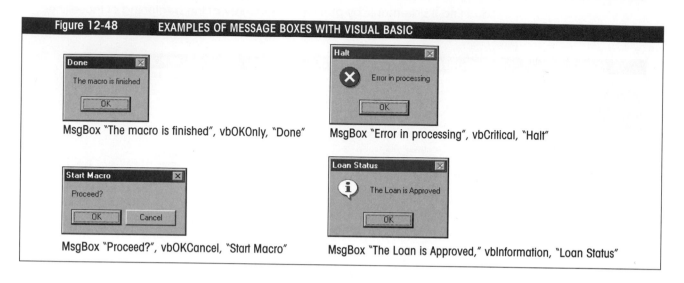

Figure 12-48 EXAMPLES OF MESSAGE BOXES WITH VISUAL BASIC

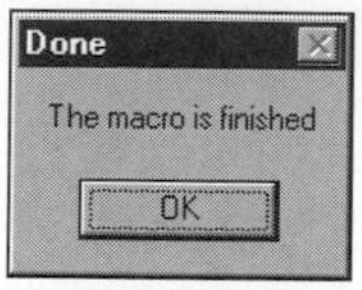

MsgBox "The macro is finished", vbOKOnly, "Done"

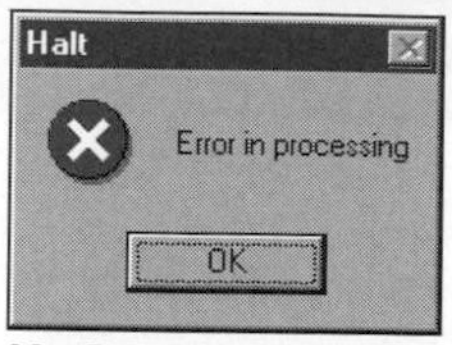

MsgBox "Error in processing", vbCritical, "Halt"

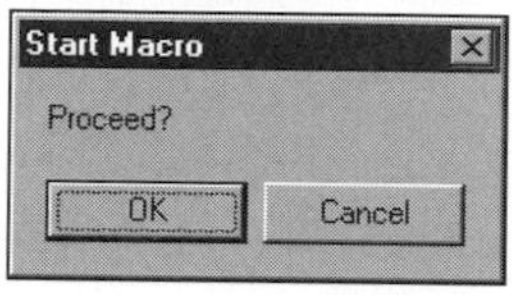

MsgBox "Proceed?", vbOKCancel, "Start Macro"

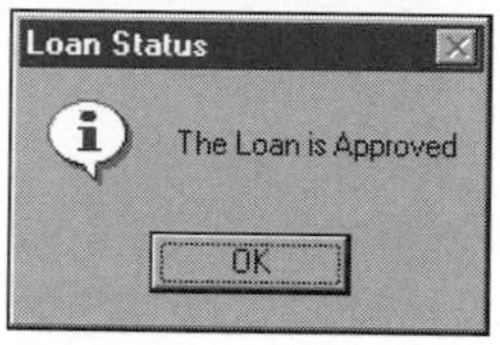

MsgBox "The Loan is Approved," vbInformation, "Loan Status"

Some button styles merely inform, some ask a question, and others provide an alert to a problem of some kind. You don't have to learn the names of these different buttons and message styles; the Visual Basic Editor will provide pop-up Help as it did when you wrote the InputBox function in the last session.

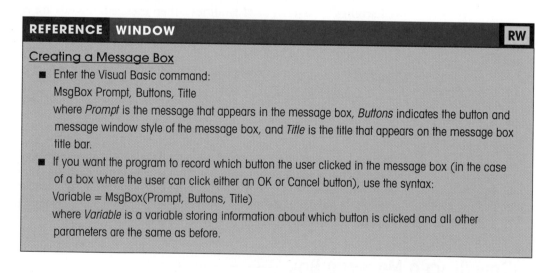

REFERENCE WINDOW RW

Creating a Message Box

- Enter the Visual Basic command:
  MsgBox Prompt, Buttons, Title
  where *Prompt* is the message that appears in the message box, *Buttons* indicates the button and message window style of the message box, and *Title* is the title that appears on the message box title bar.
- If you want the program to record which button the user clicked in the message box (in the case of a box where the user can click either an OK or Cancel button), use the syntax:
  Variable = MsgBox(Prompt, Buttons, Title)
  where *Variable* is a variable storing information about which button is clicked and all other parameters are the same as before.

Now that you've seen the syntax of the MsgBox function, you can use it in the Financial_Reports macro. Because the message box will be reporting an error on the part of the user, you'll use the vbCritical button style to indicate this fact.

To enter the MsgBox function:

1. Select the comment line you entered as a placeholder in the previous set of steps, and press the **Delete** key.

2. Type **MsgBox** and then press the **Spacebar**. The Visual Basic Editor displays the syntax for the MsgBox function, with the word "Prompt" bolded.

   You'll first enter the prompt or message that you want to show the user.

3. Type **"Please type General, Earnings, Assets, or Liabilities",**

   After typing the comma, the editor displays a pop-up list box showing all the possible button styles.

4. Double-click **vbCritical** from the pop-up list box, and then type **a comma**.

   The next parameter you need to enter is the text for the message box title bar.

5. Type **"Invalid Report Name"** and press the **Down Arrow** key. The completed macro is shown in Figure 12-49.

   TROUBLE? If you see an error message, study Figure 12-49 and try retyping the MsgBox command to match the command shown there.

Figure 12-49 THE COMPLETED FINANCIAL_REPORTS MACRO

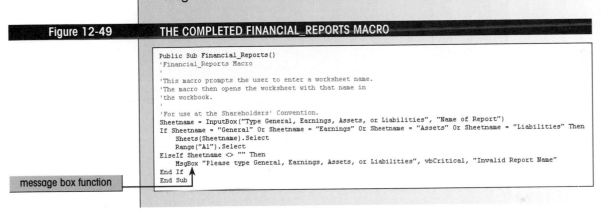

```
Public Sub Financial_Reports()
'Financial_Reports Macro
'
'This macro prompts the user to enter a worksheet name.
'The macro then opens the worksheet with that name in
'the workbook.
'
'For use at the Shareholders' Convention.
Sheetname = InputBox("Type General, Earnings, Assets, or Liabilities", "Name of Report")
If Sheetname = "General" Or Sheetname = "Earnings" Or Sheetname = "Assets" Or Sheetname = "Liabilities" Then
    Sheets(Sheetname).Select
    Range("A1").Select
ElseIf Sheetname <> "" Then
    MsgBox "Please type General, Earnings, Assets, or Liabilities", vbCritical, "Invalid Report Name"
End If
End Sub
```

message box function

You've finished the Financial_Reports macro. You only need to print a hard copy of the macros in your module, close the Visual Basic Editor, and test the macros. If the macros work, you'll then modify a few elements of the workbook to make it ready for use at the convention.

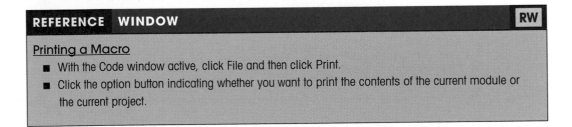

REFERENCE WINDOW RW

Printing a Macro

- With the Code window active, click File and then click Print.
- Click the option button indicating whether you want to print the contents of the current module or the current project.

Before you print your macro, be sure to save it.

To print and test your macros:

1. Click the **Save** button.

   Excel saves the current version of the Kiosk workbook along with the macros it contains.

2. Click **File** on the menu bar, and then click **Print**.
3. Make sure that the **Current Module** option button is selected, and then click the **OK** button.
4. Click **File** on the menu bar, and then click **Close and Return to Microsoft Excel**.
5. Click the **Main Menu** sheet tab.
6. Click the **View Financial Reports** button. The dialog box you created asks you to name a report.

   First, test how the macro responds to an incorrect entry.
7. Type **Libelities** (the spelling mistake that Steve made earlier) and click the **OK** button. Excel displays the message box shown in Figure 12-50.

Figure 12-50 THE ERROR MESSAGE BOX YOU CREATED IN VISUAL BASIC

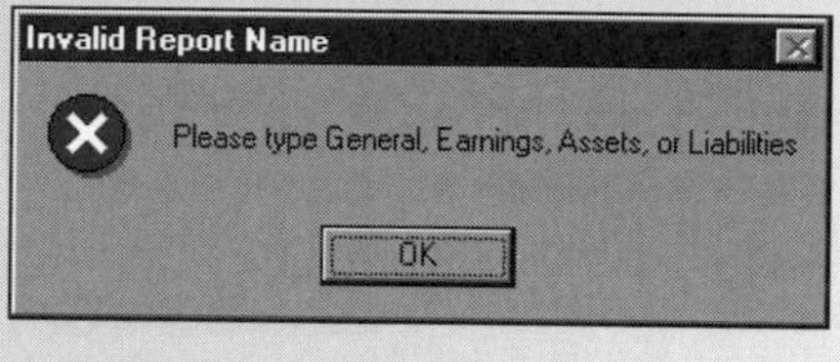
Invalid Report Name
Please type General, Earnings, Assets, or Liabilities
OK

   TROUBLE? If you get an error message from Excel when running your macro, compare the printout of your macro with the one shown in Figure 12-49, and then return to the editor to correct any typing mistakes.
8. Click the **OK** button.

Now you'll test the situation in which you enter nothing and click Cancel.

To test the macro with no user input:

1. Click the **View Financial Reports** button again, and then click the **Cancel** button. You should be returned to the Main Menu worksheet without seeing the message box.
2. Click the **View Financial Reports** button one last time.
3. Type **Liabilities** (spelling it correctly this time) and click the **OK** button. The Liabilities worksheet appears.

   TROUBLE? If the Liabilities worksheet does not appear, check your typing. The worksheet name should begin with a capital "L."
4. Click the **Return to the Main Menu** button on the worksheet to display the Main Menu worksheet.
5. Save your changes to the workbook.

The macro now appears to work properly. You contact Steve to show him the new features of the macro and to ask him if there are any more changes he wants you to make.

Finishing Your Customized Application

When you are finished creating your macros, you will want to think about other aspects of your workbook. Will users be allowed to change any of the values in the worksheets? What elements of the document window do you want them to see? Do you want them to see the toolbars or menu commands? Which, if any, of the worksheets do you want to hide from them?

You discuss these issues with Steve. Steve looks over the Kiosk workbook and suggests that you make the following changes:

1. Modify the properties of the workbook so that it describes the nature and purpose of the document.
2. Protect the contents of all the worksheets so they can't be changed by one of the convention attendees. Also password-protect the entire document.
3. Hide all sheet tabs, gridlines, row and column headers, and scroll bars from each of the financial report worksheets.
4. Hide the formula bar, status bar, and any toolbars in the document window.
5. Alter the worksheet menu bar so that it displays only the File menu and menu commands for the macros you created.

Viewing your Workbook's Properties List

You'll start Steve's checklist by working with the properties of your document. Excel allows you to store information about your document in a Properties dialog box. The Properties dialog box fulfills many of the same needs that your Documentation sheet does. The advantage of the Properties dialog box is that you can easily access these property values from outside of Excel. To do this, you right-click the workbook file from within Windows Explorer and choose "Properties" from the pop-up menu. Thus, you can view documentation on your workbook without having to go through the process of starting up Excel. An additional advantage is that these properties can be accessed by Visual Basic programs, allowing them to be modified by customized macros. To see how the Properties dialog box works, add information about the Kiosk workbook now. First, you'll save the workbook under a new name.

To edit your workbook's list of properties:

1. Go to the **Documentation** sheet and change the workbook name in cell B7 to **Kiosk 4** and save the workbook as **Kiosk 4** in the Tutorial folder for Tutorial.12 of your Data Disk.
2. Click **Properties** from the File menu.
3. Click the **Summary** dialog sheet tab.
4. Type **Shareholders' Report** in the Title box of the Kiosk 4 Properties dialog box and press **Tab**.
5. Type **An interactive report of Imageon's financial condition** in the Subject box and press **Tab** three times.
6. Type **Imageon** in the Company box. See Figure 12-51.

Figure 12-51 THE PROPERTIES DIALOG BOX FOR YOUR WORKBOOK

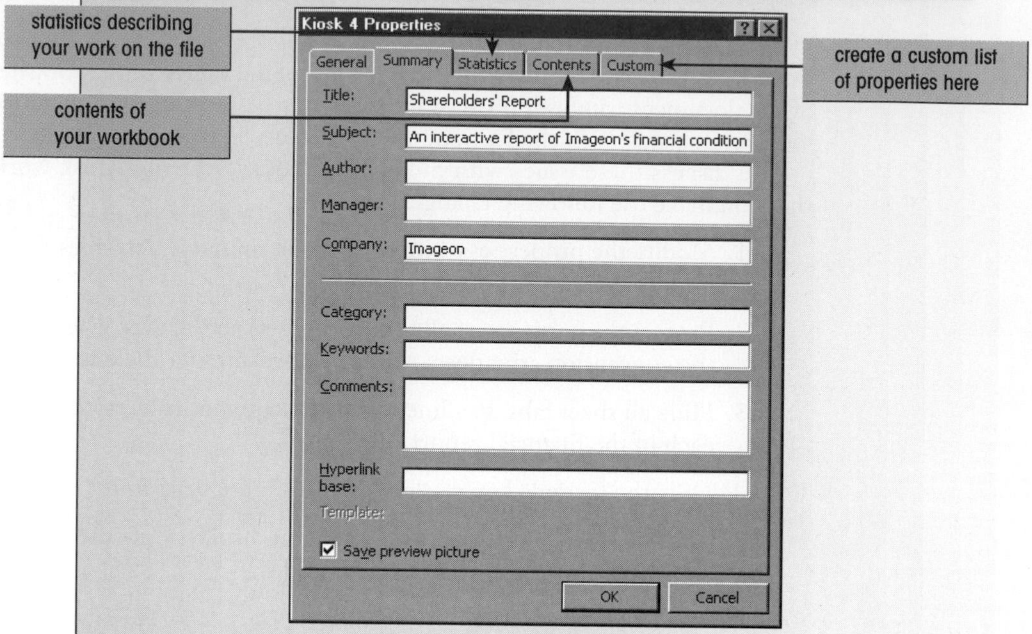

7. Click the **OK** button.

The Properties dialog box has other dialog sheets where you can view additional properties about your document, including the amount of time you've spent editing the file. You can also create your own customized list of properties. Excel's online Help contains additional information about document properties.

Protecting your Workbook and Worksheet

Now that you've edited the list of properties for the Kiosk 4 workbook, your next task will be to protect your workbook from changes from unauthorized users. You can protect each individual worksheet and the entire workbook itself.

To password-protect each worksheet:

1. Click **Tools**, point to **Protection** and click **Protect Sheet**.

2. Make sure that the Contents, Objects, and Scenarios check boxes are selected.

If you want to add a password so that other users can't unprotect the sheet, you could enter one now in the Password text box. For now though, protect the sheet without a password and leave the Password text box blank.

3. Click the **OK** button.

4. Repeat this process for the remaining sheets in the workbook.

When you protected each worksheet, you kept other people from changing the values in those sheets. Now add further protection to your workbook by adding password-protection to the document itself. Adding a password to the workbook prevents other users from hiding or removing sheets, or even adding new worksheets.

REFERENCE WINDOW RW

Protecting your Workbook and Worksheet

- To protect a worksheet, point to Protection from the Tools menu and then click Protect Sheet. Determine whether you want to protect the sheet's content, objects and/or scenarios.
- To unprotect your worksheet, point to Protection from the Tools menu and then Unprotect Sheet. Enter the worksheet's password.
- To protect a workbook, point to Protection from the Tools menu, and then click Protect Workbook. Determine whether you want to protect the structure of the workbook and/or the workbook's windows.
- To unprotect your workbook, point to Protection from the Tools menu and then Unprotect Workbook. Enter the workbook's password.

To password-protect the workbook:

1. Click **Tools**, point to **Protection** and click **Protect Workbook**.
2. Verify that the **Structure** check box is selected in order to protect the structure of the workbook, and the **Windows** check box is selected so that unauthorized users cannot move, resize, hide, or close your workbook's windows. As before, you'll leave the password box blank.
3. Click the **OK** button.

Hiding Screen Elements

Now that you've gone through the process of protecting your workbook from other users, you'll next work on fulfilling the other set of Steve's request: hiding certain screen elements like scroll bars, sheet tabs, and menus from the user. These screen elements fall into two general categories: those that are native to Excel itself and those that are native to a worksheet. The difference is important. When you hide screen elements that are native to Excel, those elements will be hidden in *all* Excel workbooks that you'll open; screen elements that are native to the worksheet will be hidden in that worksheet only. Other worksheets and workbooks will be unaffected. Figure 12-52 displays the screen elements that you'll hide and to which category they belong.

Figure 12-52 SCREEN ELEMENTS OF EXCEL

NATIVE TO EXCEL	NATIVE TO A WORKSHEET
Toolbars	Gridlines
Formula bar	Row & column headers
Status bar	Horizontal and vertical scrollbars
Menus	Sheet tabs

Steve wants all of the elements listed in Figure 12-52 either hidden or modified. You can hide some of these elements now using Excel's Options dialog box. The **Options dialog box** contains a list of features that you can modify to control how Excel behaves on your system.

You'll use it now to determine what Excel displays and what it hides. First though, you'll group your worksheets, so that when you hide screen elements that are native to individual worksheets, these changes will be reflected in all of the sheets in the group.

To hide certain Excel screen elements:

1. Click the **Main Menu** worksheet tab and then group the worksheets from the Main Menu to the Liabilities sheet (refer to Tutorial 8 if you are unsure how to group these sheets).
2. Click **Tools** and then **Options**.
3. Select the **View** dialog sheet from the Options dialog box. The dialog sheet contains a list of the screen elements you'll be hiding from the shareholders. Note that some of these are native to Excel itself and will be hidden in all Excel workbooks, and some will apply only those sheets that you've just grouped.
4. Deselect the following elements by clicking the appropriate check boxes: **Formula bar**, **Status bar**, **Gridlines**, **Row & column headers**, **Horizontal scroll bar**, **Vertical scroll bar**, and **Sheet tabs**. See Figure 12-53.

Figure 12-53 HIDING SCREEN ELEMENTS THROUGH THE OPTIONS DIALOG BOX

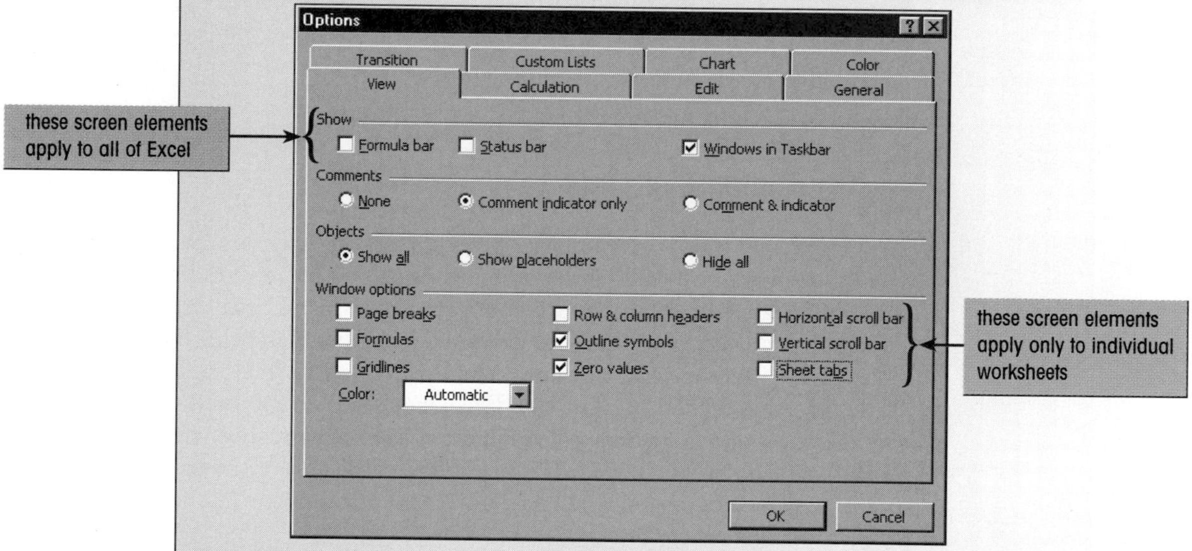

5. Click the **OK** button. The view of your workbook is changed, with several screen elements hidden from the user. See Figure 12-54.

Figure 12-54 THE KIOSK 4 WORKBOOK WITH SEVERAL FEATURES HIDDEN

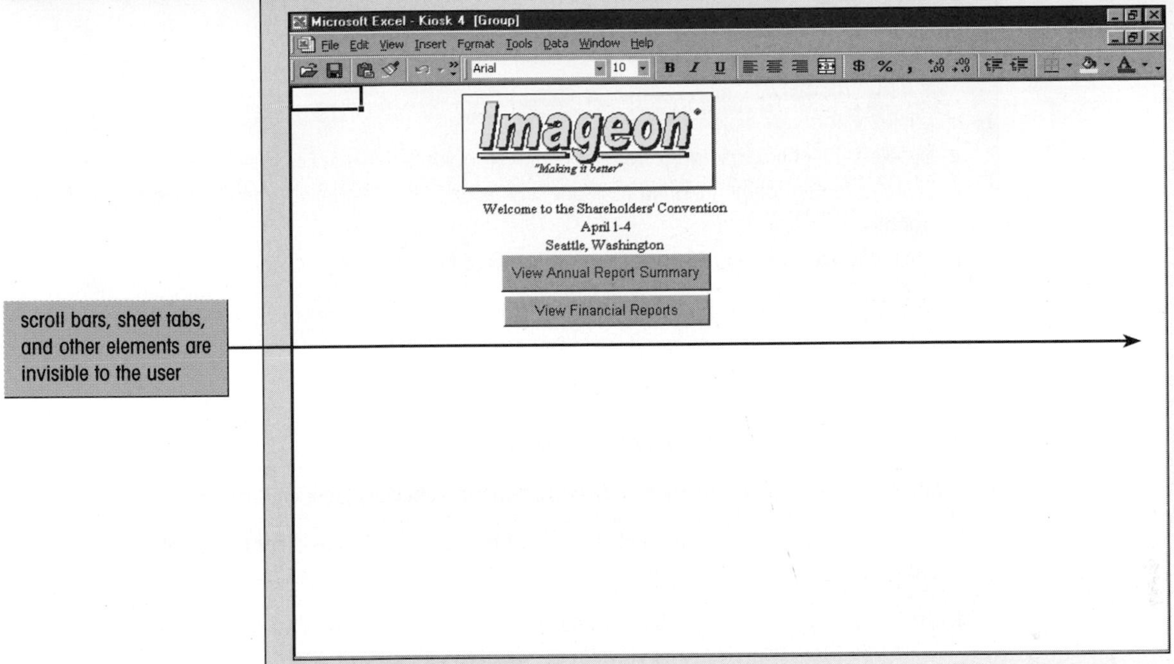

You've managed to hide several elements of the screen and now the shareholders will only see the contents of each worksheet and the Excel menu. If users want to move from one worksheet to another, they'll have to use the buttons you've created. You still have to edit the menus and toolbars to simplify the appearance of your application even more. You'll do this task next.

Customizing Excel Menus

Excel allows users to edit menus and toolbars, remove them, or create new ones. You'll learn about these techniques in editing the main Excel menu. Steve is concerned that all of the options listed on the menu will be confusing to the shareholders. When the convention is going on, he wants the shareholders to see only the File menu and three menu commands to display the main menu, the Annual Report, and a financial report. To make these changes, you have to open the Customize dialog box.

One important point though: the changes you make affect the entire Excel working environment, not just the workbook or worksheet you happen to have open. If you want to have custom menus that change based on what workbook is active, you can do so using Visual Basic, but this is a more advanced topic. For now, you can only make changes to the entire Excel working environment. For that reason, you'll make changes to the menu and toolbars for now, but then you'll restore them back to their original form before you close Excel. This will allow other Excel users who may be working on different workbooks to view the default Excel settings.

REFERENCE WINDOW RW

Customizing Excel Menus

- Click Customize from the Tools menu (or right-click the Excel menu bar and click Customize from the pop-up menu).
- Click the Toolbars dialog sheet tab.
- Deselect the check box in front of the menus or toolbars you want to hide in the Toolbars list box.
- Select a toolbar or menu in the Toolbars list box and click the Reset button to reset it to its default condition.
- Click the New button to create a new menu bar or toolbar.
- Click the Close button to save your changes.

To open the Customize dialog box:

1. Click **Tools** and **Customize**. The Customize dialog box opens up.
2. Click the **Toolbars** dialog sheet tab if necessary to display the Toolbars dialog sheet.
3. Deselect all toolbars in the Toolbars list, except the Worksheet menu bar. If you had the Standard and Formatting toolbars showing, they should now be removed from your screen.

Removing Menu Items

Now the only thing remaining on your screen should be the document window and the Excel menu bar. You'll remove all of the items from the menu bar except the file menu. Don't' worry, you'll reset the menu bar later.

To remove items from the menu:

1. With the Customize dialog box still open, click **Help** on the menu bar.
2. Drag **Help** off the menu bar onto the display area so that the pointer changes to a .
3. Release the mouse button. The Help menu is now removed from the menu bar.
4. Continue removing the remaining menus from the menu bar *except* the File menu. Your menu should now only display the File menu and nothing else.

You can use this same technique to remove buttons from toolbars or menu commands from menus. In each case, open the Customize dialog box and drag the item off its menu (or toolbar) onto the display area. When you release the mouse button, the item will be removed. Next you'll learn how to add new items to your menu.

Inserting Menu Commands

To insert a menu command, you drag a command *from* the Customize dialog box *to* the menu or toolbar. The Customize dialog box contains a list of all Excel commands and menus, as well as the macros you've created. In this example, you create three new menu commands on the Excel menu bar to run the three macros you created. Start with the macro to display the main menu worksheet.

REFERENCE WINDOW RW

Creating a New Menu or Toolbar Item

- Open the Customize dialog box.
- Click the Commands dialog sheet tab.
- Locate the type of command you want to create from the Categories list box.
- Drag the command from the Commands list box to the menu bar or toolbar you want to change. (If you want to create a new item based on a macro, locate the Macros category in the Categories list box and drag the "Custom Menu Item" or "Custom Button" to the menu bar or toolbar.)

To create a menu command:

1. With the Customize dialog box still open, click the **Commands** dialog sheet tab. The commands available to you appear in the Commands list box on the right side of the dialog box. Commands are organized into categories, many of which correspond to the various menus on the original Excel menu bar.

   You want to create commands based on your macros.

2. Scroll down the Categories list box and click the **Macros** entry. See Figure 12-55.

Figure 12-55 CHOOSING A MACRO COMMAND FROM THE CUSTOMIZE DIALOG BOX

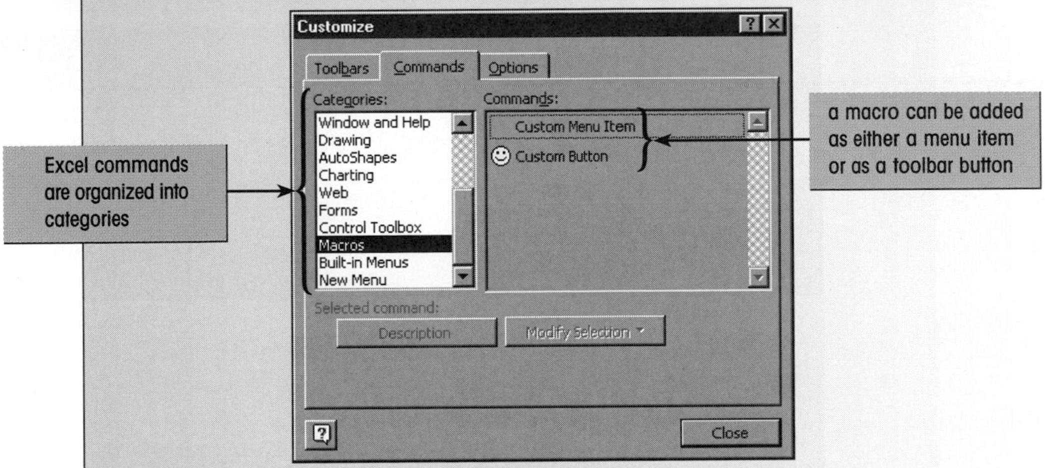

Your macro can be added to a menu (or toolbar) in one of two ways: as a menu item or as a button. Both will operate in the same way. In this case, because you're modifying the Excel menu bar, you'll create a menu item.

3. Click **Custom Menu Item** from the Commands list box and drag it to the Excel menu bar just to the right of the File menu, until your pointer becomes a . Release the mouse button. Now you have a new menu item, named "Custom Menu Item", as shown in Figure 12-56.

Figure 12-56 ADDING A COMMAND TO THE EXCEL MENU BAR

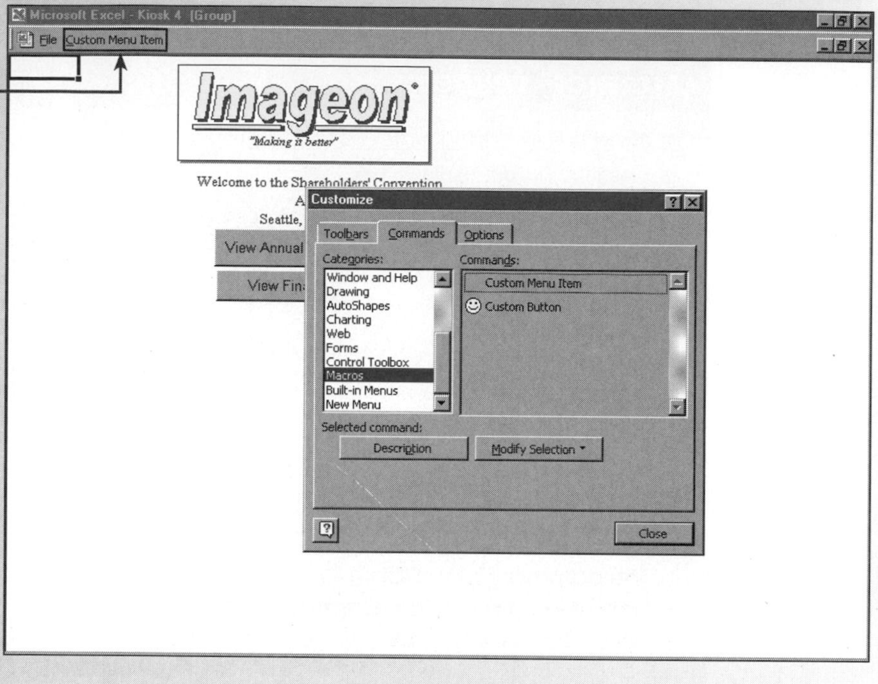

You now have to edit the menu item so that it will run the "Main_Menu" macro when clicked, and so that it has a more descriptive name.

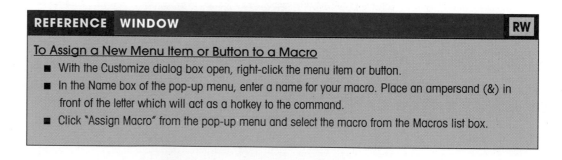

REFERENCE WINDOW RW

To Assign a New Menu Item or Button to a Macro

- With the Customize dialog box open, right-click the menu item or button.
- In the Name box of the pop-up menu, enter a name for your macro. Place an ampersand (&) in front of the letter which will act as a hotkey to the command.
- Click "Assign Macro" from the pop-up menu and select the macro from the Macros list box.

To edit a menu command:

1. Right-click **Custom Menu Item** from the Excel menu bar.
2. Select the Name box and enter the text, **&Main Menu** but do *not* press the Enter key. The "&" indicates which of the letters in the menu will act as a hotkey. Just as you can access Excel's File menu by typing Alt+f, you'll be able to access this new menu item by typing Alt+m. See Figure 12-57.

Figure 12-57 ADDING A COMMAND TO THE EXCEL MENU BAR

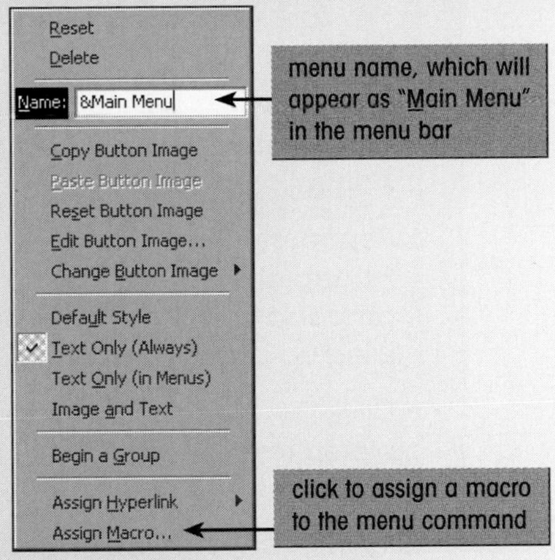

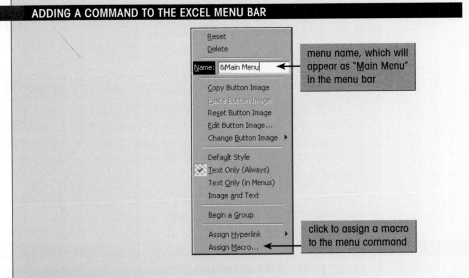

3. Click **Assign Macro** from the pop-up menu.

TROUBLE? If you accidentally closed the pop-up menu earlier, you can always get it back by right clicking the menu item on the menu bar.

4. Double-click **Main_Menu** from the list of macros in the Assign Macro dialog box.

5. Click the **Close** button on the Customize dialog box.

Note that the new menu item is "Main Menu" with the initial M underlined. This is because of the "&" character you entered into the Name box in step 2 and indicates that the "M" is a hotkey to this command.

Now test your new menu command.

To test the Main Menu command:

1. Click the **View Annual Report Summary** button located on the Main Menu sheet. The display window shows the Annual Report Summary.

2. Click **Main Menu** on the Excel menu bar. You should now be returned to the Main Menu sheet.

Using the same techniques, add menu commands for the remaining two macros. Because you've removed the Tools menu from the menu bar, you'll have to run the Customize command using the pop-up menu.

To create the final two menu commands:

1. Right-click the Excel menu bar and click **Customize** from the pop-up menu.

2. Click **Macros** from the Categories list box in the Commands dialog sheet.

3. Drag the **Custom Menu Item** to the Excel menu bar.

4. Right-click **Custom Menu Item** in the menu bar, click **Name:** on the pop-up menu, and type **&Annual Report** in the Name box.

   In this case, the & symbol is in front of the letter "A", so the hotkey for the menu item is Alt+a.

5. Click **Assign Macro** from the pop-up menu and then double-click **Annual_Report** from the list of macros.

6. Repeat steps 3–5 to create a menu item for the Financial Reports macro. Enter **Financial &Reports** in the Name box for this new menu item (you'll put the ampersand next to the letter "R" in this case because the "F" hotkey is already used up by the File menu.)

7. Click the **Close** button in the Customize dialog box. Figure 12-58 shows the completed revised Excel menu bar.

Figure 12-58 THE REVISED EXCEL MENU

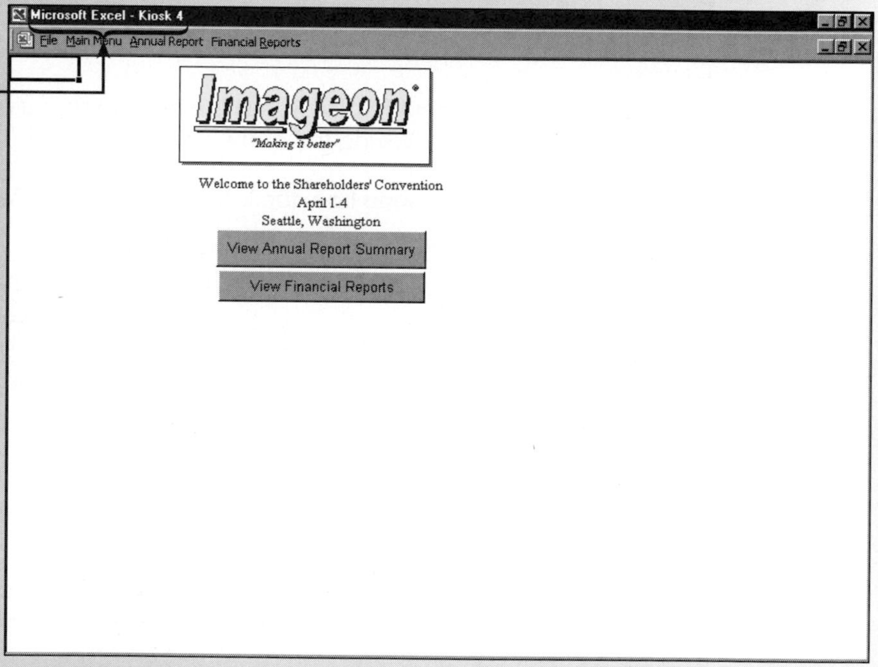

8. Test out the new menu commands by using them to display the Main Menu, Annual Report, and various financial reports. Try clicking the menu command to run the macros as well as using the keyboard shortcuts (Alt+m for the Main Menu, Alt+a for the annual report, and Alt+r for the financial reports.

It's a good idea to review what you've done here. You've hidden all of the various screen elements that Steve doesn't want the user to see, and you've revised the main Excel menu bar, adding your own custom menu items. One problem with this setup is that your new menu bar will be used by *all* Excel workbooks, not just Kiosk 4. This means that you should reset the menu bar before closing the workbook, as well as unhiding those screen elements that are native to Excel (and not just specific worksheets.)

Resetting Menu Options

You can reset the menu bar using the same Customize dialog box you used to modify it in the first place. You'll also restore the Standard and Formatting toolbars that you hid earlier.

To restore the Excel menu bar and other toolbars:

1. Click **File** and **Save** to save the Kiosk 4 workbook.
2. Right-click the Excel menu bar and click **Customize** from the pop-up menu.
3. Click the **Toolbars** dialog sheet tab.
4. Click the **Standard** and the **Formatting** check boxes in the Toolbars list box.
5. Scroll down and highlight the **Worksheet Menu Bar** from the Toolbars list box and click the **Reset** button.
6. Click **OK** when prompted to reset the changes you've made.
7. Click the **Close** button.

Now restore the other screen elements.

To restore the other screen elements:

1. Click **Tools** and then **Options**.
2. In the Options dialog box, select the **View** dialog sheet tab and then select the **Formula bar** and **Status bar** check boxes to restore these screen elements. You do not have to restore the other screen elements because they are native to each individual worksheet and will not affect the appearance of other, unrelated, workbooks.
3. Click the **OK** button.

If you want to return the customized menu bar you created, you'll have to go through the editing process again. You can also use the Customize dialog box to create your own menu or toolbar that will be attached to the workbook or use Visual Basic to automate the process of editing the Excel menu bar; but those are more advanced topics. You can finish your work.

To finish your work:

1. Close the **Kiosk 4** workbook and save your changes.
2. Exit Excel.

Steve is very pleased with the job you've done, and looks forward to using your workbook at the shareholders' meeting. He feels that your Excel workbook is user-friendly, and that it will help shareholders find the information they want easily, even if they aren't familiar with Excel. This will then free up the convention staff for more substantive discussions with the shareholders.

Session 12.3 Quick Check

1. What is a control structure and why might you need one in your Visual Basic procedure?
2. Define the following terms:
   a. comparison operator
   b. logical operator
3. What is the syntax of the If-Then-Else control structure?
4. What control structure would you use if you had multiple conditions from which to choose?
5. What is the syntax of the MsgBox function?
6. What command would you enter to display a message box with the following elements: The text "File Status" in the title bar, the message "File Saved", and a single OK button in the dialog box.
7. Indicate which of the following screen elements are native to Excel and which are native to an individual worksheet:
   a. toolbars
   b. sheet tabs
   c. gridlines
   d. status bar
   e. row & column headers

You've completed your customized application. You've seen how you can write Visual Basic macros that prompt users for information and evaluate the information they enter. You've seen some of the basic features of the Visual Basic Editor and you've observed how the editor can assist you in writing and interpreting the Visual Basic language. The shareholders' convention is still a month away—plenty of time for you to learn more about the powerful capabilities of the Visual Basic Editor and the Visual Basic language.

REVIEW ASSIGNMENTS

Steve has worked with the Kiosk 4 workbook you completed in the tutorial. He has added four chart sheets to the workbook. He would like to have you create another button on the Main Menu worksheet with the caption "View Financial Charts". When the user clicks this button, an input box will appear asking for the name of the chart. There are four names the user can enter: Orders, Revenue, Total Assets, and Debt. Steve wants you to put in the usual error control structure so that if the user types an incorrect name, or clicks the Cancel button, the sub procedure can respond to it properly. To create Steve's custom application, do the following:

1. If necessary, start Excel, and make sure your Data Disk is in the appropriate drive. Open the **Kiosk 5** workbook in the Review folder for Tutorial 12, enable macros, and save it as **Kiosk 6**.

2. Enter the new workbook name, your name, and the date in the Documentation worksheet.
3. Use the Macro Recorder to record the act of clicking the Orders chart sheet, but do not select any object within the chart sheet. Name the macro you've recorded "Show_Charts" and include the description "This macro displays financial charts from the Kiosk workbook."
4. Start the Visual Basic Editor. Rename the project "Imageon_Convention" and rename Module1 "Chart_Macros."
5. Edit the Show_Charts macro in the Code window, and create an input box that will prompt the user for the name of the chart sheet they want to view. Name the variable that stores this information as "Chartname." Make the prompt of the input box read, "Chart: Orders, Net Revenue, Total Assets, or Debt." Let the title bar of the input box read "View Financial Chart."
6. Replace the occurrence of "Orders" (including the quotation marks) in the macro with "Chartname."
7. Create a control structure for the Show_Charts macro that tests whether the user has entered one of the four chart sheet names. If the user has not entered one of the four allowed names, have the macro display a message box with the text "Please enter: Orders, Net Revenue, Total Assets, or Debt." The title bar of the message box should read "No Chart Found." Use the vbInformation button style for the message box. (Use the Financial_Reports macro in this tutorial as a guide.)
8. Print your macro.
9. Return to Excel and create a macro button on the Main Menu worksheet with the Show_Charts macro attached to it. Name the macro button "View Financial Charts."
10. Copy and paste the "Return to Main Menu" button on each of the four chart sheets.
11. Test your macros and verify that they work properly.
12. Make the Main Menu worksheet the active sheet, and group the remaining worksheets (aside from the Documentation sheet). Then remove gridlines, sheet tabs, row & column headers, and toolbars from the grouped worksheets.
13. Edit the properties of the Kiosk 6 workbook, defining the title, subject, author (your name), and company (the name of your class).
14. Protect the structure of the Kiosk 6 workbook, but do not specify a password.
15. Save and close the workbook. Reset the view option for Excel.

CASE PROBLEMS

Case 1. Creating a Print Macro at Casey's Flowers Barbara Twain works in the finance department of Casey's Flowers, a nationwide distributor of flowers and greeting cards. Part of Barbara's job is to create and print the company's financial statements.

Barbara has entered the statements in an Excel workbook in three worksheets: Finance, Income, and Balance, representing the financial summary, income statement, and balance sheet.

The workbook also has a Documentation sheet in which Barbara would like to place macros to quickly print any sheet in the workbook. The macro would display an input box and prompt Barbara for the name of the report she wants to print. It will also verify that she's entered one of three financial worksheets in the workbook. She's asked you for some help in creating her macro. Do the following:

1. If necessary, start Excel, open the **Casey** workbook in the Cases folder for Tutorial.12 on your Data Disk and save it as **Casey Print Macro**.
2. Enter the new workbook name, **your name**, and the **date** on the Documentation worksheet.
3. Using the Macro Recorder, record a macro named Print_Macro in which you click the Finance sheet tab, print the worksheet, and then return to the Documentation worksheet, selecting cell A1.
4. Edit the Print_Macro sub procedure in the Visual Basic Editor. Add an input box to the macro in which the user is prompted to "Enter sheet to print." Give the input box the title "Print a financial report." Save whatever the user enters in the input box into a variable named "Sheetname."
5. Use the Edit and Replace command to replace the occurrence of the word "Finance" (including the quotation marks) with the variable name, "Sheetname."
6. Add an If-Then-ElseIf control structure that checks to see whether the user has entered either Finance, Income, or Balance. If the wrong name is entered, have the procedure display a message box informing them of the error. Use the Exclamation style for the message box and button and give it a title. If they've pressed the Cancel button in your input box, have the procedure end without doing anything.
7. Place a button on your Documentation worksheet that runs the macro when the user clicks it.

Explore

8. When the macro runs, it flickers as it goes through the process of selecting a sheet, printing it, and reselecting the Documentation worksheet. One of the properties of the Excel application is screen updating. Return to the Visual Basic Editor to continue editing the Print_Macro sub procedure. Enter a new line at the beginning of the procedure (directly after the Sub Print_Macro statement) to turn off screen updating for the Application object. Turn screen updating back on in the last line of the macro before the End Sub statement. (*Hint*: You have to enter a Visual Basic statement that turns the ScreenUpdating property of the Application object to FALSE to turn off screen updating and TRUE to turn screen updating back on.) You can learn more about the ScreenUpdating property using the online Help.
9. Print your Print_Macro sub procedure.
10. Edit the properties of the workbook, defining the title, subject, author (your name), and company (the name of your class.)
11. Save the workbook.

Case 2. Creating a Break-Even Function for Brakdale Skis Clyde Mason analyzes monthly sales figures at Brakdale Skis, a manufacturer of cross-country skis in Green Bay, Wisconsin. One of the most important pieces of information he looks at each month is the break-even point for the company. The break-even point is the point at which sales revenue equals the total fixed and variable expenses of producing the product (for a full discussion of break-even analysis, see Tutorial 9.) The break-even point is equal to:

Total Fixed Expenses / (Average Unit Price — Average Unit Cost)

Clyde uses this function so frequently that he wishes Excel included it in its list of financial functions. He asks you to help him create a customized function named "breakeven" that would calculate the break-even point when given the total fixed expense, unit price, and unit cost.

To create a customized function, you have to create a function procedure in the Visual Basic Editor. The syntax for a Function procedure is:

Function Function_Name(Parameters)

<Visual Basic Statements>

Function_Name=Expression

End Function

Here, *Function_Name* is the name of your function. Note that it is listed twice, once in the first line in the macro where the name of the function is declared, and then later when it gets its value from an expression in the last line of the procedure before the End Function statement. The *parameters* are the list of variables, separated by a comma, that are used in calculating the function. Clyde's break-even function has three variables: Fixed_Expense, Unit_Price, and Unit_Cost. To create Clyde's break-even function, do the following:

1. If necessary, start Excel, open the **Brakdale** workbook in the Cases folder for Tutorial.12 on your Data Disk, and save it as **Brakdale Break-even**.
2. On the Documentation worksheet, enter the new workbook name, your name, and the date.
3. Open the Visual Basic Editor.
4. **Explore** Use the Insert Module command on the menu bar to insert a new module in the project.
5. **Explore** Use the Insert Procedure command to insert a public function procedure into the module you just created. Name the function "breakeven."
6. In the set of parentheses on the first line of the breakeven function, enter the list of parameters to be used in the function, separated by commas. These are: Fixed_Expenses, Unit_Price, and Unit_Cost.
7. Insert a line into the function procedure that calculates the value of breakeven, in terms of the three parameters you entered into the function breakeven line.
8. Save your work and print a copy of your function procedure.
9. Exit the Visual Basic Editor and return to the Brakdale Break-even workbook.
10. In cell C17 of the Break-even worksheet, use the Function Wizard to enter your new customized function. Look for the function in the User-Defined category of functions provided by the Paste Function button. Label the cell appropriately.
11. Using your breakeven function, determine how many units per month Brakdale Skis must sell to break even. Confirm your estimate by entering this value into cell C3, the number of units sold. What is the resulting operating income? Print and save your workbook.

Case 3. Viewing Stock Information at Davis & Larson Victoria D'Allesandro at the investment company of Davis & Larson has created a workbook with information on 26 different industrial stocks. She wants to make this worksheet available to coworkers and clients. A list of the stocks is at the front of the workbook. Victoria wants you to create a macro that will allow users to click the ticker symbol from the list of stocks, press a key, and then have the macro display the worksheet for that stock. You suggest using an input box, but with 26 ticker symbols, the prompt for the box would be very long.

The macro you create will use an Excel object with the object name "ActiveCell." The ActiveCell object is simply the cell that happens to be currently selected in the workbook. The macro will then extract whatever value has been entered into the active cell and then open a worksheet whose name is equal to that value.

Victoria also wants the user to be able to go back to the list of stocks by pressing a single key or key combination. Finally, you should modify the workbook's appearance. Remove the column and row headings, the sheet tabs, the status bar, and the formula bar. To create Victoria's customized application, do the following:

1. If necessary, start Excel, open the **Stocks** workbook in the Cases folder for Tutorial.12 on your Data Disk, and save it as **Stock Information Macro**.
2. On the Documentation worksheet, enter the new workbook name, your name, and the date.
3. **Explore** Use the Macro Recorder to create two new macros: one named Stock_Info that displays the AA worksheet, selecting cell C2 in the process, and the other named Stock_List that displays the Stock List worksheet, selecting cell A1. Within the Macro Recorder dialog box, assign the keyboard combination Ctrl+t to the Stock_Info macro and Ctrl+m to the Stock_List macro.
4. **Explore** Edit the Stock_Info macro in the Visual Basic Editor, adding a line at the beginning of the macro that retrieves the value from the active cell and stores it in a variable named "Stockname." (*Hint*: Use the Value property of the ActiveCell object.) Edit the macro further so that it opens the worksheet referenced by the Stockname variable.
5. Print the macros in your module.
6. Test your macro by clicking a ticker symbol in the Stock List worksheet and pressing Ctrl+t. Verify that the macro displays the worksheet for that stock. Also test that pressing Ctrl+m takes the user back to the Stock List worksheet.
7. Group the Stock List and each stock sheet of the workbook together and hide the row and column headers, the worksheet tabs, and the scrollbars.
8. Edit the properties of the workbook, defining the title, subject, author (your name), and company (the name of your class).
9. Protect the structure of the workbook so that other users cannot change it. Do not use a password.
10. Save the changes to your workbook, with the Stock List worksheet as the active sheet.

Case 4. Creating a Documentation Sheet at BG Software Sally Crawford works at BG Software, an educational software company. Sally uses Excel workbooks to track product plans, schedules, marketing, and sales. Sally knows that Documentation sheets are an important element of an Excel workbook which allow others to quickly see its purpose and contents. The steps Sally takes to create the Documentation sheets are always the same. She could save herself time if she had a macro that automated the process of creating a Documentation sheet, prompting her for information.

Figure 12-59 shows the general form of Sally's Documentation sheet.

Figure 12-59

	A	B	C	D
1	**BG Software**			
2				
3				
4	Workbook:			
5	Created by:			
6	Date:			
7				
8	Purpose:			
9				
10				

Only cells A1, A4-A6, and A8 of this sheet will remain constant for each workbook. Sally would like the macro that generates the title sheet to always include those elements in the proper locations. She would also like to have a dialog box that prompts her for this information:

Workbook name	to place in cell B4
User name	to place in cell B5
Date	to place in cell B6
Purpose	to place in cell B8

Sally asks you to write such a macro for her. To create Sally's macro, do the following:

1. If necessary, start Excel, and create a new workbook with the name **Documentation Sheet Macro** in the Cases folder for Tutorial.12 on your Data Disk.
2. Use the Macro Recorder to record the steps you take to create the Documentation sheet, using a mock workbook name, user name, and date. Include a step to format the width of column A and B to 20 characters and to bold the title, "BG Software," in cell A1. Name the macro appropriately.
3. Edit the macro you create with the Macro Recorder, replacing the mock names you entered with variables whose values are entered by the user via an input box.
4. Print a copy of your macro.
5. Go through the macro line by line and using Excel online Help, write a short description of what each line in the macro does. Identify any objects, properties or methods in your sub procedure.
6. Save and test your macro and verify that it works properly.

INTERNET ASSIGNMENTS

The purpose of the Internet Assignments is to challenge you to find information on the Internet that you can use to create effective spreadsheets. The actual assignments are updated and maintained on the Course Technology Web site. Log on to the Internet and use your Web browser to go to the Student Online Companion to accompany this text at **www.course.com/NewPerspectives/office2000**. Click the Excel link, and then click the link for Tutorial 12.

QUICK CHECK ANSWERS

Session 12.1

1. Define your needs; decide on the application's appearance; use the Macro Recorder to create the initial Visual Basic code for the macros; modify the Visual Basic code; and finalize the appearance of your application.
2. **a.** The Project Explorer gives a hierarchical view of the objects in your project.
   b. The Properties window gives you a view of the properties of the individual objects.
   c. The Code window displays the Visual Basic code for your project's macros.
3. **a.** a collection of macros, worksheets, forms for data entry, and other items that make up the customized application you're trying to create

b. an element of an application, such as a worksheet, a cell, a chart, a form, or a report

c. an attribute of an object that defines one of its characteristics, such as its name, size, color, or location on the screen

d. a collection of macros

e. the set rules specifying how you must enter certain commands

4. Select the property and press the F1 key.
5. sub, function, and property
6. Sub Procedure_Name( )
   <Visual Basic commands and comments>
   End Sub
7. to organize macros based on their content or purpose

Session 12.2

1 **a.** a programming language that performs tasks by manipulating objects

b. an object that is composed of a group of other objects

c. an action that can be performed on an object

d. a piece of information that controls how the method or function is used

e. a named storage location containing data that you can retrieve and modify as the program is running

2. Sheets("Assets").Name="Assets Table"
3. Sheets("Assets").Select
4. Sheetname = Sheets("Assets").Name
5. Type an apostrophe at the beginning of the line.
6. Optional parameters are parameters in methods or functions that are not required for the method or function to work. They appear in brackets.
7. Last name=InputBox("Enter your last name", "Log In")

Session 12.3

1. A control structure is a series of commands that evaluates conditions in your program, and then directs the program to perform certain actions based on the status of those conditions.
2. **a.** is a word or symbol that is used to compare values or expressions within a condition

   b. used to combine expressions within a condition
3. If <condition> Then
   <Visual Basic Statements>.
   Else
   <Visual Basic Statements>
   End If
4. If-Then-ElseIf control structure
5. MsgBox(Prompt,Buttons,Title)
6. MsgBox("File Saved", vbOKOnly,"File Status")
7. **a.** Excel **d.** Excel

   b. worksheet **e.** worksheet

   c. worksheet

OBJECTIVES

In this case you will:

- Create a template worksheet
- Format a worksheet to improve its appearance
- Enhance a worksheet with varied fonts and borders
- Embed a graphic object in a worksheet
- Protect worksheet cells
- Use TODAY, IF and VLOOKUP functions
- Create and edit a print macro

SALES INVOICING FOR ISLAND DREAMZ SHOPPE

CASE

Island Dreamz Shoppe

Like many entrepreneurs, Nicole Richardson discovered the old-fashioned way to make money: choose something you like to do, keep costs low and quality high, and make teamwork a priority. This principle led to the success of her Island Dreamz Shoppe, a gift gallery featuring crafts of artists from the Caribbean whose jewelry, paintings, and embroidered giftware capture the spirit of the islands.

Since the gallery opened two years ago, business has been brisk. Responding to requests from many of her customers, Nicole expanded her business to include mail orders. When customers visit the Shoppe, Nicole gives them a catalog to take home. Many customers find it more convenient to order items after they return home than to cram extra gifts into an already overstuffed suitcase.

On a good day, Nicole receives about a dozen phone calls from customers who want to place orders. With so few calls, she doesn't need a full-blown order-entry system, but she would like to automate her invoice preparation. She decides to create an Excel template for her sales invoices. After she creates the template, all she needs to do is enter data for each order and print the invoice.

Nicole recently completed a paper invoice for an order from Rachel Nottingham, shown in Figure AC-1. Using this invoice as a model for the labels, formulas, and format that she wants to use in her template worksheet, Nicole prepares her planning analysis sheet (Figure AC-2). The calculations she needs in the template include the current date, the unit price of each item ordered times the quantity ordered (the extended price), the total amount for all items, the sales tax, the shipping cost, and the total amount of the order.

Figure AC-1 ISLAND DREAMZ SHOPPE SALES INVOICE

Island Dreamz Shoppe
1001 Anchor Cove
Montego Bay, Jamaica, B.W.I.

Date	24-Nov-01
Invoice No	1097

Name: Rachel Nottingham
Address: 2741 Landsdowne Road
City: Victoria, BC Postal Code: V8R 3P6
Country: Canada

Item #	Description	Quantity	Unit Price	Extended Price
21	Summer Beach Scene	3	$25.00	$75.00
27	Sea Scape Watch	2	36.00	72.00
47	Spanish Ducat Key Chain	1	12.00	12.00
63	Raindrop Crew Neck T-shirt	2	14.00	28.00
67	Stone-washed Twill Jacket	3	54.00	162.00

Total Sale	$349.00
Sales Tax	24.43
Shipping	25.00
TOTAL	$398.43

Payment Method	
	Check
	Visa
X	MasterCard
	Discover
	American Express
Credit Card #	4799123456789000

Expiration	03/99

Thank you for your order!

Figure AC-2 NICOLE'S PLANNING ANALYSIS SHEET

Planning Analysis Sheet

My goal:
Develop a template worksheet for preparing sales invoices

What results do I want to see?
A sales invoice for each order

What information do I need?
Customer name and address
Item number and quantity to be shipped
Lookup description in product table ❶
Lookup unit price for item in product table ❷
Method of payment

What calculations will I perform?
1. Extended price ❸ = quantity * unit price
2. Total sale ❹ = sum of extended price
3. Sales tax ❺ = total sale * 7%
4. Shipping ❻ = if total sale is less than $200 then $15, otherwise $25
5. Total ❼ = total sale + sales tax + shipping

Using her planning analysis sheet and the original paper invoice, Nicole sketches the template she wants to create using Excel (Figure AC-3). For each item ordered, she plans to enter the item number, description, quantity, and unit price. She wants Excel to do the calculations described in her Planning Analysis Sheet (Figure AC-2). The circled numbers are guides to help you relate Nicole's sketch to the required calculations.

Figure AC-3 NICOLE'S SKETCH OF HER TEMPLATE WORKSHEET

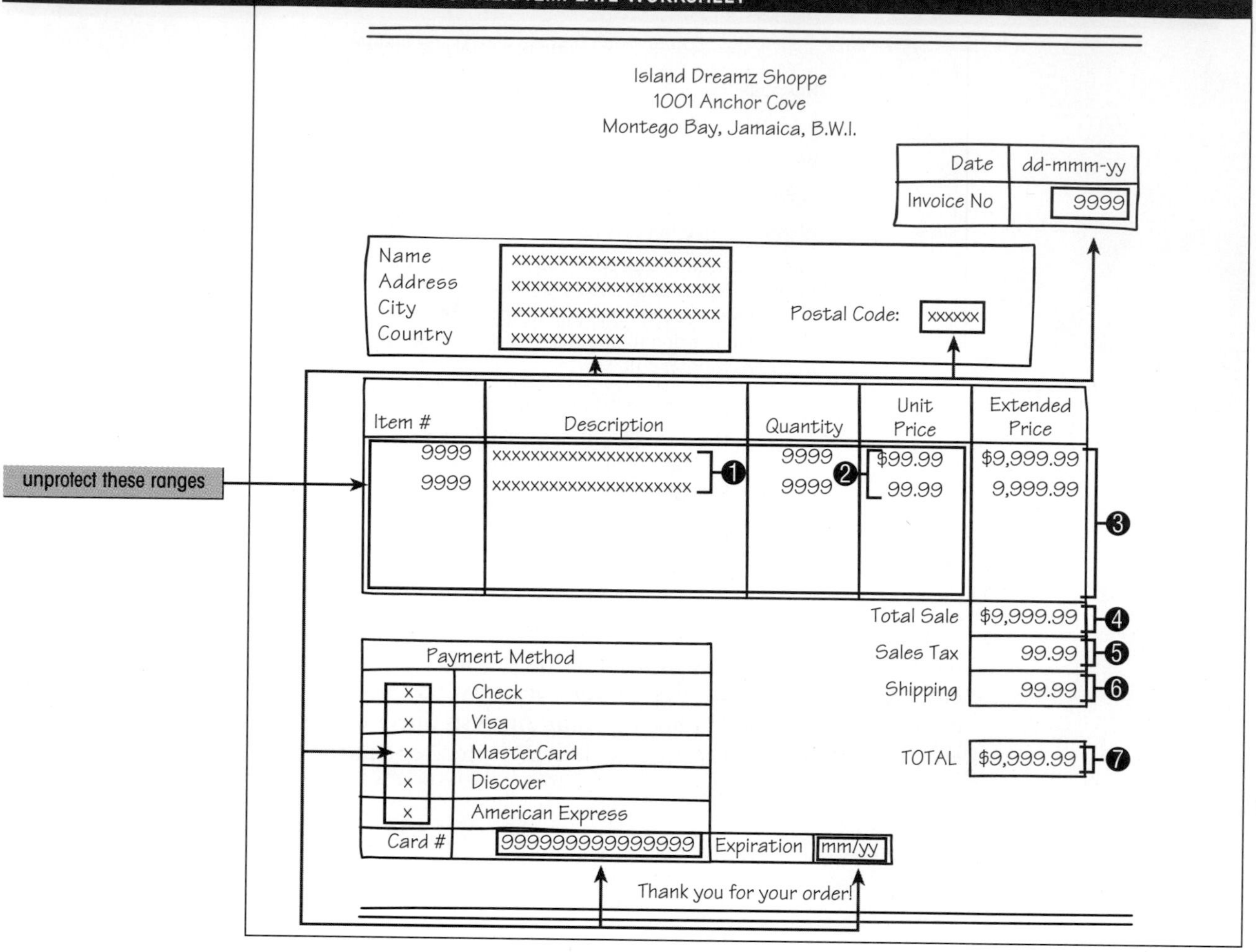

Nicole also sketches a table that lists the items Island Dreamz sells (Figure AC-4). The table includes the number, description, and unit price of each product.

Figure AC-4 ISLAND DREAMZ PRODUCT TABLE

Item #	Description	Unit Price
21	Summer Beach Scene	25.00
27	Sea Scape Watch	36.00
31	Victorian Walking Stick	28.00
47	Spanish Ducat Key Chain	12.00
63	Raindrop Crew Neck T-shirt	14.00
67	Stone-washed Twill Jacket	54.00
78	Island Can Coolers	6.00

Nicole has asked you to help her create the invoice worksheet. To create the sales invoice worksheet, do the following:

1. Start Excel with a blank workbook and insert a Documentation sheet at the beginning to explain the purpose and content of the document. Include your name and the date in the Documentation sheet.
2. On a new worksheet named **Invoice**, start creating the sales invoice. Begin by inserting the invoice labels, corresponding to placement of the labels shown in Figure AC-3 (it does not need to match Nicole's sketch exactly.) Adjust column widths as necessary.
3. Enter the calculations specified in Figure AC-2 in the worksheet. Use the TODAY function to enter the current date in the appropriate location in the invoice.
4. Format the cells as shown in Figure AC-1. Also note that the first cell in the Unit Price and Extended Price columns is formatted differently than the rest of the cells in those columns.
5. Add fonts and borders as shown in Figure AC-1 (try to match the figure as near as possible.) Add any color combinations that you think enhance the readability and appearance of the invoice.
6. Embed the **Logo.bmp** file located in Case1 folder of TutAdd on your Data Disk, at the top of the invoice as shown in Figure AC-1.
7. Print the worksheet and save the current version of the workbook as **Island Dreamz** in the Case1 folder of TutAdd on your Data Disk.
8. Use the Macro Recorder to create a macro that prints the Invoice worksheet. Add a button, labeled "Print," at the bottom of the Invoice worksheet to run the macro.
9. Unlock those cells in which data is entered (but not cells containing formulas or text), and then protect the worksheet for contents, objects and scenarios. Do not specify any password.

10. Test the operation of the worksheet by entering data for the order shown in Figure AC-1. Note how the values in the Extended Price column are calculated automatically as you enter the data. Use the macro to print this invoice.
11. Delete the data for Rachel's order, and then save the workbook as **Island Dreamz 2**.
12. Turn off the worksheet protection so you can continue to modify the workbook. Insert a new sheet after the Invoice sheet and name it **Product**. Create a product table that contains the product information shown in Figure AC-4. Excluding the column titles, give this table the range name "Products". Print a copy of this worksheet.
13. Nicole wants Excel to automatically look up the description and unit price in the product table when an item number is entered in the worksheet. Use the VLOOKUP function to determine the description and unit price values in the invoice sheet based on what item number the user enters.
14. The invoice will show #N/A values for the description, quantity and extended price columns, if no item number is entered. Correct this problem by modifying the formulas in these columns using an IF function so that if no item number is entered (i.e. the item number = "") then the value in these columns are blank (i.e. ""), otherwise the values are calculated as before.
15. Enter a test order into your invoice using some of the item numbers from the Products table. Be sure to leave some of the rows of the invoice blank to show that you have corrected the problem noted in question 14. Print the Invoice and the Product worksheet.
16. Lock the Description and Unit Price columns since they now contain formulas. Protect the Invoice worksheet.
17. Save the workbook as **Island Dreamz 3**.
18. Save the workbook as **Island Dreamz Invoice** in template format to the Case1 folder in TutAdd of your Data Disk (*not* to the Templates folder of your hard drive).
19. Close your workbooks and save your printouts.

OBJECTIVES

In this case you will:

- Create and use a multiple sheet workbook
- Enhance worksheets with formatting
- Consolidate worksheet files
- Link worksheets
- Create macros for displaying and printing sheets
- Edit your macros so they prompt the user for information and check user input
- Create charts from summary data
- Use Microsoft Word as a destination application

PERFORMANCE REPORTING FOR BOSTON SCIENTIFIC

CASE

Boston Scientific[1]

Boston Scientific is on the cutting edge of medical cost reduction. The company develops and manufactures catheters and other products that are used as alternatives to traditional surgery. As described by CEO Peter Nicholas: "We were one of the first companies to articulate the concept of less invasive procedures." Less invasive procedures are possible because current medical imaging techniques let physicians see inside the body and manipulate instruments through a natural opening or a tiny incision. Boston Scientific aggressively markets its products for these medical procedures. For example, a traditional coronary bypass operation often costs $50,000 to $70,000, including the hospital stay and weeks of recovery time. By contrast, clearing a clogged artery with one of Boston Scientific's catheters, which is inserted under the skin of a patient's arm, takes just a few hours and costs around $12,000.

Although many of Boston Scientific's products are expensive relative to the cost of a scalpel, they enable a patient to leave the hospital much sooner and avoid huge hospital bills. For this reason, Boston Scientific's products are popular and sales continue to increase rapidly. Another important element in its growth is the company's ability to leverage technology across its four largely autonomous divisions: Medi-Tech (radiology), Mansfield (cardiology), Microvasive Endoscopy (gastroenterology), and Microvasive Urology.

Willow Shire joined Boston Scientific last year as a junior accountant. Her responsibilities include preparing the quarterly performance report that consolidates the financial results for the four divisions. She also needs to add an interface to the workbook to make it easier to view reports for each division and the overall total. To help Willow prepare the statement, do the following:

1. Open the **Boston** workbook located in the Case2 folder of TutAdd on your Data Disk. Add a Documentation sheet describing the purpose and content of the workbook. Include your name and the date.
2. Add a consolidation sheet named **All.** Insert formulas in the consolidation worksheet that add the division results to determine the corporation total.
3. Enhance the appearance of the five accounting worksheets with special formatting, colors and borders.
4. Print a copy of the consolidation sheet.
5. Save the workbook as **Boston Scientific** to the Case2 folder in TutAdd of your Data Disk.
6. Create a worksheet named **Earnings** that displays the operating Earnings for each division by quarter. Insert a column titled Total that displays each division's overall earnings for the year. Format the worksheet to give it a pleasing appearance.
7. Create a chart sheet containing a clustered column chart that compares the operating earnings for each division by quarter. Add appropriate titles to the chart. Name the chart sheet **Column Chart.**
8. Create a chart sheet containing a pie chart that compares the operating earnings for the year (the value in the Total column from the Earnings worksheet) for the four divisions. Add appropriate titles. Name the chart sheet **Pie Chart.**
9. Print copies of the Earnings worksheet, and the two chart sheets.
10. Save the workbook as **Boston Scientific 2.**
11. Use the Macro Recorder to record a macro that displays the All worksheet, selecting cell A1. Name the macro Show_Report.
12. Edit the macro in the Visual Basic Editor so that it prompts the user for the name of the sheet to view (telling them that they can select "All", "Urology", "MediTech", "Mansfield" or "Endoscopy") and then displays that worksheet. Include an If-Then-Else control structure to detect errors. If the user enters an incorrect name, the macro should display a message box informing the user of the error.
13. Insert a new worksheet after the Documentation sheet worksheet named **Menu.** Place a macro button named "View Report" on the Menu worksheet that runs the Show_Report macro when clicked.
14. Create a second macro named Show_Chart that displays one of the two charts in the workbook. Include the necessary code to prompt the user for the name of the chart and to check the user's input, informing the user of any errors. Create a button named "View Chart" on the Menu worksheet that runs the Show_Chart macro.
15. Open the Visual Basic Editor and print the macros you created.
16. Save the workbook as **Boston Scientific 3.**
17. Start Microsoft Word and create a memo to Mr. Nicholas that summarizes your results. Copy and paste the pie chart you created earlier as a picture in the Word document. Also paste the table from the Earnings worksheet. Save the document as **Boston Scientific Report.** Print the memo.
18. Close the memo document and the workbook. Hand in your printouts.

OBJECTIVES

In this case you will:

- Create a query data source
- Retrieve data from a data source with a query
- Edit the properties of a query
- Create a PivotTable and PivotChart using external data
- Save a worksheet as a Web page

NEGOTIATING SALARIES FOR THE NATIONAL BASKETBALL ASSOCIATION

CASE

National Basketball Association

When Dr. James Naismith nailed a peach basket to a pole, he could not possibly have envisioned the popularity of the sport that he founded. Since those early days of peach baskets and volleyballs, basketball has become one of the most popular sports in the world—especially in America.

The National Basketball Association (NBA) is home to some of the world's greatest athletes. The popularity of the NBA soared in the 1980s, thanks to players like Michael Jordan, Julius Erving, "Magic" Johnson, and Larry Bird. This popularity resulted in larger attendance at games, larger television viewing audiences, and an increase in advertising sponsorships that, in turn, led to increased player salaries. While growing up, Troy Jackson wanted to be a professional basketball player. However, during his senior year of college, Troy had reconstructive knee surgery, ending his chances of ever playing competitive basketball. But Troy was still determined to make it to the NBA one way or another. Upon graduation, he was offered a job in the NBA head offices in New York, working on the staff of the commissioner.

The commissioner and his staff are concerned with the large number of player salaries being decided through arbitration. Salary arbitration is the process of negotiating a contract when both sides cannot agree to a specific dollar amount. The arbitration process is conducted through an independent third party who listens to arguments from both sides and then makes a final determination about the terms of the contract. During the past several years, the number of contracts decided through arbitration has more than tripled. To help the NBA head office understand what has been happening in the arbitration process, Troy suggests viewing the results in an Excel workbook.

The commissioner agrees that this would be useful in overseeing salaries being decided through arbitration. The arbitration data has been placed in an Access database. Retrieve that data and analyze it doing the following:

1. Start Excel with a blank workbook and insert a Documentation sheet at the beginning to explain the purpose and content of the document. Include your name and the date in the Documentation sheet.
2. Create a blank worksheet named **Player List**.
3. Create a new data source pointing to the Players database located in the Case3 folder of TutAdd in your Data Disk. Name the data source **NBA Salaries**.
4. With the NBA Salaries data source, create a query that retrieves the last and first name of each player in the database (from the Player table), the player's position (from the Position table), the player's team (from the Team table) and the bid that the player settled for (from the Bids table).
5. Have the query sort the retrieved data in descending order of the settled bid.
6. Retrieve the data from the query to cell A1 of the Player List worksheet. Print the player list.
7. Edit the properties of the data you retrieved so that they are refreshed automatically whenever the workbook is opened.
8. Remove any blank worksheets from the workbook and then save it as **NBA** to the Cases3 folder of TutAdd on your Data Disk.
9. Create a PivotTable and PivotChart report, retrieving the data from the NBA Salaries data source.
10. Retrieve the following fields from the database:

    PID, PosID and TeamID from the Player table
    Position from the Position table
    Team from the Team table
    Player Bid, Team Bid and Settle from the Bids table
11. Place the Team field in the Page area of the PivotTable, the Position field and the average Player Bid in the Row area, and Team Bid and Settle Bid in the Data area.
12. Set up the PivotTable so that it refreshes whenever the workbook is opened.
13. Place the PivotTable on a worksheet named **Bid Table** and the chart on a chart sheet named **Bid Chart**.
14. Calculate the average percent increase of the settled bid over the original team offer. For which position is the % increase the largest?
15. Print the PivotTable and Bid Chart.
16. Save the workbook as **NBA 2**.
17. The commissioner would also like to have a copy of the PivotTable to place on the association's internal office Web. Save the Bid Table worksheet as a Web page named **Arbitrate**. Do include any interactivity in the page.
18. View the Arbitrate Web page in your browser and print it out from there.

OBJECTIVES

In this case you will:

- Create macros to sort a list
- Ask what-if questions about a completed worksheet
- Filter data
- Link worksheets
- Use Goal Seek
- Create scenarios
- Create a data table
- Include worksheet data in a Word document

MANAGING TOURS FOR ETS

CASE

Executive Travel Services

Executive Travel Services (ETS) of San Diego is a travel agency that specializes in selling packaged tours to business executives from Fortune 500 companies. Tom Williams, a retired executive from a Fortune 500 company, started ETS in 1982. As an executive, Tom often wished he could socialize with other top executives in an informal setting for several days. Acting on his idea, Tom founded ETS. ETS books tours that last from one to three weeks. The tours' design lets executives enjoy a variety of activities while becoming acquainted with one another.

In the last several months, the number of executives requesting tours has nearly doubled. ETS accidentally overbooked several of its more popular tours, such as the Orient Express. Tom discussed the overbooking problem with Melissa Merron, a recently hired travel associate. They agreed that an Excel list could be used to develop a tour management system that would provide them with the necessary information to avoid overbooking problems in the future. Melissa worked with Tom and the other ETS associates to develop the field definitions shown in Figure AC- 5.

Figure AC-5 DATA DEFINITION FOR TOURS DATABASE

Field Name	Description
Tour	Tour name
Start	Date the tour starts
Stop	Date the tour stops
Type	Type of tour: Fish, Golf, Photo, or Relax
Sold	Number of seats sold for tour
Open	Number of seats still open for sale
Price	Price of tour

Melissa used Excel to set up the list. Tom would like her to make several changes to improve the operation of the tour management system. To help Melissa improve her list, complete the following:

1. Develop a planning analysis sheet for creating, modifying, and operating the tour management system. Use your planning analysis sheet to develop your Excel solution.
2. Open the **Travel** workbook from the Case4 folder in TutAdd on your Data Disk. Insert a Documentation sheet to explain the purpose and content of the document. Include your name and the date.
3. Review the Tours list on the Travel workshet and the named ranges. What is missing?

4. Add the appropriate field names in the order they are listed in Figure AC- 5. Center and bold each field name. Create range names for each field in the list.
5. Enhance the appearance of the report title and subtitle. Bold both titles. Italicize the subtitle. Increase the point size of the title to 14 points.

   Add any appropriate formatting to give the workbook a professional appearance. Print the **Tours** database.
6. Print a copy of the **Travel** worksheet.
7. Save the workbook as **Executive Travel** in the Case4 folder of TutAdd on your Data Disk.
8. Sort the list in ascending order of the Start field. Preview and print the sorted list.
9. Create a macro named Sort_Data to do the sort described above, then add a button to run the macro.
10. Open the Visual Basic Editor and edit the Sort_Data macro so that it prompts the user for the name of the first field by which to sort the data.

Explore

11. Edit the Sort_Data macro so that it uses whatever the user has entered as the Key1 sort field (*Hint:* If you store the user's response in a variable named "FieldName" the value of the Key1 parameter in the Sort method should be equal to Range(FieldName).)
12. Include code that will validate the user's response (one of the seven field names shown in Figure AC- 5) and display a message if the user enters a wrong field name.
13. Test and print your macro.
14. Save the workbook as **Executive Travel 2**.
15. Tom wants to know how much revenue the tour produces. Add a Total Revenue field to the list, and place it immediately to the right of the Price field (total revenue is calculated as the number of seats sold for a tour multiplied by the price charged for the tour.)
16. Change the definition of the Database range name to incorporate the new field you created. Give the new field the range name "Total."
17. Edit the Sort_Data macro so that it will accept "Total" as a sort field.
18. Add a formula to calculate the total revenue for all tours. Place the formula in a cell that will not be in the way of records that may be added to the list.
19. Print the worksheet sorted in ascending order of total revenue.
20. Save the workbook as **Executive Travel 3**.
21. Open the **Travel2** workbook, ETS's projected income statement. Add a Documentation sheet to this workbook including your name and the date.
22. What is missing from the Project Income worksheet? How can you solve this problem?
23. Using a linking formula, include the total revenue for all tours from the Tours list in ETS's projected income statement.
24. Add a rental expense of $12,000 in a new row inserted below administrative expense.
25. Print the **Project Income** worksheet.
26. Save the workbook as **Executive Travel 4**.
27. Based on the expected revenue from the Tours list and the added rental expense, what commission rate could ETS pay and still show a net income of $15,000? Print this solution.
28. Develop high-cost and low-cost scenarios for expenses that involve changing the rates for the commission, administration, reserve system or supplies. What is the effect on net income under each scenario? Create a scenario summary report on a separate worksheet and print the report.
29. Save the workbook as **Executive Travel 5**.
30. Create a table on its own worksheet that shows the effect on net income if the commission rate varies from 20% to 30% in increments of 1% and the administrative rate varies from 35% to 45% in increments of 1%. Print the resulting table.
31. Save the workbook as **Executive Travel 6**.
32. Start Word and create a memo to Tom that includes the table you created in the projected income statement and the results of your scenarios. Print the document and save it as **Executive Travel 7**.

OBJECTIVES

In this appendix you will:

- Use PMT, PPMT, IPMT functions
- Use AND function
- Use nested IF function
- Use YEAR function

EXCEL FUNCTIONS

SESSION A1.1

In this session you will develop a loan calculator using the PMT function and an amortization schedule using the PPMT and IPMT functions.

Financial Functions

Many people need to make loans for expensive items such as automobiles, sound systems, or home improvements. Often, they may not have the cash on hand at one time to make such purchases. Asking for a loan may cause anxiety for people who do not understand the full picture of how loans and interest rates are calculated.

At a local financial institution, which makes such loans, Jerry Angelo wants to develop a loan calculator worksheet for the institution's customers. The loan calculator would be made available to potential customers so that they can begin some calculations before meeting with a loan officer. His plan will allow the customer to use a computer to experiment with different loan scenarios. The calculator would determine the customer's monthly payment using varying loan amounts, interest rates, and time periods. In addition, the worksheet would also display an amortization schedule, a report that shows the details of each monthly payment—how much of each payment goes to paying off the loan and how much applies to interest. Jerry believes this service will help educate the loan applicant and reduce some of the applicant's anxiety.

Jerry asks you to develop the loan calculator and amortization schedule worksheet using data from an old loan application. Use as an example a loan of $20,000 at 7% interest being paid off monthly over three years.

Introduction to Financial Functions

Excel has fifteen financial functions that are related to money. Figure A1-1 shows four financial functions used to analyze loans and annuities.

Figure A1-1 FINANCIAL FUNCTIONS USED TO ANALYZE LOANS AND ANNUITIES

FUNCTION AND ARGUMENTS	DESCRIPTION
PMT(rate,nper,pv)	Calculates the payment for a loan based on constant payments and a constant interest rate.
IPMT(rate,per,nper,pv)	Returns the interest payment for a given period for an investment based on periodic, constant payments and a constant interest rate.
PPMT(rate,per,nper,pv)	Returns the payment on the principal for a given period for an investment based on periodic, constant payments and a constant interest rate.
PV(rate,nper,pmt)	Returns the present value of an investment. The present value is the total amount that a series of future payments is worth now.

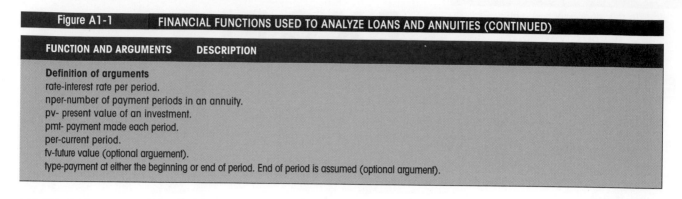

Figure A1-1 FINANCIAL FUNCTIONS USED TO ANALYZE LOANS AND ANNUITIES (CONTINUED)

FUNCTION AND ARGUMENTS	DESCRIPTION
Definition of arguments rate-interest rate per period. nper-number of payment periods in an annuity. pv- present value of an investment. pmt- payment made each period. per-current period. fv-future value (optional arguement). type-payment at either the beginning or end of period. End of period is assumed (optional argument).	

You will use the functions in Figure A1-1 to develop the loan calculator and amortization schedule.

Calculating a Loan Payment Using the PMT Function

The PMT function calculates the periodic payment of a loan assuming a constant interest rate and constant payments over the life of the loan. It is based on three factors: amount of the loan (principal), interest rate, and length of the loan (term). Now, develop the loan calculator section of the worksheet.

To develop the loan calculator:

1. Open the **Loan Analysis** workbook in the Tutorial folder for Appendix.01 and save it as **LoanCalculator**. Review the row and column labels.

   Enter the rate, term, and principal for the loan.

2. Type **7%** in cell B2, **3** in cell B3 and **20000** in cell B4 (Do not use the comma when typing 20000.)

   Enter the function to calculate the loan payment.

3. If necessary, click **B5**, click **Paste Function** [fx], click **Financial**, and then double-click **PMT** to open the PMT formula palette. See Figure A1-2.

Figure A1-2 PMT FORMULA PALETTE

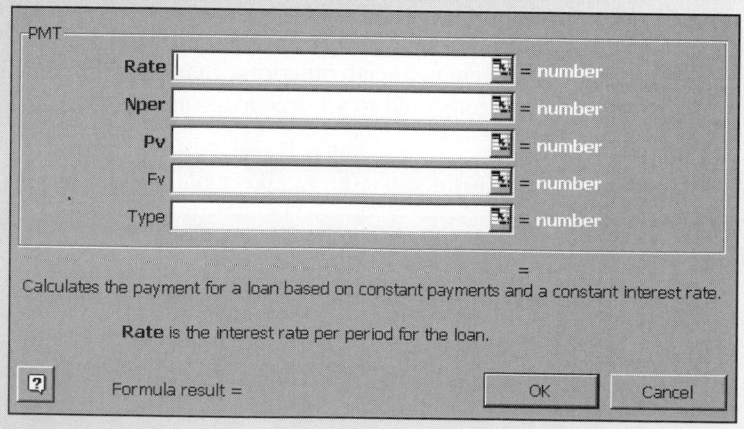

4. In the Rate text box, type **B2/12**. The interest rate entered in cell B2 was an annual rate so you need to divide it by 12 to get the rate per month.
5. In the Nper (number of periods) text box, type **B3*12**. The entry in cell B3 is expressed in years, you need to multiply the years by 12 to compute the number of monthly payments.
6. In Pv text box, type **B4** and click **OK**. The monthly payment appears as a negative number ($617.54).

   Display the monthly payment as a positive number.
7. Double-click cell **B5**. Position the insertion point to the right of the equal sign (=), type **-**, and then press the **Enter** key. The monthly payment appears as $617.54.
8. Click cell **B5**. See Figure A1-3.

Figure A1-3 COMPLETED LOAN CALCULATOR

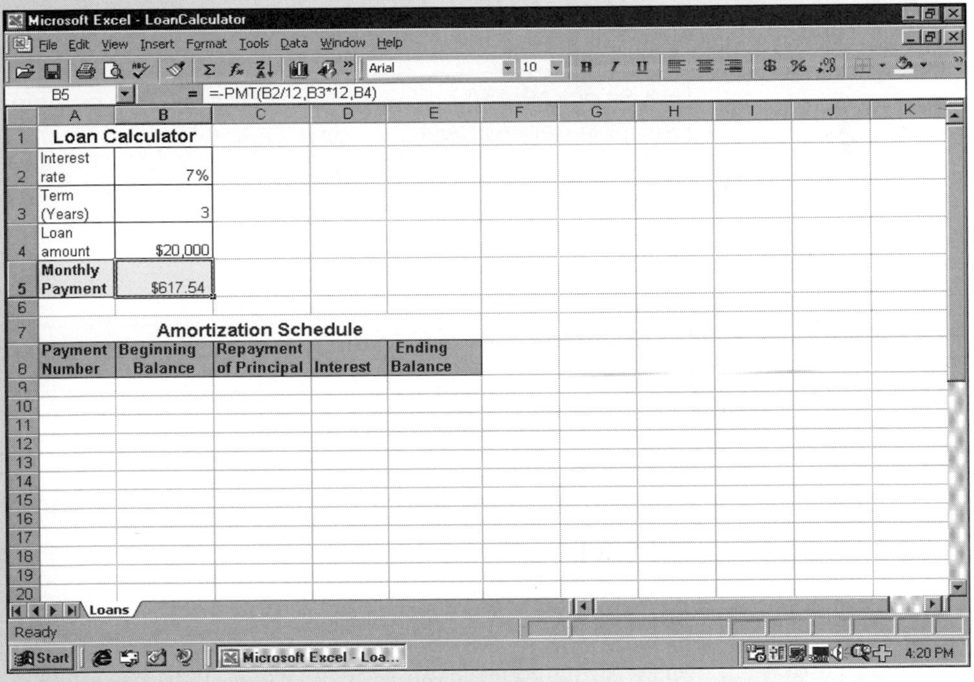

The loan calculator portion of the worksheet is complete.

Developing the Loan Amortization Schedule

Now prepare the **loan amortization schedule**, a report that shows the details of each loan payment. This schedule shows how much of each month's payment is applied to the repayment of principal, and how much is applied toward interest. The schedule also shows the ending loan balance after each loan payment. Figure A1-4 describes the calculations you'll use to prepare the amortization schedule.

Figure A1-4 **CALCULATIONS FOR AMORTIZATION SCHEDULE**

COLUMN IN AMORTIZATION SCHEDULE	NOTES ABOUT FORMULA
Payment number	In cells A9:A44 enter values 1 to 36
Beginning Balance	In cell B9, enter the amount of loan In cells B10:B44, enter ending loan balance from previous period
Repayment of Principal	In cells C9:C44, use PPMT function
Interest	In cells D9:D44, use IPMT function
Ending Balance	In cells E9:E44, use beginning balance less repayment of principal

Use Excel's AutoFill feature to enter the numbers 1 to 36 to represent the 36 payments.

To enter the numbers 1 to 36 using AutoFill:

1. Type **1** in cell A9 and **2** in cell A10.
2. Select **A9:A10** and use the AutoFill feature to complete the sequential series 3 to 36 in cells A11:A44.

Now, enter the beginning loan balance. Before the first payment is made, the beginning balance equals the amount of the loan.

To enter the beginning balance for period 1:

1. In cell B9, type **=B4**.

Calculating the Principal Paid in Each Period Using the PPMT Function

The column labeled Repayment of Principal in the amortization schedule shows the amount of the monthly payment that is applied to repaying the principal. This amount varies throughout the life of the loan and depends on the interest rate, total number of payments, amount of the loan, and the specific period. These are the arguments used with PPMT function to compute the principal paid for a specific period.

To calculate the repayment of principal using the PPMT function:

1. Click **C9**, click **Paste Function** [fx], click **Financial**, and then double-click **PPMT** to open the PPMT formula palette. See Figure A1-5.

Figure A1-5 PPMT FORMULA PALETTE

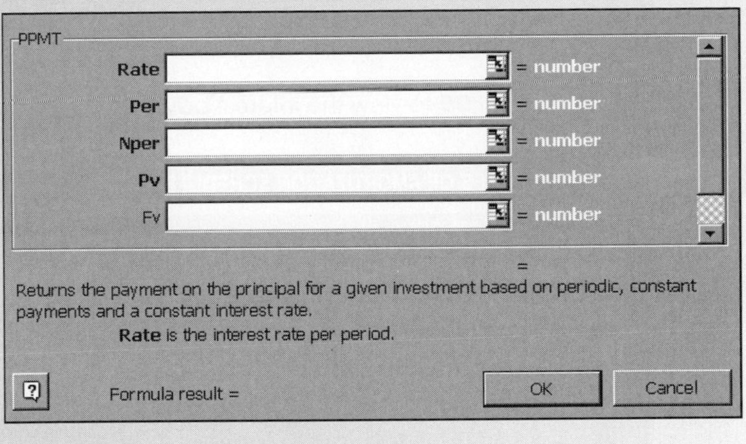

2. In the Rate text box, type **$B$2/12** to compute the monthly interest. Because you will be copying Rate to other rows in the amortization schedule, you add the dollar signs to the cell reference to make this portion of formula an absolute cell reference.
3. In the Per (current period) text box, type **A9.** Because this portion of the formula references the payment period it needs to vary as it is copied to other cells. Leave this portion of the formula as a relative cell reference.
4. In the Nper (number of periods) text box, type **$B$3*12** to determine the number of monthly payments.
5. In Pv text box, type **$B$4** and click **OK**. The repayment of principal amount appears as a negative number. Display this amount as a positive number. Double-click cell **C9**. Position the insertion point to the right of the equal sign (=), type -, and then press the **Enter** key. The repayment of principal for payment number 1 appears as $500.88. The formula in cell C9 is =-PPMT($B$2/12,A9,$B$3*12,$B$4).

Calculating the Interest Paid in Each Period Using the IPMT Function

The interest column in the amortization schedule shows the amount of the monthly payment that is applied toward interest for each period. The IMPT function is used to calculate this amount.

To calculate interest payment for a given period using IPMT function:

1. Click **D9**, click **Paste Function** [fx], click **Financial**, and then double-click **IPMT** to open the IPMT formula palette.
2. In the Rate text box, type **$B$2/12**.
3. In the Per text box, type **A9.**
4. In the Nper text box, type **$B$3*12**.

5. In Pv text box, type **$B$4** and click **OK**. The interest amount appears as a negative number. Double-click cell **D9**. Position the insertion point to the right of the equal sign (=), type **-**, and then press the **Enter** key. The interest appears as $116.67.

6. Click cell **D9** to view the interest payment formula. See Figure A1-6.

Figure A1-6 EARLY STAGES OF AMORTIZATION SCHEDULE

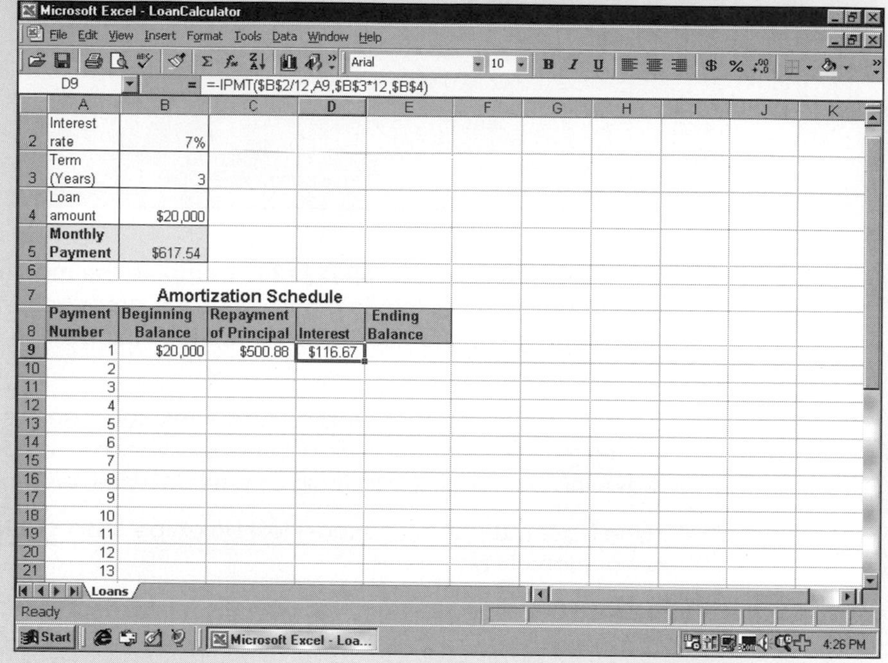

Now, complete the amortization schedule.

Completing the Amortization Schedule

First, compute the ending balance for the first month, this represents the amount of the principal that still needs to be repaid.

To complete the amortization schedule:

1. In cell E9, type **=B9-C9,** the formula to compute the ending balance. The amount is $19,499.12.

   For the remaining payment periods, the ending balance for the current month is also the beginning balance for the next month.

2. In cell B10, type **=E9**.

   Copy the formulas in C9:E9 down one row.

3. Select **C9:E9,** then click and drag the fill handle in cell **E9** down one row to row 10.

   Now copy the formulas in row 10 to the other rows of the amortization schedule.

4. Select **B10:E10**, then click and drag the fill handle in cell **E10** to row 44.

5. When finished, your amortization schedule should look like Figure A1-7. Check that the ending balance in period 36 equals zero.

Figure A1-7 COMPLETED AMORTIZATION SCHEDULE

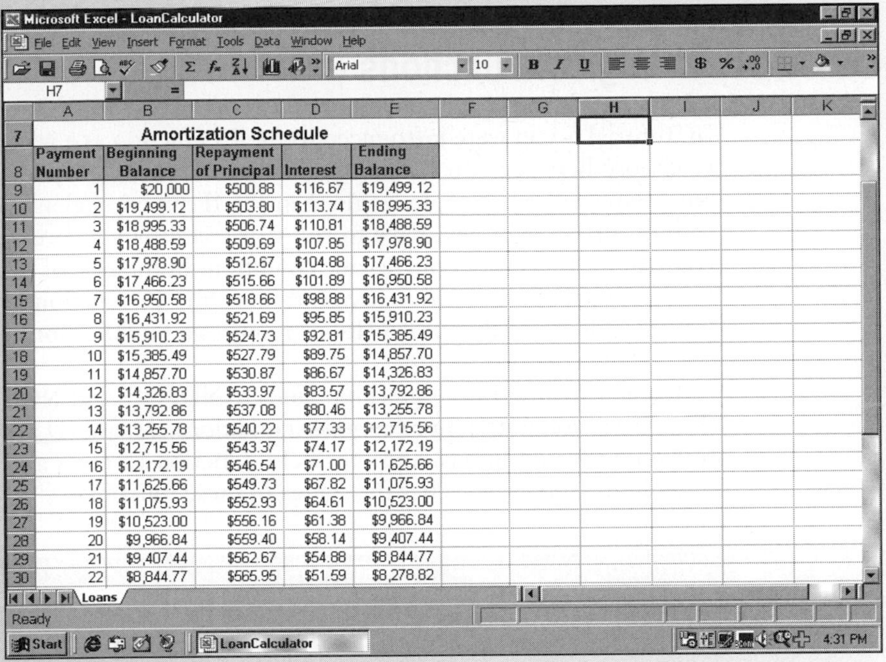

Amortization Schedule				
Payment Number	Beginning Balance	Repayment of Principal	Interest	Ending Balance
1	$20,000	$500.88	$116.67	$19,499.12
2	$19,499.12	$503.80	$113.74	$18,995.33
3	$18,995.33	$506.74	$110.81	$18,488.59
4	$18,488.59	$509.69	$107.85	$17,978.90
5	$17,978.90	$512.67	$104.88	$17,466.23
6	$17,466.23	$515.66	$101.89	$16,950.58
7	$16,950.58	$518.66	$98.88	$16,431.92
8	$16,431.92	$521.69	$95.85	$15,910.23
9	$15,910.23	$524.73	$92.81	$15,385.49
10	$15,385.49	$527.79	$89.75	$14,857.70
11	$14,857.70	$530.87	$86.67	$14,326.83
12	$14,326.83	$533.97	$83.57	$13,792.86
13	$13,792.86	$537.08	$80.46	$13,255.78
14	$13,255.78	$540.22	$77.33	$12,715.56
15	$12,715.56	$543.37	$74.17	$12,172.19
16	$12,172.19	$546.54	$71.00	$11,625.66
17	$11,625.66	$549.73	$67.82	$11,075.93
18	$11,075.93	$552.93	$64.61	$10,523.00
19	$10,523.00	$556.16	$61.38	$9,966.84
20	$9,966.84	$559.40	$58.14	$9,407.44
21	$9,407.44	$562.67	$54.88	$8,844.77
22	$8,844.77	$565.95	$51.59	$8,278.82

6. Change the input values (Interest rate, Term, and Loan amount) to see the effect on both the Monthly Payment and Amortization Schedule.

7. Save, then close the workbook.

The loan calculator and amortization schedule are complete and can now be used by the bank's customers.

SESSION A1.2

In this session you will learn to develop complex conditional formulas. You will nest the AND function within the IF function. You'll also learn how to nest IF functions.

AND, OR, NOT, and Nesting IF Functions*

Maria Abba, vice president of administration for Branco, Inc., is compiling Branco's budget estimates for two of Branco's employee benefits: costs for matching employee contributions to the 401(k) retirement plan and the cost of health insurance.

Maria provides you with information on each benefit program.

401(k) plan: Branco matches dollar-for-dollar up to 3% of an eligible employee's salary into the employee's 401(k) account. The company policy specifies that only *full-time regular* employees, employed for *one or more years* are eligible for the 401(k) plan.

*Before reading this section, you may find it helpful to review the IF function on page EX 7.13.

Health insurance costs: Branco pays 100% of the health insurance cost for all employees. The amount Branco pays per employee depends on the level of an employee's coverage: $5000 for family coverage, $4000 for individual coverage, and $0 if the employee has coverage elsewhere.

Maria asks you to help her develop these cost estimates for each employee.

Introduction to Logical Functions

In Tutorial 7 you were introduced to the IF function as a way of applying conditional logic to choose between two alternative formulas. The calculations for 401(k) and health insurance require more complex logic than the IF function alone is capable of handling. In the case of 401(k) plan, you have to test two conditions before you can determine the 401(k) cost; the IF function evaluates one condition. In the case of health insurance cost, you need to choose from three alternative formulas; the IF function only evaluates two alternative formulas. Each of these calculations requires a modification of the IF function in order to resolve the conditional logic.

Excel provides three logical functions (AND, OR, and NOT) that are typically used with the IF function to test more complex conditions. The AND and OR functions enable you to test multiple conditions, and the NOT function reverses a condition that returns true or false. Figure A1-8 describes the syntax of these functions.

Figure A1-8 SYNTAX OF AND, OR, AND NOT FUNCTIONS

FUNCTION	DESCRIPTION	EXAMPLE	RESULT
AND(logical condition1, logical condition2, ...logical condition30)	Returns TRUE if all logical conditions (up to 30) are TRUE; returns FALSE if one or more logical condition is FALSE	IF(AND(B2>=10000,B2<=4000), B2*1.05,B2) Assume B2=30000 Assume B2=50000	 31500 50000
OR(logical condition1, logical condition2, ...logical condition30)	Returns TRUE if any logical condition (up to 30) is TRUE; returns FALSE if all logical conditions are FALSE	IF(OR(C2="Finance",C2="Accounting") "Eligible","Ineligible") Assume C2=Accounting Assume C2=Marketing	 Eligible Ineligible
NOT(logical condition)	Reverse the value of its argument, if logical condition is FALSE, NOT(logical condition) returns TRUE, if logical condition is TRUE, NOT(logical condition) returns FALSE.	IF(NOT(A2="Married"),"Other","Joint") Assume A2=Sales Assume A2=Married	 Other Joint

The AND, OR, and NOT functions are typically placed within the IF function to create a **nested function**, a function that is used as an argument within another function.

Using the AND Function to Compute the 401(k) Costs

First, review the company's 401(k) policy.

The company policy specifies that only full-time employees employed with the company for one or more years are eligible for a 401(k) plan. Both conditions must be met to be eligible for the plan. Maria developed a flowchart to represent the logic to calculate the 401(k) costs. See Figure A1-9.

Figure A1-9 FLOWCHART SHOWING EMPLOYEE ELIGIBILITY FOR 401(K) RETIREMENT PLAN

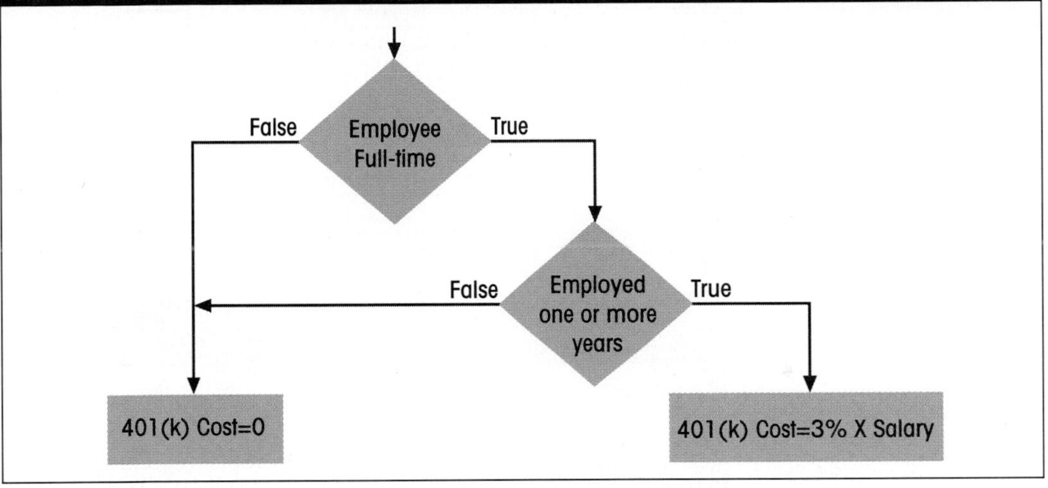

As you see in the flowchart, both conditions must be TRUE for an employee to be eligible for the 401(k) plan, in which case the company contributes 3% of the employee's salary; otherwise the employee is not eligible and the company's contribution is zero.

The IF function evaluates a single condition. To create the formula to determine the cost of the 401(k) plan for each employee, you use the AND function along with the IF function.

Now open the workbook that contains the employee data.

To open the Employee workbook:

1. Open the **Employee** workbook in the Tutorial folder for Appendix .01 and save it as **Employee Benefits**. See Figure A1-10.
   Data on each employee is stored in separate rows. There are seven fields for each employee. The Job Status codes for the employees' current status, are FT= full-time, PT= part-time, and CN= consultant. Heath Plan codes for type of coverage are F=family, I=individual, and N=no coverage. Notice two fields: 401(k) Cost and Health Insurance Cost have no values.

Figure A1-10 **EMPLOYEE DATA WORKSHEET**

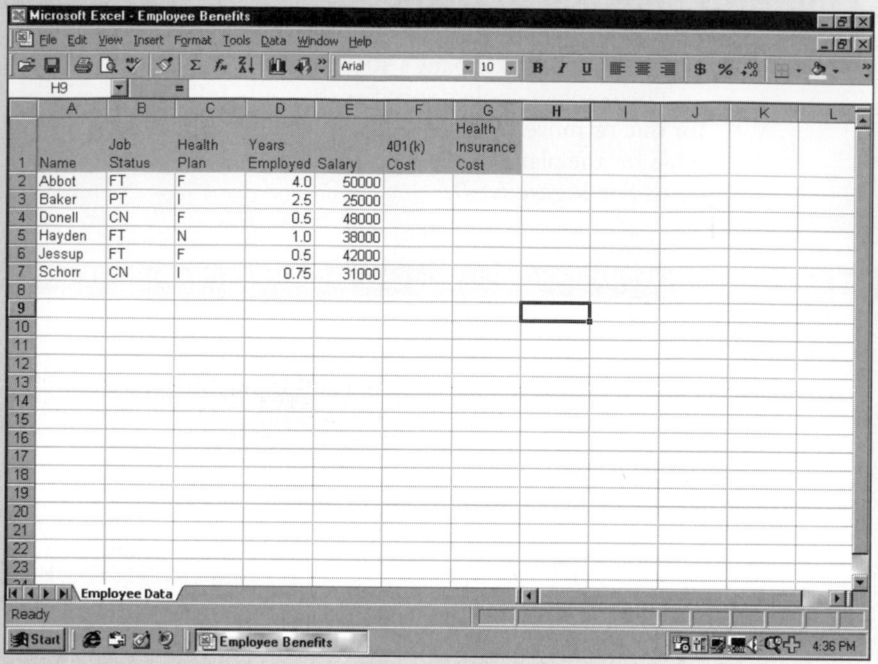

To create a formula to determine the cost of matching an employee's contribution to the 401(k) plan, you nest the AND function within the IF function. The Excel formula for the first employee has the following syntax

`=IF(AND(B2="FT",D2>=1),E2*0.03,0)`

`where red = condition, green = value-if-true, and blue = value-if-false.`

Now enter the formula for each employee.

To enter a formula using an AND function, nested within an IF function:

1. Click cell **F2** to make it the active cell.
2. Type **=IF(AND(B2="FT",D2>=1),E2*0.03,0)** and press **Enter**. Notice, 1500 appears in cell F2.
3. Copy the formula in cell **F2** to the range **F3:F7**.
4. Click cell **F7**. When finished your output should be similar to Figure A1-11.

Figure A1-11 **401(K) COST ESTIMATES COMPLETED**

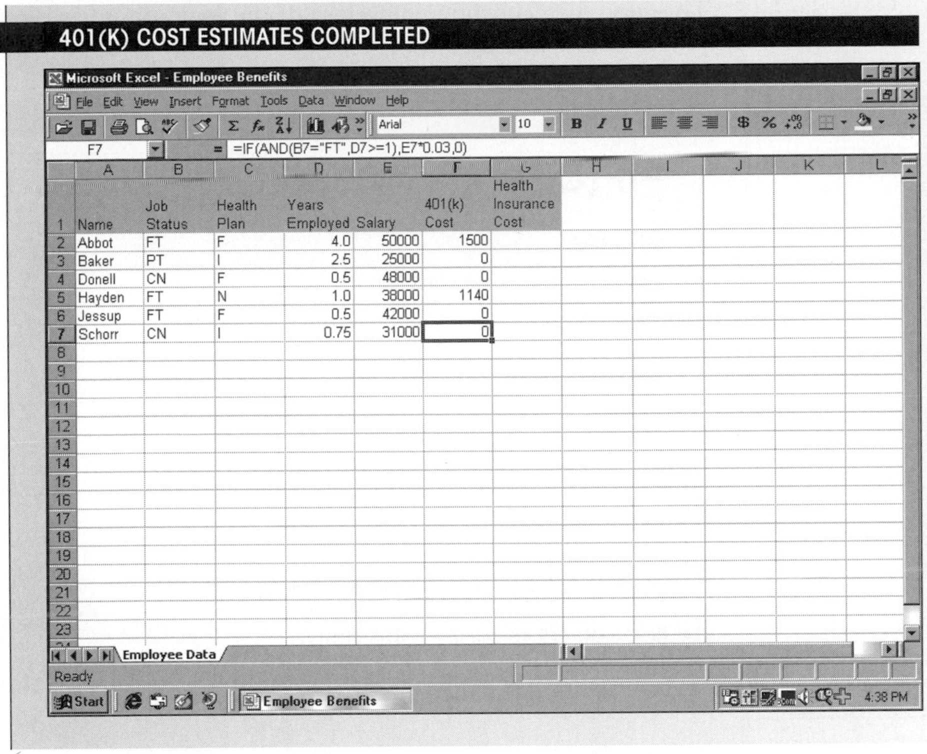

The formulas you created will calculate the 401(k) costs. Now build the formula to compute the health insurance costs.

Nesting IF Functions to Compute Health Insurance Costs

There are decisions in which the AND and OR functions cannot resolve the conditional logic for certain computations. In these cases, you may find that placing the IF function within another IF function, or *nesting* the IF function, creates a hierarchy of tests and is a good way to resolve the conditional logic. For example, determining the health insurance cost for each employee requires a formula to choose from among three cost options: $5000 for family coverage, $4000 for individual coverage, and $0 if the employee has coverage elsewhere. The employee database contains a Health Plan code that is used to determine the level of coverage. Figure A1-12 illustrates the logic to determine the health insurance cost.

Figure A1-12 **FLOWCHART SHOWING HEALTH INSURANCE COST OPTIONS**

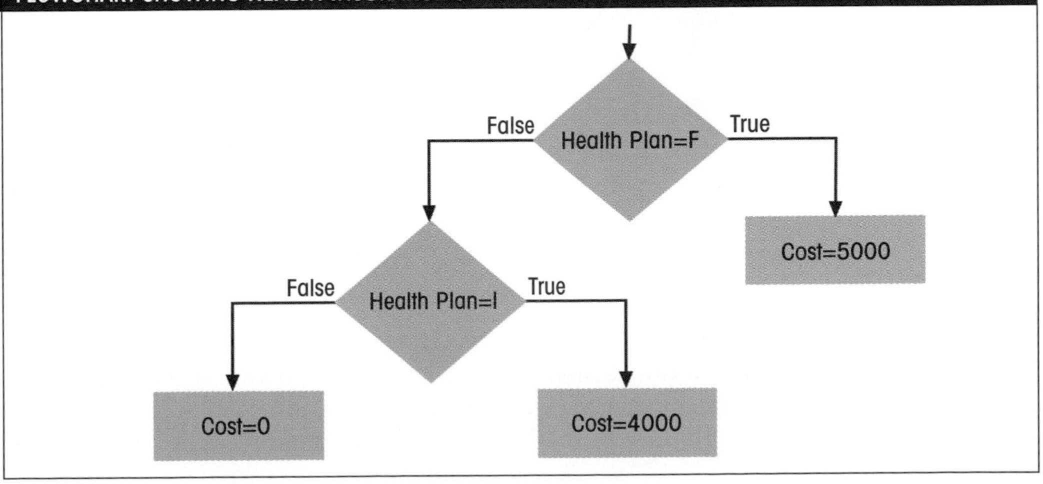

The nested IF function equivalent of the logic illustrated in the flowchart for the first employee shown in figure A1-13.

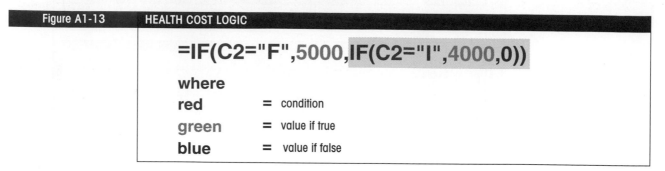

Figure A1-13 HEALTH COST LOGIC

=IF(C2="F",5000,IF(C2="I",4000,0))

where

red = condition

green = value if true

blue = value if false

Now enter the nested IF function needed to calculate the cost of health insurance for each employee.

To enter the nested IF function:

1. Click cell **G2** to make it the active cell.
2. Type **=IF(C2="F",5000,IF(C2="I",4000,0))** and press **Enter**. The IF function returns 5000.
3. Copy the formula in cell **G2** to the range **G3:G7**.
4. Click cell **G7**. When finished, your output should be similar to Figure A1-14.
5. Save, then close the workbook.

Figure A1-14 HEALTH INSURANCE COST ESTIMATE COMPLETED

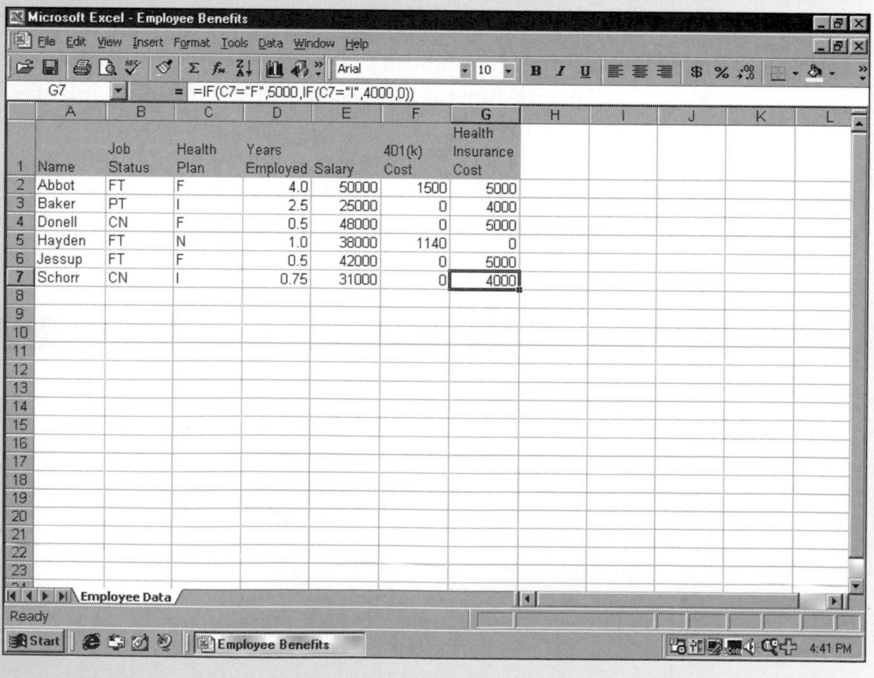

Name	Job Status	Health Plan	Years Employed	Salary	401(k) Cost	Health Insurance Cost
Abbot	FT	F	4.0	50000	1500	5000
Baker	PT	I	2.5	25000	0	4000
Donell	CN	F	0.5	48000	0	5000
Hayden	FT	N	1.0	38000	1140	0
Jessup	FT	F	0.5	42000	0	5000
Schorr	CN	I	0.75	31000	0	4000

In this session you used the AND function within an IF function to develop the conditional logic needed to calculate the 401(k) costs. Then you nested IF functions to develop a conditional formula to calculate the health insurance cost.

SESSION A1.3

In this session you will learn how Excel stores date and time values and uses the YEAR function to calculate the number of years between dates.

Date and Time Functions

Century, Inc. recognizes employees for their longevity of employment by providing service awards at one-year, five-year, ten-year and twenty-year time intervals. Millie Fenton subtracts the employee's hire year from the current year to compute the number of years an employee has been employed. She uses this information to determine which employees receive service awards.

Introduction to Date and Time Values

Excel stores dates and times as values. Each date between January 1, 1900 and December 31, 2078 is stored as a sequential serial number. January 1, 1900 is assigned the value 1, January 2, 1900 is assigned the value 2, January 1, 1901 is 367, January 1, 2000 is the value 36526, and so on.

Excel works with time values as fractions of a 24-hour day. For instance, midnight is stored as 0.0, noon (12 PM), is stored as 0.5, and 6 PM is stored as 0.75. Time is treated as an extension of the serial number Excel uses with dates. So January 1, 2000 at 12 PM is represented by the value 36526.5.

Because dates are stored as serial numbers, you can perform calculations with dates (sometimes referred to as date arithmetic.) For example, you can add integers to dates or calculate the number of days between two dates. You can also perform arithmetic with time values. For example, you can calculate the number of hours between two times.

Excel has many functions to assist you with dates and times. Figure A1-15 lists some of these functions.

Figure A1-15 DATE AND TIME FUNCTIONS

FUNCTION	DESCRIPTION
TODAY() *Notice that although parentheses are included, no arguments are used in this function*	Returns the current date
NOW() *Notice that although parentheses are included, no arguments are used in this function*	Returns the current date and time
DATE(year, month, day)	Returns the date based on its three arguments: year, month, and day
DAY(date)	Extracts a day of the month from a date
MONTH(date)	Extracts a month number from a date
YEAR(date)	Extracts a year (yyyy) from a date
WEEKDAY(date)	Returns a day of the week (Sunday =1) from a date
DATEVALUE(date_text)	Converts a date from text to a date
DATEDIF(start_date, end_date, unit)	Calculates the number of days, months, or years between two dates. Units are entered as "Y" (complete years), "M" (complete months), or "D" (days).
HOUR(time)	Extracts the hour part from a time
MINUTE(time)	Extracts the minute part from a time
SECOND(time)	Extracts the second part from a time

Using the YEAR Function to Calculate Years Employed

Now calculate the number of years an employee has been employed at Century, Inc. The data Millie has about employees includes the date hired. You will extract the year from the date hired using the YEAR function so you can subtract the year hired from the current year.

To calculate years employed:

1. Open the **Service** workbook in the Tutorial folder for Appendix.01 and save it as **YearsEmployed**.
2. Enter the current year. Type **2001** in cell B1.
3. Type **=$B$1-YEAR(B4)** in cell C4. Notice the cell is formatted with date and time.
4. Return to cell C4, click **Format**, click **Cells**, and click **General** format in the **Numbers** tab. Click **OK**. 15 appears in cell C4.
5. Copy the formula to the cells in the range **C5:C7**.

Figure A1-16 CALCULATION OF YEARS EMPLOYED COMPLETED

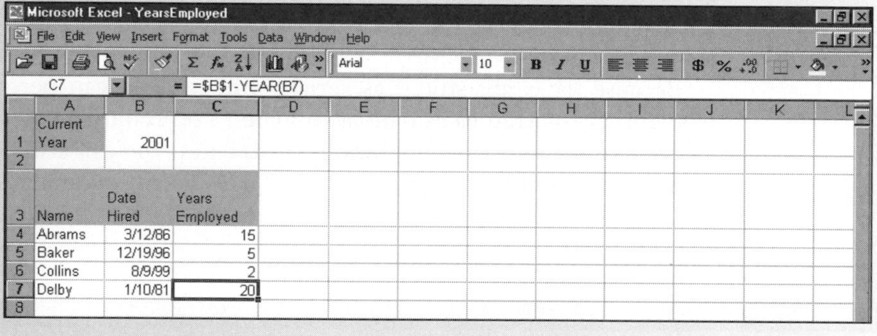

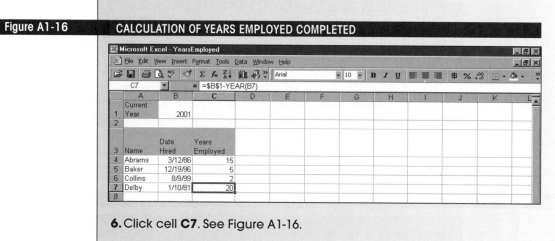

6. Click cell **C7**. See Figure A1-16.
7. Save, then close the workbook.

Text and Statistical Functions

Excel has several hundred functions that perform a wide range of calculations. Figure A1-17 lists a few text and statistical functions that you may find useful. For more information on these and other functions consult the online help system.

Figure A1-17 ADDITIONAL STATISTICAL AND TEXT FUNCTIONS

FUNCTION	DESCRIPTION	EXAMPLE USING FIG A1-18	RESULT
COUNT(value1,value2,...)	Counts the number of values in a range.	=COUNT(A1:A6)	3
COUNTA(value1,value2,...)	Counts the number of nonblank characters in a range.	=COUNTA(A1:A6)	6
COUNTIF(range,criteria)	Counts the number of cells within a range that meet the given criteria.	=COUNTIF (A1:A6,"Rhode Island")	2
SUMIF(range,criteria,sum_range)	Adds the cells specified by a given criteria.	=SUMIF(A1:A6,">20")	56
LEFT(text,# of leftmost characters)	Returns leftmost characters of a string.	=LEFT(A1,5)	Rhode

Figure A1-17 ADDITIONAL STATISTICAL AND TEXT FUNCTIONS (CONTINUED)

FUNCTION	DESCRIPTION	EXAMPLE USING FIG A1-18	RESULT
MID(text,position of first character you want to extract, # of characters to extract)	Returns a specific number of characters from a text string starting at a position you specify.	=MID(A1,7,2)	Is
RIGHT(text, number of characters to extract)	Returns rightmost characters in text string.	=RIGHT(A1,4)	Land
LEN(text)	Returns the number of characters in a text string.	=LEN(A1)	12
CONCATENATE(text1,text2,...)	Joins several text strings into one text string.	=CONCATENATE(A3,A4)	Massachusetts24

Figure A1-18

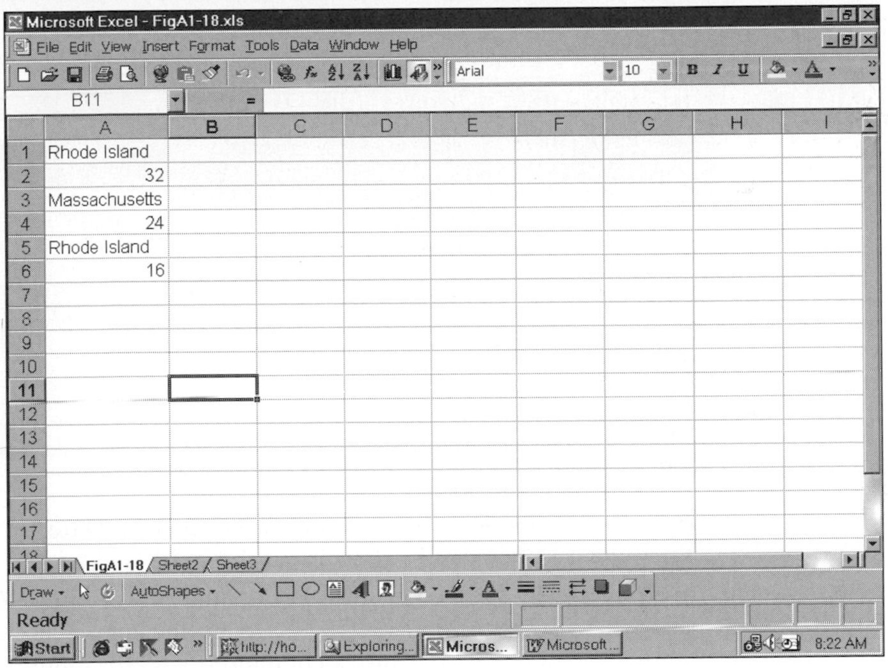

REVIEW ASSIGNMENTS

1. Open the **LoanAnalysis2** workbook in the Review folder of Appendix.01 and save it as **LoanAnalysis3**.
2. Change the interest rate to 8%. Print the results.
3. Insert two formulas to calculate total payments made during the entire loan (monthly payment times number of payments) and total interest (total payments – loan amount). Place the formula to calculate Total Payments in cell B6 and the formula to calculate Total interest in cell B7. Print only the loan calculator section of the worksheet.

Explore

4. In a separate sheet, develop a worksheet to determine the number of periods needed to pay off a loan assuming a potential borrower knows the interest rate, the loan amount, and the amount the borrower wants to repay each month. How many months will it take to pay off a $10,000, 9% loan paying $100 a month? (*Hint*: Look up the NPER function in Help. Enter the payment amount as a negative number.) Develop an attractive worksheet. Print the results.

5. Save and close the workbook.
6. Open the **Employee2** workbook in the Review folder of Appendix .01 and save it as **Employee3**.

Explore

7. a. The company is considering changing its 401(k) policy to include eligibility for all of its employees, both full-time and part-time, regardless of their years of service. Create a formula in column F to reflect these changes.
   b. Another possible revision to the plan specifies that both full-time and part-time employees employed with the company for one or more years are eligible for a 401(k) plan. Both conditions must be met to be eligible for the plan. Create a formula in column G to calculate 401(k) cost based on this new policy.

Explore

8. Develop the health insurance formula so you display the label "invalid code" in the Health Insurance Cost column if an invalid code is entered in the Job Status field.
9. Include your name in a custom footer, then print the results. Save and close the workbook.
10. Open a blank workbook and calculate how many days until you graduate. Follow the steps in Figure A1-19.

Figure A1-19 STEPS FOR CALCULATING DAYS UNTIL GRADUATION

CELL	ENTER
A1	Enter the label **Graduation Date**
B1	Enter your date of graduation
A2	Enter the label **Today's date**
B2	Enter a function to display today's date
A3	Enter the label **Number of days until graduation**
B3	Enter a formula to compute the number of days from today's date until you graduate

11. Print the results. Save the workbook as **GraduationDate**.
12. Microsoft has developed a rule to interpret dates entered with a two-digit year occurring in either the 20th or 21st century. For example, if you enter 4/24/99, does Excel store this date as 4/24/1999 or 4/24/2099? Determine how Excel treats dates entered using a two-digit year (mm/dd/yy instead of mm/dd/yyyy) by inputting the dates in Figure A1-20 into Sheet2. Format the six cells using the date format m/d/yyyy. Briefly explain how Excel treats dates entered with a two-digit year.

Figure A1-20 DATES TO INPUT

A2	7/1/00
A3	7/1/28
A4	7/1/29
A5	7/1/30
A6	7/1/31
A7	7/1/99

13. a. Open the **Service2** workbook in the Review folder of Appendix.01 and save it as **Service3**.
    b. Enter the TODAY function in cell B1 and then format that cell using the format type m/d/yyyy. Use the same format type to format cells B4:B7.
    c. Apply the DATEDIF function in cells C4:C7 to calculate the number of complete years of service. If necessary, use Help to learn more about the DATEDIF function.
    d. Print and save the workbook.

CASE PROBLEMS

Case 1. Depreciation at Imat Helen Fayer is an accountant at Imat Corporation. One of her responsibilities is to maintain information about the assets that the company owns. This information is used to compute depreciation for the financial reports and identify new assets that need a property identification tag stamped on the asset.

1. Open the **Asset** workbook in the Cases folder for Appendix.01, and save it as **AssetData**. Notice data has been entered in all columns except the Depreciation and Needs Tag columns. You need to develop formulas for each of these columns.
2. Accountants use different methods to calculate depreciation. Excel provides functions that calculate depreciation for each of these depreciation methods. Figure A1-21 describes each function.
   Use the IF function to develop a formula to compute depreciation for each asset. Within the IF function test the depreciation method code (SLN is straight-line-code, SYD is sum-of-years-digits, DDB is double-declining balance) to determine the appropriate depreciation function to use to compute depreciation.

Figure A1-21 DESCRIPTION OF FUNCTIONS

DEPRECIATION METHOD	FUNCTION AND ARGUMENTS	DESCRIPTION
Straight Line	SLN(cost,salvage,life)	The SLN function calculates straight-line depreciation for a single period. This method distributes the depreciation evenly over the life of the asset.
Double-declining balance	DDB(cost,salvage,life,period)	The DDB function uses the double-declining balance method to calculate the amount of depreciation for a specified period. This method computes depreciation at an accelerated rate. Depreciation is highest in earlier periods and decreases in successive periods.
Sum of years digits	SYD(cost,salvage,life,period)	The SYD function uses the sum-of-the-years'-digits method to calculate an asset's depreciation for a specified period. This method concentrates depreciation in earlier periods.
	where cost=purchase price of the asset salvage=value of the asset at end of useful life life=number of periods over which the asset is being depreciated period=period for which to calculate depreciation	

3. Print a report that includes the Asset description, Cost, Date purchased, and Depreciation.

4. In the Needs Tag column, enter a formula that displays "Yes" or "No" depending on whether the asset needs a property tag. The criteria for tagging is as follows:
   - Asset purchased in current year. Use 2001 as the current year.
   - Cost of asset is $3000 or more

   Both criteria must be met to place "Yes" in the Needs Tag column, otherwise place "No".
   First, enter the current year in cell B2 and the Tag cutoff amount in cell B3. Use the information in cell B2 and cell B3 to develop an IF function in the Needs Tag column.
5. Use the information in the Needs tag column to print only those assets that need to be tagged. Show only the columns Asset description, Date purchased, and Needs Tag on the printout.
6. Save and close the workbook.

Case 2. North State University Revisited Dean Long of the College of Business Administration has to prepare a summary report for a presentation to advisory council. She has prepared a sketch of the information to summarize from the faculty list. See Figure A1-22.

Figure A1-22 SKETCH OF SUMMARY REPORT

GROUP	NUMBER	TOTAL SALARY
All faculty		
Female faculty		
Full professor		

1. Start Excel and make sure your Data Disk is in the appropriate disk drive. Open the workbook **FacultyRevisited** in the Cases folder for Appendix.01, and then save it as **FacultySummary**.
2. Complete the summary report, cells A2:C5. Use the appropriate functions in Figure A1-17 to develop formulas for the summary report.
3. Print only the summary report. Remember to include your name in the custom footer.

Explore

4. North State University has changed servers for their email and every faculty, staff, and student has a new email address. The dean wants to include the new address in column M of the faculty list. The email address can be generated by using text functions. A new address consists of the following:

   The user id portion of the email address is formed from the
   - First letter of your first name, plus the
   - First three letters of your last name, plus the
   - Last four digits of your social security number, then

     add @nsu.edu to complete the address.

   For example, Alicia Smith's social security number is 000-10-9999. Her email is AS9999@nsu.edu. (*Hint*: Review the CONCATENATE function.)

   Print the faculty list.
5. Save the workbook.

OBJECTIVES

In this tutorial you will:

- Create a data map
- Modify titles and legends on a data map
- Resize a data map
- Change the format of a data map
- Display multiple sets of data in different formats on a single map
- Magnify an area of a data map
- Display labels on a data map
- Create a custom pin map
- Remove map features from a data map

USING DATA MAPS

Creating a Data Map for a Presentation

CASE

Morning Glory Naturals

As a marketing major at the local college, you have the opportunity to intern with Morning Glory Naturals, a specialty tea company with corporate headquarters in New York City. You have been assigned to work with the company's director of marketing and sales, Miguel Sanchez.

When the company introduced its unique products two years ago, Morning Glory conducted an aggressive marketing campaign. Now, Miguel must present to the company's stockholders the results of this marketing campaign in terms of Morning Glory's sales.

Miguel has already created an Excel worksheet with data on the sales in each state in which Morning Glory does business. For his presentation, Miguel would like one of his slides to be a map showing sales by state and region. Your task is to help Miguel create this map by using Excel's data mapping feature, Microsoft Map.

SESSION A2.1

In this session you'll learn how to create a data map. Then you'll customize it by changing titles and legends, as well as by improving the data map's overall appearance. You'll also learn about the data map formats available with Microsoft Map and how to change data map formats.

Introducing Data Mapping

Before you begin creating the data map for Miguel, you should understand what data mapping is. **Data mapping**, like charts, helps you to visualize and analyze your data. When data in a worksheet is categorized by geographic regions, such as countries, states, census tracts, or zip codes, that data can be presented in the form of a color-coded map to help clarify relationships and trends in the data. For example, you can use a data map of demographic data to better understand market potential or to plan sales and marketing efforts. Data maps also can be used effectively for political campaigns: A data map shaded according to where support is strong, nonexistent, or marginal can aid in the decision on where to concentrate advertising and fund-raising efforts.

Creating a data map in Excel is easy: You select a worksheet range that includes geographic regions and then click the Map button on the Standard toolbar to start Excel's add-in module Microsoft Map.

Creating a Data Map

Microsoft Map, developed by MapInfo Corporation, consists of predesigned maps that form the basis for automatically transforming your worksheet data into data maps. Microsoft Map includes maps of Australia, Canada, Europe, Mexico, North America, Southern Africa, UK standard regions, United States with Alaska and Hawaii insets, United States in North America, and world countries. Additional maps can be ordered directly from the MapInfo Corporation.

REFERENCE WINDOW RW

Creating a Data Map

- Organize data in columns. Usually, the first column includes geographic regions such as states or countries, and other columns include data associated with each geographic region.
- Select the range containing the data you want to include in a data map.
- Click the Map button on the Standard toolbar.
- Click and drag the mouse pointer to size the map frame.
- Release the mouse button.

Now, you're ready to use Microsoft Map to create Miguel's data map. Your first step is to make sure the worksheet that Miguel has created is organized correctly.

Organizing a Worksheet for a Data Map

The first step in creating a data map is arranging, if necessary, your worksheet data in columns. One column must contain geographic data that Microsoft Map can match with one of its predefined lists of geographic names. The geographic names can be full state names, standard state abbreviations, provinces, countries, or other geographic regions recognized by Microsoft Map. You'll find a list of the standard spellings and abbreviations for all geographic names that Microsoft Map can use to create maps in the Excel workbook Mapstats (located in the C:\Program Files\Common Files\Microsoft Shared\Datamap\Data folder). If your worksheet contains additional data, such as population statistics, you should include a value for each geographic name. Mapstats also contains various demographic data corresponding to each state, province, and country.

Now that you know how a worksheet must be organized, you're ready to open Miguel's Excel worksheet.

To start Excel, open the StSales workbook, and rename it:

1. Start Excel as usual, and make sure your Data Disk is in the appropriate drive.
2. Open the **StSales** workbook from the Appendix.02 folder on your Data Disk, and then save it as **State Sales**.
3. If necessary, click the **Sales-U.S.** sheet to display it. See Figure A2-1.

Figure A2-1 STATE SALES WORKSHEET

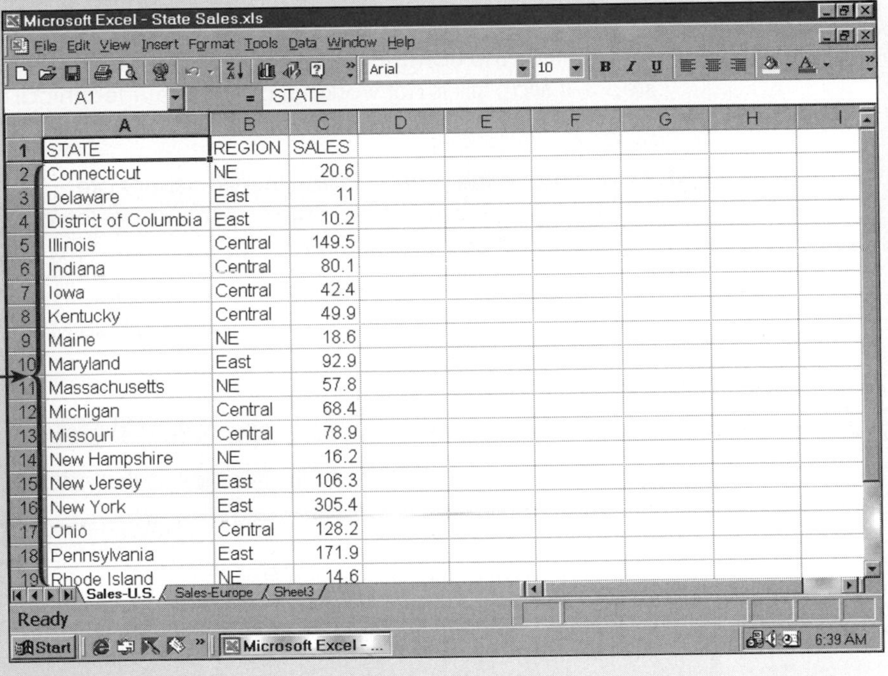

State names in correct format for Microsoft Map

As you look at Miguel's worksheet, you notice that the first column contains the full names of the states in which Morning Glory sells its products. Microsoft Map will recognize full state names and will use these names to determine which map to automatically create. The second column identifies the region into which the Morning Glory marketing group has assigned each state, and the third column represents sales within each state. Notice that the State Sales worksheet includes sales data for every state listed.

You determine that the State Sales worksheet is organized correctly for a data map. Now you're ready for the next steps: selecting the data map range and sizing the frame.

Selecting the Data Map Range and Sizing the Frame

Your first step in creating a map is to select the range of data you want to include in the map. The range will include the geographic ranges, as well as any other map data you want displayed. For Miguel's data map of Morning Glory's sales, the data map range you select will include the column headings, which Microsoft Map will use to label both the map legend and columns of data, as well as all the other worksheet data. After you select the data map range, you'll size the frame in which the map will appear (also on the Sales-U.S. worksheet). Don't worry about the initial size of the map frame; you can resize the frame later as needed.

To select a data map range and size a data map frame:

1. Select the range **A1:C22**, the range containing the data you want to include in the map.
2. Scroll down the worksheet, until row **24** appears as the first row in the worksheet.
3. Click the **Map** button.

   Trouble? If the Map button doesn't appear on any toolbar, you may add the button to a toolbar. Click Tools, click Customize, and then click the Commands tab. In the categories list, click Insert. Scroll down to find Map and click and drag it from the command list to the toolbar. Click the Close button. Return to step 3. If Map still is not working, consult your technical support person or instructor for help.

4. As you move the pointer inside the worksheet area, the pointer changes to a crosshair +. Position the crosshair in the upper-left corner of cell **A24** to mark the upper-left corner of the map.
5. Click and drag down to the right to cell **G36**, to draw the data map frame. When you release the mouse button, the Multiple Maps Available dialog box opens. See Figure A2-2.

Figure A2-2 MULTIPLE MAPS AVAILABLE DIALOG BOX

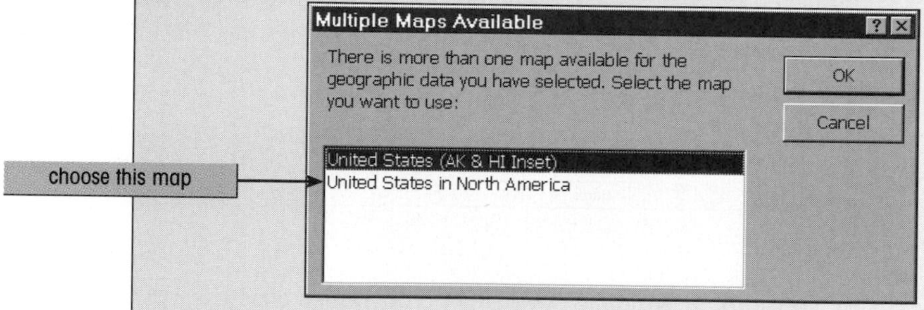

Trouble? If the Resolve Unknown Geographic dialog box opens, Excel didn't recognize one or more geographic names in the worksheet. Click Cancel, correct the error, and then repeat step 1. Remember that geographic names must be spelled correctly and included in the range.

Microsoft Map analyzes the geographic names in the first column of the range you selected and determines that two different maps can be used—United States (AK & HI Inset) or United States in North America, which includes only the 48 contiguous states. Because your data doesn't include sales for Alaska or Hawaii, you'll choose the United States in North America map.

6. Click **United States in North America**, and then click the **OK** button. Microsoft Map builds a map based on the selected data. The map of North America, as well as the Microsoft Map Control dialog box, are visible. See Figure A2-3.

Figure A2-3 DATA MAP OF NORTH AMERICA

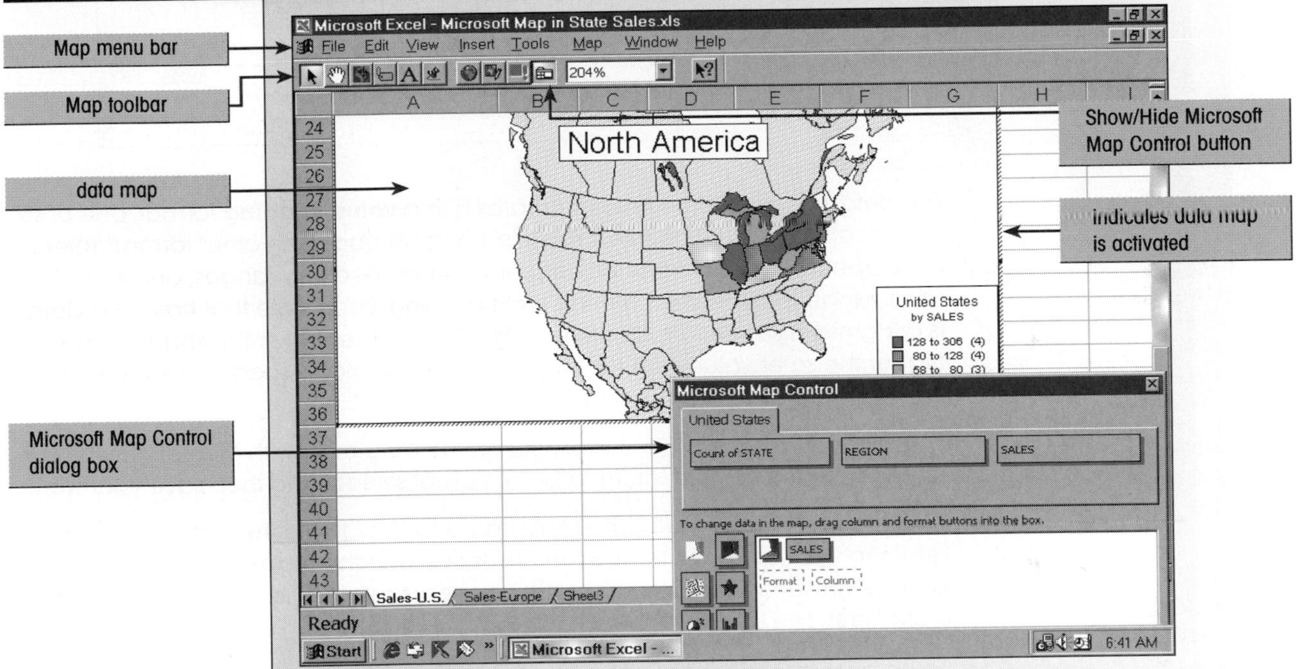

Notice that a special Map menu bar and Map toolbar replace the usual Excel menu bar and toolbars. The Map menu bar and Map toolbar enable you to easily customize the data map. You'll have a chance to use some of the Map menu bar commands and Map toolbar buttons later in this tutorial.

Because you won't need to use the Microsoft Map Control dialog box at this time, you will close it so you can get a better view of the data map.

7. Click the **Show/Hide Microsoft Map Control** button on the Map toolbar (or click the **Close** button in the Microsoft Map Control dialog box). See Figure A2-4.

Figure A2-4 **VALUE SHADING FORMATTED DATA MAP**

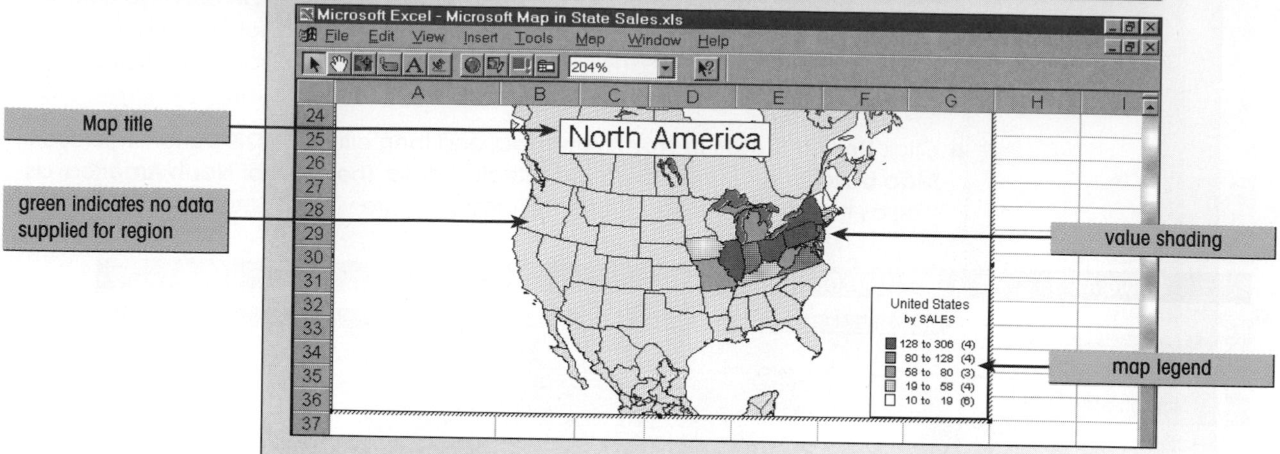

The default map Microsoft Map creates is in a **value shading** format, one of six data map formats available. (You'll learn more about the other formats later in this appendix.) In this map format, sales are divided into ranges, and each sales range is associated with different shading. Each state that has sales data is assigned a shade to indicate its level of sales. The darker the shading, the higher the sales value (see the map legend). The states shaded green are those that have no sales data supplied.

You're ready to discuss your progress on the data map with Miguel. Now, you'll exit Microsoft Map and return to Excel's usual screen, and then save your work.

8. Click any cell outside the data map frame to deactivate the data map and return to the worksheet. Notice the border around the map and the Map toolbar are removed. The data map now appears as an embedded object in the worksheet. See Figure A2-5.

Figure A2-5 DATA MAP APPEARS AS AN EMBEDDED OBJECT

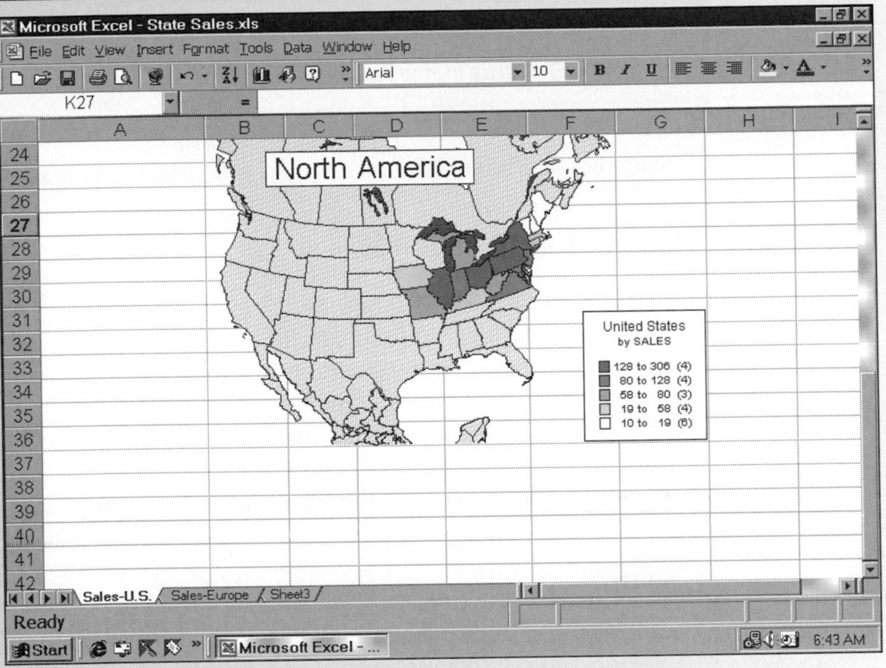

9. Save your worksheet.

As you review the data map with Miguel, you both agree that several changes would improve the data map's appearance and readability. For instance, the map title and legend could be more informative, and the map area is too small. Miguel asks you to make these changes.

Customizing the Data Map

With Microsoft Map, it's easy to change titles, legends, colors, and symbols associated with your data map. To make changes to a data map, however, Microsoft Map must be activated. You do this by double-clicking the map object. (Clicking the map object once displays only the sizing handles, which allow you to move, resize, or delete the map, but not to make any changes to it.)

To activate a data map:

1. With the mouse pointer over the data map, double-click the **map object** to activate it. The diagonal-lined border around the map indicates the data map is activated.

With Microsoft Map activated, you're ready to make your first change: editing the title of the data map. Microsoft Map automatically assigns a title to your map but Miguel would like it to be more descriptive. He asks you to change the title to U.S. Sales.

To edit a data map title:

1. Double-click the **map title** to open an Edit Text Object input box.
2. Type **U.S. Sales** in the text box and then click **OK**.

Now that you have changed the map title, you're ready to modify the map legend.

Modifying Map Legends

The **map legend** describes how the colors and styles on the map represent data values. Each legend includes a title and subtitle, and for a value shading formatted map, the legend also includes the shade and value range for each level of shading in the map. When you look at the map legend for the data map you just created (see Figure A2-5), you can easily see which shade indicates states with the highest sales and how many states (the numbers in parentheses) fall into each value range.

Miguel asks you to change the map legend so its title is the same as the map title.

To edit a data map legend title:

1. Move the mouse pointer over the map legend, and then double-click the **map legend title** to open the Format Properties dialog box. If necessary, click the **Legend Options** tab to select it. See Figure A2-6.

   Trouble? If the Microsoft Map dialog box opens after you double-click the mouse pointer, click the OK button to refresh the map and then repeat step 1.

Figure A2-6 CHANGING MAP LEGEND TITLE

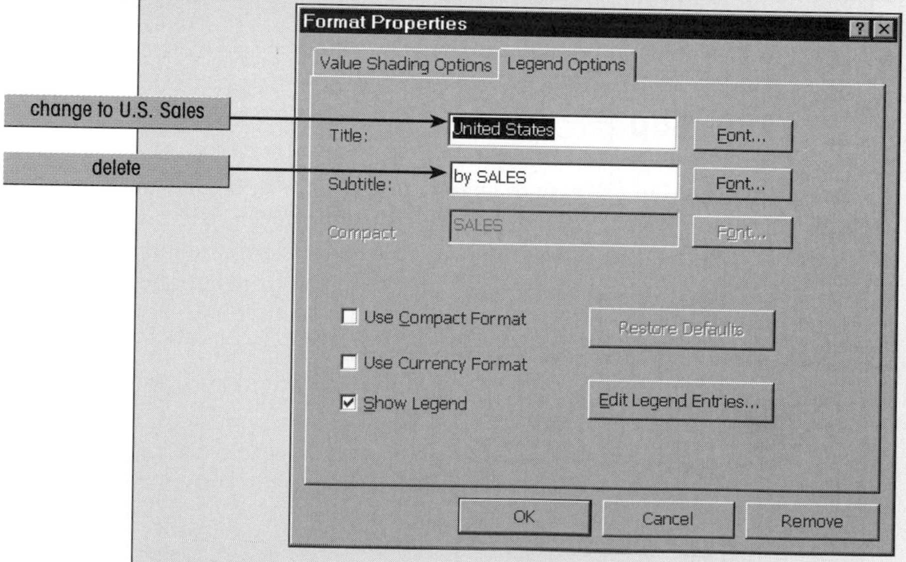

   You can use this dialog box to change the text of the legend title and subtitle, as well as the font used for each of these elements.

2. Type **U.S. Sales** in the Title text box.
3. Delete the entry in the Subtitle text box, and then click the **OK** button.

With the map title and legend title edited, your next change is to resize the data map.

Resizing the Data Map

After you have created a data map, you can easily move or resize it. In this case, Miguel asks you to increase the size of the map so it fills the entire worksheet window.

To resize a data map:

1. Make certain row **24** is the first cell in the worksheet window, then place the mouse pointer over the lower-right corner of the map so that its shape changes to ↘. Click and drag down and to the right until the map fills the range **A24:H42**. See Figure A2-7.

Figure A2-7 RESIZED DATA MAP

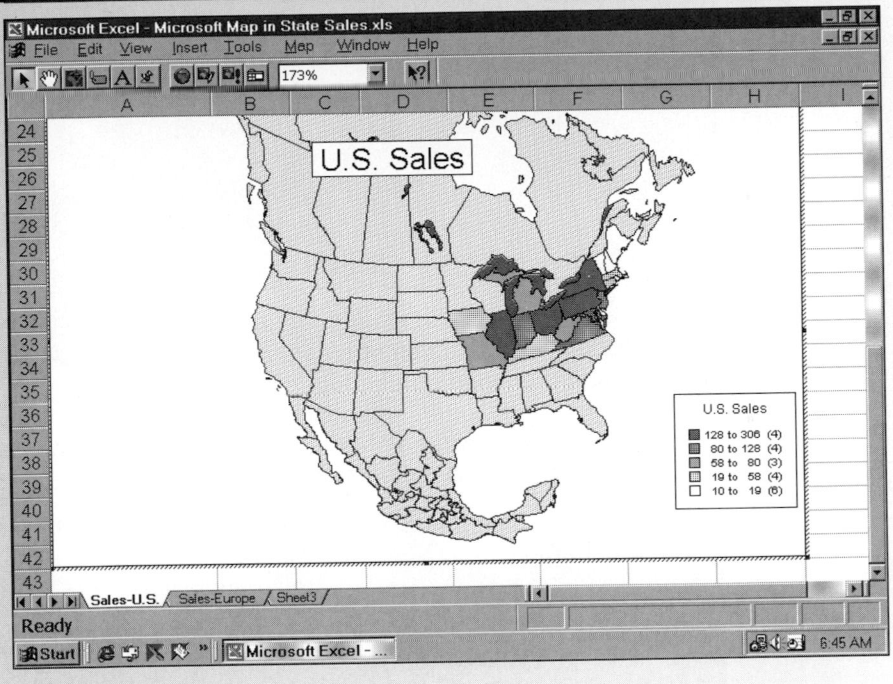

You show the data map to Miguel, who agrees that the changes you have made improve it. However, he thinks the data map can be further enhanced by using fewer value ranges and changing the shading color. You'll make these changes now.

Modifying the Value Shading Data Map

You can customize the appearance of a value shading map, for example, by changing the number of ranges into which data is segmented as well as the color used to shade the different value ranges. Also, you can specify whether ranges should be defined by an equal number of items or by an equal spread of values.

Miguel asks you to adjust the number of value ranges so that there are only three levels of shading, and to change the shading color from black to blue.

To change the number of value ranges and color for the value shading map format:

1. Click **Map** on the menu bar, and then click **Value Shading Options** to open the Format Properties dialog box. See Figure A2-8.

Figure A2-8 CHANGING THE VALUE SHADING OPTIONS

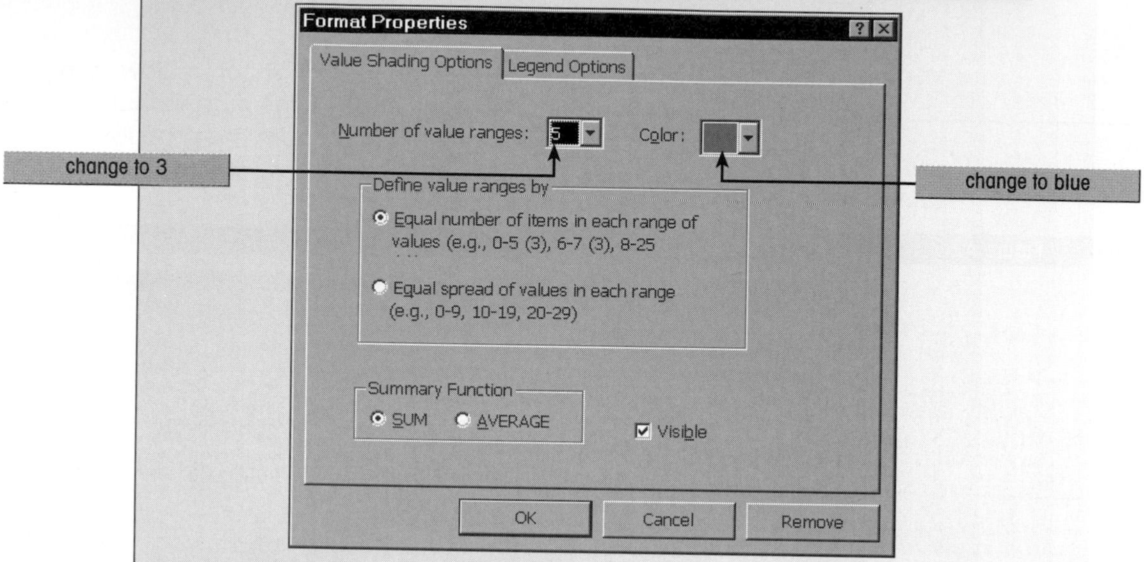

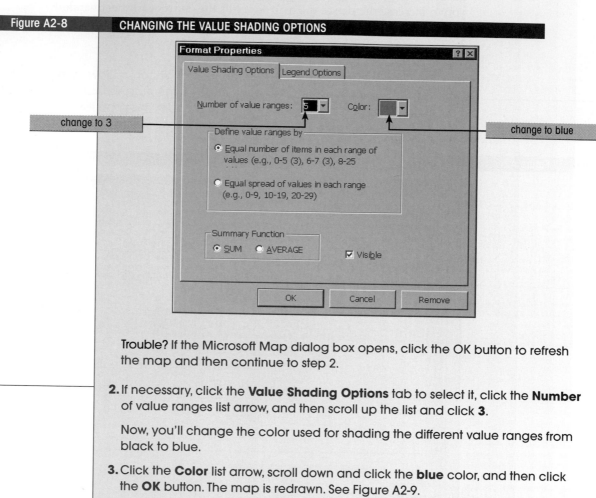

Trouble? If the Microsoft Map dialog box opens, click the OK button to refresh the map and then continue to step 2.

2. If necessary, click the **Value Shading Options** tab to select it, click the **Number** of value ranges list arrow, and then scroll up the list and click **3**.

   Now, you'll change the color used for shading the different value ranges from black to blue.

3. Click the **Color** list arrow, scroll down and click the **blue** color, and then click the **OK** button. The map is redrawn. See Figure A2-9.

Figure A2-9 VALUE SHADING DATA MAP AFTER CHANGES

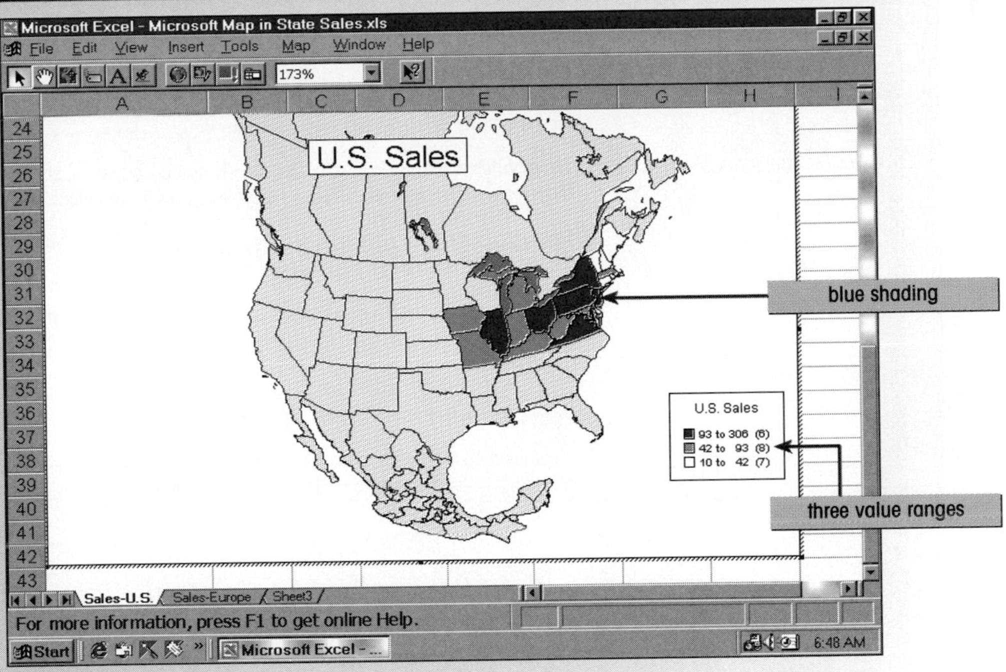

Sales are now divided into only three value ranges, and each sales range is associated with a different shade of the color blue. Before you show your progress on the data map, you realize it's time to save your work.

4. Save the worksheet.

You show the data map to Miguel, and he agrees that it looks attractive and readable. However, he's not sure it's in the best data map format for presenting the sales data. He asks you to experiment and change the data map format.

Changing the Format of a Data Map

The value shading format is one of six data map formats available for creating a data map (see Figure A2-10). To change the format from one data map type to another, you must first open the Microsoft Map Control dialog box.

Figure A2-10 MAP FORMATS

BUTTON	MAP FORMAT	DESCRIPTION
	Value shading	Divides the values in specified data column into ranges, and assigns a different shade of a single color to each map region based on which range a region's value falls into; darker shades represent higher values.
	Category shading	Visually differentiates geographic regions into subgroups that share a common characteristic; each map region is assigned a different color based on a data value.
	Dot density	Displays a pattern of dots in each map region, with each dot representing a specified number of items; the more dots in a region, the higher the value.
	Graduated symbol	Displays different sized symbols in each map region, proportionate to the region's data value; the larger the symbol size, the higher the data value.
	Pie chart	Displays a pie chart over a geographic region that has category or value shading; the pie chart shows the relative value of each data category to a whole.
	Column chart	Displays a column chart over a geographic region that has category or value shading; the column chart shows the comparison between values of two or more numbers.

To open the Microsoft Map Control dialog box:

1. Click the **Show/Hide Microsoft Map Control** button on the Map toolbar.
2. If necessary, center the Microsoft Map Control dialog box (shown in Figure A2-11) on the screen by clicking its **title bar** and dragging the dialog box until it's in the center of the map.

Figure A2-11 MICROSOFT MAP CONTROL DIALOG BOX

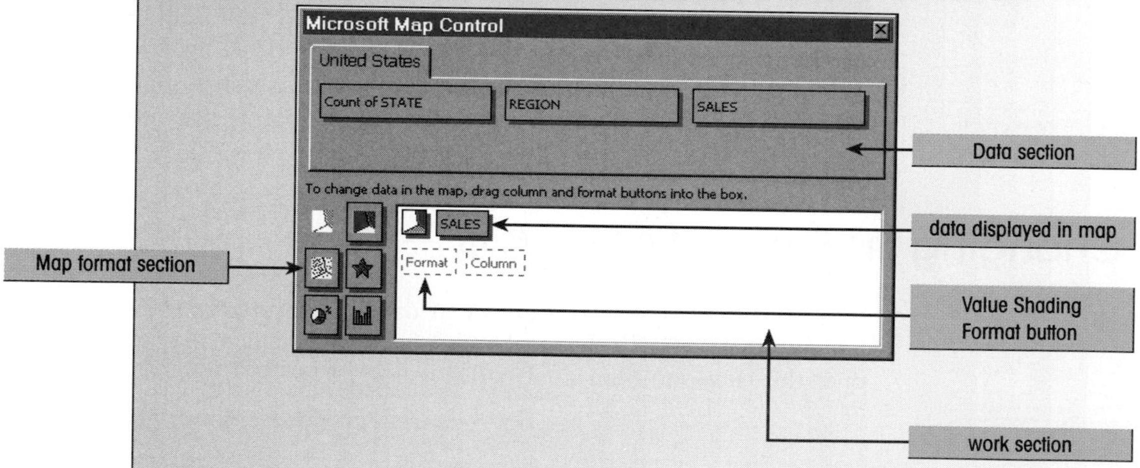

The Microsoft Map Control dialog box consists of three sections: the Data section, which includes the column titles you have selected from the worksheet; the Map Format section, which includes the six data map formatting options available; and the Work section, where you specify the map format and data column(s) that Microsoft Map uses to create the map.

After reviewing the data map formats available, Miguel asks you to experiment with the graduated symbol and the dot density map formats.

To change the data map to the graduated symbol and dot density formats:

1. Position the mouse pointer over the **Graduated Symbol** button in the Map Format section of the dialog box. The mouse pointer changes to .
2. Click and drag the **Graduated Symbol** button into the Work section, and place it over the **Value Shading** button .
   When you release the mouse button, the map is redrawn.

   Trouble? If the Microsoft Map dialog box opens as you begin to drag the mouse pointer, click the OK button to refresh the map and then repeat step 2.
3. Click the **Show/Hide Microsoft Map Control** button on the Map toolbar to close the dialog box so you can view the graduated symbol format map. See Figure A2-12. Notice that with a graduated symbol format, the size of the symbol that appears in each state corresponds to the sales in that state. The higher the sales, the larger the symbol.
   Now, you're ready to try the dot density map format.

Figure A2-12 **GRADUATED SYMBOL FORMATTED DATA MAP**

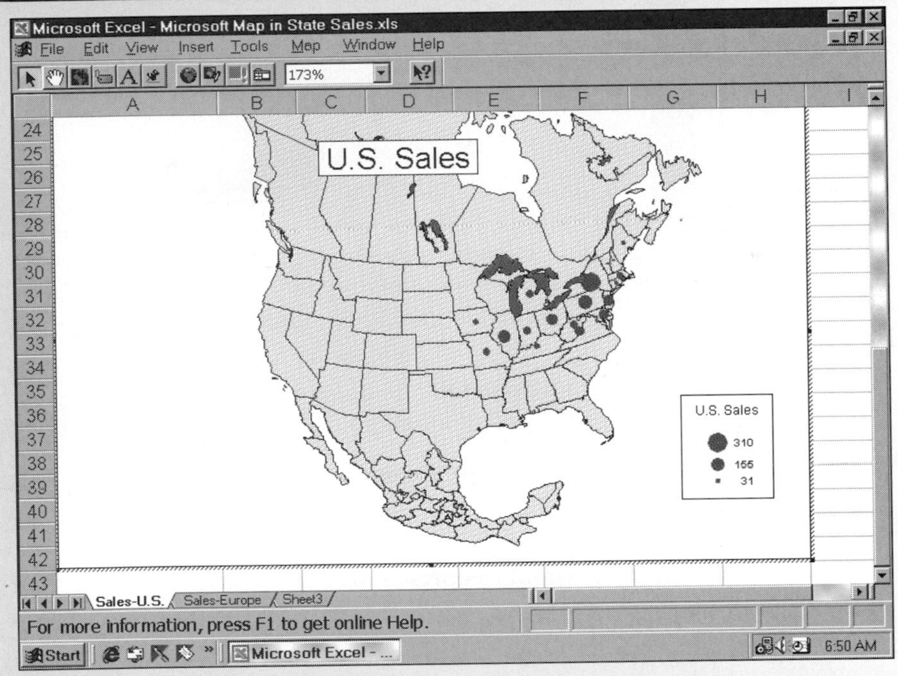

4. Click the **Show/Hide Microsoft Map Control** button on the Map toolbar to open the dialog box again.
5. Position the mouse pointer over the **Dot Density** button in the Map format section of the dialog box. The mouse pointer changes to .
6. Click and drag the **Dot Density** button into the Work section over the **Graduated Symbol** button . When you release the mouse button, the map is redrawn.

7. Click the **Show/Hide Microsoft Map Control** button on the Map toolbar to close the dialog box so you can view the dot density data map. See Figure A2-13. The dot density format shows a series of dots that represent the level of sales in each state. Each dot represents a fixed amount of sales. The denser the pattern of dots in a state, the higher that state's sales. The choice between these map formats is one of personal preference.

Miguel asks you to keep the dot density format, you do so and save your work.

Figure A2-13 DOT DENSITY FORMATTED DATA MAP

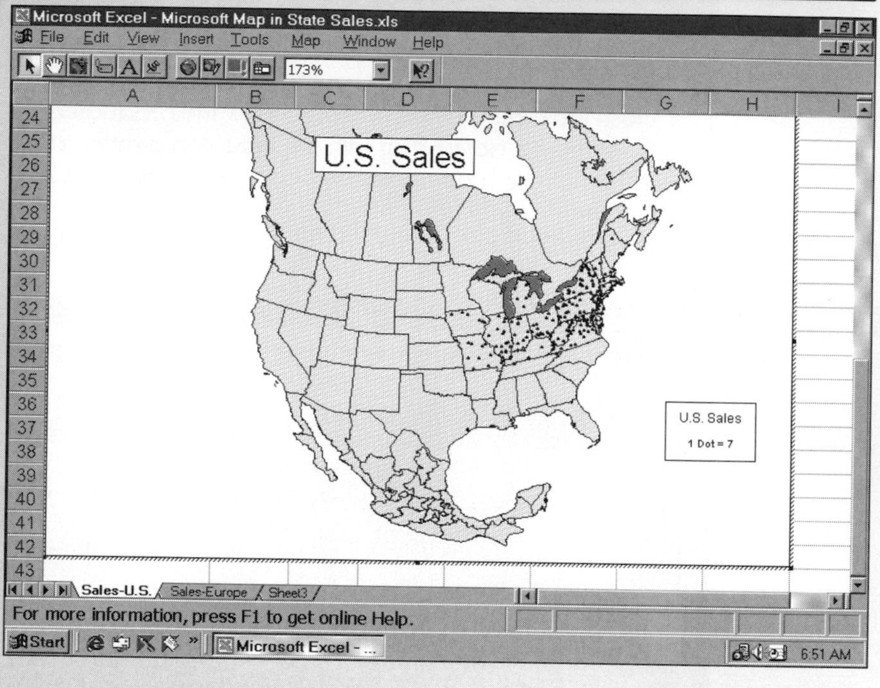

8. Save the worksheet.

Session A2.1 QUICK CHECK

1. Why would you present data in the form of a color-coded data map?
2. You have collected population data on 10 provinces in Canada. Describe how you would organize your worksheet so you can prepare a data map of Canada.
3. For a value shading data map format, what does a green shade indicate?
4. After creating a data map, how do you exit Microsoft Map and return to Excel's usual screen?
5. How do you edit a data map legend title?
6. What dialog box must be open in order to change the format of a data map?
7. Describe how to interpret the dot density data map format.
8. There are 30 major league baseball teams, divided into two leagues, located in the United States and Canada. What map format would you use to show the distribution of teams by league, and why?

In this session you've created a data map and customized it. In the next session you'll finalize Miguel's data map by adding an overlaid data map showing sales by region, displaying state labels, and inserting a pushpin to identify Morning Glory's headquarters.

SESSION A2.2

In this session you'll learn how to overlay a data map over an existing one, thereby placing two formats on a single map. You'll also use the Map toolbar to magnify and reposition an area of the data map and to display labels on the map. Finally, you'll learn how to insert a pushpin in a map to identify a specific location.

Overlaying Maps

You can overlay multiple map formats for different data on a single map, which allows you to display more information on a map. For example, you could have a value shading format showing sales divided into five categories, overlaid with the graduated symbol format showing the states that have sales and customer service offices.

For Miguel's data map, he wants to present sales of Morning Glory products (using the dot density format) as well as show the concentration of sales by region (East, Central, and NE). To do this, you'll need to create a category shading data map, which will color-code each sales region (based on the Region column of the State Sales worksheet), and then overlay this map over the dot density data map you've already created. Then you'll have created a map that will show the relationship of sales among sales regions as well as within states.

REFERENCE WINDOW RW

Overlaying data maps

- Activate the current data map, and open the Microsoft Map Control dialog box.
- Click and drag the desired format button into the Format position in a new row of the Work section.
- Click and drag the name of a data column into the Column position of the same row in the Work section.

Now, you'll create and overlap a category shading data map on Miguel's data map.

To overlay a data map:

1. If you took a break after the last session, make sure Excel is running, the **State Sales** workbook is open, and the **data map** is activated.
2. Click the **Show/Hide Microsoft Map Control** button on the Map toolbar to open the Microsoft Map Control dialog box.
3. Click the **Category Shading** button in the Map Format section of the Microsoft Map Control dialog box, and then drag it over the outlined word **Format** in the Work section. Release the mouse button.
4. Click the **Region** column button in the Data section of the dialog box, drag it over the outlined word **Column** in the Work section, and then release the mouse button.

5. Click the **Show/Hide Microsoft Map Control** button on the Map toolbar to close the dialog box. See Figure A2-14.

Figure A2-14 CATEGORY SHADING MAP OVERLAID ON DOT DENSITY MAP

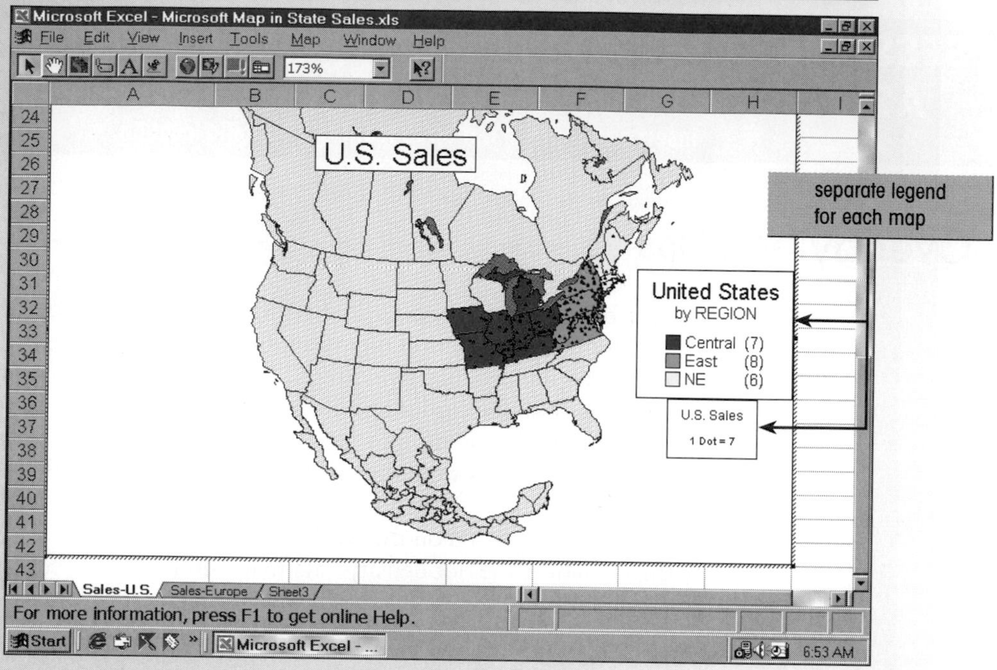

Now you have created a category shading map, with each sales region appearing in a different color. In addition, sales in each state continue to be shown in a dot density data map format. Notice that each map has its own legend.

If you change your mind and want to remove one of the map layers, you would simply click and drag the data column button out of the Work section and then release the mouse button when you see the pointer change to a recycle bin.

Miguel is pleased with how well the map overlay presents the sales data. However, he points out the large geographic area displayed in which Morning Glory has no sales. Because Morning Glory has sales in only 21 states, Miguel wants to limit, as much as possible, the map to only those states. He asks you to magnify and reposition the map so that it focuses on those 21 states.

Magnifying an Area of the Data Map

If you want a more detailed view of a certain area of a map, you can zoom in on that specific portion. You can easily change the magnification of an area by assigning a zoom percentage other than the default (usually 100%) to the Zoom Percentage of Map list box on the Map toolbar. A zoom percentage greater than 100% will increase the magnification; a value less than 100% will reduce the magnification.

Because you want to zoom in on only a portion of Miguel's data map, you'll now increase the magnification level to 400%.

To magnify a portion of the data map:

1. Click the **Zoom Percentage of Map** list arrow on the Map toolbar, and then click the magnification level **400%** to redraw the map.

   Notice that because you've zoomed in on one area, the map is no longer centered within the map frame. You'll correct that problem now by using the Grabber tool to reposition the map within the map frame.

2. Click the **Grabber** button on the Map toolbar. As you move the pointer inside the map frame, the pointer changes to . Click and drag the map to the left, as shown in Figure A2-15.

Figure A2-15 DATA MAP AFTER REPOSITIONING AND MAGNIFICATION

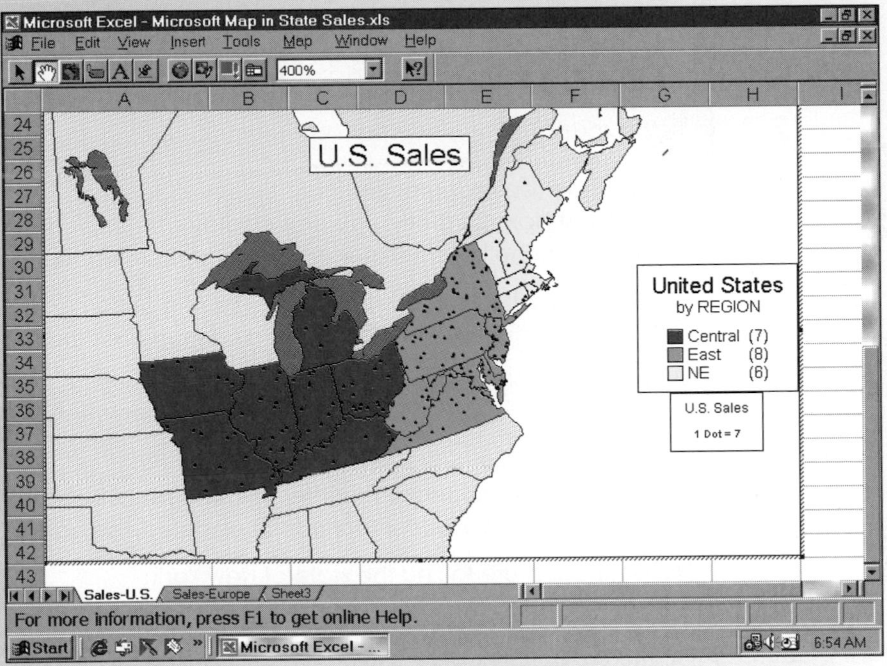

3. Click the **Grabber** button on the Map toolbar to turn off the Grabber tool.

Miguel is pleased with how the data map is progressing. He decides, though, that it would be helpful to identify Morning Glory's headquarters in New York City with a push-pin and label on the map. Like many of us, Miguel isn't certain where each geographic region is exactly located on the map. To make sure New York is identified correctly, he asks you to first display the state labels on the data map.

Displaying Labels on the Data Map

Data maps provide you with an overall perspective, which allows you to see relationships, not the details. To view the details, such as the geographic name or the data value that corresponds to a specific map region, you can have a label appear as you move the mouse pointer over a map region. (If you want the label to be permanently added to the map, click the mouse button immediately after the label appears.) You'll use this feature of Microsoft Map to display the label for the state of New York.

To display map labels on a data map:

1. Click the **Map Labels** button on the Map toolbar. The Map Labels dialog box opens. See Figure A2-16.

Figure A2-16 MAP LABELS DIALOG BOX

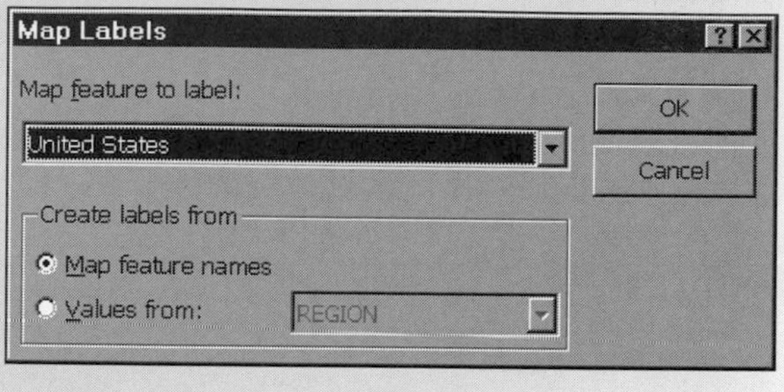

Trouble? If the Microsoft Map dialog box opens, click the OK button to refresh the map.

The map features that you can display labels for are listed in the Map feature to label list box. Currently, you can display names or data values related to map regions in the United States. You want to display the names of the states.

2. Make sure the Map feature names option button in the Create labels from section of the dialog box is selected, and then click the **OK** button.

   If you want the data value from the worksheet to pop up on the map, instead of the name of state, select the Value from option button and select a category from the list.

3. As you move the mouse pointer over the map, it changes to +. As you move + over a map feature that can be labeled, the name of the state appears.
4. Use this feature to find the state of New York.
5. Click the **Select Objects** button to turn off the Map Labels tool.

Now that you're sure where New York state is located, you're ready to insert a pushpin on the data map to identify the company's headquarters.

Identifying Special Points Using a Custom Pin Map

You can create custom pin maps to mark specific elements on your map, such as the location of manufacturing plants, warehouses, or sales offices. Microsoft Map's **Custom Pin Map feature** allows you to place one or more pushpins on a map. Once you have placed a pushpin on a map, you can easily change its size, shape, or color. You also can add a descriptive label to the right of the pin.

Miguel asks you to insert a pushpin on the data map to identify Morning Glory's New York City headquarters. Before you add one or more pushpins to a map, however, you must first assign a name to the custom pin map you are about to create. This allows you to create more than one pushpin collection, which you can then switch between by selecting the appropriate pin map name. For example, you can create a pushpin map of warehouses and another of sales offices.

To assign a name to a custom pin map:

1. Click the **Custom Pin Map** button on the Map toolbar to open the Custom Pin Map dialog box. See Figure A2-17.

Figure A2-17 CUSTOM PIN MAP DIALOG BOX

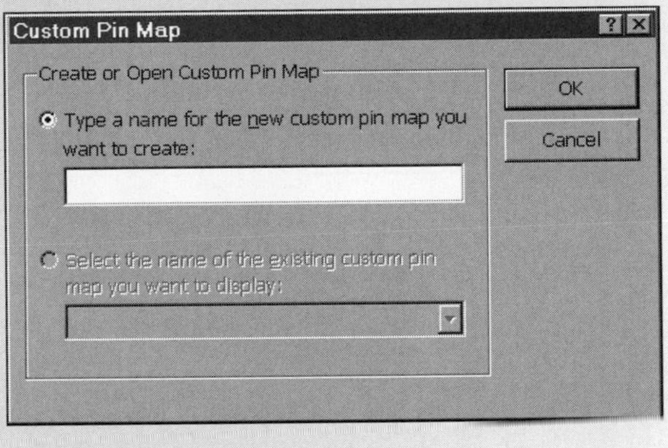

2. Type **SiteLocation** in the Type a name for the new custom pin map you want to create text box, and then click the **OK** button. Notice the mouse pointer changes to when you move it over the map.

   Now, every time you click the mouse, you'll add a pushpin to the map.

You're now ready to add the pushpin to identify Morning Glory's headquarters. Then you'll add a label to the right of the pin.

To add a pushpin and pin label to a data map:

1. Click at the approximate location of New York City to open the Edit Text Object input box.

   Trouble? If you accidentally added an additional pushpin, click the Custom Pin Map button to turn off the pushpin tool, make sure the pushpin you want to delete is selected, press the Delete key, click the first pushpin to select it, and then continue to step 2.

   Notice the pushpin is surrounded by a thick border, and a blinking insertion bar appears immediately to the right of the pushpin. The insertion bar indicates that Microsoft Map is waiting for you to add a descriptive label to the pushpin, which you'll now do.

2. Type **Headquarters** and click **OK** to insert a label next to the pushpin. See Figure A2-18. Notice that the label and the symbol for the pin are linked: If you move the symbol, the label moves with it.

Figure A2-18 **DATA MAP WITH PUSHPIN INSERTED**

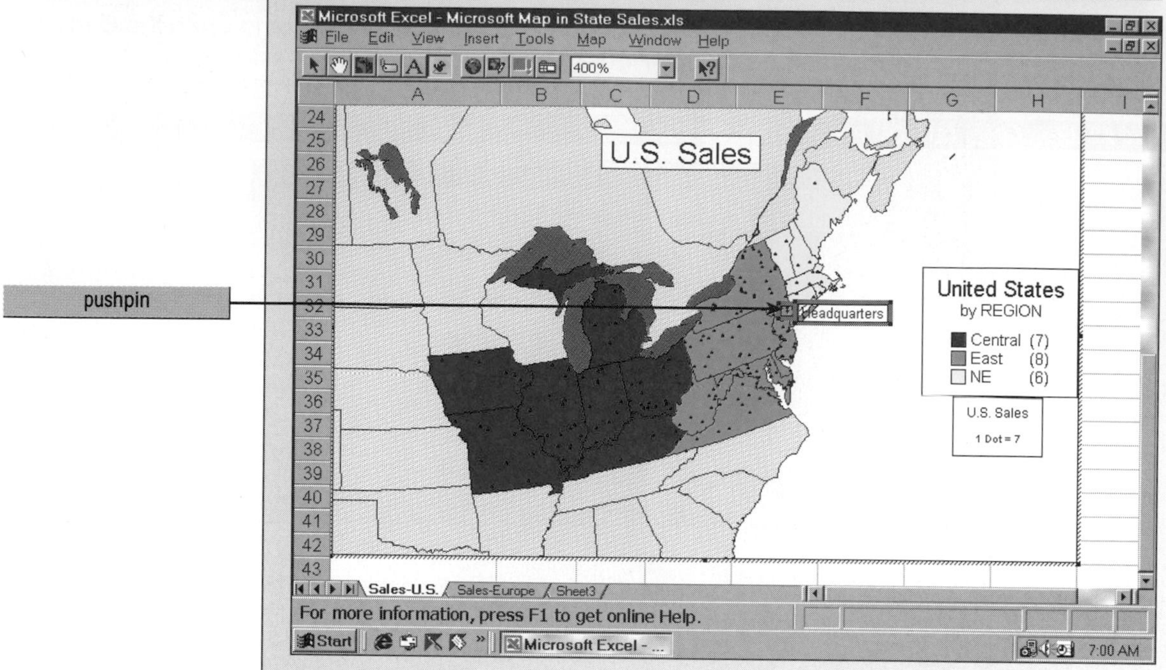

3. Click the **Custom Pin Map** button on the Map toolbar to turn off the pushpin tool.

4. Click anywhere within the map frame to deselect the push pin border.

Miguel likes how the pushpin identifies Morning Glory's headquarters but thinks the pushpin is too small. He asks you to increase its size.

To change the size of the pushpin:

1. Move the mouse pointer over the pushpin, right-click the **pushpin** to display the Shortcut menu, and then click **Format** to open the Symbol dialog box.
2. Click the **Font** button to open the Font dialog box, click **24** in the Size list box, and then click **Bold** in the Font style list box.
3. Click the **OK** button twice to display the data map with a larger pushpin.

   Trouble? If you need to reposition the pushpin, move the mouse over the pushpin and then drag the object to the correct location. Click anywhere within the map frame to deselect the pushpin.

4. Move the mouse pointer over the pushpin label **Headquarters**, right-click the mouse, click **Format Font** to open the Font dialog box, and then click **Bold** in the Font style list box.
5. Click the **OK** button to display the map with a bold label next to the pushpin.
6. Click anywhere within the map frame to deselect the pushpin and its label. See Figure A2-19.

Figure A2-19 DATA MAP WITH PUSHPIN SHOWING LOCATION OF MORNING GLORY'S HEADQUARTERS

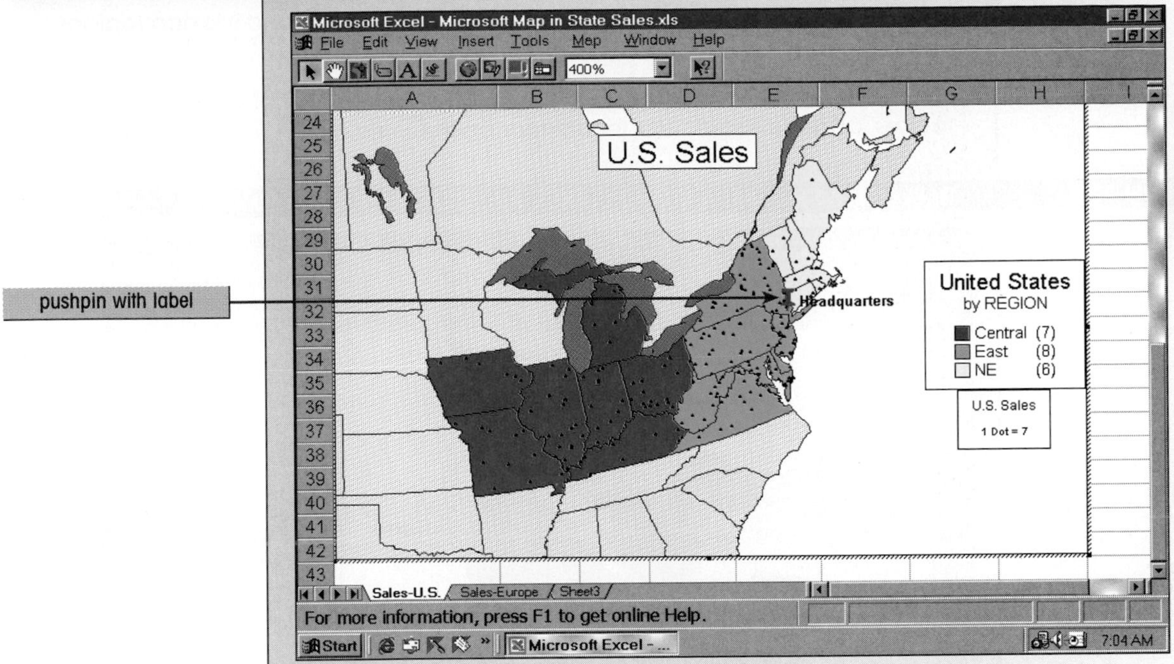

As you review the data map with Miguel, you both agree one final change is necessary: removing unnecessary map features.

Removing **Map Features**

You can remove (or add) features in your map, such as lakes, cities, airports, and highways, if they aren't needed (or if they provide excessive detail). Miguel and you agree that you should remove the map regions of Canada and Mexico, because Miguel's presentation will focus on only U.S. sales.

To remove features from a data map:

1. Click **Map** on the Map menu bar, and then click **Features** to open the Map Features dialog box. See Figure A2-20.

Figure A2-20 MAP FEATURES DIALOG BOX

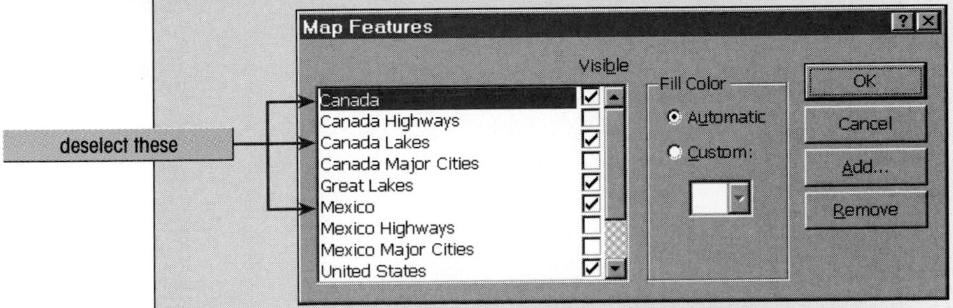

2. Click the **Canada** check box to remove the check.
3. Use the same procedure to remove the Canada Lakes and Mexico regions from the map.
4. Click the **OK** button. See Figure A2-21. Notice the regions of Canada, Canada Lakes, and Mexico no longer appear on the data map.

Figure A2-21 DATA MAP WITH CANADA, CANADA LAKES, AND MEXICO FEATURES REMOVED

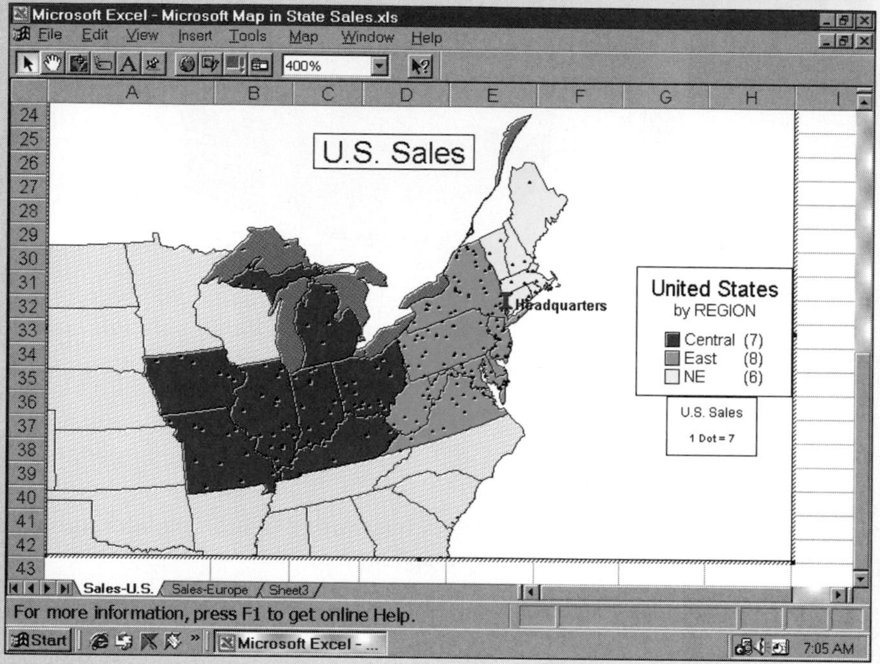

Miguel is pleased with the appearance of the data map and asks you for a printout. First, you'll save the worksheet and then print the data map along with the worksheet data.

To save and print the worksheet:

1. Click anywhere outside the data map frame to exit Microsoft Map and return to the usual Excel screen.
2. Click the **Save** button on the Standard toolbar.
3. Click the **Print** button to print the State Sales worksheet and data map.

   Your work is completed. You're ready to exit Excel.
4. Click the **Close** button on the Excel program window to exit Excel.

Session A2.2 Quick Check

1. What is an advantage of overlaying maps?
2. How do you remove a map overlay?
3. If you want the map of North America to focus on the U.S. western states, what tool(s) on the Map toolbar would you use, and why?
4. You created a data map of Europe but cannot recall where Belgium is located. How would you use the Map toolbar to find this country?
5. How do you permanently add a display label to a data map?
6. Your company has sales offices in Los Angeles, California, and Dallas, Texas. What Microsoft Map feature would you use to identify these offices on a data map?
7. How do you change the size of a pushpin on a data map?
8. How do you display the Map Features dialog box?

In this appendix you learned how to use Microsoft Map to create a data map from an Excel worksheet and how to customize that data map. The data map you created allowed Miguel to effectively present Morning Glory's sales information to the company's stockholders.

REVIEW ASSIGNMENTS

After seeing how effective the data map was in showing the distribution of Morning Glory's U.S. sales, Miguel asks you create a data map of the company's Canadian sales. Do the following:

1. If necessary, start Excel and make sure your Data Disk is in the appropriate disk drive. Open the **StSales2** workbook in the Review folder for Appendix.02 on your Data Disk, and save it as **State Sales 2**. If necessary, display the **Sales-Canada** worksheet.
2. Create a data map of Canada on the Sales–Canada worksheet using the value shading format. Choose the map for Canada.
3. Change the map title to "Sales in Canada."
4. ***Explore*** Click and drag the map title to the upper-left corner of the map.
5. Change the number of value ranges to three. Change the value shading color to yellow.
6. Increase the map magnification to 100%.
7. ***Explore*** Insert the label for the provinces with the highest sales (darkest shade) in the appropriate region on the map. (*Hint:* Click the left mouse button when the display label appears.)
8. ***Explore*** Add the "Canadian major cities" feature to the map. Insert the label for Montreal next to its marker.
9. Save your workbook, print the **Sales–Canada** worksheet and data map, and then close the **State Sales 2** workbook.

CASE PROBLEMS

Case 1. Expansion at Linens & the Likes As the marketing research assistant for Linens & the Likes, a specialty linen and accessory company that is expanding its retail operation throughout the United States, you have accumulated U.S. demographic data and entered it into an Excel worksheet. The Site Location team must select the best locations for new stores. As a first step in the selection process, they have asked you to create a data map showing the distribution of per capita income by state. Do the following:

1. If necessary, start Excel and make sure your Data Disk is in the appropriate drive. Open the **PCI** workbook in the Cases folder for Appendix.02 on your Data Disk, and save it as **USPCI**.
2. Create a graduated symbol data map showing the distribution of per capita income in the United States. Choose the map with Alaska and Hawaii insets. Place the map below the data.
3. Edit the map to make it more attractive, such as changing the color used for the symbol and adding a more descriptive title. Make any other appropriate changes.
4. **Explore** Create a category shading data map overlay showing the seven regions of the country. Change the colors assigned to each region, and then resize the map legends so they don't cover the map. Print the data map.
5. **Explore** Remove the graduated symbol data map, and then insert a pushpin in the state with the largest per capita income. Include a descriptive label.
6. **Explore** Print the worksheet on one page and the data map on another. (*Hint*: Use Page Break Preview.)
7. Save the workbook, and then close it.
8. **Explore** Create a pie chart map format that compares sales of linens with sales of pillows for each state in the FarWest region. (*Hint:* This map format requires using two columns of data from the PCI workbook.)
9. Improve the appearance of the map as you think necessary, save the workbook as **USPCI2**, print the data map, and then close the workbook.

Case 2 U.S. Environmental Protection Agency The U.S. Environmental Protection Agency (EPA) has divided the U.S. into ten regions. Each state is assigned to one region. Prepare a data map that will show the regions and the states within the regions.

1. Open the file **EPA.xls** in the Cases folder for Appendix.02 and save it as **EPAMAP.xls**.
2. Choose the U.S. map with AK & HI insets. Select the most appropriate format to prepare a data map showing the ten regions into which the EPA is divided.
3. Change the title and legend to more descriptive captions.
4. Save, then print only the map.

Case 3. Pepper-Eton North America To show their presence in North America, the company provides information about where its various facilities are located. The following information showing the type of operation and location of these facilities appears in its various publications:

- Manufacturing: Sonora, Mexico, Michigan
- Sales Offices: British Columbia, Canada, Massachusetts
- Customer Service: Texas, Georgia
- Training: Quebec, Canada

To improve the visual impact of this information, you have been asked to display this information in a data map. Do the following:

1. If necessary, start Excel and make sure your Data Disk is in the appropriate drive.
2. In a blank sheet in the workbook, create a blank map of North America. (*Hint:* Click the Map button without highlighting a worksheet range. Select the map for North America.)
3. Create a custom pin map. Insert a pushpin and label in each location that identifies the activity performed in that location. (*Hint:* Use the Map Labels button to help identify map locations. Increase the pushpin size and label font size, as necessary.)
4. Modify the custom pin map by color-coding each pushpin based on function (manufacturing, sales, customer service, and training). (*Hint:* Select and double-click each pushpin individually.)
5. Improve the appearance and readability of the map as you think appropriate, then save the workbook as **Operations** in the Appendix.02 Cases folder on your Data Disk.
6. Name the sheet **Pin Map** and then print the data map.
7. Save your work, and then close the workbook.

Case 4. Population and Census Data Mapstats is an Excel file that contains census data for many countries. It also contains data from states, provinces, and counties. Locate the **Mapstats** workbook on your computer (*Hint:* Use the Find command), and then select one of the worksheets and use the Clipboard to copy this data to a new workbook. Create a data map with your choice of map format and data, and then improve the appearance and readability of the map. This could involve changing the title, editing the legend, magnifying a map area, resizing the map frame, or removing map features. After you've completed your data map, save the workbook as **ExploreMapStats** in the Appendix.02 Cases folder on your Data Disk, print the data map, and then close the workbook.

QUICK CHECK ANSWERS

Session A2.1

1. Data mapping helps you to visualize and analyze your data, as well as to better understand relationships in geographic data.
2. place names of provinces in the first column and population data in the second column
3. Green shading means no value is given for the geographic area.
4. click anywhere outside the map frame to return to Excel's normal view

5. double-click the map legend to open the Format Properties dialog box, click the Legend Options tab, and then type the new title in the Title text box
6. Microsoft Map Control dialog box
7. Dot density format shows a series of dots in each map area. Each dot represents a fixed amount of the value being represented. The denser the pattern of dots in each map area, the higher the value.
8. Use the category shading format to color code the map regions by league. Your data would include a column for League; values would be AL and NL.

Session A2.2

1. Overlaying map formats enable you to display more information on a single map.
2. make sure the Microsoft Map Control dialog box is open; click and drag the format and column buttons (one at a time) from a row of the Work section of the dialog box
3. click the Zoom Percentage of Map list arrow to increase the zoom on a specific portion of the map, and then use the Grabber tool to position the western states in the center of the map
4. click the Map Labels button, and then move the pointer over each map area until the label for Belgium appears
5. click the Map Labels button, and then move the pointer over a map area; once the label appears, click the mouse to add the label to the map
6. use the Custom Pin Map button to add pushpins to locate each sales office
7. move the mouse over the pushpin, right-click to display the Shortcut menu, and then click Format to open the Symbol dialog box; click the Font button to open the Font dialog box, and then click the desired size in the Size list box; click the OK button twice to return to the data map
8. click Map on the Map menu bar, and then click Features

OBJECTIVES

In this tutorial you will:

- Trace dependent and precedent cells in a workbook
- Uncover and correct worksheet errors
- Create and apply a style
- Create and apply custom formats for numbers and dates
- Save and edit a worksheet template
- Share workbooks

AUDITING, CUSTOM FORMATTING, AND SHARING WORKBOOKS

CASE

Suzanne Bouchard, Financial Planner

Suzanne Bouchard, a financial planner, wishes to expand her business. Therefore, she needs to spend more time developing new client relationships and less time administering her current client investments. To grow her business, Suzanne has hired a temporary employee to develop an Excel workbook. The workbook will include a separate worksheet for each client's investment portfolio, as well as a summary worksheet that gives an overview of each client's investment status.

Suzanne has asked you to take over the maintenance responsibilities. She has also pointed out that the workbook's appearance and readability could be improved. You decide your first task is to familiarize yourself with the workbook details. You'll use Excel's Audit feature to examine the relationships among the workbook's cells and formulas.

SESSION A3.1

In this session you'll learn how to trace relationships among cells in a worksheet, as well as how to uncover errors. In addition, you'll improve the workbook's appearance by creating and applying styles and custom formats. Finally, you'll learn how to insert a template into an existing workbook and then edit that template.

Auditing a Worksheet

As you develop complex worksheets, your chances of making a mistake increases as the size and complexity of the worksheet increases. To help review your worksheets, Excel provides an **Audit** feature, which inspects the overall logic of a worksheet by locating and analyzing formulas. The Audit feature works by drawing, directly on your worksheet, **tracer arrows**, which show relationships between the active cell and related cells.

This feature is especially helpful when you're using a workbook someone else created because these tracer arrows can show you how the other person set up formulas and values. Tracer arrows can also help you to find the source of errors in worksheets that you develop.

In order to use tracer arrows to examine Suzanne's workbook, you first need to open the workbook and then display the Auditing toolbar.

To start Excel, open the Stock workbook, and rename it:

1. Start Excel as usual, insert your Data Disk in the appropriate drive, and then open the file **Stock** from the Appendix.03 folder on your Data Disk. See Figure A3-1.

Figure A3-1 SUMMARY WORKSHEET FROM STOCK WORKBOOK

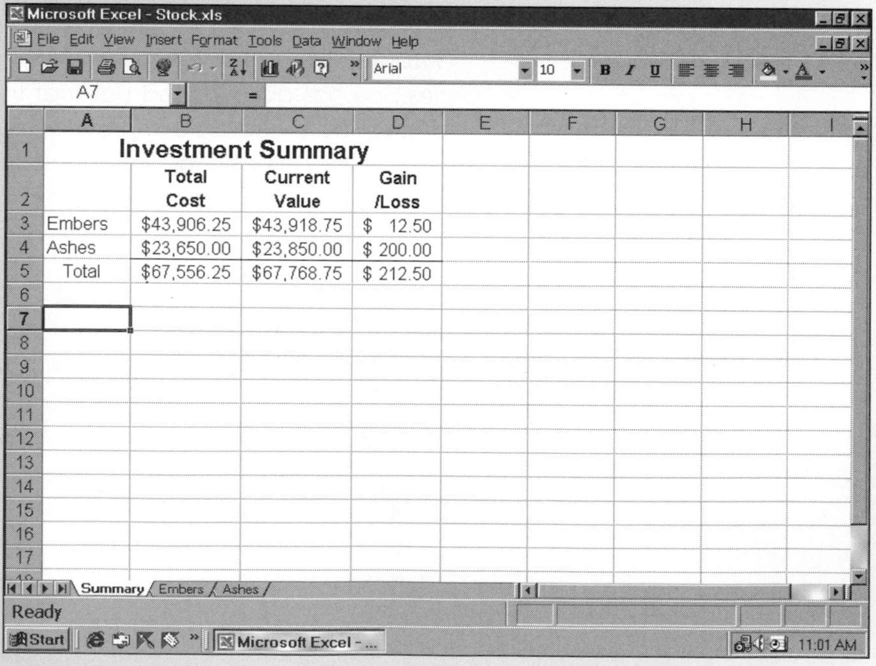

Notice that the workbook consists of three sheets—a Summary sheet and two client sheets (Embers and Ashes). The Summary sheet displays an overview of each client's investment results; the other sheets list the financial information for each stock in the client's portfolio.

2. Save the workbook as **Stock Portfolio**.

Your next step is to display the Auditing toolbar.

The **Auditing toolbar** allows you to examine the relationships among cells and formulas on your worksheet by drawing (and removing) tracer arrows. You also can use the toolbar to help identify worksheet errors. You'll display the Auditing toolbar now.

To display the Auditing toolbar:

1. Click **Tools**, point to **Auditing**, and then click **Show Auditing Toolbar** to display the Auditing toolbar. See Figure A3-2.

Figure A3-2 AUDITING TOOLBAR

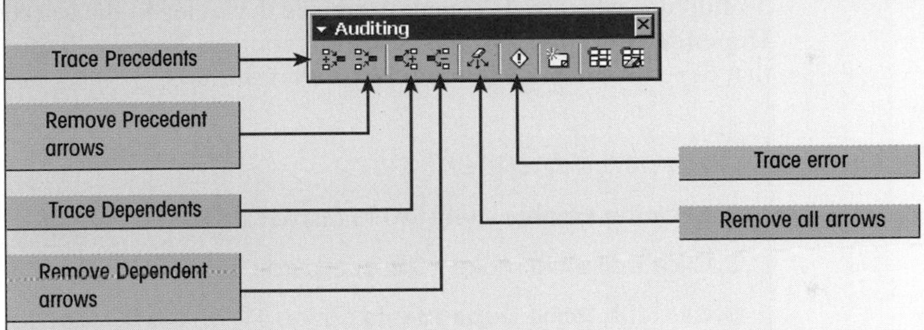

With the Auditing toolbar in view, you can now easily use the tracer arrows to point out all cells that provide data to a formula as well as all cells that contain formulas using the selected cell. That is, you can identify dependent and precedent cells.

Dependent and Precedent Cells

Precedent cells are those whose values are used by the formula in the current cell, and **dependent cells** are those that use the value in the current cell. For example, in Figure A3-1 if cell D3 is the active cell with the formula =C3-B3, cells C3 and B3 are precedent cells. That is, the value in cells C3 and B3 are used by the formula in cell D3. On the other hand, if cell C3 is the active cell, cell D3 would be a dependent cell because it uses the value from cell C3.

REFERENCE WINDOW RW

Tracing the Flow of Data and Formulas

- Select the cell you want to trace.
- To identify precedent cells, click the Trace Precedents button on the Auditing toolbar to see which cells the formula uses. Click the Trace Precedents button again to see the next level of precedents.
- To identify dependent cells, click the Trace Dependents button on the Auditing toolbar to see which formulas reference this cell. Click the Trace Dependents button again to see the next level of dependents.

Now that you understand what dependent and precedent cells are, you're ready to use the Auditing toolbar to trace the relationships among formulas in the Stock Portfolio workbook. You'll begin by finding all cells that depend on the number of IBM shares Embers owns.

Tracing Dependent Cells

To find out which cells contain formulas that refer to the selected cell, you use the **Trace Dependents** button on the Auditing toolbar. Now you'll use this button to find the cells that depend on cell B4 in the Embers worksheet.

To trace dependent cells:

1. Click the **Embers** sheet tab to display it.
2. Click cell **B4** to make it the active cell.
3. Click the **Trace Dependents** button on the Auditing toolbar. Excel draws a line with blue tracer arrows from the active cell B4 to dependent cells D4 and F4. The arrows in cells D4 and F4 indicate these cells contain formulas that use the value in cell B4. See Figure A3-3.

Figure A3-3 **TRACE ARROWS INDICATE DEPENDENT CELLS**

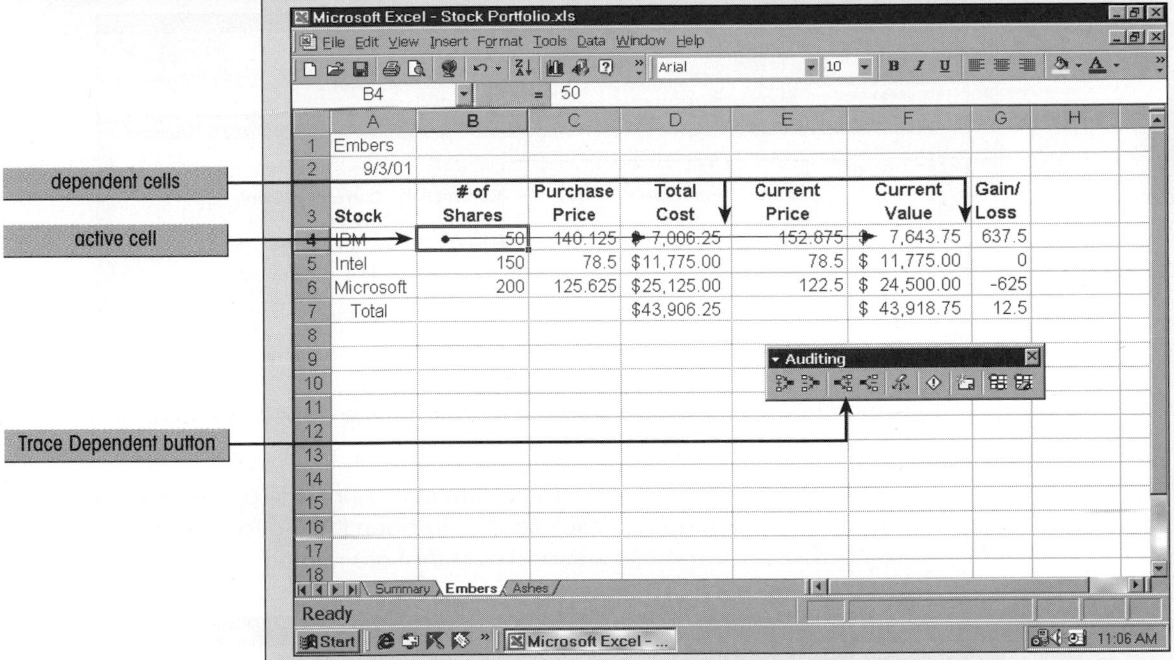

You'll continue to trace the next level of dependent cells.

4. Click the **Trace Dependents** button again. Another set of arrows appear to indicate the next level of dependencies, which are referred to as **indirect dependencies.** Notice the blue tracer arrow indicates that cell B4 is indirectly used in cells D7, F7, and G4. See Figure A3-4.

Figure A3-4 **TRACER ARROWS SHOW DIRECT AND INDIRECT DEPENDENCIES**

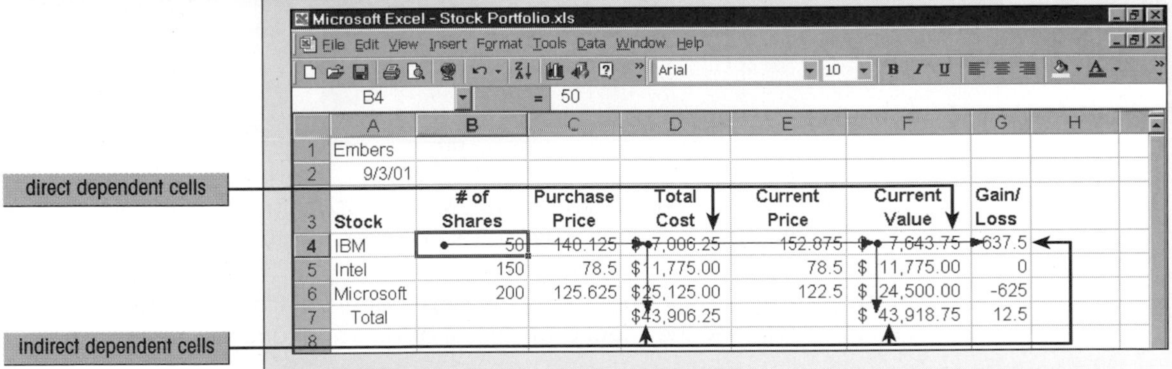

Continue to trace the next level of dependent cells.

5. Click the **Trace Dependents** button again. The black dashed tracer arrow and worksheet icon indicate that there are formulas on another worksheet or workbook that depend on the value in cell B4. The direction of the arrow, toward the worksheet icon in this case, indicates that the active cell (B4) indirectly feeds the cell in a related worksheet. See Figure A3-5.

Figure A3-5 **TRACER ARROWS INDICATE DEPENDENT CELLS ON ANOTHER WORKSHEET**

indicates formulas on another worksheet depend on active cell

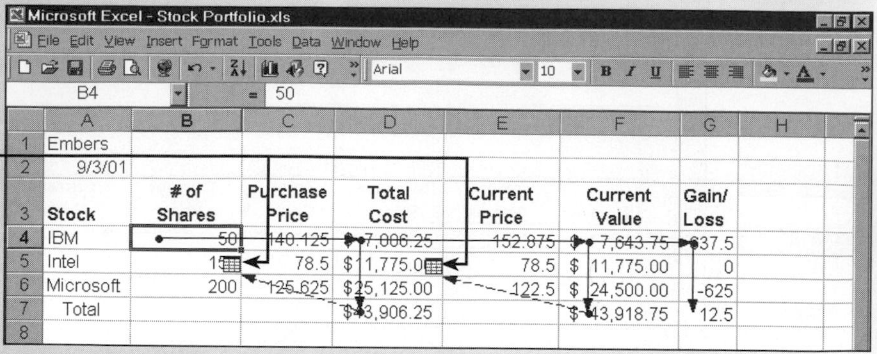

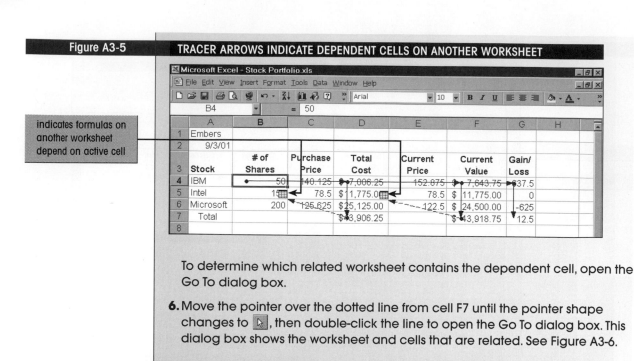

To determine which related worksheet contains the dependent cell, open the Go To dialog box.

6. Move the pointer over the dotted line from cell F7 until the pointer shape changes to [pointer icon], then double-click the line to open the Go To dialog box. This dialog box shows the worksheet and cells that are related. See Figure A3-6.

Figure A3-6 **GO TO DIALOG BOX**

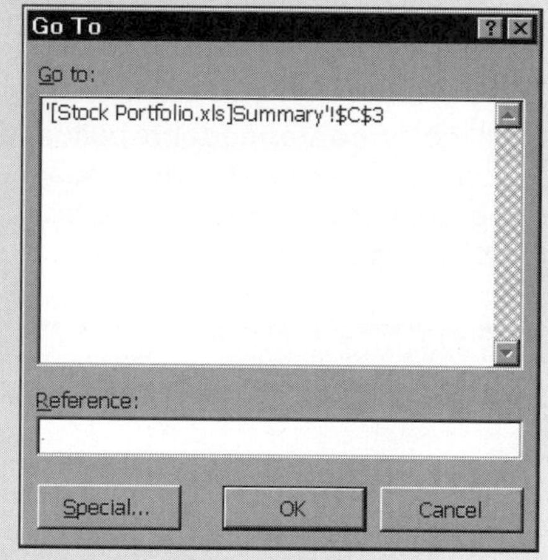

7. Click **(Stock Portfolio.xls)Summary!$C$3** in the Go to list box, and then click the **OK** button. Excel automatically jumps to the Summary sheet. Cell C3 in the Summary sheet is now the active cell.
Now that you've examined some of the dependent cells in the Embers worksheet, you'll return to the sheet and clear it of the tracer arrows.

8. Click the **Embers** sheet tab to display it, and then click the **Remove All Arrows** button [button icon] on the Auditing toolbar to remove all tracer arrows from the worksheet.

Using the Trace Dependents button, you were able to trace the flow of data from the cell containing the number of IBM shares throughout the workbook. Similarly, you can use the **Trace Precedents** button [button icon] on the Auditing toolbar to find the cells that provide data to a formula.

Tracing Precedent Cells

You'll use the Trace Precedents button to identify the cells that provide data to calculate the Gain/Loss formula in cell G4 in the Embers worksheet.

To trace precedent cells:

1. If necessary, click the **Embers** sheet tab to display it, click cell **G4**, and then click the **Trace Precedents** button on the Auditing toolbar. Notice that the blue tracer arrows indicate cells D4 and F4 provide data directly to the formula in cell G4. See Figure A3-7.

Figure A3-7 TRACER ARROWS INDICATE CELL PRECEDENTS

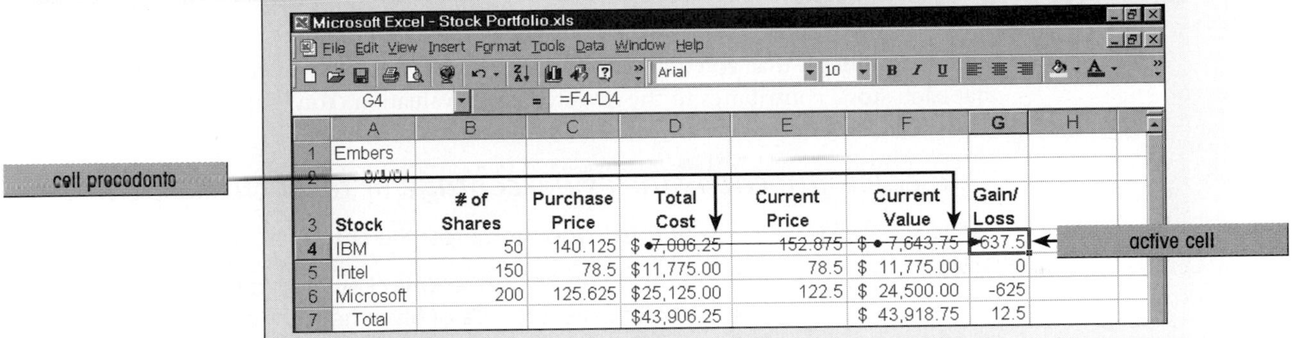

Continue tracing the precedents.

2. Click the **Trace Precedents** button again. The blue tracer arrows extend from G4 to show indirect precedents—cells B4, C4, and E4. See Figure A3-8.

Figure A3-8 EXCEL EXTENDS TRACER ARROWS TO INDIRECT CELL PRECEDENTS

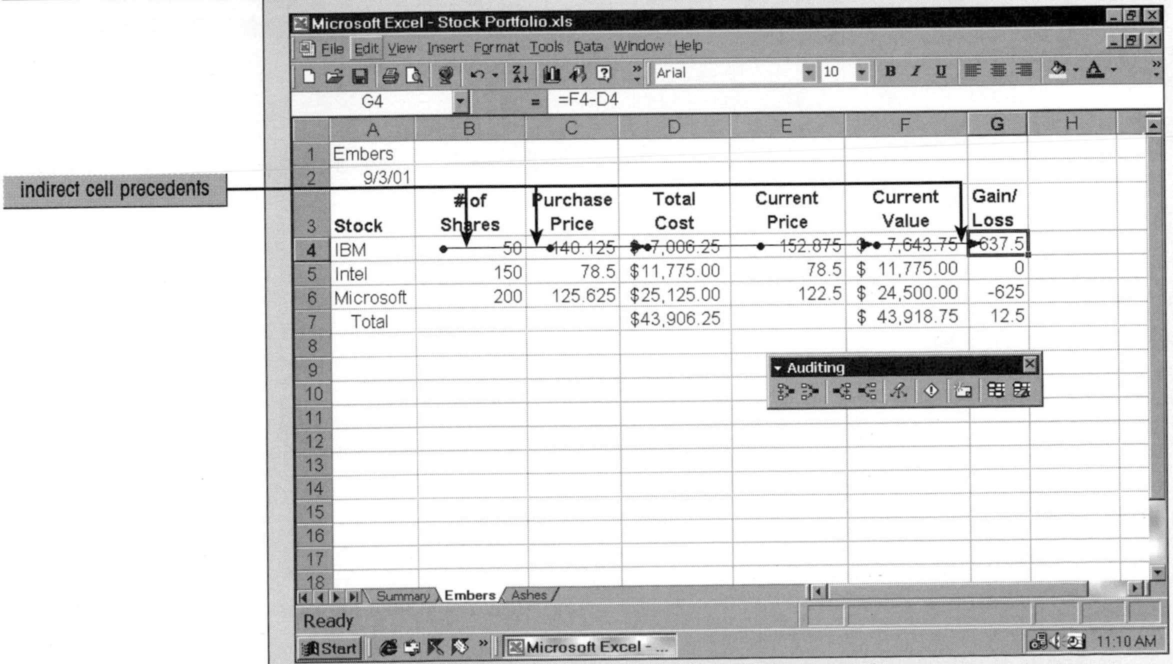

3. Click the **Trace Precedents** button again. You'll hear a beep, indicating that there aren't any additional indirect precedents.

4. Click the **Remove All Arrows** button on the Auditing toolbar to remove all tracer arrows.

Using the Trace Precedents button, you were able to see a visual representation of the cells that are used (directly and indirectly) by the formula in cell G4.

Suzanne stops by to ask about your progress, and to see if you would interrupt your work to add new information to the workbook.

Modifying the Worksheet

Suzanne requests that you add a column to Embers' worksheet that shows the percentage that each stock contributes to the investor's total valuation. You'll modify the worksheet now.

To calculate each stock's percentage of total current value:

1. Click cell **H3**, type **% of Total**, and then press the **Enter** key.

2. In cell **H4**, type **=F4/F7**, and then press the **Enter** key. The value 0.174043 appears, indicating that Embers has 17% of his or her portfolio in IBM stock.

   You now need to copy the formula to cells H5 and H6.

3. Click cell **H4**, and then move the pointer over the fill handle in H4 until the pointer changes to +. Click and drag the pointer to **H6**. The error value #DIV/0! appears in cells H5 and H6. See Figure A3-9.

Figure A3-9 **ERROR VALUES IN WORKSHEET**

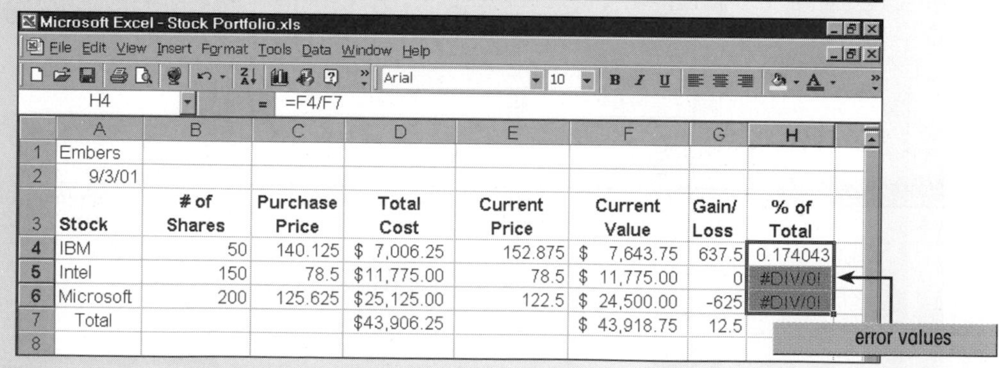

	A	B	C	D	E	F	G	H
1	Embers							
2	9/3/01							
3	Stock	# of Shares	Purchase Price	Total Cost	Current Price	Current Value	Gain/ Loss	% of Total
4	IBM	50	140.125	$ 7,006.25	152.875	$ 7,643.75	637.5	0.174043
5	Intel	150	78.5	$11,775.00	78.5	$ 11,775.00	0	#DIV/0!
6	Microsoft	200	125.625	$25,125.00	122.5	$ 24,500.00	-625	#DIV/0!
7	Total			$43,906.25		$ 43,918.75	12.5	
8								

Apparently, you've introduced an error in the worksheet. To discover the source of your error, use Excel's Trace Error feature.

Tracing Errors

If your worksheet displays error values, such as #DIV/0!, you can click the **Trace Error** button on the Auditing toolbar to help find the source of the errors. Figure A3-10 describes various error values that may appear in a worksheet.

Figure A3-10 EXPLANATION OF ERROR VALUES

ERROR VALUE	DESCRIPTION
#DIV/0!	A formula is divided by 0 (zero).
#NAME?	Excel doesn't recognize text in a formula, for example, misspelling the name of a function.
#NA	A value is unavailable to a function or formula, for example, an inappropriate lookup value argument in the VLOOKUP function.
#NULL!	An intersection of two areas that do not intersect is specified.
#NUM!	A problem with a number in a formula or function, for example, using an unacceptable argument in a function that requires a numeric argument.
#REF!	A cell reference is invalid, for example, deleting cells that are referenced by other formulas.
#VALUE!	Wrong type of argument or operand is used, for example, supplying a range to an operator or function that requires a single value, not a range.

Now you'll use the Trace Error button to help identify the cell that is causing the error value to appear.

To trace an error value appearing in the worksheet:

1. Activate the cell that contains the error by clicking cell **H5**.
2. Click the **Trace Error** button on the Auditing toolbar to display tracer arrows that point to the cells (in this case, cells F5 and F8) that feed the formula in cell H5. See Figure A3-11.

Figure A3-11 TRACER ARROWS AFTER CLICKING THE TRACE ERROR BUTTON

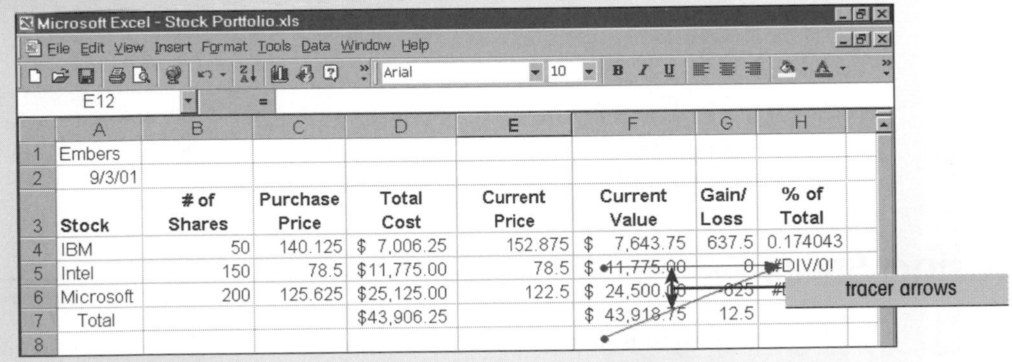

The Trace Error button doesn't correct the error; it only draws tracer arrows to precedent and dependent cells. You are responsible for determining the reason for the error and correcting it.

As you review the worksheet, you realize the error value #DIV/0! occurred because the formula in cells H5 and H6 attempted to divide by a cell that is empty (treated by Excel as zero). To correct the problem in your worksheet, you need to use an absolute reference, instead of a relative reference, to indicate the location of the total current investment (cell F7) when the formula is copied. That is, you need to change the formula from =F4/F7 to =F4/$F$7. The easiest way to correct the error is in Edit mode.

To change a cell reference to an absolute value:

1. Click cell **H4**.
2. In the formula bar, click to the right of the / (division) operator. Press the **F4** key to change the reference to $F$7, and then press the **Enter** key to update the formula in cell H4.
3. Click **H4**, and then copy the formula to cells **H5** and **H6**. Notice that the error value #DIV/0! and the tracer arrows no longer appear. See Figure A3-12.

Figure A3-12 TRACER ARROWS AND ERROR VALUES REMOVED AFTER FORMULA IS CORRECTED

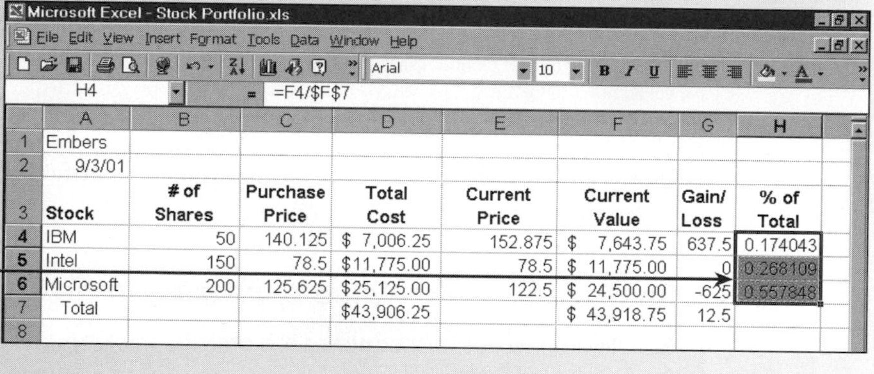

error values and tracer arrows removed

4. Click any cell to deselect the range. You've corrected the error and completed examining the relationships among cells and formulas in the Stock Portfolio workbook.

   You no longer need to display the Auditing toolbar.

5. Click the Auditing toolbar **Close** button ☒ to close it.

Now that you have a better grasp of the Stock Portfolio workbook, your next task is to improve its appearance. You decide your first change will be to create a style for the client name and then apply it to all client worksheets.

Using Styles

A **style** is a saved collection of formatting, such as font, font size, pattern, and alignment, that you combine, name, and save as a group. A style can include from one to six attributes—Number, Font, Alignment, Border, Pattern, and Protection. Once you have saved a style, you can apply it to a cell or range to achieve consistency in formatting. Excel has six predefined styles—Comma, Comma [0], Currency, Currency [0], Normal, and Percent. By default, every cell in a worksheet is automatically formatted with the Normal style, which you use whenever you start typing in a new worksheet.

For the Stock Portfolio workbook, Suzanne asks you to create a special style for the client name to make it stand out on the worksheet.

Creating Styles

You can create a style in two ways: by using an example of the cell that has the formats you want associated with the style; or manually, by choosing formats from the Style dialog box and selecting the formats you want associated with the style.

REFERENCE WINDOW RW

Creating a style by example

- Select a cell containing the formats you want to include in the style.
- Click Format from the menu bar, and then click Style to open the Style dialog box.
- Select the Style name text box, and then type a new name for the style.
- Click the OK button.

Suzanne asks you to use the following attributes to format the client name: Bookman Old Style font in bold, size 12, red font color, and yellow fill color. For the Stock Portfolio workbook, you'll create a style by providing an example. That is, you'll first format the cell with the client name on the Embers worksheet, then create a style based on the cell, and finally apply the style as necessary to the other worksheets in the Stock Portfolio workbook.

To format the client name:

1. If necessary, click the **Embers** sheet tab, and then click cell **A1**.
2. Click the **Font** list arrow on the Format toolbar, and then click **Bookman Old Style**.

   TROUBLE? If Bookman Old Style isn't included in the Font list box on your computer, choose another font of your choice.

   TROUBLE? You might have to click the Move Buttons button to select the Font, Font Color, and Fill Color.

3. Click the **Font Size** list arrow, and then click **12**.
4. Click the **Bold** button B to boldface the client name.
5. Click the **Font Color** list arrow A, and then click the **Red** color tile (third row, first column).
6. Click the **Fill Color** list arrow, and then click the **Yellow** color tile (fourth row, third column).
7. If necessary, increase the width of column A so the entire client name fits within cell A1.

Now that you have formatted the cell with the client name exactly the way you want, you'll use it to create a style (which you'll call ClientName) by example.

To create a style by example:

1. Click cell **A1**, the cell containing the formatting you want to use as the example.
2. Click **Format** from the menu bar, and then click **Style** to open the Style dialog box. See Figure A3-13. Notice the attributes of the Normal style are listed in the Style includes section of the dialog box.

Figure A3-13 STYLE DIALOG BOX

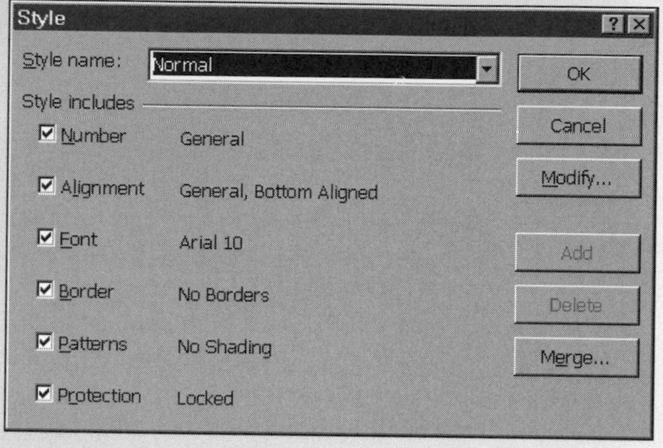

You want to add a new style and save it as ClientName.

3. Type **ClientName** in the Style name list box.
4. Click the **OK** button.

The style is created based on the formatting in cell A1. Now you can apply it to the other client worksheet (Ashes) in the Stock Portfolio workbook.

Applying Styles

Whenever you want a cell or range formatted using a style, select the item you want to format, and then select the style you want to apply from the Style dialog box.

To apply a style:

1. Click the **Ashes** sheet tab to select it, and then click cell **A1**, the cell you want to format.
2. Click **Format** from the menu bar, and then click **Style** to open the Style dialog box.

   You're ready to select the style.

3. Click the **Style name** list arrow, and then click **ClientName**.
4. Click the **OK** button to apply the style. See Figure A3-14.

Figure A3-14 WORKSHEET WITH CLIENTNAME STYLE APPLIED

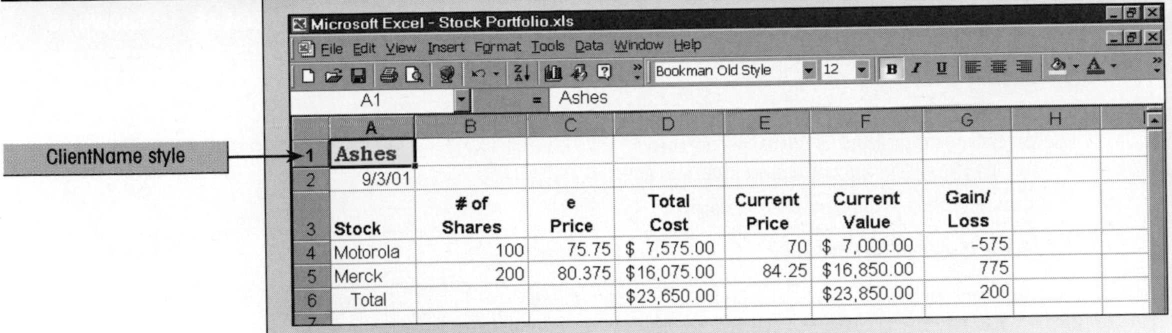

5. Save the workbook.

You're pleased with how easy it is to use styles to improve the workbook's appearance. Now you're ready to continue making changes by creating custom formats.

Creating Custom Formats

You've probably already used Excel's predefined formats to improve the appearance and readability of your worksheets by, for example, formatting currency values with dollar signs, large numbers with commas, and percentages with trailing percent signs. (If you haven't already worked with Excel's predefined formats, you'll have a chance to work with its accounting format in Case Problem 2.) For these purposes, the formats provided by Excel work well. However, for some situations, you may want to create your own custom format to better fit your needs.

To create a custom format, you specify **format codes**, a series of symbols, which describe how you want to display a number, date, time, or text value. For example, ##.# consists of placeholders for digits and a decimal place. The symbols tell Excel to display the value stored in a cell with one digit to the right of the decimal place. Figure A3-15 lists the formatting symbols you can use to create custom formats.

Figure A3-15 NUMERIC FORMAT SYMBOLS

SYMBOL	MEANING	CUSTOM FORMAT	ENTERED IN CELL AS	SHOWN AS
0	Determining number of decimal places shown; displays leading and trailing 0s (zeros)	##0.00	.2	0.20
#	Same as 0 (zero), except only significant digits are shown; insignificant 0s (zeros) are not shown	###.00	.2	.20
?	Same as 0 (zero); insignificant 0s removed, spaces inserted to align numbers correctly	# ??/??	5.2	5 1/5
.	Marks location of decimal point	##.00	2	2.00
,	Thousand separator	#,###	3535.25	3,35
%	Displays % sign and treats number as percentage	###%	.02	2%
/	Sets the location of the fraction separator	# ??/??	5.3	5 3/10
E+	Displays numbers in scientific notation and inserts E or e in displayed value if format contains one or more 0s or #s to the right of E- or E+ to indicate the power of the exponent	0.000E+000	5678	5.678E+003
"Text"	Displays entry within quotes as text	### "Dollars"	325	325 Dollars
*	Repeats the character following the asterisk enough times to fill the cell	*$###	35	$$$$$$$$$35
\	Character following the \ is text	###\@	325	325@
:$_+()-/-	Characters shown	000-00-0000	067421113	067-42-1113
@	Indicates where user input text will appear	@*.	Chapter 1	Chapter 1........
[color]	Displays characters in cell in indicated color	[Blue]##0	325	325
_ (underscore)	Inserts a blank space the width of the character following the underscore; aligns positive values with negative values enclosed in () so numbers and commas align	#,##0_);(#,##0)	325	325

When you design your own custom format, it can consist of up to four sections, each separated by a semicolon, in the following structure:

positive format; negative format; zero format; text-value format

The first section defines the format for positive numbers, the second section defines the format for negative numbers, the third section defines how zero values will appear, and the fourth section defines how text will be treated.

For example, the following format code:

#,###; (#,###);0;"Enter a number!"

specifies that positive numbers appear as whole numbers with a comma, negative numbers appear in parentheses as whole numbers, zero values appear as 0 (zero), and the text "Enter a number!" appears if anything but a number is entered in the cell. If your custom format includes only one part, Excel applies that format to all positive, negative, and zero values.

REFERENCE WINDOW RW

Creating a Custom Number Format

- Select the cells you want to format.
- Click Format, and then click Cells to open the Format Cells dialog box.
- Click the Number tab, and then click Custom in the Category list box.
- Type or edit the number format code in the Type text box.
- Click the OK button.

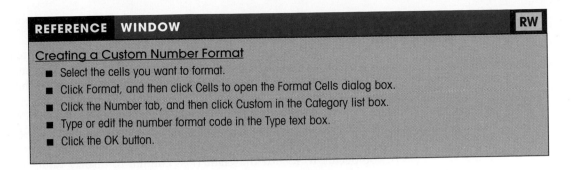

As you review the Stock Portfolio workbook, you decide that the stock prices should appear with a fraction, instead of with a decimal, because stock prices are shown with fractions in most financial publications. Excel doesn't include the exact format in which you want to display the prices, so you'll create your own custom format.

To create a custom format for displaying fractions:

1. Make sure the **Embers** sheet is selected.
2. Select the ranges **C4:C6** and **E4:E6**.
3. Click **Format**, and then click **Cells** to open the Format Cells dialog box.
4. Click the **Number** tab if necessary to select it, and then click **Custom** in the Category list box.
5. Select the existing format code in the Type text box, and then type **$#,##0 ??/??** to replace it.
6. Click the **OK** button to display the stock prices with a fraction.
7. Click anywhere in the worksheet to deselect the range. See Figure A3-16.

Figure A3-16 STOCK PRICES SHOWN WITH FRACTIONS

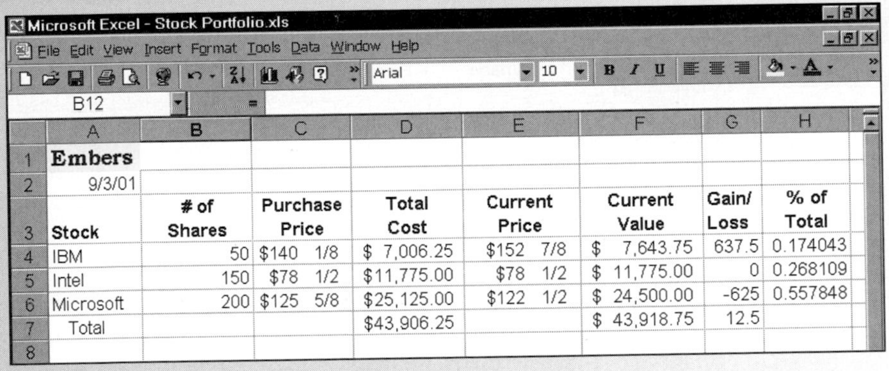

	A	B	C	D	E	F	G	H
1	**Embers**							
2	9/3/01							
3	**Stock**	**# of Shares**	**Purchase Price**	**Total Cost**	**Current Price**	**Current Value**	**Gain/ Loss**	**% of Total**
4	IBM	50	$140 1/8	$ 7,006.25	$152 7/8	$ 7,643.75	637.5	0.174043
5	Intel	150	$78 1/2	$11,775.00	$78 1/2	$ 11,775.00	0	0.268109
6	Microsoft	200	$125 5/8	$25,125.00	$122 1/2	$ 24,500.00	-625	0.557848
7	Total			$43,906.25		$ 43,918.75	12.5	
8								

After reviewing the worksheet, you determine that the workbook would be more readable if different colors were used for the values in the Gain/Loss columns, to indicate gains, losses, or no changes. To do this, you'll again use custom formatting.

Custom Formatting Data with Color

You also can use the numeric custom format codes to display the contents of the selected cell or range in a different color, depending on the value in the cell, by adding a specific color code to a custom format. To change the color of an entry, type the name of the color in square brackets for each section of the format code in front of the definition of the custom format for the section. The valid color codes are [BLACK], [CYAN], [MAGENTA], [WHITE], [BLUE], [GREEN], [RED], and [YELLOW]. For example, the format code $#,##0;[RED]($#,##0) displays positive values in black (default color) and negative values in red.

You decide to format the Gain/Loss column to display values in blue if the investment shows a gain (positive number), red if a loss (negative number), and the words "No Change" if the gain or loss is zero.

To assign color to a custom format:

1. Select the range **G4:G7**.
2. Click **Format**, and then click **Cells** to open the Format Cells dialog box.
3. If necessary, click the **Number** tab to select it, and then click **Custom** in the Category list box.
4. Select the current format code in the Type text box, and then type **[BLUE]$#,##0.00;[RED]$#,##0.00;"No Change"** to replace it.
5. Click the **OK** button to return to the worksheet.
6. Click any cell to deselect the highlighted range. See Figure A3-17.

Figure A3-17 FORMATTING GAIN/LOSS VALUES USING COLOR

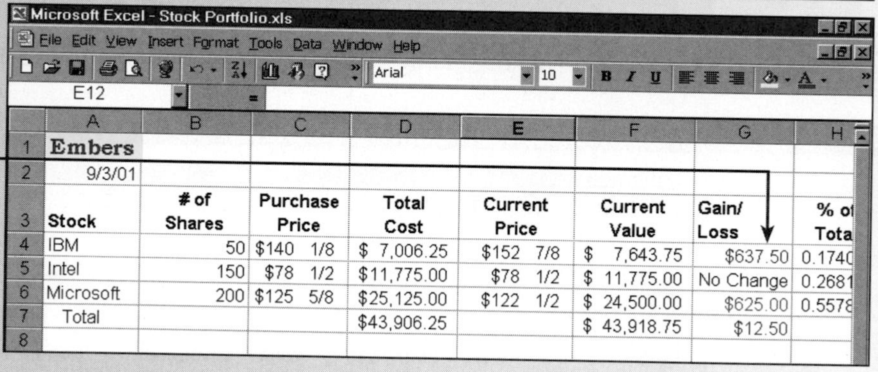

	A	B	C	D	E	F	G	H
1	Embers							
2	9/3/01							
3	Stock	# of Shares	Purchase Price	Total Cost	Current Price	Current Value	Gain/ Loss	% of Tota
4	IBM	50	$140 1/8	$ 7,006.25	$152 7/8	$ 7,643.75	$637.50	0.1740
5	Intel	150	$78 1/2	$11,775.00	$78 1/2	$ 11,775.00	No Change	0.2681
6	Microsoft	200	$125 5/8	$25,125.00	$122 1/2	$ 24,500.00	$625.00	0.5578
7	Total			$43,906.25		$ 43,918.75	$12.50	
8								

column custom formatted with color code

One last change is needed: changing the format of the date.

Custom Formatting Dates

When your workbook displays dates and/or times, you'll most likely use one of Excel's predefined date and time formats to display them in a readable format. Although the predefined time and date formats are usually fine, you also can create custom formats. Figure A3-18 illustrates the format codes used for dates and times.

Figure A3-18 FORMAT CODES USED FOR TIME AND DATES

SYMBOL	TO DISPLAY
m	Months as 1–12.
mm	Months as 01–12.
mmm	Months as Jan–Dec.
mmmm	Months as January–December.
d	Days as 1–31.
dd	Days as 01–31.
ddd	Days as Sun–Sat.
dddd	Days as Sunday–Saturday.
yy	Years as 00–99.
yyyy	Years as 1900–9999.
h	Hours as 1–24.
mm	Minutes as 01–60 (when immediately follows h signifies minutes; otherwise, months).
ss	Seconds as 01–60.

You decide to change the worksheet date so it displays the date in the format "As of Day of week, Month Day, Year" instead of mm/dd/yy. For example, 07/09/99 would appear as "As of Wednesday, July 9, 1999".

To create a custom date format:

1. Click cell **A2**.
2. Click **Format**, and then click **Cells** to open the Format Cells dialog box.
3. If necessary, click the **Number** tab to select it, and then click **Custom** in the Category list box.
4. Select the current format code in the Type text box, and then type **"As of " dddd, mmmm d, yyyy**. Check the Sample box, above the Type text box, to see if the code you're entering is working as expected.
5. Click the **OK** button.
6. If necessary, increase the width of column A to display the date. See Figure A3-19.

Figure A3-19 WORKSHEET AFTER CUSTOM FORMAT APPLIED TO TIME AND DATE FIELD

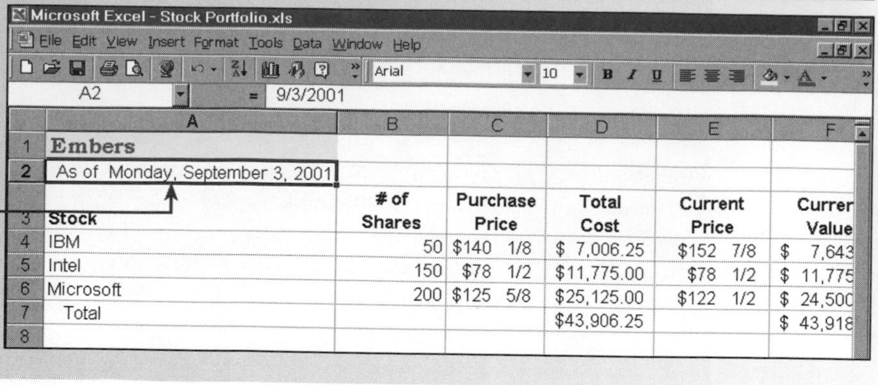

Now that you've created custom formats for the Embers worksheet, you realize that you should apply these same formats to the Ashes worksheet.

Applying Custom Formats

Once a custom format is defined, it is stored in the workbook and can be applied like any other predefined format. The custom format is only available in the workbook in which it was created. (If you no longer want the format, you can delete it by selecting the custom format in the Custom Category list box of the Format Cells dialog box and then clicking the Delete button.)

Now you'll apply the custom formats you've already created for the stock prices, Gain/Loss column, and date to the Ashes sheet.

To apply the custom formats:

1. Click the **Ashes** sheet tab to select it.
2. Select the ranges **C4:C5** and **E4:E5**.
3. Click **Format**, and then click **Cells** to open the Format Cells dialog box.
4. If necessary, click the **Number** tab, and then click **Custom** in the Category list box.
5. Click the **Type** list arrow, and then scroll down and click the format code **$#,##0 ??/??**.
6. Click the **OK** button to display the stock prices with a fraction.
7. Click anywhere in the worksheet to deselect the range.
8. Select the appropriate cell or range, and then repeat steps 3–7 to format the Gain/Losses and Date cells.
9. Save, and then print the workbook.

When you show Suzanne your changes to the Stock Portfolio workbook, she's impressed by your work and thanks you for your help. Because she plans to sign many new clients, she decides to save the Embers worksheet as a template.

Inserting a Worksheet Template

Usually, when you open a template, Excel opens a new workbook with the formatting and content identical to its predefined template. Sometimes, however, you may want to insert a worksheet into an existing workbook based on another template. That's what Suzanne wants to do: Each time she signs a new client, she'll need to add a new sheet to the Stock Portfolio workbook with the same labels, formatting, and formulas as the other client sheets (Embers and Ashes). As a result, Suzanne created a template, named NewClient, by modifying the Embers sheet and deleting all the other sheets in the Stock Portfolio workbook. (Because creating templates involves placing a file in the Microsoft Office Templates folder, you won't step through the following tasks but will instead only read about how to accomplish them.) See Figure A3-20.

Figure A3-20 NEWCLIENT TEMPLATE

indicates template

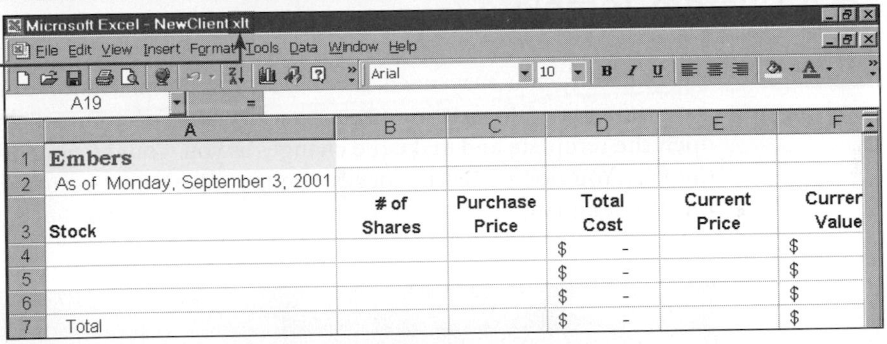

REFERENCE WINDOW RW

Inserting a sheet from a template into the current workbook

- Right-click the mouse button on the sheet tab where you want to insert the worksheet.
- From the Shortcut menu, click Insert to open the Insert dialog box.
- Click the General tab if necessary, click the desired template, and then click the OK button.

After creating the template, Suzanne decided to test it by adding a fictitious client. Figure A3-21 shows the sheet after being inserted into the Stock Portfolio workbook. As she reviewed the new sheet, Suzanne realized cell A1 still had the name "Embers." The new client sheet should not have a client name; instead, it should be blank. Suzanne needs to edit the template.

Figure A3-21 NEWCLIENT WORKSHEET INSERTED

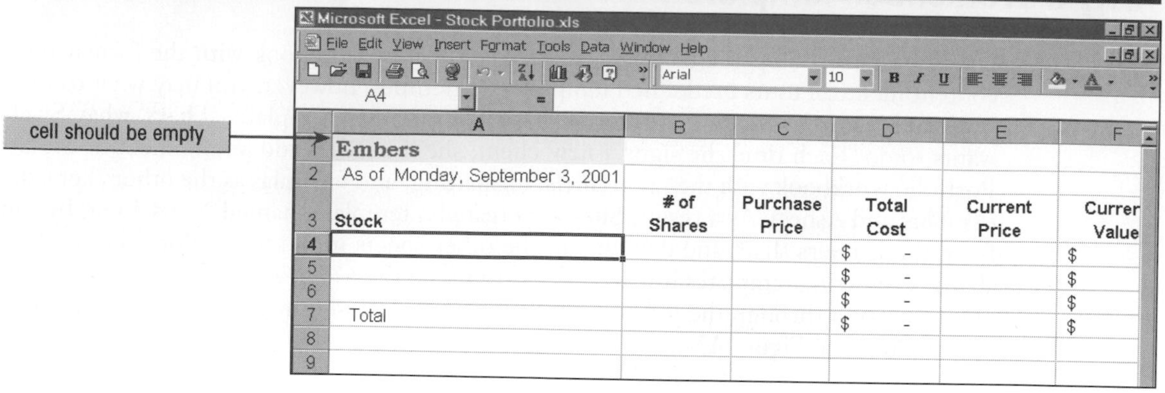

Editing a Custom Template

Occasionally, you may need to revise your template, for example, to reflect changes in requirements or formatting preference. When you want to change a template, you simply open the template and make the changes as you would to any other workbook, and then save the file. You don't need to specify the template type because Excel automatically saves the file as a template.

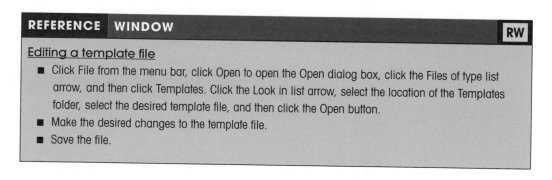

REFERENCE WINDOW RW

Editing a template file

- Click File from the menu bar, click Open to open the Open dialog box, click the Files of type list arrow, and then click Templates. Click the Look in list arrow, select the location of the Templates folder, select the desired template file, and then click the Open button.
- Make the desired changes to the template file.
- Save the file.

Suzanne revised the template and then tested it again by adding a fictitious client. See Figure A3-22. The NewClient template was edited successfully.

Figure A3-22 EDITED NEWCLIENT WORKSHEET TEMPLATE

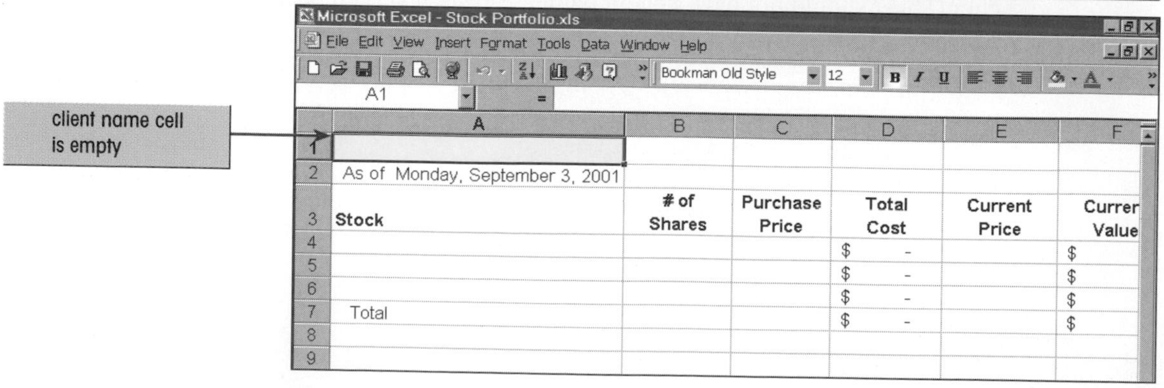

Session A3.1 Quick Check

1. What is the purpose of Excel's Audit feature?
2. Which button on the Auditing toolbar do you use to find out which cells contain formulas that reference the selected cell?
3. After clicking one of the trace buttons on the Auditing toolbar, you notice that the worksheet icon appears. What does this mean?
4. What is an advantage of using styles in a workbook?
5. What is the difference between a predefined format and a custom format?
6. What is the purpose of the # symbol? How does it differ from 0 (zero) as a format symbol?
7. What date symbol would you use to indicate that the day of the week should be spelled out?
8. How do you edit a worksheet template?

In this session you used tracer arrows to audit the Stock Portfolio workbook and then used styles and custom formats to improve its appearance. Then you learned how to save a worksheet as a template and how you can easily edit that template. In the next session you'll learn about sharing workbooks.

SESSION A3.2

In this session you'll learn how to set up a shared workbook and then how to use it for monitoring, commenting, sharing, and resolving conflicts. You'll also find out how to merge shared workbooks.

Sharing Workbooks

In today's business environment, working in groups is common. With Excel, you can use its Shared Workbook feature to share files with coworkers and work on data collaboratively. A **shared workbook** is a workbook that has been set up to allow multiple users on a network to view and make changes at the same time. (Because sharing workbooks involves working on a network in groups, you won't actually step through the following tasks but will instead only read about how to accomplish them.)

Setting Up a Shared Workbook

To share a workbook on a network, you use the Share Workbook command on the Tools menu to open the Share Workbook dialog box (see Figure A3-23). By clicking the Allow changes by more than one user at the same time check box, you enable multiple users to access and make changes to the workbook at the same time. In order for users to share the workbook, it must be placed on your network.

Figure A3-23 SHARE WORKBOOK DIALOG BOX

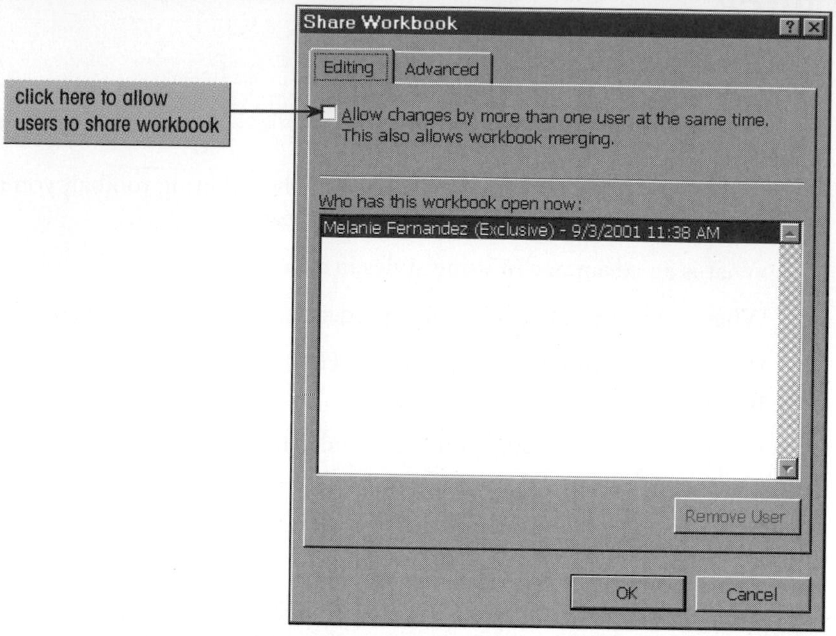

REFERENCE WINDOW RW

Creating a shared workbook

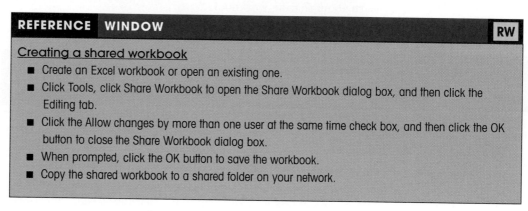

- Create an Excel workbook or open an existing one.
- Click Tools, click Share Workbook to open the Share Workbook dialog box, and then click the Editing tab.
- Click the Allow changes by more than one user at the same time check box, and then click the OK button to close the Share Workbook dialog box.
- When prompted, click the OK button to save the workbook.
- Copy the shared workbook to a shared folder on your network.

To confirm that you've set up a shared workbook correctly, you would open up the workbook (in the usual procedure) and look for the word "Shared" in brackets added to the workbook's title bar (see Figure A3-24). Once you've set up a shared workbook and placed it on the network, you can work with it like any other workbook, and you can monitor its use, track changes, resolve conflicts, and merge it with other shared workbooks.

Figure A3-24 **SHARED WORKBOOK**

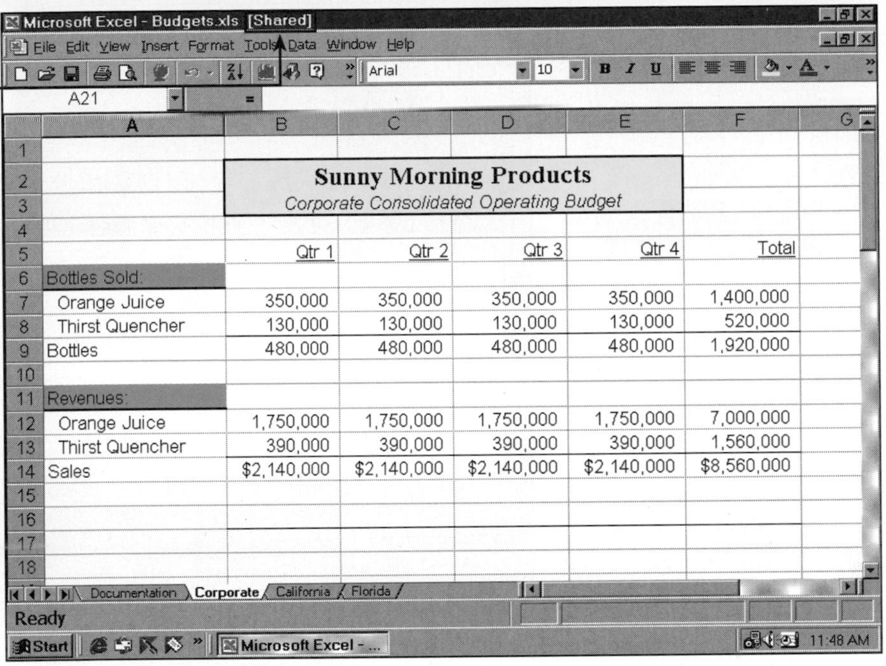

Working with a Shared Workbook

Using a shared workbook is similar to using any workbook: You can enter numbers and text, edit cells, move data around the worksheet, insert new rows and columns, and perform other tasks. In a shared workbook, however, there are some features of Excel that aren't available, such as not being able to delete worksheets, define conditional formats, set up or change data validation, insert or change a chart, or use the drawing tools.

Monitoring a Shared Workbook

Once a shared workbook is active, you can find out who is currently accessing a shared workbook by selecting the Share Workbook command on the Tools menu. The Editing tab in the Share Workbook dialog box shows a list of all users currently using the file. Figure A3-25 shows a list of users who currently have the shared workbook open.

Figure A3-25 SHARED WORKBOOK WITH TWO USERS

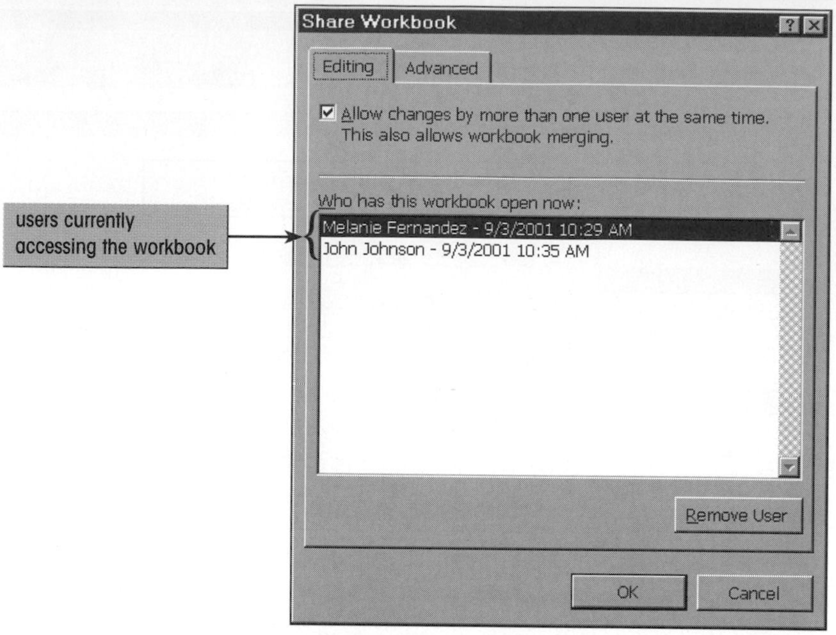

Adding Comments to a Shared Workbook

While working with a shared workbook, you may want to provide explanations for changes you made by attaching comments to cells that others can view. To include a comment, click the Comment command on the Insert menu, and then type the comment. You can view each comment, along with the name of the user who wrote it, when you move the pointer over the cell. If more than one user adds a comment to the same cell, the text of all saved comments for the cell appears. Figure A3-26 shows a shared workbook with two comments added to a cell.

Figure A3-26 SHARED WORKBOOK WITH COMMENTS

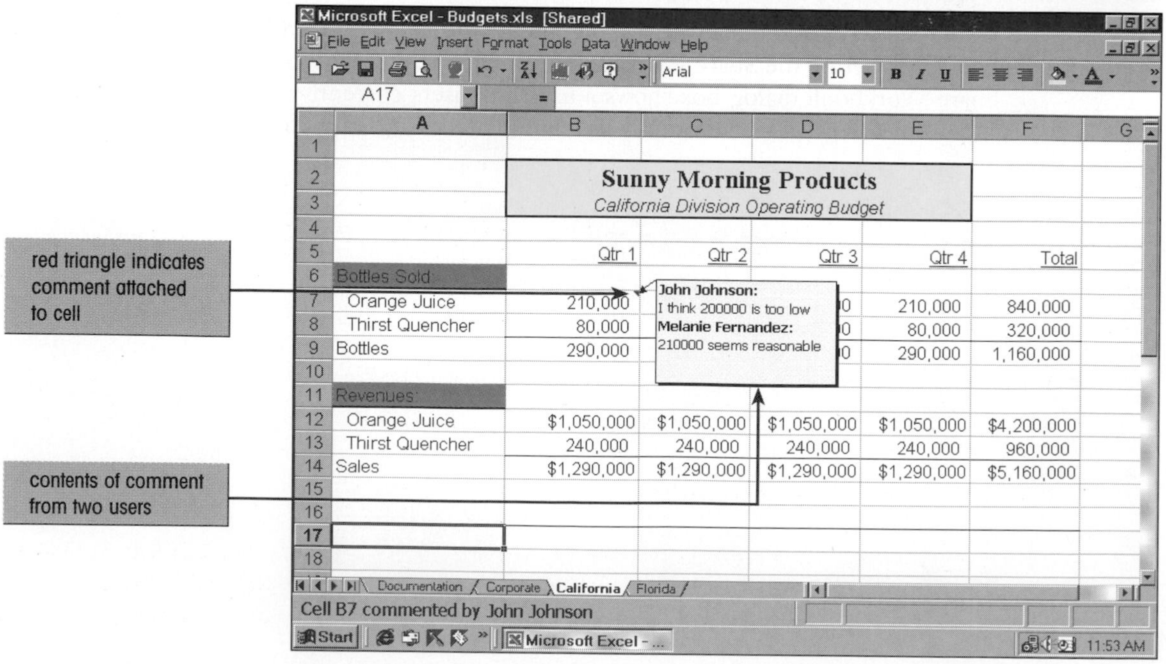

REFERENCE WINDOW RW

Adding a comment to a cell
- Click the cell to which you want to add the comment.
- Click Insert, and then click Comment to display a comment box.
- Type your comment.
- Click outside the comment box.

Tracking Changes to a Shared Workbook

To update a shared workbook with your changes, use the Save command from the File menu, just as you do when saving any workbook. Each time you save the workbook, the changes you've made update the shared workbook. In addition, all the saved changes made by other users since the last time you saved the workbook are also uploaded into your workbook. A message "The workbook has been updated with changes saved by other users" informs you that other users' changes have been updated into your workbook. These changes will be outlined with a different colored border, and a mark in the upper-left corner of the cell will indicate a comment. When you move the pointer over the cell, a comment box opens, informing you who made the change, the date and time of the change, and the substance of the change. Figure A3-27 shows a coworker's changes marked in blue (after you saved the workbook).

Figure A3-27 TRACKING CHANGES TO A SHARED WORKBOOK

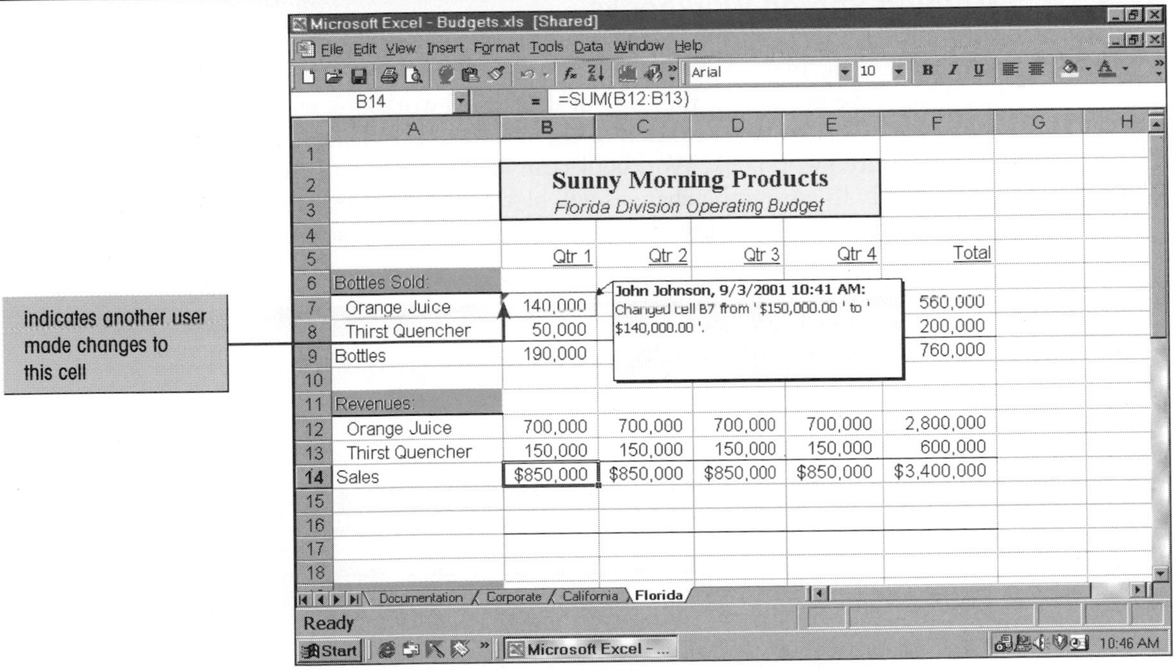

Resolving Conflicts in a Shared Workbook

As long as each person makes changes to a different cell in the workbook, Excel can automatically integrate these changes into the shared workbook. Sometimes when you save a shared workbook, changes may conflict, for instance, when two or more users enter different values in the same cell. When this occurs, someone needs to decide which changes to keep. Excel's default approach allows the first person who saves the workbook after the conflict occurs to decide which changes to accept. Figure A3-28 shows the dialog box that opens after you have saved a workbook where a conflict exists. You decide if you want to accept your changes or another user's changes.

Figure A3-28 RESOLVE CONFLICTS DIALOG BOX

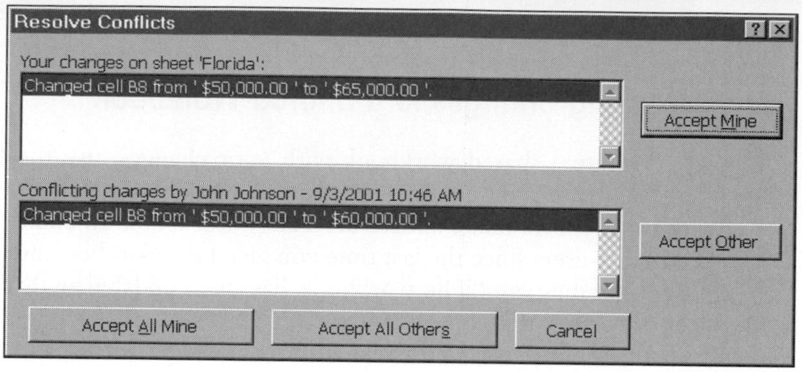

If you don't want to "resolve conflicts" when you save a shared workbook, you can set it so that the current changes being saved will be accepted automatically. To implement this strategy, select the Changes being saved win option button in the Advanced tab of the Share Workbook dialog box.

Merging Shared Workbooks

Sometimes you may need to make a copy of a shared workbook, perhaps because a user needs to make changes to the copy of the shared workbook while on a business trip. When the copied workbook is returned to the network, the changes need to be merged into the original shared workbook. Workbooks can be merged as long as the change history has been maintained. To ensure the changes will be tracked, you open the Highlight Changes dialog box by clicking Tools on the menu bar and pointing to Track Changes. See Figure A3-29.

Figure A3-29 HIGHLIGHT CHANGES DIALOG BOX

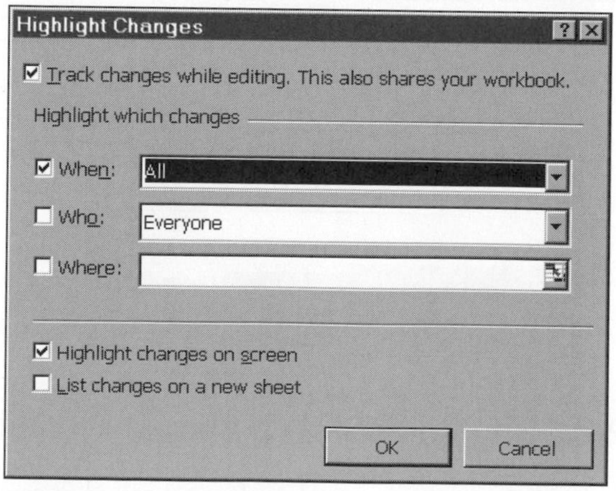

REFERENCE WINDOW RW

Distributing a copy of a shared workbook

- Open the shared workbook.
- Click Tools from the menu bar, point to Track Changes, and then click Highlight Changes to open the Highlight Changes dialog box.
- If necessary, click the Track Changes check box to select it, and then click the OK button.
- Click the OK button to save the workbook.
- Make a copy of the workbook using a different filename, and then copy the file to a disk.

When you're ready to merge workbooks, you simply click Tools on the menu bar, and then click Merge Workbooks.

REFERENCE WINDOW RW

Merging Shared Workbooks

- Open the copy of the shared workbook into which you want to merge the changes from another workbook.
- Click Tools from the menu bar, and then click Merge Workbooks to open the Select Files to Merge into Current Workbook dialog box.
- Select the copy of the Excel file that has changes to be merged with the current file.
- Click the OK button to merge the files.
- Save and close the workbook.

A few words of caution when merging workbooks:

- The workbook must be shareable.
- You cannot merge files with the same name.
- The change history must be maintained, and the changes must be tracked until the workbooks are merged.

Session A3.2 Quick Check

1. What is a shared workbook?
2. Where does a shared workbook need to be located?
3. How can you tell if a workbook is being shared?
4. Answer true or false for each question regarding shared workbooks:
   a. You can make changes to a cell.
   b. You can create a chart.
   c. You can save a workbook.
   d. You can find out who is accessing the workbook.
5. How do you find out which users are currently accessing a shared workbook?
6. Describe what happens when you save a shared workbook.
7. When does the Resolve Conflicts dialog box open?
8. Why would you merge shared workbooks?

In this session you learned about Excel's Shared Workbook feature. You observed how to set one up, work with it, as well as use it for monitoring, commenting, sharing, and resolving conflicts. You learned how to merge shared workbooks as well.

REVIEW ASSIGNMENTS

Suzanne Bouchard has added a partner, Chuck Kim, to her firm. Chuck is impressed with your work on the Stock Portfolio workbook and asks you to help him confirm the accuracy and improve the appearance of his workbook.

1. If necessary, start Excel and make sure your Data Disk is in the appropriate drive. Open the **Stock1** workbook in the Review folder for Appendix.03 on your Data Disk and save it as **Stock Portfolio 1**.
2. Make cell B5 on the Summary sheet the active cell. What happens when you click the Trace Dependents button on the Auditing toolbar? Why?
3. Make cell D6 the active cell, click the Trace Precedents button on the Auditing toolbar twice. Print the worksheet. What happens? Why? Remove all tracer arrows.
4. Create a custom format for the # of Shares column of the Graham worksheet so that as you enter a number, the word "shares" automatically appears after the number. For example, if you enter "100", "100 shares" appears.
5. Create a style with the following attributes that you can apply to each stock name in the worksheet: font style bold italic; font color indigo; (row 1 column 7); and fill color light turquoise (row 5 column 5). Name the style StockName.
6. Apply the custom format and style you created for the Graham worksheet to the other sheets in the Stock Portfolio 1 workbook.
7. Save, print, and then close the workbook.

CASE PROBLEMS

Case 1. Groceries to Go Yolanda Brown is the National Sales Manager for Groceries to Go, which delivers frozen and nonperishable foods to customers across the country. The annual stockholders' meeting will be held next month, and the company president has asked Yolanda for a sales update. Yolanda has compiled the data in an Excel worksheet and asks you to confirm the worksheet's accuracy. Do the following:

1. If necessary, start Excel and make sure your Data Disk is in the appropriate drive. Open the **GrowGo** workbook in the Cases folder for Appendix.03, and save it as **Groceries to Go**.
2. The values in column F should display each region's share of sales to total sales. The values in cells F4:F7 are incorrect. Select cell F6 and use the Trace Error button on the Auditing toolbar to help determine the reason for the error. What is the source of the problem? After you determine the source, correct the problem on the worksheet.
3. Click cell F4 and use the Trace Error button on the Auditing toolbar. What happened? What does this tell you about the use of the Trace Error button?
4. Identify all the direct and indirect cells that use the Gross Sales in the Northeast value (cell B3). Print the worksheet with tracer arrows and then remove the tracer arrows.
5. Use the Trace Precedents button on the Auditing toolbar to identify all cells (direct and indirect) that feed cell G3. Print the worksheet with tracer arrows and then remove the tracer arrows.
6. Edit the formula in cell B10 so MAX(B3:B7) is changed to MIX(B3:B7). Explain why the error value appears in cell B10 and then change the formula back to the original.

Explore

7. Use the Trace Error button on the Auditing toolbar on cell G7. Print the worksheet with tracer arrows. How do you think the error value #NAME? in cell G7 occurred? (*Hint:* Review your results from Question 6.)
8. Save your worksheet, and then close it.

Case 2. Absolute Accounting Marla Tower, the proprietor of Absolute Accounting, prepares tax worksheets for local small businesses. She has just created a tax worksheet for Crazy Carl's Used Cars and needs to verify it. She asks you to do the following:

1. If necessary, start Excel and make sure your Data Disk is in the appropriate drive. Open the **Tax** workbook in the Cases folder for Appendix.03, and save it as **TaxSchedule**.

Explore

2. Improve the appearance of each sheet by using the Accounting format. (*Hint:* Click Format on the menu bar, and then click Cells.)
3. Use the Auditing toolbar to find where the supporting information for automobile expense listed on the Schedule C worksheet is located. Reduce the magnification to 50%. Print the worksheet with tracer arrows and then remove them. Change the magnification back to 100%.
4. Use the Auditing toolbar to determine what cells in the Schedule C sheet telephone expense feeds. What are the direct and indirect cells? Remove the tracer arrows.
5. Start with cell B4 in the Schedule C workbook, and identify all direct and indirect precedent cells related to this cell. Print the worksheet with tracer arrows and then remove them.

Explore

6. Modify the formula in cell G14 in the Sch C Details sheet so it is =Sum(G2:G14). What happens? Identify and explain the problem.
7. Save your worksheet, and then close it.

Case 3. Marketing Magic Jamil El-Tobqui is the director of public relations at Marketing Magic, an advertising and marketing firm. He's in charge of preparing the company's Annual Report, which will be distributed to stockholders and customers. Because Jamil wants the Annual Report to look as striking as possible, he has asked you to experiment with custom formatting the data. He asks you to do the following:

1. If necessary, start Excel and make sure your Data Disk is in the appropriate drive. Open the workbook **Format** in the Cases folder for Appendix.03, and save it as **Custom Formats**.
2. In cell B2, create a format that will display a negative percentage as (85.2%) instead of –0.852.
3. In cell B3, create a custom format so the negative percentage appears as (13.2%) in red.
4. In cell B4, create a custom format that will display the day of the week instead of the date. For example, you enter 7/31/99, and "Saturday" appears.
5. In cell B5, create a custom format that will display the word "Dollars" following the amount. For example, if you enter 25, then "25 Dollars" appears.
6. In cells B6, B7, and B8, create a custom format that displays a positive number to two decimal places. If a negative value is entered, the message "Enter a positive number" appears, and if zero is entered, 0 (zero) appears.
7. Save, print, and then close your worksheet.

Case 4. Grading the Introduction to Business Course The Introduction to Business course at City College of Buffalo is team-taught by four instructors, one each from the Accounting, Marketing, Management, and Finance Departments. Each instructor gives two quizzes, all equally weighted and used to compute a numeric average for the students' final grades.

This semester, the City College is offering six sections of Introduction to Business with approximately 25 students per section. Professor Terry Smith, the course coordinator, has received the six rosters listing the students in each section.

Terry Smith plans to put the information for the students into an Excel workbook into which each faculty member can enter quiz grades. You'll help Professor Smith with this workbook by doing the following:

1. Develop (sketch) a design for a spreadsheet to track each student's quiz scores, quiz average, and final grade. Remember that you are planning a spreadsheet that will include all students (25 per section) for all six sections.
2. List the steps you would take to set up your workbook as a shared workbook into which each of the four faculty can enter data.
3. The marketing instructor has scores ready to enter for the first marketing quiz that students took in Section 3. The finance instructor has scores for the first finance quiz students took in Section 5. Assuming that you now have a shared workbook, establish a set of instructions as to how each instructor should enter the exam grades in the workbook.
4. As the marketing professor was entering grades, the professor wanted to know if anyone else was using the workbook. What can the professor do to determine who else is currently accessing the shared workbook?
5. The marketing professor finishes entering the grades and saves the workbook. Ten minutes later, the finance professor finishes entering grades and saves the workbook. What will the finance professor observe after saving the file?
6. After entering the quiz grades, the marketing instructor informs the course coordinator that student Jesse Graverly's name is missing from the workbook, so no grade can be entered. What can you do?
7. The accounting instructor made a copy of the workbook and took it home over the weekend to enter the accounting quiz grades of Section 1. The instructor's home computer cannot connect to the network. What needs to be done when the faculty member returns to the office to get the accounting grades for Section 1 into the workbook on the network?
8. Sketch the layout of a template to simplify the administrative setup for this course. Explain how the template would simplify the course coordinator's work.

QUICK CHECK ANSWERS

Session A3.1

1. Excel's Audit feature helps you to inspect the overall logic of a worksheet by locating and analyzing formulas, as well as uncovering errors.
2. Trace Dependents button
3. There are formulas on another worksheet or workbook that depend on or feed the selected cell
4. They provide consistency in formatting, especially if the format includes several attributes.
5. A predefined format is one Excel provides; you create a custom format if a predefined format doesn't fit your needs.
6. The # symbol means a significant digit will appear; however, an insignificant digit will not. The 0 (zero) symbol displays leading and trailing zeros.
7. dddd
8. open the template: click File, click Open, change the Files of type list arrow to Templates, locate the Templates folder and the Template file you want to edit, and then click Open; then make the desired changes to the template, and save the file

Session A3.2

1. A shared workbook is set up to allow multiple users on a network to view and make changes at the same time.
2. You place the workbook on a shared folder on a network.
3. The title bar has the word "Shared" in brackets following the worksheet name.
4. **a.** True; **b.** False; **c.** True; **d.** True
5. click Tools, click Share Workbook, and then examine the Editing tab on the Share Workbook dialog box
6. When you save your workbook, all saved changes other users made since the last time you saved the workbook will be uploaded. These changes will be outlined in color, and a mark will appear indicating a comment is available.
7. When two users have made changes to the same cell.
8. If a copy of the shared workbook has been updated "offline," you would want to incorporate those changes into the copy on the network.

OBJECTIVES

In this tutorial you will:

- Learn about different ways Excel can create Web pages
- Learn about interactive and noninteractive Web pages
- Create a Web page based on a pivot table
- Edit a pivot table from within a Web page
- Export a pivot table from the Web to an Excel workbook

SAVING PIVOTTABLES IN HTML FORMAT

Creating Interactive PivotTables for the Web

CASE

GP Golf Gloves

GP Golf is a manufacturer of golf apparel located in Argyle, Maine. The company's specialty is golf gloves. They sell three brands: the Regular glove, the Pro and the SoftGrip glove. Each of these gloves comes in four sizes: small, medium, large and extra large. GP Golf creates separate versions of its gloves for women and men, and for right handers and left handers.

The company has created an Excel workbook that contains monthly sales figures for each model, size and version of its gloves. Peter Boyle, the director of sales, would like to make this information easily available to his sales staff. The company has recently installed an Intranet in order to facilitate the sharing of documents and information among its employees. Peter has asked you to help him in placing his workbook on the Intranet.

You and Peter discuss the issue with the network group and are told that documents on the company's Intranet must be saved in HTML format—the standard format for Web pages. Peter objects, feeling that this would remove the workbook's functionality. Unable to convince them to change their policy, Peter asks you to find out whether Excel can create Web pages that will preserve some of the features of workbooks.

SESSION A4.1

In this session you'll learn about the different ways Excel workbooks can be exported as Web pages. You'll learn how to create a Web page containing an interactive PivotTable. You'll have a chance to work with the PivotTable and learn how to perform many of the same operations in your Web browser that you perform from within Excel.

Saving Workbooks as Web Pages

Excel provides many different possibilities for creating Web pages based on your Excel workbook. These pages fall into two main categories: noninteractive and interactive. A **noninteractive Web page** contains the data from the workbook and some of the formatting, but it does not allow users to work with the data as they would from within Excel. Creating a noninteractive Web page is like creating a "snapshot" of the data in the workbook. Every time the workbook changes, it has to be resaved to the Web page, or else the page will be out of date.

An alternative is to create an **interactive Web page** which preserves some (but not all) of the workbook's functionality. When you publish your workbook in an interactive format, users can still do the following:

- Enter data
- Format data
- Enter formulas and functions
- Sort and filter a data list

If your interactive Web page contains data from an external data source, which may occur when publishing a PivotTable or chart, you can refresh the page to retrieve the most current data. Thus there is no need to resave the workbook whenever new data is entered.

With all of these advantages, you may wonder why you would ever want to save your Web page in a noninteractive format. One reason could be that you want your page to be only a snapshot of the workbook at a specific moment in time (as may occur in a page displaying annual report information.) Also, while interactive Web pages can be powerful, their features are not necessarily going to be supported by every type and version of Web browser. You might create a fancy Web page only to discover that your users lack the ability to view and use it. Thus before publishing your workbook on the Web, you need to understand the needs and capabilities of your audience.

Excel provides three ways of producing interactive Web pages: pages with spreadsheet functionality, interactive PivotTables, and interactive charts.

Web Pages with Spreadsheet Functionality

A Web page with **spreadsheet functionality** works like an Excel spreadsheet. The spreadsheet appears within the Web page along with several Excel tools. With these tools users can sort and filter the data, format cells, insert functions, and copy, cut and paste data. Figure A4-1 shows a worksheet you might create for GP Golf to analyze cost, volume and profit for the SoftGrip model. Figure A4-2 shows the same worksheet as it would appear on a Web page with spreadsheet functionality.

Figure A4-1 AN EXCEL WORKSHEET

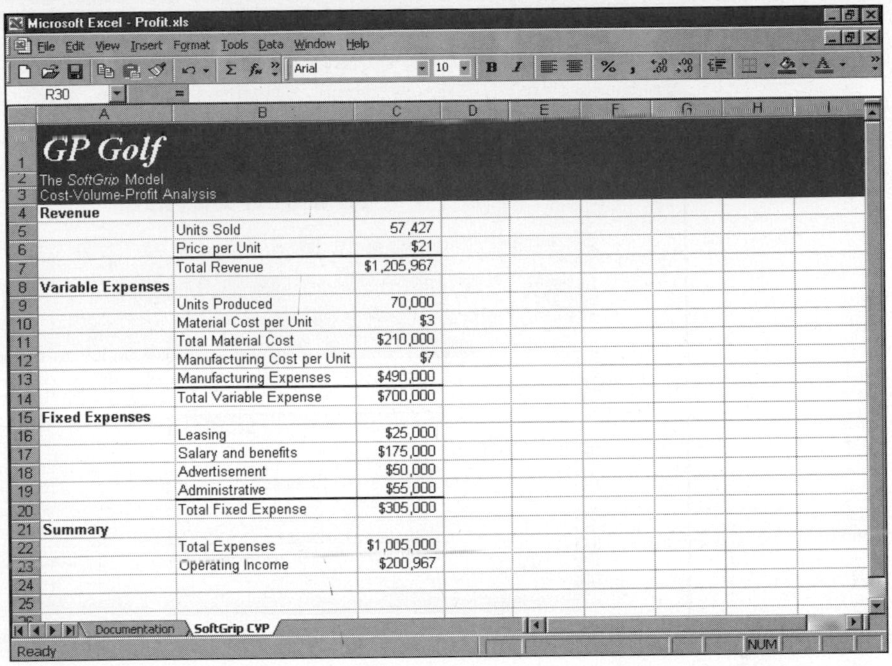

Figure A4-2 THE SAME WORKSHEET VIEWED AS WEB PAGE WITH SPREADSHEET FUNCTIONALITY

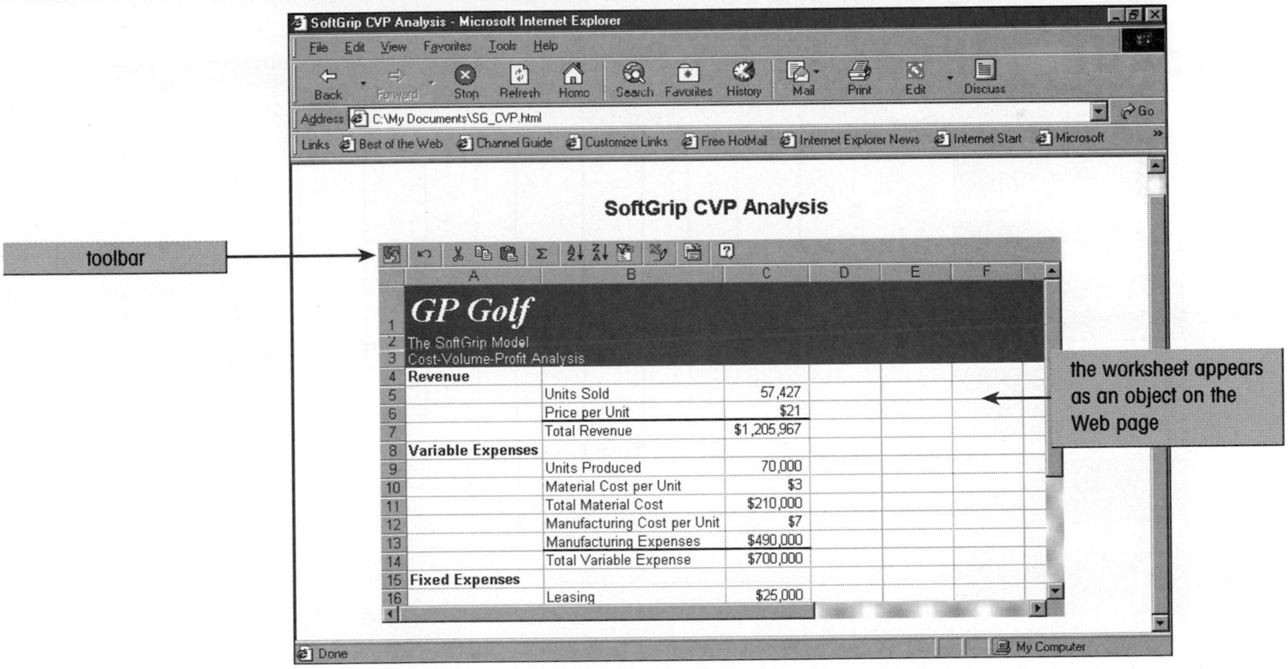

Though it may appear that the worksheet is an embedded object on the Web page, that's not the case. The Web page is not linked to the original worksheet and any changes that a user makes to the page will not be reflected in the original workbook. This leaves the user free to perform several "what-if" analyses on the data without having to worry about changing the source workbook. In this example, a user on GP Golf's Intranet could use the Web page to explore the effects on the SoftGrip's total revenue if the price had been dropped to $20 per unit (see Figure A4-3).

Figure A4-3 WORKING WITH THE DATA ON THE WEB PAGE

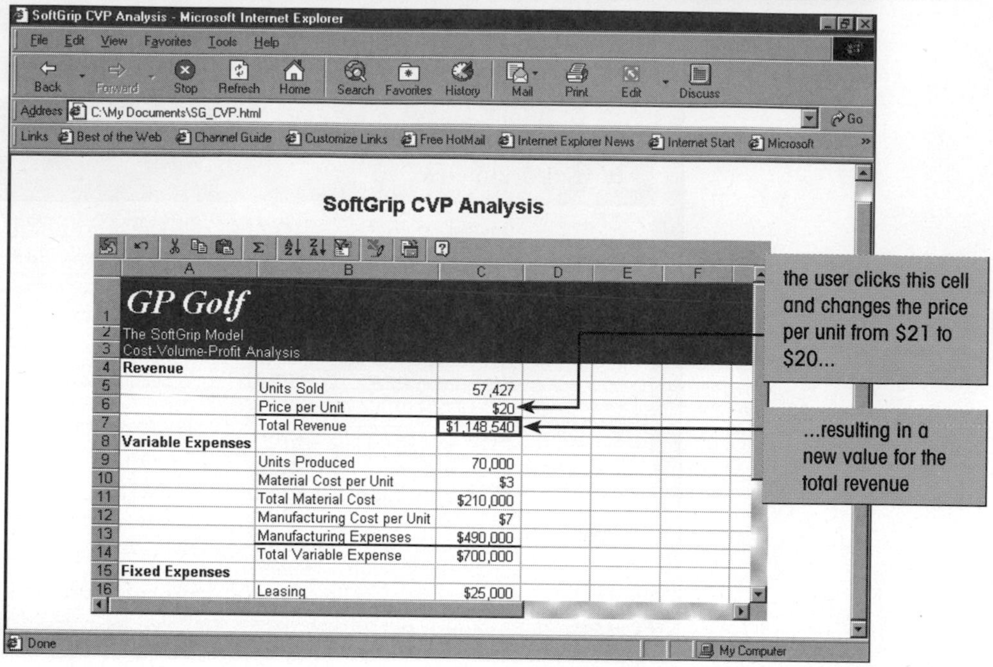

The spreadsheet toolbar, shown in Figure A4-4, provides the user with a subset of the features available in Excel. Note that many Excel features are not included.

Figure A4-4 THE SPREADSHEET TOOLBAR

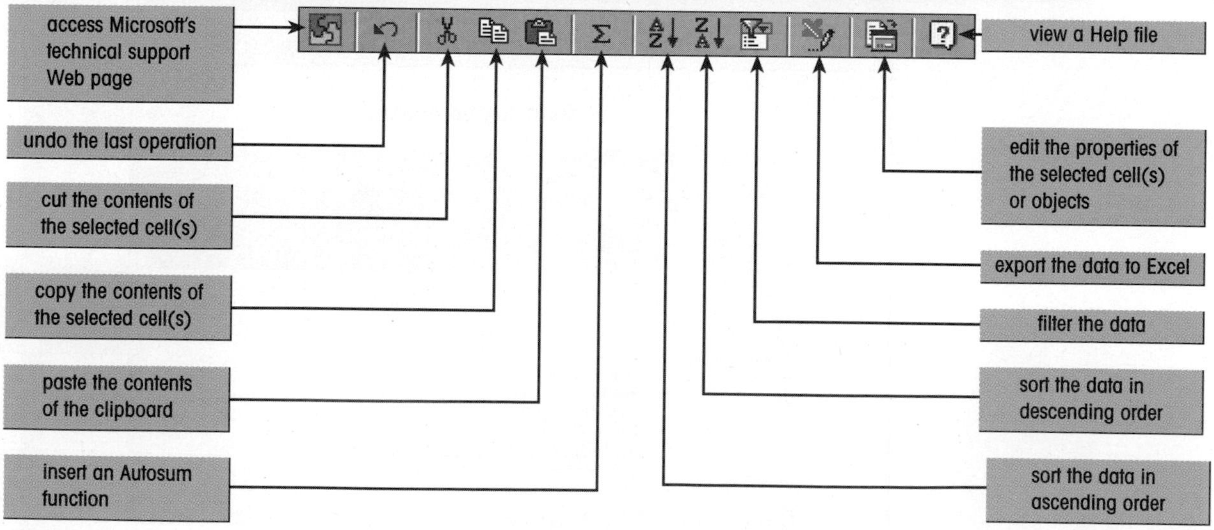

Some formatting elements will not be transferred to your Web page. Among those features that will be lost when saving the worksheet to the Web are:

- Pattern fills
- Dotted or broken borders
- Graphics
- Named cells or ranges

- Drawing object layers
- Wrapped text within a cell
- Multiple fonts within a cell
- Conditional formatting
- Outlining
- Cell comments

And there are other features, such as auditing, which are not available on the Web page. Review the online help for a complete list of features and formatting that are changed or removed when creating a Web page with spreadsheet functionality.

Web Pages with PivotTable Lists

The Web version of a pivot table is called a **PivotTable list**. PivotTable lists can be published with or without PivotTable functionality. **PivotTable functionality** allows the user to perform basic tasks like data filtering; but more importantly it enables the PivotTable list to be connected with the source data. The user can refresh the Web page at any time and be assured that the most current data is displayed in the PivotTable. A PivotTable list without PivotTable functionality behaves like a worksheet saved with Spreadsheet functionality. You can work with the pivot table, but the table is not connected to the data source. There are differences between the appearance of a PivotTable list and an Excel pivot table. Figure A4-5 and Figure A4-6 show the same pivot table viewed from within Excel and from within the Web browser.

Figure A4-5 **AN EXCEL PIVOT TABLE**

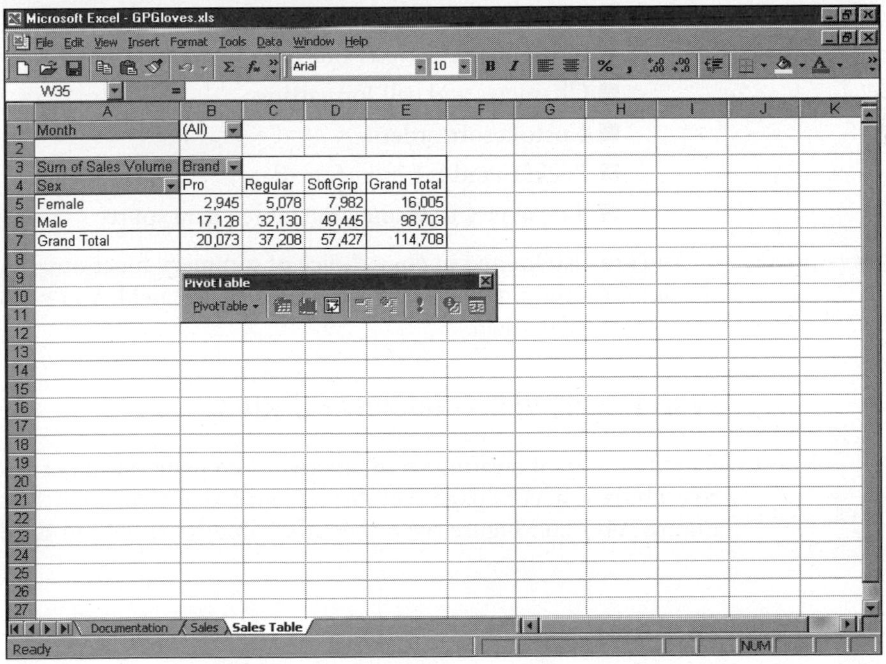

Figure A4-6 A WEB PAGE PIVOTTABLE LIST

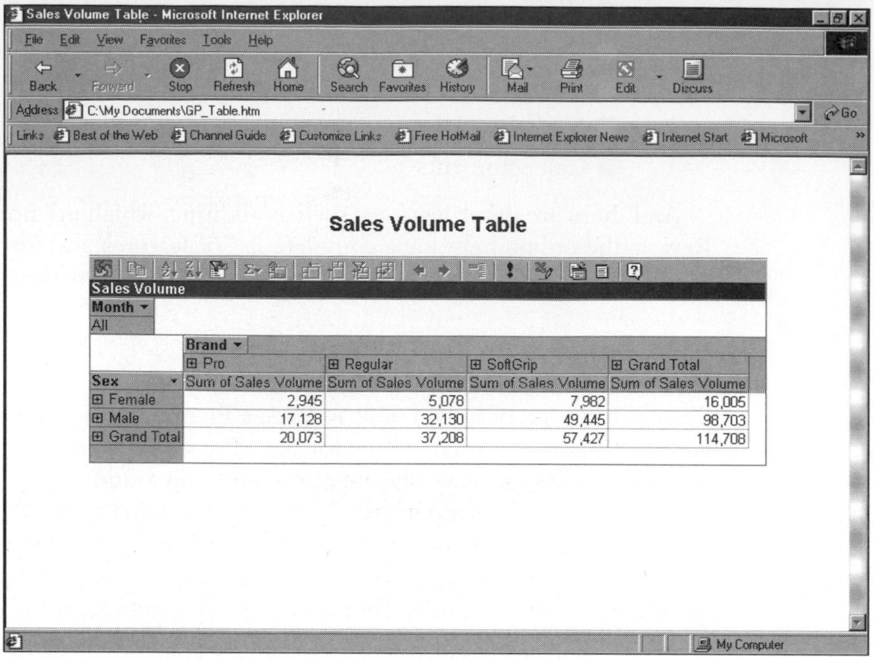

As with Excel's pivot tables, you can move fields around to alter the view of the table. You can also expand the table to view the underlying data. There are several features that Excel does not export to a PivotTable list. These include:

- Calculated fields and items
- Custom calculations and subtotals
- Character and cell formatting
- Custom sort orders
- Background refresh of the data
- The ability to change the table's data source

You are also limited in your choice of summary functions. The PivotTable list can display the sum, minimum, maximum or count of data field. You cannot, for example, display the average of a data field.

Web Pages with Interactive Charts

The final way of creating an interactive Web page is with an interactive chart. The **interactive chart** is a Web page that displays an Excel chart that the user can update and modify. Figure A4-7 and Figure A4-8 show the same chart both in Excel and on the Web.

Figure A4-7 AN EXCEL CHART

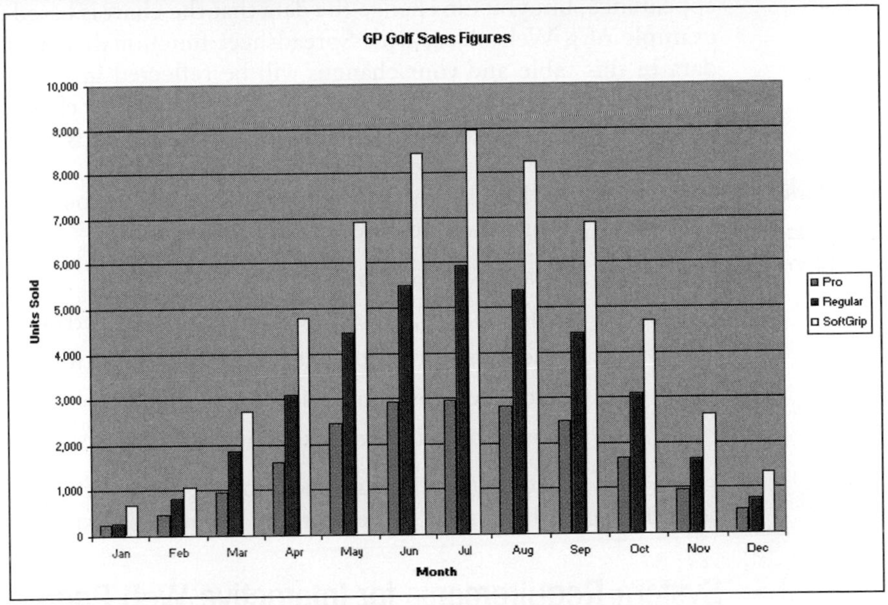

Figure A4-8 AN INTERACTIVE WEB CHART

the chart can be viewed but not edited or moved

the data table is displayed on the Web page below the chart

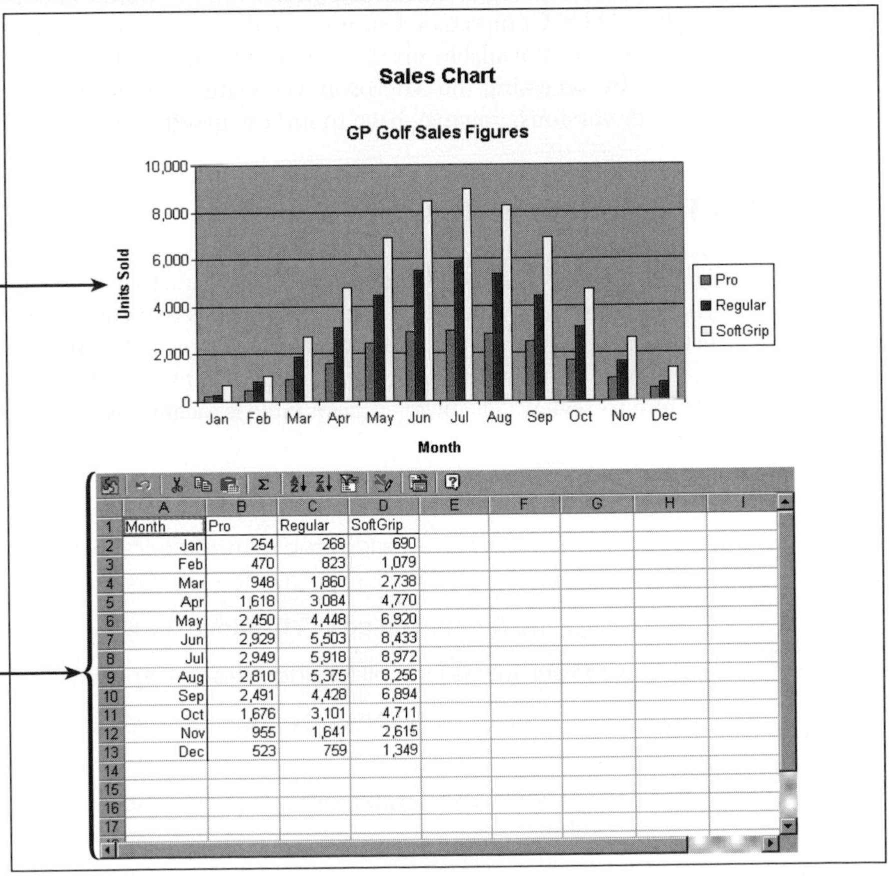

	A	B	C	D
1	Month	Pro	Regular	SoftGrip
2	Jan	254	268	690
3	Feb	470	823	1,079
4	Mar	948	1,860	2,738
5	Apr	1,618	3,084	4,770
6	May	2,450	4,448	6,920
7	Jun	2,929	5,503	8,433
8	Jul	2,949	5,918	8,972
9	Aug	2,810	5,375	8,256
10	Sep	2,491	4,428	6,894
11	Oct	1,676	3,101	4,711
12	Nov	955	1,641	2,615
13	Dec	523	759	1,349

Note that the Web page includes the data for the chart. You can't change the chart's appearance, but you can change the data that the chart is based on. The data table is another example of a Web object with Spreadsheet functionality. You can sort, filter and edit the data in this table and your changes will be reflected in the chart. The chart and the data table are not connected to the original workbook, so any changes you make to the Web page are not reflected in the workbook, and if the workbook is changed, you'll have to republish its contents if you want the Web page to be current.

Many of the Excel features are not retained when you convert a chart to an interactive Web page. Among those features which are lost are:

- 3-D and Surface chart types
- High-low lines, series lines, trend lines and error bars
- Shadows, semitransparent fills and autoscale fonts
- Customized positioning and sizing of chart objects
- Drawing objects, text boxes and pictures placed on the chart

If you want to edit the size and position of the chart within the Web page, you have to edit the page using an HTML editor like Front Page Express.

System Requirements for Interactive Web Pages

Not every Web browser can display a Web page containing these interactive components. You must be using Internet Explorer 4.01 or higher and you must have the Microsoft Offline Web Component feature installed on your system. The Microsoft Offline Web Component is available on the Microsoft Office 2000 installation disk or can be downloaded by accessing the Microsoft Web site. If your users are running other browsers or browser versions, you may have to limit yourself to creating noninteractive Web pages.

Creating an Interactive PivotTable

Having reviewed some of the material on interactive components, you return to Peter with your information. Peter feels that he only needs to create a Web page containing a PivotTable list. This will provide his sales staff with quick access to the most current sales data and give them most of the functionality of an Excel pivot table. He asks you to create such a Web page for him to review. The original pivot table is located on a workbook named "GPGloves."

To open the GPGloves workbook:

1. Open the file, GPGloves located in the Tutorial folder of Appendix.04 on your Data disk.
2. Change the filename in cell B2 to **Glove Sales**.
3. Enter **(Your Name)** in cell B3 and **(The Date)** in cell B4.
4. Save the workbook as **Glove Sales** to the Tutorial folder in Appendix.04 of your Data Disk.
5. Click the **Sales Table** tab to view the pivot table.

To convert this pivot table to an interactive PivotTable list, you first use Excel's File Save As command, specifying Web Page as the file type.

To start creating the interactive PivotTable list:

1. Click **File** and then **Save As** from the Excel menu bar.
2. Select **Web Page (*.htm; *.html)** from the Save as Type list box. See Figure A4-9.

Figure A4-9 SAVING A WORKBOOK AS A WEB PAGE

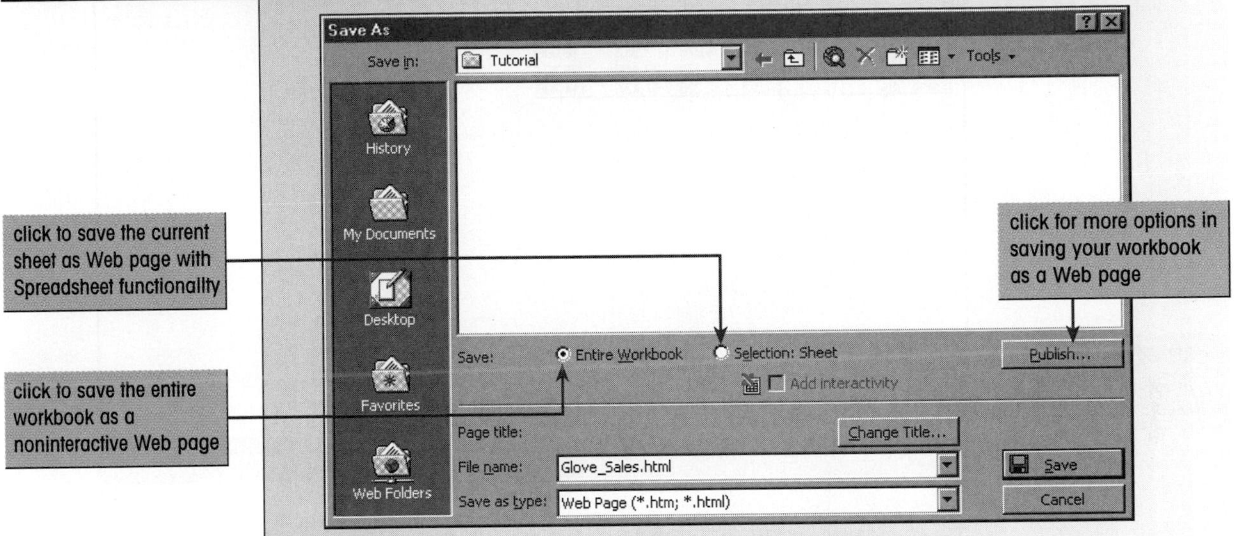

At this point you have several options for saving this worksheet. If you click the Entire Workbook option button, Excel will save the entire workbook as a noninteractive Web page with separate sheets for each worksheet as shown in Figure A4-10. If you click the Selection:Sheet option button along with the Add Interactivity checkbox, Excel will save the entire Sales Table worksheet as an interactive Web page using Spreadsheet functionality. It will not, however, create a PivotTable list with PivotTable functionality—which is what Peter wants you to do.

Figure A4-10 A COMPLETE WORKBOOK AS A NONINTERACTIVE WEB PAGE

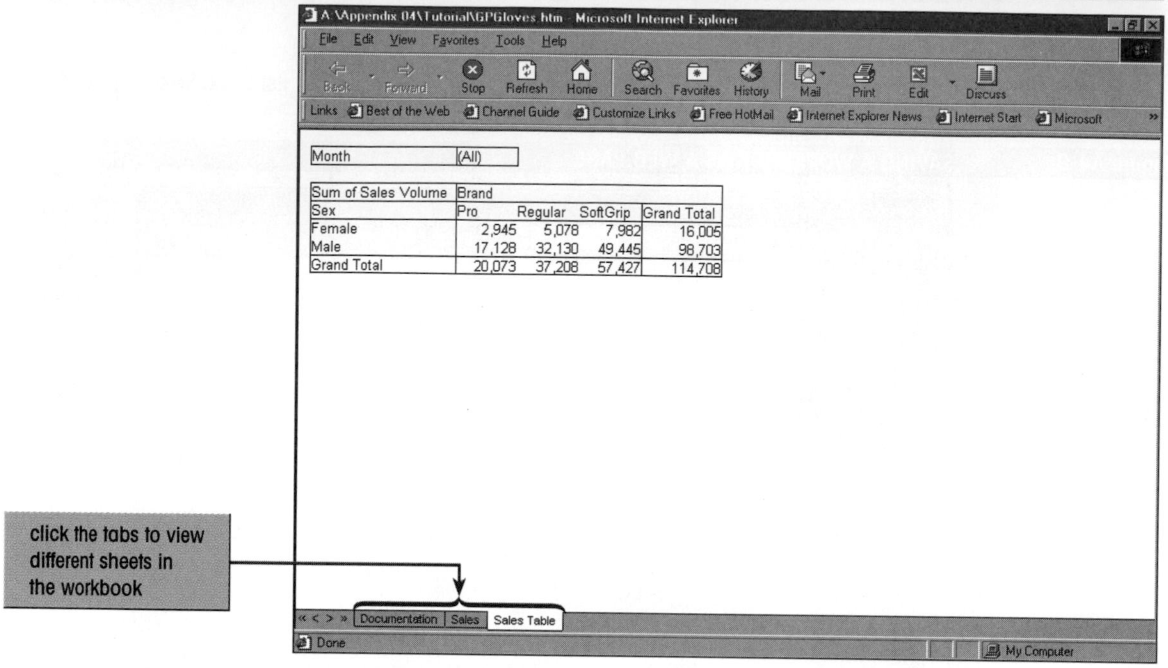

To create your Web page, you need additional options.

To view other options for your Web page:

1. Click the **Publish** button.

   The Publish as Web Page dialog box appears as shown in Figure A4-11.

Figure A4-11 THE PUBLISH AS WEB PAGE DIALOG BOX

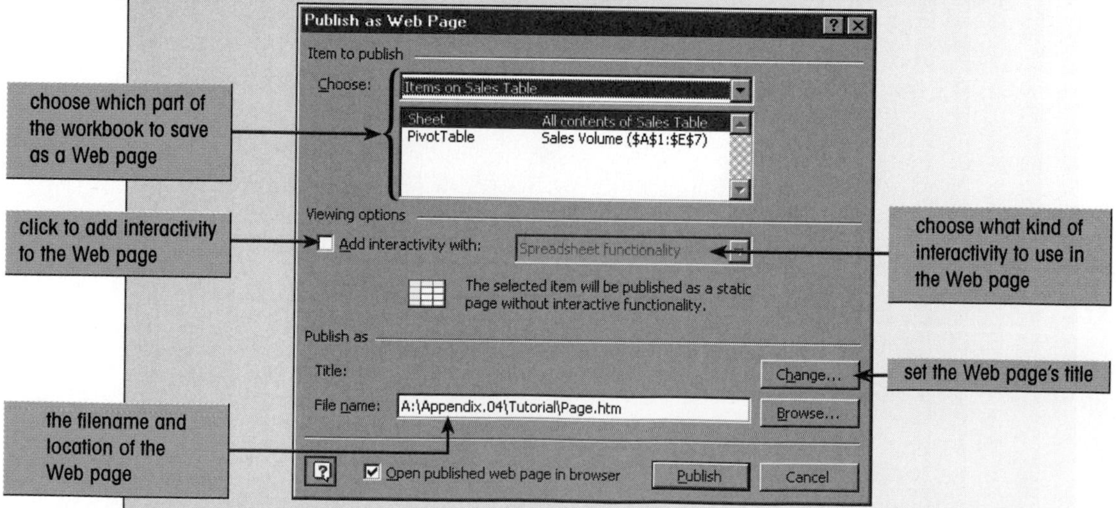

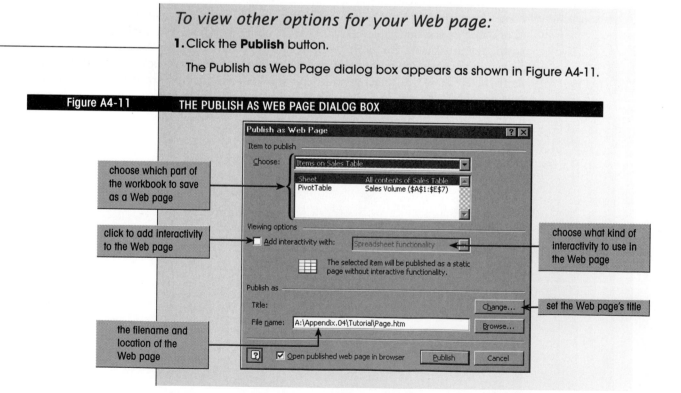

From this dialog box you can specify which part of the current workbook you wish to save as a Web page. As you can see from Figure A4-11, you could save the entire Sales Table worksheet or just the pivot table on that worksheet. You can also specify whether the Web page will be interactive or not, and if so, whether it employs Spreadsheet functionality or PivotTable functionality. You can also enter a title and filename for the Web page. You have all the options you need to create the Web page Peter envisions.

To enter options for the Web page:

1. Verify that **Items on Sales Table** is selected in the Choose drop-down list box.
2. Select **PivotTable** from the list of items so that only the pivot table is sent to the Web page.
3. Click the **Add interactivity with** checkbox and verify that **PivotTable functionality** is selected in the drop-down list box.
4. Click the **Change** button and type **GP Golf Sales Figures** in the Title box. Click the **OK** button.
5. Enter **Glove_Sales.html** in the File name box, located in the Tutorial folder of Appendix.04.
6. Verify that the **Open published web page in browser** checkbox is selected, so that your browser will open your Web page automatically after you save it.

   Figure AC4-12 shows the completed dialog box.

Figure A4-12 THE COMPLETED PUBLISH AS WEB PAGE DIALOG BOX

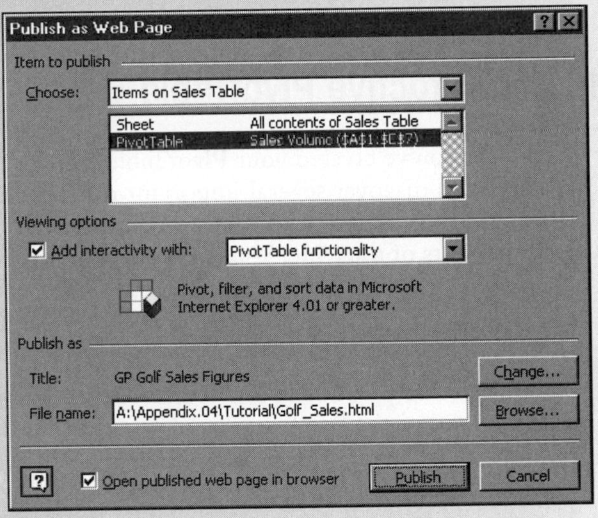

7. Click the **Publish** button.

   Figure A4-13 displays the completed Web page.

Figure A4-13 THE INTERACTIVE PIVOTTABLE FOR GLOVE SALES

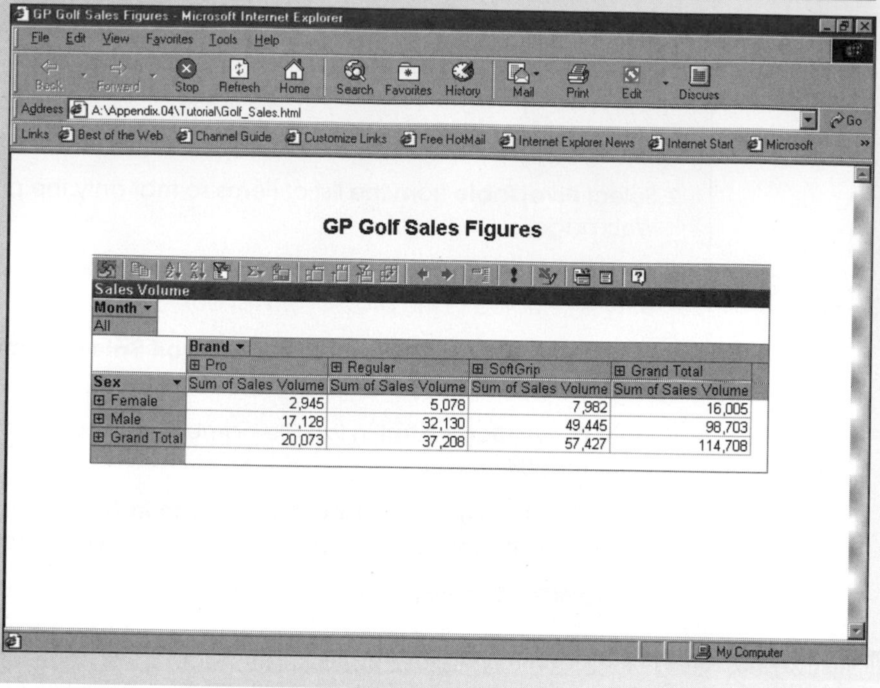

Working with an Interactive PivotTable

Now that you've created your PivotTable list, you'll find that it operates like an Excel pivot table. You'll discover several important differences as well. You can manipulate the placement and type of fields. You can format the table's values and labels, and you can hide certain elements of the table. You'll start by working with the table's fields.

Modifying PivotTable Fields

This particular pivot table has four areas: a Page area containing the Month field, a Row area containing the Sex field, a Column area displaying the Brand field and the Data area displaying the sum of the Sales Volume field for each combination of the other three fields. As with an Excel pivot table, you move these fields around. Try this now by moving the Month field to the Row area of the table.

To move the Month field:

1. Click the **Month** field button and move it down to the left of the Sex field button until a vertical line appears by the mouse pointer.
2. Release the mouse button.

   The new pivot table, shown in Figure A4-14, now shows a Row area that has both the Month and the Sex field.

Figure A4-14 **THE PIVOT TABLE WITH THE MONTH FIELD IN THE TABLE'S ROW AREA**

drop box for the table's Page area

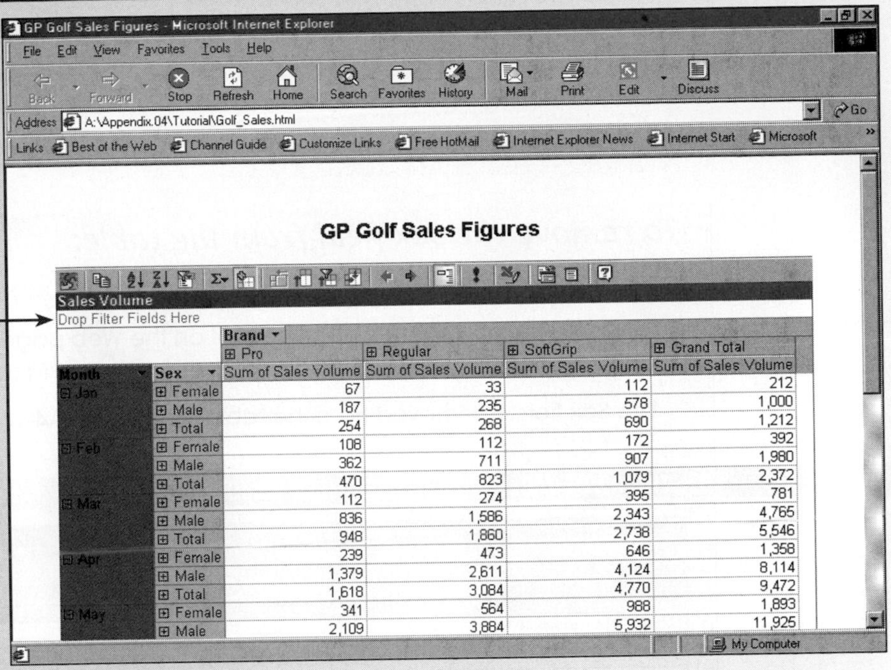

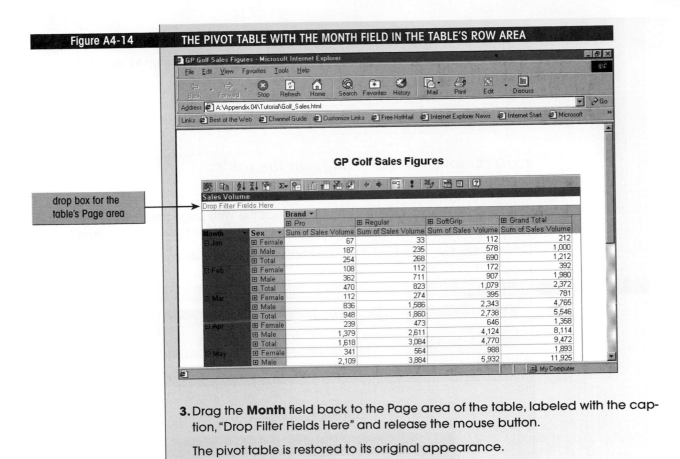

3. Drag the **Month** field back to the Page area of the table, labeled with the caption, "Drop Filter Fields Here" and release the mouse button.

The pivot table is restored to its original appearance.

To display only a few levels of a field, you can select those levels from the field's drop-down checkbox—just as you would with a pivot table in Excel. Try this now by changing the table so that it displays sales figures for only the SoftGrip glove.

To display only the SoftGrip sales figures:

1. Click the **Brand** drop-down list button.

2. Deselect the **Pro** and **Regular** checkboxes as shown in Figure A4-15.

Figure A4-15 **REMOVING THE PRO AND REGULAR BRANDS FROM THE PIVOT TABLE**

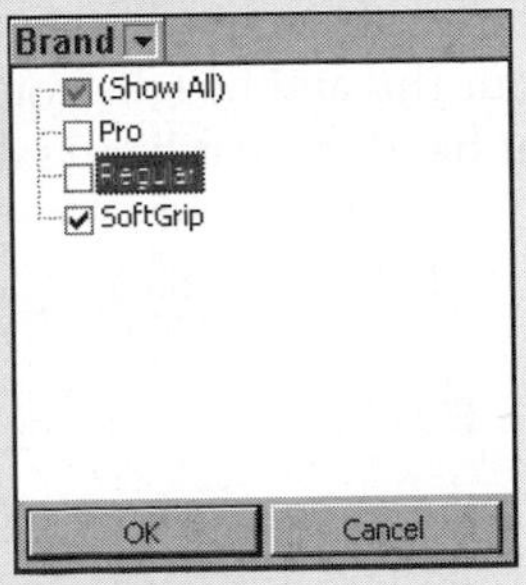

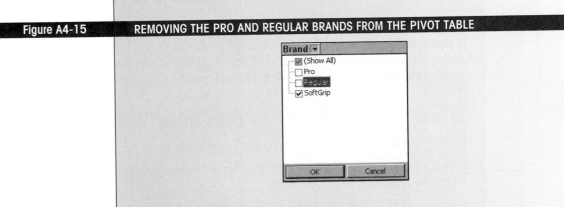

3. Click the **OK** button.

The pivot table now displays only the sales results for the SoftGrip brand.

4. Click the **Brand** drop-down button again.
5. Click the **(Show All)** checkbox and then click the **OK** button to restore the table.

If you want to remove a field, drag its button off of the table.

To remove the Sex field from the table:

1. Click the **Sex** field button.
2. Drag the field button to an empty spot on the Web page and release the mouse button so that the mouse cursor changes to a [cursor] and release the mouse button.

   The Sex field is removed from the table. See Figure A4-16.

Figure A4-16 THE PIVOT TABLE WITH THE SEX FIELD REMOVED

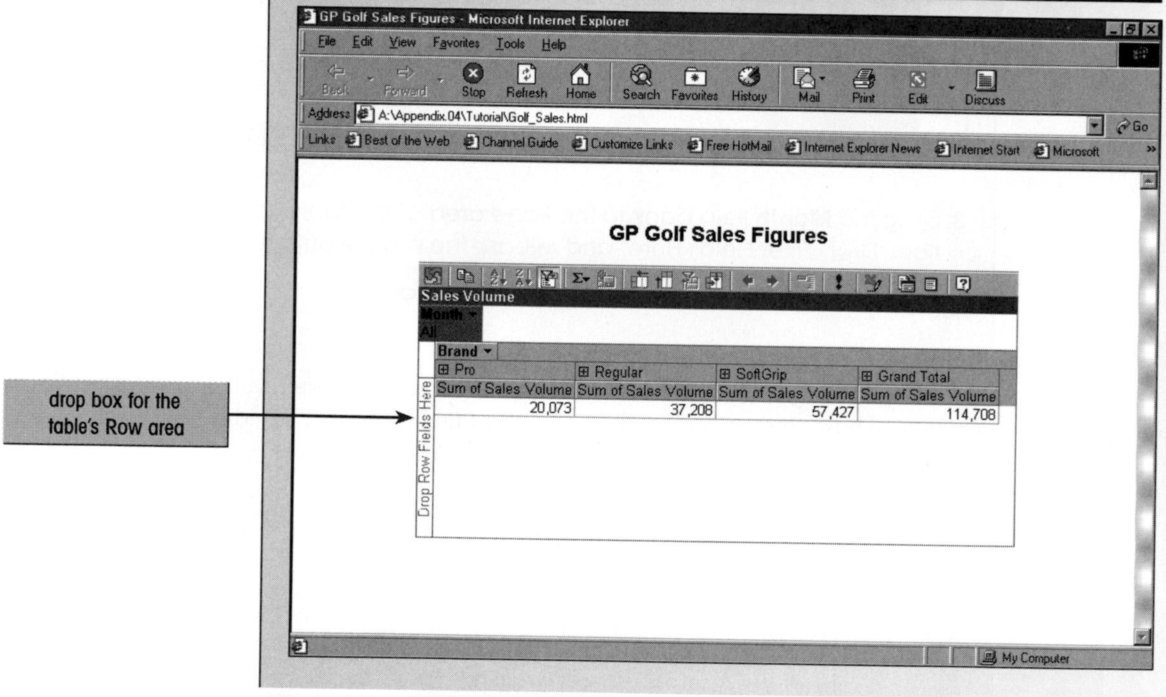

If you want to add a new field to the table, you must first display the table's field list. You ask Peter about this and he tells you that he would like to see the sales figures broken down between right hand and left hand sales. This information requires the use of the Hand field.

To add the Hand field to the pivot table:

1. Click the **Field List** button [button] on the pivot table toolbar.
2. Drag the **Hand** field from the field list to the Row area drop box and release the mouse button.
3. As shown in Figure A4-17, the table now displays sales figures broken down by brand and hand.

Figure A4-17 ADDING THE HAND FIELD TO THE PIVOT TABLE

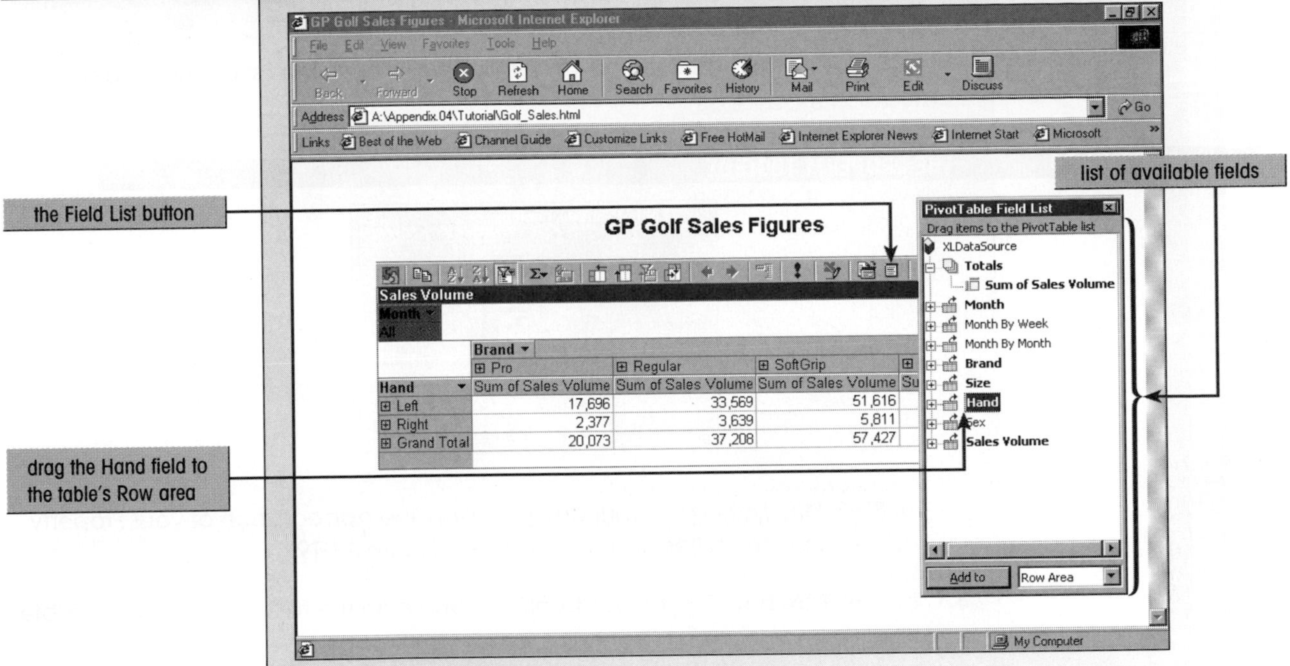

4. Click the **Close** button to close the Field List window.

Formatting PivotTable Elements

You can also change the appearance of your pivot table by hiding and displaying the different parts of the table. These include the title bar, toolbar, expand indicators and the drop areas or drop boxes. See Figure A4-18.

Figure A4-18 PIVOT TABLE ELEMENTS

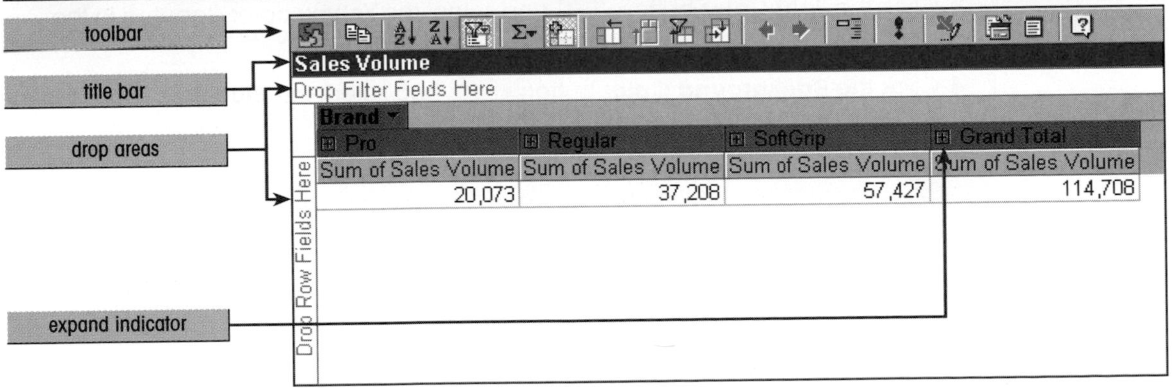

To view or hide these elements you need to use the Property Toolbox. The **Property Toolbox** gives you complete control over the appearance of all elements of your pivot table. Open the toolbox now and use it to hide the pivot table's title bar.

To hide the title bar:

1. Click the **Property Toolbox** on the pivot table toolbar.
2. Click the **Show/Hide** title bar, if necessary to display the list of pivot table elements. See Figure A4-19.

Figure A4-19 THE PROPERTY TOOLBOX

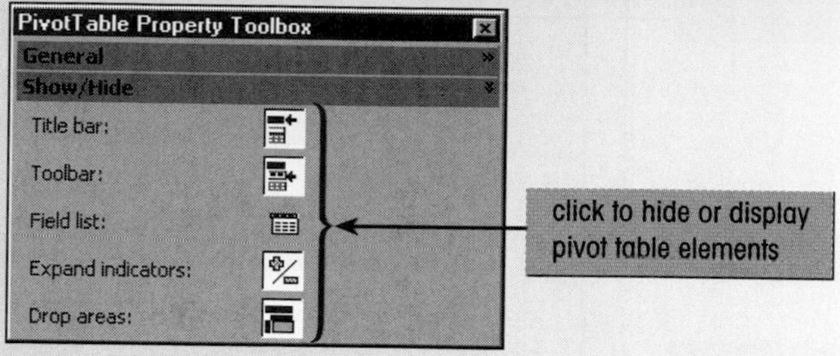

TROUBLE? Depending on your configuration, the appearance of your Property Toolbox may look different from the one in Figure A4-19.

3. Click the **Title bar** element to deselect it and hide the title bar in the pivot table.

As you select different items in the pivot table, the Property Toolbox displays a different list of properties. For example, you can use the Property Toolbox to format the appearance of values and labels in the table. To see how this works, you decide to format the labels of the pivot table to display yellow text on a solid blue background.

To format the pivot table labels:

1. With the Property Toolbox still open, click the **Hand** field button in the pivot table.
2. If necessary, click the **Format** title bar in the Property Toolbox to display its list of properties.
3. Click the **Font Color** button and select the **Yellow** color (located in the fourth row and third column of the color matrix).
4. Click the **Background Color** button and select the **Blue** color (located in the second row and sixth column of the color matrix).

   Figure A4-20 displays the revised pivot table.

Figure A4-20 **CHANGING THE COLOR OF PIVOT TABLE LABELS**

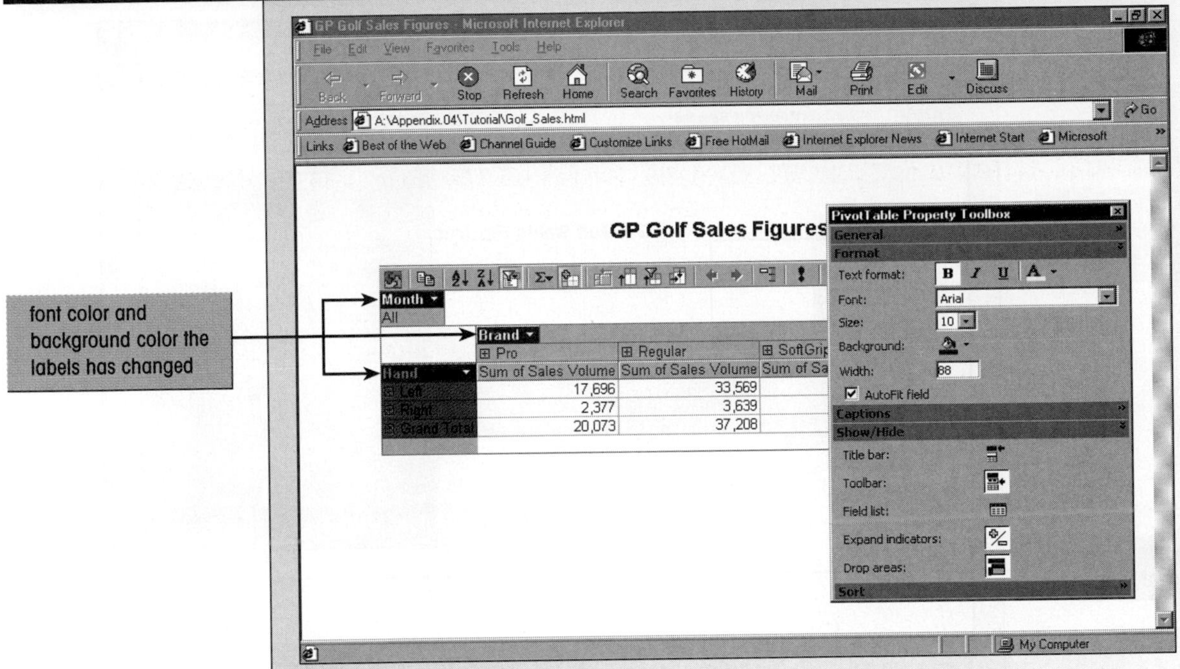

Another use of the Property Toolbox is to change the summary function used in the pivot table. By default the Sum function is used, but you can change that to the Count, Minimum or Maximum function. To see how this works, you decide to change the summary function from Sum to Maximum in order to display the maximum number of sales for each combination of hand type and brand.

To display the maximum sales figure:

1. Click any one of the **Sum of Sales Volume** labels in the pivot table.

2. Click the **Total Function** title bar in the Property Toolbox, if necessary, to display the Function drop-down list box.

3. Select **Max** from the Function drop down list box.

4. The pivot table now displays the maximum sales volume for pivot table cell as shown in Figure A4-21.

Figure A4-21 **CHANGING THE SUMMARY FUNCTION USED BY THE PIVOT TABLE**

the pivot table displays the maximum sales volume for each cell

selecting the Max summary function

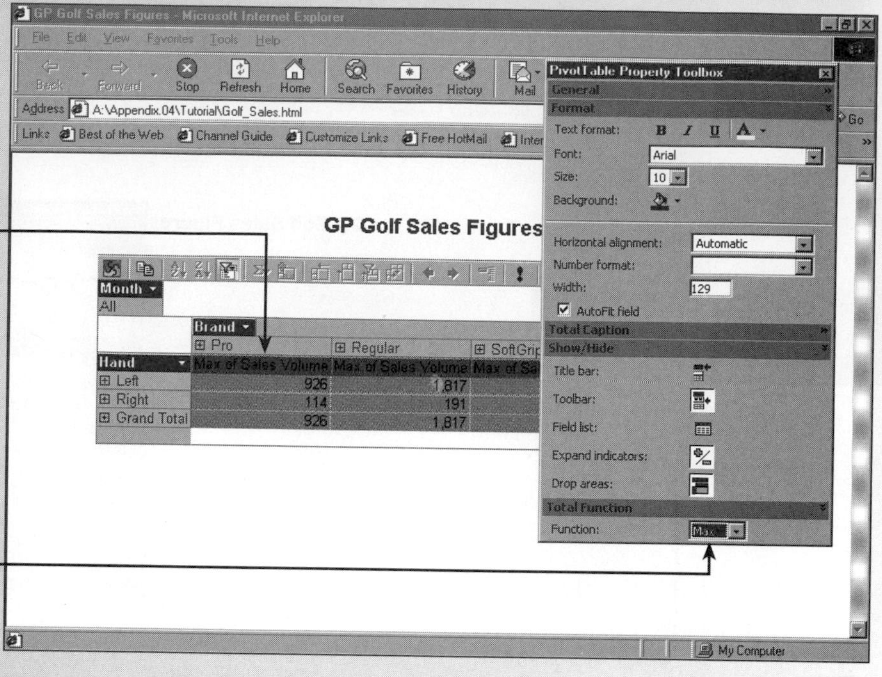

5. Click **Sum** from the Function drop down list box to restore the pivot table.

6. Click the **Close** button to close the Property Toolbox.

You've completed your work with the Property Toolbox. You may wonder what permanent affect these changes have had on the Web page. The answer is none. When you change the layout of the pivot table or format the appearance of one or more pivot table elements, those changes are present only for the time you're viewing the page. If you close your browser and reopen the page, it returns to its original state (the one displayed in Figure A4-13). Also, if someone else opens the Web page, they won't see any of your changes either. The changes you make to that page affect your browser only and only for that period of time that you're viewing the page.

Exporting a Pivot Table to Excel

If you want to save your pivot table in a more permanent format, you can export it back to Excel. The changed pivot table won't replace the original table; rather a new workbook will be created containing the new pivot table along with the underlying source data.

To export your pivot table to Excel:

1. Click the **Export to Excel** button on the pivot table toolbar.

Excel opens a new workbook similar to the one shown in Figure A4-22 containing the pivot table with your revised formatting.

Figure A4-22 THE PIVOTTABLE LIST SAVED AS AN EXCEL PIVOT TABLE

pivot table retains the formatting and layout of the Web page's PivotTable list

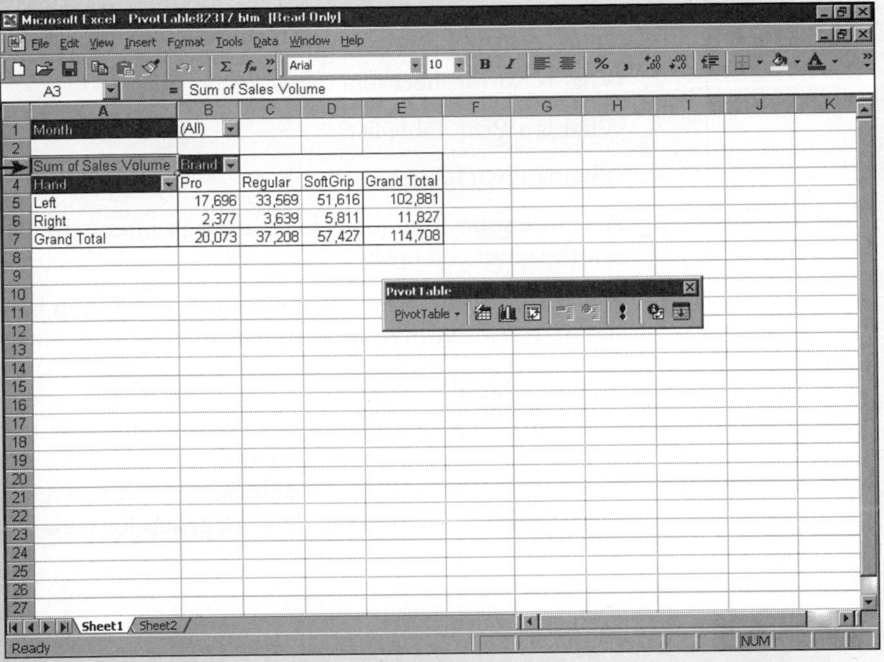

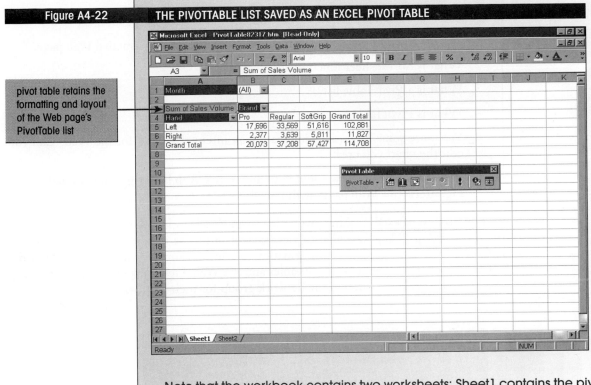

Note that the workbook contains two worksheets: Sheet1 contains the pivot table and Sheet2 contains the underlying data values.

TROUBLE? The filename of the workbook is generated automatically by Excel. Your filename may be different from the one shown in Figure A4-22.

2. Save the workbook as **Glove Sales 2** in Excel Workbook format to the Tutorial folder of Appendix.04 on your Data Disk.

You've completed your work on pivot tables and the Web. You can save and close your applications now.

To finish your work:

1. Close the Glove Sales and Glove Sales 2 workbooks, saving them to the Tutorial folder of Appendix.04 on your Data Disk.

2. Close your Web browser.

Session A4.1 Quick Check

1. What is the difference between an interactive and noninteractive Web page?
2. What is Spreadsheet functionality?
3. What is a PivotTable list?
4. What is PivotTable functionality?
5. What are some limitations in creating an interactive chart for the Web? Can you edit the chart you create?
6. What should you know about your audience's Web browsing software before creating interactive Web pages with Excel?

The process of exporting the pivot table to an Excel workbook will be useful to people in the Sales group. They'll be able to view sales data on the company's Intranet, and if they wish, they can easily export that information to Excel for further work. Peter is pleased with what you've shown him about pivot tables and the Web. He'll look over your work and present the page you've created to the network group for their approval.

REVIEW ASSIGNMENTS

Peter has worked some more with the pivot table Web page you created. He's very enthusiastic about it and would like to see you do the same thing for GP Golf's line of golf shoes. GP Golf makes three styles of shoes: the American, the Fairway model and the Standard model. Shoes come in two types: soft spikes and hard spikes. There are also different models for men and women. He's stored the sales data in an Excel workbook that contains a pivot table that he wants you to export to a Web page. Like the page you created earlier, this PivotTable list should utilize PivotTable functionality.

1. Open the workbook **GPShoes.xls** located in the Review folder of Appendix.04 on your Data Disk.
2. Save the pivot table located on the Shoe Sales Table worksheet to a Web page named **GP_Shoes.html** located in the Review folder of Appendix.04 on your Data Disk. Use PivotTable functionality in the Web page. Give the page the title **GP Golf Shoe Sales.**
3. Print the initial version of the Web page.
4. Add the Month field to the Page area of the pivot table and have the pivot table display sales data for only the month of April.
5. Add the Gender field to the Row area of the table so that values of the Spikes field are nested within the Gender field.
6. Edit the properties of the field labels and field values so that they appear as black text on a white background.
7. Hide the pivot table's title bar.
8. Print the revised version of the Web page.
9. Export the pivot table to Excel. Insert a Documentation sheet containing your name and the date. Save the workbook as **GPShoes2.xls** in the Review folder of Appendix.04 on your Data Disk.
10. Close your workbooks and Web browser.

CASE PROBLEMS

Case 1. Creating an Interactive Spreadsheet for Davis Blades Davis Blades is a leading manufacturer of roller blades. One of their most popular models is the Professional. Anne Costello, a sales analyst at Davis Blades, is examining the cost-volume-profit relationship of sales of the Professional for her region. She's preparing for an online sales conference over the Web and would like to create a Web page containing her CVP analysis. Because there will be different scenarios discussed at the online meeting, she would like to create a Web page to provide interactivity for the participants, allowing them to change Anne's assumptions online and view the results. You tell Anne that you can create such a Web page using Excel and utilizing Spreadsheet functionality.

1. Open the workbook **Davis.xls** located in the Cases folder of Appendix.04 on your Data Disk.
2. ***Explore*** Save the contents of the CVP Data worksheet to an interactive Web page using Spreadsheet functionality. The Web page filename should be **Davis_CVP.html** and should be stored in the Cases folder of Appendix.04 on your Data Disk. Give the Web page the title **Davis Blades CVP Analysis**. Print the Web page.
3. On the resulting Web page, change the number of units produced and sold from 1200 to 1500 units. What affect does this have on the operating income?
4. Format the background color of the cells in the first row of the spreadsheet, changing the color from green to red. Change the color of the text in cells A2 and A3 to red.
5. ***Explore*** Hide the column and row headers, the title bar, the cell gridlines and the toolbar.
6. Print the resulting Web page.
7. Close your workbooks and Web browser.

Case 2. Creating an Interactive Chart for the Bread Bakery It's time for the stock holders meeting for the Bread Bakery, a company specializing in finely baked breads. Your supervisor, David Keyes, would like to have some of the sales figures available on the Web for the stock holders before the convention. He's saved the information in a workbook and would like you to save the chart included in that workbook to the Web. He would like the chart to be interactive rather than static.

1. Open the workbook **Bread.xls** located in the Cases folder of Appendix.04 on your Data Disk.
2. ***Explore*** Locate the chart sheet **Sales Chart** and save the chart as a Web page with Chart functionality named **Sales_Chart.html** in the Cases folder of Appendix.04. Give the Web page the title **Bread Bakery Sales**.
3. Print the resulting Web page as it appears in your Web browser.
4. ***Explore*** Edit the data table on the Web page Q:, and using the AutoSum formula, calculate the total sales for each brand of bread for each quarter and for all sales over the entire year. Print the Web page.
5. ***Explore*** Filter the data table so that it displays the sales only for the third and fourth quarters. Print the Web page.
6. Hide the following elements in the data table: the toolbar, gridlines, title bar, row headers and column headers. Print the resulting Web page.
7. Close your workbooks and Web browser.

QUICK CHECK ANSWERS

1. A noninteractive Web page contains data from a workbook and some formatting, but does not allow the user to work with the data. An interactive Web page does allow the user to work with the data and perform some of the tasks of a spreadsheet.
2. The capability of a Web page to work like an Excel spreadsheet (in a limited fashion).
3. A Web version of the pivot table with some of the features of an Excel pivot table.
4. The capability of a Web page to work like an Excel pivot table, including the ability to link to a data source and refresh the appearance of the table with current data.
5. You cannot edit the chart or format it. Several features of the chart are lost when exported to the Web.
6. Is the browser Internet Explorer 4.01 or higher, and has the user installed the Microsoft Online Web Component feature? If this is not the case, the user will not be able to work with the interactive Web page created by Excel.

ADDITIONAL EXCEL PROJECTS

Projected Budget for Cape Cod Arts Council

The Cape Cod Arts Council is a small, nonprofit organization that teaches arts and crafts classes in a converted boathouse located in the Cape Cod area. You will create the Cape Cod Arts Council's budget for the first six months of 2001, based on figures obtained from the 2000 budget, and then ask a series of "What if?" questions to determine realistic planning goals for the second half of 2001.

The following four activities are required to complete the six-month budget for the Cape Cod Arts Council:

Project Activities

Enter and Enhance Labels

You can quickly present worksheet data in an attractive and easy-to-read format. In Figure P1-1, the labels in the top five rows are centered across columns and enhanced with various font styles and sizes, while a white-on-black effect is used to highlight two of the worksheet titles.

Calculate Totals

You can either use the AutoSum button or enter a formula when you need to add values in a spreadsheet. You use the AutoSum method when you want to add the values in cells that appear consecutively in a column or row and when you are entering the total directly below or to the right of the added values. You enter a formula when you want to calculate values that do not appear in consecutive or adjacent cells. For example, you would enter the formula =A1+A3 if you wished to add the values in cells A1 and A3. You can also use the SUM function. For example, you would enter the formula =SUM(A1:A6) if you wished to add all the values in cells A1 through A6 and enter the result in a nonadjacent cell.

Ask "What if?" Questions

One of the most useful tasks you can perform with a spreadsheet program is to change values in a worksheet to see how the totals are affected. For example, you can ask yourself: "*If we spend $2,000 a month on payroll instead of $4,500, how much money will we save over six months?*" As soon as you change the values entered in the Payroll row, the totals are automatically updated. To complete Project 1, you will ask three "What if?" questions.

Format and Print the Budget

You will use a variety of the features in the Page Setup dialog box to produce an attractive printed version of your budget that includes a customized header.

When you have completed the activities above, your budget will appear as shown in Figure P1-1.

FIGURE P1-1: Cape Cod Arts Council projected budget

Cape Cod Arts Council | Six-Month Budget | January to June 2001

Header text

Cape Cod Arts Council

North Shore Boathouse, R.R. #2, Mattapoisett, MA 02739

Labels centered across columns

Projected Budget
January to June 2001

White text on black background

5/6/99

	January	February	March	April	May	June	Totals
Income							
Course Fees	$ 26,041.67	$ 26,041.67	$ 26,041.67	$ 26,041.67	$ 33,854.17	$ 33,854.17	$ 171,875.00
Grants	1,000.00	1,000.00	1,000.00	1,000.00	1,000.00	1,000.00	6,000.00
Donations	400.00	400.00	400.00	400.00	400.00	400.00	2,400.00
Total Income	$ 27,441.67	$ 27,441.67	$ 27,441.67	$ 27,441.67	$ 35,254.17	$ 35,254.17	$ 180,275.00
Expenses							
Payroll	$ 5,520.83	$ 5,520.83	$ 5,520.83	$ 5,520.83	$ 5,520.83	$ 5,520.83	$ 33,125.00
Lease	600.00	600.00	600.00	600.00	600.00	600.00	3,600.00
Course Supplies	1,200.00	1,200.00	1,200.00	1,200.00	1,200.00	1,200.00	7,200.00
Maintenance	400.00	400.00	400.00	400.00	400.00	400.00	2,400.00
Computer Lease	400.00	400.00	400.00	400.00	400.00	400.00	2,400.00
Advertising	700.00	700.00	3,000.00	700.00	700.00	700.00	6,500.00
Total Expenses	$ 8,820.83	$ 8,820.83	$ 11,120.83	$ 8,820.83	$ 8,820.83	$ 8,820.83	$ 55,225.00
Profit	**$ 18,620.83**	**$ 18,620.83**	**$ 16,320.83**	**$ 18,620.83**	**$ 26,433.33**	**$ 26,433.33**	**$ 125,050.00**

Currency style

Comma style

Border styles

activity:

Enter and Enhance Labels

You need to enter and enhance the name and address of the organization, the worksheet title, the current date, and the first series of labels.

Hint

If a button does not appear on the Formatting toolbar, click the More Buttons button on the toolbar to view a list of additional buttons.

steps:

1. Start Excel, open a new worksheet, click the blank box to the left of the **A** at the top left corner of the worksheet to select the entire worksheet, click the **Font Size list arrow**, then click **12**
   A font size of 12 is selected for the entire worksheet.

2. Click cell **A1**, type **Cape Cod Arts Council**, press **[Enter]**, type the remaining labels as shown in Figure P1-2, then save your worksheet as **Projected Budget for Cape Cod Arts Council** on the disk where you plan to store all the files for this book

3. Click cell **A1**, click the **Font list arrow** on the Formatting toolbar, select **Comic Sans MS**, if it is available, or select **Britannic Bold**, click the **Font Size list arrow** on the Formatting toolbar, then select **24**

4. Select cells **A4** and **A5**, click the **Font Size list arrow**, then select **18**
   Although the text extends into columns B and C, you only need to select cells A4 and A5 — the place where the text originated.

5. Select cells **A1** to **H5**, as shown in Figure P1-3, **right-click** the selection, click **Format Cells**, click the **Alignment tab**, click the **Horizontal list arrow**, click **Center Across Selection**, click **OK**, select cells **A4** to **H5**, click the **Fill Color list arrow** on the Formatting toolbar, click the **black box**, then click away from the cells to deselect them
   You can no longer see the labels in cells A4 and A5.

6. Select cells **A4** and **A5**, click the **Font Color list arrow** on the Formatting toolbar, then click the **white box**

7. Click cell **A7**, click the **Paste Function button** on the Standard toolbar, select **Date & Time** from the list under Function category, select **Today** from the list under Function name (you'll need to scroll down), click **OK**, click **OK** again, select cells **A7** to **H7**, then click the **Merge and Center button** on the Formatting toolbar

8. Click cell **B9**, type **January**, press **[Enter]**, click cell **B9** again, position the mouse pointer over the fill handle in the lower right corner, drag the + to cell **G9**, then click the **Center button** on the Formatting toolbar
   The six months from January to June appear and are centered.

9. Click cell **A10**, enter the labels required for cells **A10** to **A25** and cell **H9**, as shown in Figure P1-4, click the **Spelling and Grammar button** on the Standard toolbar, correct any spelling errors, then save your worksheet

FIGURE P1-2: Labels for cells A1 to A5

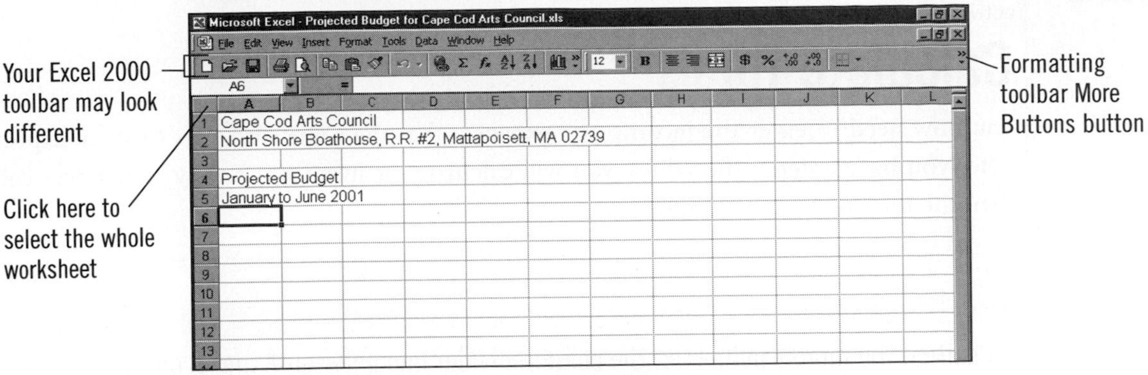

FIGURE P1-3: Cells A1 to H5 selected

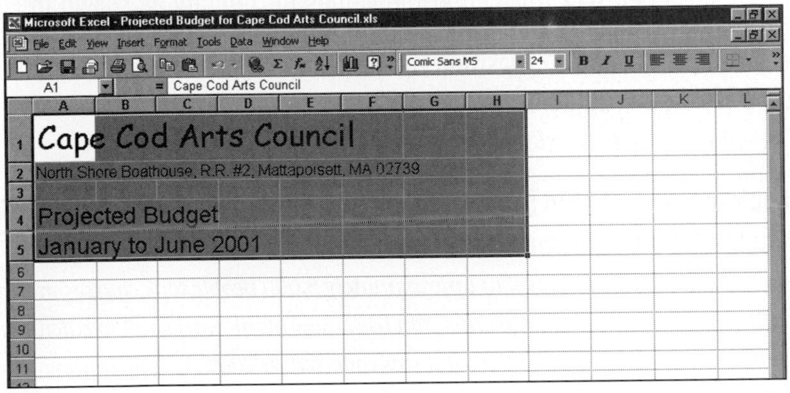

FIGURE P1-4: Labels for cells A10 to A25 and H9

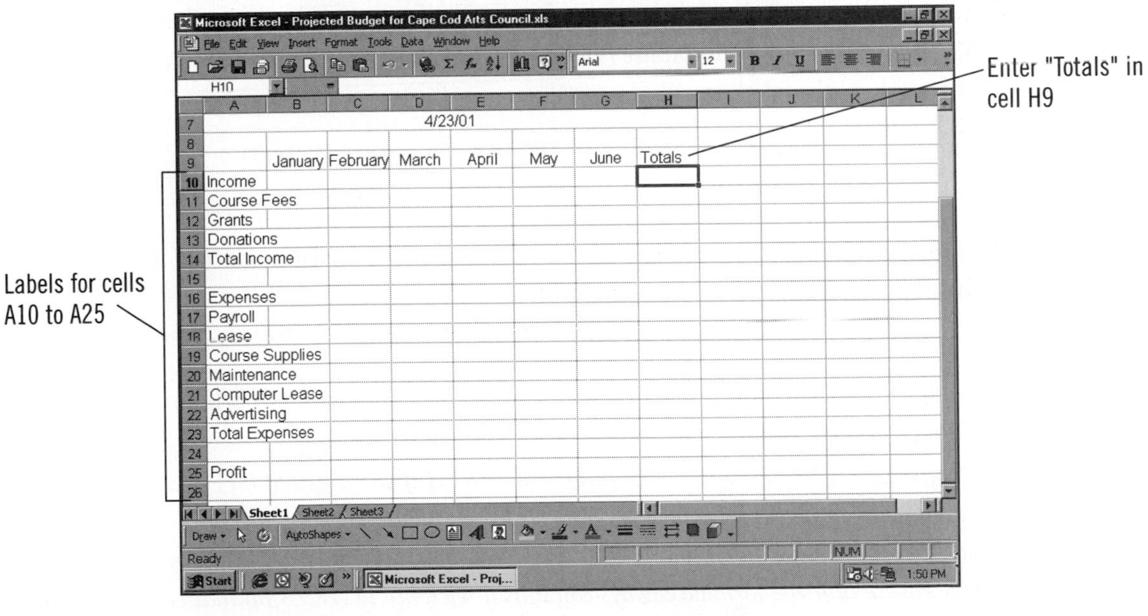

Clues to Use

Merging Cells

A merged cell is a single cell created by combining two or more cells. The cell reference for the merged cell is the upper-left cell in the original selected range. When you merge a range of cells, only the data in the upper-left cell of the range is included in the merged cell. You use the Alignment tab in the Format Cells dialog box to center several rows of data across columns and you use the Merge and Center button on the Formatting toolbar when you want to center the data in only one cell across several columns.

activity:

Calculate Totals

You now need to enter the income and expenses that the Cape Cod Arts Council expects in 2001. After you have entered the values, you will calculate the average monthly course fees collected and then the total income and expenses.

steps:

1. Position the mouse pointer on the column divider line between **A** and **B** on the worksheet frame so it changes to ✛, double-click to increase the width of column A to fit all the labels in cells A10 to A25, click cell **B12**, then enter the values for January as shown in Figure P1-5
2. Select cells **B12** to **B22**, position the mouse pointer over the fill handle in the lower-right corner of cell **B22**, then drag across to cell **G22**

   The values in cells B12 to B22 appear in cells C12 to G22.
3. Double-click the **Sheet1 tab** at the bottom of your worksheet, type **Budget**, press **[Enter]**, double-click the **Sheet2 tab**, type **Fees**, then press **[Enter]**

   In the year 2000, you know that approximately 5,000 people took courses in three payment categories: adults, children/seniors, and school groups. You use a new blank worksheet to calculate the average course fee in each category for 2001, based on the total fees collected in 2000. You use a new worksheet to avoid cluttering the current worksheet with data that won't be printed. You named the two worksheets you will be using.
4. Enter and enhance the labels and values in the Fees worksheet, as shown in Figure P1-6

   You will need to use your mouse to widen column A so that the labels are clearly visible and then center and bold the labels in cells A1 to E1.
5. Click cell **E2**, enter the formula **=B2*C2*D2**, then press **[Enter]**

   You should see 110000 in cell E2. If not, check your formula and try again.
6. With cell **E2** selected, drag the fill handle down to cell **E4**, click cell **E5**, then double-click the **AutoSum button** Σ on the Standard toolbar

   The course fees collected should be 156250 or $156,250.
7. Click the **Budget tab**, click cell **B11**, enter the formula **=Fees!E5/6**, press **[Enter]**, then drag the fill handle of cell **B11** across to cell **G11**

   Ooops! Cells C11 through G11 contain zeroes. Why? If you click cell C11 and look at the formula entered in the formula bar at the top of the worksheet, you will see =Fees!F5/6. But cell F5 of Fees! worksheet does not contain a value! You need to enter a formula that designates cell E5 as an absolute value. By doing so, you ensure that the formula always contains a reference to cell E5 no matter where in the worksheet the formula is copied.
8. Click cell **B11**, drag I across **E5** in the formula bar, press **[F4]**, press **[Enter]**, then fill cells **C11** to **G11** with the new formula

   You will see 26042 in cells B11 to G11. Don't worry if decimal places appear. You will format the cells in a later activity.
9. Select cells **B11** to **H14**, click Σ, select cells **B17** to **H23**, then click Σ again

   The total income in cell H14 is 164650, and the total expenses in cell H23 are 46800, as shown in Figure P1-7.

FIGURE P1-5: **Values for cells B12 to B22**

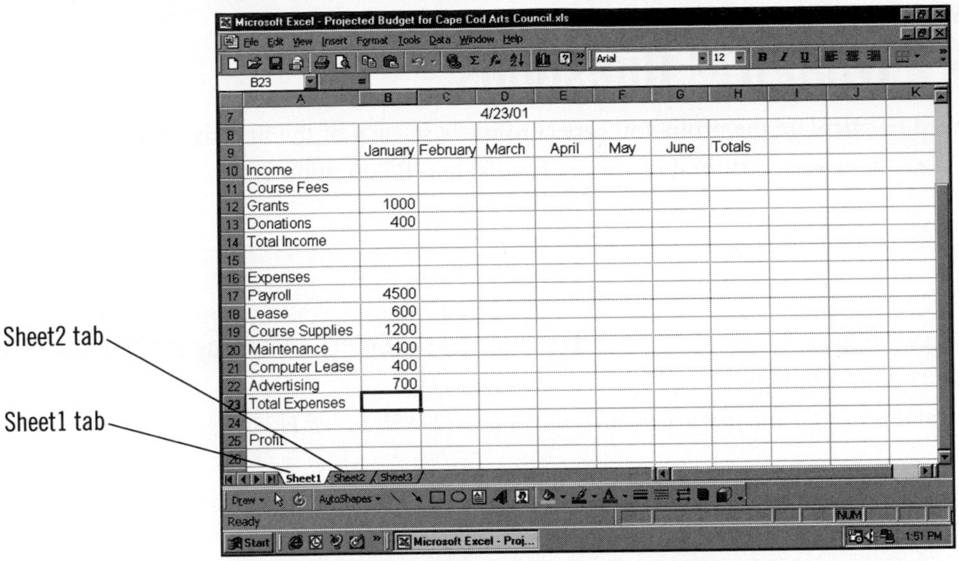

FIGURE P1-6: **Fees sheet labels and values**

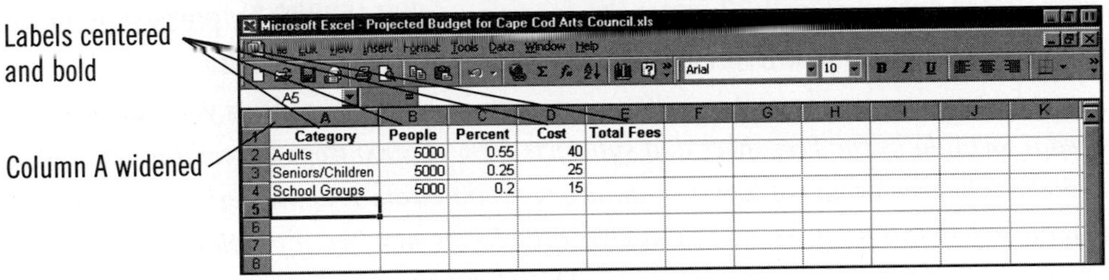

FIGURE P1-7: **Worksheet completed with totals**

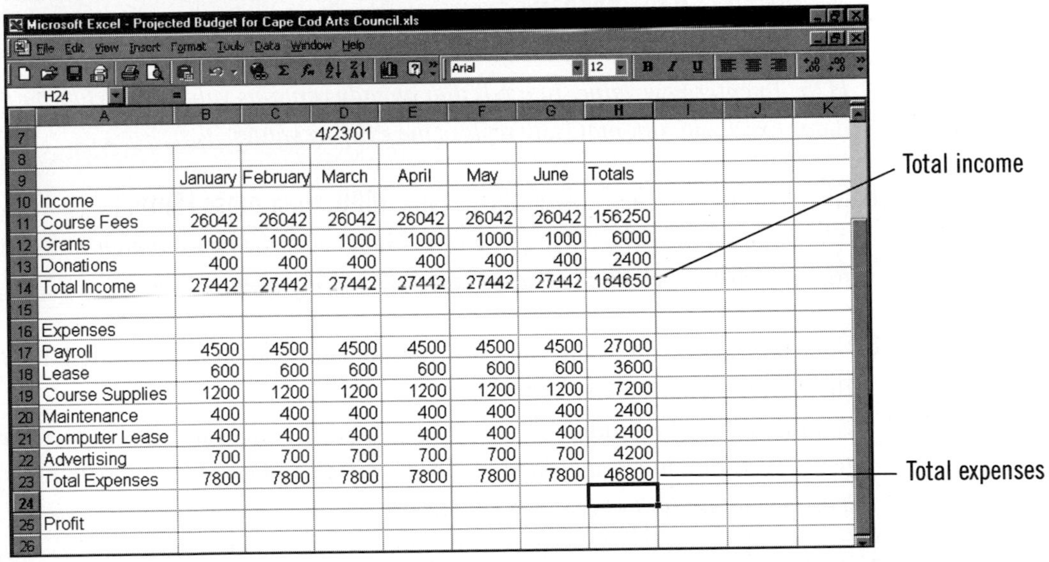

Clues to Use

Relative and Absolute References

By default Microsoft Excel considers all values entered in formulas as relative values. That is, Excel will change all cell addresses in a formula when you copy it to a new location. If you do not want Excel to change the cell address of a value when you copy it, you must make the value absolute. *To do this, you enter a dollar sign ($) before both the column and row designation in the address. You can also press [F4] to insert the symbol. For example, $C$26 tells Excel that the reference to cell C26 must not change, even if you copy the formula to a new location in the worksheet.*

activity:

Ask "What if?" Questions

You need to calculate the profit you expect to make in each of the first six months of 2001, then perform the calculations required to answer two "What if?" questions.

steps:

1. Click cell **B25**, enter the formula **=B14-B23**, press **[Enter]**, then copy the formula across to cell **H25**, as shown in Figure P1-8
   The total profit for the first six months of 2000 is 117850 in cell H25.
2. Click the **Fees tab**, click cell **D2**, type **60**, press **[Enter]**, then click the **Budget tab**
   The first "What if?" question is, "What if you raise the adult course fee to $60? The answer is that your total profit in cell H25 is 172850. Good news!
3. Click the **Fees tab**, click cell **B2**, enter the formula **=5000-(5000*.2)**, press **[Enter]**, copy cell **B2** to cells **B3** and **B4**, as shown in Figure P1-9, then click the **Budget tab**
   A course fee increase could result in a 20% drop in the number of students you can expect in 2000. You entered a formula in the Fees sheet that subtracts 20% of 5000 from the total number of adult course fees (5000).The new profit is 130600 — quite a reduction from 172850! Perhaps you shouldn't raise the adult course fees to $60, if the result is a 20% drop in the number of people who take courses!
4. Return to the Fees sheet, change the cost of the adult course fee to **40** and the number of people in cells **B2** to **B4** to **5000**, then return to the Budget sheet
   The results of the first "What if?" question led you to return to your original profit of 117850 in cell H25. To enter new values in a cell that already contains values, just click on the cell and type the new data. Excel will automatically replace the existing values.
5. Click cell **D22** in the Budget sheet, type **3000**, then press **[Enter]**
   The question is, "What if you launch a $3,000 advertising campaign in March?" Your total profit for the six months (cell H25) is now reduced to 115550 from 117850.
6. Click cell **F11**, click at the end of the formula entered on the formula bar, type ***1.3**, press **[Enter]**, then copy the formula to cell **G11**
   A major advertising campaign launched in March could lead to a 30% increase in revenue from course fees in May and June. You edited the formula in cells F11 and G11 to reflect this projected 30% increase. The new total profit in cell H25 is 131175.
7. Click cell **B17**, enter the formula **=(24500/12)+4500**, press **[Enter]**, then copy the formula across to cell **G17**
   The "What if?" question is, "What if you hire a full-time administrative assistant for $24,500 per year?" You divide this amount by 12 to determine the monthly rate, then add the total to the values entered in the Payroll row. Your total profit is now 118925.
8. Change the formula in cell **B17** so that it adds **4500** to half of **24500** divided by **12**, press **[Enter]**, copy the formula across to cell **G17** and compare your worksheet with Figure P1-10
   The value in cell B17 will be 5520.8, and the total profit in cell H25 will be 125050. If your results are different, ensure that your formula in cell B17 adds 4500 to 24500 divided by 2 and 12.

FIGURE P1-8: **Formula in cell B25 copied to cell H25**

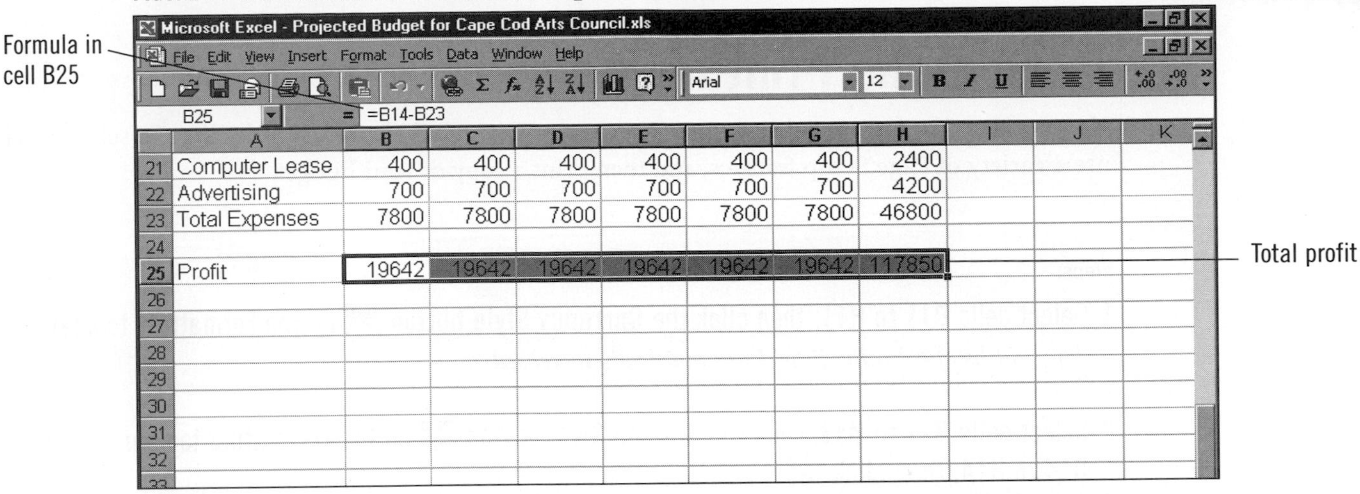

FIGURE P1-9: **Formula in cell B2 copied to cells B3 and B4**

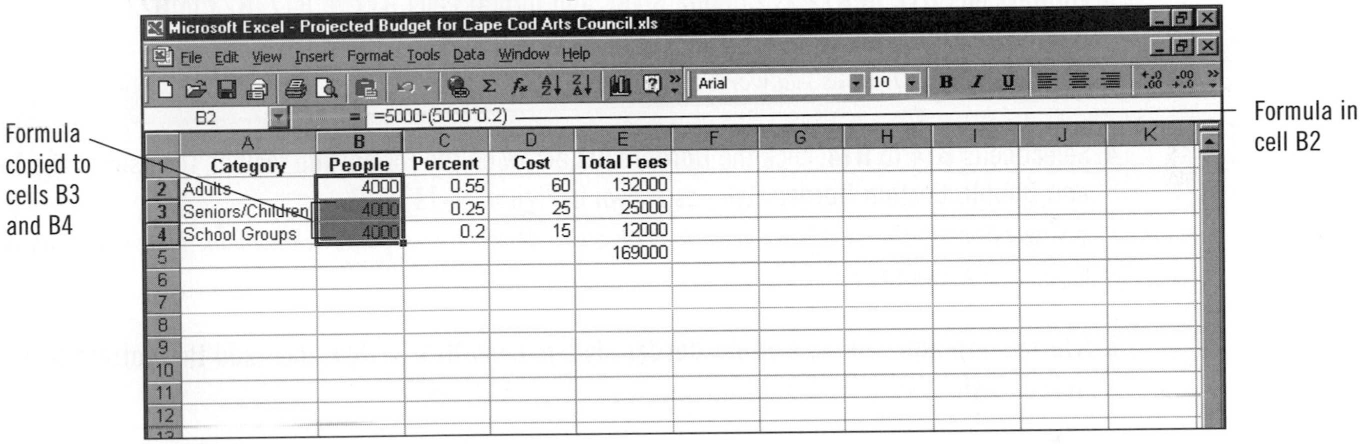

FIGURE P1-10: **Worksheet with completed budget**

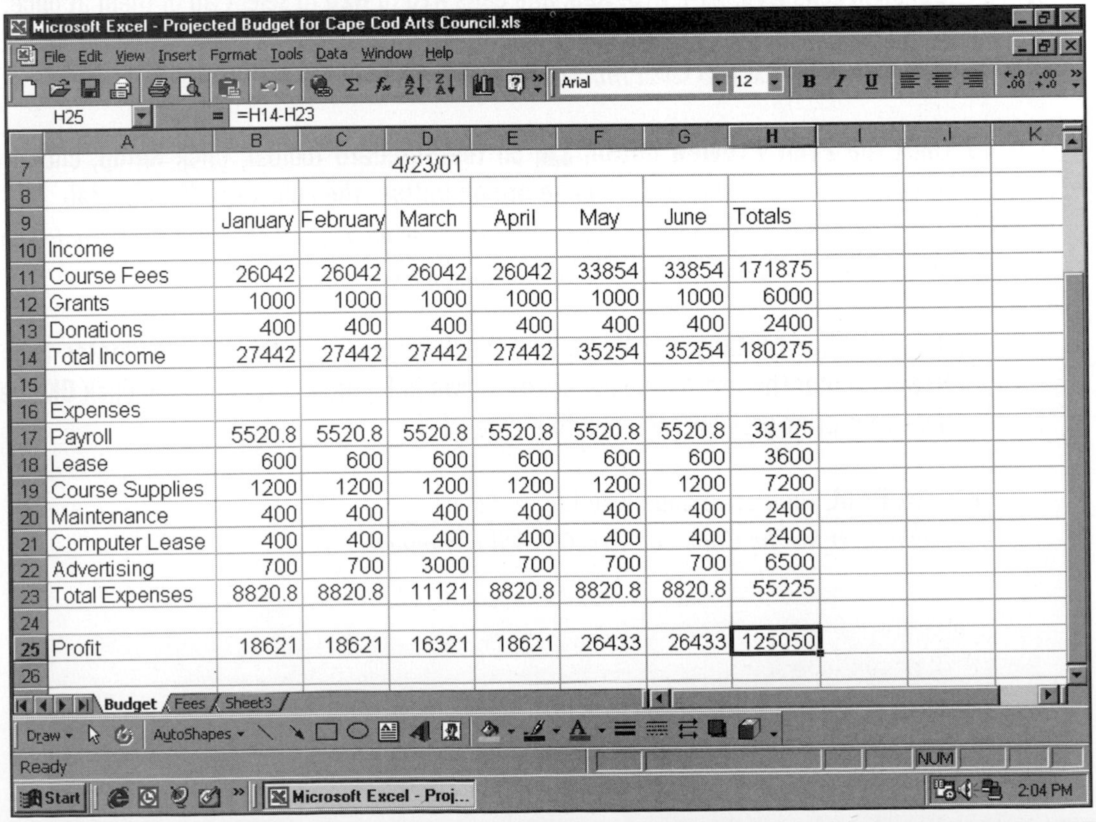
Microsoft Excel - Projected Budget for Cape Cod Arts Council.xls
File Edit View Insert Format Tools Data Window Help
H25 =H14-H23
7 4/23/01
9 January February March April May June Totals
10 Income
11 Course Fees 26042 26042 26042 26042 33854 33854 171875
12 Grants 1000 1000 1000 1000 1000 1000 6000
13 Donations 400 400 400 400 400 400 2400
14 Total Income 27442 27442 27442 27442 35254 35254 180275
16 Expenses
17 Payroll 5520.8 5520.8 5520.8 5520.8 5520.8 5520.8 33125
18 Lease 600 600 600 600 600 600 3600
19 Course Supplies 1200 1200 1200 1200 1200 1200 7200
20 Maintenance 400 400 400 400 400 400 2400
21 Computer Lease 400 400 400 400 400 400 2400
22 Advertising 700 700 3000 700 700 700 6500
23 Total Expenses 8820.8 8820.8 11121 8820.8 8820.8 8820.8 55225
25 Profit 18621 18621 16321 18621 26433 26433 125050
Budget Fees Sheet3
Ready NUM
Start Microsoft Excel - Proj... 2:04 PM

activity:

Format and Print the Budget

Now you need to format values in the Currency or Comma Styles, add border lines to selected cells, use a variety of Page Setup features, and then print a copy of your budget.

steps:

1. Select cells **B11** to **H11**, then click the **Currency Style button** on the Formatting toolbar
   The widths of columns B to H automatically increased.
2. Select cells **B12** to **H13**, click the **Comma Style button** on the Formatting toolbar, select cells **B14** to **H14**, then click
3. Format cells **B18** to **H22** as **Comma Style**, and format cells **B17** to **H17**, **B23** to **H23**, and **B25** to **H25** as **Currency Style**
   Refer to Figure P1-13 as you work.
4. Select cells **B14** to **H14**, click the **Borders list arrow** on the Formatting toolbar, then select the **Top and Double Bottom Border** style, as shown in Figure P1-11
   A single line appears above cells B14 to H14, and a double line appears below them. Note that you need to deselect the cell to see the borders.
5. Add the **Top and Double Bottom Border** style to cells **B23** to **H23**, then add the **Bottom Double Border** style to cells **B25** to **H25**
6. Center and bold the heading "Totals" in cell **H9**, press and hold the **[Ctrl]** key, select cells **B9** to **G9**, click cells **A10**, **A14**, **A16**, **A23**, and cells **A25** to **H25** to select all of them at once, then click the **Bold button** on the Formatting toolbar
   Using the [Ctrl] key to select multiple non-adjacent cells saves you time.
7. Click the **Print Preview button** on the Standard toolbar, click **Setup**, click the **Landscape option button** and the **Fit to 1 page option button**, then click the **Margins tab**
   You select a variety of options in the Print Preview mode from the Print Setup dialog boxes in order to format your budget attractively on the printed page.
8. Click the **Horizontally** and **Vertically check boxes**, click the **Header/Footer tab**, click **Custom Header**, enter the text for the header as shown in Figure P1-12, click **OK**, click **OK** again, then compare your print preview screen with Figure P1-13
9. Click **Print**, then save and close the workbook
   The budget for the Cape Cod Arts Council is complete.

FIGURE P1-11: Border styles

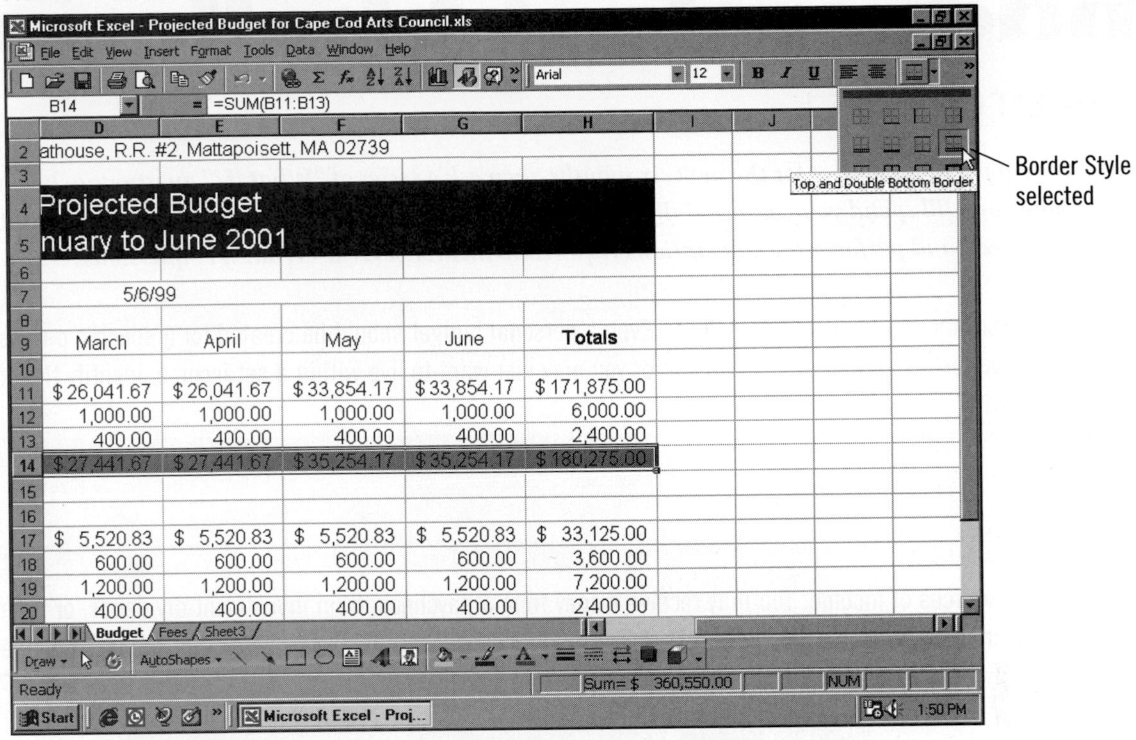

FIGURE P1-12: Custom header

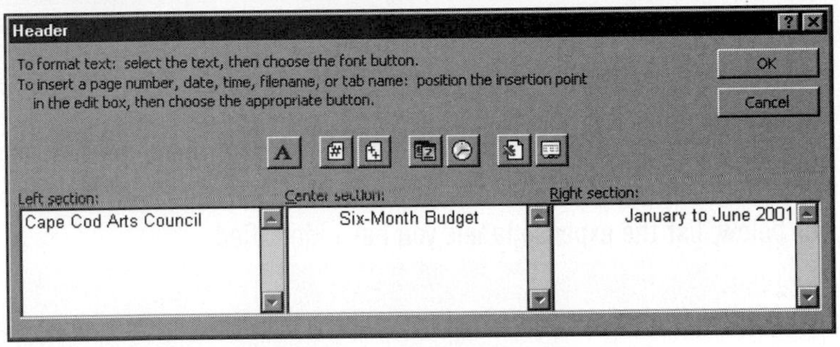

FIGURE P1-13: Completed worksheet

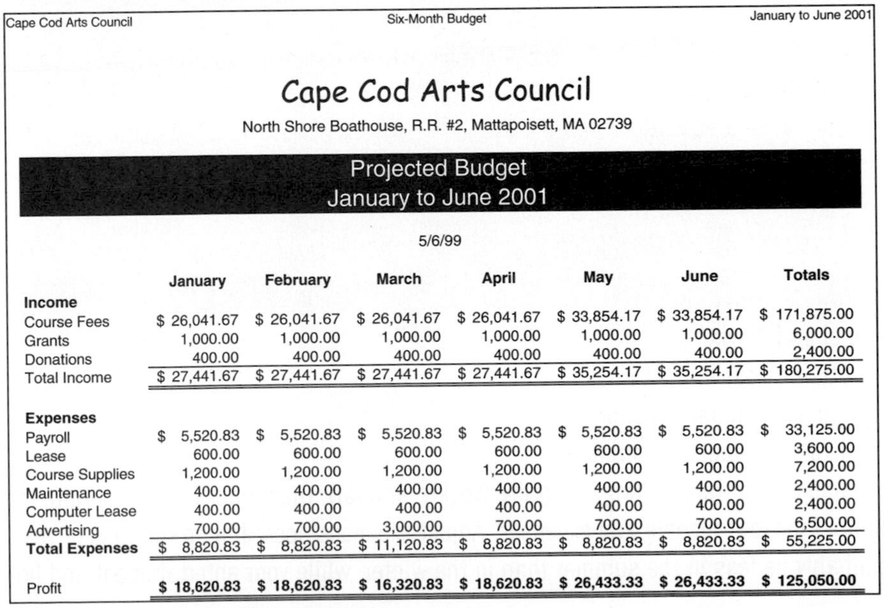

Cape Cod Arts Council | Six-Month Budget | January to June 2001

Cape Cod Arts Council

North Shore Boathouse, R.R. #2, Mattapoisett, MA 02739

Projected Budget
January to June 2001

5/6/99

	January	February	March	April	May	June	Totals
Income							
Course Fees	$ 26,041.67	$ 26,041.67	$ 26,041.67	$ 26,041.67	$ 33,854.17	$ 33,854.17	$ 171,875.00
Grants	1,000.00	1,000.00	1,000.00	1,000.00	1,000.00	1,000.00	6,000.00
Donations	400.00	400.00	400.00	400.00	400.00	400.00	2,400.00
Total Income	$ 27,441.67	$ 27,441.67	$ 27,441.67	$ 27,441.67	$ 35,254.17	$ 35,254.17	$ 180,275.00
Expenses							
Payroll	$ 5,520.83	$ 5,520.83	$ 5,520.83	$ 5,520.83	$ 5,520.83	$ 5,520.83	$ 33,125.00
Lease	600.00	600.00	600.00	600.00	600.00	600.00	3,600.00
Course Supplies	1,200.00	1,200.00	1,200.00	1,200.00	1,200.00	1,200.00	7,200.00
Maintenance	400.00	400.00	400.00	400.00	400.00	400.00	2,400.00
Computer Lease	400.00	400.00	400.00	400.00	400.00	400.00	2,400.00
Advertising	700.00	700.00	3,000.00	700.00	700.00	700.00	6,500.00
Total Expenses	$ 8,820.83	$ 8,820.83	$ 11,120.83	$ 8,820.83	$ 8,820.83	$ 8,820.83	$ 55,225.00
Profit	**$ 18,620.83**	**$ 18,620.83**	**$ 16,320.83**	**$ 18,620.83**	**$ 26,433.33**	**$ 26,433.33**	**$ 125,050.00**

Independent Challenges

INDEPENDENT CHALLENGE 1

Create your own personal budget for the next six months, then ask a series of "What if?" questions to help you make decisions regarding how you will spend your money. Fill in the boxes below with the required information, then set up your budget in an Excel worksheet, and perform the calculations required to answer several "What if?" questions.

1. You need to determine the goal of your budget. Even a personal budget should be created for a specific purpose. For example, you may wish to save for a vacation or to buy a car, or you may just want to live within a set income. Identify the goal of your budget in the box below:

Budget goal: ______________________________

____

2. Determine your sources of income. You may receive money from a paycheck, from investment dividends, or from a student loan. Each income source requires a label and a row on your budget worksheet. In the box below, list the income labels you will require:

Income labels:

1. ______________________ **3.** ______________________

2. ______________________ **4.** ______________________

5. ______________________

3. Determine your expenses. At the very least, you will probably need to list your rent, food, utilities, and phone. You may also need to list transportation costs such as car payments, gas, insurance, and bus fares. In addition, include labels for entertainment, incidentals, and savings. In the box below, list the expense labels you have identified:

Expense labels:

1. ______________________ **6.** ______________________

2. ______________________ **7.** ______________________

3. ______________________ **8.** ______________________

4. ______________________ **9.** ______________________

5. ______________________ **10.** ______________________

4. Set up your budget in Excel as follows:
   a. Enter and enhance a title for your budget in cell A1.
   b. Enter the current date (use the Today function).
   c. Enter the Income and Expense labels in column A.
   d. Determine the time frame of your budget (e.g., monthly, weekly, annual), then enter the appropriate labels starting in column B.
   e. Enter the values required for your income and expenses. Adjust expenses according to the time of year. For example, your utilities costs will probably be less in the summer than in the winter, while your entertainment and holiday expenses may rise in the summer.
   f. Calculate your total income and expenses.

g. Ask yourself at least five "What if?" questions, and then make the calculations required to answer them. Here are some sample "What if?" questions:
   - What if I move in March to a new apartment where my rent is 30% more than the current rent?
   - What if I eat out in restaurants only twice a month?
   - What if I take the bus or subway to work twice a week?
   - What if I join a fitness club with monthly dues?
   - What if I buy a car with payments of $250/month? Remember to factor in costs for insurance and gas.
   - What if I start taking violin lessons?

   Try to formulate questions that will help you plan your finances to achieve the goals you have set.
h. Save your worksheet as "Personal Budget".
i. Format and print a copy of your budget.

INDEPENDENT CHALLENGE 2

You have been working all term as a teaching assistant for a course of your choice. The instructor you work for has given you the grade sheet she has kept "by hand" and has asked you to transfer it to Excel and then calculate each student's grades. Complete the steps below to create a course grades analysis for a course of your choice.

1. Determine the name of the course. For example, the course could be English 100, Psychology 210, or International Business 301.
2. Determine the grade categories and the percentage of scores allocated to each category. For example, you could allocate 40% of the total grades to Assignments, 30% to Exams, and 30% to Oral Presentations. Allocate at least three grade categories and make sure the percentages you assign add up to 100%.
3. Set up the worksheet called Grades with the name of the course, a list of at least 20 students, and labels for the various assignments, exams, quizzes, etc. You determine the number of items in each of the three grade categories you have selected.
4. Determine the total scores possible for each item in each score category and enter the totals one row below the list of names. To check the set up of your Course Grades Analysis, refer to the Course Grades Analysis you created for Project 2.
5. Enter the points for each student. Make sure you refer to the totals you entered to ensure that each score you enter for each student is equal to or less than the total points possible.
6. Calculate the total points for each score category, divide the total points by the total of the possible points, then multiply the result by the percentage you assigned to the mark category. The formula required is: Sum of Student's Points/Sum of Total Points*Percentage. For example, if the Assignment points are entered in cells C4, D4, and F4, the total possible points are entered in cells C25, D25, and F25, and the percentage of Assignments is 40%, the formula required is: =(C4+D4+F4)/($C$25+$D$25+$F$25)*.4
7. Calculate the total points out of 100 earned by the first student on your list.
8. Copy the formulas you used to calculate the first student's weighted score in each category for the remaining students.
9. Sort the list of students alphabetically by name.
10. Create a Lookup table in a worksheet called Lookup that lists the letter grades and ranges.
11. Enter the LOOKUP formula in the appropriate cell in the Grades worksheet, then copy the formula down for the remaining students.
12. Create a Pivot table that counts the number of times each letter grade appears.
13. Create a Column chart from the data in the Pivot table to show the breakdown of scores by letter grade.
14. Copy the Column chart to the Grades sheet.
15. Save the workbook as Course Grades Analysis for [Course Name], format the Grades sheet and Column chart attractively, print a copy, then save and close the workbook.

APPENDIX: TECHNOLOGY TOOLS

Enhance your learning experience with technology tools

The New Perspectives team and Course Technology pride themselves on developing quality learning tools—not just textbooks. There's a lot more to the textbook you're holding than these pages. Here are just a few of the highlights.

CBT (Computer-Based Training)/WBT (Web-Based Training)

Explore!

In the back of this textbook you will find a FREE sample of Explore!, an exciting new learning product. Explore! places you, the student, as an intern in a working company, AdZ, Incorporated. You will gain computer skills through helping the other AdZ employees solve their business problems. The CD contained in your textbook contains a CBT that teaches you the basic operating system and file management skills of Microsoft Windows 2000 Professional. (You do not need Microsoft Windows 2000 Professional to run Explore!, but the content may not match what you see on your computer if it is running Windows 95, 98, or NT.)

Explore! is also available for Word, Access, Excel, PowerPoint, and Office 2000. Each Explore! CBT is organized to match your New Perspectives textbook, so it makes an excellent companion study tool or independent learning system.

For more information, or to use the WBT version of Explore!, go to *www.npexplore.com*. (Instructors: Go to www.npexplore.com for all support materials.) Or, continue with this appendix for step-by-step instructions on how to use Explore!

MyCourse.com

www.mycourse.com

MyCourse.com allows you to enhance and supplement your classroom learning through additional course content made available online. You can use MyCourse.com to go beyond traditional learning by accessing and completing online readings, tests, and other assignments. A complete description of MyCourse.com and step-by-step instructions on how to us it are provided later in this appendix.

On the Web

The Office 2000 Student Online Companion
http://www.course.com/NewPerspectives/office2000/

The Internet Assignments at the end of each tutorial point you to the Student Online Companion for your textbook. These assignments give you an opportunity to combine the skills gained in the tutorial with Web research. But the Student Online Companion provides more than just additional case projects. You also can obtain your data files and updates to the text. And the Additional Resources section is constantly updated to bring you the latest news and tips on using Office 2000. A helpful and comprehensive Computer Buyer's Guide is also available on the Student Online Companion; just click the link for the guide.

Welcome to Explore!

Explore! is a system of discovery learning.

Explore! challenges you to take control of your own learning. You'll participate in solving realistic business problems and discover skills along the way. Through videos, animations, interactive graphics, guided work in the live application, and a wealth of resources online, Explore! puts the fun back in learning.

Launching the CD and Logging into the Web

You can use Explore! either via the Web or through this CD. You can even switch between the two versions at any time! All your information will be saved on your tracking disk (explained on pages 2 and 3).

To take the course over the Web

- You will need the keycode at the back of this folder and an active e-mail account.
- Get connected to the Internet through your ISP, and go to www.npexplore.com.
- Click **Take a Course** and follow the onscreen instructions.

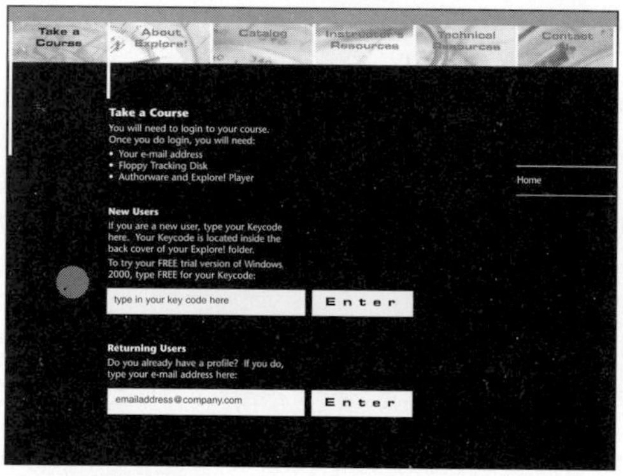

To take the course from the CD

- Put your CD into the CD-ROM drive, label side up.
- If your machine supports AutoPlay, insert this CD into the CD-ROM drive. The course will start automatically. Follow the onscreen instructions.
- If your machine does not support AutoPlay:
  1. Click **Start**.
  2. Click **Run**.
  3. Type **d:\IST_Player.exe** (where "d" is your CD-ROM drive).
  4. Click **OK**.

Logging In and Setting Up Your Tracking Disk

- Once you enter the course (either via the Web or CD), you will need to log in if you want your progress tracked.

  As a new user, you will be required to set up your profile. You'll do this by entering your First Name, Last Name, Student ID number, and Class section number in the appropriate fields. Your Student ID must be unique to you.
- Then you will be asked to choose and confirm a password.

■ Once you've set up your profile, you only need to put your tracking disk in your floppy drive to access your profile every time you start the course. This disk will bookmark where you are in the course and save your quiz results.

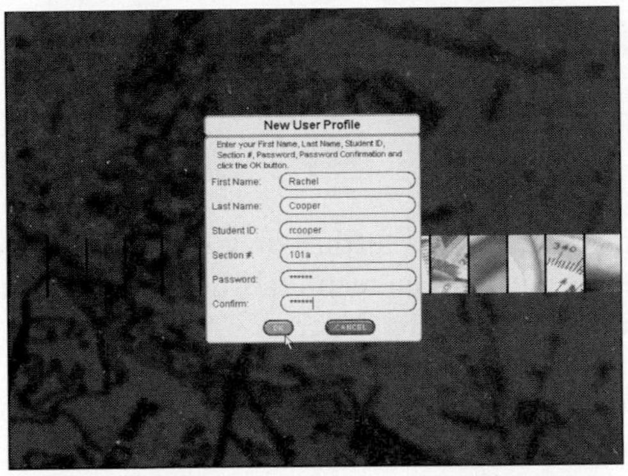

Much of the work you do will be recorded on your tracking disk and your instructor will be checking it from time to time. This disk will be proof of the work you do. So please be sure to save your disk and keep any other files (such as Portfolio Project files, explained on pages 4 and 5) on a separate disk.

Navigating Explore! Getting Started

Explore! will take you inside a working company—AdZ, Inc. As an intern at this fictional Seattle-based advertising agency, you will participate in training, listen to voicemails, and create project files for clients live in the application. If you are using Explore! in a public setting (such as a computer lab), we recommend you use headphones.

Explore! is divided into Tutorials, each of which is designed to be completed in about 90 minutes. Each Tutorial consists of several learning objectives or lessons.

■ To launch a Tutorial, click the name of that tutorial in the menu screen.

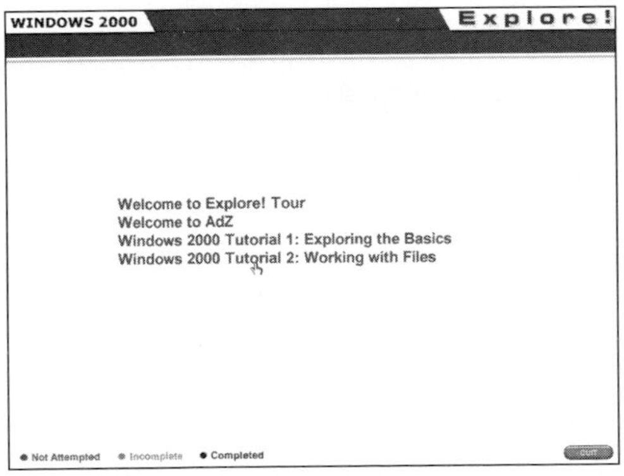

Navigating Explore! Courses, Tutorials, Lessons, and Sections

Once inside the Tutorial, you can navigate your way through the course using the navigation box at the lower-right corner of your screen.

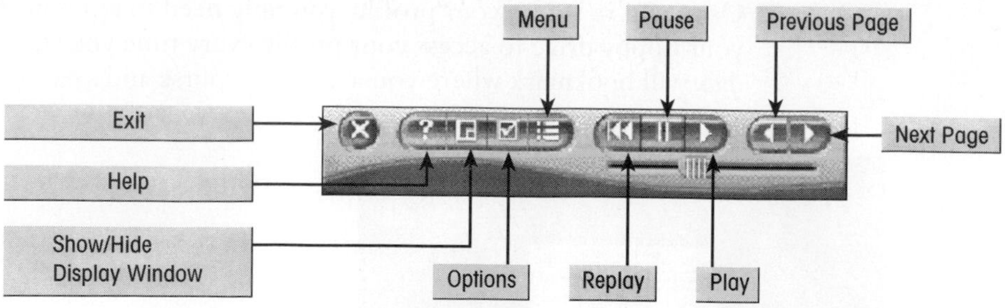

Each Lesson (learning objective) is further divided into Sections. You can move through the Sections of a Lesson by clicking the menu tab, and then clicking the link. We highly recommend you follow the Tutorial in the order in which topics are presented, at least for the first time through.

When navigation buttons are gray, they are inactive. This typically means you need to complete a task on screen before the course will proceed. Often this task is not stated outright—you need to figure it out on your own based on the information provided. But don't worry if you aren't 100% sure—just try something! Explore! will often supply hints and help if you get it wrong. And if you ever need it, help is accessible just by clicking the Help button.

Self-evaluation and Quick Checks

At the end of every Tutorial, you will be prompted to do a self-evaluation that checks whether you are confident enough to take the quiz on this Tutorial.

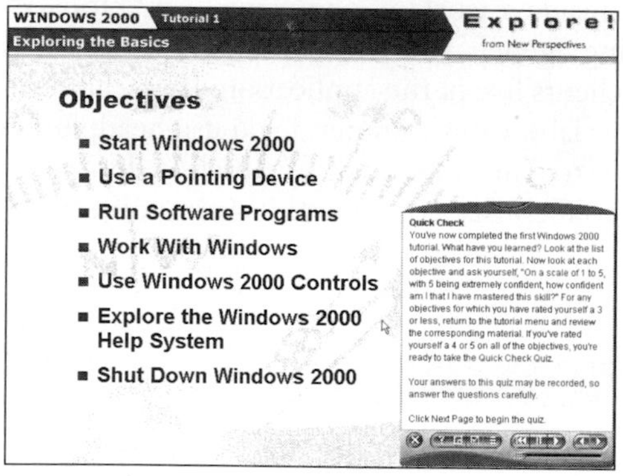

Each quiz consists of 20 questions, designed to test your understanding of the concepts and mastery of the skills included in the lessons. Before you start the quiz, be sure your tracking disk is in the floppy drive. Quizzes are scored upon completion, and encoded on your tracking disk. You can review a quiz as many times as you like, until you feel confident of your skills.

Portfolio Projects and Turning in Files

Most Tutorials include work in the live application throughout the instruction, but all include a live application Portfolio Project at the very end of the Tutorial.

This Portfolio Project allows you to apply what you've learned in the Tutorial to another situation at AdZ, Inc. Unlike total simulation products, the Portfolio Project gives you and your instructor tangible proof of your progress.

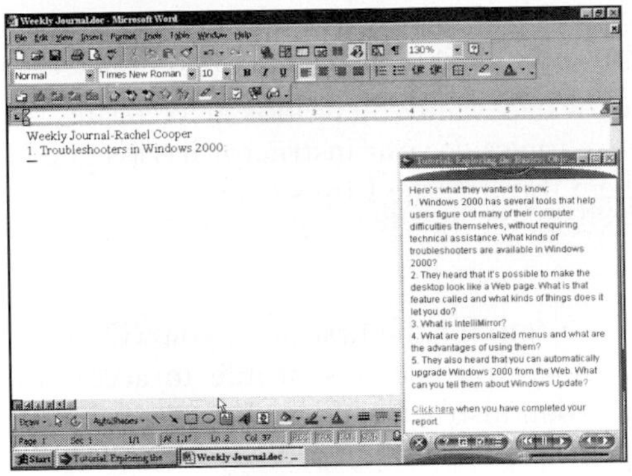

You can hand in tutorial data files, portfolio project files, and tracking disk files on a floppy disk or send them via e-mail to your instructor.

- To e-mail any data or project files, simply attach the *student ID*.txt file from your project disk to the e-mail message, where *student ID* is the same student ID number you used to set up your profile (see pages 2 and 3).

Explore! on the Web

Our community of users is always accessible on the Web at www.npexplore.com. Here you'll find FAQs for any technical support questions, information about Discovery Learning, an online demo, and much more!

AdZ, Inc. also has a Web site for you to explore. Go to the intern's corner for additional resources and data to work on your project and to interact with other users of Explore!. Or just browse the company background, client list, description of services, and more.

We're excited about Explore! and we think that after you work with it, you will be too.

It's time to Explore!

MyCourse.com

MyCourse.com offers instructors and students an opportunity to supplement classroom learning through additional course content online. As a student, you can use MyCourse.com to expand your traditional learning by accessing and completing short readings, Practice tests, and other assignments through this customized, comprehensive Web site.

MyCourse.com provides five types of course content: Objectives, Case Projects, Assignments, Practice Tests, and Links. Your instructor may choose to assign any combination of these activities.

- **Objectives** outline the material to be covered within the tutorial. Topic Reviews, which are listed below each Objective, guide you to the area of the tutorial you need to focus on in order to achieve the given objective.
- **Case Projects** are detailed assignments that let you apply the knowledge gained in the tutorial. There are typically two case projects per tutorial. The first case project provides hands-on practice and application of the concepts, whereas the second case project is more research-based.
- Your instructor may choose to create **Assignments** specifically for your course that build upon previous exercises or assignments, or that investigate completely new areas of the subject matter. Your instructor will direct you to turn in the completed Assignments either in class or by e-mail.
- The **Practice Tests** allow you to test your knowledge with brief quizzes that directly correspond to the Objectives. Practice Tests are graded as soon as you complete them, so you know instantly how well you're doing. Practice

Tests are for self-testing only—results are not tracked or consolidated, although you can e-mail your results to your instructor.

- Your instructor may want you to look at Web sites that have content relevant to your course topics. If your instructor has assigned these sites, you can easily access them through the **Links** feature.

Getting Started

If you are using MyCourse.com for the first time, you will need to create an individualized MyCourse.com user profile. You use this profile to access the course information and assignments created by your instructor. In order to reach the User Profile page, go to http://www.mycourse.com and click the New User link.

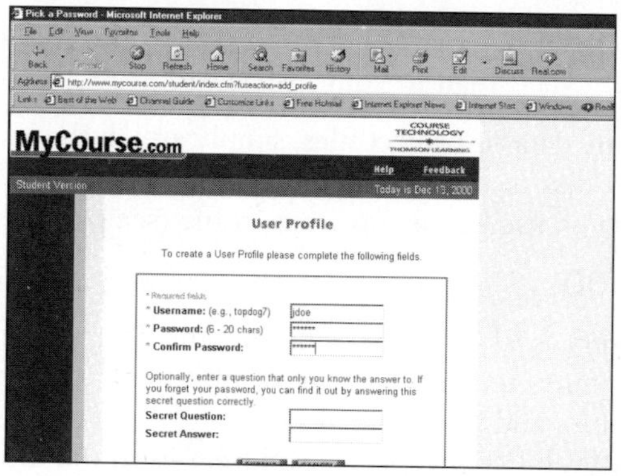

The User Profile page summarizes specific information about you and creates your username and password, which you will need in order to access your MyCourse.com account. There are five fields on this page:

Username (required)	Create a username that consists of at least six characters. It is recommended to use a combination of your first and last names. For example, if your name is Sally Student, you would enter Sstudent. You will use this username to log in to MyCourse.com on subsequent visits.
Password (required)	Enter a password that contains at least six characters. You will use this password to log in to MyCourse.com on subsequent visits.
Confirm Password (required)	Re-enter the password for confirmation.
Secret Question (optional)	Enter a question that has an answer only you would know.
Secret Answer (optional)	Type the answer to the secret question.

You must complete the first three fields. Completing the optional fields for the Secret Question and Secret Answer will provide MyCourse.com with an easy way to help you if you forget your username and password. Once you have completed the User Profile fields, click Submit. The next screen, the Student Information page, prompts you to provide your contact information. After completing the required fields on this page, click Submit.

You will now need to enroll in your MyCourse.com course. Each course has its own Access Key, which is a coded password. Your instructor will provide you with the appropriate Access Key for your course. To enroll in your course, type the appropriate Access Key in the Access Key field, and click Submit.

Another way to enroll in a MyCourse.com course is to enter your textbook's ISBN in the Access Key field. This option is available for students who want to access the extra course content available in MyCourse.com, even if their instructor is not using MyCourse.com to supplement the course.

Once you enroll in your MyCourse.com course, you are launched into your MyCourses home page, which is your customized starting point for all of the MyCourse.com features.

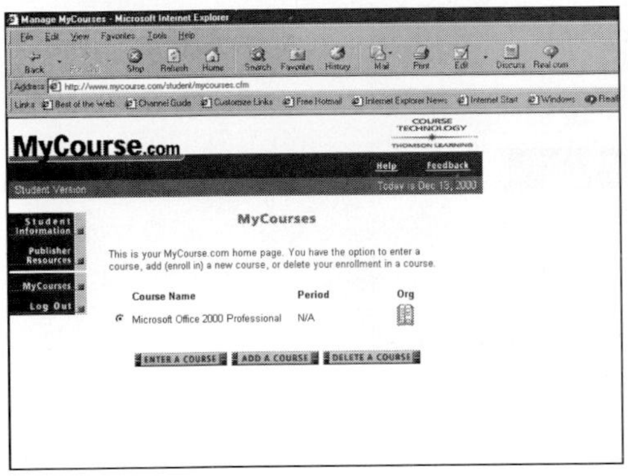

Once you have registered for at least one course, MyCourse.com creates an individualized MyCourse.com home page for you, called MyCourses. From this page, you can use the buttons at the bottom of the screen to enter a course, add or enroll in a new MyCourse.com course, or delete an existing course. Any time you log on to MyCourse.com as a returning user to view your assignments, update your student information, or revise your registration information, you will be launched into your MyCourses home page. Once you have entered your course, you have the option to return to your MyCourses home page at any time by clicking the MyCourses link in the left-hand navigation bar.

Navigating Around MyCourse.com

The left-hand navigation bar in any MyCourse.com screen provides navigation options based on your current location. For example, when you are in the Day at a Glance page of a Calendar-Organized course, the left-hand navigation bar shows eight options:

- Zoom Calendar – When you are working in a Calendar-Organized course, you can click Zoom Calendar to enlarge the Day at a Glance calendar for easier readability.
- Announcements – Your instructor may broadcast information such as classroom changes or assignment reminders using the Announcement feature. Any time you enter a course, you will see announcements for that course displayed on the course's opening screen. You can click the Announcement link in the left-hand navigation bar to display the announcement dates.
- Course Syllabus – The Course Syllabus page lists details about the course for which you are registered, including the course name, instructor, Access Key, course number, semester, start and finish dates, office hours, class times, course description, texts, grading policies, and any other policies specified by the instructor.
- Instructor Information – The Instructor Information page shows you all of the information the instructor included in his or her user profile. The page includes his or her name and school, and might also include phone numbers, e-mail address, office location, and other information.
- Student Information – You can use the Student Information link to update your user profile name and contact information.
- Publisher Resources – Clicking Publisher Resources loads the Course Technology Web page that provides an overview of the textbook you are using in your MyCourse.com online course, as well as access to any additional materials you may need such as data files.

- MyCourses – This link returns you to your MyCourses home page, your starting point for entering, adding, or deleting online courses.
- Log Out – This link exits you from the MyCourse.com Web site.

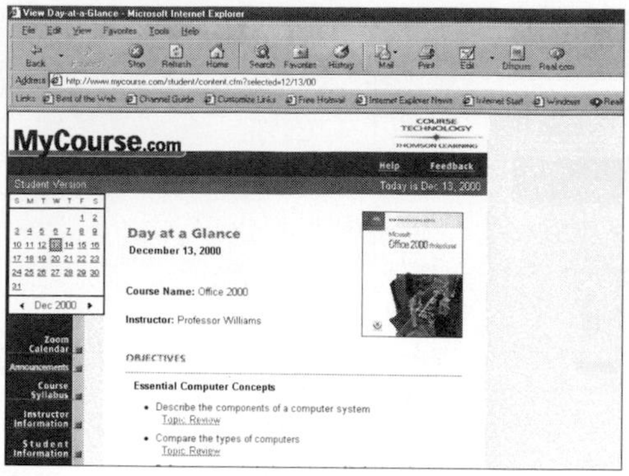

Course Organization Methods

Each course is organized either by Textbook Chapter, Calendar, or Session. Your instructor selects the method of organization. The way you enter a course varies with the way your course is organized, although the course content and the way you add and delete courses are the same, regardless of how the course is organized. The icon in the Org column to the right of each course's period indicates the course organization method.

A **Textbook Chapter-Organized course** is typically used for courses using only one textbook. You can view the content of each chapter that is assigned to the course. Assignments are not tied to a date or any other information. To enter a Textbook Chapter-Organized course, select the option button to the left of the appropriate course. Click the Enter a Course button at the bottom of the page. You are now launched into the Chapter at a Glance page for your selected course. The course name and instructor are shown in addition to the list of assigned content for the first chapter of the textbook. To access the Chapter at a Glance page for another chapter, click the Table of Contents link on the left-hand navigation menu, and then select the chapter whose content you want to see.

The **Calendar-Organized course** option is the default organizational method for MyCourse.com online courses. It allows your instructor to assign readings, projects, or other work based on your class calendar. The MyCourse.com Day at a Glance calendar is the primary tool you use to manage your Calendar-Organized courses. You can click a date to see that day's assignments. Days that have work assigned to them appear on the Day at a Glance calendar with a gray background. To enter a Calendar-Organized course, select the option button to the left of the appropriate course. Click the Enter a Course button at the bottom of the page, which launches you into the Day at a Glance page for your selected course. The course name, instructor name, and a graphic of the textbook are shown in addition to the Day at a Glance calendar. Click a date to see the content assigned for that day.

If your instructor is simultaneously teaching more than one session of your course, he or she may choose to designate different content for each session using the **Session-Organized course** option. To enter a Session-Organized course, select the option button to the left of the appropriate course and click the Enter a Course button at the bottom of the page. You are then launched into the Session at a Glance page for the selected course. This page automatically defaults to Session 1, which is indicated by the red 1 in the Sessions box in the upper-left corner of the page. If you are not enrolled in Session 1, click the appropriate session number in the Sessions box. The currently selected session number appears in red with a box around it. The Session at a Glance page shows information about your course, including course name and instructor name, and also lists the content assigned for each session.

INDEX

D

E

F

G

N

Q

R

S

T

U

V

X

Y

Z

TASK REFERENCE

TASK	PAGE #	RECOMMENDED METHOD
3-D cell reference, create	EX 8.18	(When entering a function into a worksheet cell) select a sheet or sheet range, then select cell range within those worksheets.
AutoComplete, use	EX 1.15	To accept Excel's suggestion, press Enter. Otherwise, continue typing a new label.
AutoFill, create series	EX 7.17	Enter first or first two values in a series. Select this range. Click and drag fill handle over cells you want series to fill.
AutoFilter	EX 5.19	Click any cell in list. Click Data, point to Filter, then click AutoFilter. Click list arrow in column that contains data you want to filter, then select value with which you want to filter.
AutoFilter, custom	EX 5.22	Click any cell in list. Click Data, point to Filter, then click AutoFilter. Click list arrow in column that contains data you want to filter. Click Custom then enter criteria in Custom AutoFilter dialog box.
AutoFormat, use	EX 2.28	Select range to format, click Format, then click AutoFormat. Select desired format from Table Format list, then click OK.
AutoSum button, use	EX 2.07	Click cell where you want sum to appear. Click . Make sure range address in formula is the same as range you want to sum.
Border, apply	EX 3.21	*See* Reference Window: Adding a Border.
Cancel action	EX 2.26	Press Esc, or click Undo .
Cell contents, clear	EX 1.29	Select cells you want to clear, then press Delete.
Cell contents, copy using Copy command	EX 2.10	Select cell or range you want to copy, then click .
Cell contents, copy using fill handle	EX 2.10	Click cell(s) with data or label to copy, then click and drag fill handle to outline cell(s) to which data is to be copied.
Cell reference types, edit	EX 2.14	Double-click cell containing formula to be edited. Move insertion point to part of cell reference to be changed, then press F4 until reference type is correct, then press Enter.
Chart, activate	EX 4.11	Click anywhere within chart border. Same as selecting.
Chart, add data labels	EX 4.17	Select chart, then select a single data marker for series. Click Chart, click Chart Options, then click Data Labels. Select type of data labels you want, then click OK.
Chart, adjust size	EX 4.11	Select chart and drag selection handles.
Chart, apply a pattern to a data marker	EX 4.20	*See* Reference Window: Selecting a Pattern for a Data Marker.
Chart, apply a texture	EX 4.32	Click Format Chart Area on Chart toolbar, click Patterns tab, click Fill Effects button, and then click Texture tab. Select desired texture.
Chart, create	EX 4.06	Select data to be charted. Click , then complete steps in Chart Wizard dialog boxes.
Chart, delete data series	EX 4.14	Select chart, select data series, then press Delete.

TASK REFERENCE

TASK	PAGE #	RECOMMENDED METHOD
Chart, explode pie slice	EX 4.29	Select pie chart, then click slice to explode. Drag selected slice away from center of pie.
Chart, format labels	EX 4.31	Select chart labels, then use Formatting toolbar to change font type, size, and style.
Chart, move	EX 4.11	Select chart and drag it to a new location.
Chart, rotate a 3-D chart	EX 4.30	Select a 3-D chart. Click Chart, then 3-D View. Type values you want in Rotation and Elevation boxes.
Chart, select	EX 4.11	Click anywhere within chart border. Same as activating.
Chart, update	EX 4.13	Enter new values in worksheet. Chart link to data is automatically updated.
Chart, use picture	EX 4.36	Create column or bar chart. Select all columns/bars to be filled with picture, then click Insert, point to Picture, then click From File. Select picture from Insert Picture dialog box, then click Insert.
Chart title, add or edit	EX 4.16	Select chart. Click Chart, then click Chart Options. In Titles tab, click one of title text boxes, then type desired title.
Chart Wizard, start	EX 4.07	Click .
Clipboard contents, paste into range	EX 2.15	Click .
Code Window, view	EX12.17	Start Visual Basic Editor. Click View and Code.
Colors, apply to a range of cells	EX 3.24	*See* Reference Window: Applying Patterns and Color.
Column width, change	EX 2.23	*See* Reference Window: Changing Column Width.
Conditional formatting	EX 5.24	Select cells you want to format. Click Format, then click Conditional Formatting. Specify condition(s) in Conditional Formatting dialog box. Click Format button and select formatting to apply if condition is true.
Copy formula, use copy-and-paste method	EX 2.14	Select cell with formula to be copied, click , click cell you want formula copied to, then click .
Data source, define a	EX11.16	Click Data, point to Get External Data and click Create New Query. Click <New Data Source> and click OK.
Data, validation	EX 7.05	Select cell for data validation. Click Data, then click Validation. Use tabs in Data Validation dialog box to specify validation parameters (Settings tab), input message (Input Message tab), and error alert message (Error Alert tab).
Data form, add record	EX 5.14	Click any cell in list, click Data, then click Form. Click New button, type values for new record, then click Close.
Data form, delete record	EX 5.17	Click any cell in list, click Data, then click Form. Click Criteria button, enter criteria, then click Find Next. After finding record to delete, click Delete button.
Data form, search	EX 5.17	Click any cell in list, click Data, then click Form. Click Criteria button, enter criteria, then click Find Next.

TASK	PAGE #	RECOMMENDED METHOD
Delimited text files, import	EX11.05	Click Delimited option button in Step 1 of Text Import Wizard and specify delimiter.
Embed, object	EX 6.16	In Excel, select object and click Copy button. Switch to another program and open document. Select location where document will appear and click Edit, click Paste Special. Click the Paste option button, click Microsoft Excel Worksheet Object, then click OK.
Excel, exit	EX 1.34	Click File, then click Exit, or click Excel Close button.
Excel, start	EX 1.05	Click Start button, point to Programs, if necessary click Microsoft Office, and then click Microsoft Excel.
Fixed width text files, create column break for	EX11.06	In Step 2 of Text Import Wizard, click spot where you want column break to appear.
Fixed width text files, import	EX11.07	Click Fixed Width option button in Step 1 of Text Import Wizard.
Fixed width text files, move a column break in	EX11.06	In Step 2 of Text Import Wizard, click column break and drag to new location.
Fixed width text files, remove column break from	EX11.07	In Step 2 of Text Import Wizard, double-click column break line.
Font, select	EX 3.17	Select cell or range you want to format. Click Format, click Cells, and then click Font tab. Select desired font from Font List box.
Font, select size	EX 3.16	Select cell or range you want to format. Click Format, click Cells, and then click Font tab. Select desired font size from Font List box.
Footer, add	EX 2.32	In Print Preview window, click Setup, then click Header/Footer tab in Page Setup dialog box. Click Custom Footer and edit existing footer in Footer dialog box.
Format, apply to several worksheets at once	EX 8.14	Group worksheets to be formatted and then apply formatting commands. Ungroup sheets after formatting.
Format, bold	EX 3.16	Select cell or range you want to format, then click , which toggles on and off.
Format, center in cell	EX 3.12	Select cell or range you want to format. Click , which toggles on and off.
Format, center text across columns	EX 3.14	Select cell or range with text to center. Click Format, click Cells, then click Alignment tab. Click Horizontal Text alignment arrow and select Center Across Selection.
Format, comma	EX 3.11	Select cell or range of cells you want to format, then click .
Format, copy	EX 3.09	Select cell or range of cells with format you want to copy. Click , then select cell or range of cells you want to format.
Format, currency	EX 3.06	Select cell or range of cells you want to format. Click Format, then click Cells. Click Number tab, click Currency in Category box, then click desired options.
Format, font	EX 3.16	Select cell or range you want to format. Click Font arrow and select desired font.

TASK REFERENCE

TASK	PAGE #	RECOMMENDED METHOD
Format, indent text	EX 3.15	Select cell or range you want to indent. Click .
Format, italic	EX 3.18	Select cell or range you want to format, then click , which toggles on and off.
Format, percent	EX 3.11	Select cell or range of cells you want to format, then click .
Format, wrap text	EX 3.13	Select cell or cells you want to format. Click Format, click Cells, then click Alignment tab. Click Wrap text check box.
Formula, enter	EX 2.08	Click cell in which you want result to appear. Type = and then type rest of formula. For formulas that include cell references, type cell reference or select each cell using mouse or arrow keys. When formula is complete, press Enter.
Formulas, display	EX 2.37	Click Tools, then click Options. Click View tab, then click Formulas check box.
Formulas, enter into several worksheets at once	EX 8.11	Group worksheets to contain formulas and then enter formulas.
Freeze rows and columns	EX 5.06	Select cell below and right of row or column you want to freeze. Click Window, then click Freeze Panes.
Function, enter	EX 1.18	Type = to begin function. Type name of function in either uppercase or lowercase letters, followed by an opening parenthesis. Type range of cells you want to calculate using function, separating first and last cells in range with a colon, as in B9:B15, or drag pointer to outline cells you want to calculate. *See also* Paste Function button, activate.
Goal Seek, use	EX10.11	Click Tools and Goal Seek. Enter cell containing goal in Set Cell box and intended value in To Value box. Enter cell that should be changed to reach that goal in By Changing Cell box.
Gridlines, add or remove	EX 3.32	Click Tools, click Options, then click View. Click Gridlines check box.
Header, add	EX 2.32	In Print Preview window, click Setup, then click Header/Footer tab in Page Setup dialog box. Click Custom Header button to add a header in Header dialog box.
Help, activate	EX 1.26	*See* Reference Window: Using the Office Assistant, and Figure 1-23
Hyperlinks, insert	EX 6.24	Select text or graphic to serve as hyperlink, then click Insert Hyperlink button. Click File, Web Page or Bookmark, select file you want to link to, and then click OK.

If-Then-Else control structure, Visual Basic syntax for creating a	EX12.42	If <Condition> Then
		   <Visual Basic Statements>
		Else
		   <Visual Basic Statements>
		End If

TASK	PAGE #	RECOMMENDED METHOD

If-Then-ElseIf control structure, Visual Basic syntax for creating a	EX12.43	If <Condition> Then
		<Visual Basic Statements>
		ElseIf <Condition 2> Then
		<Visual Basic Statements>
		ElseIf <Condition 3> Then
		<Visual Basic Statements>
		Else
		<Visual Basic Statements>
		End If

Input Box, Visual Basic syntax for creating a	EX12.34	Variable = InputBox(Prompt, Title)
Labels, enter	EX 1.14	Select cell, then type text you want in cell.
Link, update	EX 6.15	In Excel, edit data. Switch to other program to view changes in destination document.
Linked Workbook, open	EX 8.38	Click Edit, click Links, click workbook name from list of links.
Linked workbook, retrieve data from	EX 8.39	Click Edit, click Links, click workbook name from list of links and click Update Now.
Links, objects	EX 6.11	In Excel, select object and click copy. Switch to another program and open document. Select location where object will appear and click Edit, and then click Paste Special. Click Paste Link option button, click Microsoft Excel Worksheet Object, then click OK.
Links, view list of	EX 8.37	Click Edit and Links on Excel menu bar.
Lookup Tables, create	EX 8.44	Create a table on a worksheet. Insert compare values in first row or column of table. Insert values to be retrieved in rows or columns that follow.
Macro, assign shortcut key	EX 7.37	Click Tools, point to Macro, click Macros. Select name of macro, click Options, enter shortcut key letter in Shortcut key text box, click OK.
Macros, assign to a button	EX12.06	Display Forms toolbar. Click button tools and draw button image on worksheet. Click macro name in Macros list box that appears and type text that describes button's purpose on button image.
Macro, assign to button	EX 7.43	*See* Reference Window: Assigning to a Button Object in a Worksheet.
Macro, recording	EX 7.31	Click Tools, point to Macro, then click Record New Macro. In Record Macro dialog box, enter a descriptive name in the Macro Name box, select location where you want to store macro, assign a shortcut key, click OK. Perform tasks in macro. Click Stop Recording button.
Macro, run from Tools menu	EX 7.35	Click Tools, point to Macro, then click Macros. Select name of macro you want to run, then click Run button.
Macro, run using shortcut key	EX 7.38	Press Ctrl + shortcut key.
Macros, edit	EX12.09	Click Tools, point to Macro and click Macros. Click macro name and click Edit.

TASK	PAGE #	RECOMMENDED METHOD
Macros, print	EX12.49	Open Code Window in Visual Basic Editor. Click File and Print. Specify current module or project.
Macros, record	EX12.05	Click Tools, point to Macro and click Record New Macro. Enter macro name and description. Perform actions, then click  on Macro toolbar.
Menus, customizing	EX12.56	Click Tools and Customize. Make modifications to menus in Customize dialog box and by typing directly in menus themselves.
Menu item, assigning to a macro	EX12.58	Open Customize dialog box. Right-click menu item and click Assign Macro on the menu. Select macro from list box.
Menu item, creating	EX12.57	Open Customize dialog box. Click Commands dialog sheet and locate type of command you want to create. Drag command from Commands list box to menu bar or toolbar.
Menu item, removing a	EX12.56	Open Customize dialog box. Drag menu item off menu bar.
Menu, restoring a	EX12.61	Open Customize dialog box. Click Toolbars dialog sheet tab. Select menu from Toolbars list box and click Reset button.
Message box, Visual Basic syntax for creating a	EX12.48	MsgBox Prompt, Buttons, Title
Methods, Visual Basic syntax for applying a	EX12.29	Object.Method
Non-adjacent ranges, select	EX 4.25	Click first cell or range of cells to select, then press and hold Ctrl key as you select other cell or range of cells to be selected. Release Ctrl key when all non-adjacent ranges are highlighted.
Numbers, enter	EX 1.15	Select cell, then type number.
One-Variable Data Table, create	EX 9.11	Set up One-Variable Data Table structure, click Data and Table. Enter cell reference for input cell in Row Input Cell box or Column Input Cell box.
Page Break, insert	EX 5.31	Click row selector button where you want to start new page. Click Insert, then click Page Break.
Paste, graphic object	EX 6.06	Select cell where you want to place object. Click Insert, point to Picture, then click from File. Select object, then click Insert.
Paste Function button, activate	EX 2.19	*See* Reference Window: Using the Paste Function button.
Patterns, apply to a range of cells	EX 3.24	*See* Reference Window: Applying Patterns and Color.
PivotTable, create	EX 5.34	Select any cell in list. Click Data, then click PivotTable and PivotChart Report. Identify source, location, layout of data, and placement of pivot table.
PivotTable, retrieve external data for a	EX11.34	Start PivotTable Wizard. Click External Data Source, click Get Data, choose a data source, and use Query Wizard to define a query for PivotTable.
Print Preview window, open	EX 2.30	Click .

TASK	PAGE #	RECOMMENDED METHOD
Printout, center	EX 2.31	In Print Preview dialog box, click Setup button. Click Margins tab, then click Horizontally and/or Vertically check boxes.
Printout, landscape orientation	EX 3.34	In Print Preview window, click Setup button. Click Page tab in Page Setup dialog box, then click Landscape option button in Orientation box.
Project Explorer, view	EX12.11	Start Visual Basic Editor. Click View and Project Explorer.
Projects, changing the name of	EX12.12	Open Visual Basic Editor, click Tools and name of project. Enter new name in Project Name box along with a project description.
Properties Window, view	EX12.13	Start Visual Basic Editor. Click View and Properties Window.
Properties, change with the Properties Window	EX12.14	Select an object in Project Explorer. View Properties Window and select a property from Properties list. Enter a new value for property.
Property, Visual Basic syntax for changing a	EX12.27	Object.Property = Expression
Protection, cell	EX 7.25	Select cells you want to remain unprotected. Click Format, click Cells, click Protection tab and remove check from Locked check box. Click Tools, point to protection, then click Protect Sheet. Click OK.
Query Wizard, start	EX11.17	Click Data, point to Get External Data and click Create New Query. Select data source, select Use Query Wizard checkbox, and click OK.
Query, choose columns for a	EX11.18	Start Query Wizard. Click plus box in front of table name containing columns. Double-click each column to add it to query.
Query, edit a	EX11.30	Click a cell in external data range. Click on External Data toolbar.
Query, filter data for a	EX11.21	Start Query Wizard. Choose columns for query. Select column you want to filter in Column to Filter list box. Specify comparison type and filter value in two list boxes to right of Column to Filter list box.
Query, refresh a	EX11.28	Click a cell in external data range. Click on External Data toolbar.
Query, save	EX11.33	Start Query Wizard and select columns for query, any filters and sort options. In final dialog box, click Save Query. Enter location and name for file containing query.
Query, set properties for a	EX11.28	Click a cell in external data range. Click on External Data toolbar.
Query, sort data for a	EX11.21	Start Query Wizard, select columns and any filters for query. In Sort Order dialog box, select columns to sort by in Sort By list box and click either Descending or Ascending.
Range, highlight	EX 1.30	Position pointer on first cell of range. Press and hold mouse button and drag mouse through cells you want, then release mouse button.
Range, move	EX 2.27	Select cell or range of cells you want to move. Place mouse pointer over any edge of selected range until pointer changes to an arrow. Click and drag outline of range to new worksheet location.
Range, nonadjacent	EX 4.25	*See* Non-Adjacent ranges, select.
Range, select	EX 1.30	*See* Range, highlight.

TASK	PAGE #	RECOMMENDED METHOD
Range name, defining	EX 7.10	Select cell or range you want to name. Click Insert, point to Name, then click Define. Type name in Names in workbook box, then click OK.
Report, using Report Manager to create a	EX 9.36	Click View and Report Manager. Click Add button. Specify views and scenarios to include on report.
Report, adding a section to a	EX 9.37	Open Add Report dialog box. Click Add button.
Row or column, delete	EX 2.26	Click heading(s) of row(s) or column(s) you want to delete, click Edit, then click Delete.
Row or column, insert	EX 2.24	Click any cell in row/column above which you want to insert new row/column. Click Insert and then click Rows/Columns for every row/column in highlighted range.
Scenario Reports, create	EX 9.35	Click Tools and Scenarios to open Scenario Manager. Click Summary. Click Scenario Summary option button and specify the result cells and click OK.
Scenarios, create	EX 9.28	Click Tools and Scenarios. Click Add and enter a scenario name.
Scenarios, edit	EX 9.34	Click Tools and Scenarios. Click scenario name and click Edit.
Scenarios, view	EX 9.32	Click Tools and Scenarios. Click scenario name and click Show.
Sheet, activate	EX 1.10	Click sheet tab for desired sheet.
Sheet tab, rename	EX 2.15	Double-click sheet tab for desired sheet.
Shortcut menu, activate	EX 3.10	Select cells or objects to which you want to apply command, click right mouse button, then select command you want.
Solver, add constraints to	EX 10.20	Start Solver and click Add. Specify constraint cells and type of constraint.
Solver, add integer constraints to	EX10.24	Start Solver and click Add. Select INT from constraint list arrow.
Solver, create an Answer Report for	EX10.26	Start Solver and click Solve. Click Answer in the Reports list box.
Solver, set a target cell for	EX10.19	Start Solver and specify cell reference for target cell and whether Solver should minimize, maximize, or set cell to a specific value.
Solver, start	EX10.18	Make sure that Solver add-in is installed. Click Tools then click Solver.
Sort, more than one sort field	EX 5.12	Select any cell in list. Click Data, then click Sort. Specify sort fields and sort order, then click OK.
Sort, single sort field	EX 5.10	Select any cell in column you want to sort by. Click Sort Ascending or Sort Descending button on Standard toolbar.
Spell check	EX 2.22	Click Tools, click Spelling.
Sub procedure, insert	EX12.20	Click Insert and Procedure from Visual Basic Editor menu bar. Type procedure name, click Sub and Public option. Click OK.
Subtotals, insert	EX 5.28	Sort list on column you want to subtotal. Select any cell in list, then click Data, then click Subtotals. Specify criteria for subtotals, click OK.

TASK	PAGE #	RECOMMENDED METHOD
Templates, create	EX 8.27	Create a workbook. Click File and Save As. Enter template filename and select Template from Save As Type drop-down list box.
Templates, open	EX 8.25	Click File and New. Double-click icon of template you want to open.
Text box, add	EX 3.27	Click  on Drawing toolbar. Position pointer where text box is to appear, then click and drag to outline desired size and shape. Type comment in box.
Text files, import	EX11.05	Click File and Open and select Text Files from Files of Type list box. Locate text file and click Open. Complete steps of Text Import wizard.
Text files, remove columns from	EX11.09	Open text file. In Step 3 of Text Import wizard, click column and click Do Not Import Column (skip) option button.
Text files, specify starting row for	EX11.07	Open text file, click Starting Row list arrow in Step 1 of Text Import wizard.
Text Import Wizard, start the	EX11.05	Open any text file from within Excel.
Toolbar, add or remove	EX 3.26	Click any toolbar with right mouse button. Click name of toolbar you want to use/remove from shortcut menu.
Two-Variable Data Table, create	EX 9.18	Set up Two-Variable Data Table structure, click Data and Table on menu. Enter row input cell and column input cell values.
Undo button, activate	EX 2.26	Click .
Web Query, create a	EX11.45	Click Data, point to Get External Data and click New Web Query. Enter options for retrieving information from Web site.
Web Query, refresh a	EX11.42	Click a cell in external data range. Click on External Data toolbar.
Web Query, run a	EX11.40	Click Data, point to Get External Data and click Run Web Query. Select a Web Query file and click Get Data. Enter any values when prompted.
WordArt, embedding	EX 6.07	Click , then click . Select WordArt style, enter text, specify font, then click OK.
Workbook, adding a password to a	EX12.53	Click Tools, point to Protection and click Protect Workbook. Specify which elements of workbook are to be protected and enter a password.
Workbook, changing the properties of a	EX12.51	Click File and Properties. Edit Properties dialog box.
Workbook, open	EX 1.10	Click  (or click File, then click Open). Make sure Look in box displays name of folder containing workbook you want to open. Click name of workbook, then click Open.
Workbook, save with a new name	EX 1.21	Click File, then click Save As. Change workbook name as necessary. Specify folder in which to save workbook in Save in box. Click Save.
Workbook, save with same name	EX 1.21	Click .
Worksheet, adding a password to a	EX12.52	Click Tools, point to Protection and click Protect Sheet. Specify which elements of worksheet are to be password protected. Type a password.

TASK	PAGE #	RECOMMENDED METHOD
Worksheet, close	EX 1.33	Click File, then click Close, or click worksheet Close button.
Worksheet, delete	EX 7.29	Click sheet tab of sheet you want to delete. Click Edit, click Delete Sheet, then click OK.
Worksheet, insert	EX 8.04	Right-click Sheet tab of a worksheet in workbook and click insert on Shortcut menu. Double-click Worksheet icon in dialog box.
Worksheet, move	EX 8.06	Click worksheet tab and drag tab along row of sheet tabs, dropping tab at desired location.
Worksheet, print	EX 1.31	Click to print without adjusting any print options. Use Print command on File menu to adjust options.
Worksheet, screen elements hiding	EX12.54	Click Tools and Option. Deselect checkboxes for screen elements you want to hide.
Worksheet, screen elements restoring	EX12.61	Click Tools and Option. Select checkboxes for screen elements you want to restore.
Worksheet labels, formula	EX 5.26	Use column headers and row labels in place of cell references to build formulas.
Worksheets, group	EX 8.10	For a contiguous sheet range: click first sheet tab in range, hold down Shift key and click last sheet tab in range. For a noncontiguous sheet range: hold down CTRL key and click sheet tab of each sheet in range.
Worksheets, ungroup	EX 8.10	Click a sheet tab of a sheet not in group, or right-click tab of a sheet in group and click Ungroup Sheets on Shortcut menu.
Workspace, create	EX 8.46	Open all workbooks in the workspace, click File and Save Workspace.
Workspace, open	EX 8.46	Click File and Open and select Workspace file.

Standardized Coding Number	Certification Skill Activity	Tutorial Pages	End-of-Tutorial Practice: End-of-Tutorial Pages	End-of-Tutorial Practice: Exercise	End-of-Tutorial Practice: Step Number
XL2000.1	**Working with cells**				
XL2000.1.1	Use Undo and Redo	2.24			
XL2000.1.2	Clear cell content	1.30–1.33	1.35	Review Assignment	6
			1.38	Case Problem 4	7
XL2000.1.3	Enter text, dates, and numbers	1.16–1.17	1.35	Review Assignment	5, 7
			1.36	Case Problem 1	3, 4
			1.36	Case Problem 2	3, 4
			1.37	Case Problem 3	3, 6, 7
			1.38	Case Problem 4	1, 2, 3, 4, 7
		2.04–2.07	2.37–2.38	Review Assignment	4, 10
			2.39	Case Problem 1	1, 5
			2.40	Case Problem 2	1
			2.42	Case Problem 4	1
		8.05	8.40	Review Assignment	2
XL2000.1.4	Edit cell content	1.23–1.24	1.35	Review Assignment	4
		1.26	1.37	Case Problem 2	7
XL2000.1.5	Go to a specific cell	1.08–1.09			
XL2000.1.6	Insert and delete selected cells	3.18			
XL2000.1.7	Cut, copy, paste, paste special and move selected cells, use the Office Clipboard	2.10–2.14 6.14	2.38	Review Assignment	12,17
XL2000.1.8	Use Find and Replace	5.09			
XL2000.1.9	Clear cell formats	3.17	3.36	Review Assignment	12
XL2000.1.10	Work with series (AutoFill)	7.17–7.18	7.38	Review Assignment	1
XL2000.1.11	Create hyperlinks	6.33–6.37	6.42	Review Assignment	8, 9, 10
			6.44	Case Problem 2	14
			6.45	Case Problem 3	7, 8
			6.45	Case Problem 4	6
XL2000.2	**Working with files**				
XL2000.2.1	Use Save	1.34	1.37	Case Problem 2	5
			1.37	Case Problem 3	8
			1.38	Case Problem 4	5
		2.35	2.38	Review Assignment	14
			2.39	Case Problem 1	8
			2.40	Case Problem 2	7
			2.41	Case Problem 3	6
			2.42	Case Problem 4	6
			3.41	Case Problem 4	6
XL2000.2.2	Use Save As (different name, location, format)	1.22–1.24	1.35	Review Assignment	2
			1.36	Case Problem 1	2
			1.36	Case Problem 2	1
			1.37	Case Problem 3	2
			1.38	Case Problem 4	5

Standardized Coding Number	Certification Skill Activity	Tutorial Pages	End-of-Tutorial Practice		
			End-of-Tutorial Pages	Exercise	Step Number
			2.37	Review Assignment	3
			2.41	Case Problem 3	1
			3.36	Review Assignment	1
			3.37	Case Problem 1	1
			3.38–3.39	Case Problem 2	1, 8
			3.40	Case Problem 3	1
XL2000.2.3	Locate and open an existing workbook	1.11–1.12	1.35	Review Assignment	1
			1.36	Case Problem 1	1
			1.36	Case Problem 2	1
			1.37	Case Problem 3	1
XL2000.2.4	Create a folder	1.22			
XL2000.2.5	Use templates to create a new workbook	8.24–8.28	8.50	Case Problem 1	10, 11
XL2000.2.6	Save a worksheet/workbook as a Web Page	6.37–6.40	6.41	Review Assignment	5
			6.43	Case Problem 1	9
			6.45	Case Problem 3	5
XL2000.2.7	Send a workbook via email	6.11			
XL2000.2.8	Use the Office Assistant	1.27–1.29	1.35	Review Assignment	11
			2.38	Review Assignment	9, 16
			2.42	Case Problem 3	10
			4.40	Case Problem 1	11
XL2000.3	**Formatting worksheets**				
XL2000.3.1	Apply font styles (typeface, size, color and styles)	3.14–3.17	3.36	Review Assignment	3
		3.27	3.37	Case Problem 1	3
			3.38	Case Problem 2	4
			3.40	Case Problem 3	3
			3.41	Case Problem 4	3
XL2000.3.2	Apply number formats (currency, percent, dates, comma)	3.06–3.10	3.37	Case Problem 1	3
			3.38	Case Problem 2	4
			3.40	Case Problem 3	3
			3.41	Case Problem 4	3
		5.41–5.42			
		A1.14			
XL2000.3.3	Modify size of rows and columns	2.22			
		3.24	3.36	Review Assignment	3
XL2000.3.4	Modify alignment of cell content	3.11–3.13	3.36	Review Assignment	5
			3.37	Case Problem 1	2
			3.38	Case Problem 2	4
			3.40	Case Problem 3	3
			3.41	Case Problem 4	3
XL2000.3.5	Adjust the decimal place	3.09–3.10			
XL2000.3.6	Use the Format Painter	3.09			
XL2000.3.7	Apply autoformat	2.26–2.27	2.39	Case Problem 1	6
			2.41	Case Problem 2	9
			2.41	Case Problem 3	4
			2.42	Case Problem 4	4

Standardized Coding Number	Certification Skill Activity	Tutorial Pages	End-of-Tutorial Practice		
			End-of-Tutorial Pages	Exercise	Step Number
XL2000.3.8	Apply cell borders and shading	3.19–3.23			
XL2000.3.9	Merging cells	3.13	3.37	Review Assignment	14
XL2000.3.10	Rotate text and change indents	3.11–3.13	3.37	Review Assignment	14
XL2000.3.11	Define, apply, and remove a style	3.17			
XL2000.4	**Page setup and printing**				
XL2000.4.1	Preview and print worksheets & workbooks	1.32 2.28–2.30 3.31–3.34	1.35 1.36 1.37 1.37–1.38 1.38 2.38 2.41 2.41 2.43	Review Assignment Case Problem 1 Case Problem 2 Case Problem 3 Case Problem 4 Review Assignment Case Problem 2 Case Problem 3 Case Problem 4	9 6 6 9, 12 6, 8, 9 15 8, 11 7 7
XL2000.4.2	Use Web Page Preview	6.38–6.40	6.43 6.45 6.45	Case Problem 1 Case Problem 3 Case Problem 4	9 5 7
XL2000.4.3	Print a selection	2.33	2.41	Case Problem 3	7
XL2000.4.4	Change page orientation and scaling	2.36 3.32–3.33			
XL2000.4.5	Set page margins and centering	2.29–2.30 3.33	2.40 2.41 2.41 2.43	Case Problem 1 Case Problem 2 Case Problem 3 Case Problem 4	9 11 7 7
XL2000.4.6	Insert and remove a page break	5.31–5.33	5.51 5.51	Review Assignment Case Problem 1	16 3
XL2000.4.7	Set print, and clear a print area	2.33	2.42 4.41	Case Problem 3 Case Problem 3	11 7
XL2000.4.8	Set up headers and footers	2.30–2.32 3.33	2.40 2.41 2.43 3.36 3.37 3.38 3.41 4.40	Case Problem 1 Case Problem 3 Case Problem 4 Review Assignment Case Problem 1 Case Problem 3 Case Problem 4 Case Problem 2	9 7 7 7 5 5 7 5
XL2000.4.9	Set print titles and options (gridlines, print quality, row & column headings)	2.36 3.30–3.31 5.32–5.33	2.40 2.41 2.41	Case Problem 1 Case Problem 2 Case Problem 3	11 8, 11 7

Standardized Coding Number	Certification Skill Activity	Tutorial Pages	End-of-Tutorial Practice: End-of-Tutorial Pages	End-of-Tutorial Practice: Exercise	End-of-Tutorial Practice: Step Number
XL2000.5	**Working with worksheets & workbooks**				
XL2000.5.1	Insert and delete rows and columns	2.22–2.24	2.38 2.40	Review Assignment Case Problem 2	8, 9 3, 4
XL2000.5.2	Hide and unhide rows and columns	3.34–3.35	5.51	Review Assignment	15
XL2000.5.3	Freeze and unfreeze rows and columns	5.06–5.07	5.51 5.52 5.53	Case Problem 1 Case Problem 2 Case Problem 3	2 3 2
XL2000.5.4	Change the zoom setting	5.08–5.09			
XL2000.5.5	Move between worksheets in a workbook	1.07 1.12	1.37 1.38	Case Problem 3 Case Problem 4	7 2
XL2000.5.6	Check spelling	2.21			
XL2000.5.7	Rename a worksheet	2.14	2.38 2.39 2.40	Review Assignment Case Problem 1 Case Problem 2	5 7 6
XL2000.5.8	Insert and Delete worksheets	7.23–7.24 8.04–8.05	7.39 7.41	Review Assignment Case Problem 1	13 12
XL2000.5.9	Move and copy worksheets	8.06–8.07			
XL2000.5.10	Link worksheets & consolidate data using 3D References	6.03–6.05 8.32–8.40	8.48 8.49 8.50 8.52	Review Assignment Case Problem 1 Case Problem 2 Case Problem 4	6 5 3, 4, 5, 6, 7 3, 7
XL2000.6	**Working with formulas & functions**				
XL2000.6.1	Enter a range within a formula by dragging	2.19–2.20	2.38	Review Assignment	12
XL2000.6.2	Enter formulas in a cell and using the formula bar	1.17–1.18 2.07–2.08	1.36 1.36 1.37 1.38 2.38 2.39 2.40 2.41 2.42	Case Problem 1 Case Problem 2 Case Problem 3 Case Problem 4 Review Assignment Case Problem 1 Case Problem 2 Case Problem 3 Case Problem 4	3 2 4, 5 1 11 2, 3, 4 2, 3 2 2
XL2000.6.3	Revise formulas		2.41	Case Problem 3	9
XL2000.6.4	Use references (absolute and relative)	2.10–2.12	2.38 2.40 2.41	Review Assignment Case Problem 2 Case Problem 3	8 3 2
XL2000.6.5	Use AutoSum	2.06–2.07	2.40	Case Problem 2	2
XL2000.6.6	Use Paste Function to insert a function	2.17–2.18	2.38	Review Assignment	13

Standardized Coding Number	Certification Skill Activity	Tutorial Pages	End-of-Tutorial Practice: End-of-Tutorial Pages	Exercise	Step Number
XL2000.6.7	Use basic functions (AVERAGE, SUM, COUNT, MIN, MAX)	1.19–1.20 2.15–2.20 5.40–5.41	 2.38 2.40 2.41 2.42 5.50 5.52	 Review Assignment Case Problem 2 Case Problem 3 Case Problem 4 Review Assignment Case Problem 2	 13 2 3 1 8 3
XL2000.6.8	Enter functions using the formula palette	2.17–2.18			
XL2000.6.9	Use date functions (NOW and DATE)	A1.14–A1.15	A1.18	Review Assignment	10,11,12
XL2000.6.10	Use financial functions (FV and PMT)	7.19–7.21 A1.02–A1.03	7.51 A1.17	Case Problem 2 Review Assignment	4 4
XL2000.6.11	Use logical functions (IF)	7.13–7.16 A1.08–A1.14	7.47 7.53 7.54 A1.18	Review Assignment Case Problem 3 Case Problem 4 Review Assignment	11 4 4 8, 9
XL2000.7	**Using charts and objects**				
XL2000.7.1	Preview and print charts	4.23	4.39 4.40 4.40 4.41 4.41	Review Assignment Case Problem 1 Case Problem 2 Case Problem 3 Case Problem 4	9 7, 9, 11 5, 7, 8 7 4
XL2000.7.2	Use Chart Wizard to create a chart	4.07–4.12 4.26 4.36 5.48–5.49 7.22–7.25	4.39 4.40 4.40 4.41 4.41	Review Assignment Case Problem 1 Case Problem 2 Case Problem 3 Case Problem 4	5 2, 8, 11 2 2, 3, 4 2, 3, 4
XL2000.7.3	Modify charts	4.14–4.19 4.27–4.29	4.39 4.40 4.40 4.41 4.41	Review Assignment Case Problem 1 Case Problem 2 Case Problem 3 Case Problem 4	6, 8, 10, 11, 12 3, 4, 5, 6 4 2, 3, 4 2, 3, 4
XL2000.7.4	Insert, move, and delete an object (picture)	4.36–4.38	4.39	Review Assignment	14b
XL2000.7.5	Create and modify lines and objects	4.19–4.21	4.39	Review Assignment	8

Expert Skills

Standardized Coding Number	Certification Skill Activity	Tutorial Pages	End-of-Tutorial Practice		
			End-of-Tutorial Pages	Exercise	Step Number
XL2000E.1	**Importing and exporting data**				
XL2000E.1.1	Import data from text files (insert, drag and drop)	11.03–11.10	11.49 11.50	Review Assignment Case Problem 1	2 1, 2
XL2000E.1.2	Import from other applications	6.06–6.10			
XL2000E.1.3	Import a table from an HTML file (insert, drag and drop - including HTML round tripping)	11.46–11.48 A4.03–A4.04 A4.13–A4.14			
XL2000E.1.4	Export to other applications	6.11–6.14 6.17–6.19	6.44 6.45	Case Problem 2 Case Problem 4	3 2
XL2000E.2	**Using templates**				
XL2000E.2.1	Apply templates	8.24–8.26			
XL2000E.2.2	Edit templates	8.27–8.28 A3.16–A3.17			
XL2000E.2.3	Create templates	8.27–8.28			
XL2000E.3	**Using multiple workbooks**				
XL2000E.3.1	Using a workspace	8.46–8.47	8.52	Case Problem 4	10
XL2000E.3.2	Link workbooks	8.11–8.13			
XL2000E.4	**Formatting numbers**				
XL2000E.4.1	Apply number formats (accounting, currency, number)	5.42	A3.24 A3.25	Review Assignment Case Problem 2	6 2
XL2000E.4.2	Create custom number formats	A3.12–A3.15	A3.23 A3.26	Review Assignment Case Problem 3	4 2, 3, 4, 5, 6
XL2000E.4.3	Use conditional formatting	5.24–5.26	5.53 5.54 5.55 5.56	Case Problem 1 Case Problem 2 Case Problem 3 Case Problem 4	5 4 6 5
XL2000E.5	**Printing workbooks**				
XL2000E.5.1	Print and preview multiple worksheets	8.22–8.23	7.55	Case Problem 4	8

Standardized Coding Number	Certification Skill Activity	Tutorial Pages	End-of-Tutorial Practice		
			End-of-Tutorial Pages	Exercise	Step Number
XL2000E.5.2	Use the Report Manager	9.35–9.38	9.40 9.42	Review Assignment Case Problem 2	14 10
XL2000E.6	**Working with named ranges**				
XL2000E.6.1	Add and delete a named range	7.10–7.13	7.47 7.49 7.51	Review Assignment Case Problem 1 Case Problem 2	9 3 4
XL2000E.6.2	Use a named range in a formula	7.12–7.13	7.49	Case Problem 1	5
XL2000E.6.3	Use Lookup Functions (Hlookup or Vlookup)	8.40–8.46	8.49 8.50 8.51	Review Assignment Case Problem 2 Case Problem 3	13 6, 7 4, 6
XL2000E.7	**Working with toolbars**				
XL2000E.7.1	Hide and display toolbars	12.53–12.56			
XL2000E.7.2	Customize a toolbar	12.57–12.60			
XL2000E.7.3	Assign a macro to a command button	12.06–12.08			
XL2000E.8	**Using macros**				
XL2000E.8.1	Record macros	7.30–7.35 7.40–7.42	7.47 7.50 7.52 7.54 7.54–7.55 12.63 12.64 12.66 12.67	Review Assignment Case Problem 1 Case Problem 2 Case Problem 3 Case Problem 4 Review Assignment Case Problem 1 Case Problem 3 Case Problem 4	12, 15 10 8 8 5, 6, 7, 8 3 3 3 2
XL2000E.8.2	Run macros	7.35–7.36	12.63 12.64 12.66	Review Assignment Case Problem 1 Case Problem 6	11 8 6
XL2000E.8.3	Edit macros	12.45–12.47	7.52 12.63 12.64 12.66 12.67	Case Problem 2 Review Assignment Case Problem 1 Case Problem 3 Case Problem 4	14 5 4, 8 4 3

Standardized Coding Number	Certification Skill Activity	Tutorial Pages	End-of-Tutorial Practice: End-of-Tutorial Pages	End-of-Tutorial Practice: Exercise	End-of-Tutorial Practice: Step Number
XL2000E.9	**Auditing a worksheet**				
XL2000E.9.1	Work with the Auditing Toolbar	A3.03–A3.04	A3.25 A3.25	Case Problem 1 Case Problem 2	7 3, 4
XL2000E.9.2	Trace errors (find and fix errors)	A3.08–A3.09	A3.24	Case Problem 1	2, 3
XL2000E.9.3	Trace precedents (find cells referred to in a specific formula)	A3.06–A3.07	A3.23 A3.24	Review Assignment Case Problem 1	3 5
XL2000E.9.4	Trace dependents (find formulas that refer to a specific cell)	A3.05–A3.06	A3.23	Review Assignment	2
XL2000E.10	**Displaying and Formatting Data**				
XL2000E.10.1	Apply conditional formats	5.24–5.26	5.53 5.54 5.55 5.56	Case Problem 1 Case Problem 2 Case Problem 3 Case Problem 4	5 4 6 5
XL2000E.10.2	Perform single and multi-level sorts	5.10–5.13	5.52 5.54	Review Assignment Case Problem 2	4, 15 2
XL2000E.10.3	Use grouping and outlines	5.30–5.31 8.14	5.52 5.55 8.49 8.50	Review Assignment Case Problem 3 Review Assignment Case Problem 1	11 8 12 6, 7
XL2000E.10.4	Use data forms	5.13–5.18	5.56	Case Problem 4	3
XL2000E.10.5	Use subtotaling	5.28–5.31	5.52 5.54 5.54 5.55	Review Assignment Case Problem 1 Case Problem 2 Case Problem 3	5, 10 7 3 7
XL2000E.10.6	Apply data filters	5.19–5.24	5.52	Review Assignment	6, 7, 14
XL2000E.10.7	Extract data	6.11–6.14 6.17–6.19	6.44 6.45	Case Problem 2 Case Problem 4	3 2
XL2000E.10.8	Query databases	11.15–11.20	11.49 11.51 11.52 11.53	Review Assignment Case Problem 2 Case Problem 3 Case Problem 4	6 2 2, 3, 4, 12 1, 2

Standardized Coding Number	Certification Skill Activity	Tutorial Pages	End-of-Tutorial Practice		
			End-of-Tutorial Pages	Exercise	Step Number
XL2000E.10.9	Use data validation	7.06–7.10	7.46 7.49 7.51	Review Assignment Case Problem 1 Case Problem 2	3, 4, 5, 6, 7 4 3
XL2000E.11	**Using analysis tools**				
XL2000E.11.1	Use PivotTable autoformat	5.34–5.49	5.53 5.54 5.54 5.55 5.56	Review Assignment Case Problem 1 Case Problem 2 Case Problem 3 Case Problem 4	12 9 7 11 7
XL2000E.11.2	Use Goal Seek	10.10–10.13			
XL2000E.11.3	Create pivot chart reports	5.50–5.51	5.55 5.55 5.56	Case Problem 2 Case Problem 3 Case Problem 4	8 12 9, 10
XL2000E.11.4	Work with Scenarios	9.26–9.34	9.40 9.42 9.44 9.45	Review Assignment Case Problem 2 Case Problem 3 Case Problem 4	11, 12, 13 4, 6, 7, 9 7, 8, 9 8, 9
XL2000E.11.5	Use Solver	10.18–10.28	10.31 10.31–10.32 10.32 10.33 10.34	Review Assignment Case Problem 1 Case Problem 2 Case Problem 3 Case Problem 4	9, 10, 11, 12, 13, 14 2, 3 2, 3 3, 4 6
XL2000E.11.6	Use data analysis and PivotTables		9.42	Case Problem 2	9
XL2000E.11.7	Create interactive PivotTables for the Web	A4.07–A4.09	A4.15 A4.16 A4.17	Review Assignment Case Problem 1 Case Problem 2	2 2 2
XL2000E.11.8	Add fields to a PivotTable using the Web browser	A4.09–A4.13	A4.15 A4.17	Review Assignment Case Problem 2	4, 5, 6 4
XL2000E.12	**Collaborating with workgroups**				
XL2000E.12.1	Create, edit and remove a comment	A3.19–A3.20			

Standardized Coding Number	Certification Skill Activity	Tutorial Pages	End-of-Tutorial Practice: End-of-Tutorial Pages	End-of-Tutorial Practice: Exercise	End-of-Tutorial Practice: Step Number
XL2000E.12.2	Apply and remove worksheet and workbook protection	7.25–7.29	7.46 7.50 7.54 12.63 12.66	Review Assignment Case Problem 1 Case Problem 3 Review Assignment Case Problem 3	2 11 10 14 8
XL2000E.12.3	Change workbook properties	12.51–12.52	12.63 12.64 12.66	Review Assignment Case Problem 1 Case Problem 3	13 10 9
XL2000E.12.4	Apply and remove file passwords	12.52–12.53			
XL2000E.12.5	Track changes (highlight, accept, and reject)	A3.20–A3.21			
XL2000E.12.6	Create a shared workbook	A3.18–A3.19	A3.27	Case Problem 4	2, 3, 4
XL2000E.12.7	Merge workbooks	A3.21–A3.22			

File Finder

Location in Tutorial	Name and Location of Data File	Student Saves File As...	Student Creates New File
WINDOWS 98 LEVEL I			
Tutorial 2			
Session 2.1			Practice Text.doc
Session 2.2 *Note:* Students copy the contents of Disk 1 onto Disk 2 in this session.	Agenda.doc Budget98.wks Budget99.wks Exterior.bmp Interior.bmp Logo.bmp Members.wdb Minutes.wps Newlogo.bmp Opus27.mid Parkcost.wks Proposal.doc Resume.doc Sales.wks Sample Text.doc Tools.wks Travel.wps Practice Text.doc (*Saved from Session 2.1*)		
Tutorial Assignments	*Note:* Students continue to use the Student Disks they used in the tutorial. For certain Assignments, they will need a third blank disk.	Resume 2.doc (*saved from Resume.doc*)	Letter.doc Song.doc
EXCEL LEVEL 1, DISK 1			
Tutorial 1			
Session 1.1	Tutorial.01\Tutorial\Inwood.xls		
Session 1.2	Tutorial.01\Tutorial\Inwood.xls	Tutorial.01\Tutorial\Inwood 2.xls	
Review Assignments	Tutorial.01\Review\Inwood 3.xls	Tutorial.01\Review\Inwood 4.xls	
Case Problem 1	Tutorial.01\Cases\Enroll.xls	Tutorial.01\Cases\Enrollment.xls	
Case Problem 2	Tutorial.01\Cases\Budget.xls	Tutorial.01\Cases\BudgetSol.xls	
Case Problem 3	Tutorial.01\Cases\Medical.xls	Tutorial.01\Cases\Medical 2.xls	
Case Problem 4			Tutorial.01\Cases\ CashCounter.xls
Tutorial 2			
Session 2.1			Tutorial.02\Tutorial\MSI Sales Report.xls
Session 2.2	Tutorial.02\Tutorial\MSI Sales Report.xls (*Saved from Session 2.1*)	Tutorial.02\Tutorial\Report.xls MSI Sales Report.xls	
Review Assignments	Tutorial.02\Review\MSI 1.xls	Tutorial.02\Review\	MSI Sales Report 2.xls
Case Problem 1			Tutorial.02\Cases\MJ Income.xls
Case Problem 2			Tutorial.02\Cases\Airline.xls
Case Problem 3	Tutorial.02\Cases\Fresh.xls	Tutorial.02\Cases\Fresh Air Sales Incentives.xls	
Case Problem 4			Tutorial.02\Cases\Portfolio.xls

Note: The "NP on Microsoft Windows 98-Level I" Make Student Disk Program must be installed to obtain the student files for the Windows 98 tutorials.

File Finder

Location in Tutorial	*Name and Location of Data File*	*Student Saves File As...*	*Student Creates New File*
Tutorial 3			
Session 3.1	Tutorial.03\Tutorial\Pronto.xls	Tutorial.03\Tutorial\ Pronto Salsa Company.xls	
Session 3.2	Tutorial.03\Tutorial\ Pronto Salsa Company.xls *(Saved from Session 3.1)*	Tutorial.03\Tutorial\ Pronto Salsa Company.xls	
Review Assignments	Tutorial.03\Review\Pronto 2.xls Tutorial.03\Review\Explore3.xls	Tutorial.03\Review\Pronto 3.xls Tutorial.03\Review\Pronto 4.xls Tutorial.03\Review\Explore3 Solution.xls	
Case Problem 1	Tutorial.03\Cases\Running.xls	Tutorial.03\Cases\Running2.xls	
Case Problem 2	Tutorial.03\Cases\Recycle.xls	Tutorial.03\Cases\Recycle2.xls Tutorial.03\Cases\Recycle Data.xls Tutorial.03\Cases\Recycle3.xls	
Case Problem 3	Tutorial.03\Cases\StateGov.xls	Tutorial.03\Cases\State Government.xls	
Case Problem 4			Tutorial.03\Cases\Payroll.xls
Tutorial 4			
Session 4.1	Tutorial.04\Tutorial\Concepts.xls	Tutorial.04\Tutorial\Cast Iron Concepts.xls	
Session 4.2	Tutorial.04\Tutorial\Cast Iron Concepts.xls *(Saved from Session 4.1)* Tutorial.04\Tutorial\Stove.pcx		
Review Assignments	Tutorial.04\Review\Concept2.xls Tutorial.04\Review\ ElectronicFilings.xls	Tutorial.04\Review\Cast Iron Concepts 2.xls Tutorial.04\Review\Filing Solution.xls	
Case Problem 1	Tutorial.04\Cases\Tekstar.xls	Tutorial.04\Cases\TekStar Electronics.xls	
Case Problem 2	Tutorial.04\Cases\DowJones.xls	Tutorial.04\Cases\Dow Jones Chart.xls Tutorial.04\Cases\Dow Jones 2.xls	
Case Problem 3	Tutorial.04\Cases\California.xls	Tutorial.04\Cases\California Economic Data.xls	
Case Problem 4			Tutorial.04\Cases\ RealtorCharts.xls
EXCEL LEVEL II			
Tutorial 5			
Session 5.1	Tutorial.05\Tutorial\Faculty.xls	CBA Faculty.xls	
Session 5.2			
Session 5.3			
Review Assignment	Tutorial.05\Review\Faculty2.xls	CBA Faculty 2.xls	
Case Problem 1	Tutorial.05\Cases\Office.xls	Office Supplies.xls	
Case Problem 2	Tutorial.05\Cases\Medical.xls	Med Tech.xls	
Case Problem 3	Tutorial.05\Cases\TeaHouse.xls	TeaHouse Revenue.xls	
Case Problem 4	Tutorial.05\Cases\NBA.xls	NBA Salaries.xls	
Tutorial 6			
Session 6.1	Tutorial.06\Tutorial\Baskets.xls Tutorial.06\Tutorial\Letter.doc Tutorial.06\Tutorial\NPA.xls	New Baskets.xls Customer Letter.doc	
Session 6.2	*(Continue from Session 6.1)*		
Session 6.3	Tutorial.06\Tutorial\New Baskets.xls	New Baskets.xls	
Review Assignment	Tutorial.06\Review\CustLtr2.doc Tutorial.06\Review\NPA.xls Tutorial.06\Review\NewBask2.xls Tutorial.06\Review\AdvLetr.doc Tutorial.06\Review\MonSales.xls Tutorial.06\Review\AdvLetr.doc Tutorial.06\Review\MonSales.xls	Customer Letter 2.doc NPA.htm New Baskets 2.xls Advisory Board Letter.doc MonSales2.xls Advisory Board Letter2.doc Advisory Board Letter2.xls	

File Finder

Case Problem 1	Tutorial.06\Cases\ToyStore.xls Tutorial.06\Cases\ToyLtr.doc	Toy Store Sales.xls Toy Memo.doc	
Case Problem 2	Tutorial.06\Cases\StSales.xls Tutorial.06\Cases\StMemo.doc Tutorial.06\Cases\StMemo1.doc	State Sales Memo.doc State Sales Memo1.doc	
Case Problem 3	Tutorial.06\Cases\AlumProd.xls Tutorial.06\Cases\Alumltr.doc	Alumni Products.xls Alumni Letter.doc HorzPrc.htm	
Case Problem 4	Tutorial.06\Cases\Inwood.xls	Inwood 1.xls	Inwood Memo.doc
Tutorial 7			
Session 7.1	Tutorial.07\Tutorial\401k.xls	401kPlan.xls	
Session 7.2	*(Continue from Session 7.1)*		
Session 7.3	*(Continue from Session 7.2)*		
Review Assignment	Tutorial.07\Review\401kPlan2.xls	401kPlan3.xls	
Case Problem 1			Travel Expense.xls
Case Problem 2			Sales Agreement.xls
Case Problem 3			Apex Rental.xls
Case Problem 4	Tutorial.07\Cases\Invoices.xls	Sales Invoices.xls	
Tutorial 8			
Session 8.1	Tutorial.08\Tutorial\Grades2.xls Tutorial.08\Tutorial\Grades4.xls	Grades3.xls Grades4.dot	Grades.xls
Session 8.2	Tutorial.08\Tutorial\White.xls	Summary Grades.xls	
Session 8.3	Tutorial.08\Tutorial\TA1.xls	TA1Lookup.xls	
Review Assignment	Tutorial.08\Review\Calc223.xls	Calc223 Grades.xls	
Case Problem 1	Tutorial.08\Cases\Copiers	Copier Sales.xls	
Case Problem 2	Tutorial.08\Cases\Kitchen.xls	Kitchen Warehouse.xls	
Case Problem 3	Tutorial.08\Cases\Index.xls	NYSE Index.xls	
Case Problem 4	Tutorial.08\Cases\R1.xls Tutorial.08\Cases\R2.xls Tutorial.08\Cases\R3.xls	North.xls South.xls Southwest.xls	Bread Bakery
EXCEL LEVEL 3			
Tutorial 9			
Session 9.1	Tutorial.09Tutorial/Davis.xls	Tutorial.09Tutorial/Break-even Analysis.xls	
Session 9.2	Tutorial.09Tutorial/Davis.xls	Tutorial.09Tutorial/Scenario Report.xls	
Review Assignment	Tutorial.09/Review/LowCost.xls	Tutorial.09/Review/Low Cost Scenario 2.xls	
Case Problem 1	Tutorial.09/Cases/HomeEd.xls	Tutorial.09/Cases/HomeEd Analysis.xls	
Case Problem 2	Tutorial.09/Cases/Prints.xls	Tutorial.09/Cases/Sales Mix.xls	
Case Problem 3	Tutorial.09/Cases/Bakery.xls	Tutorial.09/Cases/Bakery Analysis.xls	
Case Problem 4			Tutorial.09/Cases/Chen.xls
Tutorial 10			
Session 10.1			Tutorial.10/Tutorial/Refrigerator Order.xls
Session 10.2	Tutorial.10/Tutorial/GoldStar.xls	Tutorial.10/Tutorial/Appliance Order.xls	
Review Assignment	Tutorial.10/Review/Dryers.xls	Tutorial.10/Review/Dryer Order.xls	
Case Problem 1	Tutorial.10/Cases/Couches.xls	Tutorial.10/Cases/Furniture Order.xls	
Case Problem 2	Tutorial.10/Cases/Pontoon.xls	Tutorial.10/Cases/Pontoon Boat Order.xls	
Case Problem 3	Tutorial.10/Cases/Pizza.xls	Tutorial.10/Cases/Chipster Employee Schedule.xls	
Case Problem 4			Tutorial.10/Cases/Southland Furniture.xls

File Finder

Location in Tutorial	Name and Location of Data File	Student Saves File As...	Student Creates New File
Tutorial 11			
Session 11.1	Tutorial.11/Tutorial/History.txt	Tutorial.11/Tutorial/Sunrise Fund.xls	Tutorial.11/Tutorial/Sunrise Portfolio.dqy
Session 11.2	*(Continued from Session 11.1)*		
Session 11.3	*(Continued from Session 11.2)*		
Review Assignment	Tutorial.11/Review/NYA2000.xls	Tutorial.11/Review/NYSE Index Analysis.xls	
Case Problem 1	Tutorial.11/Cases/Invoice.txt	Tutorial.11/Cases/Invoice Data.xls	
Case Problem 2	Tutorial.11/Cases/EZNet	Tutorial.11/Cases/"EZNet" Tutorial.11/Cases/Inventory Data.xls	
Case Problem 3	Tutorial.11/Cases/Arts	Tutorial.11/Cases/EuroArts Tutorial.11/Cases/Home Catalog.xls Tutorial.11/Cases/Regional Sales.xls	
Case Problem 4			Tutorial.11/Cases/Web Query Data.xls
Tutorial 12			
Session 12.1	Tutorial.12/Tutorial/Imageon.xls	Tutorial.12/Tutorial/Kiosk 1.xls	
Session 12.2	*(Continued from Session 12.1)*	Tutorial.12/Tutorial/Kiosk 2.xls	
Session 12.3	*(Continued from Session 12.2)*	Tutorial.12/Tutorial/Kiosk 3.xls Tutorial.12/Tutorial/Kiosk 4.xls	
Review Assignment	Tutorial.12/Review/Kiosk 5.xls	Tutorial.12/Review/Kiosk 6.xls	
Case Problem 1	Tutorial.12/Cases/Casey.xls	Tutorial.12/Cases/Casey Print Macro.xls	
Case Problem 2	Tutorial.12/Cases/Brakdale.xls	Tutorial.12/Cases/Brakdale Break-even.xls	
Case Problem 3	Tutorial.12/Cases/Stocks.xls	Tutorial.12/Cases/Stock Information Macro.xls	
Case Problem 4			Tutorial.12/Cases/Documentation Sheet Macro.xls
Appendix 2			
Session A2.1	Appendix.02/Tutorial/StSales.xls	Appendix.02/Tutorial/State Sales.xls	
Session A2.2	*(Continued from Session A2.1)*		
Review Assignment	Appendix.02/Review/StSales2.xls	Appendix.02/Review/State Sales 2.xls Appendix.02/Cases/USPCI.xls	
Case Problem 1	Appendix.02/Cases/PCI.xls	Appendix.02/Cases/USPCI2.xls	
Case Problem 2	Appendix.02/Cases/SalesEur.xls	Appendix.02/Cases/BalanceSalesForce.xls	
Case Problem 3			Appendix.02/Cases/Operations.xls
Case Problem 4			Appendix.02/Cases/ExploreMapStats.xls
Appendix 3			
Session A3.1	Appendix.03/Tutorial/Stock.xls	Appendix.03/Tutorial/Stock Portfolio.xls	
Session A3.2	*(Continued from Session A3.1)*		
Review Assignment	Appendix.03/Review/Stock1.xls	Appendix.03/Review/Stock Portfolio 1.xls	
Case Problem 1	Appendix.03/Cases/GrowGo.xls	Appendix.03/Cases/Groceries to Go.xls	
Case Problem 2	Appendix.03/Cases/Tax.xls	Appendix.03/Cases/TaxSchedule.xls	
Case Problem 3	Appendix.03/Cases/Format.xls	Appendix.03/Cases/Custom Formats.xls	
Case Problem 4			
Appendix 4			
Session A4.1	Appendix.04\Tutorial\GPGloves.xls	Appendix.04\Tutorial\Glove Sales.xls Appendix.04\Tutorial\Glove_Sales.html Appendix.04\Tutorial\Glove Sales 2.xls	
Review Assignment	Appendix.04\Review\GPShoes.xls	Appendix.04\Review\GP_Shoes.html Appendix.04\Review\GPShoes2.xls	
Case Problem 1	Appendix.04\Cases\Davis.xls	Appendix.04\Cases\Davis_CVP.html	
Case Problem 2	Appendix.04\Cases\Bread.xls	Appendix.04\Cases\Sales_Chart.html	